Saguenay River

Chicoutimi

Grand Baie

Roi

Tadoussac

Domaine du

St. Lawrence River

LaMalbaie

Les Éboulements

Kamouraska

Baie St Paul

Petite Rivière

Île aux Coudres

St. Joachim

St. Anne

Château Richer

ge Gardien

auport

ourg

ye

Lévis

Cap Tourmente

Île d'Orléans

**Selected communities
in the St. Lawrence
and Saguenay River Valleys**

ke

Phantoms of the French Fur Trade

Twenty Men
Who Worked in the Trade
Between 1618 and 1758

Volume II

Timothy J. Kent

Silver Fox Enterprises
Ossineke, Michigan
2015

Copyright © 2015 by Timothy J. Kent
Published by Silver Fox Enterprises
P.O. Box 176
11504 U.S. 23 South
Ossineke, MI 49766

All drawings by the author unless otherwise noted
All photographs by Timothy and Dorothy Kent
Typeset by Model Printing, Alpena, Michigan
Printed by Thomson-Shore, Inc., Dexter, Michigan

Publishers Cataloging-in-Publication Data
Kent, Timothy J.
Phantoms of the French Fur Trade, Twenty Men Who Worked in the Trade Between 1618 and 1758
2,450 pp. in three volumes, 6.125 by 9.25 inches
Includes two indexes, by subjects and by proper nouns

Contents:
1. Fur Trade, U.S. and Canada, 1600-1760. 2. Settlement, U.S. and Canada, 1600-1813. 3. Biographies of twenty French fur trade employees/settlers and their wives, U.S and Canada, 1589-1813. 4. Commerce, U.S. and Canada. 5. Transportation, U.S. and Canada. 6. Exploration, U.S. and Canada. 7. Indians/Native Americans, U.S. and Canada. 8. North American History, 1600-1800. 9. U.S. History, 1600-1760. 10. Canadian History, 1600-1800.

Library of Congress Catalog Card Number 2015900460
International Standard Book Number 978-0-9657230-7-7

Front Cover of Volume I: "Quebec" etching by Alain Manesson Mallet, in *Description de l'Universe* (Paris, 1683), 5:277; in the possession of the author.

Front Cover of Volume II: Artist's reconstruction of Ft. Michilimackinac in 1749, based upon drawings and observations by Lotbinière from that year. (Courtesy of Mackinac State Historic Parks)

Front Cover of Volume III: The author (left) and his son Ben, portaging their birchbark canoe before departing on the Tahquamenon River.

Table of Contents

Volume One

Volume Two

Volume Three

IX

François Brunet dit Le Bourbonnais, Sr. and his wife Barbe Beauvais

*One of the earliest recorded voyageurs during the 1670s,
one of the very earliest documented voyageur-traders to be
hired after the license system was implemented in 1682,
then an independent voyageur-trader partnered with other traders*

The son of the farm worker Antoine Brunet and his wife Philippe David, François Brunet dit Le Bourbonnais was born in about 1644 or 1645, in the parish of Bardais (also spelled Barday) within the province of Bourbonnais. (In the census which was conducted in New France in 1681, François gave his age as 37. Later, at the time of his funeral on June 24, 1702, one of his family members indicated to the priest that the deceased had been 57 years old. Thus, his year of birth has been calculated as about 1644 or 1645.) His family name "Brunet," meaning "brown-haired lad," had probably originated as a nickname that had been applied to one of his ancestors back in medieval times. It was only in the New World that the young man acquired the nickname "Le Bourbonnais" or "The One From Bourbonnais."

The province of Bourbonnais, in which François Brunet grew to adulthood, encompassed an area that measured about eighty miles in length by some fifty miles in width. It was located slightly to the east of the geographical center of France, and just north of the large range of rough highlands called Le Massif Central. (After the French Revolution, when the ancient provinces were divided into *Départements* in 1790 and were renamed, the former Bourbonnais generally corresponded with the new Department of Allier.) This area lay to the east of the section of France from which the vast majority of the colonists of New France originated, which was the northwestern one-third of the country. Only a minute number among the 9,066 identified settlers of the colony who remained there permanently originated from this province of Bourbonnais. Among the 8,483 colonists whose places of origin have been identified, only 21 of them (.25 percent) came from Bourbonnais. These included five individuals who arrived before 1670 (the period of François' arrival), an additional two others who immigrated between 1670 and 1699, and another fourteen who came between 1700 and 1759. Thus, Monsieur Brunet's province of origin was a great rarity in the St. Lawrence settlements; this made the expression "Le Bourbonnais" a logical choice for his nickname, which would distinguish him from any other colonists who also had the family name of Brunet. During the course of the entire history of New France, only two other permanent settlers besides François are known to have borne the sobriquet "Le Bourbonnais." These were Maïeul Dumay, who married and had children, and François Dubois, who had neither spouse nor children. Clearly, this nickname would only have been applied to François Brunet, and to these other two men, after they had emigrated from the mother country to the colony; technically, back in France, every one of the residents of the entire province of Bourbonnais would have rightly earned this nickname.

The village of Bardais was located in the northwestern area of the province, about eighteen miles southeast of the boundary line which separated Bourbonnais from the adjacent province of Berry. (Oddly enough, in Francois' 1672 marriage contract, the notary recorded the place of origin of Monsieur Brunet as "the parish of Barday in Berry," although his home parish had actually been located some 18 miles away from the edge of that latter province.) In Blaeu's 1665 atlas of France, each of the communities on the various maps were portrayed, in descending order of size, as a *ville* (city or town), a *bourg* (market town), a *village* (small village), or a *hameau* (hamlet). On his detailed map of the province of Bourbonnais, the cartographer depicted Bardais as belonging to the second-largest category. As a *bourg*, it would have been the community to which the self-sufficient farming residents of the far-flung villages, hamlets, or *lieus-dits* (named places), scattered for many miles around, would have traveled to participate in the weekly market, or to conduct business with the merchants or the notary, or to attend functions at the church. According to Blaeu's detailed chart from 1665, the *ville* or town which was nearest to Bardais would have been Ainay-le-Chateau, which was located about four miles to the west. Since François stated in 1672 that he was from the parish of Bardais, he had hailed from one of the scattered smaller settlements that utilized the market town of Bardais as their center of orbit. His statement clearly indicated that he had not originated in the *bourg* itself. The solitary church in this centralized market community, dedicated to St. Laurent, had been constructed in the XII century. (In 1844, for administrative purposes, this parish and that of St. Pierre in the nearby community of Isle, about 1 1/2 miles to the southeast, were joined together to create Isle-et-Bardais. Thus, the combined parish and community thereafter boasted two very similar churches, both of which dated from the 1100s and both of which still stand to this day.)[1]

François Brunet's parish of Bardais was located about 200 miles from the Atlantic port of La Rochelle, and some 230 miles from the English Channel port of Honfleur. Thus, he may have sailed for New France from either of these two locales, or from another coastal port in one of these two regions. Whatever his point of embarcation, he made the transatlantic voyage either during the summer of 1669 or within a few years preceding that summer.

There is no surviving documentation to indicate whether or not François had signed a contract as an indentured laborer before his departure for the New World. Such agreements usually involved three years of service for an employer in the colony, in return for a free transatlantic passage plus room and board and a modest salary during each of the three years of work. In the 1666 census of Montreal Island, 31 of the 106 enumerated family households contained one or more male *engagés* (hired laborers), who worked for the family members and resided with them. In addition, another 28 men were listed as *engagés* working for the Seigneurs of the Island (the Sulpician order), while two were listed for the Hospital Nuns, twelve for La Grange, and three for the Sisters of the Congregation of Notre Dame (nuns who taught school to native girls).[2] It is highly likely that a large percentage of these workers were indentured laborers working off their three-year contracts. However, even when work contracts were signed in France by indentured laborers who were destined for Montreal, those binding agreements were sometimes cancelled early and the men were granted parcels of land, in order to induce them to remain permanently in the Montreal community, where settlers were sorely needed.

During this period, according to the census of 1667, the inhabitants of Montreal Island numbered 750. This figure reflects the corrected number after the multiple listings of various colonists had been rectified by modern scholars. Nearly all of these individuals resided at or within a few miles of Montreal, along a five-mile stretch of the western shoreline of the St. Lawrence River.[3] It was in this same year of 1667 that the extended period of Iroquois attacks and lighting raids, which had terrorized the native allies and the St. Lawrence settlers for a full quarter-century (ever since 1641) had finally drawn to a close, upon the signing of various peace treaties. These accords would remain in effect for nearly two decades, until the Iroquois would shatter them in about 1686.

The earliest surviving documentation for François Brunet's presence in New France is his first marriage contract, which was drawn up on December 9, 1669 at the home of the Montreal notary Bénigne Basset. At this time, Francois was about 24 or 25 years old; he was identified in the document as a resident of Montreal Island. According to this *promesse de mariage*, he agreed to marry at some time in the future Marie Marthe Thibodeau, the daughter of Mathurin Thibodeau and Catherine Avrard, who were also residents of Montreal Island. On the day of the nuptial agreement, the bride-to-be was amazingly young to be taking this major step in life: she was ten weeks short of her ninth birthday! However, it is abundantly clear that neither François nor young Marie Marthe and her parents intended that this marriage would take place until at least three more years had passed. According to the laws of the Catholic Church at this time, a young woman was obliged to have reached the age of twelve, and a young man the age of fourteen, to legally marry. However, each individual had to have reached puberty to be wed, no matter what age they had attained. Marie Marthe was the only surviving child of the Thibodeau couple, who had originated in the port town of La Rochelle. More than a decade before this agreement was drawn up, back in June of 1659, Mathurin had hired on to become a settler in Montreal, and the couple and their four children had eagerly set sail for the colony. However, during the course of the long ocean voyage, all three of their older children had perished. Then, to top off the couple's series of terrible misfortunes, their baby had died on October 8 at the age of nine months, just ten days after they had arrived at Montreal! Sixteen months later, little Marie Marthe had been born there, and she had been baptized in the Montreal church on February 21, 1661; thereafter, the Thibodeau couple had produced no more children.

In spite of the official document which the notary penned on December 9, 1669, the marriage that François had promised to undertake with Marie Marthe did not ultimately come to pass. In fact, the *promesse* was annulled a number of months after the December agreement. Afterward, Monsieur Brunet would remain single for another two years.

On November 4, 1670, eleven months after her first nuptial agreement, Marie Marthe Thibodeau, at the ripe old age of 9³/4 years, would commit to a second marriage contract, this time with François Chartier dit Laforest. However, this contract would likewise be annulled, at some point during the following two years. Finally, she would sign a third nuptial agreement on February 2, 1673, three weeks before celebrating her twelfth birthday. In this instance, the contract would be fulfilled as specified: nine weeks after the signing, on April 9, in front of the altar of the Montreal church, young Marie Marthe would become the wife of 29-year-old Jean Boursier dit Lavigne.

Interestingly, Jean Boursier and François Brunet would be closely linked during most of their adult lives. Jean would stand as the godfather at the baptism of the first child of François and his wife, three days before Jean and Marie Marthe's own wedding. In addition, from 1676 on, the Boursier couple would live as very close neighbors of François and his wife in the Lachine seigneury, separated by only a single farm. Finally, Jean and François would work closely together as a voyageur team in the western interior for many years.[4]

François' *promesse de mariage*, drawn up in December of 1669, clearly indicates that he had arrived in New France either during or some time before the transatlantic sailing season of 1669. The fact that he made an official agreement to marry an underage girl at least three years into the future may imply that he had arrived in the colony as a *"trente-six mois,"* an indentured laborer who had signed a thirty-six month work contract before embarking from the mother country. He may have made this marriage arrangement with the long-range plan that, after the passage of three years' time, his obligations as a contracted worker would draw to a close at about the same time that Marie Marthe would reach the legal minimum age for becoming a bride. The fact that he eventually received his first grant of land in 1673 also supports this hypothesis, since individuals were usually not permitted to either marry or receive land grants in the colony until they had completed their period of indentured labor.[5]

His presence in New France by at least the summer of 1669 also implies that François was a member of the militia of Montreal. Orders from the King announcing the obligatory establishment of such civilian forces throughout the colony arrived with the sailing vessels of 1669. According to the royal decree, all able-bodied men between the ages of sixteen and sixty were obligated to join the militia. However, a full 6^1/2 years before this decree arrived, back in the winter of 1663, the Governor of Montreal and the male inhabitants of the settlement there had organized their own civilian fighting forces. By February of 1663, these forces had consisted of twenty squads, each of which contained seven men. Thus, out of a total population of scarcely 400 persons in the community, 140 men had volunteered as fighters in Montreal's "Militia of the Blessed Virgin."[6]

At some point during the summer or autumn of 1670, François was embroiled in a physical altercation with Philippe Pothier dit Lafontaine, a fellow resident of Montreal Island. Since the latter man received bodily injuries in the course of the fracas, he registered a complaint against François with the Court of Montreal, by which he hoped to receive reparation payments from his opponent. After the Judge had rendered his decision in the case, Messieurs Brunet and Lafontaine met at the office of the Montreal notary Basset on November 14, 1670, in order to officially settle their dispute. According to the document that was drawn up, François had already paid to his opponent "the sum of forty-two livres for damages, interests, board and lodging, and medicines and surgeon's services which were administered to treat the said Lafontaine until his recovery, as well as for legal expenses, including the efforts which he knows the said Lafontaine sustained in acquiring the aforementioned information that comprised the report of the said surgeon." At the conclusion of the document, the notary added the following sentence: "The said Bourbonnais is unable to and does not know how to sign, having been questioned according to the ordinance."[7] A similar statement would appear at the end of each of the notary documents that François would generate throughout his entire life, clearly indicating that he never did learn to read or write.

During this same autumn of 1670, a second dispute developed between François and a fellow resident of Montreal Island. In this case, his antagonist was Mathurin Thibodeau, whose nine-year-old daughter he had promised to marry back in December of 1669. This time, it was Monsieur Brunet who took the complaint to the Montreal Court, with the intention of receiving a financial settlement. At issue was "one gun and a blanket which the said Bourbonnais is said to have lost in the [St. Lawrence] River after having overturned the said canoe." However, the arbitration that was decreed by Pierre Godin dit Châtillon and another individual named Limousin was not accepted by the two opponents. But a few months later, on January 14, 1671,

François and Monsieur Tibodeau met with the notary Basset, who was also the recorder of the Montreal Court, in order to officially register their resolution of the issue. Also present at this gathering was Monsieur Godin, one of the two original arbitrators in the case. According to their settlement, Thibodeau agreed that he owed and would pay to François 100 livres for the lost gun and blanket, creating a resolution that was in accord with both of the protagonists.[8] Unfortunately, in his short document describing the details of the settlement, the scribe did not include a full description of the capsize incident, nor the events which had led up to it. However, Monsieur Thibodeau's willingness to pay out a moderate sum of money to François clearly implies that, at the time of the accident, the paddler had been engaged in a voyage for Thibodeau's benefit. Whatever the details of the situation had been at the time of the capsize, the latter man obviously felt that he was financially responsible for replacing the lost equipment.

Considering the esteemed reputation and career that François eventually developed as a voyageur and a voyageur-trader in the west, it is fascinating to note that one of the very earliest pieces of documentation concerning his presence in New France related to one of his canoe voyages. He had initially submitted this case involving his capsize and loss of property to the Court of Montreal in the autumn of 1670. That was less than a year after François' earliest documented presence in the colony, which was his *promesse de mariage* from December of 1669. This particular court case provides an example of how young men transplanted from France learned to embrace and master the challenges and demands of the new ways of life in New France, acquiring new skills which were necessary for their very survival. Some of their newly-mastered talents included traveling by native methods in all seasons, involving snowshoes in winter and canoes in the unfrozen months.

Nine months after the settlement concerning his lost gun and blanket, on October 18, 1671, François stood for the first time as the godfather at a christening ceremony. In this instance, the baby to whom he bequeathed his own name in the Montreal church was the newborn son of the Montreal mason Étienne Campeau and his wife Catherine Paulo. Standing beside him as the godmother was Marguerite Gervaise, the wife of the Montreal gunsmith Jean Baptiste Gadois.[9]

The spring of 1672 brought with it not only fine weather but also momentous times for François. Now about 27 or 28 years old, he had finally found the mate of his life. She was Barbe Beauvais, 15$^1/2$ years old, the second child and eldest daughter of the immigrants Jacques Beauvais dit Saint Gemme and Jeanne Soldé. Having been born at Montreal on August 28, 1656, Barbe had been baptized in the church there on the following day, and she had later been confirmed in the same edifice on July 11, 1664, six weeks before she had reached her eighth birthday. Barbe had been enumerated with her family members in the colony-wide censuses of 1666 and 1667; in both instances, the family had been residing either in or near to Montreal. (In 1684, her younger sister Charlotte would become the second wife of Alexandre Turpin, whose biography has already been presented in this work.)[10]

On April 18, 1672, François and Barbe gathered with various family members and friends at the home of the notary Basset to draw up their marriage contract. In this document, the prospective groom was described as "François Brunet dit Le Bourbonnais, son of the deceased Antoine Brunet, farm worker, and of Philippe David, from the parish of Barday in [the province of] Berry, in the diocese of Bourges," while the future bride was recorded as "Barbe Beauvais, daughter of Jacques Beauvais and of Jeanne Soldé, from Montreal." For their part, the latter couple promised to bequeath to the prospective bride a dowry of 400 livres tournois (the currency of France, which was worth 25 percent more than the currency that was used in the colony); they would deliver this sum to their daughter over the course of five payments. The official witnesses on this lively occasion were Jean Gervaise, Jean Baptiste Gadois, Nicolas Godé, and Louis Chevalier.[11]

Eleven weeks after their contract-signing event, on July 11, the bride and groom pronounced their wedding vows in the Notre Dame de Montreal church. This day, the four official witnesses included Zacharie Dupuis, the Sieur de Verdun (Major of the garrison stationed at Montreal), Jean Baptiste Gadois (gunsmith at Montreal), Jean Dubreuil (resident of Montreal since at least May of 1668, where he would marry in 1682), and __ Dechaunière (probably Desaulnièrs).[12]

At first, the new couple resided in or near to Montreal. It was there that their first child was born, in a worrisome but eventually joyous event which took place eight months and three weeks after Barbe and François had celebrated their wedding. At his baptism on April 6, 1673, the little lad received his name from his godfather Jean Boursier dit Lavigne (who would marry twelve-year-old Marie

Marthe Thibodeau three days later, in the same Montreal church). The baby's godmother was Jacqueline Aubry, the wife of Antoine Gros dit Laviolette. (The Boursier and Gros families would relocate to the Lachine seigneury in 1676 and 1678, respectively.)[13]

On May 28, 1673, François received a grant of property in the seigneury of Lachine, about eight miles south-southwest of Montreal. (Technically, Montreal Island represented a single huge seigneury, and each of the settlement areas on the island, such as Lachine, was either a fief or a sub-fief. However, for the sake of clarity and continuity, in this work, many of the settled areas on Montreal Island are referred to as seigneuries. Normally, this term designated a large plot of land that had been granted to an individual, who then bore the responsibility of enlisting settlers to reside upon that land. However, the Sulpicians based at Montreal were the seigneurs of the entire island. They granted relatively small lots to hundreds of individual colonists, and also ceded larger plots of land, which were true fiefs and sub-fiefs, to certain individuals. The use of the word seigneury by the present author for many of the Montreal Island communities meshes well with the rest of the settlement areas throughout the St. Lawrence Valley, most of which were true seigneuries, although many of them had a number of small fiefs and sub-fiefs within them.)

The new settlement area of Lachine was located on the lands which stretched out along the St. Lawrence shoreline from both sides of the southern end of the eight-mile-long portage road. This overland passage, called Le Chemin de Lachine or the Lachine Road, extended along a gently curving route between Montreal and the southeastern corner of Montreal Island, skirting the Sault de St. Louis (the St. Louis or Lachine Rapids) and their powerful downstream whirlpools. In this violently turbulent section of the St. Lawrence, the water level dropped a full forty feet in elevation. About $1^1/2$ miles west of the southern terminus of the portage road (and $1/2$ mile east of the end of the future Lachine Canal) the community of Lachine had been established (it is now called La Salle). At this place, the Sulpicians had granted in 1667 a rather extensive plot of land, a sub-fief, to René Robert Cavelier, Sieur de La Salle. It was here that the stockaded village of Lachine (also called Ft. Rémy from 1680 onward) had been gradually constructed. After two years, La Salle had abandoned his plans to develop this community, instead deciding to focus on his ambitious plan to establish a series of posts in the central and southern interior. Thus, in 1669, he had sold his land at Lachine, along with the few structures there that belonged to him, to Jean Milot.

Over the next several years, the quarter-mile-long community had grown to include a seigneurial manor house (which had on its ground floor a well, a blacksmith's shop, and a bakery with an oven that extended out to the exterior); a wind-powered grist mill (built in 1671 of field stones so it could serve as a round-tower redoubt); several barracks buildings to house soldiers; a number of storage buildings; and the homes of various settler families. In 1676, a wooden church measuring 36 by 20 feet would be constructed in the village area, by the master carpenter and Lachine settler Pierre Godin dit Châtillon (a direct ancestor of the present author). At first, this edifice would be served by visiting priests, so that the register for the Paroisse des Saints Anges (Holy Angels Parish) would commence in that year of 1676. Four years later, in 1680, a *presbytère* (rectory or priest's residence) would be built beside the church, on the side opposite the cemetery, to accommodate the first resident parish priest, Father Pierre Rémy, who would be appointed in that year.

From 1668 onward, colonists gradually settled along the St. Lawrence shoreline in the Lachine seigneury. In the process, they developed farms on the lands that extended for about $1^3/4$ miles to the west of the village site (to the adjacent seigneury of La Présentation or Côte St. Gilles), and for about $4^1/4$ miles to the east of the village site (to the adjacent seigneury of Verdun). Thus, the entire stretch of river frontage that was encompassed by the Lachine seigneury measured some $6^1/4$ miles in length. The western two-thirds of this span was called the Côte de Lachine, while its eastern one-third was dubbed the Sault St. Louis. These two sections were separated by the Commons land.[14]

Over the years, as the long, slender lots fronting on the St. Lawrence were granted to the individual settlers, a rather large area immediately east of the end of the portage road was left unassigned. This area commenced at the Baie de Quenneville (the terminus of the portage road) and extended eastward along the shoreline for a full half-mile (fifteen arpents). This parcel would serve as the Commons area of the seigneury. As such, it would be reserved for the usage of many of the residents for such tasks as pasturing animals and cutting wood; it would also be for the use of those numerous individuals who utilized the portage road.

The fourth lot to the east of the Commons area was the elongated rectangular piece of property that was granted to François Brunet dit Le Bourbonnais in the spring of 1673, just six years after La Salle had been granted the first land in the seigneury. During the thirteen years following La Salle's concession, a total of thirty men received lots fronting on the river's shoreline in the eastern and central sections of the seigneury. The frontage of these plots covered five miles, extending eastward from a spot $1/2$ mile west of the village site (commencing at the end of the future Lachine Canal). Most of these pieces of property stretched inland away from the river for $7/10$ mile or more. To understand how François' grant fit into this series of land concessions, here follows the sequence in which these river-fronting lands were distributed: 1 lot in 1668, 1 in 1669 (plus Milot's purchase of La Salle's property), 1 in 1670, 9 in 1671, 3 in 1672, 10 in 1673 (including the lot which was granted to Monsieur Brunet), none in 1674, 1 in 1675, 1 in 1676 (this lot was granted to François' close neighbor and paddling partner Jean Boursier dit Lavigne), 1 in 1677, none in 1678, none in 1679, and 2 in 1680. (Besides François Brunet, five other direct ancestors of the present author were among the men who received these long, slender lots: Louis Fortin, Jean Quenneville, Léonard Girardin, Pierre Godin dit Châtillon, and Vivien Magdelaine dit Ladouceur.) Seven years later, in 1687, the land of the Commons area would be jointly granted to fourteen of the property-owning men of the seigneury, including François Brunet.[15]

The St. Lawrence frontage of François' elongated, rectangular piece of property commenced about 1700 feet ($1/3$ mile) east of the Commons area, and about $8/10$ mile east of the southern end of the portage road. Three decades after he received this concession, in the 1703 inventory of the possessions which had jointly belonged to him and Barbe, the notary would thus summarize the document of the land grant:

"One contract of concession of the said sixty arpents [51 acres] of surface area, located at the said place of Lachine, with three arpents [575 English feet] of frontage [on the St. Lawrence River] by twenty arpents [$7/10$ mile] of depth, having on one side [the land of] Jacques Cardinal, on the other side [that of] Pierre Couillard [sic, a misreading by the notary; it was actually Pierre Cardinal], in the front the St. Lawrence River, and behind the lands of the Côte Saint Paul, granted by the deceased Monsieur Dollier [de Casson], Superior of the [Sulpician] Seminary of Montreal, on the date of the twenty-eighth of May, 1673."[16]

As it extended off toward the northwest, the rear portion of François' plot of land crossed the Montreal-to-Lachine portage road. During this same year in which he received his property, Pierre

Cardinal was granted the lot adjacent to the east side of the Brunet land, while Pierre's father Simon Jean Cardinal and Pierre's elder brother Jacques were jointly granted the lot which lay 1,150 feet to the west of the Brunet land. Four years later, in 1680, the intervening two lots positioned between the latter (western) Cardinal lot and the Brunet lot were granted to Jean Vincent Chamaillard dit Lafontaine (adjacent to François) and Jean Horieux dit Lafleur, respectively.

In order to retain ownership of their property, each owner was obliged to annually pay a modest set of fees, in both wheat and cash, to the seigneurs (the Sulpicians, who owned Montreal Island); these payments were due each year on or before the Feast Day of St. Martin, November 11. In addition, the *censitaires* were also obliged to have their grains ground at the seigneurial mill, where the miller retained $1/40$ of the ground flour as the obligatory fee for the seigneurs. In François' case, his trek to haul his grains westward to the mill in the stockaded village and then to haul his resulting flour back home would entail a jaunt of about $5^1/2$ to 6 miles, for the round trip.[17]

Shortly after acquiring their land in the Lachine seigneury, François and Barbe began the strenuous tasks of clearing and developing the property and constructing its buildings, while they continued to reside for a time in or near to Montreal. Over the following decades, the results of their efforts in these demanding tasks would be documented in two instances. First, in the census of 1681, the portion of their 51 acre parcel that had been cleared and was under cultivation would be estimated at 12 arpents (10 acres). More than two decades later, in the inventory of their possessions which would be drawn up in 1703, the amount of land in this parcel which was under cultivation would be estimated at 40 arpents (34 acres). The latter document would also record the presence of a house, a stable, a granary, and a separate root cellar.[18]

During the summer of 1674, while François and Barbe were continuing to develop their future home in the Sault St. Louis section of the Lachine seigneury, a tragic accident took place just offshore from the general area of their farm. In the thrashing, foaming waters of the Lachine Rapids, the canoe which was carrying Louis Jolliet, two other Frenchmen, and a young native slave capsized, resulting in major losses. During the previous summer of 1673, Monsieur Jolliet, Fr. Jacques Marquette, and five other Frenchmen had carried out a ground-breaking voyage of exploration. Traveling in two canoes, the party had paddled southward from St. Ignace at the Straits of Mackinac to the foot of Green Bay on Lake Michigan, up the Fox River, down the Wisconsin River, and then down the Mississippi River as far as the mouth of the Arkansas River. On their return voyage northward, they had deviated from their outbound route by paddling up the Illinois, Des Plaines, and Chicago Rivers, to reach Lake Michigan at the future site of Ft. Checagou. By about mid-October, Jolliet and his five colleagues had returned to Sault Ste. Marie, while Fr. Marquette had traveled back to the mission at the foot of Green Bay. Over the course of the following winter, Jolliet had polished both his trip journal and the map illustrating the party's ground-breaking trek; for safety's sake, he had also made an extra copy of these two documents. In the late spring of 1674, after leaving the backup copies of the journal and the map with the Jesuit missionaries at the Sault, he and two of his colleagues, along with a young native slave who had been given to him in the Mississippi Valley, departed in one canoe for the St. Lawrence settlements. Jolliet was eagerly anticipating sharing his newfound knowledge with the administrators of the colony at Quebec. However, he was apparently overly eager. In latter June, when the paddlers reached the Lachine Rapids, rather than hiking over the portage road to Montreal, they decided to make a run down the torrential rapids. In the process, the canoe capsized, and both of Jolliet's French colleagues, as well as the native boy, all drowned. Monsieur Jolliet, the only survivor, was saved "after being four hours in the water." However, the box containing his journal and map from the voyage of exploration, as well as his other personal papers, were lost in the waters of the river. To top off this huge loss of invaluable information, the spare copies of the map and the journal that he had deposited for safekeeping with the priests at the Sault were destroyed when the mission buildings there burned down shortly afterward; in addition, Father Marquette's journal of the Mississippi voyage was not preserved. Thus, the maps which were later prepared to reflect the newly acquired knowledge were based upon Jolliet's memories and Marquette's map.[19]

On July 1, 1675, Barbe and François were elated and proud to bring their brand new baby and first daughter to the Montreal church to celebrate her christening. On this day, the two sponsors of little Barbe were Raphaël Beauvais, Barbe's 21-year-old unmarried brother, and Michelle Picard (the eldest daughter of Hugues Picard dit Lafortune), who would turn age 14 in five days and was still single; both the godfather and the godmother were residents of Montreal.

In the church ledger, the parents of the baby girl were described by the priest as "of this parish," meaning the parish of Montreal. However, this statement is not to be interpreted as evidence that the little Brunet family was still residing in or near to Montreal. It is possible that they had already relocated from the area of the town to their slowly-developing farm in the Lachine seigneury. In fact, if they had moved the eight miles toward the south, they would still have been obliged to travel that distance to Montreal in order to have their child baptized by a priest. The only other churches in the greater Montreal region which had been established by the summer of 1675 included Boucherville (well to the northeast of the town and across the river, begun in 1668), Laprairie (well to the southeast of Montreal and across the river, begun in 1670), and Pointe aux Trembles (near the northeastern tip of Montreal Island, begun in 1674). The church at Montreal would have been much closer and easier for the Brunet family to reach from Lachine than any of these other three churches. Monseigneur Laval would not establish the parish of Lachine until April of 1676, and even at that time he would not announce the appointment of one specific priest to permanently tend this fledgling parish. Such an appointment would be postponed until 1680; during the intervening four years, the Lachine parish would be tended by periodic visits of traveling priests. It is impossible to determine from the surviving evidence whether Barbe, François, and their two babies were still living in or near Montreal in the summer of 1675 (a full 25 months after François had been granted his land in the Sault St. Louis section of the Lachine seigneury), or whether they had already moved southward to their new farm beside the Lachine Rapids. However, by the time their third child would arrive in early September of 1677, there would be no doubt as to the family's permanent location. The baptism records of the Montreal parish would indicate that this newest baby, having been born at Lachine, had been christened at the Montreal church.[20]

On October 9, 1675, Barbe was present in the Montreal church for another significant ecclesiastical ceremony, this time the wedding of her next-younger sister. Some $3^1/2$ years earlier, at the age of $13^2/3$, Marguerite Beauvais had signed a marriage contract, but this nuptial agreement had been later annulled. Now 17 years old, she was taking as her husband Jacques Tétu, who had arrived in the colony a decade earlier as a soldier in the Carignan Regiment. Barbe's presence among the official witnesses listed in the parish register on this cheerful

October day was quite unusual during this era; customarily, only men served in this capacity at this time.[21]

It was during this very period that François Brunet's activities as a voyageur involved in the fur trade were first clearly documented. Some five years earlier, back in October of 1670, he had submitted to the Montreal Court a suit against Mathurin Thibodeau, in order to gain compensation for the gun and the blanket which he had lost in a canoe capsize accident while paddling on the St. Lawrence. However, no specific details of François' actions during that particular incident had been recorded in the notary's settlement document. In contrast, during the period of 1675-1676, the paddling activities of Monsieur Brunet and his voyageur partner Jean Boursier dit Lavigne were very clearly identified. Probably during the autumn of 1675, and definitely during the paddling season of 1676, they hauled freight back and forth on the upper St. Lawrence River between Lachine and Ft. Frontenac, in the employ of René Robert Cavelier, Sieur de La Salle.

Back in 1673, Governor Frontenac and about 400 Frenchmen had traveled up the St. Lawrence to the outlet of Lake Ontario. There, on the northern shore beside the mouth of the Cataraqui River (at the present Kingston, Ontario), they had cleared a plot of land and had constructed two log buildings surrounded by a crude stockade. This facility, the first to be built in the west, was intended to serve as a commercial outlet dealing with the Iroquois populations, in direct competition with English and Dutch traders. However, Minister Colbert back in France had later refused to reimburse the Governor for the expenses which he had incurred in both building and maintaining this fort. In addition, he had refused to approve it as an outlying trade center, wishing instead that the peltries commerce would remain concentrated in the St. Lawrence communities. Two years later, in May of 1675, with Frontenac's considerable support, La Salle had been granted this fortification and the surrounding lands, by Louis XIV; the new owner was to utilize them as his own seigneury. As part of the plan, La Salle would both repay Frontenac's debts and finance the operations of the facility, which he would name Ft. Frontenac in honor of his patron. As generous compensation, both of these men intended to profit handsomely from the commerce that would be conducted at the post, as well as throughout the entire region.

After receiving his grant at the Court and sailing back to the colony, La Salle arrived at Quebec in September of 1675. Shortly thereafter, he hired voyageurs and workmen in the St. Lawrence settlements to haul materiel westward to Ft. Frontenac, rebuild and expand the facility (again building mostly with wood), and actively commence trading in the surrounding region.[22]

In the "Statement of Expenses Incurred by de La Salle," which the new owner apparently drew up at about the end of 1676, one of his expenditures for transporting building materials, equipment, supplies, and trade merchandise westward and peltries eastward was thus described:

"For 4 journeys made to the fort by the men named [Jean Boursier dit] Lavigne and [François Brunet dit] Le Bourbonnais, at the rate of 110 livres for each trip [for the two men together] to carry there from Montreal the required stores .... 440 livres."

Another ten voyageurs were also hired to make this same journey, but only twice instead of four times, at the same wage of 55 livres per paddler per trip:

"For two journeys made by the men named Violette de Lyon, Charles Diels, Picard, Pigoret, La Rivière de Tours, Charles Ptolomée, Jean Brossard, Nicolas Bonhomme, Nicolas Gaigner, Laforge...at the rate of 55 livres [per man] for each journey .... 1,100 livres."

Besides paying these twelve men to make a number of round-trip journeys between Lachine and Ft. Frontenac, La Salle also hired ten voyageurs on one occasion to haul freight by canoe up the St. Lawrence from Quebec to Montreal, utilizing some of the same above-mentioned paddlers:

"For the journey of the men named St. Croix, La Rivière de Tours, Jean Brossard, Nicolas Bonhomme, La Douceur, La Verdure, La Fleur, Charpentier, Bon Jacques, and Chambly from Quebec to Montreal, to carry there the food supplies which are required at the fort, at the rate of 20 livres each .... 200 livres."

(One of these lattermost paddlers, who was listed simply as "La Douceur," was Vivien Magdelaine dit Ladouceur, a fellow resident of the Lachine seigneury along with the voyageur partners Brunet and Boursier; he is also a direct ancestor of the present author. About 34 to 40 years old in 1675, Vivien had been granted his long lot at the extreme eastern end of the Sault St. Louis section of the seigneury in 1671, and he had been married at the church in Montreal in November of the following year. After the safe arrival of their first child in October of 1673, the couple had lost their second son at Lachine on March 17, 1676, at the age of nine days. By the spring or early summer of 1681, when the colony-wide census would be enumerated, Vivien, his wife Marie Godin dite Châtillon, and their three surviving children would be listed on their Lachine farm, which was located about $1^1/2$ miles northeast of the Brunet property.)[23]

For the voyageurs who were working for La Salle during his initial development of Ft. Frontenac, their activities apparently took place during the autumn of 1675 and the spring, summer, and autumn of 1676. Various of the other men who served in his employ at the fort during this period, and were thus recorded on his list of expenditures, worked for the commandant for a year or less. For example, those who were hired for a full year included two carpenters, one joiner or interior woodworker, two blacksmiths, and one cooper; those whose term of employment was shorter than a year included three masons, who each served at the fort for just $3^1/2$ months. Thus La Salle's "Statement of Expenses" seems to date to the latter months of 1676, since he had commenced his development of the trading facility in September of 1675.

The canoes which were utilized by the voyageurs to haul freight to and from Ft. Frontenac during this particular period were bought by La Salle in the St. Lawrence settlements on several different occasions, as was noted in his expense account. The following entries were the four specific notations that he made concerning these watercraft:

"Paid to Monsieur [Charles] Bazire [a very prominent Quebec merchant]...for supplies, clothing, and canoes which were furnished to carry provisions necessary for the maintenance of the said fort .... 6,300 livres
Paid to Brother [Charles] Boquet [Quebec-based *donné*, guide, and interpreter for the Jesuits] for 3 canoes .... 135 livres
For 3 canoes purchased from the Hurons [near Quebec]....... 48 livres
For one canoe purchased from Monsieur [Joseph Godefroy, Sieur de] Vieuxpont [a Trois-Rivières peltries merchant]................. __ livres"[24]

The canoes that were used by the French during this era of the fur trade were usually manned by crews of either two or three paddlers.[25] The expense account entry concerning François Brunet and Jean Boursier recorded them as an independent two-man team; these partners were each paid 55 livres per round trip from Lachine to the fort and back again. Since the other ten paddlers enumerated in the expense account each received the same wage of 55 livres per trip, it is highly likely that they, too, were employed by La Salle in two-man crews. However, since they were all listed in a single group, it is not possible to determine just how these ten individuals were paired together for carrying out their journeys.

Eight years later, in 1684, La Salle discussed various aspects of the work of the voyageurs who were then handling the transportation for his Ft. Frontenac operations:

"The [paired] canoe men now get [as a team] eight francs [livres] per hundredweight [of cargo hauled] in place of twelve [livres], the price which was paid before the barques were constructed. Two men carry, on each voyage, twelve or thirteen hundredweight, and ordinarily take twelve to fifteen days in going up [against the current] and four or five [days] in coming down [with both the current and the prevailing westerly winds]. Thus, they can make ten or twelve voyages [per paddling season], and, consequently, transport from twelve to thirteen thousand weight from the opening of navigation in the month of April until the end of November, when it is closed by the ice at Montreal. When they are returning, they are obliged to bring back as much peltry as the canoes can hold without [additional] payment, so that the return voyage does not increase the expense."[26]

This document supports the assertion that the majority of the canoes which were utilized on these Ft. Frontenac runs were handled by only two men. The decrease in the wages of these latter paddlers, following the slightly better-paid voyages that Messieurs Brunet and Boursier and their colleagues had made back in 1675-1676, was related to the construction at the fort of four *barques*, relatively small ships that were propelled by sails. The first of these wooden vessels had been built at the post in 1674, while the latter three had been constructed after the commandant's arrival in the late autumn of 1675. Costs related to the initial one were mentioned in La Salle's 1676 "Statement of Expenses," along with the information that this particular vessel was sometimes utilized in making trips along the uppermost portion of the route between the fort and Montreal: "[Paid] To Sieur [Jean] Gitton [a prominent Quebec merchant] for the rigging and equipment for the *barque* [named *Frontenac*] which was built to facilitate communication with Montreal and to hold the Iroquois in check .... 1,700 livres."[27]

Apparently, the *barques* were sometimes sailed eastward from the fort for about eighty miles, on St. Lawrence waters that lacked rapids, to a place where they met and took on the cargo of westbound voyageurs traveling in canoes from Lachine. These trips by the *barques* had shortened the distance that was covered by the paddlers, which in turn had enabled La Salle to negotiate a decrease in the canoe handlers' wages. As a result, the new pay scale encouraged the two-man voyageur teams to transport more cargo on each journey, since they were now paid per hundred pounds of weight hauled. Formerly, François Brunet and his single colleague Monsieur Boursier had together earned 110 livres per round-trip run (covering the entire distance between Lachine and Ft. Frontenac). Eight years later, if a pair of paddlers hauled 1200 pounds of cargo, they would together garner 96 livres; if they could manage 1300 pounds, their combined take would increase to 104 livres. In comparison, during this same period, voyageurs making a round-trip journey to the Straits of Mackinac and back during a single summer season could each earn 100 livres in salary, along with permission to trade another 100 livres worth of merchandise for their own considerable profit.[28]

La Salle's assertion that a pair of voyageurs could carry out ten or twelve round-trip journeys to Ft. Frontenac in a seven-month paddling season was an exaggeration. According to his own information, an average round trip required three weeks to complete. Thus, it would have been technically possible to carry out about ten trips during the period between the spring thaw and the fall freeze, between April and November. However, such an intensely grueling schedule, with virtually no rest days during the entire period, would not have been sensible for any paddlers who intended to sustain long-term careers. Allowing for a few days of rest between voyages, during which the men would recuperate in the St. Lawrence settlements, would have created a time frame of nearly one month per trip. This would have allowed a maximum of about seven or eight journeys during the unfrozen months, at the most. However, the work schedule of the Brunet-Boursier team, completing four-round trip journeys over the course of one paddling season, may have been more typical. Even the voyageurs who made round trips to the distant west during a single summer, laboring over the span of six months, usually had a short period of lighter duty at their destination point in the interior, before they commenced their grueling return leg of the trip.

The commandant's writings of 1684 pointed out the slightly different seasonal schedule that was utilized by voyageurs making runs on the upper St. Lawrence River between Lachine and Ft. Frontenac, compared to those men who traveled to and from the distant interior via the Ottawa River. For the paddlers on the more southerly route along the St. Lawrence, their work season could commence several weeks earlier in the spring (in April rather than

May), and it could safely extend several weeks later into the fall (into November instead of October). This difference in scheduling was due to the differences in the timing of the seasonal changes in the two areas. On the upper St. Lawrence River and Lakes Ontario and Erie, the ice broke up and cleared considerably earlier in the spring, and solid ice reformed several weeks later in the autumn, compared to the departure and arrival times of the ice on the more northerly waterways, including the Ottawa River. Nevertheless, on the more southerly route, safety was a major concern during the month of November, when freezing weather could suddenly descend upon the paddlers.

In 1684, La Salle described a number of the articles which were traded at Ft. Frontenac, along with their prices of exchange. In the process, he enumerated some of the merchandise that the Brunet-Boursier team had hauled in to the fort:

1 pair of stockings	2 beaver pelts
1 white shirt	$1^1/4$ beavers
1 yard of woolen stroud fabric	2 beavers
1 yard of woolen Iroquoise fabric	2 beavers
1 yard of blue woolen serge fabric from Poitou	$1^1/2$ beavers
1 pound of large glass beads	2 beavers
3 trade axes	$1^1/8$ beavers
1 gun	6 beavers
2 pounds of gunpowder	1 beaver
4 pounds of balls or bulk lead	1 beaver
1 pound weight of small kettles	1 beaver
$1/2$ pound of tobacco	1 beaver
1 *pot* [1.64 English quarts] of brandy	4 beavers
1 *pot* of wine	$1/2$ beaver

According to La Salle's comments following this list, smaller articles which were traded at the fort, including clasp knives, fire steels, vermilion paint pigment, and large mirrors made of tin plate, were proportionately higher in price markup than the above items; however, he did not indicate their specific trading prices.[29]

Each of the round-trip journeys that François Brunet and Jean Boursier made between the terminus of the Montreal portage road, close to their respective homes at Lachine, and their destination of Ft. Frontenac covered, in each direction, the entire length of the upper St. Lawrence River. The one-way distance of this trip, from the men's home seigneury beside the Lachine Rapids to the outlet of Lake Ontario, encompassed about 210 miles of waterway. Over the course of this distance, the elevation of the river rose 173 feet. Along the route, traveling in a generally southwesterly direction at all times during the westbound leg, the paddlers encountered six major obstacles. The first one, about twenty miles southwest of Lachine, was called Les Cascades; here, they portaged their canoe and cargo for $1/3$ mile. It was actually possible to line up this rapids, but at its head was the Cataracte de Trou (Waterfall of the Hole), which did required a portage. Thus, it seemed easier to cover the entire distance in a single carry, rather than lining up the rapids and then unloading, portaging, and reloading at the Cataracte. Twelve miles further upriver came two more falls in quick succession, first the Sault des Cèdres (Cedar Falls) and then the Sault du Buisson (Falls of the Bush). Each of these obstacles required a portage of about 500 paces. Now came the broadened section of the river that was dubbed Lac St. François; it was 38 miles long and often as much as three miles wide. Just above its head, the voyageurs reached the obstacle that was termed the Long Sault (Long Falls), which was divided by two midstream islands into a side-by-side line of three rapids. On the westbound trip, the men portaged both the canoe and the cargo here, for $3/4$ mile along the north bank; or instead, they carried only the cargo, and lined the empty craft up the north channel. On their eastbound return trip, if the water level was sufficient, they usually ran down this rapids using its south channel. After managing the Long Sault, the partners paddled some forty miles upriver to the next obstruction, which was named Rapide Plat (Shallow Rapids). When the water level was adequate, it was possible for them to line and pole the loaded canoe up this section. About twenty miles further, Les Galops (The Gallops) provide their sixth and final major obstruction along the route. This stretch of the river could be lined up in all water levels. After this, the final eighty miles of the river offered no obstructions. Thus, at Anse aux Perches (Setting Poles Bay), the men happily threw into the woods their long poles, which they had earlier needed to work their way up the various shallows and rapids. In the lattermost forty miles of the ever-widening river, they encountered only a gentle current and a huge maze of islands, which was termed Mille Îles (Thousand Islands). This section finally led the voyageurs to their destination, the fort on the north shore of Lake Ontario near its outlet.[30]

In about 1709-1710, Antoine Raudot, the Intendant of New France, described in one of his letters this same water route. In his account, he presented the various obstructions as they were encountered during the eastbound downstream passage from Ft. Frontenac out to Lachine, traveling with both the current and the prevailing westerly winds:

"One sails easily for thirty leagues on this great river, which is at least a league in width and has no discernible current. About four leagues from this fort and for a distance of twelve leagues, it is dotted with so many islands that it is called the Thousand Islands. Among these is Toniata, with abundant eel fishing from spring until autumn; it is from here that come all of the eels that are caught in this colony. Ships can sail from Niagara Falls [near the western end of Lake Ontario] to [the community of] La Galette, a distance of thirty leagues [on the upper St. Lawrence], to where the rapids begin.

The Galots [sic, instead of Galops] are really two rapids, one right after the other. At five leagues from Galots is the Shallow Rapids. It is a great current of water, separated into two channels by an island that is a half-league in length. Six leagues lower is the Long Sault, three-quarters of a league in length. There are three channels with a strong current of water and some waterfalls. From the lower part of the Long Sault to Lac St. François, a distance of six leagues, the country is the most beautiful that one can see along both sides of the river. Two leagues below here, we find Les Cèdres, where there is another rapids that is joined to one called Cotteau [at the present Cotteau Landing]. There are some cascading waters falling one upon the other and about a league long. One league from this rapids there are three more, one after the other. The first is called Du Buisson, a falls that leads by degrees into another named Le Trou, and finally this one leads into the third, called Les Cascades. Here the rapids end, and one enters into Lac St. Louis, about five or six leagues long. This lake receives the waters from the great Ottawa River on the north side and all of the waters from the [St. Lawrence] rapids that I have described."[31]

The two paddling partners who together faced and overcame the challenges along this route on numerous voyages, François Brunet dit Le Bourbonnais and Jean Boursier dit Lavigne, had personal lives that were in many respects very similar and parallel, and were also highly interconnected. Both men had emigrated from the mother country to become settlers at Montreal. During the paddling season of 1676, while working in the employ of La Salle, François was about 31 or 32 years old, while Jean was about 32 years of age. François had married Barbe Beauvais at the Montreal church on July 11, 1672; Jean had celebrated his wedding there with Marie Marthe Thibodeau nine months later, on April 9, 1673 (his bride was the twelve-year-old girl whom François had promised to marry three years earlier). Three days before the latter wedding, Jean had stood as the godfather at the baptism of François and Barbe's first child, and he had bequeathed to the baby his own given name. By July of 1676, François was the father of two children, who were 39 and 12 months old; at that same time, Jean's two children were 24 and 7 months of age. Monsieur Brunet had been granted his long, slender lot fronting on the St. Lawrence in the seigneury of Lachine in 1673, while Monsieur Boursier received his own lot there in 1676; the two plots were separated only by the property of Pierre Cardinal, which was just 575 feet wide.[32]

These two men were not only close friends and close neighbors. At some point, they had also decided to join forces to create a professional voyageur duo, working together as a closely-knit unit in an occupation that regularly defied injury and death. After completing the four journeys to and from Ft. Frontenac that were documented in La Salle's 1676 expense account, it is quite likely that they continued to make these moderately profitable runs as a two-man team. Eventually, they may have decided against continuing this particular job when the wages that were paid for these trips were reduced, as La Salle noted in his report of 1684. However, there is no surviving documentation concerning their ongoing career as a voyageur team from the end of the 1676 season until they would travel to the Ottawa Country during 1685-1686 and again in 1686-1687. Then, in partnership with four other voyageur-traders, they would labor in the Illinois Country during 1688-1689. During the course of the latter three ventures, they would be working as wintering voyageur-traders; thus, they would earn much more money than they had garnered for their trips as voyageurs paddling on the upper St. Lawrence.

It is important to acknowledge that, during the seven paddling seasons between 1678 and 1684, instead of making runs for La Salle on the upper St. Lawrence River, there is a distinct possibility that François and Jean conducted illegal trading voyages to the distant interior, without official permission. During this period, hundreds of men from the St. Lawrence communities were doing this very thing. Back in 1672, Jean Baptiste Patoulet, a deputy of the Intendant Jean Talon, had noted that an estimated 300 to 400 residents of the colony were trading in the interior without the legal approval of the authorities.[33] Seven years later, the Intendant Duchesneau complained bitterly in a 1679 letter to the Court about what he perceived as an out-of-control situation:

"I refer to what relates to the disobedience of the coureurs de bois [unlicensed traders in the interior]...It has at last reached such a point that everyone boldly contravenes the King's interdictions. There is no longer any concealment; even parties are gathered with astonishing insolence to go and trade in the native country.

I have done all that is in my power to prevent this misfortune, which may lead to the ruin of the colony. I have enacted ordinances against the coureurs de bois; against the merchants who furnish them with goods; against the gentlemen and others who harbor them; and even against those who have any knowledge of them and will not inform the justices nearest to the spot. All of that has been in vain, inasmuch as several of the most considerable families in this country are interested therein, so that the Governor lets them go on, and even shares in their profits...

The coureurs de bois do not only act openly, they [also] carry their peltries to the English [at Albany], and endeavor to direct the native trade there... The natives complained to the Governor, in the council which was held at Montreal, that the French were in too great numbers at the trading posts [in the interior]; he [the Governor] curtly rebuffed them...There is an almost general disobedience throughout this country. The number of those in the woods is estimated at nearly five or six hundred, exclusive of those who set out every day...

In 1676, His Majesty interdicted the Governor from giving licenses to trade in the interior and in the native country...Meanwhile, the Governor, in order to elude the prohibitions which had been laid down in the King's ordinance, and yet not to appear in contravention of them, issued licenses to hunt, which served as pretext to nullify those orders. His Majesty, as was just, again remedied this by his last ordinance [of 1678]."[34]

Again in the following year of 1680, Duchesneau fumed about the situation to his superiors across the ocean:

"There is not a family of any condition and quality whatsoever [in the St. Lawrence settlements] that has not children, brothers, uncles, and nephews among them...There are eight hundred persons or more in the bush, whatever may be stated to the contrary. I have not been able to obtain the precise number, inasmuch as all those who are involved with them conceal it."[35]

It is clear that François Brunet and Jean Boursier did not paddle off to the distant interior preceding the winter of 1676-1677, since François impregnated Barbe at about the beginning of December, and Jean impregnated his wife less than four months later. During the first week of September in 1677, little Marie Jeanne Brunet was born on the family's farm in the Lachine seigneury. On the fifth day of that month, they traveled the eight-mile distance to the Montreal church for her baptism, at which François Xavier Prudhomme, a Montreal resident with two tiny boys of his own, served as the godfather. Standing beside him as the godmother and the grantor of the baby's name was Jeanne Descaries, the twelve-year-old unmarried daughter of the Montreal charcoal burner Jean Descaries dit Le Houx. Interestingly, the entry for this ceremony in the Montreal church register was signed by both "Guyotte, priest of Lachine" and "Gilles Perot, priest of this parish." This indicates that Étienne Guyotte, a Sulpician who had arrived from the mother country exactly two years before, was at this time the cleric who was periodically tending to the flock at the Lachine church, which would not have its own resident priest until 1680.[36]

This particular church document, from September 5 of 1677, provides the earliest surviving evidence that François, Barbe, and their young children had by this point permanently relocated from Montreal southward to the Lachine seigneury. François had been granted his property here $4^1/3$ years earlier, back in May of 1673. For the rest of his life, except for the stints while he would be absent on long voyages into the interior, and during a particularly sad period between late 1689 and 1694, François would reside here on the family farm beside the Lachine Rapids, in the Sault St. Louis area of the seigneury.

About $3^1/2$ months after Marie Jeanne's christening, two days after Christmas in 1677, the little Brunet family again made the long trip to town, for a similar ecclesiastical ceremony in the same church. On December 27, Barbe appeared as the godmother of the newborn Barbe Boursier, the second daughter and third child of their close-by neighbors, Jean Boursier dit Lavigne (François' paddling partner) and his wife Marie Marthe Thibodeau. Joining Barbe as the co-sponsor on this occasion was Alexis Buet, a Lachine tailor who would marry in the Lachine church in just a few weeks.[37]

The next time that Barbe Beauvais gave birth, on April 29, 1680, the number of members of her family increased not by just one but by two at the same time. The arrival of twin girls was heralded at their respective baptisms on the following day, in the Holy Angels Church at Lachine, which was located about $2^3/4$ miles west of the Brunet farm. Tiny Catherine was sponsored by Jean Baptiste Jarry, an unmarried Montreal resident who was 25 years old, and Catherine Cuillerier, age 7^1/2, the daughter of René Cuillerier of Montreal and Lachine.[38] On the same day, twin sister Anne's godfather was the same Jean Baptiste Jarry, while her godmother was Jeanne Richecourt dite Malteau, the former widow of Jean Foucher and the present wife of Jean Roy dit Lapensée.[39]

About a year later, the colony-wide census of 1681 was conducted, during the spring or early summer months. The enumerator recorded the following family at the Lachine seigneury in household 217:

"François Brunet, age 37, married

Barbe Beauvais, 24, married

Jean, 8

Barbe, 6

Jeanne, 4

Catherine, 1

Anne, 1

12 arpents [10 acres] of land cleared and under cultivation

7 horned cattle

1 gun"[40]

In each instance, the listed age of the two parents and their five offspring was either accurate or quite close to being correct. According to their baptismal records, Barbe would turn age 25 in latter August of this year of 1681, while Jean had turned 8 at the beginning of April. Barbe would turn 6 at the beginning of June, and Marie Jeanne would celebrate her fourth birthday in the first week of September. Finally, the twin girls had turned 1 on April 29 of this year.

To fill out the details of the Brunet family at this time, living on their farm beside the St. Lawrence River, one can turn to the following information which was recorded 22 years later:

"One house situated on the land of the said place of Lachine, measuring forty-five feet in length by twenty feet in width, solidly built in pièce-sur-pièce style [with widely-spaced vertical framing elements and horizontal infill logs], consisting of two large rooms with two hearths and chimneys of stone, plus two side rooms [sleeping and storage rooms], all on the ground floor, and a large attic, entirely roofed with boards, the doors framed and the windows of its doors containing fixed wooden frames.

One granary built in pièce-sur-pièce style, measuring fifty feet in length by twenty-five feet in width, without additional roof covering [besides the chinked logs].

[One stable.]

One root cellar [a separate subterranean structure]."[41]

Immediately to the east of the Brunet family, in household 218, the census-taker recorded the family of Léonard Girardin, living on the single farm that separated the Brunet property from the Boursier property. With Monsieur Girardin (age 36) was listed his wife Charlotte Jolivet (33) and their children Anne (8), Hilaire (6), Charles (4), and Catherine (2). (This couple and their youngest child Catherine are also direct ancestors of the present author.)

At this time, in the eastern and central five miles of the Lachine seigneury, from the Verdun boundary on the east to a half-mile west of the village site, the settlers numbered about 115 to 125. By this point, they had cleared and planted about 400 arpents (340 acres) of land, and they owned a total of 85 horned cattle.[42] On the entire Montreal Island, the population consisted of 778 males and 610 females, bringing the total number of residents to 1,388 persons. This number represented just 14 percent of the 9,742 people who were living in the various communities of the colony at this time. These numerous individuals were spread out along both sides of the St. Lawrence River in a swath more than two hundred miles long, which extended northeastward from the area of Lachine all the way to Cap Tourmente, at the eastern end of the Côte de Beaupré. The greatest portion of this population was concentrated in the three regions of Montreal, Trois-Rivières, and Quebec. Besides these residents, a small number of people resided at Tadoussac, some ninety miles beyond Cap Tourmente toward the northeast. Two years earlier, providing further details about the colony, the Intendant had reported to the Court that, in addition to some 9,400 French residents who owned 2,000 firearms (1,840 guns and 159 pistols), New France also contained 21,900 arpents (25,765 acres) of land which was cleared and under cultivation. In addition, the residents owned a total of 6,983 horned cattle, 719 sheep, 145 horses, 33 goats, and 12 donkeys.[43]

On January 6, 1682, Barbe stood beside the baptismal font in the Lachine church, as the godmother of the two-day-old boy who had been born on the next-door farm, immediately west of the Brunet family's property. The fourth child of Vincent Chamaillard (a maker of wooden shoes) and Catherine Renusson, little Vincent was named by his godfather, Vincent Dugas, who was a domestic servant in the service of François Marie Perrot, the Governor of Montreal. In the record of this day's activities, the godmother was listed as "Barbe Beauvais of this parish, wife of François Brunet of this parish." This information was penned into the ledger by Fr. Rémy, who had been appointed as the first resident priest of the Holy Angels Parish back in 1680. By good fortune, none of the well-wishers at this encouraging baptismal ceremony could foresee that Vincent would die of smallpox just three weeks after his 21st birthday, in January of 1703.[44]

At the time of the Chamaillard christening, Barbe was about halfway through her sixth pregnancy. Some $4^1/2$ months later, on May 26, 1682, she gave birth to their second son, Jean François. Two days later, he was baptized by Fr. Rémy at the Lachine church, with two fellow residents of the Lachine seigneury as his sponsors. These were Jean Cardinal, about age 24 and still single, and Marie Roy, the wife of André Merlot dit Laramée. (Jean François would grow up to marry Françoise David, and thus provide the direct ancestral linkage between Barbe and François and the present author.)[45]

In the following year of 1683, the church leaders in the colony created a master list which was entitled "Account of the Parish Priests and Missions, Which Has Been Drawn Up This Year in Canada." This document sheds considerable light on how the population had been gradually spreading out beyond the bounds of the main towns, during this period of peace with the Iroquois nations. Within the greater Montreal region, the roster included six separate groupings of settlements, churches, and missions:

"The town of Montreal, of which the parish extends one and one-half leagues along the coast toward the southwest and a little more along the coast toward the north, and is joined with the Seminary of Saint Sulpice; there are 641 souls.

Lachine, at the [southeastern] end of the Island, which extends three leagues along the coast toward the southwest and one league along the coast toward the north[east]; there are 314 souls.

La Pointe aux Trembles, at the [northern] foot of the Island, to which is joined the Island of Ste. Thérèse at a distance of a half-league, which extends along the coast toward the southwest one league and toward the north two short leagues; including the said Island of Ste. Thérèse, there are 427 souls.

La Prairie de la Madeleine and the Côte St. Lambert [on the mainland immediately to the east of Montreal Island], which extends for two and one-half leagues, to which is joined Chambly, called Fort St. Louis, at an overland distance of four leagues [to the east]; there are 304 souls.

Boucherville, to which are joined the seigneuries of Tremblay and of Longueuil, about two leagues distant [toward the south]; there are 200 souls at Boucherville, 30 at Tremblay, and 90 at Longueuil. Likewise is joined Cap Varennes, one league distant [north] from the said Boucherville in descending the river; there are 55 souls. The seigneury of Petit Moine, which is very near, contains 12 souls, and Cap St. Michel, which is two leagues from Boucherville, contains 16 souls. In total [within this particular grouping of settlements], 403 souls.

Repentigny [on the western shore of the St. Lawrence, north of Montreal Island], where there are 118 souls, to which is joined the seigneury of Tilly, distant one league, where there are 70 souls; Jesus Island is likewise distant one league along the coast toward the southwest, where there are 30 souls. The Côte de St. Sulpice is distant two leagues along the coast toward the north, where there are 12 souls. In total [within this particular grouping of settlements], 230 souls."[46]

According to this list, a grand total of 2,319 people resided in the greater Montreal region at this time. Since the 1681 census had recorded 1,388 individuals living on Montreal Island itself, this roster showed that an additional 930 people resided in the outlying areas which extended beyond the Island.

By this point, settlement along the southern shoreline of Montreal Island had extended westward for about six or seven miles from the southeastern corner of the island. Thus, the single parish which was tended by Fr. Rémy from his base at the Lachine church stretched over a total of about nine miles, extending westward from Verdun to La Présentation, at the present community of Dorval.[47] This span measured considerably less than the generalized distance of four leagues that was expressed in the parishes roster of 1683. Over the next few years, colonists would settle upon lands further to the west along this southern shoreline, including the area of Pointe Claire and the area of Bout de l'Île, the area at and near the western tip of the island. In fact, the church register of the lattermost place would commence just three years later, in 1686.[48]

In 1683 and 1684, Barbe became related through marriage to two members of the Turpin family, of which the Montreal trader-outfitter-investor Alexandre Turpin was the patriarch (his biography has already been presented in this work). First, on May 24, 1683, Barbe's brother Raphaël (who was 22 months older than Barbe) married Élisabeth Turpin, Alexandre's daughter. Seventeen months later, on October 30, 1684, Barbe's sister Charlotte (who at age 17$^{1}/_{3}$ was nearly eleven years younger than Barbe) joined in matrimony with Alexandre himself, who was 42 or 43 years old.[49]

In addition to his other occupations, Alex Turpin also operated as a private *financier*. His records indicated that both François Brunet and his paddling partner Jean Boursier had either borrowed cash from him or had made purchases at his Montreal store on credit. On March 30, 1684, Alex drew up a roster of all those individuals who owed him money at that point. His list included these two entries, representing minute unpaid balances:

"By [François Brunet dit Le] Bourbonnais, son-in-law of Monsieur [Jacques Beauvais dit] Saint Gemme ....18 sols [8/10 *livre*] By [Jean Boursier dit] Lavigne, son-in-law of [Mathurin] Thibodeau .... 2 *livres* 1 sol 10 *deniers*"⁵⁰

By the time Barbe attended the second Turpin-Beauvais nuptial ceremony in Montreal in the autumn of 1684, she was nearly six months pregnant. On February 17, 1685, she and François were pleased to welcome their seventh child into the world. At little Élisabeth's christening on the following day at the Lachine church, her godfather was recorded as Étienne Renaud, a joiner (probably Antoine Renaud, who would marry at Lachine in November of 1687). The godmother on this occasion was Élisabeth Turpin, the baby's aunt, who had married Barbe's brother Raphaël back in 1683 and lived in Montreal.⁵¹

It is interesting to note that, in the church ledger on this February day, Fr. Rémy identified the father of the baby, François Brunet, as a *laboureur*, a farm worker. Indeed, François had received his grant of land at Lachine in May of 1673, and he and his family members had cleared and developed the farm and then had moved onto it. However, he had been clearly documented as a voyageur working for La Salle during 1675-1676, and he most likely had continued to be employed in this occupation, at least intermittently, during the period from 1677 through 1684. But his participation in the peltries commerce during these latter years may have been unlicensed, and thus not written into public records. Three months after the baptismal ceremony of his newest daughter in 1685, François would sign a contract to work in the western interior as a legal fur trade employee. His career is a typical example of the mixing of multiple occupations that was so usual in New France. It was exceedingly common for an individual to combine farming with at least one other occupation that would provide cash income, including working in various capacities in the fur trade business, in operations that were sometimes legal and at other times illicit.

On May 24, 1685, François made the eight-mile trip from his farm northward to Montreal, in order to officially approve the following contract, by which he would work in the distant west as a voyageur-trader: "Before Hilaire Bourgine, notary of the Island of Montreal, and the undersigned witnesses was present in person François Brunet, son of Antoine Brunet, habitant of this island, at present in this city, who, of his own free will and voluntarily, has bound and engaged himself and has promised to well and faithfully serve Michel Messier, Sieur de Saint Michel, residing at present in this said city, who has specified and accepted him for the voyage of about eighteen months which he is going to make to the Ottawa Country. During this period, [Brunet] will do all that the Sieur de Saint Michel commands or will command of him which seems honest and lawful. In consideration of which, the said Sieur promises and obliges himself to give and pay to the said Brunet, upon his return from the said voyage, the sum of three hundred livres for wages, and he has permission to trade, for his own profit, his gun and his blanket. The beaver pelts derived therefrom will be brought down with those of the Sieur, without any deductions from his wages. Thus, everything having been willfully specified and agreed upon by the said parties, who have the intention of being obligated to mortgage all of their possessions, present and future, they have promised, waived, and obligated themselves.*

[This agreement] made and drawn up at Villemarie in the office of the notary, in the afternoon of the twenty-fourth day of May, 1685, in the presence of François Pougnets and Claude Tardy, merchants of the said place, as witnesses, as required, who have signed with the said Saint Michel and the notary. The said Brunet has declared that he does not know how to write or sign, having been questioned according to the ordinance.

Signed,

C. Tardy, F. Pougnets, Michel Messier, and Bourgine"[52]

This document represents one of the very earliest known records of the hiring of a legal voyageur-trader after the new licensing system had been initiated. During the latter 1660s and throughout the 1670s, the number of traders working in the interior without permission had absolutely burgeoned. By 1680, Intendant Duchesneau had estimated that "There are eight hundred persons or more in the bush, whatever may be stated to the contrary." From the administrators' point of view, something had to be done to change this situation, in which the laws were being so flagrantly disobeyed. Thus, in May of 1681, following the suggestions of the Intendant, the King's Minister had issued a decree which established a system of legal trading licenses or *congés*. In addition, the ordinance had granted a general amnesty to all of the illicit traders who would come out from the interior regions. As a result, instead of the former ban on traders operating in the west, the Governor or Intendant of the colony could now issue up to 25 official licenses each year. These were to be distributed at the price of 600 livres apiece, or they were to be given at no charge to deserving widows, orphans, charities, or churches, in order to finance charitable works. Some were also to be granted, at no cost, to individuals who needed to generate capital in order to initiate some worthy private enterprise. No recipient could receive a license two years in a row. The recipients were not required to utilize the trading license themselves. They could hire voyageur-traders to carry out the work for them, or they could instead sell the *congé* outright (such sales often generated considerably more cash than the official fee of 600 livres, with the price often reaching 1,000 to 1,200 livres or more). Each license authorized the departure of a single canoe, staffed by a crew of three men and loaded with equipment, provisions, supplies, and merchandise. In addition to the 25 licenses, the administrators could also issue an unspecified number of free permits, to worthy traders who had performed some special service for the government. After this system had been officially declared by the Crown, Governor Frontenac had decided to postpone its implementation until the following year, to 1682.[53]

After the establishment of this program of legal licenses and permits, the term *voyageur* or traveler had come into common usage. It was applied to differentiate those individuals who had received official permission to trade in the interior from the *coureurs de bois* or illicit traders, who would continue to operate outside of the legal system during the entire French era. However, during the eighteenth century, the term *voyageur* would come to apply to all canoemen who were hired by a licensed employer.

The new system of licenses had been designed to drastically reduce the number of traders who were operating in the interior. The 25 official licenses were intended to involve only 75 voyageur-traders each year; the pool of such individuals in the interior was to be rotated annually. However, no limit had been placed upon the number of special trading permits which could be issued. This omission from the ordinance led to considerable abuses. In addition, few of the *coureurs de bois* ultimately heeded the amnesty announcement of 1681. Instead, they continued to carry out their clandestine operations beyond the reach of the law, defying the threatened confiscation of their merchandise and canoes and the penalty of being sentenced to serve as rowers on the King's galleys in the Mediterranean. In spite of these threatened punishments, the new license system would ultimately do very little to reduce the number of participants in the interior trade, or diminish the amounts of merchandise flowing in and peltries flowing out.

In order to handle the outgoing eastbound cargo of furs and hides, which were generally bulkier than the incoming westbound merchandise had been, the down-bound journey toward the east often required additional canoes and sometimes extra paddlers, both coming from interior sources. During the era of the 1670s-1690s, six voyageur-traders typically paddled two canoes loaded with merchandise into the interior, with three men per craft. After trading their goods and acquiring another canoe, they then would come out with three canoes of peltries, with two paddlers in each craft. As an alternative, traders sometimes hired native paddlers and their canoes in the interior, in order to transport out the excess amount of furs and hides which would not fit into the canoes of the Frenchmen.[54]

A survey of the voyageur hiring contracts which were recorded with Montreal notaries during this period reflects the considerable increase in the number of legal traders who traveled to the western interior after the license system was implemented. The following is a summary by the present author of the men who were hired each year, and the destinations which were recorded in their contracts, based upon the documents which have been located in notarial records. This partial survey covers the first twelve years between 1682, when the license system was first instituted, and 1693. It is important to note that many hiring contracts were arranged privately, and were thus not recorded with a notary. In addition, considerable numbers of other contracts were recorded with notaries in Quebec and Trois-Rivières, while a great many voyageurs were not officially licensed and recorded at all; instead, they operated as illegal *coureurs de bois*. However, the contracts that were recorded in the offices of the Montreal notaries are informative and of considerable significance.[55]

1682: 1 man to the Ottawa Country (in each instance, this denotes based at St. Ignace) has been located.

1683: 2 men to the Ottawa Country have been located.

1684: 1 man to the Ottawa Country has been located.

1685: 13 men to the Ottawa Country, 1 man to Sault Ste. Marie.

1686: 1 man to the Ottawa Country, 6 men with Henri de Tonty to the Illinois and Mississippi River region.

<u>1687</u>: 1 man to the Ottawa Country.

<u>1688</u>: 49 men to the Ottawa Country, 1 man to Green Bay, 3 men to the Mascoutens and Dakotas with Nicolas Perrot, 8 men to Illinois or Ft. St. Louis (on the Illinois River).

<u>1689</u>: 3 men to the Ottawa Country, 8 men to Ft. St. Louis.

<u>1690</u>: 13 men to the Ottawa Country, 4 men to Michilimackinac (St. Ignace), 10 men to Illinois.

<u>1691</u>: 9 men to the Ottawa Country, 11 men to Illinois.

<u>1692</u>: 28 men to the Ottawa Country, 2 men to Michilimackinac (St. Ignace).

<u>1693</u>: 27 men to the Ottawa Country, 2 men to Michilimackinac (St. Ignace), 7 men to Illinois.

In this extensive survey of voyageur hiring contracts in the notary records of Montreal, only four have been found which predate 1685, the year in which François Brunet dit Le Bourbonnais was engaged by Michel Messier. Interestingly, one of those previous four men was Barbe Beauvais' younger brother Jean Baptiste, who had been hired by Pierre Chesne dit Saint Onge and Laurent Benoît on April 8, 1683; at the time, Monsieur Beauvais had been 20 1/2 years old.[56]

Between March 25 and May 24, 1685, a total of ten men were engaged individually to make voyages to the west. One of them was to travel to Sault Ste. Marie, while the other nine would work in the Ottawa Country, which was the term of the French denoting the entire region surrounding Lakes Huron, Michigan, and Superior. (On Franquelin's 1688 *Map of North America*, portraying all of the territory that was known to the French at the time, the cartographer applied the huge label "Nations sous le nom d'Outaouacs" across the massive region of the upper three Great Lakes as well as a considerable area toward the north, well beyond Lake Nipigon. In this manner, he indicated that all of the native groups who resided within this large area were identified by the catch-all term "Ottawas.")[57] Within this vast region, the community of St. Ignace, located on the north shore of the Straits of Mackinac (which was usually called Michilimackinac) served as both the primary place of rendezvous and the main depot for storing westbound supplies and merchandise as well as eastbound peltries. It was here, too, that the traders acquired birchbark canoes, paddles, long birchbark panels to be spread over a framework of poles to form a traveling shelter, and provisions, all of which were produced by the native populations of the region. This community had been first settled by native and French residents in 1671, and the first French troops had arrived here in 1683.

The ten men who were engaged during March, April, and May of 1685 presumably all departed for the west in the May brigade. In a number of these cases, only a single individual was recorded in the contract as the hirer. This was true for the four men who were individually engaged by Claude Greysolon, Sieur de Tourette (who was the brother and business associate of Daniel Greysolon, Sieur DuLhut. By this year, Claude was in charge of their two brand-new posts, Ft. Tourette on Lake Nipigon north of Lake Superior and Ft. Kaministiquia at the mouth of the Kaministiquia River on Lake Superior).[58] Having only a solitary boss was also the case for François Brunet, with his single hirer Michel Messier; Charles Détaillis with his hirer Antoine Bazinet; and Léonard Simon with his hirer the Sieur de Beauvais (probably Lieutenant René Legardeur). In most of these instances, it is not possible to identify all three of the individuals who would together comprise the three-man crew in a given canoe. Such was not a problem in two of the other hiring contracts: Gilles Deniau was engaged to paddle with his two hirers Simon Guillory and Étienne Campeau, while Jacques Chaperon and Robert Janot were engaged to travel with their single hirer Michel Dagenais.

Later in this same summer of 1685, four additional voyageur-traders would be engaged, three of them for a single hirer on June 26 and one with two hirers on August 7. It is assumed that these latter four men, all bound for the Ottawa Country, departed from Lachine as members of the September brigade.[59] Presumably, all of the men who were engaged for service in the west during this period were selected because they were already highly experienced in this line of work, and could be counted upon to carry out their duties with diligence.

In the case of François Brunet and Michel Messier, a document from 1686 would clearly identify the third voyageur-trader who filled out the crew in their canoe: François' close neighbor, long time paddling partner, and business associate Jean Boursier dit Lavigne.[60] However, a thorough search of the notary records of the Montreal region has not yielded any hiring contract for Jean. Such a contract would have guaranteed for him a salary, such as the one that Monsieur Messier had promised to François; however, it would also have bound him to work on behalf of the hirer. Jean may have made a private agreement with Messier, in which he agreed to paddle to and from the west in Messier's canoe, but while he was at the destination in the interior, he would labor only on behalf of the partnership between himself and François.

Likewise, there is no surviving documentation concerning the source of the merchandise that Jean and François exchanged with native customers during this trading voyage. Perhaps the two partners paid cash for all of their westbound goods, utilizing the profits that they had earned from previous work and had saved. In that case, there would have been no debt incurred with a merchant outfitter, and thus there would have been no notary document generated to record the transaction. During this era, according to the highly experienced Nicolas Perrot, three voyageur-traders typically loaded their canoe with merchandise and supplies worth about 3,000 livres for a westbound voyage. Then they "usually resorted to Michilimackinac, or else went among those natives who, they believed, had the most peltries."[61]

During François' period of service in the interior on this trip, which could last for up to eighteen months, he would earn 300 livres in wages, and he would also be fed at his employer's expense. This amount of pay may be compared to the total of 220 livres that he had personally garnered as a voyageur back in 1675-1676, for making four round-trip voyages between Lachine and Ft. Frontenac with his partner Jean Boursier; each of these three-week journeys had entailed about 420 miles of paddling and portaging. For the sake of comparison, the following were the typical annual salaries that were earned by men in various occupations in the colony during this era: blacksmith, 360 livres; carpenter, 300 livres; surgeon, 300 livres; cooper, 200 livres; joiner, 180 livres; tailor, 180 livres; and day laborer, 180 livres. Thus, voyageur-traders who were working on a fixed salary for another individual (and were not participating in the enterprise as an investor sharing in the overall profits) were relatively well-paid men during this period.[62] However, the real money was to be made as one of the co-investors, the individuals who would earn a major share of the profits of the enterprise (while also sharing the risk of potential financial losses in case of a disaster). That is the reason why, during this venture of 1685-1686, François Brunet and Jean Boursier would also have their own separate enterprise in play on the side, with their own supplemental goods to trade.

At the time of departure from Lachine of the Brunet-Boursier-Messier crew, in May of 1685, François was about 40 or 41 years old, Barbe was three months short of age 29, and their seven children ranged in age from 12, 10, $7^1/2$, 5, 5, and 3 years down to 3 months. Jean Boursier was about 41, his wife was 24, and their six offspring ranged in age from 11, 10, 7$^{1}/2$, 5, and 3 years down to 16 months. Michel Messier, the Sieur de Saint Michel, about 43 to 48 years old, had arrived in Montreal by the summer of 1651. In 1658, he had married Anne Lemoine, the sister of Charles Lemoine, who was one of the wealthiest and most powerful peltries merchants in Montreal. Over the following 24 years, the couple had produced twelve children, of whom three had died as tiny infants while a fourth had perished at the age of ten. In 1685, their three oldest daughters were already married, while the remaining five living children were 15, 11, 9, 6, and 4 years old. Back in 1668, Messier had been granted the seigneury of Cap St. Michel (on the eastern shore of the St. Lawrence, just east of the northern tip of Montreal Island, where the community of Varennes had later developed); a decade later, he had purchased the small seigneury of La Guillaudière.[63] According to the details of François' contract, these three comrades intended to spend about eighteen months in the interior, from about May of 1685 until October of 1686.

During this period of 1$^{1}/2$ years, their work probably entailed some three to four months of total traveling time during the outgoing and return trips, with the rest of the time spent in trading. Their westbound voyage involved paddling on the Ottawa, Mattawa, and La Vase Rivers, then Lake Nipissing, the French River, and along the northern shorelines of Georgian Bay and Lake Huron. This brought them to their initial destination, the community of St. Ignace at the Straits of Mackinac, which served as their primary base of operations. However, they may have traveled anywhere within the upper Great Lakes region to carry out their commerce over the course of the following year. Finally, somewhat ahead of their original projected schedule, the trio returned to the Montreal area in about August of 1686.

Writing in 1685, just a year before Francois' return, the French officer Lahontan had described various aspects of the convoy whose arrival at Lachine he had observed that summer. This was his account from Montreal, penned with his own distinctive style and spellings: *"The pedlers [voyageur-traders], call'd coureurs de bois, export from hence every year several canows full of merchandise, which they dispose of among all the savage nations of the continent, by way of exchange for beaver skins. Seven or eight days ago, I saw twenty-five or thirty of these canows return with heavy cargoes. Each canow was manag'd by two or three men, and carry'd twenty hundred weight [2,000 pounds of cargo], i.e. forty packs of beaver skins [weighing about fifty pounds apiece], which are worth a hundred crowns [300 livres] apiece. These canows had been a year or eighteen months out. You would be amaz'd if you saw how lewd these pedlers are when they return; how they feast and game [gamble], and how prodigal they are, not only in their cloths but [also] upon women. Such of 'em as are married [such as the Brunet-Boursier-Messier crew members] have the wisdom to retire to their own houses; but the batchelors act just as our East India men and pirates are wont to do. For they lavish, eat, drink, and play all away, as long as the goods [money] holds out; and when these are gone, they e'en sell their embroidery, their lace, and their cloaths. This done, they are forc'd to go upon a new voyage for subsistence."[64]*

The enterprise of 1685-1686 had indeed been productive for the partners François Brunet and Jean Boursier. In fact, it had been so productive that, at the time of their departure from the Straits, they had not been able to fit their entire take into their canoe (or the canoe belonging to Monsieur Messier). As a result, they had been obliged to temporarily leave either all of it or a considerable portion of it at St. Ignace, in the hands of a trusted friend. This left-behind supply had consisted of 26 packs of beaver pelts, which could have contained anywhere from 520 to 650 individual pelts. Writing in 1685, Lahontan had observed that each canoe of Frenchmen, manned by two or sometimes three paddlers, typically carried out 40 packs of beaver pelts.[65] Thus, the partners' stored amount probably represented a full 2/3 of a canoe load. Instead of paying other voyageurs or native paddlers to transport this cargo down to Montreal, accompanying them in the summer brigade of 1686, the partners had decided to save money, planning to use their own time and effort during a future voyage to haul out the stored peltries. They intended to make a return trip to the Straits during September and October of 1686, after which they would retrieve their laid-aside furs and also carry out additional trading over the following winter and spring.

Obviously, the generous supply of peltries that the two partners had garnered during their year of trading had been the result of much more than the exchange of François' gun and blanket, as had been permitted according to his employment contract with Monsieur Messier. In return for his salary of 300 livres, François had been obligated to work for Messier during their time in the west. Thus, either his employer had been very generous in allowing François to spend part of his time and energy trading for his own profit in partnership with Jean Boursier, or else Jean was the one who had generated all of the peltries for the Brunet-Boursier partnership. Perhaps François' wages had been utilized to cover a portion of the expenses that were generated by their partnership. There is even a possibility that the entire stock of 26 packs of stored beaver pelts represented the entire yield that the latter partnership had gathered during the year, and that these had not been allowed in Messier's down-bound canoe.

Not long after their return home, the two partners received a jolting blow. Other voyageurs from St. Ignace who had followed them on the eastbound route brought out disheartening information. Immediately upon receiving this news, with their well-laid plans now in total disarray, the two men hastened to the office of the notary Bourgine in Montreal. Since François could not even sign his name, much less write, the partners urgently requested that the scribe write out and officially submit their complaints for them, as follows:

"Today, the ninth day of September, 1686, in the afternoon, appeared before the recorder of leases of the Island of Montreal [Louis Chambalon] and the recorder, notary, and scribe of the said island [Hilaire Bourgine] the Sieurs François Brunet dit [Le] Bourbonnais and Jean Boursier dit Lavigne, habitants of the said Island, at present in this town, who have said and declared that they left at Michilimackinac in the hands of Sieur Latour the quantity of twenty-six packs of beaver pelts, containing twenty to twenty-five pelts in each one. They had intended to return to recover them this autumn, going up as a twosome, leaving tomorrow the tenth, with permission. But they have learned from the voyageurs who arrived in this town this very day that Monsieur [Henri] de Tonty has taken and withdrawn from Sieur Latour the said twenty-six packs of beaver pelts, and has disposed of them to pay some individuals whom he owes. Therefore, they wish to arrange their voyage [to Michilimackinac] for next spring, which they cannot do as long as Milord the Marquis de Denonville, Governor and Lieutenant General for the King in this country, orders them to leave [this autumn] to take up the Reverend Fr. Enjalran, to whom [the Governor] has promised and has given hope to embark on the route in their canoe. [Permission to depart next spring would] give them, who have lost everything, the opportunity to go up on their own schedule. Since they are obliged to go up [this autumn], and thus will make the voyage in vain, they have protested and protest against the said Sieur de Tonty concerning all of the expenses, damages, and interests which they have suffered and will suffer for his having taken the said beaver pelts, for all of their setbacks, and the loss of their voyage. They have requested that I record their declaration and protestation, which I have granted to them due

to their service and valor in the time and place, by which reason it has been done for them by the notary of the said Montreal on the day and year noted above, in the presence of the Sieurs François Pougnet and Louis Chambalon, witnesses, residing at the said place, who have signed with the said Boursier and me, the notary. The said Bourbonnais has declared that he does not know how to write or sign, having been questioned according to the ordinance. Signed,

F. Pougnet, Chambalon, and Bourgine, notary [but not by Boursier]"[66]

The frustrating situation which faced the two partners at this time had been caused by Henri de Tonty, a military officer who was about 36 or 37 years old and had been been a Captain for at least the previous nine years. Since the summer of 1678, he had served as the faithful confidant and lieutenant of René Robert Cavelier de La Salle, in all of the latter man's undertakings. In September of 1679, the two officers had supervised the construction of Ft. Miami at the mouth of the St. Joseph River, and in January of 1680 the building of Ft. Crèvecoeur on the Illinois River. In 1682, Captain Tonty had traveled down the Mississippi River to its delta region with La Salle's party of discovery, and during the following winter and spring of 1683 he had helped construct Ft. St. Louis atop Starved Rock beside the Illinois River; he had then commanded this new facility until February of 1686. At that time, he had received word that La Salle had sailed with a large party from France to the Gulf of Mexico, with the intention of establishing a colony at the mouth of the Mississippi. Departing from Ft. St. Louis with 25 Frenchmen and four native men, the Tonty party had paddled down the Mississippi, reaching its mouth area in about mid-April. Since some native people had seen the La Salle vessels sailing off toward the southwest, Tonty had sent out search parties, but they had been unable to make any contact. Thus, running short of fresh water, Tonty had been obliged to lead his men back northward to Ft. St. Louis, arriving on June 24. Almost immediately, upon learning that he had been summoned to Montreal to confer with Governor Denonville, he had departed from the post. While traveling along the main water route between the Illinois Country and the St. Lawrence settlements, he had arrived at the Straits of Mackinac. It was here at St. Ignace, while en route to Montreal, that he had seized the 26 packs of beaver pelts which the Brunet-Boursier partners had left in the hands of Sieur Latour. (The latter man, about 35 years old, had been a domestic servant of the Jesuits at their mission here at the Straits since at least 1681.) Tonty had then utilized the 520 to 650 beaver pelts contained within these packs "to pay some individuals whom he owes."[67] Scanning ahead into the future, the two partners apparently would not have to resort to either a notary agreement with the officer or court proceedings against him in order to retrieve their property. It seems that Tonty would willingly repay them in a rather timely manner for all of the beaver pelts that he had "borrowed" from their stored resources, using proceeds from his profitable commercial operations at Ft. St. Louis, which he would continue to command.

However, in the early autumn of 1686, the situation was discouraging for François and Jean. They were under strong pressure from Governor Denonville to immediately travel back to the Straits of Mackinac, even though their peltries stored there had been dispersed. The administrator wanted the pair of paddlers to transport Fr. Jean Enjalran back to his post at Michilimackinac. This Jesuit priest, 46 years old, had been in New France for a decade and at the Straits mission since at least 1679; by 1686, he had become the Superior of all of the missionary stations in the interior. At Mackinac, he tended to the Ottawas who resided at both St. Ignace and at Gros Cap, three miles to the west. Early in this summer of 1686, Fr. Enjalran had traveled out to the St. Lawrence Valley, to personally explain to the Governor the complex events that had been taking place between the native allies of the French and the Iroquois nations, and the various tensions that had been growing as a result. Considering the priest's crucial role as an observer and reporter in the west for the government, Denonville felt that he should be returned to his post as soon as possible.[68]

It is to be assumed that François and Jean had previously gathered the needed equipment and provisions for their upcoming venture, as well as the supply of merchandise which they would trade in the interior over the following winter and spring. There are no notary documents indicating that these acquisitions created any debts for them, or required that they share the investment in this trip with any other individuals. During this enterprise, they would apparently be operating as independent investors, with no other individuals sharing in either the profits or the possible financial losses. Even before the disheartening turn of events concerning their stored pelts had suddenly arisen, they had planned to travel back in to the Straits with the September convoy, in order to retrieve those packs and to carry out additional commerce; in fact, they had previously obtained permission from the Governor to do so. According to their own statement of protest, "They had intended to return to recover them [the stored peltries] this autumn, going up as a twosome, leaving tomorrow the tenth [of September], with permission." Obviously, they had planned to winter over in the west; there would not have been sufficient time to paddle in to Mackinac, retrieve their beaver pelts, and safely return to the St. Lawrence settlements before the freezing of the waterways. No information was provided in their protest document to indicate that the administrator offered them some reward for transporting the priest about 700 miles toward the west. However, the Governor may have agreed to grant them their permit for this particular voyage free or charge; or he may have promised to issue them a no-cost permit at some future time, for another trading journey. On the other hand, to compensate them for transporting the cleric on this trip, he may have provided them with generous amounts of food supplies and equipment drawn from official government stores, enabling the partners to save their own stocks for use during a later voyage.

It was not unusual that the Brunet-Boursier partners had intended to paddle into the western interior as a two-man crew. From the 1680s through the first decade of the following century, French trade canoes were manned by crews of three, and sometimes only two, voyageurs. Later, during the 1710s and 1720s, crews of three, and more often four or five men, would be the norm. Over the course of these five decades, the canoes which were utilized would range up to a maximum of 32 feet in length; this latter size had been documented as early as 1670. Then, in about 1729, the largest eight-place (nine-thwart) craft would be increased by a maximum of four feet, so that the very longest examples would measure 36 feet, while retaining the pattern of nine thwarts. Beginning with the transport season of 1730, licenses would be sometimes issued for crews of seven to ten paddlers, to handle these expanded craft. However, most of the licenses which would be issued for the largest canoes over the years would specify crews of only seven men. This number would be the usual maximum complement of voyageurs in the largest trade canoes on standard cargo runs during the 1730-1760 period, although instances of eight to ten-man crews would be sometimes recorded. Crews manning canoes of moderate size would typically consist of four, five, or six voyageurs in the 1730s. Then, during the final two decades of French rule, the men in these moderately-sized craft would typically number five or six, with the latter crew size predominating in the 1750s.[69]

Near the beginning of September in 1686, shortly before François departed to spend another year or more in the west, Barbe became pregnant for the eighth time. On June 4, 1687, she safely delivered little Marie, who was baptized on the following day at the Lachine church. At the joyful ceremony, the godfather was Jean Baptiste Pothier, a chanter, school master, and secretary for the Sulpicians, who were the seigneurs of Montreal Island. The godmother was Barbe's younger sister Marie Étiennette Beauvais, 18³/4 years old and still single. One year and a week later, these two sponsors would be wed at the Montreal church, after which they would settle at Lachine and the groom would become the notary there.[70]

It is interesting to note that Fr. Rémy, who had been the permanent priest residing at Lachine for the previous eight years (ever since his appointment in 1680), recorded the father of newly-christened Marie as "François Brunet, *laboureur* (farm worker)." The cleric had utilized this same designation for François while recording the baptism of the couple's previous baby, back in February of 1685. Since the birth of that first child, François had spent the period between May of 1685 and August of 1686 working as a voyageur-trader in the west, based at Michilimackinac. In addition, at the time of this lattermost christening, he was again absent in the interior on another voyage, laboring in the same capacity. The local priest would certainly have been aware of these extended absences, and of their purpose. It appears that he made it a point to avoid any specific mention of his parishioners' journeys to the interior in the church records, since some of the men would have been gone with legal permission while others would have been running illicit operations, without official approval. This omission of data in the church ledger would avoid the documentation of their voyages in public records, which could be held against them in a court of law if the notations specifically described the unauthorized business that was often being conducted. The priests often felt that it would be helpful to avoid the terms *voyageur*, *voyageur-marchand*, and *voyageur-negociant* in their official records.

When François finally returned to his family during the summer of 1687, he most likely did so after participating in a major military campaign in the home territory of the most westerly of the Iroquois nations. Three years earlier, Iroquois warriors had begun making attacks against the Illinois and Miami nations in the west, disrupting what had generally been peaceful relations ever since the treaties of

1666 and 1667. Their intentions had been to vanquish these two allies of the French. Afterward, they intended to crush the Ottawas, Hurons, and Tionontates at the Straits of Mackinac, in order to seize complete control of the fur trade business in the entire midwest region. This serious threat had obliged the French to mount a military expedition to Lake Ontario during the summer of 1684. By this means, they had hoped to intimidate the warring Iroquois nations, by showing them that the French could attack their home villages (which were located south and east of the lake) if they did not restore the former situation of peace. However, Spanish influenza had swept through the eastern half of the army composed of Frenchmen and native allies, the portion that had been traveling westward from the St. Lawrence communities. This had forced Governor Labarre to negotiate a peace agreement that had been very humiliating for the French.

Now, three years later, matters had come to a head, and Governor Denonville intended to lead a massive campaign against the Iroquois homelands lying south of Lake Ontario. In this manner, he intended to cause all of the Iroquois nations to cease their raids against the settlements along the St. Lawrence, as well as against the native nations living far to the west who were allied with the French. The thrust of the two attacking French and native armies would be brought to bear upon the Senecas, who were the most westerly and the most numerous and powerful of the Iroquois nations. As had been done three years earlier, back in the abortive campaign of 1684, the western army consisted of French and native forces gathered from throughout the Great Lakes region, and from as far southwest as the Illinois Country. Messieurs Perrot and Boisguillot, trading in the upper Mississippi area, assembled nearly all of the Frenchmen there and paddled to St. Ignace, where Olivier de Morel, Sieur de La Durantaye, the commandant there at the Straits, had gathered the Frenchmen from his region (where the Brunet-Boursier partners had been working) plus some Ojibwa warriors. These combined forces traveled southward on Lake Huron to the one-year-old Ft. St. Joseph on the St. Clair River, where they were joined by Daniel Greysolon, Sieur DuLhut and his soldiers from that post. Further to the south, the entourage was again augmented, this time by French and native forces from Illinois, who had made their way to the Detroit River. It is highly likely that this lattermost group of fighting men, in order to cross the Michigan Peninsula, had traveled up the Grand River and then down a tributary of the Saginaw River, which were connected by a portage path (this well-known detour passage was first depicted and labeled on French maps in 1684 and 1688).[71] As a combined unit, the huge aggregate of fighting men assembled at the Detroit River then paddled eastward to Lake Ontario, to join ranks with the eastern army from the St. Lawrence. In the meantime, the Ottawa and Huron/Tionontate warriors from the Straits of Mackinac had traveled by way of Georgian Bay and the Toronto Portage to join their comrades on the south shore of Lake Ontario.

The eastern army, assembled in the St. Lawrence Valley, was composed of 832 regular troops, 1,300 militia fighters, and 300 allied native warriors. Oddly enough, these eastern forces arrived on July 10 at the appointed place of rendezvous, on the southern shore of the massive lake, at virtually the exact time as the western forces! This was purely coincidental, yet it bore great and clearly positive significance to the native allies within both groups.

When the combined armies approached the first Seneca village overland, they were ambushed in thick forest by a large contingent of Iroquois warriors. In the ensuing battle, some 100 Frenchmen and ten allied warriors were killed. In addition, many others were wounded, including Fr. Enjalran, whom the two partners had transported to Michilimackinac during the previous autumn. After this initial clash, the Senecas burned their own nearest village and fled with their families. During the next nine days, the French and native forces destroyed huge amounts of standing corn crops at three or four deserted Seneca villages, along with an estimated 50,000 bushels of parched corn. Then, as dysentery began to spread through the men, the two armies left the area and returned to their respective home areas, having fought a total of one battle with uncertain results. However, instead of traveling back to the west, François Brunet and Jean Boursier made their way eastward, to return to their respective families and homes in the Lachine seigneury.

In the aftermath of this Seneca campaign, attacks by Iroquois war parties actually increased rather than decreased, in both number and intensity. Their fierce raids fell not only upon the communities of the St. Lawrence Valley, but also upon the Ottawa River route leading to and from the Upper Country.[72]

However, another threat, even more insidious than marauding Iroquois warriors, also endangered the lives of the people living in the St. Lawrence Valley at this time. When the annual fleet of vessels from France had arrived during this summer of 1687, beginning on the first day of June, their cargoes had included not only people, merchandise, and supplies, but also fatal germs. Shortly after their arrival, a terrible epidemic of both measles and smallpox began to sweep through the French and native communities that lined the shores of the river, ranging from Tadoussac all the way upstream to the Montreal area. This scourge of sickness and death would continue unchecked for nearly a year, extending well into 1688. By the time it would finally abate, over a thousand residents, both French and native, would be dead.[73]

In the midst of these multiple woes, along came a positive event. On November 28, 1687, fourteen of the land-owning inhabitants of the Lachine seigneury, including François, were granted joint ownership of its Commons area. This plot of land, which commenced immediately east of the terminus of the Montreal-to-Lachine road, extended eastward for a half-mile along the St. Lawrence shoreline, and stretched a half-mile toward the north. On this day, the concession of the Commons property was made by "the Seminary of St. Sulpice in Montreal, legal representative of the Seminary of St. Sulpice in Paris, seigneur and proprietor of Montreal Island." The new joint owners of the communally-owned plot were listed in the document in the following order: Jean Fournier, [Catherine Godin] the widow of Louis Fortin dit Lagrandeur [who had died seven weeks earlier, on October 5], Pierre Cardinal, Pierre Tabault dit Léveillé, André Merlot dit Laramée, René Cuillerier, Claude Cécire, Vincent Dugas, René Horieux dit Lafleur de Nantes, Vincent Chamaillard, François Brunet dit Le Bourbonnais, François Lory, Jean Boursier dit Lavigne, and Jean Paré. These fourteen individuals, all of whom were identified in this notarial record as residents of Lachine, owned the long strips of farmland which extended westward from the Commons for $1\frac{1}{3}$ miles and eastward from the Commons for $1\frac{1}{4}$ miles. For some reason, the owners of the fifteen lots at the western end of the seigneury and the owners of the eight lots at its extreme eastern end were not included in this legal transfer. Technically, according to the details of the concession, the Sulpician seigneurs granted to the fourteen named individuals only the rights of usage of the property, not the full ownership of it. For these rights, which included such activities as cutting wood and grazing livestock, each of the recipients would pay an annual seigneurial fee of 20 sols (one livre). Fifteen years later, in 1702, the Sulpicians would dispense with this yearly token obligation.[74]

When the population of the colony was enumerated in the census of 1688 (probably during the spring or early summer), a number of interesting trends appeared. Although the residents of the St. Lawrence Valley are usually considered to have been primarily French at this time, it is of particular interest to note that more than 1,200 native people lived in the Valley by this period. Thus, they represented about 11 percent of the total population residing along the river, compared to the 10,038 French residents. With this number of French people living in 1,721 houses, they averaged 5.83 persons per house. In comparison, the 1,211 native people resided in 157 shelters, thus averaging 7.71 people per shelter. During the previous seven years, the French population had increased by only 296 individuals, or 3 percent. However, firearms in the hands of the civilian population, which had increased during that same period by 36 percent, now numbered 2,563 guns and 159 pistols. The new total of 2,722 firearms (almost all of them shoulder-firing, smooth-bore guns) that were present averaged 1.08 guns for each adult male, counting both the 1,978 Frenchmen and the 400 native men. This supply of enumerated firearms included only those which belonged to civilian men; it did not include the guns which were in the hands of each of the resident soldiers in the Troupes de la Marine.

In this colony in which subsistence agriculture predominated (although the fur trade provided the mainstay of the economy and the principal export), oxen were the main draft animals, since horses were still a great rarity. Cows, pigs, and chickens were the other common farm animals, since sheep were still somewhat limited in numbers. In comparing the total numbers of the various animals that were recorded in 1679-1681 and again in 1688, the following figures and increases were documented: horned cattle, now numbering 7,779 in 1688, had increased by 11 percent; sheep, now totaling 1,020, had increased by 42 percent; horses, now numbering 218, had increased by a full 50 percent, although they were still scarce; pigs, now totaling 3,701, had not been enumerated earlier; goats, having numbered 33 in the earlier count, had not been recorded in 1688; and chickens had unfortunately not been enumerated at all.[75]

During this same year of 1688, the members of the Brunet-Beauvais family were apparently touched by the miraculous powers of Kateri (Catherine) Tekakwitha, an Algonkin-Mohawk woman who had spent the latter years of her life on the opposite shore of the St. Lawrence, at the mission community of Kahnawake. This young woman (who would be canonized as a saint of the Roman Catholic Church on October 21, 2012, during the writing of this biography of the Brunet family) had died in April of 1680 at the age of 24, and had been initially interred in the mission cemetery. Within about nine months of her death, commencing in January of 1681, apparently miraculous healings had begun to occur among the French residents of the Lachine seigneury and at other nearby locales, in each instance after the recipients had made prayerful appeals to Kateri. In 1684, her body had been removed from the cemetery and had been reburied beneath the floor of the mission church. As her intercessions in times of great physical need continued to take place throughout the 1680s and into the 1690s, Fr. Rémy of the Lachine parish would pen a description of many of these inspiring phenomena in 1696. He would entitle his report *Certificat des miracles faits en sa paroisse de Lachine par l'intercession de la B. [Béni] Catherine Tegakouita*. The following is a summary of his description of the apparently miraculous events that took place in the Brunet household beside the Lachine Rapids during 1688. They occurred some time after young Barbe Brunet, the eldest daughter and second child of François and Barbe, had celebrated her thirteenth birthday on July 1.

"In 1688, Barbe Brunet, aged thirteen, had been ill for two months of the tertian [recurring] fever, which had gone into the double tertian. No remedy was found to reduce the fever, which had emaciated her until she was like a skeleton. Thus unable to either stand up [or] take remedies or food, she was ready to die, and was given up by the doctor. Then, she was told to have recourse to Catherine Tekakwitha. In fact, she promised to have a novena [a devotion of nine days duration] made at the tomb [of Catherine] and to go there to offer her devotions. Two days later, she began to feel better, her fever left her, and she recovered her health."[76]

By the summer of 1688, François and his paddling partner Jean Boursier had been back in the St. Lawrence settlements for some nine or ten months. However, the time was fast approaching for them to again leave their families, to depart on yet another trading trip. This time, they decided to move the focus of their efforts somewhat southward: during their next enterprise, they would work in the Illinois Country, to the south and southwest of Lake Michigan. It is highly likely that the partners made this decision due to the sheer numbers of voyageur-traders who were now flocking to the upper Great Lakes region. In this year of 1688 alone, in the hiring contracts that were registered with Montreal notaries, a total of 53 men were engaged to labor in this northern region. Their contracts specified that 49 of the men would work in the Ottawa Country, one man would labor at La Baye (at the foot of Green Bay), and three men would travel with Nicolas Perrot a bit further to the west, into the lands of the Mascoutens and the Dakotas. In contrast, only eight men were engaged to travel to the Illinois Country or to Ft. St. Louis. One of these voyageur-traders was hired by the Montreal merchant Antoine Pascaud, while the other seven were engaged by François Dauphin de La Forest; he shared with Henri de Tonty the trade monopoly of Ft. St. Louis, which was located atop Starved Rock beside the Illinois River. These latter two men had been the lieutenants of La Salle during his various enterprises in the west.[77]

The furs that were harvested by the native groups living in this more southerly region, with its warmer climate, were generally of lesser quality than the thicker, richer pelts which were gathered by other groups residing further to the north, in the colder climates. However, by good fortune, both higher and lower qualities of beaver pelts were utilized in the manufacture of hats. In fact, the recipe for the most marketable *chapeaux de feutre* (felt hats) consisted of three parts of higher-quality *castor gras* and one part of lower-quality *castor sec*. The inferior pelts which were graded as *castor sec* (dry beaver), having thinner fur, were harvested from beavers in the more southerly areas during all seasons or in the northern areas during the summer. In contrast, the pelts which were graded as *castor gras* (greasy beaver) had thicker and richer fur, since they were grown by beavers in the cold north during the winter. In addition, these latter pelts were sewn together by the native people to create robes, which they used as outer garments and as bedding before they were traded. In the course of their usage, the outer guard hairs on these pelts were shed, leaving only the soft underfur that was utilized in making felt. This eliminated the labor and expense of removing the guard hairs, a step which was necessary when processing the pelts of *castor sec* quality.[78]

In spite of the inferior quality of the beaver pelts that were available in the Illinois Country, François and Jean apparently reasoned that, at this particular time, they could generate greater profits by working in this more southerly area than in the upper Great Lakes region. To their way of thinking, having fewer competing French traders would allow them to garner many choice peltries, and thus earn substantial profits. However, there was one main drawback to working in the

Illinois Country: the longer canoe voyage in and out, which often involved paddling on waterways that were less cooperative, and thus more challenging.

François and Jean, along with their other colleagues, would travel the customary westbound route to the Straits of Mackinac, via the Ottawa, Mattawa, and La Vase Rivers, then Lake Nipissing, the French River, and the north shorelines of Georgian Bay and Lake Huron. From Michilimackinac, they would paddle southward over the full length of Lake Michigan; near the southern end of the lake, they would take one of two routes to reach the Illinois River. From the southeastern corner of Lake Michigan, they could travel along the St. Joseph River-Kankakee Portage-Kankakee River route; or from the southwestern corner of the lake, they could take the Chicago River-Chicago Portage-Des Plaines River route. This latter passage was immensely more challenging whenever the water levels were moderate or low. Since François and his colleagues would be making their journey in the autumn, a season of typically low water levels, they would most likely avoid the daunting Chicago River route and take the more amenable St. Joseph River passage. This route would entail paddling up the St. Joseph for about fifty miles, hiking over the four-mile Kankakee Portage, and then descending the Kankakee River for about 150 miles. However, unfortunately, the latter watercourse was nearly as susceptible to drops in water levels during dry seasons as the Chicago and Des Plaines Rivers. Whichever route they chose, the men knew that their journey into the heart of the Illinois Country would definitely not be an easy one.[79]

On the map of North America that the cartographer Franquelin created in this same year of 1688, he clearly depicted both of the water routes that extended from the southern end of Lake Michigan to the Illinois River. He labeled the St. Joseph River as "Rivière des Miamis," the Kankakee River as "Rivière Theakiki," and the Kankakee Portage that connected these two watercourses as "Portage." On the alternate route that ran toward the south, he portrayed at its beginning "Fort Checagou," beside the mouth of the Chicago River (this facility had been established in 1684). He labeled the Des Plaines River as "Rivière Checagou," he depicted "Fort S. Louis" well toward the southwest on the eastern bank of the "Rivière des Illinois" (on the Illinois River at the present Starved Rock State Park), and he portrayed "Fort Crèvecoeur" further down this waterway on the same eastern shore (near the present Peoria, established in 1680 and utilized only that year). The mapmaker also indicated the locations of twelve major native villages within this area, half of them positioned beside or very close to the Illinois-Des Plaines water highway. This, then, was the general region in which François, Jean, and their colleagues would labor during the following year.[80]

During their previous ventures to the west, Messieurs Brunet and Boursier had usually worked as a two-man team, except for the one voyage which they had made with Michel Messier back in 1685-1686. Now, they decided to take on four additional partners, all of whom were much younger men. These six associates would share equally in both the expenses of the enterprise and its profits; likewise, if disaster struck, they would share jointly in the resulting financial losses. One of the young men, Michel Descaries, was already in the Illinois Country. Commencing in the Montreal area, François, Jean, and the other three partners would assemble the outfit, travel westward, and join Michel for a year of trading.

In July, the men assessed the amounts of equipment, provisions, and trade merchandise that they already had on hand. As Nicolas Perrot recorded, during this era of the trade, a three-man crew usually invested about 3,000 livres in their total outfit. Thus, a six-man partnership like the one formed by François and his five colleagues could spend as much as 6,000 livres in their preparations. In late July, they took delivery on the additional materiel that they had decided they needed to conduct their enterprise. This supplemental outfit, including a second canoe, cost them a total of 1,886 livres. On August 2, they assembled in the office of the Montreal notary Adhémar, to acknowledge their shared debts for the additional supplies. Two days later, two of the men returned to the scribe's office, to record that they had acquired the above-mentioned second canoe from the same source:

"Before Antoine Adhémar, notary and scrivener of the Island of Montreal, residing at Ville Marie, and the witnesses named at the end were present in person Sieur Antoine Pascaud, merchant living in this town, in the name of and as the legal representative of Claude [Bouchard dit] Dorval, heir of the deceased Charles [sic, was Claude Bouchard dit] Dorval, based upon the power of attorney which was passed before Master Bénigne Basset, notary of this Island, on February 23 last, which he has granted and has afterward taken back except for the transaction which follows, François Brunet dit [Le] Bourbonnais, Jean Boursier dit Lavigne, Joseph Aubuchon, and Jean [sic, was René, Jr.] Cuillerier, acting both for themselves and for Michel Descaries,

their partner, at present in the Illinois Country. Of their own free will and voluntarily, [these six individuals] including the said Sieur Pascaud in the said name [of Dorval], have acknowledged and admitted that they well and truly owe to the Sieur Hilaire Bourgine, merchant living in this town, present and assenting, the sum of 1,706 livres 3 sols 6 deniers, for good merchandise and used clothing which was delivered to them six days ago, as expressed in the invoice which he has given to the said debtors and which they have signed. This said sum of 1,706 livres 3 sols 6 deniers the said Sieur Pascaud, in the said name of and as the legal representative of the said Dorval, and the said Brunet, Boursier, Aubuchon, and Cuillerier promise and in solidarity are obliged to give and pay to the said Sieur Bourgine or to the bearer of these presents and in this town in good beaver pelts at the prices set by the office [of the export monopoly company] at Quebec in the year 1689, under the bond and mortgage of all and each of the possessions, both moveable and real estate, present and future, of the said Brunet, Boursier, Aubuchon, and Cuillerier, and the said Pascaud in the name of the possessions and belongings of the said Dorval. For the execution of these presents, the said debtors have selected as their [temporary] legal residence [to which writs may be delivered], the house and residence of the said undersigned notary [Adhémar], situated on Rue Saint Paul. Thus have they promised and in solidarity have they obligated themselves. [This agreement] drawn up at the said Ville Marie in the office of the said notary on the second day of August, 1688 in the afternoon, in the presence of the Sieurs Pierre Cabazier and Silvain Guerin, witnesses living at the said Ville Marie, who have signed below with [the Sieurs Pascaud, Boursier, Bourgine,] Aubuchon and the notary. The said Brunet and Cuillerier have said and declared that they do not know how to sign, having been questioned after the reading was done, according to the ordinance.

Signed,

Pascaud, Jean Boursier, J. Aubuchon, Bourgine, Cabazie, Sillevain Guerin, and Adhemar, notary.

In addition, the said Sieur Pascaud, in the said name [of Dorval], and the said Joseph Aubuchon, acting for the individuals named in the said obligation, have acknowledged that they [also] owe the sum of 180 livres to the said Sieur Bourgine for one canoe [which he has provided to them], which they promise to pay as noted above, according to the same terms which were agreed upon by the parties in the said obligation and under the same penalties. Thus have they promised and obligated themselves. [This agreement] drawn up on the fourth of August, 1688 in the morning, in the presence of the

Sieurs Cabazier and Guerin, who have signed below with the said Pascaud, Aubuchon, Bourgine, and the notary, according to the ordinance.
Signed,
Pascaud, J. Aubuchon, Bourgine, Cabazie, Sillevain Guerin, and Adhemar, notary"[81]

When these financial arrangements were concluded, the five partners residing in the St. Lawrence Valley were within weeks of setting out for the west. At this time, François was about 43 or 44 years old, Barbe was about to turn 32, and their eight children (six girls and two boys) ranged in age from 15 years down to 14 months. Living close by on the second farm toward the east, Jean Boursier was about 44, his wife was 27, and their seven living children (five girls and two boys) ranged from 14 down to $2^1/2$ years; their next daughter and last child would arrive on September 28, just weeks after the departure of the brigade. These two long-time paddling partners, both of them highly experienced voyageur-traders, were the senior members of the six-man team; the other four partners were much younger.

René Cuillerier, Jr., a fellow resident of the Lachine seigneury, was $21^1/2$ years old and single; as the eldest child in the Cuillerier family, he had lived with his parents and younger siblings about $1^1/2$ miles west of the Brunet farm since about 1670. In 1676, his merchant father, René, Sr., had built a fortified house there, which he had called Ft. Cuillerier; this wooden edifice had served as a combination trading post, storehouse, and fortress. René, Sr. had also been associated with La Salle's commercial enterprises in the west. Partner Joseph Aubuchon, 24 years old, was the second son of the Montreal merchant Jean Aubuchon, Sieur de Lespérance, who had been assassinated at home in his bed $2^2/3$ years earlier, on December 3, 1685. Joseph had married Élisabeth Cusson (about 23 years old) at the Montreal church on March 20, just $4^1/2$ months before signing on with the crew for the Illinois Country; the newlyweds were expecting their first child around Christmas. Partner Claude Dorval, about 28 years old, the son of a surgeon, had been raised at Château-Richer on the Côte de Beaupré; he was still single, but he would finally take a bride in February of 1694. The sixth partner, Michel Descaries, already in the Illinois Country, was age 31; he was the son of a Montreal charcoal burner. Two years after the completion of this trading venture, in August of 1691, Michel would marry Marie Cuillerier, the young sister of his partner René, Jr., when she would be 16 years old. In summary, the two elders in this trading association were each about 43 or 44 years old, and they had a total of fifteen living children between their two families (very soon to be sixteen, including twelve girls and four boys). Among the other four partners, ages 21, 24, 28, and 31, only one of them (the 24-year-old) was married; he and his wife were awaiting the arrival of their first child in about five months.[82]

Interestingly, Hilaire Bourgine did not usually function as a merchant or an outfitter, even though the text of Adhémar's document presented above described him as a "merchant living in this town." Normally, he worked with information, and its recording in handwritten documents. By this point in the summer of 1688, he had been present in the colony for two decades, first appearing in records drawn up at Quebec back in February of 1669. Beginning in December of 1684, he had become the clerk or registrar of the Montreal Court, and in 1685 he had commenced his tenure as a notary in Montreal. In January of 1688, seven months before handling this transaction with François and his trading associates, he had taken on the additional functions of the fiscal attorney for the seigneury of Montreal, a position within the court system.[83] However, during July of 1688, Monsieur Bourgine had somehow arranged to supply this Illinois-bound crew with the numerous articles that they needed for their upcoming venture, even though he himself did not have an outfitting business. He had apparently taken on the role of middle-man in this transaction, arranging for the delivery of the outfit to François and his colleagues from some other source. This outside source was not mentioned in the document that officially recorded the monetary debt of the six partners to him. Presumably, he had generated for himself a certain degree of profit from this triangular business arrangement.

The invoice of the specific articles that Hilaire Bourgine supplied to François Brunet and his partners in late July, to equip them for their upcoming enterprise in the Illinois Country, has not been discovered. However, the invoice for a comparable outfit which was supplied at about the very same time by the Montreal merchant Charles de Couagne to three other voyageurs who were bound for the same destination has been preserved.[84] These latter partners were the brothers Joseph and Michel Pelletier dit Antaya (ages 33 and 14, respectively) and François Coutu dit Le Picard (about 34 to 37 years old). While preparing for their venture in the Illinois Country, François and his colleagues acquired from their merchant-outfitter materiel that was valued at 1,886 livres; for their part, the Pelletier-Coutu partners acquired articles that were valued at 2,084 livres. Since these two outfits appear to reflect two very similar enterprises, an examination of the specific items that were provided to the latter crew may shed considerable light on the articles which were supplied to François and his associates. In the following outfitting roster, the order of the items has been rearranged, and they have been grouped into categories of daily-life activities. It is not possible to determine which of these articles were intended for the use of the three men themselves, and which of them were destined to become trade merchandise for native customers. It is highly likely that various of the items which are missing from this outfit were supplied by the Pelletier-Coutu partners themselves; thus, it was not necessary for them to purchase these articles from their merchant-outfitter. However, many of the missing items were probably not required for this particular trading trip. (In the French monetary system, twelve deniers equals one sol, and twenty sols equals one livre.)

"Invoice of the merchandise delivered for the account of Madame Antaya [Marguerite Madeleine Morisseau, widow of François Pelletier dit Antaya, resident of Sorel, and mother of Joseph and Michel] to the Sieur François Coutu dit Le Picard from Lavaltrie, Joseph Pelletier, and Michel Pelletier, to be paid in beaver pelts at the prices set by the office of the King at Quebec [the peltries exporting company] for letters of exchange on France, the third of August, 1688, upon their return from the Illinois Country, where they are going to trade.

[Transportation category]
1 canoe, for 160 l. (livres)
1 towing line, for 4 l.
1 towing line from the shop of Monsieur Dupré, for 3 l.
1 sponge, for 8 s. (sols)
2 boxes (or chests), at 35 s. apiece
1 box (or chest) covered with black leather, for 6 l.
1 tumpline, for 35 s.
2 tumplines at Lachine, at 50 s. apiece
[No mention of paddles; setting poles; sailing rig; canoe-bottom poles; canoe repair kit (although the list does include crooked knives, butcher knives, axes, awls, and numerous kettles, one of which could have been utilized for melting repair gum, a mixture of pine pitch, fat, and pulverized charcoal);

supplies of extra birchbark, sewing roots, and gum for making canoe repairs;
long birchbark panels for covering traveling shelters; tarpaulins; ice creepers;
or snowshoes]

[Foods, beverages, tobacco, and medicines category]
2 bushels of peas, at 50 s. per bushel
60 pounds of side pork, at 8 s. per pound
$^1/_4$ bushel of salt, for 15 s.
12 [units not given; ounces?] of nutmeg, at 2 s. 8 d. per unit
167 pounds of galette [thick, hard pancakes], at 14 s. per 5 pounds
6 bags to carry the galette, at 35 s. apiece
24 half-gallons of brandy, at 50 s. per half-gallon
1 half-gallon of brandy, for 50 s.
2 casks [for the brandy], at 50 s. apiece
46 pounds of tobacco, at 45 s. per pound
18 pounds of tobacco, at 45 s. per pound
2 calf skins to protect the tobacco, at 15 s. apiece
2 ounces of theriac [a mixture of various drugs and honey, formerly thought
to be an antidote to poison], for 3 l.
[No mention of wine or containers for the peas, side pork, or salt]

[Hunting, warfare, and fishing category]
6 guns, at 22 livres apiece
2 utility guns, at 20 livres apiece
8 gun sheaths, at 30 s. apiece
100 pounds of gunpowder, at 25 s. per pound
3 casks to carry the powder, at 2 l. apiece
200 pounds of [bulk] lead, at 6 s. per pound
40 pounds of balls, of which 8 pounds are of royal lead, at 6 s. per pound
30 pounds of balls from Monsieur Cuillerier, at 6 s. per pound
1 pound of balls, at 6 s.
200 gunflints, at 10 s. per hundred
60 gun worms, at 3 l. per hundred
100 iron arrow points, at 2 s. apiece
3 dozen [36] large butcher knives, at 3 l. per dozen
23 dozen [276] butcher knives, at 2 l. per dozen
8$^1/_2$ pounds of cord for [fishing] nets, at 25 s. per pound
[No mention of pistols, gunsmithing tools, powder flasks or horns, powder
measures, shooting bags, shot and ball pouches, ball molds, snare wire,
sword blades to be hafted as spears, harpoon heads, fish hooks, fishing line,
or ice chisels]

[Fire-starting and cooking category]
24 fire steels, at 4 s. apiece
15 1/4 pounds of [brass or copper] kettles, at 45 s. per pound
50 pounds of [brass or copper] kettles, at 40 s. per pound

[Woodworking category]
6 large axes, at 45 s. apiece
6 small axes, at 20 s. apiece
30 axes, at 18 s. apiece
2 dozen [24] clasp knives, at 3 s. apiece
6 dozen [72] canoe [crooked] knives, at 22 s. per dozen
[No mention of adzes, augers, gimlets, drills, drawknives, chisels, wedges, froes, hammers, nails, or building hardware such as hinges, latches, and locks]

[Clothing items and blankets category]
10 pairs of stockings from Poitou, at 3 l. 10 s. per pair
12 pairs of trade stockings, at 45 s. per pair
7 trade shirts, at 3 l. apiece
6 shirts made of Meslis linen [hempen sailcloth], at 3 l. apiece
4 camisoles [rather tight-fitting overshirts or sleeping shirts with long sleeves], at 50 s. apiece
10 blue hooded coats, at 8 l. 10 s. apiece
3 hooded coats, at 3 l. apiece
5 large lined dress coats, at 15 l. apiece
1 large dress coat, for 10 l.
1 dress coat, for 3 l.
9 pairs of sleeves, at 50 s. per pair
2 large blankets, at 16 l. apiece
2 blankets, at 10 l. apiece
3 blankets from Normandy, at 8 l. apiece
[No mention of shoes, breeches, waistcoats, kerchiefs, caps, hats, gloves, or mittens]

[Bulk fabrics category]
15 yards of woolen stroud fabric, at 9 l. 10 s. per yard
1 1/4 yards of red woolen limbourg fabric, 7 l. 10 s per yard
19 1/2 yards of woolen serge fabric for making hooded coats, at 4 l. 5 s. per yard
18 1/2 yards of red [woolen] fabric for making hooded coats, at 4 l. 5 s. per yard

1^1/2 yards of woolen Iroquoise fabric, at 4 l. per yard
10 yards of linen fabric, at 35 s. per yard
5 yards of linen fabric from the shop of Monsieur Arnaud, at 28 s. per yard
10 yards of linen fabric from the shop of Monsieur Arnaud, at 22 s. per yard
[Used by native customers to produce their own moccasin liners, leggings, knee garters, breechclouts, belts, sleeves, mantles, hoods, mittens, scarves, and turbans. No mention of silk or cotton fabrics, ribbons, binding tapes, or gartering material]

[Sewing and leather-working category]
30 awls, at 10 s. per dozen
200 needles, at 16 s. per hundred
8 pounds of sewing thread, at 3 l. per pound
[No mention of straight pins, thimbles, scissors, or hide scrapers]

[Ornaments category]
5 pounds of glass beads, at 2 l. per pound
[No mention of copper, brass, or iron wire, or bells. Native metalworkers fashioned finger rings, wrist bands, arm bands, ear bobs, nose rings, gorgets, pendants, head bands, hair pipes, tubular beads, and tinkling cones from copper and brass salvaged from pots and kettles]

[Grooming category]
1^3/4 pounds of soap, at 14 s. per pound
12 mirrors, at 5 s. apiece
4 dozen [48] combs, at 8 s. apiece
12^1/4 pounds of azure blue paint pigment, for 9 l.
[No mention of razors, wire for making spring tweezers, or vermilion pigment]

[Writing and recreation category]
1 writing set (or ink stand), for 1 l.
Some paper
[Tobacco and brandy listed earlier. No mention of pipes, snuff tobacco, snuff boxes, jews harps, playing cards, or dice]

Paid by my note to Monsieur [Alexandre] Turpin for expenses, 114 l.
In money paid for them to [Monsieur] Champagne, 4 l.

Amounting to the sum of two thousand eighty-four livres,
six sols.. 2,084 livres 6 sols

[Three days later, additional purchases made by each of the two sons]
Joseph Pelletier owes on the 6th of August, 1688 the following, on the
account of Madame Antaya
1 pair of shoes from the shop of Monsieur Arnaud, for 6 l.
1 pair of stockings, for 8 l.
As formerly on August 3, in money, 1 l. 12 s.
In money, 1 l. 15 s.
Total, 17 l. 7 s.

Michel Pelletier owes on the 6th of August, 1688, on the same current
account
1 pair of shoes from the shop of Monsieur Arnaud, for 6 l. 15 s.
1 pair of stockings, for 8 l.
1 cap, for 1 l.

[Grand total of these additions] 32 livres 7 sols"

Between August 6, 1688 and July 17, 1689 (when the Pelletier-Coutu crew returned and paid off their outfitting invoice with the merchant), Monsieur Couagne furnished to Madame Antaya the following articles, many of which had not been taken by her two sons on their trading voyage: gunpowder, lead, salt, vinegar, a hogshead of eels, wine, woolen serge fabric, woolen frieze fabric, painted linen fabric, cotton indienne fabric (bearing hand-painted or block-printed designs), silk thread, ribbons, a boxwood comb, a dress coat, a scarf, and two dressing gowns.

It is certain that the outfit that François Brunet and his five colleagues assembled in July of 1688 was much larger than the one represented by the above invoice. The above- listed equipment, supplies, and trade merchandise was intended to support the activities of three voyageur-traders for a year. In contrast, the Brunet-Boursier team consisted of two three-man crews (counting Michel Descaries, who was already in position in the west). Thus, during the course of their year-long enterprise in the Illinois Country, they would require about twice the amount of equipment and supplies, and they would be able to exchange about twice the amount of merchandise with native customers. Thus, the single canoe that Hilaire Bourgine provided to the six partners was obviously their second craft, having been added to one which they already owned.

It was not surprising that François, Jean, and their fellow partners waited until the latter part of this summer of 1688 to complete their preparations and eventually travel west with the September convoy. In fact, only a few voyageur-traders had headed off with the May brigade, due to events of the previous year. During the summer of 1687, the majority of the French and native traders living in the west had been involved in the campaign against the Seneca nation. As a result, they had not been able to bring out their accumulated supplies of peltries from Michilimackinac. To remedy this situation, in the autumn of that same year, Governor Denonville had sent in a large number of men from the St. Lawrence communities, to supposedly aid in hauling out those furs and hides during the following summer; these were individuals who had served in the summer expedition as militia fighters. As compensation for their martial services, each of them had been allowed to go up without a permit, and each one had been allowed to take a supply of 500 livres worth of trade goods. (However, their return from St. Ignace with the accumulated peltries would be by no means rapid; these individuals would remain in the interior for a full two years of trading, finally descending in 1689.)[85]

These events from 1687, which had drawn off numerous men and a huge amount of materiel from the St. Lawrence settlements, had caused a slow start in the spring of 1688. Gradually, however, preparations were commenced by other individuals who were interested in launching commercial ventures in the west. In examining the hiring contracts for voyageur-traders which were registered with the notaries in Montreal, the only engagements that were finalized in April included one man who was destined for the Illinois Country and another two who were headed for the Ottawa Country. Then, on May 13, 14, 15, 18, and 20, an additional eight men were hired for the upper Great Lakes region. Ten of these individuals were presumably part of the small convoy that shoved off in May. It is unknown whether the eleventh man, engaged by Antoine Pascaud to work in Illinois, departed with this first brigade of the year, or whether he waited until September to travel with his other Illinois-bound colleagues.

As the summer progressed, the action gradually picked up, including the preparations that the Brunet-Boursier team and their new youthful partners carried out. The hiring contracts that were drawn up over the course of the summer reflected the steady increases in the activity levels. In June, only five voyageur-traders for the Ottawa Country were engaged at Montreal, on June 3, 6, 17, and 27. During July, however, twenty men were hired to work in this region (including a few who were assigned to La Baye and the area slightly to the west), while seven others were contracted to labor for Monsieur La Forest in the Illinois Country; these contracts were registered on July 3, 4, 5, 20, 23, 24, 26, 27, 29, 30, and 31. The engagements from August were nearly as numerous, with 17 men being hired to work in the Ottawa Country on August 1, 2, 4, 6, and 8, plus one final man being engaged belatedly on the 19th. Thus, over the summer months, a total of 43 voyageur-traders had been contracted at Montreal for the Ottawa Country, while seven others had been engaged for the Illinois Country.[86]

Among the numerous men who left for the west with this September brigade, François Brunet dit Le Bourbonnais was not the only one who was a direct ancestor of the present author. Pierre Cadieux, born and raised in Montreal, had turned 22 in the spring of 1688. As the second child and first son of the locksmith Jean Cadieux and Marie Valade, he had been baptized in the Montreal church back on April 7, 1666. Among his nine siblings, his older sister Marie Jeanne and one of his younger sisters Marie Nicole had already died, at the ages of $15^1/2$ years (in 1680) and $3^1/4$ years (in 1677), respectively. Then, when Pierre had been $15^1/2$, his father had died at Montreal in September of 1681, at the untimely age of about 45 to 47, leaving seven other living children besides Pierre. Five months later, in February of 1682, his mother had remarried at Montreal, and within four years she had produced three more children with her new husband. On August 2, 1688, (the same day that François Brunet and his five partners acknowledged their debt to their outfitter) Pierre was hired by Claude Greysolon, Sieur de Tourette, to work as a voyageur-trader in the Ottawa Country. Along with the other nineteen men who were contracted by Monsieur Greysolon at Montreal between April 16 and August 6, he would work in the Lake Superior region. His employer, along with Greysolon's brother Daniel Greysolon, Sieur DuLhut, had recently established Ft. Kaministiquia on the western shore of Lake Superior, as well as Ft. Tourette to the north of this massive lake, on the northern shore of Lake Nipigon. At these two posts, which had been erected during 1684 and 1685, the Greysolon employees had been carrying on a brisk commerce; Pierre and his nineteen colleagues had been hired to continue these activities. On Jaillot's 1685 map entitled *Partie de la Nouvelle France*, the cartographer applied the following label to the Tourette facility: "Post of the Sieur Duluth (sic) to prevent the Assiniboins and other natives from going down to Hudson's

Bay."[87] After this particular stint of labor in the Lake Superior area during 1688-1689, there is no known documentation which indicates that Pierre worked in the fur trade during the following sixteen years, until his voyage to Detroit in the summer of 1705, when he was 39 years old. However, considering how many individuals participated illegally in the peltries commerce each year during this era, there is a distinct possibility that he was among their numbers, working as a *coureur de bois*. Circumstantial evidence supporting this premise is the fact that Pierre would not marry until eight years after he had completed this 1688-1689 contract for Monsieur Greysolon, when he would be $30^1/2$ years old. (The present author is descended from his daughter Jeanne, who would be born in February of 1703 to Pierre and his second wife, Jeanne Marsan.)[88]

In September of 1688, the brigade launched onto the waters of the St. Lawrence River at Lachine, headed for the west. At this seigneury, located at the terminus of the Montreal-to-Lachine portage road, various support facilities were gradually developing to facilitate the regular departures and arrivals of canoe convoys. These activities were related to virtually all of the fur trade, military, and missionary expeditions of the French that were focused on the interior, as well as the ventures of native traders and warriors who resided in those distant interior regions. The facilities that were sometimes required at Lachine included shelters for canoes, cargoes, paddlers, and passengers, and sometimes the feeding of those people as well.

The men of the 1688 brigade hoped that their extensive numbers would deter Iroquois attacks en route, which were most likely to occur along the Ottawa River. In addition, these raids would most likely be inflicted upon any canoes that forged too far ahead of their group, or any that lagged too far behind their group. Unfortunately, it was not possible for the entire massed convoy to remain close together. It was necessary that the total number of canoes be divided into smaller groups, and that some distance be allowed to form between these miniature brigades. Otherwise, if all of the craft within the entire convoy were to remain bunched into a single assemblage, major delays would be caused at the numerous portage landings, due to overcrowding. In addition, very few of the camping places along the route could accommodate the entire massed group.

During the following eleven-month absence of François Brunet and Jean Boursier from their homes, their respective wives Barbe Beauvais and Marie Marthe Thibodeau may have felt, in certain respects, like widows. However, after all these years of their paddler spouses being away on numerous long-distance ventures, the two wives had likely become accustomed to the situation. In fact, long before this, they must have learned how to handle the myriad challenges that invariably arose during the long absences of their husbands. In all likelihood, one of their most useful coping mechanisms had been to support one another. This was made easier by the proximity of their two properties, which were only separated by a span of 575 feet, containing a single farm.

However, on the opposite (west) side of Barbe and François' land, Catherine Renusson did actually become a widow within weeks of the departure of the September brigade. On November 13, 1688, her husband Vincent Chamaillard passed away, at the untimely age of about 42 to 48, leaving three living children who were ages 11, 8, and 6. Previously, the couple had endured major portions of heartache. First of all, their fifth child had died on the day of her birth, back in December of 1683. More recently, their newest baby had died at the age of twelve days in August of 1687; two months later, in October, another of their children had passed away at the age of nine; and their second-youngest child had perished in January of 1688, two weeks before his third birthday. Thus, within the span of the previous thirteen months, Catherine had lost three of her sons and her husband, each one in a separate incident. Barbe, living immediately next door to the Chamaillards, as she had done ever since Vincent and Catherine had settled here with their children in 1680, probably assisted the family as best she could in each of these mournful situations. As was quite typical in New France, Catherine remarried within four months of the death of her first husband. Her new spouse, Augustin Alonze dit l'Espagnol (Augustino Alonzo called the Spaniard), originally from Santiago de Compostella in Spain, had come to New France a few years earlier as a French soldier in the Dumesnil Company; he had never been married. Following their nuptial ceremony, which was held at the Lachine church on March 7, 1689, the new husband joined his spouse on her farm, adjacent to the property of the Brunet family.[89]

When it was time for François, Jean, and their four youthful associates to haul out the peltries that they had gathered during most of a year of trading in the Illinois Country, it is almost certain that they paddled three canoes, with two men per craft. In fact, their accumulated furs may have even required the hiring of a fourth canoe and its pair of native paddlers. If their overage cargo was less than a fourth canoe load, the partners may have paid other traders a freighting fee, in order to have them transport the partners' extra packs amid their own cargo. In 1685, the officer Lahontan observed that the eastbound canoes were typically manned by only two or sometimes three paddlers. He also explained one aspect of the multiplier factor as it related to incoming merchandise and outgoing peltries:

"The lading [trade goods] of two canows, computed at a thousand crowns [3,000 livres in outfitting expenses], is a purchase [which has the trading potential] for as many beaver skins as will load four canows. Now, four canows will carry a hundred and sixty packs of skins, that is, forty apiece; and reckoning each pack to be worth fifty crowns [150 livres], the value of the whole amounts to eight thousand crowns [24,000 livres]."[90]

In addition to this issue of monetary value, there was also a second aspect involved in the increased size of outgoing cargoes. Furs and hides were generally much bulkier than the articles of merchandise which were traded to acquire them. This second aspect of the multiplier factor likewise led to the need for extra watercraft in order to haul out the products of a trading season.

Hoping to ward off any Iroquois onslaughts that might crop up during their eastbound journey in 1689, large numbers of French and native traders gathered at Michilimackinac in the early summer, intending to form a massive convoy. Included among the paddlers, who had come from both the upper Great Lakes region and the Illinois Country, were the many men who had been sent in by the Governor two years earlier, to retrieve the accumulated furs and hides at St. Ignace. This impressive flotilla of canoes brought out to Montreal a huge supply of peltries which was worth some 800,000 livres.[91]

By the last week of July, François and his five partners, having returned home from their Illinois venture, were settling up their accounts. During their lengthy absence, the Lachine merchant René Cuillerier, who was the father of their partner René, Jr., had paid off the debt that they had owed to the notary-outfitter Hilaire Bourgine, for the invoiced articles that he had supplied to the men. Thus, after disposing of their supply of pelts, the partners repaid Monsieur Cuillerier, Sr. and then divided among themselves the remaining proceeds from the enterprise. Finally, to officially register this payoff and to dissolve their joint partnership, Michel Descaries, representing all six of the trading associates, along with René Cuillerier, Sr., visited the Montreal notary Adhémar on July 29, and had the scribe draw up the following document:

"Account settled between the Sieurs Cuillerier [Sr. and] Descaries, etc., [his] associates in the partnership for the Illinois Country.

Before etc. [Antoine Adhémar, notary] were present the Sieurs René Cuillerier, [Sr.,] merchant, and Michel Descaries, acting for and in the name of his other associates in the partnership and voyage which they had to the Country of the Illinois, they being [Jean Boursier dit] Lavigne, [François Brunet dit Le] Bourbonnais, René Cuillerier, Jr., Joseph Aubuchon, and others [Claude Bouchard dit Dorval, legally represented by Antoine Pascaud], who have said and declared that they are respectfully quit of all matters whatever that they have had in common due to the said partnership, declaring that the said Cuillerier [Sr.] has been paid for the contents of the invoice of the Sieur [Hilaire] Bourgine. Concerning this and in all matters, the said parties are in accord. [This agreement] made and drawn up at the said Ville Marie in the office of the said notary on July 29, 1689 in the morning, in the presence of the Sieurs Louis Chevalier and Georges Michelet, witnesses residing at the said Ville Marie, who have signed below with the said parties and the notary, according to the ordinance.

Signed,

René Cuillerier, Michel Descaris, L. Chevalier, Michellet, and Adhémar, notary"[92]

At this point, François Brunet was 44 or 45 years old. After this record from 1689, no surviving documents have been found which indicate that he participated in any further business dealings related to the peltries commerce, either as an active voyageur-trader or as a stay-at-home investor financing other traders. However, even if he did not actively take part in the furs-and-hides business, he most likely kept abreast of current events. This would not have been difficult to do, since his farm was located about 8/10 mile east of the end of the Montreal-to-Lachine portage road, the scene of virtually all of the departures and arrivals of French and native convoys. This span between his property and the terminus of the portage road contained three farms next to his and then the half-mile-wide Commons land.

When François returned to his life in the St. Lawrence Valley, two topics seemed to be salient in nearly everyone's mind. One of these subjects was the high level of danger from lightning raids by Iroquois warriors. Back in 1687, after the military campaign by French and native forces into the lands of the Senecas, Iroquois war parties had resumed their sporadic attacks against the St. Lawrence settlers, breaking two entire decades of peace. The next year, due to Iroquois blockades around their two forts in the southwest, the French had been forced to abandon their distant and highly exposed new post at Niagara, near the western end of Lake Ontario. (The task of maintaining Ft. Frontenac, at the eastern end of this same lake, would soon become untenable, and it would likewise be closed in the autumn of 1689.) Close to home, stockades of refuge had been constructed at each of the exposed seigneuries during 1688. Along the southern shoreline of Montreal Island, from east to west, these had included the fortifications at Verdun (about $1^1/2$ miles northeast of the Brunet farm), Ft. Cuillerier on the property of René Cuillerier, Sr. ($1^3/4$ miles west of the Brunets), Ft. Rémy at the village of Lachine ($^3/4$ mile further toward the west), and Ft. Rolland ($1^3/4$ miles further west, at the western end of the Lachine seigneury). The residents of the seigneury of La Présentation or Côte St. Gilles, extending for about $2^1/4$ miles west of Ft. Rolland (to about the present community of Dorval), would use the latter stockade as needed. Thus, the settlers who were spread out along some nine miles of the shoreline in this southeastern section of the island, from the eastern end of Verdun to the western end of La Présentation, had four palisades to which they could flee for protection in case of attacks.

Across the Atlantic, in the spring of 1689, war had broken out between France and the combined countries of England, Spain, the Dutch Netherlands, and the Hapsburg Empire. By late spring, ships had brought this news to the English colonies; unfortunately, word of it would not reach New France via French vessels until September. During the summer, the Iroquois nations had been elated to receive this information, which meant that in their upcoming war with the French, they would have the military support of both England and her colonies. However, unaware of these perilous events, the colonists along the St. Lawrence had no idea of the fierce onslaught that would soon descend upon many of them.[93]

Lacking any knowledge of these grave events which were transpiring both to the south and across the ocean, the residents of Montreal Island were much more intrigued with the exciting project of the Lachine Canal. Going back a full decade, Fr. Dollier de Casson, the Superior of the Sulpicians of Montreal (the seigneurs of Montreal Island), had proposed the construction of such a waterway, running in a northeasterly direction between Lachine and Montreal. According to his ambitious plans, the project would entail widening and deepening the eastward-flowing branch of the small Rivière St. Pierre (which flowed northeastward from Lac St. Pierre to Montreal, along a course that was generally parallel to the St. Lawrence), and also digging a canal southwestward from Lac St. Pierre to the St. Lawrence River. Upon its completion, water diverted from the St. Lawrence would flow northeastward over the full distance of $8^1/2$ miles to Montreal. This canal would serve two important functions. First, it would allow westbound canoes and bateaux to be loaded at Montreal, saving both the expense and the heavy labor of hauling watercraft and cargoes overland to Lachine, which now had to be done either by hand or by cart. Second, its flow would provide a steady and reliable source of water power, to operate an entire series of grist mills located along its banks. In this manner, the local millers would no longer have to rely only upon wind power to rotate their grinding wheels. In this year of 1689, Fr. Dollier had proposed to the Intendant that those residents of the Lachine seigneury who had not paid the Sulpicians their seigneurial fees should be obliged to work off those unpaid fees by laboring on the canal project. On June 5, the Intendant had issued an ordinance turning this proposal into law, and one week later, work had commenced on the project, the first canal in North America. However, this ground-breaking labor (both literally and figuratively) would come to an abrupt halt just seven weeks later, for reasons that had been entirely unforeseen.[94]

Six days after François, Jean, and their four youthful partners had settled their accounts and had officially dissolved their fur trade association, came the night of August 4-5. That night, under the cover of darkness and a violent hailstorm, a massive force of about 1,500 Iroquois warriors crossed northward over the broad St. Lawrence. Silently spreading out along eight miles of shoreline, from the Sault St. Louis area (beside the Lachine Rapids, where the Brunet and Boursier families lived) westward to La Présentation, the raiders remained undetected by the sentries in the various forts throughout the entire night. Waiting until dawn to launch their ferocious strike, the Iroquois, who numbered nearly 200 attackers per mile of shoreline, took the French completely by surprise. Soon, they had slain at least 24 French residents and had captured an estimated 79 others. They also destroyed by fire 56 of the 77 houses in the area, along with numerous stables, granaries, and other outbuildings, and killed a large portion of the livestock.

In the immediate aftermath, most of the survivors of this first onslaught sought refuge within the four stockades. But some of them made their way to Montreal, where Governor Denonville was visiting at the time. Immediately, he sent Philippe Rigaud, Sieur de Vaudreuil, the acting governor of Montreal, to the raided area with a force of about 300 soldiers. Their orders were to bolster the troops who had been manning the four forts, and enforce the Governor's orders that all of the residents of the attacked area were to gather within these stockades of refuge and remain there. After reaching Ft. Rolland, Vaudreuil sent word back to the Governor requesting additional reinforcements. In response, on August 6, the administrator dispatched about fifty soldiers and some thirty allied native warriors, under the command of Lieutenant Labeyre and Charles Lemoyne. This party covered the ten miles to Ft. Rémy without incident; however, after they departed from the fortified village, heading west toward Ft. Rolland ($1^3/4$ miles away), they were attacked by an Iroquois party. During the skirmish that followed, the enemy warriors killed and scalped about twenty of the native allies and captured about half of the soldiers, including Labeyre and four of his subaltern officers. In the fray, Lemoyne was wounded, but he and some of his companions managed to return to Ft. Rémy. During this debacle, which was taking place within sight of Ft. Rolland, the officers inside pleaded with Vaudreuil to be permitted to go to the aid of their comrades. But the commander refused, since his orders specifically stated that he and his forces were to remain within the forts! Previously, again taking his orders literally, Vaudreuil had denied permission to one of his officers to conduct a counter-attack upon a large party of Iroquois warriors. These enemies would have been easy prey, since they had become drunk on the liquor that they had seized in the homes. Thus, by remaining entirely in a defensive mode, the commander had lost at least two opportunities to fight back against the Iroquois raiders and inflict heavy casualties on them.

Numerous scholars have sought to identify the colonists who either died or were captured in this horrific raid, which was soon afterward dubbed the Lachine Massacre. The primary document for identifying those who perished on site in the attack was the official list that was drawn up by Fr. Rémy, who had been the resident priest of the Lachine parish since 1680. Not long after the raid, the deceased were hastily buried in the very places in which they had each been found. Five years later, Bishop Saint-Vallier declared that these bodies were to be exhumed and reburied in the consecrated ground of the

Lachine cemetery. These mournful reburials were conducted during the last week of October in 1694. It was during this process that Fr. Rémy made a list of those 24 individuals who had perished in the raid of 1689. (This roster was signed by the priest; by Jean Paré and André Rapin, members of the church council; and by Guillaume Daoust, the chanter of the parish and a direct ancestor of the present author.) Among the listed victims, nine of them had originally been buried in the area of the Lachine seigneury, while the other fifteen had been initially interred further to the west, in the adjacent seigneury of La Présentation, which was also called Côte St. Gilles.

Somehow, François, Barbe, and their eight children all survived the attack and evaded capture. However, on the Boursier farm, just 575 feet toward the east, their close neighbors and close friends were not so fortunate. Fr. Rémy reported that he and his parishioners reburied little Madeleine Boursier, who had been drowned by Iroquois attackers. At the time of the raid, she had been seven weeks short of her first birthday, having been born just weeks after the Brunet-Boursier team had departed for the Illinois Country, back in September of 1688. Three of the other members of her family fared little better. The parents Jean and Marie Marthe, as well as their nine-year-old daughter Marie Élisabeth, were taken captive; afterward, the girl may have died in captivity, or she may have been adopted into the Iroquois world and remained there for the rest of her life. At the time of little Madeleine's reburial in October of 1694, Jean was recorded as being dead. Some four years later, a Lachine document from February 25, 1699 indicated that Marie Marthe had passed away some time previous to that date, presumably while in Iroquois hands. But the couple's other five children, ages 15, 11, 7, 5, and 3, escaped death and capture during the raid. (Eventually, François would become their legal guardian.)

Madeleine Boursier was the only resident to die on site within the eastern two-thirds of the Lachine seigneury, in the stretch of about $4^1/4$ miles that extended eastward from Ft. Rémy. However, six other settlers who lived in this area are known to have been captured. These included two members of the Jean Roy household (one mile northeast of the Brunet's land), two people in the Jean Paré home ($^1/2$ mile east of the Brunets), Catherine Renusson (on the farm immediately west of François and Barbe), and Pierre Pérusseau's wife Marie Leroy, in their home by the eastern end of the stockaded village site. A short distance west of the village, Jean Fournier was wounded but escaped, while his wife Marie Crépin was captured; in addition, two soldiers died and were later buried there. These latter men, having been part of the supplemental contingent of troops led by Labeyre, had been killed in the skirmish after they had left the fortified village site of Lachine (Ft. Rémy), headed for Ft. Rolland. In addition, the dead buried within this area included about twenty native allies, who had also been felled in the same fight west of Ft. Rémy.

According to the priest's list of reburials, the other 21 victims (twenty French and one native) had been initially interred in 1689 in the western portion of the Lachine seigneury and in the adjacent La Présentation seigneury (which was also called Côte St. Gilles). It was in this area, extending along the shoreline for some four miles, that the raiders had directed their greatest fury. The deceased individuals here included seven men, three women, nine children, one soldier, and a fifteen-year-old native slave who had belonged to René Chartier.[95]

A span of 1³/4 miles of river frontage comprised the western section of the Lachine seigneury. This area extended westward from Ft. Rémy (the stockaded Lachine village site) to Ft. Rolland, at the edge of the La Présentation seigneury. In this particular area, residents in at least nine of the households suffered either death or capture at the hands of the Iroquois raiders. Three of these families included direct ancestors of the present author, while a fourth family contained a daughter and sibling of ancestors.

One of the hardest-hit households here, in terms of sheer numbers of dead or captured individuals, was that of Pierre Barbary (or Barbarin) dit Grandmaison, about 38 years old, and his wife Marie Lebrun, about 35 (both of whom are direct ancestors of the present author). Their home was located about one mile west of Ft. Rémy, about ³/4 mile east of Ft. Rolland (on the seventh lot east of the latter stockade), and some 3³/4 miles west of the Brunet home. Pierre had originally come to New France in 1665 as a soldier in the Carignan Regiment, while Marie had arrived some time during the following two years as a *fille du Roi*. During the attack, both of these parents and all five of their living children were captured, while one of their two sons-in-law was slain. (Three months earlier, on April 28, the heavy-hearted Barbary couple had lost two of their other young children, in a tragic house fire; these little ones had been 4²/3 and 2¹/2 years old, respectively.) On August 5, the living Barbary children included their only surviving son, age twelve, and their two young daughters, who were seven years old and nine weeks old, respectively. Of the couple's two married daughters, their eldest, who was about age twenty and had no children, had been living a short distance to the west with her husband André Danis dit Larpenty. In the raid, he was killed on site, while she was seized. The other married daughter, Marie Madeleine, was about to turn sixteen; she had wed the retired soldier Pierre Jamme dit Carrière back in February, less than six months before the attack. (This Jamme couple would eventually provide the first generation of genealogical linkages between the Barbary couple and the present author.) The newlyweds had apparently been residing with the Barbary family; during the attack, she was captured, but he escaped (or he may have been fortunately away from the seigneury at the time of the onslaught).

At some point, both of the Barbary parents died while in captivity; for her part, the eldest married daughter was never again documented in New France, so she presumably also passed away while in Iroquois hands. The two youngest daughters would remain permanently in Iroquois country, willingly spending their lives there. (By the time the war ended in 1697 and this information reached the colony in 1698, and prisoner exchanges were eventually negotiated during the following years, the older of these two young daughters would have spent the majority of her life as an Iroquois; the younger one, captured at the age of just two months, would have known only Iroquois ways all of her life.) Among the seven captured Barbary family members, only Marie Madeleine and her younger brother Pierre would return to the colony, in about 1700, to resume their lives as French colonists after some eleven years of living as native captives. Marie Madeleine, then about 27 years old, would return to her waiting husband, after which they would produce seven children between September of 1701 and September of 1716 at Lachine, Bout de l'Île, and Pointe aux Trembles. Her brother Pierre, age 23 in 1700, would be married at Lachine in October of 1701 and would afterward settle there.[96]

One other captive from the Lachine raid of 1689, Suzanne Aly (or Alix), is known to have spent this long a period in Iroquois captivity before returning to the St. Lawrence settlements. Seized at the age of seven weeks, this girl was returned to New France some eleven years later, in about 1700. During the fierce attack, both of her parents and all three of her siblings had been killed on site; thus, she would have had no memories of her family of origin.[97] One other person who was seized in the raid resided with the Iroquois for about a year longer than the Barbary and Aly captives, before finally returning to his former life among the French. This was François Davaut, whose family had resided two lots to the east of the Aly household. Captured at the age of six (when his mother and his two-year-old brother were killed on site and his father was seized, to later die while in captivity), François returned to the colony some twelve years later, in about 1701. Unfortunately, the young man would perish of smallpox in January of 1705, five weeks before he would have celebrated his 22nd birthday. Besides these four individuals, another four captives are known to have returned during the 1690s, including one in about 1694, two in about 1698, and one without a documented year.[98]

The household immediately west of the Barbary home, that of Jean Michel (or Michau) and his wife Marie Marchessault (the former widow of Pierre Boutin), was the scene of bloody carnage on the morning of August 5, 1689. On that fateful day, Jean (about 49 years old), the couple's stepson Albert Boutin (age 18), and their eldest child Pierre (16) were all killed on site. Marie, who was about 50 years old at the time, was taken captive, as was possibly their second-oldest child, François (age 15, who disappeared from the documentary record after March of 1689). Somehow, the two young daughters of the family eluded capture; these were Marie Renée (age 12, who would eventually marry Pierre Sauvé and become the direct ancestral link between the Michel couple and the present author) and Marie Madeleine (age 8). Twelve years after the attack, in July of 1701, the matriarch Marie was cited in a Montreal document; thus, she apparently made her way back to the colony at some point during that span of time.[99]

In the dim dawn light of August 5, Iroquois warriors also attacked the nearby Maupetit family. They resided two lots west of the Michel home, on the fourth farm east of Ft. Rolland. The father of the family, Pierre Maupetit dit Poitevin, was a retired soldier, and also a master handler of woolen fabrics. The mother, Marie Louise Beaune, about 21 years old, had grown up on the Beaune family farm immediately east of the Barbary household. At the time of the onslaught, the couple, having been married for $5^2/3$ years, had three young children. These offspring were $3^1/2$ years, $2^2/3$ years, and 9 months old, respectively. (The middle child, Pierre, Jr., would eventually grow up to marry Angélique Villeray and provide the familial link between the Maupetit couple and the present author.

Their dual biography is presented later in this work.) At some point after Pierre, Sr. was seized by the attackers, he either died or was killed while in Iroquois captivity. Nine years after the raid, in June of 1698, Marie Louise would finally remarry at the Lachine church, to Louis Lory; however, she would bear no children by her second husband. By 1702, he would be listed as owning property at Pointe Claire, about three miles west of the La Présentation seigneury.[100]

Although the horrific raid of 1689 has been called for centuries the Lachine Massacre, the adjacent seigneury located immediately to the west suffered as many or more casualties than did the residents of the Lachine seigneury. In at least twelve of the households in La Présentation (also called Côte St. Gilles), many of the settlers were either slain or taken captive. In one of these homes, located about a quarter-mile west of Ft. Rolland, lived Michel Prézeau (or Prézot) dit Chambly, about 41 years old, and his wife Marie Chancy, about age 32. At the time of the attack, the couple had four living children, having earlier lost three others at very young ages. Their surviving offspring in 1689 included Marie (10 years old, who would eventually marry Pierre Clément and provide the ancestral linkage between the Prézeau couple and the present author), Marguerite (8), Madeleine (4), and André (age unknown). During the raid, both of the parents and little Madeleine were taken captive, and thereafter disappeared from the documentary record. The other three children in the household apparently eluded the Iroquois warriors, since each of them later grew up, married, and produced families of their own.[101]

The known casualties of the raid (both the killed and the captured individuals) were stricken along a stretch of at least $6^1/2$ miles of St. Lawrence shoreline. This area extending westward from the Jean Roy household ($^1/2$ mile west of Verdun) to at least the René Chartier home ($^3/4$ mile west of Ft. Rolland). In addition to the 24 individuals who were killed (plus about twenty allied native warriors who were also slain), an estimated 79 settlers living in the attacked area were captured during the raid. However, an estimated 27 of these latter individuals (about one-third of them) eventually made their way back to their homes, either by escaping or by being later exchanged or released. One of these fortunate returned souls was Catherine Renusson, François and Barbe's neighbor who lived on the adjacent farm immediately to the west, with her new second husband Augustino Alonzo; she was cited in a document in April of 1691. Another returnee was Pierre Gauthier dit Saguingoira, who had been sixty years old when both he and his wife Charlotte Roussel had been seized. She would die while in captivity, while he would remain among the Iroquois for at least 8$^{1}/2$ years before eventually making his way back to Lachine.[102]

The reburials of the 24 victims of the 1689 raid, ordered by Bishop Saint-Vallier, took place in the cemetery of the Lachine church in late October of 1694. This has misled many historians of the past into thinking that all of the surviving residents of this portion of Montreal Island abandoned their homes and farms for five years after the raid, before eventually returning in fear and uncertainty. It is undoubtedly true that the horrible events of death and destruction that occurred in August of 1689 must have scarred their psyches for the rest of their lives. However, a number of period documents clearly show that, soon after the horrific attacks, many of the residents of the area began courageously repairing and rebuilding both their farms and their lives.

As a testament to these activities, between August and the end of December in 1689, the priest performed five marriages, one baptism, and two burials at the parish church in Lachine. (One of these marriages, the one celebrated on December 2, involved Marie Madeleine Bourgery, a direct ancestor of the present author. The 38-year-old widow of Jean Beaune, also a direct ancestor, she had been a widow since January of 1687. She was residing with her four unmarried children in the western section of the Lachine seigneury, on their farm immediately to the east of the Barbary property. On this December day, she married Jacques Chasle dit Duhamel, a retired soldier.) During the following year, Monseigneur de Saint-Vallier came to the same edifice to conduct confirmation ceremonies. In addition, land grants in the Lachine seigneury were ceded to six individuals during the year of 1690; and within the space of just a few more years, all of the interior lands (in back of the original grants fronting on the St. Lawrence) were settled, as were also those of the Côte St. Paul, which lay immediately north of the Sault St. Louis section of the seigneury, where the Brunet farm was located.[103]

It is a documented fact that a great number of the homes, stables, granaries, and other outbuildings along the shoreline in this area of Montreal Island had been destroyed in the deadly raid, and that innumerable farm animals had also been killed. In addition, it would have probably been many weeks after the attacks, stretching into September of 1689, before those families who had lost their assets could safely commence rebuilding, due to the continued threat of Iroquois strikes. As a result, with winter approaching, many of the families who now lacked homes and other buildings, livestock, and stored foods left for Montreal. They intended to spend the first frozen season in town, before returning in the following spring to begin their rebuilding efforts in earnest.

It is not known whether François and Barbe's farm and livestock had remained intact during the raid. Fortunately, all ten members of their family had survived the onslaught (at least physically), including the eight children, who ranged in age from $15^2/3$ down to $2^2/12$ years. In any case, they decided to move to the security of Montreal for the present time. Since François had recently reaped substantial profits from his trading enterprise in the Illinois Country, he had considerable financial resources on hand. As a result, he could apparently purchase a home outright, without needing to take out a loan (there is no known documentation of any loan or debt for him during this period). On September 13, 1689, five weeks after the August raid, he and Barbe purchased a lot on Rue St. Paul in Montreal, on which stood both a house and a shop. The neighbors flanking this property were the Montreal merchant Jean Milot dit Le Bourguignon and the notary Hilaire Bourgine. (The former individual had purchased the original Lachine land grant from La Salle back in 1669. The latter man, expecting to become a father for the first time in the coming December, had arranged the partial outfit that François and his colleagues had required before their departure for the Illinois Country, back in August of 1688.) The sellers of the property were Pierre Lusseau dit Desruisseaux, bourgeois of Montreal and formerly a sergeant in the Troupes de la Marine, and his wife Marguerite Sédilot. This young couple, who had been married for $2^1/2$ years, had one child, a toddler son who was thirteen months old. According to the sales agreement, the price for the lot and buildings was 2,000 livres, "which the said Brunet and his said wife are obliged to pay to the said sellers within fifteen days from today." Nicolas Perrot, the highly respected trader, interpreter, and liaison with the native nations in the Wisconsin-Minnesota region, appeared as one of the signing witnesses at the bottom of the notary document. After completing this transaction, the sellers relocated with their son to Pointe aux Trembles, near the northern tip of Montreal Island.[104]

Twelve days after purchasing their town property, on September 25, the Brunet couple visited a different notary in Montreal, this time to arrange a lease on a piece of land which was located at a distance south-southwest of town. The sub-fief which included this property, called Pointe St. Charles, commenced immediately southwest of the town; it extended along the St. Lawrence shoreline for about 3^1/2 miles, to the eastern edge of the Verdun fief. François apparently intended to farm this parcel of leased land, which belonged to Catherine Thierry dite Primot, the widow of the distinguished interpreter and peltries merchant Charles Lemoyne, Sieur de Longueuil; she was leasing it out both in her name and in the names of her minor children. In the notarial document which spelled out the details of this agreement, the leasing couple were identified as "François Brunet dit Le Bourbonnais, habitant, and Barbe Beauvais, his wife, of Montreal."[105]

Several weeks after completing this transaction, in mid-October, François was deeply saddened to learn that one of his former partners in the Illinois trading venture, young René Cuillerier, Jr., had drowned in a canoe-capsize accident. This tragic incident had taken place on the St. Lawrence in the Quebec area, some three months before René would have celebrated his 22nd birthday. However, his body would not be interred in the Lachine cemetery until December, after it had been finally found in the river. Until about ten weeks before the accident, young René had been François' business partner and colleague. Together, they had safely paddled and portaged many hundreds of challenging miles, while traveling both into and out from the Illinois Country via Michilimackinac. During their journeys, they had often been under the threat of attack by Iroquois war parties. Thus, this strange accident, back in their home territory and apparently unrelated to any Iroquois depredations, must have provided Monsieur Brunet with considerable food for thought about the unpredictable vagaries of life and death.[106]

It was also during this same autumn that François learned that René Robert Cavelier, Sieur de La Salle, his employer on those upper St. Lawrence cargo runs to and from Ft. Frontenac back in 1675-1676, was dead. He had been assassinated by one of his own men more than two years earlier, back in 1687, while the commander and his party had been attempting to establish a colony near the mouth of the Mississippi River, having sailed from France to the Gulf Coast. However, news of his murder had been withheld by his own colleagues, and it had not reached the St. Lawrence communities until French traders from the Arkansas post had traveled out to the eastern settlements during this autumn of 1689.[107]

During the dead of winter in 1690, three separate forces of French and native fighting men marched southward from the three main towns on the St. Lawrence, headed in slightly different directions. In each case, they were intent upon inflicting retaliation upon the English colonists, whose leaders had been largely responsible for the havoc that the Iroquois had been wreaking upon the French settlers. The first group, consisting of 114 Canadians plus 96 warriors from the native communities near Montreal, traveled overland to the Mohawk River Valley and the stockaded community of Schenectady, in the New York colony. On February 18, in their surprise attack at dawn upon the thirty-odd houses, they killed about sixty settlers and seized about fifty others as prisoners. Another fifty or sixty managed to escape, probably fleeing from the homes that had been attacked by the French rather than by the native allies, who would not have spared anyone. After loading some fifty horses with plunder and burning all of the houses in the settlement, the attackers prepared to head north. Before departing, however, they released about half of the prisoners, those who were not fit enough to endure the long winter journey, and left with 27 captive men and boys.

The second retaliatory force, bound for the New England frontier, departed from Trois-Rivières with about fifty men, half of them French and the other half native. By late March, they had reached the settlement of Salmon Falls on the Atlantic coast, near Portsmouth. Although the colonists there lived in three small stockaded forts, they had posted no guards. Thus, no one raised an alarm before the attackers fell upon all three forts at the same time at the crack of dawn. In the fighting, 34 English colonists were slain and another fifty or so, most of them women and children, were captured. After burning the farms and slaughtering the livestock, some of the raiders headed northward on their long march home, with their captives in tow.[108]

The third group of retaliatory fighters, departing from Quebec, were likewise bound for the New England area. This force, containing about fifty Canadian militiamen and four to five hundred Abenaki warriors, was joined en route by most of the men who had completed their attack on Salmon Falls. Making their way to Ft. Loyal on Casco Bay (on the Atlantic coast near the present Portland, Maine) by May, they laid siege to this stockade, to which the local settlers had fled during the previous night. After the attackers had dug European-style trenches up to the palisade walls and the defenders had surrendered, the French and native forces destroyed the fort. Then, nearly all of the prisoners were placed in the charge of the native attackers, who killed those who had been wounded, as well as all of those individuals who could not keep up with the pace during the return march.[109]

In this manner, the Canadian version of offensive guerrilla warfare was inaugurated, during the winter and spring of 1690. When Barbe, François, and the other survivors of the Lachine Massacre heard the news of these three retaliatory expeditions, they may have had mixed reactions. On the one hand, they knew that these raids had been inflicted upon the English, whose leaders were encouraging and equipping the Iroquois nations in their depredations against the French colonists. On the other hand, the members of the Brunet family, as well as all of the other Lachine survivors, were intimately familiar with the horrors and losses that these English settlers had recently suffered, at the hands of the French and native fighters.

In the early spring of 1691, Barbe's father died. Jacques Beauvais dit Saint Gemme was laid to rest in the Montreal cemetery on March 20.[110]

Less than a month later, Barbe and François' ninth child was warmly welcomed into the Brunet family. At the baptism of little Angélique in the Montreal church on April 16, her godmother and name-giver was Angélique Labrie, while the baby's godfather was Jacques Lanthier, a fellow resident of Lachine who would marry at Montreal three years later.[111]

Three months after this baptism, on July 13, the Brunet clan again returned to this same church for another jubilant christening ceremony. On this occasion, the one-day-old baby was Barbe's niece Charlotte Turpin, the fourth child of her sister Charlotte Beauvais and her husband of nearly seven years, Alexandre Turpin, Sr. (whose dual biographies have already been presented in this work). The godfather was Alexandre Turpin, Jr., age 21, while the godmother was Barbe Beauvais, the baby's proud aunt.[112]

In spite of the optimistic mood that the settlers attempted to maintain, by means of these and other upbeat celebrations, the dangers of sickness, injury, and death were always close at hand. Two dramatic reminders of this omnipresent aspect of daily life in the colony flared out of the blue during the summer of 1691.

First, on June 26, enemy forces attacked the western area of the Lachine seigneury and the adjacent seigneury of La Présentation, killing six men; these victims included three settlers and four soldiers.

One of these deceased colonists, René Huguet (age 38), had lived a short distance west of Ft. Rolland, in La Présentation. Back in the 1689 raid, he had lost his wife (age 22), one son (6), and one daughter (3) when these three loved ones had been taken captive by Iroquois warriors. Both René Huguet and another of the settlers killed in 1691, Jean Gourdon (age 45, who resided 1 1/2 miles away toward the east, on the opposite side of Ft. Rolland in Lachine) had been brothers-in-law of Vincent Aly. This latter man (age 40), along with his wife (23) and three of his children (9 years, 6 years, and 2 months old), had all been killed at their home in the La Présentation seigneury during the 1689 attack. In that earlier raid, his youngest daughter, Suzanne (age 2), had been seized, but she would survive in Iroquois captivity for some eleven years, before being finally returned in about 1700.[113]

Six weeks after the June raid, at dawn on August 11, 1691, a combined force of about 400 English and Iroquois fighting men attacked at Laprairie. This village and seigneury, located directly across the St. Lawrence from the Verdun fief, was about seven miles southeast of the Lachine village site, some six miles southeast of the Brunet farm, and about five miles south-southeast of Montreal. In this instance, by good fortune, the French had been forewarned; thus, in advance of the attack, they had been able to gather hundreds of defenders in the area. As a result, they were able to drive off the raiders, in the process killing 37 of them and wounding 31 others. However, the French casualties from this fighting were considerably worse: 45 dead and 60 wounded.[114]

On June 1, 1692, some fourteen months after Barbe's father had passed away, Barbe and François joined her widowed mother Jeanne Soldé, her older brother Raphaël, Raphaël's wife Élisabeth Turpin, and the Montreal surgeon Jean Martinet, Sieur de Fonblanche, in the office of the Montreal notary Adhémar. They gathered on this day to officially register the Beauvais clan's mutual agreements concerning their joint inheritance. Madame Soldé, the matriarch, and her eldest son Raphaël Beauvais had been declared the legal guardians of the youngest Beauvais child, Jeanne, who was by this time 19 1/3 years old (thus of minor age) and still single. Monsieur Martinet had been named as her supplemental or deputy guardian. For this official document, François Brunet represented all five of the other living Beauvais children, including Marguerite and her husband Jacques Tétu, Charlotte and her husband Alexandre Turpin, Marie-Étiennette and her husband Jean Baptiste Pothier, and the unmarried brothers Jean and Jean Baptiste.[115]

The generous piece of land in the Lachine seigneury which was ceded to François on April 5, 1693 provides clear evidence that he and Barbe intended to permanently move back to this seigneury in the future. Upon their return, they planned to reside with their numerous children on their farm beside the Lachine Rapids, where they had lived for many years before the Iroquois raid of 1689. The new land concession, which had been surveyed by Gédéon de Catalogne on March 30, was granted by Fr. Dollier de Casson, the Superior of the Sulpicians (the seigneurs of Montreal Island). It was registered on this fifth day of April with the Lachine notary Jean Baptiste Pothier, who also happened to be Barbe and François' brother-in-law. The new property, in the form of a long slender rectangle, angled northward from the inland end of Monsieur Brunet's St. Lawrence-fronting land. Measuring four arpents (768 English feet) in width by twenty arpents ($7/10$ mile) in length, it contained a total of eighty arpents (68 acres) of surface area. Compared to his original land grant from 1673, this additional lot had the same length, but it was one arpent (192 feet) wider; thus it contained 17 acres more than his river-fronting lot.[116]

In spite of receiving this land concession, the Brunet family would not return to their farm at Lachine for at least another year or more (probably not until the summer or autumn of 1694). On April 12, 1693, one week after officially registering their new rear lot behind their Lachine farm, François and Barbe signed an agreement to rent a farm in the fief of Verdun. This latter fief lay immediately south-southwest of the sub-fief of Pointe St. Charles; it occupied the riverside space between the Pointe St. Charles lands and the Sault St. Louis section of the Lachine seigneury. Some $3^1/2$ years earlier, back in September of 1689, the Brunet couple had first leased a piece of land south-southwest of Montreal, in the sub-fief of Pointe St. Charles. They had eventually allowed that first rental agreement to run out, and had not renewed it. Now, in a document in which they were described as "living near to the town of Ville Marie," the couple leased from Sister Marguerite Bourgeois and the Congregation of Notre Dame of Montreal a farm in the Verdun area that belonged to this order. According to the notary document, François and Barbe would supply to the Notre Dame Sisters "three finished harvests, terminated and completed." In each of these three harvest seasons, they would deliver to the nuns sixty bushels of wheat, ten bushels of peas, and two bushels of oats. In addition, each year they would fatten two pigs for the nuns, and haul six cords of firewood to the parish of Saint Charles. During this three-harvest period, the renters would have the use of the house, stable, granary, and garden on the property, as well as the use of a pair of oxen. It is particularly interesting to note that this second leased farm was located just three miles or less away from their own Lachine property; that was the total distance between their Lachine farm and the eastern boundary of the Verdun fief.[117]

All of the articles that the Brunets could produce on the leased farm which were beyond the promised rental amounts in the agreement would remain the property of the family. At this point, the two sons were 20 and 11 years old, respectively. Thus, along with François, they would have been able to provide a great deal of outdoor labor for this family enterprise. For their part, the six older daughters (ages $18^3/_4$, $16^2/_3$, 13, 13, 8, and 6) could have assisted Barbe very much, both indoors and outdoors. Two-year-old Angélique's main job would have been to generate smiles on the faces of her siblings and parents. It is possible that, over the course of the three-harvest period of $2^1/_2$ years, François and Barbe may have hired additional workers as necessary for this farming operation, particularly after they moved back to their original farm in the Lachine seigneury. However, after most of the family members returned to their own property at Lachine (which appears to have taken place in about the summer or autumn of 1694), certain of the children may have remained on this Verdun property until the conclusion of the lease, after the harvests of the summer and autumn of 1695 had been completed.

It is to be remembered that, during the entire five-year period while Barbe and François were absent from the Lachine seigneury, they continued to own their home on St. Paul Street in Montreal. They had purchased this town property in September of 1689, within five weeks of the Iroquois attacks. However, they apparently wished to raise their own foods and other products, instead of living as traditional town-dwellers. Thus, during the planting, tending, and harvesting seasons, they probably divided their time between one or the other of the successive leased farm properties and their home in town. During the winters, they probably resided entirely on Rue St. Paul in Montreal, having made arrangements for the care of the farm animals in the countryside during their absence.

About two weeks after they had arranged to lease the Verdun farm, Barbe safely delivered their tenth child and third son. For his christening ceremony at the Notre Dame de Montreal church on April 30, baby Joseph's sponsors were Georges Beau and Barbe Baitournai.[118]

Until now, Barbe and François had been extremely fortunate concerning the survival of their offspring. They had earlier produced nine children, and all nine of them were continuing to thrive. This survival rate, however, was an anomaly in New France, where about a quarter of all children died before they had completed their first year, and almost 45 percent of them perished before they reached the age of ten. Unfortunately, the run of good luck of the Brunet family suddenly halted at this point in the summer of 1693, plunging them into deep grief. After living for only four months, little Joseph died; he was laid to rest in the Montreal cemetery on August 30.[119]

About seven weeks later, on October 20, Barbe and all seven of her siblings, along with the spouses of the five married ones, divided between themselves the ownership of a portion of the Beauvais family land. This property was located a short distance south of Montreal in the area that was called the St. Joseph Quarter.[120]

As winter weather approached in the autumn of 1693, François agreed to rent out certain portions of a house that was located within the stockade at Verdun. This building was probably associated with the farm in the Verdun fief that he had leased in April from Sister Marguerite Bourgeois. In fact, it is highly likely that this house was intended to be the residence of the renters of the nuns' farm whenever they would seek refuge within the Verdun palisades during enemy attacks. On November 14, according to the Montreal notary's document, Monsieur Brunet agreed to rent out, until the end of the following year of 1694, "one room with a fireplace and one room behind the hearth where there is a fireback, a cellar space beneath the said rooms, the attic, [and] two stables, one for the said Buet and the other for the said Roy." The two renters were Alexis Buet and Jean Roy dit La Pensée, fellow residents of the Lachine seigneury with François and Barbe. Monsieur Buet, about age 48 to 54, had a wife and two children. Monsieur Roy, about age 46 to 55, had a wife and three surviving children; their youngest, Marie Anne, had been captured in the 1689 raid when she had been two years old. These two families, like the Brunet clan, were still displaced more than four years after the raid on their Lachine farms. Thus, the two renters apparently intended to use the two rooms plus the entire attic of the house to shelter themselves and their combined five children during the following 13 1/2 months. In the contract, Messieurs Buet and Roy agreed that, at the end of the following March, they would each pay François 40 livres to cover this entire rental period.[121]

During the first week of April in 1694, Jean Brunet dit Le Bourbonnais, Barbe and François' eldest child and first son celebrated his 21st birthday. Ten weeks later, on June 14, he signed a contract to serve as a voyageur-trader in the west. According to this notary document, Jean, along with Louis Roy and a number of other men, were engaged by the Montreal merchant Antoine Pascaud to make a journey to the Ottawa Country. Between May 24 and September 21 of this year, according to the notary records of the Montreal region, a total of 59 men were hired for such labor, either in the Ottawa Country or at Michilimackinac; two others were hired to work in the Illinois Country. Jean's engagement in mid-June represented the young man's initial entry into the world of the fur trade. This first step would eventually lead him to spend his entire adult life in the Illinois Country, where his father had traded during 1688-1689. In about 1700, Jean would marry the native woman Élisabeth Deshayes at Kaskaskia, after which the couple would produce at least three children there. It is highly likely that Barbe and François would never meet this daughter-in-law, or these three granddaughters. In 1724, Jean would be recorded as the Lieutenant of the Kaskaskia militia forces, indicating that he had become a well-respected member of the community there.[122]

Over the course of his many years of working in the peltries commerce, François had set a strong and positive example for his children, which eventually spread to the spouses of his daughters as well. As a result, over the span of more than three decades, commencing in this year of 1694 and extending to at least 1725, all three of his surviving sons, as well as five of his seven sons-in-law, would be employed at some point in the fur trade in the western interior.

About eight months after they had buried baby Joseph Brunet back in August of 1693, Barbe again became pregnant. This time, the expectant parents, having lost their previous child after just four months of life (which had been a unique and tragic experience for them), were probably a bit more apprehensive than they had been during any of the previous ten pregnancies. It was apparently during this eleventh gestation period, which started at about the end of April in 1694, that Barbe, François, and most of their nine children moved permanently back to their farm beside the Lachine Rapids, in the Sault St. Louis section of the Lachine seigneury. This relocation from their Rue St. Paul home in Montreal and their leased farm in the Verdun fief probably took place during the summer or autumn of 1694, about five years after they had endured and survived the horrific Iroquois raid of 1689.

As a result of this move, by the time of the baby's arrival at Lachine on January 30, 1695, the family was firmly ensconced on their old familiar farm. Two days later, on February 2, they assembled at the Holy Angels church in Lachine for the baptism of the little lad, whom the parents had decided to again name Joseph. On this hopeful occasion, the baby's godmother was his sister Marie Jeanne Brunet, who was $17^1/2$ years old and still single, while the godfather was recorded in the parish register as René Tabault. This must have been an incorrect identification of one of the three sons of the Brunet's long time neighbor Pierre Tabault, who had received his land grant in the Lachine seigneury back in 1672, a year before François had been granted his own riverfront land. Among the three Tabault sons, Pierre, Jr. (age $20^2/3$ at this time) would marry the Brunet's daughter Catherine in April of 1703; Alexis was $18^3/4$ years old at this time; and Jean (age $13^2/3$ at this time) would marry the Brunet's daughter Angélique in 1710. Thus, since no one in the neighboring Tabault family was called René, the name "René Tabault" in this particular baptismal record was most likely either a mis-writing or a later misreading of the name "Pierre Tabault."[123]

Sadly, all of the heart-wrenching emotions that had been generated by the loss of their first baby named Joseph came rushing back to the Brunet family just three days after the christening of their second Joseph. The tiny lad passed away on February 5, having survived for only seven days; he was buried in the Lachine cemetery on the following day.[124]

In spite of this poignant death in the Brunet clan, and the deaths of so many other infants and youngsters which occurred in New France on a very regular basis, the population of the colony continued to grow at a steady pace. In this year of 1695, the people residing on Montreal Island included 1,114 males and 1,047 females, totaling 2,161 settlers. However, this number represented just 17 percent of the total of 12,786 colonists who lived in all of New France, strung out along the St. Lawrence shorelines from the Montreal area downriver to Tadoussac.[125]

During the summer of 1696, after they had spent about two years back on their old farm in the Lachine seigneury, François and Barbe executed three land transactions. These dealings, which involved one acquisition and two sales, further concentrated their holdings in the seigneury and liquidated their distant properties. First, on July 24, they purchased the entire lot that lay immediately to the west of their riverfront property, from Augustin Alonze dit L'Espagnol and Catherine Renusson. At this point, the latter couple was residing in Montreal, as they may have done ever since Catherine's escape from Iroquois captivity, which took place some time before she was cited in a document by a Montreal notary on April 22, 1691. (However, they would eventually return to live at Lachine, where Augustin would die in January of 1709.) The transferred lot, fronting on the St. Lawrence, measured 575 feet in width by 7/10 mile in depth, exactly the same dimensions as the Brunet's original riverfront property next door. On this July day, François and Barbe acquired this new land from the Alonze couple for the sum of 120 livres.[126]

One month later, on August 26, the Brunets liquidated their two pieces of property which were not in the Lachine area. The first one was located a short distance south of Montreal, in the area that was called the St. Joseph Quarter. Barbe and François had acquired ownership of this piece of land when each of the Beauvais siblings and their spouses had divided this particular Beauvais property among themselves back in October of 1693. On this August day, the Brunets agreed to sell their portion of this family land to Barbe's older brother Raphaël, for the sum of 200 livres. However, the transaction would only be finalized "upon his return from the Ottawa Country." In other words, it would be postponed until at least the autumn of the following year of 1697. That would be the earliest time that Raphaël could complete his upcoming trading voyage to the western interior and return to Montreal.[127]

The second property which François and Barbe sold on this same day of August 26, 1696 (in front of the same notary, their brother-in-law Jean Baptiste Pothier) was their lot and buildings on St. Paul Street in Montreal. In this second instrument of sale, the sellers were described as "of the Holy Angels Parish of Lachine and Montreal Island." The purchasers, again close family members, were Barbe's youngest sister Jeanne Beauvais and her husband of eight months, the Montreal innkeeper Guillaume Boucher. The transferred property, which the Brunets had owned for nearly seven years, since September of 1689, was thus described: "a house located at Ville Marie on Rue

Saint Paul, adjoined on one side by [the property of] the Sieur René Cuillerier [Sr.], on the other side by [that of] the Sieur Charles Milot, in back by [that of] the Sieur Jean Milot...the sale made for the sum of three thousand livres in three equal payments, plus eighty livres for the gratuity."[128]

Less than a week after these two property sales, at about the beginning of September, Barbe became pregnant for the twelfth time. Both of their previous babies had died as tiny infants, the first Joseph at the age of four months and the second Joseph at the age of just seven days. These two disheartening losses, in 1693 and again in 1695, must have planted some apprehensions that would prey upon the minds of the expectant parents during the course of this latest pregnancy.

During this same autumn, a case which was heard by the Montreal Court involved several members of the Brunet family. On September 27, 1696, the Montreal butcher Paul Bouchard (age 33, who had a wife and three children) introduced a suit against the Lachine settler Antoine Beaudrias or Beaudry(who was about 46 years old, and likewise had a wife and three children). The land belonging to the latter man, an interior lot at the extreme eastern end of the Lachine seigneury, had been granted to him during the previous year. It abutted against the interior lot of the Brunets, which had been granted to them back in 1693. According to Monsieur Bouchard's accusations, he had entrusted a cow into the care of François Brunet dit Le Bourbonnais; however, Monsieur Beaudrias had purportedly mistreated and provoked this poor animal to the point of death. On October 1, a number of witnesses were called to testify in this case, including Barbe Beauvais and the Brunet's daughter Catherine, who was 16 years old. Other witnesses included Françoise Bouet, the wife of Alexis Buet, to whom François had rented two rooms in the Verdun house during 1693-1694; the Montreal residents Pierre Lécuyer, his wife Marie Juillet, and their daughter Catherine, who was about to turn age 13; and René Mallet, age 28, the son-in-law of the Lécuyer couple. Nine days later, on October 10, the Court completed its deliberations and announced its verdict. According to Jacques Alexis Fleury, Sieur Deschambault (the Chief Judge), the Court had dismissed the suit against Beaudrias, claiming that there was insufficient evidence that the death of the cow had been caused by the defendant.[129]

Six weeks later, on November 25 and 26, Barbe and François

reveled in a number of novel and pleasurable experiences. These were the drawing up of the marriage contract and then the wedding celebration of Barbe, their second child and eldest daughter, who was $21^5/12$ years old. On the 25th, the members of the Brunet clan and friends of both the prospective bride and groom assembled before the Lachine notary Jean Baptiste Pothier, who also happened to be the brother-in-law of the bride's parents. Georges Brault dit Pomainville, who was about to become François and Barbe's first son-in-law, was 28 years of age, and the second-oldest among fourteen children of the Brault clan of Lauson, directly across the St. Lawrence River from Quebec. He and his younger brothers Jean Baptiste (age 23) and Joseph (21) had recently moved westward to the Montreal region, so they could more readily participate in the fur trade action. All three siblings would eventually marry and settle in the Lachine seigneury. (In fact, seven years into the future, Jean Baptiste would marry the Brunet's daughter Élisabeth, when she would be 18 years old. On these festive occasions in 1696, she was $11^1/2$ years of age, and probably dreaming of who would some day become her husband.)

At the nuptial ceremony that was celebrated at the Lachine church on the following day, November 26, an unusually large number of official witnesses were recorded in the parish ledger by Fr. Rémy. Another rare element was the considerable number of females among these fourteen individuals. The witnesses on the bride's side included Barbe's sisters Marie Jeanne (age 19) and the twins Catherine and Anne ($16^1/2$), her brother Jean François ($14^1/2$), her unmarried cousin Marguerite Tétu (17), her aunts Jeanne Beauvais and Élisabeth Turpin, and her uncle the notary Jean Baptiste Pothier. Family friends included Louis Mallet (age 23, who would marry Marie Jeanne, the next-oldest Brunet daughter, nine months later) and his older brother René Mallet, both from Montreal, the brothers Jacques and Nicolas Boyer from Montreal, François Roy, and Jean Chicout. After the wedding, the couple would settle in the Lachine seigneury, where they would produce eight children over the span of some fifteen years. This would also serve as Georges' home base during his years of working as a voyageur-trader in the west.[130]

In most instances, before a wedding ceremony could be performed, it was obligatory that the banns of the upcoming marriage be posted or announced on three separate occasions. These public announcements, made on three Sundays or Holy Days, were to be carried out in the home parishes of the prospective bride and groom.

During the 1690s, the fee that was paid to the priest for posting the three successive banns in the parish was 6 livres. In addition, he charged another 6 livres for performing the wedding ceremony. These official rates for ecclesiastical services, as well as those which were charged for saying high and low masses and for burying individuals in either a cemetery or a church, had been established six years earlier, back in 1690.[131]

On February 20, 1697, Barbe and François sold an 8½-acre piece of land in the Montreal region which they had inherited from her family's estate. On this date, they registered with their brother-in-law, the notary Jean Baptiste Pothier, that they had transferred the property, measuring 96 feet in width by $7/10$ mile in length, for the sum of 100 livres in cash. The purchaser was Jean Roy, who lived in the area called Les Argoulets, immediately northeast of the Verdun stockade.[132]

A jubilant day was celebrated in the Brunet household about 3½ months later, on May 29, when the tenth living child joined the family. For little Louis' christening ceremony on the 31st, Louis Mallet, who would marry Barbe and Francois' second daughter Marie Jeanne five months later, was chosen to serve as the godfather. Logically, the future bride Marie Jeanne stood as the godmother of her new baby brother. In the parish register, the priest identified the occupations of both the father and the godfather as "farm worker," the same designation that the pastor had applied to François during the earlier years, when he had been very actively working as a trader in the west.[133]

This twelfth birth would be the final one for Barbe and François. During the 24-year span between their first delivery in April of 1673 and this arrival in May of 1697, the couple had welcomed a dozen babies into the world. However, two of them, the two Josephs preceding little Louis in 1693 and 1695, had not survived infancy. The arrival of their first child had taken place one week short of nine months after their wedding; thereafter, the other ten deliveries had been separated by 27, 26, 32 (the twin girls), 25, 33, 28, 46, 24, 21, and 28 months, respectively. The one long interval of 46 months, between June of 1687 and April of 1691, had taken place while the family's normal life at their Lachine farm had been interrupted by the 1689 massacre. During the second half of that period, from September of 1689 onward, they had lived in their Montreal house and at the first of their leased farms southwest of town. During the couple's 24 childbearing years, Barbe had aged from 17 to 41, while her husband's age had increased from about 28 or 29 to about 52 or 53.

The arrival of Louis, their tenth living child, finally qualified Monsieur and Madame Brunet for the royal "baby-bonus" payments, which the King and his Minister had inaugurated back in 1669 to promote population growth in the colony. According to the regulations, parents who had ten living legitimate children, none of whom had entered the clergy, would receive an annual payment of 300 livres. Those families with twelve living offspring would be paid an even higher pension, 400 livres each year.[134]

Nine days after Louis' baptismal festivities, on the morning of June 9, 1697, François visited the office of the Montreal notary Adhémar. He had traveled the eight miles from Lachine to collect a debt, and then to officially register the following information:

"François Brunet dit Le Bourbonnais, habitant of the said Island of Montreal, at present at the said Ville Marie, has acknowledged that he has received from François Guillemot [dit] Lalande of the said Ville Marie the sum of two hundred livres, which had been owed to him according to a bond passed before the deceased Master Claude Maugue, royal notary of this Island, on the year and day [not stated, but the notary had died seven months earlier, on November 9, 1696]."

Monsieur Guillemot, a Montreal baker and retired soldier, had lived with his wife at Lachine from 1685 until at least 1688, and quite possibly until the Iroquois raid in 1689; since then, the couple had resided at Montreal. They were expecting their ninth child in about three months; however, they had lost their first two babies at the ages of three weeks and eleven months, respectively. Upon receiving this payment, François issued a paid-in-full receipt to his former debtor.[135]

The Lachine settler Antoine Beaudrias may have been a rather contentious fellow, especially when it came to the subject of cattle. Back in the previous September, the Montreal butcher Paul Bouchard had sued him in the Montreal court, for supposedly tormenting to death a cow that the butcher had entrusted to the care of François Brunet (the case had been dismissed, for insufficient evidence). About nine months later, on June 15, 1697, Beaudrias lodged charges of assault and battery in the same court against Monsieur and Madame Brunet and their nineteen-year-old daughter Marie Jeanne, who would marry in four months. The land of the plaintiff, which had been granted to him in 1695, was an interior lot at the extreme eastern end of the Lachine seigneury. The western end of his property abutted at a perpendicular angle against the side of the interior lot of the Brunets, which had been granted to them back in 1693. At some point during the early summer of 1697, cattle belonging to the Brunet family had apparently strayed onto Beaudrias' property; this had occurred after the latter man had supposedly requested that this not be allowed to happen. As a result, tempers had flared and the situation had erupted into violence, in the course of which Beaudrias had supposedly suffered physical injuries from certain members of the Brunet clan. On June 15, the Court summoned a pair of witnesses to appear before the bench in two days time. On the 17th, the testimony of Joseph Cuillerier (age 18, son of the Lachine resident René Cuillerier, Sr.) and Michel Trottier (age 26, from Batiscan) was heard. In addition, the Court ordered that the Montreal surgeon Jean Martinet, the Sieur de Fonblanche, examine the plaintiff and issue a medical report on his condition. A summons to appear was also issued for François Brunet, which was delivered to him by the Court bailiff Georges Pruneau.

At this point, before the official proceedings could advance any further, François arranged a private settlement with Monsieur Beaudrias. Four days after he had been issued the subpoena to appear before the Court, in the afternoon of June 21, François joined his accuser in the notary's office, to officially register their joint agreement and to terminate the legal action which Boudrias had initiated against him. "The said parties desiring to live in peace...the said Brunet promises and is obliged to pay all of the legal expenses, as well as the expenses for the said [Sieur de] Fonblanche in bandaging and medicating the said Boudrias and for the said [medical] report and its delivery to the Court."[136]

This agreement was very similar to the one which François had reached nearly 27 years earlier with Philippe Pothier dit Lafontaine, back on November 14, 1670. In that instance, during the course of a fracas, Monsieur Brunet had inflicted physical injuries on the latter man, and the Montreal Court had decided Lafontaine's suit in favor of the injured party. As a settlement, François had then paid his opponent "the sum of forty-two livres for damages, interests, board and lodging, and medicines and surgeon's services which were administered to treat the said Lafontaine until his recovery, as well as for legal expenses, including the efforts which he knows the said Lafontaine sustained in acquiring the aforementioned information that comprised the report of the said surgeon."[137]

Ten weeks after settling the 1697 suit out of court, on September 6, Barbe and François were overjoyed to welcome their first grandchild. He arrived at Lachine 9 months and ten days after their daughter Barbe and Georges Brault dit Pomainville had been married there. The beaming grandmother was doubly pleased to be chosen as the godmother of baby Nicolas, for his christening ceremony which was held in the Lachine church on the same day as his birth. On this occasion, the little lad was given his name by his godfather Nicolas Boyer, an 18-year-old farm worker who had been one of the official witnesses at the wedding of the young couple during the previous November.[138]

Further family festivities brightened the lives of the Brunet clan during the following month of October, when Marie Jeanne, at age 20 the couple's second-oldest daughter, joined Louis Mallet in marriage. At the drawing up of their marriage contract on October 13, the prospective bride was identified by the notary as "Jeanne Brunet, daughter of François Brunet dit Le Bourbonnais and of Barbe Beauvais, from the Sault St. Louis and the Lachine Parish on Montreal Island." The future groom, age 24, had been born and raised in Montreal. When the couple pronounced their nuptial vows at the Holy Angels Church in Lachine sixteen days later, on the 29th, the seven official witnesses included four close relatives. These were Marie Jeanne's maternal uncles Jean Baptiste Pothier and Raphaël Beauvais (the latter man having returned from his westward trading venture), and Louis' mother Marie Anne Hardy and his younger brother Pierre (age 21 and still single). The other three witnesses were the bride and groom's friends Jean Ducharme, Madeleine Dufresne, and Catherine Legras. The newlyweds would first settle at Montreal, then at Lachine between 1700 and 1708, and finally at Bout de l'Île from about 1710 on; during these years, they would produce seven children. These three communities would also serve as Louis' home base during his years of laboring as a voyageur-trader in the western interior.[139]

Barbe's younger brother Jean Baptiste Beauvais married Marie Madeleine Lemoine at Batiscan on November 12, 1697. He had waited a particularly long time to tie the knot, since he was 37 years old at the time. In the parish record of this wedding, Barbe and Jean Baptiste's mother Jeanne Soldé was described as still living. However, this would be the last documentation concerning her to be recorded in the colony.[140]

Various events which took place during the year 1698 produced very mixed emotions for the members of the Brunet clan. First came the encouraging ceremony of Confirmation for three of Barbe and François' younger children. Among the 21 persons who received this sacrament in the Lachine church on June 6 were Jean François Brunet (age 16), Élisabeth Brunet (13), and Marie Brunet (11). The other two children in the family, Anglélique (7) and Louis (13 months) would have to wait a number of years before they could participate in this faith-strengthening religious training and then the final ceremony of Confirmation.[141]

Nine weeks later, on August 10, François and his son-in-law Georges Brault dit Pomainville traveled to Montreal to visit the notary in his office. At that time, they had the scribe draw up two related documents. The first one was a receipt indicating that Georges and his wife Barbe Brunet, residents of the Sault St. Louis area at Lachine, had received from François and his wife Barbe Beauvais the sum of 360 livres *en avancement d'hoirie,* as an advance on the future bequests of inheritance which young Barbe would some day be entitled to receive from the family estate, after the eventual deaths of her parents. This money would be utilized to pay for the adjacent pair of long riverfront lots which lay immediately west of the Brunets' Alonze lot. This pair of lots, with a total St. Lawrence frontage of 6 arpents (1,150 feet), had belonged to the deceased René Horieux dit Lafleur. This unlucky man, an unmarried retired soldier, had drowned in the local area more than five years earlier, back on March 30, 1693, when he had broken through the ice while returning from hunting moose. The second document from this August day spelled out the obligation for this same amount of money, which Georges now owed to his father-in-law François.[142]

Unfortunately, their trip back to Lachine did not unfold without incident. Just two days after the above appointment with the notary, on August 12, the Lachine resident Léon Girard submitted to the Montreal Court charges of assault and battery against François Brunet dit Le Bourbonnais. According to the plaintiff's accusations, he had been physically attacked by Monsieur Brunet after an exchange of words had taken place between the two men. This had occurred on the previous Sunday evening while they, along with Brunet's son-in-law Georges Brault and Brunet's other adjacent neighbor François Lory, had been together returning home to Lachine from Montreal. (Monsieur Girard, who lived immediately east of the stockaded village site of Lachine, had been a settler here for at least a decade, since at least 1688, when he had married a young local woman; they were expecting their fifth child in the coming October. He was apparently a well-respected man in the area, since he would be cited as the Captain of the Lachine militia forces seven years later, in 1705.) On August 13, the Court officials heard the testimony of François Lory dit Gargot, age 52, the royal bailiff and sergeant of the Court, who resided immediately east of the Brunet land. On the following day, they listened to the deposition of Georges Brault, age 28 (who lived immediately west of the Brunets), after which they issued a summons to François Brunet to appear before the Court. Unfortunately, the outcome of the case was not preserved with the rest of the Court's documents. However, there was no subsequent notary record describing any financial settlement. Thus, it is likely that the suit was dropped or the case was dismissed, so that François was not obliged to pay any reparations to Monsieur Girard for this physical altercation.[143]

When the vessels from the mother country arrived during this summer of 1698, they brought word that the war between France and a number of European nations had ended during the previous year. It was also in this year of 1698 that the raids by Iroquois warriors against both the French colonists and their native allies finally ceased once and for all. However, treaty negotiations between the latter three groups would drag on for another three years, until the Great Treaty would ultimately be signed in Montreal during the summer of 1701. When a new war would break out between France and other European nations in 1702, the Iroquois would remain neutral, not siding with the English as they had previously done for decades.[144]

The days of September 1 and 2 in the autumn of 1698 were joyful ones for the entire Brunet clan. The first date witnessed the safe arrival in Montreal of Barbe and François' first Mallet grandchild, nine months and three days after their daughter Marie Jeanne and Louis Mallet had been wed. On the following day, little François Marie was baptized in the Notre Dame de Montreal church, with his maternal grandfather François Brunet and his paternal grandmother Marie Anne Hardy as sponsors. Also in attendance was the midwife Jeanne Richecourt dit Malteau (the wife of Jean Roy dit Lapensée), who had assisted in the baby's delivery. Back in 1693-1694, François had rented out two rooms in the Verdun house to this Roy couple and their three remaining children (their youngest, Marie Anne, had been captured in the 1689 Iroquois raid). However, to the deep grief of the entire extended family, the little Mallet lad survived for only two short weeks. He passed away on September 15, and he was buried in the Montreal cemetery that same day.[145]

One month later, on October 13, an altercation took place on the Brunet property, during which tempers flared and blows were apparently delivered. On this day, Paul Lécuyer, 22 years old, was about to marry Françoise Lecomte, who would soon turn age 16. As the young man passed in front of the Brunet household, traveling westward from his parents' home (on the boundary of Verdun) to the Lachine church for his wedding celebration, harsh words and physical violence must have erupted between him and several members of the Brunet family. Four days later, on the 17th, Paul's father Pierre Lécuyer appeared before the Montreal Court. He was there to register, in the name of his son, charges of assault and battery against François Brunet dit Le Bourbonnais, his wife Barbe Beauvais, and their daughter Barbe Brunet, who was married to Georges Brault dit Pomainville. (The latter couple lived on the adjacent double lot immediately west of the Brunet property.) According to the plaintiff's statements, these three individuals had attacked his son while he was passing in front of their home, while he was going to his wedding at Lachine. On the same day on which the complaint was lodged, the Court officials ordered that Barbe Beauvais be summoned to appear before the bench on the 19th. They also subpoenaed three witnesses to support the claims of Monsieur Lécuyer: André Roy, Françoise Roy, and Jean Cardinal. No results of this case have been preserved in the records of the Court. However, the decision either went in favor of the plaintiff and against the members of the Brunet family, or else the involved parties reached their own private settlement outside of court. Three days after leveling the charges, on October 20, Pierre and Paul Lécuyer joined François in the office of the Montreal notary Antoine Adhémar, where they officially registered their mutual agreement and settlement.[146]

In summary, on three separate occasions during the previous sixteen months, François had been accused in Criminal Court of assault and battery, in two of those instances along with certain of his family members. In the first case, in which charges had been leveled on June 15, 1697, he, Barbe, and their soon-to-be-married daughter Marie Jeanne (who would soon turn age 20) had been involved in a fracas with an adjacent neighbor, after their Brunet cattle had strayed onto the man's property; Monsieur Brunet had settled this case out of court. Fourteen months later, on August 12, 1698, François alone had been charged with attacking a fellow traveler while returning from Montreal to Lachine; no court decision or notarial settlement concerning this second case have been located, so the suit may have been dropped. After two months had passed, on October 17, Monsieur and Madame Brunet, along with their married daughter Barbe (age 23), had been accused of attacking a young man who had been passing in front of their home; no documents reflecting the Court's decision in this case have been located, but an agreement and settlement between the parties had been recorded by a Montreal notary.

February 8 and 9 in 1699 marked two heartwarming occasions for Barbe and François. On the first day, the proud parents, along with various family members and friends, watched their daughter Anne Brunet and Louis Couillard sign their marriage contract in front of a notary. The bride-to-be, who was the twin sister of Catherine, was three months short of age 19, while the prospective groom, hailing from the area of Trois-Rivières and about 26 years old, was a joiner (a builder of furniture and interior woodwork). On the second day of nuptial festivities, the couple pronounced their vows in the Lachine church before eight official witnesses. These included the bride's uncles Raphaël Beauvais and Jean Baptiste Pothier and her aunt Anne Marie Beauvais, as well as five friends of the bride and the groom: Marguerite Chorel, Jean Baptiste Crevier dit Duvernay, Pierre Trottier, the army officer Bernard Alexandre Deschevert, Sieur de Rochemont, and Claude or François Tardif. Following the wedding, the young couple would settle at Lachine until at least 1717, where they would produce seven children; afterward, they would relocate a few miles toward the west, to Pointe Claire, where their eighth child would be born in 1724.[147]

Less than a month after this jubilant wedding celebration, on March 6, François was obliged to participate in a rather unpleasant court procedure. This legal task must have triggered in him a flood of memories, many of which were wonderful, but some of which were horrendous. Some time earlier, he had been designated as the legal guardian of the five Boursier children who had survived the Lachine Massacre of 1689, which had taken place nearly a decade earlier. In the raid, Jean Boursier dit Lavigne (François' close friend, paddling and trading partner, and adjacent neighbor for many years) and his wife Marie Marthe Thibodeau (whom François had once promised to marry), as well as their nine-year old daughter Marie Élisabeth, had been captured by Iroquois warriors and had never been heard from again. In addition, the baby of the family, little Madeleine, who had been seven weeks short of her first birthday, had been drowned by the attackers. These events had taken place on the farm that was slightly east of the Brunet land, separated from their property by a distance of just 575 feet, the width of a single farm lot. At the time of the onslaught, the five Boursier children who eluded capture and death had been ages 15, 11, 7, 5, and 3.

In March of 1699, the seigneurs of Montreal Island (the Sulpician order), represented by Pierre Raimbault, the collector of seigneurial fees for the Sulpicians, initiated legal procedures for collecting the overdue monies that were owed on the Boursier land. The fees of *cens et rentes* for this property had not been paid during the previous twelve years, not since 1687, two years before the raid. In this civil case before the Montreal Court, François served as the legal representative of the Boursier children, since he was their official guardian. On March 6, the Court ordered that an official survey of measurement was to be carried out on the property under consideration at Sault St. Louis, which had been granted to Jean Boursier back in 1676.[148]

When this case was continued almost seven months later, on September 24, the eldest Boursier son, Alexandre, was 25 years old and still single. His siblings, all of whom were unmarried, included Barbe (age 21), Anne (17), Jeanne Catherine (15), and Jean (13). Alexandre and Jean, as the two male heirs, officially requested that they be permitted to hold an assembly of their relatives. In this manner, they hoped to recover from their family estate the 400 livres which had belonged to their mother Marie Marthe Thibodeau as her prefixed dower, as had been expressed in her marriage contract. They also asked that they be shown the accounts of the administration of their estate, which had been managed by their guardian François Brunet dit Le Bourbonnais. Permission for both of these requests was granted on this date by the Chief Judge of the Court, Jacques Alexis Fleury, Sieur Deschambault. However, the five underage heirs were apparently not successful in their efforts to raise the needed funds, by which they had hoped to pay off the long-overdue seigneurial fees and retain ownership of their familial property. On November, 3, upon the directive of the Court, an official posting was made ordering the seizure of the concession of land at Sault St. Louis which had belonged to the Boursier heirs.[149]

Shortly afterward, this property was divided into three parcels and was acquired by three different individuals. The westernmost two arpents (384 feet) of frontage went to François and Barbe's son-in-law Louis Mallet and his wife Marie Anne Brunet; the middle 384 feet was acquired by Jean Baptiste Brault dit Pomainville (Georges' brother, who would marry Élisabeth Brunet in 1703); and the easternmost 575 feet went to Louis Roy. Following these three transfers, the lots extending to the east from the Commons of the seigneury were owned by the following men, in sequence from west to east: Georges Brault dit Pomainville, 1,150 feet of St. Lawrence frontage; François Brunet dit Le Bourbonnais, 1,150 feet; François Lory, 575 feet; Louis Mallet, 384 feet; and Jean Baptiste Brault dit Pomainville, 384 feet. (After Jean Baptiste's marriage to Élisabeth in 1703, the eventual purchaser of Monsieur Lory's lot would be the only landowner within this stretch of 7/10 mile of frontage who would not be a member of the extended Brunet clan.)[150]

By the time Barbe and François' daughter Marie Jeanne delivered her second child in the spring of 1700, the young Mallet couple had relocated from Montreal to their newly-acquired property in the Lachine seigneury. Now, all three of their married daughters lived with their husbands rather close to the Brunet family (although the Couillards were not nearly as close as the Braults and the Mallets). At the birth of little Catherine on April 2 and her baptism that same day at the Lachine church, everyone was probably a bit apprehensive, since the Mallets had lost their first baby back in September of 1698, at the age of two weeks. However, as the little lass thrived during the following weeks and months, the family must have breathed a collective sigh of relief.[151]

Nearly seventeen months after their daughter Anne had married Pierre Couillard, Barbe and François were elated to welcome their first Couillard grandchild into the world. Marie Anne was born at Lachine on June 29, 1700, and she was christened at the church there two days later, on the first of July. However, the baby lived for less than four days; she died on July 2, and was buried the same day in the cemetery beside the Lachine church.[152]

About six months later, on Christmas Day, Barbe's sister Marie Charlotte Beauvais passed away at Montreal, at the age of 33 1/2. She had been married to the Montreal outfitter and trader Alexandre Turpin for sixteen years, during which time they had produced eight children.[153]

It was in about this year of 1700 that Jean, the Brunets' eldest child and first son, married Élisabeth Deshayes, a native woman, at Kaskaskia in the Illinois Country, and soon began his own family there. However, it is not known when Barbe and François eventually received the wonderful news of his wedding and the later arrival of his three children, via letters or messages transported by voyageur-traders.[154]

A major topic of conversation in both Lachine and throughout the entire Montreal region in 1700 was the resumption of work on the Lachine Canal. This man-made watercourse, when completed, would extend for $8^1/2$ miles in a northeasterly direction from Lachine all the way to Montreal. Work had commenced on the southwestern section of the project eleven years earlier, back in the summer of 1689. However, after seven weeks of labor, those efforts had been suddenly halted by the Iroquois raid of August 5. Now, on October 30, 1700, the Sulpicians (as the seigneurs of Montreal Island) entered into a construction contract with Gédéon de Catalogne, the primary surveyor, cartographer, and engineer of the colony. According to their agreement, with the Sulpicians supplying the tools and provisions, Catalogne's workers would excavate a canal which would be twelve feet wide and nine feet deep. According to their overly optimistic plans, the workmen would complete it by June of 1701. The owners of the four slender lots of farmland at the southwestern end of the proposed waterway, fronting on the St. Lawrence for $1/3$ mile, agreed that the canal could cross their properties at a diagonal. Their acceptance was recorded in a notary document which they approved on the same date of October 30 as Catalogne's contract. Two of these property owners were the retired soldier and master shoemaker Guillaume Roussel dit Sans Souci and his wife Nicole Filiatrault, the former widow of Étienne Lalande dit Langliche (both Monsieur Roussel and Madame Filiatrault are direct ancestors of the present author). The owners of the other three lots, in sequence from west to east, were Louis Fortier; François Legantier, the Sieur de La Vallée et de Rané; and Pierre Gauthier dit Saguingoira. Their document of approval was officially witnessed by Alexandre Turpin (whose biography has already been presented in this work) and Guillaume Daoust, both of whom are direct ancestors of the present author.

With the highest of hopes, Fr. Dollier de Casson, the Superior of the Sulpicians, paid Monsieur Catalogne 9,000 livres to carry out the project. However, after about half of the excavation had been completed (the section running southwestward from Lac St. Pierre all the way to the St. Lawrence shoreline, plus the canalized Lac itself), work was halted. Less than a year after the commencement of the project, this stoppage occurred when the excavators moved to the area east of Lac St. Pierre. In this latter area, the engineer had intended to create the eastern one-third of the canal. However, as the excavators attempted to widen and deepen the eastward-flowing branch of the Rivière St. Pierre, they were unable to dig through the sandstone and limestone bedrock which lay beneath this natural waterway. The completed southwestern section of the slender canal, as well as the canalized Lac St. Pierre at about the midpoint of the proposed waterway, were both depicted on Vachon de Belmont's 1702 land ownership map of Montreal Island. The southwestern terminus was located about 3^1/2 miles west of the Brunet farm. On the key of the 1702 map, the westernmost parcel at the terminus, the Roussel-Filiatrault lot, was labeled "[Property of] Langliche, where the beginning of the canal is, as marked on the map, [the lot measuring] two arpents [384 feet] in frontage by 20 arpents [^{7}/10 mile] in depth."

This stage of progress was as far as this long-dreamed watercourse would reach during the French regime. And this was after some 20,000 livres had been expended on the attempt, more than double the cost that had been originally proposed by Catalogne. Years later, the engineer Chaussegros de Léry would try on two occasions to persuade the administrators of New France to complete the work. But these efforts would be in vain; the colony still lacked the financial resources, the professional skills, and the specialized equipment which such a project demanded.

Some twenty months after Guillaume Roussel and Nicole Filiatrault had granted permission for the construction of the canal across the riverfront area of their long slender lot, on June 26, 1702, the Sulpicians would grant them a special financial dispensation. In return for no longer having to pay the annual seigneurial fees on their property, the couple would relinquish all rights to the forty-foot-wide strip of land running across their concession where the canal had been excavated.

For many decades after 1701, the completed section of ditch would be utilized as a crude canal (without the entire eastern section of the proposed waterway, which had been planned to encompass the widened and deepened Rivière St. Pierre). It was useful mainly to the residents of the Côte St. Paul and Côte St. Pierre fiefs, which flanked the former Lac St. Pierre (on its southeastern and northwestern sides, respectively). Then, during the Anglo period in 1783, with the installation of a number of locks, this same ditch would become the first canal operating with locks in North America. Between 1821 and 1825, the entire length of the canal would finally be completed. It would have a width of 28 feet and a depth of $4^1/2$ feet, with six sets of locks to offset the drop of more than 40 feet of the Lachine Rapids which it bypassed. This depth would be increased to nine feet between 1843 and 1848, and ultimately to its final depth of fourteen feet in 1885, to accommodate steamboat traffic on the St. Lawrence and Ottawa Rivers.[155]

By 1701, the Holy Angels Church within the stockaded village at Lachine (nearly three miles west of the Brunet farm) had been in use for a quarter-century. Built of stout timbers by the carpenter Pierre Godin dit Châtillon (a direct ancestor of the present author) during the winter of 1675-1676, this first edifice measured about 36 by 20 feet. In the spring of 1701, plans were finalized for the construction of a much larger church here, which would be built of field stones; this new one would measure 60 by 30 feet.

In pleasant anticipation of attending services in this much grander edifice during the remainder of his life, as would also his family members, François arranged to permanently lease a specific pew within it. In the afternoon on April 11, he joined the parish priest Fr. Rémy and the three members of the parish council, Pierre Cardinal, François Dubois dit Brisebois, and Jean Roy dit La Pensée, in the public meeting hall in the rectory building. François' brother-in-law the notary Jean Baptiste Pothier was also present, to officially record their agreement. According to his document (the specific details of which had been earlier approved by Fr. Dollier de Casson, the Superior of the Sulpicians, back on January 22), the five men jointly acknowledged the following details:

"The Sieur parish priest and the parish council members have acknowledged and declared that they have leased and assigned to François Brunet dit [Le] Bourbonnais, habitant living in the said parish, here present and assenting for both himself and for Barbe Beauvais, his wife, their children and descendants from legitimate marriage, and no others, a pew in the said church, which is the third one from the front on the Epistle side [the right side when looking toward the altar], between that of Sieur Jean Cuillerier and that of Simon Guillory [both of them peltries merchants at Lachine and

Montreal], in consideration of the [annual] price and sum of forty livres, which the said Cardinal named above has acknowledged and declared that he has received from the said Brunet [for the coming year] in card money utilized in this region."

In a number of parishes, the right to occupy a specific pew in the church was maintained down through multiple generations in some families. Certain of the pews were reserved for the seigneur, the current members of the parish council, the sexton, and sometimes representatives of certain informal religious brotherhoods. The other pews could be leased for an annual fee, the details of which were spelled out in notary contracts such as this one from 1701.[156]

It is worth contemplating what might have been passing through François and Barbe's minds at this point. What thoughts, pious ideas, or regrets, or possibly fears of eternal damnation (or at least a stint in Purgatory) may have prompted them to permanently lease this pew in a prominent location within the parish church? Now about 56 or 57 and 45 years of age, respectively, they had both been involved in physical altercations with local residents during recent years, once in 1697 and twice in 1698. These scuffles had resulted in multiple charges of assault and battery being lodged against both François and Barbe (as well as their two eldest daughters) in the Criminal Court. At this stage of their lives, could the Brunets have been attempting to move "closer to God?" Or was their permanently acquiring this pew prompted by more worldly ideas, their own public acknowledgement of their prominent and respected position within the community, as some of its earliest settlers?

Card money, which François used to pay the pew-leasing fee to the church, had been first introduced within the colony sixteen years earlier. At that time, there had been a serious shortage of currency in New France. This had been a problem for decades before 1685, and it would continue to be a problem over many years afterward. The coins from various countries which did appear in the colony were constantly being drained off, to either France or Albany. In addition, the pelts of beavers and other animals, as well as hides, were often awkward to use as a portable medium of exchange. As an antidote to this situation, in 1685, Intendant Jacques De Meulles had created card money from packs of playing cards. He had accomplished this by writing the particular denomination on the face of each card and then affixing his signature to it, to make it legal tender. In the ensuing years, other Intendants also resorted to the issuance of card money. In each instance, the cards were redeemable when currency sent from the King arrived with the vessels from the mother country. This ingenious system of producing money, which substituted for actually printing currency, helped to facilitate internal commerce within the colony.[157]

This year of 1701 marked the uplifting arrival of two new grandchildren at Lachine for Barbe and François. The first one, Marie Josèphe Brault, joined the world on June 14; she was baptized in the local church on the 16th. Now, three young grandchildren resided on the farm immediately west of the Brunets; this new baby had older brothers who were 3 3/4 years and 23 months old, respectively. On the land immediately east of the Brunets' property lived an additional granddaughter, Catherine Mallet, who had celebrated her first birthday on April 2. The second infant to join the extended Brunet clan arrived on September 11, amid some apprehension on everyone's part. The young Couillard couple had lost their first baby back in July of 1701, when their new daughter had lived for only four days. However, this time, little Pierre seemed to be hale and hearty. (No one could foresee that he would perish at the age of 33 months, in June of 1704.)[158]

Between the encouraging arrival dates of these two new babies, construction commenced on what would be known as "*la grande église de pierre*," the field stone church within the palisaded village. On July 21, witnessed by the commandant of Ft. Rémy (Jean Brouillet, the Sieur de la Chassagne), the three members of the parish council, the architect-businessman Michel Lefebvre, the two local master masons who would be building it (François Martin and Alexis Tabault), and a large number of parishioners, Fr. Rémy blessed the site and laid the first stone. It would take a full two years to complete the edifice (it would finally be inaugurated in July of 1703). Then, it would serve the parish for 162 years, until it would finally be replaced in 1865 and demolished four years later.[159]

By the spring of 1702, Barbe and François had only two sons residing close by: Jean François, who would turn 20 on May 26, and Louis (the baby of the family), who would turn 5 three days later. Jean, their eldest son, age 29, was away living and working in the Illinois Country. Their other seven children were all girls: Barbe, Marie Jeanne, and Anne who were married (ages 26, 24, and 22, respectively) and Catherine, Élisabeth, Marie, and Angélique who were still single (ages 22, 17, 15, and 11, respectively). Other than

Jean and his family in distant Illinois, the entire clan all lived in the Lachine seigneury, including the Brunet couple, their nine children, their three sons-in-law, and their five grandchildren.[160]

It probably pleased François greatly when his middle son, on the very date of his 20th birthday (May 26, 1702), signed a contract to work as a voyageur hauling freight in both directions between Lachine and Ft. Frontenac, just as his father had done for La Salle a quarter-century earlier, back in 1675-1676. According to the details of the contract, the two paddling colleagues of "François Brunet dit [Le] Bourbonnais, Jr." would be the Brunets' son-in-law Georges Brault dit Pomainville and Pierre Tabault. (The latter man, who lived in the adjacent seigneury of La Présentation, some $3^1/2$ miles west of the Lachine village, would soon become the Brunets' son-in-law, in the following April of 1703, when he would marry their daughter Catherine.) It is highly likely that at least the latter two partners were highly experienced in dealing with the challenges of hauling freight by canoe, since their profitable labor agreement specified the following:

"The said hirees will begin to do the said transporting from this day [May 26] forward, and they will continue without interruption as long as they have cargo to transport. The said lessors promise to the hirees first preference in doing the said transporting to the said Ft. Frontenac, as much during the present summer and autumn as during the navigation seasons of the following years, as much as it will be in their power."[161] (The biographies of François Brunet, Jr. and his wife Françoise David, direct ancestors of the present author, are included later in this work.)

For some time, François, Sr. had been afflicted with pleurisy, an inflammation of the pleura, the thin membrane that covers the lungs and also lines the chest cavity. Sufferers of this disease usually experienced difficult and painful breathing, which was often accompanied by the exuding of liquid into the chest cavity. Finally, on the last day of his life, François was struggling to take in each painful breath. He mercifully passed away on June 23, 1702.

After conducting his funeral on the following day, the priest of the Lachine parish penned the following entry into the church ledger: *"June 24, 1702. Buried François Brunet dit Le Bourbonnais, age 57. Died the previous day in his bed, of pleurisy. Burial was done in the presence of his wife, his children, relatives, and friends. Witnesses [probably Jean] Cuillerier and [Guillaume] Daoust [chanter of the parish]."*[162]

One of his family members had obviously provided the

information that Monsieur Brunet had been 57 years old at the time of his demise. However, back in the spring or early summer of 1681, François himself had reported to the census-taker that he had been 37 at that time; this would have made him about 58 at the time of his death. From these two statements, his year of birth has been extrapolated as about 1644 or 1645.

Eighteen days after his interment, the day of July 11 must have been an especially difficult one for Barbe. On that day, the Brunet couple would have celebrated the 30th anniversary of their wedding. Having become a bride six weeks before her sixteenth birthday, Barbe now found herself widowed with ten living children before she had reached the age of 46. At this point, she could not have foreseen that she had thus far lived only about half of her life, that she would never remarry, and that she would live as a widow at Lachine for $43^1/2$ more years, until January of 1746![163]

The fees that the family paid to the priest for conducting François' burial service (6 livres), and for any Masses that they may have requested that the priest perform for the repose of his soul (6 livres for Low Masses, 8 livres for High Masses), had been standardized throughout the colony back in 1690. At that time, the following ecclesiastical fees had been established:

Publishing the three banns of marriage, together...6 livres

Wedding ceremony...6 livres

Standard Low Mass...6 livres

High Mass...8 livres

Cemetery burial in the country districts...6 livres

Burials within churches:

In country parishes...40 livres

At Trois-Rivières...60 livres

At Montreal...100 livres

At Quebec...120 livres

(However, the rates for children's burials were to be at half of these standard rates)[164]

Less than half a year after burying her husband, Barbe suffered additional deep grief, with the deaths of even more close family members. These losses were the result of the horrendous epidemic of smallpox that swept through the St. Lawrence settlements during the latter part of 1702 and continued until at least the spring of 1703. First, at the Brault household immediately west of the Brunet farm, the disease caused her daughter Barbe to deliver her male baby two months early, on December 18, after just seven months of gestation (according to the priest's notations in the parish ledger). The tiny lad was either stillborn or he died after just a few hours; he was buried in the Lachine cemetery on the same day, a week before Christmas. Eighteen days later, on January 3, 1703, little Marie Josèphe Brault, the youngest member of the same family, was felled by smallpox at the age of $18^1/2$ months; her funeral was held two days later. This scourge continued at least through the following spring. On April 22, the priest recorded in the parish ledger that he had just interred baby Louis Roy, age $4^1/2$ weeks, a victim of smallpox. His parents, François Roy and Marie Cécire, lived about $1^1/2$ miles northeast of the Brunet farm, near the border of the Verdun fief. Two days later, on the Mallet farm immediately east of the Brunet home, Barbe's daughter Jeanne delivered a baby girl, who was either stillborn or she died after a very short time; she was buried on the following day, April 25. The priest did not indicate whether or not the death of this child had been caused by the raging smallpox epidemic. During this span of just four months, the matriarch Barbe had suffered the loss of one of her five living grandchildren, and she had also witnessed the deaths of two other grandchildren on the same day that each of them had been born. In addition, she had been saddened by the smallpox-caused death of her godson Vincent Chamaillard, Jr. on January 22, three weeks after he had celebrated his 21st birthday. Barbe had watched him grow up on the farm next door to the west, where the little Brault family now lived (Catherine Renusson and Vincent Chamaillard, Sr. had raised their brood of five children there). During the course of this vicious epidemic, some 250 residents of Montreal Island died of the disease, and about a quarter of the population of the town of Quebec.[165]

Although this scourge was still tormenting the colonists when spring arrived in 1703, they summoned the courage to continue on with their lives. In this vein, Barbe and François' daughter Catherine and her fiancé Pierre Tabault proceeded with their wedding plans. First, on April 15, the prospective couple stood before the Montreal notary Michel Lepailleur, along with various family members and friends, to create their marriage contract. At this time, the bride-to-be was two weeks short of her 23rd birthday (her twin sister, Anne, had married more than four years earlier). The prospective groom, $27^1/2$ years old, had been born and raised in the Lachine seigneury, about $^4/10$ mile east of the palisaded village; thus, these two young people had lived about $2^1/4$ miles apart nearly all of their lives. (More than five years earlier, Pierre's mother Jeanne Françoise Roy had died; in January of 1688, his father had remarried, to Marie Barbant, the widow of Jean de Lalonde. The biographies of two of Marie's voyageur sons, Jean Baptiste Lalonde and Guillaume Lalonde, are presented later in this work. Throughout the St. Lawrence Valley, the residents of many of the communities were just as highly interconnected.) The Tabault-Brunet couple was married in the Lachine church on the following day, April 16, with numerous relatives on both sides serving as the twelve official witnesses. They then settled on Pierre's property, which was located about $3^1/2$ miles west of the Lachine village, in the seigneury of La Présentation; there, they would produce three children within the next five years.166

Three months after this lively nuptial celebration, which was held in the old wooden church at Lachine, the brand new church built of field stones was dedicated, amid considerable festivities. Unfortunately, François had not lived long enough to enjoy the prominently-located pew that he had leased in perpetuity for his family within the new edifice.167

By the autumn of 1703, Barbe had been without her husband for more than fifteen months. Thus, the official selection of the guardians of their minor-age children, as well as the drawing up of the inventory of the family's estate (the future inheritance of all ten of their surviving children), had been postponed long enough. On October 8, the Montreal Court officially registered that Barbe Beauvais, widow of François Brunet dit Le Bourbonnais, had been chosen as the primary guardian, by means of a family meeting; her older brother Raphaël Beauvais, an innkeeper in Montreal, had been selected to serve as the supplemental or deputy guardian. In addition, the Court ordered that an official inventory of the couple's joint possessions be conducted in a timely manner.168

Eight days later, on October 16, Barbe was joined on the farm by her brother Raphaël, the notary Lepailleur from Montreal, and three men from the neighborhood. They had gathered to enumerate the Brunet-Beauvais belongings, in compliance with the Court's decree. *"In the year 1703, on the sixteenth day of October at nine o'clock in the morning, at the request of Barbe Beauvais, widow of the deceased François Brunet dit [Le] Bourbonnais, who while living was an habitant of the Island of Montreal at the place called Lachine, and as ordered by the Court of the royal jurisdiction of Montreal on the eighth of the present month, concerning the issue of the estate which there was between her and the said deceased her husband, as the mother and guardian of the minority-age [and unmarried] children who were produced by her and the said deceased individual, her husband, who are Jean François Brunet, twenty years old [actually 21], Élisabeth, eighteen years old [and about to marry Jean Baptiste Brault in six weeks], Marie, sixteen years old, Angélique, thirteen years old [actually 12], and Louis, six years old, who are present in person, as well as Jean Brunet, thirty years old, who is absent [in the Illinois Country], and in the presence of Raphaël Beauvais, uncle of the said minority-age children and their supplemental guardian as well as representing [the married children of the Brunet family and their spouses] Georges Brault, the husband of Barbe Brunet; Jeanne Brunet, the wife and legal representative of [her husband] Louis Mallet; Pierre Couillard, the husband of Anne Brunet; and Pierre Tabault, the husband of Catherine Brunet, all and each of them children and inheritors of half of the estate of the said deceased Brunet, their father.*

For the creation of the present inventory and the sharing and dividing of the belongings of the said estate, a true and accurate inventory and description of all of the belongings, furnishings, animals, implements, utensils of the residence, titles, papers, and instructions, together with the real estate of the said estate, was drawn up by me, Michel Lepailleur, royal notary on the Island of Montreal, residing at Ville Marie, and the undersigned witnesses. The said furnishings were found at the house where the said guardian is residing at the said place of Lachine, all of which were shown and described by her, without any belongings being hidden, under the penalties of the ordinance which we presented to her hearing. The said furnishings were priced and appraised according to their correct values at the present time by the Sieurs René Cuillerier, Charles Caillé, and Jacques Petit, her neighbors living at the said place, men of integrity, who have appraised and priced them to the best of their knowledge and according to the sums as required. The said witnesses [except Caillé] have signed with the said mother-guardian and the supplemental guardian, the said Cuillerier, and the notary after the reading was done, according to the ordinance.
Signed,
Barbe Bauves, Raphel Bauvais, Rene Cuiler, and J. Petit

At this moment, on the said day and hour, upon the above-noted request, and in the presence of the said above-named individuals, we proceeded with the said inventory, which thus follows.
The following are the immovables [real estate portion] of the said estate
One concession [of land] situated at the said place of Lachine upon which the

said widow is living, containing six arpents of frontage [on the St. Lawrence River, including three arpents from the grant of 1673 and three arpents from the purchase of 1696, measuring in total 1,150 English feet] by twenty arpents [7/10 mile] of depth, of which there are [fifty crossed out] forty arpents [of surface area, equal to 34 acres] worked with the plow and around [space left blank] arpents worked with the pickaxe, adjoined on one side by [the land of] Jean Roy [François Lory had died in 1702], on the other side by [Georges Brault dit] Pomainville, in front by the [St. Lawrence] River, and at the other end by separated lands. Charged by the seigneurs [the annual fees of] three bushels of wheat and eight livres in currency...........................
...[No valuation listed]

One other concession [of land] at the said place [of Lachine, angling northward from the inland end of the above-described main lot] containing four arpents [768 English feet] of frontage by twenty arpents [7/10 mile] of depth, of which there are twelve arpents [of surface area, equalling 10 acres] cleared to stubble, adjoined on one side by [the land of] René Cuillerier, on the other side by wild land, at one end by the Commons land, and at the other end by [that of] Antoine Beaudrias [Beaudry]. Charged by the seigneurs [the annual fees of] two bushels of wheat and forty sols [two livres] in currency. [No valuation listed]

One house situated on the land of the said place of Lachine [on the primary, first-listed lot], measuring forty-five feet in length by twenty feet in width, solidly built in pièce-sur-pièce style [with widely-spaced vertical framing elements and horizontal infill logs], consisting of two large rooms with two hearths and chimneys of stone, plus two side rooms [for sleeping and storage], all on the ground floor, and a large attic, entirely roofed with boards, the doors framed and the windows of its doors containing fixed wooden frames, estimated in its entirety at one thousand livres......................... 1,000 livres

One granary built in pièce-sur-pièce style, measuring fifty feet in length by twenty-five feet in width, without additional roof covering [besides the chinked logs], estimated at [five crossed out] four hundred livres .... 400 l.

[One stable]

One root cellar [a separate subterranean structure], estimated at .... 75 l.

[In the granary were found]
25 bushels of white peas, estimated at...37 l. 10 s.
200 small sheaves of wheat which will be threshed, the said [resulting] wheat
will be appraised at 2 livres per bushel, thus it has been appraised at...........
....*no valuation listed]*
45 sheaves of oats which will be threshed, the said [resulting] oats will be
appraised at 1 livre per bushel ....*[no valuation listed]*

1 plow, equipped with its cutting blade [plowshare], moldboard, long
connector unit which attaches it to the wheeled pulling unit, wheeled pulling
unit, and other items... 23 l.
1 cart with its [two] wheels with iron hub reinforcement bands............ 20 l.
2 iron hub reinforcement bands for cart [wheels]...................................... 2 l.
2 connector units for a sled [or sledge] .... 4 l.

In the stable were found
4 oxen, three years old, estimated at 60 livres apiece............................ 240 l.
8 adult cows, estimated at 30 livres apiece .... 240 l.
2 young milk cows, estimated at 25 livres apiece .... 50 l.
2 yearling calves, estimated at 12 livres apiece.. 24 l.
8 medium-sized pigs, estimated at 15 livres apiece .... 120 l.
10 sheep, estimated at 5 livres apiece.. 50 l.
2 1/2 dozen [30] chickens, estimated at 8 sols apiece.............................. 12 l.
2 stacks of firewood, three or four years' worth, estimated at 40 livres
apiece .... 80 l.

In the kitchen room of the said house were found
1 iron pot hanger
1 fire shovel
1 iron-bound [wooden] bucket
1 iron grill [or gridiron]
1 copper kettle
1 brass kettle
1 old large copper kettle
2 old small kettles, entirely broken
1 large pot with its cover
1 copper pot with its cover
2 small copper pots with their tinned-interior covers
1 low-walled saucepan of copper
1 wretched low-walled saucepan of tin plate

1 frying pan
1 large cooking spoon
1 copper skimmer
1 tin plate larding needle
1 pair of solid-construction flatirons [for pressing clothing and other fabric items]

1 oval folding table
51 pounds of pewter in 17 basins [of various sizes, and presumably other vessels as well]
29^1/2 pounds of old ceramic wares plus one [very large] plate, totalling 40 pounds of crockery
1 porcelain cup
1 stoneware jug
1 earthenware jug
1 faience [tin-glazed earthenware] carafe
1 earthenware pitcher
1 lidded food-carrying vessel for traveling, of pewter

[In other areas of the large kitchen room, or much more likely in the adjacent small room, were found]
1 old gun without a cock ....6 l.
2 pairs of snowshoes with rawhide lashings
1 chest of pine wood, closing [locking] with a key
1 old chest, closing [locking] with a key
1 horse collar with a complete harness
1 old broken saddle for a horse
1 old hewing axe
1 large crosscut saw with its [wooden] frame
1 double-bitted mortise chisel
2 small chisels
1 auger
1 gimlet
1 old wood rasp
1 knife for scraping hides
1 small anvil and one hammer

In the large room [parlor] at the side of the said kitchen room were found
1 large table of cherry wood, with its [two] benches
6 plain chairs with caned seats

4 turned and footed chairs [probably with wooden seats]
1 armchair of cherry wood, upholstered with velour fabric
1 small footstool of walnut wood
1 small oval table
1 large armoire [or wardrobe] with two doors, closing [locking] with a key
1 chest of medium size, of cherry wood with flat panels
1 bed frame of turned cherry wood
1 pillared bed canopy covered with linen fabric
1 set of bed curtains of velour fabric
1 old [straw-filled] mattress
1 linen blanket
1 blue [woolen] blanket from Toulouse
3 curtains of [woolen] serge fabric from Saint Pierre, containing four yards of fabric
10 small tablecloths of various coarse linen fabrics, each one containing about 3 1/2 yards of fabric, plus one that is partly worn out
16 tablecloths of various linen fabrics, each one containing 1 yard of fabric
3 dozen [36] small napkins of various linen fabrics, partly worn out

[In other areas of this second large room, or much more likely in the adjacent second small room, were found]
[François' surviving articles of clothing]
15 men's shirts of various linen fabrics, partly worn out
2 white shirts
1 camisole [long-sleeved overshirt or sleeping shirt] of red woolen fabric
1 hooded coat for springtime
1 old cloak of white woolen fabric, heavily worn out

Pieces of a Spanish pistol which has been broken into various pieces
2 old axes
2 old broken pickaxes
120 pounds of butter

Here follow the papers, titles, and instructions of the said estate
The contract of marriage of the said deceased Brunet and the said Beauvais, made and drawn up before the deceased Bénigne Basset, royal notary at Montreal and witnesses on the date of the eighteenth of April, 1672, by which it appears that the said Beauvais has brought to the said estate the sum of four hundred livres [the dowry provided by her parents]. She is to retain half of the estate as her own property and the other half is to remain

with the said estate [for the children]. In addition, according to her choice, the said Beauvais is endowed with the sum of [either the] the prefixed dower or the customary dower. [This document] is hereby numbered and entered into the inventory with the number 1.

One contract of concession [land grant] of the said sixty arpents [51 acres] of surface area, located at the said place of Lachine, with three arpents [575 feet] of frontage by twenty arpents [7/10 mile] of depth, having on one side [the land of] Jacques Cardinal, on the other side [that of] Pierre Couillard [sic, actually Pierre Cardinal], in front the St. Lawrence River, and behind the lands of the Côte Saint Paul, granted by the deceased Monsieur Dollier [de Casson], Superior of the Seminary of Montreal, on the date of the twenty-eighth of May, 1673. Inventoried as number 2.

One contract of concession [land grant] granted by the said deceased Monsieur Dollier [de Casson], passed before [Jean Baptiste] Pothier, royal notary, on the date of the fifth of April, 1693, containing eighty arpents [68 acres] of surface area, with four arpents [768 feet] of frontage by twenty arpents [7/10 mile] of depth, located at the said place of Lachine, with the said frontage commencing behind the Commons of the said place of Lachine, having on one side ungranted lands, on the other side the Lake of Nicolas Gasnier [Gagné], and at the back ungranted lands. Inventoried as number 3.

One declaration of adjudication of land containing three arpents [575 feet] of frontage by twenty arpents [7/10 mile] of depth located at the said place of Lachine above the Sault St. Louis, adjoined on one side by the land of the said Commons [actually, that of François Brunet] and on the other side by [that of] Georges Brault dit Pomainville, sold to the said deceased Brunet by Catherine Renusson, present wife of Augustin Alonze and former wife of Vincent Chamaillard, for 120 livres on the date of the eleventh of August, 1696, the said sum (illegible text). Inventoried as number 4.

One contract of sale by the said deceased Brunet and the said Beauvais to Guillaume Boucher and Jeanne Beauvais his wife [Barbe's sister] of a house located at Ville Marie on Rue Saint Paul, adjoined on one side by [the property of] the Sieur René Cuillerier, on the other side by [that of] the Sieur Charles Milot, in back by [that of] the Sieur Jean Milot, the said contract having been passed before [Jean Baptiste] Pothier, royal notary, on the twenty-sixth of August, 1696, the said sale made for the sum of three thousand livres plus eighty livres for the gratuity. The said contract was inventoried as number 5.

One report of surveying the land containing four arpents [768 feet] of frontage at the said place of Lachine [the rear concession of Brunet land, granted on April 5, 1693], conducted by the Sieur [Gédéon de] Catalogne on the date of the thirtieth of March, 1693. Inventoried as number 6.

One discharge receipt from Georges Brault [dit] Pomainville and Barbe Brunet his wife for the sum of three hundred sixty livres which the said [François] Brunet and his wife [Barbe Beauvais] had given as an advance on the inheritance [of their daughter Barbe Brunet], passed before Master Antoine Adhémar, royal notary, on the tenth of August, 1698. Inventoried as number 7.

The following are the debts which are owed to the said estate
By the Sieur Guillaume Boucher [Barbe's brother-in-law], the sum of two thousand livres according to an act of the sale of a house [document 5 above] located at Ville Marie on Rue Saint Paul, mortgaged specifically for the said sum .... 2,000l.
By the said [same] Sieur Boucher, the sum of two hundred livres for two years of payments against the principal sum, as well as 127 livres from old reckonings [previous transactions].. 327l.
By Georges Brault [dit] Pomainville [her son-in-law], nine bushels of loaned wheat [at 2 livres per bushel].. 18l.
By Louis Mallet, her son-in-law, six bushels of loaned wheat [at 2 livres per bushel].. 12l.
By Joseph Brault [dit] Pomainville [Georges' brother; Joseph would lease Barbe's farm on the following day] ....nine bushels of loaned wheat [at 2 livres per bushel].. 18l.

[Grand total of assets]...5,134l. 7s. 4d.

The following are the liabilities which are owed by the estate
To the Sieur Desauniers, surgeon, for bandages and medicines............. 28l.
To Sieur Desauniers [probably Pierre Trottier, Montreal merchant]..7l. 5s.
To Claude Caillé, for seven thick planks..4l. 4s.
To Pierre Couillard [her son-in-law].. 4l.
To Sieur Ca____ .... 2l.

These are all of the furnishings and real estate [and documents] which were found to be inventoried, as submitted by the said widow as the things of which she is aware that pertain to the said estate, to be included and added to *the present inventory. All of the furnishings have remained in the care and possession of the said widow, who has been charged with producing them when she will be so ordered.*

This [inventory] was closed and settled at the said place of Lachine at the house where the said widow is residing, in the morning in the presence of Sieur Jean Petit, royal bailiff, and of Vincent Lenoir as witnesses who have been called, who have signed with the said guardian, the said supplemental guardian, [the primary assessor,] and the notary.
Signed, Barbe Bauves, Raphel Bauvais, J. Petit, Vincent Lenoir, Rene Cuiler, and Lepailleur, notary"[169]

The land ownership map of Montreal Island which was drawn up by Vachon de Belmont during the previous year of 1702 verified that, by this point, the family's riverfront property had a total St. Lawrence frontage of six arpents, or 1,152 English feet. This property was listed on the key of the map as belonging to "Bourbonnais."[170] Back in 1681, at the time of that particular census, the family had owned only half of this land, just the eastern portion with three arpents of frontage that had been granted to François in 1673. By the time of the 1681 census, the family had cleared and put into cultivation ten acres of this property; in addition, they had owned seven horned cattle and one gun.[171] Now, 22 years later, the family owned the adjacent lot (purchased from the Alonze couple in 1696) as well as an interior lot that touched the inland end of their riverfront lot (granted to François in 1693). The combined riverfront lots contained 34 acres which were under cultivation with the plow, plus an unspecified number of acres that were under cultivation with the pickaxe; in addition, the interior lot had 10 acres "cleared to stubble." During the intervening 22 years since the census of 1681 had been enumerated, the family's total number of horned cattle had increased from seven to sixteen.

The primary difference between acreage which was worked with the plow and that which was worked with the pickaxe was whether the tree stumps had been removed or whether they were still in place. The oxen-drawn plow was not usually employed on a piece of ground until all of its stumps, as well as their associated root systems, had been cut and burned to a depth beneath the surface which would not hinder the cutting blade and moldboard of the plow (or else the stumps and their roots had been pried and pulled entirely out). It is to be noted that the inventory of the farm listed one plow with all of its equipment as well as two pickaxes.

The family's combined riverfront lot contained 120 square arpents of surface area. The annual fees that they paid to the Sulpicians, the seigneurs of Montreal Island, for the *cens* and the *rente* on this property totaled eight livres in currency plus three bushels of wheat. The interior lot had 80 square arpents of area; their annual seigneurial fees on this latter land totaled two livres in currency plus two bushels of wheat. Thus, in total, the Brunets annually paid out ten livres (200 sols) in money for the *cens*, plus five bushels of wheat (ten livres worth) for the *rente*. In return, they possessed two pieces of property that together contained ten arpents in total frontage and 200 square arpents (170 acres) in total area. (Throughout the entire colony, the usual seigneurial rates involved a token *cens* fee of 1 or 2 sols per arpent of frontage, and a slightly more substantial *rente* fee of about 1 livre per arpent of frontage.)

The Sulpicians typically charged their *censitaires* 1/4 to 5/6 sol per square arpent of area for the *cens* (the Brunets were charged 1 sol, on average). In addition, they charged one or two capons, or 1/2 to 1 bushel of wheat, per 20 square arpents for the *rente* (the Brunets were charged 1/2 bushel). These were the standard fees for the colonists of Montreal Island, according to rates which had been established by the Sulpician Seminary at Montreal. Besides the seigneurial fees of the Brunet family, the following is another example of the fees which were paid by settlers in the Lachine seigneury. In 1670, Louis Aumeau was "charged with paying to them [the seigneurs] six deniers tournois [1/2 sol] in *cens* each year for each [square] arpent of the said land, and a seigneurial *rente* of two bushels of wheat, [these fees to be] annual, perpetual, and unredeemable, payable on the Day and Feast of St. Martin [November 11]." In addition, the colonists relinquished to their seigneurial miller 1/40 of their grain when it was ground at the seigneurial gristmill. Besides these fees which went to the seigneur, each family was also obligated to hand over to the Church a tithe of 1/26 of the threshed wheat which they produced each year; however, new lands were exempt from this charge during their first five years of cultivation.[172]

One aspect of this Brunet inventory of 1703 which was rather rare was its inclusion of the buildings which stood on the property, along with their estimated valuations. This information was made all the more valuable by the addition of the descriptions of their methods of construction, and within the house information, the description of its room divisions plus the number of hearths and chimneys and their building material.

It is particular interesting to note that the family's belongings included "one horse collar with a complete harness," as well as "one old broken saddle for a horse." At the time of the inventory in 1703, the Brunets did not own a horse. However, based upon the complete array of horse gear that was in their possession, it is almost certain that they had earlier owned such an animal. In the present work, this is the ninth biography to be offered. Among these nine studied couples, the Brunets represent the very first instance in which evidence of horse ownership by the subjects has been encountered. The very first horse in New France had been transported from the mother country in 1647, as a special gift for Governor Montmagny from the monopoly company. However, after that date, no others had been imported for eighteen years, until 1665, when a dozen horses had arrived; these had still been a great rarity. Five years later, in 1670, about sixty mares and at least two stallions had been brought in, providing the first real breeding stock in New France. Until that time, all transport and farming tasks in the colony had been carried out by humans, oxen, and dogs. Even by the time of the 1688 general census of the colony (eighteen years after the arrival of the primary breeding stock), when 10,038 French settlers had resided in the St. Lawrence settlements, there had still been a grand total of only 218 horses present. In the Montreal region, the rural populace had often endured raids by marauding Iroquois warriors, with the accompanying slaughter of their livestock, during the 1680s and 1690s. Thus, horses had been even more scarce in this area, compared to the settlements further downriver, which had been attacked less often. These unrelenting attacks had only ceased in 1698. François and Barbe had probably acquired their horse during the fourteen-year period between the 1688 census and the patriarch's death in 1702. At that time, this helpful animal (which was usually utilized for transport, rather than for plowing) must have still been quite a rarity among the colonists of modest means.[173]

It was probably a reflection of the permanent peace accords which had been finalized with the Iroquois nations two years before the inventory, back in 1701, that the only gun inventoried in Barbe's home was not in functioning condition. It was described by the enumerator as "one old gun without a cock," and it was valued at the rather modest sum of six livres. There may have been one working gun in the family's possession at this time. However, her son Jean François may have been carrying it during his regular voyageur runs between

Lachine and Ft. Frontenac, which would have still been ongoing at this date in mid-October. The family also owned a Spanish-made pistol, but it had been dismantled at some point into a number of pieces. Civilian-owned pistols were quite scarce in the colony by this period; back at the time of the 1688 census, fifteen years earlier, only 159 pistols had been enumerated in the entire colony. However, this number had not included the pistols which were in the possession of the officers of the Troupes de la Marine.[174]

When an estate inventory was drawn up, it was customary for the surviving spouse to keep aside his or her clothing, other personal possessions, and a bed with its set of bedding. As a result, these articles were not listed with the other communally-owned belongings of the couple. Thus, in addition to the single canopy bed, one mattress, and two blankets that were enumerated in the Brunets' home, they most likely also owned at least one additional bed, plus considerable amounts of bedding.

It comes as no surprise that few of the garments that had belonged to François at the time of his death fifteen months earlier were still present in the family home. Besides the clothing that he had worn into his grave, most of his other garments had probably been distributed in the meantime among his adult son Jean François and his three sons-in-law (the possessions of his children were not listed in the inventory). No mention was made of any shoes, boots, stockings, breeches, waistcoat, dress coat, hooded coat for winter use, cap, hat, gloves, mittens, or scarf, all of which he had undoubtedly owned at the time of his demise.

In the inventory, no values were assigned to the two rather large parcels of property, or to the stable, or to the crops of wheat and oats which had been harvested and stored in the granary but had not yet been threshed. Without these items being included, the grand total of valuation of the listed articles came to 5,134 livres. Dividing this total figure into a number of categories is informative, since this shows how the value of the Brunet estate was generally distributed. The three listed buildings (minus the stable) were worth 1,475 livres (29 percent of the estate), while the livestock totaled 656 livres (13 percent). Since the harvested wheat and oats had not yet been threshed and valued by the bushel, the only threshed crop to be listed was 25 bushels of white peas, worth 37 livres. Without having the valuations of the wheat and oats to consider, no meaningful percentage may be figured comparing the crop values to the total estate value. The remaining listed possessions of the estate (including 80 livres worth of cut and stacked firewood) were valued at 591 livres, just 12 percent of the grand total.

The debts which were owed to the Brunet estate by the four individuals (two of whom were sons-in-law and a third was a brother-in-law of Barbe) came to 2,375 livres; interestingly, this figure represented fully 46 percent of the grand total value of the enumerated estate. However, 2,327 livres of this indebtedness (all but 48 livres) was owed by a single couple, Barbe's youngest sister Jeanne and her husband Guillaume Boucher. Their debt alone (for the purchase of François and Barbe's house in Montreal back in 1696, for the sum of 3,000 livres) equalled 45 percent of the value of all of the possessions that had been recorded in the inventory. In contrast, the other three debtors owned only the small amounts of 18, 12, and 18 livres, respectively. On the other side of the ledger, the debts which were owed by the estate to other individuals totaled only 45 livres, representing less than one percent of the value of the estate's listed possessions.

Immediately after concluding the inventory at the Brunet farm, Barbe, Raphaël, and the notary, with the same two witnesses Cuillerier and Petit standing by, drew up the official statement of division of the estate. In this document of October 16, they delineated the rights of inheritance of all of the legal heirs. These included Barbe, the five underage children who were present, son Jean who was away in the Illinois Country, and the four daughters along with their husbands. After separating off the large amount which was owed by Barbe's sister Jeanne Beauvais and her husband Boucher, which would be settled at a later time, the parties factored into the division the amounts of wheat that the two sons-in-law and Joseph Brault owed, as well as the 45 livres worth of debts which were owed by the estate to other individuals. As usual, Madame Brunet penned her signature at the bottom of this document as "Barbe Bauves."[175]

On the following day, before the same notary, Barbe leased out the family farm to Joseph Brault dit Pomainville, the younger brother of her son-in-law Georges. (This young man had already developed a working relationship with the family, since he had owed the estate for nine bushels of loaned wheat. In fact, it is entirely possible that he had already been working the Brunet farm.) Now 28 years old, Joseph had married Marie Anne Marchand at the Lachine church six months earlier, on April 10, after she had lost both her three-week-old daughter and her husband to smallpox on March 1 and 2, respectively. Nine days after their wedding, her four-year-old daughter had died of the disease as well, leaving the newly remarried mother with four living children between the ages of 14 and 5 years. Commencing with the lease agreement, these six people in the blended family of Joseph Brault would become additional members of the Brunet household. Among the unmarried Brunet children at this time, Jean François (age 21) was very often away working as a voyageur, while Élisabeth (18) would marry in about six weeks and move to her husband's farm close by. Thus, only Marie (age 16), Angélique (12), and Louis (6) were truly living at home. So the addition of a second resident family would not cause much crowding in a home that had once teemed with an entire array of active Brunet offspring. Since Barbe contracted this lease of the farm in the name of herself, her five underage children, and her son Jean who lived permanently in the Illinois Country, all seven of them would share in the payments that would be made by Joseph Brault as the lease proceeded over time.[176]

During the following month of November, the drawing up of Élisabeth's marriage contract, followed by her wedding the next day, were the main subjects of focus for the members of the extended Brunet family. On the 25th of the month, the prospective couple gathered with the Montreal notary Raimbault and various friends and relatives to dictate their nuptial agreement. Élisabeth, $18^3/4$ years old, was preparing to spend the rest of her life with Jean Baptiste Brault dit Pomainville, age 30, who was a brother of both Georges (who had married Barbe Brunet back in 1696) and Joseph (who had just leased the Brunet family farm). Shortly after the nearby Boursier farm had reverted to the Sulpicians for unpaid seigneurial dues back in 1699, Jean Baptiste had acquired within it a plot with two arpents of St. Lawrence frontage. It was located immediately east of the portion that had been purchased by Louis Mallet, another son-in-law of the Brunets. Thus, within a stretch of $7/10$ mile that started at the Commons of the seigneury and ran toward the east, lay the long slender farms of Georges Brault (and his wife Barbe Brunet), Barbe Beauvais (leased to Joseph Brault), Jean Roy (not a Brunet clan member), Louis Mallet (and his wife Marie Jeanne Brunet), and Jean Baptiste Brault (and his wife Élisabeth Brunet). On their farm, Jean Baptiste and Élisabeth would produce six children within the next 22 years; during a number of those years, he would be away working as a voyageur. At the couple's wedding celebration on November 26,

1703, the 22 official witnesses named in the church register included an entire spate of relatives as well as numerous friends; among these named individuals were twelve women.[177]

The year of 1704 brought to Barbe two financial transactions, plus the safe arrival of two babies. The first transaction took place on February 16, when Georges Brault acknowledged in an official notary document that he had received a loan from his mother-in-law Barbe Beauvais, the widow of François Brunet dit Le Bourbonnais. Seven months later, Barbe received a payment from Madeleine Dupont, the widow of François Guillemot dit Lalande, and on September 28 she registered a paid-in-full discharge receipt for her with the notary. Seven years earlier, back in June of 1697, Monsieur Guillemot (a Montreal baker and retired soldier) had repaid François 200 livres for a debt. Now, three years after his death, his widow was paying off an additional sum.[178]

The arrival of two babies within the first week of May in this spring of 1704 brought much joy to Barbe. Her daughter Catherine, having been married to Pierre Tabault for $12^1/2$ months, delivered her first child on May 3. Barbe was pleased to serve as the godmother of little Catherine, whose baptism was held on the same day in the Lachine church. This newly-started family lived about six miles to the west of the Brunet farm, in the seigneury of La Présentation or Côte St. Gilles.[179]

Five days later, on the 8th, a new baby was born in the Brunet home, an event which had probably not taken place there in a number of years. This day marked the arrival of the first child of the farm-leasing couple, Joseph Brault and Marie Anne Marchand. At the christening ceremony of Marguerite Angélique in the church on the following day, Barbe stood as the godmother. Future offspring of this couple, who already had four surviving children from Marie Anne's first marriage, would arrive in 1706, 1709, and 1711.[180]

But this season also brought a great portion of sadness to the Brunet clan. Back in September of 1701 and then on April 25 of this year of 1704, daughter Anne and her husband Pierre Couillard had joyously welcomed the arrival of their first two living children at Lachine, after having lost their first baby on her fourth day of life. Now, within the span of three days in June, the young parents were crushed by the deaths of both of their little ones. First, little Pierre passed away on the 16th, at the age of $2^3/4$ years; he was laid to rest in the cemetery beside the church on the following day. Then baby

Jean Baptiste died on the 18th, when he was just seven weeks old; he was interred beside his brother on the same day.[181]

In the wake of these tragic losses, the family members supported and encouraged one another as best they could, and life continued. Their spirits were lifted somewhat by the arrival of little Jean Baptiste Brault, Jr. on October 30, 1704. This little lad was the first child of daughter Élisabeth and her husband Jean Baptiste Brault, Sr., who had been married for eleven months.[182]

During the summer of 1705, Barbe appeared as the baptismal sponsor for the new baby of Jean Paré and Marguerite Picard. At little Joseph's christening ceremony on July 4, the godmother, who was soon to turn age 49, stood at the baptismal font with this couple's thirteenth and penultimate child. Monsieur Paré was an example of a man who had continued to serve as a soldier in the colony even after his marriage, while also working as a master carpenter. Married at Montreal in October of 1681, Jean had been documented as the Sergeant of the garrison at Montreal in 1681, 1683, and 1684, and later as the commandant of the habitants at Ft. Rémy in the village of Lachine in May of 1693 and January of 1695.[183]

At this point, Barbe's voyageur son Jean François was $23^1/2$ years old. During the course of his travels, he had met and become infatuated with Françoise David, a resident of the seigneury of Champlain, which was located to the east of Trois-Rivières. (She was the granddaughter of Claude David and Suzanne Denoyon, whose biography has already been offered in the present work.) This young woman, who had turned age 20 in November of 1704, lived some ninety miles northeast of Lachine. After the young couple became engaged, Fr. Rémy published two banns of marriage at the Lachine church, after which he dispensed with the third bann. However, Barbe was not able to watch them exchange their wedding vows, since the ceremony was held at Champlain on January 25, 1706, in the bride's home parish of Notre Dame de la Visitation. On this lighthearted occasion, the official witnesses included the bride's grandfather Pierre Couillard, her brother Jean David, and her brother-in-law Jacques Levalois, since both of her parents were already deceased. Later, the record of their marriage was officially copied and registered by the Lachine notary Jean Baptiste Pothier, Barbe's brother-in-law. Settling in the Lachine seigneury, the couple would produce seven children there over the span of eighteen years, before moving to Bout de l'Île, the area at and near the western tip of Montreal Island. During many of these years, Jean François would labor as a voyageur-trader in the western interior. (Jean François and Françoise [whose dual biography is presented later], along with their daughter Marie Angélique, would provide the ancestral linkages between Barbe and François and the present author.)[184]

Some eight months after this family wedding, on October 6, 1706, Barbe's brother-in-law Guillaume Boucher, an innkeeper in Montreal and the widower of her sister Jeanne Beauvais, transferred the ownership of the Brunet home on Rue St. Paul in Montreal back to Barbe. The young couple had purchased the house and lot from Barbe and François more than a decade earlier, back in August of 1696. However, within the first seven years after this transaction (before the Brunet inventory in October of 1703), they had only been able to pay 1,000 livres toward the purchase price of 3,000 livres. Eventually determining that he was unable to pay off the remainder of the owed amount, Monsieur Boucher had decided to return the home to Barbe and the Brunet estate. The Boucher couple had not been blessed with good fortune. Having married in December of 1695, their first child had arrived $7^1/2$ months later; however, he had only survived for six weeks. Their second baby had been born in November of 1697, but he had passed away after just thirteen weeks. Their third child and only daughter had arrived in the following year; but she had died at a young age, and had disappeared from the documentary record. Finally, after just seven years and two months of marriage, Jeanne Beauvais had died in February of 1703, three weeks after having celebrated her 30th birthday.[185]

In December of 1706, Barbe welcomed into the world the first Brunet-named grandchild that she had ever held. (Earlier, their eldest son Jean Brunet and his wife had produced one child in the Illinois Country; but it is very unlikely that Barbe and François had ever had the opportunity to meet this distant daughter-in-law and granddaughter.) Five weeks before they would celebrate their first wedding anniversary, Françoise David and her husband Jean François Brunet delivered their first child, on December 18. Little Françoise was baptized in the Lachine church on that same day.[186]

About six weeks later, celebrations were again in order for the members of the extended Brunet clan: this time, they were for the marriage of daughter Marie, who was $19^2/3$ years old. On February 5, 1707, she and her soon-to-be-husband Pierre Caillé dit Biscornet gathered with the notary, family members, and friends to draw up their marriage contract. Pierre, age 26, had been born and raised at Laprairie, on the eastern shore of the St. Lawrence about seven miles east of the Brunet farm. Two days later, the couple recited their vows in the Lachine church. On this occasion, the official witnesses included the bride's unmarried sister Angélique Brunet (age 15^1/2), her aunt Marguerite Beauvais, her brother-in-law Georges Brault, and the couple's friend Anne Dubois. After settling at Laprairie, the couple would produce six children over the next nineteen years. (They would thus be the second couple within the extended Brunet clan to settle in some other seigneury than Lachine; Catherine and Pierre Tabault resided about 3^1/2 miles west of the Lachine village in the seigneury of La Présentation or Côte St. Gilles.)[187]

During the summer, Barbe performed a layman's provisional baptism on the newborn daughter of the Lachine blacksmith Jean Bizet and his wife Catherine Louise Gros, shortly after the baby's arrival on June 14. However, the tiny lass survived but a few hours, before passing away on the same day. She was interred in the cemetery beside the Lachine church on the 15th, with Barbe Beauvais and the elderly resident Jean Malherbeau dit Campillion as the official witnesses.[188]

About 10^1/2 months after Barbe had heartily joined in the festivities of her daughter Marie's marriage to Pierre Caillé, the young couple added a brand new member to the extended clan. December 19, 1707 marked the arrival of Pierre, Jr. at Laprairie; he was christened there on the following day.[189]

In the summer of 1708, Barbe acquired ownership of a lot with a home that was located within the village of Lachine. On June 15, she and René Cuillerier, Sr. (a merchant of Lachine and Montreal, and since 1670 one of the original settlers of the Lachine seigneury) jointly purchased a piece of property within the palisaded village, which was still called Ft. Rémy. This they acquired from the nuns of the Congregation of Notre Dame of Montreal, with the consent of the Sulpician seigneurs. Then, on the same day, Barbe and René officially divided between themselves the lots and houses that they had just acquired in the village.[190]

It was during the year 1708 or a bit earlier that Barbe's only younger brother, the Montreal merchant Jean Baptiste Beauvais, passed away. During eleven years of married life in Montreal, he and his wife had produced four children; however, each of these babies had died within a month of its birth. In January of 1709, when Jean

Baptiste would have been 46 years old if he had lived, his widow remarried; she later bore five more children.[191]

During the winter of 1710, the severe weather was offset by a warmhearted celebration in the Brunet family: the wedding of the youngest daughter, who was also the last one to be married. First, on February 12, Angélique (who would turn 19 in April) and her fiancé Jean Tabault (27^1/$_2$ years old, born and raised at Lachine) stood before the Montreal notary to create their marriage contract. (They were already in-laws, since Jean's older brother Pierre had wed Angélique's older sister Catherine nearly seven years earlier, back in April of 1703.) Five days after signing their contract, on February 17, the bride and groom were joined in marriage at the Lachine church, with four official witnesses present. These were the bride's uncle Jean Baptiste Pothier (the notary) and friends François Morel, Pierre Perthuis, and Paul Dumouchel. Before long, the newly wedded couple would relocate to Montreal, where they would produce two children within the next seven years.[192]

For Barbe, her responsibilities for her children had now been lifted, for the most part. Over the course of the previous fourteen years, since the winter of 1696, nine out of ten of the Brunets' living children had found soul mates and had married. At long last, their two older sons and all seven of their daughters had spouses, and all but the newly-married Angélique had offspring of their own. Only their youngest child, Louis, who would turn 13 in May, was still living at home. (He would remain single for another eleven years, until January of 1721.)[193]

Near the end of this summer of 1710, Barbe was pleased to be selected as the godmother of the first baby born to the Lachine residents Nicolas Robillard and Françoise Cécire. On August 13, little Nicolas, Jr. was both born and baptized.[194]

However, the optimistic mood that was engendered by the safe arrival of this local infant was dashed two months later, when the second child of Jean François Brunet and Françoise David arrived. The tiny girl was born on October 17, but she died and was buried beside the Lachine church on the same day.[195]

Eight months and one week later, on June 23, 1711, these same parents were elated to deliver a healthy granddaughter for Barbe to coddle. Little Marie Angélique was baptized at the Lachine church on the same day.[196] After another eight months had elapsed, Barbe sold a portion of the family farm to Jean François (who was now sometimes called François Brunet, Jr., even in legal documents). This transfer of property was officially registered with the Montreal notary on February 22, 1712.[197] Now, four of Barbe's married children resided very close by, within the 7/10 mile stretch of land that extended eastward along the St. Lawrence shoreline from the Commons land. In sequence from west to east, these offspring were Barbe and her husband Georges Brault, François, Jr. and his wife Françoise David, Marie Jeanne and her husband Louis Mallet, and Élisabeth and her husband Jean Baptiste Brault.

The autumn of 1713 delivered to Barbe heart-wrenching sensations that she had never before experienced. September 7 was the bleak date on which her daughter Catherine, one of the twins, was laid to rest in the Montreal cemetery at the untimely age of $33^{1}/3$ years. She had been married to Pierre Tabault for a decade; during that time, the couple had produced three children, who were now 9, 7, and 5 years old. Fourteen months after her death, Pierre would remarry in 1714; afterward, he and his second wife would produce six additional offspring at Montreal, Lachine, and Pointe Claire.

It was in the year 1714 that Barbe sold her lot within Ft. Rémy, the stockade-enclosed village site of Lachine, along with its house and outbuildings. She transferred this property to the Lachine flour merchant Gabriel Gibault on August 16, six years after she had acquired it back in June of 1708.[198]

By this point, the wooden palisade walls which surrounded the town of Montreal had been standing for nearly three decades, and they were in need of a major upgrade. The initial stockade had been erected in 1685 or 1686, after which this first set of log walls had been reinforced in 1699. Over the course of the following nine years, the inhabitants had outgrown the area of this initial enclosure. This expansion of the population had required a commensurate expansion of the stockade perimeter, which had been carried out during the years from 1708 to 1710. Now, however, the King's Minister determined that all of the wooden walls of the palisade were to be replaced with much more durable ones, constructed of cut stone.

On November 6, 1714, Intendant Bégon decreed that these new and improved walls encircling the town would be built with contributions from all of the colonists who resided within the governmental district of Montreal (which extended to a point some thirty miles northeast of the town itself). This massive construction project would be carried out by means of the *corvée* system. This term referred to the amount of unpaid labor which each household was obliged to contribute every year to the seigneurs (in this instance, the Sulpicians), since the inhabitants were their *censitaires* or property-holders. In his pronouncement, the administrator declared that there would be drawn up "an allotment and tax of the number of days of labor which each of the said habitants will be obliged to furnish for the said *corvées*, in proportion to their possessions and abilities." The various tasks which they would carry out were planned to take place during those seasons in which most of the people were less busy, particularly after the autumn harvests had been completed. Thus, during the autumn seasons, they would be assigned to transport the rough-cut stones from the quarries to the assembly points, and during the winters they would haul these crude blocks to the workshops for further shaping. Other tasks of the habitants would entail hauling lime and sand to appropriate locales, for the fabrication of mortar.

However, instead of carrying out these assigned labors themselves, with their own teams of horses, each of the habitants had the option of paying for another individual to substitute for him. For each day of labor of a man, the levied tax was to be three livres, and for each day of labor of a pair of harnessed horses, the tax would be eight livres. These funds would be utilized to pay for replacement workers and teams of horses. For anyone who did not participate as ordered, with either direct labor or payments for substitutes, "the penalty for disobedience will be five hundred livres in fines for each of the contraventions, applicable to the King to be utilized for the expenses of the fortifications."

Between December 16, 1714 and March 25, 1715, the master roster of all of the colonists who were expected to contribute to this immense building project was drawn up. This document was entitled "List of the habitants of Montreal Island, Jesus Island, and the neighboring seigneuries who have been requisitioned to work on the fortifications of Montreal in 1715." After the 344 designated residents of the town and outlying areas of Montreal were listed, there followed the inhabitants (in this sequence) of Longue Pointe (37 listings), Côte de Vertus (27), Notre Dame de Liesse (42), Saint Michel (20), Saint Ours (50), Ménagerie des Pauvres (5), Boucherville (78), Côte de Verchères (25), Île Bouchard, Seigneury of Monsieur Dejordy (15), Côte de Varenne (21), Côte St. Michel (23), Côte Ste. Thérèse (15), Côte de Lachine (56), Côte St. Paul (14), Côte St. Pierre (5), Lachenaie (32), Rivière des Prairies (55), Île Jésus (46), Les Mille Îles (16), and Haut [Bout] de l'Île (74).

In the section of the roster pertaining to the Lachine seigneury, called "Côte de Lachine," a total of 56 land owners were recorded. They were headed by the Captain of the parish militia forces here, Claude Caron. Within the eastern or Sault St. Louis section of this seigneury, where the majority of the Brunet clan members resided cheek by jowl, four of the clan's families were listed. These included "The Widow Bourbonnais" (Barbe Beauvais, widow of François Brunet dit Le Bourbonnais, Sr.), "Brunet [dit] Bourbonnais" (Barbe's son François Brunet dit Le Bourbonnais, Jr.), "Jean [Baptiste] Pomainville" (husband of Barbe's daughter Élisabeth Brunet), and "The Widow Pomainville" (Barbe's daughter Barbe Brunet, the widow of Georges Brault dit Pomainville).

After a number of years of ongoing construction, the entire set of encircling walls would be completed. Rising more than twenty feet in height, they would feature a total of sixteen gates, most of which would be positioned in the south wall, which faced the St. Lawrence River. The western wall of the town enclosure was located at the present Rue McGill, while the eastern wall was positioned just to the east of the present Rue Berri; the north wall extended along the present Rue St. Jacques, and the south wall ran parallel to the St. Lawrence. These ponderous barriers of mortar-laid stone would protect the community for more than eight decades, until they would be razed in 1804.[199]

In 1715, two of Barbe's Caillé grandsons died at Laprairie, about five miles east of the Brunet farm on the eastern shore of the St. Lawrence. First, Antoine, who had been born to Marie Brunet and Pierre Caillé 34 months earlier, passed away on January 2; he was buried on the same day. Six months later, on the first day of July, this youngster was followed to the grave by his older brother Pierre, Jr.; the eldest child of the family, Pierre was $7^{1}/_{2}$ years old. These two poignant losses left the young couple with two children: Marie, who was $5^{1}/_{2}$, and the toddler Joseph, who was 13 months old.[200]

It was during this same summer and in the same area of Laprairie that Barbe's next-younger sister Marguerite Beauvais died on June 28; in two months, she would have celebrated her 57th birthday (Barbe was two years and two days older than her). Over the course of forty years of marriage, Marguerite had borne thirteen children at Laprairie.[201]

When the vessels from France arrived during this summer of 1715, they brought the shocking news that caused the people to cry out, "*Le*

Roi est mort! Vive le Roi! (The King is dead! Long live the King!)." Their monarch Louis XIV had died at the age of 77, after having worn the Crown for 72 of those years. His reign had extended from 1643, when he had been five years old, until this year of 1715. However, during that period, his mother Anne of Austria had ruled in his stead for the first eight years, after which Cardinal Jules Mazarin had ruled for another decade. Only in 1661, when Louis had been 23 years old, had he finally assumed the role of the true leader of the realm. In 1711, when the King had been 73 years old, his son Louis had died at the age of 40, struck down by smallpox. In the following year, measles had felled Louis de France, Le Grand Dauphin (who was the King's grandson), at the age of 30; this same epidemic had also taken the Dauphin's wife and his eldest son. As a result of this series of three deaths in the direct line of male succession, the Dauphin's second son ascended to the throne in 1715. At this time, the deceased Louis XIV's *arrière-petit-fils*, his great-grandson, became Louis XV when he was five years old. Ultimately, the new King would come rather close to matching the record length of time that his great-grandfather had ruled. Louis XV's reign would extend for 59 years, from 1715 until 1774, during which time his age would increase from 5 to 64. During the first eight years of his reign, he would rule through the regency of Philippe d'Orléans, Louis XIV's nephew, and then for twenty more years through the regency of the Duc de Bourbon. Louis would finally assume full control of the realm in 1743, when he would be 33 years old. The successive reigns of these two Louis monarchs would span a full 131 years, from 1643 until 1774. In comparison, the period of permanent settlement in New France would extend from 1608 to 1760 (technically, until the treaty of 1763). Thus, during all but its first 35 years of permanent settlement, the colony would be ruled by one of these two Kings.[202]

At some point during 1715 or earlier, Georges Brault dit Pomainville, Barbe's oldest son-in-law, passed away. His departure left her daughter Barbe, then forty years old, with six living children who ranged in age from 18 down to about 4 years. On January 16, 1716, the younger Barbe signed a marriage contract at Lachine with Martial Dumoulineuf; in their subsequent years together, the new couple would produce no additional children.[203]

In the summer of 1716, Barbe rented out the family home on Rue St. Paul in Montreal. Since 1703, it had belonged to the entire Brunet clan, as a major portion of their joint inheritance, and in 1706 it had been transferred back into Barbe's name by Guillaume Boucher, her widowed brother-in-law. On August 20, 1716, she signed a rental contract for the house with Marguerite Lepage, the wife of the soldier Simon Gilbert dit Sanspeur, who was away at the time. This young couple, having been married since February of 1713, had produced children at Montreal in 1713, 1714, and 1715; however, their first baby had survived for just eleven days.[204]

It was in the autumn of 1716 that Barbe received the melancholy news that another of her grandchildren had passed away. Angélique and Jean Tabault's eldest child, Marie Josèphe, was laid to rest in the Montreal cemetery on November 4, at the age of four years. The couple's only other offspring was their son Jean Hippolyte, who had been born six weeks earlier.[205]

Death struck the clan again on two occasions during the following summer of 1717. First, little Jean Hippolyte Tabault passed away in Montreal, at the age of eleven months; he was buried there on August 17.[206] Then, Barbe received word that her son-in-law Louis Mallet had died on July 18 at Detroit, when he had been 43 years old. He, Marie Jeanne, and their children had relocated from Lachine westward to Bout de l'Île some seven years earlier. At the time of her husband's demise, Marie Jeanne was age fifty; during their two decades of marriage, they had produced seven children. Four years into the future, Marie Jeanne would remarry at Bout de l'Île, in September of 1721. However, she and her second husband, 22-year-old Philibert Couillaud dit Larocque, would produce no additional offspring.[207]

Even more deaths plagued the family during 1718. The first to die was Barbe's youngest daughter Angélique. Four days after celebrating her 27th birthday, on April 20, she left this world and was interred in the Lachine cemetery. During their eight years of married life, she and Jean Tabault had produced two children; however, both of them had died at a young age. The first one, a daughter, had passed away in 1716 at the age of four years, while the second one, a son, had died in 1717 at the age of eleven months. The widowed Jean would remarry six years later, but he and his second wife would not produce any offspring, and he would perish after just four years.[208]

The second loss to befall the extended Brunet clan in 1718 was the newest Caillé grandson, who was born across the St. Lawrence at Laprairie on October 22. Seven weeks later, he died on December 16.[209] Although Barbe could not have known it at the time, Dame Fortune would smile on the clan during the following six years, sparing them from any additional deaths during that time.

A ceremony which was conducted in the Ste. Anne Church at Bout de l'Île during the summer of 1719 brought with it a novel experience for Barbe: the marriage of a grandchild. On July 3, she was one of the three official witnesses at the wedding of her granddaughter Catherine Mallet, the eldest child of her daughter Marie Jeanne and her deceased husband Louis Mallet. The bride was 18^1/4 years old, while the groom, Charles Duquet, was 27^1/2 years of age. The three witnesses recorded in the parish ledger on this joyful day were the groom's brother Étienne Duquet, Jacques Milot (a merchant of Bout de l'Île), and "Barbe Beauvais of Lachine, maternal grandmother of the bride and widow of François Brunet." Having attended so many forlorn funerals in recent years, this ceremony must have generated within the matriarch a great deal of joy and encouragement.[210]

Three months later, Barbe received the payoff of a loan from Marie Madeleine Lemoine (the remarried widow of her brother Jean Baptiste Beauvais) and her second husband René Godefroy, the Sieur de Linctot, who was an officer in the Troupes de la Marine. Shortly thereafter, on October 6, Barbe visited the notary to issue to her a discharge receipt for this payment; it was apparently the payoff of a loan that Barbe had granted to her merchant brother and Marie Madeleine some sixteen years earlier, back on July 20, 1703.[211]

Within the first week of January in 1721, two joyous events buoyed Barbe's spirits. The first of these events took place on the 4th, when Louis, her youngest child and third son, stood before the notary Michel Lepailleur with his fiancée Marie Madeleine Girard to draw up their marriage contract. The prospective groom was 23 years and seven months old, while the bride-to-be (whose parents were both deceased) was five months older than him. Interestingly, 22^1/2 earlier (back on Sunday, August 10, 1698), Louis' father François Brunet had physically attacked Marie Madeleine's father Léon Girard, while they had been returning to Lachine following a visit to Montreal. After registering charges of assault and battery against Monsieur Brunet in the Montreal Court, either Monsieur Girard had dropped the charges against him or the Court had dismissed the case, since no settlement had ever been recorded with a notary. Now, nearly a quarter-century later, both of these fathers who had exchanged angry words and had then escalated their conflict into a fight, were resting quietly in their graves, while their two offspring were planning to join one another in loving matrimony.[212]

The priest at Lachine had published the banns of this impending marriage of Louis Brunet dit Le Bourbonnais and Marie Madeleine Girard on December 29, January 1, and January 5. Thus, on January 7, he penned the following notations into the church register:

"All of the habitants of this parish having found no impediment, I, the undersigned priest of the parish of the Holy Angels at Lachine, have received their mutual consent of marriage, and I have given to them the nuptial benediction with the ceremonies proscribed by the Holy Church, in the presence of and with the consent of Barbe Beauvais, mother of the groom, of Jacques Chasle, guardian and grandfather of the bride, of Raphaël Beauvais, uncle of the groom, of Jean [Brault dit] Pomainville, brother-in-law of the groom, of Marie Anne Beaune, aunt of the bride on the maternal side, of Jean and Marguerite Charlotte Girard, brother and sister of the bride, of Jean and Jacques Chasle, maternal uncles of the bride, all from this parish except for Raphaël Beauvais, the guardian of the groom, from Ville Marie, and Jean and Jacques Chasle from Pointe Claire. All of them have said that they do not know how to sign, except for these undersigned.
Signed,
Barbe Bauves, Raphel Bauvais, Jacque Chale, and J. Letessier, priest of La Chine"[213]

A month later, Barbe was pleased to attend the wedding at Lachine of another granddaughter, Marie Anne Couillard, who was the oldest surviving child of her daughter Anne and Pierre Couillard. At the age of 15$^{1}/_{2}$ years, the bride was joining in nuptial partnership with Pierre Primot from Châteauguay, who was 24$^{1}/_{2}$ years old. After the priest had dispensed with the third published bann of marriage, the young couple pronounced their vows on February 10. One of the official witnesses recorded on this day in the church ledger was "Barbe Beauvais, grandmother of the bride, of this parish."[214]

Eleven months after Barbe had witnessed her son Louis' wedding to Marie Madeleine Girard, this young couple delivered their first child. This cheerful event took place on December 11, 1721 at Lachine, where they had settled; on the following day, little Marie Josèphe was baptized at the local church.[215]

Two weeks later, on the day after Christmas, Barbe traveled to Montreal to officially record with the notary the sale of the family's home there. The purchaser of their lot and buildings on Rue St. Paul was Marie Anne Legras, identified in the document as a *marchande*. Age 42 at this point, she was the wife of the Montreal merchant bourgeois Charles Delaunay; they had married a quarter-century earlier, and had produced fourteen children within 24 years, between

April of 1697 and March of this year of 1721. Since the home belonged to the joint estate of the Brunet family, Barbe would be sharing the proceeds from the sale with five of her children, who were listed in the document. These would include Jean in the Illinois Country (described in the document "at present on the Mississippi"), François, Jr. and his wife Françoise David, Élisabeth and her husband Jean Brault, Angélique and her husband Jean Tabault, and Louis and his wife Marie Madeleine Girard.[216]

The inclusion of these five offspring in the sharing, plus the exclusion of the other five, must have reflected the divisions of the estate as they had been negotiated between the various family members back in the autumn of 1703, following the inventory of Barbe and François' joint possessions. The children excluded from a share of the sale proceeds in 1721 included Barbe and her second husband after the death of Georges Brault; Marie Jeanne and her second husband after the death of Pierre Mallet; Catherine, who had died in 1713, leaving her husband Pierre Tabault and three offspring; and Anne and her husband Pierre Couillard. Interestingly, these sharing arrangements did not include Marie and her husband Pierre Caillé, who had been married for fourteen years and had produced seven children at Laprairie. At the time of the estate division back in 1703, she had been only six years old; thus, she would certainly have been included at that time in the terms of division which would have guaranteed for her a fair share in the future. Equally interesting is the fact that Angélique, who had died in 1718 without any living children, was granted a share of these sale proceeds; these monies would go to her widowed husband Jean Tabault, a resident of Lachine and Montreal, who had not yet remarried. Back in 1703, François, Élisabeth, Marie, Angélique, and Louis (in descending order of their ages) had been the five unmarried and underage Brunet children whose inheritance rights had been specifically protected at the time of the estate proceedings (along with those of Jean, the eldest child, who had relocated to the Illinois Country).

July 19, 1722 brought a unique experience for Barbe, when she stood in the Lachine church as the godmother of a tiny native girl. Anne Angélique, whose native parents resided at the mission of Lac des Deux Montagnes, about twenty miles west of Lachine, had been born two days earlier. On this occasion, the godfather was Noël Legault dit Deslauriers, a fellow resident of the seigneury who had eight living children.[217]

Eighteen months later, on January 31, 1724, Barbe and Monsieur Legault again appeared as official witnesses at an ecclesiastical ceremony in the Holy Angels Church at Lachine. This time, Barbe's granddaughter Françoise Angélique Brault, the oldest surviving daughter of her daughter Barbe Brunet and the deceased Georges Brault, was marrying the Lachine voyageur Pierre Noël Legault, who was the eldest son of Noël. The bride was $17^2/3$ years old, while the groom was age 23. After conducting the nuptial ceremony, the priest recorded in the church ledger the names of the fourteen official witnesses, nearly all of them relatives of the newlyweds, including Barbe Beauvais.[218]

But the lighthearted mood was shattered just nine weeks later, when Barbe's son-in-law Pierre Couillard, the husband of her daughter Anne, passed away. He was laid to rest in the cemetery at Pointe Claire, some nine miles west of the Brunet farm, on April 5. The couple had been married for 25 years; during the first eighteen of those years, they had borne seven children in the Lachine seigneury, three of whom had died at very young ages. The widowed Anne, who was now 44 years old, had two to four living children, one of whom was already married. Three years into the future, Anne would remarry, but she would have no additional children with her second husband.[219]

The summer of 1726, when Barbe was about to turn age 70, brought with it two heart-wrenching losses. However, just before they befell the family, the matriarch officially took two young charges into her home, under rather unusual circumstances. According to a notary document from June 9, Pierre Raimbault, the King's Councilor and Attorney for the Provost Court at Montreal, bound on this date an eighteen-year-old named Pierre, who was recorded without a family name and as a "found child," to Barbe Beauvais, the widow of François Brunet dit Le Bourbonnais. Less than a month later, on July 4, Councilor Raimbault bound an additional "found child" to Barbe; this time, the young charge was identified as Françoise, six months old (again without a family name). Since the authorities were aware of the respective given names and ages of these two young people, they had apparently each been anonymously abandoned by their parent or parents shortly after their births, and had been raised since then as orphans in private homes, under the care of the state.

In New France, the colonists were strongly encouraged by the administrators to take care of any orphans who were present within their own families. However, in the case of parent-less children who had no relatives, and of foundlings, the ultimate responsibility for their upkeep usually rested upon the state, especially from the 1720s onward. In 1717, the King's Attorney of the Provost Court at Montreal had registered a complaint with the Council of the Marine Department at Versailles. This official had objected to the fact that an out-of-wedlock French child had been given to a native woman at Lorette (near Quebec) to raise as her own. The Attorney had requested that, in the future, he and all of the other Crown Attorneys be granted the authority to place all foundlings with French families. In this manner, according to his view, "this abuse" of French children being raised by native families would be reduced, since this practice was contrary to the monarch's intention to Frenchify the native populations. The Council had referred the issue to the Intendant of the colony, Michel Bégon, who in 1720 had outlawed the practice of French children being given to native people to raise. Thereafter, foundlings and illegitimate children would be regularly placed in French homes, where they would typically serve as either household servants or apprentices of their hosts. In return for taking in these *enfants du Roi* (children of the King), the informally adopting parents were usually paid a gratuity by the state. The expenses of these court-arranged adoptions were covered by some of the proceeds from the Domaine du Roi, the region in the lower St. Lawrence Valley which was leased out by the administrators to generate revenues for operating the colony.[220]

On the same day in which the second foundling child came to live with Barbe at the Brunet farm in 1726, the sixth offspring of her daughter Élisabeth and her husband Jean Baptiste Brault was born on their farm, which was located $2/10$ mile east of the Brunet land. Little Marie Charlotte was christened by the pastor on the very same day, July 4, in the Lachine church. However, after just three weeks of life, the little one passed away on July 25; she was interred on the same day. This would be the last baby whom this couple would produce.[221]

On the day before little Marie Charlotte departed, on July 24, 1726, Barbe's daughter Marie died, seven weeks after she had celebrated her 39th birthday. She and Pierre Caillé had been married for nineteen years, residing all the while at Laprairie, across the St. Lawrence and about seven miles east of the Brunet farm. This couple had borne eight children, three of whom had died young; the surviving ones were now 16, 14, 12, 6, and $3^1/2$ years old. Just $2^1/2$

years into the future, in February of 1729, widowed Pierre would also perish, having never remarried.[222]

By 1728, Barbe must have marveled when she realized that her François had already been gone for more than a quarter-century. During the course of this particular year, she recorded two financial transactions before Montreal notaries. First, on September 3, she issued a discharge receipt to Claude Saint-Olive, an apothecary in Montreal, for the payoff of a debt which he had owed to her.[223]

Two months later, on November 6, Barbe sold the inheritance rights which had belonged by law to Jean Tabault, the widower of her daughter Angélique Brunet, to his own widow, Françoise Pilet. Six years after Angélique's death (they had produced no surviving children), Jean and Françoise had been married, in 1724. However, the couple had produced no additional children, and he had passed away in Montreal after just $4^{1}/2$ years, on September 24, 1728, the day before he would have turned age 36. Barbe settled his portion of the Brunet family estate with this document of transfer on November 6. (Back in December of 1721, he had been listed as one of the rightful recipients of a part of the monies which had been generated by the sale of the Brunet family home on Rue St. Paul in Montreal.)[224]

In the depths of winter in 1733, on January 7, Barbe must have counted her blessings when she witnessed the marriage of yet another of her granddaughters at the altar of the Lachine church. Marie Angélique Brault, the eldest daughter of Élisabeth Brunet and Jean Baptiste Brault dit Pomainville, had just turned age 23 a week before. Her fiancé, fellow Lachine resident François Roy, would soon turn 29. When the priest recorded the event in the parish ledger, he noted the presence of "Barbe Beauvais, grandmother of the bride."[225]

More than seven years later, in the spring of 1740, the matriarch of the clan was forced to suffer another poignant loss. This time, it was the death of Jean François (also called François, Jr.), her middle son. He was laid to rest in the Ste. Anne cemetery at Bout de l'Île on March 13, ten weeks before he would have celebrated his 58th birthday. In the church ledger, the priest recorded that the parents of the deceased had been *"anciens habitants de la paroisse de Sts. Anges de Lachine* (early settlers of the Holy Angels parish at Lachine)." Jean François and Françoise David had been married for more than 36 years; during the first eighteen of those years, the couple had borne seven children on the Lachine farm not far from Barbe. After moving westward some fifteen miles to Bout de l'Île in about 1724, their final offspring had arrived five years later. At this point, their six surviving children ranged in age from 28 down to $10^3/4$ years. Now, Barbe knew that she was aging considerably, when she realized that four of her ten adult children had already preceded her in death. It is not known whether this most recent loss had been related to the epidemic of yellow fever that raged through the St. Lawrence settlements during this year of 1740.[226]

The day of August 28, 1745 marked Barbe's 89th birthday. Neither she nor the many loved ones who had gathered around her could have known that this would be the matriarch's last such celebration. However, everyone was definitely aware how very unusual it was for residents of New France to live as long as she had. On average, the age at death of adults who passed away in the colony was 61.6 years for women and 61.9 years for men.[227]

Barbe had already exceeded those average death ages by more than a quarter-century. As a result, she was acutely aware that one of the greatest burdens of living to such an advanced age was having to suffer the losses of so many beloved family members and friends. For Barbe, these had already included an entire series of close family members, including both of her parents, at least six of her siblings, her husband François, four of her adult children (plus the two tiny babies, both of them named Louis), a number of sons-in-law and daughters-in-law, numerous grandchildren, and even some great-grandchildren. In addition, innumerable cousins, in-laws, nieces, and nephews had also departed before her.

Nearly two months before her birthday festivities, back on June 4, Barbe had requested that an official document be drawn up, one which would transfer to her daughter Élisabeth and her husband Jean Brault dit Pomainville (who lived just $2/10$ mile east of Barbe's farm) the annual payments that Barbe received from a certain long-term loan. This document was officially registered on September 23, 1745.[228]

Four months later, Barbe exhaled her last breath on January 25, 1746, at the Lachine seigneury. On the following day, she was laid to rest in the cemetery beside the church, joining her husband who had preceded her by $43^1/2$ years. Since his departure back in 1702, she had spent nearly half of her lifetime as a widow on their Lachine farm. After her funeral, the priest recorded in the ledger of the Holy Angels Parish that the matriarch of the Brunet clan had been 89 years and five months old (in fact, she had been three days older than that).

At her burial, the official witnesses had been Alexis Tabault and Jean Baptiste Dubois.[229]

During their respective lifetimes, François and Barbe had both observed and taken part in innumerable significant events within the colony. Over the course of those many decades, they had each day borne what had come their way, and in the process had made the best of it. This would have been life as they had viewed it from their own personal perspective. However, in the overall picture, they had also been creating a portion of the history of New France.

Signature barbe bauves, October 16, 1703.

François Brunet dit Le Bourbonnais, Sr.-Barbe Beauvais
Lineage of Timothy Kent

I. François Brunet, Sr.   11 July, 1672   Barbe Beauvais
(Antoine/   Montreal, QC   (Jacques/
Philippe David)   Jeanne Soldé)

II. Jean François Brunet, Jr.   25 Jan, 1706   Françoise David
(François, Sr./   Champlain, QC   (Claude, Jr./
Barbe Beauvais)   Marie Jeanne Couillard)

III. Angélique Brunet   16 Jan, 1730   Guillaume Lalonde #2
(Jean François, Jr./   Bout de l'Île (Mtl.), QC   (Jean Baptiste/
Françoise David)   Jeanne Gervais)

IV. Guillaume Lalonde #4   2 Feb, 1761   Marie Charlotte Sauvé
(Guillaume #2/   Bout-de-l'Île (Mtl.), QC   (François Marie/
Angélique Brunet)   Élisabeth Madeleine)

V. Angèle Lalonde   27 Jan, 1812   Hyacinthe Achin
(Guillaume #4/   Vaudreuil, QC   (Jacques/
Marie Charlotte Sauvé)   Marie Amable Trottier)

VI. Élisabeth/Isabelle Achin   17 Feb, 1835   Joseph Lalonde
(Hyacinthe/   St. Polycarpe, QC   (Joseph/
Angèle Lalonde)   Geneviève Daoust)

VII. Joseph Lalonde   ca. 1873   Josephine Chatelain
(Joseph/   Curran, ON   (Étienne/
Élisabeth Achin)   Marie Madeleine Taillon)

VIII. Élisabeth Lalonde   30 Jan, 1893   Joseph Bouchard
(Joseph/   Carrollton, MI   (Philéas Joseph/
Josephine Chatelain)   Adelaide Barbeau)

IX. Frances L. Bouchard   28 Apr, 1945   S. George Kent
(Joseph/   Detroit, MI   (George Kapantais/
Élisabeth Lalonde)   Eugenia Papadakis)

X. Timothy J. Kent   5 Sept, 1970   Dorothy J. Minton
(S. George/   Ossineke, MI   (Garnet J./
Frances L. Bouchard)   Elaine A. Reece)

Notes for Brunet dit Le Bourbonnais, Sr.

1. Notary Bénigne Basset, April 18, 1672, Archives Nationales du Québec à Montréal (ANQ-M); R. Jetté, 1983, p. 180, and Corrections et Additions, 1996, p. 6; Michelin detailed maps of France; R. Harris, 1987, pl. 45; G. Robb, 2007, pp. xi-xiii; J. Bleau, 1665, pls. 58-59, 73, 130-131; Carte de Cassini No. 11, 1756; P. Larousse, 1980, pp. 133, 1194; Collection de Patrimoine Des Communes de France, France, 1999, p. 70; R. Jetté, 1983, pp. 1164, 382, 367.
2. G. Lanctôt, 1969, pp. 218-233.
3. A. Lafontaine, 1985, p. 327; M. Trudel, 1973b, pp. 255-256.
4. Notary Bénigne Basset, December 9, 1669, November 4, 1670, and February 2, 1673, ANQ-M; R. Jetté, 1983, pp. 1078, 234, 155; H. and J. Tardif, 1993, pp. 122-123)
5. L. Dechêne, 1992, p. 30.
6. G. Lanctôt, 1969, pp. 145, 209.
7. Notary Bénigne Basset, November 14, 1670, ANQ-M.
8. Notary Bénigne Basset, January 14, 1671, ANQ-M.
9. H. Charbonneau and J. Légaré, 1978-1990, Vol. 6, Notre Dame de Montreal recs; R. Jetté, 1983, pp. 194, 447.
10. R. Jetté, 1983, pp. 180, 70; H. Charbonneau and J. Légaré, 1978-1990, Vols. 5 and 6, Notre Dame de Montreal recs; A. Lafontaine, 1985, Montreal household No. 79 in 1666 and household No. 53 in 1667.
11. Notary Bénigne Basset, April 18, 1672, ANQ-M.
12. H. Charbonneau and J. Légaré, 1978-1990, Vol. 6, Notre Dame de Montreal recs; R. Jetté, 1983, pp. 390, 447, 371, 1092.
13. H. Charbonneau and J. Légaré, 1978-1990, Vol. 6, Notre Dame de Montreal recs; R. Jetté, 1983, pp. 155, 531; F. Stanislas, 1950, pp. 28, 33 and map inside back cover.
14. L. Dechêne, 1992, pp. 65-66; F. Stanislas, 1950, pp. 13-17, 34, 37-38, 41-43, and maps on inside front and back covers; R. Harris, 1987, pl. 46. 1702 Montreal Island land ownership map by Vachon de Belmont: in Nos Racines, Vol. 22, 1979, pp. 430-431; M. Trudel, 1973a, pp. 172-173; recreation by G. Gallienne, 1977; and L. Dechêne, 1992, p. xxi. On the lattermost map in Dechêne, the Sault St. Louis section was portrayed as extending about $1^1/2$ to 2 miles too far to the west, not conforming to the 1702 original.
15. F. Stanislas, 1950, pp. 25-26, 35, and maps inside front and back covers; 1702 Vachon de Belmont map in L. Dechêne, 1992, p. xxi.
16. Notary Michel Le Pailleur, October 16, 1703, ANQ-M.
17. F. Stanislas, 1950, pp. 26-28, and map inside back cover; Notary Michel Le Pailleur, October 16, 1703, ANQ-M; F. Dollier, 1672, pp. 8, 28; W. Eccles, 1964, p. 50.
18. A. Lafontaine, 1986, Lachine area; Notary Michel Le Pailleur, October 16, 1703, ANQ-M.

19. A. Vachon, 1966d, pp. 394-395; J. Donnelly, 1968, pp. 208-229. Maps: A. Vachon, 1982, p. 90; Nos Racines, Vol. 11, 1979, pp. 210, 215; M. Trudel, 1973a, pp. 92-93; W. Eccles, 1983, p. 108; B. Dunnigan, 2008, p. 17; J. Donnelly, 1968, p. 333.
20. H. Charbonneau and J. Légaré, 1978-1990, Vol. 6, Notre Dame de Montreal recs; R. Jetté, 1983, pp. 70, 911; R. Harris, 1987, pl. 46; F. Stanislas, 1950, pp. 37-38.
21. H. Charbonneau and J. Légaré, 1978-1990, Vol. 6, Notre Dame de Montreal recs; R. Jetté, 1983, pp. 70, 1072.
22. E. Osler, 1967, pp. 49-68; C. Dupré, 1966, p. 175; A. Vachon, 1982, pp. 94-95, 238.
23. R. Jetté, 1983, pp. 1169, 749; F. Stanislas, 1950, p. 32, and map inside back cover; A. Lafontaine, 1986, Lachine household No. 208.
24. Statement of Expenses: P. Margry, 1876-1886, Vol. 1, pp. 293-296; English translation in R. Preston and L. Lamontagne, 1958. Bazire and Godefroy suppliers: R. Jetté, 1983, pp. 59-60, 509. Bouquet supplier: J. Monet, 1966e, p. 108.
25. T. Kent, 1997, p. 89.
26. R. La Salle, 1684, pp. 218-219.
27. E. Osler, 1967, pp. 65-67.
28. C. Skinner, 1996, p. 310.
29. R. La Salle, 1984, p. 220.
30. C. Skinner, 1996, pp. 293-296.
31. A. Raudot, 1709-1710; I. Dixon, pp. 193-194; W. Kinietz, 1965, pp. 335-336.
32. R. Jetté, 1983, pp. 180, 155; H. Charbonneau and J. Légaré, 1978-1990, Vol. 6, Notre Dame de Montreal recs; F. Stanislas, 1950, pp. 27-28, and map inside back cover.
33. W. Eccles, 1983, p. 110.
34. J. Duchesneau, 1679, pp. 131-135.
35. J. Duchesneau, 1680, pp. 140-145.
36. H. Charbonneau and J. Légaré, 1978-1990, Vol. 6, Notre Dame de Montreal recs; R. Jetté, 1983, pp. 951, 338, 551.
37. H. Charbonneau and J. Légaré, 1978-1990, Vol. 6, Notre Dame de Montreal recs; R. Jetté, 1983, pp. 155, 183.
38. H. Charbonneau and J. Légaré, 1978-1990, Vol. 5, Sts. Anges de Lachine recs; R. Jetté, 1983, pp. 594, 295.
39. H. Charbonneau and J. Légaré, 1978-1990, Vol. 5, Sts. Anges de Lachine recs; R. Jetté, 1983, p. 1019.
40. A. Lafontaine, 1986, Lachine household No. 217.
41. Notary Michel Le Pailleur, October 16, 1703, ANQ-M.
42. F. Stanislas, 1950, p. 19.
43. L. Dechêne, 1992, p. 292; J. Duchesneau, 1679, p. 136.
44. H. Charbonneau and J. Légaré, 1978-1990, Vol. 5, Sts. Anges de Lachine recs; R. Jetté, 1983, pp. 218, 378; F. Stanislas, 1950, pp. 27, 38, and map inside back cover.

45. H. Charbonneau and J. Légaré, 1978-1990, Vol. 5, Sts. Anges de Lachine recs; R. Jetté, 1983, pp. 197, 801.
46. P. Dubé, 1993, p. 88.
47. F. Stanislas, 1950, p. 38.
48. R. Harris, 1987, pl. 46.
49. R. Jetté, 1983, pp. 70, 1101.
50. Notary Claude Maugue, May 13, 1684, ANQ-M.
51. H. Charbonneau and J. Légaré, 1978-1990, Vol. 5, Sts. Anges de Lachine recs; R. Jetté, 1983, p. 976.
52. Notary Hilaire Bourgine, May 24, 1685, ANQ-M.
53. W. Eccles, 1978, pp. 109-110; C. Skinner, 1996, pp. 49-50.
54. T. Kent, 2004, pp. 49-54.
55. ibid., pp. 55-56.
56. E. Massicotte, 1929-1930, p. 195; R. Jetté, 1983, pp. 70, 245, 82.
57. A. Vachon, 1982, p. 107.
58. T. Kent, 2004, p. 83.
59. E. Massicotte, 1929-1930, p. 195.
60. Notary Hilaire Bourgine, September 9, 1686, ANQ-M.
61. E. Blair, 1911, Vol. 1, pp. 229-230.
62. C. Skinner, 1996, p. 310.
63. R. Jetté, 1983, pp. 180, 155, 802, 710.
64. L. Lahontan, 1703, Vol. 1, p. 55.
65. ibid., pp. 99-100.
66. Notary Hilaire Bourgine, September 9, 1686, ANQ-M.
67. C. Dupré, 1966, pp. 175-180; E. Osler, 1967, pp. 233-234; T. Kent, 2004, p. 71; R. Jetté, 1983, pp. 1083, 660.
68. T. Kent, 2004, pp. 39-40, 97-98; R. Jetté, 1983, p. 406.
69. T. Kent, 2004, p. 94.
70. H. Charbonneau and J. Légaré, 1978-1990, Vol. 5, Sts. Anges de Lachine recs; R. Jetté, 1983, pp. 937, 70.
71. T. Kent, 2003, pp. 10-35.
72. E. Blair, 1911, Vol. 1, pp. 249-252 and Vol. 2, pp. 20-23; L. Lahontan, 1703, Vol. 1, pp. 124-131, 144 and n. 1; W. Eccles, 1964, pp. 150-156; T. Pease and R. Werner, 1934, pp. 132-133; L. Kellogg, 1968, pp. 234-236; L. Kellogg, 1967, p. 311; P. Charlevoix, 1866, Vol. 3, pp. 280-287; W. Kane, 2002, p. 130.
73. W. Eccles, 1964, pp. 150, 155.
74. Notary Jean Baptiste Pothier, November 28, 1687, ANQ-M; F. Stanislas, 1950, pp. 25-26, and maps inside front and back covers; R. Jetté, 1983, p. 431.
75. 1679 and 1681 figures: J. Duchesneau, 1679, p. 136. 1688 figures: A. Vachon, 1982, p. 152; L. Dechêne, 1992, p. 292.
76. P. Rémy, 1696; S. Summerville, October 2012, pp. 181-184, including translation on p. 184.
77. E. Massicotte, 1929-1930, pp. 195-198; E. Osler, 1969, pp. 634-635.
78. W. Kenyon and J. Turnbull, 1971, p. 16.
79. C. Skinner, 1996, pp. 288-289.

80. A. Vachon, 1982, p. 107; T. Kent, 2004, p. 71; H. Tanner, 1987, pp. 32-33; R. Harris, 1987, pls. 37-38.

81. Notary Antoine Adhémar, August 2, 1688, ANQ-M.

82. R. Jetté, 1983, pp. 180, 155, 295, 28-29, 132, 134, 338; F. Stanislas, 1950, pp. 17-19, 24, and maps inside front and back covers and outside back cover; T. Pease and R. Werner, 1934, p. 179, n. 1.

83. R. Jetté, 1983, p. 153.

84. Registered with Notary Claude Maugue, July 17, 1689, ANQ-M; O. L. Schmidt Manuscript Collection, Chicago Historical Society; T. Pease and R. Werner, 1934, pp. 162-176; R. Jetté, 1983, pp. 888, 287; E. Massicotte, 1929-1930, p. 197.

85. W. Eccles, 1964, p. 156.

86. E. Massicotte, 1929-1930, pp. 195-198.

87. A. Vachon, 1982, p. 240.

88. R. Jetté, 1983, pp. 189, 1107, 642, 775, 142; E. Massicotte, 1929-1930, pp. 196-198; T. Kent, 2004, p. 65; Y. Zoltvany, 1969, p. 261.

89. R. Jetté, 1983, pp. 218, 11; F. Stanislas, 1950, p. 27, and map inside back cover.

90. L. Lahontan, 1703, Vol. 1, p. 100.

91. W. Eccles, 1978, p. 166.

92. Notary Antoine Adhémar, July 29, 1689, ANQ-M.

93. W. Eccles, 1964, pp. 155, 157-158, 163-165; F. Stanislas, 1950, pp. 17-19, 24, 42, 45; 1702 Montreal Island land ownership map by Vachon de Belmont: in Nos Racines, Vol. 22, 1979, pp. 430-431; M. Trudel, 1973a, pp. 172-173; recreation by G. Gallienne, 1977; and L. Dechêne, 1992, p. xxi.

94. W. Eccles, 1964, p. 208; L. Dechêne, 1992, p. 66.

95. W. Eccles, 1964, pp. 164-165; F. Stanislas, 1950, pp. 44-50; Y. Zoltvany, 1969b, p. 566; P. Moogk, 2000, p. 256; S. Colby, 2003, pp. 137-138; H. Lamarche, 1999, pp. 189-228; H. Lamarche, 2002-2003, pp. 1-4; R. Jetté, 1983, pp. 307, 155, 808, 44, 305-306, 590. 1702 Montreal Island land ownership map by Vachon de Belmont: in Nos Racines, Vol. 22, 1979, pp. 430-431; M. Trudel, 1973a, pp. 172-173; recreation by G. Gallienne, 1977; and L. Dechêne, 1992, p. xxi.

96. R. Jetté, 1983, pp. 44, 590, 305-306; H. Lamarche, 2002-2003, p. 2; F. Stanislas, 1950, pp. 47-48; A. Lafontaine, 1986, Lachine household No. 240; 1702 Montreal Island land ownership map by Vachon de Belmont: in Nos Racines, Vol. 22, 1979, pp. 430-431; M. Trudel, 1973a, pp. 172-173; recreation by G. Gallienne, 1977; and L. Dechêne, 1992, p. xxi.

97. R. Jetté, 1983, p. 11; H. Lamarche, 2002-2003, p. 3.

98. R. Jetté, 1983, p. 311; H. Lamarche, 2002-2003, pp. 2-3.

99. R. Jetté, 1983, pp. 808, 158; H. Lamarche, 2002-2003, p. 2; F. Stanislas, 1950, pp. 47-48; A. Lafontaine, 1986, Lachine household No. 241; 1702 Montreal Island land ownership map by Vachon de Belmont: in Nos Racines, Vol. 22, 1979, pp. 430-431; M. Trudel, 1973a, pp. 172-173; recreation by G. Gallienne, 1977; and L. Dechêne, 1992, p. xxi.

100. R. Jetté, 1983, pp. 792, 70, 744; H. Lamarche, 2002-2003, p. 3; F. Stanislas, 1950, p. 48; A. Lafontaine, 1986, Lachine household No. 239; 1702 Montreal Island land ownership map by Vachon de Belmont: in Nos Racines, Vol. 22, 1979, pp. 430-431; M. Trudel, 1973a, pp. 172-173; recreation by G. Gallienne, 1977; and L. Dechêne, 1992, p. xxi.

101. R. Jetté, 1983, pp. 946, 258; H. Lamarche, 2002-2003, p. 3; F. Stanislas, 1950, pp. 47-48; A. Lafontaine, 1986, Lachine household No. 264; 1702 Montreal Island land ownership map by Vachon de Belmont: in Nos Racines, Vol. 22, 1979, pp. 430-431; M. Trudel, 1973a, pp. 172-173; recreation by G. Gallienne, 1977; and L. Dechêne, 1992, p. xxi.

102. In Lamarche's analysis of the casulties of the 1689 raid (2002-2003, pp. 1-3), she presented the named of the 24 individuals who had been killed on site, as well as 66 others who had been apparently captured at the time. She also studied the documentary evidence concerning 23 other individuals who, at various times, have been described as having been captured in the 1689 raid. Although Lamarche implied that all 23 of these latter names ought to be eliminated from the roster of captives, fully thirteen of these people, according to her own presented evidence, could very well have been seized and later returned to the colony. Among these are individuals who were cited in documents $3^{1}/2$ weeks, ten weeks, almost three months, and almost five months after the raid, plus three individuals who were cited in 1690, two in 1691, one in 1695, one in 1698, one in 1699, and one in 1705. Thus, it is definitely possible that all thirteen of these people could have been captured, and later returned to the colony and the documentary record. Even among her list of "actual or presumed" captives, she included two individuals who were "briefly captured," three who were cited in documents in 1691, 1692, and 1701, and one person who died in or some time before 1699. Thus, the total number of captives has been expressed in the present work as 79 (66 on Lamarche's list, plus the other 13 candidates who were quite likely also seized). Renusson: R. Jetté, 1983, p. 11; H. Lamarche, 2002-2003, pp. 1-2; F. Stanislas, 1950, pp. 48-49. Gauthier: R. Jetté, 1983, p. 475; H. Lamarche, 2002-2003, p. 2; S. Colby, 2003, pp. 137-138; F. Stanislas, 1950, p. 48.

103. F. Stanislas, 1950, pp. 46, 50; R. Jetté, 1983, pp. 70, 238; A. Lafontaine, 1986, Lachine household No. 239.

104. Notary Claude Maugue, September 13, 1689, ANQ-M; R. Jetté, 1983, pp. 815, 153, 746.

105. Notary Bénigne Basset, September 25, 1689, ANQ-M; R. Jetté, 1983, pp. 719-711; L. Dechêne, 1992, map p. xxi.

106. R. Jetté, 1983, p. 295.

107. E. Osler, 1967, pp. 199-244.

108. W. Eccles, 1964, pp. 172-174.

109. ibid., pp. 175-176.

110. R. Jetté, 1983, p. 70.

111. H. Charbonneau and J. Légaré, 1978-1990, Vol. 5, Notre Dame de Montreal recs; R. Jetté, 1983, p. 649.

112. H. Charbonneau and J. Légaré, 1978-1990, Vol. 5, Notre Dame de Montreal recs; R. Jetté, 1983, p. 1101.

113. H. Lamarche, 2002-2003, pp. 2-3; 1702 Montreal Island land ownership map by Vachon de Belmont: in Nos Racines, Vol. 22, 1979, pp. 430-431; M. Trudel, 1973a, pp. 172-173; recreation by G. Gallienne, 1977; and L. Dechêne, 1992, p. xxi.

114. W. Eccles, 1964, pp. 186-187.

115. Notary Antoine Adhémar, June 1, 1692, ANQ-M; R. Jetté, 1983, p. 70.

116. Notary Jean Baptiste Pothier, April 5, 1693, ANQ-M; Notary Michel Le Pailleur, October 16, 1703, ANQ-M, inventory containing a description of both the 1693 concession document (document No. 3) and the property itself, as well as its earlier survey (document No. 6); F. Stanislas, 1950, map inside back cover.

117. Notary Antoine Adhémar, April 12, 1693, ANQ-M; L. Dechêne, 1992, map on p. xxi.

118. H. Charbonneau and J. Légaré, 1978-1990, Vol. 5, Notre Dame de Montreal recs.

119. ibid.; R. Jetté, 1983, p. 180; L. Dechêne, 1992, p. 59.

120. Notary Antoine Adhémar, October 20, 1693, ANQ-M; M. Trudel, 1973c, map opp. p. 414.

121. Notary Claude Maugue, November 14, 1693, later copied by Notary Pierre Raimbault under the same date, ANQ-M; R. Jetté, 1983, pp. 183-184, 1019, 1021; H. Lamarche, 2002-2003, p. 2.

122. R. Jetté, 1983, pp. 180-181, 862; E. Massicotte, 1929-1930, pp. 201-203.

123. H. Charbonneau and J. Légaré, 1978-1990, Vol. 5, Sts. Anges de Lachine recs; R. Jetté, 1983, p. 1060; F. Stanislas, 1950, p. 23, and maps inside front and back covers.

124. R. Jetté, 1983, p. 180.

125. L. Dechêne, 1992, p. 292.

126. Notary Claude Maugue, July 24, 1696, ANQ-M; Notary Antoine Adhémar, August 11, 1696 adjudication, ANQ-M; Notary Michel Le Pailleur, October 16, 1703 inventory, described in document No. 4, ANQ-M; F. Stanislas, 1950, p. 27, and map inside back cover; Notary Jean Baptiste Pothier, April 22, 1691, ANQ-M; R. Jetté, 1983, p. 11; H. Lamarche, 2002-2003, p. 1.

127. Notary Jean Baptiste Pothier, August 26, 1696, ANQ-M; R. Jetté, 1983, p. 70.

128. Notary Jean Baptiste Pothier, August 26b, 1696, ANQ-M; Notary Michel Le Pailleur, October 16, 1703 inventory, document No. 5; R. Jetté, 1983, pp. 70, 139.

129. J. Holzi, 1995, Vol. 1, 1693-1703, Jud. Civ., October 10, 1696, Case No. 003-0178b; F. Stanislas, 1950, map inside back cover; R. Jetté, 1983, pp. 133, 142, 180, 183-184, 681, 758-759.

130. Notary Jean Baptiste Pothier, November 25, 1696, ANQ-M; H. Charbonneau and J. Légaré, 1978-1990, Vol. 5, Sts. Anges de Lachine recs; R. Jetté, 1983, pp. 180, 165-166, 1072, 70, 759, 161.

131. W. Eccles, 1964, p. 226.
132. Notary Jean Baptiste Pothier, February 20, 1697, ANQ-M; 1702 Montreal Island land ownership map by Vachon de Belmont: in Nos Racines, Vol. 22, 1979, pp. 430-431; M. Trudel, 1973a, pp. 172-173; recreation by G. Gallienne, 1977; and L. Dechêne, 1992, p. xxi.
133. H. Charbonneau and J. Légaré, 1978-1990, Vol. 5, Sts. Anges de Lachine recs; R. Jetté, 1983, pp. 180, 759.
134. W. Eccles, 1964, p. 48; A. Vachon, 1982, pp. 144-145, 154.
135. Notary Antoine Adhémar, June 9, 1697, ANQ-M; R. Jetté, 1983, pp. 543, 791.
136. J. Holzi, 1995, Vol. 1, 1693-1703, Jud. Crim., June 15, 1697, Case No. 004-0213; F. Stanislas, 1950, map inside back cover; Notary Antoine Adhémar, June 21, 1697, ANQ-M.
137. Notary Bénigne Basset, November 14, 1670, ANQ-M.
138. H. Charbonneau and J. Légaré, 1978-1990, Vol. 5, Sts. Anges de Lachine recs; R. Jetté, 1983, pp. 165. 161.
139. Notary Antoine Adhémar, October 13, 1697, ANQ-M; H. Charbonneau and J. Légaré, 1978-1990, Vol. 5, Sts. Anges de Lachine recs; R. Jetté, 1983, pp. 180, 759.
140. R. Jetté, 1983, pp. 70-71.
141. H. Charbonneau and J. Légaré, 1978-1990, Vol. 6, Sts. Anges de Lachine recs; R. Jetté, 1983, p. 180.
142. Notary Antoine Adhémar, August 10, 1698a and 1698b, ANQ-M; Notary Michel Le Pailleur, October 16, 1703 inventory, document No. 7, ANQ-M; F. Stanislas, 1950, p. 27, and map inside back cover; R. Jetté, 1983, p. 570; 1702 Montreal Island land ownership map by Vachon de Belmont: in Nos Racines, Vol. 22, 1979, pp. 430-431; M. Trudel, 1973a, pp. 172-173; recreation by G. Gallienne, 1977; and L. Dechêne, 1992, p. xxi.
143. J. Holzi, 1995, Vol. 1, 1693-1703, Jud. Crim., August 12, 1698, Case No. 005-0297 (one short portion of text, the summons of Brunet, was incorrectly included in the papers of Case No. 005-0282), plus the original text of the complaint as recorded by Fleury, Sieur Deschambault; R. Jetté, 1983, pp. 500, 744.
144. W. Eccles, 1964, pp. 201, 220-221.
145. H. Charbonneau and J. Légaré, 1978-1990, Vol. 5, Sts. Anges de Lachine recs; R. Jetté, 1983, p. 1019, 759.
146. J. Holzi, 1995, Vol. 1, 1693-1703, Jud. Crim., October 17, 1698, Case No. 005-0307, plus the original text of the complaint as recorded by Fleury, Sieur Deschambault; R. Jetté, 1983, pp. 681, 678; Notary Antoine Adhémar, October 20, 1698, ANQ-M; 1702 Montreal Island land ownership map by Vachon de Belmont: in Nos Racines, Vol. 22, 1979, pp. 430-431; M. Trudel, 1973a, pp. 172-173; recreation by G. Gallienne, 1977; and L. Dechêne, 1992, p. xxi.
147. Notary Antoine Adhémar, February 8, 1699, ANQ-M; H. Charbonneau and J. Légaré, 1978-1990, Vol. 5, Sts. Anges de Lachine recs; R. Jetté, 1983, pp. 279-280, 1062.

148. J. Holzi, 1995, Vol. 1, 1693-1703, Jud. Crim., March 6, 1699, Case No. 006-0326; R. Jetté, 1983, p. 155; F. Stanislas, 1950, map inside back cover.
149. J. Holzi, 1995, Vol. 1, 1693-1703, September 24 and November 3, 1699, Case No. 007-0370; R. Jetté, 1983, p. 155.
150. 1702 Montreal Island land ownership map by Vachon de Belmont: in Nos Racines, Vol. 22, 1979, pp. 430-431; M. Trudel, 1973a, pp. 172-173; recreation by G. Gallienne, 1977; and L. Dechêne, 1992, p. xxi.
151. R. Jetté, 1983, p. 759.
152. ibid., p. 280.
153. ibid., p. 1101.
154. ibid., p. 181.
155. Notary Jean Baptiste Pothier, October 30, 1700, ANQ-M; Notary Antoine Adhémar, June 26, 1702, ANQ-M; Nos Racines, Vol. 29, 1979, pp. 571-572; R. Jetté, 1983, p. 1014; W. Eccles, 1964, pp. 208-209; L. Dechêne, 1992, p. 66; F. Stanislas, 1950, pp. 44, 54, and maps inside front and back covers and outside back cover; D. Lanken, 1983, p. 49; 1702 Montreal Island land ownership map by Vachon de Belmont: in Nos Racines, Vol. 22, 1979, pp. 430-431; M. Trudel, 1973a, pp. 172-173; recreation by G. Gallienne, 1977; and L. Dechêne, 1992, p. xxi.
156. Notary Jean Baptiste Pothier, April 11, 1701, ANQ-M; F. Stanislas, 1950, pp. 38, 43; R. Jetté, 1983, pp. 295, 545; H. Lafortune and N. Robert, 1994, pp. 37-40.
157. W. Eccles, 1964, p. 36; A. Vachon, 1982, pp. 280-281.
158. R. Jetté, 1983, pp. 165, 280.
159. F. Stanislas, 1950, pp. 38, 43.
160. R. Jetté, 1983, p. 180.
161. Notary Pierre Raimbault, May 26, 1702, ANQ-M; R. Jetté, 1983, p. 180; 1702 Montreal Island land ownership map by Vachon de Belmont: in Nos Racines, Vol. 22, 1979, pp. 430-431; M. Trudel, 1973a, pp. 172-173; recreation by G. Gallienne, 1977; and L. Dechêne, 1992, p. xxi.
162. N. Webster, 1984, "pleurisy;" H. Charbonneau and J. Légaré, 1978-1990, Vol. 14, Sts. Anges de Lachine recs; R. Jetté, 1983, pp. 295, 307.
163. H. Charbonneau and J. Légaré, 1978-1990, Vol. 14, Sts. Anges de Lachine recs; R. Jetté, 1983, p. 180.
164. W. Eccles, 1964, p. 226.
165. R. Jetté, 1983, pp. 165, 1020, 759, 218;1702 Montreal Island land ownership map by Vachon de Belmont: in Nos Racines, Vol. 22, 1979, pp. 430-431; M. Trudel, 1973a, pp. 172-173; recreation by G. Gallienne, 1977; and L. Dechêne, 1992, p. xxi; F. Stanislas, 1950, p. 27, and map inside back cover; L. Blair, 2000, p. 11; D. Hunter, 2002, p. 92.
166. Notary Michel Le Pailleur, April 15, 1703, ANQ-M; H. Charbonneau and J. Légaré, 1978-1990, Vol. 14, Sts. Anges de Lachine recs; R. Jetté, 1983, pp. 181, 1060;1702 Montreal Island land ownership map by Vachon de Belmont: in Nos Racines, Vol. 22, 1979, pp. 430-431; M. Trudel, 1973a, pp. 172-173; recreation by G. Gallienne, 1977; and L. Dechêne, 1992, p. xxi.
167. F. Stanislas, 1950, p. 38.

168. J. Holzi, 1995, Jud. Civ., October 8, 1703, Case No. 015-0710; R. Jetté, 1983, pp. 70-71.

169. Notary Michel Le Pailleur, October 16, 1703, ANQ-M.

170. 1702 Montreal Island land ownership map by Vachon de Belmont: in Nos Racines, Vol. 22, 1979, pp. 430-431; M. Trudel, 1973a, pp. 172-173; recreation by G. Gallienne, 1977; and L. Dechêne, 1992, p. xxi.

171. A. Lafontaine, 1986, Lachine household No. 217.

172. F. Stanislas, 1950, pp. 24, 33; F. Dollier de Casson, 1928, p. 28; W. Eccles, 1964, pp. 15, 49-51.

173. R. Douville and J. Casanova, 1968, p. 100; Louis Nicolas illustration and text from 1670s in Nos Racines, Vol. 10, 1979, p. 195; 1688 census in A. Vachon, 1982, p. 152.

174. A. Vachon, 1982, p. 152.

175. Notary Michel Le Pailleur, October 16, 1703b, ANQ-M.

176. Notary Michel Le Pailleur, October 17, 1703, ANQ-M; R. Jetté, 1983, pp. 166, 435, 181.

177. H. Charbonneau and J. Légaré, 1978-1990, Vol. 14, Sts. Anges de Lachine recs; R. Jetté, 1983, pp. 165-166.

178. Notary Pierre Raimbault, September 28, 1704, ANQ-M; Notary Antoine Adhémar, June 9, 1697, ANQ-M; R. Jetté, 1983, p. 543.

179. H. Charbonneau and J. Légaré, 1978-1990, Vol. 14, Sts. Anges de Lachine recs; R. Jetté, 1983, p. 1060; 1702 Montreal Island land ownership map by Vachon de Belmont: in Nos Racines, Vol. 22, 1979, pp. 430-431; M. Trudel, 1973a, pp. 172-173; recreation by G. Gallienne, 1977; and L. Dechêne, 1992, p. xxi.

180. H. Charbonneau and J. Légaré, 1978-1990, Vol. 14, Sts. Anges de Lachine recs; R. Jetté, 1983, p. 166.

181. R. Jetté, 1983, p. 280.

182. ibid., p. 166.

183. ibid., pp. 873-874.

184. H. Charbonneau and J. Légaré, 1978-1990, Vol. 12, Notre Dame de la Visitation de Champlain recs; R. Jetté, 1983, pp. 181, 312.

185. Notary Michel Le Pailleur, October 6, 1706, ANQ-M; R. Jetté, 1983, pp. 139, 70.

186. R. Jetté, 1983, pp. 181-182.

187. Notary Antoine Adhémar, February 5, 1707, ANQ-M; H. Charbonneau and J. Légaré, 1978-1990, Vol. 14, Sts. Anges de Lachine recs; R. Jetté, 1983, pp. 181, 191-192.

188. H. Charbonneau and J. Légaré, 1978-1990, Vol. 14, Sts. Anges de Lachine recs; R. Jetté, 1983, pp. 111, 758.

189. R. Jetté, 1983, p. 192.

190. Notary Antoine Adhémar, June 15, 1708a and b, ANQ-M; F. Stanislas, 1950, pp. 17-19, 24, and map inside front cover.

191. R. Jetté, 1983, pp. 70-71, 510.

192. Notary Michel Le Pailleur, February 12, 1710, ANQ-M; H. Charbonneau and J. Légaré, 1978-1990, Vol. 14, Sts. Anges de Lachine recs; R. Jetté, 1983, pp. 181, 1060.

193. R. Jetté, 1983, pp. 180-181.
194. H. Charbonneau and J. Légaré, 1978-1990, Vol. 14, Sts. Anges de Lachine recs; R. Jetté, 1983, p. 996.
195. R. Jetté, 1983, p. 182.
196. ibid.
197. Notary Michel Le Pailleur, February 22, 1712, ANQ-M.
198. Brunet-Tabault data: R. Jetté, 1983, p. 1060. Property sale: Notary Pierre Raimbault, August 16, 1714, ANQ-M; R. Jetté, 193, p. 494.
199. Exhibits in Pointe à Callières Archaeological Museum, Montreal, 1994; ANQ, Ordonnances des Intendants, 1713-1720, Vol. 6, p. 54v., Archives des Colonies, C11A, Vol. 35, folios 330-352.
200. R. Jetté, 1983, p. 192.
201. ibid., p. 1072.
202. P. Larousse, 1980, pp. 1491-1492.
203. R. Jetté, 1983, pp. 165, 384. G. Robb, 2007, p. 359.
204. Notary Antoine Adhémar, August 20, 1716, ANQ-M; R. Jetté, 1983, p. 497.
205. R. Jetté, 1983, p. 1060.
206. ibid.
207. ibid., pp. 180, 759, 281.
208. ibid., pp. 180, 1060.
209. ibid., p. 192.
210. H. Charbonneau and J. Légaré, 1978-1990, Vol. 14, Ste. Anne de Bout de l'Île recs; R. Jetté, 1983, pp. 759, 392-393.
211. Notary Jacques David, October 6, 1719, ANQ-M; Notary Pierre Raimbault, July 20, 1703, ANQ-M; R. Jetté, 1983, pp. 510, 70-71.
212. Notary Michel Le Pailleur, January 4, 1721, ANQ-M; R. Jetté, 1983, pp. 180, 183, 500.
213. H. Charbonneau and J. Légaré, 1978-1990, Vol. 14, Sts. Anges de Lachine recs. plus microfilm copy of the original parish register.
214. H. Charbonneau and J. Légaré, 1978-1990, Vol. 14, Sts. Anges de Lachine recs; R. Jetté, 1983, pp. 280, 947.
215. R. Jetté, 1983, p. 183.
216. Notary Michel Le Pailleur, December 26, 1721, ANQ-M; R. Jetté, 1983, pp. 700, 320-321, 180-183.
217. H. Charbonneau and J. Légaré, 1978-1990, Vol. 14, Sts. Anges de Lachine recs; R. Jetté, 1983, p. 698.
218. H. Charbonneau and J. Légaré, 1978-1990, Vol. 14, Sts. Anges de Lachine recs; R. Jetté, 1983, pp. 165-166, 698.
219. R. Jetté, 1983, pp. 280, 339.
220. Notary Antoine Adhémar, June 9 and July 4, 1726, ANQ-M; R. Jetté, 1983, pp. 180, 962; P. Moogk, 2000, pp. 40, 218, 288 n. 65, 314 n. 9.
221. R. Jetté, 1983, p. 166.
222. ibid., pp. 180, 192.
223. Notary Joseph Raimbault, September 3, 1728, ANQ-M.

224. Notary Nicolas Augustin Guillet de Chaumont, November 6, 1728, ANQ-M; R. Jetté, 1983, p. 1060.
225. H. Charbonneau and J. Légaré, 1978-1990, Vol. 14, Sts. Anges de Lachine recs; R. Jetté, 1983, pp. 166, 1021.
226. H. Charbonneau and J. Légaré, 1978-1990, Vol. 25, Ste. Anne de Bout de l'Île recs; R. Jetté, 1983, pp. 180, 182; L. Blair, 2000, p. 11.
227. H. Charbonneau et al, 1993, p. 184, Fig. 27.
228. Louis Claude Danré de Blanzy, September 23, 1745, ANQ-M.
229. H. Charbonneau and J. Légaré, 1978-1990, Vol. 25, Ste. Anne de Bout de l'Île recs.

X

Pierre Girard and his wives
Suzanne de Lavoie and Élisabeth Lequin

*Trader from the Quebec area who hauled merchandise upriver
in his own vessel, to exchange it with native customers
and/or French outfitters at Trois-Rivières or Montreal*

Neither Pierre Girard's place of origin in France nor the names of his parents have been identified. These invaluable pieces of information are usually documented in notarial marriage contracts and in church marriage records. However, the marriage contract of Pierre Girard and Suzanne de Lavoie, which was drawn up by the Quebec notary Gilles Rageot on August 11, 1669, has been lost from the notarial documents of New France. By good fortune, the date of this document, the name of the Quebec notary who penned it, and a very short summary of its contents were all included in an inventory of the couple's possessions that was conducted on June 22, 1700. No record of the marriage ceremony of this Girard couple has been preserved in the church records of the colony. However, the same inventory of 1700 described Pierre's land grant document from July 28, 1669, and indicated that this grant had been issued fifteen days before their wedding. This statement revealed that Pierre and Suzanne's marriage had taken place on August 12, 1669, on the day following the signing of their marriage contract.

In determining Pierre's year of birth, three separate documents which recorded his age may be examined. These are the census of 1666 (in which he was recorded as age 23), the census of 1681 (when his age was documented as 40), and the church record of his second wedding in 1688 (at which time he indicated that he was 43 years old). From these three documents, his year of birth has been estimated as between 1641 and 1645.

In numerous records in New France, Pierre's family name was spelled in a wide variety of ways. He usually signed it, in laboriously printed letters, as PiERRE GiRART; however, in one case he printed it as GiRAT. Virtually all of the notaries who drew up documents concerning him spelled his name Girard. In the records of the Hôtel

Dieu hospital at Quebec, in one instance the registrar nun wrote his name as Gerar. Over the decades, at least five variants of his family name were penned by priests into various church records: these included Girar, Girard, Gerar, Gerard, and Gyrat.

Pierre Girard was present in New France by at least the autumn of 1663. This information was recorded in a document more than seven years later, in February of 1671, when a colonist officially acknowledged in front of a Quebec notary that he had received a loan from Monsieur Girard back in October of 1663. The borrower was now taking steps to settle that long-overdue debt.

"Before the said notary [Gilles Rageot] was present in person Noël Jérémie dit La Montagne, living at Batiscan, who has acknowledged and declared that he fairly and truly owes to the Sieur Joseph Boursier, cleric of the Company of Jesus at the [Jesuit] College in Quebec, for and as a payoff of Pierre Girard, absent, the sum of fifty [livres] as the remainder of a debt of 94 livres, according to a promise which he [La Montagne] had made to him [Girard] on October 15, 1663, which was duly recorded with the said notary. This money has been given to the said La Montagne, the said sum having been paid with the promise that it will be entirely repaid to the said creditor at his discretion. Thus have they promised, obligated themselves, and waived. [This agreement] made and drawn up at the home of the said notary in the afternoon of February 4, 1671, in the presence of Pierre Biron, bailiff, and Jacques de La Touche, who have signed with the parties.
Signed, N. Jeremie de La Montagne, Jacques de la Tousche, Biron, and G. Rageot"[1]

When Pierre had granted the loan of 94 livres, back in the autumn of 1663, he had been about 18 to 22 years old and residing in the Quebec area. The borrower, Noël Jérémie dit La Montagne, had worked as an interpreter and clerk at the trading posts of the *Domaine du Roi*, the Domain of the King. This huge region encompassed the lands extending northward from the St. Lawrence River, and northeastward along the river's shore from just below Île aux Coudres (an island near the later community of Baie St. Paul) for nearly 300 miles downriver to below Sept Îles, a little beyond the mouth of the Moise River. The revenues which were derived from the fur trade, hunting, fishing, and agriculture in this massive region helped to defray the expenses of the colony. Monsieur Jérémie, some 13 to 17 years older than Pierre, had married at Quebec in January of 1659; by the time of Pierre's loan to him in October of 1663, $4^3/4$ years later, he and his wife had produced two children in the Quebec area. Through at least the year 1669, this ever-growing family had lived at Sillery, a short distance southwest of Quebec. However, by February of 1671, when Monsieur Jérémie borrowed the 50 livres from the Jesuit, in order to pay off Pierre's overdue loan to him from $7^1/4$ years earlier, he had moved with his family to Batiscan, northeast of Trois-Rivières.

Joseph Boursier, the Jesuit Brother who loaned this money to Noël Jérémie, had been sent to proselytize among the Hurons in the Georgian Bay region of Lake Huron back in the 1640s. Two decades later, in the census of 1666, he had been recorded as residing at the Jesuit College at Quebec, and still working at the level of a Brother. Interestingly, Pierre Girard had been enumerated in this same census as living in the same College, engaged as a laborer working for the Jesuits. Thus, at the time when the cleric loaned 50 livres to Monsieur Jérémie to repay the overdue loan, he had known the eventual recipient of the money, Pierre Girard, for at least five years (since at least the census of 1666).[2]

In this particular census, the enumerator listed 35 men under the heading "The Reverend Jesuit Fathers at the College of Quebec, with the names of the brothers and the domestic servants there." The ten priests who were residing in this facility at the time included Fathers François Lemercier (the Superior), Claude Dablon, Jérôme Lalemant, Claude Pijart, Pierre Chastelain, Joseph Marie Chaumonot, Claude Bardy, Thierry Beschefer, Pierre Raffeix, and Julien Garnier. The seven Brothers living at the College included Ambroise Brouart, Florent Bonnemer (pharmacist, surgeon, and doctor), Louis Gaubert, Pierre Masson, Joseph Boursier (who would later loan Monsieur Jérémie 50 livres to pay off Pierre Girard), Guillaume Lauzier, and Louis Leboesme. In addition, there were eight resident *donnés* there, men who had dedicated their lives to laboring in the Grey Brothers order of lay workers. These were Charles Boivin, Guillaume Boivin, Martin Boutet dit Saint Martin, Jacques Lévrier, Jacques Aubry, Charles Pavie, Charles Bocquet, and François Poisson.

The residents of the Jesuit College in 1666 also included ten employees. These men included René Voisin, age 20, tailor of suits; Thomas Pageau, age 21, tailor of suits; Thomas Trigalon, age 50, joiner, married in France; Pierre Hot, age 23, worker (*travaillant*); Pierre Girard, age 23, worker (*travaillant*); Mathurin Legras, age 20, cooper; Pierre Rollandeau, age 22, mason; Jacques Blais, age 30, joiner, married in France; Urbain Champlain, age 32, Master of the School; and François Dumoussard, age 23, Master of Music.

The enumerator also recorded one final category of residents: "There are at the said College twenty-one lodgers, of whom four are from France and the others were born in this country." Among these men, the six who have been identified thus far include Pierre Paul Gagnon, Fr. Charles Amador Martin (son of Abraham Martin, whose biography is the first one to be presented in Volume I), Louis Soumande, Pierre Terrier de Francheville, Charles Poupeau, and Jean Caignet.[3]

It is certain that the majority of the ten residents of the Jesuit College who were listed in the employees category were actually indentured laborers, men who were working off their respective three-year employment contracts. This assemblage of men, for the most part, was made up of very young adults. In fact, seven of the ten were only from 20 to 23 years old (the ages of the ten were 20, 20, 21, 22, 23, 23, 23, 30, 32, and 50). Among the entire group of ten employees living at the Jesuit College at this time, only Pierre Girard, Pierre Hot, and Thomas Pageau (two laborers and a tailor), are known to have remained permanently in the colony, where they would eventually marry and establish families of their own.

Indentured laborers were typically recruited in France to serve in the colony for a period of three years; thus, the hirees were often termed *trente-six mois*, "thirty-six monthers." According to their hiring contracts, which the workmen signed in the mother country before departure, they would be first transported across the Atlantic, then they would be fed, housed, and paid a specified modest salary during their period of servitude. The wages for each individual (paid by the person or group who ultimately purchased their work contract in the colony) usually ranged from 60 to 75 livres per year, but they were sometimes as high as 100 livres; the specific fee depended upon the given man's previous employment and training. In addition, if the workers decided not to remain in the colony at the conclusion of their service, they would be given a no-cost trip back to the mother country, with the expenses of the return voyage covered by the original hirer. (Typically, about one-third of these contract workers did return to France.) The hiring agents in the mother country were allowed to give each indentured worker an advance of up to 35 livres from the man's first year's wages. In addition, the hirer often provided food and housing for the hiree from the time the contract was signed until the time the ship departed on its transatlantic journey.

In New France, the legally binding contracts of the indentured workmen were sold to administrators, seigneurs, religious orders (such as the Jesuits), and colonists, who would from then on assume the costs of the men's upkeep and wages for the duration of the service period. As one would expect, the selling price for each contract was considerably higher than the sum of up to 100 livres or more that the hiring agent in France had expended on that given individual, in the course of recruiting him, giving him an advance on his wages, feeding him, housing him, and finally transporting him across the ocean. Each indentured workman who was safely delivered to New France brought a measure of profit to the hiring agent; thus, the more workmen who were recruited, the greater the amount of profit. The maximum number of indentured men per ship was not limited or restricted; only the minimum number of men, prorated at one man per 15 tons of internal capacity of a given vessel, was expressed in the license of each specific ship. In the colony, indentured laborers were not permitted to either marry or receive land grants until they had completed their obligatory period of service.[4]

Among Pierre Girard's nine fellow residents at the College who were employed by the Society of Jesus (the Jesuit Order), only two of them (besides Pierre) appear to have remained in New France on a long-term basis. Thomas Pageau or Pageot, described as a 21-year-old tailor of suits in 1666, was similarly listed at the College in the census of the following year. In November of 1675, some $9^1/2$ years after he had been initially enumerated with Pierre at the College, he married a young woman at Quebec and settled at the nearby seigneury of Charlesbourg. There, the couple produced eleven children over the span of 25 years, between 1678 and 1703, before Pageau's death at Charlesbourg in March of 1706. The other eventually-permanent settler among the group of Jesuit employees in 1666 was Pierre Hot or Hotte, who was described at that time as a 23-year-old "worker." He was similarly listed at the College in the enumeration of the following year; after that, he waited to become a married man even longer than Monsieur Pageau had waited. Hotte's wedding day at the Quebec church finally arrived in April of 1676, a full decade after he and Pierre had appeared on the roster of Jesuit employees living at the College. (He had earlier signed two different marriage contracts, one in September of 1669 and the other in August of 1670; but each of these respective contracts had been annulled, for some reason.) After his wedding, he and his wife settled in the Petite Auvergne area of the Charlesbourg seigneury, where they produced ten children in seventeen years, between 1676 and 1693. He died at Charlesbourg some time before January of 1696.[5] Messieurs Pageau and Hotte, plus Pierre Girard, clearly represent three instances in which an indentured laborer did remain in New France on a permanent basis, becoming a lifelong colonist and establishing a family.

Among the other seven of Pierre's Jesuit-employed colleagues in 1666, two of them had left spouses back in the mother country, while the other five were still single. Most of these men seem to have returned to France, utilizing the cost-free ship passage back to the mother which had been promised to them when they had originally signed on as indentured laborers. René Voisin and Urbain Champlain were never again documented in the colony after the census of 1666. For their part, Mathurin Legras and Jacques Blais (the latter man had a wife back in France) were listed at the College in the census of the following year, but thereafter in no additional records in the colony. The mason Pierre Rollandeau signed a marriage contract in July of 1668, but it was later annulled and he then disappeared from the documentary record. François Dumoussard, the musician, was cited in a Quebec document in July of 1670, but he did not appear afterward in any additional records. The joiner or interior woodworker Thomas Trigalon, who had been the oldest employee of the Jesuits in 1666, was already fifty years old at that time; in addition, he had a wife back in the mother country. He was mentioned six years later in a Quebec record from February of 1672, but that was his last appearance in the documents of the colony.[6]

As was noted above, Pierre Girard was enumerated in the 1666 census as a *travaillant*, a worker or laborer, in the employ of the Jesuit Order. He was further described in this document as residing at the Jesuit College in Quebec, in the company of nine other employees of the Order. These fellow workers included two tailors of suits, a mason, two joiners, a cooper, another laborer, a school master, and a musician. The lattermost individual, Thomas Dumoussard, had come to the colony in 1665 as a drummer in the La Tour Company of the Carignan Regiment. However, he had soon been bound to the Jesuits by Captain La Tour as a lay worker of the Order, "since he was an excellent musician, but he had plans to do charity and to study."[7]

It is not possible to determine the wide range of tasks that Pierre probably carried out for the Jesuits. However, based upon the types of work that he performed in subsequent years, he may have often labored for them by working their farm, and by clearing the forest cover from the property near the farm. The Jesuits' farming operation was located about $2^1/2$ miles north of the College, on their Notre Dame des Anges seigneury. The fact that Pierre was described in the census as a resident of the College at Quebec does not rule out the possibility that he spent a great deal of time at this moderately distant farm, and on the adjacent forest-covered lands. In fact, he may have often slept over at the farm, rather than traveling $2^1/2$ miles to return to the College at the end of a work day.

Ever since 1626, the Society of Jesus had owned the rather large seigneury of Notre Dame des Anges (Our Lady of the Angels), which was located immediately north of Quebec, directly across the wide mouth area of the Rivière St. Charles. It extended along the St. Lawrence shoreline toward the northeast for nearly three miles, from the St. Charles River on the west to the Beauport River on the east. The latter waterway formed the boundary with the adjacent seigneury of Beauport, which had been granted to Robert Giffard back in 1634. The Beauport seigneury extended northeastward along the St. Lawrence for another span of nearly three miles, from the Beauport River on the west to the Rivière Montmorency on the east. The latter watercourse formed the boundary with the adjacent seigneury of L'Ange Gardien, which was the westernmost portion of the Côte de Beaupré.

In the southeastern corner of the Jesuits' seigneury of Notre Dame des Anges, spread out along the St. Lawrence shoreline for about $1^1/2$ miles, was the area called La Canardière (The Duck Pond). In this settled area, which extended northeastward to end at the Beauport River, was the farm of the Jesuits plus the lands of a few colonists. The clearings and buildings of the priests and the settlers were strung out in a long line, a short distance back from the edge of the river. One of the men who was hired by the Society of Jesus to work on their farm property during this period, and who was clearly identified as such, was Michel Durand. In the census of 1667, he was described as a 25-year-old resident of Beauport and an "employee at the farm of the Jesuits at Notre Dame des Anges." Two years later, he would be married at Beauport. After another thirteen years, in 1682, both he and his wife Cécile Valet would be identified as domestic servants of the Jesuits at the Notre Dame des Anges seigneury.[8]

Over time, other than the rather small southeastern corner area of their seigneury, the rest of the Jesuits' seigneury of Notre Dame des Anges became the seigneury of Charlesbourg. Thus, the lands which extended toward the northeast from Quebec and the St. Charles

River included, in sequence from west to east, the seigneuries of Charlesbourg, Beauport, and (within the Côte de Beaupré) L'Ange Gardien, Château Richer, and Ste. Anne de Beaupré. The massive Île d'Orléans, also a part of the Côte de Beaupré seigneury, lay one to two miles south of the mainland area of the Côte; it extended downriver toward the northeast for some eighteen miles.[9] This was the overall region in which Pierre Girard, as well as his future wife Suzanne de Lavoie, would reside during the next several years.

In the census of 1667, Monsieur Girard was not enumerated as a resident of the Jesuit College. His absence from the Jesuits' primary place of residence may be interpreted as evidence that he had completed his three years of indentured labor for them, and that he had then struck out on his own, to forge his new independent life. This would be logical, since he had by this point been in New France for at least $3^1/2$ years, since at least October of 1663. Unfortunately, his name has not yet been located anywhere in the 1667 census, in any variant spelling.[10] There is a complete lack of documentary evidence concerning him during the three-year period following the enumeration of 1666.

It was during these very years that a highly welcome period of peaceful relations with the Iroquois nations commenced. Ever since 1641, Iroquois war parties had attacked the various native nations in the interior who were allied with the French. From the early 1650s on, these warriors had expanded their raids to also include the French and native settlements in the St. Lawrence Valley. In 1666 and 1667, after the campaigns of the Carignan-Salières Regiment into the Iroquois homelands, each of the Iroquois nations ratified a peace treaty with the French officials. Until this point, over the course of a full quarter-century, the colonists and their native allies had endured, and had been held back by, nearly constant scourges of marauding Iroquois warriors. Now, with this constant danger finally removed from their daily lives, the French would be able to clear and occupy many new areas along the St. Lawrence, and successfully expand their farming activities.

It was in this milieu, during the summer of 1669, that Pierre acquired a long, slender lot in the seigneury of Maure (which was also called Cap Rouge). This rather large swath of land, located on the north shore of the St. Lawrence, had been granted to the seigneur Jean Juchereau, Sieur de Maure, back in 1647. Commencing about seven miles southwest of Quebec, it fronted on the St. Lawrence for nine miles and extended inland toward the north for five miles. It is interesting that Pierre would wish to acquire a piece of river-fronting property in this particular area, a long plot entirely covered with forest, when he had the intention of establishing a pioneer farm. Beginning at Quebec and stretching for about twenty miles toward the southwest along the north shore of the St. Lawrence, the lands fronting on the river and extending for about a mile toward the north had virtually no agricultural capabilities. Starting about a mile inland, the land became fair or better, in terms of its farming and gardening productivity. However, the river-fronting lots which were granted to the settlers here typically extended inland for only about $1^1/10$ mile. This was the discouraging situation in the entire seigneury of Maure, and to the west in the adjacent six miles that comprised almost half of the neighboring seigneury of Neuville (which was also called Dombourg and Pointe aux Trembles). Throughout all of the settled portions of the St. Lawrence Valley, this particular twenty-mile stretch was the only place in which extremely poor-quality riverfront land was occupied by colonists during the French regime. And it was in this minimally productive locale that Pierre Girard planned to eventually settle, with the intention of supporting himself and his future family as productive farmers and gardeners! The only logical explanation for his choice of property at this place is that he, along with all of the other land-grant recipients in the area, were unaware of the extremely poor quality of the land, as it related to agriculture.[11]

On June 22, 1700, when an inventory would be conducted of the belongings of Pierre Girard, the notary would thus summarize the document by which the young colonist had officially received his property at Maure:

"A contract passed before the said Sieur [Gilles] Rageot on July 28, 1669 of a lot granted to the said Pierre Girard on the Coast and seigneury of Maure, containing three arpents [575 English feet] of frontage [on the St. Lawrence River] and thirty arpents [$1^1/10$ mile] of depth, along with the rights of hunting and fishing. The said lot was at that time entirely covered with standing timber. Granted only fifteen days before the first marriage of the said Girard [which was celebrated on August 12, 1669]; for this reason, it belongs to the estate between him and the said de Lavoie, his first wife."[12]

The document of concession did not mention it, but the long, rectangular plot that Pierre received on this July day was located in the Rivière des Roches (Rocky River) area of the seigneury (this information would be included in later documents). This small watercourse, only six or seven miles in total length, was positioned in the westernmost portion of the seigneury. It flowed into the St. Lawrence 1^1/4 miles east of the western boundary line of the seigneury. Thus, the St. Lawrence frontage of Pierre's lot, in the area of the Rocky River, was probably located some fifteen miles southwest of Quebec.[13]

Two weeks after acquiring this forest-covered property, on August 11, Pierre and his bride-to-be Suzanne de Lavoie visited the notary at Quebec, in the company of various friends. There, the engaged couple drew up their contact of marriage. At this time, Pierre was about 24 to 28 years old, while Suzanne was about age 18. Years later, when the inventory of Pierre's possessions would be conducted in June of 1700, the notary would summarize their nuptial agreements document in this manner:

"The marriage contract between the said Pierre Girard and the said deceased [Suzanne] de Lavoie, his first wife, indicating, among other stipulations, that they will own their possessions in common according to the Customary Laws of Paris, passed before the deceased notary Master Gilles Rageot on August 11, 1669."[14]

Since the actual contract is now missing from the notarial records of New France, this minimal summary is all that remains of the nuptial agreements that Pierre and Suzanne made on this festive day. Likewise, no record of their marriage ceremony has been located in the surviving church records of the colony. However, in the notary's summary of the land grant that had taken place on July 28, 1669, he mentioned that the property concession had been officially registered "fifteen days before the first marriage of the said Girard." This clearly indicated that the couple had exchanged their nuptial vows on August 12, 1669, on the day following their signing of the marriage contract.

Before reaching her joyful wedding day with Pierre, Suzanne had lived through a considerable number of adventures and hardships. The eldest child of Pierre de Lavoie and Jacquette Grinon, she had been born and raised in the parish of St. Étienne at Aytré (also spelled Estré); this village was located about four miles southeast of the port city of La Rochelle, on the western coast of France. In about 1665, when she had been about age 14, she had emigrated from this port with her widowed father (about 33 or 34 years old) and her three siblings, the youngest of whom was apparently a tiny infant at the time. Settling in the Quebec region, Suzanne had been married during the following year, at the beginning of the autumn in 1666. The engaged couple had dictated their marriage contract to the Quebec notary Romain Becquet on August 24, after which they had been married in the Quebec church three weeks later, on September 13.

Suzanne's husband, Jean Tesson, had been twenty years old at the time of their wedding. The eldest child of a tailor of suits from Cognac (about fifty miles southeast of La Rochelle), Jean had immigrated to New France some four years earlier, in about 1662, in the company of his father (about age 41) and his three younger siblings. His mother had remained behind at La Rochelle, where she had passed away in May of 1664. In the colony-wide census that had been conducted in the spring or early summer of 1666, Jean and his family had been enumerated in the Ste. Famille Parish on Île d'Orléans (which encompassed the northeastern quarter of the island). In this census, the eldest son had been listed as a 20-year-old laborer, along with his tailor father and his two younger brothers; his only sister had died some time earlier. Within a few months of this enumeration, the Tesson family had relocated to the Petite Auvergne section of the Charlesbourg seigneury, just north of Quebec. By the time Suzanne and Jean had drawn up their marriage contract on August 24, 1666, Jean and his family had already made this move to the Petite Auvergne area. In their nuptial contract, Suzanne's place of residence was simply recorded as "the parish of Notre Dame at Quebec," with no specific details.

During their subsequent years together, the young couple had lived in the seigneury of Charlesbourg. In February of 1667, five months after their nuptial ceremony, they had exchanged their original lot there for another one which belonged to a fellow resident of the seigneury. However, their span of time as a couple had been destined to be short. Probably in about early-to-mid 1669, Jean had died, before they had produced any children.[15]

In the meantime, Suzanne's father Pierre de Lavoie (who had appeared as one of the official witnesses at her wedding in September of 1666), had been working as a farmer in the seigneury of Maure (also called Cap Rouge), some distance southwest of Quebec. In the census of 1667, he had been recorded in this capacity at this locale, in the employ of the widower François Pelletier. It is possible that he had met Pierre Girard at some point during the spring or early summer of 1669, while Monsieur Girard had inspected the lot at Maure which would be ceded to him on July 28 of this year. It is not possible to discern at the distance of $3^1/2$ centuries just how Pierre

Girard met Pierre de Lavoie's widowed and childless daughter Suzanne, probably in the spring or early summer of 1669. At this point, Monsieur Girard had not yet been granted his property at Maure; he was still living in the area of Quebec and Charlesbourg. It was in the latter seigneury that Suzanne had resided for some three years with her former husband, on land which the young couple had acquired there by trading their original piece of property there for another one. Thus, in all likelihood, it was in the Charlesbourg and Quebec region, rather than in the Maure area some distance to the southwest, that Pierre and Suzanne had met and had eventually become engaged, preceding their wedding in September of 1669.[16]

After their marriage ceremony, the Girard couple first settled in the seigneury of Charlesbourg, probably in the La Canardière area near the Beauport River. It would be only after a number of years had passed, after they had gradually cleared a substantial amount of their property in the Rocky River area of the Maure seigneury and had constructed the necessary buildings there, that the couple would relocate to their pioneer farm. According to the later inventory of 1700, they would have on this latter land "one house by the edge of the shore" and "one house in the upper clearing," in addition to a stable, a granary, and other outbuildings.[17] It is highly likely that the second house, the one which they built "in the upper clearing," was located about a mile north of the St. Lawrence shoreline. This would have been the area in which the land was of higher quality, more conducive to raising field crops and garden produce, compared to the portions of their property that lay closer to the St. Lawrence.

Near the end of the summer in 1670, Suzanne's father Pierre de Lavoie remarried, at the age of about 38 or 39, having been in the colony for some five years. On August 25, a visiting Quebec notary drew up the couple's marriage contract at the Maure seigneury. At this time, his new bride, Isabelle Aupé, was about 23 or 24 years old, while Pierre's two unmarried daughters were about 13 and 5, respectively. The newly blended family settled in the Rocky River section of the Maure seigneury, in the same area in which Pierre and Suzanne had been granted their fully-wooded property a year earlier.[18]

Happy celebrations were in order for Suzanne and Pierre in the late summer of 1671, when their first child safely entered the world at Beauport, which was adjacent to the seigneury of Charlesbourg. This event took place a full two years after the couple had exchanged their wedding vows. On August 9, when little Jeanne was one day old, she was baptized in the Quebec church with two residents of La Canardière as her sponsors. The godmother who bequeathed her name to the infant was Jeanne Chalifou, 17^1/2 years old, the daughter of Paul Chalifou, a carpenter of large projects who resided at La Canardière in the Notre Dame des Anges (Charlesbourg) seigneury. This young godmother was eagerly anticipating the celebration of her own wedding, which would be held in the very same edifice just eight days later. Standing beside her as the godfather at this heartwarming christening was Jean Rasset, a young and unmarried joiner (a builder of interior woodwork or furniture) who now lived at La Canardière (formerly at Beauport); he would prove to be a sometime work colleague and a lifelong friend of Pierre. Over the course of the coming decades, Monsieur Girard would be one of the official witnesses at Monsieur Rasset's own wedding (in November of 1678; before this, the latter man would have settled on the lot adjacent to the Girard property at Maure), and Pierre would later appear as an official witness for the marriage of one of the Rasset children. For his part, Jean Rasset would stand as a witness at the first wedding of a Girard child, as well as at the wedding of a Girard stepson; in addition, Rasset's wife Jeanne Chapeau would appear as the godmother of Suzanne and Pierre's sixth child.[19] Considering the woodworking occupations of their 1671 baby's godfather (Monsieur Rasset, a joiner) and the father of the baby's godmother (Monsieur Chalifou, a carpenter), there is a distinct possibility that Pierre worked with these two men, as a laborer and assistant supporting their more highly skilled talents.

On February 2, 1672, Jean Juchereau, the Sieur de Maure, who had been Pierre's seigneur ever since he had been granted his lot back in 1669, passed away at Beauport; he was interred two days later in the Quebec cemetery. About five weeks earlier, on January 4, the ownership of the Maure seigneury had been transferred from Jean to his eldest son Jean Juchereau, Jr., the Sieur de La Ferté, who was about 51 years old at this time. Now, Pierre would pay his annual seigneurial fees to Jean, Jr. rather than to Jean, Sr.[20]

On November 30 of this same year, Suzanne stood beside the baptismal font of the Quebec church, where she served as the godmother of the two-day-old son of Vincent Croteau and Jeanne Godequin. This young couple lived in the Rocky River section of the Maure seigneury, in the vicinity of the Girards' property, and it was there that their second and third children would arrive in 1672 and 1674. The request by the Croteau couple, that Suzanne would appear as the sponsor of their new baby in the autumn of 1672, reflected the personal relationships that Suzanne and Pierre were developing in this outlying seigneury southwest of Quebec. These friendships were growing as the Girards slowly carried out the challenging tasks of clearing portions of their land and constructing their buildings, in anticipation of eventually moving there from their present location in the Charlesbourg seigneury, some eighteen miles away. On the occasion of this christening, the baby's godfather was Louis de Lahaie, who lived in the area of Charlesbourg and Quebec.[21]

Five weeks later, on January 8, 1673, Pierre officially accepted a forest-clearing job, in order to earn ready cash. Joining him in this endeavor was his friend Jean Rasset and François Dolbec, both unmarried young men who resided in the La Canardière area of the Charlesbourg seigneury. (Monsieur Rasset had stood as the godfather of the Girards' first child seventeen months earlier, back in August of 1671.)

"Before Romain Becquet, royal notary, were present in person Jean Rasset and François Dolbec, living at La Canardière, both for themselves and equally firmly for Pierre Girard. These said named individuals have promised, promise, and obligate themselves, in solidarity one for the other, to the Sieur Nicolas Follin, merchant bourgeois living in the city of Paris, present and assenting, the following. They will cut down and clear the forest, according to the customs of this region, on ten arpents [8^1/2 acres] of the lands above the Petit Village at the aforementioned place of La Canardière, clearing the forest and completing the said work by the next Day and Feast of Easter, under the penalty of all expenses, damages, and interests. This present agreement is made in consideration of the sum of eighteen livres for each of the said ten arpents of forest, which the said Sieur Follin has promised and promises to pay to the aforementioned individuals according to the manner in which the said work will advance. The said Rasset and Dolbec acknowledge and declare that they have received today as an advance from the said Sieur Follin the sum of sixty livres, to be deducted from the first work which they will carry out on the said ten arpents. Thus have they promised, obligated themselves in solidarity, and waived. [This agreement] made and drawn up at the said Quebec in the office of the said notary in the afternoon on the eighth day of January, 1673, in the presence of Étienne Marandeau and Louis Baston, living at the said Quebec, who have signed with the said Sieurs Follin, Rasset, and the notary. The said Dolbec has declared that he does not know how to

write or sign, having been questioned according to the ordinance. Just now has appeared the said Girard, who has accepted the present agreement after it was read, and he has declared that he does not know how to sign, having been questioned according to the ordinance.
Signed,
Jean Rasset, Nicolas Follin, Marandeau, L. Baston, and Becquet."[22]

During the next twelve to fifteen weeks of winter and spring, before the arrival of Easter in this particular year, the three colleagues could potentially earn a total of 180 livres (60 livres for each of them), if they could complete the clearing tasks on the entire plot of $8^1/2$ acres. Twelve years after the three partners carried out their forest-clearing work, in 1685, Robert de Villeneuve created a highly detailed map of the Quebec region. On his chart, he depicted several large cleared areas that were located inland from the settled riverfront area of La Canardière. These clearings extended from $3/4$ to $1^1/2$ miles northwest of the shoreline of the St. Lawrence. It is possible that Pierre and his two colleagues had removed the forest cover from a portion of one of these very areas in 1673.[23]

At the time of their forestry employment, Monsieur Dolbec was about 25 to 29 years old. He and Monsieur Rasset were accumulating funds so that each of them could eventually establish his own pioneer farm, marry, and raise a family. (They would each accomplish these goals within a few years. Dolbec would marry in August of 1675, and before September of 1678 he would be settled at Neuville, the seigneury immediately west of Maure. Rasset would marry in November of 1678, and before August of 1679 he would be settled at Maure.)[24]

Clearing forested land for wages was one of the methods that young men in the colony utilized to lay aside cash for the purpose of establishing themselves. Another method that many of them chose was laboring in the fur trade, particularly as a voyageur or a voyageur-trader in the distant interior. This latter work was more dangerous and unpredictable than forest-clearing, but it paid higher wages. Clearing land in the St. Lawrence Valley had its inherent risks and dangers, but in a number of ways, it was less risky and dangerous than paddling off into the wilderness to work for many months at a time. In addition, laboring close to one's home, friends, and loved ones was less challenging than leaving these familiar places and faces, for as long as a year or more, while on a trading expedition. Within a few years, Pierre Girard would devise his own method of participating in the peltries commerce. His activities would involve their own inherent challenges and dangers, but they would enable him to remain in the St. Lawrence Valley, and they would only take him away from his family for a number of weeks or months each summer.

During Pierre's months of felling trees near La Canardière for cash, Suzanne was completing her second pregnancy. Finally, on April 5, 1673, their second child and first son arrived in good health. One week later, at his christening ceremony in the Quebec church on April 12, his godfather and name-giver was François Dolbec, Pierre's land-clearing partner. (More than four decades into the future, Pierre's son Pierre Girard, Jr. would marry as his second wife François' daughter Marie Angélique Dolbec.) Standing beside François as the baby's other sponsor was Marie Thibault, the ten-to-twelve-year-old daughter and eldest child of Michel Thibault and Jeanne Soyer, who lived next door to the Girard's property at Maure.[25]

Twenty months later, a third child joined the ever-growing Girard family. After the arrival of Marie Madeleine, Suzanne and Pierre waited for fourteen days, until December 16, 1674, to have her baptized at Quebec. This two-week delay is strong evidence that the couple had by this point permanently settled on their farm in the Rocky River section of the Maure seigneury, some fifteen miles southwest of Quebec. More than five years had elapsed since the lot there had been ceded to Pierre, back in the summer of 1669. At this optimistic christening ceremony, the infant's sponsors were Jean Thibierge, age 17, the son of a Quebec tanner, and Madeleine Chapeau, the unmarried 17-year-old daughter of Pierre Chapeau, a linen weaver and settler in the Maure seigneury.[26]

The Gerard family of five only had to wait 25 months before they became a family of six. On January 4, 1677, little Jean Pierre came into the world at the Rocky River farm. This specific locale of his birth, in the westernmost section of the Maure seigneury, was recorded by the priest at the Quebec church when the baby was christened there on January 13, nine days after his arrival. The godfather on this day was Jean Pierre Jouineau, an unmarried 22-year-old neighbor in the Rocky River area. The godmother was Suzanne's younger sister Marie de Lavoie, who had married Pierre Grenon eleven months earlier and had settled at Neuville, the seigneury immediately west of Maure.[27]

Ten months later, although the Girard couple did not produce another child at this time, their family size still increased by one person. In this instance, the additional child who came to live with them did so under the terms of a legal contract, as was recorded by one of the official scribes in Quebec on October 19, 1677:

"Before Gilles Rageot, recorder and royal notary, etc., was present in person Renée de Laporte, wife of Michel Duveau [dit] Descormiers, absent from the region, formerly the wife of Jacques Arrivé [dit Delisle], mother and guardian as it is said of [Marie] Madeleine Arrivé [8³/4 years old], daughter of her and the deceased [Jacques Arrivé]. The said named individual [Renée de Laporte], while firmly including the said Descormiers, her husband, has made a promise to agree and consent to these presents, and with him is obligated, in solidarity one for the other, one for both of them, without division or discussion or renunciation. She has acknowledged and declared that she fairly and truly owes to Pierre Girard, habitant of the Rivière des Roches [area of the seigneury of Maure], present and assenting, the sum of 120 livres for three years of feeding and maintaining the said daughter [Marie] Madeleine Arrivé, commencing as of today. After an accounting had been made between the parties, the said Laporte has promised and is obliged to pay the said sum to the said creditor in six weeks, under the penalty of all expenses, damages, and interests, in valid payments of money or of saleable articles at the current prices. Thus have they promised, obligated themselves, and waived, etc. [This agreement] made and drawn up at the said Quebec in the office of the said notary in the morning of October 19, 1677, in the presence of Jean Baptiste Gosset, bailiff, and Jacques Rivet of Quebec, witnesses who have signed with the creditor and the notary. The said Laporte has declared that she does not know how to sign.
Signed,
Pierre Girart, J. Gosset, J. Rivet, and G. Rageot."[28]

Renée de Laporte had married her first husband, the candle maker Jacques Arrivé, in July of 1663 on Île de Ré, just offshore from La Rochelle. After the young couple had immigrated together to New France, they had produced four children in the Quebec region between August of 1665 and March of 1671. Jacques had died in the Charlesbourg area some time before their inventory of August 17, 1673. About four months after this enumeration of her belongings, in January of 1674, Renée had married the Quebec resident Michel Duveau. She would not become pregnant with their first Duveau child until about late December of 1677 (delivering the child on the following September 22, 1678). About two months before the commencement of this first pregnancy with Monsieur Duveau, on October 19, 1677, Renée and he made the above arrangements with the Girard couple. Their plans entailed hiring Suzanne and Pierre to take in the third Arrivé child, Marie Madeleine, who was $8^3/4$ years old at the time. Besides her, the other three Arrivé youngsters from Renée's first marriage included two older daughters, who were ages $12^1/4$ and $10^1/2$, and a boy who was $6^1/2$ years old. Perhaps Marie Madeleine was less cooperative than her three siblings, and her mother and step-father were seeking some relief, by hiring out her care to the Girard family for the interval of three years. By the time of the arrival of the second Duveau baby in February of 1680, the blended Duveau-Arrivé family would move from Quebec to the Neuville seigneury. It would be there that Marie Madeleine, two weeks before her 19th birthday in January of 1688, would marry a 22-year-old retired corporal. The couple would then settle at Neuville, and later at Montreal, producing seven children. Thus, the three years that Marie Madeleine would spend with the Girard family on their farm, from the autumn of 1677 until the autumn of 1680, would apparently work out well for both the girl and her family of origin.[29]

On February 24, 1678, Suzanne stood as the godmother for one of the twin boys who had been born on the previous day to Pierre Vallière and Anne Lagou, neighbors who lived five farms away. This time, the christening ceremony was conducted by a visiting priest at the adjacent seigneury of Neuville. Suzanne and the unmarried Quebec carpenter Rémi Dupil were the sponsors for baby Rémi, while two other individuals sponsored the other twin, named Jean. Unfortunately, the latter lad would only survive for three weeks; he would die on March 20, after which he would be buried four days later in the cemetery at Quebec. It was good that tiny Jean's family members and their friends could not peer into the future: about $3^1/2$ years and two babies later, the twins' father, Pierre Vallière, would die at the untimely age of about 34, shortly before October of 1681.[30]

The Girard family made the fifteen-mile trip from their home to Quebec on two occasions during November of 1678, to take part in important ecclesiastical celebrations at the church. The first instance took place on the first day of the month, when Pierre served as the godfather for little Vincent de Lavoie, Suzanne's fifteen-day-old half-brother. He was the third baby to be produced by her father Pierre de Lavoie and Isabelle Aupé, who lived thirteen farms away from the Girards. Interestingly, the godmother on this day was Renée de Laporte, who, thirteen months earlier, had transferred the care of her daughter Marie Madeleine Arrivé to Madame and Monsieur

Girard for the span of three years. It is highly likely that the estranged mother (who was still residing in the Lower Town area of Quebec) and her daughter, now three months short of being ten years old, encountered each other during this special occasion at the church.[31]

Three weeks later, Pierre again appeared as an official witness at the Notre Dame church in the Upper Town area of Quebec. This time, it was for the wedding of his friend and former land-clearing colleague Jean Rasset and his bride Jeanne Chapeau, who had just celebrated her 21st birthday. After their nuptial ceremony on November 21, the young couple would settle in the Maure seigneury, on Jean's farm adjacent to that of Pierre and Suzanne.[32]

Four months after this wedding, on March 28, 1679, Suzanne, Pierre, and their ever-growing brood again traveled to Quebec, this time to have their four-day-old son Jean Baptiste baptized. They had asked two friends to serve as sponsors: the Quebec carpenter Jean Marchand, and the Girards' neighbor Françoise Amiot, who was married to Charles Gingras, had two toddlers of her own, and lived four farms away from the Girards.[33]

Of particular interest is the fact that this would be the last time that Suzanne and Pierre would be obliged to make the fifteen-mile voyage eastward to Quebec to have their children christened, or to take part in many other important ecclesiastical functions. From now on, to attend such festivities, they would usually travel westward to the adjacent seigneury of Neuville. There, the parish and church of St. François de Sales (with its edifice located some seven miles west of the Girard farm) would be established in this year of 1679; its church ledger would commence in July. The parish and church of Ste. Foy would also be established in 1679, about eight miles to the east of the Girard property. However, in the decades ahead, the Girard family, along with most of their fellow residents of western Maure, would usually make the trip westward to Neuville for the majority of their church functions, rather than going eastward to Ste. Foy.[34]

But the Girards did travel to the Quebec church in the spring of 1680, to joyfully join in the nuptial celebrations of Marie Thibault, the eldest child of their next-door neighbors Michel Thibault and Jeanne Soyer. The bride was about 17 to 19 years old, while the groom, Jean Rollandeau, was age 25 to 29. On this day of April 24, the two official witnesses recorded in the parish ledger were Pierre Girard from Maure and Jean Delastre dit Lajeunesse from Neuville.[35]

Ten months later, Pierre again found himself standing as a witness at the marriage of a daughter of the same Thibault family. This time, however, he was in the new church at Neuville, and the bride was the family's second daughter, Louise, who would celebrate her 14th birthday in three months. At the time of their wedding on February 17, 1681, the groom, René Alarie dit Grandalarie, was 34 years old. The two official witnesses on this day were Pierre Girard and Jean Rasset, formerly land-clearing partners and now adjacent neighbors (the Thibaults lived on one side of the Girard farm, while the Rassets resided on the other side). After their ceremony, the newlyweds would settle in the Maure seigneury.[36]

An official colony-wide census was drawn up during the spring or the beginning of summer in 1681. At household 33 within the seigneury of Maure, the following information was recorded:
"Pierre Girard, age 40
Suzanne Lavoie, his wife, 30
Children:
Jeanne, 7 [was actually 9]
François, 8
[Marie] Madeleine, 5 [was actually 7]
Jean [Pierre], 6
Jean Baptiste, 3
1 gun
5 horned cattle
12 arpents [10 acres] of land cleared and cultivated"[37]

Oddly enough, according to their baptismal records, nearly all of the children's ages were recorded incorrectly by the enumerator. The eldest child Jeanne would turn 10 on August 8, but she was listed as being only 7 years old. François had celebrated his 8th birthday on April 5, so his age was correct; however, Marie Madeleine would turn 8 at the beginning of December, but her age was recorded here as only 5. Jean Pierre had turned 4 back on January 4th of this year, yet he was listed here as age 6. Jean Baptiste's age was likewise recorded as much older than was true: he had turned 2 on March 24, but he was listed here as a three-year-old. It is of interest to note that the family members had by this point cleared and brought under cultivation a total of ten acres of their property, twelve years after it had been granted to Pierre back in July of 1669.

On each side of the Girard farm, the enumerator documented their adjacent neighbors: Jean Rasset (age 35) and Jeanne Chapeau (24) in household 32, and Michel Thibault (40) and Jeanne Soyer (45) in household 34. Evidence concerning just when this census was drawn up in the Maure seigneury was included with the age of the younger of the two Rasset children. Little Pierre, who had been born on January 8, 1681, was recorded as six months old, which would imply a census time of about the beginning of July. However, it must have been drawn up at least a month earlier: Suzanne de Lavoie delivered her next child on June 6, but this new infant had not arrived by the time the members of the Girard family were enumerated.

Thirteen farms away from the Girards, in household 20, lived Suzanne's father Pierre Lavoie (age 50), his second wife Isabelle Aupé (here recorded as Élisabeth Aubert, 34), and their children Marie Anne (9), Madeleine (8), Pierre (6), Vincent (3), and François (2). Strangely, all but one of these Lavoie offspring (who were half-siblings of Suzanne) were listed as being one year older than their true ages; in addition, daughter Marie, age 5, was omitted entirely from the record. Like the Girard farm, the Lavoie farm also had ten acres of land cleared and under cultivation. At the time of this enumeration, Suzanne's one unmarried sister, Marie Olive (17 years old), was listed as a domestic servant at the home of Jacques Samson and his family at Lauson, directly across the St. Lawrence from Quebec.[38]

When the Girard family was documented in this census, in the spring or the beginning of the summer, Suzanne had nearly completed her sixth pregnancy; she safely delivered little Jeanne on June 6, 1681. Two days later, at the infant's baptism in the Neuville church, the godmother and name-giver was their adjacent neighbor Jeanne Chapeau, the wife of Michel Thibault; the godfather was Jean Mezeray from nearby Neuville. The fact that Suzanne and Pierre chose to have this newborn infant be named Jeanne, after her sponsor, may indicate that their oldest child Jeanne had died in the short interval between the taking of the census and the new baby's arrival in early June. No documentation concerning the elder Jeanne has been found in the colony after the census records of 1681, not even her burial record. Thus, it is not possible to determine just when Suzanne and Pierre suffered the grievous loss of a daughter who had graced their lives for nearly ten years or more.[39]

The next time that Pierre appeared as a sponsor and bequeathed his name to a baby at a christening, it was a very poignant affair. In the Neuville church on November 1, 1681, he held the week-old son of Anne Lagou and Pierre Vallière, their neighbors who lived just five farms away. Monsieur Vallière had died a short time earlier, at about age 34; his widow Anne was left with six living children, who ranged in age from nine years down to this brand new boy. At his baptism, the little lad's godmother was Marguerite Thibault, who lived next door to the Girards and would turn age 13 in three weeks. About $2^3/4$ years earlier, back in February of 1678, Suzanne had served as the christening sponsor for one of the twin boys of the Vallière couple, one of whom had lived for only three weeks. By good fortune, the farm which was adjacent to that of the widowed Anne Lagou was owned and occupied by the forty-year-old, unmarried carpenter Rémi Dupil, who had relocated to this property from Quebec. He and Anne would be married on January 8, 1682, ten weeks after the baptism of her latest child.[40]

By this point in his life, when he was 37 to 41 years old, Pierre had already been involved in the fur trade for a number of years. As did a great many other individuals in the colony, he had determined how he could best participate in this commerce. In his case, Monsieur Girard owned his own sailing vessel, a *barque* named *The Samuel*, which he utilized to haul merchandise up the St. Lawrence from the Quebec area to the towns of Trois-Rivières and/or Montreal. Both of these upriver communities hosted annual trade fairs, to which large numbers of visiting native traders paddled out from their home regions in the distant interior, bringing canoeloads of furs and hides to exchange for European goods with the French residents. It is not known whether Pierre traded directly with the native customers, or whether he instead sold his hauled merchandise to French outfitters. In all likelihood, he participated in both of these avenues of commerce, both the retail and the wholesale options. In this manner, he could generate maximum profits while remaining with his family for most of the year, on their farm about fifteen miles southwest of Quebec. By working as a combination shipper and merchant, he was only obliged to be absent from home for a limited number of weeks or months each summer. He did not have to be away for many months or even years at a time, as did the voyageurs and the voyageur-traders. Nor did he have to relocate to one of the two upriver towns in order to conduct his business.

For shuttling inbound and outbound cargos up and down the St. Lawrence, and for much of the other transport which was conducted on the river during the entire French regime, the colonists utilized two types of watercraft that were constructed from sawn lumber and hewn timbers. These were the bark (*barque*) and the shallop (*chaloupe*), each of which came in a variety of sizes. (Birchbark and dugout canoes, which were also regularly used by the French, are not included in the present discussion.)

Numerous art works dating from the French era, from Champlain's drawings onward, portrayed both categories of vessels.[41] The larger craft, the bark (the type which Pierre Girard owned and used), was well suited for hauling a considerable amount of heavy freight, as well as livestock. A 1698 contract between a Montreal boat builder and the Montreal merchant Antoine Pascaud described the *barque* under construction as measuring forty feet in length, $13^1/2$ feet in beam, and seven feet in depth, built entirely of white oak except for the decking, which was to be of pine.[42] Some period sources referred to such vessels as having an internal capacity ranging from forty to seventy tons (a ton of capacity represented 100 cubic feet or 2.83 cubic meters of space).[43] However, certain versions were much smaller, as was documented by Champlain when he arrived at Tadoussac after his ocean crossing in 1618. Switching to smaller craft for the journey upriver to Quebec, the commander and his party traveled in "a little bark of ten or twelve tons" as well as "a little shallop."[44] Barks had either two or three masts, each of which was fitted with one or two sails, usually square but sometimes lateen (a triangular sail suspended from a boom that is angled obliquely to the mast).[45] In 1754, two barks were based at Ft. Frontenac, near the eastern end of Lake Ontario, for hauling military and fur trade cargos back and forth along the full length of the lake; each of these vessels was manned by a crew of seven sailors plus the master.[46] *Barques*, armed when necessary with a number of light cannons, were not limited to voyages between Tadoussac and the upper St. Lawrence communities or on the Great Lakes. In some instances, they sailed on the Atlantic between Quebec and New England or New Holland/New York, while they sometimes even traveled across the span of ocean between New France and the mother country.[47]

Shallops, smaller in all dimensions, were best suited for hauling lesser amounts of freight of more moderate weight, and as general working boats for traders, seal hunters, whalers, and fishermen, besides their use as vehicles for general transportation. Various period illustrations depicted their dimensions as ranging from about eighteen to twenty feet in length and some five to seven feet in beam, often manned by only one or two persons. Diminutive enough to be carried on the deck of a transatlantic ship, or to be towed across the ocean, these vessels were powered by both sails and oars. The single mast or pair of masts were each rigged with a single sail, either square or lateen, while a tiller at the stern controlled the vessel's course. Multiple pairs of oars either supplemented the wind power or provided the only propulsion when the wind slackened. When necessary, *chaloupes* were armed with one or more swivel guns.[48]

Simply hauling merchandise upriver from Quebec before selling it generated a certain degree of profit for a merchant. By good fortune, a list of the prices that were charged for certain selected goods at Quebec, Trois-Rivières, and Montreal back in 1665 has been preserved.[49] This document, although it only included nine items, clearly illustrates the price mark-ups that occurred the further up the St. Lawrence that merchandise was hauled. Transport from Quebec up to Trois-Rivières entailed a journey of about 75 miles, while hauling from there up to Montreal involved a trip of about 80 additional miles. Some of this transport was done with oxen-drawn sleighs on the frozen river during winter, while the rest was done with watercraft during the unfrozen seasons. The price increases which resulted from the hauling procedures enabled merchants and traders to make a significant profit simply by transporting the commodities upriver before selling them. This was especially true if they carried out the hauling themselves (as did Pierre Girard in his own vessel), rather than hiring out this task to others.

In the 1665 list, the selling prices at each of the three more progressively distant locales were thus presented (expressed in livres, sols, and deniers, or l, s, and d):

1 keg of brandy:............*140l.* [Qc.]..............*154l.* [T-R.]............ *168l.* [Mtl.]
1 keg of wine:...........................*51l.*...........................*56l.*...........................*61l.*
1 yard of woolen serge fabric from Poitou:
...............................*4l. 5s. 10d.*...............*4l. 14s. 6d*.....................*5l. 3s.*
1 yard of fine Meslis linen fabric [sailcloth]:
...............................*1l. 9s. 9d.*.....................*1l. 13s.*.....................*1l. 16s.*
1 yard of coarse Meslis linen fabric [sailcloth]:
...............................*1l. 8s. 1d.*.....................*1l. 11s.*...............*1l. 14s. 2d.*
1 large Biscayan axe:....*1l. 11s. 5d.*...............*1l. 14s. 2d.*...............*1l. 17s. 9d.*
1 small Biscayan axe: ...*1l. 1s. 10d.*.......................*1l. 2s.*.......................*1l. 4s.*
1 keg of vinegar:.......................*30l.*...........................*49l.*...........................*54l.*
1 keg of salt:.............................*14l.*...........................*15l.*...........................*16l.*

As may be observed from this list, for both brandy and wine, the mark-ups on stocks which were sold at Trois-Rivières were 10 percent higher than their selling prices at Quebec. For those supplies of brandy and wine which were transported twice the distance upriver, all the way to Montreal, the mark-ups were 20 percent above the Quebec prices. For various of the other listed articles, the amounts of mark-up at both of the distant markets were considerably less. The excessive amounts of increase in the prices of vinegar, which were the highest rates of mark-up on the entire roster, must represent an error, either in the original recording of the prices or in a later transcription of the original information.

In considering the issue of price mark-ups, one must also note the amounts of mark-up which were added to the imported articles upon their initial arrival in New France. Two years before the above roster of prices was drawn up, back in 1663, the Sovereign Council in the colony had set the maximum prices at which various articles imported from France could be sold at Quebec. These regulations had allowed a 65 percent mark-up over the rates which were paid for similar goods back in the mother country, and a 100 percent mark-up on liquor compared to selling prices back in France. At the same time, the rate that could be charged by shippers for transporting merchandise across the Atlantic had been set at a straight eighty livres per ton, regardless of the type of cargo being hauled.[50] As a result of these official policies, Pierre Girard was probably charged a 65 percent mark-up on his supplies of tobacco and most of the other trade items that he acquired from his importer at Quebec; in addition, he probably paid to him a 100 percent mark-up on his stocks of brandy. These mark-ups covered the costs of transporting the merchandise across the Atlantic and up the St. Lawrence to Quebec.

During the 1680s, this transport was usually carried out each year by some seven or eight ships from France. On their return voyage back to the mother country, only two or three of these vessels hauled peltries, while the others sailed back virtually empty, with either little or no cargo at all in their holds.[51]

At the upriver towns of Trois-Rivières or Montreal, Pierre traded his merchandise with native customers from the distant interior, and/or with French outfitters who lived in or near to these two St. Lawrence communities. Whenever he received furs and hides from these customers (instead of receiving letters of exchange, also called promissory notes, from some of the Frenchmen), he was obliged to eventually pay an export tax on certain of them. He paid this tax when he handed over the peltries to the warehouse of the monopoly company, which handled the exporting of peltries to France.

In March of 1657, the King had issued a decree by which a *droit du quart*, an export tax of 25 percent, had been levied on the value of all furs and hides which would be turned in to the monopoly company. These revenues had been utilized by the company to help defray the expenses of running the colony and conducting the peltries-export business.[52] Six years later, in 1663, the monarch had declared that New France would thereafter be a royal colony, and a Sovereign Council had been established in the colony to carry out its operations. In the following year, the newly-established Council had passed certain regulations concerning commerce and the fur trade. As before, all residents of the colony would be permitted to engage in the peltries trade, and, as before, they would be allowed to sell their acquired furs and hides only to the monopoly company.[53] However, a change was made at that time concerning the tax or export duty of 25 percent which since 1657 had been levied on all peltries when they were accepted by the company. Now, there would be a tax of 25 percent on only all beaver pelts (plus a 10 percent tax on all moose hides, termed the *droit du dixième*, which would be added in 1666); no export taxes would be charged for the various other types of furs and hides that were taken in by the company. (These export duties on beaver and moose would continue to be charged to the individuals providing peltries until the year 1717.)[54]

Pierre Boucher in 1663 had noted the primary usages of moose hides and beaver pelts in Europe, thus explaining why these two peltries, so numerous in the trade at this time, had been singled out for the levying of income-generating export duties:

"Let us begin then with the most common and the most widely distributed of all the animals in this country, which is the elk, called here [in Canada] the moose...The skin [hairless hide] is taken to France to be made into buff leather [which has a soft, velvety surface, popular for making coats, uniforms, belts, baldrics, absorbent polishing cloths, etc.]...

The beaver...its fur is used in the manufacture of hats, and is the staple article of the trade of this country...

The bears are black...The skins of the cubs are of some value for muffs [a warm tubular covering for both hands]"[55]

Besides the moose hides and beaver and bear pelts that had been mentioned by Boucher, large quantities of various other furs and hides, termed *menus pelleteries* or minor peltries, were also brought to the company storehouse. During this period, these other furs and hides were overshadowed by beaver and moose. However, from the

1690s on, the focus would begin to change. Shortly after 1701, more than half of all peltries acquired would be those other than beaver, with the full range of peltries figuring prominently in the trade. This pattern would continue until the 1730s, when the percentage of beaver pelts involved in the commerce would reduce even further. In Europe, many of the furs were utilized as trim on robes and other garments, while large numbers of hides (of moose, elk, caribou, and deer) were fashioned into military and civilian saddles as well as a wide range of other leather goods. Whatever beaver pelts were deemed to be surplus in France were sold to Dutch merchants; from Holland, many of these furs were shipped to Russia.[56]

Several laws had been enacted by the Sovereign Council in 1663 to protect consumers in the colony. One of these changes involved the 10 percent duty that had formerly been levied on all imported items. In 1663, it had been reduced to a 10 percent tax on just imported wines, spirits, and tobacco.[57] It was a series of requests by Pierre Girard in 1682, asking for an elimination or at least a reduction of these import duties on certain articles of his merchandise, which provides the only surviving documentation concerning his commercial operations. The story of his specific activities will continue shortly.

In 1684, Governor de La Barre would compose a short historical summary for his superiors in France, entitled "Memoire Concerning the Peltries Commerce and its Tax Collection in Canada or New France." In this document, he would summarize a number of important subjects related to the fur trade:

"The proprietary seigneurs of the said country [the directors of the monopoly company before 1663] granted the freedom to participate in the [peltries] commerce to the habitants as well as to the merchants, with the stipulations that they pay one-quarter of the value of all of the beaver pelts and one-tenth of the moose hides [as export duties]...

The West Indies Company, which took possession [of the peltries export business] of the said country [in 1664] enjoyed the same rights as had been enjoyed by the original seigneurs until the revocation of the said company by the King [in 1674]...including the said right to collect the [export] taxes of one-quarter of the beaver pelts and one-tenth of the moose hides, and the [import duties] of ten percent of the value on the wines, brandies, and tobacco which entered the said country...

By an ordinance of May 11, 1675, His Majesty ordered that beaver pelts would be accepted [by the new holder of the monopoly] at the rate of 4 livres 10 sols per pound of weight, which would be paid to the habitants in letters of exchange [promissory notes] on Paris or La Rochelle...

His Majesty leased out [in 1675] to Monsieur Jean Oudiette [the representative of a group of French financiers known as The Company of the Farm] all of the rights which had belonged to the West Indies Company. These included [the exclusive right to market Canadian beaver pelts in France,] the collection of the one-quarter tax on beaver pelts and the one-tenth tax on moose hides, and the trade of Tadoussac, as well as the collection of the [import] duties of ten percent on the wines, brandies, and tobacco entering the said country...for the sum of 47,000 livres...

[The control of this leased or "farmed" monopoly was thereafter transferred a number of times]

Beaver pelts of all qualities having been [earlier] set at 4 livres 10 sols per pound, it was ordered by a declaration of the [Sovereign] Council on May 10, 1677 that greasy beaver pelts would be [thereafter] accepted at 5 livres 10 sols per beaver instead of 4 livres 10 sols, and dry beaver at 3 livres 10 sols, instead of the said [former standard] price of 4 livres 10 sols with no regard for the different qualities. This was done since the natives had found no advantage in providing greasy beavers compared to dry ones, and had neglected to acquire the [different] qualities which are necessary for the composition of [felt for making] hats.

One must observe that, of all the quantities of beaver pelts which are traded in Canada, only about 40,000 are needed for the manufacture of hats in France. Thus, three-quarters of these must be greasy beavers and the other quarter dry beavers [for the 3-to-1 recipe which produces the highest quality felt]. The remainder of the beaver pelts which come from Canada are sent to Holland and to Moscow..."[58]

Among the various subjects which were addressed in this report, one was the manner in which the King's right to collect certain taxes had been leased out or "farmed out" to a "tax farmer," a private contractor. In this procedure, the royal government would collect a single payment, all at once and in advance, from the private contractor who had submitted the highest bid for this privilege. Afterward, this "farmer" (typically an association of businessmen or investors, such as the Company of the Farm) would then recover the paid amount by gradually collecting the actual taxes, with the hope that the collected revenues would be greater than the amount that he had paid to the Crown for the privilege of "farming" the taxes. The private contractor often generated a considerable profit from this procedure, since he typically paid the government only a fraction of the total taxes which had been levied in the name of the King and had been collected by the "farmer."[59]

A price roster from the Trois-Rivières trade fair of 1683, the very period of Pierre Girard's active participation in the commerce, included many of the articles that he most likely hauled upriver in his sailing vessel. These items were in addition to the considerable amounts of brandy which he is known to have transported (along with large amounts of tobacco, which does appear on the roster). The prices on the list were expressed in beaver pelts, but the equivalent values in other furs and hides were equally acceptable in the exchanges.

"*2 pairs of black trade stockings --1 beaver*

1 large shirt -- 1 beaver

2 medium-sized shirts -- 1 beaver

3 small shirts -- 1 beaver

1 large hooded coat -- 3 beavers

1 medium-sized hooded coat -- 2 beavers

1 small hooded coat -- 1 beaver

1 cloak containing 1^1/2 yards of woolen stroud fabric -- 4 beavers

1 cloak containing 1^1/2 yards of woolen Limbourg fabric -- 4 beavers

1 cloak of woolen coat fabric, decorated with braid -- 3 beavers

1 cloak containing 2 yards of woolen Iroquoise fabric -- 2 beavers

1 blanket from Normandy worth 20 livres -- 6 beavers

1 blanket from Normandy worth 16 livres -- 5 beavers

1 blanket from Normandy worth 13 livres -- 4 beavers

1 blanket from Normandy worth 9 to 10 livres -- 3 beavers

1 blanket from Normandy worth 6 to 7 livres -- 2 beavers

1 pair of large sleeves of woolen penistone fabric, decorated with braid --
   1 beaver

2 pairs of medium-sized sleeves of woolen penistone fabric, decorated with
   braid -- 1 beaver

3 caps worth 1.5 livres apiece -- 1 beaver

1 tapabord cap -- 1 beaver

72 awls -- 1 beaver

200 sewing needles -- 1 beaver

6 scrapers -- 1 beaver

1 pound of glass beads -- 1 beaver

72 brass finger rings -- 1 beaver

6 bracelets -- 1 beaver

24 hawk bells -- 1 beaver

6 large mirrors -- 1 beaver

12 medium-sized mirrors -- 1 beaver

2 ounces of vermilion paint pigment -- 1 beaver
6 combs worth 4 to 5 livres apiece -- 1 beaver
1 large axe worth 4 livres -- 1 beaver
1 large biscayan axe worth 1.5 livres -- 1 beaver
3 axes -- 1 beaver
3 small biscayan axes -- 1 beaver
12 large butcher knives -- 1 beaver
18 medium-sized butcher knives -- 1 beaver
12 large clasp knives -- 1 beaver
15 iron arrow points -- 1 beaver
3 sword [blades] to be hafted [as spears] -- 1 beaver
100 catfish hooks -- 1 beaver
3 poids weight of net thread from Holland -- 1 beaver
1 gun worth 30 livres -- 10 beavers
1 gun worth 10 livres -- 6 beavers
1 ordinary gun -- 5 beavers
1 carbine -- 4 beavers
2 powder horns -- 1 beaver
6 pounds of lead of all sorts [balls, shot, or bulk] -- 1 beaver
200 gunflints -- 1 beaver
12 gun worms -- 1 beaver
12 fire steels -- 1 beaver
2 pounds weight of kettles -- 1 beaver
1 medium-sized box [traveling trunk] -- 4 beavers
2 fathoms [totaling $10^1/2$ English feet] of [twist] tobacco -- 1 beaver"[60]

Many of the traders who worked the annual peltries fairs at Trois-Rivières or Montreal (both those individuals who resided in one of these towns and those who traveled from elsewhere to participate in the commerce, such as Pierre Girard) left in their wake a trail of official documents. This paper trail typically concerned the trader's need to borrow funds, to take on partners and/or investors, and to purchase trade merchandise on credit from an outfitter. In some cases, these early stages were later followed by his appearance in court, if he did not pay off his debts in a timely manner and was thus sued by his creditors. The notarial and court documents which resulted from these activities typically included a rich trove of information concerning the man's business operations, waiting to be mined centuries later by some avid historian. (The biography of Alexandre Turpin, which appeared earlier in this work, includes examples of these various types of data-rich documents concerning the career of a trader at the Montreal fair.)

However, in the case of Pierre Girard, he generated almost no surviving documentation during his years of working in the peltries commerce at Trois-Rivières and/or Montreal. He carried out these activities while residing at a considerable distance away, about fifteen miles upriver from Quebec on the family farm in the seigneury of Maure. From the perspective of a historian, this nearly complete lack of documents engenders considerable disappointment. However, the very scarcity of official records clearly implies that Monsieur Girard conducted his business affairs in a conservative, frugal, and rather profitable manner, saving the proceeds from one venture and investing them into later ventures. During the course of his entire career as a merchant, there are no surviving notarial documents which indicate that he ever borrowed money, took on associates or investors for his trading ventures, or bought merchandise on credit. He owned his own sailing vessel for hauling trade goods and peltries up and down the St. Lawrence, and he apparently paid cash for all of his acquisitions and for the services of his employees. In addition, he seemingly conducted each of his transactions based upon a handshake and the good word of the participants, with no accompanying written records.

This manner of handling business by no means implies that Monsieur Girard hewed to the ancient adage *"Qui ne risque rien, n'a rien."* This expression translates literally as "He who risks nothing, has nothing;" for centuries, it has been expressed in English as "Nothing ventured, nothing gained." Pierre's attitude must have been quite the opposite of this sentiment. Each time he departed on a trading trip with his *barque,* he risked his cargos of westbound merchandise and eastbound peltries to the vagaries of wind, weather conditions, hidden boulders, shoals, and river currents. His commercial activities seem to have been closely aligned with the old saying *"Ne vendez pas la peau de l'ours avant de l'avoir tué."* The ancient French version, translated as "Don't sell the pelt of the bear before you've killed it," fits the outlook of a shrewd peltries merchant far better than the English version "Don't count your chickens before they're hatched."

Unfortunately, at the distance of one-third of a millennium, the virtually complete lack of documentation concerning Pierre's business dealings eliminates the possibility of recreating many of the details of his commercial operations. Which merchants at Quebec supplied him with his trade goods, both those articles which were imported from France and the Caribbean colonies and those which were manufactured in New France? Who aided him in sailing his bark called *The Samuel* upriver from Quebec to the trade fairs with the merchandise, and afterward back downstream with the resulting furs and hides? Who assisted him during his exchanges with native customers and/or French outfitters at Trois-Rivières and Montreal?

The few facts which are known about Pierre Girard's commercial activities in the St. Lawrence Valley come from a single, three-page document.[61] Penned by the Quebec notary Gilles Rageot on September 15, 1682, this document was a verified copy of several edicts which had been issued by Jacques Duchesneau, the Intendant of the colony, during the previous eleven days. The administrator had issued these declarations in response to a series of requests from Monsieur Girard, which the trader had commenced at about the end of August. These supplications had urged that the import duties on the stocks of tobacco and brandy which Pierre regularly imported or bought, transported upriver, and traded might be either eliminated or at least reduced considerably. Although Pierre presumably dealt in a wide array of trade merchandise, there were no duties charged on any other imported articles besides tobacco, brandy, and wine. Thus, his other goods, both those which were imported from the mother country and those that were produced by French and native residents of the St. Lawrence settlements, were not mentioned in either Pierre's requests or the Intendant's responses.

"Jacques Duchesneau, Chevalier, Councilor of the King in his Councils, Intendant of justice, police, and finance in Canada and the region of North America, considering the request which was presented to us by Pierre Girard, master of the barque named The Samuel, *relating to its motives and contents, he wished that we would order that the Sieur Durand, agent of the Gentlemen interested in the service of His Majesty in this region, would grant to him [eliminate for him] the duties on the brandies and tobacco which he had brought from the [Caribbean] Islands, or instead, that he would reduce the duties for him, based upon their [lower] value. Our edict at the bottom of the said request, from the fourth of this month [September], which was communicated to the said Sieur Durand, was that his response should be ordained based upon this reasoning. Thus, the response of the said Sieur Durand was as follows. He declared that, regarding the tobacco sold by the said Girard, who thought it to be of lesser value, he was prepared to reduce the duty for him to two sols instead of the five sols that he is accustomed to paying for each pound. Although he maintained that Girard ought to pay the ordinary duties [of 60 livres per barrel] on the said brandy, since it would*

all be sold at the price which is charged in France or a little less, he himself accepted the rate of forty-four livres per half-hogshead.

There was [then] another request which was presented to us by the said Girard, that we would order that he would be exempt from the said duties, considering the low value of the said merchandise, and having regard for the opening of the commerce [with the French colonies in the Caribbean Islands], which he would not be able to do favorably in this region, offering to deliver the merchandise which remained, if the [duties on] tobacco were five sols per pound and on brandy sixty livres per hogshead. Our edict of communication to the said Sieur Durand, on the 12th of this month, was that his response was to be as follows. Considering that [Monsieur Girard] had persisted at this, at the request of the said Girard on the date of the said 12th day of this month [September], [Monsieur Durand] made another response to him on that day...He consented that the said Girard would only need to pay two-thirds of the amount that the brandy from France was levied in duties for each barrel [thus reducing it to 40 livres], unless his [Durand's] consent would be detrimental for the future.

After having listened to the said parties and having considered everything, we ordain, with the confirmation and consent of the said Sieur Durand, that a reduction will be made for the said Girard of one-third of the duties which he is accustomed to paying [reducing it to 40 livres] for each barrel of brandy which comes to this region from France, likewise [a reduction to] two sols per pound [down from 5 sols] for the tobacco which the said Girard sells here. [This document] drawn up at Quebec on September 15, 1682. Signed Duchesneau, and lower down is written by Milord, Signed, Chevalier followed by a flourish.

Verified copy from the original, rendered just now on the fifteenth day of September, 1682, in the presence of Joseph Vandandaigue and of Jean Meunier of the said Quebec, witnesses who have signed with the said Girard and the notary.

Signed,

Pr. Girart, Joseph Vandandaigue, Jean Munier, and G. Rageot"

The first of the two listed witnesses, Monsieur Vandandaigue, was one of the rare Belgians who settled in New France. Hailing from Brussels, the joiner was about 29 to 35 years old at this time, living at both Quebec and nearby Beauport. Having been married for four years, he and his wife had already produced three children.[62]

The wording in the final paragraph of the Intendant's 1682 edict is particularly interesting. According to this text, the reductions in the duties on both tobacco and brandy would apply to Pierre's imports whether they came from the Caribbean or from the mother country. These reductions certainly allowed our merchant to reap greater profits from his upriver trading ventures.

It is unfortunate that no further records have survived pertaining to Pierre Girard's overseas importing business, associated with the island colonies far to the south. French entrepreneurs had first begun settling in the West Indies in about 1625, in time laying claim to various of the islands at the far eastern end of the Caribbean. These islands, in a long chain which was termed Les Îles Caribes (now called the Lesser Antilles), extend in a broad southward arc from east of Puerto Rico down to nearly the coast of Venezuela. Composed of the Leeward Islands in the north and the Windward Islands in the south (down to Grenada, the southernmost one), the Lesser Antilles chain separates the eastern end of the Caribbean Sea from the Atlantic Ocean. Initially, the main export crop that the French settlers had grown on their island farms had been tobacco. However, beginning in 1642, they had begun to develop the production of cane sugar, which had been a food plant of the indigenous populations of the islands long before the arrival of Europeans. Commencing in 1665, the French had also settled on Saint Domingue (now called Haiti), the western portion of the island of Hispaniola, and Île de la Tortue (now called Tortuga), a little to the north. Hispaniola, along with Cuba, Jamaica, and Puerto Rico, form the Greater Antilles.

In about 1669 (thirteen years before Pierre Girard's documented association with the island colonies), a trade triangle had been developed between Quebec, the West Indies, and France. In this profitable long-distance commerce, the goods most often flowed in a counter-clockwise direction. Lumber, barrel staves, fish, eels, peas, grain, and corn were shipped from New France southward to the French-held islands; sugar, molasses, and tobacco from the islands were transported eastward to France; and European manufactured goods were hauled westward from France to the St. Lawrence Valley. However, as the 1682 Girard document revealed, tobacco and brandy were also sometimes brought northward from the island colonies to New France, thus causing the triangular flow of goods to run in this instance in a clockwise direction. It was the further development of this commerce to which Pierre had referred in his second appeal to the Intendant, when he had requested a complete elimination of the duties on his goods which were imported from the Caribbean.[63]

As was noted earlier in the 1683 price roster for the Trois-Rivières fair, tobacco was one of the many articles that were officially approved for exchange with native traders in the St. Lawrence settlements. It also happens to be one of the two items that Pierre Girard is known to have acquired, transported upriver, and exchanged in the peltries commerce. At this time, tobacco was officially priced at the Trois-Rivières fairs at one beaver pelt (or an equivalent value in other furs and hides) for a strip of twist tobacco that measured two fathoms ($10^1/2$ feet) in length. When this same product was transported into the distant interior, its price increased as much as eight times or more. For example, one fathom of tobacco (half of the amount on the price roster) was traded at Michilimackinac in 1698 for four beaver pelts (four times the price).

The tobacco that was both used and traded by the French was grown and prepared in a variety of locations. Much of it was raised in the French colonies in the West Indies and in the Portuguese colonies in Brazil; in addition, some of it was grown by local farmers in the St. Lawrence Valley. The imported version was typically called black tobacco (*tabac noir*), while the local product was usually termed white or light-colored tobacco (*tabac blanc*). Farmers in France were forbidden to raise tobacco; this policy allowed the government to farm out the monopoly on its manufacture and distribution for a considerable revenue, and it also protected the interests of their planters in the West Indies. Large amounts of tobacco grown in Brazil were also imported to New France. These shipments involved Portuguese merchants, since Portugal had been developing colonies in Brazil since 1530. Considerable amounts of tobacco were also cultivated by farmers along the St. Lawrence, particularly in the region between Montreal and Trois-Rivières; some of this crop was sold to outfitters for use in the fur trade.

All of the tobacco that was used and traded by the French was twisted into a rope-like form, whether it was imported or grown locally, and whether it was intended for use in a pipe or as snuff. In France, dried leaves imported from the West Indies were first moistened with sprinkled water and stripped of their fibrous midline stem. Then, one of two different methods was used to twist the stripped leaves into a rope. The "French" method was done entirely by hand, with the spinner manually twisting a small bunch of leaves into an arm-long rope about one inch in diameter, and then wrapping it with a moistened complete leaf. In the "Dutch" method, a reel or spindle mechanism was utilized to manufacture a continuous tobacco rope of about the same one-inch diameter. From the reel, the rope twist was later wound several layers thick onto a wooden bobbin, to form a completed roll; this was then encased in linen fabric and aged to create finished pipe tobacco. Very similar steps were carried out by Brazilian or Portuguese workers, using a reel or a spindle, to produce ropes of Brazil tobacco. In New France, the local growers also twisted their pipe tobacco into a continuous rope-like form and wound it upon a central wooden stick. These latter rolls each weighed an average of 52 pounds, including their wooden center. However, some tobacco rolls, either produced locally or imported, weighed considerably more, sometimes as much as 150 to 200 pounds.[64]

The officer Lahontan made this observation at Montreal in 1685: "The barques which carry [from Quebec up to Montreal] dry commodities, as well as wine and brandy, are but few in number; but then they make several voyages in one year from the one city to the other."[65] He noted this phenomenon during the very period in which Pierre Girard was conducting such transport on the river in his own *barque*.

As was clearly noted in the edicts of the Intendant during September of 1682, one of Pierre's articles of hauled trade merchandise was *eau de vie* (brandy). This highly alcoholic beverage, distilled from grape wine and aged in wooden casks, was clear and colorless when it was freshly distilled. However, during the aging process, the liquid dissolved some coloring matter from the wood, and thus acquired a light brownish or amber-colored hue. Possibly the most famous brandy was cognac, which was named after the town of Cognac, located about fifty miles southeast of La Rochelle. Certain other "brandies" were produced not from grape wine but from the fermented juice of black cherries; these beverages, termed *kirsch*, were produced in the Alsace region of France, in Switzerland, and in the Black Forest region of western Germany. However, this cherry-flavored drink, as well as all of the other alcoholic beverages which were distilled from fruits besides grapes, were correctly termed cordials or liqueurs, rather than brandy.[66]

By the time Pierre Girard began dealing in *eau de vie*, during the 1670s or the first two years of the 1680s, it had long been a highly controversial article of trade with the native populations. During the first two decades after the founding of Quebec, between 1608 and 1629, the French had not provided brandy to the natives, who had had no taste for it. However, during the period of 1629-1632, while the Kirke brothers and their English forces had occupied the colony, the Anglos had dealt freely in this intoxicating beverage. Thus, upon the return of the French in 1633, they had discovered that their native customers had developed a strong thirst for *eau de vie*. But the amount of unbridled violence that many native people committed while under its influence had soon led Champlain to prohibit the distribution of brandy to them, in that same year of 1633. This highly problematic situation, and the resulting edict by the commandant of the colony, had been recorded by the Jesuit priests at Quebec. In spite of the decree, however, brandy had continued to be sold freely at both Quebec and at the deepwater port of Tadoussac downriver. Thus had been sown the seeds of the conflict, over whether to provide to or withhold from the native populations this highly alcoholic drink, for which the natives had not developed any immunities during the preceding centuries. This contentious issue between the authorities and the sellers would rage for more than a century thereafter.

In 1663, the chronicler Pierre Boucher had recorded the following observations:

"All of the native people in contact with Europeans become drunkards...The natives only drink to make themselves drunk; and when they have begun to drink, they will give anything that is asked for a bottle of brandy, in order to complete their intoxication...Since they are glad to have opportunities for revenging themselves upon their enemies without being blamed for it, that is one of the reasons why they are so passionately fond of getting drunk, thinking that when they have struck or killed anyone in a drunken fit, that is no disgrace to them, because they can say that it was the liquor did it, not they...Thus it happens that a native seldom or never drinks except to get drunk and then to execute revenge upon someone who has displeased him, or to gratify some other brutal passion, as for instance to ravish a girl or a woman."[67]

As soon as French residents of the St. Lawrence Valley had begun traveling into the interior specifically to trade, commencing in 1653, the problem had become much more widespread. From this point onward, the administrators and clergymen in the St. Lawrence settlements had not been able to supervise the distribution of brandy in the distant home regions of the native allies, far to the west and north. This beverage had been a staple item among the stocks of provisions of virtually all expeditions that were bound for the interior. Departing traders, and later the soldiers stationed at interior posts, had carried considerable amounts of brandy in their canoes, along with their other stocks of supplies. From the official viewpoint of the colonial administrators, the intoxicating beverage was to be utilized only for the personal enjoyment of the French; theoretically, it was not to be distributed to the native populations. For example, when the Governor of the colony would issue orders for the dispatching of a special convoy to the upper Great Lakes region in the early spring of 1711, he would observe: "In view of the somewhat [early] season and the coldness of the water, each voyageur shall be permitted to take four *pots* [totalling 6¹/2 quarts] to drink on the journey, on the condition that they do not give any to the natives." Two decades later, however, the official policy would have changed somewhat. The 1730 "Plan of War," concerning the campaign against the Fox nation living west of Green Bay on Lake Michigan, would propose a monthly ration of four *pots* (each one containing 1.64 gallons) of brandy for each soldier and native warrior on the expedition. This official military plan would include overtly distributing this drink to the native fighters. The ration of 6¹/2 quarts of brandy per month would have yielded a little less than ¹/2 pint per day for each man. For their part, voyageurs would often imbibe rather regular treats of spirits while en route on trading trips. Thus, from 1653 onward, large stocks of brandy had been transported into the interior, and no officials had been able to prevent a considerable portion of it from being traded to the native populations there.[68]

Whenever native traders had paddled out to the St. Lawrence to participate in the annual peltries fairs, the administrators and clergymen there had attempted to control the sale of brandy to them. At the request of these leaders in the colony, the King had decreed in March of 1657 that the sale of alcoholic beverages to natives was to be forbidden, under the penalty of corporal punishment. Nine weeks later, before this royal edict had reached New France, the residents of Montreal had decided to prohibit such sales except "through the means agreed upon by the said Community." This wording clearly indicated that certain representatives of the "Community" had been authorized to carry out this commerce. Just a few weeks later, two permanent residents of Montreal (who had obviously not been authorized to carry out such trade) had been each fined fifty livres for illegally trading in alcohol with native customers. In spite of the King's ordinance against it, commerce in brandy had then continued to be carried out throughout the colony. Not only did it help the French maintain control of the commercial relationships with their native allies, it also aided the French in establishing alliances with additional native groups.

This simmering issue had heated up considerably beginning in 1660. On May 5 of that year, Bishop Laval had issued a decree of excommunication against any individual for "giving in payment to the natives, selling, trading, or giving for nothing and through gratitude, either wine or spirits in any manner whatsoever, and under any pretext whatsoever." This was a serious penalty for committing such offenses. Any Catholic who was excommunicated would be excluded from all church and parish life; in addition, when he died, he would not receive absolution of his sins and the last sacraments from a priest, and he would thus face eternal damnation. The following year, the Bishop had lifted his threat of excommunication; but the prohibited commerce in alcohol had resumed almost immediately, so he had reinstated the penalty shortly thereafter. In addition, at about this same time, the King had made "trafficking in spirits with native people" punishable by death, and in the autumn of 1661, the administrators at Quebec had ordered two executions for such offenses. Daniel Vuil had been executed by gunshot on October 7, and a man named La Violette had received the same punishment four days later. However, this royal edict had generated such a furor in the colony that it had been later revoked.

Within months of the two executions, the excessive zeal that had been exhibited by various church and administrative leaders had been suddenly blocked. This had occurred in January of 1662, after Father Jérôme Lalemant had attempted to seek mercy for a woman who had been found guilty of the crime of brandy-peddling. In response, Governor Pierre Dubois Davaugour had declared that, if it was not to be a crime for her, then it should not be for anyone, and he had authorized the sale of liquor to any individuals, whether they be native or French. After this reversal of policy, the pros-and-cons wrangling had continued.

In 1663, after His Majesty had declared New France to be a royal colony and the Sovereign Council had been established at Quebec, certain reforms had been instituted concerning this issue. On September 28, 1663, the Council had forbidden the sale of intoxicating beverages to native people, either directly or indirectly, in both the St. Lawrence Valley and in the distant interior regions. Punishments for infractions would be a fine of 300 livres for the first offense, and flogging or banishment from the colony in case of a second offense.

For his part, Bishop Laval had agreed to lift his declaration of excommunication for this crime. However, frictions between Church and State concerning this issue had continued, as trading in brandy had persisted and certain administrative officials had continued to support it as being vitally necessary, for both commercial and diplomatic purposes.

At the beginning of 1667, a number of residents of Trois-Rivières and the adjacent seigneury of Cap de la Madeleine had petitioned the Sovereign Council to halt the sale of brandy to the resident and visiting natives in their area. By this means, they had hoped to stop the terrible disorders that typically accompanied such commerce. To ascertain the facts concerning this trade, an inquiry had been convened by the Court at Trois-Rivières, which had run from January to May of that year. In the process, considerable light had been shed on just how this clandestine commerce was often carried out, in the homes of the local residents as well as in outdoor settings.

In one instance, a native man had exchanged a pair of mittens and an old shirt for a half-pint of brandy; he had also traded a quilled belt and a necklace for additional supplies of the drink. While preparing to depart on a military expedition, a Frenchman had acquired a pair of moccasins and five pounds of suet in return for four cupfuls of brandy. In another case, a Frenchman had sold a pint of brandy diluted with an equal amount of water to a native customer for two louis and four francs (totaling ten livres). A fourth example involved the exchange of two bottles of brandy for one pelt. During the course of the investigations, many individuals had been named by other French residents as participants in this commerce. Also, in one instance, a native woman who lived in a nearby native village had been persuaded to testify. She had described seeing seven Frenchmen, some of whom were militia members and others were civilians, meeting by the bank of the St. Lawrence at Trois-Rivières with a number of men from her village. In the ensuing exchange, the latter men had acquired various containers of alcoholic beverage, including a small gourd, an earthenware flask, a moose hide bottle holding one pint, and other vessels that each held a half-pint. After the Court had gathered testimony for five months, on June 20 the Sovereign Council had finally declared seven men to be guilty of trafficking in brandy with natives; but it had not convicted these individuals of encouraging drunkenness or causing a public scandal. Thus, the Council had only condemned the specific infraction that the law described, and it had done so only under considerable pressure from the clergy.

Seventeen months later, on November 10, 1668, the Council had completely rescinded the ban, and it had granted to all of the residents of the colony the freedom to sell and trade brandy openly with the native populations in the St. Lawrence settlements. This compromise measure had involved permitting such commerce in the colony, where it might be supervised, but prohibiting it in the distant interior regions, which were virtually impossible to police. During the following spring, when a census had been conducted at Trois-Rivières and in the adjacent seigneuries of Cap de la Madeleine and Champlain, some of the settlers who were present had revealed that other settlers, traders, and soldiers from their area were out trading brandy with native groups who lived some 120 to 150 miles away. Thus, numerous colonists had already stretched the lenient policy beyond its original intent, to involve trading at locales that were moderately distant from the St. Lawrence communities.

In spite of the 1668 decision of the Sovereign Council, the dispute had continued throughout the colony, as the clergymen and certain of the administrators, merchants, and traders had sought to renew the ban on all sales of brandy to native people. Over the years, opposition to them had been voiced by other Governors, Intendants, outfitters, traders, and tavern keepers, as well as the King's Minister Colbert himself, all of whom had supported the open barter of alcohol, and had even encouraged the expansion of its commerce into the interior regions. In 1678, His Majesty had ordered a meeting of twenty prominent citizens to consider this issue, at gatherings to be held in the Governor's residence at Quebec. Governor Frontenac, who had been in favor of unrestricted brandy trading, had chosen for these meetings primarily men who were of like mind with him. Thus, at the October meetings, the majority had voted in favor of free trade in brandy, asserting that it should be considered the same as any other article of merchandise. They had also stated that alcohol played an important role in attracting native people to the St. Lawrence settlements, where they could be exposed to civilized life and the Catholic religion.

The following are excerpts from the summaries of certain of the testimonies which had been presented during these meetings:

"The Sieur [Sidrac Michel] Dugué [Sieur de Boisbriant]: The brandy trade is absolutely necessary to attract the natives to the French colonies and to

prevent them from taking their peltries to foreigners [Dutch and English merchants at Albany and New York]. This can in no way prejudice the conversion of the natives or the increase of religion. On the contrary, if this permission is not granted, the natives, who can find spirits elsewhere, will not come back to the French, but will go to the English and the Dutch, who instead of instructing them in the Gospel will make them fall into heresy or leave them in their state of superstition...

The Sieurs [Jean Baptiste Legardeur, Sieur] De Repentigny and [René Robineau, Sieur] De Bécancour: Trading liquor to the natives is necessary, and must be permitted in order to prevent coureurs de bois and vagabonds from taking it to the places where the natives hunt, under pain of very severe consequences. It is very important for the establishment of commerce and religion that we give them drink; for if we refuse, they will assuredly draw away from us and go to the Dutch and the English, taking their peltries there and depriving the French inhabitants of the benefits that they derive from them. This commerce [in highly watered-down brandy] is the only one which yields some profit, because of the high cost of the other merchandise that we trade with the natives. Furthermore, by going to foreigners, they will remain idolatrous or will be instructed in a false religion...

The Sieur [Louis] Jolliet: Going into the woods with liquor to meet the natives coming to trade with the French must be prohibited under pain of death, and the natives must likewise be forbidden to take it back with them. But the inhabitants should be allowed to give them something to drink in their homes and places of trade, with moderation and without making them drunk, and they [the French suppliers] should be punished in case of disorder. It is not true to say that all natives get drunk. A few, like those who live among us, use liquor properly. Others use it as an object of trade. They buy it in our habitations and take it into the woods to exchange it for beaver pelts...It is true, however, that there are not many of these, not three in two hundred...

The Sieur [Jacques] Le Ber: The liberty to trade in spirits in houses with moderation could be granted, but the French and the natives should be forbidden to take it into the woods or to the native villages...

The Sieur [Jean François Bourdon, Sieur de] Dombourg: ...If this trade is permitted, coureurs de bois will spring up everywhere to engage in it. It is a great sin to give spirits worth twenty sols [one livre] in exchange for a beaver pelt worth six to seven livres."[69]

In response to the sentiments that had been expressed at these gatherings of prominent merchants and outfitters, the King had issued a decree on May 24, 1679. In his edict, he had forbidden anyone from transporting liquor to the distant native villages, but he had permitted it to be sold to native people, in moderate quantities, in the St. Lawrence settlements. The penalties for infractions were to be a fine of 100 livres for the first offense, a fine of 300 livres for the second offense, and corporal punishment for the third offense. (Considering the large profits that could be reaped by violating the law and carrying the brandy trade to the native populations in the distant countries, these were by no means severe punishments.) In addition, the Monarch had ordered the Bishop to withdraw his interdiction against the brandy trade. This royal ruling had been issued against the opposition of both Governor Frontenac and His Majesty's own Minister Colbert, neither of whom favored any restrictions at all on the commerce in brandy. However, during the following years, the King's edict was generally ignored by the various Governors and Intendants of New France. Only by permitting the brandy trade could the French retain their native customers and allies, and compete with their Dutch and English competitors.

This then was the situation in the colony during the latter 1670s and the beginning of the 1680s when Pierre Girard commenced his trading operations, hauling his merchandise to the upriver towns of Trois-Rivières and/or Montreal. He was legally allowed to trade any and all of his goods, including his stocks of brandy, directly with the native people at the annual trade fairs, as well as in a wholesale manner with French outfitters. There was a high demand for his goods, especially for his stocks of brandy and tobacco. Some idea of the amounts of brandy and wine which were utilized in the colony each year during this period may be derived from the import quotas which were placed on such articles. The annual imports of brandy were limited to 4,000 barrels, while the maximum limit on wine was 8,000 barrels.

Shortly after Governor Denonville arrived in New France during the summer of 1685, he made an inspection tour of the communities all along the St. Lawrence. In the process, he noted the immense number of taverns that were in operation; these facilities catered to not only the local French settlers but also to the resident and visiting native populations. In some instances, according to his observations, in seigneuries that had only about twenty homes, fully half of them were taverns. The situation was even worse in the three towns. Trois-Rivières had 25 houses, of which 18 to 20 were grog shops; the houses in Montreal and Quebec represented nearly the same ratio of homes to taverns.[70]

However, rather than buying alcohol by the glass or the bottle, thrifty French colonists instead purchased their supplies of brandy and wine in bulk for the entire year from merchant-outfitters. Typically, when the farmer-settlers bought their entire year's worth of goods in about November (paying their bills with wheat, peas, pork, or firewood from their own farms), their stocks of purchased brandy and wine represented about 8 and 9 percent, respectively, of their total expenditures. In comparison, visiting native traders usually spent about 4 percent of their peltries on supplies of brandy, which they then transported back to their home regions in the interior, to trade some of it and to consume the rest of it themselves.[71]

The very fact that Pierre Girard had requested from the Intendant a reduction in the amounts of import duties that he had been paying on his stocks of tobacco and brandy, plus the fact that he had indeed received from the administrator significant reductions in those import taxes, clearly indicates that our merchant-trader was handling a considerable amount of trade merchandise. It also implies that he had already been doing so for a number of years.

Due to the nearly complete lack of documentation concerning Pierre's fur trade operations, it is not possible to determine just how long after 1682 he continued to conduct his commerce at Trois-Rivières and/or Montreal. By the time an inventory of his possessions would be drawn up in June of 1700 (when he would be about 55 to 59 years old), he would no longer own the sizeable sailing vessel with which he had earlier transported merchandise and peltries up and down the St. Lawrence. In its stead, he would own one birchbark canoe, whose size was not recorded. However, its stated valuation of only 12 livres strongly implies that it was a craft of rather modest dimensions. Thus, in all likelihood, he had halted his river-borne business operations some time before 1700, and had afterward sold his *barque*.[72]

About three weeks before Pierre had commenced his series of petitions to the Intendant in 1682, requesting an elimination or at least a reduction of the duties on his imported brandy and tobacco from the West Indies, a major catastrophe had struck the town of Quebec, which lay some fifteen miles northeast of the Girard farm. On August 4, a ferocious fire had swept through the Basse Ville (Lower Town) area of the community, destroying 55 structures (almost all of the buildings in the area) in less than seven hours. Most of these lost buildings, which had included a number of warehouses, had been made of wood. This destructive conflagration would lead to the rebuilding of the area in more fire-resistant stone rather than in wood, as well as the eventual construction of the church of Notre Dame des Victoires (beginning in 1688 and opening for worship in 1691).[73]

Eight days after the Intendant Duchesneau made his final decision concerning Pierre's import-duties requests, the settler-trader of the Maure seigneury appeared as the godfather of a new baby. This child had been recently born to one of his and Suzanne's neighbors in their Rocky River area of the seigneury, which was its westernmost section. On September 23, 1682, Monsieur Girard imparted his first name to the five-day-old son of Jacques Martineau and Antoinette Dumontier, at the christening ceremony that was held at the nearest church, which was located in Neuville, the adjacent seigneury to the west. The child's other sponsor was Marie Anne Agathe, the wife of Laurent Armand, who were also residents of Maure.[74]

The first day of March in 1683 brought with it a jubilant celebration for several of the families of Maure. On this day, Marguerite Thibault, $14 1/3$ years old (who had grown up on the farm adjacent to the Girards) took as her husband Étienne Gilbert, age 30. The three official witnesses for this ceremony at the Neuville church (which was located about seven miles west of the Girard land) were Pierre Girard, Jean Rasset (Pierre's neighbor on the opposite side, and one of his two land-clearing partners at La Canardière back in 1672), and Louis Doré. Each of these three men had been settled with their families at Maure for a number of years; the new couple would join them in the seigneury, to eventually produce their own brood of thirteen children.[75]

Speaking of offspring, at the time of the above wedding, Suzanne was already about five months pregnant with their seventh Girard child. On July 4, little Françoise was both born and baptized at the Neuville church, with Michel Thibault, their next-door neighbor, and Marie Madeleine Masse, the wife of Jean Mezeray (residents of the Neuville seigneury) as her sponsors.[76]

It was in this year of 1683 that the clergymen of the colony drew up their "Account of the Parish Priests and Missions," recording each of the parishes and their total number of inhabitants. According to this report, it was not only the settlers of the Neuville and Maure seigneuries who attended the church of St. François de Sales at Neuville. "Neuville, to which is joined La Pointe aux Écureuils [the seigneury immediately west of that of Neuville], which is two leagues away, and Vilieu, which is one league away on the other side of the St. Lawrence; there are [a total of] 394 souls."[77]

In the following year, the Girard and de Lavoie families happily made the seven-mile trip westward from Maure to the Neuville church on June 26, 1684. On this day, Suzanne's younger sister Marie Olive de Lavoie (who was about 19 to 21 years old), married Michel Fernet. This unmarried farmer and wooden-shoe maker, who was about age 39 to 43, had settled in the Neuville seigneury some years earlier. After the ceremony, the officiating priest recorded in the church ledger the names of the three official witnesses: Pierre Girard, Pierre Grenon (Suzanne and Marie Olive's brother-in-law, who was married to their other sister, Marie), and Guillaume Lefebvre (a young married colonist of Maure or Neuville). Following the wedding, the new couple settled on the groom's farm at Neuville.[78]

Six months later, on January 16, 1685, Monsieur Girard again found himself standing as an official witness for an ecclesiastical celebration in the Neuville church. In this instance, he served as the godfather for the two-day-old son and second child of René Alarie dit Grandalarie and Louise Thibault, fellow settlers in the Maure seigneury. The baby's other sponsor was Marguerite Thibault, the wife of Étienne Gilbert, who was the aunt of the child and also a resident of Maure.[79]

When five-day-old Élisabeth Marchand was christened in the church at Neuville on May 2, 1685, the priest penned into the ledger the names of her parents, Charles Marchand and Bonne Guerrier (residents of Neuville or Maure) and then her godparents, Valentin Moreau and Élisabeth Marié, after which he signed below the entry. He then added the name of Pierre Girard to the record, since Monsieur Girard had apparently christened the child provisionally, shortly after her birth.[80]

Suzanne and Pierre were pleased to welcome their eighth and final child into the world on June 10, 1686. On the following day, at his christening celebration in the church at Neuville, his godfather was Louis Doré, who had moved with his wife and four children to the Maure seigneury at least six years earlier. Little Pierre Louis' godmother was Madeleine Mezeray, the daughter of Jean Mezeray of Neuville; she would celebrate her twelfth birthday in six weeks. (Nearly 28 years later, a grown-up Pierre Louis would marry as his second wife Marguerite Tardif, and this couple would provide the ancestral linkage between Pierre and Suzanne and the present author.)[81]

Over a span of fifteen years, between 1671 and 1686, Monsieur and Madame Girard had produced eight children, four girls and four boys. Their first one had arrived in August of 1671, a full two years after the couple had exchanged their nuptial vows. Thereafter, the intervals between the babies' births had been 20, 20, 25, 27, 26, 25, and 35 months, respectively. During this period of childbearing, Suzanne had aged from about 20 or 21 to 35 or 36, while Pierre's age had increased from about 26 to 30 up to 41 to 45. The couple had been especially fortunate in the survival rate of their offspring, in an era in which the rates of infant and childhood mortality were staggeringly high. They had only lost one child, Jeanne, their first, and she had lived to be at least ten years old.

It was at about this time in the mid-1680s that the Iroquois nations resumed their hit-and-run attacks against the settlements of the St. Lawrence Valley. Preceding this, both the French colonists and their native allies had enjoyed a period of generally peaceful relations with these nations who lived south and southeast of Lake Ontario. These years of peace had commenced with the treaties of 1666 and 1667, and had continued for nearly two decades.

In the depths of winter in 1687, Suzanne was honored to stand beside the baptismal font in the Neuville church as the godmother of a tiny infant. Little Marie Valin had been born six days earlier, on February 19. However, at her christening on the 25th, the mother, Marie Madeleine Valin, refused to identify the father of the child, and she gave to the girl her own name. Standing beside Suzanne at the ceremony was the godfather, Marc Thouin.[82]

Just five months later, Suzanne de Lavoie was dead. It is highly likely that she had been felled by the terrible epidemic of both smallpox and measles that had been sweeping through the French and native communities that lined the shores of the St. Lawrence, ranging from Tadoussac all the way upstream to the Montreal area. The fateful germs had come to the colony with the vessels from France, which had begun to arrive on June 1. From that point on, the scourge of sickness and death would continue unchecked for nearly a year, extending well into 1688. By the time it would finally abate, over a thousand residents of the colony, both French and native, would be dead.[83]

Suzanne was laid to rest in the cemetery beside the Neuville church on July 24, 1687. After the grief-filled ceremony, the priest recorded in the ledger that the two official witnesses had been François Garnier and Michel Harbour, residents of Neuville. He also indicated that the deceased had been 37 years old at the time of her demise. Six years earlier, back in 1681, Suzanne had reported her age to the census enumerator as 30 years. Thus, she had been born in about 1650 or 1651.[84]

With Suzanne's untimely passing, a very disheartened Pierre (who was about 42 to 46 years old) was left with seven children, who ranged in age from 14 years down to just 15 months. For some reason, he eventually moved with his family about eighteen miles toward the northeast, to the seigneury of Notre Dame des Anges (which was also called Charlesbourg). This was the area flanking the St. Lawrence in which he and Suzanne had lived during the early years of their marriage, where they had produced their first three children before moving westward to their farmland at Maure.

Over time, Pierre realized that he needed to find a new life partner, a woman who would provide companionship and support as well as assist him in running the household and raising his children. To fulfill these multiple roles, he eventually found Élisabeth Lequin, a widow whose age was close to his own and who was living in the Neuville seigneury. About 40 years old, she had four living children; she had been a widow since early December of 1687, about four months less than Pierre had been a widower.

In fact, Élisabeth had already endured numerous challenges and hardships in her life, including bearing eight children within fourteen years, watching four of those children die, and outliving not one but two husbands. She had been born in about 1648 to Pierre Lequin and Catherine Boldieu, in the St. Germain l'Auxerrois parish of Paris. In about 1668, she had immigrated to New France as a *fille du Roi* (daughter of the King), with the hope of finding a suitable mate and starting a new life. On July 5 of that year, Élisabeth had married at Quebec the newly-retired Carignan-Salières soldier Jean Gaigneur dit Laframboise, who had been 25 years old. Settling in Quebec, the couple had produced two children, with the first one arriving one year and eight days after their wedding day. However, this first child had died in July of 1670, one week before her first birthday; the second one, a boy, had passed away in December of that same year, at the age of eleven days. In between these two deaths, Élisabeth's husband had also perished, on September 29, at the untimely age of 27 years.

Surprisingly, the burial records of the Quebec church had not reflected an unusually high number of deaths during this particular period. The interments in the cemetery there during the last three months of 1669, the twelve months of 1670, and the first five months of 1671 had consisted of the following:

1669: 3 in October, 5 in November, and 10 in December

1670: 14 in January, 2 in February, 2 in March, 2 in April, 1 in May, 3 in June, 4 in July (including Élisabeth's first child), 1 in August, 2 in September (including her husband), 5 in October, 5 in November, and 5 in December (including her second child)

1671: 2 in January, 6 in February, 2 in March, 0 in April, and 0 in May

The two months during this twenty-month interval which had experienced the greatest number of deaths and burials had been December of 1669 and January of 1670, with 10 and 14 interments, respectively. The fact that Élisabeth Lequin's personal losses had fit into the usual ebb and flow of life and death in the colony had probably not brought any consolation to the bereaved widow.

In late December of 1670, three months after her husband had died and one week after the death of her second child, Élisabeth had acceded to the courting efforts of the immigrant upholsterer Étienne Léveillé, who had been about 28 or 29 years old. The couple had drawn up a marriage contract at Quebec on December 27, and they had been married in the church there six weeks later, on February 8, 1671. Settling on his pioneer farm in the Neuville seigneury, some 18 to 20 miles southwest of Quebec, they had borne six children there in the decade between September of 1672 and July of 1682. Of these offspring, the eldest had died in September of 1677, nine days before his fifth birthday, while the youngest had passed away on October 1, 1687, nearly three months after having celebrated his fifth birthday. Three months after this second boy's death, Élisabeth's second husband had also died; he had been laid to rest in the Neuville cemetery on December 6, 1687. It is highly likely that the deaths of both the boy and his father during the latter months of this year had been caused by the horrific double epidemic of measles and smallpox which was raging through the St. Lawrence population at this time. This wave of disease had also most likely killed Pierre Girard's wife Suzanne de Lavoie, in the adjacent seigneury of Maure, a few miles to the east.

By the spring of 1688, the widower Pierre Girard and the widow Élisabeth Lequin had decided to join forces and become a married couple, blending their two families together. On April 16, they stood before the Quebec notary Gilles Rageot to draw up their marriage contract. In this document, the prospective groom was identified as "habitant of the Coast of Notre Dame des Anges," while his fiancée was identified as "from Neuville, widow of Étienne Léveillé."[85] Ten days later, the couple exchanged their wedding vows in the Church of St. François de Sales at Neuville. In the priest's records, the groom was described as "Pierre Girard, of Maure, age 43, widow of Suzanne Lavoie;" his new bride was described as "Élisabeth Dequin (sic), age 40, of this parish [of Neuville], widow of Étienne Léveillé." The three official witnesses on this day (in which the mood was probably a mixture of ambivalence and cautious optimism) included Jean Hardy, his sixteen-year-old son Pierre Hardy, and Pierre Piché, all of whom were residents of the Neuville seigneury. (In exact parallel with her reported age of 40 at this time, Élisabeth's age would be documented four years later in the records of the Hôtel Dieu hospital in Quebec as 44, thus making her birth year about 1648. Considering these two ages in two different documents which mesh together perfectly, her reported age of 48 back in the 1681 census must certainly represent an error, either in the original recording or in some later transcription; this latter record implies a birth year of 1633, a full fifteen years earlier than the birth year derived from the other two documents.)[86]

At the time of their wedded union, Élisabeth brought four Léveillé children to the blended family unit: Pierre ($13^3/4$ years old), Élisabeth ($11^2/3$), Jean ($9^1/2$), and Étienne ($7^2/3$). Pierre's seven Girard children included François (age 15), Marie Madeleine ($13^1/3$), Jean Pierre ($10^3/4$), Jean Baptiste (9), Jeanne (two months short of 7), Françoise ($4^3/4$), and Pierre Louis (ten weeks short of 2). Neither of the newly married parents could have imagined at this point that, a dozen years into the future, one of her Léveillé sons would marry one of his Girard daughters.[87]

As they worked to create a combined family, the two adults and their eleven children settled together on the Girard farm, in the westernmost section of the Maure seigneury that was called Rivière des Roches or Rocky River. However, during the following years, they would also continue to maintain and work the Léveillé property and its buildings, which were located in the adjacent Neuville seigneury, immediately to the west. In the process, they would clear more forest cover from the Léveillé land, and convert this additional acreage into agricultural property. Shortly before his remarriage, Pierre had hired two local Maure estimators to draw up a generalized valuation of the Girard property, its buildings, and the moveable possessions which had belonged to the Girard family. These men had declared a value of 1,000 livres for the land and its structures, and a value of 500 livres for the Girard belongings. Likewise, in January of 1689, he engaged three local estimators from Neuville to determine the generalized value of the Léveillé holdings there. These men assessed the value of the property and its buildings at 900 livres, and the value of the Léveillé belongings at 190 livres. In neither case were any structures, livestock, harvested crops, or individual possessions specifically documented. However, a dozen years into the future, these generalized figures would assist the members of the family in their division and distribution of the combined assets of the blended family.[88]

Nineteen months after their wedding, Pierre served as one of the three official witnesses at the burial in the Neuville cemetery of one of the long time settler-farmers from Neuville or Maure. On November 28, 1689, he helped lay to rest Charles Marchand, about 45 years old, who had left behind a wife and five children. The other two witnesses on this occasion were Jacques Marié (from Maure) and François Garnier (from Neuville).[89]

It was in the autumn of 1690 that European-style warfare arrived within hearing distance of the Girard-Léveillé family and their neighbors living southwest of Quebec, in a conflict that involved virtually all of the militiamen of the region. At this time, Pierre was 45 to 49 years old, his eldest son François had turned 17 in April, and his eldest stepson Pierre Léveillé had turned 16 in July. Thus, each of them fell within the 16-to-60 age bracket of militia service which was obligatory for all able-bodied men of the colony.

A decade later, the inventory of the family's possessions would indicate that there were two guns in the household. Back in 1682, Joseph Antoine Lefebvre, Sieur de Labarre and Jacques De Meulles, the new Governor and Intendant of the colony, respectively, had issued a joint edict which would enable the settlers of New France to better defend themselves. Each of the male residents who was fit to bear arms was to have a gun or a firearm in his home. During the coming winter, each habitant who was capable of bearing arms but did not own a gun was to acquire one, under the penalty of a fine during the following spring. To facilitate these purchases, the two administrators ordered that the Quebec merchant Charles Aubert de La Chesnaye and the Montreal merchant Jacques Le Ber were to take good and marketable wheat, corn, peas, and salted pork meat as payment for these weapons. These farm products were to be valued at the following rates: wheat was to be valued at 50 sols (2.5 livres) per bushel, the other two field crops were to be rated in proportion, and salted pork was to be valued at the customary price.[90]

Since a state of war had broken out between France and England in 1690, a fleet of some 32 ships carrying more than 2,000 Massachusetts militia fighters sailed from Boston in August of this year, under the command of William Phips. Intending to invade and capture New France, these vessels traveled up the St. Lawrence River, finally arriving in the Quebec area on October 16. Eight of the ships, including the largest ones, anchored in front of the town itself, while other smaller vessels anchored to the east, off the nearby community of La Canardière and along the Beaupré coast. To bolster his defenses, Governor Frontenac gathered nearly 3,000 fighting men, most of whom were militiamen, in the area of Quebec; these defending forces included a large party of militia fighters and regular troops who had marched overland from Montreal in four days. The Governor confidently answered Phips' demand for surrender with the statement that he had no reply "save from the mouths of my cannon and from my musketry." On the 18th, two days after their arrival, English forces totaling about 1,200 men landed on the Beauport shore east of the St. Charles River, intending to cross the St. Charles and attack Quebec from the side. However, they were strongly opposed by militia fighters from Beauport and the Côte de Beaupré plus numbers of native allies, and these English forces were also ravaged by smallpox. Being unable to cross the small river and having suffered heavy losses, the invaders were finally evacuated three days later, having made little impact. In the meantime, the four large vessels in the English fleet had bombarded the town for two days, until they had used up most of their ammunition and had sustained considerable damage themselves, from the cannons of the French. With the prospect of approaching frigid weather trapping their fleet in ice, it was clear to Phips and his officers that their campaign had totally failed, and that they would be forced to abandon it. Three days later, after an exchange of prisoners had been carried out, the English fleet departed; en route downriver, some of the ships were wrecked on shoals and islands in the lower St. Lawrence. Thus, before reaching New England, hundreds of men among the invaders had lost their lives, some to sickness and others to shipwreck. In grateful thanksgiving for their own deliverance, the French changed the name of the church that was under construction in the Lower Town from L'Enfant Jésus to Notre Dame de la Victoire. (Twenty-one years later, in 1711, after the massive British invasion fleet of Hovenden Walker would be forced to turn back after storms and thick fogs had caused a number of devastating shipwrecks in the lower St. Lawrence, the name of the edifice would again be altered. This time, the word Victory would be changed to the plural form, becoming Notre Dame des Victoires.)[91]

Within weeks of the departure of the enemy fleet from the Quebec area, Pierre's brother-in-law Jean de Lavoie (Suzanne's only brother) was married in the Neuville church. Some years earlier, he had joined the army and had served in the garrison stationed at Quebec, during at least 1684 and 1685. Now retired from the military life, he married Barbe L'Homme on November 28, 1690, after which the new couple settled in the Maure seigneury. At this point, all of Suzanne's family members resided at either Maure or Neuville. Her father with his second family and her newly-married brother lived at Maure, while her sister Marie (married to Pierre Grenon) and her sister Marie Olive (married to Michel Frenet) resided at Neuville.[92]

In the middle of the summer of 1691, the Girard-Léveillé household was plunged into deep melancholy, upon the death of Jean Baptiste Girard. This boy had lived his entire twelve years and three months on the family farm at Maure, except for the few months after his mother's death back in 1687, when his father had relocated the family for a time to Notre Dame des Anges seigneury, northeast of Quebec. This was the first child whom Pierre had lost since little Jeanne had passed away, some time after the census of 1681, when she had been about ten years old. At the lad's funeral in the Neuville church on July 8, 1691, the official witnesses were his older brother François, at age 18 the oldest child of the family, and Michel Harbour.[93]

Life in New France entailed a continuous cycle of death followed by a renewal of hope and movement forward. Four months later, the members of the family strove to elevate their spirits, in order to properly celebrate the first marriage of a Girard child. On November 6, while standing in front of the Quebec notary, Marie Madeleine (who would turn 17 in a month) signed a marriage contract with Daniel Jean Denevers dit Brantigny from Sillery near Quebec, who would turn 35 in December. Two weeks later, on the 19th, they were wed in the Neuville church. On the latter occasion, the six official witnesses were the bride's brother Jean Pierre Girard, her uncles Pierre Grenon and Michel Frenet, her next-door-neighbor Jean Rasset, the groom's brother Guillaume Denevers, and their Neuville friend Ignace Liénard.[94]

In the following spring of 1692, Élisabeth, the matriarch of the blended family, fell seriously ill, and she required hospitalization at Quebec, some fifteen miles from the farm. On the roster of patients which was drawn up on May 22 at the Hôtel Dieu hospital, individual number 12 was thus described: "Élisabeth Quin, age 44, from St. Germain l'Auxerrois parish, Paris, wife of Gerar, nine days in hospital."[95]

Eight months later, Pierre was honored to serve as the godfather for the newest baby of their next-door neighbors, Jean Rasset and Jeanne Chapeau. On January 26, 1693, he stood at the baptismal font of the Neuville church to sponsor two-day-old Marie Louise, along with his co-sponsor Louise Desgranges, the wife of Louis Delisle, who lived in the Neuville seigneury.[96]

Commencing in December of 1693, records began to document ecclesiastical ceremonies that were held in the Maure seigneury itself. These were celebrations of baptisms and marriages which were sometimes conducted by visiting priests at the newly-formed parish of St. Augustin, whose first chapel was built in 1694.[97] However, for many years thereafter, numerous of the residents of the seigneury still continued to travel west to the Neuville church for important occasions.

One such event at the latter church took place on November 22, 1694, when Élisabeth's only daughter (and Pierre's only stepdaughter) Élisabeth Léveillé married Adrien Piché from Neuville. At this time, the bride was 18 years old, while the groom was age 26. For this hopeful and encouraging ceremony, the two official witnesses were Pierre Léveillé, brother of the bride, and Nicolas Langlois. After the wedding, the couple would settle in Les Écureuils, the seigneury immediately west of Neuville, where they would eventually produce four children.[98]

On July 15, 1695, Élisabeth again traveled to the Neuville church, this time to appear as the godmother and grant her name to the one-day-old daughter of Marie Madeleine Berthelot and her husband, the retired soldier and surgeon François Circé, the Sieur de Saint Michel. This couple had relocated to the Neuville seigneury about three years earlier. For this christening, the godfather was Simon Lefebvre dit Angers, also a resident of Neuville.[99]

Seventeen months later, Pierre was chosen to stand as the sponsor of the newborn daughter and tenth child of Charles Gingras and Françoise Amiot, neighbors of theirs in the Rocky River section of the Maure seigneury. At the christening ceremony, which was conducted in the local St. Augustin parish on December 18, 1696 (the same day as the baby's birth), Pierre's fellow sponsor was Élisabeth Marié.[100]

By the summer of 1697, Pierre's youngest stepson, Étienne Léveillé, was about to turn age 17, and he wished to learn a trade. Thus, Pierre arranged a four-year apprenticeship for him with Antoine Girard, a maker of edged tools who lived and worked in the Lower Town area of Quebec. This craftsman, not a relative of Pierre, was 33 years old. He and his wife had been married for nearly a decade, but the only child whom they had thus far produced had died three years earlier, at the age of 21 months. They were expecting their next baby in about five months. On June 24, Pierre, Étienne, and the craftsman visited one of the Quebec notaries, to officially register the young man's contract of apprenticeship.

"Before [Nicolas Métru,] the undersigned royal notary of the Provost Court of Quebec, residing there, and the witnesses named at the end was present Pierre Girard, habitant of the seigneury of Maure, who had acknowledged and declared that he has bound [his stepson] Étienne Léveillé, son of the deceased Étienne Léveillé and of Élisabeth Lequin, his father and mother, the said Girard having married the said Lequin in his second marriage, to Antoine Girard, edged-tool maker living in this town [of Quebec]. The said Étienne Léveillé, present and assenting, is around sixteen [ten weeks short of 17] years old. He is to be engaged for the time and space of four years, entire and consecutive, to commence on the seventeenth of the month [of August] and to end on the same day in the year 1701, to serve as a shop boy and to labor during the entire time in the occupation of edged-tool maker, that of the said Antoine Girard, and to be obliged to do as much as he will be able. The said Étienne Léveillé will be bound to serve and obey the said Antoine Girard in everything that will be commanded of him that is honest and legal during this time. The said Antoine Girard will lodge, feed, and maintain the said Léveillé and have his laundry washed during the said time according to his usual condition, providing to the said Léveillé during the said time all of the clothing that will serve him, either new or used. The said Pierre Girard has promised that, in case the said Léveillé...leaves the service of the said Antoine Girard, he will be obligated, as much as he will be able, to search for him and

make him return to his assignment. The said Antoine Girard has promised to treat him humanely during the entire said time. Thus have they promised and obligated themselves. [This agreement] made and drawn up at the said Quebec in the office of the said notary in the afternoon of June 24, 1697, in the presence of the witnesses, who reside at the said Quebec, who have signed with the said notary and the said Pierre Girard. The said Léveillé and Antoine Girard have declared that they do not know how to write or sign, having been questioned.

Signed, Pierre Girat, J. Lajus, and Métru."[101]

Oddly, although Pierre signed this document in his usual manner, with laboriously printed individual letters, he did not utilize his customary spelling of PiERRE GiRART; instead, he wrote PiERRE GiRAT.

In the spring of 1698, Pierre was honored to appear as one of the official witnesses at the wedding of his niece Marie Grenon, who was the twenty-year-old daughter of Suzanne's sister Marie de Lavoie and her husband Pierre Grenon. At the celebration in the Neuville church on April 14, she took as her husband André Bergeron, age 24, from the St. Nicolas parish. Besides her uncle Pierre Girard, the other two recorded witnesses were Jean Demers, the maternal grandfather of the groom, and Jacques Brin dit La Pensée.[102]

In the autumn of the same year, Pierre undertook a much sadder task when he served as one of the witnesses at the funeral in Neuville of one of his Maure neighbors, Jeanne Dufossé, who was about 59 or 60 years old. She had lost her husband Louis Doré two years earlier, when he had been about age 57 to 60. This couple had relocated with their children from Quebec to the Maure seigneury some time before 1680. Besides Monsieur Girard, the other recorded witness at the burial ceremony on November 7 was Jean Juneau, a fellow resident of Maure.[103]

Death struck much closer to home on two occasions during 1699. First, in the spring, the family's next-door-neighbor Jeanne Soyer died at the age of about 61 or 62. She and Michel Thibault had moved with their children from Quebec to the Rocky River area by at least 1672. At this point, their two older children were already married and established (their younger two would marry in 1699 and 1703). At Jeanne's burial, besides Pierre, the other two official witnesses were Jean Juneau and Antoine Marié; all three of these men were settlers of Maure.[104]

Tragedy struck the Girard-Léveillé family in the autumn of 1699, when Élisabeth's youngest son (and Pierre's youngest stepson) Étienne Léveillé passed away in the Hôtel Dieu hospital in Quebec on September 7. He had celebrated his 19th birthday just nine days earlier. This was the young man for whom Pierre had arranged an apprenticeship in July of 1697; he had only been able to complete two years of the four-year training program before he had perished.[105]

Two marriage ceremonies at the Neuville church during November of this year helped to buoy the spirits of the family members somewhat. First came the wedding on the 9th of Pierre's niece Marguerite Grenon (18 years old) and Jean Bergeron (age 23); nineteen months earlier, the bride's older sister Marie had married the groom's older brother André. On this occasion, the two recorded witnesses were Pierre Girard, uncle of the bride, and Michel Demers, uncle of the groom.[106]

Two weeks later, on the 24th, Pierre again stood as an official witness at a wedding that was held in the same edifice. This time, the nuptial celebration involved Louis Doré, at age 27 the eldest son of Pierre's deceased Maure neighbors Louis Doré and Jeanne Dufossé, who had passed away in 1696 and 1698, respectively. The bride was Catherine Coquin, 21 years old, the daughter of the Neuville residents Pierre Coquin and Catherine Badin. In addition to Pierre Girard, the other recorded witnesses were Michel and Étienne Doré, brothers of the groom, and Antoine Marié, brother-in-law of the bride.[107]

Having rung in the brand new century on *Ignolée* (New Year's Eve), Pierre and Élisabeth were patiently making their way through the long winter months of 1700 on the farm. In the process, they were looking forward to their twelfth wedding anniversary, which they would celebrate in late April. However, Madame Girard did not live to see that happy day. Pierre was obliged to lay to rest the mortal remains of his second wife in the cemetery at Neuville on February 12. On this bleak day, he was flanked by the witnesses Pierre Coquin and Jean Jeantin.[108]

At the time of her demise, Élisabeth had been about 51 or 52 years old, and during those years, she had endured a great many hardships. Over the course of her adult life, she had buried two husbands as well as five of her eight children. However, one of her surviving offspring, Élisabeth, had married Adrien Piché in 1694, and the couple had produced three grandchildren while living to the west in the seigneury of Les Écureuils. Arriving in December of 1695, December of 1697, and November of 1699, these three babies had each been baptized at the Neuville church within one to six days of their respective births. It is hoped that these youngsters had brought much joy to the matriarch during her final years.[109]

It was especially unfortunate that Élisabeth did not live long enough to witness the marriage of her eldest son, Pierre Léveillé. He and his fiancée drew up their marriage contract with a Quebec notary on April 14, 1700, just eight weeks after Élisabeth's funeral. Perhaps she would have smiled knowingly on that occasion, when her son contracted to marry Jeanne Girard, her second-youngest stepdaughter, whom she had helped to grow to womanhood for nearly twelve years. Back in April of 1688, when the Girard and Léveillé children had been blended into a single large family by the marriage of Pierre and Élisabeth, Jeanne Girard had been $6^{10}/12$ years old, while Pierre Léveillé had been $13^3/4$ years old. Now, in April of 1700, after a dozen years of being stepsiblings, she was seven weeks away from turning age 19 and he was $25^3/4$. The tale of the various stages of their relationship over those twelve years, advancing from newly-met stepsiblings to eventual spouses, would have made fascinating reading if its details had been recorded for posterity.

Five days after signing their marriage agreement, on April 19, the couple recited their vows at the St. Augustin church at Maure. After the ceremony, the officiating priest recorded the two official witnesses: Jean Rasset (the next-door neighbor beside the Girard farm at Maure) and Jean Mezeray (a family friend at Neuville).[110]

Since all of these family members and friends had gathered at the Maure church for these clan festivities, they also joined in the nuptial celebrations of another couple there as well. On this same day, the widower Michel Boucher (who was two weeks away from his 39th birthday) took as his second wife Geneviève Amiot dite Neuville (who was $16^3/4$ years old). For this second ceremony, the witnesses were Pierre Girard, Jean Mezeray, and Michel Guyon.[111]

Two months later, on June 21, the Provost Court of Quebec declared that Pierre Girard was to be the legal guardian of his three unmarried and minority-age children: Jean Pierre (age $23^1/2$), Françoise (13 days short of turning 17), and Pierre Louis (14). This declaration did not include his unmarried son François, since he was 27 years old, thus having reached his majority; his daughter Marie Madeleine, age $25^1/2$, who had been married to Daniel Denevers since 1691; or his daughter Jeanne, age 19, who had been wed to Pierre Léveillé for two months. At the same time, the Court determined that Adrien Piché, the husband since 1694 of Pierre's stepdaughter Élisabeth Léveillé (23³/4 years old), would be the legal guardian of Pierre's stepson Jean Léveillé, who was age 21²/3. The Court also ruled that Pierre's eldest stepson, Pierre Léveillé (who was five weeks short of turning age 26), would be the supplemental guardian of the three minority-age Girard children, who were his stepsiblings, and of Jean Léveillé, his younger brother. These decisions by the Provost Court, reached some four months after the death of Élisabeth Lequin, were some of the initial steps involved in the settlement of the estate of the Girard-Léveillé clan.

On the following day, June 22, 1700, Pierre, along with his Girard children, Adrien Piché, and Pierre Léveillé, traveled the fifteen miles from Maure to Quebec. Their goal was to have the notary François Genaple make an official copy and register the inventory which had been recently drawn up of the belongings at the Girard farm. This enumeration had been recently conducted by the long time priest at the Neuville church, Fr. Jean Basset, and three local appraisers. Also to be examined and registered by the notary were all of the documents that Pierre had amassed over the years, concerning the legal and financial affairs of himself and his two deceased wives. In advance of this meeting, the notary had located and assembled various other documents from the records of certain Quebec notaries and merchants, especially those which pertained to the old debts of Élisabeth's former husband Étienne Léveillé. In some instances, these records were simply borrowed temporarily from the files of the notaries and merchants, while in other cases they were copied.[112]

"In the year 1700, on the twenty-second of June at five o'clock in the evening, before François Genaple, notary and registrar of the King in the town and Provost Court of Quebec in Canada, undersigned with the witnesses named at the end, appeared Pierre Girard, habitant of the coast and seigneury of Maure, widower from the most recent marriage of the deceased Élisabeth Lequin, who had previously been the widow of the deceased Étienne Léveillé, her former husband, who while living was an habitant of the seigneury of Dombourg, presently called Neuville. The said Girard appeared both in his name and as the chosen guardian, according to a ruling yesterday of a session of the Provost Court of this town, of Jean Pierre Girard, twenty-three years old, Françoise [Girard], sixteen years old [twelve days short of seventeen], and Louis Pierre [Pierre Louis Girard], fourteen years old, all minors, children of him and of Suzanne de Lavoie, his first wife from a former marriage. Also appeared Pierre Léveillé [five weeks short of age 26,

*who had wed Pierre's daughter Jeanne Girard, age 19, two months earlier],
the chosen supplemental guardian of the said minors; Adrien Piché, both as
the husband of Élisabeth Léveillé [age 23³/4] and as the chosen guardian of
the minor Jean Léveillé, twenty-two [actually 21²/3] years old; and again
the said Pierre Léveillé, both in his name and as the chosen supplemental
guardian, according to the same Court ruling, of the said Jean Léveillé,
his full brother. These Pierre, Jean, and Élisabeth Léveillé are children of
the said Étienne Léveillé and the said Lequin, their father and mother, of
whom they are each heirs of one-third [of the Léveillé share of the estate].
The said parties have jointly declared with one accord of consent to pay the
expenses, and [earlier] had the kindness to have an inventory drawn up in
their presence, with estimations and appraisals by habitants of these places,
of the possessions remaining after the death of the said widow Lequin which
belonged to the estate of the said [two] marriages, continuing up to the day
of estimation and appraisal. Thus have they agreed, assented, and consented
among themselves. For the description, estimation, and appraisal of the
entire contents as is required for the one part and the other part [Pierre
Girard plus the Girard and Léveillé heirs], a report and description has just
now been drawn up by me, the said notary, in genuine form conforming
to a memorial which was [earlier] drawn up by private writing of the said
estimators [the priest at Neuville, relatively near to the Girard farm, and
three local men of that area], to serve and be held instead of an inventory
[conducted by me] of the said possessions, to be afterward utilized for the
division which they will together carry out of the possessions of the said
estate. This has been undertaken by the said notary, in the presence of the
said parties and witnesses, for the description of the said possessions and
all of the associated titles and papers, which have been placed in our hands
by the said Girard, after he had sworn that the contents thereof is all that
is related and that he has not held back or diverted anything. This has been
done at the joint request of all of the said parties. The following is in the same
order which conforms to the said [earlier] privately written appraisal, which
is as follows.*

*First, the lot of the first estate of the said Pierre Girard and the said deceased
de Lavoie, his first wife, situated on the Coast of Maure............ 1,400 livres
One raised framework for a granary, completely uncovered................ 160 l.
One stable .... 40 l.
All of the said buildings, together adding up to the sum of 630 livres, were
built during the said most recent estate [of Pierre and Élisabeth Lequin], as
has been declared by the said parties*

Then followed the moveable possessions

A bunch of thick planks, estimated at .... *12 l.*

One pair of working oxen, valued at .... *150 l.*

One young ox .... *40 l.*

Two very small oxen .... *60 l.*

Five cows at 30 livres apiece .... *150 l.*

Four pigs, together .... *48 l.*

Twenty bushels of good-quality wheat, at six livres per bushel .... *120 l.*

Thirteen bushels of poor-quality wheat, at four livres per bushel .... *52 l.*

Four bushels of peas, at five livres per bushel .... *20 l.*

Seventy pounds of sidepork, at six sols per pound .... *21 l.*

One wretched moldboard of a plow .... *8 l.*

One wretched cutting blade [plowshare] of a plow .... *2 l. 10 s.*

Two wheeled pulling units of plows .... *8 l.*

All of the implements [furnishings and equipment] of the said house, estimated at .... *30 l.*

Three wretched chests .... *5 l. 10 s.*

Three wretched kettles and one small kettle, with one low-walled saucepan and a wretched grill [or gridiron], together estimated at .... *12 l.*

One iron pot, estimated at .... *5 l.*

One frying pan .... *1 l. 10 s.*

The dishes, estimated at .... *10 l.*

One iron oil lamp, estimated at .... *15 s.*

One keg .... *1 l.*

One sieve for sieving flour, estimated at .... *10 s.*

One bread kneading and raising box .... *2 l.*

Two flatirons for pressing linens, estimated at .... *7 l.*

Two yards of skimpy fabric, estimated at .... *5 l.*

Two guns, together .... *25 l.*

One birchbark canoe .... *12 l.*

[Total of the moveable items] .... *808 l. 15 s. [actually, 832 l. 10s.]*
All of the said moveable possessions, together adding up to eight hundred eight livres fifteen sols, have remained with the said Girard since the said [earlier] description and appraisal of them was conducted by the said estimators, with the consent of all of the above-named individuals. The said Girard has acknowledged and promises to be held accountable to the said parties, that each of these possessions will be found upon their return. The said [earlier] privately written document was certified by Monsieur [Jean] Basset, priest of the place [St. François de Sales church at nearby Neuville], and was signed by him and by Jean Mezeray, Claude Carpentier, and Jean

Juneau, the appraisers, the third one of whom declared that he did not know how to sign. This document [written with a decidedly phonetic style of spelling] is attached to the present inventory [but it has not been included in the present translation].

The following are the owed debts which are to be paid by the most recent estate
To Sieur [Lucien] Bouteville, [Quebec] merchant, for merchandise furnished by him according to his note from last October 20 [1699] ....260 l. 18 s.
To Monsieur [Jean] Basset, priest, 13 livres and to Monsieur Têtu 9 livres 12 sols, for the feeding of the said Lequin .... 22 l. 12 s.
To Jean Baptiste Thibault, for nineteen days of work at 30 sols per day 28 l.
To one named [Pierre Louis] Doré, for fifteen days [of work] at 30 sols per day..22 l. 15 s.
To Sieur [François] Grégoire, for linen fabric furnished by him .... 8 l. 8 s.
The said owed debts together add up to 342 livres 13 sols. These do not include the cost of the expenses which all of the said parties have been obliged to incur during their stay in this town [of Quebec]. The said Girard is in agreement with them that he will be charged with paying these costs, as well as the expenses of the present inventory, the examination [of the documents] which was carried out, the papers which it was necessary to obtain, and the expense of collecting several contracts to bring them here. In addition, he will pay for the [official] division which will be conducted of the possessions of the estate after the drawing up of the said present inventory. The total of these costs and expenses which the said Girard will be obliged to cover will be figured into the act of their said division. It is not yet possible to known the said amount [of these expenses].

Here follows the declaration of the owed debts of the estate of the said deceased Léveillé and the said Lequin, which were paid off by the said Pierre Girard during his subsequent marriage with the said Lequin, at the expense of their estate, which have been accounted for with proofs and paid receipts. These are to be figured in by the heirs of the said Léveillé and the said Lequin.
Paid to Nicolas Juchereau, Sieur de Saint Denis, the sum of 196 livres which was owed from a transaction of the said Léveillé on the date of March 20, 1680, [in a contract] passed before the notary Master [Michel] Fillion, in response to a court order which was rendered against the said Girard on February 28, 1689 and again on April 18, 1690 .... 196 l.
Paid to Claude Bourget, as the husband of Marie Couture, widow of François Vessier, according to a court order which was rendered against the said

deceased Léveillé on September 5, 1680 and was later ordered to be fulfilled by the said Girard according to another court order of June 8, 1694, the sum of 39 livres 4 sols plus three livres in court costs ....42 l. 4 s.

Paid to Monsieur [Claude Bermen, Sieur] de La Martinière according to a bond of the said deceased Léveillé passed before the said notary [Michel] Fillion on March 8, 1680 and the court order [against Girard] rendered on June 24, 1689, at the bottom of which is a receipt for the sum of 45 livres.. 45 l.

Paid in expenses which were incurred on this subject......................5 l. 13 s.

Paid to Pierre Normand [dit] La Brière, according to a court order of June 25, 1678 [against Léveillé] which the said Girard was ordered to fulfill by another court order of June 18, 1694, followed by the payoff which was finally made of both the principal and the court costs ....39 l.

Paid to Guillaume Guillot, according to a court order [against Girard] of June 18, 1694, as the remainder on a debt owed by the deceased Léveillé... 20 l.

Paid to Monsieur [Fr. Jean] Basset for the interment of the said deceased Léveillé [on December 6, 1687] and one of his sons [Jean Baptiste, on October 1, 1687], for burial services, Masses, and overdue interests on these charges ....31 l. 10 s.

Paid to Monsieur [François Madeleine Fortuné Ruette, Sieur] d'Auteuil for the payoff of a debt of the said Léveillé, according to his receipt of April 19, 1695 for six bushels of wheat at three livres per bushel..........................18 l.

The following are the papers, titles, and instructions
The marriage contract between the said Pierre Girard and the said deceased [Suzanne] de Lavoie, his first wife, indicating, among other stipulations, that they will own their possessions in common according to the Customary Laws of Paris, passed before the deceased notary Master Gilles Rageot on August 11, 1669. The said contract has been paraphrased by us, the said notary, and inventoried here as the first item with the mark of the letter A.

A contract passed before the said Sieur [Gilles] Rageot on July 28, 1669 of a lot granted to the said Pierre Girard on the Coast and seigneury of Maure, containing three arpents [575 English feet] of frontage [on the St. Lawrence River] and thirty arpents [1^1/10 mile] of depth, along with the rights of hunting and fishing. The said lot was at that time entirely covered with standing timber. Granted only fifteen days before the [August 12, 1669] first marriage of the said Girard; for this reason, it belongs to the estate between him and the said de Lavoie, his first wife. This contract has been paraphrased by us and inventoried as the second item with the mark B.

Another marriage contract, passed between the said Girard and the said deceased Élisabeth Lequin before the said Sieur [Gilles] Rageot on April 16, 1688, containing certain stipulations and conditions, indicating, among other conditions, that they will also own in common their possessions, moveable belongings, and acquired real estate according to the Customary Laws of Paris, and that they will not be held accountable for the debts of either one of them which had originated previously. This contract has been paraphrased by us, the said notary, and inventoried here as the third item with the mark and letter C.

A privately written copy made in the form of an inventory which was deposited in the office of the deceased Master Gilles Rageot on the said day of August 16, 1688 [along with the second marriage contract], containing only two articles. The first, [the description of] the said lot of the said Girard, situated on the said Coast of Maure, [its value] estimated at the sum of one thousand livres by Michel Thibault and Charles Gingras, habitants of the place, who were chosen for this purpose. The second of these articles consists of the estimation which was briefly made [in 1688] of all of the animals and implements belonging to the said Girard and the said deceased de Lavoie, [valued at] the sum of five hundred livres. The said copy has been derived from the certified copy of Master Gilles Rageot on the date of yesterday, June 21, 1700. It has been paraphrased by us, the notary, and inventoried here as the fourth piece with the mark D.

The official document of the election of the guardians and supplemental guardians of the said minors mentioned and named in the heading of the present inventory on the date of yesterday, the 21st of the month of June [1700]. It has been paraphrased by us, the said notary, and inventoried as the fifth item with the mark and letter E.

One sheaf containing twenty items of legal proceedings, made at the request of the Sieur [Nicolas] Juchereau, Sieur de Saint Denis, which were taken out against the said deceased Léveillé during his lifetime and [later] against the said Girard. Among these items are two discharge receipts from the Sieur de Saint Denis, indicating that payments had been made to him by the said Girard in order to pay off the said debt of the said Léveillé, as was mentioned above in the list of his owed debts which were paid off by the said Girard. The said sheaf was paraphrased by us, the notary, and inventoried here as the sixth item with the mark F.

Another sheaf of legal proceedings, made at the request of Claude Bourget against the said Pierre Girard for the payment of the overdue debts of the said deceased Léveillé, which were likewise mentioned in the owed debts. The said sheaf paraphrased by us as the seventh item and inventoried with the mark G. The said sheaf contains several items.

Another sheaf containing four items, of which one is a bond [of Léveillé] and a court order in favor of the deceased [Monsieur de La Martinière] for merchandise, mentioned in the owed debts, paraphrased by us and inventoried as the ninth item with the mark H.

Another sheaf with four items, concerning the legal pursuit of the said [Pierre Normand dit] La Brière [against Léveillé], which was mentioned above in the owed debts. Paraphrased and inventoried as the ninth item with the mark J.

Two other items at the request of Guillaume Guillot, paid off by the said Girard in the discharge for the said Léveillé, which is likewise mentioned in the owed debts, paraphrased and inventoried as the tenth item with the mark K.

Items concerning the said children heirs of the said deceased Léveillé, which are to be returned to them by the said Girard in the process of the division of their possessions:

The marriage contract between the said deceased Étienne Léveillé and the said Élisabeth Lequin, passed before the said notary Master Gilles Rageot on December 27, 1670, containing certain conditions and stipulations, which has been paraphrased by us, the notary and inventoried here as the eleventh item with the mark L.

A contract of concession made to the deceased Léveillé of a lot with two arpents [384 English feet] of frontage by forty arpents [1 1/2 miles] in depth situated in the seigneury of Dombourg, presently called Neuville, passed before the said notary Sieur [Gilles] Rageot on the last day of May, 1672, along with the right of fishing in the St. Lawrence River in front of it. The said contract paraphrased by us and inventoried as the twelfth item with the mark M.

A verified copy of a privately written document in the form of an inventory made of the belongings of the said deceased Léveillé and the said Lequin, estimated and appraised by Pierre Coquin, Jean Hardy, and Michel Langlois in the following manner. The [value of the] said lot estimated at nine hundred livres, and the moveable possessions therein estimated together at one hundred ninety livres. The said document dated January 14, 1689. The original had been deposited in the office of the notary [Gilles Rageot], from which a verified copy was made by us, the notary, paraphrased and inventoried as the thirteenth item with the mark N.

A privately written document of the new estimation of the said lot of the said Léveillé, conducted since the decease of the said Lequin, dated last April 10 [1700], by J[ean] Mezeray, Léonard Faucher, and Jean Hardy. The two former [witnesses] signed with Monsieur [Jean] Basset, the parish priest; the said Hardy did not know how to sign. [The value] of the said lot has been estimated at the sum of sixteen hundred livres. The said document paraphrased by us, the notary, and inventoried here as the fourteenth item with the mark O.

Two discharge receipts from Monsieur [Nicolas] Dupont [Sieur de Neuville], seigneur of the seigneury of Neuville, for the previous ten years of rents, which were paid to him by the said Girard for the lot of the said deceased Léveillé, of which the last one is dated last November 11, 1699. Paraphrased and inventoried as the fourteenth item with the mark P.

Another discharge receipt, signed by Charlotte de La Combe [widow of Antoine Caddé of Quebec, who had died between August of 1688 and March of 1689], for all that the said Léveillé had owed [which was paid off by Pierre Girard], dated January 31, 1690, paraphrased and inventoried as the sixteenth item with the mark Q.

A certificate from the Sieur [François] Hazeur, merchant [of Quebec], which contains a promise from July 8, 1682 to repay him for the cost of a house, a debt owed by the said Étienne Léveillé and the Sieur [Jean] Dubuc [of Neuville]. Monsieur Hazeur testified that he paid to Monsieur [Nicolas] Dupont [Sieur de Neuville, the seigneur of Neuville] sixty-six livres for the said deceased Léveillé and one hundred livres for the said Dubuc. These two same sums were entered into the great record book of accounts of the said Sieur Dupont. The said certificate is dated March 12, 1693. Hazeur has initialed in the margin [of the present inventory], and the item has been inventoried as the seventeenth item with the mark R.

The said Girard has said that he is not aware of anything further to be inventoried. With the consent of the said parties, all of the said papers have been returned and placed in his hands, of which he will remain in charge, likewise for all of the contents of the said inventory which are in his possession.

This has been done, finished, and closed on the said day at seven o'clock in the evening on the twenty-second of June, 1700, in the presence of the Sieurs Jacques Barbel, attorney for civil cases, and Adrien Legris, habitant of this town on St. Nicolas Street, as witnesses who have signed with the said notary. The said parties have declared that they do not know how to write or sign, after being questioned. The said Girard has said that he could formerly write his name in printed letters but that he is no longer able to do so, having been prohibited by Monsieur the Lieutenant General [the Chief Judge of the Quebec Court], who was surprised that he did not know how to read.

Signed,

Adrien Legris, Barbel, and Genaple

Received payment for having examined the papers of the present inventory and for having written out the documents.

On the eleventh of October in the said year of 1700, in the afternoon, appeared before the said notary in his office the said [Pierre] Girard and Pierre Léveillé, who have stated that the said Girard had omitted to declare and to have included in the above inventory the used clothing left by the said deceased Isabelle (sic) Lequin, his wife, which they have estimated between them [in value] at 45 livres. In addition, he omitted one old scythe and one old [small] building estimated at five livres, together adding up to the sum of fifty livres. They have requested that these said articles be included in the present inventory, to be figured as a portion for the children heirs. [This supplement] made and drawn up by the said notary in the presence of the Sieur de La Pierrotière, lieutenant in the troops of the King, and of Coeurballe, manager of the residence of Milord the Intendant, as witnesses, who have signed with the said notary. The said Girard and Léveillé have declared that they do not know how to sign, having been questioned according to the ordinance.

Signed,

Coeurballe, De la Pierrottière, Hallouin, and Genaple."[113]

After the total value of the moveable possessions has been corrected (increasing the sum by 23 livres 10 sols, to reflect the listed values of the individual articles), the total value of the entire estate of Pierre Girard and Élisabeth Lequin amounts to 2,912 livres 10 sols. It is of considerable interest to break this overall amount down into its separate components. First, the Girard property itself was worth 1,400 livres, a full 48.1 percent of the estate. Then, its buildings (including one house by the river, a second house at the inland clearing, a stable, the raised framework for a granary, the planks to cover that framework, and a small building which was mentioned in the addendum to the inventory) were together valued at 647 livres, or 22.2 percent of the total sum. The livestock (oxen, cows, and pigs) were together worth 448 livres, or 15.4 percent of the estate, while the harvested crops and produce (wheat, peas, and sidepork) were valued at 213 livres, or 7.3 percent of the total. Finally, the other possessions (both inside and outside the home, including Élisabeth's clothing and the scythe that were mentioned in the addendum) were worth a total of 204.5 livres, or 7 percent of the estate. Not included in the enumeration were Pierre's clothing and his other personal belongings. In addition, no mention was made of the separate Léveillé property in the adjacent seigneury of Neuville, along with its associated structures and possessions.

In comparison, the outstanding debts of the estate totaled 342 livres 10 sols, which sum was equivalent to 11.8 percent of the family's total assets at the Girard farm. It is quite likely that the debt of 261 livres that the family owed to the Quebec merchant Lucien Bouteville, for merchandise which had been provided by him eight months earlier (back in October of 1699), had not been related to Pierre's former commerce in the fur trade. At this stage of his life, when he was about 55 to 59 years old, Monsieur Girard had probably halted his participation in the upriver trade; he had apparently sold his *barque*, and he now owned only a birchbark canoe of modest value. The goods from the Quebec merchant had probably been the customary articles that were utilized by most of the farmer-settlers in the colony.

From the roster of debts, it appears that Father Basset from the Neuville church and a Monsieur Têtu had assisted in caring for Élisabeth during her final illness. For these services, "for feeding the said Lequin," they were to be paid 13 livres and 9 livres 12 sols, respectively. It is not clear from this entry just what aid these men had provided. Had they supplied to the family, or had they personally prepared, special foods which were easier for her to digest? Or had one or both of these men traveled to the Girard farm to actually feed her? Or had she been transported to Neuville to spend her final days or weeks in their care? A later document would indicate that Pierre's son François Girard had loaned 12 livres toward her care during "the sickness of his mother." Perhaps this money had paid for medicines, or surgeon's visits, or other related expenses. (At this time, Fr. Basset, who was about 53 years old, had been in the colony for a quarter-century. He would eventually die at Neuville in November of 1715.)[114]

According to his financial accounts, Pierre had hired two young men, Jean Baptiste Thibault and Pierre Louis Doré, to work for him on the farm. It is quite likely that their labors, at the rate of 1.5 livres per day per man, had been focused on clearing the forest cover from additional areas of the long, slender lot. This activity had probably been carried out at the inland end of the property, where the quality of the soil was considerably better than in areas that were closer to the St. Lawrence shoreline. The first of these laborers, Monsieur Thibault, had been born and raised on the farm next door to the Girard family. At this point, he was nearly 28 years old, and he had been married since the previous November 24 (to a local 23-year-old woman, in a ceremony at the Maure church); the couple was expecting their first child in latter August. The second workman, Monsieur Doré, also a resident of the Maure seigneury, was almost 29 years old. Pierre had served as an official witness at the Neuville church for the funeral of his mother, Jeanne Dufossé, back in November of 1698, and as a witness in the same edifice for the wedding of Pierre Louis Doré himself on November 24 of 1699. (Coincidentally, this had been the very same day on which his colleague Jean Baptiste Thibault had been married, some miles away in the Maure church.) The Doré couple was expecting their first child in about February of 1701.[115] Over time, Monsieur Thibault had worked a total of nineteen days for Pierre, while Monsieur Doré had labored for him for a total of fifteen days. These were two examples of young men from the St. Lawrence Valley who had chosen to work as laborers in the local region, instead of hiring on as voyageurs to make long-distance trips. Both groups of men, especially those who chose to work as paddlers for only one or just a few voyages, wished to amass some money in order to finance and establish their own fully equipped farms. Quite often, they had not yet married, or they had been wed for only a short time.

According to the inventory, Pierre had paid off a total of 397 livres in debts which Élisabeth's former husband Étienne Léveillé had owed to six different individuals. It is of particular interest to note that, in their marriage contract from April 18, 1688, Pierre and Élisabeth had publicly and officially agreed (according to the notary's summary) "that they will not be held accountable for the debts of either one of them which had originated previously." However, the numerous creditors of the deceased Léveillé had doggedly pursued Pierre in court, pressing him to pay off these old debts. And apparently in each instance, the judges had decided that it was Pierre's responsibility to settle these long-overdue accounts. The various court decisions against him, forcing the new husband to cover the unpaid debts of the departed husband, had commenced just ten months after Pierre and Élisabeth's wedding. These decrees had been announced by the court officials on February 28, 1689; June 24, 1689; April 18, 1690; June 8, 1694; and twice on June 18, 1694.

In the closing paragraph of the inventory, the notary penned first a very common sentence and then an extremely unusual and particularly disturbing statement:

"The said parties have declared that they do not know how to write or sign, after being questioned. The said Girard has said that he could formerly write his name in printed letters, but that he is no longer able to do so, having been prohibited by Monsieur the Lieutenant General [the Chief Judge of the Quebec Court], who was surprised that he did not know how to read."

At the end of the short addendum to this same document, which was written some 3$^{1}/_{2}$ months later, the scribe then noted these facts: *"The said Girard and Léveillé have declared that they do not know how to sign, having been questioned according to the ordinance."*

This was the last in a series of stages of declared literacy through which Pierre Girard had passed, over the course of more than a quarter-century. Back in January of 1673, the notary Romain Becquet had written the following statement at the end of Pierre's forest-clearing contract: "Just now has appeared the said Girard, who has accepted the present agreement after it was read, and he has declared that he does not know how to sign, having been questioned according to the ordinance." At some point during the next 4$^{3}/_{4}$ years, Monsieur Girard had learned to sign his name, although it was in laboriously printed letters, with a combination of capital and small-case figures. At the bottom of the notary contract from October 19, 1677 (by which Pierre and Suzanne had agreed to house and care for young Marie Madeleine Arrivé for three years), he had penned PiERRE GiRART. Five years later, in September of 1682, the notary Gilles Rageot had produced a verified copy of certain decrees of the Intendant Duchesneau, concerning the reduction of Monsieur Girard's import duties on brandy and tobacco. In this copy, the scribe had replicated the supplicant's signature as Pr. Girart, written in the notary's own flowing cursive penmanship rather than in Pierre's crudely printed letters, and with capitalization on only the first letter of each word. This was obviously not an exact and faithful copy of his actual signature, as he had penned it onto the original document, but it at least indicated Monsieur Girard's spelling. Fifteen years later, on June 24, 1697, Pierre had again signed his name on a contract (in which he had arranged an apprenticeship program for his stepson Étienne Léveillé). However, in this instance he had omitted the final R from his family name, writing it as PiERRE GiRAT. This oversight of one of the six letters in his family name must have reflected just how very seldom he needed to pen his signature during the course of each decade.

Some time between this document from June of 1697 and the Girard-Léveillé estate inventory of June 22, 1700, a span of four years, some strange event had obviously taken place. On that as-yet-unidentified occasion, the Lieutenant General of the Quebec Court, its Chief Judge, had been surprised to learn that Pierre was unable to read. As a consequence, this judicial figure had imperiously declared that Monsieur Girard would no longer be permitted to affix his signature to official documents. Thereafter, he would be obliged to declare that he was did not know how to sign. Pierre did just that with the addendum of the inventory on October 11, 1700. In this particular instance, the Judge had indeed done something that was very bizarre. It is most certain that "literacy policeman" was well beyond the bounds of his official duties as an arbiter of legal cases.[116]

On June 23, 1700, the day following the official drawing up of the estate inventory, the notary recorded the details of the division of the Girard-Léveillé estate.[117] In advance of this day, Pierre had arranged the various details with his six living Girard children and his three living Léveillé stepchildren. This time (unlike the notary's record from the previous day), the second document listed not only the three minority-age and unmarried Girard offspring (Jean Pierre, Françoise, and Pierre Louis) but also "jointly with François Girard, the eldest son [age 27] of the said Girard and the said de Lavoie, his first wife, of majority age, and Daniel Denevers, as the husband of Jeanne Girard, his daughter." In the process of recording these various Girard heirs, however, the notary bungled the text. The eldest daughter

Marie Madeleine, now 25 years old, had been married to Monsieur Denevers for nearly nine years; the other wedded daughter of the family, Jeanne, age 19, had married Pierre Léveillé in April of this year. It was presumably the patriarch's intention that both of these married Girard heirs were to be included in the estate settlement, as was their legal right. However, the notary mistakenly included just one married daughter's name, and he matched it with the name of the other married daughter's husband. This accidental mis-recording of information garbled somewhat the details of the official document, but not its intent.

After listing the participants in the division of the estate, a number of facts were then entered into the record. First, after the death of Suzanne de Lavoie, Pierre's first wife, the widower had not arranged for an inventory to be drawn up which listed their communal possessions in detail. He had only acquired a generalized statement by two local appraisers, indicating that the value of the Girard lot and its buildings at Maure had been estimated at 1,000 livres and the moveable belongings therein at 500 livres. After the death of Étienne Léveillé and the subsequent marriage of his widow Élisabeth Lequin to Pierre Girard four months later, a generalized statement by three local appraisers had indicated that the Léveillé lot and its buildings at Neuville had been estimated at 900 livres and the moveable possessions therein at 190 livres. Since that time, the Léveillé heirs had cleared more forest cover and had developed the Léveillé land and its buildings considerably; as a result, it had recently been appraised at 1,600 livres. During their nearly twelve years of marriage, Pierre and Élisabeth had produced no additional children.

In the settlement, it was agreed that the entirety of the Léveillé property at Neuville (measuring 384 feet in St. Lawrence frontage by $1^1/2$ miles in depth), along with all of its assets, would belong to the three Léveillé heirs, in three equal portions. Likewise, the Girard property at Maure would belong to Pierre and his Girard heirs. However, 630 livres worth of structures had been erected on this latter land during the period of the Girard-Lequin marriage. Thus, the Girard-Léveillé estate (which was to be divided into three equal parts, for Pierre, the Girard heirs, and the Léveillé heirs) would be credited with this same amount of valuation. In addition, to the total estate would be added the 808 livres worth of moveable possessions that had been jointly owned by Pierre and Élisabeth; these had been enumerated in the recent inventory. These two sums (not including the 1,400 livre value of the Girard land itself) totaled 1,438 livres; this was the value of the estate that was to be divided into three equal portions.

However, from this amount was first subtracted the debts which the estate owed to five individuals (totalling 342 livres 13 sols), as well as the costs of settling the estate (totaling 85 livres 14 sols, which are detailed below). Thus, 428 livres 7 sols was subtracted from the total assets of 1,438 livres, leaving a sum of 979 livres.

This sum was then divided into three equal parts, each one worth 326 livres 11 sols; these portions were assigned to Pierre Girard, the six Girard heirs as a unit, and the three Léveillé heirs as a unit. In addition to their one-third portion, the three Léveillé offspring also received half of the 189 livre value of Pierre and Élisabeth's belongings, equal to 94 livres 10 sols. These two sums for the Léveillé children totalled 420 livres 11 sols. Subtracted from this amount, however, was the entire 397 livres of listed debts which their father Étienne Léveillé had incurred during his lifetime but had not paid off. Pierre Girard had settled these debts himself, and he was now being reimbursed for these expenses. Thus, the final remainder in assets for the three Léveillé heirs was the paltry sum of 23 livres 11 sols. This tiny sum was awarded to Pierre in good faith, as a gratuity for all of his travels and the expenses that he had incurred while settling the overdue debts of their late father.

In the end, the three Léveillé children received only the original Léveillé property and all of its associated assets (the buildings and the possessions therein). However, they were absolved from all debts of the estate, both those which Pierre had already settled years before and the remaining five which he would soon pay off. In closing, Pierre handed over to Adrien Piché, the husband of Élisabeth Léveillé, all seven of the Léveillé family documents which had been identified in the recent inventory as items L through R.

Affixed to the notary's settlement document was a detailed list of the various expenses which had been incurred during the inventorying and dividing of the estate. These costs had been subtracted from the overall estate before any divisions of assets had been conducted.
"Statement of the expenses to be paid along with the owed debts
For the expense of feeding in this town Pierre Girard, his children, Pierre
Léveillé, and Adrien Piché .... 13 livres
For the delivery of four [notary] contracts to be included
in the inventory...18 l. 14 s.

For the official document of the guardianship declarations ....4 l.
For the inventory and the division of the estate.....................................32 l.
For the closing of the said inventory...5 l.
For three quarter-pints of brandy, for everyone.......................................1 l.
Twelve livres owed to François Girard, loaned by him for the
[treatment of the] sickness of his mother ....12 l.
Sum total...85 l. 14 s."

During the course of the inventorying and dividing of the accumulated assets of the clan, no protests or indications of dissatisfaction had been recorded in any of the documents. There seems to have been a sense of fairness pervading the various proceedings. This equitable mentality may have been encouraged by the old adage *Contentement passe richesse* (Contentment is better than riches). In addition, the fact that the eldest Léveillé son had recently married the second-youngest Girard daughter probably engendered a considerable amount of civility and objectivity into the entire procedure, and most likely increased the solidarity among the members of the blended family.

Three weeks after the estate had been settled, Pierre appeared at the Neuville church as the godfather for the one-day-old daughter of Sébastien Migneron and Catherine Tru, fellow residents of the Maure seigneury. Joining Pierre as the co-sponsor was another Maure neighbor, Françoise Doré, the 22-year-old unmarried daughter of Louis Doré.[118]

The entire Girard-Léveillé clan seems to have evaded the grip of death that swept through the St. Lawrence Valley late in 1700 and again during the latter months of 1701. The second of these two epidemics was especially devastating: by the week before Christmas, smallpox had carried off more than a thousand residents of the settlements, both French and native.[119]

Between these two scourges, in February of 1701, Pierre was pleased to serve as the baptismal sponsor for the brand new baby of René Alarie dit Grandalarie and Louise Thibault, fellow residents of Maure. At the ceremony at the Neuville church on the 6th, his co-sponsor was Marie Françoise Hayot, the unmarried daughter (age 26) of the deceased Jean Hayot. This was an extremely bitter-sweet occasion for everyone, since the baby's father René had passed away about ten weeks before her arrival.[120]

Again on September 26 of 1702, Pierre was chosen to be a godfather, this time for a young couple who lived in the Maure seigneury and in a ceremony that was conducted at the Maure church. Little Marie Madeleine had been born on this same day as the second child of Charles Tinon dit Desroches and Marie Bonnodeau. This baby's godmother was Pierre's next-door neighbor Madeleine Rasset, age 16 and still unmarried. According to the priest's records, the child had been baptized provisionally by the midwife shortly after her birth.[121]

A much more heart-rending ceremony took place about ten weeks later, when Pierre's young brother-in-law Vincent de Lavoie was laid to rest in the cemetery at Neuville. Just 24 years old and still single, he had been born to Suzanne's father Pierre and his second wife Isabelle Aupé. The two official witnesses at Vincent's burial on December 12 were his nephew Pierre Girard, Jr. (Pierre and Suzanne's son, who was three weeks short of age 26) and his brother-in-law Pierre Grenon (who had married Suzanne's sister Marie).[122]

It is highly likely that Vincent had perished as a result of the fierce epidemic of smallpox that raged through the settlements of the St. Lawrence during the latter part of 1702 and continued until at least the spring of 1703. During the course of this horrendous wave of disease, the losses were very high; for example, about a quarter of the population of the town of Quebec perished, as well as some 250 residents of Montreal Island.[123]

On April 4, 1703, Pierre stood before one of the Quebec notaries to acknowledge that he owed a debt to the Quebec merchant Lucien Bouteville. In the document, Monsieur Girard was identified as residing in the Rocky River section of the Maure seigneury. Since the actual record is now missing from the Archives Nationales du Québec at Quebec, it is not possible to determine if this debt was a new one for Pierre, or whether he had still not paid off the sum of 260 livres 18 sols which he had owed to the merchant back at the time of the inventory in June of 1700 (for merchandise that Monsieur Bouteville had supplied to the family in October of 1699).[124]

On July 10, 1703, Pierre's eldest son, François Girard, approved a hiring contract by which he agreed to serve as a voyageur, on a round-trip journey between Lachine and Ft. Pontchartrain at Detroit (this post had been founded two years earlier). François, 28 1/2 years old, was one of 42 paddlers who were engaged for this voyage on this same day, in a mass contract which was drawn up by the Montreal notary Antoine Adhémar.[125] It is not known whether this action kindled in his father Pierre a wish that he himself had traveled to the distant west to trade, rather than carrying out his fur trade business in the St. Lawrence Valley. However, by choosing to remain in the area of the settlements, the patriarch had been able to remain at home with his family for most of the months of the year. In addition, he had been able to work for himself and generate his own profits (and also hire other men to assist him with his moderately large sailing vessel), rather than earning a salary from an employer, such as his son François would now earn from the Company of the Colony of Canada.

Five months after this hiring contract, celebrations were in order for the Girard-Léveillé clan. On December 28, various family members and friends gathered before a Quebec notary to witness the drawing up of the marriage contract of Pierre and Suzanne's youngest daughter, Françoise, who was now 20^1/2 years old. Her fiancé, Noël Berthiaume, six months younger than her, was from the seigneury of Ste. Foy, some five or six miles east of Maure. Oddly enough, when the young couple was married in the church of St. Augustin at Maure two weeks later, on January 15, 1704, only the bride, the groom, and Hilaire Desthilaire, "Recollet priest of this parish," were recorded in the parish register, with no additional witnesses being listed. After the ceremony, the newlyweds settled in the groom's home seigneury of Ste. Foy, where they would produce nine children over the next two decades.[126]

The first one of Pierre Girard's numerous Berthiaume grandchildren arrived twelve months and three weeks after the wedding, on February 8, 1705. At the baptism of tiny Pierre in the Notre Dame church at Ste. Foy on the following day, the boy's godparents were his uncle Pierre Girard (Pierre's son Jean Pierre, who was generally called Pierre Girard, Jr., now age 28, still unmarried and living in the Maure seigneury) and the baby's aunt Catherine Bonhomme, the wife of Jacques Berthiaume, of Ste. Foy. Officiating at the ceremony was Fr. Charles Amador Martin, the son of Abraham Martin (the first subject in this series of biographies), who was the parish priest of Ste. Foy at this time.

Nearly two years later, Pierre was pleased to be present as one of the official witnesses at the wedding of his youngest stepson, Jean Léveillé. On November 24, 1706, the groom, who was 28 years old, took as his bride Marguerite Auger of Neuville, who would celebrate her 15th birthday in three months. When the couple exchanged their vows in the Neuville church, the official witnesses included "Pierre

Girard, stepfather of the groom; Pierre Léveillé of Neuville, brother of the groom; René Auger of Neuville, brother of the bride; and Ignace Liénard dit Boisjoli of Neuville." The newlyweds would settle in the Neuville seigneury, where they would produce eight offspring between 1711 and 1724. Now, all three of Pierre's living Léveillé stepchildren were married. His other stepson, Pierre Léveillé, also resided in the Neuville seigneury with his wife Jeanne Girard, as they had done ever since they had married back in 1700. Since they would have ten children between 1702 and 1723, there would be plenty of Léveillé youngsters growing up during the coming decades in the seigneury which was adjacent to Maure.[127]

During the summer of 1708, Pierre lost his father-in-law, Pierre de Lavoie. About 76 to 80 years old, he had lived in the Rocky River section of the Maure seigneury since at least 1667, even before he had married his second wife, Isabelle Aupé, in 1670. It was there that the couple had produced eight children, between 1673 and 1688. Old Monsieur de Lavoie was buried in the Maure cemetery on July 9, the day following his death, after having been a widower the second time for 21 years.[128]

In about 1709, Pierre and Suzanne's eldest son, François, was wed at Lotbinière, some twenty miles southwest of Maure. Afterward, the groom, about 33 years old, and his bride Antoinette Lemay, about age 26, settled at Trois-Rivières, where they would produce two children in about 1709 and 1725. (It was this son who had worked as a voyageur traveling to and from Detroit during the summer of 1703.)[129]

The year of 1710 brought with it the encouraging nuptial ceremony of yet another Girard son. This time, the festivities revolved around Jean Pierre (commonly called Pierre, Jr.), who was now $33^1/2$ years old. At the recording of his marriage contract by a Quebec notary on July 18, he agreed to join in partnership with Angélique Houard, who was about age 26 and from Lauson, across the St. Lawrence from Quebec. Just $2^1/2$ weeks after their contract-signing, on August 4, the couple was married in the bride's home parish at Lauson, which was called St. Joseph de la Pointe. Pierre, Sr., who was about 65 to 69 years old at this time, apparently did not make the fifteen-mile journey to the church to join in the celebrations. However, it is very clear that he was not recorded in the priest's ledger as deceased, as were the groom's mother (Suzanne de Lavoie) and the bride's father (Jean Houard). The official witnesses who were recorded in the parish ledger included Noël Berthiaume, brother-in-law of the groom; Philippe Amiot, uncle of the groom; Pierre Joli, cousin of the groom; Mathieu, Étienne, and Jacques Huard, three brothers of the bride; Eustache Couture and Jean Baptiste Grenet, two brothers-in-law of the bride; and Pierre Vallière.[130]

Since the newly-wedded Girard couple settled in the seigneury of Maure, Pierre, Sr. was handily close by and ready to serve as the godfather of their first child when the tiny lad arrived on May 23, 1711, nine months and three weeks after the wedding. His christening took place in the Neuville church on the day following his birth. After Pierre, Sr. had granted his own first name to the baby, the priest recorded in the register that the godparents were "Pierre Girard of St. Augustin, grandfather of the child, and Françoise Amiot of St. Augustin, maternal great-aunt [sister of the grandmother] of the child and widow of Charles Gingras." The latter man, a neighbor in the Rocky River section of the Maure seigneury, had passed away back in January of 1710.[131]

The youngest of Pierre and Suzanne's children, Pierre Louis, searched farther afield from Maure to find his soul mate than had any of his siblings or stepsiblings. In the spring of 1711, about two months before he would turn age 24, Pierre married Rosalie Tremblay (24 years old) of La Petite Rivière St. François Xavier. This little village was located some 60 miles northeast of Maure, isolated in a very long stretch of the north shore of the St. Lawrence. The scene of their wedding on April 21 was about ten miles further toward the northeast, at Baie St. Paul, which offered the nearest church to be found in the entire region; this parish had been established in 1681. However, to the great sadness of everyone, Rosalie only lived for four months and one week after their wedding. She died on August 27, and was buried in the cemetery at Baie St. Paul on the following day. In his grief, Pierre Louis would live as a widower in the northeastern area for the next three years.[132]

About eighteen months after his wife's untimely death, on March 11, 1713, Pierre Louis agreed to sell his one-twelfth share of the Girard property at Maure to his next-older brother Pierre Girard, Jr. (officially named Jean Pierre). According to the notary document, the younger brother was living at Baie St. Paul, while his older sibling was residing in the seigneury of Maure. The property being transferred was a portion of the family land which had a total St. Lawrence frontage of 575 feet and a depth extending off toward the north of 1 ^{1}/10 miles. The two parts which belonged to these two sons had been inherited from the family estate. Pierre, Sr. had retained ownership of half of the lot, while his six adult children had divided the ownership of the other half into equal portions.

A month after this transaction had been officially registered with the notary, on April 8, the cemetery at Neuville offered a poignant scene. Jean Baptiste Thibault (who had been born and raised on the farm next door to the Girard family) and his wife Marie Françoise Amiot had just lost their ten-year-old son and eldest child, Jean Baptiste, Jr. Besides the two parents from Maure and the priest who conducted the funeral, the only other witness who was recorded in the parish ledger was Pierre Girard. From this entry, it is not possible to determine whether this individual was Pierre, Sr., about 68 to 72 years old, or Pierre, Jr., age 36. Both the father and the son were living in the Maure seigneury at this time.[133]

After three full years of living as a widower, Pierre's son Pierre Louis Girard again found someone with whom he could share his triumphs and his disappointments in life. On April 10, 1714, this young man, now about to turn age 27, married Marguerite Tardif of L'Ange Gardien on the Côte de Beaupré, who would celebrate her 23rd birthday in two months. (She was a granddaughter of Olivier Le Tardif and Barbe Émard, whose biographies have been presented earlier in this work.) According to the priest's notations in the L'Ange Gardien church register, the groom was identified as "of St. François Xavier, widow of Rosalie Tremblay." The following four men were the official witnesses at the ceremony, according to the information in the same ledger entry: "Pierre Girard, father of the groom, Charles Vézina, René Mathieu, and Noël ___." These four witnesses, plus the father of the bride, were all listed as being present at the nuptial celebration. Thus, Pierre, Sr., who was at this time about 69 to 73 years old, had made the journey of about 25 miles to the home parish of his new daughter-in-law. He had exerted this effort in order to watch as his youngest son made a fresh start in life, and to join in the jubilant festivities which launched that bright new beginning. (The present author is descended from this new Girard-Tremblay couple, who provided the direct linkage between Pierre Girard, Sr. and Suzanne de Lavoie and himself.)[134]

The priest's notations in the L'Ange Gardien parish ledger of 1714 represent the last known documentation in the colony for Pierre Girard. Sr. No further mentions concerning him have been found in any later documents, and his burial information has not been located in any of the surviving church records. Thus, it is not known whether he was still living when his son Pierre, Jr. lost his young wife in the following year of 1715.

While residing in the Maure seigneury, Pierre, Jr. and Angélique Houard had produced four children after their 1710 wedding; these youngsters had arrived in May of 1711, July of 1712, March of 1714, and March of 1715. However, four months after delivering their fourth baby, Angélique died on the second day of August, at about age 31; she was laid to rest in the cemetery at Maure on the following day. Eventually, after two years and two months of raising his children as a widower, Pierre, Jr. finally remarried at the Maure church, on October 24, 1717. Joining him as his new life partner was Marie Angélique Dolbec of Neuville, age 20. She was the fifth daughter and twelfth child of Anne Masse and François Dolbec dit Dufresne. By coincidence, this new father-in-law had been one of the two forest-clearing partners of Pierre, Sr. back in the winter of 1673, nearly 45 years earlier. At the Girard-Dolbuc nuptial celebrations, the two official witnesses were Jean Thibault, uncle of the groom, and Louis Doré, cousin of the groom. No information concerning the groom's parents was included in the priest's entry, since this was Pierre, Jr.'s second marriage. If the patriarch Pierre Girard, Sr. had been still living at this time, he most likely would have been listed in the parish register as being present at this festive occasion, which took place in his own home church.[135]

Although no burial record for Pierre Girard, Sr. has ever been located in any church documents, it is quite possible that he had been laid to rest in the Maure cemetery. However, both his first wife Suzanne de Lavoie and his second wife Élisabeth Lequin had been buried at the Neuville cemetery (some ten miles west of the Maure funerary grounds), in July of 1687 and February of 1700, respectively. Thus, he might have been interred beside one or the other of these spouses, rather than being separated from them in the Maure cemetery.

Signature PiERRE GiRART, October 19, 1677.

Pierre Girard-Suzanne de Lavoie Lineage of Timothy Kent

I. Pierre Girard
(parents not identified)

12 August, 1669
Quebec, QC

Suzanne de Lavoie
(Pierre/
Jacquette Grignon)

II. Pierre Louis Girard
(Pierre/
Suzanne de Lavoie)

10 April, 1714
L'Ange Gardien, QC

Margueritie Tardif
(Guillaume/
Marguerite Godin)

III. Scholastique Girard
(Pierre Louis/
Marguerite Tardif)

22 April, 1737
Les Éboulements, QC

Pierre Gagnon
(Joseph/
Marie Madeleine Tremblay)

IV. Marie Anne Victoire Gagnon
(Pierre/
Scholastique Girard)

21 Nov, 1771
Les Éboulements, QC

Louis Basile Bruno Tremblay
(Basile/
Marie Anne Gonthier)

V. Françoise Tremblay
(Louis Basile Bruno/
Marie Anne Victoire Gagnon)

13 Nov, 1798
Les Éboulements, QC

André Perron
(Joseph/
Madeleine Bouchard)

VI. Rosalie Perron
(André/
Françoise Tremblay)

31 Jan, 1831
Les Éboulements, QC

Joseph Bouchard
(Joseph Marie/
Marie Anne Tremblay)

VII. Philéas Joseph Bouchard
(Joseph/
Rosalie Perron)

20 Sept, 1859
Grande Baie, QC

Adelaide Barbeau
(André/
Agathe Gagné)

VIII. Joseph Bouchard
(Philéas Joseph/
Adelaide Barbeau)

30 Jan, 1893
Carrollton, MI

Élisabeth Lalonde
(Joseph/
Josephine Chatelain)

IX. Frances L. Bouchard
(Joseph/
Élisabeth Lalonde)

28 Apr, 1945
Detroit, MI

S. George Kent
(George Kapantais/
Eugenia Papadakis)

X. Timothy J. Kent
(S. George/
Frances L. Bouchard)

5 Sept, 1970
Ossineke, MI

Dorothy J. Minton
(Garnet J./
Elaine A. Reece)

Notes for Girard

1. Notary Gilles Rageot, February 4, 1671, Archives Nationales du Québec at Quebec (ANQ-Q).
2. Domaine du Roi: T. Kent, 1997, pp. 58-59; R. Jetté, 1983, pp. 597, 155.
3. A. Lafontaine, 1985, pp. 3-4, Quebec household No. 2 (he incorrectly listed the age of Pierre Girard as 25 rather than 23); R. Jetté, 1983, all of the enumerated individuals except the paying lodgers.
4. G. Perron, October 1991, pp. 44-48; G. Perron, 1998, pp. 122-133, 151; P. Moogk, 2000, pp. 93-97, 103-109; L. Dechêne, 1992, p. 30.
5. R. Jetté, 1983, pp. 864, 570-571.
6. ibid., pp. 1131, 221, 700, 112, 384, 1091.
7. Journal des Jésuites, July 23, 1665, in Jesuit Relations, 1896-1901, Vol. of 1665.
8. R. Harris, 1987, pls. 46, 51; R. Jetté, 1983, p. 394.
9. R. Harris, 1987, pls. 46, 51; M. Trudel, 1973c, maps opp. pp. 86, 112, 100, 88.
10. A. Lafontaine, 1985, records of entire 1667 census.
11. R. Harris, 1987, pls. 46, 51; M. Trudel, 1973c, maps opp. pp. 262, 304.
12. Notary François Genaple, June 22, 1700, ANQ-Q.
13. M. Trudel, 1973c, maps opp. pp. 262, 304.
14. Notary François Genaple, June 22, 1700, ANQ-Q.
15. Notary Romain Becquet, August 24, 1666, ANQ-Q; Notary Gilles Rageot, February 13, 1667, ANQ-Q; R. Jetté, 1983, pp. 667, 1069-1070, 108; H. Charbonneau and J. Légaré, 1978-1990, Vol. 1, Notre Dame de Quebec recs; J. Blaeu atlas of 1665, pp. 174-178; Michelin detailed maps of France; R. Harris, 1987, pl. 51. Census of 1666: A. Lafontaine, 1985 and H. Charbonneau and J. Légaré, 1978-1990, Vol. 6, census of Île d'Orléans, household No. 21.
16. H. Charbonneau and J. Légaré, 1978-1990, Vol. 1, Notre Dame de Quebec recs; R. Jetté, 1983, p. 667.
17. Notary François Genaple, June 22, 1700, ANQ-Q.
18. R. Jetté, 1983, p. 667.
19. H. Charbonneau and J. Légaré, 1978-1990, Vol. 1, Notre Dame de Quebec recs; R. Jetté, 1983, pp. 217, 99, 967, 333; Notary Romain Becquet, January 8, 1673, ANQ-Q.
20. R. Jetté, 1983, p. 612.
21. H. Charbonneau and J. Légaré, 1978-1990, Vol. 1, Notre Dame de Quebec recs; R. Jetté, 1983, pp. 294, 631.
22. Notary Romain Becquet, January 8, 1673, ANQ-Q.
23. R. Harris, 1987, pl. 52; N. Webster, 1984, "Easter" and "vernal equinox." Easter falls on the first Sunday following the full moon that appears on or after the vernal equinox. This equinox, the time in the spring when the length of day and night are equal everywhere, falls on about March 21 each year. According to the definition of its placement, the date of Easter varies widely in different years, falling during the period of the last week of March through the first three weeks of April.

24. R. Jetté, 1983, pp. 355, 966.
25. H. Charbonneau and J. Légaré, 1978-1990, Vol. 1, Notre Dame de Quebec recs; R. Jetté, 1983, pp. 355, 499-500, 1074.
26. H. Charbonneau and J. Légaré, 1978-1990, Vol. 1, Notre Dame de Quebec recs; R. Jetté, 1983, pp. 1077, 223.
27. H. Charbonneau and J. Légaré, 1978-1990, Vol. 1, Notre Dame de Quebec recs; R. Jetté, 1983, pp. 608, 527.
28. Notary Gilles Rageot, October 19, 1677, ANQ-Q.
29. R. Jetté, 1983, pp. 21, 400, 353.
30. ibid., pp. 1110, 385; A. Lafontaine, 1986, Maure census, p. 48.
31. H. Charbonneau and J. Légaré, 1978-1990, Vol. 1, Notre Dame de Quebec recs; R. Jetté, 1983, pp. 667, 21, 400.
32. H. Charbonneau and J. Légaré, 1978-1990, Vol. 1, Notre Dame de Quebec recs; R. Jetté, 1983, pp. 966, 223.
33. H. Charbonneau and J. Légaré, 1978-1990, Vol. 1, Notre Dame de Quebec recs; R. Jetté, 1983, pp. 763, 497.
34. R. Harris, 1987, pl. 46.
35. H. Charbonneau and J. Légaré, 1978-1990, Vol. 1, Notre Dame de Quebec recs; R. Jetté, 1983, pp. 1074, 1004-1005.
36. H. Charbonneau and J. Légaré, 1978-1990, Vol. 3, St. François de Sales de Neuville recs; R. Jetté, 1983, pp. 1074, 6.
37. A. Lafontaine, 1986, seigneury of Maure census, pp. 47-49; H. Charbonneau and J. Légaré, 1978-1990, Vol. 6, Maure census.
38. A. Lafontaine, 1986, seigneury of Maure census, pp. 47-49; R. Jetté, 1983, p. 667.
39. H. Charbonneau and J. Légaré, 1978-1990, Vol. 3, St. François de Sales de Neuville recs; R. Jetté, 1983, pp. 1074, 806, 499.
40. H. Charbonneau and J. Légaré, 1978-1990, Vol. 3, St. François de Sales de Neuville recs; R. Jetté, 1983, pp. 1110, 1074, 385-386; A. Lafontaine, 1986, census of Maure, p. 48.
41. For example, S. Morison, 1972, pp. 65, 279; J. Peyser, 1997, p. 116; R. Chénier, 1991, p. 60; A. Vachon, 1982, p. 295.
42. Notary Antoine Adhémar, December 19, 1698, ANQ-M (Montreal).
43. S. Champlain, 1929, Vol. 6, p. 61; C. Goodrich, 1940, p. 141; J. McDermott, 1941, p. 20. Ton: N. Webster, 1984, p. 1497. Muddying the period descriptions is the fact that, when describing the carrying capacity of a vessel, instead of its internal capacity, a ton usually represented only 40 cubic feet, a 60 percent reduction in the size of the unit of measure.
44. S. Champlain, 1929, Vol. 3, p. 203.
45. S. Morison, 1972, p. 279; R. Séguin, 1973, p. 585.
46. J. Peyser, 1997, p. 115.
47. Jesuit Relations, 1896-1901, 1640-1641, p. 61 (cannons); J. Marshall, 1967, pp. 234, 294-295; S. Champlain, 1929, Vol. 2, pp. 24, 27 and Vol. 6. p. 50.
48. R. Séguin, 1973, p. 585; S. Morison, 1972, pp. 278-279; C. Martijn, 2009, pp. 69-71; Journal des Jésuites for 1646-1647, pp. 176-177, 182-183 in Jesuit Relations, 1896-1901; Jesuit Relations for 1641-1642 in Jesuit Relations, 1896-1901, pp. 60-61.

49. Documents Relatifs à L'Histoire de la Nouvelle-France, 1883-1885, Vol. 1, Nos. 31 and 187.
50. W. Eccles, 1964, pp. 15-16; A. Vachon, 1982, p. 275; Y. Zoltvany, 1966, p. 29.
51. W. Eccles, 1964, p. 100.
52. M. Trudel, 1973b, pp. 227-229.
53. A. Vachon, 1982, p. 271; G. Lanctot, 1969, pp. 150-151.
54. A. Vachon, 1982, pp. 271, 275; Y. Zoltvany, 1966, pp. 27-29, 32; W. Eccles, 1964, pp. 16, 36, 62.
55. P. Boucher, 1664, pp. 35-36, 39.
56. T. Kent, 2004, pp. 48, 150, 163, 272-274; W. Eccles, 1964, p. 60.
57. W. Eccles, 1964, pp. 15-16; A. Vachon, 1982, p. 275; Y. Zoltvany, 1966, p. 29.
58. P. Dubé, 1993, pp. 121-123; Y. Zoltvany, 1966, p. 29.
59. P. Moogk, 2000, p. 55; W. Kenyon and J. Turnbull, 1971, p. 11.
60. Archives du Séminaire, Trois-Rivières, Chemise Traite des Fourrures, D 4 T82, following a document by Notary Séverin Ameau dated March 10, 1683.
61. Notary Gilles Rageot, September 15, 1682, ANQ-Q.
62. R. Jetté, 1983, p. 1112.
63. G. Perron, 1998, pp. 118-126, 223-225; V. Tapié, 1984, pp. 256-257; *Isles Antilles* map by Pierre Du Val, in 1660 *Le Monde ou la Géographie Universelle*, Paris, in private collection; exhibits in the Musiale du Perche, the Museum of Emigration to New France, in Tourouvre, France, summer of 2010 (museum first opened in September of 2006); A. Reid, March 1953, pp. 31-32; Funk and Wagnalls, 1990: "West Indies," Vol. 27, pp. 248-254; "Saint Kitts or Saint Christophe," Vol. 23, pp. 77-78; "Dominica," Vol. 8, p. 282; "Guadelouple," Vol. 12, p. 253; "Martinique," Vol. 17, p. 39; "Saint Lucia," Vol. 23, pp. 82-83; "Saint Martin," Vol. 23, p. 83; "Grenada," Vol. 12, pp. 229-232; "Tortuga Island," Vol. 25, p. 407; J. Marshall, 1967, p. 362, 414 n. 3. W. Eccles, 1964, p. 53.
64. T. Kent, 2001, pp. 780-785.
65. L. Lahontan, 1703, Vol. 1, p. 96.
66. Funk and Wagnalls, Vol. 4, p. 304.
67. G. Lanctot, 1969, p. 140; Jesuit Relations, 1896-1901, 1632 Vol., pp. 9-10 and 1633 Vol., p. 32; P. Boucher, 1664, pp. 61-62, 52.
68. T. Kent, 2001, pp. 110-111.
69. Y. Zoltvany, 1969, pp. 79-80.
70. W. Eccles, 1964, pp. 36, 72, 87-89, 142; A. Vachon, 1982, p. 373; M. Trudel, 1973b,, pp. 277, 280; G. Lanctot, 1969, pp. 141-143, 151, 160; T. Pease and R. Werner, 1934, p. 263; P. Moogk, 2000, p. 39; R. Douville and J. Casanova, 1968, pp. 160-162; L. Lahontan, 1703, Vol. 1, p. 94 n. 1; J. Saintonge, 1988, pp. 10-13; J. Marshall, 1967, p. 273-274; C. Ferland, 2008, pp. 81-82; W. Eccles, 1966, pp. 587-588; A. Vachon, 1966d, p. 396; A. Vachon, 1966k, p. 201; A. Vachon, 1966n, pp. 665-666.
71. L. Dechêne, 1992, pp. 96-107, 307.

72. Notary François Genaple, June 22, 1700, ANQ-Q.

73. Y. Zoltvany, 1966, p. 31; W. Percival, 1941, pp. 51-52.

74. H. Charbonneau and J. Légaré, 1978-1990, Vol. 3, St. François de Sales de Neuville recs; R. Jetté, 1983, pp. 783, 19.

75. H. Charbonneau and J. Légaré, 1978-1990, Vol. 3, St. François de Sales de Neuville recs; R. Jetté, 1983, pp. 1074, 496, 966, 356.

76. H. Charbonneau and J. Légaré, 1978-1990, Vol. 3, St. François de Sales de Neuville recs; R. Jetté, 1983, pp. 1074, 806.

77. P. Dubé, 1993, pp. 88-89; R. Harris, 1987, pl. 51.

78. H. Charbonneau and J. Légaré, 1978-1990, Vol. 3, St. François de Sales de Neuville recs; R. Jetté, 1983, pp. 667, 443, 527, 688.

79. H. Charbonneau and J. Légaré, 1978-1990, Vol. 3, St. François de Sales de Neuville recs; R. Jetté, 1983, pp. 6, 1074.

80. H. Charbonneau and J. Légaré, 1978-1990, Vol. 3, St. François de Sales de Neuville recs; R. Jetté, 1983, p. 763.

81. H. Charbonneau and J. Légaré, 1978-1990, Vol. 3, St. François de Sales de Neuville recs; R. Jetté, 1983, pp. 356, 806, 500-501.

82. H. Charbonneau and J. Légaré, 1978-1990, Vol. 3, St. François de Sales de Neuville recs.

83. W. Eccles, 1964, pp. 150, 155.

84. H. Charbonneau and J. Légaré, 1978-1990, Vol. 3, St. François de Sales de Neuville recs; R. Jetté, 1983, pp. 467, 556.

85. R. Jetté, 1983, pp. 456, 731; J. Reisinger and E. Courteau, 1988, p. 9; H. Charbonneau and J. Légaré, 1978-1990, Vol. 1, Notre Dame de Quebec recs.1688 marriage contract: Notary Gilles Rageot, April 16, 1688, ANQ-Q.

86. H. Charbonneau and J. Légaré, 1978-1990, Vol. 3, St. François de Sales de Neuville recs; R. Jetté, 1983, pp. 557, 913; H. Charbonneau and J. Légaré, 1978-1990, Vol. 6, Hôtel Dieu de Quebec recs. and 1681 census of Neuville.

87. R. Jetté, 1983, pp. 667, 731.

88. Notary François Genaple, June 22 and June 23, 1700, ANQ-Q.

89. H. Charbonneau and J. Légaré, 1978-1990, Vol. 3, St. François de Sales de Neuville recs; R. Jetté, 1983, pp. 763, 770, 467.

90. P. Dubé, 1993, pp. 52-53.

91. C. Stacey, 1966, pp. 544-545; W. Percival, 1941, pp. 51-57; L. Lahontan, 1703, Vol. 1, pp. 246-249; La Côte des Beaux Prés, p. 6.

92. R. Jetté, 1983, pp. 667-668, 527, 443.

93. H. Charbonneau and J. Légaré, 1978-1990, Vol. 3, St. François de Sales de Neuville recs; R. Jetté, 1983, p. 499.

94. Notary Gilles Rageot, November 6, 1691, ANQ-Q; H. Charbonneau and J. Légaré, 1978-1990, Vol. 3, St. François de Sales de Neuville recs; R. Jetté, 1983, pp. 499, 329-330, 735.

95. H. Charbonneau and J. Légaré, 1978-1990, Vol. 6, Hôtel Dieu de Quebec recs.

96. H. Charbonneau and J. Légaré, 1978-1990, Vol. 3, St. François de Sales de Neuville recs; R. Jetté, 1983, pp. 966, 322.

97. H. Charbonneau and J. Légaré, 1978-1990, Vol. 3, St. Augustin de Maure recs.

98. H. Charbonneau and J. Légaré, 1978-1990, Vol. 3, St. François de Sales de Neuville recs; R. Jetté, 1983, p. 913.
99. H. Charbonneau and J. Légaré, 1978-1990, Vol. 3, St. François de Sales de Neuville recs; R. Jetté, 1983, pp. 256-257, 686.
100. H. Charbonneau and J. Légaré, 1978-1990, Vol. 3, St. Augustin de Maure recs; R. Jetté, 1983, p. 497.
101. Notary Nicolas Métru, June 24, 1697, ANQ-Q; R. Jetté, 1987, pp. 731, 499-500.
102. H. Charbonneau and J. Légaré, 1978-1990, Vol. 3, St. François de Sales de Neuville recs; R. Jetté, 1983, pp. 527, 86, 325-326, 171.
103. H. Charbonneau and J. Légaré, 1978-1990, Vol. 3, St. François de Sales de Neuville recs; R. Jetté, 1983, p. 356.
104. H. Charbonneau and J. Légaré, 1978-1990, Vol. 3, St. François de Sales de Neuville recs; R. Jetté, 1983, pp. 1074, 771.
105. R. Jetté, 1987, p. 731.
106. H. Charbonneau and J. Légaré, 1978-1990, Vol. 3, St. François de Sales de Neuville recs; R. Jetté, 1983, pp. 527, 86, 325-326.
107. H. Charbonneau and J. Légaré, 1978-1990, Vol. 3, St. François de Sales de Neuville recs; R. Jetté, 1983, pp. 356, 269.
108. H. Charbonneau and J. Légaré, 1978-1990, Vol. 10, St. François de Sales de Neuville recs.
109. R. Jetté, 1983, p. 913.
110. Notary Charles Rageot, April 14, 1700, ANQ-Q; H. Charbonneau and J. Légaré, 1978-1990, Vol. 10, St. Augustin de Maure recs; R. Jetté, 1983, pp. 499, 731, 966, 806.
111. H. Charbonneau and J. Légaré, 1978-1990, Vol. 10, St. Augustin de Maure recs; R. Jetté, 1983, pp. 136, 139, 13.
112. Notary François Genaple, June 22, 1700, ANQ-Q.
113. ibid.
114. R. Jetté, 1983, p. 54.
115. ibid., pp. 1074-1075, 356.
116. Notary Romain Becquet, January 8, 1673, ANQ-Q; Notary Gilles Rageot, October 19, 1677, ANQ-Q; Notary Gilles Rageot, September 15, 1682, ANQ-Q; Notary Nicolas Métru, June 24, 1697, ANQ-Q; Notary François Genaple, June 22, 1700, ANQ-Q.
117. Notary François Genaple, June 23, 1700, ANQ-Q.
118. H. Charbonneau and J. Légaré, 1978-1990, Vol. 10, St. François de Sales de Neuville recs; R. Jetté, 1983, pp. 812, 356.
119. B. Weilbrenner, 1966b, p. 583; T. Kent, 2004, pp. 163-164.
120. H. Charbonneau and J. Légaré, 1978-1990, Vol. 10, St. François de Sales de Neuville recs; R. Jetté, 1983, pp. 6, 560.
121. H. Charbonneau and J. Légaré, 1978-1990, Vol. 10, St. Augustin de Maure recs; R. Jetté, 1983, pp. 1082, 966.
122. H. Charbonneau and J. Légaré, 1978-1990, Vol. 10, St. François de Sales de Neuville recs; R. Jetté, 1983, p. 667.
123. L. Blair, 2000, p. 11; D. Hunter, 2002, p. 92.

124. Notary Florent de La Cetière, April 4, 1703, ANQ-Q, which is now missing from the archives; however, it is present in an abstract in the Parchemin Project records. Notary François Genaple, June 22, 1700, ANQ-Q.

125. E. Massicotte, 1929-1930, p. 208.

126. H. Charbonneau and J. Légaré, 1978-1990, Vol. 10, St. Augustin de Maure recs; R. Jetté, 1983, pp. 499, 93.

127. H. Charbonneau and J. Légaré, 1978-1990, Vol. 10, St. François de Sales de Neuville recs; R. Jetté, 1983, pp. 731, 32-33, 735.

128. R. Jetté, 1983, p. 667.

129. ibid., pp. 499-500, 705.

130. H. Charbonneau and J. Légaré, 1978-1990, Vol. 10, St. Joseph de la Pointe de Lévis recs; R. Jetté, 1983, pp. 499-500, 574.

131. H. Charbonneau and J. Légaré, 1978-1990, Vol. 10, St. François de Sales de Neuville recs; R. Jetté, 1983, pp. 500, 497.

132. H. Charbonneau and J. Légaré, 1978-1990, Vol. 10, Baie St. Paul recs; R. Jetté, 1983, pp. 499-500, 1088; R. Harris, 1987, pl. 46.

133. H. Charbonneau and J. Légaré, 1978-1990, Vol. 10, St. François de Sales de Neuville recs; R. Jetté, 1983, pp. 1074-1075, 499-500.

134. H. Charbonneau and J. Légaré, 1978-1990, Vol. 10, L'Ange Gardien recs; R. Jetté, 1983, pp. 499-500, 1063.

135. H. Charbonneau and J. Légaré, 1978-1990, Vol. 10, St. Augustin de Maure recs; R. Jetté, 1983, pp. 500, 355.

XI

Mathieu Brunet dit Létang
and his wife Marie Blanchard

*Voyageur-trader in the upper Great Lakes region
during the early and mid 1680s, the first decade
in which the license system was in effect*

Mathieu Brunet dit Létang emigrated from France to the colony of New France during the summer of 1657, under contract as an indentured laborer. He had been born to Jacques Brunet and Jacqueline Recheine (according to a deciphering of the handwritten church record of his wedding in 1667) or Jacqueline Prohuie (according to a deciphering of the handwritten marriage contract, which was drawn up 11 1/2 years after the wedding, in 1679).

His year of birth has been estimated as about 1637 to 1641. (At the time of Mathieu's hiring contract in March of 1657, he gave his age as 20, which was most likely either correct or close to being accurate. At the time of his death in December of 1708, one of his family members would report that he had been 70 years of age. When he was ordered to testify in a court case in January of 1701, he indicated that he was 60 years old. These three instances of reported ages imply a birth year for him of about 1637, 1638, and 1641, respectively. However, at the time of the 1681 census, Monsieur Brunet indicated that he was age 35, which would imply that his year of birth had been about 1646. Since this date is considerably later than the other three reported birth years, it appears that the colonist may have reduced his age considerably (by as much as eight or nine years) when reporting his information to the census enumerator. He had certainly not been eleven years old at the time of his indenture contract back in 1657. Thus, in the present biography, the span of 1637 to 1641 has been utilized as the estimated period of his birth.)

According to his marriage contact from April 14, 1679, Mathieu Brunet was a "native of St. Jean [parish] at Rai, near the town of L'Aigle, in the diocese of Evreux in Normandy." According to Joan Blaeu's detailed 1665 maps of France and its various provinces, L'Aigle (sometimes written as Le Aigle, The Eagle) was a *ville* (town) of considerable importance in the area. Located some 85 miles due west of Paris, this community served as the locus of activity for a number of smaller *bourgs* (market towns), even smaller *villages* (villages), tiny *hameaux* (hamlets), and many scattered, miniature *lieux-dits* (named-places). Rai, positioned about two miles southwest of L'Aigle, was a small village or hamlet whose inhabitants sometimes traveled to the much more substantial town, in order to participate in the market or to conduct business with the merchants or the notary. Both of these communities were located just a few miles north of the southern border of Normandy, in the southeastern area of this province.

At some point, Mathieu relocated from Rai about eleven miles toward the south-southeast, moving into the adjacent County or region of Perche. Apparently relocating with his parents, he settled in the market town of Tourouvre. Thus, years later, at the time of Mathieu's marriage in November of 1667, the priest would record in the parish register of the Quebec church that the groom had been from Tourouvre. During the 1630s through the 1660s, nearly two hundred colonists would emigrate from Tourouvre, as well as from Mortagne nine miles to the southwest (the largest city in Perche, with sufficient population for three parish churches), and from numerous other communities in the region of northwestern Perche. Traveling across the Atlantic to the colony, these settlers would remain permanently in the New World. The recruitment program for New France had begun in earnest in this particular area of Perche back in 1634, when Robert Giffard had engaged settlers here for his seigneury at Beauport, just northeast of Quebec.

However, Mathieu did not emigrate directly from Perche to the colony. At some point, he moved westward from Tourouvre all the way to the Atlantic coast. In this manner, he joined the steady movement of poor people who relocated during the seventeenth and eighteenth centuries from the countryside and the small villages to the towns and cities of France, in an effort to find employment. Major contributors to this mass movement of land-less people were the provinces of Normandy and Flanders, as well as the region of the Massif Central, where the respective populations had long before outgrown the capacity of the soil to feed its residents. The majority of these internal emigrants gravitated to the areas that bordered on the Atlantic Ocean and La Manche (the English Channel), and to the province of Île de France (of which Paris was the center). It was in these western and northwestern provinces and in the Paris region that recruiters worked the most assiduously to enlist colonists for New France. Thus, it was in the capital city and in the western and northwestern seaports that a large percentage of the early settlers were engaged, after they had found little or no work at the end of their relocations within the mother country itself. For many of these people, moving across the ocean to the colony was simply another stage in their travels away from their homes, as they sought employment in distant places.

In the case of Mathieu Brunet, instead of relocating some 60 to 70 miles northward from Tourouvre to the ports of Honfleur or Le Havre on the English Channel, he moved about 180 miles southwest to Olonne, on the Atlantic coast. This town, located two miles north of the port of Les Sables d'Olonne, was positioned $2^1/2$ miles inland from the seacoast. These two seafaring communities were located about 40 miles northwest of the very prominent port city of La Rochelle. On March 19, 1657, when Mathieu was engaged at La Rochelle to work as an indentured laborer in New France, he was residing at Olonne.[1]

At the time of his indenture contract, which was drawn up by a La Rochelle notary, the prospective colonist's name was recorded as simply Mathieu Brunet. Thus, it appears that he acquired his nickname *dit Lestang* or *dit Lestan* ("called The Pond") after his arrival in the colony, as a means of distinguishing him from the various other Brunet families and individuals who resided in New France. In Cotgrave's 1611 work entitled *A Dictionarie of the French and English Tongues*, the French term *estang* was defined as " a great pond, poole, or standing water." Later, in the modernization of French spelling, the *es* in the first syllable was transformed into *é*, thus giving rise to the spelling *Létang*.[2]

Throughout the history of the colony, only two other men besides Mathieu are known to have utilized this nickname. One of these individuals was Michel Belenfant dit Létang, an unmarried soldier who died at Trois-Rivières in 1664. The other one was Jean Douhet, Sieur de La Rivière et de L'Étang, a recently-married immigrant who resided at Verchères. This man was killed by Iroquois warriors in 1687, before he and his wife had produced any children. In contrast, the nickname "dit Létang" was applied to Mathieu Brunet throughout his entire life in New France, which spanned more than half a century. In the 26 notary documents (the primary legal records of the period) which are known to have related to him, he was identified with this nickname in 23 of them. These ranged from the very first such document in 1669 through the final one in 1703. The only instances in which the various notaries in the colony did not utilize the addendum "dit Lestang" occurred in June of 1673, November of 1673, and May of 1690. In complete contrast, his nickname was very seldom recorded by priests in the church records. Within the series of at least 34 entries in parish ledgers that are known to have involved Mathieu, his nickname was included in only three cases. These occasions were the baptism of his second child Pierre in 1676, the wedding of his second son Jean in 1694, and the remarriage of his eldest son Michel in 1713. Interestingly, Monsieur Brunet's name was written in the church record of his own wedding in 1667 as simply Mathieu Brunet. Likewise, his name was recorded in the very same manner, without the nickname, in the official colony-wide census of 1681.[3]

By the spring of 1657, Mathieu had been residing for some time in the seafaring community of Olonne, on the western coast of France. On March 19, the Feast Day of St. Joseph, he was engaged at La Rochelle (forty miles to the southeast) to work as an indentured laborer in New France. On this day, as he stood before a notary in the city, his hirers were Antoine Grignon, Pierre Gaigneur, and Jacques Massé. Over the span of two months during this late winter and early spring, between February 3 and April 5, these three prominent Catholic merchants of La Rochelle hired a total of forty men to serve in the colony. Monsieur Grignon, who had a wife and six children in the port city, would be documented at Quebec on various occasions between September of 1654 and August of 1664, during his numerous transatlantic business trips to the colony. Pierre Gaigneur, some two decades younger than his first colleague, had married Monsieur Grignon's daughter Jeanne in 1654, but they had not yet produced any children; their four offspring would be born in the port city between 1658 and 1670. This second *marchand bourgeois* would serve as one of the primary recruiters of colonists for New France during the two decades between 1648 and 1668.

For this particular venture in 1657, the second year in which these partners had been working together, they had leased on January 20 the ship called *Les Armes d'Amsterdam*; this was a vessel with an internal capacity of 250 tons. (It would only be a decade later, in 1667, that the partners Grignon and Gaigneur would finally purchase their own ships to carry out their transatlantic ventures. Until that time, they would utilize leased vessels.) According to the records of

La Rochelle notaries, Messieurs Gaigneur and Massé served as the outfitters of *Les Armes d'Amsterdam* for her 1657 voyage, of which Quebec was recorded as the destination. In the autumn of that same year, the vessel would return with a moderate cargo of beaver pelts, which would be sold for the total sum of 16,491 livres 5 sols. Additional income had been generated for the partners from the sale in the colony of the employment contracts of the forty indentured workers whom they had recruited and had dispatched to Quebec, including Mathieu Brunet.[4]

At the time of his hiring contract, Mathieu indicated that he was twenty years old, which was a rather typical age for indentured laborers who signed on for service in New France. Since these *engagés* were typically recruited by the merchants to serve in the colony for a period of three years, they were often termed *trente-six mois*, "thirty-six-monthers." According to their hiring contracts, which the workmen signed in France before departure, they would be first transported across the ocean, then they would be fed, housed, and paid a modest salary during their period of servitude. The wages of each individual (paid by the person or organization in the colony who purchased their work contract) usually ranged from 60 to 75 livres per year but were sometimes as high as 100 livres, depending upon the given man's previous employment and training. In addition, if they decided not to remain in the colony at the conclusion of their service, they would be given a no-cost trip back to the mother country, with the expenses of the return voyage covered by the original hirer (typically, about one-third of these contract workers did return to France). The hiring merchants in the mother country were allowed to give each indentured worker an advance of up to 35 livres from the man's first year's wages. In addition, the hirer often provided food and housing for the hiree from the time the contract was signed until the time the ship departed.

In New France, the legally binding contracts of the indentured workmen were sold to administrators, seigneurs, religious orders, and colonists, who would from then on assume the costs of the men's upkeep and wages for the duration of the service period. As one would expect, the selling price for each contract was considerably higher than the sum of up to 100 livres or more that the hiring merchant in France had expended on that given individual, in the course of recruiting him, giving him an advance on his wages, feeding him, housing him, and finally transporting him across the ocean.

Each indentured workman who was safely delivered to New France generated a measure of profit for the hiring merchant; thus, the more workmen who were recruited, the greater the amount of profit. The maximum number of indentured workmen per ship was not limited or restricted; only the minimum number of men, prorated at one man per 15 tons of internal capacity of a given vessel, was expressed in the license of the ship and its captain.[5]

After Mathieu completed his term of indentured service, in about the summer of 1660, no surviving documents have yet been located which might shed light on his activities in the colony from that time until the autumn of 1667. Unfortunately, he was not enumerated in the censuses of either 1666 or 1667. In the first of these colony-wide enumerations, a total of 3,182 French residents were recorded. These included 539 individuals at Quebec, 583 in the area around Quebec, 13 across the St. Lawrence at Lauson, 521 on the Côte de Beaupré, 440 on Île d'Orléans, 462 at Trois-Rivières and in the nearby area, and 624 on Montreal Island. In the following year's census, which was considerably more accurate, the total number of colonists was recorded as 3,877 (representing an increase of fully 22 percent). These recounted individuals included 438 residents at Quebec, 930 in the area around Quebec, 111 across the river at Lauson, 670 on the Côte de Beaupré, 426 on Île d'Orléans, 552 at Trois-Rivières and in the surrounding area, and 750 on Montreal Island. In both of these censuses, the numbers of reported colonists which are noted here reflect the corrections that have been made by modern scholars concerning the multiple listings of certain individuals in different locales.[6]

During much of the seven-year period in which documentation for him is lacking, there is a distinct possibility that Monsieur Brunet dit Léstang may have been in the interior regions, participating in trading ventures that had not been officially approved by either the Governor or the Intendant. The fact that his name was not recorded in any church or civil records from the summer of 1660 until the autumn of 1667 does indicate that he remained beyond the notice of those individuals who penned public documents during that particular period.

By the autumn of 1667, Mathieu had found his soul mate, Marie Blanchard, the daughter of Jean Blanchard and Martine Lebas. (Her family name was sometimes also spelled Blanchart and Blanchar in various records of New France; however, each of the three versions was pronounced the same.) Hailing from the parish of St. Michel or St. Nicaise in Rouen, Normandy, Marie was about 18 to 20 years old. (In the census of 1681, her age was recorded as 32; at the time of her death in July of 1722, one of her family members indicated that her age had been 75. From these two records, her year of birth has been extrapolated as about 1647 to 1649.) She had emigrated from France as a *fille du Roi* (daughter of the King), hoping to find a good husband and begin a new life in the colony. After the priests at the Quebec church had published the first bann of marriage for the Brunet-Blanchard couple and had dispensed with the other two banns, the bride and groom pronounced their wedding vows in the church on November 10, 1667. At the festive ceremony, three of their friends, all of whom were from the Quebec parish, served as the official witnesses. These were Michel Morel (about 37 years old, who would soon move to Trois-Rivières; he would be married there some three years later, in about 1670), André Poutré dit Lavigne (about age 24 to 29, a recently-retired soldier of the Carignan-Salières Regiment and also a cobbler; he had been married one week earlier in the Quebec church, and he would soon be established at Sorel), and Pierre Peré. In anticipation of their wedding, Mathieu and Marie had not visited a notary to have an official marriage contract drawn up; they would eventually take care of this detail eleven years and five months after having celebrated their wedding.[7]

It was during this very period of 1666 and 1667 in which treaties with the various Iroquois nations brought about a cessation of surprise attacks by their warriors. For a full quarter-century, ever since 1641, the French colonists and their native allies had endured, and had been held back by, nearly constant scourges of Iroquois war parties. Now, with this ever-present danger finally removed from their daily lives, the French would be able to clear and occupy many new areas along the St. Lawrence, and successfully expand their farming activities.

The newly-married Brunet-Blanchard couple must have been imbued with this expansive spirit, since they decided to leave the Quebec area and settle in the outlying seigneuries near Trois-Rivières. They must have undertaken this move shortly after their wedding, probably in late 1667 or during 1668. According to the census of 1667, only 552 colonists (just 14 percent of the total French population in the St. Lawrence Valley) resided in the small town of Trois-Rivières itself and the seigneuries which were slowly developing in the areas nearby. These settled areas extended along the north shore of the St. Lawrence over a span of about eleven miles, from a spot three miles southwest of the town to eight miles northeast of the town. Commencing at the eastern bank of the St. Maurice River (just beyond Trois-Rivières), the land that stretched off to the northeast for seven miles comprised the seigneury of Cap de la Madeleine. It was here, and in the area to the northeast of this seigneury, in which Mathieu and Marie chose to settle, on lands which were being newly granted to colonists at the time. In a west-to-east sequence beyond Cap de la Madeleine (which had been established in 1636), covering a span of some twenty miles of St. Lawrence shoreline, these new seigneuries were Champlain (created in 1664), Batiscan (1636), Ste. Marie (1672), and Ste. Anne de la Pérade (1672).[8]

It was in about the year 1668, the first year following their wedding, in which Marie and Mathieu produced their first child. However, no baptismal record for tiny Michel has been located in any ecclesiastical records of the colony. The church at Trois-Rivières would have been the nearest one to the young couple, but neither the parish ledger there nor that of any other parish contains a record of this lad's christening. But the year of 1668 may be projected as the general time of his birth, since he was listed as being 13 years old in the census of 1681.[9]

As spring approached in 1669, Mathieu joined forces for the purposes of work with Louis Bercier, a local settler who was about 36 to 38 years old. This man, a joiner or maker of finished carpentry and furnishings, had married in about 1668, either at Batiscan or back in France; he and his wife were expecting their first child in this year. These two recently-wedded husbands, both of whom were relatively new to the area, struck an agreement with a man who owned properties in the seigneuries of both Cap de la Madeleine and Batiscan. Michel Pelletier, the Sieur de La Pérade, about 38 or 39 years old, was a rather wealthy merchant whose business was based out of Trois-Rivières. In the afternoon of March 30, Mathieu and Louis, along with the notary Jacques de la Touche of Trois-Rivières, traveled to Monsieur Pelletier's home at Cap de la Madeleine. There, the scribe documented the details of the agreement of the two workmen and their employer.

"Louis Le Bercier and Mathieu Brunet dit Lestang, land clearers, each one of them for the both of them, have obligated themselves on this day to the noble man Michel Pelletier de La Pérade, habitant of the said Cap and in

the seigneury of Batiscan, to clear for him on his property at Batiscan the quantity of eight arpents [6³/4 acres] of land...in consideration of the sum of twenty livres for each arpent, of which the aforesaid sum the said Sieur de La Pérade will pay in good articles."

Commencing with the spring of 1670 and each year thereafter, if the two workmen so chose, they could plant the cleared land in corn or wheat. After they had completed the harvest each year, they would be obliged to deliver to Monsieur Pelletier's home at Cap, at their own expense, five bushels of good and valid wheat for each arpent of land that they had cultivated. They would be permitted to retain for themselves the remainder of the crops which they would raise on the cleared land.

"The said Le Bercier and Brunet not knowing how to write or sign, having been questioned according to the ordinance, have made their marks. Present were Master Martin Carpentier of this said seigneury and Nicolas Dupuis, who have signed with us, the said notary. In addition, the said Sieur de La Pérade is obliged to give to them [Messieurs Bercier and Brunet] one pint of brandy [to seal the bargain].

Signed, Michel Peltier, + the mark of the said Brunet, vvvvv the mark of the said Bercier, Carpantier, Nicollas Dupuis, and Jacques de la Tousche."[10]

The seigneury of Batiscan, in which Mathieu and Louis agreed to clear the piece of land, contained a frontage of seven miles along the St. Lawrence shoreline. This stretch of land commenced about fourteen miles northeast of Trois-Rivières.[11]

Five months after arranging the details of the forest-clearing and farming project, Mathieu acquired his first known piece of property in New France. On August 24, 1669, the Trois-Rivières notary Ameau recorded that Monsieur Brunet had purchased a lot in the sub-fief of Prairies Marsolet. This sub-fief, having a total St. Lawrence frontage of about 1³/4 miles, had been granted to the interpreter and trade ambassador Nicolas Marsolet, the Sieur de Saint Aignan, back in 1644. It was located in the extreme southeastern corner of the Cap de la Madeleine seigneury, commencing about seven miles northeast of Trois-Rivières. In return for his long, slender plot within the sub-fief, which measured three arpents (575 feet) of frontage on the St. Lawrence by 40 arpents (1¹/2 miles) in depth toward the north, Mathieu paid the carpenter Étienne Gélinas fifty livres. This rather modest price must have reflected that very little of the land had been cleared of its forest cover, since the seller had only owned it for eighteen months. As his annual seigneurial fees for this property,

Mathieu was to pay to the representative of Monsieur Marsolet (since the seigneur himself resided at Quebec) one-half bushel of wheat, one capon, and one denier in cash, which were to be due on the Feast of St. Martin (November 11) each year. According to his later testimony, Mathieu soon built a home and a granary on this purchased land, which was flanked on the east side by the property of Pierre Gaillou and on the west side by that of the seller's son Jean Gélinas.[12]

The ships which came from the mother country during this summer of 1669 brought an edict from the King and Minister Colbert which ordered the establishment of an official militia in the colony. All able-bodied men between the ages of sixteen and sixty were required to participate in the activities of this informal military body. By means of monthly training sessions and drills, the appointed Captain of each local unit would see to it that the men of his unit were equipped with properly functioning firearms, and that they were instructed in the use of those weapons, as well as in the basic elements of military organization, discipline, and activities. At all times, each man in the militia forces would be equipped with sufficient supplies of gunpowder and shot. This year, Mathieu was about 28 to 32 years old, well within the age bracket of the men who were obligated to join the militia. Since he had hired himself out as a land-clearer and farmer just five months earlier, it is to be assumed that he was in sufficiently able-bodied condition to participate in the associated activities of the militia forces.[13]

Probably during the following year of 1670, Marie and Mathieu joyfully welcomed their second child and first daughter into the world. However, as with their first baby about two years earlier, no record has been found in any church ledger in the colony for the baptism of little Jeanne. She was listed in the census of 1681 as being eleven years old; thus, it is likely that her safe arrival occurred in about 1670.[14]

Less than eighteen months after he had purchased his lot in the Prairies Marsolet from the carpenter Gélinas, Mathieu was granted another plot within the same sub-fief, one that was twice as wide. On February 8, 1671, Nicolas Marsolet's representative granted to Mathieu a plot that had 6 arpents (1,150 feet) of frontage along the St. Lawrence and 40 arpents (1 1/2 miles) of depth. His adjacent neighbor on the east side was Martin Foisy, while his immediate neighbor on the west was Louis Tétreau. Upon this land, Monsieur Brunet was to develop two farms, each of which would contain three arpents of river frontage. With this new double lot, he also received the rights of hunting and fishing, on both his own granted property and on the Marsolet lands which stretched off to the north behind it for another five miles. As with the three-arpent plot that he had earlier purchased, Mathieu would be obliged to pay each year to the representative of his seigneur one half-bushel of wheat, one capon hen, and one denier in cash for each of the two new three-arpent parcels.[15]

It is to be assumed that the year 1672 brought with it the heartening arrival of the third child of the Brunet-Blanchard couple. However, as with their previous two offspring, no official baptismal record has ever been located for Marie Anne in any of the church records of the colony. Again, her year of birth has been extrapolated from the data in the census of 1681, in which she was reported as being 9 years old.[16]

In June of 1673, Mathieu and Louis Bercier, his former land-clearing and farming partner from four years earlier, reached a private settlement concerning a dispute that had arisen between them. On the 26th day of the month, Mathieu and the notary from the adjacent seigneury of Ste. Anne de la Pérade met at Monsieur Bercier's home in the seigneury of Batiscan. In their joint settlement, the two antagonists agreed that Louis would pay to Mathieu, within three days of this meeting, four bushels of good and valid wheat plus thirteen livres in cash. They had reached this accord "in order to avoid the expenses [of a court suit]...The parties have dropped all of the differences which they had between themselves, one against the other."[17]

Interestingly, in this document Mathieu Brunet was described as an "habitant of Arbre à la Croix." This was the sub-fief, about $1^3/4$ miles wide, that was located in the southwesternmost corner of the seigneury of Champlain. It lay immediately east of the sub-fief of Prairies Marsolet in Cap de la Madeleine, in which Mathieu owned two parcels of land. No other surviving documents reveal why or on which property the Brunet family was residing at Arbre à la Croix at this time. This particular place of residence for them was recorded on only one other occasion, $7^1/2$ years later, in a notary document from December of 1680. However, during that intervening period of $7^1/2$ years, Mathieu and his family would be consistently described as residents of Prairies Marsolet, in two notary records from 1676 and three others from 1679. After the record from December of 1680, the Brunet-Blanchard family would then be regularly described as living in the seigneury of Champlain. This latter information would appear in a series of six notarial documents which extended from December of 1682 until October of 1687. After this period of residence at Champlain, they would relocate to the Montreal region.

On October 30, 1673, the seigneur Nicolas Marsolet submitted a request to the Chief Judge of the Trois-Rivières Court, and two weeks later, on November 13, the Judge responded with his affirmation and his edict. All of the habitants of Prairies Marsolet were to show and register with the notary their land titles, which described the respective properties that had been granted to each of them in the sub-fief. In the meantime, an official survey of the granted lands within the Marsolet sub-fief would be conducted.

This survey was carried out by Jean Le Rouge, licensed surveyor of New France, on November 17. According to his report, the properties were measured in the presence of all of the land-owners except Laurent Pinard. In the notary document which was based upon the surveyor's report, the lots were thus listed, in sequence from east to west: Jean Gaillou, three arpents or thereabouts of frontage along the edge of the St. Lawrence; François Bigot, three arpents of frontage; Mathieu Brunet, three arpents of frontage; Laurent Pinard, two lots, each of them containing three arpents of frontage; Martin Foisy, six arpents of frontage; Mathieu Brunet, three [actually six] arpents of frontage; and Louis Tétreau, nine arpents of frontage.[18]

The first listing pertaining to Monsieur Brunet represented the lot that he had purchased from Étienne Gélinas back in 1669, which contained a frontage of three arpents along the St. Lawrence shoreline. The second Brunet listing pertained to the double lot which Mathieu had been granted by the seigneur in 1671. In the latter case, the statement of three arpents of frontage instead of six arpents was simply a clerical error, which was apparently made by the notary when he copied the surveyor's notes into the finished document. This mistake was corrected when Mathieu reported to the notary's office in Trois-Rivières ten days later, on November 27, 1673, and showed to him the actual titles that he held for the two parcels of land.

After reading the first title, concerning the land grant of February 8, 1671, the notary reiterated all of its details, including the correct dimensions of the parcel (six arpents of frontage by forty arpents of depth, for the creation of two adjacent farms), its location in relation to the adjacent neighbors, the hunting and fishing rights, and the annual seigneurial fees. At the conclusion of this newly-written document, the notary penned the following sentence: "The said [Brunet dit] Lestang has declared that he has not yet been able to make or build a house on the said two farm sites, and that he will work unceasingly at the clearing of the land and afterward build on it." Then, in a separate section, the scribe noted that Jean Le Rouge had conducted a survey of this property on November 17. At the end of each of these two sections, the notary indicated that "He has made his mark." In each instance, after Mathieu had applied his moderately large + mark below the text, the scribe added, "Mark of the said Brunet."

In the third section of the document, the notary reiterated all of the details of the Brunet lot purchased on August 24, 1669, which were expressed in the title that Mathieu produced for him. This was the parcel that actually did contain three arpents of St. Lawrence frontage. At the end of this section, the scribe wrote, "Upon this *habitation* (farm site) the said Mathieu Brunet declares that he has built a granary and a house." Again, the fourth section of the new document consisted of a statement concerning Monsieur Le Rouge's survey of the latter property on November 17. As before, beneath both the third and the fourth sections, Mathieu applied his bold + mark. The statement at the end of the third section of this document clearly indicated that Mathieu and Marie had established their primary place of residence on the three-arpent lot which Mathieu had purchased in the summer of 1669. On this land, they had constructed both a house and a granary.[19]

Five weeks after the official registration of their land documents, Marie and Mathieu were elated at the safe arrival of their fourth child, on January 3, 1674. Now, their ever-growing brood contained two girls and two boys. Six days after the baby's arrival, on the ninth day of the month, the tiny lad was christened at Cap de la Madeleine by a visiting priest from Trois-Rivières. (The first records of this new parish of Ste. Marie Madeleine had commenced only a few weeks earlier, in the previous November.) The godfather who bequeathed his first name to the boy on this happy day was Jean Peré, while the godmother was Marie Bouchard.[20]

Offspring number five, Pierre Brunet, arrived 25 months later. When he was christened at Cap de la Madeleine on February 13, 1676, the priest recorded that the little lad had been born in the Marsolet sub-fief to "Mathieu Brunet dit Lestan and Marie Blanchart." At his inspiring baptism, the sponsors were Pierre Girardeau and Marie Madeleine Provencher. This young godmother, a resident of Cap de la Madeleine who about sixteen years old, would marry Aubin Maudou in the Cap church nine months later.[21]

Well before his marriage to Mlle. Provencher, Aubin Maudou dit Potdevin, who was about 24 to 32 years old, became a business partner of Mathieu Brunet. On April 4, seven weeks after Aubin's fiancée had stood as the baptismal sponsor for Mathieu's latest child, these two men leased a plot of land in the La Touche section of the Champlain seigneury, with the intention of farming it. They made these arrangements with the owner of the lot, René Blanchet, who lived in the adjacent seigneury of Cap de la Madeleine with his wife and three children. The La Touche name for this particular section of Champlain had been derived from the name of the seigneur himself, Étienne Pezard, Sieur de La Touche et de Champlain. This highly respected soldier, who had served as the Captain of first the garrison at Trois-Rivières and then of the garrison at Montreal, had been granted this seigneury twelve years earlier, back in 1664.[22]

During the summer of 1676, a physical altercation broke out between Mathieu and Marie on the one side and the woman who often resided on the farm immediately east of the Brunet's double lot at Marsolet on the other side. This action led to charges being leveled against the Brunet couple in the Trois-Rivières Court, after which a settlement was finally reached between all of the parties in front of the Trois-Rivières notary on August 3.

Unfortunately, the cause of the conflict was not described in this settlement document. *"Before Antoine Adhémar, royal notary and registrar of the Court of Trois-Rivières, residing at Champlain, and the witnesses named at the end were present Martin Foisy, habitant of Arbre à la Croix, of the one part, and Mathieu Brunet dit Lestang, habitant of Prairies de Marsolet, and Marie Blanchard, his wife, who has duly authorized the facts which follow, of the other part...The said Foisy had registered a complaint before Monsieur [Gilles] Boisvinet [Sieur de Saint Marguerite], Councilor of the King and Lieutenant General [Chief Judge] of the town of Trois-Rivières, on account of blows which were committed on the person of Marie Madeleine Beaudoin, his wife, by the said Brunet and Blanchard, his wife...Desiring to nourish peace and friendship between them through the agency of their mutual friends, they have agreed and conceded that which follows...The said Brunet and Blanchard, his wife, in solidarity, one for the other and each of them only for the whole, without discussion or dissension, renouncing any such said divisions, have faithfully promised and obligated themselves to pay and discharge for the said Martin Foisy all of the expenses*

which were incurred by him, both the legal expenses of traveling and arranging witnesses as well as the pains and travels which were required of the surgeon who has come and visited the said Beaudoin, which expenses of the said plaintiff up to this day and in their entirety will be discharged for the said Foisy...[This agreement] made and drawn up at Prairies de Marsolet in the home of Louis Tétreau, habitant of the said place [immediately west of the six-arpent property of the Brunets], on the third day of the month of August, 1676 in the afternoon, in the presence of [Jean-]Guy Vacher, the Sieur de Lacerte, master joiner living at Trois-Rivières, with the said Foisy, Jean Larue, Antoine Roy, habitant of Batiscan, and Bernard Dumouchel dit Laroche, habitant of the said Prairies [Marsolet]. Since it was said that the said Brunet and his wife did not know how to sign, having been questioned according to the ordinance, they have made their mark, after having heard a reading of these presents by the said notary.
Signed,
Martin Foysid, + mark of the said Brunet, X mark of the said Blanchard, Vacher, + mark of the said Larue, + mark of the said Roy, + mark of the said Dumouchel, and Adhémar"[23]

In the autumn of 1677, celebrations were in order for the Brunet-Blanchard family when their seventh child arrived safely on October 25. At Marie's baptismal festivities in the Cap de la Madeleine church on the following day, the godfather was none other than Martin Foisy. (The Brunet and Foisy couples had apparently restored their neighborly friendship during the previous fifteen months, after their mutual grievances had been resolved by the official settlement back in 1676.) The baby's other sponsor on this cheerful occasion was Barbe Duchesne.[24]

In the spring of 1679, Mathieu and Marie conducted two property transactions at Marsolet: one of these was a sale, while the other one was a lease with the intention to farm. In this sub-fief, their immediate neighbor to the east was François Bigot, about 35 years old, who owned a lot with three arpents of St. Lawrence frontage. Here he lived with his wife Catherine Baillargeon, about age 26 or 27, and their two children who were $3^1/2$ years and twelve months old, respectively. Their plot was the same size as the lot on which the Brunets lived next door, where Mathieu and Marie had built a house, a granary, and various outbuildings. Almost a half-mile to the west of the Brunets' farm was their wooded double lot, which contained six arpents of river frontage. Six years earlier, back in 1673, the couple had promised their seigneur Nicolas Marsolet that they would clear portions of this latter property and build one or two houses upon it. However, it is not known whether they had accomplished much toward these goals by the spring of 1679. On April 14 of this year, Mathieu and Marie visited the notary Adhémar, along with Monsieur Bigot, to register that the Brunets had sold their six-arpent lot to him. In addition, they had leased from Bigot his three-arpent property, which lay adjacent to their place of residence, with the intention of farming it themselves.[25]

During this same visit to the notary, the Brunet-Blanchard couple requested that the scribe draw up a marriage contract for them, which they had not done eleven years and five months earlier, when they had been married back in November of 1667. On this occasion, Monsieur Adhémar recorded that Mathieu Brunet dit Lestang, living at Prairies de Marsolet, was a native of St. Jean parish at Rai, near the town of L'Aigle, in the diocese of Évreux in Normandy, while Marie Blanchard was a native of the parish of St. Nicaise in the town and diocese of Rouen. He also added, *"Mariés depuis environ douze ans* (Married for about twelve years)." For this document, the two official witnesses were François Bigot and Martin Foisy. The latter settler was the neighbor who lived immediately east of the six-arpent lot which the Brunets had just sold. He was also the man who had stood as the godfather of the most recent Brunet child in October of 1677, and the irate husband who had registered charges in court against Mathieu and Marie for having struck his wife during the summer of 1676. As is often the case, the passage of time had apparently smoothed the ruffled feathers of the former antagonists.[26]

In the early summer of 1679, Mathieu was honored to stand beside the baptismal font in the Cap de la Madeleine church, and there grant his name to the four-day-old son of Nicolas Milet dit Marandais and Michelle Lesdiller. The godmother on this occasion was Madeleine Dufan. At the conclusion of this christening, the priest neglected to record the date with the rest of the information in the parish ledger. However, based upon the records that preceded and followed it, this ceremony took place some time between May 23 and June 26.[27]

It was during the latter part of this year that the parish of Notre Dame de la Visitation was established in the seigneury of Champlain. The records of this parish commenced with the first entry in October of 1679. It would be in this new church that the vast majority of the ecclesiastical celebrations of the Brunet family would be held during the next eight years, through the autumn of 1687.[28]

On January 15, 1680, Mathieu (who was described in the notarial document from Trois-Rivières as a resident of the sub-fief of Marsolet) purchased a piece of land across the river from Cap de la Madeleine, "on the other shore of the great St. Lawrence River." The lot that he acquired, located in the sub-fief of Villiers in the seigneury of Bécancour, had been owned by Jean Mouflet dit Champagne and his wife Anne Dodin, a young couple who had four children. Shortly after conducting this property transfer, the Mouflet family moved upriver about ninety miles, to settle at Lachine.[29]

The seigneury of Bécancour (whose residents attended the Cap de la Madeleine church across the river) was owned by Charles Legardeur, Sieur de Villiers. It was here that Nicolas Perrot, the distinguished trader, interpreter, and liaison with the native nations of the upper Great Lakes region, settled with his wife and five children at about this time. Two of the Perrot couple's later children would be born at the other sub-fief of Bécancour, called Lintot, in July of 1680 and in February of 1683, while a third would be born in the sub-fief of Villiers in January of 1684. It is possible that Mathieu Brunet first met Monsieur Perrot late in 1679 or at the beginning of 1680, when he inspected and then purchased his new lot at Villiers. The close relationship that eventually developed between these two men will be discussed later in this story. In addition to Nicolas Perrot, Claude David (who had spent the years from 1660 to 1663 in the western Great Lakes, as one of the very earliest Frenchmen to travel into the interior specifically to trade) may have also inspired in Mathieu a deep interest in the peltries commerce. Claude (whose biography has already been presented in this volume) resided during this same period (in sequence) in the seigneury of Champlain, then across the St. Lawrence in the south-shore seigneury of Gentilly, and finally in the adjacent seigneury of Bécancour to the west. After his stint as an active trader in the west, Monsieur David had also served as an investing partner in Nicolas Perrot's trading ventures. These two residents of the same areas in which Mathieu lived may have had a considerable influence on his decision to participate seriously in the peltries business.[30]

Six months after they had acquired the across-the-river property, Marie and Mathieu's family size expanded by one, with the arrival of baby Jacques on July 30, 1680. For his baptism a week later at the new Champlain church, on August 6, the couple chose Jacques Leuraux of Trois-Rivières to serve as the boy's godfather and name-giver, and Marie Tétreau of Prairies Marsolet to stand as his godmother. This latter sixteen-year-old, the eldest child of their neighbors Louis Tétreau and Noëlle Landeau, would marry during the following year.[31]

By the end of 1680, the Brunet family was again residing in the Arbre à la Croix sub-fief of the Champlain seigneury, as they had once been previously documented, back in June of 1673. (Yet they had been very consistently described as living in the Prairies Marsolet sub-fief of the Cap de la Madeleine seigneury, a few miles west of Arbre à la Croix, during the following interval of 7 1/2 years, until this particular document.) On December 10, 1680, Mathieu visited the notary to record his purchase of a rather extensive parcel of land in the Champlain seigneury. (This seigneury, commencing some eight miles northeast of Trois-Rivières, contained about five miles of St. Lawrence frontage.) The sellers of the lot, François Lory dit Gargot and his wife Perrette Paremant, had four children. This family wished to relocate upriver to Montreal and Lachine (which they would do following this transaction). The property being transferred to Mathieu, measuring 4 1/2 arpents (865 feet) in frontage along the St. Lawrence and 40 arpents (1 1/2 miles) in depth, was being sold with all of its buildings for 500 livres. This sum was to be paid in four equal payments, the first of which would be due on the Day of the Feast of Noël (Christmas Day) in the following year of 1681. The other three payments were to be delivered on that same day in each of the following years, until the purchase price had been fully paid off. It was on this farm in the Champlain seigneury that the Brunet-Blanchard family would reside for the next seven years, until their eventual move to the Montreal region in the autumn of 1687. However, oddly enough, Mathieu would only pay a total of 36 livres against this debt, during the entire period of their seven years of living on this farm as well as the first four years of their residence in the Montreal area. His lack of payments would eventually lead to a court suit and an eventual settlement between Messieurs Brunet and Lory, in December of 1701.[32]

By the time the colony-wide census was conducted during the spring or early summer of 1681, Marie was a few months pregnant with their eighth child. When the enumerator visited household number 11 at Champlain (which Mathieu had purchased during the previous December), he recorded the following information:
"Mathieu Brunet [dit Lestang], age 35

Marie Blanchard, his wife, age 32
Children:
Michel, 13
Jeanne, 11
Marie Anne, 9
Jean, 8
Pierre, 6
Marie, 4
Jacob [Jacques], 1
One cow, 21 arpents [17.9 acres] of land cleared and under cultivation"[33]

It is quite likely that Mathieu may have reduced his age by as much as eight or nine years when supplying the family's information to the census-taker; this assertion is based upon three other sources of information concerning his probable year of birth. Since no baptismal records exist for the three oldest Brunet children, their ages listed here are the primary surviving evidence upon which projections of their years of birth may be based. Thus, their respective arrivals appear to have taken place in about 1668, 1670, and 1672. By examining the christening records for the rest of the children, it is clear that the ages of the next two younger sons were inflated somewhat for this census. Jean would not turn eight until the following January of 1682, while Pierre would not celebrate his sixth birthday until February of 1682. In comparison, the ages of the two youngest children were only slightly elevated. Marie would turn four in October of this year, while little Jacques, not yet walking, would celebrate his first birthday in August of this year. In examining these numbers, it is possible that the enumerator may have asked how old the children would be upon reaching their next birthday. Interestingly, the youngest child of the family was identified in the roster as Jacob, rather than by the customary French name of Jacques.[34]

After this enumeration, no further documentation concerning little Pierre has survived anywhere in the colony, not even the boy's burial record. Thus, it is not possible to determine just when Marie and Mathieu had to suffer the poignant loss of this child, their first such loss. All that can be said for certain is that they were able to enjoy at least $5^1/4$ years of his presence in the family.

According to the census information, the Brunet-Blanchard family owned only one cow and no oxen, yet they had nearly eighteen acres of land under cultivation. (Presumably, all of this cultivated acreage had been cleared and worked by the previous owners.) Thus, at those times in the future when oxen would be needed for the heavy labor of working the fields, Mathieu must have either borrowed or rented these cooperative beasts of burden from his neighbors, or instead hired out this demanding work to others. Two households away on one side of the Brunet farm lived the merchant Jacques Babie and his wife Jeanne Dandonneau, along with their six children, one female household servant, and a 50-year-old hired hand. This family owned eight horned cattle (presumably a combination of oxen, cows, and young cattle), had 40 arpents (34 acres) of land cleared and under cultivation, and owned one gun and a pistol. The Brunets' adjacent neighbors on the other side were Jean Arcouet dit Lajeunesse, his wife Élisabeth Pépin, and their two children. This latter family owned two oxen, had 9 arpents (7 2/3 acres) of land under cultivation, and owned one gun. One or both of these neighboring households might have been the source of oxen that were utilized for working the Brunet fields in future years, unless the Brunets eventually acquired their own team.[35]

Within months of the census, baby Catherine safely arrived on November 5, 1681. Two days later, she was christened at the Champlain church, with adjacent neighbor Jean Arcouet dit Lajeunesse standing as her godfather and Catherine Guérard, the wife of Julien Dubord dit Lafontaine, standing as her godmother and granting the baby her name.[36]

Near the close of 1682, on December 6, Mathieu visited the notary Adhémar to officially acknowledge a debt. At this time, he agreed that he owed François Chorel, the Sieur de Saint Romain, the sum of 229 livres 4 sols 8 deniers, for goods that the merchant had previously delivered to him. He acknowledged this debt "under the bond and mortgage of all and each of the possessions of the said debtor, both moveable and real estate and at present and in the future, in submission to all of the rigors of the law." Monsieur Chorel, a well-established businessman based at both Trois-Rivières and Champlain, had a wife and nine children residing in the couple's home at Champlain. It is highly likely that Mathieu had generated at least part of this debt in the process of amassing goods that he intended to exchange with native customers during his upcoming voyage to the west. In addition, another portion of the charges may have been for supplies that he would need during his sojourn in the upper Great Lakes region. At this point, Mathieu could not have imagined that, due to a series of misfortunes which would be entirely beyond his control, this indebtedness would remain unpaid for the next several years. It would again be mentioned in a new financial transaction between Messieurs Brunet and Chorel in April of 1685, when Mathieu would again be assembling merchandise and making preparations, this time for his second documented voyage to the west. But this latter venture would likewise suffer unforeseen setbacks. Finally, Mathieu would eventually be able to make payments against the two owed amounts in August of 1688, after he and Nicolas Perrot would reap some profits from their joint commercial venture in the Upper Country. In other words, the six-year period of 1683 through 1688 would present daunting challenges for Mathieu Brunet and his colleagues.[37]

It is very likely that Mathieu had been trading at the local peltries fair in Trois-Rivières for many years, dealing with the convoys of native traders who paddled out from their home regions each summer, laden with furs and hides to exchange. This commerce, which was conducted just miles west of the Brunet farm, was open to all residents of New France. In addition, this close-to-home trade generated modest-to-moderate profits for all of the French participants, without their having to expend the considerable time, energy, and resources that were required to take part in the distant interior commerce. However, ever since 1653, certain of the French residents of the St. Lawrence communities had been paddling off to the far-flung regions of the west and north, in order to trade. At these distant locales, the prices which they charged for merchandise were many times higher than the rates that were charged for the very same articles at the peltries fairs of Trois-Rivières and Montreal. Thus, if all went well (and everyone knew that events did not always play out as planned), the far-traveling traders could potentially garner much more extensive profits, as a result of their much greater efforts and also their more extensive risks. Late in 1682, Mathieu Brunet dit Létang saw an opportunity to take part in this distant business, and he leaped at the chance. (As a matter of fact, he may have previously made one or a number of trading trips to the interior. However, those voyages would have probably been carried out without official permission, and thus would have generated no documentation in public records.)

In the year 1682, in an attempt to dissuade and deter the hundreds of Frenchmen who were traveling without permission into the interior each year to carry out illicit commerce with the native nations, the license system had been inaugurated. In fact, its implementation had been postponed from 1681. In that earlier year, following the suggestions of the Intendant of New France, the King's Minister had issued a decree which had established a system of legal trading licenses or *congés*. In addition, the ordinance had granted a general amnesty to all of the *coureurs de bois* who would come out from the interior regions. Thus, instead of the former ban on traders operating in the west, the Governor or the Intendant could now issue up to 25 official licenses each year. These were to be distributed at the price of 600 livres apiece, or they were to be given at no charge to deserving widows, orphans, charities, or churches, in order to finance charitable works. Some were also to be granted, at no cost, to individuals who needed to generate capital in order to initiate some worthy private enterprise. No recipient could receive a license two years in a row. The recipients were not required to utilize the trading license themselves. They could hire voyageur-traders to carry out the work for them, or they could instead sell the *congé* outright (such sales often generated considerably more cash than the official fee of 600 livres, with the price often reaching 1,000 to 1,200 livres or more). Each license authorized the departure of a single canoe, staffed by a crew of three men and loaded with provisions, supplies, and merchandise. In addition to the 25 licenses, the administrators could also issue an unspecified number of free permits, to worthy traders who had performed some special service for the government. After this system had been officially declared by the Crown, Governor Frontenac had decided to postpone its implementation until the following year of 1682.

After the establishment of this program of legal licenses and permits, the term *voyageur* or traveler came into common usage. It was applied to differentiate those individuals who had received official permission to trade in the interior from the *coureurs de bois* or illicit traders, who continued to operate outside of the legal system during the entire French era. However, during the eighteenth century, the term *voyageur* came to apply to all canoemen who were hired by a licensed employer.

During the 1670s, the French traders working in the interior had developed certain systems of supply and distribution; these would continue to be employed, by both legal and illicit traders, throughout the remainder of the entire fur trade era. One of the primary organizational features involved *hivernants* or winterers, who remained in the interior while trading for several years at a time. These individual were served by colleagues from the St. Lawrence Valley, who transported fresh supplies of merchandise in to them, meeting at a primary rendezvous point such as the Straits of Mackinac, and then carried out their accumulated furs and hides. These commodities were sold in the eastern settlements, to pay off the outfitter and the investors and generate the profits, which were then shared appropriately among the various partners. Another configuration consisted of a number of voyageur-traders who paddled into the interior during the early part of a summer, traded over the following twelve to fifteen months, and then transported out their own peltries. The documented ventures of Mathieu Brunet would follow this latter plan.

The eastward journey to the St. Lawrence settlements often required additional canoes and sometimes extra paddlers, both coming from interior sources. These were needed in order to handle the outgoing cargo of furs and hides, which were generally bulkier than the incoming merchandise had been. During the era of the 1670s-1690s, six voyageur-traders typically paddled two canoes loaded with merchandise into the interior, with three men per craft. After trading their goods and acquiring another canoe, they then came out with three canoes of peltries, with two paddlers in each craft. As an alternative, traders sometimes hired native paddlers and their canoes in the interior, in order to transport out the excess amount of furs and hides which would not fit into the canoes of the Frenchmen. Or the traders sometimes paid freighting costs to other traders, hiring them to transport out their excess packs.

For westbound or eastbound canoes that were ascending or descending the Ottawa River (including Monsieur Brunet's known trips), the season of travel usually extended from the spring breakup of the ice in May until the freeze-up in November or December, at the latest. These were the seasonal constraints within which the paddlers were obliged to operate.[38]

In addition to the inauguration of the system of permits and licenses, other events were also changing the commercial landscape at this same time. It was these latter alterations which encouraged Mathieu and his colleagues to undertake licensed (and thus documented) ventures to the upper Great Lakes region during the following years. In 1682, Governor Frontenac was dismissed from his post by the King, and he was ordered to return to France. In his place, the Monarch dispatched in the same year Joseph Antoine Le Febvre de La Barre, who arrived at Quebec at the end of September, along with the new Intendant Jacques De Meulles. Within three weeks of their arrival, these two new administrators issued an ordinance that strictly prohibited all persons from leaving the St. Lawrence settlements without a trading permit. This interdiction was to apply to both those individuals who actually made the canoe voyages and those merchant-outfitters who supplied them with the needed merchandise and supplies.

During his decade as Governor, Frontenac had strongly favored certain interior traders, particularly Daniel Greysolon, Sieur DuLhut (operating in the region of Lakes Huron, Michigan, and Superior) and René Robert Cavelier, Sieur de La Salle (laboring in the region of Lakes Erie and Ontario and in the Illinois Country). The rival faction that was pitted against the Governor and his camp of favored associates consisted of most of the merchants and outfitters who were based at Montreal. After the departure of Frontenac and the arrival of La Barre, the latter administrator developed close associations with many of the prominent businessmen of Montreal, particularly Jacques Le Ber and Charles Lemoine, as well as with Charles Aubert de La Chesnaye and Philippe Gauthier de Comporté of Quebec; these four individuals would together form the Compagnie du Nord in 1682. Also among the new Governor's favored associates were the Quebec businessmen François Hazeur, François Viennay dit Pachot, Charles Catignon, Guillaume Chanjon, Guillaume Bouthier, François Ruette Sieur d'Auteuil, Jean Baptiste Peuvret, Jean Gobin, Pierre Soumande, Charles Macard, and François Provost.

Late in 1682 or during the first months of 1683, Monsieur Le Barre decided that he would dispatch troops during the following summer to take control of La Salle's two facilities in the west, and to order the trader-explorer back to Quebec. His two interior posts were Ft. Frontenac, located at the eastern end of Lake Ontario, and Ft. St. Louis. The latter facility was constructed atop Le Rocher (Starved Rock) beside the Illinois River late in 1682 and very early in 1683, after La Salle and his party had explored southward to the mouth to the Mississippi River.[39]

This sudden lifting of La Salle's monopoly on the peltries commerce in the Illinois Country, which was located to the south and southwest of Lake Michigan, inspired a number of men to make preparations to travel to this region. One of these motivated individuals was Mathieu Brunet dit Létang. Early in 1683, he and his thirteen associates amassed the licenses, canoes, supplies, provisions, and merchandise which they would need for their trading venture. For their total outfit, the men spent more than 15,000 livres.[40]

By May of 1683, it was time for the fourteen partners to assemble at Montreal. At this time, Mathieu was about 42 to 45 years old, while Marie (who was roughly six months pregnant at this point) was about age 34 to 36. Their eight children included Michel (about 15 years old), Jeanne (about 13), Marie Anne (about 11), Jean ($9^1/3$), Pierre ($7^1/4$), Marie ($5^1/2$), Jacques ($2^3/4$), and Catherine ($1^1/2$). The interval in which Marie would shoulder the responsibilities of running the farm and household at Champlain by herself would probably extend for about seventeen months or more, if everything played out according to the general plan. Since they had purchased the place $2^1/2$ years earlier, it was presumably in good operating condition by this point. In addition, five of the eight children were old enough to provide a great deal of assistance in its day-to-day operations.

Among Mathieu's thirteen colleagues, six were from the area of Trois-Rivières and its outlying seigneuries, while another one had been raised nearby in the seigneury of Ste. Anne de la Pérade (east of Champlain) but had recently relocated to the Montreal area. Another of the men hailed from Contrecoeur, about halfway between Trois-Rivières and Montreal; two others were from the Montreal region; and three hailed from the area of Quebec. Thus, eight of the fourteen traders, 57 percent of them, were truly from the Trois-Rivières region.

Within this party, Mathieu was definitely the senior member, according to his age, his marital status, and the total number of children in his family. Half of the partners were married, while half of them were still single. In addition to Mathieu (age 42 to 45, with his ninth child due in August), the other married associates were, respectively, 42 years old with two children, 40 with two children, 37 with one child, 28 with no children yet, 26 with his third child due in August, and 26 with one child. The ages of six of the unmarried partners were 37, 28, 25, 23, 22, and 19, while the age of the seventh individual is unknown. In summary, the ages of the seven married men ranged from about 42-to-45 down to 26 (averaging about 34), while the ages of the seven unmarried men (not including the one individual whose age is not known) ranged from 37 down to 19 (averaging about 26).

Among the seven partners who currently lived in the region of Trois-Rivières, the second oldest (and also the third oldest among the entire party) was Martin Foisy. This was Mathieu and Marie's former neighbor in the Prairies Marsolet sub-fief of Cap de la Madeleine, who had at one point charged the Brunet couple in court for having struck his wife. He had later become their friend again, so that they had chosen Martin to be the godfather of their seventh child. Now about 40 years old, Martin had a wife and two children on their farm at Champlain, who were 4 and about to turn 2 years of age. Besides Mathieu and Martin, the other married man from the Trois-Rivières area was Jean Desrosiers dit Dutremble. Soon to turn 26, he had been born at Trois-Rivières and had grown up there, then at Cap de la Madeleine, and finally at Champlain. Having been wed at Champlain $1^1/2$ years earlier and having settled there with his new wife, the couple's only child was six months old.

Besides these three married men, four of the unmarried trading associates also hailed from this same region. The oldest of these was Jean Lahaise, about 37 years old, a farm worker who labored at both Champlain and across the St. Lawrence at Gentilly. The next oldest was François Lucas dit Dontigny, age 25, who had grown up at Trois-Rivières and then Cap de la Madeleine; he was now a farm worker in the seigneury of Batiscan, immediately east of Champlain. Another unmarried partner from the same area was Antoine Desrosiers dit Lafresnière, the younger brother of Jean Desrosiers dit Dutremble who was described above. Soon to celebrate his 19th birthday, Antoine had been born and raised at Trois-Rivières, then at Cap de la Madeleine, and finally at Champlain. The fourth single man from this same area was Jacques Baston, whose age is not known. He had been documented at Trois-Rivières five years earlier, back in 1678.

One of the fourteen trading colleagues, Eustache Prévost, hailed from Contrecoeur, which was located about halfway between Trois-Rivières and Montreal. Having been married for five years, this man (who was about age 37) and his wife had thus far produced one child, who was now $1^1/2$ years old.

Among the three partners from the Montreal area, two were married while one was still single. The oldest of these, Joseph de Montenon, the Sieur de Larue, was about age 42; thus, he was the second-oldest member of the entire party, after Mathieu Brunet. He and his wife, who resided at Pointe aux Trembles near the northern tip of Montreal Island, had just one child, who was $2^3/4$ years old; they had lost their first baby at the age of just three weeks. The other married associate from the Montreal area, Jean Haudecoeur, was about 28 years old; he and his wife had only been married for seven months at this point. This young man had been raised at Ste. Anne de la Pérade, to the east of Champlain; thus, he was in actuality from the Trois-Rivières region. However, he and his new wife now lived at Boucherville, about six miles northeast of Montreal on the eastern side of the St. Lawrence. Partner Laurent Benoît dit Livernois, age 22, was still single; having been born at Montreal, he had been living in recent years at Boucherville and also a couple miles to the south at Longueuil.

Among the three trading associates from the Quebec area, only Jean Pilote was married. About 26 years old, he had grown up at Beauport and then Quebec. Jean and his wife had been married for five years; they were expecting their third child to arrive in the coming August. The little Pilote family, including their $3^1/2$ and $1^1/2$-year-old offspring, resided directly across the St. Lawrence from Quebec, in the seigneury of Lauson. Partner Jacques Mongeau, 28 years old and having been raised at Quebec, was still single. Likewise, René Legardeur, the Sieur de Beauvais, was also a resident of Quebec and still unmarried. Age 23, René was the son of Charles Legardeur, the Sieur de Tilly, who was a very prominent Quebec businessman and administrator and for decades a member of the Sovereign Council. It was René's cousin, Charles Legardeur, the Sieur de Villiers (27 years older than René, and a resident of both Cap de la Madeleine and across the St. Lawrence at Bécancour), who had owned the latter seigneury of Bécancour ever since 1668. It is abundantly clear that René was the most well-connected among the fourteen men who had formed this partnership in 1683 to trade in the Illinois Country.[41]

Near the end of May, it was about time for the convoy to depart for the west. Having assembled at Montreal some weeks earlier, those among the fourteen associates who hailed from distant communities had been residing at various inns and boardinghouses in the town during this period of final preparations. In Mathieu's case (he was some ninety miles from home), he had been both residing and taking his meals at the inn of the Montreal butcher and innkeeper Michel Lecours. This man, about 46 or 47 years old, had been married for eighteen years; he and his wife had produced nine children, of whom three had passed away at young ages. (Monsieur Lecours would die $2^1/2$ years later, in September of 1685, when his wife would be about six weeks pregnant.) Shortly before the departure of the brigade, Joseph Lemire promised to pay Mathieu's accumulated bill for accommodations, which totaled 61 livres. This was done with the understanding that Monsieur Brunet would reimburse him upon his return from the trading trip. On May 28, Messieurs Brunet and Lemire met the notary at the home of Monsieur Lecours to officially register these arrangements.

"Before Claude Maugue, royal notary in New France, residing at Montreal, was present Mathieu Brunet dit Lestang, living at Champlain, who has acknowledged that he fairly and rightly owes to the Sieur Joseph Lemire, here present and assenting, the sum of sixty-one livres for room and board, which he [Monsieur Lemire] has paid as his discharge to the Sieur Michel Lecours, merchant butcher and innkeeper in this town. The said sum of sixty-one livres will be paid by the said Lestang to the said Sieur Lemire upon his return from the voyage to the Ottawa Country which he is going to make presently, which [return] will be around the beginning of October next [1684], this in beaver pelts at the current price at the time at the office of the King at Quebec [the Compagnie de la Ferme, which held the peltries export monopoly], under the penalty of all expenses, damages, and interests. Thus have they promised, obligated themselves, and waived. [This agreement] made and drawn up at the said Montreal in the house of the said Sieur Lecours, who has declared that he has received from the said Sieur creditor [Lemire] a promise that he will pay the above sum as it stands at the present time, as ordered by the Sieur [Nicolas] Dupré [domestic servant of the Montreal merchant Jacques Le Ber], who has signified to him that he is content, on the 28th of May, 1683 in the afternoon, in the presence of the Sieurs Gilles Carré and Maximilien de Chefdeville [dit La Garenne], witnesses residing here, who have signed below with the said creditor and the notary. The said Lestang and Lecours have declared that they do not know how to write or sign, having been questioned according to the ordinance. The said Lestang has made a cross as his mark. One word [of this document] which is crossed out has no meaning.
Signed,
Joseph Lemire, + [the mark of Lestang], and Maugue, notary [but not by the two witnesses]."[42]

On the same afternoon, Mathieu was obliged to pay more than half of the rooming expenses which had been incurred by one of his colleagues in the same inn belonging to Monsieur Lecours. To support Mathieu's protest of this matter, the innkeeper agreed to make an official statement concerning this issue to the same notary.

"Today, the 28th of May, 1683 in the afternoon appeared before the undersigned notary residing at Montreal the Sieur Michel Lecours,

merchant butcher and innkeeper in this town of Villemarie. Upon the request and verbal summons of Mathieu Brunet dit Lestang, the said Lecours has declared, certified, and affirmed, on his soul and conscience according to the account book which he represents, that the said Lestang has paid to him 26 livres for and as the discharge of Jacques Sauvage, to reduce to 20 livres 17 sols 6 deniers the charges for the room which he [Sauvage] rented from the said Lecours where he lodged. The Sieur [Jacques] Le Ber was not willing to pay for them, which has forced the said Lestang, being his comrade, to pay for him, without which he would not be able to depart. In view of the complaint which he [Lestang] has lodged with Milord the [Governor] General, he [Lecours] has affirmed this to be true, which has left the said Lestang without recourse against the said Sauvage to recover the said sum which he rightly owes to him [Lestang]. Thus has he [Lecours] affirmed, which is supported by his said [account] book in each particular. [This statement] made in the presence of Sieurs Claude Tétreau and Jean Armand, witnesses who have signed below with the said notary. The said Tétreau, Lecours, and Lestang have declared that they do not know how to write or sign, having been questioned according to the ordinance. The present act was granted to the said Lestang to serve in this matter.
Signed,
Jean Armande and C. Maugue, notary"[43]

These two documents provide a number of pieces of valuable information. First, the Montreal resident Jacques Le Ber dit Larose, one of the wealthiest merchants in all of New France, had served as the outfitter for Mathieu and his colleagues. However, their financial arrangements had not included Le Ber's paying the room and board expenses of the fourteen associates during their period of preparations in Montreal, and adding these amounts to their total debt to him. But Le Ber did arrange for someone to cover these costs, an individual who would be later reimbursed by each of the partners, upon their return to the east in 1684. The fourteen partners had apparently hired an additional paddler to join them for the first leg of their westbound voyage. This was Jacques Sauvage, a young and unmarried man who would be wed at Champlain in 1690 and then would settle there. His presence implies that the partners intended to make the inbound trip as far as Michilimackinac in five canoes, with three men per craft. This was the crew size which had been decreed by the license system. Apparently, Monsieur Le Ber felt that he had no responsibility to assist in the payment arrangements of Sauvage's rooming expenses, since this man was a hired employee of the fourteen traders. Thus, it fell upon Mathieu to cover more than half of those costs.[44]

During the early summer of 1683, Daniel Greysolon, Sieur DuLhut arrived at the Straits of Mackinac at the head of a convoy of fifteen canoes from Montreal. Although the party contained militia forces, and possibly a number of regular soldiers, it was the leader's intention that these men would also serve as traders. Bearing a three-year commission from Governor de La Barre, the commandant had been ordered to discipline certain of the native nations of the upper Great Lakes region, and to prevent all of the allied groups there from taking their furs and hides northward to the English traders on Hudson's Bay. His activities were to include the construction of several fortifications, first at the Straits in 1683, and during the following two years on Lake Nipigon north of Lake Superior and at the mouth of the Kaministiquia River on Lake Superior. The latter two facilities would be ultimately left under the command of his younger brother, Claude Greysolon, Sieur de Tourette. In addition to these various official activities, DuLhut and his personnel were licensed to trade for peltries.

In June, Olivier Morel, the Sieur de La Durantaye, arrived at Michilimackinac to assume command of the brand new post. With the arrival of the DuLhut and La Durantaye parties at St. Ignace during this summer, along with the construction of the initial fortified buildings there, the functions of this important community (which had been occupied by native and French residents since 1671) expanded even further. In addition to its former position as the center of commercial and missionary activities in the interior regions, St. Ignace now also became the focal point of French military and diplomatic activities in these regions.[45]

It is not known whether Mathieu Brunet and his fourteen colleagues traveled with one or the other of these two large convoys to reach the Straits of Mackinac. In any case, they followed the customary westbound route to the Straits via the Ottawa, Mattawa, and La Vase Rivers, then Lake Nipissing and the French River, and finally the north shorelines of Georgian Bay and Lake Huron. After leaving their hired paddler Jacques Sauvage at St. Ignace, they departed from there on August 10, 1683, headed toward the south. As was mentioned earlier, it was the customary practice to travel westbound from the St. Lawrence into the interior with three men per craft (as the licensing laws specified), and then return to the east in a greater number of canoes with two paddlers in each. This was done to accommodate the bulkier outbound peltries, compared to the smaller and more concise inbound merchandise. However, these fourteen men decided that, for their voyage from Michilimackinac southward to the Illinois Country, and then back northward to the Straits and eastward to the St. Lawrence a year later, they would paddle in seven canoes with two men per craft. The decision to increase the number of canoes before leaving the Mackinac Straits and heading south was dictated by one primary reality: birchbark canoes were manufactured in considerable numbers in the Straits area. In contrast, these craft were in short supply in the Illinois region, which was far to the south of the areas in which white birch trees grew to a sufficiently large size to produce canoe-quality bark.

The route which they would cover from Michilimackinac to Illinois would first entail paddling along the full length of Lake Michigan. Near the southern end of the lake, travelers could take one of two routes to reach the Illinois River. From the southeastern corner of Lake Michigan, they could travel along the St. Joseph River-Kankakee Portage-Kankakee River route; or from the southwestern corner of the lake, they could take the Chicago River-Chicago Portage-Des Plaines River route. This latter passage was immensely more challenging whenever the water levels were moderate or low. Since Mathieu and his colleagues were making their journey in the latter summer, a season of typically low water levels, they had decided to avoid the daunting Chicago River route and take the more amenable St. Joseph River passage. This route would entail paddling up the St. Joseph River for about fifty miles, hiking over the four-mile Kankakee Portage, and then paddling down the Kankakee River for about 150 miles. However, unfortunately, the latter watercourse was nearly as susceptible to drops in water levels during dry seasons as the Chicago and Des Plaines Rivers.[46]

On the map of North America that the cartographer Franquelin would created five years later, in 1688, he would clearly depict both of the water routes that extended from the southern end of "Lac des Illinois" (Lake Michigan) to the Illinois River. He would label the St. Joseph River as "Rivière des Miamis," the Kankakee River as "Rivière Theakiki," and the Kankakee Portage that connected these two watercourses as "Portage." On the alternate route that ran toward the south, he would portray at its beginning "Fort Checagou," beside the mouth of the Chicago River (this facility would be established in 1684). He would label the Des Plaines River as "Rivière Checagou," he would depict "Fort St. Louis" well toward the southwest on the eastern bank of the "Rivière des Illinois" (on the Illinois River at the present Starved Rock State Park), and he would designate "Fort Crèvecoeur" further down this waterway on the same eastern shore (near the present Peoria, a facility built and used only in 1680). The mapmaker would also indicate the locations of twelve major native villages within this area, half of them positioned beside or very close to the Illinois-Des Plaines water highway. This, then, was the general region in which Mathieu and his partners intended to labor during the following year.[47]

However, returning safe and sound would be easier said than done. In retrospect, their well-laid plans certainly did not come to fruition. The many harrowing challenges that the party faced during the following nine months was thus reported by four of the men, on May 28 of the following year:

"We the undersigned René Legardeur, esquire, Sieur de Beauvais, Eustache Prévost, Jean Desrosiers dit Dutremble, and François Lucas [dit Dontigny], both for ourselves and for Joseph de Montenon, Sieur de Larue, Antoine Desrosiers dit Lafresnière, Jacques Baston, Jean Pilote, Martin Foisy, Laurent [Benoît dit] Livernois, Jean Lahaise, Jacques Mongeau, [Mathieu Brunet dit] Lestang, and Jean Haudecoeur, all partners in going to trade in the Illinois Country with the licenses and permission of Milord the [Governor] General, having departed from Michilimackinac on the 10th of August last [1683, and after traveling southward along the eastern shore of Lake Michigan, up the St. Joseph River, and over the Kankakee Portage,] we arrived on the 4th of December at the Rivière Teakiky [Kankakee River], where we were held back by the ice, which forced us to winter at the said place on the Kankakee. On the following 23rd of February [1684, after ten weeks of being icebound], we sent four of our men, namely Jacques Baston, François Lucas [dit Dontigny], [Mathieu Brunet dit] Lestang, and Laurent [Benoît dit] Livernois, to go hunting along the same Kankakee River in the Illinois Country about six leagues downriver from us, to try to acquire some provisions of meat so that we could go do our trading. They were discovered by sixteen Iroquois and a woman who was disguised in the manner of the Illinois, both in her language and in her clothing, carrying a white tent, who cried out to them [the four Frenchmen] that they should not have any fear, that they were all their brothers, and that they could sleep the night together. Being informed by our four Frenchmen where our cabins were and how many Frenchmen there were, they knew that we numbered fourteen. They [the Iroquois] suggested that they go along the route with our four Frenchmen, to come to our said cabins, where they arrived on the 26th of the

said month of February. They always remained on their guard, constantly looking to see whether we had with us any Illinois, or Miami, or other nations of these said places. We answered them and assured them that they had all departed to go to the Great [Mississippi] River. Upon seeing us there, they gave us a speech, telling us the news of the voyage of Monsieur Lemoine on behalf of Milord the [Governor] General, giving us a thousand praises, and telling us that we were all brothers and that they had orders from him [the Governor] to give us food to eat when we would need it, and that we would reciprocate, which we did, giving them half of a buffalo to boil that same night. They asked us if they could remain for two days in our cabins to rest, saying they they were tired, to which we willingly assented, having understood the agreement that they had made with Milord the [Governor] General. On the next day, the 27th of the said month, they claimed that they were going hunting, [but actually] they wanted to discover if it was true that we had no [native] nations near us. For this reason, they asked us for some guns with some ammunition of powder and lead, because, they said, their own were not in good condition, and that we could not refuse them, saying that we did not need to go hunting, that we had enough meat to feed ourselves. However, after they had been gone for two hours, during that time the elders among them told us that we should assemble in our cabins and that they wanted to speak to us. We all did this, and being assembled, they brought to us three presents of seven beaver pelts. The first one, of two beaver pelts, was to thank us for the good reception and good treatment that we had provided to them. The second present, of two beaver pelts, was to pray that we would have pity on them and trade with them for some necessary items which they needed. The third present, of three beaver pelts, was so that we would not give any information to Milord the [Governor] General nor to any other nation, whether they were from this region or not, and in case we would find ourselves with the nations whom they were against, that we would not take any part in the fighting. When we asked them what they could do, being only sixteen men, they told us that they had 200 men six days overland travel away and 100 men along the shores of the lake [Lake Michigan], and another 500 men on the Great Mississippi River below the Illinois [Country]. However, as it was, we refused their third present, saying to them that we could not accept these conditions, and if we would find ourselves among them and their said enemies came to attack, we would take their side as being their brothers, and in the same manner if we found ourselves amid their said enemies who were also our brothers, then we would be obliged to defend them [the allies of the French]. Thus understood, we left the [third] present, with the freedom to do what we would like, with the assurance that we could go in complete safety along the Kankakee River, and that if we encountered their men we would have nothing to fear, that they would bid us to smoke with their young men. That being concluded, they traded with us about the value of two packs of beaver pelts, and sold to us one of their guns, to cause us less suspicion of the treason that they wanted to commit against us.

On the 28th of the said month of February, they left our cabins, saying to us that they were returning to their land, and that they would take their men and depart two days after we had repaired our canoes. During this time [of their temporary absence], there arrived four Mascoutens, who had come to find, on behalf of the chief of the Outagamis [Mesquakie or Fox nation], three women who had been captured, to save them from the hands of the Iroquois, since the said Iroquois had gone to war against them. This we confirmed for them, by showing them the shelters that the said Iroquois had built like ours, in which they easily recognized some signs [of the captured women], which they carried to their village to assure their men. We made use of this occasion to write to the Reverend Father [Claude] Allouez, the Jesuit missionary [in the Green Bay-Fox River region], to warn the nations and likewise the French who might be in those places there to be on their guard. We gave them information concerning all that had taken place.

On Sunday, the 5th of March, we set out to descend along the Kankakee River and reach Fort St. Louis, where we hoped to do our trading. But our surprise was great when, after two hours of traveling, we noticed the said Iroquois numbering 200, who were waiting for us at the passage of a rapids where there was no opportunity to defend ourselves. However, we decided to cross to the other side of the said river, so that we could use our bales of merchandise and our canoes to fortify ourselves in some manner in case of an attack, and to be able to defend ourselves. But this was in vain, since there was a drop of 60 feet of water in the rapids. They shouted to us, have no fear, we are your brothers, we would like to trade with you. We responded that we were going to land below the rapids to speak with them, since our plan was to get away and reach a small island, which would offer us an opportunity to defend ourselves. But 60 of the said men having stopped two of our canoes in the rapids, they patted us and told us not to worry, that they wanted to trade. The rest of our men, seeing that we had been stopped, soon came to us, to see what had happened. But as soon as they arrived, they were taken and stopped like us. For their part, the Iroquois kept shouting to us, have no fear, we are your friends and your brothers, and we would like to trade with you. At this same moment, they seized our weapons and pulled our seven canoes onto land, where they generally pillaged all of our merchandise and canoes. *They did not want to hear for any reason that we were going up with licenses from Milord the [Governor] General, and with letters from my said seigneur [the Governor] for Monsieur [Olivier Morel, Sieur] de la Durantaye [at St. Ignace] and Monsieur the Chevalier [Henri] de Baugy [at Fort St. Louis], which they tore up with much contempt. We asked them why they were treating us in this manner, and also why they had pillaged all of our merchandise. They responded that you came looking here, this here is our land. Don't you know that Monsieur Lemoine told us to make war against the nations of this region, and that if we were to encounter any Frenchmen we were to pillage them, and that if they defended themselves we were to kill them. We told them that they were not treating us like brothers, and that they had misspoken when they came to tell us to have no worries. But they told us proudly that they had no ears to hear us, that our word was full of pride, and that one word should have silenced us. We asked them, more or less, what they wanted to do with us. They said to us, at first, that we were their slaves, and that they wanted to take us to their land.*

They kept us with them for nine days, traveling overland toward the area of Fort St. Louis with 150 men, with the rest of them in our canoes with our merchandise. Each day, they asked us if Monsieur [Henri] de Tonty, whom they called The Cut Arm, was in the fort, and how many men he might have there with him, and if Monsieur de La Salle was also there. We told them that Milord the [Governor] General had recalled Monsieur de La Salle, and that he had sent another commander in his place. They said that they knew this, and had asked us only to see if we would tell them the truth. They said that they were going to attack the said fort, and that when we had traveled fifteen leagues [further down the Kankakee River], we would reach a river which is called Chicagou [the present Des Plaines River]. There, they would send us off wherever we might want to go, but with the warning that we were not to go to the area of the fort. If they found us there, they would break our heads.

Having thus arrived at the said Chicagou [Des Plaines] River, they actually did allow us to go, but without provisions or canoes or weapons, except for two wretched guns and a little powder and lead, which we requested from them to try to subsist during our march. We then departed from this place on the 14th of March with our miserable equipment of two guns, which could not keep us from starving until the 19th of the said month, when we encountered 30 Mascoutens. Among them were the four [from the Green Bay-Fox River region] whom we had seen earlier, who had come to make war against the said Iroquois. We prayed that they would have pity on us and give us something to eat, and some guides to lead us, since we did not

know where we were going. They did this with good will, and gave us four
old men to lead us to an Outagami [Mesquakie or Fox] village [in the Green
Bay-Fox River region]. They [the Mascoutens] asked us to inform Monsieur
le [Governor] General of the pleasure that they had given to us, saying that
they are very obedient to their father.

In this same place [the Mesquakie village], we received the letters from
Monsieur the Chevalier de Baugy [who had taken over the command of Fort
St. Louis from La Salle's associate Henri de Tonty], which we have brought
with diligence and have given to Milord the [Governor] General at Quebec
on the 28th of May, 1684.

Signed,

Beauvais Le Gardeur, Eustache Prevost, Jean Desrosiers, and François
Lucas"[48]

The route of the party during the late summer and autumn of
1683, traveling southward along the eastern shoreline of Lake
Michigan from St. Ignace to the mouth of the St. Joseph River, entailed
a paddling distance of roughly 310 miles. This portion of the voyage
took place on the side of the lake which was generally exposed to the
lashings of the prevailing westerly winds. After completing this leg
of the trip, they then traveled up a stretch of about fifty miles on the
St. Joseph River and made the four-mile Kankakee Portage. During
this journey, the men may have experienced excessive delays due to
uncooperative weather, especially on the open lake water. However, it
certainly should not have taken them a full $16^1/2$ weeks, from August
10 until December 4, to reach the Kankakee River. According to this
timetable, they averaged less than $3^1/4$ miles per day during their
entire 116 days of traveling. There can be only one logical explanation
for their extremely slow progress and their tardy arrival at the entry
to the Illinois Country: they must have halted on numerous occasions
to trade. However, the four men made no mention of this fact in their
recitation of the events which had transpired.

Following their icebound sojourn on the Kankakee, the rough
encounters that Mathieu and his colleagues experienced with a large
force of Iroquois warriors must not have come as a complete surprise
to them. Although the Iroquois nations had been generally peaceful
since the treaties back in 1666 and 1667, there had been some warning
signs of unrest on their part. On May 7, 1684, Fr. Jean Enjalran, the
head of the mission at Michilimackinac, wrote to the Governor:

"[Last August,] I gave advice to [René Legardeur, the] Sieur de Beauvais
and the others who went toward the Illinois quarter, conforming to your

primary orders that they were to be watchful for assaults from the Iroquois. And Monsieur de Chevalier de Baugy was at least able to receive from the Sieur D'Autray, who departed from here very late last fall, many days before the last news arrived, that which I wrote to him, that he should be on his guard and that you desired that he should avoid as much as possible entering into warfare with the Iroquois."[49]

As it turned out, this Iroquois expedition into the Illinois Country during the winter and spring of 1684 was the beginning of their concerted campaign to vanquish the Illinois and Miami nations. Afterward, they planned to crush the remaining Ottawas, Hurons, and Tionontates who were based at the Straits of Mackinac, in order to seize complete control of the fur trade business in the entire midwest region.

The question of who had authorized Iroquois parties to pillage the canoes of French traders during this period has long been considered. The above report quoted the raiders themselves as saying that they had been authorized by the Governor, who, at the time of these particular events in 1684, was Monsieur La Barre. However, on November 13 of this same year, La Barre included the following sentence in his report to the King, describing a conference that the administrator had conducted with Iroquois delegates at Montreal back in 1683:

"I gave to them a wampum belt to make them cease causing any more trouble for all of the French, no matter who, and by this present revoking the order that had been given to them by my predecessor, Monsieur le Comte de Frontenac, to pillage all of the Frenchmen who were not the bearers of his seal."[50]

From this text, it appears very clear that Frontenac, and not La Barre after him, had conveyed the dangerous signal to the Iroquois. That order had encouraged them to pilfer merchandise and canoes from any traders in the interior who had not been approved by the Governor himself, and who did not carry a passport that had been issued by him.

It is unfortunate that the four men who described the trading party's misadventures did not continue their detailed narrative beyond their meeting the thirty Mascoutens along the route. This chance encounter took place after the party had slowly made its way on foot along the Des Plaines River for five days. From this group of Mascoutens, four old men were generously loaned, who lead the party northward to an Outagami (Mesquakie or Fox Nation) village.

This village would have been located in the region of Green Bay and the lower Fox River, some 200 miles toward the north as the crow flies. Since the report did not provide any details, it is not possible to determine whether this entire trip was accomplished on foot, or by what routes the men and their four guides traveled. Since the party was not equipped with canoes at the beginning of their journey with the four elderly Mascoutens, it is quite possible that they did not travel by way of the Chicago Portage and the adjacent Chicago River to reach Lake Michigan before turning northward. Instead, they may have traveled north on foot along pathways, either for the first portion of the trip or for the entire journey.[51]

After they arrived at the Mesquakie village, the party received from a messenger letters which were intended for La Durantaye, the commandant at St. Ignace, and Governor La Barre in the St. Lawrence settlements. These missives had been hastily penned by Henri de Baugy at Fort St. Louis. (During the previous summer of 1683, this officer had been dispatched by Governor La Barre to assume command of La Salle's facility atop Le Rocher, which had until then been under the control of the trader-explorer's lieutenant Henri de Tonty.) While Mathieu and his partners had been slowly making their way on foot up the Des Plaines River (before meeting the Mascoutens), their former Iroquois captors had continued along the remaining forty miles of distance to Fort St. Louis. Arriving there on March 21, they commenced their attack. Ensconced within the fort, the 46 French and native defenders repulsed many assaults by the enemy forces over the span of six days. Halfway through this series of fights, on March 24, Baugy dispatched a messenger with his letters for La Durantaye and La Barre. When these missives reached the party of fourteen traders at Green Bay, at least some of the men carried them over the route of about 220 canoe miles toward the northeast to St. Ignace. In response to the news from Baugy, the commandant led a relief party of about sixty Frenchmen southward to Fort St. Louis, but they arrived there long after the enemy raiders had departed.[52]

By April 20, at least René Legardeur from among the fourteen partners was present at Michilimackinac. It was on this day that La Durantaye requisitioned supplies for the canoe that Legardeur and several other men would paddle out to the St. Lawrence, carrying the latest news to Governor La Barre. Shortly before their departure, Monsieur Boisguillot, the second in command at St. Ignace, wrote to the administrator on May 5:

"Having returned today from Sault Ste. Marie with the Reverend Father Superior [Enjalran], we were not very surprised to find Monsieur de Beauvais with four Frenchmen, who had still more news which they brought to us, about that which has happened in the Illinois Country...It is of very great importance not to suffer with impunity the insolent robbery that the Iroquois committed on the fourteen Frenchmen [on the Kankakee River]. Otherwise, Milord, what would the natives say, and how would they hope for the protection from Onontio [the native name for Governor La Barre] if they persuade themselves that he does not resent the injuries that were done to his own children...[P.S.] Monday, May 8. Our men will depart when the weather is good. They must take advantage of it."[53]

The paddlers in the two canoes certainly did take advantage of what must have been outstanding traveling conditions. After an amazingly speedy voyage, Legardeur and his five colleagues reported to the Governor just twenty days later, on May 28.

It is not entirely clear whether all four of the partners who composed the Kankakee misadventures report for the Governor traveled out to the St. Lawrence, and dictated their narrative there upon their arrival. It is entirely possible that Messieurs Prévost, Desrosiers, and Lucas had joined René Legardeur in composing the report at La Baye or at St. Ignace, and only the latter man transported it out to the authorities. At any rate, the members of the party seem to have taken pains to represent themselves rather democratically in this document, including among the four testifiers both married and single men, and also residents of several geographical areas. René Legardeur, the Sieur de Beauvais (age 23 and single) hailed from Quebec, while François Lucas (25 years old and single) was from Batiscan (east of Trois-Rivières). Jean Desrosiers dit Dutremble (age 26, married with one child) resided at Champlain, while Eustache Prévost (about 37 years old, married with one child) was from Contrecoeur. None of the three men who lived in the Montreal area were among the four testifiers; however, one of these Montreal-area individuals had only recently moved there from Ste. Anne de la Pérade (east of Trois-Rivières). Since more than half of the party consisted of men from the Trois-Rivières region, it apparently seemed appropriate that two of the four contributors to the narrative should have hailed from that area.

Eight days after receiving their report, on June 5, 1684, Governor La Barre included the following statement in his missive to the King's Minister at Versailles: "The Iroquois, who pretended to be our friends, having attacked during the last days of February a party of fourteen of our men who had gone toward the Illinois Country to trade, entirely pillaged them of the sum of more than 15,000 livres." Nicolas Perrot noted during this same period that a three-man crew typically spent about 3,000 livres in the course of assembling their complete outfit, including the cost of the canoe. Thus, it was rather usual that the fourteen partners (who, along and their hired paddler Jacques Sauvage, comprised five three-man crews) had expended more than 15,000 livres in their preparations for their trading venture. These expenditures had apparently included the costs of their five craft, which had become seven in number at St. Ignace, before the party had left Monsieur Sauvage there and had headed south toward Illinois.

The majority of the fourteen partners, including Mathieu Brunet, had remained behind at La Baye (Green Bay) or at Michilimackinac in May of 1684. Their return to the St. Lawrence settlements would be postponed until the conclusion of the retaliatory campaign that would be conducted during this summer against the westernmost nations of the Iroquois. These were the Senecas and the Onondagas, who resided south of Lake Ontario. If Mathieu had not previously known Nicolas Perrot, it was most likely during this spring and summer (at La Baye and Michilimackinac and during the military campaign) that the two men laid the foundation of friendship and trust that would encourage them to work together during the coming years.

According to the plans of the Governor, the campaign was intended to intimidate each of the Iroquois nations, by showing them that the French could attack their home villages if they did not restore the former situation of peace. Two separate armies would converge on Lake Ontario. The one departing from Montreal consisted of regular soldiers, about 700 militia fighters, and some 400 allied warriors from the St. Lawrence settlements. The other force, coming from the upper Great Lakes region, contained about 150 voyageur-traders (including Mathieu Brunet and most of his partners) and more than 500 allied native fighting men. This second army included Nicolas Perrot and the many warriors with whom he held sway in the west.

Unfortunately, as the eastern forces traveled up the St. Lawrence to the lake, "tertian ague" (Spanish influenza) swept like wildfire through the men, laying most of them low. Before the western army had reached the rendezvous point on the south shore of Lake

Ontario, where Governor La Barre and his forces were waiting in pitiful condition, Iroquois emissaries arrived there to negotiate a peace treaty. Upon seeing the state of their adversaries, the leaders of the Iroquois party dictated the terms of the agreement, which were very humiliating for the French. In the process, the Iroquois did agree not to harm the Miami nation, but they vowed to complete their extermination of the Illinois. After the treaty sessions had been concluded, a ship was sent westward on the lake from Ft. Frontenac, to intercept the army from the upper Great Lakes and instruct the men to return to their home areas. This they did, retracing their route along the Niagara River (including its grueling six-mile portage around Niagara Falls) and along the lengths of Lakes Erie and Huron. However, Nicolas Perrot and a number of the men (including Mathieu) from the western forces did not travel back with the group; instead, they paddled eastward via the St. Lawrence River to return to their homes and families. (Perrot returned to his family at Bécancour, across the river from Trois-Rivières, some time shortly before August 20. On that date, he penned a letter to his financial backer the notary Antoine Adhémar, which has survived.) Many of the men of the eastern army died while en route back to the St. Lawrence communities, and those who did survive brought the scourge of the disease with them; it would ravage the colonists throughout the entire autumn and early winter.[54]

Remembering the terrible quarter-century of Iroquois attacks which they had earlier endured, the French and native residents of the St. Lawrence settlements were now quite apprehensive about the future. During the previous summer of 1683, one of the King's new edicts which had arrived ordered every able-bodied Frenchman in the colony to own a gun. The local merchants had been instructed to accept wheat, peas, or corn as payment for these weapons, at certain established prices. Considering the new potential menace of marauding warriors, this regulation concerning owning firearms was followed much more avidly from 1684 onward.[55]

When Mathieu returned to his home and family, some time shortly before August 20, 1684, he was presumably quite disheartened by the financial results of his fifteen-month odyssey. He and his thirteen partners still owed many thousands of livres to their outfitter, Jacques Le Ber, and they had not garnered a single fur or hide that they could hand over to the Montreal merchant. Obviously, Mathieu would be obliged to make another commercial voyage to the west, to settle his debts. But that could be postponed for a time.

Now, he avidly listened as his family members described the many joyous events that he had missed during his absence. Nearly three months after Mathieu had departed, on August 19, Marie had safely delivered their ninth child, Marguerite. She had been baptized two days later in the church at Champlain, with Marguerite Provencher of Cap de la Madeleine, the eighteen-year-old wife of Antoine Cottenoir and the mother of a six-month old baby, as her godmother. The other sponsor had been Bernard Dumouchel, master cobbler and the father of three, who lived in the Brunet's former sub-fief of Prairies Marsolet in Cap de la Madeleine.[56]

The other event of great significance during his absence had been the marriage of one of their children, which had been a first-time experience for Marie (and later for Mathieu, when he belatedly learned of it). On April 12, 1684, daughter Jeanne, who was about fourteen years old, had wed François Huard dit Laliberté, who was about age thirty and had not been previously married. The bride was the Brunet's second-oldest child and their eldest daughter. At the ceremony in the Champlain church, there had been three official witnesses in attendance, including Pierre Durand from the Champlain parish and two from Ste. Anne de la Pérade: Marie Gouin, the wife of Monsieur Gendron, and Antoine Guibord. Unfortunately, during their twenty-year marriage, the Huard-Brunet couple would not produce any children. This was a rather unusual occurrence in the St. Lawrence settlements.[57]

By the spring of 1685, some eight months after Mathieu had returned from his first documented trading trip to the west, he was already concluding preparations for another such voyage. Notarial records from the Montreal area show that, besides Mathieu, five of the other partners from his failed venture of 1683-1684 definitely made legal, licensed trading journeys to the west in later years. These five other men included four who had been single at the time of the 1683-84 venture, as well as one who had already been married at that time. Two of these men were hired as voyageur-traders working for other individuals (one in 1688 and the other in 1689). In addition, three of the former partners hired other individuals to labor for and with them (one of the men did so in 1688, another in 1693, and a third one in various years between 1685 to 1694). The lattermost individual, who hired voyageur-traders to work for and with him over the course of a number of years, was René Legardeur. Others among the fourteen partners from 1683-1684 may have also participated in the interior trade in later years. However, if they did so, their arrangements were recorded by notaries in the regions of Trois-Rivières or Quebec, or else the men participated in illicit, unlicensed ventures that left no paper trails in public documents.[58]

During his upcoming venture commencing in 1685, Mathieu would work in partnership with Nicolas Perrot, in the region of Green Bay and westward from there. This area, well to the north of the Illinois Country, would be much more likely to be free of marauding Iroquois war parties. In addition, this region, with its colder temperatures and longer winters, would produce beaver and other pelts which were of considerably higher quality than those that were harvested in warmer areas further to the south.

During April of this year, as part of his preparations, Mathieu acquired a considerable stock of articles from the Champlain merchant François Chorel, the Sieur de Saint Romain. Back in December of 1682, before his first documented trading voyage, he had likewise received merchandise from Monsieur Chorel; at that time, he had acknowledged that his debt to the merchant had totaled 229 livres 4 sols 8 deniers. During the ensuing $2^1/2$ years, due to the financial failure of the 1683-1684 venture, he had not been able to repay any portion of that owed amount. At this point in the spring of 1685, he added another 222 livres 10 sols 14 deniers worth of goods to his bill; this virtually doubled his debt, bringing it to a total of 452 livres 3 sols 2 deniers. Thus, on April 27, he and Marie traveled to the home of Martin Desmilliers (two farms away in their seigneury of Champlain), along with the local notary plus Nicolas Perrot and their adjacent neighbor Louis Demiromont as witnesses, to officially update their statement of indebtedness to the trusting merchant.

"Before Antoine Adhémar, royal notary and registrar of the [Governmental] Jurisdiction of Trois-Rivières, residing at Cap de la Madeleine, and the witnesses named at the end were present in person Mathieu Brunet dit Lestang and Marie Blanchard, his wife, living at Champlain. The said Blanchard and the said Brunet her husband have duly authorized of their free will the facts and stipulations which follow, showing solidarity and indivisibility with each other, one for the other and each of them for the whole, without division, discussion, or disloyalty, renouncing any such said divisions. They have acknowledged and admitted that they fairly and truly owe to François Chorel, Sieur de Saint Romain, merchant of Champlain, absent, with the aforementioned and undersigned notary stipulating and assenting for him, the sum of 452 livres 3 sols 2 deniers, as the balance of

generally any and all of the reckonings which they have passed with him. This includes the sum of 229 livres 4 sols 8 deniers owed to the said Sieur de Saint Romain and agreed to by the said Brunet on December 6, sixteen hundred eighty [two], which was passed before the said undersigned notary and which by this present agreement will be voided, and this former debt will not serve the said Sieur de Saint Romain as the basis for a mortgage claim. The said Brunet and Blanchard his wife promise to pay and deliver the said sum of 452 livres 3 sols 2 deniers to the said Sieur de Saint Romain at his home at Champlain in good beaver pelts upon the first request which will be made by the said Sieur de Saint Romain, under the bond and mortgage of all and each of the possessions of the said debtors, both moveable and real estate, at present and in the future, subject to all the rigors of the law. For the execution of these presents, the said debtors have selected as their legal residence [to which writs may be delivered] their home and residence located at the said Champlain. Thus have they promised, obligated themselves in solidarity as noted above, and waived.

[This agreement] made and drawn up at the said Champlain in the home of Martin Desmilliers in the year 1685, on the 27th day of April in the afternoon, in the presence of Sieur Nicolas Perrot of Rivière du Saint Michel [the Bécancour seigneury] and of Louis Demiromont, royal bailiff and sergeant for all of Canada at Cap de la Madeleine, at present at Champlain, witnesses who have signed the certified copy of these presents with the said notary. The said debtors [Mathieu Brunet and Marie Blanchard] have declared that they do not know how to sign, having been questioned after the reading was done of everything, according to the ordinance. Thus have they signed this certified copy N. Perrot, Demiromont, and Adhémar, the aforementioned and undersigned royal notary.
Signed,
Adhemar, notary"[59]

Eighteen days later, on May 17, Mathieu and Marie again met with the same notary, along with Monsieur Perrot. However, this time the three gathered at the scribe's own office, in his home at Cap de la Madeleine. Mathieu and Nicolas had been completing the final preparations for their upcoming venture, which might last as long as $2^1/4$ years or more. With this long duration in mind, they had decided to make an important arrangement, one that would be crucial for the sake of Marie and the nine Brunet children during Mathieu's extended absence.

"Before Antoine Adhémar, royal notary and registrar of the [Governmental] Jurisdiction of Trois-Rivières, living at Cap de la Madeleine, and the

witnesses named at the end were present in person Mathieu Brunet dit Lestang, living at Champlain, and Marie Blanchard, his wife, who have authorized of their free will the facts and stipulations which follow, showing solidarity and indivisibility with each other, one for the other and each of them for the whole, without division or discussion, renouncing any such said divisions. They have acknowledged and declared that they fairly and truly owe to Nicolas Perrot, living at Rivière Saint Michel, present and assenting, the sum of six hundred livres, which sum has been furnished to the said debtors to provide for the food and maintenance of the said Blanchard and their children during the voyage which the said Brunet is going to make with the said Sieur Perrot to La Baie des Puants [Bay of the Winnebagos, Green Bay], the Mascoutens, and the Nadouessioux [Sioux or Dakotas]. The said Sieur Perrot will take the said sum of six hundred livres from the portion of the peltries belonging to the said Brunet which will be derived from the said voyage. By these presents the said creditors assign, obligate, and mortgage to the Sieur Perrot, in preference to all other creditors, generally all of their other possessions, both moveable and real estate, present and future, subject to all the rigors of the law, without any special obligations and generally derogating one for the other. For the execution of these presents, the said debtors have selected as their legal residence [to which writs may be delivered] their irrevocable domicile at their home located at the said Champlain. They consent and agree to all of the acts and deeds of the law which may be carried out...Thus have they promised, obligated themselves in solidarity as noted above, and waived.

[This agreement] made and drawn up at the said place of Cap de la Madeleine in the office of the said notary, in the year 1685 on the seventeenth day of May in the afternoon, in the presence of Louis Demiromont, royal bailiff, and Antoine Trottier, living at the said place of Cap de la Madeleine, who have signed below with the said Sieur Perrot and the notary. The said debtors have declared that they do not know how to sign, having been questioned after the reading had been done, according to the ordinance.
Signed,

N. Perrot, Demiromont, At. Trotier, and Adhemar, notary"[60]

This cash advance of 600 livres by Perrot, which would cover the needs of Marie and the Brunet offspring during the next couple of years, was thus officially registered with the notary, and definite arrangements were made for the repayment of this loaned sum. In contrast, it is of particular interest to note that Messieurs Brunet and Perrot did not draw up an official notary document which spelled out the details of their own partnership as traders. This omission clearly implies that their personal arrangements were sealed with simply a handshake, backed by the weight of their respective reputations.

The loan document specifically mentioned three of the native nations who resided in the Wisconsin Country, where Monsieur Perrot had been laboring for some seventeen years and where he and Mathieu Brunet would soon be working together. These mentioned groups were the Winnebago, Mascouten, and Dakota nations. In fact, documents and maps from this specific period identified at least nine separate native groups who lived in the region of Green Bay and the areas extending off to the west and southwest for some 300 miles. (This was the very sphere in which the Perrot-Brunet party would trade during their 1685-1687 venture.) In a generally east-to-west sequence, these resident groups included the Menominees, who occupied the land west and northwest of southern Green Bay; the Winnebagos, who resided in the area of the southern end of Green Bay and the adjacent lower reaches of the Fox River; and the Potawatomis, who lived around the southern portion of Green Bay. The villages of the Sauk and Mesquakie (the latter were also called the Outagami or Fox) nations were located on the lower Fox River and on its northward-reaching tributary the Wolf River (which was termed the "Rivière des Mascoutens" during this period). The Mascoutens resided along the upper reaches of the Fox River, as did also the Kickapoos. The Miamis located their villages along the upper Fox River and on the upper Wisconsin River. Finally, the Dakotas occupied the area around the junction of the Mississippi and Minnesota Rivers, and up both of these watercourses.61

On his 1688 *Carte de l'Amérique Septrionnalle*, Jean Baptiste Franquelin would portray in considerable detail the primary water route which ran into and through this region, along which Mathieu Brunet and Nicolas Perrot were about to travel during the early summer of 1685. Green Bay, the long arm of "Lac des Illinois" (Lake Michigan) extending from the lake toward the southwest, would be labeled "Baie des Puans" (Bay of the Winnebagos). Oddly enough, at the southern end of the Bay, by the mouth of the Fox River, the cartographer would not depict the facility of "La Baye," at which French traders had been residing and trading with the local native populations ever since 1670. However, from the foot of Green Bay, the Fox River (called "Rivière des Outagamis" by the French, but not thus labeled on his map) would be shown extending southward to Lake Winnebago. On this lake would be portrayed the "Mission St.

François Xavier," which had been in operation since 1669. From Lake Winnebago (dubbed "Lac St. François" or "Lac des Mascoutens" by the French, but not so labeled here), the upper Fox River, extending off toward the southwest, would be labeled "Lacs des Folles Avoines" (Wild Rice Lakes). This name aptly fit its depiction as a river that was interrupted at regular intervals by three relatively small lakes. The $1^1/2$-mile overland carry between the upper Fox River and the upper Wisconsin River would be labeled "Portage," while the latter waterway, flowing toward the southwest, would be called "Rivière Ouisconsing." At the mouth of the Wisconsin, where it flowed into the "Fleuve Mississippi," would be located "Fort St. Nicolas," the facility which Perrot would establish in 1688. Some 75 miles northward up the Mississippi River would be depicted the mouth of the "Rivière Noire" (Black River), flowing in from the northeast. The locale on the east bank of the Mississippi just north of this mouth would be labeled "La Place Hivernement" (The Wintering Place). About 60 miles further up the Mississippi from the mouth of the Black River, the "Rivière des Saulteurs" (Chippewa River) likewise would be shown as flowing in from the northeast. At the junction of the Chippewa and the Mississippi, Franquelin would portray "Fort St. Antoine," which the Perrot party would construct in 1686, during Mathieu's tenure with the group. (Perrot also called this facility the "Poste des Nadouessioux," the Sioux Post.)

This same map would also include the daunting secondary route which was occasionally utilized by the French during this period to reach the upper Mississippi River and the Dakota people living there. Near the western end of Lake Superior, this route would be shown extending southward via "Rivière Nesualsicoton" (the present Bois Brulé River) and over the $2^1/2$-mile carry at its headwaters, which was labeled "Portage." At the terminus of this path would be depicted "Fort Ste. Croix," which had been established in 1683. Here, "Lac de la Providence" formed the headwaters of the "Rivière de la Madeleine" (also dubbed the "Rivière Ste. Croix," but it was not so labeled on this chart), which flowed toward the southwest and then toward the south to reach the Mississippi. The mouth of the Ste. Croix/Madeleine River was located some 40 miles up the Mississippi from the mouth of the Chippewa River and Fort St. Antoine.

On Franquelin's map, about 30 miles further up the Mississippi from the Ste. Croix mouth, by the "Saut St. Antoine" (St. Anthony Falls), he would portray the "Rivière Nadouessioux (the present

Minnesota River, which the French also called "Rivière St. Pierre") branching off toward the southwest, while the Mississippi extended further toward the northwest. In this region and well to the north, he would depict numerous villages of the "Nations des Issatis ou des Sioux," as well as the "Poualacs" to the southwest of them (a different group of Sioux or Dakotas).[62]

In this spring of 1685, as Nicolas Perrot completed the preparations for his next trading venture in this region west of Lac des Illinois, he was about 41 to 45 years old. (In comparison, Mathieu was about 44 to 48 years of age, and he had either eight or nine living children, who ranged in age from 17 down to $1^3/4$ years. Marie, braced to handle the household on her own during his long absence, was about 36 to 38 years old.) Starting a quarter-century earlier, Nicolas had worked as a *donné* or lay employee of the Jesuit priests between 1660 and 1663, and then in the same capacity for the Sulpician priests from 1666 to 1667. This employment, in the Montreal area and possibly also at other locales, had enabled him to become familiar with native languages and customs, and to keep abreast of events which transpired at both the St. Lawrence trade fairs and in the western interior. Since at least the summer of 1667, he had been involved in the peltries commerce. On August 24 of that year, he and his partner Toussaint Beaudry had formed an association with two Montreal investors, Jean Desroches and Isaac Nafrechon. These latter two men had provided the canoe, equipment, provisions, and trade merchandise so that Perrot and Beaudry could carry out their journey to the west. Upon the return of the two voyageur-traders from the interior, they had split the profits in equal halves with the two financial backers. This had been one of the earliest fur trade contracts in which it was clear that the Frenchmen had paddled together in their own canoe, instead of being distributed singly in a native convoy among separate craft which were both owned and manned by native traders. Starting in 1668, at the invitation of a group of Potawatomis, Messieurs Perrot and Beaudry had commenced trading in the region of Green Bay, the Fox River, and the Wisconsin River. Over the course of the following seventeen years, Nicolas had become highly trusted and respected, by both the native populations of the west and the colonial administrators and military leaders of New France. During that interval, he had been called upon numerous times to serve as an official interpreter and ambassador, acting as a liaison between the native and French worlds in commercial, political, and military affairs.

At this point, having been married to Madeleine Raclos for 13$^1/_2$ years, the Perrot couple now had eight living children, who ranged in age from thirteen years down to sixteen months. Sadly, they had lost one of their children, little Marie Madeleine, 1$^3/_4$ years earlier; she had died back in August of 1683, at the age of 5$^1/_2$ months. After their wedding in the Cap de la Madeleine church in the autumn of 1671, Monsieur and Madame Perrot had settled in the seigneury of Bécancour (across the St. Lawrence from Trois-Rivières), by at least the summer of 1675. It was on June 24 of that year that Jean Boutilly had contracted to work for Nicolas for the rest of his life. On December 2, 1677, Nicolas had been granted a long, slender plot of land at Bécancour.

In the spring of 1685, Nicolas was appointed by Governor La Barre as the commandant of the Baie des Puants area and the neighboring regions to the west. Since he was not actually an army officer, he certainly could not have held the rank of Oliver Morel, Sieur de La Durantaye or Henri de Tonty. However, due to Monsieur Perrot's powerful influence with the native populations of this region, the administrator fully realized the importance of officially placing him in charge of this sector. Beneath the surface, having Nicolas in command of this area probably increased the Governor's profits from the fur trade that was conducted there as well.

It was most likely this administrator who provided the new commandant with the impressive silver monstrance that Nicolas eventually presented to the Jesuit missionary at La Baye during this voyage (probably to encourage the cooperation of the priest concerning his fur trading operations in the region). This resplendent implement, standing fifteen inches high, was used during certain special ceremonies in the church, to display the consecrated Host for the adoration of the faithful. These words were engraved around the outer edge of its oval base: *CE SOLEIL A ESTE DONNE PAR Mr NICOLAS PERROT A LA MISSION DE St FRANCOIS XAVIER EN LA BAYE DES PUANTS 1686* (This monstrance was given by Monsieur Nicolas Perrot to the mission of St. Francis Xavier at the Bay of the Winnebagos, 1686). Not long after Nicolas presented it, this ornate article would be buried for safekeeping about five miles above the mouth of the Fox River, probably in 1687. It would be found in 1802, and would eventually be preserved in the collections of the State Historical Society of Wisconsin.

In the early summer of 1685, the Perrot party (including Mathieu

Brunet) arrived at La Baye, at the foot of Green Bay. There, the commandant learned that war had broken out between the Mesquakie (Fox) nation on the one side and the Ojibwas, Ottawas, and Dakotas on the other side. In his efforts to restore peaceful relations between these various allies of the French, Perrot discovered the root of the conflict. The daughter of an Ojibwa leader had been held prisoner by the Fox nation for a year, and during that time, her captors had refused the gifts that all of the nations of the Bay had offered for her release. In fact, the Fox leaders had recently decided that the young girl would be burned, in retaliation for the death of one of their important leaders who had been killed by the Ojibwas in the fighting. Accompanied by his party of fifteen to twenty men and the girl's father, Perrot visited the Fox village where she was being held, and he convinced the residents to release the girl to her parent. This was done on the condition that the Ojibwa man would intervene with his people and their current allies, and convince them to cease their hostilities against the Fox people, which he soon did.

Having settled this diplomatic matter, Perrot and his men commenced their voyage up the Fox River and down the Wisconsin River, intending to reach the *Missi-sippi* or Great River. (The total paddling distance from the Straits of Mackinac to the junction of the Wisconsin and the Mississippi was about 600 miles.) The Fox and Wisconsin, comprising the canoe route between La Baye and the Mississippi, were relatively large rivers; they both contained sufficient water depths to allow canoe travel throughout the entire year. However, during the winter, ice presented considerable problems in traveling along this route. Between the foot of Green Bay and Lake Winnebago, a distance of 42 miles, the lower Fox fell a full 169 feet in elevation; this created a steeper gradient than that of both the Ottawa and the Mattawa Rivers. Along the lower Fox, the paddlers faced five or six major obstacles, the first of which was located about eight miles upstream from the mouth. In times of sufficient water, the Rapide de Père could be lined up, by pulling the loaded canoes up the rapids with towing lines. Seven miles further up, the men reached the Petite Kakalin, which could also be lined up in times when there was enough water depth. After another fifteen miles of paddling, they were obliged to portage for more than a mile around the Rapide de Kakalin. The next twelve miles presented an almost continuous rapids with a fast current, in which Mathieu and his colleagues had to alternately pole, line, and wade against the fast water. At the end of this stretch came the Grande Konomee waterfall, which required a mile-long carry. Nine miles further, the paddlers arrived at the Rapides des Puants, a $1^1/2$-mile stretch of rapids which could be lined up except during times of extremely low water levels. This led the party to Lake Winnebago, where they coasted along its western shore for some fourteen miles to reach the outlet of the upper Fox River.

After making a short carry at its mouth, the men reveled in this unobstructed passageway, which presented no rapids at all along its entire length. However, after traveling up the river for about eighty miles, through areas of marsh grass and wild rice with minimal current, they approached the area of the height-of-land portage. Here, the channel became narrower, and it even sometimes disappeared entirely amid the tall grasses. A few miles before they reached the beginning of the portage, the watercourse became a swamp that was too shallow to be paddled; it was also choked with wild rice that towered over the men's heads. Here, the voyageurs had to wade in the mud, dragging and pushing the craft along while grabbing the stalks of the rice plants to gain some purchase. Finally reaching the portage, Mathieu and the others were treated to a flat and unobstructed path, one which ran for $1^1/2$ miles across a prairie. At the end, they reloaded and happily pushed off onto the broad waters of the Wisconsin River, which they descended for 182 miles. The only potential difficulties along this latter passage were the scattered sand bars, and the small islands that sometimes presented difficulties in locating the channel. In the lower reaches of the river, the speed of the current slowed, and the broad channel was flanked by tall limestone outcroppings. If the party was blessed with cooperative weather conditions, the Wisconsin River section of their journey probably only took them three or four days to complete.

At the junction of this river with the Mississippi, the canoes turned right and headed northward up the massive watercourse. After covering about 75 miles, the party came to the mouth of the Rivière Noire (Black River), flowing in on the right from the east. On Franquelin's map of 1688, he would label the eastern bank of the Mississippi just above this river mouth *La Place Hivernement*, The Wintering Place. (After Monsieur Perrot would complete this two-year venture in the west, he would meet with Franquelin in 1687, and the trader would provide the latest information for the official cartographer of the colony to add to his chart.) It is highly likely that this "Wintering Place" label indicated the specific locale at which the party was forced to halt late in 1685, due to cold weather and dangerous ice accumulation on the river. Temporarily blocked by the forces of nature from reaching the Dakota country, the men constructed a wintering post here. The commandant later described its location as "at the foot of a mountain, behind which was a great prairie abounding in wild animals."

The mountain to which he referred was Trempealeau Mountain, located two miles above the present community of Trempealeau Landing, Wisconsin (within Nicolas Perrot State Park). The Winnebago name for this dramatic, isolated ridge of limestone capped with sandstone, rising some 400 feet above the level of the adjacent waters of the river, was *Haymeashan* (Soaking Mountain), while the Dakota dubbed it *Minnay-chonkahah* (Bluff in the Water). Thus, the French called it *Mont Qui Trempe à l'Eau* (Mountain Which Soaks in the Water), which was eventually shortened to "Trempealeau." The remains of an early French post which were unearthed in this area in 1888, about a mile north of the present community of Trempealeau, are most likely the remnants of the Perrot party's wintering facility of 1685-1686.

After spending the winter months here (and in the process forming commercial alliances with the local native groups), the party disembarked in the spring of 1686, headed northward toward the territory of the Dakota nations. After paddling some sixty miles further up the Mississippi, they passed on the right the mouth of the Rivière des Saulteurs (the Chippewa River), flowing in from the east. North of here on the eastern bank of the Mississippi, the men constructed Fort St. Antoine, which the commandant named in honor of his patron, Governor Joseph Antoine Lefebvre de Labarre.

Unbeknown to the commander of the party, within weeks of his departure from the St. Lawrence settlements in the previous year, a new Governor of New France had arrived: Jacques René de Brisay, Marquis de Denonville. This new administrator had been ordered by the King's Minister to oppose any new expeditions that were aimed at discovering new lands in the interior. Thus, Denonville had written to him at Versailles in September of 1685: "There are some of our Frenchmen who are among the Ottawas [meaning the various native nations of the west] who say that they have orders from Monsieur de Labarre to go to the Mississippi. I know that it is not your intention to allow our Frenchmen to ramble so far away; and

I will do my best to bring them back." That October, after the canoe route to the west had been closed for the winter, he had decided to place all of the Frenchmen who were in the west under the command of La Durantaye at St. Ignace. This move had effectively removed Monsieur Perrot from his command of the Wisconsin Country. However, the letters expressing these changes of orders would not be delivered to the interior until the summer of 1686.[63]

Nicolas Perrot later recorded in his memoirs numerous events from this period. Many of these events also involved Mathieu Brunet, who was his close colleague during this span of 2^1/$_2$ years:

"I was sent to that Bay [Baie des Puants, Green Bay], carrying a commission to be commander in chief there, and in the regions further toward the west, and even of those which I might be able to discover. Monsieur de La Durantaye then relieved Monsieur de La Valtrie, who had been commandant there [in Wisconsin] during the Iroquois campaign [of 1684]. I had no sooner arrived in the region where I was to govern [in the area of the Dakotas, during the summer of 1686] than I received orders from Monsieur Denonville to go back with all the Frenchmen whom I had. I was unable to do so without abandoning the goods which I had been compelled to borrow [take on credit] from the merchants for my voyage. At that time, I was in the country of the Sioux [Dakotas], where the ice had broken up all of our canoes, and I was compelled to spend the summer there. Meanwhile, I devoted myself to procuring watercraft so that I could go to Michilimackinac [and also to carrying out plenty of profitable trading], but the canoes [built by native groups living further to the east] did not reach me until the autumn [of 1686, too late to travel out to the Straits of Mackinac].

In the beginning of the winter [of 1687] I received other orders, to call together all of the Frenchmen and natives whom I should find within my reach and along my route, in order to go with them to [a place] near the lake [Lake Ontario] where the Tsonontouans [the Senecas, the westernmost Iroquois nation] are settled. Immediately, I set out, and I invited the Miamis [to go] to this war, which they promised me to do. But the Loups [Kickapoos], who were their neighbors, dissuaded them from it, making them believe that the French intended to betray them, and to make the Iroquois eat them when they joined the former [the French].

I went by land to the village of the Miamis, who were about sixty leagues distant [toward the southeast] from my post; and I returned by land, the same as I had gone. I learned on the road that, before arriving there [back at my post], a body of fifteen hundred men from the nations of the Bay -- Foxes, Mascoutens, Kickapoos -- who were going to war against the Sioux, intended to pillage my stock of merchandise, knowing that I was not there. And that they were planning to do the same to the Frenchmen who were further up, and to kill them. Some of them had come, therefore, as spies to my post, to find out the condition of affairs there, under the pretext of trading for powder. They carried back to the camp [of the above-mentioned warriors] the information that within the fort they had seen only four persons.

When I returned there [to my fort] the next day, two others of those natives came to the fort, who found me there. I told them that I must talk with their leaders, of whom I named to them seven or eight of the more prominent. They returned to their camp, and the very men whom I had named to them came to visit me.

The sentinel who was on duty notified me of their arrival. I had always taken care to keep the gate of the fort closed; I had it opened in order that they might enter, and conducted them to my cabin. They saw there many guns in good condition, provided with good flints and locks. The two spies who had previously come had likewise seen the guns. I made them believe that we [Frenchmen] numbered forty men, not counting those whom I had sent out to hunt. They believed this, just as I said it, because the men whom they had seen there, going into a cabin, quickly changed their clothing and again appeared before them.

I had some food given to them, and meanwhile I reproached them for their treacherous purposes of trying to plunder my goods and kill the Frenchmen. I told them of every point of their conspiracy. I also made them understand that they were at that moment at my disposal, but that I was not a traitor, like them; and that my only demand from them was to give up the war [against the Sioux] that they were on the way to undertake, and rather to turn their arms against the Iroquois. [I added that] two sentinels were at all times stationed at the two bastions of the fort, both having many guns at hand, and relays [of guards] were on duty all night long. These natives confessed to me that they had been plotting. I made them presents, in order to induce them to obey me, and received from them, verbally, all sorts of amends.

The next day, the main body of that band arrived, and they thought that they could enter [the fort] all at once. I held the leaders in my power within it, and I warned them that they were dead men at the first act of violence that their men should commit, for we would begin with them. My Frenchmen, under arms, kept well on their guard. There were some of the leaders whom I had detained, who climbed up on the gate of the fort and called out to their men that matters had been amicably settled between them and us. They entreated me to buy their peltries in exchange for ammunition, so that they could go *hunting for buffalo. I had them enter by turns, and after I had traded with them for what [peltries] they had, they separated, each to his allotted place, to carry out their hunt. A few days afterward, I set out with two Frenchmen, to go across the country to La Baye. And at every turn I encountered some of those natives, who showed me the best routes and entertained me very hospitably. When I reached La Baye, I held conferences with the nations there.*

In the spring [of 1687, I stored in the buildings of the Jesuits at La Baye all of the peltries that my party had amassed, and] I set out with all of the young [native and French] men, and arrived at Michilimackinac one afternoon. Monsieur de La Durantaye had gone away in the morning with the Frenchmen, who had not been able to make the Ottawas [of the Straits area] resolve to go on the warpath. As soon as they [the Ottawas] saw me, they told me to wait for them a few days, since they were intending to go away with me [on the campaign]. They said that their canoes were not in good condition, and that when these were ready, they would follow the French. I believed them, and waited for them for a week.

Monsieur de La Durantaye [and his contingent of fighting men, traveling southward along Lake Huron,] arrested thirty Englishmen [and Dutchmen, led by Johannes Roseboom and the French deserter Abel Marion dit Lafontaine,] who had come [from Albany] to trade with the Ottawas, and confiscated all of their goods; and he caused the best part of these, and especially their brandy, to be [sent back to St. Ignace and] distributed among the Ottawas. Those natives had preserved a keg of it, containing 25 pots [half-gallons], in order to get my men drunk and contrive to entice them away; they did what they could, and gave my men a keg full. But I was informed of it, and had the keg staved in in front of me, and the brandy poured out upon the ground.

I embarked with my people [the French traders plus about 100 Potawatomi, Winnebago, and Menominee warriors, since the Miamis had gone on ahead and the Kickapoo, Fox, and Mascouten warriors had traveled overland], after I had sharply upbraided the Ottawas. I joined [on western Lake Erie] Monsieur de La Durantaye, who had met Monsieur [Henri] de Tonty [and his forces from the Illinois Country] at the fort of Monsieur DuLhut located at Detroit [Fort St. Joseph on the upper St. Clair River, near the present Port Huron]. They had arrested [on western Lake Erie] thirty more Englishmen [and Dutchmen from Albany, led by Major Patrick McGregory], and [the French fighting men] were on the point of going back [to the Straits] if I had not arrived. For sixty Englishmen had already become too many enemies for them, and they had narrowly escaped being killed by the very natives who had accompanied them, inasmuch as the Frenchmen had become intoxicated on the liquor that they had plundered from the Englishmen; and that would have occurred, if the officers had not kept the prisoners under guard. They feared that the Iroquois, having information of their advance, would prepare ambushes for them; and that, if the English joined the enemy, they might be defeated. My arrival caused them to resume their voyage the next morning, without any fear, on account of the assistance that was furnished to them by my party.

At the end of two days, we reached Niagara [on June 27], where we threw up an entrenchment to defend ourselves from the Iroquois if they came to attack us. We spent several days in that place. The Ottawas and Hurons [from Michilimackinac] joined us there, having reached us by land from Thegegagon [the Toronto Portage], having left their canoes [on the] opposite [end of the portage route] at [Georgian Bay of] Lake Huron. They had decided to follow [us] when they saw that the nations of La Baye had refused to believe them [and had refused to turn back when they had arrived at the Straits with me]. For it would have been a cause for shame to them, not to be present in an encounter with the enemy, if any such had occurred, when they had seen their allies pass by their place of abode [at Michilimackinac]. We there received orders from Monsieur Denonville, and advanced toward the Tsonontouans [Senecas]."[64]

The eastern army in this campaign, assembled in the St. Lawrence Valley, was composed of 832 regular troops, 1,030 militia fighters, and 300 allied native warriors. Oddly enough, these eastern forces arrived on July 1 at the appointed place of rendezvous, on the southern shore of Lake Ontario at Irondoquoit Bay, at virtually the exact same time as the western forces. This was purely coincidental, yet it bore great positive significance to the native allies within both groups.

The Jesuit Fr. Thierry Bechefer, who accompanied the eastern army, penned a report of the events which then ensued. (A later document from 1688 would confirm that Mathieu Brunet had participated in these martial events.)

"Great precautions had been taken to effect the landing [at Irondoquoit Bay], because it was thought that the Iroquois would oppose it. It was, however, carried out very peacefully. And by great fortune, 180 Frenchmen -- who had come by order of Monsieur de Denonville from the Ottawa Country, where they had been engaged in trading -- arrived at the same time, with 300 or 400 natives from various nations, whom they had induced to follow them. Everyone set to work at once to build a fort for the protection of the boats and canoes of the army, which was to march overland [toward the south] to seek

the enemy in his own country. As this post was of great importance, 400 men were left in it under the command of [Rémi Guillouet,] Sieur Dorvilliers, an old officer of great ability and very distinguished merit. While they were working at [constructing] this fort, some Iroquois made their appearance on a height, and called out to our people that it was useless to waste time in erecting palisades. They said that an advance should be made as soon as possible, for they were extremely impatient to fight the French. And, after uttering loud yells and discharging their guns beyond range, they fled.

On the 12th [of July] at noon, the army began its march, and proceeded only 3 leagues [about nine miles] that day. On the 13th, they started very early [with three companies totaling 170 Frenchmen at the front, led by La Durantaye, de Tonty, and DuLhut, with Captain Louis Hector de Callières at the head and western natives on their flanks, followed by Governor Denonville with the regular troops and the militia fighters, and the remaining native warriors at the rear], and advanced with all possible dispatch. After they had passed 2 very dangerous defiles [narrow passages], there remained but one, a short quarter of a league from the plain. Our army was attacked there, when it least expected it. The scouts had beaten [scoured] the country on all sides, and even quite near the place where the enemy lay in ambush in the defile, without discovering them. 200 or 300 of them, those who were the farthest at the front, after uttering their yells which were usual on such occasions, fired on our advance guard, which consisted mostly of Canadians [the 170 men described above] and of our natives, who were on the flanks. Monsieur de Callières, who led them, made them charge in such a manner that the enemy did not long stand before them. Meanwhile, from 500 to 600 other Iroquois tried to take our men at the rear, at the same time that the head of the column was attacked. But Monsieur de Callières, who perceived their plan, threw forward some battalions, and caused so heavy a fire to be directed at that them that they at once fled.

All of our troops were so fatigued after the long and forced march over bad roads, during extraordinarily hot weather, in a country which is in the same latitude as Marseilles, that it was not deemed advisable to pursue the enemy -- especially since, in order to do so, it would have been necessary to leave the road and enter woods of which they had no knowledge, and wherein the Iroquois might have laid ambushes for our people and made them fall into them. This was all the more to be feared, since it was impossible to march in a body while pursuing foes who run through the woods like deer. Moreover, as our natives who could be most relied upon on this occasion spoke 7 or 8 different languages, there was reason to fear that they might [accidentally] attack one another, for lack of mutual understanding and recognition. It was therefore deemed advisable to encamp upon the very spot where the action had taken place.

We had 7 men killed, both French and native, and about 20 wounded, among whom [these wounded] was one of our Fathers [Jean Enjalran from St. Ignace], who was with the natives when our army was attacked. 28 of the enemy remained [dead] on the field. A Shawnee slave who had fought with them, and who surrendered to us a few days afterward, assured us that the Iroquois had suffered 50 killed and over 60 mortally wounded, besides many others who received less severe wounds; and that many slaves had taken advantage of it to escape.

Due to the heavy rain that fell on the following day, camp was struck only about noon. After it had emerged from the woods, the army marched in battle array directly to the first [two] villages, which were only half a league distant. They found them abandoned, and almost reduced to ashes, for the enemy had set fire to the cabins before retreating from them. Since our people found no one with whom to fight, they set to work destroying the native corn in the fields. They also burned that which was stored in the villages, and that which had been transported to a fort built of large stakes on a height, in a very commanding position, where the enemy had intended to defend themselves. We afterward proceeded to the other [two] villages, about 4 leagues distant from the first, which we found abandoned but not reduced to ashes. Our natives, who arrived there first, secured a considerable amount of booty from all of the goods that the enemy had not been able to carry away in a very precipitous flight. While they were occupied in destroying the corn, various parties went in every direction, without finding any of the enemy -- except in the case of one Huron who went along toward [the village called] Goiogouen, who met a man and a woman, whom he killed and whose scalps he brought back. The destruction of the native corn is calculated to entail great inconvenience upon the Iroquois, and hunger is sure to cause many to perish. For it is impossible for the other [Iroquois] nations who, united together, are not as numerous as that of the Tsonontouan [Senecas], to supply it with food for 14 months without themselves suffering greatly. Those who will disperse through the woods, to live by fishing and hunting, will be liable to be captured and killed by our natives, their foes, who are resolved to seek them everywhere. Since it was by this means that Monsieur de Denonville could do most injury to the Iroquois, he devoted every attention to it; it occupied 9 whole days. Afterward, he resumed his march [back] to the fort [on Irondoquoit Bay] where the boats [and canoes] and equipment of the army had been left; for they were so fatigued that they were no longer in a condition to undertake anything of any consequence.

Nevertheless, he thought it was of the highest importance to build a fort at the entrance of the Niagara River...30 leagues from Tsonontuan [toward the west]...After placing it in a state of defense, Monsieur de Denonville left therein a garrison of one hundred men...and started to go to Montreal with the militia fighters, and while on the way to escort a convoy [eventually arriving at Montreal on August 13.]"[65]

The leaders La Durantaye and Perrot, as well as many of the voyageur-traders from the interior (including Mathieu Brunet), did not travel back to Michilimackinac with the returning western forces. Instead, they traveled with the eastern army out to the St. Lawrence settlements. (Within weeks of their return, by about mid-September, Madame Perrot would become pregnant, safely delivering their next child on June 14, 1688.)

In the aftermath of the Seneca campaign, attacks by Iroquois war parties actually increased, in both number and intensity. Their raids fell not only upon the communities of the St. Lawrence Valley, but also upon the Ottawa River route leading to and from the Upper Country. However, even more fatalities among the St. Lawrence inhabitants were caused by the epidemic of measles and smallpox which swept through the eastern settlements, having been imported by the ships from France that summer. At this point, the total population of the colony along the St. Lawrence River, including the soldiers, totaled just over 11,000. By the time the scourges of the diseases would subside, over one thousand of the residents would have died.[66]

In addition to their grave concerns over the health of their family members, Nicolas Perrot and Mathieu Brunet dit Lestang also found themselves in serious financial difficulties. The disaster which had befallen them (which they had learned about only after returning home) was reported some years later by the historian La Potherie, who based his work mostly on Monsieur Perrot's writings:
"The French voyageurs who had been among the allies [having remained in the west, instead of participating in the Seneca campaign] came to Montreal in order to purchase new merchandise there. At the same time, the news came [with them] that the church of the [Jesuit] missionaries at La Baye, and a part of their buildings, had been burned. There were some Frenchmen who met great losses in this fire; Sieur Perrot lost in it more than forty thousand francs [livres] worth of beaver pelts."[67]

Thus, Mathieu's second laborious and time-consuming venture into the Pays d'en Haut, like his first one, had resulted in a total financial loss! Again, after a danger-filled absence of 27 months, he was unable to repay the debts that he had accrued, with both the trading party's outfitter and the Champlain merchant François Chorel.

At this point, Mathieu and Marie made a major decision: they would relocate to the Montreal area. Nearly five years earlier, back in December of 1680, they had bought their rather extensive property and its buildings, located in the Champlain seigneury, from François Lory dit Gargot and his wife Perrette Paremant. However, as later documents would reveal, the Brunets had only paid a paltry 36 livres toward the purchase price of 500 livres. This lack of payments would eventually lead to a court suit and an eventual settlement between Messieurs Brunet and Lory, in December of 1701. However, at this time in the autumn of 1687, Mathieu and Marie were fully aware that they had paid virtually nothing for the use of the farm for nearly seven years, and that they were probably going to remain in deep financial trouble for the foreseeable future. Thus, in their minds, the most logical solution was to abandon the farm and move upriver to an entirely new region, one which annually witnessed a great deal of action in the peltries business. In this new locale, the Montreal area, they would make a fresh start.[68]

On October 4, 1687, the Montreal notary Bénigne Basset recorded that "Mathieu Brunet dit Lestang and Marie Blanchard, his wife, from Champlain," had leased land to farm in the sub-fief of Hautmesny, which was located about two miles south-southwest of Montreal "on the bank of the Rivière St. Pierre." This watercourse, which was the outlet of Lac St. Pierre, had two branches. One of them flowed northeastward to Montreal, while the other branch (the one under discussion here) ran eastward and into the St. Lawrence. The mouth of this latter branch was located opposite the midpoint of the offshore Île St. Paul, which lay close by. This branch of the St. Pierre River formed the southern boundary of the area of St. Lawrence frontage which was called Pointe St. Charles. The Brunets would reside in the area of this river branch and the adjacent Pointe St. Charles (which encompassed some 2 1/2 miles of curving St. Lawrence frontage) for at least the next twelve years. Mathieu and Marie arranged their lease of farmland at Hautmesny with the Montreal peltries merchant Jean Vincent Philippe, Sieur du Hautmesny. He was the seigneur of this sub-fief, which had been granted to him by the Sulpicians back in 1665.[69]

A month later, Mathieu visited the Montreal notary Adhémar to officially record that he had leased a cow from a resident of the town of Montreal, Marie Pacreau. About 53 to 57 years old, she had first married Fiacre Ducharme dit Lafontaine back in 1659, and after his death she had wed Antoine Pichou dit Duverney in 1678; this latter husband had also passed away at some point. On November 6, 1687, she and Mathieu struck a bargain, one which would hopefully be beneficial to both parties.

"Was present Marie Pacreau, widow of the Sieur Pichou dit Duverney, living in this town, who has acknowledged and declared that she has leased out a milk cow, as a rental from this day until five years after the following details are finished and completed, to Mathieu Brunet dit Lestang, living on this Island, present and assenting. The said Pacreau promises to lease and deliver to the said renter the said cow, which will be brought from the woods where she is at present. This lease is transacted in consideration of eight pounds weight of butter for the first year of the present lease, and in the other four years nine pounds of butter for each of the said years for the lease of the said cow, which the said renter promises and is obliged to deliver to the said Pacreau at her home in this town in good condition during each of the said years of the present lease on the Day and Feast of Saint Michel, the 29th of September. Everything which will be provided to the said cow will be divided in halves between the said parties during three years [and Brunet will provide them at his own expense during the other two years]. At the end of the present lease, the ownership of the aforementioned cow will be divided in halves between the said parties. The said renter promises to feed, lodge, and house the said cow, even during the winter, in a manner which is good and appropriate. In case the said cow should die during the present lease, whether it be a natural death or due to some accident, the said renter will be held accountable to pay the said Pacreau one half of the value of which the said cow will be estimated."[70]

During the same afternoon and before the same notary, Mathieu and Madame Pacreau also arranged a second business deal.

"Mathieu Brunet dit Lestang, living in the Rivière Saint Pierre area of this Island, of his own free will has promised and is obliged to furnish and deliver at the end of March [1688] to Marie Pacreau, widow of Antoine Pichon dit Duverney and [Jean] Lagrange, her son-in-law, the quantity of twenty cords of good wood of maple, cherry, beech, ash, and elm, in front of the door of the said Pacreau in this town [of Montreal]. He will deliver the said cords, which will be eight feet long and four feet tall [the width was not specified], to the said place according to the custom of the region. The said Pacreau, here present and assenting, has promised and is obliged to pay to the said Brunet the sum of five livres for each of the said twenty cords."[71]

Mathieu had nearly five months time in which to cut and haul this rather extensive supply of wood, which he apparently intended to harvest on the property that he had recently leased. For these months of laborious work, he would earn a total of 100 livres.

Some six weeks after Mathieu had arranged the details of his woodcutting project, in latter December of 1687, Marie became pregnant for the tenth time. Their previous baby had arrived back in August of 1683, not long after Mathieu had departed on his 1683-1684 trading venture.

Apparently, the property that Mathieu and Marie had leased for farming purposes on the bank of the Rivière St. Pierre in October of 1687 was not sufficient for all of their plans. Thus, less than five months later, on February 25, 1688, the couple leased additional land in the nearby Pointe St. Charles area. This plot belonged to Jacques Le Ber, the very wealthy Montreal merchant who had outfitted Mathieu and his colleagues in the Perrot party for their 1685-1687 trading venture, $2^{1}/2$ years earlier. (Since all of the accumulated peltries from their efforts had been destroyed in the burning of the Jesuit buildings at La Baye, their outfitting debt to Monsieur Le Ber was still unpaid at this point.) The 1702 land ownership map of Montreal Island, compiled by Vachon de Belmont, portrayed this property of the merchant, which fronted on the St. Lawrence about a half-mile northeast of the mouth of the Rivière St. Pierre. (Le Ber also owned one-third of the nearby Île St. Paul, which lay a short distance offshore.)[72]

According to this second lease agreement, the Brunets apparently did not intend to utilize this additional piece of land for farming. They may have planned to use it for cutting wood, harvesting hay, and grazing livestock; however, they did ultimately farm it. Just $3^{1}/2$ months after arranging this second property lease, on June 3, Mathieu leased an additional third parcel; according to the text of the notary document, the Brunets did intend to farm this particular plot. In this instance, the individual who was leasing out the land was the Montreal resident Mathurin Jousset dit Laloire, who was about 55 to 62 years old; he and his wife had lost seven of the twelve children whom they had produced during their 27 years of married life.[73]

Over the span of eight months, from October of 1687 to June of 1688, Mathieu and Marie had leased the rights to utilize three parcels of land on Montreal Island. These three transactions apparently reflected Monsieur Brunet's intentions to remain ensconced in the Montreal area, at least for the present time, rather than heading out on another trading voyage to the west. Thus, when Nicolas Perrot was carrying out his preparations during the summer of 1688 for another venture in the *Pays d'en Haut*, he and Mathieu made certain arrangements, which reflected Mathieu's decision to remain behind in the St. Lawrence Valley. In the process, the two partners worked out a series of details which spelled out just how they intended to eventually settle their joint business affairs. In the morning on August 1, the two associates visited a notary in Montreal, to officially register the various agreements which they had made.

"Before [Antoine Adhémar] etc. was present Mathieu Brunet dit Lestang of this Island [of Montreal], who has acknowledged and declared that he has ceded and conveyed by these presents, without any guarantee of monetary restitution nor any recourse in any manner except for only the following facts and promises of the Sieur Nicolas Perrot, seigneur of Rivière du Loup, present and assenting, all of the rights and advantages which he [Brunet] has and which belong to him due to the [private or verbal] contract of partnership which he had made with the said Sieur Perrot, his partner on a voyage to the Mascoutens and Nadoussioux [Dakotas]. These rights include all that belongs to him according to an agreement between them [concerning Perrot's cash advance which maintained Marie Blanchard and the Brunet children during the 1685-1687 trading venture] which was passed before the said undersigned notary on the year and day [of May 17, 1685], whose contents have been this day placed into his [Brunet's] hands [as being paid off]. Of this promissory note, he [Brunet] has been made the bearer, requester, and receiver, and he has paid off that which he had taken [the 600 livres in cash] and subrogated in its place the rights, names, reasons, and actions for everything which has been arranged by the said Sieur Perrot as he wishes, by means of these presents, without him having any recourse, as it has been said, being truly resigned to the losses and fortunes of the said Sieur acceptant [Perrot].

In addition, the said Brunet dit Lestang has ceded and conveyed, as above without guarantees from the said Sieur Perrot, all such permits which have been provided or are to be bestowed by [Governor] Milord the Marquis de Denonville to the said cedant [Brunet] as gratuities which he was pleased to grant to him, as one of those who came down from the said region [of the Mascoutens and Sioux in 1687] for the war against the Tsonontouans [Senecas].

The said cedant [Brunet] has reserved for himself all of the beaver pelts and other peltries which he had in the aforementioned region of the Mascoutens and Nadouessioux, which originated with these nations and were for his own profit. The said Perrot has granted those to him, since he [Brunet] had gained them during the time in which he had been in the aforementioned region and they belonged to the said Lestang, the cedant, who will be permitted to dispose of the said articles however he wishes.

The aforementioned conveyance and transfer is thus made in consideration of the sum of one thousand livres, which the said Sieur Perrot has agreed that he will pay to the said Brunet, the cedant, or upon his order, as follows. Nine hundred livres in beaver pelts at the price of the office [of the export monopoly company] at Quebec upon his return, when the beaver pelts and [other] peltries of the said partnership will arrive in this said town [Montreal], which will be at the latest in the autumn of 1689, and the remaining one hundred livres in this town in merchandise at the store of the Sieur [Jean François] Charron [the later co-founder of the Charon Brothers order of hospital brothers], merchant, according to the promissory note which the said Sieur Perrot will issue to him [Charron] according to the current prices at the time of the delivery of the said merchandise. In addition, the said Sieur [Perrot] has agreed to pay off for the said cedant [Brunet] his part of the merchandise which they had purchased for the said partnership only. Thus have they promised, obligated themselves, and waived. [This agreement] made and drawn up at the said Villemarie in the office of the said notary on the first day of August, 1688 in the morning, in the presence of the Sieur Pierre Cabazier and of Silvain Guerin, witnesses living at the said Villemarie who have signed below with the said Perrot and the notary. The said Brunet has declared that he does not know how to write or sign, having been questioned according to the ordinance after the reading [of the document] was done by the said notary in the presence of the said parties and witnesses.

Signed,

N. Perrot, Cabazie, Sillevain Guerin, and Adhemar, notary"[74]

According to their joint agreement, Mathieu would receive 1,000 livres in payments from Nicolas Perrot, including 100 livres worth of merchandise from a Montreal merchant as soon as it could be delivered, plus 900 livres in beaver pelts during the year 1689. In addition, his cash advance loan of 600 livres was declared as having been paid off, as was also his portion of the outfitting expenses from the 1685-1687 venture. Besides these three considerable assets, Mathieu would also be allowed to retain ownership of the beaver pelts and the other peltries that he had garnered during their voyage in the Wisconsin Country. Unfortunately, these had been destroyed in the conflagration of the Jesuit buildings at La Baye, along with all those which had belonged to the other associates. However, Monsieur Perrot promised, in effect, to replace them during his upcoming sojourn in the west, and to transport these replacement ones out to Montreal. These latter two facts were not directly stated in the document, but they were understood; in their stead, the text indicated that Mathieu was to retain ownership rights to these various peltries. In return for these numerous and generous concessions, Mathieu relinquished his rights to any future commercial profits which Nicolas Perrot would generate in his western endeavors. He also agreed to hand over to Perrot any free trading permit which the Governor would grant to him in the future, in return for the services that he had rendered during the campaign against the Seneca nation.

In this document, the notary identified Nicolas Perrot as the "seigneur of Rivière du Loup." The trader had purchased this seigneury, which was also sometimes called Louiseville, only about two months earlier. However, a few years later, he would be obliged to return it to its former owner, having been unable to make the payments on the purchase price of the land, which totaled 4,000 livres.[75]

Two days after officially registering their business agreements, Mathieu again visited the office of the same notary on August 3. There, he promised that, when Monsieur Perrot would return in 1689 with his supply of peltries and hand over 900 livres worth of beaver pelts to him, he would in turn transfer 650 livres worth of them to François Chorel, Sieur de Saint Romain. Mathieu had owed a debt to this merchant of Champlain ever since December of 1682, before Mathieu's 1683-1684 trading voyage to the west. Later, in the spring of 1685, this trusting man had again supplied Mathieu with additional merchandise and supplies, before his second documented commercial venture, which had spanned the years from 1685 to 1687. Monsieur Brunet's promise to repay the overdue sum in the autumn of 1689 was received by Marie Anne Aubuchon, Chorel's wife, who had been granted a power of attorney by her husband before his departure. At this time, Madame Chorel was seven months pregnant, awaiting the arrival of the couple's fourteenth child.[76]

The above document listing the various business agreements between Messieurs Brunet and Perrot contained clear evidence that Mathieu had indeed been a participant in the Denonville campaign against the Senecas during the summer of 1687. The actual fighting of that expedition, and the subsequent destruction by the French and allied native forces of four Seneca villages and their corn crops, had taken place in the area of Seneca Lake and the present community of Genesee River, New York. As compensation for this martial service, the Governor and Intendant had afterward proposed to the King that all such participants should be granted a trading license at no cost. However, as much as five years into the future, by September of 1692, no such licenses would yet have been issued. But this delay would not concern Mathieu, since he had transferred any rights that he had held to such a license to his former partner.[77]

By the summer of 1688, Nicolas Perrot had been appointed by Governor Denonville as the commandant of the Wisconsin Country, holding virtually the same authority there that he had earlier received from the former Governor Labarre. During his 1688-1689 trading venture, Perrot and his party would establish Fort St. Nicolas, at the junction of the Wisconsin and Mississippi Rivers. Before his departure in August or September of 1688, the commandant must have notified the cartographer Franquelin of his intention to construct this facility, so that this brand-new information could be incorporated into the map-maker's up-to-date chart of North America, which he produced in this same year of 1688. For this particular trip to the west, Perrot had hired six voyageur-traders at Montreal: one man for "the Mascoutens and Nadouessioux" on May 14, another one for "the Ottawa Country" on May 20, two men for "the Ottawa Country" on July 30, and two others for "the Mascoutens and Nadouessioux" on July 31. These six hiring records indicate that the commandant possessed two trading licenses at this time, and that he was dispatching the three-man crew of one license to the region that was based out of St. Ignace and the Straits of Mackinac, and was sending the crew of the other license to the Wisconsin Country, west and southwest of the foot of Green Bay. (As the commandant of this latter western region, he was not included as one of the obligatory three men in each licensed canoe.) Nicolas did not complete his six hiring contracts until the end of July, and he drew up his business agreement with Mathieu on the first day of August. Thus, the brigade of canoes in which these six men traveled westward with Monsieur Perrot in this year of 1688 did not depart from Lachine until mid-to-latter August or early September. On May 8 of the following year, while at his post of Fort St. Antoine (which had been established during the expedition with Mathieu Brunet), the commandant would claim possession of the Wisconsin Country and the adjacent region of the upper Mississippi River for the King of France. The proclamation that he would read on that day would be entitled "Record of the Taking Possession, in His Majesty's Name, of the Bay of the Winnebagos, of the Lake and Rivers of the Outagamis and Mascoutens, of the River Ouiskonche and that of the Mississippi, the Country of the Nadouessioux, the Rivers Ste. Croix and St. Pierre, and other places more remote."[78]

During this same period of 1688-1689, the voyageur-trader Jacques Denoyon and his party would become the first documented Frenchmen to venture far westward from Lake Superior. Traveling inland from Ft. Kaministiquia, they would reach Rainy lake, where they would erect a small post and spend the winter trading. During the following summer of 1689, the men would advance down the Rainy River to reach Lake of the Woods, before returning to Superior with their rich cargo of peltries.[79]

In the middle of September in 1688, Marie and Mathieu, along with the rest of the family, had a wonderful reason to celebrate: their tenth child was delivered safely. Little Mathieu, Jr. was baptized at the Notre Dame de Montreal church on September 17, with his eldest brother Michel (about age 20) serving as his godfather and Marguerite Denis appearing as his godmother. Although this was the tenth offspring to be produced by the Brunet couple, the little lad's arrival may not have qualified them for the royal baby bonus. Their fifth child, Pierre, had been last documented in the census of 1681; since no record of his death has been preserved in the colony, he may have already perished by the time of the arrival of his youngest sibling in 1688. According to the official regulations, which the King and his Minister had inaugurated back in 1669 to promote population growth in the colony, parents who had ten living legitimate children, none of whom had entered the priesthood, would receive an annual payment of 300 livres. However, unfortunately, Marie and Mathieu may have had only nine living children by this time.[80]

Mathieu, Jr. would be the final child to be born to the couple. Between about 1668 and September of 1688, a span of two decades, they had produced ten babies. The birth years of the first three Brunet offspring can only be estimated, based upon their listed ages in the census of 1681. However, after the arrival of the fourth child Jean in January of 1674, the intervals between the births of the latter six children were 25, 22, 34, 15, 21, and 61 months. The lattermost interval (between August of 1683 and September of 1688) included the two extended periods during which Mathieu had been away trading in the interior. These were his documented commercial voyages of 1683-1684 and 1685-1687. During their two decades of childbearing, Marie's age had increased from about 19 to 21 up to 39 to 41, while Mathieu's age had gone from about 27 to 31 up to 47 to 51. Of their ten offspring, only Pierre may have passed away at a young age; at the time of the 1681 census, the last record which exists for him, he had already celebrated his fifth birthday. This survival record of the family was an especially fortunate one during this period, when the mortality rates for both infants and young children were exceedingly high.

Three months after the arrival of baby Mathieu, Jr., the Montreal Court announced its decision against Mathieu, Sr. Ever since he had agreed to purchase the farm at Champlain from François Lory dit Gargot, back in December of 1680, he had paid only the miniscule sum of 36 livres against the selling price of 500 livres. Thus, Monsieur Lory, who had relocated with his family to the Montreal area shortly after transferring the property to Mathieu, had sued him in the Montreal Court, with the hope of forcing him to pay off the debt. It was the Chief Judge's decision in this case, in favor of the plaintiff and against Mathieu, which the Court decreed on December 14, 1688. But Monsieur Brunet did not respond to these legal pressures; he refused to make any additional payments toward the farm, which he and Marie had abandoned more than a year earlier, when they had moved to the Montreal area.[81]

Two weeks after the Court's pronouncement, Mathieu contracted to supply wood to the Montreal master carpenter Léonard Paillé, who had recently moved there from the area of Charlesbourg and Beauport. According to their contract from January 2, 1689, Mathieu would provide him with 300 "good and saleable" thick planks of pine. One hundred of these were to have the standard ten-foot length, while the other two hundred were to be eleven feet long; all of the planks were to be ten inches wide and two inches thick. These products were to be delivered to a Montreal location of the craftsman's choice, some time before the Feast of St. Jean (June 23). If Mathieu could produce more than the requested number of 300 planks, Monsieur Paillé would be obliged to accept them, up to an overall total of 500 units. For the standard ten-foot ones, the carpenter would pay him 60 livres per hundred, while the eleven-foot versions were to be prorated accordingly; any additional planks beyond the ordered 300 would be paid at these same two rates. Carpenter Paillé also agreed that, as an advance toward the eventual total payment, he would hand over to Mathieu 100 livres within the next three days; the remainder would be paid upon the delivery of the completed products. For some reason, seven weeks later, on February 23, the two men returned to the notary to mutually cancel their agreement.

Interestingly, in this document the notary identified Mathieu as "an habitant living in this town [of Montreal]," and he described the place at which the original transaction was recorded as "at the said Montreal in the house and residence of Mathieu Brunet." This is the only known record in which a place of residence in Montreal was recorded for our Monsieur Brunet. Perhaps Marie and the children were residing on one of their three leased properties south of town, while he was temporarily living in the town itself, seeking employment for cash until his supplies of peltries would arrive during the coming summer or autumn.[82]

January 10, 1689 brought with it a very out-of-the-ordinary event for the Brunet family, when the third oldest child and second oldest daughter was married in the Montreal church. Mathieu had been away in the west when Jeanne, their eldest daughter, had been wed nearly five years earlier, back in the spring of 1684. That event had taken place when she had been about 14 years old. This time it was daughter Marie Anne, who would turn age 17 this year; she was joining in partnership with Antoine Pilon, $24^1/2$ years old. The wedding itself was conducted eight days after the couple had drawn up their marriage contract with the Montreal notary Claude Maugue. After the nuptial ceremony, oddly enough, the priest recorded only one official witness in the church ledger: Pierre Chantereau, the beadle or sexton of the parish. Only this solitary man, a minor functionary at the church, and not a single relative or identifiable friend of either the bride or the groom, appeared in the official record as a listed witness. This may imply that the family members and friends of the two engaged people had not approved of their union. Premarital pregnancy was apparently not an issue in this instance; the first child of the newlyweds would not arrive until eleven months after their church ceremony. This baby would be the first of thirteen whom the couple would produce in the Montreal area during the span of 22 years. (Marie Anne and Antoine Pilon would provide the direct ancestral linkage between Mathieu and Marie and the present author, via the Pilon couple's fifth child, Élisabeth.)[83]

Late in July, an impressive flotilla of canoes, manned by both native and French traders, brought out to Montreal a huge supply of furs and hides. These products of the interior regions were worth the fantastic sum of about 800,000 livres. This brigade included the many Frenchmen who had been sent in two years earlier, following the Seneca campaign of 1687, to retrieve the accumulated peltries at St. Ignace. At that time, each of these men had been equipped with up to 500 livres worth of trade merchandise, as well as permission to remain in the interior and trade.[84]

Presumably, upon their arrival, Nicolas Perrot and his party delivered to Mathieu the 900 livres worth of beaver pelts that the commandant had promised to hand over to him, to settle and close out the affairs of their partnership. In addition, the men probably also handed over to Mathieu other peltries to replace those that he had stored at La Baye back in 1687, which had been destroyed in the burning of the Jesuit buildings there. These deliveries took place some time in late July. About a month later, on August 28, Monsieur Perrot would hire three more voyageur-traders at Montreal. According to their contracts, these three men would be poised to conduct a trading voyage to the Ottawa Country.[85]

However, well before the engagement of these men, within about a week of the arrival of the huge convoy from the west, terrifying events occurred on Montreal Island which occupied the full attention of the French and native populations of the entire Montreal region. These horrifying activities took place only a few miles southwest of the Brunet's leased farm on the Rivière St. Pierre. During the night of August 4-5, 1689, under cover of darkness and a violent hailstorm, a massive force of about 1,500 Iroquois warriors crossed northward over the broad St. Lawrence. Silently spreading out along eight miles of shoreline, from the Sault St. Louis area of the Lachine seigneury westward into the seigneury of La Presentation, the raiders remained undetected by the sentries in the various forts throughout the entire night. Waiting until dawn to launch their ferocious strike, the Iroquois, who numbered nearly 200 attackers per mile of shoreline, took the French completely by surprise. Soon, they had slain at least 24 French residents and had captured an estimated 79 others. They also destroyed by fire 56 of the 77 houses in the area, along with numerous stables, granaries, and other outbuildings, and killed a large portion of the livestock. The easternmost end of this swath of death and destruction was located about three miles southwest of the Brunet's leased farm on the bank of the St. Pierre River.[86]

In the aftermath of this terrible onslaught, life in the region very gradually returned to its normal ebb and flow of daily activities. Four months after the Iroquois raid, Marie was elated to stand as the godmother of her and Mathieu's very first grandchild. Whatever ruffled feelings might have kept family members and friends from appearing as official witnesses at the marriage ceremony of their daughter Marie Anne and Antoine Pilon eleven months earlier seem to have faded away by this point. Quite possibly, the genuine sufferings of the residents of the two attacked seigneuries had burnished everyone's perspective on the value of family relationships and the beauties of the normal events of *la vie quotidienne* (daily life). In any case, on December 9, baby Jeanne Pilon was baptized in the Montreal church with Marie Blanchard and Jean Legras as her sponsors. The latter man, interpreter for the King in the Iroquoian languages (including the Huron dialect), was also a merchant bourgeois of Montreal. From this point onward, Marie and Mathieu would relish being called *Grand-maman* or *Mémé* and *Grand-papa* or *Pépé*.[87]

Three months later, on March 12, 1690, Marie again found herself standing beside the baptismal font within the same edifice in Montreal, this time for the christening of Marie Marguerite Lemoine. Born to Nicolas Lemoine and Marguerite Jasselin, the baby's godfather on this occasion was Pierre Cavelier. The young parents, having been married for nearly seven years, had settled in the Lachine seigneury. Their second child had died there in December of 1687 at the age of eight months; their third and fourth children, twin boys, had passed away in October of 1688, having lived for only 20 and 25 days, respectively. Following the Iroquois raid in August of 1689 (when the wife Marguerite had been about two months pregnant), the young couple and their eldest child (their sole surviving offspring) had relocated from Lachine to Montreal, where they would reside for the rest of their lives.[88]

In September of 1691, Marie and Mathieu welcomed their third grandchild into the world. However, this latest addition to the clan arrived under less usual circumstances than had their two Pilon grandchildren, who had been born to daughter Marie Anne and her husband Antoine Pilon. (Their daughter Jeanne and her husband François Huard would never produce any children.) Back on October 23, 1690, the Brunets' third-oldest daughter, Marie, had celebrated her 13th birthday. Some two months later, in about mid-to-latter December, she had become pregnant by an individual named Jean

Piron. On September 18, 1691, the baby was both born and christened in the Montreal church. At the time of the infant's baptism, Jean Piron was registered by the priest as his birth father, and the newborn lad was given the name Jean. No other information besides this birth record has been located in the colonial documents for the man named Jean Piron. Likewise, no data other than the baptismal information has been located for baby Jean in the records of the colony.[89]

By this point, Mathieu and Marie's financial situation must have been reasonably comfortable, sufficiently so for them to make plans to build a home of their own in Montreal (they only held leases on each of their farm properties, rather than ownership). With this intention in mind, on March 4, 1692, Fr. François Dollier de Casson, who was the Superior of the Sulpicians (the seigneurs of Montreal Island), conveyed and transferred to Mathieu Brunet dit Lestang, habitant of Montreal Island, a piece of property which fronted on the Place d'Armes (which was also called Place de l'Église), near the western edge of the walled community. In the contract of transfer, the lot was thus described:

"an emplacement *(living site) of land on the Commons of this town, consisting of eighteen feet along the street called Chegouamigon and twelve feet in length, along the street and encirclement of posts [stockade] of the town, the back of which is 12^1/$_2$ feet long. It is bounded on one side by the said Chegouamigon Street and on the other side by the property of [Marie Anne Drouard,] the widow of [Jean François Hazeur, Sieur de] Petit Marais, at one end by the property of one named [Claude] Robillard, a butcher, and at the other end by the said street and encirclement of posts [stockade] of the town...It is understood that this is to be used to build a house according to the ordinances, beginning with the year and day of the present contract."*

The one-time purchase price for this lot was to be 450 livres, payable to Fr. Dollier, while the annual seigneurial fees thereafter were to be 22 livres 10 sols in cash for the *rente* and 5 sols for the *cens*; these fees were to be due each year on the Day and Feast of St. Martin, November 11. As one of the accompanying obligations of ownership of this property, Mathieu was to have his grains ground at the seigneurial mill of Montreal Island and nowhere else, under the penalty of confiscation of the said grains. As collateral for this transaction, Mathieu put up "the house which will be built upon the said living site."[90]

Ten weeks later, on May 18, Mathieu and Marie officially transferred a portion of their newly-acquired lot, *un morceau de terre situé en la ville de Villemarie vers la Place d'Armes* (a piece of land located in the town of Montreal toward the Place d'Armes), to Michel Brunet, their eldest son. This transaction was carried out with the *bon plaisir* (approval) of the Seminary of Sulpice of Montreal (the Sulpicians).[91]

The Brunet couple apparently gifted this small piece of property to their eldest child Michel, whose age was recorded on this occasion as 25, since he was soon to be married. Two days after his parents had registered the land transfer, on May 20, the young man signed a contract by which he agreed to serve as a voyageur, traveling to the Ottawa Country with two other men. These three individuals, forming the crew of a single canoe for one license, were hired by Joseph Loisel, Antoine Bazinet dit Tourblanche, and Pierre Janot dit Lachapelle, three Montreal-area traders or investors. On the previous day, these three latter individuals (who had obviously acquired two trading licenses) had also hired three voyageur-traders to labor for them in the Ottawa Country, to be based out of Michilimackinac.[92]

Michel's voyage entailed a run of about four months duration, departing in late May and returning by the end of September at the latest (since he was back in time for his wedding in the Montreal church on October 7). This was apparently a trip in which the three men hauled new infusions of provisions, supplies, and trade merchandise westward to St. Ignace, delivering this cargo to associates of the three hirers (associates who were remaining at work in the interior). For their eastbound return trip, the three paddlers then brought out the accumulated furs and hides that the associates had gathered in the course of their trading in the upper Great Lakes region. This is the only voyage to the west that Michel Brunet dit Lestang is known to have made; however, this was just the sole trip for which public documents were drawn up. He may have made other journeys as an illegal *coureur de bois*, without official approval and license. If this trip in 1692 was indeed his only voyage, it represents one of those instances in which a young man made just one or a few journeys so that he could earn sufficient cash to pay for the expenses of setting up his own pioneer farm. Since Michel was married in October of this year, immediately following his trip, there is a high likelihood that this was the case for this particular young man.

Michel and his fiancée Marie Moison were wed in the church at Montreal on October 7. The bride, who had been christened Marie Madeleine but was called Marie, was $17^2/3$ years old; she had been living with her parents and siblings at Lachine. The two official witnesses on this festive day were two very prominent merchants bourgeois of Montreal: François Lemaître, the Sieur de La Morille, and Jacques Le Ber dit Larose. (It was the latter man who had outfitted the party of Mathieu Brunet and his thirteen colleagues for their trading voyage to the Illinois Country back in 1683.) Oddly, it was six weeks after their nuptial celebration that the newly-wedded couple visited the Montreal notary Maugue, to belatedly draw up their marriage contract.[93]

Certain documents from this period imply that Mathieu Brunet was not an excellent farmer. In particular, two records dating from December 2, 1692 and February 24, 1693 shed light on this aspect of his life. They refer to the farm in the Pointe St. Charles area, fronting on the St. Lawrence about a mile south of Montreal and about a half-mile northeast of the Rivière St. Pierre, which he had been leasing for the previous 4³/4 years. On February 25, 1688, Mathieu had officially arranged to lease this particular piece of property from the prominent Montreal merchant Jacques Le Ber (who had outfitted him and his thirteen colleagues for their Illinois trading trip in 1683, and had later stood as an official witness at his son Michel's wedding ceremony in October of 1692). By this point late in 1692, ownership of the land had been transferred from Le Ber to the former Montreal peltries merchant Jean François Charron, Sieur de La Barre, who had already owned the adjacent property immediately to the northeast of the Le Ber lot. (In this year of 1692, Monsieur Charron, in association with Jacques Le Ber and Jean Fredin, had founded the Hôpital Général de Montréal and the Frères Charon, the order of hospital brothers who operated this residential facility for indigent men and boys just south of the town.) On December 2, 1692, Monsieur Charron cancelled the lease on the land which was held by Mathieu, who was identified in the notary document as a "farmer of the Pointe St. Charles area."[94]

After demanding this lease cancellation, Monsieur Charron assessed the damages and losses which he perceived that Mathieu had caused at the formerly leased farm, and he then sued him for damages in the Montreal Court. In response, the Court appointed two well-respected members of the community, Nicolas Boyer (a carpenter living in the St. Pierre River area) and Claude Robillard (a master butcher in Montreal, and also a direct ancestor of the present author), to serve as arbitrators in this case. The resulting agreements between the parties were pronounced by the Bailiff on February 7, 1693. Seventeen days later, on the 24th, Mathieu visited Monsieur

Charron at his home in Montreal, along with the two assigned arbitrators and the notary Adhémar, to officially register the details of their settlement. In this document, Mathieu Brunet dit Lestang was again identified as a "farmer of the Pointe St. Charles area," since he was still farming the land fronting on the Rivière St. Pierre which he had leased back in October of 1687.

According to their agreement, Monsieur Charron would take the three oxen which remained from the four that had been provided to Mathieu, the four milk cows that had likewise been supplied to him, one five-year-old ox, one two-year-old black bull, one three-year old red cow, one one-year-old heifer, one sow and three piglets, eighteen chickens and one rooster, the cart with its wheels, the sled, and the two plows with their implements. For his part, Mathieu would take one five-year-old club-footed ox, one three-year-old red cow with white at the base of its two rear legs, one other red cow with a half-white neck, and another small one-year-old red cow. Concerning the forty bushels of wheat which Monsieur Charron had received from Mathieu as lease payments, he would keep all of these as compensation for the dead cattle, for which Mathieu had been responsible; however, he would deliver to Mathieu nine bushels of wheat and eight bushels of corn. All of the hay and the straw which were at the farm would belong to Monsieur Charron, except for one hundred bundles of straw which he would give to Mathieu. The latter man would receive no compensation for the various improvements which he claimed to have wrought on the farm and its buildings during his tenure there; in addition, he would be obliged to cover the court costs of the suit which Monsieur Charron had taken out against him. One month later, Mathieu again visited the Charron home in Montreal, along with the same notary. At this time, the two former antagonists jointly registered that all of the above transfers had been carried out, to the satisfaction of both of the parties.[95]

Commencing with the last day of August in 1693, three more of Marie and Mathieu's children celebrated their marriages within the span of fifteen months. The first of these joyful celebrations, the one conducted in the Notre Dame de Montreal church on August 1, joined in matrimony their daughter Marie, who was $15^1/2$ years old, and François Bigras, who would turn age 28 in five weeks. (The bride-to-be, the sixth child of the Brunet family, had given birth to an out-of-wedlock boy nearly two years earlier, back in September of 1691.) In the parish ledger, the officiating priest did not record any official witnesses as being present at this ceremony.[96]

Fig. 70. First Habitation at Quebec, built in 1608; artist's reconstruction based upon Champlain's drawing of 1612, redrawn after Jeffrys.

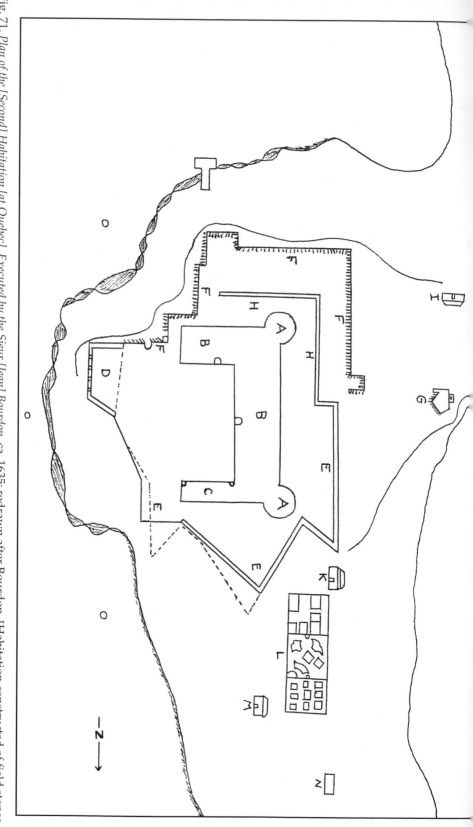

Fig. 71. *Plan of the [Second] Habitation [at Quebec]. Executed by the Sieur [Jean] Bourdon, ca. 1635; redrawn after Bourdon.* [Habitation constructed of field stones from 1624 to 1626.] A. two towers, B. two buildings of the storehouse, C. two rooms for lodging the clerk and others, D. platform where the cannons are, E. high thick walls [zigzag walls of squared horizontal timbers] with their ditch [dry moat], F. palisades [of vertical posts], G. redoubt where there is a small detached house and some cannons, H. Ditch [dry moat], I. bake house, K. the forge, L. gardens, M. hut of the timber sawyers, N. building of Sieur [Jean] Juchereau, O. the St. Lawrence River [pier at shoreline to the south portrayed but not identified].

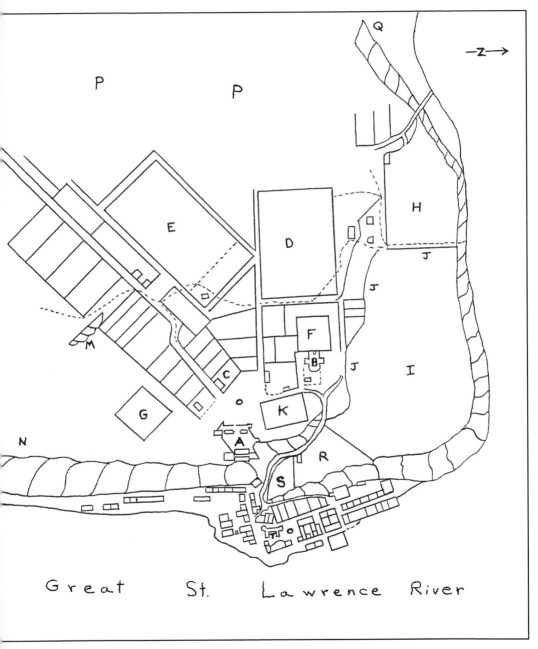

72. *True Plan of the Upper and Lower Town of Quebec, As It Is in the Year 1660* [by Jean Bourdon]; redrawn after Bourdon. A. Ft. St. Louis, B. Great Church, C. Palace of the Seneschal, D. the Reverend Jesuit Fathers, E. Ursulines, F. Grand Place, G. garden of the Fort, H. Hospital, I. the Sieur [Guillaume] Couillard, J-J-J. Hill of the Sieur Couillard, K. Fort of the Hurons, L. Great Road to Cap Rouge, M. Mount Carmel, N. Windmill, O-O. Place D'Armes, P-P. workable forest, Q. Ste. Geneviève Hill, R. [Denis Joseph Ruette] the Sieur Dauteuil, S. Cemetery, T. Storehouse. [Note brook shown flowing across entire Upper Town area.]

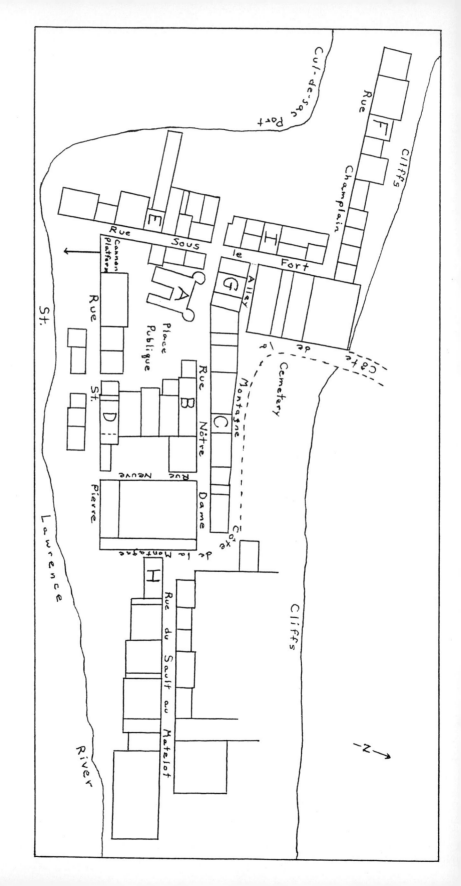

Fig. 73. Early Landholders of Lower Town area of Quebec, redrawn after Trudel. A. Old Habitation and Storehouse (both the wooden and stone versions), and future site of Notre Dame des Victoires church, built from 1688 to 1691, B. New Storehouse, C. Sevestre house, D. Gagnon-Gravel store, E. Perron-Suire store, F. Turpin house rented from Pré, G. Turpin house rented from Toupin, H. Turpin house rented from Toupin and Gloria, I. Turpin house rented from Gauvreau.

74, Upper. Quebec, Basse Ville: Notre Dame des Victoires church and Place Publique in front. Top of front wall rebuilt after 1759 Anglo bombardment and fire.

75, Lower. Quebec: Closeup view of front of the church, with outline of northeast tower of the excavated stone Habitation outlined in green paint on pavement.

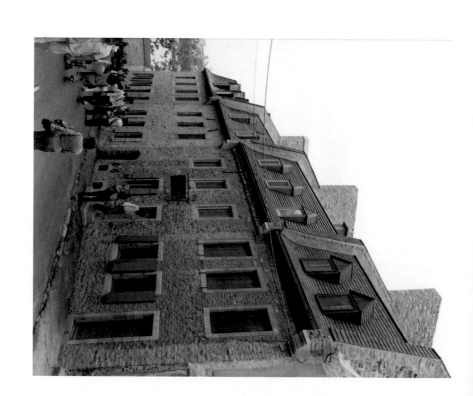

Fig. 76, Left. Quebec: Interior view of the church, including ex voto model of the ship which brought Marquis de Tracy to the colony in 1665 to command Carignan-Salières Regiment.

Fig. 77, Right. Quebec, Basse Ville: Rue Sous le Fort, Perron-Suire store stood on the second lot in the right foreground.

. 78, Upper. Quebec, Basse Ville: Rue Champlain, on which Alexandre Turpin rented a house from Monsieur Pré.

. 79, Lower. Quebec, Basse Ville: Site of first cemetery, on Côte de la Montagne, with heights of Upper Town in background.

Fig. 80, Upper. Quebec, Upper Town: Street scene including Jacquet House built on the corner in 1675, one of the oldest surviving buildings in New France.

Fig. 81, Lower. Southwesterly view from Cap Tourmente, showing entire St. Lawrence coastline of Côte de Beaupré (with its exposed tidal flats) extending off toward Quebec in the distance, with d'Orléans lying offshore. Original alignment of long slender lots is still visible via the hedgerow and fence lines.

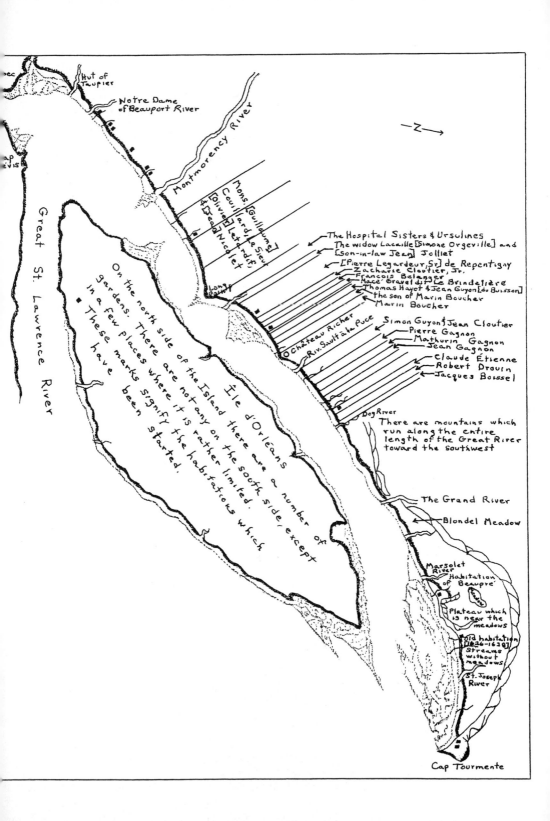

Hut of
Taupier

Notre Dame
of Beauport River

Montmorency River

−Z→

Great St. Lawrence River

Quebec

Cap Levis

Mons. [Guillaume]
Couillard [le Sieur
[Olivier] Le Tardif]
& [Jean] Nicolet

Long Point

Château Richer
○ Riv. Sault à la Puce

Île d'Orléans

On the north side of the Island there are a number of
gardens. There are not any on the south side, except
in a few places where it is rather limited.
These marks signify the habitations which
have been started.

The Hospital Sisters & Ursulines
The widow Lacaille [Simone Orgeville] and
[son-in-law Jean] Jolliet
[Pierre Legardeur, Sr.] de Repentigny
Zacharie Cloutier, Jr.
François Belanger
Macé Gravel dit Le Brindelière
Thomas Hayot & Jean Guyon [du Buisson]
the son of Marin Boucher
Marin Boucher

Simon Guyon & Jean Cloutier
Pierre Gagnon
Mathurin Gagnon
Jean Gagnon
Claude Étienne
Robert Drouin
Jacques Boissel

Dog River

There are mountains which
run along the entire
length of the Great River
toward the southwest

The Grand River

Blondel Meadow

Marsolet
River
Habitation
of Beaupré

Plateau which
is near the
meadows

Old habitation
[1626-1628?]
Streams
without
meadows

St. Joseph
River

Cap Tourmente

82. *Map from Quebec to Cap Tourmente, 1641*, by Jean Bourdon. Redrawn after Bourdon.

Fig. 83, Left. L'Ange Gardien: Small family chapel, constructed of stone as miniature church.
Fig. 84, Right. Château Richer: Stone home built in seventeenth century by Joseph-Macé Gravel dit Brindelière, store partner of the Gagnon brothers.

g. 85, Upper. Château Richer: Moulin du Petit Pré, water-powered grist mill built for the seigneury of Beaupré in 1695. Destroyed by invading Anglo troops in 1759, rebuilt in 1763.

g. 86, Lower. Petite Rivière St. François Xavier: Setting of the community in the distance, at the foot of forest-covered slopes descending nearly to the St. Lawrence shoreline.

Fig. 87, Upper. Petite Rivière: St. François Xavier church, built in 1738 of closely spaced upright squared timbers set upon a sill log, with rubble and clay infill in the spaces between the upright members. Utilized until stone church built in 1903, then demolished.

Fig. 88, Lower. Tadoussac: Reconstruction of Pierre Chauvin's home and storehouse, constructed in 1600 in *pièce-sur-pièce* style. Framework of squared timbers had horizontal squared timbers as infill between the widely spaced upright elements.

9. 89, Upper. Tadoussac: Church built from 1747 to 1749 of squared timbers in *pièce-sur-pièce* style, later covered with clapboard siding.

9. 90, Lower. Trois-Rivières: Stone house built by military officer François Châtelain in 1729.

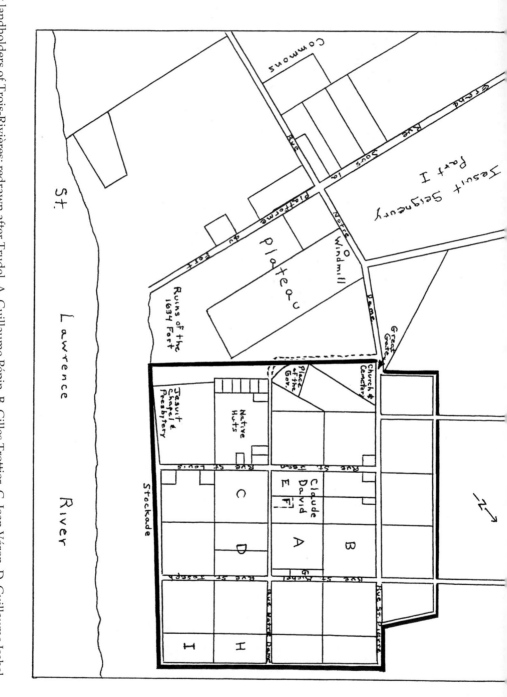

Fig. 91. Early landholders of Trois-Rivières; redrawn after Trudel. A. Guillaume Pépin, B. Gilles Trottier, C. Jean Véron, D. Guillaume Isabel, E. Claude Jutras, F. Jacques Brisset, G. Jean Denoyon, H. Médard Chouart, I. Marie Marguerie, widow of Jacques Hertel.

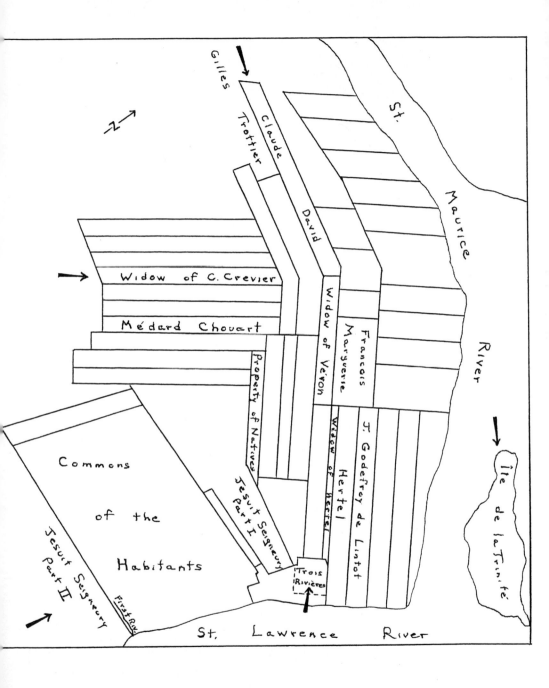

g. 92. Early landholders of outskirts around Trois-Rivières; redrawn after Trudel. The five broad arrows indicate properties which belonged to Claude David.

Fig. 93, Upper. Cap de la Madeleine: Notre Dame du Cap church, built of stone in 1714, the oldest surviving church in Canada which is still in its original form.

Fig. 94, Lower. Batiscan: Presbytery of St. François Xavier parish, built of stone in 1696.

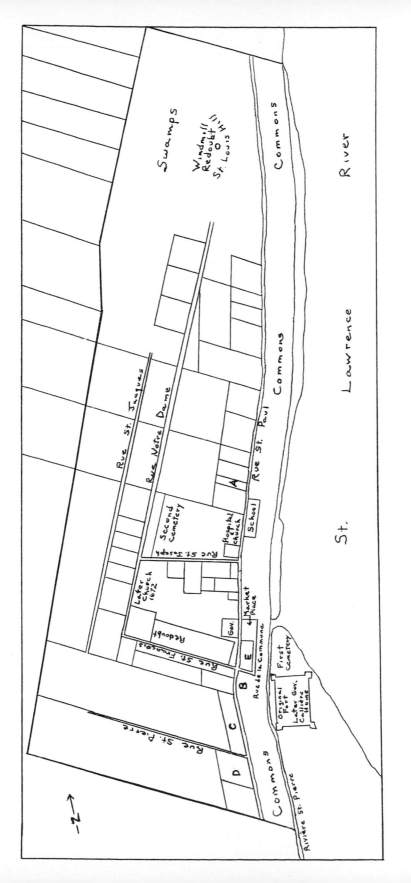

Fig. 95. Early landholders in the place reserved for the town of Montreal; redrawn after Trudel. A. Turpin house rented from Charly, B. Turpin house rented from Descaries, C. Turpin house rented from Migeon, D. Gadois-Beauvais house, E. Turpin house, hired out construction.

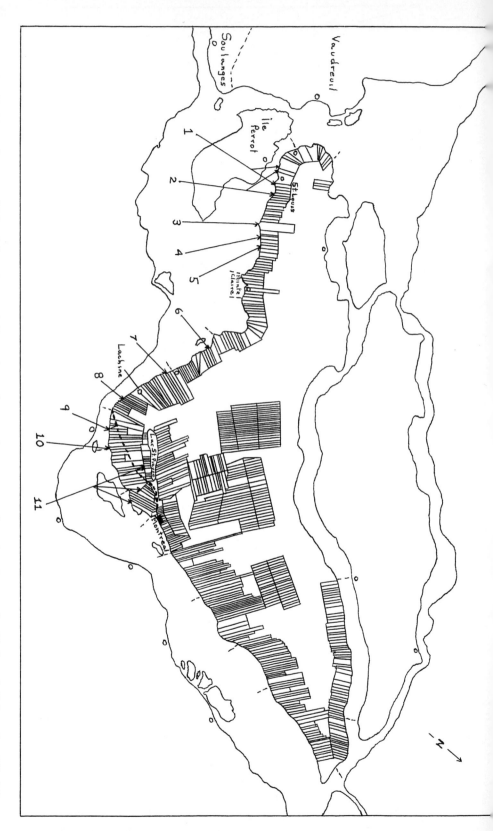

Fig. 96. Early landholders of Montreal Island (locations and dimensions of properties are approximate); redrawn after Vachon de Belmont and Dechêne.
1. Lalonde, 2. Maupetit, 3. Quenet, 4. Villeray, 5. Lory, 6. Robert Réaume, 7. Maupetit, 8. Tabault/ Lalonde, 9. Brunet dit Bourbonnais, 10. Simon Réaume (Legros), 11. Brunet dit Létang.

g. 97, Upper. Montreal: Obelisk at the site of the Market Place.

g. 98, Lower. Montreal: View from the former open interior area of Sulpician Seminary, built in 1685 in the form of protective fortress. Two of the four corner towers and two of the connecting buildings still remain, forming the oldest surviving structure in Montreal; clock added in 1710.

Fig. 99, Upper. Montreal: Truteau House, the oldest standing house in the town, built in 1698 on foundations of 1668 house.

Fig. 100, Lower. Just west of Ft. Chambly: Ancient farmstead, with stone house and wooden outbuildings.

ʒ. 101, Upper. Île Perrot: Stone windmill constructed on Pointe du Moulin in round tower style in 1705 for grinding grain, and stone miller's home built in 1785.

ʒ. 102, Lower. Île Perrot: Chapel of St. Jeanne Chantal parish, built of field stones in 1740.

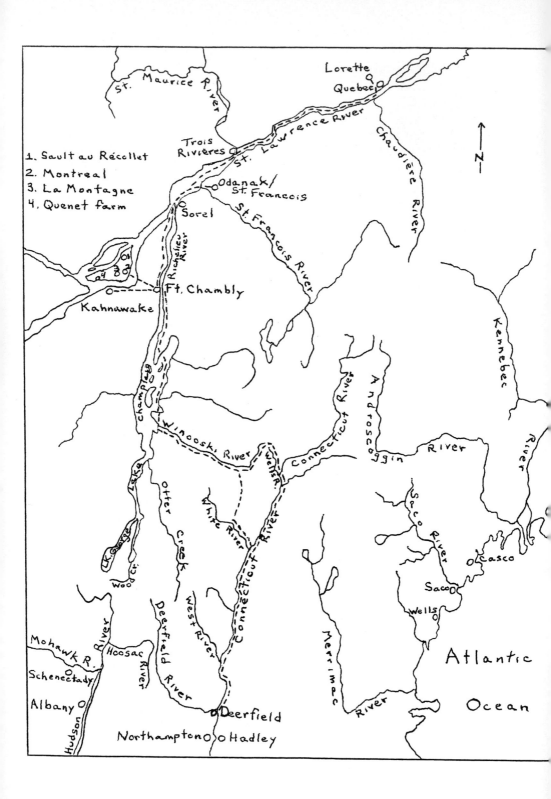

Fig. 103. Primary water highways between New France and New York/New England. Broken lines indicate routes of travel of Deerfield captives and their captors during the winter of 1704. Redraw after Haefeli and Sweeney.

g. 104. *Canadian Going to War on Snowshoes Over the Snow*, Militiaman of New France on a winter
campaign during the 1690s, illustration by La Potherie; redrawn after La Potherie.

Fig. 105, Upper. Deerfield, Massachusetts: Kent family outlining the Allyn family burial plot in the Old Burying Ground, final resting place of Sarah Allyn's siblings and relatives. Headstone beside Doree is that of Sarah's brother Samuel, killed in 1746 during attack by French-allied native warri

Fig. 106, Lower. Deerfield, Massachusetts: House built in 1707 for Reverend John Williams, after his release from captivity in New France. His first home, where he and his family members had been either killed or captured, had stood upon this lot; it had been burned down during the 1704 raid.

More than thirteen months after Marie's wedding, on October 19, 1694, Jean, the second-oldest son and fourth child of the family, took as his bride Marie Perrier. When this ceremony was conducted in the Lachine church, the groom was ten weeks short of age 21, while the bride was 24 years old. She had first married Guillaume Loret dit Lafortune back in December of 1683, and they had settled at Lachine. Their first baby had died in November of 1686, after living for only five days; it is not known what became of their second child, who had been born in March of 1688. At some later time, her husband had passed away as well. Following the Brunet couple's nuptial celebration, the priest recorded the four official witnesses who were present: Marie Gaillard, mother of the bride, Jean Sabourin, step-father of the bride, Catherine Brunet (13-year-old sister of the groom), and Barbe Duchesne. The newlyweds would first settle at Lachine, living there until at least 1702, after which they would relocate westward to Bout de l'Île; they would produce six children between 1695 and about 1708. Just $4^1/_2$ months before his wedding, on June 7, Jean had hired on as a voyageur to make a round-trip summer run to Michilimackinac. At various times during the next nine years, he would continue to work in this occupation, through his trip to Detroit in the summer of 1703.[97]

The very next wedding to be conducted at the Lachine church after that of Jean Brunet and Marie Perrier was the nuptial ceremony of Marie's next-younger sister, Catherine. On November 15, ten days after having celebrated her 13th birthday, she was joined in matrimony with Honoré Danis, a master carpenter from Montreal who was 25 years old. On this occasion, the officiating priest recorded that the occupation of the father of the bride was *laboreur* (farm worker), and that nine individuals had appeared as official witnesses. Those on the bride's side were her brother Michel Brunet, her brother Jean Brunet and his wife Marie Perrier, her sister Marguerite (age 11), and her brother-in-law François Bigras. On the groom's side were his brother Jean Danis, his brother-in-law Pierre Gougeon, his brother-in-law Étienne Badel, and the couple's friend Barbe Duchesne, who had also witnessed Marie Brunet's wedding in this same church one month earlier. After the wedding, the couple would settle in the Lachine seigneury, where they would produce seven children between 1699 and 1711.[98]

Now, at this point near the end of 1694, six of Marie and Mathieu's nine living children were married. The three remaining offspring who still resided at home with them were Jacques (age 14), Marguerite (11), and Mathieu, Jr. (6).

With the arrival of the following spring, sadness descended upon the clan when the Brunets' fourth Pilon grandchild died after only five weeks of life. Antoine had been born on March 11, 1695 at Laprairie, on the eastern shore of the St. Lawrence. This seigneury was located about five miles south-southeast of the Brunet farm on the bank of the Rivière St. Pierre. On April 17, the tiny lad died at home, after which he was laid to rest the same day. Until this point, Marie and Mathieu had been especially blessed with a high survival rate among both their children and their grandchildren.[99]

Near the end of the summer, on August 23, Mathieu and two other men from the Montreal area were sued in the Montreal Court for unpaid debts. Mathieu Brunet dit Lestang, Ignace Durand, and Paul Desmarais together owed money to the 30-year-old Quebec merchant bourgeois Nicolas Pinguet, Sieur de Targis (who was still single and would remain so for another thirteen months). The plaintiff, in order to submit his suit to the Court at Montreal and then to have representation there in the ensuing legal proceedings, sent as his attorney his 29-year-old brother. This was the Quebec businessman Jacques Pinguet, Sieur de Vaucours (who had already been married for six years, and whose wife was expecting their fifth child in about a month). One of Mathieu's fellow defendants in this suit, Ignace Durand, about 28 years old, had been married for six years, but the couple's only child had been stillborn back in December of 1691. He and his wife had moved to Montreal from Quebec in 1691 (and within months after this court case, they would return to the Quebec area to live). The other co-defendant, Paul Desmarais, about age 41, had been wed for sixteen years; he and his wife had already produced seven children. This couple had relocated to Montreal from Champlain (east of Trois-Rivières) some time between 1685 and 1687. Both of these defendants, like their colleague Mathieu (who had moved to the Montreal area with his family in the autumn of 1687), had relocated from other areas of the St. Lawrence Valley to settle in the Montreal region. It is quite likely that each of them had done this with the intention of actively participating in the peltries commerce, either at the annual Montreal trade fair or in the distant interior, or possibly in both of these venues. If the trio had become involved in the western commerce, they may have taken part as either voyageur-traders themselves or as investors backing other men, who did the actual traveling and trading for them. The fact that the three Montreal-area defendants were sued together for unpaid debts clearly implies that they had become indebted to the Quebec merchant while operating as a trio of united partners. In all likelihood, this debt had been generated when they had acquired from the merchant either a cash loan or provisions, supplies, and merchandise which had been utilized for a trading venture. Interestingly, the Court records only noted the submission of the suit on August 23. They did not report any additional days of hearing testimony and viewing evidence, or any announced verdict. Thus, the three defendants must have settled the case out of court, by paying off their creditor without protest. Unfortunately, no additional documentation concerning the partnership of these three men, or this legal case and its apparently quiet settlement, has been located in the notarial records of the colony.[100]

Nearly two years later, during the summer of 1697, Mathieu again found himself being sued in the Montreal Court. Back in March of 1692, he had purchased from the Sulpicians for 450 livres a house-building lot on Rue Chegouamigon and the Place d'Armes, near the western edge of the stockade-enclosed town. In the process, he had agreed that he would pay the customary seigneurial fees, 5 sols for the *cens* and 22 livres 10 sols for the *rente*, on the Feast Day of St. Martin (November 11) each year. However, during the ensuing five years, Mathieu had neither built a house on the lot nor paid the annual fees to his seigneurs. Thus, in early May of 1697, Jean Dionet dit Lafleur, the collector of seigneurial fees for the Sulpicians, submitted to the Court a suit against Mathieu. His goal was to force Monsieur Brunet to pay the sum of 115 livres 15 sols, which was the total amount of the accumulated unpaid fees for the previous five years. On May 16, Mathieu officially engaged the services of Antoine Galipeau, a *practicien* (attorney for civil cases), to represent him in this case and to supervise the sale of the lot. According to the agreement between the two men, after the liquidation of the property would be carried out, Monsieur Galipeau would be authorized to use the proceeds from the sale to pay off the overdue fees.

In this notary document, Mathieu was identified as "an habitant of the Rivière St. Pierre area," indicating that he and the family were still residing on their leased farm in this locale. However, on May 16, when he visited the notary to officially record his arrangements with the attorney, Mathieu indicated that his temporary residence at the moment was "the home of Sieur Claude de Devoir, located at the said Villemarie on Rue Chagouamigon." If at some point during the previous five years Mathieu had built a home on his lot on this same street, he would have listed it as his domicile.

According to the records of the Court, a judgement against Mathieu was announced on May 20, in which he was ordered to pay the overdue amount to Jean Dionet; in addition, an evaluation of the building lot was also ordered. Ten days later, on June 1, the ordered payment had still not been remitted. Thus, the Lieutenant Général (Chief Judge) ordered that an auction of the property was to be conducted; three public postings of this information were then carried out. On June 5, the Court's final order was issued: Mathieu was to either pay the overdue sum or default on the lot, after which bids on it would be received. Monsieur Brunet apparently chose the latter option, to default on the property. Six weeks later, on July 19, after the auction had been completed, the Chief Judge ordered that the sum of 300 livres which had been paid by the highest bidder was to be distributed between the various creditors who had come forward.[101]

May 4, 1698 was an especially happy day for Marie Blanchard. She had been chosen by her daughter Marie and her son-in-law François Bigras to serve as the godmother of their daughter Françoise, who had arrived on this same day as the fourth child of the family. At the christening ceremony in the couple's home church of Lachine, Marie was joined by the Lachine resident Jean Cuillerier, who stood as the godfather.[102]

Eleven days later, on May 15, Mathieu traveled to the office of the Montreal notary Adhémar, to officially register a debt. On this particular afternoon, he acknowledged that he owed Fr. Pierre Rémy, the parish priest of the Lachine church, 21 livres in money plus two bushels of wheat, which the cleric had apparently loaned to him.[103]

After another three weeks had passed, the two youngest offspring of the Brunet family received the sacrament of Confirmation in the Lachine church, at special festivities that were held there on June 6. These two children were Marguerite, who would turn fifteen in ten weeks, and Mathieu, who would turn ten in September.[104]

Once the long spell of good fortune concerning the survival rate of the family's younger members had been broken, death and anguish seemed to haunt the clan. Starting in March of 1699, over the course of the next thirteen months they would lose three of the members of the two younger generations. First came the death of Marie and Mathieu's sixth Pilon grandchild, Antoine, who perished at Lachine on March 6 at the age of five months. This unfortunate couple had also lost their first Antoine at this same age, four years earlier.[105] Five months after the burial of baby Antoine, on August 3, the Brunets' second-youngest child, Marguerite, passed away. Sixteen days short of her sixteenth birthday, she was laid to rest in the Lachine cemetery on August 4, with two official witnesses present. These were the Lachine notary Jean Baptiste Pothier and the Lachine and Montreal peltries merchant Jean Cuillerier.[106] Just six months later, additional grief befell the clan, when the third child of their son Michel died at Lachine on February 3, 1700, having survived for only six weeks. Grandson Joseph was interred in the cemetery beside the Lachine church on the following day.[107]

Two months after the melancholy departure of tiny Joseph, Mathieu helped to restore some of the clan's optimism, in a ceremony that was conducted on April 5 in the Lachine church. On that day, he appeared as the godfather and granted his own name to their next Pilon grandchild to be born, with Catherine Danis standing beside him as the godmother. By good fortune, little Mathieu Pilon would both survive and thrive during the following decades; he would grow up to become a voyageur in 1722, and he would marry two years later.[108]

Some time between the spring of 1698 and the spring of 1700, Mathieu, Marie, and their sons Jacques and Mathieu, Jr. (their only two surviving children who were still unmarried and living at home) relocated, moving from the farm which they had been leasing since 1687 to their own property. In the spring of 1698, Jacques was 17^3/4 years old, while Mathieu, Jr. was 9^3/4 years of age. At some point during the two-year interval following this particular spring, Mathieu, Sr. was granted a long slender lot in the sub-fief called Côte St. Paul. This sub-fief was located immediately southeast of Lac St. Pierre, and its individual farm plots abutted at their back ends against the southeastern shoreline of the long, narrow lake. Mathieu's property was located about 1^1/2 miles toward the west from the Rivière St. Pierre area, where the family had leased land for more than a decade. His new lot measured 20 arpents (385 English feet) in frontage by 20 arpents (^{3}/4 mile) in depth, extending southeastward away from the high-water mark of Lac St. Pierre. On the east side of his land was the lot of André Carrière, while the adjacent property on the west side belonged to their eldest son Michel. These three pieces of property, located at about the midpoint of the lake, would all be identified and located on the land-ownership map of Montreal Island which would be created by Vachon de Belmont in 1702. The Montreal-to-Lachine portage road ran to the east of the southeast ends of each of these elongated plots.[109]

Back on May 15, 1698, Mathieu had acknowledged that he had received from Fr. Rémy, the parish priest of the Lachine church, a loan of 21 livres in cash plus two bushels of wheat. In that notarial document, he had been identified as a resident of the Rivière St. Pierre area; an addendum penned at the bottom of the record indicated that he had later handed over the two bushels of wheat. About two years after this acknowledgement of indebtedness, on June 26, 1700, Mathieu and this same cleric made additional financial arrangements, this time for a long-term loan. In their agreement, the notary recorded that Mathieu still owed Fr. Rémy the former loaned sum of 21 livres, and to this unpaid balance the priest had now loaned to him and Marie an additional 79 livres. The total indebtedness of 100 livres was to be repaid at the rate of five livres per year in perpetuity, with the annual payments to be due on or before June 26 each year. The couple would also pay the customary seigneurial fees to the Sulpicians, the seigneurs of Montreal Island. As collateral for this loan, the Brunet couple, who were now identified as residents of the sub-fief of Côte St. Paul in the Holy Angels Parish of Lachine, mortgaged their property in that sub-fief, along with "their domicile of their home located on the said concession in the Côte St. Paul...and all of their possessions, both moveable and real estate." Mathieu and Marie declared that these holdings were free and clear of all debts, except for the sum of 320 livres which they owed to the widow Babie (Jeanne Dandonneau, the former wife of the deceased Champlain merchant Jacques Babie). They were paying her in annual installments, in accordance with a court order which had been previously decreed against them. This particular loan document from the spring of 1700 was the first one to record that Mathieu had been granted his own lot in this sub-fief, and that the couple had already lived there sufficiently long to have constructed a home on the land. It is to be presumed that they had also constructed the other standard outbuildings there, including a stable, a granary, an outhouse, and the other necessary structures as well. Quite probably it was the couple's expenses in finally establishing their own new farm, instead of leasing a pre-existing farm which belonged to someone else, that required this new loan of 79 livres from Fr. Rémy. Later notary documents would indicate that the Brunet couple would reside on this property in the Côte St. Paul for the rest of their married life together.[110]

On January 11, 1701, Mathieu was summoned to appear before the Montreal Court, to testify in a case which involved the issue of a certain laborer being paid for his days of work. During the course of his testimony, Monsieur Brunet stated that he was sixty years of age, which would imply a birth year for him of about 1641.[111]

A month later, on February 10, Marie was pleased to appear as the baptismal sponsor of their second Danis grandchild, who had been born at Lachine three days earlier. At the christening ceremony of Jean Baptiste in the local church, the co-sponsor was the Montreal resident Jean Danis, the baby's uncle. However, to the great sadness of all, the little lad would only survive for five weeks; he was buried in the Lachine cemetery on March 14.[112]

At this time in 1701, a major topic of conversation in both the local area and throughout the entire Montreal region was the resumption of work on the Lachine Canal. This man-made watercourse, when completed, would extend for $8^1/2$ miles in a northeasterly direction from Lachine all the way to Montreal. Work had commenced on the southwestern section of the project twelve years earlier, back in the summer of 1689; however, after seven weeks of labor, those efforts had been suddenly halted by the Iroquois raid of August 5. Back on October 30, 1700, the Suplicians (as the seigneurs of Montreal Island) had entered into a construction contract with Gédéon de Catalogne, the primary surveyor, cartographer, and engineer of the colony. According to their agreement, with the Suplicians supplying the tools and provisions, Catalogne's workers would excavate a canal which would be twelve feet wide and nine feet deep; according to their overly optimistic plans, the workmen would complete it by June of 1701.

With the highest of hopes, Fr. Dollier de Casson, the Superior of the Sulpicians, had paid Monsieur Catalogne 9,000 livres to carry out the project. However, after about half of the excavation had been completed, work was halted during the summer of 1701. At this point, the laborers had completed the section running southwestward from Lac St. Pierre all the way to the St. Lawrence shoreline, as well as the canalization of much of the Lac itself (which lay at the back end of Mathieu and Marie's lot). Less than a year after the commencement of the project, this stoppage now occurred after the excavators moved to the area east of Lac St. Pierre, a short distance to the east of the Brunets' land. In this latter area, the engineers had intended to create the eastern one-third of the canal. However, as the excavators attempted to widen and deepen the northeastward-running branch of the Rivière St. Pierre, they were unable to dig through the sandstone and limestone bedrock which lay beneath this natural waterway. The completed southwestern section of the slender canal, as well as the canalized Lac St. Pierre at the back of the Brunet lot (their property lay at about the midpoint of the entire proposed waterway) were both depicted on Vachon de Belmont's 1702 land-ownership map of Montreal Island. The southwestern terminus of the canal was located about four miles southwest of the Brunet farm.

This stage of progress was as far as this long-dreamed-of watercourse would reach during the French regime. And this was after some 20,000 livres had been expended on the attempt, more than double the cost that had been originally proposed by Catalogne. Years later, the engineer Chaussegros de Léry would try on two occasions to persuade the administrators of New France to complete the work. But these efforts would be in vain; the colony still lacked the financial resources, the professional skills, and the specialized equipment which such a project demanded.

For many decades after 1701, the completed section of the ditch would be utilized as a crude canal (without the entire eastern one-third of the proposed waterway, which had been planned to encompass the widened and deepened northeastern branch of the Rivière St. Pierre). It was useful mainly to the residents of the Côte St. Paul (such as the Brunet family) and the Côte St. Pierre, the two sub-fiefs which flanked the former Lac St. Pierre on its southeastern and northwestern sides, respectively. Eight decades later, during the Anglo period in 1783, with the installation of a number of locks, this same ditch would become the first canal operating with locks in North America. Between 1821 and 1825, the entire length of the canal would finally be completed. It would have a width of 28 feet and a depth of $4^1/2$ feet, with six sets of locks to offset the drop of more than 40 feet of the Lachine Rapids which it bypassed. This depth would be increased to nine feet between 1843 and 1848, and ultimately to its final depth of fourteen feet in 1885, to accommodate steamboat traffic on the St. Lawrence and Ottawa Rivers.[113]

On November 13, 1701, Marie and Mathieu's son Jacques and

his fiancée Jeanne Verret drew up their marriage contract with a Montreal notary, and they were married in the Lachine church on the following day. At this lighthearted and optimistic time, the groom (who was the Brunets' seventh child) was 20^2/3 years old, while the bride, hailing from Charlesbourg (just east of Quebec), was a month away from her 26th birthday. All of the official witnesses at the ceremony who were listed by the priest in the parish ledger were members of Jacques' family: his brothers Michel and Mathieu, his sisters Marie Anne and Catherine, and his brothers-in-law Antoine Pilon and Honoré Danis (husbands of Marie Anne and Catherine, respectively). After settling in the Côte St. Laurent sub-fief, about four miles northwest of the Brunet parents, the young couple would produce four children between 1702 and 1708. By good fortune, no one who was present at the wedding could see into the future and realize that three of these four babies would die within days of their respective arrivals.[114]

Five weeks after this celebration (which would be the last time that Marie and Mathieu would together watch a wedding of one of their children), on December 19, 1701, Mathieu finally reached a monetary settlement with François Lory. Back in December of 1680, a full 21 years earlier, Mathieu had purchased the farm at Champlain from this man and his wife, agreeing to deliver to them a total of 500 livres in four annual payments. However, he had only paid them the paltry sum of 36 livres. After waiting years to collect the unpaid sum of 464 livres, Monsieur Lory had finally sued Mathieu in the Montreal Court late in 1688. In response, the Chief Judge had decreed on December 14 of that year that Monsieur Brunet was obliged to pay the debt. However, within months, the case had become more complicated when Jeanne Dandonneau, the widow of the deceased Champlain merchant Jacques Babie, had seized the property and had sold it for 300 livres. She had done this in order to recover some of the money that Lory had owed to her and her deceased husband. Thereafter, Mathieu had refused to make any payments to Lory.

Now, twelve years later, at the end of 1701, Messieurs Brunet and Lory had finally reached a settlement between themselves. To officially document and record the various details, they visited the office of the Montreal notary Antoine Adhémar. First, they recounted to him the complicated history of the series of events and transactions which had taken place. Then they agreed that the former man owed the latter man the sum of 291 livres 16 sols (instead of the full unpaid balance of 464 livres from the farm sale). To settle this debt, Mathieu would pay 109 livres 16 sols directly to Lory, and he would dispense the remaining 182 livres in the following manner. The sum of 130 livres would be paid to the Montreal merchant Pierre Trottier, the Sieur Desaulniers, who was the legal representative of Étienne Charet, his deceased father-in-law. Another 30 livres would be handed over to the heirs of the deceased Jacques Le Marchand, who had been a farm worker in the area east of Trois-Rivières. Finally, the sum of 22 livres would be given to Jacques Aubuchon of Cap de la Madeleine or Trois-Rivières.[115]

In the afternoon of the following day, December 20, Mathieu returned to the office of the same notary, along with the merchant Pierre Trottier. The two men had worked out a method by which Monsieur Brunet, who was identified in the agreement record as "habitant of the Côte St. Paul of this Island," would pay the owed money in deliveries of cord wood.

"The said Brunet has promised, promises, and obligates himself to give and pay to the said Sieur Trottier Desaulniers or to the bearer the said sum of 130 livres in good and saleable cord wood, rendered in this town in front of the door of the said Sieur Desaulniers at the rate of six livres per cord in the following manner. Ten cords will be delivered around the end of the next year of 1702 and the beginning of 1703. Upon commencing, he will haul well and continuously until the said ten cords of wood have been rendered in front of the door of the said Sieur Trottier Desaulniers. The said Brunet will bring the remainder [11²/3 cords] of the said cord wood worth the said total sum of 130 livres to this said town in front of the door of the said Sieur Desaulniers, at the rate of six livres per cord, around the end of the said year 1703 and the beginning of 1704. This he will haul well and continuously, as noted above."[116]

To fulfill this contractual obligation, during the following years of 1702 and 1703, Mathieu cut, stacked, and hauled to Montreal a total of 21²/3 cords of firewood. (A standard piled cord of wood measured 4 feet in width, 4 feet in height, and 8 feet in length.) He presumably harvested this considerable amount of wood from his own property, which was ³/4 mile long by 385 feet wide, and contained a total of 34 acres. As a point of interest, Mathieu was about 60 to 64 years of age at the time he made these arrangements to work off this particular debt. And the only child who was still at home to assist him was Mathieu, Jr., who had turned 13 in September of that year. The labors of Mathieu in this two-year-long operation were, in effect, the price that he belatedly paid for the seven years of residence that he and his family had enjoyed on their farm at Champlain. That period, between December of 1680 and the autumn of 1687, had included his two documented trading voyages to the west, the first one in 1683-1684 and the second one in 1685-1687. Thus, the Champlain farm had served as a solid base for the family during those two extended absences.

After reaching the above financial agreement with Mathieu Brunet, François Lory only lived for about seven more weeks; he died at Lachine on February 4, 1702 (at the age of about 55), and was buried there two days later. Nearly five months after his demise, both his son François Lory, Jr. (about 31 years old) and Mathieu Brunet dit Lestang were sued in the Montreal Court by the Lachine and Montreal merchant René Cuillerier. On June 26, the court recorder noted that Monsieur Lory, Jr. had earlier been ordered to pay the sum of 22 livres to Monsieur Cuillerier. On this date, however, the Court learned that Lory had already given to the merchant a promissory note for the sum of 40 livres which had been signed by Monsieur Brunet. At some point during the next seven months, Cuillerier apparently presented the note to Mathieu for payment, and he must have refused to comply. As a result, on February 7, 1703 the Court issued a summons for Monsieur Brunet to appear before the Judge, at which time he would be obliged to remit 40 livres for his promissory note.[117]

Some weeks earlier, the Brunet clan had been very pleased to welcome the first child to be born to son Jacques and his wife Jeanne Verret. Joseph had arrived on December 24, 1702, one year and six weeks after his parents had been married; he had been baptized in the Montreal church on the following day, on the Feast of Noël. However, the tiny lad had only survived for 21 days; he had been laid to rest in the Montreal cemetery on January 14, 1703.[118]

A month after these heart-wrenching events, a slender ray of brightness and hope managed to dispel the clan's gloom somewhat, upon the safe arrival of the fifth child of son Michel and his wife Marie Moison. At his christening ceremony in the Lachine church on February 13, one-day-old Jean Baptiste's godmother was his grandmother Marie Blanchard, while his godfather was Jean Deferre. By good fortune, this boy would grow up hale and hearty; he would work as a voyageur in the west between 1724 and 1726, after which he would marry in 1730.[119]

When Mathieu appeared before the Montreal notary Michel Le Pailleur some four months later, on June 26, 1703, he generated in this scribe's office his last known notary document to be preserved in the colony. On this particular afternoon, "Mathieu Brunet dit Lestang, habitant of the Côte St. Paul" acknowledged that he lawfully owed the Montreal merchant Étienne Volant the sum of 150 livres. This debt was for "good merchandise which has been supplied to him in his need by the said creditor."[120]

Over the span of the next five years, Marie and Mathieu would have to bear a long string of deeply painful losses of close family members. During this time, they would lose not only two of their grandchildren but also three of their own children. The first to depart was their eldest daughter Jeanne, their second child. She and her husband François Huard had not produced any offspring of their own. No burial record for Jeanne has been located, so the only time reference for her death is the date when her widower remarried, on September 2, 1704. This day was 20 1/3 years after he and Jeanne had married, and about 34 years after her birth.[121]

In the late spring of the following year, the matriarch and patriarch of the clan lost another of their Pilon grandchildren, the youngest one. Little Jacques had survived the most critical first year of his life, but he still perished at the age of 14 1/2 months. He was interred in the Lachine cemetery on May 11, 1705, the same day on which he had died.[122]

Nine months later, on the first day of February in 1706, the mood of the clan was brightened considerably by a joyful and uplifting event. This was the wedding of the eldest child of this same Pilon family, which was conducted at the Holy Angels Church in Lachine, nine days after the young couple had signed their marriage contract. Two months beyond her 16th birthday, Jeanne Pilon was Marie and Mathieu's oldest grandchild; on this day, she took as her husband the immigrant Jacques Prou dit Le Poitevin. In the parish ledger, the priest recorded the names of the fourteen official witnesses. Among these, the bride's family was represented by her grandfather Mathieu Brunet, Sr., her uncles Michel Brunet, Jacques Brunet, and Mathieu Brunet, Jr., and her aunts Catherine Brunet and Marie Perrier (Marie's husband Jean Brunet was not present this day). The other witnesses included Pierre Léger, François Morel, Charles Demers, Jean Gabriel Picard, Nicolas Robillard, Marie Anne Rapin, Barbe Rapin, and Élisabeth Messaguier.[123]

But in the autumn of this same year, Mathieu and Marie, as well as the other members of the clan, again fell into mourning. Sadly, the youngest child of the Brunet family, Mathieu, Jr. passed away seven weeks after he had celebrated his 18th birthday. He was buried at Montreal on November 7, 1706. The fact that he was interred in this particular cemetery, rather than in the cemetery of his home parish at Lachine, indicates that he must have died while he was in Montreal, possibly while living and working there. At his funeral, the two official witnesses were Antoine Forget, the clerk of the Seminary, and Jean Baptiste Quenneville, the *bedeau* (beadle or sexton) of the Montreal parish.[124]

Another family loss followed this one just nine months later. Back in 1704, son Jacques Brunet and his wife Jeanne Verret had reveled in the survival of their second baby, after having earlier lost their first child in 1703. However, the happiness surrounding the arrival of their third little one in the summer of 1707 was destined to last for only four days; tiny Jeanne was buried at Montreal on August 8.[125]

Sixteen months later, as deep winter was setting in during December of 1708, sickness was sweeping through the population of the Montreal region. On or just before the first day of the month, Jacques Brunet, Marie and Mathieu's seventh child, passed away at his home on the Côte St. Laurent, some four miles west of his parents' farm. Just $28^1/3$ years old, he was buried on December 1 in the Montreal cemetery. At his funeral, besides the officiating priest Yves Priat, the two official witnesses were François Vachon de Belmont, who was the Superior of the Sulpician Seminary at Montreal (and also the maker of the 1702 land-ownership map of the Island), and Jean Baptiste Quenneville, the beadle or sexton of the parish. During their seven years and one month of marriage, Jacques and his wife Jeanne Verret had produced three children, but two of them had died. Fifteen days after Jacques' burial, Jeanne would deliver their fourth baby, but he would live for only four days, and would join his father in the same burial grounds on December 21.[126]

During much or all of this terrible period of poignant loss and deep misery, Mathieu was himself very ill. In fact, he eventually became so sick that Marie or someone else transported him to the Hôtel Dieu hospital on Rue St. Paul in Montreal, which was about two miles from their farm. No records have survived which might indicate how long he was confined to his bed there, but he never recovered, and he died in this institution. Shortly thereafter, the patriarch of the

Brunet dit Lestang family was laid to permanent rest in the Montreal cemetery, on December 17, 1708. In the record of his interment in the Montreal parish ledger, the priest recorded that Monsieur Brunet had belonged to the Lachine parish, that he had passed away at the Montreal hospital, and that he had been 70 years of age. (This lattermost information, provided by one of his own family members, would imply a birth year of about 1638. However, other documents which have been previously quoted in this biography indicate that the years of his birth could have extended from 1637 to 1641. Thus, his true age at the time of his demise may have ranged from about 67 to 71.) The parish record also noted that his final ceremony had been witnessed by three priests: Yves Priat, Henri Antoine Mériel, and Pierre Rémy. The latter cleric had been Mathieu's own parish priest at Lachine, and he had loaned money to Mathieu on two occasions, first in May of 1698 and again in June of 1700.[127]

At this point, Marie was about 59 to 61 years old. Having been married for 41 years, she and Mathieu had celebrated their wedding anniversary five weeks before his death. During their span of more than four decades together, among the ten children whom they had produced, three of them had died before they could marry. These had been Pierre, who had passed away some time after his fifth birthday; Marguerite, who had died at the age of 16; and Mathieu, Jr., who had perished when he had been 18 years old. In addition, their daughter Jeanne had been married for some twenty years before her death at the age of about 34, having never had any children of her own. Their son Jacques had been married for seven years before his demise at the age of 28; of his four children, three had died at very young ages. In addition, numerous of the other grandchildren in the clan had also passed away.

But Marie Blanchard still had her farm in the Côte St. Paul, and she had more years to live. Whenever assistance would be necessary, it would be close at hand, since her son Michel Brunet, his wife Marie Moison, and their numerous children lived on the adjacent farm immediately to the west. In addition, the other four married Brunet children all lived with their spouses and families in the Montreal region, not so many miles away.

Marie had no way of knowing that she would live for another 13^1/$_2$ years. However, having already endured six decades of life, including a great many tragic losses, she must have assumed that there would be additional losses of close family members, as well as numerous times of happiness and celebration, coming in the future.

One of the first of those celebratory days came in the autumn of 1710, nearly two years after both Mathieu and their son Jacques had died. On October 19, Jacques' widow Jeanne Verret remarried in the Montreal church, taking as her second husband Guillaume Delisle dit Lardoise. This couple would settle at Montreal and produce three children; these youngsters would join the one daughter, six years old in 1710, who had survived from the four offspring whom Jeanne had earlier borne with Jacques.[128]

In the heart of the winter of 1713, Michel's wife Marie Moison died at the age of 33 at the Montreal hospital, where Mathieu had passed away $4^{1}/4$ years before. She was buried in the cemetery at Montreal on February 3. Among the seven surviving children on their farm in the Côte St. Paul, which was right next door to Marie's property, the eldest, Michel, was $13^{1}/3$ years old, while the youngest, Marie Thérèse, was age $3^{1}/4$. Even with Grand-mère Marie's able assistance, with this number of young dependents on his shoulders and two farms to operate, Michel (now about 44 or 45 years old) must have felt the imperative to remarry within a short time. And so he did on July 10, five months and one week after the demise of his beloved first wife Marie. His second spouse, Anne Élisabeth Émereau dit Bélair, was $27^{1}/3$ years old, and had never been married; both of her parents and all three of her older siblings had already passed away. At their nuptial ceremony in the Montreal church, the four official witnesses were Jean Baron, a bourgeois of Montreal; Martin Cirier dit Argenteuil, a soldier and joiner at Montreal; Jean Baptiste Quenneville, the beadle or sexton of the Montreal parish; and Yves Lucas dit Saint Venant, master cooper of Lachine. Now, Marie had a new daughter-in-law living on the adjacent farm, where the new couple would produce four additional children during the next eleven years.[129]

Looking backward from our vantage point of three hundred years into the future, it is not possible to determine for certain whether Marie Blanchard had ever personally met the last-named witness, Yves Lucas dit Saint Venant, before her son's wedding on July 10, 1713. However, at some point within this same year or slightly later, Mathieu's widow and this widower, who both attended the Lachine church, would become man and wife in a ceremony conducted in that very same edifice.

Back in March of 1705, Monsieur Saint Venant, a master barrel-maker who had emigrated from western Brittany, had been about

39 years old. At that time, in the church at Lachine he had wed Perrine Lapierre, the widow of the deceased Honoré Danis dit Tourangeau. Perrine had then been about 54 to 59 years old, and had seven or eight living children, all of whom were already grown up and married, except for the youngest one, who was a 21-year-old voyageur by the time his mother remarried in 1705. One son of the Danis couple, Honoré Danis, Jr., had married Marie and Mathieu's daughter Catherine Brunet in 1694, thus making Perrine Lapierre and Marie Blanchard mutual mothers-in-law. After just seven years of married life with Perrine and no children to care for, Yves had become a widower in the spring of 1712, when she had died in the Montreal hospital at the age of about 61 to 66; she had been buried in the cemetery of Montreal on April 24.[130]

In 1713, Marie Blanchard was about 64 to 66 years old, and she had been living as a widow for some $4^1/2$ to 5 years. Yves Lucas dit Saint Venant was about 47 years of age; he had been living as a widower for about a year or more. Although no record of their wedding ceremony has been found in the church ledgers of the colony, the new couple married and settled in the Lachine parish at about this time, most likely on Marie's own farm in the Côte de St. Paul, beside her son Michel's farm.

On November 18, 1714, Marie traveled westward about sixteen miles to the Ste. Anne church at Bout de l'Île, at the western tip of Montreal Island, to attend the wedding of her oldest grandson. Jean Pilon, 23 years of age, from the St. Louis parish of Pointe Claire, was joined in matrimony with Marie Anne Gervais, age 20, of the Ste. Anne parish. The officiating priest recorded in the church ledger that the third bann of marriage for this couple had been dispensed by Fr. Vachon de Belmont, the Grand Vicar and Superior of the Sulpician Seminary at Montreal, and he also recorded the names of the four official witnesses. These were identified as Marie Blanchard, grandmother of the bride and widow of Mathieu Brunet, from Holy Angels parish at Lachine; Jean Brunet, brother-in-law of the bride, of this parish of Ste. Anne; Pierre Barbary, uncle of the groom, from St. Louis parish at Pointe Claire; and Jean Lalonde, brother-in-law of the bride, of this parish of Ste. Anne.[131]

Three months after this heartening occasion, in February of 1715, a much sadder ceremony was conducted, the burial of Marie's son-in-law Antoine Pilon, the husband of her daughter Marie Anne. This couple (who formed the direct ancestral linkage between Mathieu and Marie and the present author) had been married for 26 years. During that time, they had produced thirteen children while living at Montreal, Laprairie, Lachine, Bout de l'Île, and Pointe Claire; of these offspring, two had died. Their youngest living child at this time was three months short of turning age 4. On February 22, the day following his death, Antoine was buried at Pointe Claire.[132]

It is interesting to note that, in the earlier church record from November of 1714, Marie had not been identified as the wife of Yves Lucas, although it is highly likely that she and Yves had already been married in the Lachine church by that point. However, at the beginning of 1716, in the record of the wedding of another of Marie's grandsons, the matriarch was so identified. On January 20, Michel Brunet, the son of Jean Brunet and Marie Perrier, was joined in partnership with Marie Louise Jamme. Both the bride (age 14) and the groom (age 20) were from the parish of Pointe Claire, where the nuptial ceremony was conducted. Only two official witnesses were recorded by the priest. These were identified as Marie Blanchard of this parish of Pointe Claire, originally from the Lachine parish, wife of Yves Lucas of this parish, widow of Mathieu Brunet of Lachine; and Michel Brunet from the Côte St. Paul, uncle of the groom (he was also Marie's eldest son). This record clearly indicated that Marie and Yves were definitely married by this point, and that they had relocated, at least for the present time, from Lachine to his property in the Pointe Claire seigneury, some eight miles southwest of Marie's farm.[133]

During the autumn of 1717, the news reached Marie that Mathieu's former partner in the peltries commerce, Nicolas Perrot, had passed away at his home in the Bécancour seigneury, across the St. Lawrence from Trois-Rivières. The demise of this highly respected trader, interpreter, and diplomat to the native nations had come some months earlier, back on August 13 of this year, when he had been about 73 or 74 years old. During his 46 years of marriage, he and Madeleine Raclos had produced eleven children over a span of eighteen years. Of these offspring, two had died young (at the ages of 6 months and 17 years, respectively), while the other nine had grown to adulthood and had married. During the summer of 1688, after exiting from the interior with a huge supply of furs and hides, Nicolas had delivered the owed amounts of peltries to Mathieu, which had officially closed out and dissolved their trading partnership.

During the following nine years, Monsieur Perrot had repeatedly traveled to the west, to both carry out his peltries business and handle diplomatic matters with the various native nations. During the first three of those years, he had hired a number of voyageur-traders at Montreal to work for him and with him in the interior. These men had included three destined for the Ottawa Country in August of 1689, two headed for the same region in May of 1690, and one in August of 1691. At the conclusion of his 1690 voyage, he had brought back to the colonial administrators information concerning the lead mines of the upper Mississippi River region, which had been pointed out to him by leaders among the Miami nation. When the closure of most of the interior posts had been imminent in 1697, he had returned permanently to the St. Lawrence Valley, to settle on his farm in the Bécancour seigneury. In September of that year, he had dispatched his three eldest sons to the west, "to go up through the Ottawa Country by the permission which Milords the Count de Frontenac and the Intendant gave to me, to take from the Miamis, the Mascoutens, and the Outagamis that which they owe me." After the death of his protector Governor Frontenac in November of 1698, Nicolas Perrot had been ruined financially. He had been not only saddled with the debts that he had incurred during his many years of service, but he had also been unable to acquire from the government any compensation for the sums that he claimed were due to him or any pension in return for his decades of faithful service. In 1701, at the ratification of the Great Treaty at Montreal, he had served as the interpreter for the various nations of the west, who had been his friends and business associates for some three decades. In his later years, he had composed a number of reports and accounts; his *Memoir on the Manners, Customs, and Religion of the Native People of North America* was the only one which had been published. However, most of his other reports (which have not survived) had been incorporated by Le Roy de La Potherie into the second volume of his *Histoire de l'Amérique Septentrionale*.[134]

Some time after January of 1716 and before February of 1719, Marie and Yves moved from his land in the Pointe Claire seigneury back to the Lachine parish, presumably returning to Marie's farm in the Côte St. Paul. The occasion at which their relocation was documented was the baptism of one of Marie's great-grandchildren in the Lachine church. On February 15, 1719, Marie Angélique Brunet, having been born on that same day as the first child of Michel Brunet, Jr. and Marie Pelletier of this parish, was christened, accompanied by four sponsors. The official godparents were Michel Brunet, grandfather of the child (and also Marie's eldest son), and Angélique Girard (age 39), the unmarried daughter of Léon Girard and Clémence Beaune. However, the priest also recorded the presence of two additional witnesses: Marie Campeau from Montreal, the midwife, and Marie Blanchard of this parish. In addition, the record noted that these christening ceremonies had been supplemental, since the baby had been baptized at home, shortly after her birth, by the midwife Marie Campeau.[135]

Having been a widow for $4^1/3$ years and having numerous children to support and raise, Marie's daughter Marie Anne (who was about age 47) finally remarried at Pointe Claire. On June 26, 1719, she joined in marriage with Laurent Godin dit Beauséjour et Châtillon, a widower whose wife had died eighteen months before. Of his five children, three were still living, and two of them were already grown and married; only his youngest daughter, about 17 years old, would remain single for another three years before celebrating her wedding.[136]

By the summer of 1722, Marie was coming to the finish of her long and fruitful life. Near the end of July, she breathed her last, after which she was lovingly buried in the cemetery beside the Lachine church on July 29. The priest who conducted her funeral recorded that Marie Blanchard, the wife of Yves Lucas dit Saint Venant, had been 75 years old at the time of her demise; this information would imply a birth year of about 1647. However, back at the time of the 1681 census, her age had been listed as 32, indicating a birth year of about 1649. Thus, at the time of her death, Marie's true age was probably about 73 to 75. According to the information in her burial record, her eldest child, son Michel Brunet, was listed as the sole official witness at her interment. The Sulpician priest who officiated on this sad occasion, Jacques Letessier, was about 46 years old; he had been transferred from the mother country to New France only five years earlier.[137]

Yves Lucas dit Saint Venant would live for nearly four more years, probably residing on his own land off to the west at Pointe Claire. He would be buried in the Pointe Claire cemetery on May 3, 1726.[138]

Thus ended the long sagas of Marie Blanchard and Mathieu Brunet dit Létang. Theirs had not been easy, comfortable lives, flush with financial abundance. In fact, they had apparently had to expend considerable energy to acquire the few material possessions that they did accumulate during their lifetimes. Hopefully, they had garnered a great deal of satisfaction from the non-material aspects of life during the many decades that they had spent on this earth.

Mark of the said Brunet, and mark of the said Blanchard, August 3, 1676.

Mathieu Brunet dit Létang-Marie Blanchard
Lineage of Timothy Kent

I. Mathieu Brunet (Jacques/ Jacqueline Recheine or Prohuie)	10 Nov, 1667 Québec, QC	Marie Blanchard (Jean/ Martine Lebas)
II. Marie Anne Brunet (Mathieu/ Marie Blanchard)	10 Jan, 1689 Montréal, QC	Antoine Pilon (Thomas/ Madeleine Ruault)
III. Élisabeth Pilon (Antoine/ Marie Anne Brunet)	7 Jan, 1715 Pointe Claire, QC	Guillaume Daoust (Guillaume/ Marie Madeleine Lalonde)
IV. Claude Daoust (Guillaume/ Élisabeth Pilon)	19 Jan, 1761 Pointe Claire, QC	Ursule Jamme (Jean Baptiste/ Marie Josèphe Clément)
V. Geneviève Daoust (Claude/ Ursule Jamme)	30 Jan, 1809 Ste. Geneviève, QC	Joseph Lalonde (Étienne/ Marie Charlotte Levac)
VI. Joseph Lalonde (Joseph/ Geneviève Daoust)	17 Feb 1835 St. Polycarpe, QC	Élisabeth/Isabelle Achin (Hyacinthe/ Angèle Lalonde)
VII. Joseph Lalonde (Joseph/ Élisabeth Achin)	ca. 1873 Curran, ON	Josephine Chatelain (Étienne/ Marie Madeleine Taillon)
VIII. Élisabeth Lalonde (Joseph/ Josephine Chatelain)	30 Jan, 1893 Carrollton, MI	Joseph Bouchard (Philéas Joseph/ Adelaide Barbeau)
IX. Frances L. Bouchard (Joseph/ Élisabeth Lalonde)	28 Apr, 1945 Detroit, MI	S. George Kent (George Kapantais/ Eugenia Papadakis)
X. Timothy J. Kent (S. George/ Frances L. Bouchard)	5 Sept, 1970 Ossineke, MI	Dorothy J. Minton (Garnet J./ Elaine A. Reece)

Notes for Brunet dit Léstang

1. Marriage contract: Notary Antoine Adhémar, April 14, 1679, Archives Nationales du Québec at Montreal (ANQ-M). Church wedding record: H. Charbonneau and J. Légaré, 1978-1990, Vol. 1, Notre Dame de Quebec records, November 10, 1667; R. Jetté, 1983, p. 180. Indenture contract: H. Charbonneau and J. Légaré, 1978-1990, Vol. 6, Immigrants hired at La Rochelle. J. Blaeu, 1665, pp. 58-59, 190, 200-201, 73; detailed modern Michelin maps of France; M. Trudel, 1966c, p. 198; R. Harris, 1987, pl. 45; P. Moogk, 2000, pp. 90-91.
2. R. Cotgrave, 1611, "estang."
3. H. Charbonneau and J. Légaré, 1978-1990, Vol. 6, Immigrants hired at La Rochelle, and Vols. 1, 4, 5, 6, 13, and 14, recs. of Notre Dame de Quebec, Ste. Marie Madeleine de Cap de la Madeleine, Notre Dame de la Visitation de Champlain, Notre Dame de Montreal, Sts. Anges de Lachine, Ste. Anne du Bout de l'Île, and St. Joachim de Pointe Claire; R. Jetté, 1983, pp. 1172, 179, 358.
4. H. Charbonneau and J. Légaré, 1978-1990, Vol. 6, Immigrants hired at La Rochelle; R. Jetté, 1983, pp. 180, 528, 456; M. Delafosse, 1951, pp. 480-481, 493-503.
5. G. Perron, October 1991, pp. 44-48; G. Perron, 1998, pp. 122-133, 151; P. Moogk, 2000, pp. 93-97, 103-109.
6. A. Lafontaine, 1985, pp. 315, 327.
7. Notary Antoine Adhémar, April 14, 1679, ANQ-M; H. Charbonneau and J. Légaré, 1978-1990, Vol. 1, Notre Dame de Quebec recs; R. Jetté, 1983, pp. 180, 831, 943; J. Reisinger and E. Courteau, 1988, p. 89.
8. A. Lafontaine, 1985, p. 327; M. Trudel, 1973b, p. 255; M. Trudel, 1973c, map opp. p. 312; M. Trudel, 1973a, pp. 168-169; R. Harris, 1987, pl. 51.
9. A. Lafontaine, 1986, Champlain Census, Household No. 11.
10. Notary Jacques de la Touche, March 30, 1669, ANQ-Trois-Rivières (ANQ-TR); R. Jetté, 1983, pp. 85, 888.
11. M. Trudel, 1973c, map opp. p. 312.
12. Notary Séverin Ameau, February 13, 1668, August 24, 1669, and November 27, 1673, ANQ-TR; R. Jetté, 1983, pp. 775, 483; M. Trudel, 1973c, map opp. p. 312; M. Trudel, 1973a, pp. 168-169.
13. E. O'Callaghan, 1853-1857, p. 61; J. Verney, 1991, pp. 42, 117-118; W. Eccles, 1964, pp. 47-48; W. Eccles, 1972, pp. 69-79; P. Moogk, 2000, pp. 70-71, 211; R. Jetté, 1983, p. 312.
14. A. Lafontaine, 1986, Champlain Census, Household No. 11.
15. Notary Séverin Ameau, February 8, 1671 and November 27, 1673, ANQ-TR; R. Jetté, 1983, pp. 424, 1070; M. Trudel, 1973c, map opp. p. 312.
16. A. Lafontaine, 1986, Champlain Census, Household No. 11.
17. Notary Michel Roy dit Châtellerault, June 26, 1673, ANQ-TR; Notary Antoine Adhémar, December 10, 1680, ANQ-M; M. Trudel, 1973c, map opp. p. 312.
18. Notary Séverin Ameau, November 17, 1673, ANQ-TR.
19. Notary Séverin Ameau, November 27, 1673, ANQ-TR.
20. H. Charbonneau and J. Légaré, 1978-1990, Vol. 1, Ste. Marie Madeleine de Cap de la Madeleine recs; R. Harris, 1987, pl. 46.
21. H. Charbonneau and J. Légaré, 1978-1990, Vol. 1, Ste. Marie Madeleine de Cap de la Madeleine recs; R. Jetté, 1983, pp. 949, 790.
22. Notary Jean Cusson, April 4, 1676, ANQ-TR; R. Jetté, 1983, pp. 790, 114, 909.
23. Notary Antoine Adhémar, August 3, 1676, ANQ-M; R. Jetté, 1983, pp. 424, 124, 1070, 1104, 658, 1018, 384.

24. H. Charbonneau and J. Légaré, 1978-1990, Vol. 4, Ste. Marie Madeleine de Cap de la Madeleine recs.

25. Notary Antoine Adhémar, April 14, 1679a and April 4, 1679b, ANQ-M; R. Jetté, 1983, pp. 101, 40.

26. Notary Antoine Adhémar, April 14, 1679c, ANQ-M; H. Charbonneau and J. Légaré, 1978-1990, Vol. 6, marriage contracts, April 14, 1679.

27. H. Charbonneau and J. Légaré, 1978-1990, Vol. 4, Ste. Marie Madeleine de Cap de la Madeleine recs; R. Jetté, 1983, p. 813.

28. H. Charbonneau and J. Légaré, 1978-1990, Vol. 4, Notre Dame de la Visitation de Champlain recs; R. Harris, 1987, pl. 46.

29. Notary Jean Cusson, January 15, 1680, ANQ-TR; P. Dubé, 1993, p. 89; R. Jetté, 1983, pp. 841-842; M. Trudel, 1973ac, pp. 168-169.

30. P. Dubé, 1993, p. 89; R. Jetté, 1983, pp. 696, 898, 312.

31. H. Charbonneau and J. Légaré, 1978-1990, Vol. 4, Notre Dame de la Visitation de Champlain recs; R. Jetté, 1983, p. 1070.

32. Notary Antoine Adhémar, December 10, 1680 and December 19, 1701, ANQ-M; R. Jetté, 1983, p. 744; M. Trudel, 1973c, maps opp. pp. 312, 318; M. Trudel, 1973a, pp. 168-169.

33. A. Lafontaine, 1986, p. 76; H. Charbonneau and J. Légaré, 1978-1990, Vol. 6, Census of Champlain.

34. H. Charbonneau and J. Légaré, 1978-1990, Vol. 4, Ste. Marie Madeleine de Cap de la Madeleine recs; R. Jetté, 1983, p. 180.

35. A. Lafontaine, 1986, p. 76; R. Jetté, 1983, pp. 37, 19.

36. H. Charbonneau and J. Légaré, 1978-1990, Vol. 4, Notre Dame de la Visitation de Champlain recs; R. Jetté, 1983, p. 370.

37. Notary Antoine Adhémar, December 6, 1682, April 27, 1685, and August 2, 1688, ANQ-M; R. Jetté, 1983, p. 252.

38. T. Kent, 2004, pp. 49, 51-52, 54.

39. P. Dubé, 1993, pp. 9-10, 14-15, 52; W. Eccles, 1959, pp. 75-98; T. Kent, 2004, p. 85; Y. Zoltvany, 1969c, p. 375.

40. P. Charlevoix, 1866, Vol. 3, p. 244.

41. R. Jetté, 1983, pp. 180, 424, 384, 631, 746, 384, 54, 945, 825, 559, 82-83, 918, 686, 823, 695-697.

42. Notary Claude Maugue, May 28, 1683a, ANQ-M; R. Jetté, 1983, pp. 680, 389, 243.

43. Notary Claude Maugue, May 28, 1683b, ANQ-M.

44. R. Jetté, 1983, pp. 1036, 670; Y. Zoltvany, 1969c, p. 375.

45. T. Kent, 2004, pp. 65-69.

46. C. Skinner, 1996, pp. 288-289.

47. A. Vachon, 1982, p. 107; T. Kent, 2004, p. 71.

48. P. Dubé, 1993, pp. 184-188; H. Tanner, 1987, pp. 32-33.

49. T. Kent, 2004, pp. 72-73.

50. P. Dubé, 1993, p. 20, n. 46; W. Eccles, 1959, pp. 162-165.

51. H. Tanner, 1987, pp. 32-33.

52. T. Kent, 2004, p. 71.

53. T. Kent, 2004, pp. 71-72, 78.

54. P. Dubé, 1993, p. 188; W. Eccles, 1964, pp. 120, 122, 133-134; E. Blair, 1911, Vol. 1, pp. 232-242, 252-253; T. Kent, 2004, pp. 74- 83.

55. A. Leduc, August-September 2000, p. 10.

56. H. Charbonneau and J. Légaré, 1978-1990, Vol. 4, Notre Dame de la Visitation de Champlain recs; R. Jetté, 1983, pp. 949, 277, 384.

57. H. Charbonneau and J. Légaré, 1978-1990, Vol. 4, Notre Dame de la Visitation de Champlain recs; R. Jetté, 1983, pp. 180, 574, 540.

58. R. Jetté, 1983, pp. 746, 384, 54, 945, 695; E. Massicotte, 1929-1930, pp. 195-203.
59. Notary Antoine Adhémar, April 27, 1685, ANQ-M.
60. Notary Antoine Adhémar, May 17, 1685, ANQ-M.
61. H. Tanner, 1987, pp. 32-33, 40-41; R. Harris, 1987, pls. 37-38.
62. A. Vachon, 1982, p. 107, inside front cover; L. Kellogg, 1968, pp. x-xi; H. Tanner, 1987, pp. 32-33; R. Harris, 1987, pls. 37-38; A. Vachon and C. Perrault, 1969, p. 518; "Memoir on the Taking Possession of the Country of the Upper Mississippi," May 8, 1689, in B. French, 1875, p. 122; Marco Coronelli map of 1688, in S. Tucker, 1942, pl. X; C. Skinner, 1996, pp. 270-272.
63. R. Jetté, 1983, p. 898; Notary Bénigne Basset, August 12, 1667, ANQ-M; Notary Guillaume Larue, June 24, 1675, ANQ-TR; T. Kent, 2004, pp. 19-20; E. Blair, 1911, Vol. 1, pp. 243-252, Vol. 2, pp. 21-43, 249-256; L. Kellogg, 1968, pp. 122-123, 231-237; A. Vachon and C. Perrault, 1969, pp. 516-520; G. Merrick, 1987, p. 301 and map after p. 67; Jesuit Relations, 1896-1901, Vol. 66, frontispiece illustration. Paddling route: C. Skinner, 1996, pp. 282-288.
64. E. Blair, 1911, Vol. 1, pp. 243-251.
65. Jesuit Relations, 1896-1901, Vol. 63, pp. 270-279. Supplemental data from P. Charlevoix, Vol. 4, pp. 280-291; L. Lahontan, Vol. 1, pp. 118-134; C. Skinner, 2008, pp. 68-71; and the official reports by Governor Denonville and Intendant Jean Bochart de Champigny in O'Callaghan, 1853-1857, Vol. 9, pp. 331-333, 336-344, 358-369.
66. W. Eccles, 1964, p. 155.
67. E. Blair, 1911, Vol. 2, p. 25.
68. Notary Antoine Adhémar, December 10, 1680 and December 19, 1701, ANQ-M; R. Jetté, 1983, p. 774.
69. Notary Bénigne Basset, October 4, 1687, ANQ-M; R. Jetté, 1983, pp. 909-910.
70. Notary Antoine Adhémar, November 6, 1687a, ANQ-M; R. Jetté, 1983, pp. 372, 914.
71. Notary Antoine Adhémar, November 6, 1987b, ANQ-M.
72. Notary Bénigne Basset, February 25, 1688, ANQ-M; R. Jetté, 1983, p. 670. 1702 Montreal Island land ownership map by Vachon de Belmont: in Nos Racines, Vol. 22, 1979, pp. 430-431; M. Trudel, 1973a, pp. 172-173; recreation by G. Gallienne, 1977; and L. Dechêne, 1992, p. xxi.
73. Notary Antoine Adhémar, June 3, 1688, ANQ-M; R. Jetté, 1983, pp. 610-611.
74. Notary Antoine Adhémar, August 1, 1688, ANQ-M.
75. A. Vachon and C. Perrault, 1966, p. 518.
76. Notary Antoine Adhémar, August 3, 1688, ANQ-M; R. Jetté, 1983, p. 252.
77. L. Frontenac and J. Champigny, September 15, 1692, p. 47.
78. E. Massicotte, 1929-1930, pp. 196-197; E. Blair, 1911, Vol. 2, pp. 27-34, 39-41, 253-254; L. Kellogg, 1968, pp. 236-237; A. Vachon and C. Perrault, 1996, p. 518; B. French, 1875, p. 122.
79. J. Denoyon, 1717, pp. 495-498.
80. H. Charbonneau and J. Légaré, 1978-1990, Vol. 5, Notre Dame de Montreal recs; R. Jetté, 1983, p. 180; W. Eccles, 1964, p. 48; A. Vachon, 1982, pp. 144-145, 154.
81. Notary Antoine Adhémar, December 19, 1701, ANQ-M.
82. Notary Claude Maugue, January 2, 1689, ANQ-M; R. Jetté, 1983, p. 864.
83. H. Charbonneau and J. Légaré, 1978-1990, Vol. 5, Notre Dame de Montreal recs; R. Jetté, 1983, pp. 180, 917, 222.
84. W. Eccles, 1964, pp. 156, 166; Notary Antoine Adhémar, July 29, 1689, ANQ-M.
85. E. Massicotte, 1929-1930, p. 198.

86. W. Eccles, 1964, pp. 164-165; F. Stanislas, 1950, pp. 44-50; Y. Zoltvany, 1969b, p. 566; P. Moogk, 2000, p. 256; S. Colby, 2003, pp. 137-138; H. Lamarche, 1999, pp. 189-228; H. Lamarche, 2002-2003, pp. 1-4; R. Jetté, 1983, pp. 307, 155, 808, 44, 305-306, 590. 1702 Montreal Island land ownership map by Vachon de Belmont: in Nos Racines, Vol. 22, 1979, pp. 430-431; M. Trudel, 1973a, pp. 172-173; recreation by G. Gallienne, 1977; and L. Dechêne, 1992, p. xxi.
87. H. Charbonneau and J. Légaré, 1978-1990, Vol. 5, Notre Dame de Montreal recs; R. Jetté, 1983, pp. 917, 700.
88. H. Charbonneau and J. Légaré, 1978-1990, Vol. 5, Notre Dame de Montreal recs; R. Jetté, 1983, pp. 711-712.
89. R. Jetté, 1983, pp. 917, 180, 924.
90. Notary Bénigne Basset, March 4, 1692, ANQ-M; Montreal maps in R. Harris, 1987, pl. 49; R. Jetté, 1983, pp. 561, 996.
91. Notary Bénigne Basset, May 18, 1692, ANQ-M.
92. E. Massicotte, 1929-1930, p. 200; R. Jetté, 1983, pp. 180, 740, 59, 591.
93. H. Charbonneau and J. Légaré, 1978-1990, Vol. 5, Notre Dame de Montreal recs; R. Jetté, 1983, pp. 180, 820, 704, 670.
94. Notary Bénigne Basset, February 25, 1688 and December 2, 1692, ANQ-M; R. Jetté, 1983, p. 233. 1702 Montreal Island land ownership map by Vachon de Belmont: in Nos Racines, Vol. 22, 1979, pp. 430-431; M. Trudel, 1973a, pp. 172-173; recreation by G. Gallienne, 1977; and L. Dechêne, 1992, p. xxi.
95. Notary Antoine Adhémar, February 24, 1693, ANQ-M; Notary Bénigne Basset, October 4, 1687, ANQ-M; R. Jetté, 1983, pp. 161, 996.
96. H. Charbonneau and J. Légaré, 1978-1990, Vol. 5, Notre Dame de Montreal recs; R. Jetté, 1983, pp. 180, 101.
97. H. Charbonneau and J. Légaré, 1978-1990, Vol. 5, Sts. Anges de Lachine recs; R. Jetté, 1983, pp. 180-181, 900, 742; E. Massicotte, 1929-1930, pp. 202, 208.
98. H. Charbonneau and J. Légaré, 1978-1990, Vol. 5, Sts. Anges de Lachine recs; R. Jetté, 1983, pp. 180, 305-306.
99. R. Jetté, 1983, p. 917.
100. J. Holzi, 1995, Vol. 1, 1693-1703, Case No. 002-0130, August 23, 1695; R. Jetté, 1983, pp. 394, 393, 343, 922-923.
101. Notary Bénigne Basset, March 4, 1692, ANQ-M; Notary Antoine Adhémar, May 16, 1697, ANQ-M; J. Holzi, 1995, Vol. 1, 1693-1703, Case No. 004-0208; R. Jetté, 1983, pp. 353, 459.
102. H. Charbonneau and J. Légaré, 1978-1990, Vol. 5, Sts. Anges de Lachine recs; R. Jetté, 1983, p. 101.
103. Notary Antoine Adhémar, May 15, 1698, ANQ-M.
104. H. Charbonneau and J. Légaré, 1978-1990, Vol. 5, Sts. Anges de Lachine recs; R. Jetté, 1983, p. 180.
105. R. Jetté, 1983, p. 917.
106. H. Charbonneau and J. Légaré, 1978-1990, Vol. 5, Sts. Anges de Lachine recs; R. Jetté, 1983, pp. 180, 937, 295.
107. R. Jetté, 1983, pp. 180-181.
108. H. Charbonneau and J. Légaré, 1978-1990, Vol. 5, Sts. Anges de Lachine recs; R. Jetté, 1983, p. 917.
109. Notary Jean Baptiste Pothier, June 26, 1700, ANQ-M; R. Jetté, 1983, pp. 180, 204; M. Trudel, 1973a, pp. 116-117. 1702 Montreal Island land ownership map by Vachon de Belmont: in Nos Racines, Vol. 22, 1979, pp. 430-431; M. Trudel, 1973a, pp. 172-173; recreation by G. Gallienne, 1977; and L. Dechêne, 1992, p. xxi.
110. Notary Antoine Adhémar, May 5, 1698, ANQ-M; Notary Jean Baptiste Pothier, June 26, 1700, ANQ-M.

111. J. Holzi, 1995, Vol. 1, 1693-1703, Case No. 010-0467, January 11, 1701.

112. H. Charbonneau and J. Légaré, 1978-1990, Vol. 5, Sts. Anges de Lachine recs; R. Jetté, 1983, pp. 305-306.

113. Notary Jean Baptiste Pothier, October 30, 1700, ANQ-M; Notary Antoine Adhémar, June 26, 1702, ANQ-M; Nos Racines, Vol. 29, 1979, pp. 571-572; R. Jetté, 1983, p. 1014; W. Eccles, 1964, pp. 208-209; L. Dechêne, 1992, p. 66; F. Stanislas, 1950, pp. 44, 54, and maps inside front and back covers and outside back cover; D. Lanken, 1983, p. 49. 1702 Montreal Island land ownership map by Vachon de Belmont: in Nos Racines, Vol. 22, 1979, pp. 430-431; M. Trudel, 1973a, pp. 172-173; recreation by G. Gallienne, 1977; and L. Dechêne, 1992, p. xxi.

114. H. Charbonneau and J. Légaré, 1978-1990, Vol. 5, Sts. Anges de Lachine recs; R. Jetté, 1983, pp. 180, 182, 1121.

115. Notary Antoine Adhémar, December 19, 1701, ANQ-M; R. Jetté, 1983, pp. 37, 1092, 763, 28.

116. Notary Antoine Adhémar, December 20, 1701, ANQ-M.

117. J. Holzi, 1995, Vol. 1, 1693-1703, Case No. 012-0593, June 26, 1702; R. Jetté, 1983, pp. 744, 295.

118. R. Jetté, 1983, p. 182.

119. H. Charbonneau and J. Légaré, 1978-1990, Vol. 5, Sts. Anges de Lachine recs; R. Jetté, 1983, pp. 181, 183.

120. Notary Michel Le Pailleur, June 26, 1703, ANQ-M; R. Jetté, 1983, p. 716.

121. R. Jetté, 1983, pp. 180, 574.

122. ibid., p. 917.

123. H. Charbonneau and J. Légaré, 1978-1990, Vol. 5, Sts. Anges de Lachine recs; R. Jetté, 1983, p. 949.

124. H. Charbonneau and J. Légaré, 1978-1990, Vol. 13, Notre Dame de Montreal recs; R. Jetté, 1983, p. 180.

125. R. Jetté, 1983, p. 182.

126. H. Charbonneau and J. Légaré, 1978-1990, Vol. 13, Notre Dame de Montreal recs; R. Jetté, 1983, pp. 180, 182, 946.

127. H. Charbonneau and J. Légaré, 1978-1990, Vol. 13, Notre Dame de Montreal recs; R. Jetté, 1983, pp. 180, 800, 974, 946.

128. R. Jetté, 1983, pp. 182, 322-323.

129. H. Charbonneau and J. Légaré, 1978-1990, Vol. 13, Notre Dame de Montreal recs; R. Jetté, 1983, pp. 181, 820, 403, 51, 257, 954, 746.

130. R. Jetté, 1983, pp. 746, 305-306.

131. H. Charbonneau and J. Légaré, 1978-1990, Vol. 14, Ste. Anne de Bout de l'Île recs; R. Jetté, 1983, p. 917.

132. R. Jetté, 1983, p. 917.

133. H. Charbonneau and J. Légaré, 1978-1990, Vol. 14, St. Joachim de Pointe Claire recs; R. Jetté, 1983, pp. 181-182.

134. R. Jetté, 1983, p. 898; E. Massicotte, 1929-1930, pp. 198-199; A. Vachon and C. Perrault, 1966, pp. 518-519; E. Blair, 1911, Vol. 2, p. 255; R. Douville, 1963, p. 58.

135. H. Charbonneau and J. Légaré, 1978-1990, Vol. 14, Sts. Anges de Lachine recs; R. Jetté, 1983, p. 182.

136. R. Jetté, 1983, pp. 917, 513-514.

137. H. Charbonneau and J. Légaré, 1978-1990, Vol. 14, Sts. Anges de Lachine recs; R. Jetté, 1983, pp. 746, 1066.

138. R. Jetté, 1983, p. 746.

XII

Robert Réaume and his wife
Élisabeth Brunet dite Belhumeur

*Important voyageur-trader, and eventually a very prominent
voyageur-merchant partnered with the first commandant of
Ft. Michilimackinac. Worked at intervals in the upper Great
Lakes region until he reached the venerable age of 51*

In the period documents of New France, Robert Réaume's family name was spelled at least seventeen different ways, all of which were pronounced generally the same. These variants included Raeome, Raiome, Rayome, Reame, Reaume, Reaulme, Reausme, Reome, Reomme, Reosme, Rehaume, Rehaumme, Reheaume, Rheaume, Riaume, Riom, and Riome. In this biography, the spelling has been standardized as Réaume.

Robert Réaume, born to René Réaume and Marie Chevreau in January of 1668, is the first male subject in this entire series of biographies who was a native of New France. Each of the previous eleven men whose life stories have been presented thus far had been born in the mother country, and had come to the colony as transplanted immigrants. Robert's father, the carpenter René Réaume, had emigrated from Notre Dame de Cougne parish in La Rochelle. According to the respective ages that were recorded for him in the census of 1681 (39) and at the time of his funeral in 1722 (88), he was born during the interval of about 1634 to 1642. Robert's mother Marie Chevreau, hailing from St. Valérien parish in Châteaudun, had emigrated from France in 1665 as a *fille du Roi*, a marriageable girl or young woman who had agreed to relocate to the colony, with the hope of marrying a settler who had already established himself there. The only known record of her age is that which was recorded in the 1681 census (29), which would imply a birth year for her of about 1652.

René and Marie were married in the mission church at Sillery, just southwest of Quebec, on October 29, 1665, twenty days after the Quebec notary Pierre Duquet had drawn up their marriage contract (which neither of them could sign); at this time, René was about 23 to 31 years old. According to Élisabeth's reported age in the one later census, she would have been about 13 years old at the time of her emigration and wedding (most of the *filles du Roi* were married within months of their arrival in the colony). However, the ages which were documented by enumerators in the various census returns were sometimes well off the mark; this may be clearly observed in those instances in which the true ages of the subjects being enumerated can be derived from their baptismal records. Thus, it is possible that Élisabeth may have been a bit older than age 13 when she experienced these major events in her early life. She had departed from France during this same year, after her father's death, with an estimated 200 livres worth of articles as her dowry. In order to clearly sanction the marriage of such a young bride, the couple's wedding record was signed by Governor Daniel Rémy de Courcelle, Intendant Jean Talon, and Alexandre Prouville, Chevalier de Tracy (the commandant of all troops in the colony, including the newly-arrived Carignan-Salières Regiment), as well as the highly-placed women Anne Gasnier (the wife of Jean Clément, the Sieur DuVault et de Monceaux, who did not immigrate to the colony) and Barbe de Boulogne (the widow of Louis d'Ailleboust, the Sieur de Coulonges).

More than two years earlier, some time before June 30, 1663, René had been granted a long, slender plot of land that fronted on the St. Charles River (which was also sometimes called La Petite Rivière or La Petite Rivière St. Charles). This lot had 2 arpents (385 feet) of river frontage, and extended off toward the north for 32 arpents ($1^1/6$ miles). This property was located in the extreme southeastern corner of the seigneury of St. Ignace, about two miles west-northwest of the Upper Town area of Quebec. It was on this land that the couple eventually settled and raised their brood of thirteen children. However, at the time of the 1667 census, this particular farm site was only identified as *une habitation àu Réaume* (a dwelling belonging to Réaume), with only one arpent (.85 acre) of land cleared and under cultivation. Since no inhabitants were listed by name at this household (as they were at various of the other nearby farms), this clearly indicated that the Réaume family had not yet moved permanently from Quebec onto their farm property. (At this time, three other *habitations* very close to Robert's were likewise not yet permanently occupied. These had, respectively, 1.7, 2.5, and 3.4 acres of land which had been cleared of forest cover and placed under cultivation.) Until the St. Charles church would be constructed at the Charlesbourg seigneury in 1679 (at a place some two miles north of the Réaume farm) and priests would begin conducting ceremonies there, the family would travel to the church in the Upper Town of Quebec to celebrate important ecclesiastical occasions.

One of the first of these celebratory times for the couple, coming about thirteen months after their wedding, was the arrival of their first child, Maurice. He was born on December 6, 1666, and he was baptized two days later at the Quebec church.[1]

Nearly fourteen months later, on January 25, 1668, our Robert joined the family. His arrival occurred about eight months after the 1667 census had been conducted, when the family farm had only contained .85 acre of cleared and cultivated land. Thus, it is quite possible that, by this point in the heart of the following winter, the family had not yet developed their farming operation sufficiently so that they could relocate there from Quebec. At Robert's christening festivities, which were held in the Quebec church on the day following his birth, the Quebec tailor of suits Robert Moussion dit Lamouche, whose farm property was four lots away from that of the Réaumes, stood as the lad's godfather and granted to him his first name. Hélène Bonneau, the wife of Jacques Desmoulins (residents of Charlesbourg or Notre Dames des Anges, just northeast of the Réaume farm), was his godmother.[2]

The number of siblings of Robert increased steadily over the course of the following 23 years, with the regular arrivals of eleven additional brothers and sisters:

Simon, born on November 7, 1669, baptized on November 9 at the Quebec church.

Étiennette, born on January 1, 1672, baptized on January 3 at the Quebec church.

René, Jr., born on October 12, 1673, baptized on October 14 at the Quebec church.

Jean Baptiste, born by the St. Charles River on September 24, 1675, baptized on the same day at the Quebec church.

Marie Renée, born by the St. Charles River on July 1, 1677, baptized on July 2 at the Quebec church.

Jacques, born on November 28, 1679, baptized on the same day at the Quebec church; he died two days later, and was buried on December 1 in the Quebec cemetery.

Pierre, born on February 8, 1681, baptized on February 9 at the Charlesbourg church (which had been established in 1679);

he passed away on December 20, 1683, and was buried on the following day in the Charlesbourg cemetery.

Jacques II, born at the locale of St. Bernard (in the seigneury of Charlesbourg) on April 22, 1683, baptized on April 25 at the Charlesbourg church.

Michel, born on December 20, 1685, baptized on December 22 at the Charlesbourg church.

Charles, born on April 15, 1688, baptized on April 17 at the Charlesbourg church.

Pierre II, born on July 26, 1691, baptized on July 28 at the Charlesbourg church.

In addition to these twelve siblings, Robert also had a half-brother as well. In about mid-to-latter October of 1668, when Robert was about nine months old, his father impregnated Renée Labastille dite Martin, an unmarried *fille du Roi* from the St. Séverin parish in Paris who was about 19 years old at the time. During the previous summer, she had arranged a marriage contract with Pierre Rollandeau on July 20, but the contract had later been annulled. Baby Jacques was both born and baptized at the Quebec church on July 26, 1669; after the ceremony, the officiating priest noted that René Réaume had been the boy's birth father. This christening ceremony was conducted ten weeks after Renée had married the shoemaker René Gauthier dit Larose, at the Ste. Famille church on Île d'Orléans. Little Jacques, although he had begun life as an *enfant naturel*, presumably grew up as the elder brother of the eleven Gauthier children whom his mother later bore with her husband. However, he may have died at a relatively young age, since no later records of him have been located under the names of Labastille, Martin, Gauthier, or Réaume.[3]

Four days before the birth of his out-of-wedlock son Jacques, René Réaume was sentenced by the *Conseil Souverain* (Sovereign Council) to publicly apologize to one of his neighbors, who resided on the St. Charles River only four lots away from the Réaume farm. For having supposedly damaged her reputation with "atrocious insults," René was ordered on July 22, 1669 to make his apology to Anne Tavernier, the wife of Robert Moussion (the latter man had stood as Robert Réaume's godfather back in January of 1668). According to his sentence, the convicted man was to appear in the chambers of the Sovereign Council on his knees, acknowledge that his accusations against Madame Moussion had been false and malicious, and concede that she was a good and honorable woman. In addition, René was to pay a fine of three livres, which was to be given to the Quebec hospital, as well as 30 sols ($1^1/2$ livres) in court costs, since it was he who had lost the case. Apparently, young Robert was growing up with a rather hot-headed father, who was also a very prominent carpenter in the Quebec area. When the young son later chose to follow in his parent's footsteps and enter the carpentry trade, it is to be hoped that he did not emulate the public relations skills of his elder. However, Robert apparently apprenticed with a different craftsman than his father; the surviving records show René taking on only one apprentice during his career, that of Pierre Gauthier in 1674, for the period of $2^1/2$ years.

In the majority of the apprenticeships that were conducted in the colony, the duration was three years, although some contracts ran for four or five years or even longer. After his first two years of training, the services which were provided by the apprentice to the master were construed as payment to the master for his having imparted the instruction. In some cases, however, the parents paid the master extra compensation for educating the boy in his trade, in addition to the youth's services in both the workplace and the home of the master. In certain instances, the total duration of the apprenticeship was only for two years, if the parents paid for certain expenses of the apprenticed son, such as his clothing. Most craftsmen would not accept any boy who was less than twelve years old, except as an unpaid servant. The only official apprenticeships which were available to girls were with dressmakers, and these arrangements of indenture were very rare.[4]

In 1672, Robert's father René Réaume carried out a building project for the Quebec and Charlesbourg joiner Jacques Lareau. In return for constructing a half-timbered house which measured 30 by 15 feet and would have cost 150 livres, Monsieur Réaume received from his client a lot on Rue des Jardins in Quebec. This street in the Upper Town area, running in a north-south direction between the estate of the Jesuits and that of the Ursulines, was located just west of the Place in front of the Notre Dame Church. After building a home on this newly-acquired lot in town, the family would thereafter split their living time between the Upper Town and their farm, which lay some two miles to the west-northwest. This pattern of dividing their residence would apparently continue until at least the year 1689, when they would still own the home and property on Rue des Jardins. In this same year, they would also own land at La Canardière, which was also called Notre Dame des Anges. This tiny seigneury belonging to the Jesuits was nestled along the St. Lawrence River between the seigneuries of Charlesbourg and Beauport. Some time after 1689, the family would move permanently to their farm in the Charlesbourg parish.[5]

On April 7, 1681, when Robert was 13 years old, he was confirmed in special ceremonies that were conducted at the Quebec church. In the records of this day, during which the sacrament of Confirmation was administered to numerous individuals, he was listed as Robert Réaume of Quebec.[6]

At about this same time in 1681, a colony-wide census was conducted. The enumerator recorded the following inhabitants in their home on Rue des Jardins, listed as household 191 in the Upper Town area of Quebec:

"René Réaume, carpenter, age 38
Marie Chevreau, his wife, age 29
Children:
Maurice, 15
Robert, 13
Simon, 11
Étiennette, 10
René [Jr.], 7
Jean, 5
Marie, 4
Pierre, 1
1 gun, 1 cow, 10 arpents [8.5 acres] of land cleared and under cultivation."[7]

This document is the only known record concerning Marie's age (implying a birth year for her of about 1652), and it is one of only two records which refer to René's age (the other was his burial record). In this enumeration, which was probably conducted during the spring or early summer of 1681, the registered ages of the eight children were mostly correct. Maurice had turned 15 during the previous December, Robert had celebrated his 13th birthday in the previous January, and Simon had turned 11 back in the previous November. However, Étiennette's age was increased a bit, since she would not turn 10 until January of 1682. In contrast, the age of René, Jr. was reduced by a full year: he had already turned 8 back in the previous October. As was recorded, Jean Baptiste would remain age 5 until the coming September, but Marie Renée would not turn 4 for a few months, not until July. Finally, baby Pierre had been born on February 8; thus, he was only a few months old, but the census indicated that he was already one year of age. In comparison, the age of the baby in the nearby Morel household was specifically listed as 5 months.

It is of considerable interest to note that the Réaume family was recorded as owning 8.5 acres of land which was cleared and under cultivation. This statement most likely referred to their farm that fronted on the St. Charles River, about two miles away from their home in the Upper Town. It is unlikely that they would have had this much property under cultivation within the town itself. However, it is quite likely that both the family's single gun and their solitary cow were kept with them wherever they resided, being transferred back and forth between their house in town and their farmstead, which were some two miles distant from each other. It is also of interest that the family did not own their own team of oxen. This implies that, on those occasions when they needed a team for heavy tasks such as plowing, they borrowed or rented oxen and the associated equipment, or instead hired out the job to others. For all of the other tasks of daily life, they seem to have relied upon human power.

This census also reveals that, just two lots away from the Réaumes lived Olivier Morel, the Sieur de La Durantaye, along with his wife Françoise Duquet and their four young children (this household also contained two guns and two cows). Two years later, during the summer of 1683, Captain Morel would travel to the Straits of Mackinac, to assume his role as the commandant at the newly-constructed facilities of Ft. De Buade at St. Ignace; after another two years, he would become the commandant of the entire Upper Country. The close proximity of this important military and fur trade personage to the Réaume home in the Upper Town area may have highly influenced Robert and four of his younger brothers, since these five individuals would all later establish for themselves careers in the fur trade business, as traders, voyageurs, interpreters, or merchants.[8]

Some fifteen months after the census, on August 4, 1682, a ferocious fire swept through the Lower Town area, destroying 55 structures (almost all of the buildings in the area) in less than seven hours. Most of these lost buildings, which included a number of warehouses, had been made of wood. This conflagration would lead to the rebuilding of the area in more fire-resistant stone rather than wood, as well as the eventual construction of the church of Notre Dame des Victoires (beginning in 1688 and opening for worship in 1691). During the course of this fire of 1682, the lower (eastern) section of the wooden retaining wall that flanked the Côte de la Montagne (the winding roadway that led from the Lower Town to the Upper Town) was destroyed. Since there was no longer a wall to hold back the earth along the steeply angled slope beside the roadway, the soil soon eroded from the hillside onto the street and eventually rendered it impassible. As a result, in the following year of 1683, René Réaume and Jean Giron (Monsieur Réaume's partner for this specific job only) were hired to rebuild the wooden retaining wall.[9]

During the spring of 1689, when Robert was $21^1/4$ years old, his older brother Maurice, at 23 the eldest child of the family, was married. On April 19, Maurice and Marie Anne Vivier (who was 18 years old) exchanged their vows in the St. Charles church at Charlesbourg. On this happy occasion, Robert appeared as one of the official witnesses, along with Étienne Roy and Thomas Pageau, two uncles of the bride, all of whom were members of the Charlesbourg parish. Four days short of nine months later, Robert proudly stood as the godfather for his newborn nephew René, the young couple's first child. At the christening ceremony in the Charlesbourg church on January 15, 1690, the baby's other sponsor was his 16-year-old unmarried aunt Jacquette Marguerite Vivier.[10]

The earliest surviving notary document concerning Robert Réaume dates from May 13, 1690, four months after he had stood beside the baptismal font in the Charlesbourg church to sponsor his nephew. At this time, the young man was $22^1/3$ years old; he had already been thoroughly trained as a master carpenter, presumably through an extended apprenticeship program. However, his first documented business venture was, oddly enough, as a cod-fisherman. After this initial stint of work, all of his later documented employment, throughout his adult life over the course of at least the next three decades, would be focused on the fur trade.

The cod-fishing industry which was carried out by residents of New France (rather than by seasonal fisherman visiting from the mother country) was focused on the lower St. Lawrence River and the Gulf of St. Lawrence. The southern branch of this harvesting was carried out from bases that were strung out along the shoreline of the Gaspé Peninsula. The products from here (including both cod and salmon) were shipped upriver toward the west, for consumption by the residents of the colony, rather than being sent across the Atlantic to France. The closest of these fishing stations to Quebec was at Matane, on the south shore of the St. Lawrence some 230 miles northeast of Quebec. This station, which had a permanent, year-round resident population, had been established in 1677. This was just thirteen years before Robert and his five colleagues joined forces to conduct a cod-fishing operation at this locale, in the employ of a young businessman of Quebec.

Their employer, Charles Damours, the Sieur de Louvières, was 28 years old at this time. The son of the distinguished Quebec merchant and administrator Mathieu Damours, the Sieur de Chaufours, he had been married for $2^1/2$ years. The couple's first child had died in November of 1688, after just ten days of life, but their second daughter was $6^1/2$ months old and healthy. This young businessman and investor had been given the sub-fief of Marsolet by his aunt, the widow of Nicolas Marsolet, back in 1684, when he had been just 21 years old. In other words, he had come from a world of considerable privilege and stature, by Canadian standards.

The six men who were contracted on May 13, 1690 to conduct a cod-fishing operation for him at Matane apparently all hailed from the Quebec area. Besides Robert Réaume, the other members of the team included Jean Debray, Sébastien Rosmadek, Jacques Desardillier, Jean Bergevin, and Jean Baptiste Roger. According to their agreement, they would depart immediately and would labor during the course of the summer for as long as the fishing season would last, processing and salting their catch at Matane. The six men would provide the scaffolding for drying and any other equipment which would be needed to process the cod, while Monsieur Damours would provide their provisions and any other needed articles (including the temporary shelters), as well as the fully-equipped and outfitted shallops. At the completion of the season, their joint settlement would involve the harvest of salted fish, as well as the oil and the offal which had been derived from them. After the costs of the provisions and the other items which had been supplied by Monsieur Damours had been removed from the overall harvest, the remainder would be divided into five equal shares. The latter man would take three of these shares, from which he would pay the group of boys who had processed the fish and the other products on land and had transported them back to Quebec. The remainder of his shares would reimburse him for the use of the shallops and the shelters that he had provided, and also serve as his profits. The other two shares would be divided equally among the six hired men, with each of them covering whatever expenses each one had personally incurred in conducting the venture.[11]

The wooden boats called shallops which were utilized by Robert and his colleagues for carrying out this industry, were the general working vehicles of traders, fishermen, seal hunters, and whalers, besides being used as vehicles for general transportation. Built of hewn timbers and sawn lumber, *chaloupes* were depicted in various period illustrations as ranging from about eighteen to twenty feet in length and some five to seven feet in beam. Often manned by only one or two persons, they were powered by both sails and oars. The single mast or pair of masts were each rigged with a single sail, either square or lateen (a triangular sail suspended from a boom that is angled obliquely to the mast). A tiller at the stern controlled the vessel's course, while multiple pairs of oars either supplemented the wind power or provided the only propulsion when the wind slackened. When necessary, shallops were armed with one or more swivel guns.[12]

It is quite likely that Robert and his five colleagues had returned to their homes in the Quebec area by mid-October in this year of 1690, in time to join their fellow militiamen in defending the colony against the naval invasion of Anglo forces from New England. Since a state of war had broken out between France and England, a fleet of some 32 ships carrying more than 2,000 Massachusetts militia fighters had sailed from Boston in August, under the command of William Phips. Intending to invade and capture New France, these ships traveled up the St. Lawrence River, finally arriving in the Quebec area on October 16. Eight of the vessels, including the largest ones, anchored in front of the town itself, while other smaller vessels anchored to the east, off the nearby community of La Canardière (where Robert's family owned land) and along the Beaupré coast. To bolster his defenses, Governor Frontenac gathered nearly 3,000 fighting men, most of whom were militiamen, in the area of Quebec; these defending forces included a large party of militia fighters and regular troops who had marched overland from Montreal in four days. The Governor confidently answered Phips' demand for surrender with the statement that he had no reply "save from the mouths of my cannon and from my musketry." On the 18th, two days after their arrival, English forces totaling about 1,200 men landed on the Beauport shore east of the St. Charles River, intending to cross the St. Charles and attack Quebec from the side. However, they were strongly opposed by militia fighters from Beauport and the Côte de Beaupré plus numbers of native allies; these English forces were also ravaged by smallpox. Being unable to cross the small river and having suffered heavy losses, the invaders were finally evacuated three days later, having made little impact. In the meantime, the four large vessels in the English fleet had bombarded the town for two days, until they had used up most of their ammunition and had sustained considerable damage themselves, from the cannons of the French. With the prospect of approaching frigid weather trapping their fleet in ice, it was clear to Phips and his officers that their campaign had totally failed, and that they would be forced to abandon it. Three days later, after an exchange of prisoners had been carried out, the English fleet departed; en route downriver, some of the ships were wrecked on shoals and islands in the lower St. Lawrence. Thus, before reaching New England, hundreds of men among the invaders had lost their lives, some to sickness and others to shipwreck. In grateful thanksgiving for their own deliverance, the French changed the name of the church that was under construction in the Lower Town from L'Enfant Jésus to Notre Dame de la Victoire. (Twenty-one years later, in 1711, after the massive British invasion fleet of Hovenden Walker would be forced to turn back after storms and thick fogs had caused a number of devastating shipwrecks in the lower St. Lawrence, the name of the edifice would again be altered. This time, the word Victory would be changed to the plural form, becoming Notre Dame des Victoires.)[13]

By the spring of 1693, some $2^1/2$ years after his season of cod-fishing, Robert Réaume was $25^1/4$ years old. At some point, although he still considered himself to be a resident of Quebec, he had made his way upriver to the Montreal area. There, he had adopted the occupation of voyageur-trader and voyageur. In fact, by 1693, he had apparently already developed a reputation as being highly competent and trustworthy in these roles. As a result, on May 2 of this year, he was hired by highly-placed persons to paddle to the western interior, to carry out an important commercial mission.

"Before Antoine Adhémar, royal notary of New France residing at Villemarie, and the witnesses named at the end were present in person Pierre d'Ailleboust, Esquire, Sieur d'Argenteuil, half-pay Lieutenant in the Detachment of the Marine Department, acting for and in the name of Monsieur [Jacques Petit, Sieur de] Verneuil, Treasurer of the [Troops of the] Marine Department [in New France], to whom he promised to agree to these presents but to which he will be exempt from the pain of all expenses, damages, and interests, of the one part, and Robert Réaume, voyageur, ordinarily living at Quebec, of the other part, who have in good faith made the bargain and contract which follows. That is, the said Réaume binds and

obligates himself to go up to Le Pays Outaouois [The Ottawa Country] for the said Sieur de Verneuil and to come down in the present year, with a native from this said town, in a canoe loaded with the beaver pelts as well as the belongings and used clothing of Zacharie Jolliet which are in the said Ottawa Country, as well as everything else pertaining to the costs and expenses of the said beaver pelts and belongings. The said Réaume will care for the said beaver pelts in the best possible manner down to this town. This bargain is made with the stipulation that, for retrieving the said peltries, the said Réaume shall have provided to him the said canoe, the provisions for him and for the said native, and everything that will be required to bring down the said peltries. In addition, in consideration for which shall be given to the said Réaume upon his return to this said town the sum of two hundred fifty livres for his wages, salaries, and cares, in good beaver pelts at the price of the office [of the peltries exporting monopoly company], which will be taken from those which the said Réaume will assist in bringing down. In case of loss [of the said retrieved cargo], nothing shall be deducted from the said two hundred fifty livres of the said wages, as agreed upon. After the peltries [and belongings] of the said deceased Sieur Jolliet in the said Ottawa Country shall be loaded into the said canoe, in case the said canoe is not loaded enough, the said Réaume will be permitted to finish the loading with such peltries as he may wish to place therein, the carrying of which will be for his profit in addition to his said wages. Thus have they promised, obligated themselves, waived, etc. [This agreement] made and drawn up at the said Villemarie in the office of the said notary on the second day of May in 1693 in the afternoon, in the presence of Monsieur [Charles] Juchereau [Sieur de Beaumarchais] and Georges Pruneau, witnesses living at the said Villemarie who have signed below with the said [Pierre d'Ailleboust,] Sieur d'Argenteuil and the notary. The said Réaume has declared that he does not know how to write or sign, upon being questioned after the reading was done, according to the ordinance.
Signed,
P. D. Dargenteuil, Juchereau, G. Pruneau, and Adhémar, notary."[14]

Zacharie Jolliet had been the youngest of the three Jolliet brothers who had lived to adulthood. In sequence from the oldest to the youngest, these were Adrien (born in about 1643), Louis (born in September of 1645), and Zacharie (born in December of 1650). Growing up in Quebec and on the Côte de Beaupré, these three siblings had each eventually entered the peltries business. Adrien, the oldest, had been one of the seven French traders, including Claude David, who had conducted the pioneering commercial expedition to Chequamegon

Bay on Lake Superior from 1660 to 1663. During a later trading trip to the west in 1668-1669, Adrien had surveyed the Lake Superior region for possible copper mine sites. In the latter year, an Iroquois guide had shown him the southern route from the interior out to the St. Lawrence settlements, by way of Lakes Huron, Erie, and Ontario and the upper St. Lawrence River. Following this venture, on December 1, 1669, Adrien had summoned Jean Cusson, the notary of Cap de la Madeleine (just east of Trois-Rivières) and two witnesses to his home in the Cap seigneury. There, the young trader, who was only about 26 years old but was very ill and bedridden, had dictated his last will and testament. Within the next couple of months, he and his younger brother Louis had drawn up a contract by which they had agreed to make a trading voyage to the west. However, Adrien had died before the party could embark on this latest venture, probably before March 22, 1670. He had been married for about seven years, and he and his wife Jeanne Dodier had produced two children. During those wedded years, they had resided at Château-Richer, Trois-Rivières, and Cap de la Madeleine.[15]

Louis Jolliet, the middle brother, had first entered the peltries commerce in about 1669 or 1670, either shortly before or just after the demise of his older brother. In 1673-1674, he had led the exploratory party (including Fr. Jacques Marquette) which had traveled southward from St. Ignace along the shoreline of Lake Michigan, along the Fox and Wisconsin Rivers, and down the Mississippi River. The men had halted their southward progress at the mouth of the Arkansas River in the lands of the Quapaw nation, more than seven hundred miles from the mouth of the Mississippi. This expedition, conducted without any government funding, had been underwritten by the profits which the seven partners had garnered from trading, both before and after the journey of exploration. After this venture, Louis had become involved in the trade that was conducted in the north shore region of the lower St. Lawrence Valley. During the summer and autumn of 1679, he led a party up the Saguenay River to Lac St. Jean and from there by various rivers to Hudson's Bay and back, in order to establish trade relations with the native nations of the region. In this year of 1679 and in 1680, he had been first granted the Mingan Islands and then Anticosti Island in the mouth area of the St. Lawrence River, where he had established both fisheries and trading facilities. Back in 1675, he had married Claire Françoise Bissot, and the couple had produced six children during the following decade.[16]

Zacharie Jolliet, the youngest of the three fur-trader brothers, had been a member of both the 1673-1674 expedition and the 1679 one, both of which had been led by his brother Louis, who was $5^1/4$ years his senior. In the case of the first venture, Zacharie had signed the notary contract on October 1, 1672 in which he and Louis had formed a seven-man partnership with François Chavigny, the Sieur de La Chevrotière, Jean Plattier, Pierre Moreau dit La Taupine, Jacques Largillier, and Jean Thiberge. At that time, when Zacharie had been $21^3/4$ years old and Louis had been age 27, each of the seven associates had been unmarried. According to their partnership document, the men had agreed "to make together the voyage to the Ottawa Country [there to] trade with the natives as profitably as possible." For this venture, the two Jolliet brothers and Monsieur Chavigny had each contributed funds toward the necessary outfitting expenses. During the actual May-to-October voyage of exploration in 1673, Zacharie had remained behind at Sault Ste. Marie, tending to the group's trading operations there. However, on the 1679 expedition which traveled from the St. Lawrence Valley northward to Hudson's Bay and back, Zacharie had been one of the actual participants.

In 1685, he had been in charge of a trading post in that northern region which the party had traversed; this facility had been located on Lake Nemiskau, to the southeast of James Bay. Previous to this assignment, he had led a trading venture with five other partners to the Ottawa Country in 1682-1683, and after the Nemiskau Lake stint he had again been present at the Straits of Mackinac, up to November of 1689. At that time, after the native nations of the Straits area had learned of the recent devastating raid by Iroquois forces on the Lachine seigneury and the ineffectiveness of the French in its aftermath, they had decided to change allegiances. They would side with the Iroquois and join in the Dutch and English trade, abandoning their former alliances with the French. The two missionaries and the commandant at the Straits had quickly penned warning letters describing this situation to the Governor. Then Zacharie and a single colleague had transported those important missives out to the St. Lawrence settlements, under very trying conditions, during the months of November and December of 1689. They had made the first part of this highly challenging journey by canoe and the remainder on foot, walking atop the frozen waterways. It is not known whether he had later returned to Michilimackinac or Sault Ste. Marie at any point during the 1690-1692 period.

In November of 1678 at the Quebec church, Zacharie had married Marie Niel, who had been $18^{1}/2$ years old at the time. During the twelve-year interval between their wedding and October of 1690, Marie had borne four children. (However, the second baby, arriving in October of 1680, had been fathered by someone other than Marie's husband; this individual had not been identified at the time of the boy's baptism.) Zacharie had died some time during the 19-month period between May 4, 1691 and November 25, 1692. During that time, he would have been about 40 or 41 years of age. On the latter date, Marie had married Jacques Petit, the Sieur de Verneuil, at Quebec. He had been appointed as the Treasurer of the Troops of the Marine Department in the colony in 1685 (a post which he would hold until his death in June of 1699). Thus, it was Monsieur Petit who had hired Robert Réaume in May of 1693 (through the intermediary Pierre d'Ailleboust of Montreal) to paddle to either the Straits of Mackinac or Sault Ste. Marie, to retrieve the belongings of the deceased Zacharie Jolliet. (The Jolliet brothers had earlier traded at the Sault, which was a common two-day commute from the Straits, under normal paddling conditions. As a result, Zacharie's possessions could have been at either or both of these locations.)[17]

To be selected to carry out this assignment with just one native colleague, Robert must have been known as a highly accomplished and respected paddler. And to already have this reputation, he must have earlier made a number of trading trips to the west. Yet there is no surviving documentation for such voyages, which strongly implies that they had been carried out without official approval, and thus had left no paper trail recorded in public documents.

Robert's wages for this retrieval venture reflected both the importance of the mission and the faith of his employers that he could handle any and all challenges that might arise along the way. For this journey, he would receive a full 250 livres worth of beaver pelts, for a trip which would take about $3^{1}/2$ to 4 months to complete. Since there was no mention in the hiring contract of the remuneration of the native partner Robert would choose to join him, it appears that Robert was obliged to pay his fellow paddler out of his own salary. If he gave his native colleague let us say 50 to 75 livres, the remaining 175 to 200 livres still represented about half of the typical salary of a highly experienced voyageur-trader working for a full twelve to fifteen months. And this particular venture would not involve any trading; it would only entail paddling westward, retrieving the cargo, and paddling eastward back to the St. Lawrence settlements. (Thus, during this particular assignment, Robert would be truly working as only a highly skilled voyageur.) In other words, he was being paid quite well for this trip. In addition to these guaranteed wages in beaver pelts, Robert was also permitted to bring out additional peltries if the retrieved cargo did not completely fill the canoe, "the carrying of which will be for his profit in addition to his said wages." It is not clear from the text of the contract whether this represented a veiled trading permit, which would allow Robert to take in trade merchandise and exchange it with native customers at St. Ignace or Sault Ste. Marie, or whether he would only be permitted to transport back out excess peltries of other traders, hauling them out as paying freight. Since no restrictions were expressed in the document, both of these options appear to have been available to him, at his own discretion.

The conditions of this voyage would not be ordinary. Ever since the convoy of 1690 had brought out a large supply of peltries, war activities and the virtual blockade of the Ottawa River by lurking Iroquois warriors had prevented nearly all other deliveries from coming out to the St. Lawrence Valley. Thus, for three years, furs and hides had been accumulating at various locales in the interior, particularly at the Straits of Mackinac. In this spring of 1693, with the economy of New France in jeopardy, Governor Frontenac decided to dispatch to Ft. de Buade a brigade of four canoes heavily manned by a total of 23 paddlers (who would later bring out as many as a dozen loaded canoes from the interior). During the first leg of their westbound journey, they would be escorted partway up the Ottawa River by another 27 men.

It is unlikely that the party of 23 men who were being sent west by the Governor to bring out peltries included the voyageur-traders who had been privately hired during the winter and spring to work for employers in the interior. These included the two men who had been hired on February 3 by Claude Greysolon, Sieur de Tourette, to labor at his posts of Kaministiquia and La Maune/Tourette in the Lake Superior region; the one man who had been engaged on April 29 by two trader partners for service in the Ottawa Country; the two men who had been hired on April 30 to work for Louis de La Porte, Sieur de Louvigny, the commandant of Ft. De Buade; and the two men who had been engaged on May 2 to work with Robert's younger brother Simon Réaume (age 23) in the Ottawa Country. In this latter endeavor, Simon's business partner was the officer Pierre d'Ailleboust, Sieur d'Argenteuil; he had represented Robert's absent employer Jacques Petit at the time Robert's contract had been drawn up on the same day of May 2.

The four canoes dispatched by the Governor, plus those of the westbound voyageur-traders along with Robert and his native colleague, safely ascended the Ottawa River and then traveled on to Michilimackinac. However, the group of 27 men who had escorted them on the lower portion of the Ottawa was attacked by an Iroquois war party during their return trip, as they approached their homes on Montreal Island.

In July, the massive flotilla that headed eastward from the Straits was a sight to behold. Made up of the 23 voyageurs sent in by Frontenac, Robert and his one colleague, some two hundred Frenchmen who had been trading in the west, and numerous native paddlers who had been hired to make the trip, the downbound convoy arrived at the St. Lawrence settlements on August 17. These canoes, numbering more than two hundred, transported out a gigantic supply of furs and hides that had a total value of about 800,000 livres. It is likely that the peltries and belongings of the deceased Zacharie Jolliet, hauled out by Robert Réaume and his single paddling partner, were included in this estimate of the total amount of cargo that was brought out at this time.[18]

Just 3^1/2 weeks after his return to Montreal, Robert was again hired to make another voyage to the west, this time as a wintering voyageur-trader. His employers in this instance included Marie Niel, the former widow of Zacharie Jolliet who had married Jacques Petit in November of 1692, as well as Monsieur Petit himself (Robert's former employer). These two spouses from Quebec, along with Joseph Després and Charles Jobin, had formed a partnership to utilize a trading license which they had received from the Governor. Monsieur Després, unmarried and about 28 years old, had been enumerated back at the time of the 1681 census as a domestic servant of the Jesuits at their Ottawa mission, which was based at Michilimackinac. Monsieur Jobin, also single and about 29 years of age, hailed from the Charlesbourg seigneury, the general area in which Robert had been raised.

On September 10, 1693, Messieurs Després and Jobin, Marie Niel (representing both herself and her absent husband), and Robert Réaume met with the notary at Montreal to draw up the details of their business agreement. The three men who stood before the scribe would travel to the interior, including "Robert Réaume, voyageur, at present in this town, who has voluntarily engaged himself to go up to the Ottawa Country, to depart from this town during this month or later, to return in the next year 1694." During his upcoming term of service, he would be fed at the expense of the four partners, and upon his return to Montreal he would receive from them 200 livres worth of good beaver pelts as his wages. In addition, he would be permitted to take to the west merchandise that would generate one half-pack of beaver pelts, and he would be allowed to transport out this pack at no cost. According to the contract, the two working associates would likewise be allowed to each bring out one half-pack of beaver pelts for their own respective private profits. These pelts would not be related to the ones that belonged to the joint partnership with Monsieur and Madame Petit. However, at the time of the engagement, Monsieur Jobin transferred this particular right to Robert, who would thus be permitted to bring out a full pack of beaver pelts for his own profit.

For the upcoming year of work as a voyageur-trader, Robert agreed to the salary of 200 livres, which, at first glance, appears to be rather low. However, this basic wage would be augmented considerably by the profits that he would generate by selling a full pack of beaver pelts upon his return. In addition, he probably felt that he had been generously paid by Jacques Petit for retrieving Zacharie Jolliet's possessions during the summer. This may have convinced him to accept this seemingly reduced wage for the upcoming twelve months of employment, working for the same hirer as well as his three associates. Combined together, Robert's overall earnings from the 15 to 16 months of labor represented an excellent rate of pay. These earnings included his wages from the summer voyage (possibly 175 to 200 livres plus his profits from hauling other peltries as space allowed) plus his salary for the upcoming wintering venture (200 livres plus his profits from one full pack of beaver pelts).[19]

At the same time that Robert and his colleagues were solidifying their plans for the upcoming season of commerce in the west, other investors and traders were also making similar arrangements. For the westbound September convoy, the hirings that were recorded by Montreal notaries included ten men to work in the Ottawa Country; two men to labor for Pierre Laporte, Sieur de Louvigny, the commandant at Ft. De Buade; seven men to work for Henri de Tonty and François Dauphin, Sieur de La Forest in the Illinois Country; and ten others who joined in partnership with Pierre Le Sueur to labor in the region of western Lake Superior and the upper Mississippi River (this lattermost contract described the men's intended destination as the Ottawa Country). All of these engagements were drawn up by scribes of the Montreal area between August 13 and September 13. Thus, the convoy of at least eleven canoes (including the one paddled by Robert and his two associates) probably departed from Lachine for the distant interior during the third or fourth week of September.

When it was time to exit from the west during the following summer of 1694, Robert and his two colleagues probably joined the large convoy of eastbound canoes which gathered at St. Ignace. These were manned not only by the usual array of French and native traders, but also by the Sieur de Louvigny (who was relinquishing his position as the commandant at Michilimackinac to Antoine Lamothe, Sieur de Cadillac) as well as the Ottawa leaders from the Straits (whom the departing commandant had convinced to travel out to Montreal in order to confer with the Governor).[20]

After this venture, during Robert's sojourn of about ten months in the St. Lawrence Valley, he may have resided with his family of origin in the area near Quebec, at least for part of that time. He had not yet moved permanently to the Montreal area, so he was still officially identified as a resident of the Charlesbourg parish (which extended eastward from the St. Charles River to the western boundary of the Beauport parish). Thus, he may have been present or near to the Charlesbourg seigneury when the joys associated with the arrival of his first niece, the third child of his older brother Maurice, suddenly turned to anguish. Little Marie Anne, who was baptized in the Charlesbourg church on January 20, 1695, was laid to rest in the cemetery beside the church just two days later.[21]

By at least the middle of the summer in 1695, Robert had returned to the Montreal area. On June 13, he accepted a contract for another stint in the upper Great Lakes region, during which he would labor as a wintering voyageur-trader in the service of two unmarried military officers.

"Before Claude Maugue, royal notary residing at Villemarie, and the undersigned witnesses was present Robert Réaume, who has acknowledged that he has bound himself for a voyage of one year to the Ottawa Country, to commence today, in the service of Augustin Le Gardeur, Sieur de Courtemanche, Esquire, and Jean Baptiste Bissot, Sieur de Vincennes, officers in the Troops [of the Marine Department]. The said Sieur de Vincennes was

present and assenting for the two of them at the time of the engagement which was made by the said Réaume, which he [Vincennes] will later arrange with him [Courtemanche]. This transaction was made in consideration of the sum of 350 livres in beaver pelts at the price of the office [of the peltries exporting monopoly company]. In addition, he will be permitted to bring out from this place one pack of beaver pelts and his belongings for his own private account [without having to pay for their transport]. In case the present agreement does not take place during the current year, it will be nullified."[22]

Augustin Legardeur, Sieur de Courtemanche, a grandson of the early interpreter and trade ambassador Jean Nicolet, was $31^1/2$ years old at this time. Born at Quebec, he had relocated to the Montreal area with his family at the age of seven. In 1690, he had been commissioned as an ensign when he had been 26 years old, after which he had been promoted to half-pay lieutenant in 1691 and to lieutenant in 1692. During the following year of 1693, Monsieur Le Gardeur had been appointed to supervise the construction of and serve as the commandant of Ft. St. Joseph (Le Poste des Miamis de la Rivière St. Joseph) on the St. Joseph River in the present southwestern Michigan. Some months later, in January of 1694 (just after his 30th birthday), he had been promoted to the rank of midshipman. He would marry in July of 1697, after which he and his wife would settle at Quebec and produce six children over the course of seventeen years. From his marriage onward, he would become deeply involved in commercial dealings to the north of the Gulf of St. Lawrence, in eastern Quebec and Labrador. In this region his business interests would include the fur trade, fishing, and the harvesting of seals and whales.[23]

Robert's other employer in June of 1695, Jean Baptiste Bissot, Sieur de Vincennes, was $27^1/2$ years old at this time. Born and raised at Quebec and across the St. Lawrence at Lauson, he was the tenth child of the very prominent businessman and administrator François Bissot, Sieur de La Rivière. One of his older sisters had married Louis Jolliet back in 1675. Jean Baptiste had been the co-owner of the seigneury of Vincennes ever since he had been four years old (sharing the ownership with his brother François Charles, who was four years his senior). In this year of 1695, he had been commissioned as an ensign in the regular troops (the rank that he would still hold five years later). In the following year of 1696, he would be appointed as the commandant of Ft. St. Joseph. In September of that same year, he would also be married at Montreal, after which he and his wife would bear eight offspring at Montreal over the span of fourteen years. He would command at Ft. St. Joseph until about 1699, after which he would spend his later life working closely with the Miami nation, first on the St. Joseph River and later on the Maumee River in the present northwestern Indiana. It would be his son François Marie Bissot who would later command at Ft. Ouiatenon and the post of Vincennes on the lower Wabash River.[24]

As is abundantly clear, Robert Réaume's labors as a voyageur-trader in the employ of the officers Legardeur and Bissot would take place at and in the region of Ft. St. Joseph. This post had been established by Lieutenant Legardeur four years earlier, back in 1691, as a combination military, commercial, and missionary facility. Within its palisade walls, the tiny settlement contained a commandant's house as well as a few other structures. Here, the commander, about eight to ten soldiers, an interpreter, some fifteen traders, and a missionary priest lived and worked. This fort, as well as Ft. De Buade at St. Ignace, would be depicted on the map of the interior regions of North America that Louis de Laporte, who had served as the commandant at Michilimackinac from 1691 to 1694, would draw in about 1697.[25]

It was a well-known fact throughout the colony that the officers who commanded at the various interior posts supplemented their military pay with a considerable amount of fur trade profits. In many cases, this commerce was conducted openly by hired employees of the officers (such as Monsieur Réaume). However, in some instances, certain of the commandants garnered a great deal of extra profits from the illegal sales of brandy to the native populations, as well as from the extortion of generous fees from the traders who operated within their domain. In 1698, Governor Frontenac would pen these comments in support of the commercial activities of the officers at the distant posts:

"I believe that it is impossible to have the commandants and soldiers at the Michilimackinac and Miami [St. Joseph] posts live on their salary alone...[The commanders] are compelled by absolute necessity to hire three Canadians [the decreed number for a single trading license], to each of whom they give from 400 to 500 livres per year in wages. They must [also] purchase a canoe for their journey [that of the three hired traders], which costs them 200 livres. Add to that about 300 livres for their provisions and supplies which are required to go only to Michilimackinac [plus more for those who proceed another 360 miles southward by canoe to Ft. St. Joseph], plus those sums which they must pay [there] to have wood dragged from two leagues

distant, which is necessary for their heat and that of their officers...How can it be possible for a Captain with his pay, and the subaltern officers with a very modest one, and especially the soldiers, to subsist and provide for their needs while engaging in no trade whatsoever?"[26]

In the spring and early summer of 1695, as preparations were carried out for the westbound convoy, the engagements of 33 men were recorded by notaries in the Montreal area. These consisted of 25 men who were specified for the Ottawa Country, 6 individuals for Michilimackinac (including two in the employ of the commandant Cadillac), one man for Henri de Tonty, the commandant at Ft. St. Louis in the Illinois Country, and one individual for "The West." Among the men who were bound for the Ottawa Country, three were hired by Ensign Bissot to work as voyageur-traders in the area of Ft. St. Joseph. Besides Robert Réaume (who was co-hired by both Bissot and Lieutenant Legardeur on June 13), his two fellow *engagés* were Louis Hus dit Paul (engaged on May 16) and Jean Séguin (hired on June 10). Monsieur Hus, who was about 25 years old and unmarried, had been engaged for a venture to the Ottawa Country back in August of 1688. He would marry in 1699, after which he and his wife would settle at Sorel and produce fourteen children in 28 years.

In addition to these three voyageur-traders, Ensign Bissot also contracted with Joseph Pillet, who would serve for two years as the blacksmith at Ft. St. Joseph. This craftsman, age 21 and single in 1695, would marry and settle at Lachine in 1700, later producing fourteen offspring within 24 years. He would again be engaged by Ensign Bissot on July 4, 1704, to work in the Ottawa Country during the period in which the majority of the posts in the interior would be closed.[27]

Eventually, the 1695 brigade of traders who were bound for the Straits and points beyond departed from Lachine on June 15. The majority of these traders were those individuals who, shortly after their departure for the west in the previous autumn of 1694, had turned around on the lower Ottawa River and had returned to Montreal, due to the very early onset of severe weather.[28]

During the latter part of the summer in 1696, when Robert returned from his period of service at Ft. St. Joseph, he found that, throughout the St. Lawrence Valley, one subject was on nearly every colonist's mind: the future of the fur trade. In 1695, the peltries market in France had become completely flooded with beaver pelts. At that time, the monopoly company had held in storage in the mother country some 3.5 million livres worth of beavers, which could not be sold at any price. Since the late 1680s, nearly four times more of this fur than could be dispersed had been shipped each year from New France to the mother country. As a result, during the 1690s, traders in the interior had attempted to focus more and more upon other furs besides beavers; however, the surplus of the latter fur had not dissipated.

To rectify the situation, Louis XIV and Pontchartrain, the Minister of the Marine and Colonies Department, had declared in May of 1696 a nearly complete withdrawal of Frenchmen from the western interior regions. No more licenses or permits were to be issued to trading personnel, and the peltries-exporting company was to accept no more beaver pelts; in addition, the interior forts were to be destroyed and the troops withdrawn. The only exception would be Ft. St. Louis in the Illinois Country, which would be kept open for military purposes. The native population would thereafter be required to travel exclusively out to the St. Lawrence communities to carry on commerce and receive presents. In response to this royal directive, Governor Frontenac had complained to the Minister, had postponed taking action until the following year of 1697, and had allowed commerce to continue. However, only seven voyageur-traders were engaged via Montreal notary contracts during 1696, including two in April, four in August, and one in September. (The lattermost individual was Jean Baptiste Lalonde dit L'Espérance, whose biography is presented later in this series.)

In 1697, as a reaction to the outcry from the Governor and the fur trade and military communities, Minister Pontchartrain would modify the edict. The posts of Ft. Frontenac, Ft. de Buade, and Ft. St. Joseph des Miamis were to remain militarily active but without commerce, while trading would be permitted to continue at Ft. St. Louis des Illinois. However, Frontenac would firmly believe that, under this plan, the three strictly military installations could not be maintained without the profits of commerce at those posts. Therefore, he would authorize trade canoes to travel in during 1697 to these four primary posts, for one final year of commercial activity. At the same time, he would order a general recall for the following year of all of the French from the interior.

Ultimately, from 1698 onward, trade would be allowed to continue at Ft. Frontenac, the post at Chicago, Ft. St. Louis, and Ft. Tourette/La Maune (at the northern end of Lake Nipigon, north of

Lake Superior), with severe limitations placed upon the number of beaver pelts which were to be accepted. Missionaries would be permitted to continue their activities throughout the interior.[29]

Although Robert Réaume could not foresee all of these events when he emerged from the interior in the late summer of 1696, he must have clearly sensed that his trading days in the west were at a close, at least for the foreseeable future. Thus, at the age of $28^2/3$, he decided that this was the right time for him to marry, settle down, and begin to raise a family.

In the area around Montreal, Robert found his life partner, a young woman who was nearly seven years his junior. This was Élisabeth Brunet dite Belhumeur, born and raised in the Montreal area, who had celebrated her 22nd birthday in July of this year. She was often called Isabelle; in fact, her given name was recorded in the couple's marriage contract as Isabelle, while the church record of their wedding three days later listed her as Élisabeth. The name Isabelle also occasionally appeared in certain of her church documents late in her life. However, for the sake of clarity, our protagonist is called Élisabeth throughout this biography, except in those specific instances in which period documents are quoted which identified her as Isabelle.

Élisabeth's father, Antoine Brunet dit Belhumeur, had emigrated from the St. Nicolas parish in La Rochelle when he had been about 16 to 18 years old. Since his ages were recorded in the Montreal census of 1666 as 22, in the enumeration of 1667 as 25, and in the census of 1681 as 36, his year of birth had apparently fallen within the period of about 1644 to 1646. Arriving in about 1662, he had made arrangements on November 21 of that year to clear land for the Sulpicians, who were the seigneurs of Montreal Island. One year later, on November 28, 1663, he had married Françoise Moisan in the Montreal church. Hailing from the St. Barthélemy parish in La Rochelle, the bride had immigrated to New France in 1663 as a *fille du Roi*, during the first year of this royal program in which young women had been transported to the colony to become wives of settlers who had already established themselves. According to her listed ages of 21 in the census of 1666, 23 in the enumeration of 1667, and 35 in the census of 1681, plus her recorded age of 75 at the time of her funeral in November of 1718, her birth had apparently taken place within the period of about 1643 to 1646. Thus, she had emigrated from her homeland when she had been about 17 to 20 years of age, after both of her parents had died.

After the couple drew up their marriage contract at Montreal on October 19, 1663 (which neither of them could sign) and celebrated their wedding six weeks later, they settled in the Montreal area. More than two years later, on December 5, 1665, Antoine was granted an elongated piece of property in the sub-fief which was called the Côte St. François. This area, commencing about $3^{1}/2$ miles north of the town itself, had a St. Lawrence frontage of about three miles. It was on their pioneer farm in this area that the Brunet couple produced four children before the arrival of baby Élisabeth and her twin sister:
François, baptized on March 17, 1665 at the Montreal church.
Marie Françoise, baptized on April 26, 1667 at the Montreal church.
Catherine, baptized on August 25, 1669 at the Montreal church.
Antoine, born and baptized on July 6, 1672 at the Montreal church;
   he was buried in the Montreal cemetery four days later, on July 10.

After the arrival of the twins Élisabeth and Geneviève, they were christened in the Montreal church on July 23, 1674. At this ceremony, Élisabeth's godfather was Louis d'Ailleboust, the unmarried 18-year-old son of the important Montreal administrator Charles d'Ailleboust, Sieur des Musseaux. Her godmother was 18-year-old Élisabeth Hubert, the unmarried daughter of Nicolas Hubert, a master tailor of suits in Montreal. Nearly two years later, Élisabeth's younger sibling Marguerite was born on Île Jésus, just to the northwest of Montreal Island, after which she was christened in the Montreal church on April 16, 1679.[30]

About two years after the arrival of baby Marguerite, the colony-wide census of 1681 was conducted. At this time, the Brunet family was thus enumerated in household number 95 in the Montreal area:
"Antoine Brunet, age 36
Élisabeth Moisan, his wife, age 35
Children:
Marie, 15
Catherine, 13
Élisabeth, 7
Geneviève, 7 (twins)
Marguerite, 3
François, 17
1 gun, 5 horned cattle, 17 arpents [14.5 acres] of land cleared and under cultivation."[31]

In this document, which was probably drawn up during the spring or early summer of 1681, the recorded ages of five of the six children were consistently elevated by one year. The family's eldest child, François, would not turn age 17 until the following March; he was recorded at the very end of the list, almost as an afterthought, implying that he was residing elsewhere at the time. Marie Françoise had turned 14 in late April, but Catherine would celebrate her 12th birthday (not her 13th) in late August. The twins would turn 7 in late July, while Marguerite had completed her second year of life in mid-April. Since each of the children's ages (except that of Catherine) was increased by one year, it appears that the census-taker had asked them what their respective ages would be upon their next birthday, rather than their current ages at the time of the enumeration.

The five horned cattle which the family owned most likely included milk cows as well as a pair of oxen, with the latter livestock being utilized for heavy hauling tasks and for plowing. During the interval of nearly fifteen years since Antoine had acquired the property on the Côte St. François, they had managed to clear and bring under cultivation a total of 14^1/2 acres. This indicates that they had averaged about one acre per year in their ongoing efforts to convert forest-covered land into agricultural property.

About a year after this census, Élisabeth's final sibling arrived. Barbe Angélique was born on June 18, 1682, after which she was baptized at the Montreal church on the following day. However, no later records for her have been located in the colony; thus, she apparently died at a young age.[32]

When Élisabeth was nine years old, her older siblings began to be married. This pattern commenced in October of 1683, when her eldest sister Marie (age 16) married Jean Patenaude in the Montreal church; afterward, the couple would settle in Montreal, where they would bear two children, in 1685 and 1686. Next came Élisabeth's other older sister, Catherine (age 16), who wed Jean's younger brother Pierre Patenaude in the Montreal church in November of 1685; they would set up housekeeping in Montreal and later across the St. Lawrence at Longueuil, and over the span of 24 years they would produce ten children. In 1686, bringing great sadness to the entire family, Élisabeth's sister Marie died a short time after the birth of her second child, who had arrived on April 7 (and would survive to grow to adulthood). Eight months after the baby had been born, in December, her widowed husband remarried at Laprairie.[33]

Two years later, brightness again prevailed, at the time of the wedding of Élisabeth's older brother François, who was married in November of 1688. Afterward, he and his wife would reside at Montreal, Boucherville, and finally at St. François on Île Jésus, producing twelve children in 22 years. This wedding record from November 15, 1688 would be the last document that would note that her father, Antoine Brunet dit Belhumeur, was still living (he was about 42 to 44 years old at this time). Some time during the next $5^1/2$ years, before a certain case in the Montreal Court would commence on July 3, 1694, the patriarch would pass away.[34]

However, even while he was still living, Élisabeth's mother Françoise, the matriarch of the clan, seems to have found a way to generate a considerable amount of supplemental income. After the death of her daughter Marie, her son-in-law Jean Patenaude had remarried on December 10, 1686, and had settled at Laprairie. This seigneury was located about five miles south-southeast of Montreal, on the opposite shore of the St. Lawrence. Jean's new bride was Romaine Robidou of Laprairie, age $17^1/2$, the widow of Jean Roux dit Laplante. When she had first married, back in October of 1683, Romaine had been 14 years old. The only child whom the Roux couple had produced had been born in April of 1686; this little lass had died in May of 1687 at the age of thirteen months, five months after Romaine had remarried.

By the autumn of 1688, the matriarch Françoise Moisan was about 42 to 45 years old. Over time, she had become friends with Romaine Robidou (her former son-in-law's second wife since December of 1686), who often visited Françoise at her home on the Côte St. François. Eventually, the local priest became concerned about the young woman's activities during her visits to the Brunet household, and he expressed these concerns to her husband, Jean Patenaude. When the latter man traveled to the Brunet house to discuss the issue with Françoise, both she and her eldest son François (who was 23 years old and about to marry) mistreated him.

Thus, since he was not able to resolve the situation on his own, Monsieur Patenaude took his case to the Montreal Court in September of 1688. He did this with the hope that the Court would force his wife to return home. Standing before the Judge on September 19, Jean accused his former mother-in-law of living a scandalous life, and of having drawn his second wife into prostitution. In his charges, he stated that "for quite some time, several people have engaged in a sinister commerce with the said Belhumeur woman, who has always been the ruin and the cause of debauchery of the youth of the entire Côte St. François, and who continues to live in such infamy." He also charged that soldiers regularly visited the Brunet home, in spite of the warnings, threats, and even beatings that they received from their officers, and that certain of the customers sometimes fought with each other. According to his information, one of the men had even treated Françoise badly when he had discovered her sleeping with other men.

During the course of the Court hearings, André Hunault provided sworn testimony, in which he stated that he and Françoise had been lovers for more than two years, living together as husband and wife. (This had apparently taken place before his wedding in November of 1686, when he had been 29 years old.) Monsieur Hunault testified that, not only did she lead a "dissolute and infamous life...she was even so brazen that, to satisfy her brutality, she had no concern if her daughters who were twelve or thirteen years old were prostitutes." Another man, Pierre Delorme dit Sanscrainte (an unmarried soldier in the Merville Company, stationed at Montreal), testified that, when Francoise's husband Antoine Brunet was away, which was quite often, she would sleep with Monsieur Delorme, and that, when Monsieur Brunet would return, the lover would hide in the barn. However, in spite of the array of apparently damning evidence which was presented, the only response of the Court was to publicly denounce Françoise's conduct, and to order her to have no further contact with Romaine Robidou.[35]

About eighteen months after this flurry of potentially embarrassing legal activities, Élisabeth stood with dignity as the godmother of her newborn niece Marie Catherine Patenaude, the second child of her sister Catherine and her husband Pierre Patenaude. At the festivities which were conducted in the Montreal church on March 6, 1690, when Élisabeth was $15^2/3$ years old, the baby's other sponsor was Jean Arnaud.[36]

More than three years later, in the early summer of 1693, Élisabeth was a month away from celebrating her 19th birthday. On June 14, she stood before the notary Adhémar to sign a marriage contract with the Montreal voyageur René Beaujean, who was $21^1/2$ years old. However, for some reason, this contract was later annulled; she would not marry for $3^1/4$ years, while he would wait an additional two years more before he would finally take a bride.[37]

During the heart of the summer in 1694, when Élisabeth and her twin sister Geneviève were about to turn age 20, the two of them and their mother were called to testify in a case which was being heard by the Montreal Court. On July 3, the records of the Court noted the statements of the Director of the Commissary of the Marine Department, who described certain events that had taken place during the changeover from the old card money to the new issue, which had been ordered by the Intendant. In the process, "he had discovered a good number of forgeries, and while investigating the reason, the names of Beaudry, Langevin, Doré, and Castillon had been brought forward by the widow Belhumeur." On the sixth of the month, the members of the Court interrogated the prime suspect, Jacques Beaudry, a surgeon and sergeant in the Crisafy Company who had originated in the town of Périgueux. The next day, Beaudry was taken into custody, while subpoenas were delivered to Françoise Moisan and her twin daughters to appear before the Court on the following day. On July 8, the statements of these three witnesses were each taken and recorded. However, the evidence contained within these three testimonies was apparently deemed to be insufficient for a conviction. Two days later, Charles Juchereau, the Sieur de Beaumarchais, who was the Chief Judge, ordered the release of Monsieur Beaudry and the closure of the case.[38]

Seven weeks before the twin Brunet sisters would celebrate their joint 21st birthdays, Geneviève married Louis Tétreau in the Montreal church. At the time of the nuptial ceremony on June 4, 1695, the groom was about 26 years old. Now, Élisabeth and her younger sister Marguerite (age 16) were the only Brunet siblings who were not yet married. Their youngest sister, Barbe Angélique, would have been 13 years old at this time, if she were still living. However, no records for her after her birth in June of 1682 have been located, so it may be assumed that she died at a young age.[39]

On April 15, 1696, Élisabeth stood beside the baptismal font of the Montreal church as the godmother of Marie Élisabeth Robidas. This infant, along with her twin brother Michel, had been born that same day to Louise de Guitre and Jacques Robidas dit Manseau, who was a shoemaker and sergeant in the Crisafy Company. (This was the same unit of soldiers as that of Jacques Beaudry, who had been acquitted of the charges of forging card money. This sponsorship by Élisabeth at a christening ceremony, plus the testimonies which had been presented in the above-mentioned forgery and prostitution cases in the Court, clearly indicated that members of the Brunet family were certainly familiar with a number of the troops who were stationed at Montreal.) Baby Robidas' other sponsor on this occasion was the Montreal merchant Claude Pothier.[40]

This joyous baptismal event took place while Robert Réaume was preparing to paddle from Ft. St. Joseph out to Montreal, after his year of service for his two officer employers. It is not known whether he and Élisabeth had met at some point before his departure for the west in June of the previous year. However, within weeks of his return in the latter summer of 1696, the two engaged individuals were preparing to draw up their marriage contract and then exchange their wedding vows.

First, they met with the Montreal notary Claude Maugue on September 19, 1696, to execute their contract of marriage. In this document, the scribe identified the prospective groom as Robert Réaume, son of René Réaume, master carpenter, and of Marie Chevreau, from the parish of Charlesbourg, by Quebec (indicating that Robert had not yet officially relocated from his place of origin to the Montreal area). The bride-to-be was listed as Isabelle Brunet, daughter of the deceased Antoine Brunet and of Françoise Moisan. Since the notary did not record a parish or place of residence for her or her parents, it was apparently understood that they were from the local Montreal area.[41]

Three days later, on September 22, the Notre Dame de Montreal church was the scene of their wedding. On this jubilant occasion, the priest recorded in the parish ledger the same names for Robert and his parents as had appeared in the marriage contract, as well as the groom's same residence in the Charlesbourg parish; but he added the information that he was 28 years old. In the case of the bride, he identified her as Élisabeth Brunet, gave the same names for her parents as had been recorded in the marriage contract, and added that she was 22 years of age and was from the Montreal parish. The cleric also penned in the names of the four official witnesses. These were Jacques Tétreau, brother-in-law of the bride (Louis Tétreau's younger brother, about age 24, who would marry Élisabeth's sister Marguerite in 1698); Pierre Hervé (about 23 years old, who would marry at Montreal in two years); Robert Giguère (age 33, voyageur of Montreal, who would not marry before his death fifteen years later); and Pierre Tessier (21 years old, Montreal voyageur who would never marry). Although Robert could not sign the ledger, Élisabeth could and she did.[42]

No surviving documents reveal where the newlyweds lived in Montreal during their first autumn, winter, and spring as a married couple. However, ten months after their wedding, on July 8, 1697, they rented a house from Martin Massé, the Montreal master blacksmith and knife maker. In their rental agreement, Robert was identified as a carpenter, and he and Élisabeth were listed as residents of Montreal. The home, in which they would reside for at least seventeen months, until they would purchase and move to their own farm, was located "in the town of Villemarie on Missillimakinac and Chagouamigon Streets." This was in the far western area of the town, near the stockade wall. It is of particular interest that Monsieur Réaume was identified as a carpenter, the occupation for which he had been trained in his younger years. It is also interesting that the two streets which flanked their rental property in Montreal were named after the important fur trade locales of Michilimackinac and Chequamegon. (The latter bay, located on the southern shore of Lake Superior near its western end, was the place where the pioneer trader Claude David and his colleagues had spent the years from 1661 to 1663.)[43]

Seventeen days after arranging this house rental, on July 27, Robert stood as the godfather at the christening of a three-day-old native girl in the Montreal church. Baby Louise, born to Jean Pakikanakouskan and Marguerite Papiskanaoua, received her given name on this day from her godmother Louise Magnan, the unmarried daughter of the deceased Jean Magnan.[44]

One week before Élisabeth and Robert were to mark their first wedding anniversary, they had an even more important reason to celebrate. On September 14, 1697, they were elated and relieved to safely welcome into the world their first child. That same day, they took little Simon to the church for his baptism, where his unmarried uncle Simon Réaume (Robert's next-younger brother, who would soon turn age 28) granted him his name. The baby's godmother was his unmarried aunt Marguerite Brunet (Élisabeth's only younger sister, who was age 18).[45]

Five months later, Robert found himself embroiled in a case in the Montreal Criminal Court, in which he was accused of physical assault. This particular case would proceed over the course of nine weeks, during which 21 witnesses would be called and 42 Court documents (containing a total of 138 pages) would be generated. During the second week of February in 1698, shortly after Robert had celebrated his 30th birthday, he became involved in an altercation with Marie Madeleine Émond, age 33, the wife of the Montreal voyageur Nicolas Dupuis dit Montauban, who was about 56 or 57 years old. This couple had been married for sixteen years; they had produced two children in 1684 and 1686, but these youngsters had both perished in the autumn of 1687, during that particular epidemic. In February of 1688, she had borne a child out of wedlock with an unnamed father, during one of her husband's trading voyages to St. Ignace; this baby had lived for only two months. Later, the Dupuis couple had produced two additional daughters, who were now ages 7 and 5 years of age. Marie Émond had grown up on Île d'Orléans; shortly before her marriage to Monsieur Dupuis in 1681 at the age of 17, she had worked as a servant for the Quebec merchant and cabaret operator Pierre Nolan. During the course of her employment for Monsieur Nolan, she had apparently become quite familiar with the procedures of operating a cabaret.[46]

The altercation between Robert Réaume and Marie Madeleine Émond, which had occurred during the second week of February in 1698, had apparently escalated into physical violence. The first appearance of this case before the officials of the Montreal Court took place on February 12. At that time, the Montreal surgeon Antoine Forestier (married for 27 years, with 17 children) presented a report concerning the injuries of Madame Dupuis, the plaintiff, who claimed that she had been assaulted and injured by Robert Réaume, the accused. On the following day, she brought witnesses to testify before the Chief Judge; during the same session, she also requested that she receive 100 livres in compensation from the accused, and she urged that he be imprisoned. On the 14th, a number of subpoenas were issued, to both Robert Réaume and various individuals who were to testify on behalf of the plaintiff. Four days later, the accused was questioned, during which he stated that he was thirty years of age, that he resided on Rue des Outaouais in Montreal, and that he was a carpenter by trade. Afterward, the plaintiff made additional statements against the accused, as well as responses to his statements. On the 20th, witnesses who were to testify on behalf of the accused were summoned, and an inquiry requested by Monsieur Réaume was conducted, during which his witnesses gave their depositions. On the following day, a similar inquiry on behalf of Madame Dupuis was held, in which her witnesses presented their depositions. February 26 brought with it the Court's decision that these proceedings had taken a different direction, in view of the scandalous life of the plaintiff; this was followed by a request from the King's Attorney that the Court hold an "extraordinary trial." At the same time, the Chief Judge convicted Robert Réaume of having committed assault and battery, and he forbade Marie Madeleine Émond from operating a cabaret, which she had been doing illegally.

Following the new direction of the case, on March 4, the Court expressed its interest in questioning the cabaret operator Madame Dupuis, concerning her reportedly scandalous conduct. Four days later, during two different questioning sessions by the Chief Judge, the accused woman refused to respond. However, on the same day, witnesses in the case against her were summoned and their depositions were recorded. After another four days had passed, on March 12, Catherine Lucos (a cabaret operator in Montreal, about 51 or 52 years old, the wife of Marin Moreau dit Laporte) was imprisoned for refusing to take the oath and to testify. On the following day, the Court bailiffs Jean Quenneville and Georges Pruneau ascertained that Madame Dupuis had disappeared. In addition, witnesses were again gathered, and Catherine Lucos (who had spent the previous night in custody) was finally questioned; afterward, the latter woman was convicted of having disobeyed the Court. On April 18, the King's Attorney registered charges against Marie Madeleine Émond for having committed public scandal. On the following day, she was convicted of these charges, and she was sentenced to pay 100 livres in fines and to be banished from the colony for five years.

One of the 21 witnesses who had testified in this double case was Jacques Denoyon, an unmarried voyageur-trader from Boucherville (about six miles northeast of Montreal) who had just turned age 30. A decade earlier, he and his party of traders had been the first documented Frenchmen to venture far westward from Lake Superior. Traveling inland from Ft. Kaministiquia, they had reached Rainy Lake, where they had erected a small post and had spent the winter trading. During the following summer of 1689, the men had advanced down the Rainy River to reach Lake of the Woods, before returning to Superior with their rich cargo of peltries.[47]

By October in this year of 1698, Robert was away on a trip, which may have involved a trading operation in some distant locale. However, there are no surviving documents recording any such ventures for him during this particular period. Thus, he may have been taking part in an illegal, unauthorized commercial journey at this time, leaving no trail of documentation in his wake. However, this was a trip which would not extend over the coming winter; Robert would be back in Montreal in time to conduct a very important business transaction there on December 3.

At any rate, since he was away during the autumn, Élisabeth visited the Montreal notary Basset on October 11, along with a man who for a long time had owed Robert a debt and who now wished to acknowledge it and officially promise to repay it. Pierre Burel dit Mouchetique ("called Mosquito"), a soldier in the Company of Captain Paul Lemoine, Sieur de Maricourt, stationed at Montreal, admitted that he owed the following:

"To Robert Réaume, living at the said Villemarie but absent, assenting for him by Élisabeth Brunet, his wife, the quantity of sixteen good and salable dry beaver pelts, due to the loan of the same quantity which the said debtor had received from him a long time before the drawing up of these presents."
Monsieur Burel promised to repay this loan during the following year of 1699, at the latest during the month of September.[48]

At the bottom of this two-page document, along with the notary and one of the two witnesses, Madame Réaume penned her signature. Although it was written in a smooth and practiced cursive hand, it appears upon first glance to read "eliabe brunet." If she had intended to write "elisabeth" as her first name, she apparently omitted the letter "s" in the middle and the letters "th" at the end. However, it is much more likely that she had instead intended and indeed wrote "elsabe," reflecting the way her name may have often been pronounced.

Four days later, on the 15th, Élisabeth was pleased to attend special ceremonies that were conducted in the Montreal church. On this day, her last remaining unmarried sibling pronounced her wedding vows. Marguerite, $19^1/2$ years old, took as her husband Jacques Tétreau, who was about 26 years of age. These two young people had apparently known each other for quite some time; Marguerite's older sister Geneviève had married Jacques' older brother Louis three years earlier, back in 1695.[49]

On December 3, 1698, after having lived in a rented house in Montreal for the previous seventeen months, Robert purchased his own farm and property. This piece of land contained four arpents (768 feet) of frontage along the St. Lawrence, and had 40 arpents ($3/4$ mile) of depth, extending off toward the north. It was located on the southern shoreline of Montreal Island, in the sub-fief that was called La Présentation or Côte St. Gilles. His river frontage, about $3^1/2$ miles west of the Lachine village site and some 5 miles west of the southern terminus of the Lachine-to-Montreal portage road, was positioned directly opposite the western end of the offshore island called Île Dorval. The seller, Jacques Morin, was about 68 to 77 years old; his wife Louise Garnier had passed away about $3^1/2$ months earlier, at the age of about 61 to 70. This couple had been married at Montreal in 1661, after which they had produced five children over the following decade (all except the first of whom had lived to adulthood). In the 1698 document of sale, Monsieur Morin was described as "living at the mountain, near the town of Villemarie," while Robert was identified as being "from Montreal." The elderly seller must have known that he was nearing the end of his life; the last documentation for him was recorded on January 1, 1699, less than a month after he had transferred this land to Robert. About four years after the purchase of this property, it would be portrayed and described by Vachon de Belmont on his 1702 land ownership map of Montreal Island, including its river frontage measurement of 4 arpents.[50]

At this time, Robert and Élisabeth must have felt relatively comfortable about relocating from the well-populated, stockade-enclosed town to the thinly-occupied, exposed southern area of Montreal Island. This portion of the Island had a few scattered forts of refuge along the shore, to which the colonists could flee when enemy attacks would take place. The closest of these defensive facilities to their newly purchased farm was Ft. Rolland, which was located about $1^3/4$ miles to the east of their land. The scourge of surprise attacks by Iroquois war parties, which had plagued the colonists for many years, had nearly faded away by this point. This had occurred as the populations of the Iroquois nations had become decimated by both diseases and battles lost to various of the native nations who were allied with the French. The newly acquired property of the Réaume couple was adjacent to the area where some of the most devastating losses had occurred during the massive Iroquois raid of August 5, 1689, $9^1/3$ years earlier. But these two optimistic people apparently felt that the threat of further attacks was now minimal. In fact, protracted peace negotiations from 1699 on would lead to a provisional treaty in 1700, and its final ratification at Montreal during the summer of 1701.

Sadness descended upon the clan in the spring of 1699, when Robert and Élisabeth received word that the new baby of Robert's younger brother René and his wife Marie Guyon had been stillborn. On April 31, the infant had been buried in the cemetery of Château

Richer, on the Côte de Beaupré. This had been the first loss of a child for this couple, since their first two children had both survived and thrived.[51]

In June of this same year of 1699, Robert acquired a permit to travel to the Ottawa Country, which also contained tacit permission to conduct trading while he was there. He was given this permission even though the only interior facilities at which commerce was still officially permitted were Ft. Frontenac at the eastern end of Lake Ontario, the Chicago Post and Ft. St. Louis in the Illinois Country, and Ft. Tourette/La Maune at the northern end of Lake Nipigon. Robert received this permit from his younger brother Jean Baptiste, who was 23[1]/2 years old at this time. This sibling had been granted it from the Governor, as compensation for official services that he had rendered as a voyageur during the previous summer.

"Before Antoine Adhémar, royal notary of the Island of Montreal residing at Villemarie, and the witnesses named at the end was present Jean [Baptiste] Réaume, voyageur, at present in the said Villemarie, who has said that, during the previous year, he descended from the Ottawa Country to this town in the service of the King, in order to carry the dispatches which were to be presented to Milord the Governor [Frontenac] from Monsieur the Commandant of the said region [Midshipman Alphonse de Tonty, who commanded at Ft. De Buade during 1697-1698], along with Louis Marchand, [René Alexandre] Lemoine [Sieur] Despins, [Jean] Nolan, [Jean] Dupré, Boutillier, Michelon, and [Gaspard] Magnan [dit Champagne]. It was promised to give to each of them, as compensation, a permit to ascend again to the Ottawa Country, in order to retrieve the possessions which they have there. Concerning the said granted permit, the said Jean [Baptiste] Réaume has transferred his, by these presents, to Robert Réaume, his brother, in order to utilize it for the profit of the said cedant [Jean Baptiste] as well as the said Robert Réaume, who will consider the amount to be turned over to him based entirely upon his good conduct. [This agreement] made and drawn up at the said Villemarie in the office of the said notary, in the year 1699 on the 19th of June in the afternoon, in the presence of Sieurs Georges Pruneau, royal bailiff, and Pierre Rivet, defense attorney for civil cases, witnesses living at the said Villemarie who have signed below with the said notary. The said Robert Réaume has declared that he does not know how to write or sign, having been questioned according to the ordinance.
It has been agreed that the two words which have been scratched out have no meaning.
Signed,
Rivet, G. Pruneau, and Adhémar."[52]

This document clearly portrayed the ease with which Governor Frontenac stretched the newly-imposed limits on traders venturing into the interior. During the summer of 1698, eight voyageur-traders had paddled down from the Straits of Mackinac, ostensibly to deliver letters from the commandant Tonty at Ft. De Buade to the Governor. However, this outbound journey, in reality, had given the party of men an opportunity to bring out a large portion of their accumulated peltries. As compensation for their governmental services, which had apparently required eight paddlers in three or four canoes to deliver one or more letters, each of the eight traders had been granted a permit to return to the *Pays den Haut*. It is significant that the above document of transfer made no mention of any prohibitions or limitations upon transporting merchandise in or bringing newly-garnered peltries out. In fact, the execution of these commercial activities was the very purpose for granting the eight permits.

During this summer of 1699, the only two hiring contracts of voyageurs which were publicly recorded by Montreal notaries were for two men who were engaged by the Jesuits on August 1 and August 22. These paddlers were hired to haul in supplies to the missionary priests in the upper Great Lakes region, particularly to their central base at St. Ignace. During the course of this summer, the royal declarations concerning illegal commerce were enforced more assiduously by the new Governor, Louis Hector de Callière, who had replaced Frontenac after his death in the previous November of 1698. To show his firm stance, the new administrator ordered the seizure of a number of canoes at Lachine, which were loaded with merchandise bound for traders at the Straits. In the aftermath, the outfitters who were carrying out this smuggling operation were sentenced to heavy fines for their aborted attempt. During the autumn, the administrator also reported that numbers of *coureurs de bois* were returning to Montreal in small groups, after their supplies of merchandise had become depleted, since they had made no arrangements for its replenishment. However, these events would be immediately followed by the establishment of the French colony on the Gulf Coast, which would breathe new life into the illicit careers of many individuals who would otherwise have been forced to exit from the west, due to a lack of trade goods. For example, in January of 1700, Henri de Tonty himself would lead 21 *coureurs de bois* in six canoes southward from his fort on the Illinois River to the Gulf Coast via the Mississippi River, in order to exchange peltries for new supplies of merchandise.[53]

At the end of July in 1699, the Réaume clan was shocked by the death of Louis Tétreau, the husband of Élisabeth's twin sister Geneviève, at the age of about 30. He had become seriously ill, after which he had entered the Montreal hospital and had passed away there. He was laid to rest in the Montreal cemetery on July 31. This couple had been married for four years and two months, but they had not produced any children.[54]

Four months later, Élisabeth and Robert's spirits were buoyed considerably by the safe arrival of their second child, little Nicolas Marie. At his November 25 christening ceremony in the Montreal church, on the day following his birth, he received his given name from the Montreal resident Nicolas d'Ailleboust, Sieur de Mantet (age 36), who was both a midshipman in the army and a peltries merchant. The baby's other sponsor was Marie Anne Lemoine (age 21), the wife of Jean Bouillet, Sieur de La Chassaigne. Her deceased father had been the distinguished Montreal peltries merchant Charles Lemoine, while her husband was a Captain in the army.[55]

When baby Nicolas was six months old, Robert was summoned before the Montreal Court to provide his testimony, in a case which had been brought by the colony's surveyor and cartographer Lieutenant Gédéon de Catalogne (who had been married for a decade and already had seven children). In this case, which extended over eight days from June 2 through June 11, 1700, Monsieur Catalogne sued the Montreal peltries merchant Joseph Guyon dit Després for a number of packs of beaver pelts which he claimed Monsieur Guyon owed to him. (The latter man, age 34, had been married for three years, but he and his wife had not yet produced any children.) In the Court documents, as one of the key witnesses, Robert Réaume was identified as an "habitant living in the Holy Angels parish of Lachine, age 32 or thereabouts." Both of these facts were correct, since he had purchased his farm west of the Lachine village site back in December of 1698, and he had celebrated his 32nd birthday $4^{1}/4$ months earlier, back on January 25.[56]

A major topic of conversation in both the Lachine area and throughout the entire Montreal region in 1700 was the resumption of work on the Lachine Canal. This man-made watercourse, when completed, would extend for $8^{1}/2$ miles in a northeasterly direction from Lachine all the way to Montreal. Work had commenced on the southwestern section of the project eleven years earlier, back in the summer of 1689; however, after seven weeks of labor, those efforts had been suddenly halted by the Iroquois raid of August 5. Now, the Sulpicians (as the seigneurs of Montreal Island) entered into a contract with Gédéon de Catalogne, the primary surveyor, cartographer, and engineer of the colony, to complete the project. (Robert had been called to testify in Catalogne's suit against Joseph Guyon back in June of this year.) During this new effort, the western half of the canal would be completed before construction would again be halted. (A detailed account of this entire project may be found in the previous biography of François Brunet dit Le Bourbonnais, Sr.) The southwestern terminus of this finished section would be located about $2^1/4$ miles east of the Réaume farm.

As autumn approached in this year of 1700, Robert apparently made his customary preparations in anticipation of another trading voyage to the west. In the afternoon on September 22, he and the Montreal merchant Charles Villiers together visited the notary Adhémar, to officially record the transaction which they had just completed. According to the document, Monsieur Réaume acknowledged that he owed Monsieur Villiers "the sum of 642 livres 11 sols 10 deniers for good merchandise which was sold and delivered to him by the said Sieur Creditor on this day, of which he [Réaume] is content." Robert promised to pay off this debt during the month of August in 1701. "For the execution of these presents, the said debtor has selected as his [temporary] legal residence [to which writs may be delivered] his residence in this town, the house and residence of Françoise Moisan, his mother-in-law, located on Rue St. Paul...and he has mortgaged all of his belongings, both moveable and real estate, present and future." However, in spite of this promised schedule of repayment, Robert would not pay off the final portion of this debt until some time after March 28, 1705, according to a rearrangement of the debt which he would make on that date.

The timing of this acquisition of a considerable amount of merchandise, and the promise that he would pay for it during the following August, nearly a year later, strongly implies that this transaction represented outfitting preparations for an impending voyage. A large number of Ottawa traders from Michilimackinac had arrived at Montreal in June, and over the course of the summer, leaders of both the Ottawa and Huron/Tionontate nations from the Straits had participated in the negotiations for the general peace treaty which had been held at Montreal. After the official signing ceremony of this preliminary agreement on September 8, 1700, the Governor dispatched Fr. Jean Enjalran and Captain Augustin Legardeur, Sieur de Courtemanche "to the Ottawa nations, to get them to accept and sign it, as well as all of the upper nations." Over the span of seven months during the winter and spring of 1700 and 1701, this officer would conduct a grueling round of treaty conferences with each of the allied nations in the north and the west. In addition to this man's efforts in working with the native nations, the Governor also sent, in latter September of 1700, the first of many representatives into the interior to urge the numerous *coureurs de bois* to come out. This first representative was Alphonse de Tonty, who had commanded at Ft. De Buade during its final year of operation, before the withdrawal of all of the military personnel from there as well as from all of the other western posts. (But for the most part, the renegade traders would be unresponsive to the various offers of amnesty.) Considering the significant amount of merchandise that Robert received from the Montreal merchant Villiers on September 22, 1700, it is highly likely that he was one of the voyageurs who paddled westward with these various officials during the month of September. It appears that he took along with him on the journey a generous stock of trade goods, so that he could conduct commercial activity on the side.[57]

On July 2, 1701, Captain Courtemanche returned to St. Ignace after his extensive round of treaty conferences. Shortly thereafter, a huge brigade of 144 canoes departed from the Straits for the east, loaded with native delegates who were bound for the treaty signing at Montreal. However, after sickness had ravaged through much of the party, thirty of the craft were obliged to turn back. On July 22, the remaining canoes of the flotilla (presumably including one that contained Robert Réaume) arrived at Montreal, bringing the total number of native delegates who were in attendance there to about 1,300. According to the Great Treaty, which was ratified on August 4, the Iroquois nations agreed to remain neutral in any future wars between France and England. They also accepted defeat in their attempt to wrest control of the western trade from the French. However, they would remain in place as a physical barrier between the nations of the western interior and Albany, thus ensuring that those western groups would continue to trade primarily with the French, rather than with the English.[58]

Six weeks before the native delegations had assembled at Montreal for the Great Treaty council, a convoy of some one hundred Frenchmen, led by Captain Antoine Lamothe, Sieur de Cadillac, had departed from Lachine for the west. Their mission was to establish Ft. Pontchartrain, on the strait between Lake Huron and Lake Erie. During the previous year, Cadillac had received permission in France for the creation of this important community, against the bitter protests of the merchants of Montreal, who were intent upon the re-establishment of Ft. De Buade and the St. Ignace community.

With virtually no troops or licensed traders present in the west, the administrators of New France had lost a great deal of their former influence and control in the interior regions. Therefore, their earlier decision, to exit from those areas in 1698, was determined to have been a mistake. However, instead of rejuvenating the various former posts, the Court decided to create several large pivotal communities, at which French power and influence would be based. These locales would include Detroit, the central Illinois River (upon which Ft. Pimetoui had already been established), and the mouth of the Mississippi River.

One of the primary reasons for the closure of most of the interior posts had been the tremendous surplus of beaver pelts which had accumulated in the monopoly company's warehouses. To rectify this problem, the company sought to halt the harvesting of such furs, and encouraged commerce in the pelts of other animals. Within a short period of time, furs other than beaver would represent more than half of the total commerce.[59]

During the spring and early summer of 1701, the Montreal notaries had been busy recording hiring contracts. Between April 13 and June 28, these had included two men who would paddle to the Ottawa Country, hauling supplies to the Jesuits at their missions; four others who would travel to the Illinois Country; and 55 men who would comprise the convoy that would establish the new facility of Ft. Pontchartrain. The lattermost 55 individuals who were bound for Cadillac's new post at Detroit included a blacksmith/gunsmith, an assistant blacksmith, a primary storekeeper, and a clerk.[60]

Nine weeks later, on September 5, these hirings were followed by the engagement of three highly reputable voyageur-trader-guides. These three men (one of whom was Robert Réaume), with the assistance of three soldiers and traveling in two canoes, would be entrusted with the task of transporting the wives and children of the two commanders, Cadillac and his second-in-command Alphonse de Tonty, westward to the brand new fort.

"Were present Sieurs Joseph Trottier [Sieur] Desruisseaux, Robert Réaume,

and Toussaint Pothier [dit Laverdure], voyageurs living in this said town [of Montreal], who voluntarily and of their own free will have engaged themselves for the service of the King to go to Detroit of Lake Erie, this agreed upon by the Sieur François Marie Picoté [Sieur] de Belestre by virtue of the power which he is said to have, to help bring from this town to the said Detroit two canoes loaded with merchandise for the King and in which will be the wives of Lamothe and Tonty, their children, the said Sieur de Belestre, and their crews [two additional soldier-paddlers besides Belestre]. They will take as much care as is possible to descend [return] this year if time permits.* In the event that they decide that they do not have enough time to descend, the said voyageurs will stay at the said Detroit until the following spring. As soon as it will be favorable to navigate, at such time they will descend, and will be obliged to take and bring to this town the peltries which will be supplied to them at the said Detroit. Except for the risks to the said voyageurs, they will not be held responsible [for this cargo]. This agreement is made upon the condition that the canoes and food supplies will be furnished to the said voyageurs during the said voyage and for the return journey for the use of the said voyageurs at the expense of the King, and also in consideration of the sum of two hundred livres of the country to each of the said voyageurs for their wages and salaries, if by chance they descend this autumn. If they are obliged to winter at the said Detroit, the sum of four hundred livres of the country will be paid to each of them as reimbursement for their trip. And it will be permitted for each of the said voyageurs to take one chest or bag to keep his clothing in, and to take also one gun. Thus have they promised, obligated themselves, waived, etc.

[This agreement] made and drawn up at the said Villemarie in the office of the said notary, in the year 1701 on the fifth of September in the afternoon, in the presence of Sieur Jacques Bertet, tailor of suits, and Pierre Rivet, attorney in civil cases, witnesses living at the said Villemarie, who have signed below with the said Sieur de Belestre, the said Sieur Trottier, and the notary. The said Réaume and Pothier have declared that they do not know how to write or sign, having been questioned [after the reading was done,] according to the ordinance.

Signed,

Joseph Trotier, Belestre, Bertet, Rivet, and Adhémar, notary.

*In the event that they descend during this year, they will not be obliged to take to this town any peltries."[61]

The officer who made these arrangements, François Marie Picoté, Sieur de Belestre, had been born and raised at Montreal; at this time, he was 24 years old and single. In 1709, he would marry, and in the following year he would be commissioned as an ensign, eventually advancing over the years to the rank of Lieutenant. Twelve years before this relocation to the new post at Detroit, his sister Marie Anne (who was five years older than François) had married the officer Alphonse de Tonty, and since that time she had borne nine children at Montreal. Of these, the first one had died at the age of fifteen months, while the sixth one had been stillborn. The seven surviving children, most or all of whom would be traveling in the two canoes with Robert and his colleagues, were Marie Françoise (age 11), Alphonse (10), Marie Hélène (8), Louis (7), Henri Hector (5^3/4), Charles Henri (4), and Claude Joseph (13 months). Since Marie Françoise would later become a nun, it is possible that, when her family left for Detroit, she remained at Montreal in the care of a convent. In addition, the younger daughter may have also stayed behind in the care of the nuns there as well.

Also on this voyage would be Cadillac's wife, Marie Thérèse Guyon, age 30, who had married her officer husband fourteen years earlier. During the ensuing years while residing in Acadia and at Quebec, they had produced Judith in about 1688, Marie Madeleine in about 1690, Antoine in 1692, Jacques in 1695 (who would apparently die at a relatively young age, since no later documentation for him would be recorded), Pierre Denis in 1699 (who had passed away in July of 1700 at the age of one year and three weeks), and Marie Anne (who had been born at Quebec on June 5, 1701, a month after Cadillac's May 8 departure from Quebec and on the very day that the commandant had left Lachine for the west, with the founding convoy; this baby had perished just four days later). During the middle of this sequence of four children, Sieur de Cadillac had served as the commandant at Ft. De Buade for three years, from 1694 to 1697. The two Cadillac daughters would not make this journey to the west; instead, they would remain in Quebec under the care of the Ursuline nuns. The eldest son, Antoine (9 years old at this time), had departed with his father and the main expedition back on June 5. Thus, the only child traveling in the canoe with Madame Cadillac would be her son Jacques, age six.[62]

Among the three experienced and trusted voyageur-trader-guides who had been hired to make this journey, Robert was the most senior member, in terms of age, number of years married, and number of children. Now 33^2/3 years old, he and Élisabeth had been married for almost five years (with their wedding anniversary coming up on

September 22), and they were expecting their third child in about six months. Joseph Trottier, Sieur Desruisseaux, a resident of the Lachine parish, was about 33 years of age. He had been married for nineteen months, and he and his wife Françoise Cuillerier were awaiting the arrival of their second child in about five months. The third and by far the youngest of the three men, Toussaint Pothier dit Laverdure, also a resident of the Lachine parish, was 26 years old. Having been trained as a maker of edged tools, he was still single; he would eventually marry in December of 1703. During the previous summer of 1700, he had been hired to make a trip to the Ottawa Country. (The only other hirings that had been recorded by Montreal notaries that year had been two men in the employ of the Jesuits in the Ottawa Country and five men working for La Forest in the Illinois Country.)[63]

When the two canoes departed from Lachine on September 10, 1701, they were paddled by Messieurs Réaume, Trottier, and Pothier, and the three soldiers Picoté, Laurret from the Company of Chaissaigne, and a third whose name has not yet been discovered. The two craft held Madame Cadillac and her one child, Madame Tonty and five to seven of her children, 200 pounds of tobacco encased in two calf skins, 300 pounds of lead encased in cloth bags, and a half-bushel of salt, in addition to the provisions and supplies which the party would consume during the journey. Other cargo items would be picked up where they had been been left behind as overflow lading by the June and August canoes which had been bound for Detroit. (Two canoes with a total of five paddlers had departed for the new fort with supplemental supplies in August, intending to make a round trip to the post and back before the winter freeze.) The first stop for cargo pickup would take place at Ft. Rolland, $1^3/4$ miles east of the Réaume farm, followed by another pickup some twelve miles further west, at Bout de l'Île, near the western tip of Montreal Island.

The vessel with the Cadillac family members was propelled by young Pothier in the stern, Réaume in the bow, and the unidentified soldier in the *milieu*, while the canoe with the Tonty family members was powered by the voyageur Trottier, the soldier Laurret, and the officer Picoté. The two canoes had together been equipped with 10 paddles, 14 yards of Méslis linen sailcloth (fashioned into two sails), 10 pounds of line or cord (for towing lines), 2 oilcloths, and 8 tumplines, as well as 10 pounds of sealant gum, 4 small axes, 1 crooked knife, and 2 bundles of fishhook leaders for repairing the craft while en route.[64]

Back in June and July, the main convoy had traveled to Detroit via the customary route to the west, along the Ottawa and Mattawa Rivers, Lake Nipissing, and the French River, after which it had traveled southward down the eastern shorelines of Georgian Bay and Lake Huron. However, since that time, the Great Treaty had been ratified by the Iroquois nations. Thus, the more southerly route, via the upper St. Lawrence River and Lakes Ontario and Erie, would be available to Robert and his colleagues, without any worry of attacks by Iroquois war parties along the way.

After ascending the upper St. Lawrence in thirteen days or less, the party reached Ft. Frontenac, at the eastern end of Lake Ontario, some time before September 23. There, they met two canoes which were returning from Ft. Pontchartrain to Montreal, carrying Lt. Chacornacle and Fr. François Vaillant de Gueslis, as well as the first reports by Captains Cadillac and Tonty. Continuing westward along the full length of the lake, the two family canoes reached the Niagara River at about the end of September, after some three weeks of total progress. Traveling with women and young children, the party may have proceeded more slowly than the usual rugged, cargo-transporting brigade, which only stopped to rest for a few hours each night.

When they arrived at the Niagara River, no post was occupied by the French there. The previous facility at that locale had been evacuated in 1688, and the next recorded French post there would not be erected until 1719. The Niagara River presented one of the greatest ordeals on the passageway to Detroit. This northward-flowing waterway, although it was only about thirty miles long, fell a full 385 feet, in a number of rapids and the tallest waterfall in all of North America. As they paddled up its lowest seven miles, the river offered only a gentle current, with the slope dropping a mere one foot per mile. But then, the water roared out of a 200-foot-tall limestone gorge, whose sheer front face had once been the site of the original Niagara Falls. Over the course of thousands of years, the flowing water had cut this sheer wall of the Niagara Escarpment back a total of seven miles, creating a deep gorge. In this gorge, the slope of the river dropped more than 100 feet, so that it was impossible to navigate it. At the upper end of the 7-mile-long gorge was the gigantic falls, where the water plunged 164 feet, creating clouds of spray with arching rainbows. Immediately above the astounding falls were the upper rapids, in which the water dropped another 51 feet of elevation in less than one mile.

The portage which confronted Robert and the rest of the party at this place commenced at the beginning of the gorge, at its north end. The path extended along the east side of the river, but one to two miles away from the watercourse itself, for seven miles. It ended at a place just above the upper rapids, some $2^1/2$ miles east of the massive waterfall. Along the way, the path included a steep climb over three hills which rose 400 feet in elevation, before the path leveled out on the plateau above the falls. (In later years, certain special voyageurs would sometimes have clauses inserted into their contracts, which guaranteed that they would be allowed to hike over this highly demanding portage without carrying any cargo.) After putting back in, the party paddled upstream for about fourteen miles around the east side of Grande Île, and then five miles more to the head of the Niagara River, to finally reach Lake Erie.[65]

With this challenging portage behind them, the little party of two canoes traveled westward along the north shore of Lake Erie, which was some 250 miles long. Compared to Lake Ontario, which was deep and not so easily riled, this body of water was much shallower, only averaging 90 feet in depth. Thus, it could be easily and quickly whipped into stormy conditions with the sudden arrival of winds. After they had covered about one-third of the length of the lake, the party reached the well-known feature of Longue Pointe, which was still about 130 miles east of Detroit. As was customary, they landed at the base of the extremely long and slender point, intending to make the usual portage across it. Thirteen years earlier, during August of 1688, the French officer Lahontan had encountered this same projecting land feature, which was typically handled by hiking across its base, rather than by paddling the laborious detour of fifty miles around its eastward-pointing tip:

"The 25th, we arriv'd at a long point of land which shoots out 14 or 15 leagues into the Lake. And the heat being excessive, we chose to transport our boats and baggage two hundred paces over-land, rather than coast about for thirty-five leagues [to round the point]."[66]

However, after completing the portage, the Cadillac-Tonty party was not able to continue on their way. In fact, strong and persistent winds forced them to remain on shore at the base of Longue Pointe for a full nine days. During that time, the steersman of the canoe carrying the Tonty family, Joseph Trottier, was joined by his English domestic servant and three voyageur colleagues from Montreal. According to their previously-arranged plans, these men arrived by canoe with a supply of trade merchandise (but without a license authorizing such trade). Trottier then arranged with a passing Algonkin man, who was also traveling to Detroit, to replace himself in the Tonty canoe. Thus, when the two craft finally continued their westward journey, the former steersman of the latter craft remained behind with his newly-arrived colleagues, in order to spend the winter on the north shore of the lake, trading with passing native parties.

The two canoes, with their Cadillac and Tonty family members and the other cargo intact, arrived at Ft. Pontchartrain in the autumn of 1701, apparently without further incident. A number of historians have contended that the party was forced to winter en route, at Ft. Frontenac, or at the Niagara Portage, or at some other location, finally arriving at Detroit in the following spring. However, during the legal proceedings against Trottier for abandoning the group, which would take place in Montreal between August 23 and August 31 of 1702, sworn testimony would clearly indicate that the families had arrived safely at the fort on schedule. Monsieur Picoté, Madame Tonty's brother and one of the three paddlers in the canoe that transported her and her children to the post, would be very clear on this point. According to the transcriptions of the Court, he would testify on August 25, 1702 that he had wintered at Detroit. "Then, the following spring, after having received orders from Monsieur de Lamothe, he had departed from the said fort and came down here," arriving in Montreal during the first week in June.[67]

Robert likewise spent the winter at the brand-new facility of Ft. Pontchartrain, thus earning his full salary of 400 livres. In May of 1702, upholding his employment contract, he and Toussaint Pothier fulfilled their duties "to take and bring to this town [Montreal] the peltries which will be supplied to them at the said Detroit." A detailed list of the actual furs and hides which Robert led out was presented in the financial report of the first year of operation of the fort. For the sake of brevity, the valuations of each of the peltries have not been included here.

"Returns which were derived from the trade and from the hunting at Fort Pontchartrain at Detroit, which were received at Quebec in this present year of 1702.

By the first convoy, which arrived at Montreal in the month of June.

Beaver pelts which were delivered to the Office of the Farm [the export monopoly company] on August 3, 1702:

Greasy, semi-greasy, and green: 579 lbs. 2 oz.

Muscovy [winter harvested, not worn by natives]: 127 lbs. 7 oz.
Dry [not worn by natives], from winter: 1,683 lbs. 10 oz.

Furs and hides which were sold at auction, October 10 and 11, 1702:
365 tanned elk: 318 lbs.
1,199 deer: 964 lbs.
598 bears: 534 lbs.
3,967 raccoons: 3,717 lbs.
495 otters: 404 lbs.
tanned moose: 51 lbs.
bobcats: 88 lbs.
29 timber wolves: 25 lbs.
54 bear cubs: 45 lbs.
12 foxes, 12 fishers, and 6 panthers: 30 lbs."[68]

In June of 1702, when Robert returned to his family on the farm west of Lachine, he was eager to hear the news of the many events that had transpired during the nine months of his absence. During the final months of 1701, a devastating epidemic of smallpox had swept through the St. Lawrence Valley, carrying off over a thousand of the residents, both French and native. The only positive aspect of this terrible wave of disease was that it had not struck the colony until well after the 1,300 native delegates at the Great Treaty council had departed for their distant homelands.[69]

Robert also learned about the legal difficulties in which a number of his fellow voyageur-traders had become embroiled. It had started with the arrest of René Mallet, Gabriel Perrin dit Dubreuil, and Étienne Vaudry, three residents of Montreal who had been found in the interior by Alphonse de Tonty during the autumn of 1701. The trio had been subsequently transferred to the Royal Prison at Quebec, to stand trial. According to the records of the Sovereign Council at Quebec, these men had been "accused of having been in the depths of the woods without permission, where they had been surprised and arrested with some trade merchandise, notwithstanding that this was prohibited by His Majesty." Monsieur Mallet, 33 years old, had been trading for the previous thirteen years, ever since 1688; he was married with eight children. Monsieur Perrin, age 32, had a wife but no offspring, while Monsieur Vaudry, the youngest of the trio, was only 16; he would never marry. After being interrogated on November 22, the men had confessed to the crime. Two weeks later, on December 9, the Council had pronounced their sentence: they would be incarcerated in the Royal Prison at Quebec. During further interrogations, the three men had relinquished the names of nine or more other men who had then been "accused of being presently in the depths of the woods in disobedience of the prohibitions of His Majesty...Dominique and Jacques Étienne, sons of Philippe Étienne; Miville; Duclos; a son of Chauvin; Filiatrault; the sons of Saint Germain, merchant of Montreal; and the one named Réaume." The lattermost individual would have been one of Robert's younger brothers, either Simon or Jean Baptiste, who were ages 31 and 25, respectively, and unmarried at this time. To complicate the case of the three convicted men, Messieurs Mallet and Perrin had managed to flee from the jail on December 19, by breaking some boards. After their escape, Perrin's wife, Jeanne Vaudry (whose brother Étienne Vaudry was the only one among the convicted trio who had not fled; she also had four other brothers who were Montreal-based voyageurs) had been questioned by the authorities. In addition, she had been ordered not to leave the Montreal area. The cases of the various individuals, both those who had been convicted and those who had been only named and accused, had apparently remained in limbo since that time.[70]

Immensely more pleasant than hearing the news about a terrible epidemic and the legal problems of fellow traders (including one of his own siblings) was Robert's meeting for the very first time his first daughter (and third child), little Marie Josèphe. She had arrived about three months earlier, on March 18, 1702. At her christening ceremony in the Holy Angels Church at Lachine one week later, on the 25th, the priest had recorded in the parish ledger that Monsieur Réaume had been "absent." (Typically, the clerics did not document publicly in the church records that an individual was working in the interior, since substantial numbers of them were doing so illegally, without official permission.) On this special day, the baby's godfather had been the Lachine resident Vital Caron, age 28, who had been married for four years and already had three children; he and his family lived two lots east of the Lachine church. The baby's godmother had been Marie Antoinette Chouart, age 41, the youngest child of the well-known trader Médard Chouart, Sieur des Groseilliers. A year after the death of her first husband, Jean Jalot, at the hands of the Iroquois in 1694, Marie Antoinette had remarried the Lachine peltries merchant Jean Baptiste Bouchard dit Dorval. With her first spouse, she had borne eight children, and with her second one she had already produced four more in the span of six years. According to the 1702 land-ownership map of Vachon de Belmont, this large blended family lived immediately west of the Réaume farm, on the adjacent property.[71]

About five weeks after Robert had returned to his family during the first week of June, it was time for him to again depart for the west. However, this next voyage would not entail an extended absence. He would return before the freeze would close the waterways, to spend the winter at home with Élisabeth and their three young children. On July 16, 1702, a total of forty voyageurs gathered at Ft. Rolland, about $1^3/4$ miles east of the Réaume farm, to ratify their hiring contracts for a round trip to Detroit and back. Fifteen of the men, including Robert, were lumped together in one contract, while the other 25 men were included in another contract. Among all of these paddlers, Monsieur Réaume was the only one who was listed as being from Lachine. According to their employment agreement with the Company of the Colony, the men would depart from Ft. Rolland on the following day: *"...to go to the said place of Detroit, and to assist in bringing and taking a canoe to the said place loaded with the cargo which the Gentlemen of the Company will provide...and to descend immediately and return during the present year, to bring to the said Montreal the cargo which will be delivered to them at the said Detroit, and to place it at the said Montreal in the storehouse of the Gentlemen of the said Company...The said employees will not engage in any trade, directly or indirectly, either in going up, upon arrival at the said place of Detroit, or in returning, under any pretext or for any reason, under the penalty of the ordinances and the loss of their wages and salaries....This contract is made with the stipulation that the said voyageurs will be fed during the said voyage as is customarily done, and in addition for the consideration of the sum of two hundred livres in currency of the region for each one, for all of their wages and salaries for the said voyage, which will be paid at the said Montreal upon their return during the present year."[72]*

The contracts specifically mentioned that the men would be required to deliver the outward-bound furs and hides to the storehouse of the Company at Montreal. Thus, their duties would include hauling the cargo over the Lachine-to-Montreal portage road.

It is of interest to note that, according to notarial records, this would be the last time that Robert Réaume would travel into the interior as a wage-earning employee working for others. After this year, during the rest of his long career, his participation in the peltries commerce would be as an independent trader generating his own profits, and sometimes hiring voyageurs to work for and with him.

As was noted earlier in the description of the outbound June brigade, the peltries that were hauled out by the October convoy were also listed in detail in the report of the first year of operations of the new post at Detroit. According to the document, the October shipment was nearly as extensive as the June one had been. The valuations of each of the peltries have not been included here.

"Returns which were derived from the trade and from the hunting at Fort Pontchartrain at Detroit, which were received at Quebec this present year of 1702.

By the second and last convoy, which arrived [at Montreal] in the month of October.

Beaver pelts which were delivered to the Office of the Farm [the export monopoly company] on November 2, 1702:

Greasy, semi-greasy, and green: 680 lbs. 2 oz.
Muscovy: 6 lbs. 14 oz.
Dry, from winter: 1,328 lbs. 14 oz.

Furs and hides which were sold at auction, October 28, 1702:
tanned elk, 341 lbs.
deer, 889 lbs.
bears: 336 lbs.
raccoons: 1,654 lbs.
otters: 317 lbs.
bobcats: 64 lbs.
bear cubs: 84 lbs.
foxes: 21 lbs.
fishers: 2 lbs.

Additional furs and hides which were sold:
tanned elk: 14 lbs.
deer: 7 lbs.
raccoons: 2 lbs.
bear cub: 1 lb.
deer: 34 lbs.
bears: 4 lbs.
deer: 106 lbs.
bears: 21 lbs."[73]

Since Robert was away from the St. Lawrence settlements during this round trip journey to and from Detroit, not returning until October, he was not present to testify in the trial of Joseph Trottier,

Sieur Desruisseaux. After returning to Montreal in June of 1702, Trottier was finally arrested in latter August. At that time, he was charged with having traded without a license during the previous autumn, winter, and spring along the north shore of Lake Erie. During the hearings, which were conducted from August 23 through August 31, 1702, the accused man himself was interrogated, as was also François Marie Picoté (Madame Tonty's brother, who had been one of the paddlers in the canoe that had transported the Tonty family members). In addition, testimony was also taken from two Seneca men who, along with numerous of their native colleagues, had exchanged peltries for merchandise with Monsieur Trottier along northern Lake Erie during the months in question. However, in spite of the considerable array of evidence against him, the accused was not convicted of the charges of trading illegally. Even more astounding, although Trottier had abandoned his contractual duties in safely transporting Mesdames Cadillac and Tonty and their children to Ft. Pontchartrain, no charges were ever leveled against him for this dereliction of duty.[74]

Robert had been away from his family, friends, and neighbors when the previous major epidemic had raged through the St. Lawrence settlements. That had occurred during the autumn of 1701, while he had been wintering at Ft. Pontchartrain. However, this time he was at home when smallpox struck, so that he could both assist the many people who were in need and comfort the grieving survivors. Among his own clan, the first death was that of his niece Charlotte Réaume, the youngest daughter of his brother René and his wife Marie Guyon. She died at the age of two years and ten months on February 3, 1703, at their home at Château Richer, on the Côte de Beaupré. Six days later, this same little family also lost their youngest child, little Basile; he was only eight months old, not even ready to attempt his first wobbly steps. On April 4, Robert's brother Maurice and his wife Marie Anne Vivier lost their second child to the sickness, at their home in the Charlesbourg seigneury. Pierre Réaume, $10^{1/2}$ years old, was buried in the Beauport cemetery on the same day as he had perished.[75]

Although these three losses of clan members occurred at a considerable distance from Robert and Élisabeth, the spector of death also hovered very close to home as well. On May 17, Jacques Jalot, the 14-year-old who lived with his family on the farm immediately west of the Réaumes, died from the disease. At his funeral in the

Lachine church on the following day, the officiating priest recorded that the specific cause of his death had been smallpox. The five official witnesses at the burial included his stepfather Jean Baptiste Bouchard dit Dorval and his sister Angélique Jalot (age 16), as well as their Lachine friends and neighbors Robert Réaume, Antoine Rapin (age 16), and Guillaume Daoust (either Sr., age 48, or Jr., age $8^{1}/2$, most likely the elder).[76]

In the aftermath of the epidemic, in spite of the widespread grief that shrouded all of the settlements, normal events of daily life gradually resumed during this same year of 1703. In about latter June, Élisabeth became pregnant for the fourth time. Some ten weeks later, Robert purchased additional land in their sub-fief of La Presentation, which was also called the Côte St. Gilles. On September 2, he bought a piece of property from the peltries merchant François Chorel, Sieur de Saint Romain, who operated at both Champlain and Montreal. In the document of transfer, Robert Réaume was identified as an "habitant of the parish of Lachine."[77]

Twenty-five days later, on September 27, Robert again visited the same notary in Montreal, this time in the company of the distinguished Montreal merchant bourgeois and outfitter Antoine Pascaud.

"Was present Robert Réaume, habitant of the parish of Lachine on this Island, at present in this town, who has voluntarily acknowledged and declared that he owes to Sieur Antoine Pascaud, merchant of this town, present and assenting, the sum of 314 livres 14 sols 6 deniers for good merchandise which was sold and delivered to him by the said creditor before today. This sum of 314 livres 14 sols 6 deniers the said debtor promises to pay to the said Sieur creditor or to the bearer in the summer of the next year 1704 in the currency of this region, under the pain of all expenses, damages, and interests, under the bond and mortgage of all of his belongings, both present and future. For the execution of these presents, the said debtor has selected as his [temporary] legal residence [to which writs may be delivered] his residence in this town, the house of the widow Belhumeur, his mother-in-law, located on St. Paul Street. Thus have they promised, obligated themselves, waived, etc.

[This agreement] made and drawn up at the said Villemarie in the office of the said notary in 1703 on the 27th day of September in the afternoon, in the presence of Sieurs Antoine Hatanville, royal bailiff, and Jacques Bertet, tailor of suits, witnesses living at the said Villemarie who have signed below with the said Sieur Pascaud and the notary. The said Réaume, debtor, has declared that he does not know how to write or sign, having been questioned after the reading had been done, according to the ordinance.

Signed,
Pascault, Hatanville, Bertet, and Adhémar, notary."[78]

Exactly three years earlier, back in September of 1700, Robert had received a consignment of merchandise from a different Montreal merchant and outfitter, one which was worth twice as much as this shipment. As was the case with that earlier transaction, the September timing and the promise to repay the debt during the following summer for this new delivery of goods in 1703 strongly implies that this, too, represented outfitting preparations for an upcoming voyage. It is possible that Robert had received a private trading permit from the colonial administrators as an acknowledgement for services rendered, when he had safely delivered the Cadillac and Tonty family members to Detroit during his 1701-1702 voyage (in spite of the abandonment of the mission by Joseph Trottier, the other veteran guide on that trip).

The voyageur hiring contracts which were penned by Montreal notaries during 1703 reveal the travel patterns of the convoys this year. They also imply how and when Robert may have traveled to the interior, and to which destinations he might have gone. During this summer, a total of 45 voyageurs had been hired on July 10 to make a round trip from Montreal to Detroit and back, returning before the end of autumn. Then, in anticipation of the late September convoy which would travel to the west via the Ottawa River route, five men had been engaged for service in the Illinois Country, two others had been hired to work for the Jesuit missions in the upper Great Lakes region, and one man had been contracted to travel to the Ottawa Country in the service of Jean Boudor. (This lattermost individual, a merchant bourgeois of Quebec, had been hiring voyageur-traders to work for him in the west for thirteen years, ever since 1690.) These hirings for the Illinois Country, the Ottawa Country, and the missionaries around the upper Great Lakes had been executed on July 27, September 7, and September 25, respectively. Even later in the traveling season, a group of five men were engaged on October 12 to make a final trip to Ft. Pontchartrain, before winter weather would finally close the waterways for the season. It is quite likely that Robert, when he acquired his supply of merchandise from Monsieur Chorel on September 22, was making preparations to join either the September convoy which was bound for the Upper Country or the October brigade which was headed for Detroit.[79]

However, there is one document which may suggest that Robert did not travel to the west to participate in the 1703-1704 trading season. On March 24, 1704, Élisabeth gave birth to their fourth child, Hyacinthe. At his baptismal ceremony in the Holy Angels Church at Lachine on the following day, Fr. Rémy recorded in the parish ledger that the boy was the son of Robert Réaume, master carpenter, and Élisabeth Brunet. However, it is not entirely clear from this record whether Robert was present or not at this ecclesiastical celebration. Two years earlier, at the christening of their previous child at Lachine on March 25, 1702, another priest had recorded that Robert had been "absent" at the time (he had been wintering at Detroit). At the 1704 ceremony, the godfather was the Lachine resident and farm worker Joseph Gauthier dit Saguingoira, who had a wife and one child. Their farm was located about $2^1/_2$ miles east of Réaume property, beside the terminus of the Lachine Canal. The baby's godmother was Madeleine Rapin, a 25-years-old resident of Lachine who had been married to Jean Gabriel Picard for eight years and had four children. This family lived on the fourth farm east of the Réaumes. Monsieur Picard had hauled freight by canoe to and from Ft. Frontenac during the previous summer and autumn of 1703, having commenced this work on May 13.[80]

Even if Robert Réaume was not among the paddlers in the small convoy that traveled from Lachine to Ft. Pontchartrain in October of 1703, another direct ancestor of the present author was definitely one of these men. This was Jean Michel dit Taillon, who had been born in the autumn of 1675 at Château Richer on the Côte de Beaupré, and had been baptized there on October 27. He was the second of four children and the eldest son of Olivier Michel dit Letardif et Taillon (the adopted son of Olivier Letardif, whose biography was presented earlier in this work) and Marie Madeleine Cauchon. When Jean was 23 years old, his mother died at the Hôtel Dieu hospital in Quebec, on December 28, 1698; four months later, his father passed away in the same institution, on April 26, 1699.

Five years after losing both of his parents, when he was still officially a resident of the Côte de Beaupré, Jean Michel was hired at Montreal to make a journey to Detroit, spend the winter there, and return in the following year. On October 12, 1703, he, along with his colleagues Raymond Jean dit Godon, Guillaume Laberge, Joseph Lauzé dit Matha, and François Dumontier, were engaged to paddle westward to Ft. Pontchartrain before the winter freeze would close the waterways. According to their contract, which was drawn up by the Montreal notary Antoine Adhémar, the five voyageurs had been hired by the Gentlemen of the Company of the Colony to make this journey.

At this time, when Jean was about to turn 28 and was still single, his colleague Raymond Jean dit Godon, originally from Charlesbourg but later from Lachine, was 30 years old and was likewise unmarried. In contrast, Guillaume Laberge, from L'Ange Gardien, was age 29 and married with five children. Joseph Lauzé dit Matha, from Charlesbourg, was 24 years of age; after $3^1/3$ years of marriage, his wife had died nine months before this voyageur contract was drawn up, before the couple had produced any children. Jean's fourth colleague, François Dumontier, hailing from Montreal, was about 35 years of age; he was married and had produced three children, but the youngest of these had died eight months earlier, at the age of nine weeks.

This employment in 1703-1704 would be the only voyageur work of Jean Michel that would be publicly documented. However, he may have been hired in this capacity on a number of occasions, but in illegal operations which did not have official permission and thus left no paper trail. On the other hand, he may have been one of those individuals who worked for only one or just a few seasons in the fur trade, in order to lay aside enough cash to establish his own pioneer farm.

Settling in the Montreal area, Jean Michel would finally marry a full decade after his journey to Detroit, at the age of $39^1/2$ years. This ceremony, taking place twelve days after he and his fiancée had drawn up their marriage contract, would be celebrated on February 5, 1714, at St. François, on the northeastern tip of Île Jésus (which lay immediately northwest of Montreal Island). His bride, Marie Forget, age $20^1/2$, hailed from nearby Lachinae (she was a great-granddaughter of Abraham Martin, whose biography is the first one offered in the present work). Ten months after their wedding, the couple would produce their first child at St. François; this baby would be followed by six more at this locale during the next $9^1/2$ years. Some time before the spring of 1726, before he would turn age 51, Jean Michel would pass away at St. François. The only surviving documentation for the general time of his death would be the record of his widow's remarriage to François Xavier Thibault, at nearby Terrebonne on May 5, 1726.[81]

In the afternoon on March 28, 1705, Robert Réaume visited the

Montreal notary Adhémar, in order to register the adjusted amount of debt which he now owed to the Montreal merchant Charles Villiers. Some 4^1/2 years earlier, back on September 22, 1700, Robert had received from this man a consignment of merchandise which had been worth 642 livres 11 sols 10 deniers. In the intervening years, he had paid off more than 90 percent of this amount. Thus, on this March day in 1705, Messieurs Réaume and Villiers (with the latter individual representing both himself and his partner, the young Montreal merchant Laurent Renaud) officially registered that the former debt agreement was to be cancelled. In its stead, this new document indicated that Robert (described as an "habitant of Lachine") now owed Villiers only the sum of 63 livres 12 sols 7 deniers.[82]

At the time of this transaction of her husband, Élisabeth was about one month pregnant; some eight months later, on December 10, she safely delivered their fifth child, who would be named Jean Baptiste. On the same day as the boy's arrival, she and Robert traveled eastward about 3^1/2 miles to the Lachine church, where the tiny lad was christened. One of his sponsors at the ceremony (and his name-giver) was the Lachine peltries merchant Jean Cuillerier, while the infant's other sponsor was Marie Catherine Thunay, the wife of the Lachine voyageur Jacques Filiatrault. In the church record of this encouraging event, the priest indicated that the baby's father was a master carpenter.[83]

As the following spring approached, the merchant Charles Villiers sued Robert in the Montreal Court, in order to force him to pay off the balance of the debt which he owed to the merchant. On March 26, 1706, the Lieutenant Général (Chief Judge) of the Court decreed that Robert was indeed obliged to repay this debt in a timely manner. Thus, on May 30, Robert borrowed a total of 518 livres 10 sols 9 deniers from his mother-in-law, Françoise Moisan, who lived on St. Paul Street in Montreal. According to the notary document which officially registered this loan, Monsieur Réaume had received this sum of money from the widow of Antoine Brunet dit Belhumeur "in order to generally pay off any and all of the accounts which he has accumulated and made in the past up to this day, including the 64 livres 19 sols 3 deniers which the said Moisan has paid to the Sieur Villiers for the said Réaume."[84]

By the heart of the winter in 1707, Élisabeth's widowed mother (and Robert's mother-in-law) Françoise Moisan was about 61 to 64 years old. Her husband, Antoine Brunet dit Belhumeur, had passed away some 13 to 19 years before, at some point between November of 1688 and July of 1694. In addition, all six of her children who had grown to adulthood had married long before, the last of them nearly a decade earlier, back in 1698. Thus, with a very empty family nest in her home on Rue St. Paul in Montreal, she welcomed the proposal of marriage that was offered to her by Pierre Perthuis dit La Lime, who had been a widower for sixteen months.

This merchant bourgeois of Montreal, about 60 or 61 years old, had arrived in New France during the summer of 1665, as a soldier in the Carignan-Salières Regiment. After his retirement from military life, he had married the *fille du Roi* Claude Damisé in 1668. Until her death in October of 1705, the couple had been married for nearly 37 years; during that time, they had produced twelve children in 22 years, of whom nine would live to adulthood. (In addition, Claude had also borne a son by another man in 1676, in the interval between her third and fourth children by Pierre.) Before 1707, all six of the older surviving daughters had married, while the youngest daughter had perished in March of 1703 at the age of $20^2/3$ years, during the smallpox epidemic. The elder of their two sons named Pierre, Jr. would die late in the following year of 1708 at Deerfield, Massachusetts, at the age of 22, having never married. Considering the place of his death, it is highly likely that he had been a *coureur de bois* who had sought refuge among the English. His passing would leave only one offspring of Pierre Perthuis, Sr. still unmarried and living at home. This was the other Pierre, Jr., who would turn age 16 in May of 1707. Three months before this birthday celebration, on February 13, Pierre, Sr. and Françoise Moisan visited the Montreal notary Adhémar to have their marriage contract drawn up. Afterward on the same day, they exchanged their nuptial vows in the Notre Dame de Montreal church.[85]

Élisabeth must have become pregnant at about the time of her mother's remarriage, since she gave birth to Judith Réaume, their sixth child, on November 6, 1707. That same day, the infant was christened in the church at Lachine, with the sponsors Étienne Massiot and Marie Anne Rapin. The latter woman, a resident of Lachine, was 25 years old and still single at this time; no marriage record or later documentation for her has been found.[86]

Élisabeth and Robert were saddened when they learned of the death of their nephew Jacques Réaume, Jr. after just two days of life, on March 19, 1708. This tiny lad had arrived nine months and eleven days after the wedding at Château Richer of his parents, Robert's 24-year-old brother Jacques and his bride Marguerite Proteau. The young couple had settled at Montmagny, northeast of Quebec on the southern shore of the St. Lawrence.[87]

During the following month, another death in the clan occurred much closer to home, after which Élisabeth's new stepfather Pierre Perthuis was buried in the Montreal cemetery on April 16. The merchant bourgeois and her mother Françoise Moisan had only been married for fourteen months. However, although the couple had only been able to enjoy a short time together, their union had introduced Robert Réaume to Pierre's youngest son Pierre Perthuis, Jr., who was at this point five weeks away from turning age 17. In the coming years, these two men, with an age span of 23 years between them, would work closely together as business partners in the fur trade.[88]

During the autumn in this year of 1708, Robert was thrown into mourning by the passing one of his own siblings. His sister Étiennette, just four years younger than himself and having never married, died on September 11 at the age of 36; she was laid to rest in the cemetery at Charlesbourg on the following day.[89]

Death continued to stalk the Réaume family during the following months. First came the passing of another of Robert's siblings in January, when his only older brother Maurice died at Charlesbourg at the age of 42. He was buried in the cemetery there on January 17, 1709, the day following his death. Just two months later, Robert's sister-in-law Marguerite Proteau, the wife of his brother Jacques, delivered their second baby on March 21 (ten months earlier, their first child had lived for only two days). In this instance, the infant died after just one day of life, after which she was laid to rest in the Montmagny cemetery on the following day. On the day after the baby's funeral, Marguerite herself passed away, two months short of her 24th birthday.[90]

The safe arrival of Élisabeth and Robert's seventh child 6 1/2 months later contributed a great deal to the restoration of the family's spirits. When 3-day-old Pierre was baptized at the font in the Lachine church on October 6, 1709, his godfather and name giver was Jean Pierre Quesnel (a resident of Lachine, age 24 and not yet married), while his godmother was the Lachine resident Marie Picard.[91]

One of the brighter highlights of Robert's year in 1710 was his participation as one of the official witnesses at a wedding in the church at Bout de l'Île, some seven miles west of his farm. On March 2, the priest of this parish presided at the marriage of Étienne Chatouteau dit Macia (who had relocated here from Lachine) and Marie Jeanne Primeau from Châteauguay. The two witnesses from Châteauguay included the seigneur, Lieutenant Zacharie Robutel, Sieur de La Noue, as well as Pierre Narlin, while the two witnesses from Lachine included Robert Réaume and Pierre Tienel.[92]

The spring of 1711 brought with it a great roller-coaster of emotions for Robert and Élisabeth. First came the poignant death of Robert's brother Jacques, at the untimely age of 31. After losing both his wife and their two children back in 1708 and 1709, Jacques had remarried late in 1709 to Agnès Gagnon, and he had welcomed the arrival of one child during the following year. However, after just sixteen months of this second marriage, he died at Charlesbourg on March 21, and was buried there on the following day.[93]

Offsetting this loss, Robert and Élisabeth were heartened by the safe arrival of their eighth child on April 11. On the following day, the tiny lad was granted his name at his baptismal ceremony in the Holy Angels Church at Lachine by his godfather, Alphonse de Tonty. This officer, whom the priest recorded as a "Captain of a detachment of the Marine Department," had been the commandant of Ft. De Buade at St. Ignace during 1697-1698, the final year of operations of that facility, and then of Ft. Pontchartrain at Detroit from the end of 1704 until January of 1706. The baby's godmother was Marguerite Chorel, the widow (since July of 1709) of Captain Guillaume Lorimier, Sieur des Bordes, who had been the commandant of Ft. Rolland at Lachine from 1700 to 1705. The lattermost couple had lost their oldest child at the age of six back in March of 1703, during the devastating smallpox epidemic.[94]

The appearance of these two individuals as the baptismal sponsors of Robert and Élisabeth's latest child apparently reflected the respect and trust that had developed over the years between Robert and the commandants of the various interior posts. By this point, Monsieur Réaume had faithfully served the commanders of Ft. De Buade, Ft. St. Joseph, and Ft. Pontchartrain. In addition, he seems to have burnished good relationships with various high-level military figures in the St. Lawrence settlements as well.

According to the surviving notary records, Robert Réaume had not worked in the fur trade for nearly a decade, not since about 1703-1704 or possibly earlier. During those nine or ten years, while the peltries commerce had been legally closed at most of the facilities in the interior, he may have been laboring as a master carpenter in the Lachine and Montreal area, as well as operating his farm west of Lachine. However, he may have also conducted a number of unlicensed (and thus undocumented) trading trips to the west or the northwest during this period.

In fact, his younger brother Jean Baptiste had done just that on at least one occasion. During the summer of 1712, when this sibling had been 36 years old, he and three of his voyageur-trader colleagues had been placed on trial at Montreal, on charges of having previously carried out illegal commerce at the Straits of Mackinac. In this instance, Jean Baptiste's three partners had been Jacques Maret dit Lépine, Jean Magnan dit l'Espérance, and Jean Magdelaine dit Ladouceur. The legal charges, declaring that the four men had departed from the St. Lawrence without either a license or a permit, in order to "make a voyage to Michilimackinac" and "to the nations of the Upper Country, against the prohibition of His Majesty," had also involved Pierre Juillet. The latter individual had been accused of having assisted the four men, by transporting from Montreal to Lachine a cart which was loaded with "considerable trade merchandise, in packing cases, bales, and boxes, plus black [imported] tobacco, three kegs of brandy, and one keg of wine." The verdict in the trial of these four illicit traders of Mackinac had decreed that each of them was to be employed on the King's galleys (working as rowers on his vessels in the Mediterranean Sea) for the rest of their lives. However, there is no evidence that this extreme sentence had ever been carried out. Amnesty declarations had been quite common during the previous fourteen years, and they would continue to be so for the next several years. Thus, it is apparent that the sentences of the four traders had been commuted at a later date. In fact, all four of them later participated in the trade legally, with their employment recorded publicly in notary contracts.[95]

By the spring of 1713, Robert decided that it was time for him to participate with even greater vigor in the legal, licensed peltries business. Now, however, he would operate as an independent trader, rather than as an employee working for other individuals, as he had often done during the earlier stages of his career. In this new role, he would be taking much greater financial risks, since he and his single partner would be hauling more than 5,000 livres worth of merchandise and supplies to the west. They would acquire this rather large consignment of materiel on credit from two different outfitters, one on June 2 and the other on June 3. In this upcoming endeavor, which would span more than a year of labor, his partner would be Pierre Perthuis, Jr., who was now 22 years old, had been married for four months, and lived in Montreal.[96]

The first and larger of the two consignments was supplied by Jacques Le Ber, Jr., one of the wealthiest and most important peltries merchants and outfitters of Montreal. (His father, Jacques Le Ber dit Larose, had been by far the most important such man in this town until his death $6^{1}/_2$ years earlier, in November of 1706.)

"Before Michel Le Pailleur, royal notary of the Island of Montreal, residing at Villemarie, undersigned with the witnesses named below, were present the Sieur Robert Réaume, habitant of this Island on the shore of Lac Saint Louis, and the Sieur Pierre Perthuis [Sieur] de La Janvry, living in this town, who upon their departure to go up to Fort Pontchartrain at the Detroit of Lake Erie have acknowledged and declared that they well and truly owe, justly and solidly one for the other and each of them for the whole, without division or discussion, renouncing any such said divisions, to Jacques Le Ber, Esquire, Sieur de Senneville, Lieutenant in the Troops of the Marine Department, present and assenting, the sum of 3,315 livres for good merchandise which the said Sieur Creditor has sold and delivered to them this day as their supplies for the commerce of the said voyage, according to the invoice which he gave to them, and with all of which they are well content and satisfied. The said sum of 3,315 livres the said debtors have promised and are obligated, solidly as noted, to render, deliver, and pay to the said creditor or upon his order during the month of August of the next year 1714, or earlier if they come down or send their belongings to this town or to other places, in good beaver pelts at the current prices [of the export monopoly company] at Quebec or in good peltries [of other animals] at the current prices of other merchants, having preference over all of the said belongings, under the penalty of all expenses, damages, and interests. To this end, they have obligated themselves and have mortgaged, solidly as above, all of their possessions, both present and future, and in particular all of the cargo which they will bring or send from the said region, as the natural wages of the said creditor for his merchandise. For the execution of these presents, the said debtors have selected as their [temporary] legal residence [to which writs may be delivered] their residence at the said Villemarie, the home of the Sieur Urbain Gervaise, situated on St. Joseph Street. Thus have they promised, obligated themselves, waived, etc.

[This agreement] made and drawn up at the said Villemarie in the house of the said creditor [Le Ber] in the afternoon on the second day of June, 1713,

in the presence of the Sieurs Jean Baptiste Hervieux and Charles Alavoine,
witnesses who have signed with the said Perthuis, the said Sieur creditor,
and the notary. The said Réaume has declared that he does not know how to
write or sign, having been questioned according to the ordinance.
Signed,
Pierre Perthuy, Alavoyne, Hervieux, and Le Pailleur."[97]

The home at Montreal which was given as the partners' temporary legal residence for this transaction was owned and occupied by Urbain Gervaise and his wife Geneviève Perthuis. There was a close connection between this couple and the two trading partners: the woman was one of the older sisters of Pierre Perthuis.

On the following day, Robert and Pierre officially acknowledged that they had received their second infusion of merchandise and supplies, this one from Robert's younger brother Simon. This second contract, written by the same notary Le Pailleur but drawn up in Simon's home, contained virtually the same terminology and phrases as had been utilized in the debt agreement with Monsieur Le Ber on the previous day. However, the creditor in this new document was identified as "Simon Réaume, merchant of this town;" the value of the received materiel was recorded as 1,979 livres 2 sols; and the two official witnesses were identified as Claude du Devoir and Jacques Héry dit Duplanty, both of them coopers.

At the bottom of the latter agreement, an addendum would be penned fifteen months later, indicating that the full amount of this debt had been paid off:

"Was present Dame Thérèse Catin, wife of Sieur Simon Réaume, who has
acknowledged that she has received from the said Robert Réaume and Sieur
Pierre Perthuis the contents of the obligation, so that nothing is left in
this agreement for the future concerning this cargo, having delivered the
discharge of the said obligation of the said Sieurs Perthuis and Réaume to
the notary on this third of September, 1714.
Signed,
Le Pailleur, notary."[98]

Simon Réaume, Robert's next-younger brother, was 42 years old, 22 months younger than Robert. Having operated as a peltries merchant and outfitter at Montreal for a considerable number of years, he and Jeanne Thérèse Catin had been married for three years at this point, and they already had two children. The second of these babies had arrived twelve days before Simon provided this consignment to Robert and his partner for their upcoming commercial venture at Detroit.[99]

The two men probably departed from Lachine in about mid-June, most likely traveling in the large convoy that was formed by other voyageur-traders who were also bound for Ft. Pontchartrain. According to the hiring contracts which had been drawn up by notaries in the Montreal area during the early summer, at least 25 men had been engaged between May 2 and June 11 to work at Detroit. Equipped with at least 5,294 livres 2 sols worth of materiel, all of which the two partners had acquired on credit, Messieurs Réaume and Perthuis expected to be absent from their families for more than a year. In fact, they apparently returned to the Montreal area at about the end of August or the very beginning of September in 1714, nearly fifteen months after leaving. Shortly thereafter, they paid off their outfitting debt to Simon Réaume at Montreal on September 3.

During their sojourn at Detroit, they had been under the rule of the two commanders there. As noted in various hiring contracts from 1713, the man in charge was "François Dauphin, Sieur de La Forest, Esquire, Captain of a company of the troops in the detachment of the Marine Department, and Commandant for the King at the Fort Pontchartrain." For many years, he had been a very close associate of Cavelier de La Salle, first as the manager of Ft. Frontenac for a decade beginning in 1675, and then as the co-proprietor with Henri de Tonty of Ft. St. Louis in the Illinois Country, where he had remained until 1702. After being promoted to the rank of Captain in 1701, he had commenced his tenure at Ft. Pontchartrain in 1705, as second-in-command to Cadillac, after which he had been promoted to commandant in 1710. His assistant commander at Detroit was "Jacques Charles Renaud, Esquire, Sieur Dubuisson, Lieutenant of a company of the troops in the detachment of the Marine Department, Second Officer to Sieur François de Laforest, Esquire, Captain of a Company of the troops..." This officer had been promoted to the rank of Lieutenant in 1698; he remained stationed at Detroit until 1714, when he was promoted to the rank of Captain and was relocated elsewhere.[100]

Upon Robert's return at the end of this summer of 1714, he learned that, during his extended absence, the seigneur of his sub-fief had sued him in the Montreal Court, for having fallen behind in his payments of the seigneurial fees. In order to force the habitant to pay these obligatory annual fees, the *cens* and *rentes*, on his two pieces of property at La Présentation, the seigneur had submitted his case to the Civil Court back on March 13. Apparently, Robert eventually settled this issue by making the appropriate payments.[101]

By this point, the wooden palisade walls which surrounded the town of Montreal had been standing for nearly three decades, and they were in need of a major upgrade. The initial stockade had been erected in 1685 or 1686, after which this first set of log walls had been reinforced in 1699. Over the course of the following nine years, the inhabitants had outgrown the area of this initial enclosure. This expansion of the population had required a commensurate expansion of the stockade perimeter, which had been carried out during the years from 1708 to 1710. Now, however, the King's Minister determined that all of the wooden walls of the palisade were to be replaced with much more durable ones, constructed of cut stone.

On November 6, 1714, Intendant Bégon decreed that these new and improved walls encircling the town would be built with contributions from all of the colonists who resided within the governmental district of Montreal (which extended to a point some thirty miles northeast of the town itself). This massive construction project would be carried out by means of the *corvée* system. This term referred to the amount of unpaid labor which each household was obliged to contribute every year to the seigneurs (in this instance, the Sulpicians), since the inhabitants were their *censitaires* or property-holders. In his pronouncement, the administrator declared that there would be drawn up "an allotment and tax of the number of days of labor which each of the said habitants will be obliged to furnish for the said *corvées*, in proportion to their possessions and abilities." The various tasks which they would carry out were planned to take place during those seasons in which most of the people were less busy, particularly after the autumn harvests had been completed. Thus, during the autumn seasons, they would be assigned to transport the rough-cut stones from the quarries to the assembly points, and during the winters they would haul these crude blocks to the workshops for further shaping. Other tasks of the habitants would entail hauling lime and sand to appropriate locales, for the fabrication of mortar.

However, instead of carrying out these assigned labors themselves, with their own teams of horses, each of the habitants had the option of paying for another individual to substitute for him. For each day of labor of a man, the levied tax was to be three livres, and for each day of labor of a pair of harnessed horses, the tax would be eight livres. These funds would be utilized to pay for replacement workers and teams of horses. For anyone who did not participate as ordered, with either direct labor or payments for substitutes, "the penalty for disobedience will be five hundred livres in fines for each of the contraventions, applicable to the King to be utilized for the expenses of the fortifications."

Between December 16, 1714 and March 25, 1715, the master roster of all of the colonists who were expected to contribute to this immense building project was drawn up. This document was entitled "List of the habitants of Montreal Island, Jesus Island, and the neighboring seigneuries who have been requisitioned to work on the fortifications of Montreal in 1715." After the 344 designated residents of the town and outlying areas of Montreal were listed, there followed the inhabitants (in this sequence) of Longue Pointe (37 listings), Côte de Vertus (27), Notre Dame de Liesse (42), Saint Michel (20), Saint Ours (50), Ménagerie des Pauvres (5), Boucherville (78), Côte de Verchères (25), Île Bouchard, Seigneury of Monsieur Dejordy (15), Côte de Varenne (21), Côte St. Michel (23), Côte Ste. Thérèse (15), Côte de Lachine (56), Côte St. Paul (14), Côte St. Pierre (5), Lachenaie (32), Rivière des Prairies (55), Île Jésus (46), Les Mille Îles (16), and Haut [Bout] de l'Île (74).

In the section of the roster pertaining to the Lachine seigneury and the neighboring La Présentation or Côte St. Gilles, here together identified as "Côte de Lachine," a total of 56 land owners were recorded. They were headed by the Captain of the parish militia forces, Claude Caron. Within the westernmost portion of this area, where the Réaume family resided, the second-to-the last entry read "Robert Réaume." The only land owner who was recorded further to the west of him was "Le Sieur Dorvalle." This was the Lachine-based peltries merchant Jean Baptiste Bouchard dit Dorval, the 57-year-old husband of Marie Antoinette Chouart. Some 24 years earlier, back in January of 1691, he had purchased the sub-fief of La Présentation from Agate de Saint Père.

After a number of years of ongoing construction, the entire set of encircling walls would be completed. Rising more than twenty feet in height, they would feature a total of sixteen gates, most of which would be positioned in the south wall, which faced the St. Lawrence River. The western wall of the town enclosure was located at the present Rue McGill, while the eastern wall was positioned just to the east of the present Rue Berri; the north wall extended along the present Rue St. Jacques, and the south wall ran parallel to the St. Lawrence. These ponderous barriers of mortar-laid stone would protect the community for more than eight decades, until they would be razed in 1804.[102]

In the spring of 1715, after Robert had been home from his latest trading venture for eight months, came tragic news. Two of his and Élisabeth's Réaume nephews at Charlesbourg had died, within ten days of each other. These were two sons of Robert's deceased brother Maurice, who had perished $6^{1}/2$ years earlier. The first of the two boys to die, the one who was $16^{1}/2$ years old, was buried in the Charlesbourg cemetery on April 23; his youngest sibling, age $6^{3}/4$, was interred there on May 3. It is highly likely that both of these youths had been felled by some epidemic raging through the population of the St. Lawrence Valley.

On the day following the latter boy's demise, Robert was called to testify before the Criminal Court at Montreal. In the transcripts of these proceedings, he was identified as a "voyageur departing for Michilimackinac." This notation by the court scribe certainly understated the high-level activities which the trader was poised to initiate.[103]

Within months of his return from the 1713-1714 commercial venture to Detroit, Monsieur Réaume had been chosen to become the official trading partner of the commandant at the Straits of Mackinac. Over the span of at least 22 years, since at least 1693, he had developed a solid reputation as a highly reliable and trustworthy voyageur-trader. Based upon those many years of high-level performance, he had now been selected to become a *voyageur-marchand*, the highest level of trader. In this capacity, he would serve as the full business partner of the commander at the most important fur trade facility in the interior, the one that operated as the very hub of the upper Great Lakes commerce. It was in this more northerly region, with its colder and longer winters, that the peltries of the highest quality were harvested, compared to the ones of lesser quality which were garnered in the more southerly areas of the Illinois Country and the region around the Detroit facility.

Efforts to reinstate the post at Michilimackinac had commenced shortly after it had been evacuated in 1698 and the facility of Ft. Pontchartrain had been approved by the King and his Minister in 1700. Interest in its re-establishment had run very high among the French residents of the St. Lawrence Valley. Before the post closures, many investors, merchant-outfitters, craft workers, laborers, traders, and voyageurs had all reaped generous profits from the trade which had been conducted annually at the Straits facility and at its far-flung dependencies. Although a number of the citizens had been able to participate in the illicit commerce after the closures, in varying degrees, the difficulties had become greater and the total amount of trade had been reduced, compared to the earlier era of open, legal commerce.

In addition, a great percentage of the furs of finest quality which were being harvested in the northern regions each year had been transported by native hunters and traders to the English on Hudson's Bay, due to the closure of most of the avenues of legal French trade in the interior. Many furs and hides had also been exchanged by the native populations with the English in the Lake Ontario region and at Albany, sometimes by direct contact, and sometimes through the Iroquois and even the supposed native allies of the French in the Detroit region. All of this had resulted in a major loss of income for a great many French inhabitants of the St. Lawrence settlements. Such losses would continue as long as trading licenses for the western interior were abolished, and the posts at Mackinac and its dependencies remained closed. These facts had finally convinced the Court that the military and commercial post at Michilimackinac must be recommissioned.

The administrators had become convinced that, having encouraged various native populations to move to the area of Ft. Pontchartrain over the previous decade, they had positioned these allied nations too close in proximity to the Iroquois and the temptations of English traders. Therefore, they had hoped that re-establishing the Straits fort would cause many of the allies to move back to the north, where they could be more effectively influenced and pressured by officers and licensed traders, in order to retain them within the French alliance.

However, even before the latter post had been recommissioned, events had taken place which had caused the relocation to the north of a considerable portion of the native populations of Detroit. During June of 1712, large numbers of the Foxes, Sauks, and Mascoutens, who had recently relocated to Detroit from the Green Bay and Fox River region, had initiated an attack upon the outnumbered French at the fort, as well as against the few native allies who had not been away hunting. With the return of several major contingents of allied forces, the tide of battle had turned, and large numbers of these three attacking nations had been decimated. Afterward, their remnants had fled back northward to the Green Bay region, to rejoin the remaining members of their respective nations.

Considering the volatile new situation in the west, Governor

Vaudreuil had requested permission from Versailles to dispatch Captain Constant Lemarchand, Sieur de Lignery and Captain Louis de Laporte, Sieur de Louvigny to the Straits with a number of soldiers. (The latter officer had served as the commandant of Ft. De Buade from 1690 to 1694.) Working from that central base, these men would gather allied forces for a campaign against the Fox nation and their supportive neighbors, as well as against the Iroquois, if necessary. Eventually, however, without even waiting for a royal reply, the Governor had dispatched Lignery with three canoes to Michilimackinac. (As far back as 1693, this latter officer had employed voyageur-traders at the Straits.)

With this three-canoe brigade of soldiers and militiamen-voyageurs, the recommissioning of the military and commercial fort at the Straits of Mackinac had been initiated, in the autumn of 1712. This small party of men had been bound for the community of St. Ignace, on the north side of the Straits, where they had then been based for the next three years. The entirely new post on the southern shoreline of the waterway would not be built until 1715-1716; these would be the first two years in which extensive numbers of Frenchmen would be available there for large-scale construction projects. Upon the establishment of the latter facility, along with the official reinstatement of the license system and legal commerce in 1716, the Straits fort would then become as important as, and actually more important than, Ft. Pontchartrain. Thereafter, these two posts would share equally the role as the central base of commercial, military, and diplomatic activities of the French in the western interior. (However, the quality of the peltries gathered at the more northerly facility would always exceed the quality of those garnered at the more southerly post.)

In April of 1713, the Treaty of Utrecht, which ended Queen Anne's War, had initiated a period of peace between France and England, which would extend for the next three decades. Even more importantly, it had instigated a new attitude at the French Court concerning the interior regions of New France. Firstly, the treaty had declared that the French were obliged to relinquish their posts on Hudson's Bay; this had interrupted the commerce which they had been conducting with a wide array of native populations via that watercourse in the north. In addition, the treaty had stipulated that the Iroquois were British subjects; it also permitted both the English and the French to trade with the native nations in the interior.

Therefore, considering this newly altered situation, the Ministers at Versailles had felt the urgent need to reoccupy the former interior posts, and to construct additional ones as well. The personnel at these facilities would strive to block any invasion by Iroquois and British traders into those regions; they would also work to retain the native inhabitants as French allies.

During 1713, Lignery's wife had dispatched voyageur-traders with new supplies of trade merchandise to her husband at the Straits. In the following year, although licenses authorizing traders to operate at the Straits had still not been officially permitted by the King, at least three parties of traders had received permission to carry out commerce there. In the autumn of 1714, the Governor had reported to Versailles that the amount of peltries which had been brought to the Straits that year had been considerably reduced. This had come about because the various allies had been in constant danger of attacks by warriors from the Fox nation, and had thus feared leaving their villages to hunt and trap. Thus, the Foxes were now actively hampering the very foundation of the economy of New France. The administrator had also reported that beaver pelts were now in short supply in the monopoly company's warehouses, in contrast to the former years when there had been an extreme surplus of them in storage.

In 1714, the Governor had postponed for another year the dispatching of Louvigny and the garrison of twenty soldiers to the Straits of Mackinac. However, he had ordered Lignery to arrange for the participation of large numbers of allied warriors and *coureurs de bois* in the upcoming Fox campaign, which was scheduled to take place during the summer of 1715. According to the planned outline of action, this campaign was to begin in the late spring, with the departure for Michilimackinac of Louvigny and twenty soldiers, along the Lake Ontario-Lake Erie route. (This number of troops appears to be very small for a major campaign. However, at this time, there were only a total of 628 regular soldiers in all of New France.) They would travel by way of Detroit, where they would pick up additional provisions en route. The party of about 200 militiamen-traders was to depart two weeks later, with their merchandise, via the Ottawa River route. The later departure of this civilian contingent would be necessitated by the delayed thawing of the northern waterways. Native forces from Detroit, as well as warriors from the Miami and Illinois nations, would join the northern allies assembled at the Straits, where the two inbound French armies and the renegade traders in the interior would also gather. As part of their amnesty arrangements, the latter men would be required to provide their own canoes, provisions, firearms, and ammunition. After leaving the supplies of trade goods and other materiel in storage at the Straits, the combined forces would paddle westward, to confront the enemies southwest of Green Bay. After the war, upon returning to the Straits, the traders would then spend the autumn, winter, and spring carrying out their commerce.[104]

This, then, was the situation when Robert Réaume was selected to serve as Captain de Lignery's business partner at the Straits, to carry out commerce for the two of them at the soon-to-be-built Ft. Michilimackinac. As the commandant of both the fort and the entire upper Great Lakes region, it would have been inappropriate and undignified for the officer to conduct trading himself. Thus, it was arranged that Monsieur Réaume would carry out this commerce for him, in return for an equal half-share of the profits. On the one hand, the commandant would provide extensive trading opportunities for Robert. On the other hand, the *voyageur-marchand* (Robert) would acquire the merchandise, transport it to Michilimackinac, exchange it for furs and hides during the following twelve months, and haul these products out to the St. Lawrence Valley, after which he would pay off their creditors and finally share the profits equally with the Captain.[105]

To take care of the necessary business arrangements of their joint operation (since the officer was at the Straits and the voyageur-merchant was in the Montreal area), the Captain's wife at Montreal made these arrangements in his stead. To facilitate such activities, before departing for the interior, Lignery had legally granted to her his power of attorney. On May 5, 1715, she and Robert visited the office of the notary Le Pailleur, to officially register the various agreements and preparations which they had together executed.

"Before the royal notary of the Island of Montreal, residing at Villemarie, who has signed below with the below-named witnesses, were present Dame Anne de Robutel, wife and procuratrice *[agent with power of attorney] of Constant Lemarchand, Esquire, Sieur de Lignery, Captain of a company of the troops of the detachment of the Marine Department, Commandant for the King at Michilimackinac, and Sieur Robert Réaume, habitant of this Island, who have together made the acts of partnership and agreement which follow. It is to be known that the said Sieur Réaume promises and obligates himself to leave immediately from this town with a canoe, to go up to the said*

place of Michilimackinac to join the said Sieur de Lignery, in order to carry to the said place the merchandise and articles which for their partnership are necessary things for the said Sieur de Lignery, all according to the general invoices of their partnership and particularly for the said Sieur de Lignery. The contracts for bringing up the articles which are charged to their partnership will be signed by both one and the other of the said associates.

The said Sieur Réaume will not be permitted to carry on any personal commerce, but will only apply himself entirely toward the profits of the said partnership. All of the expenses, such as the wages of the men, canoes, implements, wines, merchandise, and other things, will be mutually shared between them, without exception, and will be paid from the proceeds of the said merchandise, after which the profits which will be more than the sums paid out will be shared between them in exact halves. It is well understood, however, that the said Sieur Réaume may be obliged to use up all of the merchandise [supplies] in bringing here the articles with which he will be provided, that the wages of the hirees will be paid in card money, and that he will take care that the hirees deliver nothing [other than the cargo of the partnership]. Thus have they agreed, promised, obligated themselves, waived, etc.

[This agreement] made and drawn up at the said Villemarie, in the office of the said notary, in the afternoon on the fifth day of May, 1715, in the presence of the Sieurs Nicolas Perthuis, baker, and Vincent Lenoir, joiner, witnesses who have signed with the said parties and the notary after the reading was done, according to the ordinance.

Signed,

A. Robutel de Lignery, Réaume, and Le Pailleur"[106]

Within this document, in addition to the many details pertaining to the partnership, one of its most interesting features is the signatures of the two participants. First, Robert had finally learned to sign his name, after 22 years of generating documents which he had been unable to sign! Putting plume to paper, he had trained his hand to print "reaume" in separated, small-case letters. The timing of this small but significant advancement on his part was certainly not coincidental. At this point, he had been elevated to the highest level of trader in New France. He had apparently decided that, to carry out this role with the appropriate dignity, it was imperative that he be able to sign his own name.

Also of interest, at the bottom of this single-page document, Madame de Lignery wrote her own signature, "A. robutel," after which she added the latter portion of her husband's name, "de

Lignery." She apparently did this since she was operating in her husband's place, as his official and legal representative. At this time, Anne Robutel was 53 years old and had been married for 23 years. She had borne seven children during the decade of 1693 through 1703; of these, the first one had died after just fifteen days of life, while the fifth one had perished at the age of eight.[107]

One of the two men who witnessed this partnership agreement, the Montreal baker Nicolas Perthuis, was apparently related to Robert's former partner Pierre Perthuis, Jr. Both Nicolas Perthuis and Pierre's father Pierre Perthuis, Sr. had emigrated from the St. Denis parish of Amboise, in the Loire Valley. However, back in their home town, the two men had been born to different parents. In addition, Pierre, Sr. had arrived in New France in 1665 as a soldier in the Carignan-Salières Regiment. In comparison, the earliest documentary evidence of Nicolas in the colony dates from 1688, about a full generation later.[108]

The card money which was to be utilized to pay the wages of Robert's *engagés* was produced from playing cards. First introduced back in 1685, it had been designed to rectify the chronic shortage of currency in New France, which had been a problem for decades before that year of 1685 and would continue to be a problem for many decades afterward. The coins from various countries which did appear in the colony were constantly being drained off, to either France or Albany. In addition, the pelts of beavers and other animals, as well as hides, were often awkward to use as a portable medium of exchange. As an antidote to this situation, in 1685, Intendant de Meulles had created card money from packs of playing cards. He had done this by writing the particular denomination on the face of each card and then affixing his signature to it, to make it legal tender. In the ensuing years, other Intendants also resorted to the issuance of card money. In each instance, the cards were redeemable when currency sent from the King arrived with the vessels from the mother country. This ingenious system of producing money, which substituted for actually printing currency, helped to facilitate internal commerce within the colony.[109]

On the same day that Madame de Lignery and Monsieur Réaume officially registered their partnership, they also registered a major debt that they owed. At some point before this day, they had purchased on credit a very extensive amount of trade goods and supplies, from the very prominent Montreal merchant and outfitter Jacques Le Ber,

Jr. This debt was to be paid off about sixteen months later, which would allow a total of about four months for traveling to and from the fort, and about a year for trading there.

"Before the royal notary of the Island of Montreal, residing at Villemarie, who has signed below with the below-named witnesses, were present Dame Anne Robutel, wife and agent of Constant Lemarchand, Esquire, Sieur de Lignery, Captain of a company of the troops of the detachment of the Marine Department, Commandant for the King at Michilimackinac, and Sieur Robert Réaume, habitant of this Island, in partnership and community with the said Sieur de Lignery for the commerce of the said place. They have voluntarily and solidly, one for the other and each of them for the whole, without division, dispute, or disloyalty, acknowledged and admitted that they well and justly owe to Jacques Le Ber, Esquire, Sieur de Senneville, Lieutenant in the said troops, present and assenting, the sum of 5,732 livres 7 sols 6 deniers, [footnote added here: *with a deduction made of 36 livres*]. *This sum is for good merchandise which the said Sieur Creditor has furnished, sold, and delivered to them for their partnership and commerce, according to the invoice which he gave to them, and of which they are satisfied. The said debtors, solidly as noted with the said Sieur de Lignery, have given their promise and obligated themselves to return, give, and pay to said sum of 5,732 livres 7 sols 6 deniers to the said Sieur Creditor or upon his order, during all of the month of August of the next year 1716, or earlier if they return or their articles come down, in good beaver pelts at the prices of the office [of the export monopoly company] or in good peltries [of other animals] at the current prices of the merchants, in order to pay for the outfitting, under the penalty of all expenses, damages, and interests. To this end, they have, as solidly noted above, obligated themselves and mortgaged all of their possessions, both present and future. For the execution of these presents, they have selected as their legal residence [to which writs may be delivered] their residence at Villemarie, the home of the said Sieur and Dame de Lignery at the place called Predeville. Thus have they promised, obligated themselves, waived, etc.*

[This agreement] made and drawn up at the said Villemarie in the office of the said notary, in the afternoon on the fifth day of May, 1715, in the presence of the Sieurs Louis Lefebvre [Sieur] Duchouquet, merchant, and Vincent Lenoir, as witnesses who have signed with the said parties and the notary after the reading was done, according to the ordinance.

Signed,

Anne Robutel de Lignery, Réaume, Duchouquet, Vincent Le Noir, and Le Pailleur"[110]

Three days later, on May 8, Robert acknowledged his total personal debt to the Montreal merchant and innkeeper Jean Sargnat dit Lafond. In the process, the trader also agreed to pay this amount to Lafond's agent, the prominent Montreal voyageur-trader Maurice Blondeau, during Robert's sojourn at the Straits of Mackinac.

"Before the royal notary of the Island of Montreal, residing at Villemarie, who has signed below with the below-named witnesses, was present the Sieur Robert Réaume, who, being ready to depart to go up to Michilimackinac, has acknowledged and declared that he well and justly owes to Sieur Jean Sargnat de Lafond, merchant of this town, present and assenting, the sum of 197 livres 4 sols 6 deniers, for the general payoff of all of the accounts which they have had together up to today, of which he [Réaume] is content and satisfied. The said Sieur Debtor has given his promise and obligated himself to return, give, and pay to the said Sieur Creditor the sum of 197 livres 4 sols 6 deniers at the said place of Michilimackinac, into the hands of Sieur Maurice Blondeau, merchant, his agent, for him to keep in this town, in good beaver pelts at the price of the office [of the export monopoly company] at Quebec. The said debtor promises to send the said peltries from the said place of Michilimackinac to this said town, during which the said Sieur Creditor will run the risks [of any losses]. For everything pertaining to the present agreement, the debtor will be under the penalty of all expenses, damages, and interests. And to carry it out, he is obligated to offer and mortgage all of his possessions, both present and future. For the execution of these presents he has selected as his [temporary] legal residence [to which writs may be delivered] his residence at the said Villemarie [the information which was to follow was accidentally omitted from the document by the notary].

[This agreement made and drawn up] in the office of the said notary, in the afternoon on the eighth day of May, 1715, in the presence of Sieurs Claude Solvé and Jean Trullier dit Lacombe, witnesses who have signed with the said parties and the said notary after the reading was done, according to the ordinance.

Signed,

Réaume, Sargnat, and Le Pailleur [not Solvé or Lacombe]."[111]

In order to recruit a large force of militia fighters for the upcoming military campaign against the Fox nation, trade licenses had been unofficially reinstated during this spring of 1715. After participating in this campaign, these men would be permitted to trade in the interior for a year or more, based primarily at the Straits of Mackinac. After seventeen years of minimal legal commerce in the west, there was a great eagerness on the part of the French citizenry to engage in this newly legitimized trading. Likewise, the native nations in the interior happily anticipated the return of sufficient supplies of merchandise, which would be delivered to their home regions by the French. Between February 20 and May 22, at least 30 voyageur-traders were hired in the Montreal area, as recorded in notary documents there. Among these, the contracts of 17 men specified that they would be working at Michilimackinac, another 6 would be laboring in the Ottawa Country, and 7 would be conducting trade at Detroit. These 30 individuals were undoubtedly accompanied by many others who had not been registered with Montreal notaries. All of these men received a trading permit, at no cost, in return for their participation in the campaign.[112]

Although the preparations of Robert and the numerous voyageur-traders proceeded well during this winter and spring, all was not well in the military and governmental arenas. First, the officer who had been designated to lead the entire campaign, de Louvigny, had become so seriously ill during the winter and spring that he was unable to participate. Thus, Robert's business partner Captain de Lignery would serve as the overall commander of the forces once they arrived at the theater of war. In addition, the paddlers of several canoes which had been dispatched the previous autumn along the southern Great Lakes route, carrying diplomatic gifts via the Straits to the Illinois allies in their own country, had been stricken with measles while en route. As a result, they had been required to winter at the western end of Lake Ontario, and did not arrive at the Straits until May of 1715. News of a third difficulty, which would ultimately contribute to a derailment of the campaign for that year, arrived at Montreal in the spring: the corn harvest at Detroit during the previous autumn had been a complete failure. In an attempt to solve the latter problem, the French administrators quickly arranged to purchase 300 bushels of corn from the Iroquois south of Lake Ontario, as well as 130 bushels from the Miamis at the western end of Lake Erie.

In May, the large convoy of canoes, including that of Robert Réaume, departed from Lachine, bound for the Straits by way of the southern Great Lakes route. (None of them went via the Ottawa River route, as had been originally planned.) Travel along Lakes Ontario and Erie was necessary in order to pick up the corn from the Iroquois, which had been transported to the shore of Lake Ontario, and to take on at Detroit that corn which had been supplied by the Miamis. The large brigade included the 20 rank-and-file soldiers who would be stationed at Ft. Michilimackinac after the campaign, who were led by four officers. These 24 regular soldiers were accompanied by a considerable number of militiamen-traders, as well as a party of native warriors from the St. Lawrence communities. The brigade was scheduled to reach Mackinac by mid-August, at the very latest. After being joined there by many *coureurs de bois* from the interior and warriors from the northern regions, the massed forces would then travel five or six days by canoe, to reach the Fox River, southwest of Green Bay, by the end of August. In order to save as many of the scarce provisions as possible, with the arrival in Fox territory not planned until the close of August, the St. Lawrence convoy was not dispatched from Lachine earlier in May. In addition, thinking that a shortage of time was not a crucial element, the party did not proceed hastily, by any means, toward Michilimackinac.

The allied warriors who resided at Detroit, as well as those from the Miamis and Weas along the Maumee River and the Illinois nation south of Lake Michigan, were all scheduled to travel overland, converging at Chicago. From there, they would move northward for about seven days, in order to also arrive at the Fox River during the final days of August. Whichever army arrived at the theater of war first would encircle the Fox settlements, and await the arrival of the other allied forces.

From the very beginning, various unforeseen events contributed to the failure of the complex scenario. Since an epidemic of measles was then ravaging the Miami and Wea populations, very few of their warriors were able to join the expedition. When those few arrived at the pre-arranged meeting place of Chicago, accompanied by a French officer, they waited according to the plan. However, no other forces joined them, not even the canoes which were to have traveled south from the Straits, conveying to them news concerning the progress of the army from the St. Lawrence Valley. With measles continuing to strike them down, the remaining Miami and Wea warriors finally returned to their home villages. In the meantime, 450 Illinois warriors traveled to Chicago, where they likewise waited in their turn; when no one else arrived, they finally left on August 28, to also return to their settlements. The combined native forces at the Chicago rendezvous would have totaled some 800 fighting men, if events had transpired according to plan.

As was mentioned earlier, the convoy from the St. Lawrence, consisting of French and native fighters conveying provisions, munitions, and presents for the native allies, did not travel in an appropriately hasty manner. On August 30, Lignery wrote from the Straits that these forces had not yet arrived there, although they had set out during the month of May. (He was still unaware that the warrior army had not materialized at Chicago.) Therefore, when the eastern army would eventually appear, it would be too late in the season to initiate the actual invasion. As a result, the officer allowed about one hundred French traders who had previously gathered at Mackinac to depart for Montreal, upon their request.

Ultimately, the St. Lawrence brigade did arrive at the Straits in September. It was most certainly at this time that the new Ft. Michilimackinac was constructed on the southern shore of the Straits, by this considerable force of men. The numerous arriving traders (including Robert Réaume) required extensive amounts of secured and sheltered storage space for their merchandise and supplies. In addition, the garrison of 24 soldiers who were now to be permanently stationed there also required buildings in which to live, work, and store their supplies year round. Eventually, the commandant allowed many of the traders to disperse, to carry out the commerce which had been promised to them, even though their service as militia fighters had not yet been called upon.

No explanation for the tardy arrival at Mackinac of the St. Lawrence convoy was ever conveyed to Versailles, according to the official correspondence which has been preserved. However, it is to be suspected that the majority of the men in this brigade tarried long in the region of Ft. Pontchartrain, in order to carry out the commerce which was to have been postponed until after the military campaign had been completed.

But it is very highly likely that Robert and his hirees did arrive at the Straits in a timely manner, probably during the month of July. Circumstantial evidence supporting this statement was recorded in the account books of the Montreal peltries merchant and trader Jean Alexis Lemoine, Sieur Monière (age 34, married only since March 22 of this year). Back in April, he had hired two employees at Montreal to work for and with him during the following year, first at Ft. Pontchartrain and then at Michilimackinac. After traveling to Detroit with the massive convoy, he and his two men conducted transactions there as early as June 16. Even more surprising, the trio arrived at the Straits on or before July 30, at which time further transactions were recorded in his ledgers. Later ones were entered there on

August 15, 20, and 25. These various notations were all recorded by Monière at Mackinac over the span of a full month before Captain de Lignery wrote on August 30 that the long-overdue convoy had still not arrived there. Since the officer had expected the arrival of his business partner Robert and their employees at the Straits, along with their trade merchandise, in about July, it is to be assumed that they had indeed arrived there during that month, as had the trader Monière and his men.[113]

News from the Straits finally reached the St. Lawrence in early October of 1715, reporting that the Fox campaign had not been carried out and that it was to be postponed until the following year. In the meantime, however, further numbers of voyageur-traders had been hired and outfitted, and finally dispatched in September to various locales in the interior. These individuals included seven men who had been contracted for Michilimackinac, plus one man each for the Ottawa Country and the Upper Country, and eight men for Detroit. Three of the hirees who were destined for Mackinac had been engaged by Madame de Lignery on September 4, 9, and 10. These latter three men, traveling to the west by way of the customary Ottawa River route, had been employed to haul in additional merchandise and supplies for the partnership of the commandant and Robert Réaume.[114]

In the spring of 1716, while Robert and his employees were busily operating their commercial enterprise in the west, preparations were being made in the St. Lawrence settlements for the upcoming Fox campaign and the trading that would follow it. It was at this time that the license system was officially reinstated. All of the voyageur-traders who agreed to travel to the interior and participate in the military expedition were granted free trading permits, with the understanding that, after their martial service had been completed, they would be permitted to remain in the interior until the autumn of 1717. Those men who had ascended to Mackinac the previous year would be obliged to come down to the St. Lawrence settlements after the campaign, in the autumn of 1716.

On May 1, 1716, Captain Louis de Laporte, Sieur de Louvigny, and about 225 Frenchmen departed from Montreal, headed for Michilimackinac by way of the lower Great Lakes route and Detroit. Upon their arrival at the Straits, this eastern force, including the new additions from Detroit, was joined by the garrison soldiers at the fort and the legions of legal and illegal Frenchmen who were in the west.

Ottawa warriors who resided at Michilimackinac and Ojibwa fighting men from Sault Ste. Marie also joined the army. These combined forces, containing some 800 men (probably including Robert and his *engagés*), then paddled westward to the southern end of Green Bay, where they soon located the primary settlement of the Fox nation, on the Fox River. The siege of their stout fort, which contained some 500 warriors and about 3,000 women, consisted of heavily bombarding its inhabitants with four cannons and a mortar night and day, and gradually advancing a trench toward the fortifications. All the while, the French and native attackers hoped that the neighbors of the Fox nation, the Kickapoos, Mascoutens, and Sauks, would not send warriors to assist their besieged friends. Finally, the Fox leaders sought a truce, and subsequently agreed to the presented conditions. These consisted of a general peace, restoration of all of the prisoners whom they held, replacement at a future date of all casualties with captured native slaves, and payment at a future date of reparations for all governmental expenses of the expedition. These amazingly easy terms have often been explained, both at the time and since, by noting that this campaign was primarily a profit-generating one, for both the military and civilian participants and their backers in the St. Lawrence Valley. That is to say, the various participants were not as interested in subduing the Fox people as they were in benefitting from the commerce that took place in conjunction with the expedition.[115]

During the autumn of this year of 1716, Robert paddled out to the St. Lawrence, to settle the debts which he and his Lignery partners had incurred at Montreal, and to eventually split with them the profits that had resulted from their first joint venture. (Captain de Louvigny also traveled down from the Straits to the settlements, where he would spend the winter.) At the latest, Robert had returned home by the end of October, since he was involved in a case in the Civil Court at Montreal on November 2. During the following winter, Élisabeth became pregnant for the ninth time, in about mid-February of 1717.[116]

In this instance, Robert arranged the scheduling of his next commercial venture so that, if all went according to plan, he would be present to welcome this latest baby. On May 20, he hired a voyageur-trader to travel with him to the Mackinac Straits, where the two men would conduct business over the summer and then return to the St. Lawrence before the winter freeze would close the waterways. His young partner, Louis Émery dit Coderre, would turn age 23 in twelve days; he would also remain single for another 2^1/2 years.

"Was present Louis Émery, residing at Contrecoeur, who has voluntarily engaged himself to Robert Réaume to go to and return from Michilimackinac, and to assist in going up in bringing a canoe loaded with merchandise and in coming down in bringing a canoe loaded with peltries, which merchandise in going up and the said peltries in coming down the said hiree promises to take as much care as will be possible. He will obey the said Réaume, serve him faithfully, work for his profit, avoid any damage for him and warn him if any comes to his knowledge, and generally do all which will be commanded of him that is honest and lawful and that he will be able to do. He will not be permitted to leave the said service without the consent of the said Réaume, under the penalties which are carried by the ordinances, which have been presented to him by the said notary. This transaction is made with the stipulation that the said hiree will be fed at the expense of the said Réaume according to what is customarily done for voyageurs. In addition, he will receive in consideration the sum of 500 livres in currency of the country for his wages and salary during the said time, which will be paid to him by the said Réaume upon his return to this town. Thus have they promised, obligated themselves, etc.

[This agreement] made and drawn up at the said Villemarie in the office of the said notary, in the year 1717 on the 20th day of May in the afternoon, in the presence of the Sieurs Louis Lefebvre [Sieur] Duchouquet and Jacques Diel, witnesses living at the said Villemarie who have signed below with the said Réaume and the notary. The hiree has declared that he does not know how to write or sign, having been questioned after the reading was done, according to the ordinance.

Signed,

Duchouquet, Jaque Dielle, and Adhemar [but not by Réaume]."[117]

Oddly enough, even though the notary indicated that Robert had signed the agreement, he did not do so. In fact, the scribe did not even note in the text that Robert was present at the time the document was drawn up.

There are no surviving documents which might explain why Robert did not travel to the Straits this year in partnership with Captain de Lignery, as he had done in 1715-1716. Instead of his former association with the commandant, Robert seems to have made this commercial venture independently, without any financial partners or investors. Of particular interest is the rather extraordinary sum of 500 livres that he agreed to pay his single employee, for this stint of just five or six months of labor (more than double the customary salary).

In this year of 1717, Captain de Louvigny was once again traveling to the west, again focused upon the relationship between the Fox nation and the French. At the close of the peace treaty in the previous year, six Fox leaders or sons of their leaders had traveled out to the St. Lawrence. These men had been sent as a pledge that the highest-ranking leaders of their nation would travel there in 1717, to finalize the treaty and deliver the promised native slaves and reparation payments. However, during the following winter, while smallpox had raged through the eastern settlements, three of those hostages had perished. As a result, the Governor was eager to deliver to their people on the Fox River an explanation of their demise, and to enforce the peace agreement. (However, this bloody feud would simmer and sometimes flare up for another seventeen years, until the near-destruction of the Fox nation by French and native forces in 1734.) Besides this assigned task, Louvigny was also charged with delivering the latest amnesty declaration to the Frenchmen in the interior, and escorting out any compliant *coureurs de bois*.

The Governor's next letter to Versailles reported on the journey that the Captain and his convoy made to the west. This party, which also included Robert Réaume and his employee Louis Émery, made the trip in the especially short time of $4^1/2$ weeks.

"The said Sieur de Louvigny set out from the Island of Montreal at the end of May, since the length of the winter did not allow him to leave sooner. All of the canoes of the voyageurs who were going to Michilimackinac for their goods departed at the same time, and under his orders...The said Sieur was only thirty-two days in reaching Michilimackinac, arriving there on the 29th of June, in spite of the great difficulties which he had to surmount on his way. The waters were extremely high and rapid, due to the enormous quantity of snow which fell in this country last winter. His journey was a speedy one, for he returned to Montreal on the 21st of August. However, it was productive of no result, except that of bringing back to the colony all of the coureurs de bois. He was unable to settle anything with the Fox natives."[118]

It is not known whether Robert and his *engagé* traveled back to the east with the convoy that included the officer's entourage, arriving home in latter August. It appears that this schedule would not have allowed the two men sufficient time to trade all of the merchandise that they had brought with them. It is more likely that they returned home in September or October, after having conducted a long summer of profitable commerce in the Straits area.

In any case, Robert was definitely back with Élisabeth and their children in time for the arrival of little Charles Réaume on November 16, 1717. At his baptism on the following day at the Holy Angels Church at Lachine, the tiny lad's godfather was his uncle Pierre Réaume (Robert's youngest brother, a 26-year-old voyageur from Montreal who was still unmarried). His godmother was Marie Antoinette Chouart, who lived with her husband Jean Baptiste Bouchard dit Dorval and the numerous children of their blended family on the adjacent farm, immediately west of the Réaume property. (Some $14^1/2$ years earlier, back in May of 1703, Robert had stood as one of the official witnesses at the funeral of Jacques Jalot, her 14-year-old son, when a smallpox epidemic had swept like a scythe through the population.) Two additional witnesses were also present at this optimistic christening ceremony. One of these was the godmother's unmarried daughter Marie Geneviève Bouchard dite Dorval (age 21), while the other was the Lachine midwife Marie Madeleine Rapin, who was married to Jean Gabriel Picard. This lattermost woman had most likely assisted in the delivery of Élisabeth's infant on the previous day.[119]

After 21 years of spaced pregnancies and nine births, their brood was finally complete, with two girls and seven boys. Following the arrival of Simon, their first child, in September of 1697 (one week before the couple's first wedding anniversary), the intervals between their next seven offspring had been 26, 28, 24, 21, 23, 23, and 18 months. That penultimate child, Alphonse, had come to them in April of 1711. Then, final baby Charles had joined the family in November of 1717, after an interval of 6 years and 7 months. This extended period between the penultimate child and the last one had occurred while Robert had conducted his trading expedition of 1713-1714 to Detroit, his venture of 1715-1716 to Michilimackinac, and his trip of 1717 to Michilimackinac. In essence, Robert had been absent a great deal of the time during those latter years. During their total child-bearing period, Élisabeth's age had increased from 23 to 43, while Robert's age had grown from 29 to ten weeks short of 50.

However, Robert Réaume was not yet ready to retire. Six months after celebrating the safe arrival of their latest child (they may not have realized that Charles would be their final addition to the brood), he again signed a partnership agreement with Madame de Lignery, as he had previously done three years earlier, back in the spring of 1715. As was customary, Captain de Lignery's participation in the fur trade would be much less overt than that of his rank-and-file soldiers. The usual regular duties of the commandants at the interior posts (including de Lignery) involved policing the French population and handling diplomatic affairs with the native populations, rather than carrying out military activities. Their primary focus was upon maintaining peaceful relations among the various native nations, and between those nations and the French. To this end, he and the other officers conducted councils with native leaders, presented gifts to them, and served as the official representatives of the administrators in the St. Lawrence Valley.[120]

Thus, Captain de Lignery again sought out Robert Réaume to conduct commerce for the two of them, as he had done during their 1715-1716 stint as business associates. As before, the officer's wife Anne Robutel made the necessary arrangements in the east, acting as her husband's business agent and legal representative. Like the first time, Robert again agreed to spend about a year trading their jointly-owned merchandise in the interior regions, plus about three months traveling into and out from the area of the Straits. Likewise, the eventual profits from this operation would be split in equal halves by the two parties. However, this time, the commandant and his wife put up 44 percent of the outfitting costs before the expedition commenced.

"Before the royal notary of the Island of Montreal, residing at Villemarie, who has signed below, were present Dame Anne Françoise Robutel, wife and agent of Master Constant Lemarchand, Esquire, Seigneur de Lignery, Captain of a company of the troops of the detachment of the Marine Department, Commandant for the King at Michilimackinac, and by him authorized, of the one part, and Sieur Robert Réaume, habitant of this Island, voyageur, of the other part, which parties have formed a partnership together for the commerce of the said place. To that end, the said Sieur Réaume has obligated himself to depart immediately from this town, to go up to the said place of Michilimackinac in order to join the said Sieur de Lignery, and to deliver the articles sent to the said Sieur de Lignery and entrusted to him by the said Dame, with all of the articles which will constitute the said partnership for the commerce, for the profit of which he will work as advantageously as he will be able. After the [wages of the] men, canoes, wines, implements, and other necessary things have been paid for, the profit will be divided in halves between them.

It is understood that the merchandise and supplies for the exploitation of their partnership amount to 6,779 livres 9 sols, according to the invoices which were presented and furnished. Of this sum, the Sieur François Poulin, merchant of this town, has said that he furnished to the said partnership the sum of 3,774 livres 9 sols, while Madame de Lignery furnished 3,005 livres, making the said sum of 6,779 livres 9 sols.

The said partnership has acknowledged and declared that they are indebted to the said Sieur Poulin. And the said Dame de Lignery and each of them have, by their consideration, promised and obligated themselves to return, give, and pay the sums to the said Sieur Poulin and Dame de Lignery during all of the month of August of the next year 1719, or earlier if the articles of the said partnership returning to this town have arrived. Of these, the said Poulin will have the right to all of the said assets for the said sum of 3,774 livres 9 sols, while from the remainder will be taken 3,005 livres for the said Dame de Lignery, all in good beaver pelts at the price of the office [of the export monopoly company] and other good peltries [of other animals] at the current prices, to pay for the outfitting. The surplus will be divided in equal parts between the said Dame de Lignery and the said Sieur Réaume. To satisfy all of the above, the said Dame de Lignery and the said Sieur Réaume, solidly with the said Sieur de Lignery, one for the other and each of them only for the whole, without division or dispute, waiving the right of dissolution, have given their promise and obligated themselves to return, give, and pay to the said Sieur Poulin and to the said Dame de Lignery, according to their shares, the sum of 6,779 livres 9 sols, in beaver pelts and [other] peltries as was noted, according to the terms as stated. To this end, they have obligated themselves and mortgaged solidly, as was noted, all of their possessions, both present and future, and in particular all of the articles which will be brought back for the said partnership as the proceeds from the supplies which were delivered by the said invoice. For the execution of these presents, they have selected as their legal residence [to which writs may be delivered] the home of the said Sieur de Lignery near this town. Thus have they promised, obligated themselves, waived, etc.

[This agreement] made and drawn up at the said Villemarie at the home of the said Sieur Poulin, in the afternoon on the fifteenth day of May, 1718, in the presence of the Sieurs Charles Alavoine and Vincent Lenoir, called as witnesses, who have signed with the said parties and the notary after the reading was done, according to the ordinance.

Signed,

A. Robutel de Lignery, R. Réaume, F. Poulin et Comp[agni]e, Alavoine, Le Noir, and Le Pailleur."[121]

It is of interest to note that, by this point, Robert had added his first initial to his signature: a small-case "r" followed by a period (r.

reaume). Otherwise, the remainder of his signature had remained the same, since its first appearance in notarial documents three years earlier, back in 1715.

At this time in 1718, the young Montreal peltries merchant and outfitter François Poulin, Sieur de Francheville, was 24 years old. Six months later, on November 27, he would marry Thérèse de Couagne (age 21), daughter of the prominent Montreal merchant and outfitter Charles de Couagne. François' father, Michel Poulin, Sieur de Saint Maurice, had been the original seigneur of St. Maurice, just west of Trois-Rivières. After his death in 1694, this land had been inherited by his children. François, the youngest child of the family, had been only two years old at the time of his father's demise. Eventually, an immense deposit of iron ore would be discovered on the family lands of St. Maurice, and François would be the first individual to develop the famous iron foundries there, acquiring the royal permit for this operation in 1730. This would take place just twelve years after he had outfitted Robert Réaume for his final Michilimackinac venture.[122]

At the conclusion of this final expedition in the summer of 1719, both Robert and his partner Captain de Lignery descended eastward to the St. Lawrence communities. After seven years of service on both shores of the Straits, the officer had been replaced as the commandant of Ft. Michilimackinac by Louis Liénard de Beaujeu, who would serve in this capacity for the next two years. Aged 36 years, this latter officer had been married for nearly 13 years, and he and his wife had produced nine children at Montreal. Unfortunately, since this new commander had arranged his own *voyageur-marchand* to conduct the commercial activities for him in the Straits region, Robert had lost his prominent position there, at the very hub of the upper Great Lakes trade.[123]

At the age of $51^1/2$, it was finally time for Robert Réaume to retire as an active voyageur-trader working in the distant west. He had been laboring at regular intervals in the interior for at least 26 years (about half of his entire life), since at least the summer of 1693. During this extended stint, he had developed a fine reputation, living according to the ancient French proverb *"A l'oeuvre on connaît l'ouvrier"* (By the work, one knows the workman; in the English-language version, A workman is known by his work). After this long and productive run, he decided that it would be appropriate for him to spend his remaining years in the Lachine and Montreal area. However, he could not have known at this point that he and Élisabeth would be blessed with considerable longevity: he still had a full quarter-century to live, while his life partner would be granted even a few years longer.

When Monsieur Réaume returned to his family at the end of the summer of 1719, he learned that the clan had lost two close members during the previous November of 1718, while he had been wintering at the Straits. First, Élisabeth's mother had died on the second day of the month, at the age of about 72 to 75; she had been laid to rest in the cemetery at Contrecoeur on that same day. A week later, on the ninth, their niece Madeleine Réaume, who had been born at Montreal to Robert's brother Simon and his wife Jeanne Thérèse Catin, was buried in the Montreal cemetery; she had lived for just ten weeks. Both of these deaths had probably been caused by an epidemic of malignant fever.[124]

In the autumn of 1719, when Robert retired from fur trade endeavors and renewed his focus on farm life and carpentry work, the ages of his and Élisabeth's nine children spanned a full two decades. Their brood included Simon (22), Nicolas (20), Marie Josèphe (17 1/2), Hyacinthe (15 1/2), Jean Baptiste (13 3/4), Judith (12), Pierre (10), Alphonse (8 1/2), and Charles (who would turn 2 on November 16).

During Robert's final commercial voyage, back on January 10, 1719, Élisabeth had acted as the legal representative of both him and their eldest child (who at age 21 was still a minor). On that January day, the Sulpicians, who were the seigneurs of Montreal Island, had granted a piece of land to Simon, who was identified in the notary record as "son of Élisabeth Brunet and Robert Réaume, her husband, presently absent, present and assenting for her son." This property granted to Simon, located a short distance east of that of his parents, was described as being "on the coast of Lachine close to La Présentation." The long, slender lot of Robert and Élisabeth was located in the sub-fief which was called both La Présentation and Côte St. Gilles.[125]

On November 3, 1719, their daughter Marie Josèphe and her fiancé Joseph Fortier stood as the baptismal sponsors for a *panis* (native slave) at the Pointe Claire church. This individual, 7 years old, belonged to Joseph's brother Louis Fortier, who resided in the latter parish with his wife and five children. In fact, the youngest offspring of this couple was baptized on this same occasion, on the day following her birth.[126]

Ten weeks later came the nuptial celebrations of the two christening sponsors, Marie Josèphe Réaume and Joseph Fortier. These events were unique and uplifting for Élisabeth and Robert, since she was the very first of their children to be married. At this time, the bride-to-be was 17²/3 years old, while the prospective groom, a Lachine voyageur, was age 24³/4. In anticipation of these joyful events, the priest of the Pointe Claire parish (even though both the bride and the groom were from the Lachine parish) had published one bann of marriage, after which the Grand Vicar, Fr. Vachon de Belmont, had granted a dispensation of the other two customary banns. Then came the drawing up of their marriage contract on January 17, 1720, in front of the Montreal notary Pierre Raimbault. On the following day, the couple exchanged their wedding vows in the church at Pointe Claire. At this ceremony, the five official witnesses were Marie Josèphe's godfather Vital Caron (who was the Captain of the militia forces of the Lachine coast, and resided two lots east of the Lachine church), her brothers Simon and Nicolas Réaume, Jean Picard from Lachine, and Jean Beaune from Pointe Claire.

Interestingly, at both the baptism of the native slave and this wedding ten weeks later, the regular priest of the Pointe Claire parish, Fr. Debreslay, was not present, so the missionary priest Fr. Élie Déperet conducted the ceremonies. In the first instance on November 3, 1719, the cleric identified Marie Josèphe's mother in the records as "Isabelle Belhumeur," while in the second case on January 18, 1720, he described her as "Isabelle Brunet," even though her official, legal name was Élisabeth Brunet dit Belhumeur. Both of these notations point out that our protagonist was often called Isabelle, while the first record underscores the fact that *dit* names (nicknames) were often utilized in New France as one's family name.[127]

Sixteen months after witnessing for the first time a wedding of one of their children, Élisabeth and Robert reveled in another unique and moving experience, the arrival of their first grandchild. On May 19, 1721, *petite-fille* Marie Élisabeth Fortier was both born in the Lachine seigneury and baptized in the Lachine church. On this heartwarming occasion, the priest noted that the godmother was Élisabeth Brunet, grandmother of the baby, while the godfather was Jean Moison, the infant's grand-uncle (brother of Joseph's mother).[128]

The autumn of 1722 brought with it both the joy that is associated with the forward flow of life as well as the sadness that is linked to the end of life. First came the marriage of the Réaume couple's eldest son, Simon, who was about to celebrate his 25th birthday. In order to accumulate sufficient money to establish his own farm (he had been granted uncleared, forest-covered land near La Présentation 3³/4years earlier), the young man had hired on as a voyageur in April of 1720, in April of 1721, and in May of 1722. Now, he was about to join in marriage with Charlotte Turpin, the daughter of the deceased Montreal merchant and trader Alexandre Turpin and Marie Charlotte Beauvais (whose biographies have been already presented in this work), who was also the widow of Nicolas Legros. The Legros-Turpin couple had been married at Lachine back in February of 1713, after which they had produced two children there in 1718 and 1720. On the day after Christmas in 1720, Monsieur Legros had been buried in the Lachine cemetery, after which Charlotte had lived as a widow for 21 months.

On September 8, 1722, when the prospective bride Charlotte Turpin was 31 years old, the couple met with a Montreal notary to draw up their marriage contract, after which they were married in the Holy Angels Church at Lachine two days later. The three witnesses at the wedding were Simon's sister Marie Josèphe Réaume and her husband Joseph Fortier, and the groom's brother Hyacinthe Réaume, who was 18 years old. Interestingly, the Grand Vicar had granted a dispensation of all three banns of marriage for this couple. Pre-marital pregnancy had probably not been an issue in this case, since their first baby would not be born until eleven months after their wedding ceremony. (The direct linkage between Robert and Élisabeth and the present author would be forged by Simon and Charlotte, through their fourth child, Marie Josèphe, who would arrive in 1729.)[129]

Tempering the happiness of this family wedding were the weight of loss that accompanied the news of the death of Robert's father, René Réaume, although he had lived to the ripe old age of about 80 to 88. Back on August 16, 1722, Monsieur Réaume had been taken from his home at Charlesbourg to the Hôtel Dieu hospital in Quebec, where he had survived until October 30. On the following day, the ancient carpenter had been interred in the Quebec cemetery. It is not known how much time elapsed before this sad news about the Réaume patriarch was conveyed to Robert and his family, who lived some 160 miles up the St. Lawrence.[130]

The arrival of their first Réaume-named grandchild on August 14, 1723 was a cause for major celebration. Born to son Simon Réaume and Charlotte Turpin, little Marie Françoise was christened that same day in the Lachine church.[131]

Three months later, the clan was again in a celebratory mood, this time for the wedding of the second son, Nicolas, who was about to turn age 24. Like his older brother Simon, Nicolas had also hired on to serve as a voyageur, in August of 1721. Since this is the only known such work contract for him, this may have been the only journey to the west that he ever made, before establishing himself permanently in the Montreal area. By the time he was ready to marry in the autumn of 1723, he had already settled on Île Jésus, which was located immediately northwest of Montreal Island. He had chosen to live near the northeastern tip of this 21-mile-long island, in the parish of St. François de Sales. His bride-to-be, Marie Marguerite Berlouin, was a 28-year-old widow who had first married Pierre Charbonneau back in 1715. While living in the St. François de Sales parish, the couple had borne four children in 1716, 1718, 1720, and 1722. Monsieur Charbonneau had died in October of 1722, and their youngest child had perished six months later, in April of 1723. Thus, by the autumn of the latter year, Marie Marguerite had been a widow for thirteen months. On November 23, 1723, the couple drew up their marriage contact with the notary of Île Jésus, and on the same day they pronounced their wedding vows in the St. François de Sales church. The official witnesses included Jean Berlouin, the bride's father; Joseph and Michel Charbonneau, the two older brothers of her deceased first husband; Joseph Fortier, brother-in-law of the groom; and François Brunet, Joseph Brunet, and Louis Despatis.[132]

Some 1½ years after losing his father, Robert's mother died, at the age of about 72. On February 27, 1724, Marie Chevreau was laid to rest in the cemetery at Château Richer.[133]

About five months later, in the middle of the summer, Robert and Élisabeth visited the office of the Montreal notary Jean Baptiste Adhémar, in order to acknowledge the debt that they owed to Jeanne Pion, the widow of Jean Serré. Until the latter man's death at the age of about 70 in February of this year, this elderly couple had resided in the sub-fief of Côte St. Paul, some five or six miles east of the Réaume farm. About six or seven years earlier (in about 1717-1718), according to the notary agreement that was drawn up on this day of July 23, 1724, the Serré couple had loaned to Robert and Élisabeth the sum of 48 livres 15 sols in currency of France as well as forty tanned deer hides. As was written on the two promissory notes which Madame Serré produced, these two loans had been made to them on March 30 and October 5, but the respective years of the transactions had not been specified on those documents. The Réaume couple promised to repay these two debts during the month of August in the following year of 1725. If at that time they would not have the required deer hides, the creditor would be permitted to take other articles that she would choose as comparable payment. As their temporary legal residence for this transaction (to which writs could be delivered), Robert and Élisabeth gave the home of Robert's brother, the Montreal peltries merchant Simon Réaume, which was located on Rue St. Paul. As he had done previously, Robert signed this document "r reaume." However, in doing so, he omitted the letter "a" from his name, so he was then obliged to add it above the signature, above the flanking letters "e" and "u." For her part, Élisabeth signed the page "elsabe brunet," the same signature that she had applied to another notary document more than 26 years earlier, back in October of 1698.

A full seventeen years after drawing up this debt acknowledgement, on May 22, 1741, an addendum would be penned at the bottom of this 1724 document. At that time, Robert's son Simon would agree to pay off the entire owed sum of 48 livres 15 sols in currency plus forty tanned deer hides, delivering them to the creditor's son and heir, Joseph Serré.[134]

In September of 1724, 9³/4 months after Élisabeth and Robert's son Nicolas had married Marguerite Berlouin, she safely delivered a baby boy. One day after little Simon Réaume arrived, he was baptized on September 17 in the St. François de Sales church on Île Jésus.[135]

Five months afterward, another Réaume grandson joined the clan, born to Simon Réaume and Charlotte Turpin. At the February 8, 1725 christening of tiny Jean Baptiste in the Lachine church, one of the two sponsors, Robert Réaume, was described in the priest's ledger as grandfather of the infant. He was joined at the baptismal font by the Lachine resident Marie Buet (the wife of Jean Baptiste Legros, the brother of Charlotte's deceased first husband, Nicolas Legros), who served as the other sponsor.[136]

Three months later, on May 25, Robert traveled to Montreal to handle a major business transaction for his brother Jean Baptiste, who was serving at this time as the official interpreter for the commandant at La Baye (Green Bay). The notary document recording the transaction made it clear that Jean Baptiste was also working at the post as a voyageur-trader.

"Was present Robert Réaume, habitant of the coast of Lachine, at present in this city, who, in the name of and as manager of the affairs of Jean Baptiste Réaume, his brother, voyageur, at present interpreter for the King at the

Post of the Bay of the Sauks [La Baye, or Green Bay], has acknowledged and declared that he has received from Sieur Charles Nolan [Sieur] de Lamarque, merchant of this town, who was absent, his clerk Sieur Charles Benoît stipulating and assenting for the said Sieur de Lamarque and Company, the sum of 4,821 livres 14 sols 6 deniers in merchandise and belongings referred to in the invoice which has been delivered to him with the said merchandise and signed by the Sieur Pothier for the said Sieur de Lamarque and Company, to send to his said brother at the said post of La Baye according to their instructions, having stated that he is content with all of the said supplies referred to in the said invoice...He has promised...after the said term has expired, to render and pay the said sum of 4,821 livres 14 sols 6 deniers to the said Sieur de Lamarque and Company when summoned to this town or to the bearer in this town, in beaver pelts at the prices of the office [of the export monopoly company] and [other] peltries at the prices which the merchants receive for them, as payment for this outfit, in the month of August of next year [1726] or earlier if the said Jean Baptiste Réaume or his belongings come down before the said time, under the penalty of all expenses, damages, and interests. Under the bond of and for the execution [of these presents,] he has selected as his [temporary] legal residence [to which writs may be delivered] his residence in the home of Sieur [Simon] Réaume, located on St. Paul Street in this town. Thus have they promised, obligated themselves, and waived, etc.

[This agreement] made and drawn up at the said Villemarie in the office of the said notary in the year 1725 on the 25th of May in the afternoon, in the presence of the Sieurs [left blank, but they were Jacques-Pierre or Jean Paumereau and Ignace Gamelin] living at the said Villemarie, who have signed after the reading was done.

The words scratched out are null and void.

Signed,

Réaume, Charles Benoist, Paumereau, Gamelin, and P. Raimbault."[137]

On this particular document, Robert omitted his first initial from his signature, but otherwise his name appeared the same as it had on earlier records.

Four of Robert's brothers had, like himself, gone into the peltries commerce, working in various capacities. Simon (whose home on Rue St. Paul in Montreal had served as Robert's temporary legal residence for the above transaction) had become a prominent peltries merchant and outfitter, who often hired voyageur-traders to work for him in the west. He maintained close ties with the Wea nation of the Wabash River region. Brother Jean Baptiste (who received the large consignment of merchandise in this transaction) was a highly regarded interpreter and trader laboring at the La Baye post, then at the Sioux mission, and later at Ft. St. Joseph. Both of these brothers had been associated with the fur trade since the 1690s. The second-to-the-youngest sibling, Charles (born in 1688) had worked as a voyageur-trader at least from 1710 on, sometimes hiring other men to work for and with him as well. The youngest Réaume sibling, Pierre (born in 1691), had relocated to Detroit, where he was engaged in the commerce as a merchant and a voyageur-trader. At the time of his appearance as the godfather of Robert and Élisabeth's youngest child, back in 1717, Pierre had been identified as a voyageur by the officiating priest.[138]

According to the surviving records, Robert apparently did not have to make arrangements to ship this large amount of materiel to Green Bay, since Jean Baptiste seems to have traveled down to the St. Lawrence later in this summer to retrieve it. On June 27, 1725, the latter man's daughter Judith was baptized by the missionary priest at Ft. Michilimackinac, the second daughter to be borne by his native wife, Symphorose Ouaouagoukoé. Ten weeks later, on August 14, he was granted a trading permit, which allowed him to take a canoe manned by five paddlers besides himself back to the west.[139]

During a single one-week period in the heart of the winter of 1726, Robert and Élisabeth experienced both lighthearted optimism and heart-wrenching sadness. First came the marriage of their daughter Judith on February 17 at the Lachine church. At the age of 19, their sixth child (and the fourth one to be wed) joined in partnership with Jacques Lalande dit Latreille, a voyageur from Pointe Claire who was 22 years old. The official witnesses at the ceremony included Judith's brother Jean Baptiste (age 20 and still single), and three men from the Lachine parish: the merchant bourgeois Charles Milot, the voyageur Jean Legault, and Paul Mathias. The Grand Vicar, Fr. Vachon de Belmont, had granted dispensations of the second and third banns of marriage for this union, at both the Pointe Claire and Lachine churches.[140]

Seven days later, Élisabeth and Robert were thrown into grief by the loss of one of their toddler grandchildren. Jean Baptiste Réaume, the second child of their son Simon and his wife Charlotte Turpin, had survived for one year and sixteen days, living beyond the danger-fraught first year, in which the rate of infant mortality in the colony was a full 25 percent. However, the little lad's life did not continue beyond this point; he was laid to rest in the cemetery at Montreal on February 24.[141]

As the next winter began to settle in, another grandchild arrived at Lachine, brightening the outlook of her Réaume grandparents. On December 1, Marie Thérèse Lalande, the first baby of their daughter Judith and her husband Jacques Lalande, was safely born and was baptized in the Lachine church. This gladdening day came nine months and two weeks after the young couple had recited their nuptial vows in the same edifice.[142]

Alphonse, the second-youngest child of Élisabeth and Robert, turned 16 in the spring of 1727, a typical age for commencing an apprenticeship. Thus, Élisabeth traveled to the Montreal notary Adhémar on August 3, to officially register her teenage son as an apprentice of Gabriel Gibault, who was a master joiner in Montreal. Through this training program, he would learn the art of fashioning interior woodwork and furnishings. His mentor, Monsieur Gibault, was 32 years old; having been married for $4^1/2$ years, the craftsman and his wife Marguerite Demers had already produced three children and were expecting their fourth in about November.[143]

In the autumn of this year, another of their children established his own place in the world. In this case, it was Hyacinthe, at the age of $23^1/2$ already a master cobbler, who was marrying Agathe de Lacelles, age $18^1/2$. (Perhaps more than coincidentally, the bride's father, Jacques de Lacelles, was a master joiner, the occupation to which Hyacinthe's young brother Alphonse aspired.) First the young couple visited the Montreal notary Raimbault on November 16, to draw up their marriage contract. Then on the following day, they celebrated their wedding in the church at Montreal. On the latter occasion, the two official witnesses were Jacques de Lacelle (the bride's father or her older brother) and Jean Baptiste Lachapelle. The first baby of this new couple would arrive three weeks before their first wedding anniversary. Some years later, they would relocate to Detroit, where Robert's younger brother Pierre (Hyacinthe's uncle) had already settled, as early as 1722.[144]

Six weeks later, on *Ignolée* (New Year's Eve) of 1727, Élisabeth traveled to the office of the same Montreal notary whom she had visited back on August 8, when she had arranged the apprenticeship of her second-youngest son to a master joiner. This time, her goal was to officially register the apprenticeship of her youngest boy, Charles, who had celebrated his tenth birthday six weeks earlier. According to the contract (in which the youth's age was stated as twelve years, rather than the true number of ten, since most craftsmen would not accept a boy under the age of twelve), he was to be bound in an apprenticeship to the *couvreur en bardeau* (roofer in shingles) Pierre Gatien dit Tourangeau. This Montreal craftsman, 46 years old, had been married for almost 22 years; however, of the four children whom he and his wife had produced between 1707 and 1713, the youngest two had died in 1714 and 1716, respectively, while no further documentation has been located for his two older children, implying that they likewise perished at a relatively young age.[145]

Some 3^1/2 years later, in the spring of 1731, Élisabeth and Robert's son Jean Baptiste was married at the Pointe Claire church. On April 5, the groom (25^1/3 years old), having already settled on Île Jésus, joined in matrimony with Marie Louise Beaune from Pointe Claire. On this happy day, the official witnesses included Jean Baptiste's older brother Nicolas Réaume, as well as Jacques Beaune, Baptiste Beaune, and Jacques Chamaillard. Nearly a month later, on May 1, the newly-wedded couple belatedly registered their marriage contract with the Montreal notary Adhémar. Interestingly, in both the church record and the contract of marriage, the mother of the groom was identified as Isabelle Brunet, clearly indicating that she was very often called by this first name rather than by her official given name of Élisabeth.[146]

Now, six of Robert and Élisabeth's nine children were married; in addition, the youngest two were living away from home, ensconced in apprentice programs with craftsmen in Montreal. Thus, only one offspring, Pierre, who was 21^1/2 years old, was still single and possibly living with them on the farm. In time, he would move permanently to Detroit, where Hyacinthe, his older brother and master cobbler, already resided. Pierre would eventually marry at Detroit in January of 1738, and he would later become a bourgeois of this community.[147]

In the middle of the summer in 1731, Robert traveled northward some twenty miles from their farm to Lachenaie, to stand as a witness at the wedding of one of his nephews. Michel Renaud (age 28) from Charlesbourg, the son of Marie Réaume and her husband Michel Renaud dit Canard, had found his bride Élisabeth Rochon in the St. Charles parish at Lachenaie. At their nuptial ceremony on July 10, 1731, Robert was joined by four other witnesses: Germain Blondeau, Jean Rochon, Jacques Duprat, and Jean Baptiste Desormier.[148]

During the interval of 29 months following his wedding in April of 1731, son Jean Baptiste had suffered through the death of his wife

Marie Louise Beaune, he had moved from Île Jésus back to Montreal Island, to the seigneury of Pointe Claire, and there he had found a new life partner. On August 31, 1733, at the age of $27^2/3$, he remarried, this time to Marie Anne Chamaillard, age 23. On this August day, the couple first visited the notary Claude Cyprien Porlier, to draw up their marriage contract. Later in the day, they exchanged their nuptial vows in the Pointe Claire church, where the widower's first wedding had also been celebrated. The four witnesses included Joseph Charlebois, Mathieu Pilon, Thomas Richaume, and Alexandre Boison. As at his first marriage, both the notary record and the church ledger reflected that the mother of the groom was called Isabelle Brunet, rather than Élisabeth.[149]

Unfortunately, Jean Baptiste was not the only one of the Réaume sons who would lose his wife. Back in 1723, Nicolas had married the widow Marguerite Berlouin at St. François de Sales parish on Île Jésus. The couple had then produced five children there, by the northeastern tip of the island, in 1724, 1727, 1729, 1731, and 1733, before Marguerite passed away in early 1734. Needing considerable help in managing this brood, Nicolas remarried in this same year, taking as his bride the local woman Marie Catherine Labelle; he was age $34^1/2$, while she was $19^3/4$ years old. The couple first drew up their marriage contract on May 29 before the Île Jésus notary François Coron, after which they were married on June 7 at the St. François de Sales church on the Island. The witnesses at the wedding were François Hogue, Jacques Denoyer, and Jacques, Charles, Pierre, and Joseph Labelle.[150]

Some time after November 16, 1727 (when Robert and Élisabeth were described as residents of Lachine, in the marriage contract of their son Hyacinthe) and before September 22, 1734, Robert and Élisabeth relocated westward some eight to ten miles, to Île Perrot. On this 6-mile-long island, which lay to the southwest of the western end of Montreal Island, it is very highly likely that they were residing on the land that belonged to their eldest son Simon. (He had been working as a voyageur at intervals since 1720, and lived at the easternmost end of the Lachine seigneury.) In September of 1733, he had purchased property on this island, and eighteen months later, in March of 1734, he had been granted additional land there by the seigneur's widow.[151] However, he had afterward continued to live with his wife and children in the Lachine parish for a number of years, until the summer or autumn of 1741. There are no notarial documents which indicate that the aging Réaume couple either sold or leased out their two elongated lots back in the La Présentation area. Thus, one or more of their children might have been working the family farm and living there, in their absence.

On September 22, 1734, when Robert was 69²/3 years old, he traveled the considerable distance from their Île Perrot residence to Montreal, in order to dictate to the notary his testimony concerning his deceased brother Simon's business dealings. This was done in order to shed light on activities that had taken place back in 1714, 1715, and 1716, during the period of the first campaign against the Fox nation.

"Today, before the undersigned notary of the royal [governmental] jurisdiction of Montreal, residing there, appeared Robert Réaume, ancient voyageur, habitant of Île Perrot, who has said and declared that he knows that Pierre Denis and the deceased Simon Réaume had formed a partnership for one canoe-load of merchandise, which was advanced to the said Denis [by Simon Réaume] for transport by him [Denis]. Afterward, the said Denis departed by way of the Lakes [Ontario and Erie] route, on the 30th of September, 1714, in order to go and join at Michilimackinac the said [Simon] Réaume, who was traveling by way of the Grand [Ottawa] River route. The said Denis was halted by the ice in the autumn, and was obliged to winter with the hirees [probably two voyageurs] at Pointe Pelée [on the northern shore of Lake Erie, some 35 miles east of the mouth of the Detroit River] until the following spring of 1715, at which time he proceeded to the said Michilimackinac, and found the said Sieur Simon Réaume, his partner. Réaume made an accounting and inventory of the merchandise with which the said Denis had been loaded, and noted a shortage of the amount of 400 livres, which had been utilized for expenses during his wintering and expenses of the voyage, against which the said Simon Réaume seized the said merchandise.

In the autumn, the said Simon Réaume, needing a man to transport to this town [Montreal] a canoe-load of beaver pelts and other peltries, found the said Denis, and hired him for this task. The said Simon Réaume promised to him the sum of 200 livres, which was to be deducted from the sum of 400 livres, and also promised to cancel his obligation for the other 200 livres which were involved in the account of the said Sieur Simon Réaume, since he was his partner. The said Denis conducted the canoe-load safely to this town, and delivered it to the Damoiselle Réaume [Jeanne Thérèse Catin, Simon's wife], except for 30 dry beaver pelts, which the said Denis was obliged to give along the way to a native, who assisted him in descending under difficult conditions due to the lateness of the season, since he was afraid that he would be frozen in, which would have caused wrong to the said Simon Réaume.

In 1716, the said [Simon] Réaume outfitted the said Denis with one canoe-load [of merchandise], charged to his account. Upon arriving at Michilimackinac, the said Réaume seized the said merchandise from him, since he did not want to alone pay the voyageurs whom Denis was obliged to employ for Sieur [Jacques François] Quesnel [dit] Fonblanche, for wages which would fulfill their engagement contract without having to hire them. The said informant has affirmed that he was present, and that his declaration is true. According to the requirements of the act, it is granted that this declaration be made available to the said Denis at an appropriate time and place.

[This statement] made and drawn up at Montreal in the office of the said notary in the year 1737, on the 22nd of September in the morning, in the presence of Sieurs Claude Maurice [dit La Fantasie] and Arthur Laurent Guignard as witnesses, who have signed after the reading was done.
Signed,
Robert Réaume, Claude Maurice, Guignard, and Raimbault."[152]

It is of interest that, by this point, Robert had added his entire first name to his signature. Initially, after 22 years of generating documents which he had been unable to sign, he had taught himself to apply quill to paper and sign "reaume." He had mastered this skill in time to apply his signature to a document in May of 1715. Some time within the next three years (by May of 1718), he had added his first initial to the signature, a small-case "r," which was sometimes followed by a period. Finally, by the time of the above document in the autumn of 1737, he had changed the simple initial into the full given name "robert." He executed it in separated small-case letters, in the same style in which he penned his family name.

Four months after Robert had presented this testimony, their son Pierre (the seventh child in the family) was married in Detroit. Although he wed Suzanne Hubert on January 20, 1738, it would have been many months before this happy new would have reached the parents. That could only happen after the waterways were cleared of ice, and the canoes began to travel from the interior posts out to the St. Lawrence communities.[153]

On October 6 in this year of 1738, their youngest child, Charles (who was about to turn 21, and was thus still a minor until the age of 25), received a grant of land on Île Perrot. According to the official registration document, penned by the Montreal notary Jean François

Le Pailleur, the land was located "on the bank of the Catarakouis River, at Bride du Loup Point." It was ceded by Françoise Cuillerier, the widow of Joseph Trottier, Sieur Desruisseaux, the deceased seigneur of Île Perrot. Since young Charles was absent from the region at this time, the grant was accepted by his mother, who was identified in the record as "Élisabeth Brunet and Robert Réaume, her husband, his mother."[154]

Three months later, Robert and one of his sons-in-law were asked to stand as official witnesses at a wedding in the church at Bout de l'Île, by the western tip of Montreal Island. On January 7, 1739, Ursule Lalande from Pointe Claire, who was about 27 years old, married Michel Raynaud from the Vaudreuil seigneury. The bride's brother Jacques Lalande had married Robert's daughter Judith Réaume more than twelve years earlier, back in 1726. Besides Robert, another of the witnesses on this occasion was his son-in-law Joseph Fortier, who had married his daughter Marie Josèphe Réaume back in 1720. The other two witnesses at this wedding were Pierre Leduc, Sr. and Pierre Auger.[155]

On May 22, 1741, Robert and Élisabeth's eldest son, Simon, took on the responsibility of the long-standing debt which the couple owed to Jeanne Pion, the widow of Jean Serré. Back in the summer of 1724, they had acknowledged two loans which they had received some six or seven years earlier from Monsieur and Madame Serré: the sum of 48 livres 15 sols in currency of France, and forty tanned deer hides. On this May day, seventeen years after his parents had promised to repay the pair of loans, Simon traveled to Montreal to accept this responsibility, promising to deliver the owed articles to the creditors' son and heir, Joseph Serré.[156]

When Robert had presented his testimony to the Montreal notary back in October of 1737, he had been identified as a resident of Île Perrot. Some time during the seven-year period between that document and March of 1744, he and Élisabeth moved to the parish of St. Vincent de Paul on Île Jésus. This area was located on the southeastern shore of the Island, about twelve miles north of their farm at La Présentation. At this late stage of their lives, they apparently decided to permanently move to this locale so that they could reside with one of their married children, two of whom lived in this parish.

It is highly likely that this relocation had been precipitated by the move of their son Simon and his family westward from Lachine to their property on Île Perrot, on which his parents had apparently been living for a number of years. Simon's move, done with his wife and their large brood of children, took place some time after a notary contract dated June 30, 1741 and before the wedding of their daughter Marie Françoise 7^{1}/2 months later, on January 8, 1742.[157]

One of Robert and Élisabeth's married children residing at St. Vincent de Paul was Judith and her husband Jacques Lalande dit Latreille. After their wedding at Lachine back in 1726, this couple had produced eight children at Bout de l'Île between 1729 and 1743. Some time between their son Louis' baptism on August 29, 1743 and the baptism of their next child on June 8, 1745, they relocated permanently from Bout de l'Île to St. Vincent de Paul. Their last two babies would be born and baptized in this latter parish in 1747 and 1750; in addition, one of their children would be buried there on August 30, 1745.[158]

The other offspring of Robert and Élisabeth who resided in the parish of St. Vincent de Paul was son Nicolas, along with his second wife Catherine Labelle. After their wedding back in 1734 at St. François de Sales parish on Île Jésus, they had produced five children there between 1735 and 1740; these had been added to the five who had been previously born to his first wife, Marie Marguerite Berlouin. By the time of the baptism of their next baby on January 19, 1745, this family had permanently relocated to the St. Vincent de Paul parish. There, the couple would add three more members to their brood, in 1747, 1750, and 1751. Eleven years later, Nicolas himself would be interred in this cemetery, on March 22, 1762.[159]

Besides these two married children Judith and Nicolas, all of the other offspring of Élisabeth and Robert resided in the areas of Montreal, Lachine, Pointe Claire, Bout de l'Île, and Île Perrot, except for the two sons who had moved to Detroit. Thus, it appears that the patriarch and matriarch of the Réaume clan had been invited to live out the remaining years of their lives with one or both of their two married children at St. Vincent de Paul, where they could revel in the activities of their many grandchildren there. It is certain that Judith and her family had settled in this parish by some time between August 29, 1743 and June 8, 1745, while Nicolas had relocated there some time before January 19, 1745.

Thus, when it was time for the long life of Robert Réaume to finally draw to a close, in latter March of 1744, he was residing in this parish on Île Jésus. For many years while the children had been growing up, both they and Élisabeth had been accustomed to saying *"Bon Voyage," "Au Revoir,"* and *À la Prochaine Fois"* to Papa each time he had departed on his extended and arduous voyages into the distant interior. And in every instance, he had returned to them safely. However, when they saw him off this time, no amount of deft and powerful paddle strokes would be bringing him back to the family. Robert shoved off on his Celestial Journey on March 24, 1744, after which he was laid to rest in the St. Vincent de Paul cemetery on the following day. In the parish ledger, the missionary priest Fr. O. M. Semelle recorded that Monsieur Réaume had been 85 years old at the time of his demise. However, this information, supplied by a family member, made the patriarch nine years older than his true age. According to his baptismal records from the Notre Dame de Quebec church, Robert was 76 years and two months old.[160]

According to Randle Cotgrave's *A Dictionarie of the French and English Tongues* from 1611, the term "réaume" was defined as "real, essential, effectual, thorough, assured, certain."[161] Those adjectives certainly applied to Robert Réaume and the manner in which he had led his life, spending more than a quarter of a century paddling to and from the west and conducting business in those far-flung locales in an effective and trustworthy manner.

Reminiscing over their 47^1/2 years of marriage, Élisabeth most likely acknowledged that many of those times had been challenging for her, especially during the long stints when Robert's trading ventures had taken him away from home, usually for a year to fifteen months at at time. During those extended absences, she had managed both the farm and the home, with only the children and possibly hired hands sharing the labors. However, those commercial jaunts to the west had provided a considerable degree of financial support for the family, much more profitable than the work that Robert carried out as a farmer and a carpenter.

After the loss of her husband, and after nearly a half-century of marriage, Élisabeth lived as a widow in the St. Vincent de Paul parish for another 4^1/2 years, until July 19, 1748. On the day after her death, when she was interred in the cemetery there, Fr. Renoyer identified her in the parish ledger as Élisabeth Brunet dite Belhumeur, age 72, the widow of Robert Réaume. The three official witnesses on this sad occasion were Basile Bélanger, François Huguet, and Joseph David. Although one of her family members had indicated to the priest that Élisabeth was 72 years old, her true age, based upon her baptismal records at the Notre Dame de Montreal church, was 74 years and one week.[162]

re aume

Signature reaume, May 5, 1715.

elsabe brunet

Signature elsabe brunet, October 11, 1698.

Robert Réaume-Élisabeth Brunet dite Belhumeur
Lineage of Timothy Kent

I. Robert Réaume   22 Sept, 1696   Élisabeth Brunet
(René/   Montreal, QC   (Antoine/
Marie Chevreau)   Francoise Moisan)

II. Simon Réaume   10 Sept, 1722   Charlotte Turpin
(Robert/   Lachine, QC   (Alexandre/
Élisabeth Brunet)   Marie Charlotte Beauvais)

III. Marie Josèphe Réaume 7 Jan, 1749   Martin Levac dit Bapaume
(Simon/   Bout de l'Île, QC   (Pierre/
Charlotte Turpin)   Antoinette Beal)

IV. Marie Charlotte Levac 20 Jan, 1777   Étienne Lalonde
(Martin/   Les Cèdres, QC   (Albert/
Marie Josèphe Réaume)   Angélique Maupetit)

V. Joseph Lalonde   30 Jan, 1809   Geneviève Daoust
(Étienne/   Ste. Geneviève. QC   (Claude/
Marie Charlotte Levac)   Ursule Jamme)

VI. Joseph Lalonde   17 Feb 1835   Élisabeth/Isabelle Achin
(Joseph/   St. Polycarpe, QC   (Hyacinthe/
Geneviève Daoust)   Angèle Lalonde)

VII. Joseph Lalonde   ca. 1873   Josephine Chatelain
(Joseph/   Curran, ON   (Étienne/
Élisabeth Achin)   Marie Madeleine Taillon)

VIII. Élisabeth Lalonde   30 Jan, 1893   Joseph Bouchard
(Joseph/   Carrollton, MI   (Philéas Joseph/
Josephine Chatelain)   Adelaide Barbeau)

IX. Frances L. Bouchard   28 Apr, 1945   S. George Kent
(Joseph/   Detroit, MI   (George Kapantais/
Élisabeth Lalonde)   Eugenia Papadakis)

X. Timothy J. Kent   5 Sept, 1970   Dorothy J. Minton
(S. George/   Ossineke, MI   (Garnet J./
Frances L. Bouchard)   Elaine A. Reece)

Notes for Robert Réaume

1. R. Jetté, 1983, pp. 970, 257, 4; P. Gagné, 2002, pp. 148-149; M. Trudel, 1973c, p. 115 and map opp. p. 112; A. Lafontaine, 1985, p. 161 and map after p. 58; R. Harris, 1987, pl. 52; R. Chénier, 1991, pp. 215, 31.
2. H. Charbonneau and J. Légaré, 1978-1990, Vol. 1, Notre Dame de Quebec recs; R. Jetté, 1983, pp. 970, 842, 344; A. Lafontaine, 1985, p. 161.
3. R. Jetté, 1983, pp. 970, 475-476; P. Gagné, 2002, p. 149.
4. R. Jetté, 1983, p. 842; P. Gagné, 2002, p. 149; R. Chénier, 1991, p. 215. Apprenticeships: P. Moogk, 2000, pp. 206, 218-220. 315 n. 10; D. Miquelon, 1987, pp. 209-211.
5. "Les Rhéumes, 1979, inside back cover; R. Chénier, 1991, pp. 215, 23, 31; R. Jetté, 1983, pp. 654-655; R. Harris, 1987, pl. 52.
6. H. Charbonneau and J. Légaré, 1978-1990, Vol. 6, Notre Dame de Quebec confirmation recs; R. Jetté, 1983, p. 970.
7. A. Lafontaine, 1986, p. 34; H. Charbonneau and J. Légaré, 1978-1990, Vol. 6, 1681 census, Quebec, Household No. 191.
8. A. Lafontaine, 1986, p. 34; R. Jetté, 1983, pp. 831-832.
9. Y. Zoltvany, 1966, p. 31; W. Percival, 1941, pp. 51-52; R. Chénier, 1991, pp. 215, 22, 31.
10. H. Charbonneau and J. Légaré, 1978-1990, Vol. 3, St. Charles de Charlesbourg recs; R. Jetté, 1983, pp. 970, 1130.
11. Notary François Genaple, May 13, 1690, Archives Nationales du Québec at Québec (ANQ-Q); R. Harris, 1987, pl. 54; J. Marshall, 1967, pp. 361-362; R. Jetté, 1983, pp. 300-302, 907, 87, 1003.
12. R. Séguin, 1973, p. 585; S. Morison, 1972, pp. 278-279; C. Martijn, 2009, pp. 69-71; Journal des Jésuites for 1646-1647, pp. 176-177, 182-183 in Jesuit Relations, 1896-1901; Jesuit Relations for 1641-1642 in Jesuit Relations 1896-1901, pp. 60-61.
13. C. Stacey, 1966, pp. 544-545; W. Percival, 1941, pp. 51-57; L. Lahontan, 1703, Vol. 1, pp. 246-249; La Côte des Beaux Prés, p. 6.
14. Notary Antoine Adhémar, May 2, 1693, ANQ-M; R. Jetté, 1983, pp. 4, 906, 613.
15. R. Jetté, 1983, p. 603; C. Dupré, 1966, p. 173; A. Vachon, 1966d, p. 393; A. Vachon, 1966l, p. 626; L. Lamontagne, 1966, pp. 536-537; Notary Jean Cusson, December 1, 1669, ANQ-TR; J. Donnelly, 1968, pp. 153, 188, 193, 196-197.
16. R. Jetté, 1983, p. 603; A. Vachon, 1966d, pp. 392-398; J. Donnelly, 1968, pp. 174-176, 191-232.
17. R. Jetté, 1983, pp. 603-604, 243, 830, 655, 1077, 848, 906; Notary Gilles Rageot, October 1, 1672, ANQ-Q; J. Donnelly, 1968, pp. 200-205, 231; A. Vachon, 1966d, pp. 394, 396; A. Johnson, 1966b, p. 657; G. Thorman, 1966b, p. 606; T. Kent, 2004, pp. 54-55, 112-113.
18. T. Kent, 2004, pp. 124-125; E. Massicotte, 1929-1930, pp. 200-201.
19. Notary Antoine Adhémar, September 10, 1693, ANQ-M; R. Jetté, 1983, pp. 906, 346, 600-601.
20. E. Massicotte, 1929-1930, p. 201; T. Kent, 2004, p. 130.
21. R. Jetté, 1983, p. 970; R. Harris, 1987, pl. 46.
22. Notary Claude Maugue, June 13, 1695, ANQ-M; R. Jetté, 1983, pp. 697, 110-111.
23. N. Corley, 1969, pp. 383-384; R. Jetté, 1983, p. 697; J. Peyser, 1992, p. 228.
24. Y. Zoltvany, 1969d, p. 68; R. Jetté, 1983, pp. 110-111; J. Peyser, 1992, p. 228.
25. R. Juen and M. Nassaney, 2012, p. 4; J. Peyser, 1992, pp. 74-77.
26. L. Frontenac, 1698, pp. 95-96; T. Kent, 2004, p. 130.
27. E. Massicotte, 1929-1930, pp. 203-204, 209; R. Jetté, 1983, pp. 584, 1041, 916.

28. T. Kent, 2004, p. 138.

29. ibid., pp. 148, 150, 155; E. Massicotte, 1929-1930, p. 205.

30. R. Jetté, 1983, pp. 180, 902-903, 4, 575; A. Lafontaine, 1986, p. 117; P. Gagné, 2002, pp. 415-416; H. Charbonneau and J. Légaré, 1978-1990, Vol. 5, Notre Dame de Montreal recs.

31. A. Lafontaine, 1986, p. 117; H. Charbonneau and J. Légaré, 1978-1990, Vol. 6, 1681 Census, Montreal, Household No. 95.

32. R. Jetté, 1983, p. 180.

33. ibid., pp. 180, 881.

34. ibid., pp. 180-181, 1070-1071; J. Holzi, 1995, Vol. 1, 1693-1703, Case No. 001-0051a, July 3, 1694.

35. R. Jetté, 1983, pp. 881, 1017, 996, 580, 323; P. Gagné, 2002, pp. 415-416.

36. H. Charbonneau and J. Légaré, 1978-1990, Vol. 5, Notre Dame de Montreal recs; R. Jetté, 1983, pp. 881, 20.

37. H. Charbonneau and J. Légaré, 1978-1990, Vol. 6, marriage contracts; R. Jetté, 1983, pp. 180, 69.

38. J. Holzi, 1995, Vol. 1, 1693-1703, Case No. 001-0051a, July 3, 1694; R. Jetté, 1983, pp. 180, 613.

39. R. Jetté, 1983, pp. 180, 1070-1071.

40. H. Charbonneau and J. Légaré, 1978-1990, Vol. 5, Notre Dame de Montreal recs; R. Jetté, 1983, pp. 995, 936.

41. Notary Claude Maugue, September 19, 1696, ANQ-M.

42. H. Charbonneau and J. Légaré, 1978-1990, Vol. 5, Notre Dame de Montreal recs; R. Jetté, 1983, pp. 180, 1070-1071, 567 496, 1067.

43. Notary Antoine Adhémar, July 8, 1697, ANQ-M; R. Jetté, 1983, p. 785.

44. H. Charbonneau and J. Légaré, 1978-1990, Vol. 5, Notre Dame de Montreal recs; R. Jetté, 1983, p. 751.

45. H. Charbonneau and J. Légaré, 1978-1990, Vol. 5, Notre Dame de Montreal recs; R. Jetté, 1983, pp. 970, 180.

46. J. Holzi, 1995, Vol. 1, 1693-1703, Jud. Crim., Case No. 005-0268a, March 4, 1698; R. Jetté, 1983, pp. 180, 390-391, 404, 851.

47. J. Holzi, 1995, Vol. 1, 1693-1703, Jud. Crim., Case No. 005-0268a, March 4, 1698; R. Jetté, 1983, pp. 427, 829, 954, 952, 335; J. Denoyon, 1717, pp. 495-498.

48. Notary Bénigne Basset, October 11, 1698, ANQ-M; R. Jetté, 1983, p. 712.

49. R. Jetté, 1983, pp. 180, 1070-1071.

50. Notary Antoine Adhémar, December 3, 1698, ANQ-M; R. Jetté, 1983, pp. 834. 1702 land ownership map of Montreal Island by Vachon de Belmont: in Nos Racines, Vol. 22, 1979, pp. 430-431; M. Trudel, 1973a, pp. 172-173; recreation by G. Gallienne, 1977; and L. Dechêne, 1992, p. xxi.

51. R. Jetté, 1983, p. 970.

52. Notary Antoine Adhémar, June 19, 1699, ANQ-M; C. Rush, 1969, pp. 631-632; R. Jetté, 1983, pp. 970, 1083, 764, 712-713, 851, 389-390, 751.

53. E. Massicotte, 1929-1930, p. 205; W. Eccles, 1964, pp. 245, 267; C. Skinner, 1996, p. 68.

54. R. Jetté, 1983, pp. 180, 1070-1071.

55. H. Charbonneau and J. Légaré, 1978-1990, Vol. 5, Notre Dame de Montreal recs; R. Jetté, 1983, pp. 4-5, 710, 143.

56. J. Holzi, 1995, Vol. 1, 1693-1703, Jud. Civ., Case No. 008-0419a, June 2, 1700; R. Jetté, 1983, pp. 207-208, 549-550, 970.

57. Notary Antoine Adhémar, September 22, 1700, ANQ-M; T. Kent, 2004, pp. 161-162; R. Jetté, 1983, p. 697.

58. T. Kent, 2004, p. 162.
59. ibid., pp. 162-163.
60. E. Massicotte, 1929-1930, pp. 205-206; T. Kent, 2001, p. 1022.
61. Notary Antoine Adhémar, September 5, 1701, ANQ-M.
62. R. Jetté, 1983, pp. 915, 1083-1084, 639, 548; T. Kent, 2001, pp. 40-41.
63. R. Jetté, 1983, pp. 970, 1092, 936-937; E. Massicotte, 1929-1930, p. 205.
64. T. Kent, 2001, pp. 41-42, 1022, 54.
65. ibid., pp. 12, 42-43, 851; C. Skinner, 1996, pp. 296-300.
66. C. Skinner, 1996, pp. 298-300; L. Lahontan, 1703, Vol. 1, p. 138.
67. T. Kent, 2001, pp. 42-43; J. Holzi, 1995, Vol. 1, 1693-1703, Case No. 013-0608, August 24-31, 1702.
68. T. Kent, 2001, pp. 1029-1032.
69. W. Eccles, 1964, pp. 251, 262.
70. Jugements et Déliberations, 1885-1891, Vol. 4, pp. 629-631; R. Jetté, 1983, pp. 759, 901, 1115, 970.
71. H. Charbonneau and J. Légaré, 1978-1990, Vol. 14, Sts. Anges de Lachine recs; R. Jetté, 1983, pp. 199-200, 254, 590, 134. 1702 land ownership map of Montreal Island by Vachon de Belmont: in Nos Racines, Vol. 22, 1979, pp. 430-431; M. Trudel, 1973a, pp. 172-173; recreation by G. Gallienne, 1977; and L. Dechêne, 1992, p. xxi.
72. Notary Antoine Adhémar, July 16, 1702, ANQ-M.
73. T. Kent, 2001, p. 1032.
74. J. Holzi, 1995, Vol. 1, 1693-1703, Case No. 013-0608, August 24-31, 1702.
75. R. Jetté, 1983, pp. 970-971.
76. H. Charbonneau and J. Légaré, 1978-1990, Vol. 14, Sts. Anges de Lachine recs; R. Jetté, 1983, pp. 590, 966, 307.
77. Notary Antoine Adhémar, September 2, 1703, ANQ-M; R. Jetté, 1983, p. 252.
78. Notary Antoine Adhémar, September 27, 1703, ANQ-M; R. Jetté, 1983, pp. 862, 559.
79. E. Massicotte, 1929-1930, pp. 208-209; R. Jetté, 1983, p. 142.
80. H. Charbonneau and J. Légaré, 1978-1990, Vol. 14, Sts. Anges de Lachine recs; R. Jetté, 1983, pp. 477, 966, 911-912; E. Massicotte, 1929-1930, p. 208. 1702 land ownership map of Montreal Island by Vachon de Belmont: in Nos Racines, Vol. 22, 1979, pp. 430-431; M. Trudel, 1973a, pp. 172-173; recreation by G. Gallienne, 1977; and L. Dechêne, 1992, p. xxi.
81. R. Jetté, 1983, pp. 808-809, 595, 620, 663, 384, 428, 1976; E. Massicotte, 1929-1930, p. 209.
82. Notary Antoine Adhémar, September 22, 1700 and March 28, 1705, ANQ-M; R. Jetté, 1983, p. 977.
83. H. Charbonneau and J. Légaré, 1978-1990, Vol. 14, Sts. Anges de Lachine recs; R. Jetté, 1983, pp. 295, 419.
84. Notary Antoine Adhémar, May 30, 1706, ANQ-M.
85. R. Jetté, 1983, pp. 180, 902-903; P. Gagné, 2002, p. 416.
86. H. Charbonneau and J. Légaré, 1978-1990, Vol. 14, Sts. Anges de Lachine recs; R. Jetté, 1983, pp. 970, 966.
87. R. Jetté, 1983, pp. 970-971.
88. ibid., pp. 902-903.
89. ibid., p. 970.
90. ibid., pp. 970-971, 947.
91. H. Charbonneau and J. Légaré, 1978-1990, Vol. 14, Sts. Anges de Lachine recs; R. Jetté, 1983, pp. 970, 955-956, 911-912.
92. H. Charbonneau and J. Légaré, 1978-1990, Vol. 13, Ste. Anne de Bout de l'Île recs; R. Jetté, 1983, pp. 239-240, 947, 1099, 1000.

93. R. Jetté, 1983, pp. 970-971.

94. H. Charbonneau and J. Légaré, 1978-1990, Vol. 14, Sts. Anges de Lachine recs; R. Jetté, 1983, pp. 1083, 742.

95. J. Holzi, 1995, Vol. 2, 1704-1713, Jud. Crim., Case No. 025-1351, 1712; R. Jetté, 1983, pp. 970, 768, 751, 750, 614.

96. R. Jetté, 1983, p. 903.

97. Notary Michel Le Pailleur, June 2, 1713, ANQ-M; R. Jetté, 1983, pp. 670, 568, 6.

98. Notary Michel Le Pailleur, June 3, 1713, ANQ-M.

99. R. Jetté, 1983, pp. 970-971, 568.

100. ibid., pp. 310, 977; E. Massicotte, 1929-1930, pp. 214-215; plus additional Montreal notary contracts found by Gail Moreau-Desharnais in the Burton Historical Collections, Detroit Public Library.

101. J. Holzi, 1995, Vol. 3, 1714-1718, Jud. Civ., Case No. 029-1546, March 13, 1704.

102. Exhibits in Pointe à Callières Archaeological Museum, Montreal, 1994; ANQ, Ordonnances des Intendants, 1713-1720, Vol. 6, p. 54v., Archives des Colonies, C11A, Vol. 35, folios 330-352; R. Jetté, 1983, pp. 132, 134.

103. R. Jetté, 1983, p. 970; J. Holzi, 1995, Vol. 3, 1714-1718, Jud. Crim., Case No. 031-1699, May 4, 1715.

104. T. Kent, 2004, pp. 176, 178-183, 185; R. Jetté, 1983, pp. 704-705, 651; E. Massicotte, 1929-1930, pp. 200-201.

105. G. Allaire, 1987, pp. 416, 418, 422, etc.

106. Notary Michel Le Pailleur, May 5, 1715, ANQ-M; R. Jetté, 1983, pp. 902-903, 714.

107. R. Jetté, 1983, pp. 704-705, 1000.

108. ibid., pp. 902-903.

109. W. Eccles, 1964, p. 36; A. Vachon, 1982, pp. 280-281.

110. Notary Michel Le Pailleur, May 5, 1715, ANQ-M; R. Jetté, 1983, p. 690.

111. Notary Michel Le Pailleur, May 8, 1715, ANQ-M; R. Jetté, 1983, pp. 1035, 117, 1098.

112. E. Massicotte, 1929-1930, pp. 216-217; T. Kent, 2004, p. 191.

113. T. Kent, 2004, pp. 191, 197-200; R. Jetté, 1987, pp. 711, 713.

114. E. Massicotte, 1929-1930, pp. 216-217.

115. T. Kent, 2004, p. 207; E. Massicotte, 1929-1930, p. 218.

116. J. Holzi, 1995, Jud. Civ., Case No. 034-2056, November 2, 1716; R. Jetté, 1983, p. 971.

117. Notary Antoine Adhémar, May 20, 1717, ANQ-M; R. Jetté, 1983, pp. 403-404, 690, 352.

118. L. Vaudreuil, 1717, p. 588.

119. H. Charbonneau and J. Légaré, 1978-1990, Vol. 14, Sts. Anges de Lachine recs; R. Jetté, 1983, pp. 970, 134, 590, 912.

120. T. Kent, 2004, p. 220.

121. Notary Michel Le Pailleur, May 15, 1718, ANQ-M.

122. R. Jetté, 1983, pp. 938-940, 277.

123. ibid., p. 736.

124. ibid., pp. 903, 971; P. Gagné, 2002, p. 416.

125. Notary Pierre Raimbault, January 10, 1719, ANQ-M.

126. H. Charbonneau and J. Légaré, 1978-1990, Vol. 14, St. Joachim de Pointe Claire recs; R. Jetté, 1983, p. 430.

127. Notary Pierre Raimbault, January 17, 1720, ANQ-M; H. Charbonneau and J. Légaré, 1978-1990, Vol. 14, St. Joachim de Pointe Claire recs; R. Jetté, 1983, pp. 970, 430.

128. H. Charbonneau and J. Légaré, 1978-1990, Vol. 14, St. Joachim de Pointe Claire recs; R. Jetté, 1983, p. 430.

129. Notary Michel Le Pailleur, September 8, 1722, ANQ-M; H. Charbonneau and J. Légaré, 1978-1990, Vol. 14, Sts. Anges de Lachine recs; R. Jetté, 1983, pp. 971, 531.

130. R. Jetté, 1983, p. 970; Les Rhéaumes.

131. R. Jetté, 1983, p. 971.

132. Notary François Coron, November 23, 1723, ANQ-M; H. Charbonneau and J. Légaré, 1978-1990, Vol. 14, St. François de Sales de Île Jésus recs; R. Jetté, 1983, p. 88, 226, 271.

133. R. Jetté, 1983, p. 970.

134. Notary Jean Baptiste Adhémar, July 23, 1724, ANQ-M; Notary Bénigne Basset, October 11, 1698, ANQ-M; R. Jetté, 1983, pp. 1045-1046.

135. R. Jetté, 1983, p. 971.

136. H. Charbonneau and J. Légaré, 1978-1990, Vol. 14, Sts. Ange de Lachine recs; R. Jetté, 1983, pp. 971, 183.

137. Notary Pierre Raimbault, May 25, 1725, ANQ-M; R. Jetté, 1983, pp. 851, 883, 461.

138. R. Jetté, 1983, pp. 970-971. Each of these Réaume siblings deserves his own detailed biographical study; however, these are beyond the scope of the present work, which is focused primarily on brother Robert.

139. R. Jetté, 1983, p. 971; Mackinac Register of Baptisms and Interments, 1695-1821, in Wisconsin Historical Collections, Vol. 19, 1910, p. 2; E. Massicotte, 1921-1922, p. 210.

140. H. Charbonneau and J. Légaré, 1978-1990, Vol. 14, Sts. Ange de Lachine recs; R. Jetté, 1983, pp. 971, 634, 815, 698-699.

141. R. Jetté, 1983, p. 971; L. Dechêne, 1992, p. 59.

142. R. Jetté, 1983, p. 634.

143. Notary Jean Baptiste Adhémar, August 3, 1727, ANQ-M; R. Jetté, 1983, pp. 971, 494.

144. Notary Joseph Raimbault, November 16, 1727, ANQ-M; H. Charbonneau and J. Légaré, 1978-1990, Vol. 13, Notre Dame de Montreal recs; R. Jetté, 1983, pp. 971, 623.

145. Notary Jean Baptiste Adhémar, December 31, 1727, ANQ-M; R. Jetté, 1983, pp. 971, 470; P. Moogk, 2000, p. 218.

146. Notary Jean Baptiste Adhémar, May 1, 1731, ANQ-M; H. Charbonneau and J. Légaré, 1978-1990, Vol. 25, St. Joachim de Pointe Claire recs; R. Jetté, 1983, pp. 971, 70.

147. C. Tanguay, 1871-1890, Vol. 1, p. 511 and Vol. 6, p. 524.

148. H. Charbonneau and J. Légaré, 1978-1990, Vol. 26, St. Charles de Lachenaie recs; R. Jetté, 1983, p. 977.

149. Notary Claude Cyprien Porlier, August 31, 1723, ANQ-M; R. Jetté, 1983, pp. 971, 218, 935.

150. Notary François Coron, May 29, 1734, ANQ-M; H. Charbonneau and J. Légaré, 1978-1990, Vol. 26, St. François de Sales de Île Jésus recs; R. Jetté, 1983, pp. 971, 620, 271.

151. Notary Joseph Raimbault, September 8, 1732 and March 20, 1734, ANQ-M.

152. Notary Joseph Raimbault, September 22, 1734, ANQ-M; R. Jetté, 1983, pp. 971, 956, 792.

153. C. Tanguay, 1871-1890.

154. Notary Jean François Le Pailleur, October 6, 1738, ANQ-M; R. Jetté, 1983, pp. 716, 1092.

155. H. Charbonneau and J. Légaré, 1978-1990, Vol. 26, Ste. Anne de Bout de l'Île recs; R. Jetté, 1983, p. 634.

156. Notary Jean Baptiste Adhémar, July 23, 1724, ANQ-M; Notary François Simonnet, May 22, 1741, ANQ-M.

157. Notary Jean Baptiste Adhémar, May 22, 1741, ANQ-M.
158. R. Jetté, 1983, p. 634; C. Tanguay, 1871-1890, Vol. 5, p. 98.
159. R. Jetté, 1983, p. 971; C. Tanguay, 1871-1890, Vol. 6, pp. 525-526.
160. H. Charbonneau and J. Légaré, 1978-1990, Vol. 26, St. Vincent de Paul recs; R. Jetté, 1983, p. 970.
161. R. Cotgrave, 1611, "reaume."
162. H. Charbonneau and J. Légaré, 1978-1990, Vol. 26, St. Vincent de Paul recs; R. Jetté, 1983, p. 180.

XIII

Jean Baptiste Lalonde and his wives Marguerite Masta and Jeanne Gervais

Apprentice voyageur, then voyageur-trader working for Antoine Lamothe, Sieur de Cadillac, the commandant of Ft. De Buade at Michilimackinac. Captain of the Militia of Ste. Anne Parish

---

Jean Baptiste Lalonde was born on Île Perrot in the autumn of 1675, to Jean de Lalonde dit Lespérance and Marie Barbant. His father was clearly documented in New France for the first time on November 4, 1667, at the time of his first marriage contract. In this record, which was drawn up in the office of the Quebec notary Romain Becquet, the prospective groom was identified as "Jean de Lalonde, habitant living at Pointe aux Trembles in the seigneury of Dombourg, in the parish of Sillery, son of the deceased Philippe de Lalonde, master mason, and of Jeanne Duval, his father and mother, who when living resided in the Notre Dame parish at Havre de Grace, in the archdiocese of Rouen." At this time, the young colonist was about 26 years old. In the same contract, the prospective bride was listed as "Françoise Herubert, residing in this region [of Quebec], daughter of Pierre Herubert, hotel owner and operator in the said town of Havre de Grace and residing in the said Notre Dame parish, and of the deceased Marie Cocquemer, her father and mother." She was about two or three years older than Jean; both of them had emigrated from the same parish within the same town in Normandy. In this marriage agreement, Jean consented to a prefixed dower of 300 livres for his bride-to-be. However, at some point before the couple could be married, they mutually decided to annul their contract. Thus, they returned to the notary, who penned the following addendum to the end of their document: "The parties have agreed that the present contract is to be null and void."[1]

(This was not the first time that Françoise had cancelled a nuptial agreement. Just seventeen days before approving her contract with Monsieur Lalonde, on October 18, while standing before the same notary, she had arranged a marriage contract with Martin Guérard; but this first agreement had apparently lasted for only a few days.

After annulling the November contract with Jean de Lalonde, she would finally marry at third candidate, Jean Baptiste dit Saint Amour, at Quebec in the following spring, on May 3, 1668.[2])

The marriage document with Jean indicated that, in the autumn of 1667, he was residing in the seigneury of Dombourg, which was also sometimes called Pointe aux Trembles or Neuville. This swath of land, located on the north shore of the St. Lawrence, had been granted in 1653 to the seigneur Jean Bourdon, who was the colony's surveyor, cartographer, and engineer, as well as one of its important administrators. This seigneury commenced about five miles southwest of the settlement of Quebec, and its frontage extended along the river for about five miles toward the southwest.[3]

During this period, a large percentage of the male settlers came to the colony as indentured laborers. The contracts of these workers typically extended for a full three years, during which time they were not permitted to either marry or acquire land. Thus, assuming that Jean de Lalonde was not able to pay cash for his transatlantic passage, it is highly likely that he had arrived during the summer of 1664 or earlier, and had thereafter labored contractually for three years.[4]

Some time during the year following his failed marriage plans, before the autumn of 1668, Jean relocated some eighty miles further up the St. Lawrence, toward the southwest. He moved to the seigneury of D'Autray, which had been granted in 1637 to the same seigneur who held Dombourg, Jean Bourdon. This rather large stretch of land, which had a river frontage of about three miles, commenced some 35 miles north-northeast of Montreal.[5] On October 19, 1668, Jean and two of his colleagues visited the notary's office at Quebec, to officially register a labor contract with the seigneur's widow, by which they agreed to clear a considerable amount of land within the seigneury.

"Before Romain Becquet, royal notary in New France, residing at Quebec, and the witnesses signed below appeared in person Guillaume David, Jean de Lalonde, and Jacob Lheureux, who have acknowledged and declared that they rightly and justly owe to Dame Anne Gasnier, widow of the deceased Monsieur Master Jean Bourdon, who while living [he had died nine months earlier] was Esquire, Seigneur of Saint François and Saint Jean and attorney general of the Sovereign Council of this region, in the name of and as guardian of Jacques Bourdon, Esquire, Sieur D'Autray [age 16 at this point], the sums consumed and utilized according to the accounting of the reports which are transcribed below, both those which are individual and those which are in common, conforming to the said reports. These sums they

have promised to pay to the said Dame, both individually and jointly, each of them for the whole, without division or discussion, renouncing any such said divisions...For these sums, both in common and individually, the said Guillaume David, Jean de Lalonde, and Jacob Lheureux have promised and obligated themselves to carry out the labors on the said land and seigneury of D'Autray which follow. They will burn and clear, according to the customs of the region, three arpents [2½ acres] of felled trees located at the first boundary marker of the said place six arpents [²/10 mile] below the D'Autray River, in consideration of the sum of sixty livres; likewise, burn and clear three other arpents [2½ acres] of felled trees which are below the Bourdon River, in consideration of the same sum of sixty livres; likewise, fell and burn, according to the customs of the region, 3 arpents [2½ acres] of forest, measuring six arpents in frontage by two arpents in depth, adjoining the felled trees of the said D'Autray River, in consideration of the sum of sixty livres; and fell and burn as described above three other arpents [2½ acres] of forest adjoining the felled trees which are above the said Bourdon River, in consideration of the same sum of sixty livres. The said David, Lalonde, and Lheureux will be permitted to fell and saw up as noted above, if they are able, the amount of twelve [additional] arpents [10¼ acres] of trees, that is, six arpents below the Bourdon River and six others above the said D'Autray River, in consideration of the sum of twenty (sic) livres, which will likewise be deducted and removed from the aforementioned sums...The said David, Lalonde, and Lheureux will be permitted to sow the said six arpents of land which they will have burned and cleared without paying anything [in leasing fees] for the next year [1669] only. But the said Dame Bourdon has promised to give to them next spring, at no charge, all of the wheat which will be necessary to sow the said lands, the harvest of which will be for their own profit, or a lesser amount [of wheat seed] if they will not be able to sow all of the said six arpents, even with [the assistance of] Jacques David, his son....The said David and Lalonde have declared that they do not know how to write or sign, having been questioned according to the ordinance.

Report of that which Guillaume David, habitant of D'Autray, owes individually to Madame Bourdon on the 17th of October, 1668

2 shirts .... 8 livres (l.) 10 sols (s.)
1 old violet blanket .... 4 l.
1 old kettle of medium size ....2 l. 10 s.
Total .... 15 l.

Report of that which Jean de Lalonde dit Lespérance, habitant of the said place [D'Autray], owes individually to the said Dame Bourdon on the said day [October 17]

1 blanket .... 15 *l.*

2 combs .... 1 *l.*

1 power of attorney .... 1 *l. 15 s.*

Total .... 17 *l. 15 s.*

Report of that which Jacob Lheureux, habitant of the said place of D'Autray, owes individually to the said Dame Bourdon on the 19th of the said present month

3 pairs of moccasins .... 6 *l.*

1 caribou hide [for repairing and making moccasins] .... 10 *l.*

1 pair of French shoes .... 6 *l.*

1 pair of stockings .... 4 *l. 10 s.*

1 pair of underpants .... 8 *l.*

2 shirts .... 9 *l.*

Fabric for making mittens .... 2 *l.*

1 blanket .... 20 *l.*

1 pair of snowshoes .... 12 *l.*

1 gun .... 15 *l.*

3 guabettes (?) [very inexpensive items] .... 0 *l. 5 s.*

1 power of attorney .... 1 *l.*

Total .... 93 *l. 15 s.*

Report of that which the said Guillaume David, Jean Lalonde, and Jacob Lheureux owe together to the said Dame Bourdon, advanced to assist them in their setting up at the said place of D'Autray
Furnished to the said David and Lalonde on the 17th of the present month and year [October 17, 1668]

1 large towing line [for canoes] .... 4 *l. 10 s.*

1 small towing line .... 1 *l.*

1 hogshead of French flour .... 58 *l.*

3 bushels of wheat .... 12 *l.*

2 bushels of green peas .... 8 *l.*

30 pounds of side pork .... 10 *l. 10 s.*

1 hogshead of eels .... 15 *l.*

6 half-gallons of brandy .... 18 *l.*

8 pounds of tobacco .... 8 *l.*

4 pounds of gunpowder .... 6 *l.*

1 dozen gun flints .... 0 *l. 10 s.*

1 dozen catfish hooks..*0 l. 19 s.*
4 axes.. *12 l.*
1 empty hogshead and 1 empty half-hogshead................................*3 l.*
Total ....*163 l. [actually, 158 l. 9 s.]*

Furnished to the said Lheureux on the 19th of the present month
1 half-hogshead of French flour...*28 l. 18 s.*
1 bushel of green peas...*4 l.*
14 pounds of side pork..*4 l. 18 s.*
1 bushel of salt..*3 l.*
2 half-gallons of brandy ....*6 l.*
2 pounds of tobacco ....*2 l.*
1 cooking pot ....*2 l. 10 s.*
2 pounds of gunpowder...*3 l.*
10 pounds of lead [for balls and shot] ....*9 l. 10 s.*
1 mackerel-fishing line...*3 l.*
3 large axes and one small axe ....*10 l. 10 s.*
1 hoe ....*3 l.*
2 large baskets ....*2 l.*
1 small keg for the said brandy ....*1 l. 10 s.*
1 empty half-hogshead..*1 l. 5 s.*
For paying expenses...*25 l.*
For drawing up the present document and making a certified copy.........*3 l.*
Total ....*94 l. 11 s. [actually, 112 l. 16 s.]"*[6]

Not counting the individual debts of the three men (15 livres, 17 livres 15 sols, and 93 livres 15 sols, respectively), their total amount of joint indebtedness for the outfitting amounted to $257^1/2$ livres. (If the notary had done the addition correctly, the sum would have been even greater, $271^1/4$ livres.) In comparison, the total income which they would generate from many months of clearing brush, removing stumps, and burning the felled trees, brush, and stumps on five acres, and also felling the standing trees, clearing the brush, removing the stumps, and burning all of the wood on another five acres, would amount to 240 livres. According to the contract, they could add 20 additional livres of income to this amount, by felling the trees on ten additional acres, limbing those trees, and cutting the trunks into lengths for wood (without having to clear the brush, remove the stumps, and burn the waste wood on those acres). Thus, their maximum income for laboring as woodsmen throughout the winter and spring could total a maximum of 260 livres. However, although this sum was apparently appropriate for the amount of expected labor, this money would entirely disappear when they would pay off their joint outfitting debt of $257^{1}/2$ livres!

The extra potential payment of just 20 livres, for felling and sawing up the trees on the second ten acres of forest, at first glance seems to be amazingly low. This seems especially so when this sum is compared to the considerable amount of 240 livres that the men were to receive for their labors on the first ten acres. However, it was a fact of life that felling, limbing, and cutting up trees did not pay well compared to fully clearing land, making it ready for agriculture. This latter project, carried out after the trees had been felled and removed or burned and the brush had been cleared and burned, also included the very laborious task of stump removal. This entailed digging deeply around the stumps to expose their bases, and then sawing, chopping, and burning them down to a considerably distance below the surface level, beneath the reach of the plow's cutting blade and moldboard. These various steps comprised what was described in the above document as "burn and clear, according to the customs of the region."

As odd as it may seem, if the three partners were in fact not making any profits from their months of labor as woodsmen, they must have been counting on the sale of their first crop of wheat to generate their actual income. This crop would cost them nothing monetarily, just their physical labor of preparing the ground, planting, and harvesting. Their profits from these farming activities would be considerably enhanced, since Madame Bourdon had agreed that, during their first year of farming, she would not charge them any leasing fees for the use of the land, and she would also provide the wheat seed to them at no cost.

One of Jean's two partners in this endeavor was Guillaume David, about 32 years old, who had been married for some twelve years. (His older brother was the pioneering trader Claude David, whose biography has already been presented earlier in this work.) Guillaume and his wife Marie Armand had already produced five offspring, including their eldest child and only son Jacques, who would turn age 11 in four days (he would assist in the spring planting of the newly-cleared land at his father's job site). Of their four daughters, the oldest one had died at the age of three weeks, back in 1659. By 1674, six years after this land-clearing contract, the little David family would be residing at Sorel, the seigneury which was located directly across the St. Lawrence from D'Autray; their last child would be born there during the winter of 1678.[7]

Jean's other colleague, Jacob Lheureux, was about 20 to 22 years old at this time, and he was unmarried. Two years earlier, in the census of 1666, he had been listed as a domestic servant in the household of Élie Bourbeau at Trois Rivières. Five years after this contract, in 1673, he would be residing on Île d'Orléans, downriver from Quebec. Compared to the two other partners, Jacob had not previously equipped himself to undertake a long winter and spring of outdoor labor. Thus, at this time, he was obliged to lay out the considerable expenditure of $93^3/4$ livres, to outfit himself for the upcoming employment. In contrast, both Guillaume and Jean apparently already owned all or most of the necessary clothing, plus a gun, a pair of snowshoes, and the other personal articles that were needed for traveling and working outdoors during the Canadian winter.[8]

Within eleven months of arranging this forestry and farming contract, Jean de Lalonde decided that he needed to find a woman who would be his life's partner. After traveling from his work site at D'Autray some eighty miles downriver to Quebec, Jean thought that he had finally found the one. This was Jeanne Poiré, about 21 to 28 years old, who had emigrated from the St. Laurent parish in Paris. On September 27, 1669, Jean and his fiancée gathered with various friends at the home of his employer Madame Bourdon, to draw up their marriage contract. In this document, the notary identified the prospective groom with all of the same information concerning his origins as had been recorded in his first nuptial agreement, which had been written nearly two years earlier, back in 1667. However, this time he was identified as an "habitant of the seigneury of D'Autray." As in the former case, Jean again consented to a prefixed dower of 300 livres for his bride-to-be. However, the plans of this couple were not to be fulfilled: they mutually annulled the contract within a matter of days. In fact, just seventeen days after arranging this marriage agreement with Monsieur Lalonde, Jeanne Poiré arranged another one on October 14, this time with Jean Hardy. This latter couple was married in the Quebec church on October 21.[9]

But Jean was not to be deterred in his quest to find a bride to join him at D'Autray. On October 13, on the day before Jeanne Poiré arranged her new marriage contract, Jean arranged his own new nuptial agreement, again at the home of Madame Bourdon. This time, he made his commitments to Perrette Vaillant, another young woman who had emigrated from Paris. As before, he pledged the sum of 300 livres as her prefixed dower. But again, for some reason, these marriage plans did not come to fruition, and the contract was mutually annulled within a matter of days.[10] (We are left wondering why this had happened to Jean, and asking whether the problems were with him or with the three different prospective mates whom he had chosen.)

After this latest disappointment, Jean returned to the area of his base of operations, the seigneury of D'Autray. At this point, being about 28 years old, he felt that this was certainly the right time to marry, settle down, and raise a family. Since hope springs eternal, he continued his quest to find a partner with whom he could share the rest of his life. Within just a few weeks, he had located that very person, and he found himself arranging a marriage contract with her on November 14, 1669 (exactly one month after he had made his agreement with Perrette Vaillant). This was Jean's fourth nuptial contract, and the third one that he had arranged within the span of seven weeks, since September 27. It had indeed been a very busy autumn, fraught with many more uncertainties than were usually involved in his tasks of cutting trees, removing stumps, and raising wheat.

This time, the festive event of drawing up the marriage contract took place across the St. Lawrence from D'Autray, at the seigneury of Sorel, in the home of Gabriel Gibault. The document was written out by the notary Antoine Adhémar, who served during this period as the notary here at Sorel as well as in the seigneuries of Cap de la Madeleine and Batiscan, northeast of Trois-Rivières. The text did not indicate that Jean was a resident of the seigneury of D'Autray, but that fact had been included in his prior two marriage contracts a number of weeks earlier, on September 27 and October 13.

"To draw up [this agreement, appeared] in person Jean de Lalonde, son of the deceased Philippe de Lalonde and of Jeanne Duval, a native of the town of Le Havre, the parish of Notre Dame in the archdiocese of Rouen, of the one part, and Marie Baban [Barbant], daughter of Alexandre [Baban] and of Marie Le Noble, a native of the town of Dieppe, in the parish of St. Rémy in the archdiocese of Tours...The said Lalonde had declared that the said Baban, his future wife, has brought [to the marriage as her dowry] the sum of two hundred livres...And as an increase and dower, the said Lalonde has willingly and freely declared that he has voluntarily given to the said Baban, his wife, the sum of three hundred livres...

[This agreement] made and drawn up at the said Sorel in the home of Gabriel Gibault [dit Poitevin], habitant of the said place, on the fourteenth of November, 1669 in the afternoon, in the presence of Adrien Bétourné [dit Laviolette] and Vincent Morineau, habitants of the said D'Autray, Gabriel Gibault, Mathias Batachon, and Daniel Jonan, habitants of Saint Ours, Pierre Gibault and Jacques Bissonnet, habitants of the seigneury of Varennes, Méry Arpin, habitant of Contrecoeur, Pierre Armand and Michel Germain of the said Contrecoeur, Jean Bertrand dit ____ and Jean Bonan dit Labaudette, soldiers of the Company of Monsieur de Saint Ours, Marie Deshayes, wife of the said Bétourné, and Suzanne Durand, wife of the said [Gabriel] Gibault, who have signed below. The said parties [Jean and Marie] have said that they do not know how to write or sign, after being questioned according to the ordinance, but they have made their marks."[11]

Near the bottom of the second page of the document, at the place where the notary indicated "mark of the said de Lalonde," Jean drew a symbol which appears to represent a mortise chisel with a short handle, in an upright position with its sharply angled bit facing toward the left. Where the scribe wrote "mark of the said Barban," Marie drew a rather large +.

Besides the seigneury of D'Autray, the other four locales at which the numerous witnesses resided included, from northeast to southwest, Sorel, St. Ours, Contrecoeur, and Varennes. Located along the eastern shoreline of the St. Lawrence, the latter four places extended over the distance of some thirty miles, to a location directly opposite the northeastern tip of Montreal Island. These five locales appear to have been the places where the majority of Jean's friends and acquaintances lived.

When the Carignan-Salières Regiment had been recalled to France some sixteen months earlier, during the summer of 1668, hundreds of the troops had remained behind to become colonists, and large numbers of them had settled in these particular seigneuries. Back in 1665, more than 1,200 soldiers (and copious materiel to support them) had been dispatched by the King, with the intention of suppressing the marauding Iroquois once and for all. Many of these forces, along with hundreds of militia fighters from Quebec and Montreal and about a hundred allied Algonkin and Huron warriors from the St. Lawrence settlements, had conducted two major campaigns into the home territory of the Mohawk nation. The first of these had been carried out during the winter of 1666, while the second and much more effective expedition had been conducted in the following autumn. In

July of 1667, a treaty had been signed with each of the five Iroquois nations, which had established peaceful relations between them, the French, and the native allies of the French. This treaty would hold for nearly twenty years (until 1686), and during this extended period of peace, New France would experience a tremendous surge in population growth, geographical expansion, and economic progress.

Upon the return of the Carignan-Salières Regiment to the mother country, more than 400 of the 1,200 men, including the majority of the younger officers and soldiers, had decided to become settlers. As an inducement to stay on as permanent residents, each of the rank-and-file soldiers had been promised either 100 livres or 50 livres plus a year's worth of food supplies; the sergeants had been promised double these amounts of cash plus the rations. Most of the men had settled along the Richelieu River (whose mouth was located at Sorel), or along the eastern shore of the St. Lawrence from the Richelieu River up to Montreal. This was the very area in which the majority of the witnesses at the contract-signing of Jean and Marie resided. However, there is no mention in any of the surviving documents pertaining to Jean that indicated that he had himself been one of these retired soldiers.[12]

The dowry of 200 livres which Marie Barbant brought to this union was probably supplied by the government, since she had come to New France as a *fille du Roi*, a young woman who was prepared to take as her husband a settler who had already established himself in the colony. Due to the large numbers of unmarried former soldiers in this particular region (almost all of whom were seeking wives), it was logical that considerable numbers of these prospective brides made their way to this locale.[13] For many centuries back in the mother country, this proverb had been well-known: "*Qui se marie à hâte se repent à loisier* (Those who marry in haste repent later"). However, in this new land at this time, potential brides were in very short supply. As a result, it was more important to quickly find a wife among the limited number of potential candidates, than to take the time to get to know her before arranging a marriage contract.

At this time, Jean was about 28 years old; this is based upon his listed age of 40 in the 1681 census, which is the only certain record relating to his year of birth. In comparison, Marie was about age 21. Back at the time of the 1666 census, some $3^1/2$ years earlier, she had been enumerated at Beauport (northeast of Quebec) as a domestic servant in the household of Nicolas Juchereau, the Sieur de Saint Dénis, and Marie Thérèse Giffard. This man was not only a distinguished peltries merchant, he was also the Captain of the militia forces of Beauport. Besides the six children of the family (who ranged in ages from 15 down to 4) and the four unmarried hired hands (ages 45, 24, 24, and 14), the other listed member of the household was identified as *"Marie Barbant, 18 ans, servante."* She had apparently chosen to work in this capacity for a time after her arrival as a *fille du Roi*, instead of immediately becoming married and starting a family.[14]

Among the surviving church records of the colony, no entry has ever been located concerning the wedding of Jean de Lalonde and Marie Barbant. Most of the entries in the surviving register of the church at Sorel commence in 1675, some six years after the couple had exchanged their sacred vows. However, it is supposed that this parish of St. Pierre de Sorel was founded in 1669, that it was served by traveling priests from that year onward, and that many of the records from its first six years of operation have been lost.[15]

However, the record of the baptism of Jean and Marie's first child has been preserved. This joyful ceremony was conducted in the Sorel church on May 6, 1671. But little Jean would not be destined to live to adulthood; some time before the census of 1681 (when he would have been ten years old), he would perish. Jean's arrival was followed by the birth of the couple's first and only daughter, Marie Madeleine, in about 1672.[16]

These two babies arrived while the family was continuing to reside in the seigneury of D'Autray. The parents would have taken them across the St. Lawrence to Sorel to be baptized, since the St. Pierre parish there was the nearest church to their place of residence. It is possible that a portion of the property which Jean and his two partners had cleared of forest and had converted into agricultural land back in 1668-1669 had been officially granted to Jean as his own property. On the other hand, he may have been granted an entirely different parcel of land by his employer and seigneur, the Dame Bourdon, after he and his colleagues had completed their land-clearing and farming work while in her employ.

In the autumn of 1673, in anticipation of relocating to the Montreal region, the Lalonde couple sold their land to another resident of the seigneury.

"Before the said Adhémar, undersigned royal notary, and the witnesses named below were present Jean de Lalonde dit Lespérance, habitant of D'Autray, and Marie Barbant, his wife, the said Barbant duly authorizing

the said Lalonde, her husband, to execute these presents. They have sold and are presently selling and leaving that which they are releasing in perpetuity, without any reservations, to Gabriel Bérard dit Lépine, living at the said D'Autray, present and assenting for himself as well as for his heirs and successors in the future, a concession which the said sellers have that is located at the said D'Autray, with the buildings which it contains at present. The land contains two arpents (385 English feet) of frontage and the same amount of depth...the said concession having been given directly to the said sellers by the said seigneur verbally. The said concession, which fronts on the St. Lawrence River, is flanked on the northeast side by [the land of] Sieur Adrien Bétourné [dit Laviolette], separated by a short line running from southeast to northwest, and on the southwest side by [the land of] Sieur Jean Boullard, separated by a line running parallel to the previous one, marked on the two sides by Sieur Jean Lerouge, licensed surveyor in New France, according to a report which he made on October 24 last [ten days before the transfer]...The present sale has been made by the said de Lalonde and Barbant, spouses, to the said purchaser Bérard for and in consideration of the price agreed upon between them of the sum of 400 livres tournois [the currency used in France, worth 25 percent more than that of New France], of which sum the said sellers have declared that they have already received from the said purchaser the sum of 150 livres. The said purchaser promises to pay to the said sellers 100 livres on the fifteenth day of the month of next August [1674] and the remainder of 150 livres on the same day of August 15 in the year 1675...

[This agreement] made and drawn up at the said D'Autray in the home of the said sellers on the third day of the month of November, 1673 in the afternoon, in the presence of Jean Pelletier and Adrien Bétourné, habitants of the said D'Autray and Jacques Passard, Sieur de La Bretonnière, habitant of the Rivière Manereuil, undersigned with the said purchaser. The said sellers have said that they do not know how to sign, having been questioned according to the ordinance, and they have made their marks."[17]

Their two marks were very similarly to the ones that they each penned at the bottom of their marriage contract four years earlier, back in November of 1669. These consisted of a drawing of an apparent mortise chisel by Jean and a bold + by Marie. On the occasion of this land transfer, Adrien Bétourné dit Laviolette, their adjacent neighbor on the northeast side, was one of the witnesses. Four years earlier, he and his wife Marie Deshayes had been two of the residents of D'Autray who had crossed the St. Lawrence to Sorel, in order to serve as official witnesses at the Lalonde couple's nuptial contract ceremony.

Although they officially transferred ownership of their land to Monsieur Bérard on November 3, the Lalonde couple did not actually relocate with their children to the Montreal region until the following spring or summer of 1674. In preparation for the move, Jean traveled downriver to Quebec during the second week of March, to settle his financial obligations. In the afternoon on the eleventh, he visited the office of the notary Becquet, along with Anne Gasnier, the widow of his seigneur Jean Bourdon and the mother and legal guardian of Jacques Bourdon, Sieur D'Autray (age 22), who was also present. This young man would become the full seigneur of D'Autray upon reaching his 25th birthday, which was the legal age of majority in New France. According to the document which was drawn up on this March day (in which Jean was still described as an "habitant living in the seigneury of D'Autray"), he owed Madame Bourdon a total of 380 livres tournois, for various transactions from the past. The first of these was the land-clearing contract from October 19, 1668, for which he had owed $86^{1}/4$ livres as his one-third portion of the joint outfitting debt, plus $17^{3}/4$ livres for his individual outfitting debt, totaling 104 livres. Another transaction had been conducted between them on October 22, 1669, in addition to "generally all of the other things which have been loaned or advanced by the said Dame to the said named individual for the labors which he has undertaken to do on the lands of the said seigneury of D'Autray, everything which has taken place up until today." To pay off most of the owed sum, Jean transferred to Madame Bourdon the promissory note for 300 livres which had been issued to him by Gabriel Bérard, for having purchased Jean's property back in November. In addition, he promised to pay the reminder of 80 livres within the next three months. For his part, the young seigneur-to-be forgave the amount of overdue seigneurial fees, the *cens et rentes*, which Jean owed, in consideration of the various works which he had carried out on the seigneury. It is of interest that the elder seigneur's widow signed her name as "A. Gasnier Bourdon," including both her name and the family name of her husband.[18]

By July of 1674, Jean had made his way upriver to Montreal, and had struck up a partnership with Robert Henry, an unmarried man about 28 to 30 years old who had emigrated from Rouen. On the 13th of the month, the two men visited the home of Madeleine Laguide, who was the wife of François Marie Perrot, the Governor of Montreal and the seigneur of Île Perrot. She had married him about four years earlier, and the couple had already produced two children. On this day, Messieurs Lalonde and Henry contracted to lease a farm on Île Perrot for the span of two years, which would commence in four months, on the Feast Day of St. Martin (November 11). During that period, the two men would be under the charge of Louis Aumeau (who was about 44 to 46 years of age, had been married for $2^1/2$ years, but had no children). With the farm came a certain amount of cultivated acreage, some of which had been worked with the pickaxe and some with the plow; a number of buildings, including a granary; four oxen; three cows, of which two were producing milk and one was pregnant; and a three-year-old bull. The lessees would work, cultivate, and sow all of the cultivable lands of the farm, and for this privilege they would deliver annually four bushels of wheat for each acre of land that they would work with the plow, taking it to the home of René Cuillerier dit Léveillé at Lachine, along with twelve turkeys and twelve chickens each year. In addition, they would increase each year the amount of land which was ready to be worked with the plow, and they would likewise clear additional acreage of its forest cover.[19]

Eleven months after this lease had commenced, celebrations were in order for Marie and Jean, upon the safe arrival of their third child, the first one to be born in the Montreal area. Baby Jean Baptiste (the primary subject of this biography) was born on Île Perrot, after which he was taken to the church at Montreal to be baptized on October 10, 1675. On this festive day, the godfather was Robert Henry, Jean's farm-leasing colleague, while the godmother was Françoise Goupil. This 20-year-old resident of the Lachine parish, the wife of Cybard Courault, had been married for five years and had already borne two children.[20]

In the autumn of 1676, Jean and his partner completed their two-year lease of the farm. Shortly afterward, Robert Henry moved to Acadia, while Jean was verbally granted a piece of property on Montreal Island which had a surface area of 80 arpents (68 acres). This land was located on the southern shoreline of the Island, fronting on the St. Lawrence, "on the edge of Lac St. Louis between the Point of the Rapids and the Point of the Muskrat." About a year later, on September 28, 1677, he transferred this property to Barthélemy Lemaître dit Barbelin, an unmarried resident of Montreal who was about 41 or 42 years old. Jean did this in order to pay off the debt of 240 livres that he owed to Monsieur Lemaître, including the twenty bushels of wheat which he was supposed to deliver to the latter man later in the autumn. On this day, in order to facilitate this transaction, Fr. Pierre Rémy (at this time the secretary of the Sulpicians' seigneury of Montreal Island, and the priest who would be assigned to the Lachine parish three years later) signed a certificate of land ownership for Jean, verifying that this property had been verbally granted to him about a year earlier.[21]

During the depths of the winter of 1679, the size of the Lalonde family increased by one, with the addition of baby Jean. On February 7, he was born in the sub-fief which was called the Côte St. Pierre; five days later, on the 12th, he was christened at the baptismal font of the church at Lachine. This edifice, dedicated to the Holy Angels, had been consecrated nearly three years earlier, on Holy Thursday in 1676. The Côte St. Pierre, which was located on the northwest side of Lac St. Pierre, commenced about 1^7/8 miles north of the Lachine village site and extended northward for nearly two miles.[22]

In probably about 1679 or 1680, the family moved from Côte St. Pierre some 13 or 14 miles toward the southwest, to nearly the western tip of Montreal Island. Long before, this overall area had been dubbed *Le Bout de l'Île* (The End of the Island) and *Le Haut de l'Île* (The Top of the Island). But the region which was encompassed by this term was by no means limited to only the western tip area. This name, "End (or Top) of the Island," was very often utilized to denote the entire western portion of Montreal Island, extending westward from about Pointe Claire to the westernmost tip of the landmass. However, on his 1702 land ownership map of the island, Vachon de Belmont applied the name "Bout de l'Île" to only the western tip area; he gave the name "Côte St. Louis" to the remainder of the region, extending eastward all the way to the area of Pointe Claire. (Eventually, the name St. Louis, pertaining to both the Côte and the parish, would be changed to Ste. Anne.)

In this fief which was called the Côte St. Louis, the Lalonde-Barbant settled on a piece of land which had a St. Lawrence frontage of 6 arpents (1,152 feet or .22 mile) and a depth of 20 arpents (^{3}/4 mile).[23] It was on this 102 acres of property that the Lalondes were residing in the spring or early summer of 1681, when a census of the entire colony was conducted. The enumerator for the Côte St. Louis at Bout de l'Île recorded the following family in household 280:
"Jean de Lalonde, age 40
Marie Baban, his wife, age 42 (sic)

Children:
Madeleine, 9
Jean Baptiste, 6
Jean, 3
Georges, domestic servant, 16
1 gun, 4 horned cattle, and 12 arpents (10$^{1}/4$ acres) under cultivation"[24]

This document offers the only certain evidence concerning Jean's age, implying that he had been born in about 1641. Fifteen years earlier, back in the census of 1666, Marie had been listed as a domestic servant of Nicolas Juchereau's household at Beauport; at that time, her age had been recorded as 18, which was most likely correct or nearly correct. In this 1681 census, it is quite probable that the enumerator mistakenly heard *quarante deux* instead of *trente deux* when he heard her age stated, and he thus wrote 42 instead of 32. By this point, the eldest child of the family, Jean, had already perished. If he had lived, he would have been about ten years old, having been baptized on May 6, 1671. This census is the only record of daughter Marie Madeleine's age, implying that she had arrived in about 1672. Jean Baptiste, the oldest surviving son, would turn 6 in October, while toddler Jean would not celebrate his third birthday until the following February, in 1682. Thus, it appears that the enumerator probably asked the parents how old their children would be on their next birthday, rather than their current ages. Unfortunately, no family name was recorded for the 16-year-old hired hand named George who lived with and worked for the family.

Immediately next door to the west lived Antoine de Lafresnaye, the Sieur de Brucy, his wife Hélène Picoté, and their three children. This family owned two guns and three horned cattle, but they had not yet begun to cultivate any of their property.[25]

Two farms away from the Lalondes toward the west lived Cybard Courault, the Sieur de La Coste, his wife Françoise Goupil, and their four children. Much like the Lalondes, they also owned one gun and five horned cattle, and had the same amount of 12 arpents of land under cultivation. Françoise had served as the godmother at the baptismal ceremony of Marie and Jean's oldest surviving son, Jean Baptiste, 5$^{1}/2$ years earlier, back in the autumn of 1675. Both the Lalonde family and the Courault family had been living on their respective properties long enough that they had each been able to clear the forest from more than 10 acres of land and bring these acres under cultivation.[26]

The official registration of the granting of this land to Jean de Lalonde, which had been verbally ceded to him by the Sulpicians (the seigneurs of Montreal Island), was not recorded until October 26, 1681. However, Jean, his family members, and the one hired hand had already cleared and cultivated a considerable amount of this property before the census of 1681 was enumerated. This clearly shows that they had already been residing here and working on the land for quite some time before 1681.[27]

During the following winter of 1682, a deep pall of sadness descended upon the Lalonde household. This commenced on February 2, when Jean, the youngest child of the family, died five days before he would have celebrated his third birthday. Amid the shedding of many tears, he was laid to rest in the cemetery on the following day.[28]

Some 2½ years later, during the summer of 1684, the family's spirits were buoyed considerably by the arrival of a new baby. Guillaume was born on August 21, and he was baptized at home on the same day by the missionary priest from the church at Lachine. This would be the last child whom Marie and Jean would produce, so he would always be their *benjamin* (youngest child). Between May of 1671 and August of 1684, over a span of thirteen years, they had welcomed five children into the world, of whom two had died at early ages.[29]

Jean, Marie, and their two surviving sons would establish the dynasty of the entire Lalonde clan in New France. (Daughter Marie Madeleine would marry Guillaume Daoust, so her descendants would not carry the Lalonde name.) In the present work, the biographies of both sons Jean Baptiste and Guillaume Lalonde are included, since they were active participants in the fur trade of New France. (The latter individual has been designated in this study as Guillaume Number 1.) In addition, the life stories of Jean Baptiste's son the voyageur Guillaume Lalonde (Number 2), as well as this latter man's son the voyageur Guillaume Lalonde (Number 4), are also presented. Guillaume Number 1 produced a son named Guillaume Lalonde, who was likewise a voyageur; he has been designated as Guillaume Number 3. However, since he is not a direct ancestor of the present author, as are all of the other above-named Lalonde men, his biography has not been included in this study.

The peace treaties which had been arranged with the Iroquois nations back in 1666 and 1667 had been in effect for nearly two decades. Now, however, Iroquois warriors had begun making attacks against the Illinois and Miami nations, in the interior far to the west. As they had done during the period between 1641 and 1665 (that time fighting against the Algonkins, Nipissings, Hurons, Tionontates, and Ottawas), the Iroquois intended to vanquish these two allies of the French. Afterward, they planned to crush the remaining Ottawas, Hurons, and Tionontates (who were now based at the Straits of Mackinac), in order to seize complete control of the fur trade business in the entire midwest region. This serious threat obliged the French to mount a military expedition to Lake Ontario during this summer of 1684. By this means, they hoped to intimidate the warring Iroquois nations, by showing them that the French could attack their home villages, which were located south and east of the lake, if they did not restore the former situation of peace.

Two separate armies converged on Lake Ontario: the one departing from Montreal consisted of regular soldiers, about 700 militia fighters, and some 400 allied warriors from the St. Lawrence settlements, while the one coming from the upper Great Lakes contained about 150 voyageur-traders and more then 500 allied native fighting men.

Unfortunately, as the eastern army traveled up the St. Lawrence to the lake, "tertian ague" (Spanish influenza) swept like wildfire through the men, laying most of them low. Before the western army had reached the rendezvous point on the south shore of Lake Ontario, where Governor Labarre and his forces were waiting in pitiful condition, Iroquois emissaries arrived there to negotiate a peace treaty. Upon seeing the state of their adversaries, the leaders of the Iroquois party dictated the terms of the agreement, which were very humiliating for the French. In the process, the Iroquois did agree to not harm the Miami nation, but they vowed to complete their extermination of the Illinois. After the treaty sessions had been concluded, a ship was sent westward on the lake from Ft. Frontenac, to intercept the army from the upper Great Lakes and instruct the men to return to their home areas, which they did. Many of the men of the eastern army died while en route back to the St. Lawrence communities, and those who did survive brought the scourge of the disease with them; it would ravage the colonists throughout the entire autumn and early winter.[30]

Remembering the terrible quarter-century of Iroquois attacks which they had earlier endured, the French and native residents of the St. Lawrence settlements were quite apprehensive about the future. During the previous summer of 1683, one of the King's new edicts which had arrived ordered every able-bodied Frenchman in the colony to own a gun. The local merchants had been instructed to accept wheat, peas, or corn as payment for these weapons, at specific rates of exchange. Considering the new potential menace of marauding warriors, this regulation concerning firearms ownership was followed much more avidly from 1684 on.[31]

Back in 1683, the administrators of New France had drawn up an "Account of the Parish Priests and Missions" which existed at that time in the colony. On Montreal Island, the three parishes included Our Lady of Montreal, The Infant Jesus of Pointe aux Trembles (by the northeastern tip of the island), and Holy Angels of Lachine (a little to the west of the southeastern corner of the Island). These had been founded in 1642, 1674, and 1676, respectively. According to the 1683 report, the Lachine parish extended "from the top [southeastern corner] of the Island for three leagues along the coast toward the southwest and for one league along the coast toward the north; there are 314 souls." In comparison, the Montreal parish contained 641 souls, while the Pointe aux Trembles parish had 427 souls. Besides these three parishes on Montreal Island itself, there was also the parish of the Nativity of the Blessed Virgin Mary of Laprairie (about five miles southeast of Montreal, on the southeast shore of the St. Lawrence), which had been founded in 1670; it had 304 souls. In addition, Holy Family parish of Boucherville, on the same eastern side of the river and about 15 miles further north (founded in 1668), had 403 souls. Each of the parishes on Montreal Island was served by Sulpician priests from the Seminary at Montreal; they were all supervised by Fr. François Dollier de Casson, the Vicar General of this order and the Superior of the Seminary.[32]

The number of residents living along the southern shoreline of Montreal Island had increased considerably during the 1670s and the early 1680s, and their numbers were continuing to expand at a regular rate. As a result, the church leaders determined in latter 1685 that an additional parish was to be established in its western region, encompassing the area that extended westward from Pointe Claire. This area was generally called Le Bout de l'Île or Le Haut de l'Île.

In October, the following individuals made up the party which toured the newly-established parish of St. Louis and laid out the specific area upon which the church would be constructed: the

Bishop of Quebec (Jean Baptiste de La Croix de Chevrières, Sieur de Saint Vallier), Fr. Dollier de Casson, Fr. Pierre Rémy (the parish priest of Lachine), Olivier Quesnel (the churchwarden of Lachine), Jean de Lalonde (the churchwarden of St. Louis), and Jean Quenet (an important local resident, who owned the fifteenth lot east of the construction site). The place which was chosen for the new church, at the place called Pointe St. Louis, was located roughly $1/4$ to $1/2$ mile to the east of the Lalonde farm. (Some 28 years later, in about 1713, the name of the parish would be changed to Ste. Anne, and later a new edifice would be built about $1^1/2$ miles further west.) The construction of the St. Louis church would be completed during the following year of 1686, and the parish ledger would commence in that year. On Vachon de Belmont's land ownership map of 1702, the cross symbol representing this edifice, which was labeled *Église Paroisse St. Louis* (St. Louis Parish Church), was positioned on Pointe St. Louis. In addition, on the key of the map, the specific listings of the owners of each piece of property along the *Côte et Paroisse St. Louis* indicated where the *Terre de l'Église* (Land of the Church), with its 14 arpents or 2,688 feet of St. Lawrence frontage, was located. The curved bay which lay immediately west of Pointe St. Louis (toward the Lalonde farm) was labeled on this chart as *Côte d'Urfé* (also known as Baie D'Urfé). This feature was named after the first resident curé of the parish, François Saturnin Lascaris D'Urfé, who was assigned to this church in 1686. (In the coming decades, as the population residing on Montreal Island would continue to expand, one additional parish would be established on the southern shore of the island, in 1713. This would be St. Joachim at Pointe Claire, whose church would be located roughly halfway between the church at Lachine and the one at Bout de l'Île.)

Before the St. Louis parish was created in 1685, all of the French residents of the southern shoreline of Montreal Island had belonged to the parish of Lachine. Those individuals who lived at a considerable distance from the church were occasionally served by the priest from Lachine, who traveled to the far-flung areas as a missionary. Back on July 5, 1683, Fr. Durfé had traveled to the Bout de l'Île area to christen the newest member of the flock there. That had been Marie Madeleine Courault, the three-day-old daughter of Cybard Courault, Sieur de La Coste, and Françoise Goupil, who resided with their children on the second lot west of the Lalondes. After this missionary trip, the priest had recorded in the Lachine register, "This baptism was celebrated in the house of Jean de Lalonde dit Lespérance, habitant of Haut de l'Île de Montreal, being the place where I usually say Mass for this mission, which is attached to the Holy Angels parish of Lachine." Thirteen months later, after the same cleric had traveled westward to conduct the christening ceremonies for Guillaume Lalonde on August 21, 1684, he entered additional notations into the Lachine register on August 26. According to his records, the priest had been absent "at my mission at the top of this Island, to conduct the above baptism [of Guillaume Lalonde] and to celebrate the Holy Mass." In this entry, baby Guillaume's father Jean was identified as the "churchwarden of the Mission of the Top of the Island."[33]

February of 1686 brought with it new and very special sensations for Jean, Marie, and each of their children: the wedding of their eldest child and only daughter, Marie Madeleine. On the 18th, twelve days after the couple had signed their marriage contract before the Montreal notary Pierre Cabazier, they exchanged their vows in the Lachine church (since the St. Louis edifice had not yet been completed). The bride, who was about 14 years old, joined in matrimony on this gladdening day with Guillaume Daoust, a fellow resident of the Côte St. Louis who was about age 41. Between 1691 and 1712, this couple would produce nine children, at Montreal, Lachine, Pointe aux Trembles, and Bout de l'Île. Of these, the first one and the eighth one would each die at young ages.[34] (The present author is descended from this couple through their son Guillaume and his wife Élisabeth Pilon.)

It was in about this year of 1686 that lightning attacks by Iroquois warriors resumed against the settlements of the St. Lawrence Valley. This was very disconcerting for the residents, both French and native, since they had not been obliged to endure these depredations for nearly two decades.

On November 15 of this year, Jean stood as the godfather at the baptism of Pierre Maupetit, the son of Pierre Maupetit dit Poitevin and Marie Louise Beaune. This couple owned the fourth farm to the east of the construction site of the St. Louis church. On this inspiring occasion, which took place in the Lachine church, the godmother was Marie Madeleine Émond, the wife of the Lachine trader Nicolas Dupuis. (The biographies of this newborn baby Pierre Maupetit and his eventual wife Angélique Villeray are presented later in this work.)[35]

On this same day of November 15 in the afternoon, the Sulpicians granted to Jean a parcel of meadow land, which was located a considerable distance to the north of their farm "at the place which is called Lac au Renard (Fox Lake)." This plot, which was most likely to be used for cutting hay, contained 6^1/4 arpents of surface area (5.3 acres). According to the document of transfer, the newly acquired piece of meadow property was "bounded on one side by the meadow granted to [Cybard Courault,] Sieur de La Coste, and on the other side by lands which have not been granted." On the 1702 land ownership map of Montreal Island, a number of rather slender, elongated areas were marked as *prairie* (meadow). These swaths of moist grassland, aligned in a generally southwest-to-northeasterly direction, commenced some 1^1/4 to 1^3/4 miles north of the St. Lawrence shoreline.

After acquiring their parcel of meadow, the annual seigneurial fees which the Lalondes paid to the Sulpicians consisted of the following. For the 120 arpents of land, they paid each year for the *cens* 6 deniers for each arpent (totaling 720 deniers, or 3 livres), and for the *rentes* a total of 8 bushels of wheat. For the 6^1/4 arpents of meadow, they paid annually for the *cens* 6 deniers for each arpent (totaling 37.5 deniers or 3.125 sols or .16 livre), and for the *rentes* 18 deniers for each arpent (totaling 112.5 deniers or or 5.625 sols or .28 livre). Thus, their total annual payments consisted of 3.44 livres in cash and eight bushels of wheat. Each year, they delivered these monies and grain to the fees-collecting agent of the seigneurs at Montreal on the Feast Day of St. Martin, November 11.[36]

Some time between February and December of 1684, Antoine de Lafresnaye, the Sieur de Brucy, who was Jean and Marie's adjacent neighbor to the west, died. Upon his demise, he left behind his widow Hélène Picoté (about 28 years old) and their three children, who ranged in age from seven down to one year. Nearly two years later, on November 29, 1686, she remarried in the new St. Louis church, joining in partnership with Jean Baptiste Celoron, the Sieur de Blainville, who was a Lieutenant in the army.[37]

In March of 1687, Jean and Marie decided to sell their entire 102 acre farm. Over the course of the previous seven or eight years, they had expended a great deal of labor on it, clearing and bringing under cultivation at least ten acres of land (by the time of the 1681 census), and also constructing a home and all of the necessary outbuildings. However, on March 3, Jean received from the Sulpicians a grant of a new piece of land, which was located just a short distance to the east.

On this forest-covered property, the family would start anew, after garnering a generous profit from the sale of their developed farm. Their new lot, containing 4 arpents (768 feet) of St. Lawrence frontage and 20 arpents ($3/4$ mile) of depth, was positioned on Pointe St. Louis, immediately east of the new church. According to the granting document, the plot was flanked "on one side [to the west] by the lands of the church and on the lower side [to the east] by that of the Sieur Guillaume Daoust [their son-in-law for the previous thirteen months]."[38]

Jean and Marie arranged to receive a very generous price for both their developed farm and their distant meadow land from Lieutenant Celoron, who now owned the next-door property, immediately to the west of the farm. On March 21, the couple traveled to the office of the Montreal notary Basset to officially transfer ownership to the officer, who was also present. On this occasion, the notary represented Hélène Picoté, Celoron's wife, who was absent. In this document, the sellers were identified as "Jean de Lalonde dit Lespérance, habitant living *au Bout d'en Haut de la dite Île* (at the End of the Top of the said [Montreal] Island), at present in this town, and Marie Barban, his wife." The farm which they were selling, containing 6 arpents of St. Lawrence frontage and 20 arpents of depth, was described as being bordered on one side by the lands of the heirs of the deceased Antoine de Lafresnaye and his former wife Hélène Picoté, and on the other side by the lands of Pierre Cavelier. Also to be transferred to the officer was the Lalondes' $6^1/4$ arpents of meadow property, which the engineer and surveyor Gédéon de Catalogne had surveyed back on December 5, 1685, and the Lalondes had acquired in November of 1686. For the two parcels together, Lieutenant Celoron agreed to pay them a total of 1,500 livres. Of this sum, 333 livres 15 sols would be delivered to the Sulpicians as a long-term loan from Jean and Marie, for which the couple would annually receive a payment of 20 livres from the Order. In addition, the officer would pay to the Lalonde couple 501 livres "in silver louis, piastres, and other money," and he would issue to them a promissory note for the remaining 665 livres 5 sols. Finally, he would transfer to them the deed to another piece of meadow land, one which was located "below the one which was described above." At the conclusion of the agreement, Jean and Marie handed over to the purchaser the two documents which Jean had received when the farm land and the meadow parcel had been granted to him, as well as Monsieur Catalogne's survey report on the piece of meadow.[39]

It was now time to start all over again on the new property, clearing the forest-covered land, bringing it under cultivation, and constructing a house and the various outbuildings. Within the next six months, they would complete the building of their home and the other necessary structures, while they would also convert two arpents (1.7 acres) of forest into cultivated ground.[40]

Various of the Iroquois nations were now conducting sporadic raids against the settlements along the St. Lawrence, as well as against the native nations living far to the west who were allied with the French. As a result, Governor Jacques René de Brisay de Denonville and the military leaders decided to conduct a campaign against the Iroquois homelands lying to the south of Lake Ontario. This would be done in an attempt to cause all of the Iroquois nations to cease their raiding. The thrust of the two attacking French and native armies would be brought to bear upon the Senecas, who were the most westerly and the most numerous and powerful of the Iroquois nations. As had been done three years earlier, back in the abortive campaign of 1684, the western army consisted of French and native forces gathered from throughout the Great Lakes region, and from as far southwest as the Illinois Country. Messieurs Perrot and Boisguillot, trading in the upper Mississippi area, assembled nearly all of the Frenchmen there and paddled to St. Ignace, where Olivier de Morel, Sieur de La Durantaye, the commandant there at the Straits, had gathered the Frenchmen from his region plus some Ojibwa warriors. These combined forces traveled southward on Lake Huron to the one-year-old Ft. St. Joseph on the St. Clair River, where they were joined by Daniel Greysolon, Sieur DuLhut and his soldiers from that post. Further to the south, the entourage was again augmented, this time by the French and native forces from Illinois, who had traveled overland to the Detroit River. As a unit, the huge aggregate of fighting men then paddled eastward to Lake Ontario, to join ranks with the eastern army from the St. Lawrence. In the meantime, the Ottawa and Huron/Tionontate warriors from the Straits of Mackinac had traveled by way of Georgian Bay and the Toronto Portage to join their comrades on the south shore of Lake Ontario.

The eastern army, assembled in the St. Lawrence Valley, was composed of 832 regular troops, 1,300 militia fighters, and 300 allied native warriors. Oddly enough, these eastern forces arrived on July 10 at the appointed place of rendezvous, on the southern shore of the massive lake, at virtually the exact same time as the western forces.

This was purely coincidental, yet it bore great and clearly positive significance to the native allies within both groups.

When the combined armies approached the first Seneca village overland, they were ambushed in thick forest cover by a large contingent of Iroquois warriors. In the ensuing battle, some 100 Frenchmen and ten allied warriors were killed, and many others were wounded. After this initial clash, the Senecas burned their own nearest village and fled with their families. During the next nine days, the French and native forces destroyed huge amounts of standing corn crops at three or four deserted Seneca villages, along with an estimated 50,000 bushels of parched corn. Then, as dysentery began to spread through the men, the two armies left the area and returned to their respective home areas, having fought a total of one battle with uncertain results.

In the aftermath of this Seneca campaign, attacks by Iroquois war parties actually increased rather than decreased, in both number and intensity. Their fierce raids fell upon many of the communities of the St. Lawrence Valley, and also upon the Ottawa River route leading to and from the Upper Country.[41]

When the annual fleet of vessels from France had arrived in the St. Lawrence Valley during this summer of 1687, beginning on the first day of June, their cargoes had included not only people, merchandise, and supplies, but also fatal germs. Shortly after their arrival, a terrible double epidemic of both smallpox and measles began to sweep through the French and native communities that lined the shores of the river, ranging from Tadoussac all the way upstream to the Montreal area. This scourge of sickness and death would continue unchecked for nearly a year, extending well into 1688. By the time it would finally abate, over a thousand residents, both French and native, would be dead.[42]

In the early autumn of 1687, it was the scourge of Iroquois attacks rather than the one of diseases which felled Jean de Lalonde. The settlers living along the thinly-populated western end of Montreal Island knew that they were especially vulnerable to these lightning raids, which seemed to come out of nowhere, with no advance warning. The first local resident to die in such an attack during this particular period was Jean Vincent; he was killed on September 21. This 45-year-old man, who had never married, had arrived in the colony in 1665 as a soldier in the Carignan-Salières Regiment. It was the martial efforts of these troops, along with those of militia fighters and allied native warriors, which had forced the Iroquois nations to agree to peace treaties two decades earlier, back in 1666 and 1667. Monsieur Vincent was buried in the St. Louis cemetery on the same day that he perished.[43]

(This was the second funeral to be conducted at the new parish cemetery. The first one had taken place back on February 23 of this same year, when the merchant Claude Lamothe dit Le Marquis et Sourdy had been laid to rest on the day following his death, at the age of about 35 to 40. At the time, his wife Françoise Sabourin had been pregnant with their first child; the baby would arrive at about the end of September, but she would only survive for a few weeks. This couple had resided on the farm immediately to the east of the property which Jean and Marie had developed and then had sold to Lieutenant Celeron back in March.[44])

The day of great tragedy for the Lalonde family came on September 30, 1687. On that fateful day, five local men (including Jean de Lalonde dit Lespérance, the sole churchwarden of the parish) were slain by Iroquois attackers. It is not known if they had been working together on a distant project, or if they had been traveling to or from such a work detail, at the time they were ambushed. Among the five victims, Jean was the oldest and had the most children. About 45 or 46 years of age, he left behind Marie (who was about age 39), their daughter Marie Madeleine (about age 15, who had been married to Guillaume Daoust for 19 months), and their sons Jean Baptiste (who was about to turn 12) and Guillaume (who had turned 3 six weeks earlier).[45]

The other married victim was Pierre Bonneau dit Lajeunesse, about 38 to 40 years old, who had been the Corporal of the militia forces of the Lachine parish. He and Marie Madeleine Gignard had been married for six years; during that time, they had produced two children, who had been born in 1683 and 1686. This little family had lived on the eighth farm to the east of Jean and Marie's first property, which they had sold to the officer back in March.[46]

Three unmarried local men also perished at the hands of Iroquois warriors on this horrible day. These were Henri Fromageau, who was ten days short of celebrating his 29th birthday (he had come to the colony as an indentured laborer fourteen years earlier, in the summer of 1673); Pierre Perthuis, age 24; and Pierre Petiteau, age 20.[47]

All five of the heart-rending burials that were conducted by Fr. D'Urfé in the St. Louis cemetery on this day were witnessed by the same three individuals. These were Guillaume Daoust (Jean and Marie's son-in-law and Marie Madeleine's husband, who owned the farm immediately east of the Lalonde farm); Cybard Courault, Sieur de La Coste (whose farm was located two lots west of the property that Jean and Marie had sold to Lieutenant Celoron back in March); and ___ Dutartre (possibly Jean Dutartre dit Desrosiers).[48]

The depredations of the lurking war parties did not end with the deaths of these five local men on this September day. Just 2^{1}/2 weeks later, on October 18, two unmarried soldiers of the Company of Du Cruzel were slain in this same area, during a surprise attack. Jean Baptiste Lesueur dit La Hogue (who was 21 years old) and Pierre Camus dit Lafeuillade were buried in the St. Louis cemetery on the following day.[49]

One month later, on November 17, the 24-year-old unmarried miller Louis Jets was laid to rest here as well. However, since the parish records made no mention of his cause of death, it was most likely due to the epidemic of smallpox and measles that was raging through the population at this time, rather than an Iroquois raid, that had felled this young man.[50]

Eight weeks after Jean had been killed, on November 29, 1687, Marie traveled to Montreal to the Sulpician Seminary, to receive a supplemental grant of land. On this day, when she was identified as "Marie Barban, widow of the deceased Jean de Lalonde dit Lespérance, habitant of the parish of St. Louis on Montreal Island," she received 5 arpents (4^{1}/4 acres) of property as an addition to the 80 arpents of forest-covered land (measuring 4 arpents in frontage by 20 arpents in depth) that had been granted to Jean nine months earlier, back on the third day of March. The provisions concerning this new property, which was located adjacent to the front of the former grant, stated that she was to constantly work to clear it and to bring it to a state of cultivation, and to have it measured and surveyed. Likewise, she was to pay the following fees each year to the seigneurs at their seigneurial home at the Seminary of Montreal, on the Feast Day of St. Martin (November 11): for the *cens*, 6 deniers for each arpent, and for the *rente* 18 deniers for each arpent. In addition, she was to allow the construction of any roads on her property which the seigneurs or their attorney would decide to have built for the convenience of the public.[51]

Two days later, on December 1, Marie again returned to the Seminary, this time to receive a grant of a parcel of meadow land.

This plot, containing two arpents (1.7 acres), was located "at the place called Lac au Renard (Fox Lake), bordered on one side by the meadow formerly granted to Demoiselle Hélène Picoté, widow of the deceased Monsieur [Antoine de Lafresnaye, Sieur] de Brucy, and on the other side the concession of land of the said Demoiselle [Picoté]." According to the stated conditions, Madame Lalonde was to "work constantly to clear [of brush] and to fence the land, in a suitable time and season." The other conditions which had applied to her supplemental 5 arpents of land adjacent to the farm also applied to this lot of meadow as well.[52]

After nearly eighteen years of marriage, Marie Barbant was now a grieving widow. At this time, she was about 39 years of age, and she had two children at home who were ages 12 and 3. However, in spite of enduring regular doses of hardship, suffering, and sadness, she, along with the vast majority of the other colonists, found the strength to forge ahead with their lives. Less than four months from the day of Jean's death and burial, Marie decided to remarry, as was quite typical in the challenging existence of the pioneer settlers of New France.

Her new partner would be Pierre Tabault dit Lepetit Léveillé, who had come to New France 22 years earlier, back in 1665, as a soldier in the Carignan-Salières Regiment. He was now a widower at Lachine who was about 43 years old and had three living children. These were Pierre, Jr. (age 12), Alexis (8), and Jean (5). Pierre, Sr. had married Jeanne Françoise Roy at Montreal back in December of 1672, eight days after she had celebrated her twelfth birthday. Thereafter, the couple had resided in the Lachine seigneury, on the fifth farm to the east of the stockaded village site (some 13 miles east of the Lalonde farm at Bout de l'Île). In addition to their three sons who had survived, the couple had also produced Simon, their second child, who had arrived in August of 1678. He had passed away ten days after Jean de Lalonde had died, at the age of nine on October 10, 1687, a victim of the raging epidemic. Another son, Barthélemy, had died back in December of 1681, at the age of four weeks. No burial records for Jeanne Françoise Roy have been located in any church records. Her passing had taken place some time during the five-year period after the arrival of their fifth and last child on September 25, 1682; during that period, she would have been 22 to 27 years old. Perhaps the smallpox-and-measles epidemic which had ravaged the French and native populations during the summer and autumn of 1687 (and would continue well into 1688) had caused her demise, as it had for her second-oldest child.[53]

After Marie Barbant and Pierre Tabault decided to join forces and create a blended family with five sons, they determined that they would reside on the Tabault farm at Lachine. However, they would retain ownership of the Lalonde farm at Bout de l'Île; when Jean Baptiste and Guillaume Lalonde would become adults, this latter property would be part of their inheritance. With this intention, the future members of the blended family hauled the majority of the possessions of the Lalonde household eastward the thirteen miles to Lachine. There, these belongings were stored at the home of the Lachine and Montreal merchant René Cuillerier dit Léveillé, whose farm was the third one east of the Tabault farm.[54]

(Over time, this combined Lalonde-Tabault family would become heavily involved in the fur trade. Like Jean Baptiste and Guillaume Lalonde, two of their stepbrothers Pierre and Jean Tabault would also grow up to become voyageur-traders or voyageurs during their adult years. These were very common careers for young men of the Montreal region to choose during this era, especially after the license system had been inaugurated in 1682. In some cases, the men worked at these occupations for decades, while others only labored in this field for a single year or just a few years, in order to amass enough funds to establish their own pioneer farms. To illustrate the interconnectedness of the fur trade families who resided along the southern shoreline of Montreal Island during this period, the two voyageur brothers Pierre and Jean Tabault would marry two daughters of the voyageur-trader François Brunet dit Le Bourbonnais, Sr., whose biography has already been presented in this work.)[55]

On January 19, 1688, Marie and Pierre Tabault were joined at the Cuillerier home by the Lachine notary Jean Baptiste Pothier and by various other friends and relatives, all of whom were resident of the Lachine seigneury. On this day in the very heart of the winter, the prospective bride and groom would first draw up their marriage contract. After this nuptial document was completed, two of the witnesses and the notary would then conduct an inventory of most of the Lalonde family belongings.

In the marriage contract, the couple was identified as "Pierre Tabault dit Le Petit Léveillé, habitant of the Holy Angels parish of Lachine, and Marie Barban, widow of the deceased Jean de Lalonde dit Lespérance, who while living was an habitant of the St. Louis parish, located at the upper part of the said Island." The witnesses on Pierre's side included Alexis Buet, his father-in-law (his mother-in-law's second husband); André Merlot, his brother-in-law (husband of his sister-in-law Marie Agnès Roy); Pierre Cardinal, his cousin; and Jean Fournier, his friend. The witnesses on Marie's side included the host René Cuillerier, his wife Marie Lucos, and their 17-year-old son Jean Cuillerier. Among the various details which were included in the document, the couple declared that they would choose the supplemental guardians for the two underage Lalonde children and the three underage Tabault children (the two surviving single parents would serve as the primary guardian for their respective offspring). In addition, they would have inventories conducted of the respective Tabault and Lalonde households, to safeguard the legal inheritance of these five children and stepchildren. They also promised to "feed, care for, raise, and instruct them in the Catholic, Apostolic, and Roman religion...until each of them attains the age of eighteen years or thereabouts."[56]

Then, after most of the guests had departed, Messieurs Cuillerier and Fournier, along with the notary, proceeded to draw up an official inventory of the majority of the Lalonde family possessions, which had been transported from their farm at Bout de l'Île to Lachine. This detailed document would be later utilized to divide these assets between Marie and her two sons. In the present version of the inventory, the sequence of the articles has been altered, in order to better visualize the household contents by category. In addition, in most instances, the valuation of each respective item has been omitted, for the sake of clarity.

"In the year 1688 on the 19th of January and other days following, I, the undersigned notary [Jean Baptiste Pothier], transported myself to the home of René Cuillerier, merchant living at Lachine, at the request of Marie Barban, widow of the deceased Jean de Lalonde dit Lespérance, who while living was an habitant of the parish of St. Louis, located at the top of the Island of Montreal, to inventory the possessions belonging to the estate of the said deceased Lalonde, in the presence of my said Sieur Cuillerier and Jean Fournier, living at the said place of Lachine, chosen by the said widow Barban to appraise the said belongings. I have taken into consideration the appointed time [the customary interval of time following the death of the spouse] for the appraisal of the said belongings, since neither the said widow nor anyone else has elected a guardian or supplemental guardian for the preservation of the said belongings, conforming to the formalities

of justice, having been inconvenienced and hindered by bad weather and storms from being able to go to the town to make the required will in such case, and the said election of the guardian and the supplemental guardian to take care of the said belongings which may belong to Jean Baptiste de Lalonde, twelve years old or thereabouts, and Guillaume de Lalonde, three years old or thereabouts, underage children of the said deceased Lalonde. They [Messieurs Cuillerier and Fournier] representing the said widow, have taken care of all of the necessary formalities of the said inventory at the earliest convenience, she having been made aware of the obligations under the penalties carried by the ordinances to make an exact showing of all of the possessions, both moveable and real estate, that are known between her and the said deceased, her husband, which are at the home of the said Cuillerier, without diverting anything from the enumeration of the present inventory, followed by the appraisal which will be carried out by the aforementioned experts, who will take an oath with the said widow. In which case, it will be required that they be compensated for one day for going to Monsieur the Bailiff of Montreal, to state and declare that they have proceeded with the said inventory according to all fairness.

First,
1 farm with 80 arpents [68 acres] of land, located at Pointe St. Louis, estimated with all of its appurtenances and outbuildings, as it is presently, with about 2 arpents [1.7 acres] of land under cultivation, together priced at 100 livres
[1 ox still at the Lalonde farm, listed later]
1 pregnant cow with brown hide, estimated at 40 livres
2 pigs, priced together at 20 livres
74 bushels of wheat
8 bushels of corn
3 bushels of shelled beans
1 bushel of peas
1 keg of side pork
A quantity of butter and of grease
1 pot hanger
1 grill [or gridiron]
1 brazier
4 new copper kettles
2 small brass kettles
2 wretched kettles
2 cooking pots

Jean Baptiste Lalonde and his wives Marguerite Masta and Jeanne Gervais

1 brass low-walled saucepan
1 frying pan
1 brass ladle (or large cooking spoon)
8 tureens [large ceramic bowl, usually with a pouring spout]
1 brass strainer
25 pounds weight of [ceramic or pewter] dishes, together comes to 25 livres
1 faience [tin-glazed earthenware] platter
1 faience plate
1 faience salt cellar [dispensing dish placed on the table]
1 faience pitcher
6 spoons
6 forks
1 pewter cup
4 pairs of drinking glasses and 1 glass bottle
1 small liquor chest with 12 small glass flasks
20 napkins
8 tablecloths
4 cakes of soap
8 hand towels
3 flat irons of solid construction [for pressing clothing and linens]
1 copper candlestick
1 old lantern
2 straw mattresses with several wretched household articles
3 pairs of sheets
2 blankets from Normandy, half-worn
1 old blanket from Normandy
6 old blankets and some wretched bear pelts
1 sheet serving as a bed curtain
1 native-tanned hide [of deer, elk, moose, or caribou]
4 guns, together estimated at 60 livres
3 pounds of gunpowder
12 pounds of gun balls
2 bundles of fishhook binding filaments
2 pairs of new shoes
9 pairs of moccasins
1 pair of stockings for the use of the said deceased
3 pairs of stockings
1 pair of stockings
12 shirts for the use of the said deceased Lalonde
4 shirts for the use of the said deceased

1 shirt of linen fabric from Rouen for the use of men

12 shirts for the use of the elder son of the said widow

1 chemisette [short-sleeved overshirt for warmth] of woolen melton fabric for the use of the deceased

1 small camisole [long-sleeved overshirt for warmth, also used as a sleeping garment]

1 suit with breeches [matching dress coat, waistcoat, and breeches] for the use of the said deceased

1 hooded coat of woolen fabric for the use of the said deceased

1 sash of painted linen fabric

2 dressing gowns [ankle length garment for indoor wear, for men and women]

18 chemises for the use of women

2 skirts of linen fabric

1 skirt of woolen rateen fabric

1 apron of linen fabric

2 aprons

2 handkerchiefs of painted linen fabric

Another quantity of linens, in cornets (cap with two broad lappets hanging down from the headband), neckerchiefs, and other head coverings

Several articles of small linens

3 1/2 yards of hempen linen fabric

4 1/2 yards of lightweight woolen creseau fabric

A quantity of new woolen fabric, estimated at 58 livres

A quantity of woolen fabric, priced at 14 livres

1 chest with all of its locks, in which all of the above linens were stored [shirts of the deceased, chemises for women, shirts of the elder son, tablecloths, napkins, and sheets]

1 chest, in which all of the above articles were stored [pairs of shoes, pairs of stockings, stockings of the deceased, shirts of the deceased, chemisette of the deceased, camisole, suit with breeches of the deceased, hooded coat of the deceased, sash, dressing gowns, skirts, aprons, handkerchiefs, one blanket, hand towels, hempen linen fabric, woolen creseau fabric, new woolen fabric, and woolen fabric]

1 small chest, in which all of these small linens were stored [shirt for men, cornets, neckerchiefs, other head coverings, and several articles of small linens]

1 old small chest, and several inconsequential household articles which were found in the said small chest

9 axes

1 drawknife
3 augers
2 iron splitting wedges
2 old pickaxes
10 old sickles
1 scythe sharpening stone
A quantity of old scrap iron, together priced at 4 livres
9 new sacks

Following are the debts which are owed to the said widow
Le Bonhomme [the fellow Pierre Surard dit] Lafrizade owes, according to a legal administrative reckoning, 15 livres 6 sols
Legrand Minset owes, according to a legal administrative reckoning, 14 livres
Pierre Cardinal owes 4 livres
[Michel] Desrosiers [dit Désilets] owes, according to a legal administrative reckoning, 4 livres
[Cybard Courault], the Sieur de La Coste, owes 2 livres 17 sols 3 deniers
Sansoucy owes 2 livres 5 sols

[Subtotal of listed assets: 1,344 livres 3 sols 3 deniers]

Following are the titles and papers
1 case containing three contracts of concession, namely
One, of eighty arpents [68 acres] of land located at Pointe St. Louis, granted in favor of the said Lalonde on the date of the third of March, 1687
The second, of a [2 arpents or 1.7 acres of] meadow granted to the said widow Lalonde on the date of the first of December, 1687
And the third, of a concession of about five arpents [41/4 acres] to the said widow, located adjacent to the front of the said concession of eighty arpents, on the twenty-ninth of November, 1687
All of these documents were passed before me, Jean Baptiste Pothier, notary of the town of the said Montreal, which contracts have been inventoried as one, two, and three without alteration.

After all of the above possessions had been inventoried, the said widow has declared that she has several possessions originating in the possession of the said deceased, her husband, which are at the end of the said Island [Bout de l'Île] of the said Montreal, where she had lived during the life of her said deceased husband, which she promises to have brought to the said place of Lachine at the first convenient time, to have them enumerated for the said inventory according to the appraisal which will be made by the aforementioned arbiters, as well as that of an ox which is still wandering in the woods.

[This document] drawn up on the said day and year as noted above [January 19, 1688], the said Sieur Cuillerier has signed with the said notary in the presence of the Sieur Alexis Buet, habitant of Lachine, after which the said widow and the said Fournier have declared that they do not know how to sign, having been questioned according to the ordinance. The said day and year as noted above.

Signed,

Buet, René Cullerier, and J. B. Pottier, notary

[Seven weeks later, all of the participants returned to the notary, in order to finalize the document.]

On this day, the twelfth of March in the year noted above [1688], the said widow Lalonde jointly with the aforementioned experts [appraisers] have come before the said undersigned notary to state and declare that the belongings mentioned in the aforementioned declaration [those not yet inventoried], with the aforementioned ox [and the agricultural equipment left at the farm], were found to amount to the sum of one hundred forty-eight livres ten sols [148.5 livres]. These, along with the articles of the said first part, constitute the sum total of all of the belongings in the possession of the said widow Lalonde, which have been placed in the presence of the said experts to make a determination in each case of their value.

[Grand total of all listed assets: 1,492 livres 13 sols 3 deniers]

[This document] drawn up on the said day and year as the other part by the said Cuillerier, who has signed with the said notary, after which the said widow and the expert Fournier have declared that they do not know how to sign, having been questioned according to the ordinance.

Signed,

*René Cullerier and J. B. Pottier"*57

The Lalonde home on the Côte St. Louis, from which these listed possessions had been removed, was most likely a single-story building constructed entirely of wood. As was typical at this time, it was probably roofed with thatch, planks, or wooden shingles, and featured a single chimney of wattle-and-daub construction and a few windows with panes made of oiled or greased paper. The ground floor was typically partitioned into three separate chambers. Upon first entering the house, one encountered the kitchen room, which had a hearth. This room, the only area in the building to receive heat directly from a fire, was used for cooking, and for living space during the seasons of coldest weather. The next room, the *cabane* or parlor, served as the main living space when the outdoor temperatures were less frigid; heat from the kitchen hearth wafted into this chamber. The third room, which was used for sleeping and for storage, was sometimes heated with a brazier (which warmed the air somewhat with glowing embers from the kitchen fire). The *grenier* (attic) was used for sleeping space for children and farm hands, as well as the safe, dry storage of grains. This format represented the typical home of the French colonists in the St. Lawrence Valley during this period. Thus, these various features were probably also present in the Tabault home at Lachine as well, into which the three members of the Lalonde family were about to move, blending together with the four members of the Tabault family.[58]

The entire Lalonde property, with its 68 acres, the house, and the various outbuildings (such as an outhouse, a granary, and a stable), was only worth the modest sum of 100 livres. This represented just 7 percent of the total valuation of 1,492.75 livres for all of the family's listed assets. Ten months earlier, back in March of 1687, Jean and Marie had sold the farm which they had developed at Bout de l'Île for the considerable sum of 1500 livres. However, for this price, they had transferred 102 acres of land, of which at least $8^1/2$ acres had been cleared and were under cultivation, as well as a parcel of meadow located well to the north. On their new, forest-covered property, which lay immediately east of the St. Louis church, the family had only been able to labor for six months before Jean had been killed. During that time, they had managed to clear the forest from only 1.7 acres and to bring this plot under cultivation, while also constructing the various buildings.

The family's livestock included one ox, one pregnant cow, and two pigs. These animals, plus the unspecified farming implements which had been left at the Lalonde property (such as a plow, a cart, and a sledge, plus other equipment such as hoes, shovels, scythes, rakes, flails, and winnowing baskets) totaled 208.5 livres in valuation. This represented 14 percent of the total value of all of the listed possessions.

The harvested crops and food supplies of the family consisted of 74 bushels of wheat, 8 bushels of corn, 3 bushels of shelled beans, 1 bushel of peas, 1 keg of side pork, and a quantity of butter and grease. These items were worth a total of 254 livres, representing 17 percent of the valuation of the listed assets of the family.

The other 62 percent of the valuation of the listed possessions of the Lalonde parents consisted of their articles of clothing and various household items. It is significant to note that no pieces of furniture (other than the four storage chests) were enumerated in the inventory. The unmentioned pieces probably included tables, chairs, benches, and beds, as well as other items. These omissions imply that the majority of the furnishings were left at the farm at Bout de l'Île, along with most of the farming implements, for the future use of Jean Baptiste and Guillaume Lalonde, after they had grown up and had moved onto their inherited farm. In the inventory, other than Jean and Marie's clothing, no other personal possessions belonging to them were recorded. Obviously, the listings did not include the pair of stockings, the pair of breeches, and the shirt that Jean must have worn into his grave. Some of the couple's other belongings which were not enumerated probably included boots, more coats, caps, hats, and gloves, as well as knives, a pipe and tobacco, fire-starting kits, and sewing articles, as well as various other minor items of daily life of the time. Apparently, none of the belongings of the two Lalonde boys were included in the inventory, except for Jean Baptiste's twelve shirts.

Among the many household items that were listed, of particular significance were the four guns, which had a total valuation of 60 livres. The presence of these four firearms in their home certainly reflected the constant danger of Iroquois attack which pervaded the daily lives of the colonists during this period.

The private loans which Jean and Marie had made to other individuals over the years and which had not yet been entirely repaid totaled 42 livres 8 sols 3 deniers. The largest single amount among the unpaid sums, 15 livres 6 sols, was owed by Pierre Surard dit Lafrizade. It would probably require some legal procedures in the Montreal Court for Marie to regain this sum from the estate of this particular unmarried settler. He had been buried in the Lachine cemetery on the previous October 30, at the age of about 55 to 60, most likely a victim of the fierce epidemic which was still raging through the population of the St. Lawrence Valley at this time. Pierre Cardinal, age 22, owed the Lalonde estate just 4 livres; he had been married at Montreal back in September of 1685, and he and his wife

Marie Matou had produced their first child at Lachine in August of 1687. Michel Desrosiers dit Désilets, who likewise owed 4 livres, had been married at Montreal in January of 1679; he and his wife Marie Thomasse Artault were expecting their third child to be born at Montreal in about the coming September. Cybard Courault, who owed less than 3 livres, was the Lalondes' long time close neighbor at Bout de l'Île; his wife Françoise Goupil had stood as the godmother of Jean Baptiste, at his christening ceremony in the Montreal church back in October of 1675. Considering the very small amounts which were due on four of the loans, it is quite possible that they represented the unpaid balances which were still owed on loans that had originally been considerably larger.[59]

Seven days after drawing up their marriage contract and conducting the inventory of most of the Lalonde family possessions, Marie Barbant and Pierre Tabault exchanged their wedding vows. This hope-inspiring ceremony was conducted in the Holy Angels church at Lachine on January 26, 1688. During the course of their years of married life together, they would not produce any additional children.[60]

Fifteen months after the blending of the two families had commenced, it was time to settle a number of matters concerning the Lalonde estate. This business was conducted on April 23, 1689 by René Cuillerier (the neighbor who lived on the third farm to the east), since he had been designated as the supplemental or deputy guardian of Jean Baptiste and Guillaume Lalonde. Meeting at the hospital in Montreal with the Lachine notary Jean Baptiste Pothier, who would record the details, Monsieur Cuillerier first noted that he had sold the articles from the Lalonde estate which had represented the portion belonging to the two minor-age sons, for the sum of 432 livres. From this amount, he had deducted the five sums of 72 livres, 24 livres, 3 livres 10 sols, 16 livres 4 sols, and 55 livres, totaling 170 livres 15 sols. These various sums had been paid to their stepfather Pierre Tabault, to reimburse him for the specific expenses which he had been obliged to cover in settling the estate, as had been approved in an agreement between Messieurs Cuillerier and Tabault seven weeks earlier, back on February 3. After paying off this debt to Tabault, the guardian Cuillerier had transferred the remaining 266 livres to the nuns at the Hôtel Dieu de St. Joseph hospital in Montreal, in order to establish a long term loan. In return, the religious order would pay to the two male Lalonde heirs each year, via their guardian until they would reach the age of majority, the total sum of thirteen livres tournois, as the *rente annuelle et perpétuelle.*[61]

Three months later, at the beginning of August, the five boys in the household included Jean Baptiste Lalonde (age 13^{10}/12), Guillaume Lalonde (about to turn 5), Pierre Tabault (13^{10}/12, four days younger than Jean Baptiste), Alexis Tabault (9^{3}/4), and Jean Tabault (6^{10}/12).[62]

This summer, two topics seemed to be salient in nearly everyone's mind. One of these subjects was the high level of danger from lightning raids by Iroquois warriors. Back in 1687, after the military campaign by French and native forces into the lands of the Senecas, Iroquois war parties had resumed their sporadic attacks against the St. Lawrence settlers. It was during one of these raids that Jean de Lalonde had been killed, in September of that year. In the following year, due to Iroquois blockades around their two forts in the southwest, the French had been forced to abandon their distant and highly exposed new post at Niagara, near the western end of Lake Ontario. (The task of maintaining Ft. Frontenac, at the eastern end of this same lake, would soon become untenable, and it would likewise be closed in the autumn of 1689.) Close to home, stockades of refuge had been constructed at each of the exposed seigneuries during 1688. Along the southern shoreline of Montreal Island, from east to west, these had included the fortifications at Verdun (about 2^{1}/2 miles northeast of the Tabault-Lalonde farm), Ft. Cuillerier, on additional property that belonged to René Cuillerier, Sr. (^{4}/10 mile east of the Tabault-Lalonde property), Ft. Rémy at the village of Lachine (^{4}/10 mile west of their land), and Ft. Rolland (1^{3}/4 miles further to the west, at the western end of the Lachine seigneury). The residents of the seigneury of La Présentation or Côte St. Gilles, extending for about 2^{1}/4 miles west of Ft. Rolland (to about the present community of Dorval), would use the latter stockade as needed. Thus, the settlers who were spread out along some nine miles of the shoreline in this southeastern section of the island, from the eastern end of Verdun to the western end of La Présentation, had four palisades to which they could flee for protection in case of attacks.

Across the Atlantic, in the spring of 1689, war had broken out between France and the combined countries of England, Spain, the Dutch Netherlands, and the Hapsburg Empire. By late spring, ships had brought this news to the English colonies; unfortunately, word of it would not reach New France via French vessels until September. During the summer, the Iroquois nations had been elated to receive this information, which meant that in their upcoming war with the French, they would have the military support of both England and her colonies. However, unaware of these perilous events, the colonists along the St. Lawrence had no idea of the fierce onslaught that would soon descend upon many of them.

Lacking any knowledge of these grave events which were transpiring both to the south and across the ocean, the residents of Montreal Island were much more intrigued with the exciting project of the Lachine Canal. Going back a full decade, Fr. Dollier de Casson, the Superior of Montreal (the seigneurs of Montreal Island), had proposed the construction of such a waterway, running in a northeasterly direction between Lachine and Montreal. According to his ambitious plans, the project would entail widening and deepening the eastward-flowing branch of the small Rivière St. Pierre (which flowed northeastward from Lac St. Pierre to Montreal, along a course that was generally parallel to the St. Lawrence), and also digging a canal southwestward from Lac St. Pierre to the St. Lawrence River. Upon its completion, water diverted from the St. Lawrence would flow northeastward over the full distance of $8^1/2$ miles to Montreal. In this year of 1689, Fr. Dollier had proposed to the Intendant that those residents of the Lachine seigneury who had not paid their seigneurial fees should be obliged to work off those unpaid fees by laboring on the canal project. On June 5, the Intendant had issued an ordinance turning this proposal into law, and one week later, work had commenced on the project, the first canal in North America. However, this ground-breaking labor (both literally and figuratively) would come to an abrupt halt just seven weeks later, for reasons that had been entirely unforeseen.[63]

During the night of August 4-5, under the cover of darkness and a violent hailstorm, a massive force of about 1,500 Iroquois warriors crossed northward over the broad St. Lawrence. Silently spreading out along eight miles of shoreline, from the Sault St. Louis area beside the Lachine Rapids westward to La Présentation, the raiders remained undetected by the sentries in the various forts throughout the entire night. Waiting until dawn to launch their ferocious strike, the Iroquois, who numbered nearly 200 attackers per mile of shoreline, took the French completely by surprise. Soon, they had slain at least 24 French residents and had captured an estimated 79 others. They also destroyed by fire 56 of the 77 houses in the area, along with numerous stables, granaries, and other outbuildings, and killed a large portion of the livestock. In the immediate aftermath, most of the survivors of this first onslaught sought refuge within the four stockades. But some of them made their way to Montreal, where Governor Denonville was visiting at the time. Immediately, he sent Vaudreuil, the acting governor of Montreal, to the raided area with a force of about 300 soldiers. Their orders were to bolster the troops who had been manning the four forts, and enforce the Governor's orders that all of the residents of the attacked area were to gather within these stockades of refuge and remain there. After reaching Ft. Rolland, Vaudreuil sent word back to the Governor requesting additional reinforcements. In response, on August 6, the administrator dispatched about fifty soldiers and some thirty allied native warriors, under the command of Lieutenant Labeyre and Charles Lemoyne. This party covered the ten miles to Ft. Rémy (the Lachine village) without incident; however, after they departed from the fortified village, heading west toward Ft. Rolland ($1^3/4$ miles away), they were attacked by an Iroquois party. During the skirmish that followed, the enemy warriors killed and scalped about twenty of the native allies and captured about half of the soldiers, including Labeyre and four of his subaltern officers. In the fray, Lemoyne was wounded, but he and some of his companions managed to return to Ft. Rémy. During this debacle, which was taking place within sight of Ft. Rolland, the officers inside pleaded with Vaudreuil to be permitted to go to the aid of their comrades. But the commander refused, since his orders specifically stated that he and his forces were to remain within the forts! Previously, again taking his orders literally, Vaudreuil had denied permission to one of his officers to conduct a counter-attack upon a large party of Iroquois warriors. These enemies would have been easy prey, since they had become drunk on the liquor that they had seized in the homes. Thus, by remaining entirely in a defensive mode, the commander had lost at least two opportunities to fight back against the Iroquois raiders and inflict heavy casualties on them.

Somehow, Marie, Pierre, and all five of the Lalonde and Tabault sons survived the attack and evaded capture. However, numerous of their neighbors and friends were not so fortunate. (See the biography of François Brunet dit Le Bourbonnais, Sr. for a detailed discussion of those individuals who were killed or captured in the raid, and which of the captives eventually escaped or were released.) The only resident to die on site within the eastern two-thirds of the Lachine seigneury was little Madeleine Boursier, who was seven weeks short of her first birthday; she was drowned by Iroquois attackers. Both of her parents and one of her sisters were taken captive at their farm, which was located $1^1/2$ miles northeast of the Tabault-Lalonde farm. Six other settlers who lived in this area of the seigneury are known to have been captured. These included two members of the Jean Roy household ($2^1/2$ mile northeast of the Tabault-Lalondes), two people in the Jean Paré home (2 miles east of them), Catherine Renusson ($1^1/4$ mile east of them), and Pierre Pérusseau's wife Marie Leroy, in their home on the third lot to the west of the Tabault-Lalonde farm, by the eastern end of the stockaded village site. A short distance west of the village, Jean Fournier (who had served as a witness at the marriage contract ceremony of Marie and Pierre, and had also helped to draw up the inventory of the Lalonde family possessions on the same day) was wounded but escaped, while his wife Marie Crépin was captured. In addition, two soldiers died and were later buried there.[64]

A span of $1^3/4$ miles of river frontage comprised the western section of the Lachine seigneury. This area extended westward from Ft. Rémy (the stockaded-enclosed Lachine village site) to Ft. Rolland, at the edge of the La Présentation seigneury. In this particular area, residents in at least nine of the households suffered either death or capture at the hands of the Iroquois raiders. Although this horrific raid has been called for centuries the Lachine Massacre, the adjacent seigneury located immediately to the west suffered as many or more casualties than did the residents of the Lachine seigneury. In at least twelve of the households in La Présentation (which was also called Côte St. Gilles), many of the settlers were either slain or taken captive.[65]

The majority of the known casualties of this raid took place along a stretch of at least $6^1/2$ miles of St. Lawrence shoreline, extending westward from the Jean Roy household ($^1/2$ mile west of Verdun) to at least the René Chartier home ($^3/4$ mile west of Ft. Rolland). One of these stricken households in the western section of the Lachine seigneury was that of Pierre Maupetit dit Poitevin and Marie Louise Beaune. This couple lived with their three children on the fourth farm east of Ft. Rolland. They also owned the third lot to the east of the Lalondes' second farm on the Côte St. Louis, from which Marie Barbant and the two boys had moved to Lachine. Back in November of 1686, Jean de Lalonde had stood as the godfather of the second Maupetit child in the Lachine church, $10^1/2$ months before Jean had been killed. After Pierre Maupetit was seized in the raid on August 5, he either died or was killed while in Iroquois captivity. (The biography of this latter couple and their son Pierre, Jr., who are direct ancestors of the present author, is included later in this work.)[66]

It is undoubtedly true that the horrible events of death and destruction that occurred in this raid in August of 1689 must have scarred the psyches of the settlers living in this area for the rest of their lives. However, a number of period documents clearly show that, soon after the horrific attacks, many of the residents of the area began courageously repairing and rebuilding both their farms and their lives. As a testament to these activities, between August and the end of December in 1689, the priest performed five marriages, one baptism, and two burials at the parish church at Lachine. During the following year, Monseigneur de Saint Vallier came to the same edifice to conduct confirmation ceremonies. In addition, land grants in the Lachine seigneury were ceded to six individuals during the year of 1690; and within the space of just a few more years, all of the interior lands (in back of the original grants fronting on the St. Lawrence) were settled.[67]

It is not known whether the farm and livestock of the Tabault-Lalonde family had remained intact during the raid. Fortunately, all seven members of their blended family had survived the onslaught, at least physically. It is a documented fact that a great number of the homes, stables, granaries, and other outbuildings along the shoreline in this area of Montreal Island had been destroyed in the deadly raid, and that innumerable farm animals had also been killed. In addition, it would have probably been many weeks after the attacks, stretching into September of 1689, before those families who had lost their assets could safely commence rebuilding, due to the continued threat of Iroquois strikes. As a result, with winter approaching, many of the families who now lacked homes and other buildings, livestock, and stored foods left for Montreal. They intended to spend the first frozen season in town, before returning in the following spring to begin their rebuilding efforts in earnest. From the surviving documentation, it is not possible to determine whether Marie and Pierre were forced to leave for Montreal during this period, or whether they were able to remain on their farm east of the Lachine village.

Some two years after the horrific raid, Marie's first grandchild arrived, born to her daughter Marie Madeleine and her husband Guillaume Daoust $5^1/2$ years after their wedding. On September

13, 1691, baby Marie was both born at Montreal and baptized in the church there.[68]

Seven weeks later, on November 8, 1691, Marie and her eldest son Jean Baptiste visited the home of Jean Baptiste Migeon, Sieur de Branssat, and his wife Catherine Gauchet in Montreal, along with the notary Adhémar. Nearly four years earlier, back on January 26 in 1688, Marie had married Pierre Tabault. However, that relationship had apparently not worked out well. At some point during those intervening few years, she had requested that the Montreal Court grant to her a legal separation from Monsieur Tabault, and the Court had acceded to her wishes. As a result, at the time of this notarial transaction in the autumn of 1691, Marie was residing independently with her two sons in Montreal. Jean Baptiste had celebrated his 16th birthday a month before, while Guillaume was now $7^1/4$ years old.

Marie's legal action, which was invoked when a woman's material welfare was endangered, resulted in a division of the couple's communal possessions; it did not imply a physical separation. A *séparation quant aux biens* (a separation with regard to possessions) restored personal property to the wife, as well as her marital rights; in addition, its terms sometimes granted her an allowance for living expenses, provided by her husband. Petitions for the division of a couple's community of goods were typically based upon claims concerning the husband's misbehavior or mismanagement of affairs, actions which were endangering the material welfare of his wife and children. Once such a separation had been granted, neither a husband nor his creditors could touch the wife's property, and she was permitted to manage it on her own. However, she also had to have access to enough resources so that she and her children could survive. The legal separation which the Court had granted to Marie had been intended to create an official division of the Lalonde-Tabault couple's joint possessions, not to condone their physical division into two separate households. However, at some point, Marie and Pierre and their respective children had indeed separated into two distinct households. In this particular document from November of 1691, Marie was described as "wife separated from Pierre Tabault and authorized by the law." In a subsequent document from April of 1693, eighteen months later, the notary would not even mention Monsieur Tabault, or Marie's earlier marriage to him, in the record. The scribe would simply identify her as "Marie Barban, widow of Jean de Lalonde dit Lespérance, living in this town [of Montreal]."[69]

The document which the notary Antoine Adhémar penned on this November day in 1691 was exceedingly rare: the official registration of a voyageur-trader apprenticeship. Informal training in the skills of this occupation had been carried out ever since Frenchmen had begun traveling into the interior as trade ambassadors, back in 1611. Initially, this hands-on training had been offered by the visiting native traders who had transported young Frenchmen from the St. Lawrence settlements back to their home regions in the distant west and north. There, these young men had mastered the language, dress, customs, and lifestyles of their respective hosts. This had equipped them to serve as interpreters as well as cultural, diplomatic, and commercial liaisons between the native and the French worlds. In turn, these highly trained ambassadors had taught their newly-acquired native skills to other Frenchmen. This had enabled legions of these latter men to both survive and thrive in the challenging environment of the New World. It had also equipped them to operate as effective traders when Frenchmen had begun paddling into the interior regions specifically to trade, which had commenced in the summer of 1653 (although they had traveled for some time thereafter as dispersed paddlers among the native canoes, rather than in their own craft).

At this time, Jean Baptiste Migeon, Sieur de Branssat was absent from Montreal, so his business transactions were being handled by his wife, Catherine Gauchet de Belleville. Monsieur Migeon had operated as a prominent peltries merchant in Montreal for more than a quarter-century. During that time, three records of Montreal notaries had documented at least some of his hirings of voyageur-traders. On May 13 and May 18 in 1688, he and his partner Michel Messier, Sieur de Saint Michel had engaged René Deniau and Jean Baptiste Lemarché dit Laroche to work for them in the Ottawa Country. In the hiring of the latter man, there had also been a third partner operating with Messieurs Migeon and Messier, a man named Hébert. Two years later, on May 8, 1690, Jean Baptiste Migeon had hired without any partners a voyageur-trader to labor for him in the Ottawa Country; this latter *engagé* was Gabriel Lemieux. During the same quarter-century of his fur trade activities, Monsieur Migeon had also served as an important figure in the legal system, including thirteen years as the Chief Judge of the Montreal Court between 1677 and 1690. He and Catherine had been married in the Montreal church back in 1665, and during the following two decades, they had produced ten children; of these, five had already died. Jean Baptiste himself was destined to perish at Montreal in August of 1693, less than two years after his spouse presided over this voyageur-trader apprenticeship contract.[70]

"Before the notary [Antoine Adhémar] was present Marie Barban, wife separated from Pierre Tabault and authorized by the law, living at the said Villemarie, who with the consent of Jean Baptiste Lalonde, her son, has engaged him in service for one year, to commence on the said day [of his departure next year] at the command of the undersigned Monsieur Jean Baptiste Migeon, Sieur de Branssat, who is presently absent, Demoiselle Catherine Gauchet, his wife, present and accepting for him the said Lalonde into his service during the said year of work. The said Lalonde promises to well and properly work in everything that will be commanded of him and which will be done for the profit of the said Sieur Migeon, and to warn him of any damage if it comes to his knowledge. He will not be permitted to leave this service of work without the consent of the said Sieur Migeon, under the penalties carried by the ordinances, sentences, and regulations of the Sovereign Council of this region, which were presented to the hearing of the said Lalonde by the said notary in the presence of his said mother. It is agreed by the said parties that the said Lalonde will go up next spring or before the end of the said year [1692] to the Ottawa Country, to serve him until the present agreement will end. The said Sieur Migeon will pay to the said Lalonde his wages and salaries in proportion to the time which he will serve. Thus have they promised, obligated themselves, waived, etc.

[This agreement] made and drawn up at the said Villemarie in the home of Monsieur Migeon in the year 1691 on the eighth day of November in the afternoon, in the presence of [space left blank for later insertions], witnesses living at the said Villemarie, who have signed below with the said Demoiselle Migeon and the notary after the reading was done, according to the ordinance. [However, no signatures of Madame Migeon, the notary, or any witnesses were ever applied to the document in Monsieur Adhémar's ledger, nor were any names of witnesses ever inserted into the blank space.]"[71]

Jean Baptiste must have applied himself avidly to this training program, which commenced in about May of 1692 and had no expressed time limitations or rate of pay. In addition, he must have been imbued with a particular talent for this work, and with the appropriate attitudes and confidence. Just $4^1/3$ years after initiating his schooling in the skills and demands of this occupation, he would be employed by Sieur de Cadillac as a voyageur-trader working at the Straits of Mackinac. His period of service for this commandant would start one month before he would celebrate his 21st birthday.

Young Lalonde had entered the field at a time when the focus of the trade, which had for many decades been heavily fixated upon beaver pelts and native-tanned moose hides, was gradually converting to a much greater emphasis on other furs and hides. From the 1690s onward, these latter products, which were termed *menus pelleteries* or minor peltries, would become more and more important in the commerce. By shortly after 1701, more than half of all peltries acquired would be those other than beaver, with the full range of furs and hides figuring prominently in the trade. This pattern would continue until the 1730s, when the percentage of beaver pelts involved would reduce even further.[72]

In the spring of 1693, Jean Baptiste was age $17^1/2$, while Guillaume was $8^2/3$ years old. At this time, the elder brother submitted a petition to the Montreal Court, with the hope that the Chief Judge would order the nuns of the Hôtel Dieu hospital at Montreal to remit to him about one-third of the funds which the boys' supplemental guardian had earlier transferred to the nuns as a long-term loan. Four years earlier, back in April of 1689, René Cuillerier had handed over to the nuns 266 livres, with the stipulation that they would annually and perpetually pay to the two male Lalonde heirs the total sum of 13 livres tournois. Now, Jean Baptiste wished to have 87 livres of the loaned amount returned to him, so that he could purchase wheat to sow this spring, buy needed articles of clothing, and feed and care for his brother Guillaume. On the appointed day of April 23, the Judge summoned to the Court Jean Baptiste Lalonde, Marie Barbant (the underage boys' mother and legal guardian), and René Cuillerier (their supplemental guardian), as well as the Montreal residents Pierre Perthuis, François Prudhomme, Joseph Deniau dit Destaillis, Jean Mars, and Maurice Bénard dit Bourjoli, who would serve as advisors. After hearing the details of the case, the Judge ordered that the hospital nuns were to hand over to Jean Baptiste the requested sum. A notation at the end of the notary's document indicated that the Dames Religieuses Hospitalières did so on the same day.[73]

Seventeen months later, Marie stood as the godmother for the first baby to be born to Jacques Lanthier and Angélique Matou. At tiny Marie's christening ceremony on September 19, 1694 in the Montreal church, her godfather was Marin Hurtubise, another resident of Montreal. This baby had been born to the young couple $7^1/2$ months after their wedding ceremony, when Madame Lanthier was age 21. Before they would celebrate their 17th wedding anniversary, she would give birth to a total of thirteen children, of whom at least six would die at very young ages.[74]

In the spring of 1695, Guillaume was $10^2/3$ years of age. This was almost old enough to commence an apprenticeship, although most such indentures were not arranged for boys who were younger than age 12. Thus, on April 10, Marie visited the office of the Montreal notary Adhémar to arrange a contract of service for her younger son. The scribe, who identified her as "the widow of Jean de Lalonde, of the town of Villemarie," noted that young Guillaume would be working for the brothers Charles and Urbain Gervaise, businessmen of Montreal. Charles, age 26, had been married to Marie Boyer for $1^1/2$ years; their first child, Charles, Jr., was just two months old. Urbain, 21 years old, was still single at this time. During the course of the three-year period of service which was to begin on this day, the Gervaise brothers would be obliged to treat Guillaume humanely, to feed him appropriately for his station, and to clothe him. At the end of the term, they would also be obliged to provide to Guillaume a pair of French shoes, a pair of stockings, six shirts, a camisole, a hooded coat, and a cap, all of them new. These articles would represent his wages and salaries for the three years of service, in addition to the room, board, clothing, and training which he would had received during that time.[75]

By the end of the summer in 1696, it had been about $4^1/3$ years since Jean Baptiste had commenced his apprenticeship as a voyageur-trader, and he had apparently thrived during the course of this immersion training program. In addition, he was approaching his 21st birthday (which he would celebrate in early October), bringing him to about the peak of his physical development. On September 2, he was contracted of work for a year as a voyageur-trader in the western interior, during which time he would be based at the Straits of Mackinac.

The community of Michilimackinac or St. Ignace, located on the northern shore of the Straits or narrows between Lakes Huron and Michigan, had been first permanently settled by native people and Frenchmen in the autumn of 1671. Within a short time, this locale had become the very center of commercial, military, diplomatic, and missionary activities of the French in the entire upper Great Lakes region. In this capacity, it served as the central storage depot for westbound merchandise and supplies as well as eastbound furs and hides. In addition, St. Ignace was the place at which the traders acquired canoes, birchbark panels for covering their traveling shelters, and food supplies, which were produced by the native populations of the region. In 1683, the first French troops in the *Pays d'en Haut* (the Upper Country) had been stationed here, and Ft. De Buade had been constructed thereafter. The commandant of this facility served as the commander for the entire upper Great Lakes sphere. By the latter 1680s, the community had developed into four distinct segments, which were stretched out along the shoreline of the sandy cove at St. Ignace. In sequence from south to north, these consisted of the French village, the Jesuit mission, the Huron/Tionontate village, and the Ottawa village. The latter three entities each had a stockade wall surrounding their closely-spaced structures, offering protection.

In 1694, Antoine de Lamothe, the Sieur de Cadillac, had been appointed by Governor Frontenac as the commandant of Ft. De Buade. Some $2^1/4$ years later, by September of 1696 (when Jean Baptiste was hired to carry out commerce for him), Cadillac was 38 years old. This officer had advanced through the ranks of Lieutenant (1691), Captain (1693), and Midshipman (1694) before receiving the assignment of command at this post, which was the most crucial one in the entire interior. Back in June of 1687, Cadillac had married 16-year-old Marie Thérèse Guyon; during the following eight years, the couple had produced four children, in about 1688, 1690, 1692, and 1695. Thus, by the autumn of 1696, Marie Thérèse was 25 years old, and she had four children (who were 8, 6, 4, and $1^1/2$ years of age) living with her in their home at 16 Rue Notre Dame in Montreal.[76]

It was a well-known fact throughout the colony that the officers who commanded at the various interior posts supplemented their military pay with a considerable amount of fur trade profits. In many cases, this commerce was conducted openly by hired employees of the officers (such as Jean Baptiste Lalonde). However, in some instances, certain of the commandants (such as Cadillac) garnered a great deal of extra profits from the illegal sales of brandy to the native populations, as well as from the extortion of generous fees from those traders who operated within their domain but were not the commandant's own employees. In 1698, Governor Frontenac would pen these comments in support of the commercial activities of the officers at the distant posts:

"I believe that it is impossible to have the commandants and soldiers at the Michilimackinac and Miami [St. Joseph] posts live on their salary alone...[The commanders] are compelled by absolute necessity to hire three

Canadians [the decreed number for a single trading license], to each of whom they give from 400 to 500 livres per year in wages. They must [also] purchase a canoe for their journey [that of the three hired traders], which costs them 200 livres. Add to that about 300 livres for their provisions and supplies which are required to go only to Michilimackinac, plus those sums which they must pay [there] to have wood dragged from two leagues distant, which is necessary for their heat and that of their officers...How can it be possible for a Captain with his pay and the subaltern officers with a very modest one, and especially the soldiers, to subsist and provide for their needs while engaging in no trade whatsoever?"[77]

During the summer of 1696, just before Jean Baptiste arranged his employment contract with Cadillac, one subject was on nearly every colonist's mind: the future of the fur trade. During the previous year of 1695, the peltries market in France had become completely flooded with beaver pelts. At that time, the monopoly company had held in storage in the mother country some 3.5 million livres worth of beavers, which could not be sold at any price. Since the late 1680s, nearly four times more of this fur than could be dispersed had been shipped each year from New France to the mother country. As a result, during the 1690s, traders in the interior had attempted to focus more and more upon other furs besides beavers; however, the surplus of the latter fur had not dissipated.

To rectify the situation, Louis XIV and Pontchartrain, his Minister of the Marine and Colonies Department, had declared in May of 1696 a nearly complete withdrawal of Frenchmen from the western interior regions. No more licenses or permits were to be issued to trading personnel, and the peltries-exporting company was to accept no more beaver pelts; in addition, the interior forts were to be destroyed and the troops withdrawn. The only exception would be Ft. St. Louis in the Illinois Country, which would be kept open for military purposes. The native population would thereafter be required to travel exclusively out to the St. Lawrence communities to carry on commerce and receive presents. In response to their royal directive, Governor Frontenac had complained to the Minister, had postponed taking action until the following year of 1697, and had allowed commerce to continue.

However, due to the deep uncertainty concerning the future, only about nine voyageur-traders were engaged via Montreal notary contracts during this year of 1696. These included two men on April 10 and 16 (one who was specified for service in the Ottawa Country and one for Michilimackinac); two men on April 11 (who would work in the Ottawa Country after hauling in materiel for Cadillac); four men on August 21 and 24 (a three-man crew bound for the Ottawa Country and one man headed for the same destination); and Jean Baptiste Lalonde, who was hired by Cadillac on September 2 to labor for Cadillac in the Ottawa Country.[78]

Was present Jean Lalonde dit L'Espérance, residing at the said Villemarie, who has voluntarily bound and engaged himself to Antoine de Lamothe, Esquire, Sieur de Cadillac, Captain in the detachment of the Marine Department and commandant of the Ottawa Country, who was absent. Dame Thérèse Guyon, his wife, was present and assenting. [Lalonde] has agreed to go for one year to the Ottawa Country, to commence on the day of his departure from this town, during which time the said Lalonde will do all that shall be commanded of him that is honest and lawful and according to the common practice of voyageurs, for the profit of the said Sieur de Lamothe, and he will warn him of any damage if it comes to his knowledge. He is without the authority to leave the service of the said Sieur de Lamothe without his consent. This agreement is made with the stipulation that the said Dame [Lamothe] promises to furnish to him his provisions and canoe during the said time according to the common practice of voyageurs, and in addition to pay as his wages and salaries for the said year the sum of three hundred livres in the currency of this country, payable upon his return. The said Lalonde will be permitted to take for his own use two hooded coats, six shirts, two pairs of leggings, and twelve pounds of tobacco, and if they are not worn out, he will likewise be allowed to trade them. He will also be permitted to trade his gun and his blanket. Thus have they promised, obligated themselves, waived, etc.

[This agreement] made and drawn up at the said Villemarie in the office of the said notary, on the second day of September, 1696 in the afternoon, in the presence of Sieurs François Lory and Georges Pruneau, defense attorney for civil cases, as witnesses residing at the said Villemarie, who have signed below with the said Dame de Lamothe and the notary. The said Lalonde has declared that he does not know how to write or sign, having been questioned according to the ordinance.

Signed,

Marie Therese Guyon, Lory, G. Pruneau, and Adhemar, notary"[79]

In 1694, during Cadillac's first year of command at Ft. De Buade, he had hired a single voyageur-trader via Montreal notary contracts. This man had been engaged on September 10, and his agreement had specified that he would serve in the Ottawa Country. The next year, the commandant had employed two such men; in their contracts, dated June 6 and June 7, 1695, they had each been designated for service at Michilimackinac. Finally, during the officer's third and last year as the commander of the entire upper Great Lakes region, he had hired Louis Durand and Joseph Moreau on April 11, and then Jean Baptiste Lalonde on September 2; their respective agreements had described their service as taking place in the Ottawa Country. (In the following year of 1697, no voyageur-traders would be engaged for the west in Montreal notary documents. The 1697-1698 trading season would be the last one at which commerce would be legally permitted at Ft. De Buade and its subsidiary posts, such as Fts. St. Joseph and La Baye; the majority of the interior facilities would be evacuated in 1698. Thereafter, trade would be allowed to continue legally only at Ft. Frontenac, at the eastern end of Lake Ontario; at the post at Chicago and at Ft. St. Louis, in the Illinois Country; and at Ft. Tourette/La Maune, at the northern end of Lake Nipigon, north of Lake Superior.)[80]

In the spring of 1696, in preparation for the upcoming trading season, Madame Cadillac had acquired the new infusion of trade merchandise and supplies which would be needed by her husband and his employees. This was the cargo which Louis Durand and Joseph Moreau would haul in to the Straits, and some of which Jean Baptiste Lalonde would later trade with native customers over the course of the following year. The source of these goods was Antoine Pascaud, one of the most prominent merchant-outfitters of Montreal. Having earlier been a businessman and banker at La Rochelle, he had immigrated to Montreal by the summer of 1686. A decade later, when he was about age 31, he was still single; he would marry in the Montreal church in the following January of 1697.

The outfit which Marie Thérèse Guyon had purchased on credit from Monsieur Pascaud was worth the considerable sum of 3,114 livres 7 sols 6 deniers. She had carried out this transaction with the legal authority of a letter that Cadillac had signed back on August 16, 1695; this missive had authorized her to purchase merchandise from this specific merchant. According to the notarial agreement which she had signed on April 23, 1696, she and her spouse owed this sum of money

"for good trade merchandise which has been delivered by the said Sieur [Jean] Lardouin [Monsieur Pascaud's clerk] to the said Madame de Lamothe a little while ago, for the outfit which she is sending to the said Sieur de

Lamothe, her husband, with which she was and is satisfied...For the present agreement, the said Dame has chosen as her legal residence [to which writs may be delivered] the house where she presently resides, at sixteen Notre Dame Street."

In the document, Madame Cadillac agreed that she and Captain Cadillac would pay off this credit purchase during September of 1697. A later notation, which would be added to the bottom of this record on October 12, 1697, would indicate that Monsieur Pascaud had received full payment on or before that date "for the contents contained within the present obligation."[81]

Captain Cadillac had received one trading license from the Governor in 1696, which allowed him to have one canoe-load of merchandise and supplies dispatched to him at Ft. De Buade. Thus, Louis Durand and Joseph Moreau had been hired on April 11 to paddle this craft westward to Michilimackinac. For this service, they would each receive 100 livres in currency, upon their return to Montreal in September with a cargo of the officer's outbound peltries, without having to otherwise work for him. According to their contract, each of these men was to be permitted to haul in 100 livres worth of his own merchandise, which he could trade for his own profit at any destination that the men would choose, after they had delivered the westbound canoe-load to the Captain at the fort.

While the two voyageurs had been preparing for their departure, they had been notified by Madame Cadillac that they were to convey not only the legal canoe, but also a second illegal one, filled with unauthorized trade merchandise. Since the latter craft was already illegal, Messieurs Durand and Moreau had loaded an additional 400 to 500 livres worth of goods into it, which were to be traded for their own profits. Within the two craft, Cadillac's trade merchandise had included a total of 198 half-gallons of brandy, an amount which would generate some 5,000 livres worth of peltries in the Upper Country; it was also illegal as a trade item.

At the time of departure of the westbound convoy in May, under the leadership of Pierre d'Ailleboust, Sieur d'Argenteuil (second-in-command at the Straits), the commissary of the King's storehouse at Montreal had discovered the deception of Cadillac, while he was checking the license of each canoe. He had then seized the one illegal craft and its cargo; these were later auctioned off for 675 livres after expenses, which sum was given to the Hôtel Dieu hospital at Montreal, as a charitable donation. Durand and Moreau had been permitted to set off with the convoy in the one licensed canoe of the commandant.

After arriving at St. Ignace, the two paddlers, now turned voyageur-traders, had purchased from Cadillac the illegal cargo which they had brought up for him, as well as two other illicit canoe-loads which had been transported up for the commandant in the same brigade, in native craft. The two men had intended to travel westward, trade the huge cargo, and then repay on their downward journey the nearly 7,000 livres which they owed for the merchandise, plus interest on this amount. However, before the partners had been able to depart from St. Ignace, the scheme had begun to unravel.

First, Cadillac had ordered that they be arrested, for allegedly having harmed a dog which belonged to a native resident. After a month, the two men had informed Cadillac that they would not comply with their agreement to market the purchased goods on a trading voyage. Finally, while they had been officially confined to their cabin, their belongings had been confiscated, on the grounds that they had brought with them more than 100 livres of merchandise to trade for their own profit, thus violating their employment contract. Since the two men had already traded locally their supply of brandy and much of their other personal merchandise, their confiscated possessions had contained two letters of credit or promissory notes from major purchasers, which represented a considerable amount of money. However, not having in hand those letters or notes, which could have been utilized as currency, the two men had been without resources. As a consequence, Durand and Moreau had been obliged to borrow a canoe, provisions, and merchandise from other traders, after which they had made a commercial voyage to Chequamegon Bay on Lake Superior, and from there southwestward into Dakota Country.

Upon their return to Montreal, the two men would file a lawsuit against Cadillac, for the loss of their wages, personal property, and trade merchandise. In response, the commandant would file a countersuit, based upon the charge which he had brought against them at St. Ignace, for having brought in too much merchandise to sell. After considerable elapsed time, an attempted arbitration, and much deliberation, the Intendant would finally declare in July of 1698 that Cadillac was obliged to pay Moreau 1,866 livres in compensation; by then, Durand would have dropped his side of the suit. However, Cadillac would then arrange for Governor Frontenac to block this court decision, after which the case would be referred to Versailles for judgement.

Presented below is a summary of the articles which Cadillac had confiscated from Messieurs Durand and Moreau at St. Ignace on July 27, 1696. Under the Captain's orders, the items had been removed from the cabin of the two men by a sergeant and a number of soldiers of the garrison at the fort. These articles, representing both personal belongings and trade merchandise, would be mentioned in the records of the ensuing court case, and in letters concerning the related incidents which had taken place at the Straits. In all likelihood, Jean Baptiste Lalonde would have similar items at St. Ignace, either as his own personal possessions or as articles for trading, during the following year of his tenure at the Straits in 1696 and 1697.

1 pair of stockings from St. Maixent
1 dress coat
18 yards of red woolen fabric from Limbourg
blankets
guns
5 kegs of gunpowder
20 pounds of lead
18 pounds of vermilion paint pigment
canoes

1 chest containing:
1 clasp knife
1 knife
1 mirror
2 razors
6 packs of playing cards
paper
1 writing set
1 stick of sealing wax
1 seal [for impressing the sealing wax on letters]
1 promissory note for 1,600 livres value
1 promissory note for 1,500 livres value

15 sacks of shelled corn
other food supplies
salt
$^{1}/_{2}$ pound of pepper

nutmeg
brandy
wine

Supplies of peltries:
7 packs of beaver pelts
2 otter pelts
2 bull elk hides
3 cow elk hides[82]

In contrast to the deep immersion of Durand and Moreau in Cadillac's shady dealings in 1696, no personal or legal difficulties were apparently ever recorded concerning Jean Baptiste's period of service for the Captain during 1696 and 1697. However, considering the commandant's prior and later history, it is highly likely that our Monsieur Lalonde traded both legal and illicit merchandise for his employer in and around the Straits of Mackinac during that span of time.

After exiting from Michilimackinac in 1697, Captain Cadillac would pen a memoir concerning life at the Straits of Mackinac and in the wider region, as it was carried on by both the French and the native residents. Many of his observations, concerning the period of his command from 1694 to 1697, reflected the experiences that Jean Baptiste would have had during his year of working for the commandant there.

"The position of this post is most advantageous, because it is on Lake Huron, through which all of the nations from the south are obliged to pass when they go down to Montreal and in coming back [via the Ottawa River route], as well as the Frenchmen who wish to trade in the Upper Country. None of them can pass without being observed, for the horizon is so clear that canoes can be seen from the fort as far as the keenest sight can reach. In short, it may be said that this place is the center of the entirety of this farther colony, where one is in the midst of all of the other posts, and almost at an equal distance from each of them, and among all of the nations who have dealings with us...
The houses of the French are built of wood, in pièce-sur-pièce style [with the intervals between the widely-spaced vertical framework timbers filled with horizontal timbers]. However, they are roofed with cedar bark. Only the houses of the Jesuits are roofed with [split or sawn] planks...
With regard to the land, each [native] nation has its own district, and each family marks out its piece of land and its fields...Their harvest consists of corn, peas, beans, pumpkins, and watermelons [the peas having been introduced

by the French]. The great abundance of fish and the ease of catching them caused the natives to make a settlement in this region. It is a daily manna which never fails; there is not a family which does not catch sufficient fish to live on throughout the year...I ought to mention the pleasure of seeing them bring up, in one [gill] net, as many as a hundred whitefish. This is the most delicate fish in the lake...They also catch a large number of trout, weighing up to 50 pounds...Finally, sturgeon, pike, carp, herring, dory, and a hundred different kinds of fish abound in this particular part of the lake.

It may be of interest also to state on what foods the French and the natives live...Sagimity [consisting of pounded dried corn boiled with whitefish, is a mainstay]...They eat fish cooked in all sorts of ways: fried, roasted, boiled, smoked, or stewed. They have neither oil nor butter, but they have grease and marrow from the elk, moose, or buffalo, the lattermost of which is brought to Michilimackinac from the Illinois Country or from Chicago...They make bread with corn meal, which they bake under the ashes or in hot sand...

They barter their beaver pelts for our goods; this is what is called trading, or doing trade. We supply them with gunpowder, balls, firearms, cloth, tobacco, and everything else that we use.

If people could realize the labor which is involved in acquiring beaver pelts, they would not think so lightly of this commodity. For it should be known that the French trading party generally leaves Montreal at the beginning of spring, or about the 15th of September. In this country, both seasons are bad, the first because it is the time when the ice and snow melt, making the current strong and the water very cold, and the second because it is the beginning of the ice and snow...The Canadians have to make a journey of 300 leagues by this continual and laborious work [paddling and portaging] before reaching Michilimackinac...

When they arrive here, instead of trying to recover a little from their fatigue, they hasten to continue their journey, and go on as soon as possible. They generally re-equip themselves here with canoes and provisions, after which some of them go to the northwestern coast of Lake Superior and others to the south [along Lake Huron], and they follow the rivers into the back country for a distance of 200 or 300 leagues. Some of them, following Lake Michigan, go south [and west via the Fox, Wisconsin, and Mississippi Rivers] to the most distant nations. The object of all of them alike is to get beaver pelts.

When the voyageurs have sold their goods, they return to Michilimackinac, generally arriving at the beginning of July. Here they re-equip themselves anew, and go down to Montreal in a convoy, if the commandant of the country thinks it is safe. It is clear, therefore, that those who engage in this trade for beaver pelts have to travel at least 1,000 leagues [in their round trip] before getting back to Montreal. However, aside from this, it is difficult to conceive the dangers to which they are exposed in shooting whirlpools, falls, and rapids.... Nor is this all. They must also risk losing their lives at the hands of the Iroquois, who prepare ambushes in narrow passes along the route, and if a man is captured alive, he must be prepared to be burned to death by inches. It is true [however,] that all necessary precautions are taken to avoid this misfortune, and it rarely happens that our convoys are defeated."[83]

During the latter part of the summer in 1697, Jean Baptiste traveled out to the St. Lawrence settlements with a massive flotilla of canoes which were manned by French and native paddlers, arriving at Montreal on August 29. These craft transported the impressive amount of nearly 176,000 livres worth of beaver pelts, some of which had been gathered by Monsieur Lalonde through the commerce that he had carried out for his employer. Captain Cadillac also traveled out in this massed brigade, since he had requested that he be relieved of his command at the Straits. The officer soon wrote to Versailles:

"I arrived at Montreal at the beginning of September with the convoy, which I led safely to its destination. At the same time, I had persuaded three hundred natives [Hurons, Ottawas, Potawatomis, and Sauks] to follow me, upon the notification which I had received through [the Intendant] of the designs that old England had on Quebec; this small reinforcement would have inconvenienced the enemies waging the campaign [if such an invasion had taken place.]"

Upon his return, Cadillac paid Jean Baptiste his well-earned salary of 300 livres for his twelve months of employment. About six weeks later, on October 12, the officer paid off his outfitting bill with the Montreal merchant Antoine Pascaud, as he settled his financial affairs.[84] Then, Cadillac continued to plan and scheme for his next venture. In 1698, he would sail to Paris, to lobby for royal support for his bold new project, establishing a fort and a colony of French and native settlers at the strait between Lake Huron and Lake Erie, at the locale which was known as Le Détroit. He would found this community three years later, during the summer of 1701.

Back in July of 1696, some two months before Jean Baptiste had set off for the west, a massive military campaign had been conducted against the Iroquois in their own homeland. Departing from Montreal on July 4, Governor Frontenac had led a combined force of some 2,150 men, including regular troops, militia fighters, and allied warriors from the St. Lawrence settlements. Before their arrival in the central

Iroquois territory, the Onondagas had burned their own villages and had fled; thus, the French forces had only been able to destroy the fields of crops and the caches of harvested foods. When the army had proceeded eastward to the Oneida lands, the same scenario had been enacted. Therefore, by the the time of the return of the massed forces to Montreal on August 20, they had caused the death of only a single Iroquois individual, a very old Onondaga man who had been too feeble to escape; he had been slowly roasted by the allied warriors. However, the campaign had broken the spirit of offense which the Iroquois had possessed for so long. Throughout the following two years, numerous war parties of allied native nations would carry out raids in Iroquois territory, until peace negotiations would finally begin. These talks would extend from 1698 until 1701, at which time the Great Treaty would finally be ratified at Montreal by the Iroquois, the French, and all of their native allies. In this manner, the long and brutal Iroquois wars would finally draw to a close.[85]

Jean Baptiste Lalonde celebrated his 22nd birthday in early October of 1697, within weeks of his return from the Ottawa Country. He apparently decided at about this time that he ought to marry, settle down, and raise a family. Thus, he sought and finally found his life partner, living at Pointe aux Trembles, near the northeastern tip of Montreal Island, some ten miles north of Montreal. Marguerite Masta, the daughter of the deceased Mathurin Masta (who had been a master stone cutter and mason at Montreal in his day) and of Catherine or Antoinette Éloy, would turn age 17 on December 12 of this year. Marguerite had been the sixth of seven children of this family, of whom only three had grown to adulthood. One of her brothers had died by drowning in July of 1679, shortly before his tenth birthday. Then, two of her sisters had perished on the same day in November of 1687, at ages 10 and 4, during the vicious double epidemic of smallpox and measles. Finally, another brother had been killed by Iroquois warriors during July of 1690, at the age of 18. In the midst of these poignant deaths of four of her siblings, Marguerite's father had also died at Pointe aux Trembles in May of 1688, at about 44 or 45 years of age; she had been $7^1/2$ years old at the time (afterward, her mother had never remarried). Back in 1686, Marguerite's only surviving sister had married at the age of 21. Now, her only living brother was 23 years old and still single, while her mother was about age 53 to 55.[86]

On September 15, 1697, when Marguerite had been $16^3/4$ years old, she had appeared as the godmother for the one-day-old baby boy of Jean Venne and Françoise Beauchamp. At this ceremony, held in the Infant Jésus church at Pointe aux Trembles, her co-sponsor had been François Renault. Mademoiselle Masta's appearance at these festivities had followed a long-practiced custom in New France. For many decades, it had been quite common for young women who had reached marriageable age to be chosen as godmothers for christening ceremonies; this allowed them to be presented in a dignified manner to the public, especially to potential suitors.[87]

Four months later, on January 24, 1698, Jean Baptiste, Marguerite, and various of their relatives and friends assembled in the office of the Montreal notary Antoine Adhémar, to draw up their marriage contract. In the scribe's record, the prospective groom was described as "son of the deceased Jean Lalonde and of Marie Barban, his father and mother, living on this island in the St. Joseph Quarter near this said town of Villemarie [1 1/2 miles south-southwest of the stockaded town], assisted by and with the consent of Sieur René Cuillerier, his guardian [the young man would not reach the age of legal majority for another three years]." The witnesses on his side were Monsieur Cuillerier and his sister Marie Madeleine Lalonde, the wife of Guillaume Daoust. On the prospective bride's side, the witnesses were Pierre Perthuis dit Lalime, Nicolas Senet dit Laliberté, and Jean Roy. On this occasion, Jean Baptiste promised to Marguerite a prefixed dower of 400 livres. At the end of the four-page document, at the place where the notary wrote "mark of the said future husband," Jean Baptiste made a bold + mark; immediately below this line, his bride-to-be signed "Marguerite Mastas."[88]

Ten days later, on February 3, the party again assembled, this time in the bride's home church at Pointe aux Trembles. On this occasion, as the bride and the groom pronounced their wedding vows, the five official witnesses included Jean Baptiste's brother-in-law Guillaume Daoust (this couple lived in the Pointe aux Trembles parish), Marguerite's only brother Toussaint Masta, and their friends Nicolas Senet dit Laliberté, Louis Beaudry, and François Renaud dit Blanchard. After completing their nuptial ceremony, Marguerite signed the parish ledger, but Jean Baptiste was unable to do so.[89]

Settling in the Pointe aux Trembles parish, near the northeastern end of Montreal Island, the newlyweds set up housekeeping some seven miles north of Longueuil, where Jean Baptiste's mother was residing. This latter community was located on the opposite (eastern) shore of the St. Lawrence, a short distance northeast of Montreal. By the summer of 1698, J.B.'s younger brother Guillaume (who was now one month away from turning age 14) had completed his three-year contract of working for the Montreal businessmen Charles and Urbain Gervaise. On July 25, 1698, Marie Barbant visited the Montreal notary Adhémar to create a new service contract for her younger son. This time, his apprenticeship would be with only Urbain Gervaise, age 24, the younger of the two brothers. According to this new agreement, which would run for five years beginning on this day, the young trainee worker would be treated humanely, as well as being fed, housed, and clothed by his employer. At the conclusion of his service period, he would receive from Monsieur Gervaise a pair of French shoes, a pair of stockings, a pair of breeches made of woolen Mazamet fabric, six shirts, a chemisette, two cravats, a hooded coat, and a tapabord hat, all of them new items. In addition, he would also receive a young cow which had been calved during the spring of the previous year (thus making it about fifteen months old at the time of Guillaume's release from his contract in July of 1703). These various articles, in addition to his room, board, clothing, and training, would constitute his wages and salaries for his five years of labor.[90]

Four months later, Jean Baptiste and Marguerite met with the Montreal notary Adhémar, who was visiting their community of Pointe aux Trembles on November 17, to register with him a discharge receipt. Some time previously, the young couple had received a loan of 150 livres from Catherine Éloy, Marguerite's mother. On this day, they reported that they had repaid this sum in full to Madame Masta. In the scribe's document, Monsieur and Madame Lalonde were described as "living at the said market town (*bourg*) of Pointe aux Trembles." The notary could not have realized that, some 9 1/2 months later, this couple would be eagerly awaiting the arrival of their first child.[91]

On September 4, 1699, nineteen months after they had celebrated their wedding, Jean Baptiste and Marguerite were elated to deliver this baby. On the same day as his birth, little François was baptized in the Infant Jésus church at Pointe aux Trembles, with the baby's uncle Toussaint Masta standing as his godfather and Marguerite Perthuis appearing as his godmother.[92]

However, the celebratory mood of the entire family was absolutely dashed just eighteen days later. On September 22, Marguerite died as a result of complications that she had sustained during the baby's delivery. On the day following this tragic loss, she was gently laid to rest in the cemetery at Pointe aux Trembles, with the official witnesses Gilles Martin and Guillaume Daoust (Jean Baptiste's brother-in-law) in attendance. The officiating priest recorded in the parish ledger that the deceased had been 20 years old. However, she had actually been ten weeks short of celebrating her 19th birthday, having been both born and baptized on December 12, 1680.[93]

Sixteen days after Marguerite's mournful funeral, on October 9, Jean Baptiste traveled to Montreal, to the home of the merchant Pierre Perthuis, who was a friend of the Masta family. (He had been one of the witnesses on the bride's side when the couple had drawn up their marriage contract before their wedding.) At this time, J.B. acknowledged that he and the now-deceased Marguerite had previously received 150 livres worth of merchandise from Monsieur Perthuis, which had been paid for at the time by Catherine Éloy, her mother and his mother-in-law. This transaction had been recorded on pages 232 and 233 of the merchant's ledger number 9. On this October day, the notary who was present documented that Jean Baptiste and Marguerite had later repaid the 150 livres to Madame Masta. However, Monsieur Lalonde still owed Pierre Perthuis the sum of 7 livres 8 sols, for other merchandise that had been provided by the merchant.[94]

The death of Marguerite Masta, Jean Baptiste's wife of just nineteen months, was not the only sad loss that the Lalonde clan had to bear during the year of 1699. On October 18, Marie Madeleine Lalonde and her husband Guillaume Daoust lost their eldest child, Marie, who had celebrated her eighth birthday one month earlier. This couple and their four offspring had moved from the Pointe aux Trembles parish to the Lachine parish during the previous month, shortly after their two-day-old fourth baby had been baptized in the Pointe church on September 13.[95]

After Jean Baptiste had been a widower for $16^{1}/_{2}$ months, he visited the home of the Montreal notary Pierre Raimbault on February 7, 1701, to acknowledge some old debts which he still owed to one of the Montreal merchant-outfitters. Unfortunately, the scribe did not record the specific locale at which J.B. and his 17-month-old son François were permanently living at this time.

"Before the royal notaries of the Island of Montreal, residing at Villemarie and signed below, was present Jean de Lalonde, voyageur, habitant of this Island and at present in this town, who has voluntarily acknowledged

and declared that he truly and rightfully owes to Sieur Nicolas Janvrin [dit] Dufresne, merchant of this town, absent, the undersigned notaries stipulating and assenting for him, the sum of 101 livres 10 sols in currency of the country, plus 30 sols as the fee for this document, for merchandise which was earlier furnished to the said debtor for his voyages by the said Sieur Creditor, for generally all of their accounts which have been passed up to this day. He has promised and obligated himself to render, furnish, and pay the said sum of 101 livres 10 sols [plus 1 livre 10 sols in notary fees] voluntarily to the said creditor at his home in this town or to the bearer upon the first request of the said Sieur Creditor, under the penalty of all expenses, damages, and interests. For the execution of these presents, he has selected as his [temporary] legal residence [to which writs may be delivered] the residence of [Pierre] Raimbault, one of the said undersigned notaries, located on St. François Street in this town. Thus have they promised, obligated themselves, waived, etc.

[This agreement] made and drawn up at the said Villemarie in our office in the year 1701 on the seventh day of February in the afternoon. [The said Lalonde] has declared that he does not know how to write or sign, having been questioned and asked after the reading was done, according to the ordinance.

Signed,

P. Raimbault, royal notary, and Adhemar"[96]

Apparently, Monsieur Janvrin had furnished to Jean Baptiste the supplies and merchandise that he had needed for his various early trading voyages, those which he had carried out during his four-year-long voyageur apprenticeship program. The merchant may have also supplied J.B. with a number of personal articles before he had departed on his 1696-1697 venture in the employ of Cadillac.

Nicolas Janvrin dit Dufresne, 46 years old at this time, had immigrated to Quebec by at least the summer or autumn of 1684. He had been married there in January of 1689, after which he and his wife, Marie Madeleine Berson, had relocated to Montreal. There, their first child, a daughter, had died in August of 1693 at the age of 14 months. However, their second baby, a son, arriving in the summer of 1695, was growing up in good health; he would eventually marry at the age of 27.[97]

By the autumn in this same year of 1701, Jean Baptiste had been a widower for two full years. Unfortunately, his first life partner had died at a very untimely age, after just nineteen months of marriage. However, it was now time for him to move forward and find a new partner, someone with whom he could share an entire lifetime, an individual who would help him raise his two-year-old son and run their household. At some point during the previous two years, the bereaved father and his toddler had relocated south-southwestward from the community of Pointe aux Trembles to the Côte St. Pierre, which was also on Montreal Island.[98] This sub-fief, which was located on the northwest side of Lac St. Pierre, commenced about $1^7/8$ miles north of the Lachine village and extended northward for nearly two miles. Eventually, Jean Baptiste found his new love on the opposite side of the St. Lawrence, in the seigneury of Laprairie, which was located about five miles southeast of Côte St. Pierre and an equal distance south-southeast of Montreal.

Jeanne Gervais, having been born and raised at Laprairie, was the eldest child of Mathieu Gervais dit Parisien and Michelle Picard. Mathieu had arrived in the colony during the summer of 1665, as a soldier in the Carignan-Salières Regiment. (He had apparently acquired his nickname based upon his place of origin, St. Maur des Fossés, which was located about seven miles southeast of Paris.) Eleven years after his arrival, in August of 1676 (at the age of about 28 to 30), he had exchanged wedding vows in the Montreal church with Michelle, a Montreal native who had celebrated her 15th birthday two months earlier. Moving across the St. Lawrence to Laprairie, the couple had welcomed into the world Jeanne, their first child, in early August of 1679; she had been christened in the Laprairie church on August 5. This first offspring had been followed by nine others over the course of the following twenty years. This Gervais brood had been especially fortunate in their survival rate: all of them except one would grow to adulthood and be married. Only Mathieu, born in May of 1695, apparently died early, since no documentation for him other than his birth and baptism have been located in the colony's records.

On December 27, 1698, when Jeanne had been $19^1/3$ years of age, she had stood as the godmother of the fourth child of the Laprairie residents Gabriel Lemieux and Jeanne Robidou. On this occasion in the Laprairie church, the godfather of little Joseph had been Joseph Robidou, the baby's uncle. This particular church celebration had served as Jeanne's informal introduction to the wider public, since she had now reached a marriageable age.

Some $1^3/4$ years later, on September 10, 1701, Jeanne had again stood beside the baptismal font in the church at Laprairie, this time as the sponsor of her nephew Charles Marcil. He was the first baby to be born to Jeanne's next-younger sister Romaine Gervais, who had married the Laprairie voyageur Charles Marcil $9^1/2$ months earlier. On this happy day, the baby's other sponsor had been his uncle Étienne Marcil dit L'Espagnol.[99]

By this point, Jeanne (now 22) had probably already met and been courted by the widower Jean Baptiste Lalonde, who was about to celebrate his 26th birthday. The prospective groom had two legal steps to complete before the engaged couple could arrange their marriage contract and then celebrate their wedding in church. The first task would be the official designation by the Montreal Court of the legal guardian and the supplemental guardian of his son François, who was 25 months old. This step would be followed by an official inventory, being conducted by appointed individuals, of the possessions which belonged to Jean Baptiste and his deceased wife Marguerite. This latter procedure would safeguard the inheritance which would be legally due to their only child, at some point in the future.

At ten o'clock in the morning on October 21, 1701, seven individuals answered the summons of the Chief Judge of the Montreal Court to appear in his legal chamber on that appointed day. Together, they would determine who would be the guardians of François Lalonde, the minor-age son of Jean Baptiste Lalonde and the deceased Marguerite Masta. The attendees included the two principal male figures in the boy's life, his father Jean Baptiste Lalonde and his uncle Guillaume Daoust (the husband of J.B.'s sister Marie Madeleine, now living with their children in the Lachine seigneury), plus five advisors: Jean Sabourin dit Chaunière (resident of Pointe aux Trembles), Jean Cusson (royal notary at Montreal, and resident of Bout de l'Île), François Leroux, François Lory dit Gargot (royal bailiff of the Montreal Court, and resident of Lachine), and Lambert Leduc (resident of Montreal). During the course of the morning's hearing, Jacques Alexis de Fleury, the Sieur d'Eschambault, who was the *Lieutenant général civil et criminel* (Chief Judge) of the Court, heard testimony from the various individuals. Then he determined that Monsieur Lalonde would serve as the lad's *tuteur* or guardian, while Monsieur Daoust would serve as his *tuteur subrogé* (supplemental or deputy guardian).[100]

In the afternoon on the same day, the inventory of the Lalonde-Masta estate was conducted, at the place where Jean Baptiste and little François had taken up residence. This was on a lot in the Côte St. Pierre which belonged to Joseph Leduc, a long time resident of Montreal. This man, 41 years of age, had been married to Catherine Cuillerier for nearly fifteen years; they were expecting their eighth child in about four months.[101]

"In the year 1701 on the 21st day of October in the afternoon, at the request of Jean [Baptiste] de Lalonde, habitant living on this Island on a concession belonging to the habitant Joseph Leduc, located on the Côte St. Pierre on this Island, both in his name and for the estate of the possessions which there were between him and Marguerite Masta, his deceased wife, as well as being the guardian of François, underage child of him and of her, and in the presence of Guillaume Daoust, supplemental guardian of the said underage child, appointed according to the judgement of relatives and friends of this minor by an act [of the Court] which was sent this day by Master Notary Adhémar... The undersigned royal notary of Montreal Island [Pierre Raimbault], residing at Villemarie, present with Joseph Leduc and Jacques Desgagnés, habitants of the said place and witnesses who have signed below, have conducted a proper and honest inventory and description of all of the moveable possessions, titles, papers, and instructions of the said estate which were found to exist there in the said house and place upon the said land where the said Lalonde is living, the said articles having been shown, explained, and placed in evidence by the said Lalonde and Marie Barbant, his mother. For this present inventory by them, produced by the hand of the notary, they have neither held back nor diverted anything, under the penalties which were presented for their hearing. The articles have been well priced and appraised by Paul Descaries, Pierre Hurtubise, and Lambert Leduc [older brother of Joseph, who owned the property on which J.B. and his son were residing], habitants living as close neighbors to the said concession, having been appointed for this purpose by an ordinance of Monsieur the Lieutenant General [Chief Judge], clerk of the seat of the royal Court and [governmental] jurisdiction of this Island, on the date of this day, who have been permitted to carry out according to their conscience the said pricing in relation to the present time, for the sums of money which follow. They have signed, except for the said Lalonde, Pierre Hurtubise, Joseph Leduc, one of the said witnesses, and the said Barbant, who have declared that they do not know how to write or sign, having been asked according to the ordinance. They have agreed that the ten words crossed out are null and void.
Signed,
Paul Decari, Lambert Leduc, Desgagnie, and P. Raimbault, notary

First were presented 5 promissory notes, privately undersigned, of which one blank one was estimated at three crowns [6 livres], totalling..........110 livres (l.)

1 mare... 100 l.
1 small cow.. 40 l.
2 small lambs .... 16 l.
2¹/₂ dozen [30] chickens and chicks ....22 l. 10 s.

In the house were found
2 pickaxes .... 4 l.
1 axe .... 4 l.
2 old copper kettles..3 l. 10 s.
1 cooking pot with its cover .... 4 l.
1 large cooking spoon... 1 l.
1 frying pan.. 2 l.
1 low-walled saucepan .... 2 l.
1 old kettle for drinking..15 s.
6 pewter plates .... 7 l.
2 pewter basins.. 3 l.
4 pewter spoons... 1 l.
1 small tablecloth ....1 l. 10 s.
¹/₂ yard of linen fabric from Cadix .... 15 l.
2 old chemises, for the use of the said deceased .... 4 l.
1 skirt of brown woolen bunting fabric, for the use of the said deceased ...12 l.
1 skirt of black silk taffeta fabric.. 12 l.
1 apron of grey woolen bunting fabric.. 2 l.
1 cloak of brown woolen bunting fabric, for the use of the said deceased ..13 l.
1 other cloak of grey woolen bunting fabric................................... 13 l.
10 cornets [cap with two broad lappets hanging down from the headband]
   of white hempen linen fabric ....7 l. 10 s.
2 coifs [close-fitting miniature hood in the shape of a bonnet] of black
   silk taffeta fabric, of which one is very wretched................................ 3 l.
1 old scarf...10 s.
1 [straw-filled] mattress of coarse Mélis linen fabric [sailcloth........3 l. 15 s.
1 canopy bed curtain of linen fabric and 2 small feather pillows......3 l. 15 s.
3 old blankets of different sizes .... 20 l.
Several beaver pelts sewn into a robe... 2 l.
1 old box without a lock .... 1 l.
1 wretched small chest .... *estimated as having very little value*

The said de Lalonde has declared that at both the Mountain and the said Côte St. Pierre is the quantity of 500 sheaves of wheat, of which he has promised to make his declaration of the amount which it will produce in bushels, figuring it according to the price at which he will sell it after deducting the cost of the threshing [with flail, wooden shovel, and winnowing basket]

10 bushels of peas .... *11 l.*

2 bushels of corn, estimated .... *4 l.*

250 bundles of hay .... *50 l.*

He has declared that these are owed to him, according to the claims of this day

By [Pierre Beauchamp dit] Le Grand Beauchamp .... *4 bushels of wheat*

By [Jean] Gateau .... *1 1/2 bushels of oats*

By one named [Jean de Lasague dit] Le Basque, soldier in the Company of Monsieur de Lorimier, the sum of fifty livres, according to his promissory note which was inventoried afterward .... *50 l.*

Owed by the said estate

To Sieur [Nicolas Janvrin dit] Dufresne .... *100 l.*

To Sieur [Pierre] Perthuis [dit Lalime], merchant .... *38 l.*

To Sieur René Cuillerier, merchant .... *33 l.*

To Laviolette .... *25 l.*

To Sieur [Paul, Michel, or Louis, brothers] Descaries .... *24 l.*

To Messieurs the Seigneurs [the Sulpician Order], for the lease of the land which is located at the Mountain, for their part .... *15 bushels of wheat*

To Joseph Leduc, for the farming of the land which belongs to him, for the allowance which is due to him .... *11 1/2 bushels of wheat*

Then followed the titles and instructions

First, the contract of marriage between the said Lalonde and the said deceased Masta, passed before Antoine Adhémar, the undersigned notary, on the 24th day of January, 1698, specifying, among other things, that the surviving spouse shall have and take as his preciput *(preferred portion) and his part from the listings of the belongings of the said estate up to the sum of two hundred livres in moveable articles, as they will be priced when the inventory shall be drawn up. [Inventoried as One]*

An accounting and a promissory note by [Jean de La Saugue dit] Le Basque, soldier in the Company of Monsieur [Captain Guillaume] de Lorimier [the Sieur des Bordes], for the sum of fifty livres which is owed to him [Lalonde] according to an agreement which was drawn up on the second of July, 1698, marked with a cross by the said Lalonde, who does not know how to sign. Inventoried as Two.

Thus has been drawn up all of the contents inventoried above, which have been remitted and forsaken, with the consent of the said supplemental guardian, into the hands and possession of the said Lalonde, father and guardian of the said minor, who has promised to keep an accounting of everything which will belong to him after the deduction has been made of his said preferred portion as stipulated by his said contract of marriage. Everyone has signed except the said Lalonde, Marie Barbant, Pierre Hurtubise, and Joseph Leduc, who have declared that they do not known how to write or sign, having been questioned after the reading was done, according to the ordinance. They have agreed that the twenty words crossed out are null and void.
Signed,
Daoust, Paul Decari, Desgagnie, Lambert Leduc, and P. Raimbault, notary.

[Ten months later, an addendum was inserted at the end of the document.]
Today appeared before the undersigned royal notary of the Island of Montreal, residing at Villemarie, the said Jean Baptiste de Lalonde, who had stated and declared that, when the sheaves of wheat mentioned in the above inventory were threshed and all of the expenses were paid and deducted, he estimated [a final harvest of] fifty bushels of wheat, of which quantity he will keep an accounting of that which will belong to him, according to the [above] act. [This addendum drawn up] at Villemarie in the office of the said notary in the year 1702 on the 22nd day of August in the afternoon, in the presence of Antoine Latanville and Georges Pruneau, royal bailiffs living at the said Villemarie. The said Lalonde has declared that he does not know how to write or sign, having been asked after the reading was done, according to the ordinance.
Signed,
A. Latanville, G. Pruneau, and P. Raimbault, royal notary"[102]

This inventory revealed that not only had Jean Baptiste been leasing a farm at the Côte St. Pierre (which belonged to Joseph Leduc), he had also been leasing a field near the Mount Royal (to the west-southwest of Montreal) from the Sulpician seigneurs. On this combined acreage, he had already raised crops of wheat, corn, peas, and hay. For the use of the two separate pieces of land, he had apparently agreed to pay each of his landlords in specified amounts of wheat (for working Monsieur Leduc's farm, he probably handed over a certain fraction of the final yield). Considering his minimal livestock of one mare, one small cow, two small lambs, and thirty chickens and chicks, J.B. had apparently not been living on and working this land for very long. In fact, until Marguerite's death on September 22, 1699, the couple had been residing at Pointe aux Trembles; thus, at the time of this inventory, she had been gone for only 25 months. During that time, he had produced either one or two seasons' worth of wheat, corn, peas, and hay on his two leased properties, during the two possible harvest seasons of 1700 and 1701.

No valuations were expressed in the inventory for each bushel of wheat and oats. As a result, it appears to be impossible to determine the exact total value of all of the listed assets of the Lalonde-Masta estate. However, 23 years later, when father and son would officially settle this estate, J.B. would present a total figure of 669 livres for all of the listed assets.[103] Through this single statement, it becomes abundantly clear that the wheat and oats were valued at 1.25 livres per bushel at this time. (Interestingly, this price was exactly half of the valuation of the harvested wheat which had been enumerated among the possessions of Jean Baptiste's parents twelve years earlier, when the inventory of their belongings had been drawn up back in 1689.)

Thus, the recorded assets of the Lalonde-Masta couple included the following:
178.5 livres of value in their livestock
65 livres worth of peas, corn, and hay, plus 50 bushels of wheat worth 62.5 livres, in their harvested crops
146.25 livres of valuation in their listed household contents
210 livres in cash, plus 4 bushels of wheat and $1^1/2$ bushels of oats worth 6.875 livres, in the debts which were owed to the estate.
Thus, the total assets of the couple's estate came to a grand total of 669 livres.

This figure was offset by the debts of 220 livres in cash, plus $26^1/2$ bushels of wheat worth 33 livres, which the estate owed to others. These deficits had a total value of 253 livres, representing 38 percent of the value of the listed assets.

After the deficits had been subtracted from the assets, 416 livres would remain. According to the Customary Laws of Paris (which also served as the legal code in New France), from this remaining sum, J.B. would be permitted to reserve for himself up to 200 livres worth of his personal effects, as his preferred portion. This *preciput* had been promised to the surviving spouse, whether male or female, in the couple's 1699 marriage contract. Finally, the remainder of 216 livres worth of articles was to be divided in equal halves between the father and his sole heir, François. Thus, this single son would some day be personally allotted 108 livres from the estate of his father and his deceased mother.

According to this inventory, Jean Baptiste worked the land with only a pickaxe, since no plow was enumerated. This was not unusual for small-scale farming operations in the colony. In fact, land was described as being "worked with the pickaxe" or "worked with the plow." The listings did not include such implements as scythes, sickles, rakes, shovels, and hoes. However, since the young farmer was definitely raising wheat, corn, peas, and hay, he certainly did have access to and used these items; they were simply not included in the inventory. J.B.'s only true beast of burden was his single mare; but the document did not list any cart, sled, or sledge that would have been pulled by this animal. However, there is a high probability that a plow and these vehicles were indeed present at the farm, but that they belonged to the lessor Monsieur Leduc, and were thus not included in the inventory.

Since this enumeration of the couple's belongings was drawn up more than two years after Marguerite's passing, it is possible that a number of her former garments had been either given away or utilized by others in the meantime. This may explain the fact that there were no shoes, moccasins, stockings, gloves, or mittens included among her articles of clothing. As was customary, no personal belongings of hers were listed, such as her sewing articles, nor did the enumerators list many of the small pieces of kitchen equipment which she would have undoubtedly owned and used. Likewise, none of the couple's furniture was included in the inventory, even though the list did include one curtain for a canopy bed.

Among those individuals to whom Jean Baptiste had made loans over the years, Pierre Beauchamp (this man's father had been known as "The Big Beauchamp," to distinguish him from the father's younger brother Jean, "The Small Beauchamp") lived at Pointe aux Trembles. In contrast, the other two debtors, Messieurs Gateau and Lasague, both resided in or near to Montreal.[104]

Among the individuals to whom J.B. owed money, the largest debt (of 100 livres) was owed to the Montreal merchant and outfitter Nicolas Janvrin dit Dufresne. Back on February 7 of 1701, J.B. had acknowledged that he still owed 103 livres to this man, for the various outfittings that the merchant had provided to the young voyageur during his earlier years. The next largest amount was owed to the Montreal merchant Pierre Perthuis. At the time of Marguerite's death in September of 1699, Jean Baptiste and she had owed only 7 livres 8 sols to him; in the meantime, the widower had added about 30 livres worth of additional articles to this owed amount. The third listed creditor, René Cuillerier, a prominent merchant of Montreal and Lachine, had been J.B.'s supplemental guardian (assisting his mother) ever since his father had been killed by Iroquois attackers back in 1687. The elder man had continued to function in this legal capacity until early October of 1700, when Jean Baptiste had finally celebrated his 25th birthday and had thus reached the legal age of majority. Sieur Descaries, the other identified individual to whom Jean Baptiste owed money, was likewise a resident of Montreal.[105]

After all of the owed sums had been paid to the creditors and the balances on all of the loans had been collected, some 452 livres would remain in the estate of Jean Baptiste Lalonde and his deceased first wife in this year of 1701. This figure clearly indicates that his four years of apprenticing in the fur trade, followed by his laboring for Cadillac as a fully qualified voyageur-trader in the Upper Country for one year, had not proven to be particularly lucrative for the young man. No surviving documents indicate that he ever worked legally in the peltries commerce after coming out to the St. Lawrence in the autumn of 1697. If he did participate in the trade after that date, it would have been as a *coureur de bois*, being employed in ventures that did not have official approval, which were thus illegal.

Jean Baptiste had now taken care of the two necessary legal tasks, first having the Court determine the guardians of his toddler son, and then having official appointees conduct an inventory of his estate. Thus, he and Jeanne Gervais could proceed with the drawing up of their marriage contract, and finally the celebration of their wedding, which would be held in her home parish of Laprairie.

To create their nuptial contract, the future couple assembled with numerous of their relatives and friends at the home of J.B.'s twice-widowed sister-in-law, Marie Cunégonde Masta, whose abode was located on Rue St. François in Montreal. This festive gathering took place in the afternoon on October 23, 1701. On the side of the future groom (who was identified as an "habitant of this Island"), the official witnesses included his only sister Madeleine Lalonde, his only brother Guillaume Lalonde, his only brother-in-law Toussaint

Masta, his only sister-in-law Marie Cunégonde Masta, and the Montreal merchant Pierre Perthuis. (In the document, his mother Marie Barbant was specifically noted as being absent.) On the side of the prospective bride (who was listed as being "from Laprairie St. Lambert," which was directly east of Montreal, about five miles north of the village of Laprairie), the official witnesses were her parents Mathieu Gervais dit Parisien and Michelle Picard, her brother Jean Gervais, her brother-in-law Charles Marcil (husband of her sister Romaine), her nephew Charles Diel, her first cousin Julien Bariteau dit Lamarche, Jacques Picard, Mathurine Juillet (widow of the deceased Urbain Baudreau dit Graveline), and Marie Catherine Juillet. Among the details which the royal notary penned into their contract, one involved a rather generous act by Jeanne's father: "The said Sieur [Mathieu] Gervais has promised to give to the said future husband in advance of their future inheritance one cow, about four or five years of age." At the very end of the document, the notary added this statement: "It is agreed that the underage child of the said future husband and his deceased wife will be fed, brought up, and raised in the Catholic, Apostolic, and Roman Religion under the care of the said future husband and at the expense of the said future communal estate until he has reached the age of twenty years." Neither the future groom nor the future bride was able to sign the contract.[106]

On the following day, the bride and groom crossed the St. Lawrence to the Laprairie church, whose parish was called The Nativity of the Blessed Virgin Mary. In the ledger, the priest recorded the groom as Jean Lalonde (omitting his second name, Baptiste), and the cleric did not list any official witnesses.[107]

Some three months earlier, during the final days of July and the first week of August, a huge conclave of native delegates had gathered at Montreal. Some 1,300 representatives from each of the five Iroquois nations and all of the nations who were allied with the French had assembled to conclude the Great Treaty, which they had finally ratified on August 4, 1701. According to the provisions of this pact, the Iroquois nations had agreed to remain neutral in any future wars between France and England. They had also accepted defeat in their attempt to wrest control of the western trade from the French. However, they would remain in place as a physical barrier between the nations of the western interior and Albany, thus ensuring that those western groups would continue to trade primarily with the French, rather than with the English.[108]

Although the residents of the entire Montreal region had been elated at the permanent cessation of attacks by Iroquois war parties, they had an even more devastating scourge to contend with during this autumn of 1701. This was a vicious epidemic of smallpox that swept through the St. Lawrence Valley; it eventually carried off over one thousand of the residents, both French and native.[109]

Following their wedding, Jean Baptiste and Jeanne, along with little François, had settled as a family on the Côte St. Pierre. In all likelihood, they resided on the farm there which J.B. had already been leasing from Joseph Leduc for one or two years. However, during the following months, he must have begun to contemplate moving back at some point to the Côte St. Louis, near the western end of Montreal Island (which had been dubbed the Bout de l'Île area). It was there that the Lalonde family had lived for seven or eight years during his youth, until his father had been struck down by Iroquois attackers in September of 1687. In fact, the family still owned their 68-acre lot which fronted on the St. Lawrence in that area; it was located on Pointe St. Louis, immediately east of the St. Louis parish church. This plot had 4 arpents (768 feet) of river frontage, and 20 arpents ($^3/4$ mile) of depth. During the nine months that they had owned the property before Jean had been killed, they had been able to clear and bring under cultivation 2 arpents (1.7 acres) of this forest-covered land, as well as to construct a house and the various outbuildings. The Great Treaty had brought about the permanent removal of the threat of Iroquois raids upon the settlers along the thinly-populated southern coastline of Montreal Island. This must have encouraged Jean Baptiste as he ruminated about eventually relocating toward the west, returning to the Bout de l'Île area.[110]

As a first step toward that eventual goal, J.B. and his mother visited the Montreal notary Adhémar on July 24, 1702, nine months after this eldest son and his bride had exchanged their nuptial vows. On this summer day, Marie Barbant, "both in her name and as the guardian of Guillaume Lalonde, age twenty [actually, about to turn 18], her son, and Marie Madeleine Lalonde, wife of Guillaume Daoust, of Lachine on Montreal Island," sold and transferred to Jean Baptiste a portion of the family's property "at the top of Montreal Island."[111]

However, at this time, the young couple did not move onto their newly-acquired section of the Lalonde family land at Bout de l'Île. Instead, they continued to reside on the leased farm which was located on the Côte St. Pierre. It was there that they awaited the arrival of the first child whom they would produce together, during a pregnancy that had commenced at about the first of August in 1702. Having lost his first wife due to complications from the birth of their only child, this time the expectant father must have experienced a combination of happy anticipation and foreboding dread during the course of those long months of waiting. On May 1, 1703, little Jean Baptiste Lalonde, Jr. arrived safely and Jeanne survived as well, to J.B.'s considerable relief. On that same day, they traveled to the Montreal church for the tiny lad's christening ceremony. On this lighthearted occasion, the godfather was Lambert Leduc, Jr., the 20-year-old eldest son of their close neighbor Lambert, Sr. The godmother was Catherine Cuillerier, the wife of Joseph Leduc (Lambert, Sr.'s younger brother), the Montreal residents from whom Jean Baptiste had been leasing the farm.[112]

Five months later, on October 21, Jean Baptiste arranged a business transaction with a fellow farmer of the Côte St. Pierre. These two men officially registered this agreement with the Montreal notary Adhémar on this autumn afternoon, in the presence of a third individual who was also involved in this triangular transaction. Jean Cousineau, a resident of Montreal, owed J.B. 90 livres worth of labor. On this date, he settled this debt by transferring ownership of a mare to Monsieur Lalonde, who in turn transferred the animal to his fellow farmer Noël Legault, in return for receiving payments worth 90 livres from the latter man.

"Was present Noël Legault dit Deslauriers, habitant of the Côte St. Pierre in the parish of Lachine on this Island, being at present in this town, who has voluntarily acknowledged and admitted that he owes to Jean [Baptiste] Lalonde dit Lespérance, habitant residing at [the Côte] St. Pierre, present and assenting, the sum of ninety livres for the sale of a mare which the said Legault has acquired from Jean Cousineau. Concerning this acquisition from the said Lalonde, the said Legault has declared that he has the power to consent, and he consents to pay this sum. The said parties have agreed that the said Legault will pay to the said Lalonde sixty cords of good heating wood, which he will deliver to him at the rate of thirty sols [1.5 livres] for each cord [thus totalling 90 livres in value]. He will deliver thirty cords during the next winter [of 1704-1705] in the following manner: ten cords at Christmas, ten cords in mid-February, five cords on the first of March, and the other five cords on the fifteenth of the month of March next. He will deliver the remaining thirty cords during the next year [1705-1706] at the same times as above, under the penalty of all expenses, damages, and

interests, or [he will provide its value of 45 livres] in other work to which the parties will agree. By means of these presents, the said Jean Cousineau, present and assenting, is well and validly acquitted of all of the work which he was obligated to do for the said Lalonde, by the sale which he has made of the said mare, to which the said Lalonde has agreed."[113]

Noël Legault dit Deslauriers, who was about 28 or 29 years of age, had married the widow Marie Bénard nearly five years earlier. During that time, they had first produced two children at Montreal, in 1699 and 1701. Then, their third child had been born at the Côte St. Pierre (in the Lachine parish), five weeks before this transaction was conducted. The other individual in this arrangement, Jean Cousineau, was a mason and stonecutter in Montreal. He and his wife Jeanne Bénard (Marie's older sister, thus making the two men brothers-in-law) had been married for nearly thirteen years; of their seven offspring, only the third one had died at an early age. The work which this craftsman owed to J.B. must have been related to his profession of cutting and laying stone. Perhaps he had been paid by Monsieur Lalonde to carry out a certain job, but he had never done it.[114]

On July 25, 1703, J.B.'s brother Guillaume completed his five-year work contract for the Montreal businessman Urbain Gervaise. Upon his release from this labor agreement (one month before he would turn 19), the young man received his specified allotment of clothing, as well as the 15-month-old cow which had been promised to him by his employer.[115]

It had apparently been Jean Baptiste's long-range plan to establish himself as a farmer on the Côte St. Louis, in the Bout de l'Île area. This intention was reflected in his purchase of a portion of the family's property on Pointe St. Louis from his mother and his two siblings one year before, back in July of 1702. Now, in this summer of 1703, the release of Guillaume from his five-year employment contract may have prompted J.B. to take action on his dreams. These plans apparently included establishing a home base at which his brother could also settle, until he would reach adulthood and create his own farm and family.

However, the elder sibling's decision did not involve moving back onto the Lalonde land at this time; instead, it entailed leasing for six years the large farm property which belonged to Jean Quenet. According to the 1702 land ownership map of Vachon de Belmont, this plot was located 1.6 miles east of the Lalonde family's lot, separated from it by thirteen other farms. The Quenet property was by far the largest individual plot in the entire area, measuring 10 arpents (1,920 feet or .36 mile) in St. Lawrence frontage by 40 arpents (1½ miles) in depth, extending off toward the northwest. The vast majority of the other individually-owned lots along the entire southern shoreline of Montreal Island had a river frontage of either 3 or 4 arpents, and a depth of 20 arpents (such as the Lalonde lot, which measured 4 by 20). The Quenet land, which was centered on Pointe Beaurepaire (Beautiful Hide-out Point, some decades later to be called Pointe Quenet), contained a total of 400 arpents of area, or 340 acres. The upcoming relocation toward the west-southwest by Jean Baptiste, Jeanne, and their two young children, from the leased Leduc farm on the Côte St. Pierre to the leased Quenet farm at Pointe Beaurepaire, would entail a move of some 10 to 13 miles. Since their new place would be only 1.6 miles to the east of the Lalonde land, the two brothers would probably be able to work at least portions of the latter lot at the same time that they would work the leased farm.[116]

Jean Quenet, 56 years old in the latter autumn of 1703, had been married to Étiennette Hurtubise (now age 41) for nearly 28 years. During that interval, she had borne 13 children, the first four at Lachine (through September of 1685) and the latter nine at Montreal (through October of 1703). Among these offspring, five of them (the first, fourth, ninth, twelfth, and thirteenth babies) had apparently died at young ages. In addition to these mournful losses, she had also given birth to twins on May 12, 1700; these infants had either arrived stillborn or they had only lived for a very short time, since they had been buried on that same day. Thus, by the late autumn of 1703, only six of the couple's thirteen children are certain to have been living. These six included Hélène (age 24, who had already been married for three years), Marie Clémence (22, in training to become a hospital nun), Jean (14), Élisabeth (12), Jeanne (9, who would become a nun), and Marie Anne (7, who would become a hospital nun). The two youngest children of the brood, Charlotte (number 12, arriving at Montreal in October of 1701) and Marie Josèphe (arriving there on October 10, 1703) were only documented by their baptismal records. Thus, it is not known at what ages they died, only that they did not grow to adulthood and marry.

Monsieur Quenet had worked all along as a *marchand chapelier*, a maker and seller of hats, as well as a farmer. The former employment had been his listed occupation back in the census of 1681, when he, Étiennette, and their first two children had been enumerated at Lachine. At that time, their property had been located 1.1 mile northeast of the terminus of the Montreal-to-Lachine portage road, and 3.1 miles northeast of the stockade-enclosed Lachine village. The family had owned one gun and two horned cattle, and had cleared and brought under cultivation 15 arpents (12 3/4 acres) of land. Over time, Jean's business dealings had thrived, until he had advanced from the rather modest level of a hat-making farmer to a merchant bourgeois of Montreal (but all the while retaining his initial occupation). Eventually, he had acquired the position of collector of fees for the Sulpician seigneurs, and also the inspector of royal tax collections (taking on the latter role in 1700). His considerable importance in the commercial sphere of the colony was apparently reflected in the large dimensions of his country farm, which was located at Pointe Beaurepaire on the Côte St. Louis, some ten miles west of the Lachine village. It was also about 16 miles southwest of the family's Montreal residence, as the crow flies; however, it was considerably farther away by traveling along the Montreal-to-Lachine road and then the Grand Chemin route that skirted the shoreline. The Quenet family also owned a home within the stockaded village of Lachine.[117]

It was in the office of the Montreal notary Adhémar that Monsieur Quenet and Jean Baptiste Lalonde met on November 30, 1703, to officially register the many details of the lease of the Quenet farm on the Côte St. Louis. These arrangements would commence in 3 1/2 months, during the following March.

"Was present Sieur Jean Quenet, maker and seller of hats, living in this town [Montreal], who has voluntarily acknowledged and declared that he has leased and forsaken by these presents the right to farm and harvest, commencing on the fifteenth of March next [1704] and running for six years and six harvest seasons, all of the coming products that will be completed, finished, achieved, and produced during that time to enjoy, to Jean de Lalonde dit Lespérance and Jeanne Gervais, his wife, present and assenting for themselves and for each other during the said time, the said Gervais duly authorized by the said de Lalonde, her husband, for the facts which follow. This lease will include all of the lands which are cleared on the concession that belongs to the said lessor [Sieur Quenet], located at the top of this Island at the Pointe de Beaurepaire, along with the granary, the stables, and the oven or bakery, as well as one half of the attic which is in the house constructed on the said lands. This house and the other half of the attic will remain with the said Sieur Lessor, who will transfer his lodgings and

that of his family whenever they would like, and the said Sieur Lessor and his family will [sometimes] come to reside in this town [Montreal]. The said lessees [Monsieur and Madame de Lalonde] will live in the said house until the said lessor, his wife, or their children will return [and then they will live together with them].

The said lessees will work and sow the said lands in convenient times and seasons, sowing and threshing the grains which will be harvested from these said lands. The said parties will share these grains by halves after they will be threshed and winnowed, and all of the seed grain will likewise be furnished by them by halves. In case the said lessor, his wife, and their children are residing in this town [at harvest time and are thus unavailable to assist], the said lessees will carry out the work themselves and the said Sieur Lessor will give and remit to them, for his part of the said farm, the money for the salary of a man whom the said lessees will furnish during the month of the harvests. Next year [in 1704], the said Sieur Lessor will furnish to the said lessees all of the grains with which they will sow the lands of the said farm. These provided grains will be returned to him after the dividing of the [harvested] grains, in order to pay off the said seed grains, so that the seed grains will be furnished by halves, as was mentioned above.

The said Sieur Lessor will lease to the said lessees, commencing on the fifteenth of March next, four oxen, three milk cows, two bulls which will be two years old next spring, two heifers, one small bull born last spring, a plow, and all of the other implements, for which he will make a statement, including the ages of the said animals, and they will all be appraised, and by these presents they will agree at the said time. The said lessees will bring to the said farm three milk cows and two one-year-old heifers, which will likewise be appraised on the said day of March 15 next. The prices of the said animals, both those of the said lessor and those of the said lessees, will be divided by halves between them [when they are sold], and likewise the products of the said cows which will be produced will be divided by halves at the end of the three first years of the present lease. At the end of the said lease, the products will again be divided.

The said parties have agreed that when the family [of the lessor] will live in the house, the said lessor will reserve the right to whichever cow he would like to choose, and that his wife or family living there with the lessees will take this one cow in order to have its said milk. The said lessees will care for the milk and the other products of the cows, and they will make as much butter as it will be possible to make, which will all be shared by halves between the said parties every year...The said parties have also agreed that the lessor will provide six [young] pigs, five males and one female, and the lessees will provide five, four males and one female, which will be at the said farm. Each of the said parties will feed and care for them...until next year, in the season when it is customary to take the pigs which have been fattened...The said lessor will also bring to the said farm twenty-four chickens and one rooster. The said lessees will be obliged to care for the products of the said cows and the small pigs, and to feed, guard, and protect these animals. The said lessees will return them to the said lessor at the end of the present lease, and during each of the years of the present lease they will also give to him 24 chickens, one capon, and 24 dozen eggs...At the end of the present lease, all of the said pigs will be shared by halves.

The said lessees will [cut and] haul to the said lessor during each of the winters of the present lease all of the firewood which will be needed to burn in the said house, except that which the said Sieur Quenet will need for himself, taken from the said land and farm. In addition, the lessees will take from the lands of the said farm only that wood which they will need for their heating, with the stipulation, however, that all of the wood which they will acquire by clearing land will belong to the said lessees. Following this clearing, the said lessees will then be obliged to sow half [of the newly cleared land], in addition to the other [previously cleared] lands of the said farm. The said lessor will be permitted to bake in the oven which is furnished [with the farm] when the said lessees will be living there, every time and whenever it will seem good to him [the lessor] to do so.

At the end of the present lease, the lessees will leave on the lands of the said farm as many things as are there at present...All of the crops will belong to the lessees to aid them in feeding the said animals, including all four bushels of oats which the said lessees will sow on the lands of the said farm during each year of the present lease. During the period of the lease, the said lessees will be permitted to enjoy all of the hay which will be harvested on the 26 arpents [22 acres] of meadow which the said Sieur Lessor owns at the back of the lands of the said farm, in order to feed the animals of the said farm, and if the said lessees have any surplus, it will be for the profits of the said lessees. The said lessees will spend the winter on the property of the said Sieur Lessor during each of the winters of the present lease, however without being obliged to incur any risks. They will make a garden on the lands of the said farm, for which the said Sieur Lessor will furnish all of the implements to take behind the said meadow, and the said Sieur Lessor will furnish to them a man to work the said garden, [the cost of] whose pay will be shared between them. All of the herbs and vegetables which they will harvest in the said garden will be shared by halves between the said parties. At the beginning of the present lease, the said Sieur Lessor will put the ditches which will be on the lands of the said farm in good condition, and their subsequent upkeep will be shared by halves during the rest of the lease. The said lessees will feed and shelter on the lands of the said farm two horses and two bulls, and each of them will be for the profit of the said lessees. After their labors on the said farm will be done, the said lessees will be permitted to undertake any work which will seem good to them, which work will be undertaken for their own profit...The said lessees will not be allowed to transfer their rights of the present lease as they are without the consent of the said Sieur Lessor, and [during the period of the lease] they will be obliged to make repairs on the buildings of the said farm at the expense of the said Sieur Lessor, according to the customs.

For all of the above, the said lessees are obligated and obligate themselves, solidly one for the other and each of them for the whole, without division, discussion, or disloyalty, renouncing any such said divisions. Thus have these presents been agreed upon between the said parties. For the execution of these presents, they have selected as their legal residences [to which writs may be delivered] their domiciles, that is, the said Sieur Lessor his home located near the gate of the town called Lachine, and the lessees the home of the undersigned notary [Adhémar], located in this town on Rue Notre Dame. Thus have they promised, obligated themselves, waived, etc...
Signed,
Quenet, Cabazie, Latanville, and Adhemar, notary.

March 15, 1704
Appraisal made of the animals which the Sieur Quenet has leased to Jean Lalonde...drawn up by the Sieurs Paul Descaries, Jacques Cauchois, and Hubert Ranger dit Laviolette, habitants of the Côte St. Louis [residing on the 13th farm to the east, the 3rd farm to the west, and the 7th farm to the west, respectively, from the Quenet property].

4 oxen	*400 livres (l.)*
2 two-year-old bulls	*70 l.*
2 cows with black hair	*80 l.*
2 heifers and 1 small one-year-old bull	*60 l.*

Then were appraised the animals which the said Lalonde has brought to the said farm

2 small calves	*32 l.*
2 bulls	*80 l.*
3 cows	*120 l...*

Signed,
Quenet, Paul Descari, and J. Cauchois"[118]

Oddly enough, in this detail-laden document, the notary did not record the amount of acreage on Monsieur Quenet's 340-acre lot which had already been cleared and was to be cultivated by the Lalondes. However, it was made abundantly clear in the agreement that various members of the Quenet family would be sometimes residing in the house on this farm, when they would not be living in their homes at Lachine or Montreal. During those periods, the two families (lessor and lessee) would share the single house. This contractual arrangement, which was slated to run for a full six years, would extend from March 15, 1704 until the same date in 1710.

When the lease period actually commenced in the late winter of 1704, Jean Baptiste was $28^5/12$ years old, Jeanne was age $24^2/3$, François (born to Marguerite Masta) had celebrated his 4th birthday six months earlier, and little Jean Baptiste, Jr. (born to Jeanne) was six weeks away from his first birthday. J.B.'s brother Guillaume, who was $19^7/12$ years of age at this time, had most likely joined them to work on the Quenet farm as well.

Six months after the lease had begun and they had relocated to this farm in the Bout de l'Île area, Jeanne and Jean Baptiste each appeared as a godparent at two different christening ceremony in the St. Louis church. (This edifice was located about $1^3/4$ miles west of the Quenet property.) First, Madame Lalonde had her turn on September 15, 1704, when she stood beside the baptismal font to sponsor the second child of Pierre Leduc and Catherine Fortin, a one-day old boy. Besides Jeanne Gervais, the other sponsor on this occasion was Jacques Denis dit Saint Denis, another fellow resident of the parish. Both the baby's father and godfather had been soldiers in the Troupes de la Marine during the 1680s and 1690s (in two different Companies), before they each had retired from military life to marry and then to raise families on their respective farms.[119]

Twelve days after this first christening, on September 27, Jean Baptiste appeared at the same baptismal font, as the godfather of Anne, the daughter of Jacques Denis dit Saint Denis and Anne Gauthier. This baby, the seventh child to join this household, had been born on the previous day. (Their farm was located $2^1/4$ miles east of the Quenet land, and about 600 feet west of the seigneurial wind-powered grist mill on Pointe Claire, to which all of the *censitaires* were obliged to take their grains to have them ground into flour or meal.) The godmother of little Anne was Étiennette Hurtubise, the wife of Jean Quenet. Apparently, this baptism took place during one of those periods in which part or all of the Quenet family was residing at their home on Pointe Beaurepaire, along with the lessees Monsieur and Madame Lalonde, their two young children, and probably J.B.'s brother Guillaume as well.[120]

During this particular period, the conflict between France and England which has been dubbed the War of the Spanish Succession was raging, both in Europe and in the North American colonies. In this conflict, which extended from 1702 to 1713, the warfare that was directed both northward and southward between New France and New England often took the form of vicious guerrilla raids. One such military campaign had been carried out by the French and their native allies during the heart of the winter in this year of 1704. A contingent of more than two hundred fighting men, including regular soldiers, civilian militiamen, and allied native warriors from the St. Lawrence Valley, had slogged overland on snowshoes from the Montreal area toward the south. In the wee hours of the morning on March 11, 1704, this large party had attacked the British community of Deerfield, which was the most remote village in northwestern Massachusetts colony. During this raid, 50 residents had been killed and 112 others had been captured. One of the latter individuals had been 12-year-old Sarah Allyn, who had usually resided with her family some distance south of the palisade walls, but who had for some reason been in the village itself when the attack had occurred. No other members of Sarah's family had been killed, wounded, or seized during the raid. In the aftermath, the 112 captives had been taken northward over some 300 miles of frozen landscape, to eventually live in the French and native communities that were strung out along the St. Lawrence Valley.

After the arrival of the surviving captives, Sarah Allyn would be taken in by the Montreal merchant bourgeois Jean Quenet and his family. While residing with them, at their homes in Montreal and Lachine and on their farm to the west at Pointe Beaurepaire, she would learn the French language and customs, and she would be instructed in the Roman Catholic Religion. On May 30, 1705, fifteen months after being violently wrenched from her home and family, she would be baptized in a ceremony at the St. Louis church. On this day, she would be officially transformed from the English Protestant colonist Sarah Allyn into the French Catholic colonist Marie Madeleine Hélène, having willingly accepted her new role in her new French world. In the parish ledger, the officiating priest would record that she resided with the family of Jean Quenet, that her godmother was Étiennette Hurtubise, wife of Jean Quenet, and that her stand-in godfather (in the absence of the official godfather, Pierre Lamoureux dit Saint Germain) was Jean Quenet, Jr., the 16-year-old son of Jean Quenet, Sr. Sarah's christening, conducted in the church on the Côte St. Louis, would clearly indicate that she had been living with them on their Pointe Beaurepaire farm for a considerable portion of those fifteen months, along with the ever-growing family of Jean Baptiste Lalonde and Jeanne Gervais. Her other close linkages with the Lalonde clan, which would develop over the course of the following years, will be revealed in future pages, as her story unfolds.[121]

On February 20, 1705, five months after Jean Baptiste Lalonde and Étiennette Hurtubise had stood together as the godparents of little Anne Denis, J.B.'s brother Guillaume and the second-oldest daughter of the Quenet family appeared together in the same capacity in the St. Louis church. In this instance, the baby being christened was one-day-old Guillaume Lalonde, the third child to be welcomed into the family of Jean Baptiste and Jeanne. The godmother on this jubilant day, Marie Clémence Quenet, 23 years of age, was in training to become a hospital nun at Montreal. This record in the parish ledger strongly suggests that godfather Guillaume Lalonde (designated in this study as Guillaume Number 1) was living on the leased Quenet farm with his brother and his family at this time. However, it is also possible that Guillaume was residing all or part of the time on the Lalonde family property, 1.6 miles to the west. This February event in the St. Louis church took place about three months before Sarah Allyn would be baptized in the same edifice. This evidence clearly implies that she was living at this time with at least a portion of the Quenet family on their leased-out farm. (The feted infant at the 1705 Lalonde baptism has been designated in the present study as Guillaume Number 2. The biography of this individual and his wife Marie Angélique Brunet dite Bourbonnais, the couple who provide the direct linkage between Jean Baptiste and Jeanne and the present author, is included later in this work.)[122]

For some undocumented reason, at the time of the birth of Jeanne and J.B.'s next child, the fourth one in the family, they were in Montreal. Thus on the day following his arrival, little Joseph Lalonde was baptized in the Montreal church on March 7, 1707. In the parish ledger, the priest noted that the parents of the infant were residents "of the St. Louis parish at the top of this island," and that the lad's godparents were Michelle Picard and Jean Gabriel Picard. These individuals were Jeanne's own mother, a resident of Montreal, and Jeanne's uncle (her mother's brother), who lived in the Lachine parish.[123]

Fifteen months later, Jeanne was probably both amused and amazed when her younger brother, Jean Mathieu Gervais, was wed in the Montreal church and acquired an instant family. On June 11, 1708, when he was 22 years old, he married the widow Jeanne Françoise Ronceray, age 29, who had been previously married for a decade and at this time had either four or five living children.[124]

During the first week of August in 1709, Jeanne and Jean Baptiste were plunged into deep grief, when their newest baby died at the age of just one month. This was the first time that they had lost one of their children. According to the burial record for little Thomas, the fifth offspring of the family, he had died at Ft. Senneville, which was located at the westernmost tip of Montreal Island. (This four-sided stone fortification with corner bastions had been constructed some six years earlier, back in 1703, by the prominent Montreal merchant Jacques Le Ber, Jr.) The body of baby Thomas was transported about $2^1/2$ miles eastward to the church, where he was tenderly laid to rest in the cemetery on August 6.[125]

Two-thirds of a year later, the month of April in 1710 brought to the family first deep sadness and then a wonderful reason to celebrate. First, Jeanne's mother, Michelle Picard, died and was buried in the Montreal cemetery on April 15. She had been $48^3/4$ years of age at the time of her passing, after having been married for nearly 34 years and having borne ten children.[126]

Just one week after this funeral, celebrations were in order for the Lalonde clan. In the afternoon on April 22, Jean Baptiste appeared as one of the three official witnesses on the prospective groom's side when the marriage contract was drawn up for his brother Guillaume (who was now $25^2/3$ years old). This event took place in the Montreal office of the royal notary Pierre Raimbault. The other two witnesses on the Lalonde side were Jean Mathieu Gervais, Jeanne's brother, who had acquired a ready-made family by marrying a widow with numerous children two years earlier (they lived at Laprairie), and Charles Marcil, who had married Jeanne's sister Romaine a decade earlier (they resided with their children at Longueuil).[127]

The bride-to-be was none other than Sarah Allyn, the English captive from Deerfield, Massachusetts who had become the

Canadienne Marie Madeleine Hélène. By this point, she was about to turn 18 years old, and she had been living in the St. Lawrence settlements for six years (since the spring of 1704). During all or most of that span of time, she had probably resided with the Quenet family, at their homes in Montreal and Lachine and on their leased-out farm on Pointe Beaurepaire. On this happy April day, the witnesses on her side were Henri Antoine Mériel (a Sulpician priest who had already served in Montreal for two decades), Jean Fourneau dit Brandemour, and Jean's wife Marie Élisabeth Price. Like Sarah, this woman had also been captured in the Deerfield raid; however, at that time, she had already been 20 years of age and the widow of Andrew Stevens. Thus, after her conversion and baptism in April of 1705, she had married 26-year-old Monsieur Fourneau in February of 1706. They had settled in Montreal, and had already produced three daughters there, in 1706, 1708, and 1709.[128]

As the Lalonde couple exchanged their vows in the St. Louis church five days later, on April 27, 1710, four official witnesses were present. Besides the groom's brother Jean Baptiste Lalonde, the other three men were also residents of the St. Louis parish. They were Michel Brébant, Pierre Sauvé dit Laplante, and Jean Baptiste Lecomte, the latter man an unmarried son of Aimé Lecomte.[129]

The documentation of this wedding, including the April 22 marriage contract in the Montreal notary's books and the April 27 wedding record in the St. Louis parish ledger, would be the last known records concerning J.B. and Guillaume's mother, Marie Barbant, to be penned in the colony. At this point, she was about 62 years of age. Of the three Tabault boys whom she had mothered for a few years (during her short-lived marriage to their father, Pierre Tabault, beginning in 1688), all three of them had already grown to adulthood and had been married in the Lachine church. Pierre, Jr. had been wed there in April of 1703, followed by Alexis in February of 1706 and finally by Jean in February of 1710. Pierre, Sr., who had been Marie's second husband for a very few years, would die at Lachine in the beginning of May in 1723, at the age of about 79 (but his age would be embellished by his family members, who would state that it was 91 at the time).[130]

Six weeks before Guillaume's nuptial festivities, on March 15, 1710, J.B. and Jeanne's six-year lease on the Quenet farm had drawn to a close. As a result, they had relocated to his own portion of the Lalonde family land on Pointe St. Louis, which was located about 1.6

miles to the west, adjacent to the east side of the church property. For his part, on the same day that Guillaume had witnesses the drawing up of his marriage contract, this younger of the two Lalonde brothers had also been granted a lot of his own in the Bout de l'Île area. His property had a St. Lawrence frontage of 3 arpents (576 feet) and a depth of 20 arpents (³/4 mile).[131]

Within a six-week period late in this year of 1710, Jean Baptiste stood as the godfather at two different christening ceremonies in the St. Louis church. (He was geographically well positioned to serve in this capacity, since the Lalonde family's land lay immediately east of the ecclesiastical edifice.) The first occasion took place on November 2, when the celebrated infant was the four-day-old daughter and first child of René Fortin and Madeleine Perrier, fellow residents of the St. Louis parish. This day, J.B.'s fellow sponsor was Jeanne Catherine Boursier, the wife of Étienne Magdelaine dit Ladouceur.[132]

The second baptism was held six weeks later, on December 14. In this instance, it was Félicité Sauvé, sixteen days old, who was held over the baptismal font to receive the poured holy water. Her parents, Pierre Sauvé dit Laplante and Marie Michaud, resided with the survivors of their previous eight children on the second lot to the east of the Lalonde family property. J.B.'s fellow sponsor on this day was his sister-in-law of eight months. In the parish register, the priest identified her as "Marie Madeleine Saire, wife of Guillaume Lalonde," mistaking her original given name of Sarah as her family name and spelling it phonetically.[133]

Eleven months after Jean Baptiste's lease of the Quenet farm had run out and he had moved onto his portion of the Lalonde family land, he was granted an additional piece of property, which was adjacent to his holdings. In the afternoon on February 23, 1711, he appeared in one of the halls of the Sulpician Seminary at Montreal, to receive this grant from the Sulpicians, the seigneurs of Montreal Island.

"...Jean de Lalonde, habitant living at the top of this Island [of Montreal, on the Côte St. Louis], present and assenting as the recipient of the said title, for himself as well as for his heirs and assigns in the future, of a remainder of land on the point, located beyond [immediately to the west of] the concessions of the said recipient and that of [Marie] Barbant [the main parcel having been granted to his father on March 3, 1687, and then a small supplemental piece adjacent to the front of this lot having been granted to his mother on November 29, 1687]. This property contains about 3 arpents

and 7 to 8 perches of frontage [each perche being 19.2 English feet, thus totalling about 710 to 730 feet] and narrows over the course of its depth of 20 arpents [³/4 mile], according to the report of a survey which was earlier conducted by the Sieur Basset, licensed surveyor, on June 19, 1708. It has been transferred by my said Sieur [Fr. François Bastion de] Belmont to the said Lalonde without anything, except for the buildings which have been constructed at the front area of the said remnant of land [the supplemental extension formerly granted to Marie, with its buildings] having a surface area of six arpents [5.1 acres] or thereabouts, with three arpents of frontage along Lac St. Louis [the broadened St. Lawrence River] and two arpents in depth, or two arpents of frontage and three arpents in depth."

Jean Baptiste's new piece of property had apparently been carved from the eastern side of the parcel that had been previously reserved for the St. Louis church and cemetery. His new lot, having a St. Lawrence frontage of some 710 to 730 feet, represented about 26 or 27 percent of the reserved ecclesiastical land, which had contained, up until this point, a half-mile of river frontage. According to this 1711 contract of concession, the new piece of land, added to J.B.'s portion of the lot which had originally been ceded to his father back in 1687, brought his own holdings up to 6 arpents of river frontage (not counting the 5.1 supplemental acres that had been granted to his mother). In return for owning all of this land, he would be obliged to pay to the seigneurs at their residence in Montreal or at their fees-receiving locale there, each year on November 11, one livre in money and one bushel of wheat, as the annual seigneurial fees. In addition, he was to haul his grains to the seigneurial mills to be ground, and pay the appropriate fees for this service; violations would result in the confiscation of his grains as well as fines. Also, he would be obligated to work constantly and as diligently as possible to fell all of the forest cover, clear the land, and build on his *habitation*, and to reside there. Additionally, he was to submit to any and all roads across his property which the seigneurs might decide to build, and he was to construct and maintain in a practical manner his section of the Great Road along the shore of the St. Lawrence. Finally, the Sulpicians reserved the right to take from his land any wood for carpentry or heating which they might need for either their usage or for public service, without having to pay Monsieur Lalonde for it. They likewise retained the right to take back the title of the land if it were abandoned and not occupied.[134]

Jeanne and J.B. were elated to welcome their sixth child into the world just three weeks later, on March 17, 1711. When Marie Rosalie was christened in the St. Louis church two days later, her godmother was Marie Angélique Guillet, the unmarried 18-year-old daughter of Mathurin Guillet and Marie Charlotte Lemoine. The infant's godfather was François Lamoureux dit Saint Germain, the merchant and gunsmith who owned the sub-fief of Bellevue (thus, the priest identified him as "seigneur of the Top of the Island"). This rather extensive property, containing a half-mile of St. Lawrence frontage, was located on the westernmost tip of Montreal Island. Monsieur Lamoureux would marry fourteen months later; in the meantime, he had fathered twin boys with Françoise Lecomte, who lived with her family of origin on the third lot east of his land. These babies, who had been born to the 22-year-old unmarried woman nearly a year earlier, in April of 1710, had only survived for four days.[135]

Fifteen months after the arrival of their sixth offspring, Jean Baptiste again stood beside the baptismal font in the St. Louis church. This time, he was appearing as the sponsor of a native girl who had been born to the Christianized Nipissing parents Gaspard Naokigik and Madeleine Outapinanikoue. On August 15, 1713, eleven days after she had been born, baby Françoise was sponsored by Monsieur Lalonde and Marguerite Ménard, the 24-year-old former widow of Lambert Cuillerier. She had wed the seigneur François Lamoureux back in July of 1712, bringing to this new marriage her one surviving child, a daughter who had been 3 1/2 years of age at the time.[136]

Ten weeks later, the next baby of Jeanne and J.B. arrived. Little Antoine was either born at the home of his uncle and aunt Guillaume Lalonde and Sarah/Marie Madeleine Hélène (who resided some of the time about five miles toward the east, in the area of Grande Anse, east of Pointe Claire), or else he was transported to that area on his second day of life in order to receive the sacrament of Baptism. At any rate, on October 26, 1713, the one-day-old infant was christened in the Pointe Claire edifice, and was given his first name by Antoine Pilon, his godfather, with Madeleine Lalonde standing beside him as the godmother. The two parents, as well as both of the sponsors, were all identified by the officiating priest as being member of this parish; he signed the register as "P. Lesueur, missionary priest of St. Francis de Sales parish at Pointe Claire."[137]

Two weeks after this ceremony, on November 8, Jeanne and J.B.'s new niece Marie Louise Lalonde, born that day to Sarah and Guillaume (their second child), was also baptized in the Pointe Claire church. This would be the only instance in which this latter Lalonde couple would have one of their eventual twelve children christened in this parish, rather than in the Bout de l'Île church (where their first child had been baptized in May of 1712). By at least the autumn of 1714, the two brothers and their respective wives would return to celebrating their own important liturgical functions at their long-term church of St. Louis.[138]

On March 4, 1714, Jean Baptiste was chosen to be the godfather of the new son of Michel Brébant dit Lamothe and Marie Élisabeth Lafaye (their fourth child). At this celebration in the Pointe Claire church, during which J.B. bequeathed his own name to the infant, his co-sponsor was Jeanne Brunet, the wife of Louis Mallet. It was just as well that none of the people who were present on this lighthearted day could see into the future. Little J.B. Brébant would be interred in the Pointe Claire cemetery just a few weeks later, on May 5.[139]

Tragedy struck the Lalonde clan seven months later, when Sarah and Guillaume's second child died on October 24, two weeks before she would have celebrated her first birthday. On the following day, Marie Louise's heart-wrenching funeral was held at the church of the Bout de l'Île parish. The two official witnesses were Michel Brébant, whose baby J.B. had sponsored back in March, and Élie Déperet, the Sulpician who was serving as the sub-deacon of the parish (he had been a priest for only two years, and he had only arrived at Montreal two months earlier). Afterward, Fr. René Charles De Breslay, the long time resident priest stationed here, signed the ledger as "Debreslay, priest residing at Ste. Anne at the Top of the Island."

During the previous year of 1713, when the Pointe Claire parish had been first established, it had been dedicated to St. François de Sales. At about the same time, Fr. De Breslay had apparently changed the name of the Bout de l'Île church from St. Louis (which it had been named ever since its founding back in 1685) to Ste. Anne. He seems to have done this in response to a vow that he had made to this latter saint (the mother of the Blessed Virgin Mary and the patron saint of mariners, fishermen, and water travelers). Thereafter, the parish of the Bout de l'Île area would be officially dedicated to Ste. Anne. However, during this period of flux, even this veteran cleric was sometimes a bit confused when it came to the new parish names. On November 18, 1714, when he officiated at a wedding in his own parish, he identified the groom as "Jean Pilon of the St. Louis parish of Pointe Claire." Apparently, he had written the name of his parish as St. Louis for so many years that he had penned it in this case automatically; however, he had assigned the name this time to the Pointe Claire parish! Further complicating the situation, the saint to whom the parish at Pointe Claire was dedicated would later be changed from St. François de Sales to St. Joachim.[140]

At the above-mentioned wedding of Jean Pilon in November of 1714, Jean Baptiste Lalonde was one of the official witnesses. At this nuptial celebration, held in the Bout de l'Île church, the bride was Marie Anne Gervais, Jeanne's younger sister, who was age 22. Besides J.B., the other listed witnesses were Marie Blanchard, grandmother of the groom and widow of Mathieu Brunet dit Létang; Pierre Barbary, uncle of the groom; and Jean Brunet, brother-in-law of the bride. In the ledger, Fr. De Breslay identified Jean Baptiste as a member of the Bout de l'Île parish; this clearly implies that, by this time, he and Jeanne had returned to this church. His brother Guillaume and Sarah had likewise left the Pointe Claire parish to return to their former membership in the parish at Bout de l'Île.

However, these two siblings did return to the Pointe Claire church some seven weeks later, on January 7, 1715, to stand together as official witnesses at the wedding celebration of their eldest nephew. Guillaume Daoust, identified in the Pointe Claire ledger on this day as being from the Ste. Anne parish of Bout de l'Île, at age 20, was the oldest living child of their sister Marie Madeleine Lalonde and her husband Guillaume Daoust. On this festive day, the young man exchanged nuptial vows with 19-year-old Élisabeth Pilon, daughter of Antoine Pilon and Marie Anne Brunet dite Létang (she was also a sibling of Jean Pilon, who had been married just weeks earlier). The third witness on this occasion was Thomas Brunet.[141]

By this point, the wooden palisade walls which surrounded the town of Montreal had been standing for nearly three decades, and they were in need of a major upgrade. The initial stockade had been erected in 1685 or 1686, after which this first set of log walls had been reinforced in 1699. Over the course of the following nine years, the inhabitants had outgrown the area of this initial enclosure. This expansion of the population had required a commensurate expansion of the stockade perimeter, which had been carried out during the years from 1708 to 1710. Now, however, the King's Minister determined that all of the wooden walls of the palisade were to be replaced with much more durable ones, constructed of cut stone.

On November 6, 1714, Intendant Bégon decreed that these

new and improved walls encircling the town would be built with contributions from all of the colonists who resided within the governmental district of Montreal (which extended to a point some thirty miles northeast of the town itself). This massive construction project would be carried out by means of the *corvée* system. This term referred to the amount of unpaid labor which each household was obliged to contribute every year to the seigneurs (in this instance, the Sulpicians), since the inhabitants were their *censitaires* or property-holders. In his pronouncement, the administrator declared that there would be drawn up "an allotment and tax of the number of days of labor which each of the said habitants will be obliged to furnish for the said *corvées*, in proportion to their possessions and abilities." The various tasks which they would carry out were planned to take place during those seasons in which most of the people were less busy, particularly after the autumn harvests had been completed. Thus, during the autumn seasons, they would be assigned to transport the rough-cut stones from the quarries to the assembly points, and during the winters they would haul these crude blocks to the workshops for further shaping. Other tasks of the habitants would entail hauling lime and sand to appropriate locales, for the fabrication of mortar.

However, instead of carrying out these assigned labors themselves, with their own teams of horses, each of the habitants had the option of paying for another individual to substitute for him. For each day of labor of a man, the levied tax was to be three livres, and for each day of labor of a pair of harnessed horses, the tax would be eight livres. These funds would be utilized to pay for replacement workers and teams of horses. For anyone who did not participate as ordered, with either direct labor or payments for substitutes, "the penalty for disobedience will be five hundred livres in fines for each of the contraventions, applicable to the King to be utilized for the expenses of the fortifications."

Between December 16, 1714 and March 25, 1715, the master roster of all of the colonists who were expected to contribute to this immense building project was drawn up. This document was entitled "List of the habitants of Montreal Island, Jesus Island, and the neighboring seigneuries who have been requisitioned to work on the fortifications of Montreal in 1715." After the 344 designated residents of the town and outlying areas of Montreal were listed, there followed the inhabitants (in this sequence) of Longue Pointe (37 listings), Côte de Vertus (27), Notre Dame de Liesse (42), Saint Michel

(20), Saint Ours (50), Ménagerie des Pauvres (5), Boucherville (78), Côte de Verchères (25), Île Bouchard, Seigneury of Monsieur Dejordy (15), Côte de Varenne (21), Côte St. Michel (23), Côte Ste. Thérèse (15), Côte de Lachine (56), Côte St. Paul (14), Côte St. Pierre (5), Lachenaie (32), Rivière des Prairies (55), Île Jésus (46), Les Mille Îles (16), and Haut [Bout] de l'Île (74).

In the section of the roster pertaining to the Bout de l'Île region, called "Haut de l'Isle," a total of 74 land owners were recorded. They were headed by the Captain of the St. Louis/Ste. Anne parish militia forces, Jacques Arrivé dit Delisle, who was listed as "Sieur De Lisle." Within the portion of the roster which represented the area immediately east of the church property, both of the Lalonde brothers were listed. These were Jean Baptiste, who was identified as "Lalonde L'ainé," "the elder Lalonde," and Guillaume, who was listed as "Guillaume de Lalonde." The eleventh land owner to the east of these siblings was identified as "Le Sieur Quenet."

After a number of years of ongoing construction, the entire set of encircling walls would be completed. Rising more than twenty feet in height, they would feature a total of sixteen gates, most of which would be positioned in the south wall, which faced the St. Lawrence River. The western wall of the town enclosure was located at the present Rue McGill, while the eastern wall was positioned just to the east of the present Rue Berri; the north wall extended along the present Rue St. Jacques, and the south wall ran parallel to the St. Lawrence. These ponderous barriers of mortar-laid stone would protect the community for more than eight decades, until they would be razed in 1804.[142]

During the spring of 1715, Jeanne and J.B. welcomed their eighth child into the world. Marie Anne, born on April 8, was christened on the same day in the Bout de l'Île church. The infant's sponsors were her aunt Marie Anne Gervais (Jeanne's newly-wedded sister) and her voyageur cousin Augustin Daoust, age 18, nephew of the baby's father.[143]

On February 23, 1716, Jeanne's sister Marie Catherine was married in her home church of Laprairie. The bride, 26 years old, took as her partner Jean Poupard, a widower who was four months younger than her. He had a daughter who was 25 months old, and he had been a widower for just three months.

Jean Baptiste made the trip to the Pointe Claire church one month later, on March 23, to appear as the godfather of his newborn niece

Anne Geneviève Pilon, the first baby to be born to Jeanne's sister Anne and her husband Jean Pilon. On this day, the godmother was Marie Anne Brunet dite Létang, the widow of Antoine Pilon, who was the infant's paternal grandmother.[144]

Back in the Ste. Anne parish at Bout de l'Île, J.B. was again selected to stand as godfather and bequeath his name to a baby. This time, it was for the fifth child of Pierre Poirier dit Lafleur and Marie Clémence Maupetit. The other sponsor was Jeanne Martin, the wife of Joachim Merlot.[145]

One of the most important events in the household of J.B. and Jeanne in 1717 was the safe arrival of their ninth and final child on December 18. On the same day, tiny Marie was baptized in the very close-by church, with both of her sponsors having close linkages to military personnel. The godfather was Louis Hector d'Ailleboust, esquire, the unmarried 24-year-old son of Louis d'Ailleboust, Sieur de Coulonges, officer in the troops of the detachment of the Marine Department. (The elder d'Ailleboust, both an ensign in the troops and a Montreal peltries merchant, owned a sub-fief at the western tip of Montreal Island.) The godmother was Marie Josèphe Arrivé, the 17-year-old unmarried daughter of Jacques Arrivé dit Delisle, who was the Captain of the Bout de l'Île militia forces.[146]

Over the course of the previous fifteen years, Jeanne and Jean Baptiste had produced eight children of their own, while raising François, who had been born to J.B. and his first wife, Marguerite Masta. Nineteen months after the couple's wedding, their first offspring had arrived in May of 1703. Thereafter, the intervals between the birth of this baby and those of the other seven had been 22, 25, 27, 20, 31, 17, and 32 months, respectively. During these fifteen child-bearing years, Jeanne's age had increased from 23 to 38, while J.B. had advanced in age from 27 to 42. (When his first child had arrived, born to Marguerite in September of 1699, J.B. had been five weeks short of age 24.) This family had been unusually fortunate in the survival rate of their youngsters. Only their fifth baby, little Thomas, had perished at an early age --- just one month old; all of he others would eventually grow up to adulthood and marry.

Participation in the activities of the militia forces of New France had been a part of daily life for all able-bodied males between the ages of 16 and 60 for nearly a half-century, ever since the royal edict ordering the formation of these civilian military forces had arrived during the summer of 1669. Unfortunately for historians, little has survived in the way of documentation concerning the specific individuals who participated in this informal army. However, by good fortune, some information about the role which was played by Jean Baptiste Lalonde has survived, embedded in church records and notary documents.

Five weeks after the arrival of the last Lalonde baby, J.B. appeared as one of the official witnesses at a wedding that was celebrated in the Ste. Anne church, very near to his home. After conducting the ceremony on January 30, 1718, Fr. De Breslay penned into the parish ledger the names of the bride, the groom, and the witnesses on both sides. The last name that he entered was "Jean Baptiste Lalonde, Sergeant of the militia of the Top of Montreal Island." He then indicated that the Captain of these forces, Jacques Arrivé dit Delisle, was absent, and that Monsieur Lalonde was commanding at present *la milice du Haut de l'Île de Montreal* (the militia forces of the Top of Montreal Island), in the absence of Monsieur Delisle.

This wedding celebrated the union of the local resident Barbe Denis, 19-year-old daughter of Jacques Denis dit Saint Denis and Anne Gauthier, and the Île Perrot voyageur Joseph Lefebvre, son of Michel Lefebvre dit Lasisseraye and Catherine Trottier; he was a month away from celebrating his 24th birthday. Besides J.B. Lalonde, the other witnesses included, on the bride's side, her uncles Pierre Dauzat from Lachine and Joseph Poirier dit Desloges from Île Perrot, and her brother-in-law Guillaume Vinet dit La Rente from Montreal Island; those on the groom's side included his sister Marie Anne Lefebvre and his brother-in-law Pierre Hunault from Île Perrot. Near the end of the long record, listed just before the militia officer J.B. Lalonde, the other martial witness was René Godefroy, Sieur de Linctot, (age 42), "Esquire, ensign in the detachment of the Marine Department and commandant of the Fort of the Mission of St. Louis." This latter statement indicated that a protective fortification, manned by a small number of soldiers, had been established in the area.

In fact, the citizenry of the region had constructed an entire series of forts of refuge on Montreal Island. These protective facilities were strung out along the entire perimeter of the triangular-shaped landmass. Some years later, these small fortresses would be clearly portrayed by the cartographer Nicolas Bellin, on his 1744 chart entitled "Map of Montreal Island and its Environs." Seven of the forts were positioned along the southern shoreline of the island. In sequence from east to west, these were Ft. de Lachine, Ft. Rolland,

Ft. de la Grande Anse, Ft. de la Pointe Claire, Ft. de la Pointe Quenet, Ft. Ste. Anne, and Ft. Senneville. (Interestingly, there was no longer a small protective facility at Verdun, northeast of Lachine, although one had been present there during earlier periods.) Another four forts were located along the northwestern side of the island. These posts, in order from southwest to northeast, were Ft. Geneviève, Ft. du Sault au Récollet, Ft. de la Rivière des Prairies, and Ft. des Roches. Finally, along the eastern shoreline of Montreal Island (in sequence from north to south), the forts of refuge included Ft. St. Pierre, Ft. de la Pointe aux Trembles, Ft. de la Longue Pointe, and Ft. de la Montagne. In addition to indicating these fifteen protective facilities, the mapmaker also portrayed the large stone-walled town of Montreal, on the eastern shore of the island. Its rectangular fortifications included four corner bastions as well as two additional bastions, which were located at the midpoint of the elongated eastern and western walls.[147]

As was noted by the priest, Jacques Arrivé, the Captain of the Ste. Anne militia forces, was absent from the Bout de l'Île area at the time of the Lefebvre-Denis wedding in January of 1718. The reason for his absence: he was away in the Upper Country on a year-long trading venture. In fact, on July 3, 1717, he had engaged Jean Baptiste's brother Guillaume to labor for and with him in *Le Pays d'en Haut* during that year. As Monsieur Lalonde's salary, he was to receive a total of 225 livres worth of beaver pelts, of which he had received 100 livres worth before they had departed with the westbound brigade. During that summer of 1717, a total of 59 voyageur hirings had been recorded by notaries in the Montreal area. These contracts had included 33 men whose agreements indicated that they were destined for Michilimackinac, 3 others who were headed for Michilimackinac or the Ottawa Country, 9 men who were bound for the Upper Country, 1 man who was paddling to "the North," and 13 men who were traveling to Detroit.[148]

By July of this year of 1718, Jean Baptiste had been selected as the Captain of the Bout de l'Île militia forces. This fact was recorded by Fr. De Breslay in the Ste. Anne ledger when J.B. stood as a sponsor for the seventh child of Joachim Merlot and Jeanne Martin. At this ceremony, held on July 23, the godmother of the one-day-old infant was Françoise Cécire, the wife of Nicolas Robillard. The priest recorded the godfather as "Jean Baptiste Lalonde of this parish, Captain of the Côte."[149]

Ten weeks later, when recording a marriage in the Ste. Anne parish ledger, the same cleric reiterated J.B.'s highly respected status in the region. In the process, he revealed that Monsieur Lalonde also held an important position on the church council as well. This ecclesiastical event, celebrated on October 9, was the nuptial ceremony of Jeanne's sister Marguerite Gervais and Louis Neveu. At this time, the bride, from La Prairie St. Lambert, was six weeks short of turning age 34 (but she had never been married), while the groom, from Île Perrot, was 22 years old. Interestingly, she reported her age to the priest as 28 and he indicated that he was 23, which reduced the span between their ages from twelve down to five years. The witnesses on the bride's side included Jacques Denis, her uncle Jean Gabriel Picard, and "Jean Baptiste Lalonde of this parish, brother-in-law of the bride, Captain of the militia, and church warden." This latter position of *marguillier* was the designation of the member of the *fabrique* or parish council who was in charge of administering the possessions of the parish. This was the very same role that J.B.'s father Jean de Lalonde had held when this parish had been first established 33 years earlier, back in 1685.[150]

At some previous time, Jean Baptiste Lalonde had been selected to serve as the Sergeant of the Militia of the Bout de l'Île/Côte St. Louis region of Montreal Island, and then in 1718 he had been chosen to be the Captain in charge of those forces. These facts speak volumes. First of all, by the time the above series of documents were penned in 1718, he had certainly been a member of this civilian fighting force for many years. In addition, during those years of service, he must have exhibited highly-developed skills in guerrilla-style warfare, as well as considerable abilities in organization and leadership, especially in situations of duress. J.B. had first moved westward from the Côte St. Pierre area (a little north of the Lachine village) to this section of the Island on about March 15, 1704, in order to commence his six-year lease of Jean Quenet's farm on Pointe Beaurepaire. In all likelihood, he had joined the local militia at that time, as required by law for all able-bodied males between the ages of 16 and 60 (he had been age 28 1/2 when he had first arrived here). It is not possible to determine which military actions he and his fellow militiamen may have conducted over the ensuing years, from 1704 onward, including both defensive and offensive activities. However, it is thought-provoking to consider that he had settled in this area some four days after a combined force of militia fighters, regular troops, and allied native warriors had raided the stockaded village of

Deerfield in northwestern Massachusetts colony, on March 11, 1704. It was during that violent attack that his future sister-in-law Sarah Allyn had been seized, along with 111 of her friends and neighbors, after which they had all been led through some 300 miles of frozen forested land to reach the St. Lawrence settlements and their future homes. Another 50 of the Anglo settlers of Deerfield had been killed on the spot in their own community.

As first the Sergeant and eventually as the Captain of the militia forces of St. Louis/Ste. Anne, Jean Baptiste played a number of different roles. In the rural areas outside of the three primary settlements of Quebec, Trois-Rivières, and Montreal, the militia units were organized according to parishes, rather than by seigneuries. Throughout the colony, each of these local units was commanded by a local Captain of the Militia. In the larger parishes, this officer was assisted by a Lieutenant, an Ensign, and two Sergeants. However, in the smaller parishes (such as St. Louis/Ste. Anne), the only sub-officer was a single Sergeant, the role which Jean Baptiste Lalonde had first held before being eventually selected as the Captain in 1718. In the rural areas, the Captain was a highly responsible farmer-settler who was well-respected among his neighbors. This would be one of the primary reasons that he would be chosen by the Governor of the colony to serve as the officer in charge. By means of local monthly training sessions and drills, he saw to it that the men of his unit were equipped with properly functioning firearms, and that they were instructed in the use of those weapons, as well as in the basic elements of military organization, discipline, and activities. Additionally, once a year, all of the local companies mustered for joint maneuvers. At all times, each man in the militia forces was equipped with sufficient supplies of gunpowder and shot. In addition to the Captain's military role, he also served a civil function, acting as the agent in his local area for the Intendant of New France. In this capacity, he and his sub-officer(s) delivered the orders of this administrator and saw that those directives were properly carried out. He also reported to the official any unusual activities that took place in his area. Likewise, the Captain represented the habitants of his district in any disputes that might arise between them and their seigneurs (who, for all of the residents of Montreal Island, were the Sulpicians).[151]

Near the end of this summer of 1718, Jeanne and Jean Baptiste were saddened to receive word that one of their nieces, Marie Gervais, had died at the age of just nine weeks. The sixth and youngest child of Jeanne's brother Jean Mathieu and his wife Jeanne Françoise Ronceray, she had been buried in the cemetery of their home parish of Laprairie (some 20 miles due east of the Lalondes' farm) on August 18.[152]

Within the span of a single month in the autumn of 1719, Jeanne and Jean Baptiste attended three festive occasions. The first one took place on October 13 in the Ste. Anne church by their home, when J.B. stood as the godfather of the fifth child of Joseph Poirier dit Desloges and Marie Gauthier. (This mother had once been the widow of Alexandre Turpin, whose biography was presented earlier in this work.) On this occasion, the other sponsor of baby Jean was Catherine Trottier.[153]

Two weeks later, on October 30, Jeanne's brother Mathieu Gervais was married in his home church of Laprairie. At this time, he was one month short of his 20th birthday, while his bride, Marie Josèphe Robidou, had just turned 17. This young couple would settle at Longueuil and Laprairie.[154] After two more weeks had passed, another of Jeanne's siblings joined forces with his life partner in the same church. This time, it was her aging brother Pierre Gervais, a month short of turning 43, who wed Catherine Plante, 26 years old, on November 13. These colonists would establish themselves at Laprairie.[155]

The winter and spring of 1720 delivered three major doses of melancholy to the clan, when two young nieces and a nephew of Jeanne and J.B. died. First came the loss of the eighth baby of Romaine Gervais and her husband Charles Marcil. Marie Angélique Charlotte Marcil was born at Laprairie on January 21, she was christened there on the following day, and she perished and was laid to rest in the cemetery there on the 23rd.[156] Three months later, Marguerite Gervais and her husband Louis Neveu, who had been married for nineteen months, lost their first child in latter April. Baby Catherine had been born on Île Perrot, after which she had been transported eastward to the Pointe Claire church to be baptized on the 23rd. However, she survived just four more days, and was interred at Pointe Claire on April 27.[157] Four weeks after this bleak event, Jean Baptiste's sister Marie Madeleine Lalonde and Guillaume Daoust, her spouse of 24 years, were buffeted by the death of their son Alexis François Daoust. This happened in the Bout de l'Île area, two months after the boy had celebrated his tenth birthday. He was laid to rest a few miles to the east, in the Pointe Claire cemetery, on May 8. Tragically, this was not the first time that this couple had endured the passing of one of their offspring when they were long past the most dangerous period of infancy and the young years. Almost 21 years earlier, back in 1699, they had lost their eldest child, Marie, one month after she had turned eight.[158]

In strong contrast, 1721 brought with it many reasons to celebrate rather than to mourn. First, Jeanne stood in the Ste. Anne church as the sponsor of the sixth child of the voyageur Pierre Hunault dit Deschamps and Marguerite Suzanne Lefebvre of Île Perrot. At this ceremony on May 30, infant Marie Rose's other sponsor was Guillaume Vinet dit La Rente, from the Ste. Anne parish.[159] Just two weeks later, on June 13, Jean Baptiste took his turn at sponsoring a brand-new baby at the baptismal font. This was Marie Catherine Hunault, who had been born on the previous day as the third offspring of the voyageur Antoine Hunault dit Deschamps and Marie Catherine Lefebvre of Île Perrot. (These two Hunault brothers had married these two Lefebvre sisters, back in 1711 and 1716, respectively.) On this June day, the godmother was Marie Barbe Denis, aunt of the baby and wife of Joseph Lefebvre dit Lasisseraye.[160]

In the autumn of this year of 1721, Jeanne and J.B.'s eldest daughter, Marie Rosalie, was $10^2/3$ years old. Within a single week in November, she stood as the godmother of two babies in the Lachine church. The first time was on November 21, when the celebrated infant was Marie Josèphe Picard, the one-day-old daughter of Jean Gabriel Picard and Marie Madeleine Rapin of the Lachine parish. Nearly matching the youthfulness of the godmother, the godfather was Bernardin Lemaire dit Saint Germain, who was $13^1/2$ years old.[161] The next week, on November 28, Mademoiselle Lalonde again appeared as a baptismal sponsor in this same church. This time, the ceremony was for Anne Roy, the tiny daughter born on that same day to François Roy and Marie Cécire of the Lachine parish. However, it must have wrenched the young godmother's heart deeply when she learned that this infant died and was buried in the cemetery there just two days later.[162]

During the first week of January in 1722, Jean Baptiste and Jeanne were dispirited by the loss of another tiny niece. On the second day of the month, Marie Josèphe Pilon died after just four days of life. The fourth child of her sister Anne Gervais and her husband Jean Pilon, she had been born on December 30 and had been christened in the Ste. Anne church on the following day, on the holiday of *Ignolée*

(New Year's Eve). However, the tiny infant passed away and was laid to rest in the Ste. Anne cemetery two days later, on January 2.[163]

Nine weeks later, on March 9, 1722, Jeanne (along with Jean Baptiste, as her legal husband) sold a portion of the Gervais family land at Laprairie St. Lambert to her brother Mathieu, who resided in that seigneury. They made this transfer of ownership in the office of the Montreal notary Lepailleur.[164]

With the arrival of spring weather this year, it was time for J.B. and Jeanne's third son to stand in the Ste. Anne church as godfather for the brand-new baby of their close neighbors Pierre Maupetit and Angélique Villeray (direct ancestors of the present author, whose biographies are presented later in this work). The Maupetit land was located about 1500 feet east of the Lalonde family property, separated by only two farms. On May 25, Guillaume (designated as Guillaume Number 2 in this study), who was $17^1/4$ years old, sponsored little Pierre, who had been born on that very same day. Guillaume's counterpart at the baptismal font was Marie Josèphe Brébant, the 13-year-old daughter of Michel Brébant and Marie Élisabeth Lafaye. Interestingly, almost four years into the future, this young godmother would marry Guillaume's older brother Jean Baptiste Lalonde, Jr.[165]

On August 6, 1722, Jeanne's sister Marie Anne Gervais married the Île Perrot voyageur Noël Lefebvre dit Lasisseraye, who was 22 years old. At the ceremony in the Bout de l'Île church of Ste. Anne, the official witnesses were Toussaint Hunault of Île Perrot as well as Jean Baptiste Lalonde, Pierre Sauvé dit Laplante, and Nicolas Robillard of the Ste. Anne parish.[166]

By the winter of 1723, J.B. and Jeanne's second-oldest son, Jean Baptiste, Jr., was ten weeks short of reaching his 20th birthday. On February 17, the young man's uncle and aunt Guillaume Lalonde and Marie Madeleine Hélène, who were living on Île Perrot, sold him a piece of land which they owned on the south side of this latter island. However, since J.B., Jr. was still of minor age, his parents conducted the transfer of ownership for him with the Montreal notary Lepailleur. In the document of sale, the scribe identified the recipient's parents as "Jean Baptiste Lalonde and Jeanne Gervais, his wife, of Baie D'Urfé on Montreal Island." This latter name was applied to the area of Pointe St. Louis and the shallow bay that extended westward from the Point for about a half-mile.[167]

Five months after conducting this transaction, on July 15, Jean Baptiste, Sr. purchased for himself a plot of land on Île Perrot. He acquired it from the voyageur Jean Baptiste Charlebois, who was a resident of this island and was still single at this time.[168]

Jeanne and J.B. suffered an emotional low four months later, when Jeanne's sister Marguerite died on Île Perrot at the untimely age of 39. She and Louis Neveu had been married for five years and two months, and during that time, they had produced two daughters, in 1720 and 1722. The first of these had perished just four days after her baptism, while the younger girl must have also died at a young age, since she was not mentioned in any later documents. Marguerite's funeral was held in the Pointe Claire church on November 22, 1723. During their adult lives, this was just the second time that Jeanne and Jean Baptiste had been afflicted with the death of a sibling. The first time had occurred some two or three years earlier, when Jeanne's brother Pierre had passed away in his mid-30s. He had been married to Catherine Plante in November of 1719, and they had welcomed the arrival of one daughter at Laprairie in September of 1720. No record of his burial has survived in the colony, but Catherine had remarried at Laprairie in July of 1722.[169]

On March 14, 1724, J.B. traveled to Montreal to visit one of the halls of the Sulpicians (his seigneurs), in order to receive a grant of an additional piece of land from them. This new property adjoined the inland or northwestern end of the lands which he had previously acquired, one portion having come through a purchase from his mother and his two siblings in July of 1702, and an adjacent portion located immediately to the west having been granted to him by the Sulpicians in February of 1711.

"...to Jean de Lalonde, habitant of the Top of this Island [of Montreal], present and assenting as the recipient of the said title for himself as well as for his heirs and assigns in the future, the land which will be found to be not granted at the end of his habitation which has four arpents of [St. Lawrence] frontage and is located below [east of] the Baie D'Urfé, [the new land] extending to the meadow of Lac au Renard [Fox Lake], without limitations of any kind. This land has at one end the lands of the said habitation of the said recipient, at the other end the said meadows of Lac au Renard, on one [east] side the lands of the continuation of the habitation of Guillaume Daoust [his brother-in-law], and on the other side those of the habitation of Pilon."

J.B.'s annual seigneurial fees on this additional property, payable to the Sulpicians each year on November 11 (the Feast Day of St. Martin, the patron saint of France), would be 10 sols (.5 livre) plus one-half bushel of wheat for each twenty arpents (17 acres) of surface area. Otherwise, the obligations which were related to this new land would be the same as those which applied to his previously-granted land.[170]

In the afternoon on the following day, while he was still in Montreal, Jean Baptiste visited the office of the notary Raimbault, to officially register the settlement of the estate of Jeanne's deceased sister Marguerite and her widowed husband Louis Neveu. On this occasion, as the spouse of the eldest of the seven surviving Gervais siblings, J.B. was representing Jeanne, all six of her brothers and sisters (plus their spouses), and the one underage child of their deceased brother Pierre. Thus, he and Monsieur Neveu met in the scribe's office at this time to record the details of the amicable settlement that had been worked out by the Gervais clan members. The belongings at the couple's residence on Île Perrot had been appraised at 388.5 livres, from which 23.5 livres in debts owed to creditors and 6 livres owed to the appraisers had been subtracted. The remainder of 359 livres was to be divided in halves, with one half worth 179 livres remaining with Louis Neveu. The other half worth 179 was to be divided evenly between the deceased Marguerite's seven siblings and the one minor-age child of their brother Pierre, thus making 22.5 livres for each of these eight parties. Louis promised to pay the sum of 22.5 livres to the guardian of Pierre's underage son in this year of 1724, and to pay the remainder of 155.5 livres to Monsieur Lalonde in four equal payments on March 15 of the years 1725, 1726, 1727, and 1728, respectively. In addition, he would also transfer ownership of one-half of the estate's property on Île Perrot to the seven siblings. To execute this legally binding agreement, the two parties selected as their temporary legal domiciles, to which writs could be delivered, their respective residences in Montreal: "the said Neveu his residence with Sieur Antoine Perrin, royal bailiff in this town, and the said Lalonde that of Raphaël Beauvais on Rue St. Paul in the said Villemarie." According to an addendum which would be penned at the bottom of this document nearly three years later, on January 30, 1727, J.B. would acknowledge that he had received from Louis Neveu the full payment of 179 livres, and that he had accepted the responsibility of distributing the rightful shares of this total sum to each of the eight family members.[171]

In the following autumn, Jean Baptiste and his eldest offspring, François, visited the same notary Raimbault in Montreal on September 22. The timing of their 40-mile round trip to the town was significant, since it took place eighteen days after the young man had celebrated his 25th birthday and had thus reached the legal age of majority. The father and son wished to officially register the transfer of the monies which had been legally due to François, from the estate that J.B. and François' mother Marguerite Masta had owned together before her demise.

"Today appeared before the undersigned royal notary in the [governmental] jurisdiction of Montreal in New France, residing at Villemarie, François de Lalonde, majority-age son of Jean de Lalonde, habitant of the Côte St. Louis at the Top of this Island. He has acknowledged and declared that today he received an accounting from him of the management and handling which the said Lalonde, his father and guardian, had conducted of the belongings of the estate of the deceased Marguerite Masta, his mother, wife of the said Lalonde. The inventory of this estate totaled the sum of 668 livres 19 sols 4 deniers, all in currency of the country, from which the said Lalonde had taken 200 livres as his preciput *(preferred portion). In addition, he had afterward paid off the debts of the estate, leaving a remainder in the said estate the sum of 108 livres 10 sols 9 deniers in the currency of France. The said François Lalonde has said that he has received from him sufficient information, and that he is content with this accounting. He has acknowledged that he has today been paid by the said Sieur Lalonde, his father, who is present and assenting, and that he is entirely satisfied."*[172]

Back in May of 1722, Jeanne and J.B.'s son Guillaume had been chosen to serve as the godfather for the newborn baby of the Lalonde family's close neighbors Pierre Maupetit and Angélique Villeray. At that time, the young sponsor had been 17 1/4 years old. Nearly 2 1/2 years later, in the autumn of 1724, he was again selected by a local family to stand in this same capacity for their one-day-old daughter (the sponsor was now 19 2/3 years of age). On October 14, when Nicolas Robillard and Françoise Cécire brought tiny Marie Josèphe to the Ste. Anne church to be baptized, the godmother was Marie Suzanne Thérèse Brunet, from the St. Joachim parish at Pointe Claire.[173]

More than a year later, on November 3, 1725, Jean Baptiste likewise appeared as a godfather in the Bout de l'Île church. On this day, the baby being christened was Charles Daoust, the son of Charles Daoust, Sr. and Marie Angélique Laplante of Île Perrot. Standing beside J.B. at the baptismal font was Marie Michel, the maternal grandmother of the infant and the wife of Pierre Sauvé dit Laplante. The latter couple lived two farms to the east of the Lalonde family lands.[174]

During the heart of the winter in 1726, Jeanne and J.B.'s second-oldest child (the first one to have been born to Jeanne) was within months of reaching his 23rd birthday. Jean Baptiste, Jr. had found the young woman with whom he wished to spend the rest of his life. This was Marie Josèphe Brébant, who would turn 17 on March 13, the eldest child of Michel Brébant dit Lamothe and Marie Élisabeth Lafaye, fellow residents of the Côte St. Louis. On February 21, the engaged couple visited the Montreal notary Lepailleur, along with various relatives and friends, to draw up their marriage contract. In this document, the parents of the prospective groom were identified as "Jean Baptiste Lalonde, notable, and Jeanne Gervais, of Baie D'Urfé in the parish of Ste. Anne on the Island of Montreal." Ten days later, on March 3, the bride and groom exchanged their wedding vows in the Bout de l'Île church, after which the priest recorded the names of the two official witnesses. These were Guillaume Lalonde, uncle of the groom and brother of Jean Baptiste Lalonde, Sr., and Simon Mongeneau, grandfather of the bride (he was the third husband of Marie Josèphe's grandmother Marie Anne Goupil, having married the twice-widowed woman back in 1701).[175]

These events had inspired novel and hopeful emotions in Jeanne and J.B., Sr., since this was their first experience of watching one of their offspring marry. They would not have to wait long to again enjoy these feelings. In fact, two days before the celebration of the above wedding in church, their eldest son (who had been born to Marguerite Masta, J.B.'s first wife) and his fiancée had likewise visited the same notary in Montreal, to have their own marriage contract drawn up. On this day of March 1, 1726, François Lalonde was $26^1/2$ years old, while Marie Josèphe Trottier, his bride-to-be, was age 18. The youngest child of Joseph Trottier and Marie Jeanne Robillard, she had been born and raised in the sub-fief of Côte St. Paul, a short distance north of the Lachine village. Four days after arranging their nuptial contract, on May 5, the couple celebrated their wedding in the Holy Angels church at Lachine. On this occasion, the official witnesses on the groom's side were his uncle Guillaume Lalonde (designated in this study as Guillaume Number 1) and his brothers Guillaume Joseph Lalonde (Guillaume Number 2) and Joseph Lalonde. On the bride's side, the witnesses were her siblings Joseph, Pierre, and Françoise Trottier, her uncle François Morel dit Madore, and her brothers-in-law Jean (Joseph) Ducharme and Joseph Cécire.[176]

On January 30, 1727, J.B. visited the notary Raimbault in Montreal, to officially report that he had received a payment of 179 livres from his widowed brother-in-law Louis Neveu. This was in compliance with the agreement that the two men had made nearly three years earlier, back on March 15, 1724, concerning the settlement of the estate of Neveu and his deceased wife Marguerite Gervais. In that earlier contract, it had been agreed that one-half of the property which the couple had owned on Île Perrot would be transferred to the surviving siblings of the deceased Marguerite. On this January day, Monsieur Neveu sold his remaining half of this land to J.B., with the stipulation that it was to belong to the buyer's daughter Marie Lalonde, who was at this time 9 years and 2 months old.[177]

During this same year of 1727, Jeanne and Jean Baptiste reveled in additional unique sensations, which were inspired by the arrival of their first two grandchildren. Both of these babies were born on Île Perrot, where the two newly-wedded brothers resided with their wives. First came little Marie Josèphe Lalonde, born to François and Marie Josèphe Trottier on April 14, six weeks after the couple had celebrated their first wedding anniversary. The tiny lass was baptized on the following day in the Ste. Anne church, a short distance away from the farm of her Lalonde grandparents.[178]

The second grandchild to arrive was Jean Lalonde, who was welcomed by his parents, Jean Baptiste, Jr. and Marie Josèphe Brébant, on October 9. Like his cousin six months earlier, this newborn was christened on the day following his birth in the same Bout le l'Île church. At this uplifting ceremony, his godparents were his paternal grandfather Jean Baptiste Lalonde and his maternal grandmother Marie Élisabeth Lafaye. Interestingly, the priest mistakenly recorded the family name of the latter sponsor as Brébant, although that was the family name of her husband. To the great sadness of all the members of the clan, baby Jean survived for only fifteen days; he was tenderly laid to rest in the Ste. Anne cemetery on October 24.[179]

Three months later, Jeanne lost her father. Mathieu Gervais dit Parisien was buried in the cemetery at Longueuil on February 1, 1728, on the day following his death. Having been a widower for eighteen years, never remarrying, he had reached the end of his life at the age of about 80 to 82.[180]

An additional loss came to the clan eight months later, when one of Jeanne and J.B.'s nephews perished on Île Perrot. Pierre Lefebvre, the third child of Marie Anne Gervais and Noël Lefebvre dit Lasisseraye, was buried in the Ste. Anne cemetery on October 3, six days before he would have celebrated his first birthday.[181]

During this same autumn, Jeanne and J.B.'s oldest daughter, Marie Rosalie, was 17 2/3 years old, and she had caught the eye of the Lachine-based voyageur Joseph Gauthier. This future spouse, the son of Joseph Gauthier dit Saguingoira and the deceased Clémence Jarry, was age 28. In anticipation of their upcoming wedding, the priest of the Bout de l'Île parish published their banns of marriage one time, after which the Bishop granted a dispensation of the other two customary banns. At their nuptial celebration in the church on November 9, the four witnesses listed by the officiating priest were Antoine Rapin, Jacques Charbonnier, Marie Picard, and René Godefroy, the Sieur de Linctot, Lieutenant of a company of the detachment of the Marine Department. More than a decade earlier, back in January of 1718, the latter officer had also appeared as one of the witnesses at a wedding in this church. At that time, he had been identified as the "commandant of the Fort of the Mission of St. Louis."

Belatedly, eleven days after they had celebrated their wedding, the Gauthier-Lalonde newlyweds drew up their marriage contract on November 20, in the office of the Montreal notary Lepailleur. In that document, the scribe identified Marie Rosalie's parents as "Jean Baptiste Lalonde, Captain, and Jeanne Gervais, of the Côte and Parish of Ste. Anne at the Top of Montreal Island."[182]

Four days after this wedding, the widowed Lieutenant who had appeared as one of the official witnesses again stood at the altar of the same church, this time to exchange vows with his second spouse. Sixteen months earlier, back in July of 1727, his wife of eighteen years had died. He and Marie Madeleine Lemoine had produced five children during their years together, of whom at least the eldest one (now age 19) had survived. On November 13, 1728, he and Marie Catherine d'Ailleboust de Coulonges were wed, when he was 53 years old and she was age 37. (This woman, who had not been previously married, was the daughter of an ensign in the same Troupes de la Marine in which her higher-ranked fiancé was a Lieutenant). At the nuptial ceremony in the Ste. Anne church, the witnesses were Louis Gamelin, Angélique Brunet, Jacques Charbonnier, Michel Brébant, and Jean Baptiste Lalonde, Captain of the Côte. In this instance, the Bishop had granted a dispensation of all three of the banns of marriage. (However, it is highly unlikely that premarital pregnancy was an issue, since the couple's first baby would not be born until eighteen months after their wedding.)[183]

Six weeks later, on the day after Christmas, J.B. again found himself appearing in the church in an official capacity. However, this time, instead of standing at the altar, he was standing beside the baptismal font, with the three-day-old son and third child of Michel Lefebvre dit Lasisseraye and Françoise Denis. The priest recorded in the parish ledger that the godmother of little Michel, Jr. was Marguerite Lefebvre, while the godfather was "Jean Lalonde (sic), Captain of the Côte."[184]

The first month of 1729 brought an event which was at first worrisome but gradually became hopeful and encouraging. This was the arrival of Jeanne and J.B.'s third grandchild, born to Jean Baptiste, Jr. and Marie Josèphe Brébant. This couple's first baby had survived for only fifteen days. As a result, many of the members of the clan probably had some apprehensions about the prospects of this second child. At his christening in the Ste. Anne church on January 5, the same day as his arrival, little Albert's godparents were his paternal grandfather Michel Brébant dit Lamothe and his maternal grandmother. The priest identified the latter sponsor in his ledger as "Jeanne Gervais, wife of Lalonde, Captain of the Côte."[185]

Two months later, the Lalonde clan lost its most senior member. Guillaume Daoust was a brother-in-law to Jean Baptiste and Guillaume, as the husband of their sister Marie Madeleine. This couple had been married for 43 years, and had produced nine children. Their farm on the Côte St. Louis was located immediately to the east of the Lalonde family property. At the time of his funeral in the Ste. Anne church on March 9, 1729, on the day following his demise, Guillaume's age was recorded by the priest as being 84 years. Considerably younger than him, Marie Madeleine was about 67 years of age.[186]

This loss was offset by the arrival of another Lalonde grandchild for Jeanne and J.B. two months later. Marie Thérèse, the second offspring of François Lalonde and Marie Josèphe Trottier, arrived on May 11, after which she was baptized in the Bout de l'Île church on the following day. However, the settlers of New France were constantly confronted with numerous personal losses that tempered the many gains. Thus, on August 3, Jeanne and J.B. lost one of their Gervais nephews. Toussaint, the fifth child of Jeanne's brother Mathieu Gervais and his wife Marie Josèphe Robidou, died at Longueuil at the age of 21 months.[187]

Up to this point, J.B. and Jeanne had been blessed with four Lalonde grandchildren, of whom three were still living. Then, on

September 1 in this year of 1729, they rejoiced at the arrival of their first Gauthier grandchild, born to their daughter Marie Rosalie and Joseph Gauthier $9^3/4$ months after their wedding. At Marie Josèphe's christening festivities, held in the Ste. Anne church two days later, her sponsors were her paternal grandfather Joseph Gauthier, Sr. and her maternal grandmother Jeanne Gervais.[188]

The next major cause for celebration was the marriage of Jeanne and J.B.'s third offspring, Guillaume (designated in this study as Guillaume Number 2), who was one month short of age 25. He had found his life partner, Marie Angélique Brunet dite Bourbonnais, $18^1/2$ years old, in his home parish of Ste. Anne. (She was the granddaughter of Claude David, the pioneering trader whose biography has already been presented in this work. The life stories of Marie Angélique's parents, François Brunet dit Le Bourbonnais, Jr. and Françoise David, as well as the biographies of Guillaume Lalonde Number 2 and Marie Angélique Brunet themselves, are offered later.) On January 15, 1730, the betrothed couple, along with a number of their *parents et amis* (relatives and friends), had the Montreal notary Joseph Raimbault draw up their marriage contract. As usual, J.B. was identified by the scribe as "Captain of the Parish of Ste. Anne at the Top of Montreal Island." On the following day, they exchanged their vows in the church there, with the following official witnesses looking on: René Godefroy, Sieur de Linctot, esquire, Lieutenant of the troops; Jacques Charbonnier, merchant and bourgeois; and Raphaël Beauvais, innkeeper.[189]

The same Montreal notary penned a similar nuptial contract for Guillaume's younger brother Joseph (who was two months short of age 23) just two weeks later, on January 29. Joseph had likewise discovered his partner-for-life in the Ste. Anne parish, but in the seigneury of Vaudreuil, some miles to the west across the Ottawa River. Marie Jeanne Léger (called Marie), the daughter of Pierre Léger dit Parisien and Jeanne Boilard, was $20^2/3$ years old, some $2^1/2$ years younger than her fiancé. In the same manner as his older brother, Joseph and his bride celebrated their marriage in the Ste. Anne church on the day after their contract had been drawn up. Likewise, two of this couple's witnesses were the same individuals as had appeared at the previous wedding: the officer René Godefroy and the merchant Jacques Charbonnier. However, their third witness was Jean Baptiste Ménard from the Lachine parish.[190]

Less than three months later, Jeanne and J.B. lost a brother-in-law, upon the death of Jean Baptiste Poupard, the husband of Jeanne's sister Marie Catherine Gervais. At the time of his demise on April 13, 1730, he was only 40 years old. This couple, having been married for fourteen years, had produced seven children in their home area of Laprairie, besides raising the eldest child from his first marriage. Their offspring now ranged in age from 16 years down to 8 months, while Marie Catherine herself was about to turn 41.[191]

Additional sadness descended upon the clan five months later, when Jeanne's brother Jean Mathieu Gervais passed away at the age of $46^1/2$ years; he was buried at Longueuil on September 5. During his twelve years of marriage to Jeanne Françoise Ronceray, they had welcomed six children into the world at Laprairie.[192]

With five of their eight children now grown and married, Jeanne and J.B. looked forward to a wonderful influx of grandchildren, and they sincerely hoped that these new arrivals would be healthy and would survive. The first offspring of Guillaume (Number 2) and Marie Angélique Brunet arrived on May 25, 1731, sixteen months after her parents had been married. At her christening in the Ste. Anne church on the following day, Françoise Amable Lalonde had as her sponsors her paternal grandmother Jeanne Gervais and her maternal grandfather François Brunet dit Le Bourbonnais, Jr.[193]

Grand-mère Jeanne again stood as the godmother for one of her descendants three months later, on August 25. On that day, Françoise Marie Lalonde was born to François Lalonde and Marie Josèphe Trottier, and she was christened as well on the same day. Standing at the baptismal font with Jeanne Gervais was Nicolas Robillard, the newborn's godfather and the husband of Françoise Cécire.[194]

In the following spring of 1732, the latter Robillard-Cécire couple would find themselves observing the wedding which joined their eldest child and Jeanne and J.B.'s eighth child. On May 5, Nicolas Robillard, Jr., age 21, and Marie Anne Lalonde, 17, spoke their marriage vows in the Bout de l'Île church. In the parish ledger, after the priest had identified the parents of the bride and the groom (as usual, J.B. Lalonde was referred to as "Captain of the Côte and Parish of Ste. Anne"), he listed the nine official witnesses. On the bride's side, these were her uncle Guillaume Lalonde (Guillaume Number 1), her uncle Jean Pilon, her first cousin René Rivière, and family friends Jacques Charbonnier and Jacques Diel. On the groom's side, the witnesses were his brothers Lambert and Pierre Robillard, and his maternal uncles Claude and Jean Cécire.[195]

Within a three-day span in September of 1732, Jean Baptiste appeared as the godfather for two baptisms in the Ste. Anne church. The first one took place on the 7th, when he granted his own name to the baby who had been born that same day to their nephew René Rivière (a master shoemaker) and his wife Marie Françoise Diel. In this unusual instance, Jeanne joined him as the godmother, although it was very rare in the colony to have the two sponsors at a christening be husband and wife. Two days later, on the 9th, J.B. again stood at the baptismal font, this time as the godfather of the eight-day-old daughter of Philippe Arrivé dit Delisle and Marie Anne Normand, who resided in the seigneury of Longueuil. On this day, baby Agathe's godmother was her maternal grandmother, Françoise Monique Jean, the widow of Charles Normand.[196]

J.B. and Jeanne were pleased to be chosen as baptismal sponsors for two of their new grandchildren in 1733. The first of these babies, Marie Françoise Amable Lalonde, was welcomed by her parents Guillaume Lalonde (Number 2) and Marie Anglélique Brunet on March 9, after which she was taken to the Ste. Anne church for her baptism on the same day. Besides paternal grandfather J.B., the other sponsor was maternal grandmother Marie François David. Five months later, on August 6, Jeanne had her turn, when she appeared as the godmother of Jean Baptiste Robillard, son of Nicolas Robillard, Jr. and Marie Anne Lalonde. Standing beside Jeanne as the godfather on this day, the same day on which the tiny lad had arrived, was his paternal grandfather Nicolas Robillard, Sr.[197]

Less than four months later, it was time for the Lalonde clan to celebrate the marriage of one of Jeanne and J.B.'s nephews. Louis Daoust, 21 years old, was the son of J.B. and Guillaume's sister Marie Madeleine and the deceased Guillaume Daoust. Louis had chosen as his mate Marie Renée Miguet, age 26, a fellow resident of the Ste. Anne parish. On November 23, they were married in the church there with nine official witnesses looking on. On the groom's side were his uncles Jean Baptiste Lalonde ("Captain of the Côte") and Guillaume Lalonde, his brothers Guillaume and Charles Daoust, his brother-in-law Pierre Pilon, and family friend Jacques Diel (master blacksmith). The witnesses on the bride's side were her half-sister Marie Anne Crépin, and family friends Jean Baptiste Blénier dit Jarry and Jacques Charbonnier.[198]

During the year 1735, Jeanne and J.B. celebrated the safe arrival and baptism of three new grandchildren, as well as the wedding of another of their own children. First came the birth of Marie Catherine Lalonde to her parents Guillaume Lalonde (Number 2) and Marie Angélique Brunet dite Bourbonnais of Île Perrot; she was both born and christened in the Ste. Anne church on January 15. Her godmother was Marie Lalonde, Jeanne and J.B.'s only unmarried daughter, who was 17 years old, while her godfather was Joseph Trottier, the Sieur Desruisseaux, the seigneur of Île Perrot.[199]

Three weeks later, little Nicolas Robillard joined the family of Nicolas Robillard, Jr. and Marie Anne Lalonde. On the same day as his arrival, February 7, he was taken to the Ste. Anne church for his christening, at which his sponsors were his maternal grandfather J.B. Lalonde (who was identified in the parish ledger as "Captain of the Militia") and his paternal grandmother Françoise Cécire.[200]

Spring in 1735 brought with it a heartwarming family wedding, in which Jeanne and J.B.'s last remaining son, Antoine, took as his bride Felicité Sauvé dite Laplante. For many decades, Pierre Sauvé dit Laplante and Marie Michel had lived with their dozen children just two lots to the east of the Lalonde family land. Thus, the prospective bride and groom had known each other all of their lives. The young couple (he was $21^1/2$, and she was $24^1/2$) first visited the Montreal notary Jean Baptiste Adhémar on April 24, to compose their marriage contract. Two days later, they held their nuptial celebration in the Ste. Anne church, a short distance west of where both of them had grown up. On this occasion, the three official witnesses were Jean Pilon and Jacques Diel of the Côte St. Louis/Ste. Anne, and Noël Lefebvre dit Lasisseraye of Île Perrot (who was married to Jeanne's sister Marie Anne Gervais).[201]

The safe arrival of grandson Jean Baptiste Gauthier on September 20 topped off the jubilation and good fortune of this year. Born to their daughter Marie Rosalie Lalonde and her husband Joseph Gauthier, this tiny lad was given his name by his grandfather J.B. Lalonde on the day following his birth, when he was christened in the church at Bout de l'Île. On this special occasion, Marie Madeleine Lalonde served as his godmother.[202]

On March 27, 1736, Jean Baptiste sold the piece of land on Île Perrot that he had purchased nearly thirteen years earlier, back on July 15, 1723. On this March date, in front of the local notary Claude Cyprien Porlier, he transferred this property to Charles Léger dit Parisien. This young man was an habitant of the seigneury of Cavagnol, and a younger brother of Marie Jeanne Léger, who had married J.B.'s son

Joseph back in 1730. In the document of sale, the seller was identified as "Jean Baptiste Lalonde of Baie D'Urfé on Montreal Island."[203]

The year 1738 was one of considerable joy and festivities. In January came the marriage of J.B. and Jeanne's last remaining offspring, Marie, who had celebrated her 20th birthday three weeks earlier. She had caught the eye of the fellow Ste. Anne parish resident Augustin François Brébant, who was four months short of turning 22. His parents, Michel Brébant dit Lamothe and Marie Élisabeth Lafaye, had lived on the Côte St. Louis/Ste. Anne for decades; the future groom was the fifth of the eleven children whom they had produced here. On January 13, the young couple both drew up their marriage contract with the local notary Claude Cyprien Porlier and exchanged their nuptial vows in the Ste. Anne church. At the wedding, the priest noted that the official witnesses included the bride's brothers Jean Baptiste, Jr. and Antoine Lalonde, the groom's father Michel Brébant, and family friend Jacques Diel.[204]

The parishioners of Ste. Anne again gathered in August, to help another couple celebrate their festive wedding. However, this nuptial event was rather unusual, considering the relatively advanced ages of both the bride and the groom. Marie Anne Rapin, having been born in the Lachine seigneury back in April of 1682, was 56 years of age; she had never married. Her father, André Rapin, had died in 1694, when Marie Anne had been eight years old. Some $5^1/2$ years later, her mother, Clémence Jarry, had married Joseph Gauthier dit Saguingoira; their only child had been Joseph Gauthier (Marie Anne's half-brother), born in the Lachine area in 1700. He had become a Lachine-based voyageur and had married Jeanne and J.B.'s daughter Marie Rosalie Lalonde in 1728. At this late stage of his life, Jacques Charbonnier, a merchant and bourgeois who had emigrated from Blois, France and who lived in the Ste. Anne parish, decided that he wished to spend his remaining years as the partner of Mademoiselle Rapin. Thus, on August 18, 1738, many of the couple's friends and relatives assembled at the church to join in their festivities. According to the officiating priest's records, the official witnesses included Jean Baptiste Lalonde, Captain of Ste. Anne; Antoine Jean Rapin, Marie Clémence Rapin, and Joseph Gauthier, siblings of the bride; Jean Baptiste Chenier, brother-in-law of the bride (who was married to her sister Barbe); and Vital Caron, a good friend.[205]

Some $2^1/2$ months later, Jeanne and J.B.'s first Brébant grandchild came into the world. Jean Baptiste Gabriel, the first child of Augustin

Brébant and Marie Lalonde, was both born and baptized in the Ste. Anne church on November 24, $10^1/2$ months after his parents had been wed. At his christening, his godfather and name-giver was his maternal grandfather Jean Baptiste Lalonde (identified by the priest as "Captain of the Militia"), while his godmother was his paternal grandmother Marie Élisabeth Lafaye.[206]

By the winter of 1739, Jean Baptiste was $63^1/2$ years old and Jeanne was age $59^1/2$. It is of considerable interest to note Monsieur Lalonde's age at this time. The period of obligatory participation in the militia forces for all able-bodied males in the colony ranged from 16 to 60 years of age. Yet J.B. was still continuing to serve as the Captain of the forces of the Ste. Anne parish, even though he was well into his sixties. He had been elevated to this rank from that of Sergeant 21 years earlier, back in 1718.

At this point, the patriarch and matriarch decided to transfer the ownership of all of their lands to their children and their respective spouses. As a result, they all met on March 11 with Jean François Lepailleur, the Sieur de La Ferté, the royal notary of Montreal, in order to officially register this transaction. According to the scribe's document, the owners who were transferring the property were "Jean Baptiste Lalonde, ancient notable and captain of all of the militia forces of the parish of Ste. Anne, husband of Jeanne Gervais, living at the Top of Montreal Island." This transaction included two pieces of property which fronted on Baie D'Urfé, including J.B.'s portion of the Lalonde family land (which he had purchased from his mother and his two siblings on July 24, 1702) and the adjacent lot immediately to the west (which had been granted to him by the Sulpicians on February 23, 1711). The third parcel, which was described at this time as "a plot of meadow named *La Prairie Ronde* (The Round Meadow)," was located at the inland or northwestern end of his two lots that fronted on the St. Lawrence. This parcel of moist grassland had been ceded to him by the Sulpician seigneurs on March 14, 1724. In this 1739 document of transfer, the parents listed each of their five sons by name, in descending order of age, and then their three daughters (again in descending order of age) along with their respective spouses. According to the details enumerated at this time, the eight children were each to receive an equal share of the combined properties which had belonged to their parents.[207]

Nearly one year later, on February 23, 1740, J.B. and Jeanne issued a discharge receipt to Charles Léger dit Parisien, who had purchased their property on Île Perrot nearly four years earlier. According to this receipt, Monsieur Léger had finally paid off the sum that he had owed them for the land. As was customary, J.B. was identified in this document as "Captain of the Militia of the Côte Ste. Anne."[208]

Five months later, the Captain was again selected to serve as the godfather of a newborn baby in festivities that were held in the Ste. Anne church. This time, the child, who was both born and christened on August 24, was the offspring of Jeanne's sister Marie Anne Gervais and her husband Michel Lefebvre dit Lasisseraye of Île Perrot. Little Marie Josèphe's godmother was Françoise Cuillerier, the widow of Jean Quenet. Years earlier, there had been major linkages between the latter man and both J.B. and his brother Guillaume. Back in 1704, Monsieur Quenet had leased his farm on Pointe Beaurepaire to J.B. and Jeanne for six years, and shortly thereafter, he and his first wife Étienette Hurtubise had taken in Sarah Allyn after her capture at Deerfield. In January of 1718, three months after Étienette had died, he had married the widow Françoise Cuillerier, but they had not produced any children together.

Among the numerous leadership roles that Jean Baptiste Lalonde played as the Captain of the parish, one of them was serving as an official witness at not only baptisms, but also at weddings and funerals. The year 1741 brought two instances of his serving in this capacity at burials, and one case of his appearing at a much more joyful marriage ceremony. First, he witnessed the funeral of Guillaume Vinet dit La Rente on May 15. This man, about 63 years old, had married Marie Denis 26 years earlier, back in January of 1715. The couple had produced at least eight children in the Côte St. Louis/ Ste. Anne, of whom at least four had perished at very early ages.[209]

The next time he witnessed a burial was on August 28, when François Gauthier dit Saint Germain, age 25 and unmarried, was laid to rest in the Ste. Anne cemetery. This young man, who had passed away on the previous day at Pointe D'Urfé, was the son of Jean Gauthier dit Saint Germain and Marie Storer. The latter individual, the daughter of Joseph Storer and Anne Hill, had been captured in a French-and-native raid on her community in the Massachusetts colony. Over time, she had settled into the life of a Canadienne, had been baptized at Boucherville in February of 1704 (three months before turning 19), and had married there in November of 1708 (when she had been 23 years old and her husband had been 22). After bearing two children in the Boucherville area in 1709 and 1712, the couple had moved to the Montreal area, where they had increased their family size with five more babies between 1714 and 1723. The priest who officiated at the funeral of François Gauthier noted in the parish ledger that the two official witnesses were Jean Baptiste Lalonde, Captain of the Côte, and Jacques Julien, the beadle or sexton of the parish.[210]

Three months later, the mood of the ecclesiastical ceremony was quite the opposite of that of the two funerals. This was the hopeful and encouraging wedding of a local young woman and her fiancé from Montreal. On November 20, Geneviève Diel (age 22), the daughter of local residents Jacques Diel (master blacksmith and maker of edged tools) and Marie Anne Crépin, exchanged nuptial vows with Antoine Lupien of Montreal, the son of Pierre Lupien dit Le Baron and Angélique Couronne. In contrast to many weddings in New France, only two individual were listed as official witnesses on this occasion. Both of them were local men from the parish: "Jean Baptiste Lalonde, Captain of the Militia, and René Rivière." The latter man, a master cobbler or shoemaker, was a nephew of J.B. and Jeanne.[211]

More than four years later, in the heart of the winter of 1746, Jean Baptiste was pleased to serve as a witness at a special double wedding in the Ste. Anne church. At this unusual ceremony, which took place on February 7, two children of Pierre Maupetit dit Poitevin and Angélique Villeray (who had lived for nearly three decades with their six children on the third farm to the east of the Lalonde family property) were joined in marriage with their chosen partners. In one of the couples, the groom was a Lalonde nephew of J.B. and Jeanne, while in the other couple, the bride was a Daoust great-niece of theirs. In the first union, the groom was Albert Lalonde of the seigneury of Soulanges, $26^3/4$ years old, the son of Guillaume Lalonde and Sarah/ Marie Madeleine Hélène. His bride was Marie Angélique Maupetit of Île Perrot, $20^3/4$ years old, the daughter of the Maupetit-Villeray couple. Their official witnesses were Jean Baptiste Lalonde, Captain of the Militia; André Lalonde, brother of the groom; Antoine Lalonde, cousin of the groom; and Pierre Lafleur. (This couple would provide the direct ancestral linkage between Guillaume Lalonde Number 1 and Sarah Allyn and the present author, as well as the direct linkage between Pierre Maupetit and Angélique Villeray and the present author. Biographies of both of these couples are presented later in this work.)[212]

In the other couple married on this especially festive day, the bride was Marie Josèphe Daoust of Île Perrot, 18³/4 years old, the daughter of Charles Daoust and Marie Angélique Sauvé. Her groom was Pierre Maupetit of Île Perrot, age 23³/4, son of Pierre Maupetit dit Poitevin and Angélique Villeray. Their witnesses were Jean Baptiste Lalonde, Captain of the Militia, great-uncle of the bride; Antoine Villeray, grandfather of the groom; Jean Baptiste Villeray, uncle of the groom; and Jacques Prou, uncle of the groom.[213]

Some 22 months later, on December 2, 1747, J.B. again stood at an official witnesses in the church, but this time as a baptismal sponsor. In this instance, the baby had been born two days earlier to Jacques Gros dit Lecompte and Marie Josèphe Gauthier. The priest noted in the parish records that the godfather and name-giver was "J.B. (sic) Lalonde of this parish, Captain of the Militia," while the godmother was Marie Charlotte Turpin, great-aunt of the baby.[214]

A bitter-sweet celebration for the clan was conducted in the Ste. Anne church fourteen months later, on February 3, 1749. Earlier, Jeanne and J.B.'s son-in-law Joseph Gauthier, husband of their daughter Marie Rosalie since 1728, had died. Now, twenty years and three months after the Gauthier-Lalonde couple had been married, Marie Rosalie took a second husband in the same church. This was Pierre Docile dit Dubuisson, who had emigrated from the St. Martin parish in Rouen. On this day, when the bride was six weeks short of age 38, the official witnesses were Jean Baptiste Lalonde, Captain of the Militia, father of the bride; Joseph Lalonde and Antoine Lalonde, brothers of the bride; and Pierre Ranger and Joseph Tabault. Previous to the wedding, the local priest had published one bann of marriage, after which the Bishop had granted a dispensation of the other two customary banns.[215]

Since preparations had been made to hold a fine celebration in connection with this nuptial ceremony, it was decided that this would be an excellent day to also hold the wedding of one of J.B. and Jeanne's granddaughters in the same church. Both the prospective bride and groom hailed from the Ste. Anne parish. The bride was Marie Josèphe Lalonde, daughter of Joseph Lalonde and Marie Jeanne Léger dite Parisien, while the groom was Michel Sédilot, son of Jean Baptiste Sédilot dit Montreuil and Marie Barbe Rapin. The latter couple and their children had resided for at least three decades in the Le Buisson section of the seigneury of Soulanges, which was located about seven miles southwest of the church, on the north shore of the St. Lawrence. (This latter area would not have its own church for another three years, not until the parish of St. Joseph would be established there in 1752.) The identifications of the official witnesses which were recorded on this day by the priest in the parish ledger are of particular interest. These were Jean Baptiste Sédilot dit Montreuil, Captain of the Militia and father of the groom; Jean Baptiste Lalonde, Captain of the Militia and grandfather of the bride; Charles Sédilot, brother of the groom; and Joseph Tabault.[216]

Until the parish of St. Joseph would be established in the seigneury of Soulanges three years later, in 1752, the residents of that place would belong to the Ste. Anne parish, both for ecclesiastical purposes and in the organization of the militia. Since these civilian military forces were organized throughout the colony by parish, the men of Soulanges would form their own separate militia group only after 1752. Thus, the description here of Monsieur Sédilot as Captain of the Militia clearly indicates that he had been selected by this time as the officer who was truly in charge of the fighting forces of the Ste. Anne parish. He was 59 years of age in this winter of 1749, while J.B. Lalonde was $73^1/3$ years old. This document stated that Monsieur Lalonde still held the rank of Captain. However, this title, which he would retain for the rest of his life, was probably an honorary one by this point. The active leadership of the civilian fighting forces of the parish was presumably in the hands of the younger officer, Captain Sédilot, quite likely with the advice and input of his colleague Captain Lalonde.[217]

Exactly one year and one day later, on February 4, 1750, Jean Baptiste went to his grave, in the cemetery beside the Ste. Anne church. As was to be expected, Fr. Élie Depéret, the 58-year-old Sulpician priest of the parish, identified the departed parishioner in the ledger as "Captain of the Militia." The deceased had held this highly respected position in the community for 32 years, ever since 1718. At this time, one of the family members indicated to the *curé* that the venerable patriarch had been 71 years old at the time of his demise. However, based upon his baptismal records in the Montreal church, he had actually lived for 74 years and 4 months. Four men of the parish served as the official witnesses at his funeral. These were his eldest son François Lalonde (who was 50 years old), Pierre Ranger (the beadle or sexton of the parish), Michel Brébant, and Joseph Tabault.[218]

After $48^1/3$ years of marriage, Jeanne now found herself a widow, at the age of $70^1/2$ years. At this time, she could not have imagined that she would live for another fifteen more years.

As was very typical for someone who survived to this advanced age in New France, her final years brought numerous personal losses, including both family members and friends. Some eighteen months after J.B. had passed away, his brother and Jeanne's brother-in-law Guillaume Lalonde (Number 1) died. His departure took place on August 21, 1752, on the very day that he was celebrating his 68th birthday. On the following day, he was laid to rest in the cemetery of the Soulanges seigneury, where he and Sarah/Marie Madeleine had been residing for some time.[219]

Almost two years later, Jeanne lost one of her own daughters, when Marie Anne died on July 27, 1754. When she was laid to rest on the following day in the Ste. Anne cemetery, the cleric recorded that she was 43 years old; however she had actually lived for only 39 years and 4 months. Marie Anne had been married for 22 of those years to Nicolas Robillard, who was 44 years old at the time of her departure. At her funeral, the witnesses were the parish beadle or sexton Pierre Ranger, Jr. and Augustin Dubreuil.[220]

Jeanne and J.B.'s eldest son François, who had married Marie Josèphe Trottier back in 1726, finally lost his bride of many decades. Eventually, when he was nearly 58 years old and living on Île Perrot, he decided to remarry. On July 4, 1757, 31 years after his first wedding, he joined in marriage with Marie Anne Cécire dite Riberville, a fellow resident of the island. On this occasion in the Ste. Anne church, the four witnesses were Guillaume Lalonde, François Laplante, Charles Daoust, and René Rivière.[221]

Jeanne lost her sister-in-law Marie Madeleine Lalonde, the sister of J.B. and Guillaume and the widow of Guillaume Daoust, at the beginning of the year 1761, when she was about 89 years of age. She was buried in the cemetery beside the Ste. Anne church on the third day of January, nearly 32 years after her husband had been laid to rest there.[222]

Nearly four years later, on the Feast of Noël (Christmas Day) in 1764, Jeanne's sister-in-law Sarah/Marie Madeleine Hélène died, when she was $72^2/3$ years old. Having been captured in the vicious Deerfield raid during the winter of 1704, when she had been $11^{10}/12$ years old, she had then spent a full six decades in New France, living of her own free choice as a Canadienne. She had been married to Guillaume Lalonde for more than 42 of those years, and then she had been a widow for another twelve years after his death. On December 26, Sarah was laid to rest in the cemetery at Soulanges, where she had been living for a number of years.[223]

Finally, after a long and productive life of 86 years and 3 months, it was time for Jeanne Gervais herself to depart. She passed away on October 31, 1765, after which she was reverently laid to rest in the Ste. Anne cemetery on the following day. At her funeral, the official witnesses were her nephew René Rivière and Gérard Lejeune. Jeanne had been a widow for 15 3/4 years. During her lifetime, she had outlived one of her babies (Thomas, who had perished at the age of one month back in August of 1709) as well as one of her adult children (Marie Anne, who had died at the untimely age of 39 in July of 1754). The average ages at death for adults in the St. Lawrence communities were 61.6 years for women and 61.9 years for men. Considering these figures, the matriarch had certainly lived for a very extended period of time. In fact, she had survived for a full quarter-century beyond the age when adults typically passed away in the settlements of New France. Jeanne had definitely earned the lovingly-conferred title of *La Vieille*, The Old Woman.[224]

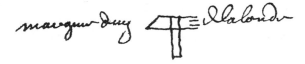

Mark of the said [Jean] de Lalonde [symbol], November 3, 1673.

Mark of the said Barban +, November 3, 1673.

Mark of the said future husband [Jean Baptiste Lalonde] +, June 24, 1698.

Signature marguerite Mastas, June 24, 1698.

Jean Baptiste Lalonde dit L'Espérance-Jeanne Gervais Lineage of Timothy Kent

I. Jean de Lalonde (Philippe/ Jeanne Duval)	14 Nov 1669 (ct. Antoine Adhémar) D'Autray, QC	Marie Barbant (Alexandre/ Marie Lenoble)
II. **Jean Baptiste Lalonde** (Jean/ Marie Barbant)	24 Oct 1701 Laprairie, QC	**Jeanne Gervais** (Mathieu/ Michelle Picard)
III. Guillaume Lalonde #2 (Jean Baptiste/ Jeanne Gervais)	16 Jan, 1730 Bout de l'Île, Mtl., QC	Marie Angélique Brunet dite Bourbonnais (Jean François, Jr./ Françoise David)
IV. Guillaume Lalonde #4 (Guillaume #2/ Marie Angélique Brunet)	2 Feb, 1761 Bout de l'Île, Mtl., QC	Marie Charlotte Sauvé dite Laplante (François Marie/ Élisabeth Magdelaine dite Ladouceur)
V. Angèle Lalonde (Guillaume #4/ Marie Charlotte Sauvé)	27 Jan, 1812 Vaudreuil, QC	Hyacinthe Achin (Jacques/ Marie Amable Trottier)
VI. Élisabeth/Isabelle Achin (Hyacinthe/ Angèle Lalonde)	17 Feb, 1835 St. Polycarpe, QC	Joseph Lalonde (Joseph/ Geneviève Daoust)
VII. Joseph Lalonde (Joseph/ Élisabeth Achin)	ca. 1873 Curran, ON	Josephine Chatelain (Étienne/ Marie Madeleine Taillon)
VIII. Élisabeth Lalonde (Joseph/ Josephine Chatelain)	30 Jan, 1893 Carrollton, MI	Joseph Bouchard (Philéas Joseph/ Adelaide Barbeau)
IX. Frances L. Bouchard (Joseph/ Élisabeth Lalonde)	28 Apr, 1945 Detroit, MI	S. George Kent (George Kapantais/ Eugenia Papadakis)
X. Timothy J. Kent (S. George/ Frances L. Bouchard)	5 Sept, 1970 Ossineke, MI	Dorothy J. Minton (Garnet J./ Elaine A. Reece)

Notes for Jean Baptiste Lalonde

1. Notary Romain Becquet, Nomvember 4, 1667, Archives Nationales du Québec at Québec (ANQ-Q); R. Jetté, 1983, pp. 634, 43.
2. R. Jetté, 1983, p. 43.
3. R. Harris, 1987, pl. 51; R. Jetté, 1983, p. 149.
4. G. Perron, October 1991, pp. 44-48; G. Perron, 1998, pp. 122-133, 151; P. Moogk, 2000, pp. 93-97, 103-109.
5. R. Harris, 1987, pl. 51.
6. Notary Romain Becquet, October 19, 1668, ANQ-Q; R. Jetté, 1983, pp. 149-150.
7. R. Jetté, 1983, p. 312.
8. ibid., p. 734.
9. Notary Pierre Duquet, September 27, 1669, ANQ-Q; R. Jetté, 1983, p. 557.
10. Notary Pierre Duquet, October 13, 1669, ANQ-Q; R. Jetté, 1983, p. 634.
11. Notary Antoine Adhémar, November 14, 1669, ANQ-M; R. Jetté, 1983, pp. 634, 3, 98, 838, 494, 109, 21.
12. W. Eccles, 1964, pp. 20, 24-26, 39-44, 47; J. Marshall, 1967, pp. 281-284, 319-330; J. Verney, 1991, pp. 37-53, 71-115; C. Skinner, 2008, p. 14.
13. M. Beaudoin, 1971, pp. 90-91; A. Lafontaine, 1985, p. 32.
14. A. Lafontaine, 1985, p. 32; R. Jetté, 1983, p., 612.
15. R. Jetté, 1983, pp. xiv-xv.
16. ibid., p. 634.
17. Notary Antoine Adhémar, November 3, 1673, ANQ-M; R. Jetté, 1983, pp. 84, 888, 98, 880.
18. Notary Romain Becquet, March 11, 1674, ANQ-Q.
19. Notary Bénigne Basset, July 13, 1674, ANQ-M; R. Jetté, 1983, pp. 564, 34.
20. H. Charbonneau and J. Légaré, 1978-1990, Vol. 5, Notre Dame de Montreal recs; R. Jetté, 1983, pp. 520, 282.
21. G. Lebel, Octobre 1940; R. Jetté, 1983, p. 564; F. Stanislas, 1950, p. 38.
22. R. Jetté, 1983, p. 634; F. Stanislas, 1950, p. 37. 1702 land ownership map of Montreal Island by Vachon de Belmont: in Nos Racines, Vol. 22, 1979, pp. 430-431; M. Trudel, 1973a, pp. 172-173; recreation by G. Gallienne, 1977; and L. Dechêne, 1992, p. xxi.
23. Notary Bénigne Basset, March 21, 1687, ANQ-M.
24. A. Lafontaine, 1986, p. 142; H. Charbonneau and J. Légaré, 1978-1990, 1681 census; R. Jetté, 1983, pp. 634, 282, 629-630, 213. For decades, scholars have realized that, when the returns of the 1681 census had been been assembled and collated, the sub-fief of Lachine had been mistakenly labeled as "Fief Verdun" (see Lafontaine 1986 pp. 134-142). However, this label of "Fief Verdun" had likewise been mistakenly applied at the time of collation to the area of Bout de l'Île, further to the west (the residents of the entire southern shore of Montreal Island all belonged to the Lachine parish at this time). This mislabeling is clearly evident when one compares these census records to Vachon de Belmont's 1702 land ownership map. It is especially obvious when observing the listings of the three neighboring households of Jean de Lalonde, Antoine de La Fresnaye, and Cybard Courault, in sequential order from east to west. These three adjacent families were not residing in the sub-fief of Verdun, northeast of Lachine, at the time of the 1681 census. Instead, they had already settled well to the west, on the Côte St. Louis in the Bout de l'Île area, on three lots in a row. The 1702 map indicated the Courault property as still being in the hands of that family, while it labeled Jean's land as belonging to "Blainville." Jean and Marie had sold it in March of 1687 to Jean Baptiste Celoron, Sieur de Blainville, who had married La Fresnaye's widow in 1686 and had thus acquired the La Fresnaye property.

25. A. Lafontaine, 1986, p. 142; R. Jetté, 1983, pp. 629-630.
26. A. Lafontaine, 1986, p. 142; R. Jetté, 1983, p. 282; H. Charbonneau and J. Légaré, 1978-1990, Vol. 5, Notre Dame de Montreal recs.
27. Notary Bénigne Basset, March 21, 1687, ANQ-M.
28. R. Jetté, 1983, p. 634.
29. ibid.
30. W. Eccles, 1964, pp. 120, 122, 133-134; E. Blair, 1911, Vol. 1, pp. 232-242; T. Kent, 2004, pp. 74, 80-83.
31. A. Leduc, August-September 2000, p. 10.
32. P. Dubé, 1993, p. 88; R. Harris, 1987, pl. 46; R. Jetté, 1983, pp. xiv-xv; F. Dollier de Casson, 1928, p. 21.
33. F. Dollier de Casson, 1928, p. 21; P. Dubé, 1993, p. 88; R. Harris, 1987, pl. 46; R. Jetté, 1993, pp. xiv-xv, 355-356; C. Hamp, 1988, p. 23; A. Yon, 1969, p. 350; D. Girouard, 1893, pp. 1-2. 1702 land ownership map of Montreal Island by Vachon de Belmont: in Nos Racines, Vol. 22, 1979, pp. 430-431; M. Trudel, 1973a, pp. 172-173; recreation by G. Gallienne, 1977; and L. Dechêne, 1992, p. xxi.
34. Notary Pierre Cabazier, February 6, 1686, ANQ-M; R. Jetté, 1983, pp. 634, 307.
35. H. Charbonneau and J. Légaré, 1978-1990, Vol. 5, Sts. Anges de Lachine recs.; R. Jetté, 1983, pp. 792, 391. 1702 land ownership map of Montreal Island by Vachon de Belmont: in Nos Racines, Vol. 22, 1979, pp. 430-431; M. Trudel, 1973a, pp. 172-173; recreation by G. Gallienne, 1977; and L. Dechêne, 1992, p. xxi.
36. Notary Pierre Cabazier, November 15, 1686, ANQ-M; Notary Béngine Basset, March 21, 1687, ANQ-M. 1702 land ownership map of Montreal Island by Vachon de Belmont: in Nos Racines, Vol. 22, 1979, pp. 430-431; M. Trudel, 1973a, pp. 172-173; recreation by G. Gallienne, 1977; and L. Dechêne, 1992, p. xxi.
37. R. Jetté, 1983, pp. 629-630, 915, 213.
38. Notary Jean Baptiste Pothier, November 29, 1687 and January 19, 1688, ANQ-M. 1702 land ownership map of Montreal Island by Vachon de Belmont: in Nos Racines, Vol. 22, 1979, pp. 430-431; M. Trudel, 1973a, pp. 172-173; recreation by G. Gallienne, 1977; and L. Dechêne, 1992, p. xxi.
39. Notary Bénigne Basset, March 21, 1687, ANQ-M.
40. Notary Jean Baptiste Pothier, January 19, 1688, ANQ-M.
41. E. Blair, 1911, Vol. 1, pp. 249-252 and Vol. 2, pp. 20-23; L. Lahontan, 1703, Vol. 1, pp. 124-131, 144 and n. 1; W. Eccles, 1964, pp. 150-156; T. Pease and R. Werner, 1934, pp. 132-133; L. Kellogg, 1968, p. 234-236; L., Kellogg, 1967, p. 311; P. Charlevoix, 1866, Vol. 3, pp. 280-287; W. Kane, 2002, p. 130.
42. W. Eccles, 1964, pp. 150, 155.
43. H. Charbonneau and J. Légaré, 1978-1990, Vol. 5, Ste. Anne du Bout de l'Île recs.; R. Jetté, 1983, p. 1129.
44. H. Charbonneau and J. Légaré, 1978-1990, Vol. 5, Ste. Anne du Bout de l'Île recs.; R. Jetté, 1983, p. 639; A. Lafontaine, 1986, p. 142.
45. R. Jetté, 1983, p. 634; A. Yon, 1969, p. 350.
46. R. Jetté, 1983, p. 128; A. Lafontaine, 1986, p. 142.
47. R. Jetté, 1983, pp. 444-445, 902, 908.
48. H. Charbonneau and J. Légaré, 1978-1990, Vol. 5, Ste. Anne du Bout de l'Île recs.; A. Yon, 1969, p. 350; A. Lafontaine, 1986, pl. 142; R. Jetté, 1983, pp. 307, 282, 397.
49. R. Jetté, 1983, pp. 725, 195.
50. ibid., p. 598.
51. Notary Jean Baptiste Pothier, November 29, 1687, ANQ-M.
52. Notary Jean Baptiste Pothier, December 1, 1687, ANQ-M.

53. R. Jetté, 1983, p. 1060; F. Stanislas, 1950, p. 23, and map inside front cover.

54. F. Stanislas, 1950, pp. 17-19, 24, and map inside front cover; R. Jetté, 1983, p. 295.

55. R. Jetté, 1983, pp. 634, 1060.

56. Notary Jean Baptiste Pothier, January 19, 1688a, ANQ-M; R. Jetté, 1983, pp. 937, 117, 197, 295, 438.

57. Notary Jean Baptiste Pothier, January 19, 1688b, ANQ-M.

58. R. Harris, 1987, pls. 55-56; P. Moogk, 1977, pp. 22-47.

59. R. Jetté, 1983, pp. 1058, 197, 348, 282.

60. R. Jetté, 1983, p. 1060.

61. Notary Jean Baptiste Pothier, April 23, 1689, ANQ-M.

62. R. Jetté, 1983, pp. 634, 1060.

63. W. Eccles, 1964, pp. 155, 157-158, 163-165, 208; F. Stanislas, 1950, pp. 17-19, 24, 42, 45; L. Dechêne, 1992, p. 66; 1702 Montreal Island land ownership may by Vachon de Belmont: in Nos Racines, Vol. 22, 1979, pp. 430-431; M. Trudel, 1973a, pp. 172-173; recreation by G. Gallienne, 1977; and L. Dechêne, 1992, p. xxi.

64. W. Eccles, 1964, pp. 164-165; F. Stanislas, 1950, pp. 44-50; Y. Zoltvany, 1969b, p. 566; P. Moogk, 2000, p. 256; S. Colby, 2003, pp. 137-138; H. Lamarche, 1999, pp. 189-228; H. Lamarche, 2002-2003, pp. 1-4; R. Jetté, 1983, pp. 307, 155, 808, 44, 305-306, 590. 1702 land ownership map of Montreal Island by Vachon de Belmont: in Nos Racines, Vol. 22, 1979, pp. 430-431; M. Trudel, 1973a, pp. 172-173; recreation by G. Gallienne, 1977; and L. Dechêne, 1992, p. xxi.

65. R. Jetté, 1983, pp. 808, 158, 946, 258, 792, 70, 744; H. Lamarche, 2002-2003, pp. 2-3; F. Stanislas, 1950, pp. 47-48; A. Lafontaine, 1986, Lachine Households No. 241, 264, 239. 1702 land ownership map of Montreal Island by Vachon de Belmont: in Nos Racines, Vol. 22, 1979, pp. 430-431; M. Trudel, 1973a, pp. 172-173; recreation by G. Gallienne, 1977; and L. Dechêne, 1992, p. xxi.

66. R. Jetté, 1983, pp. 792, 70, 744; H. Lamarche, 2002-2003, p. 3; F. Stanislas, 1950, p. 48. A. Lafontaine, 1986, Lachine Household No. 239. 1702 land ownership map of Montreal Island by Vachon de Belmont: in Nos Racines, Vol. 22, 1979, pp. 430-431; M. Trudel, 1973a, pp. 172-173; recreation by G. Gallienne, 1977; and L. Dechêne, 1992, p. xxi.

67. F. Stanislas, 1950, pp. 46, 50; R. Jetté, 1983, pp. 70, 238; A. Lafontaine, 1986, Lachine Household No. 239.

68. R. Jetté, 1983, p. 307.

69. P. Moogk, 2000, pp. 229-233; Notary Antoine Adhémar, November 8, 1691, ANQ-M; Notary Antoine Adhémar, April 23, 1693, ANQ-M.

70. R. Jetté, 1983, pp. 810, 802, 330-331, 705, 708; E. Massicotte, 1929-1930, pp. 196, 198.

71. Notary Antoine Adhémar, November 8, 1691, ANQ-M.

72. T. Kent, 2004, pp. 48, 150, 163, 272-274; W. Eccles, 1964, p. 60.

73. Notary Antoine Adhémar, April 23, 1693, ANQ-M; R. Jetté, 1983, pp. 902-903, 951, 331, 81.

74. H. Charbonneau and J. Légaré, 1978-1990, Vol. 5, Notre Dame de Montreal recs.; R. Jetté, 1983, pp. 649-650, 789, 583-584.

75. Notary Antoine Adhémar, April 10, 1695, ANQ-M; R. Jetté, 1983, p. 492; P. Moogk, 2000, p. 218.

76. T. Kent, 2001, pp. 40-41; Notary Antoine Adhémar, April 23, 1696, ANQ-M; R. Jetté, 1983, pp. 639, 548.

77. L. Frontenac, 1698, pp. 95-96; T. Kent, 2004, p. 130; Y. Zoltvany, 1966e, pp. 352-353.

78. E. Massicotte, 1929-1930, p. 205.

79. Notary Antoine Adhémar, September 2, 1696, ANQ-M.

80. E. Massicotte, 1929-1930, pp. 202, 204-205; T. Kent, 2004, pp. 148, 150, 155; R. Durand, 1997, p. 92.

81. Notary Antoine Adhémar, April 23, 1696, ANQ-M; Actes Notariés, 1974, p. 32.

82. J. Champigny, July 1698, pp. 86-94; Arbitration of Cadillac, 1697-1698, pp. 215-220; R. Durand, 1997, pp. 90-96; T. Kent, 2004, pp. 141-143.

83. A. Cadillac, 1947, pp. 3-5, 8-18, 63.

84. Y. Zoltvany, 1969e, p. 353; A. Cadillac, 1697, p.63; Notary Antoine Adhémar, April 23, 1696; Actes Notariés, 1974, p. 32.

85. T. Kent, 2004, pp. 140-141.

86. R. Jetté, 1983, p. 788.

87. H. Charbonneau and J. Légaré, 1978-1990, Vol. 5, Infant Jésus de Pointe aux Trembles recs; R. Jetté, 1983, p. 1117.

88. Notary Antoine Adhémar, January 24, 1698, ANQ-M; L. Dechêne, 1992, map p. xxi; R. Jetté, 1983, pp. 902, 1044, 1019-1020.

89. H. Charbonneau and J. Légaré, 1978-1990, Vol. 5, Infant Jésus de Pointe aux Trembles recs; R. Jetté, 1983, pp. 634-635, 307.

90. Notary Antoine Adhémar, July 25, 1698, ANQ-M; R. Jetté, 1983, p. 492.

91. Notary Antoine Adhémar, November 17, 1698, ANQ-M.

92. H. Charbonneau and J. Légaré, 1978-1990, Vol. 5, Infant Jésus de Pointe aux Trembles recs; R. Jetté, 1983, p. 635.

93. H. Charbonneau and J. Légaré, 1978-1990, Vol. 5, Infant Jésus de Pointe aux Trembles recs; R. Jetté, 1983, pp. 635, 788.

94. Notary Antoine Adhémar, October 9, 1699, ANQ-M.

95. R. Jetté, 1983, p. 307.

96. Notary Pierre Raimbault, February 7, 1701, ANQ-M.

97. R. Jetté, 1983, p. 593.

98. Notary Pierre Raimbault, October 21, 1701b, ANQ-M.]

99. H. Charbonneau and J. Légaré, 1978-1990, Vol. 15, La Nativité de la B.V.M. de Laprairie recs; R. Jetté, 1983, pp. 491, 911, 708, 996.

100. Notary Antoine Adhémar, October 21, 1701a, ANQ-M; R. Jetté, 1983, pp. 1027, 296, 720, 744, 684-685.

101. Notary Pierre Raimbault, October 21, 1701b, ANQ-M; R. Jetté, 1983, pp. 683-684, 341, 338, 584.

102. Notary Pierre Raimbault, October 21, 1701b, ANQ-M.

103. Notary Pierre Raimbault, September 22, 1724, ANQ-M.

104. R. Jetté, 1983, pp. 60, 470, 659-660.

105. ibid., pp. 593, 902-903, 295, 338-339.

106. Notary Pierre Raimbault, October 23, 1701, ANQ-M; R. Jetté, 1983, pp. 634, 788, 491, 51, 57.

107. H. Charbonneau and J. Légaré, 1978-1990, Vol. 15, La Nativité de la B.V.M. de Laprairie recs; R. Jetté, 1983, p. 635.

108. T. Kent, 2004, p. 162.

109. W. Eccles, 1964, pp. 251, 262.

110. Notary Jean Baptiste Pothier, November 29, 1687 and January 19, 1688, ANQ-M. 1702 land ownership map of Montreal Island by Vachon de Belmont: in Nos Racines, Vol. 22, 1979, pp. 430-431; M. Trudel, 1973a, pp. 172-173; recreation by G. Gallienne, 1977; and L. Dechêne, 1992, p. xxi.

111. Notary Antoine Adhémar, July 24, 1702, ANQ-M.

112. H. Charbonneau and J. Légaré, 1978-1990, Vol. 13, Notre Dame de Montreal recs; R. Jetté, 1983, pp. 683-684.

113. Notary Antoine Adhémar, October 21, 1703, ANQ-M.

114. R. Jetté, 1983, pp. 698, 506, 285.

115. Notary Antoine Adhémar, July 25, 1698, ANQ-M.

116. 1702 land ownership map of Montreal Island by Vachon de Belmont: in Nos Racines, Vol. 22, 1979, pp. 430-431; M. Trudel, 1973a, pp. 172-173; recreation by G. Gallienne, 1977; and L. Dechêne, 1992, p. xx.

117. R. Jetté, 1983, pp. 952, 584; A. Lafontaine, 1986, p. 141; F. Stanislas, 1950, p. 29, and maps inside front and back covers.

118. Notary Antoine Adhémar, November 30, 1703, ANQ-M; R. Jetté, 1983, pp. 338, 209, 965. 1702 land ownership map of Montreal Island by Vachon de Belmont: in Nos Racines, Vol. 22, 1979, pp. 430-431; M. Trudel, 1973a, pp. 172-173; recreation by G. Gallienne, 1977; and L. Dechêne, 1992, p. xx.

119. H. Charbonneau and J. Légaré, 1978-1990, Vol. 14, St. Louis/Ste. Anne du Bout de l'Île recs; R. Jetté, 1983, pp. 684, 334.

120. H. Charbonneau and J. Légaré, 1978-1990, Vol. 14, St. Louis/Ste. Anne du Bout de l'Île recs; R. Jetté, 1983, pp. 334, 952. 1702 land ownership map of Montreal Island by Vachon de Belmont: in Nos Racines, Vol. 22, 1979, pp. 430-431; M. Trudel, 1973a, pp. 172-173; recreation by G. Gallienne, 1977; and L. Dechêne, 1992, p. xx.

121. R. Jetté, 1983, p. 635; H. Charbonneau and J. Légaré, 1978-1990, Vol. 14, St. Louis/Ste. Anne du Bout de l'Île recs. A very detailed version of Sarah's life story, along with that of her eventual spouse, are offered later in the present work, with fully footnoted references.

122. H. Charbonneau and J. Légaré, 1978-1990, Vol. 14, St. Louis/Ste. Anne du Bout de l'Île recs; R. Jetté, 1983, pp. 952, 635.

123. H. Charbonneau and J. Légaré, 1978-1990, Vol. 13, Notre Dame de Montreal recs; R. Jetté, 1983, pp. 491, 911.

124. R. Jetté, 1983, pp. 491, 1005, 98.

125. H. Charbonneau and J. Légaré, 1978-1990, Vol. 14, St. Louis/Ste. Anne du Bout de l'Île recs; R. Jetté, 1983, p. 635; "Fort for Sale," 2004, p. 7. 1702 land ownership map of Montreal Island by Vachon de Belmont: in Nos Racines, Vol. 22, 1979, pp. 430-431; M. Trudel, 1973a, pp. 172-173; recreation by G. Gallienne, 1977; and L. Dechêne, 1992, p. xxi.

126. R. Jetté, 1983, pp. 491, 911.

127. Notary Pierre Raimbault, April 22, 1710a, ANQ-M; R. Jetté, 1983, pp. 634, 491, 765.

128. R. Jetté, 1983, pp. 800, 436.

129. H. Charbonneau and J. Légaré, 1978-1990, Vol. 14, St. Louis/Ste. Anne du Bout de l'Île recs; R. Jetté, 1983, pp. 167, 1037, 678.

130. R. Jetté, 1983, p. 1060.

131. Notary Pierre Raimbault, April 22, 1710b, ANQ-M.

132. H. Charbonneau and J. Légaré, 1978-1990, Vol. 14, St. Louis/Ste. Anne du Bout de l'Île recs; R. Jetté, 1983, pp. 432, 750.

133. H. Charbonneau and J. Légaré, 1978-1990, Vol. 14, St. Louis/Ste. Anne du Bout de l'Île recs; R. Jetté, 1983, pp. 1037, 635.1702 land ownership map of Montreal Island by Vachon de Belmont: in Nos Racines, Vol. 22, 1979, pp. 430-431; M. Trudel, 1973a, pp. 172-173; recreation by G. Gallienne, 1977; and L. Dechêne, 1992, p. xxi.

134. Notary Pierre Raimbault, February 23, 1711, ANQ-M.

135. H. Charbonneau and J. Légaré, 1978-1990, Vol. 14, St. Louis/Ste. Anne du Bout de l'Île recs; R. Jetté, 1983, pp. 543-544, 641. 1702 land ownership map of Montreal Island by Vachon de Belmont: in Nos Racines, Vol. 22, 1979, pp. 430-431; M. Trudel, 1973a, pp. 172-173; recreation by G. Gallienne, 1977; and L. Dechêne, 1992, p. xxi.

136. H. Charbonneau and J. Légaré, 1978-1990, Vol. 14, St. Louis/Ste. Anne du Bout de l'Île recs; R. Jetté, 1983, pp. 641, 295, 794.

137. H. Charbonneau and J. Légaré, 1978-1990, Vol. 14, St. François de Sales/St. Joachim de Pointe Claire recs; R. Jetté, 1983, pp. x, 917.

138. H. Charbonneau and J. Légaré, 1978-1990, Vol. 14, St. François de Sales/St. Joachim de Pointe Claire recs and St. Louis/Ste. Anne du Bout de l'Île recs.

139. H. Charbonneau and J. Légaré, 1978-1990, Vol. 14, St. François de Sales/St. Joachim de Pointe Claire recs; R. Jetté, 1983, pp. 167, 759.

140. H. Charbonneau and J. Légaré, 1978-1990, Vol. 14, St. Louis/Ste. Anne du Bout de l'Île recs. and St. François de Sales/St. Joachim de Pointe Claire recs.; R. Jetté, 1983, pp. xv, 167, 336, 168.

141. H. Charbonneau and J. Légaré, 1978-1990, Vol. 14, St. François de Sales/St. Joachim de Pointe Claire recs; R. Jetté, 1983, pp. 307, 917.

142. Exhibits in Pointe à Callières Archaeological Museum, Montreal, 1994; ANQ, Ordonnances des Intendants, 1713-1720, Vol. 6, p. 54v., Archives des Colonies, C11A, Vol. 35, folios 330-352.

143. H. Charbonneau and J. Légaré, 1978-1990, Vol. 14, St. Louis/Ste. Anne du Bout de l'Île recs.; R. Jetté, 1983, pp. 917, 307.

144. Wedding: R. Jetté, 1983, pp. 491, 941. Baptism: H. Charbonneau and J. Légaré, 1978-1990, Vol. 14, St. François de Sales/St. Joachim de Pointe Claire recs; R. Jetté, 1983, p. 917.

145. H. Charbonneau and J. Légaré, 1978-1990, Vol. 14, St. Louis/Ste. Anne du Bout de l'Île recs.; R. Jetté, 1983, pp. 931, 801.

146. H. Charbonneau and J. Légaré, 1978-1990, Vol. 14, St. Louis/Ste. Anne du Bout de l'Île recs.; R. Jetté, 1983, pp. 4, 21. 1702 land ownership map of Montreal Island by Vachon de Belmont: in Nos Racines, Vol. 22, 1979, pp. 430-431; M. Trudel, 1973a, pp. 172-173; recreation by G. Gallienne, 1977; and L. Dechêne, 1992, p. xxi.

147. Wedding: H. Charbonneau and J. Légaré, 1978-1990, Vol. 14, St. Louis/Ste. Anne du Bout de l'Île recs.; R. Jetté, 1983, pp. 334, 688, 311, 931, 1130, 580, 509-510. Forts: M. Trudel, 1973a, pp. 216-217.

148. Notary Antoine Adhémar, July 3, 1717, ANQ-M; E. Massicotte, 1932-1933.

149. H. Charbonneau and J. Légaré, 1978-1990, Vol. 14, St. Louis/Ste. Anne du Bout de l'Île recs.; R. Jetté, 1983, pp. 801, 996-997.

150. H. Charbonneau and J. Légaré, 1978-1990, Vol. 14, St. Louis/Ste. Anne du Bout de l'Île recs.; R. Jetté, 1983, pp. 491, 847-848, 334, 912; P. Larousse, 1980, p. 627, "marguillerier."

151. E. O'Callaghan, 1853-1857, p. 61; J. Verney, 1991, pp 42, 117-118; W. Eccles, 1964, pp. 47-48; W. Eccles, 1972, pp. 69-70; P. Moogk, 2000, pp. 70-71, 211.

152. R. Jetté, 1983, p. 491.

153. H. Charbonneau and J. Légaré, 1978-1990, Vol. 14, St. Louis/Ste. Anne du Bout de l'Île recs.; R. Jetté, 1983, p. 931.

154. R. Jetté, 1983, pp. 491-492, 996.

155. ibid., pp. 491-492, 926.

156. ibid., p. 765.

157. ibid., p. 848.

158. ibid., p. 307.

159. H. Charbonneau and J. Légaré, 1978-1990, Vol. 14, St. Louis/Ste. Anne du Bout de l'Île recs.; R. Jetté, 1983, pp. 580, 1130.

160. H. Charbonneau and J. Légaré, 1978-1990, Vol. 14, St. Louis/Ste. Anne du Bout de l'Île recs.; R. Jetté, 1983, pp. 580, 692.

161. H. Charbonneau and J. Légaré, 1978-1990, Vol. 14, Sts. Anges de Lachine recs.; R. Jetté, 1983, pp. 912, 703.

162. H. Charbonneau and J. Légaré, 1978-1990, Vol. 14, Sts. Anges de Lachine recs.; R. Jetté, 1983, pp. 1020-1021.

163. R. Jetté, 1983, p. 917.

164. Notary Michel Lepailleur, March 9, 1722, ANQ-M.

165. H. Charbonneau and J. Légaré, 1978-1990, Vol. 14, St. Louis/Ste. Anne du Bout de l'Île recs.; R. Jetté, 1983, pp. 635, 792, 167. 1702 land ownership map of Montreal Island by Vachon de Belmont: in Nos Racines, Vol. 22, 1979, pp. 430-431; M. Trudel, 1973a, pp. 172-173; recreation by G. Gallienne, 1977; and L. Dechêne, 1992, p. xxi.

166. H. Charbonneau and J. Légaré, 1978-1990, Vol. 14, St. Louis/Ste. Anne du Bout de l'Île recs.; R. Jetté, 1983, pp. 491, 688, 692, 1037, 996-997.

167. Notary Michel Lepailleur, February 17, 1723, ANQ-M.

168. Notary Michel Lepailleur, July 15, 1723, ANQ-M; R. Jetté, 1983, p. 230.

169. R. Jetté, 1983, pp. 491-492, 848, 634, 99.

170. Notary Pierre Raimbault, March 14, 1724, ANQ-M.

171. Notary Pierre Raimbault, March 15, 1724, ANQ-M.

172. Notary Pierre Raimbault, September 24, 1724, ANQ-M.

173. H. Charbonneau and J. Légaré, 1978-1990, Vol. 14, St. Louis/Ste. Anne du Bout de l'Île recs.; R. Jetté, 1983, pp. 635, 996-997.

174. H. Charbonneau and J. Légaré, 1978-1990, Vol. 14, St. Louis/Ste. Anne du Bout de l'Île recs.; R. Jetté, 1983, pp. 307, 1037. 1702 land ownership map of Montreal Island by Vachon de Belmont: in Nos Racines, Vol. 22, 1979, pp. 430-431; M. Trudel, 1973a, pp. 172-173; recreation by G. Gallienne, 1977; and L. Dechêne, 1992, p. xxi.

175. Notary Michel Lepailleur, February 21, 1726, ANQ-M; H. Charbonneau and J. Légaré, 1978-1990, Vol. 14, St. Louis/Ste. Anne du Bout de l'Île recs.; R. Jetté, 1983, pp. 635, 167, 678, 823.

176. Notary Michel Lepailleur, March 1, 1726, ANQ-M; H. Charbonneau and J. Légaré, 1978-1990, Vol. 14, Sts. Anges de Lachine recs.; R. Jetté, 1983, pp. 635, 1092, 832.

177. Notary Pierre Raimbault, March 15, 1724, ANQ-M; Notary Michel Lepailleur, January 30, 1727, ANQ-M; R. Jetté, 1983, pp. 848, 635.

178. R. Jetté, 1983, p. 635.

179. H. Charbonneau and J. Légaré, 1978-1990, Vol. 14, St. Louis/Ste. Anne du Bout de l'Île recs.; R. Jetté, 1983, pp. 635, 167.

180. R. Jetté, 1983, p. 491.

181. ibid., p. 692.

182. H. Charbonneau and J. Légaré, 1978-1990, Vol. 14, St. Louis/Ste. Anne du Bout de l'Île recs.; R. Jetté, 1983, pp. 635, 477, 480, 510; Notary Michel Lepailleur, November 20, 1728, ANQ-M.

183. H. Charbonneau and J. Légaré, 1978-1990, Vol. 14, St. Louis/Ste. Anne du Bout de l'Île recs.; R. Jetté, 1983, pp. 509-510, 4.

184. H. Charbonneau and J. Légaré, 1978-1990, Vol. 14, St. Louis/Ste. Anne du Bout de l'Île recs.; R. Jetté, 1983, p. 693.

185. H. Charbonneau and J. Légaré, 1978-1990, Vol. 14, St. Louis/Ste. Anne du Bout de l'Île recs.; R. Jetté, 1983, p. 635.

186. R. Jetté, 1983, pp. 307, 634.

187. ibid., pp. 635, 492.

188. H. Charbonneau and J. Légaré, 1978-1990, Vol. 14, St. Louis/Ste. Anne du Bout de l'Île recs.; R. Jetté, 1983, p. 480.

189. Notary Joseph Raimbault, January 15, 1730 (registered February 14, 1730), ANQ-M; H. Charbonneau and J. Légaré, 1978-1990, Vol. 25, St. Louis/Ste. Anne du Bout de l'Île recs.; R. Jetté, 1983, pp. 635, 182.

190. Notary Joseph Raimbault, January 29, 1730 (registered February 23, 1730), ANQ-M; H. Charbonneau and J. Légaré, 1978-1990, Vol. 25, St. Louis/Ste. Anne du Bout de l'Île recs.; R. Jetté, 1983, pp. 635, 699.

191. R. Jetté, 1983, pp. 941, 491.

192. ibid., p. 491.

193. H. Charbonneau and J. Légaré, 1978-1990, Vol. 25, St. Louis/Ste. Anne du Bout de l'Île recs.; R. Jetté, 1983, pp. 635, 182.

194. H. Charbonneau and J. Légaré, 1978-1990, Vol. 25, St. Louis/Ste. Anne du Bout de l'Île recs.; R. Jetté, 1983, pp. 635, 996-997.

195. H. Charbonneau and J. Légaré, 1978-1990, Vol. 25, St. Louis/Ste. Anne du Bout de l'Île recs.; R. Jetté, 1983, pp. 635, 946.

196. H. Charbonneau and J. Légaré, 1978-1990, Vol. 25, St. Louis/Ste. Anne du Bout de l'Île recs.; R. Jetté, 1983, pp. 992, 22, 854.

197. H. Charbonneau and J. Légaré, 1978-1990, Vol. 25, St. Louis/Ste. Anne du Bout de l'Île recs.; R. Jetté, 1983, pp. 635, 180, 996.

198. H. Charbonneau and J. Légaré, 1978-1990, Vol. 25, St. Louis/Ste. Anne du Bout de l'Île recs.; R. Jetté, 1983, pp. 307, 813, 115, 227.

199. H. Charbonneau and J. Légaré, 1978-1990, Vol. 25, St. Louis/Ste. Anne du Bout de l'Île recs.; R. Jetté, 1983, pp. 635, 1092.

200. H. Charbonneau and J. Légaré, 1978-1990, Vol. 25, St. Louis/Ste. Anne du Bout de l'Île recs.; R. Jetté, 1983, pp. 635, 996.

201. H. Charbonneau and J. Légaré, 1978-1990, Vol. 25, St. Louis/Ste. Anne du Bout de l'Île recs.; R. Jetté, 1983, pp. 635, 1037, 352, 692.

202. H. Charbonneau and J. Légaré, 1978-1990, Vol. 25, St. Louis/Ste. Anne du Bout de l'Île recs.; R. Jetté, 1983, p. 480.

203. Notary Claude Cyprien Porlier, March 27, 1736, ANQ-M; R. Jetté, 1983, pp. 699, 935.

204. Notary Claude Cyrpien Porlier, January 13, 1738 (registered February 7, 1738), ANQ-M; R. Jetté, 1983, pp. 635, 167, 352.

205. H. Charbonneau and J. Légaré, 1978-1990, Vol. 25, St. Louis/Ste. Anne du Bout de l'Île recs.; R. Jetté, 1983, pp. 966, 477.

206. H. Charbonneau and J. Légaré, 1978-1990, Vol. 25, St. Louis/Ste. Anne du Bout de l'Île recs.; R. Jetté, 1983, pp. 635, 167.

207. Notary François Lepailleur, March 11, 1739; Notary Antoine Adhémar, July 24, 1702, ANQ-M; Notary Pierre Raimbault, February 23, 1711, ANQ-M; Notary Pierre Raimbault, March 14, 1724, ANQ-M; R. Jetté, 1983, pp. 716, 635.

208. Notary François Simonnet, February 23, 1740 (registered March 27, 1760), ANQ-M.

209. H. Charbonneau and J. Légaré, 1978-1990, Vol. 25, St. Louis/Ste. Anne du Bout de l'Île recs.; R. Jetté, 1983, p. 1130.

210. H. Charbonneau and J. Légaré, 1978-1990, Vol. 25, St. Louis/Ste. Anne du Bout de l'Île recs.; R. Jetté, 1983, pp. 477-478.

211. H. Charbonneau and J. Légaré, 1978-1990, Vol. 25, St. Louis/Ste. Anne du Bout de l'Île recs.; R. Jetté, 1983, pp. 352, 992.

212. H. Charbonneau and J. Légaré, 1978-1990, Vol. 25, St. Louis/Ste. Anne du Bout de l'Île recs.; R. Jetté, 1983, pp. 635, 792. 1702 land ownership map of Montreal Island by Vachon de Belmont: in Nos Racines, Vol. 22, 1979, pp. 430-431; M. Trudel, 1973a, pp. 172-173; recreation by G. Gallienne, 1977; and L. Dechêne, 1992, p. xxi.

213. H. Charbonneau and J. Légaré, 1978-1990, Vol. 25, St. Louis/Ste. Anne du Bout de l'Île recs.; R. Jetté, 1983, pp. 307, 792, 1129.

214. H. Charbonneau and J. Légaré, 1978-1990, Vol. 25, St. Louis/Ste. Anne du Bout de l'Île recs.; R. Jetté, 1983, p. 531.

215. H. Charbonneau and J. Légaré, 1978-1990, Vol. 25, St. Louis/Ste. Anne du Bout de l'Île recs.; R. Jetté, 1983, p. 635.

216. H. Charbonneau and J. Légaré, 1978-1990, Vol. 25, St. Louis/Ste. Anne du Bout de l'Île recs.; R. Jetté, 1983, pp. 635, 699, 1041; R. Harris, 1987, pl. 46.

217. R. Jetté, 1983, pp. 635, 1041.

218. H. Charbonneau and J. Légaré, 1978-1990, Vol. 38, St. Louis/Ste. Anne du Bout de l'Île recs.; R. Jetté, 1983, p. 635.

219. II. Charbonneau and J. Légaré, 1978-1990, Vol. 40, St. Joseph de Soulanges recs.; R. Jetté, 1983, p. 634.

220. H. Charbonneau and J. Légaré, 1978-1990, Vol. 38, St. Louis/Ste. Anne du Bout de l'Île recs.; R. Jetté, 1983, pp. 635, 996.

221. H. Charbonneau and J. Légaré, 1978-1990, Vol. 38, St. Louis/Ste. Anne du Bout de l'Île recs.; R. Jetté, 1983, pp. 635, 212.

222. H. Charbonneau and J. Légaré, 1978-1990, Vol. 38, St. Louis/Ste. Anne du Bout de l'Île recs.; R. Jetté, 1983, pp. 635, 307.

223. H. Charbonneau and J. Légaré, 1978-1990, Vol. 40, St. Joseph de Soulanges recs.; R. Jetté, 1983, p. 635.

224. H. Charbonneau and J. Légaré, 1978-1990, Vol. 38, St. Louis/Ste. Anne du Bout de l'Île recs.; R. Jetté, 1983, pp. 491, 635; H. Charbonneau et al, 1993, p. 184, Fig. 27.

XIV
Jean François Brunet dit Le Bourbonnais, Jr. and his wife Françoise David

Voyageur and then voyageur-trader who worked over the span of thirty years, sometimes as a legal, licensed trader and at other times as an illegal coureur de bois *who was documented in court records*

Jean François Brunet dit Le Bourbonnais was born in the Lachine seigneury on May 26, 1682, to François Brunet dit Le Bourbonnais, Sr. and Barbe Beauvais. During his younger years, he was identified by his given name Jean François in church documents on four known occasions. The first time occurred at his baptism, while the second instance took place when he received the sacrament of Confirmation at age 16. The third time was when he appeared as a marriage witness at age 16, while the fourth occasion took place when he stood as the godfather at a baptism when he was 18 years old. The only other known document which named him as Jean François was the estate inventory of his parents, which was drawn up by a Montreal notary in October of 1703 (when he was $21^1/2$). From November of 1700 onward, when he was $18^1/2$ years old, he was always identified by the priests in church records as simply "François." This latter given name was also utilized in virtually all of the thirty known notary and court documents pertaining to him, which date from May of 1702 onward (from his 20th birthday on). The only exception was the above-mentioned inventory of his parents' belongings, which was penned in the autumn of 1703 (when he was identified as Jean François). Thus, in the present biography, he is always named either François, Francois, Jr., or Junior, except in those five rare instances when the documents specifically identified him as Jean François.

The nickname "dit Le Bourbonnais" was not applied to François, Jr. in any known documents until the day of his 20th birthday in May of 1702, when his first official voyageur contract was recorded. This event took place four weeks before the death of his father, François, Sr., who had been known throughout his life in New France by the family name Brunet plus the sobriquet "dit Le Bourbonnais." From May of 1702 onward, Junior was identified by this nickname in sixteen of the thirty notary and court documents. In the other half of these records, he was simply identified as François Brunet. Interestingly, in the entire series of 44 church records pertaining to him which have been located, the Bourbonnais nickname was not added to Junior's name until 1720, when he was 38 years old. This particular ecclesiastical record in 1720 was the 21st listing for him. In the 23 notations that were later penned by the priests, he was identified with his nickname of "dit Le Bourbonnais" twelve times; in the other eleven instances, he was identified as simply François Brunet.

A highly detailed picture of the earlier years of François' life, as well as the lives of his parents and siblings, has already been presented in this work, in the biographies of his parents François Brunet, Sr. and Barbe Beauvais. The information which follows in the first portion of the present biography has been extracted from that earlier chapter, in order to establish a concise foundation for François' adult years.[1]

François Brunet, Jr. was the sixth of twelve children who were born to François Brunet dit Le Bourbonnais, Sr. and Barbe Beauvais:

1. Jean (baptized on April 6, 1673 at Montreal)
2. Barbe (baptized on July 1, 1675 at Montreal)
3. Marie Jeanne (born at Lachine, baptized on September 5, 1677 at Montreal)
4. Catherine (born on April 29, 1680, baptized on the following day at Lachine)
5. Anne (born on April 29, 1680, baptized on the following day at Lachine)
6. François, Jr. (born on May 26, 1682, baptized two days later at Lachine with the given name of Jean François)
7. Élisabeth (born on February 17, 1685, baptized on the following day at Lachine)
8. Marie (born on June 4, 1687, baptized on the following day at Lachine)
9. Angélique (baptized on April 16, 1691 at Montreal)
10. Joseph I (baptized on April 30, 1693 at Montreal; he was buried on August 31, 1693 at Montreal)
11. Joseph II (born on January 30, 1695, baptized on February 2 at Lachine; he died on February 5, and was interred on the following day at Lachine)
12. Louis (born on May 29, 1697, baptized two days later at Lachine)[2]

On May 28, 1682, when François was two days old, he was christened in the Holy Angels church at Lachine. The officiating cleric on this joyous occasion was the Sulpician Fr. Pierre Rémy (age 42), who had been appointed as the first resident priest of this parish two years earlier. On this day, when the infant was given the name Jean François, two fellow residents of the Lachine seigneury stood as his sponsors: Jean Cardinal (who was about age 24 and still single) and Marie Roy (who was the wife of André Merlot dit Laramée).[3]

For at least the previous five years, since at least the summer of 1677, the steadily-growing Brunet family had been residing on their pioneer farm in the area called Sault St. Louis, which comprised the eastern one-third of the Lachine seigneury. This area, about eight miles south-southwest of Montreal, was located a short distance east of the southern terminus of the 8-mile-long Chemin de Lachine (the Lachine Road). This gently curving portage route, which connected Montreal and Lachine, bypassed the 40-foot drop in elevation of the Sault de St. Louis (the St. Louis or Lachine Rapids) in the St. Lawrence River and their powerful downstream whirlpools. Commencing at the end of the portage road and extending toward the east, the Commons area of the Lachine seigneury occupied the first half-mile of river frontage. Then began the Sault St. Louis section of the seigneury, with its series of long, slender plots of forest-covered farmland fronting on the river. The fourth of these lots east of the Commons was the elongated rectangular property of the Brunet family, which was located about 1700 feet ($1/3$ mile) east of the Commons and about $8/10$ mile east of the terminus of the portage road. The plot contained 575 feet of St. Lawrence frontage, and extended toward the northwest for $7/10$ mile.

About $1^1/2$ miles west of the terminus of the portage road, the community of Lachine had been established (it is now called La Salle). It contained the seigneurial manor house (which had on its ground floor a well, a blacksmith's shop, and a bakery with an oven that extended out to the exterior); a wind-powered grist mill, built of field stones so that it could also serve as a round-tower redoubt; several barracks buildings to house soldiers; a number of storage buildings; the homes of various settler families; and the wooden parish church measuring 36 by 20 feet, on one side of which stood the rectory and on the other side the parish cemetery. Ever since 1668, colonists had gradually settled along the St. Lawrence shoreline in this seigneury. In the process, they had developed farms on lands that extended for about $1^3/4$ miles to the west of the village site (to the adjacent seigneury of La Présentation or Côte St. Gilles), and for about 4¹/4 miles to the east of the village site (to the adjacent seigneury of Verdun). Thus, the entire stretch of river frontage that was encompassed by the Lachine seigneury measured some 6¹/4 miles in length. The western two-thirds of this span was called the Côte de Lachine, while its eastern one-third was dubbed the Sault St. Louis. These two sections were separated by the Commons land, which was utilized by many of the residents for such tasks as pasturing animals and cutting wood. It was also used by many of those numerous individuals who traveled along the portage road.

The Brunet property contained a total of 60 arpents or 51 acres. As it extended off toward the northwest, its rear section crossed the Montreal-to-Lachine road. In the year before Francois, Jr.'s birth, the census enumerator had recorded that the portions of this Brunet parcel which were cleared and under cultivation were estimated to total ten acres. The family had also owned at that time seven horned cattle and one gun. In their estate inventory of 1703, the document would indicate that the family had constructed on this land a house, a stable, a granary, and a separate root cellar. The following description of the family home and the nearby granary were recorded in this latter inventory:

"One house situated on the land of the said place of Lachine, measuring forty-five feet in length by twenty feet in width, solidly built in pièce-sur-pièce style [with widely-spaced vertical framing elements and horizontal infill logs], consisting of two large rooms with two hearths and chimneys of stone, plus two side rooms [sleeping and storage rooms], all on the ground floor, and a large attic, entirely roofed with boards, the doors framed and the windows of its doors containing fixed wooden frames.

One granary built in pièce-sur-pièce style, measuring fifty feet in length by twenty-five feet in width, without any additional roof covering [besides the chinked logs]."[4]

As was customary during this period, the window panes in the house would have consisted of oiled paper or oiled pieces of rawhide that had been scraped thin.

This inventory would also record that the family owned oxen, cows, calves, pigs, sheep, and chickens (they had also apparently owned a horse previously), as well as stacks of firewood which contained three or four years' worth of fuel. In addition, they raised crops of wheat, oats, and white peas.

Trips from the farm to the church or the grist mill, both of which were located within the stockade-enclosed village site, entailed a distance of about $2^3/4$ miles each way. The *censitaires* were obliged to take the portions of their grains which they wished to have ground to this seigneurial mill, at which they relinquished to the miller $1/40$ of their grain. In addition, they were obligated to hand over to the Church a tithe of $1/26$ of the threshed wheat which they produced each year; however, new lands were exempt from this charge during their first five years of cultivation. This was the world in which François Brunet, Jr. developed and expanded, both physically and mentally, as he grew up during most of the years of the 1680s and the 1690s.[5]

In his ever-expanding world of pioneer farms, the fur trade also loomed large, since this commerce served as the very mainstay of the economy of New France. Numerous individuals who resided in both the Lachine area and the greater Montreal region worked in this business, in a wide array of occupations. Close to home, while he was growing up, François heard tales of challenging canoe trips to and from the western interior regions, as well as stories about the many adventures and misadventures that his relatives and neighbors had experienced there. His own father's paddling partner and business colleague in these exciting ventures, Jean Boursier dit Lavigne, lived with his family just one farm away to the east. In addition, there was always plenty of activity on the Montreal-to-Lachine portage road to stimulate a boy's dreams of places hundreds of miles from the farm. The southern end of this route was located just $8/10$ mile west of the Brunet farm, and the road actually crossed the inland portion of their property. Businesses which supported this traffic were gradually developing at the Lachine end of the road, including facilities for storing cargo and for feeding and sometimes housing the travelers. This specific locale was the very place at which nearly all of the fur trade, military, and missionary personnel who carried out expeditions to the west departed and returned. As a result, the fur trade was an integral and ever-present part of life for young François Brunet.

Even before he had been born, his father François, Sr. had made numerous voyages to the western interior. During the years 1675 and 1676, Senior and his partner Monsieur Boursier had hauled freight back and forth on the upper St. Lawrence River between Lachine and Ft. Frontenac, in the employ of René Robert Cavelier, the Sieur de La Salle. During the years 1677 through 1684, the duo had most likely continued to work at this occupation, at least intermittently.

However, their participation in the peltries commerce during these particular years may have been unlicensed, since it was apparently not documented in public records. During 1685-1686, just three years after the official licensing system had been inaugurated, the two partners paddled to the Ottawa Country to trade, basing their labors at the community of St. Ignace (Michilimackinac) at the Straits of Mackinac. At the time of this fifteen-month venture, François, Jr. was 3 to 4 years old. The trading duo again returned to *Le Pays d'en Haut* (the Upper Country, encompassing the upper Great Lakes region) during 1686-1687, after which they carried out commerce in the Illinois Country during 1688-1689. During these latter two voyages, Junior was ages 4 to 5 and 6 to 7, respectively. At the time of his father's return from the Illinois Country in July of 1689, Senior was 44 or 45 years old. From then on, no surviving documents have been found which indicate that he participated in any further business dealings related to the peltries commerce, either as an active voyageur-trader or as a stay-at-home investor financing other traders. However, even if he did not take part in the furs-and-hides business, he most likely kept abreast of current events in this field. This would not have been difficult to do, since their farm was positioned only $8/10$ mile east of the portage terminus, a span which contained just three farms next to his and then the half-mile-wide Commons land.

For François, Jr., the absence of his father and many of the other local men during these formative years was by no means the only challenge that he and his family members had faced during this period. In about 1686, when he had been four years old, Iroquois war parties had resumed their attacks on the St. Lawrence settlements, as well as on the Ottawa River route, which led to and from the Upper Country. Such raids had been blessedly absent during the previous two decades, ever since a number of peace treaties had been ratified with the Iroquois nations back in 1666 and 1667. However, there was another element of daily life at this time that became even more insidious than the constant threat of lighting raids by hidden warriors. Starting in the summer of 1687, a terrible epidemic of both measles and smallpox had arrived with the vessels from the mother country. These vicious diseases, sweeping up the St. Lawrence Valley from Tadoussac all the way to the Montreal area, had continued unchecked for nearly a year, extending well into 1688. By the time the scourge of sickness and death had finally abated, over a thousand residents, both French and native, had been sent to their graves.

As protection against Iroquois depredations, stockades of refuge had been constructed during 1688 at each of the exposed seigneuries. Along the southern shoreline of Montreal Island, from east to west, these had included the fortifications at Verdun (about $1^1/2$ miles northeast of the Brunet farm), Ft. Cuillerier on the property of René Cuillerier, Sr. ($1^1/4$ miles west of the Brunets), Ft. Rémy at the village of Lachine ($3/4$ mile further toward the west), and Ft. Rolland ($1^3/4$ miles further west, at the western end of the Lachine seigneury). The residents of the seigneury of La Présentation or Côte St. Gilles, extending for about $2^3/4$ miles west of Ft. Rolland (to about the present community of Dorval), would use the latter stockade as needed. Thus, the settlers who were spread out along some nine miles of the shoreline in this southeastern section of the island, from the eastern end of Verdun to the western end of La Présentation, had four palisades to which they could flee for protection in case of attacks. However, they had no inkling of just how massive and vicious the upcoming raid would be.

During the night of August 4-5, 1689, some nine weeks after François, Jr. had celebrated his seventh birthday, a force of about 1,500 Iroquois warriors crossed northward over the broad St. Lawrence. Silently spreading out along eight miles of shoreline, from the Sault St. Louis area (beside the Lachine Rapids, where the Brunet and Boursier families lived) westward to La Présentation, the raiders remained undetected by the sentries in the various forts throughout the entire night. Waiting until dawn to launch their ferocious strike, the Iroquois, who numbered nearly 200 attackers per mile of shoreline, took the French completely by surprise. Soon, they had slain at least 24 French residents and had captured an estimated 79 others. They also destroyed by fire 56 of the 77 houses in the area, along with numerous stables, granaries, and other outbuildings, and killed a large portion of the livestock. In the immediate aftermath, most of the survivors of this first onslaught sought refuge within the four stockades. But some of them made their way to Montreal, where Governor Denonville was visiting at the time. Immediately, he sent Vaudreuil, the acting governor of Montreal, to the raided area with a force of about 300 soldiers.

Numerous scholars have sought to identify the colonists who either died or were captured in this horrific raid, which was soon afterward dubbed the Lachine Massacre. Among the 24 individuals who perished on site that day, nine of them were buried where they had been found in the area of the Lachine seigneury, while the other fifteen were interred further to the west, in the adjacent seigneury of La Présentation, which was also called Côte St. Gilles.

Somehow, the two parents and eight children of the Brunet dit Le Bourbonnais family all survived the attack and evaded capture. However, on the Boursier farm, just 575 feet toward the east, their close neighbors and close friends were not so fortunate. Little Madeleine Boursier, seven weeks short of her first birthday, was drowned by Iroquois attackers. Three other members of her family fared little better. The parents and their nine-year-old daughter were taken captive; afterward, the girl may have died in captivity, or she may have been adopted into the Iroquois world and remained there for the rest of her life. At the time of little Madeleine's reburial in October of 1694, the father of the family was recorded as being dead. Some four years later, a Lachine document from 1699 indicated that the mother had passed away some time previous to that date, presumably while in Iroquois hands. However, the couple's other five children, ages 15, 11, 7, 5, and 3, escaped death and capture during the raid.

Madeleine Boursier was the only resident to die on site within the eastern two-thirds of the Lachine seigneury, in the stretch of about $4^1/4$ miles that extended eastward from Ft. Rémy. However, six other settlers who lived in this area are known to have been captured. These included two members of the Jean Roy household (one mile northeast of the Brunet's land), two people in the Jean Paré home ($^1/2$ mile east of the Brunets), the mother of the family on the farm immediately west of the Brunet property, and Pierre Pérusseau's wife Marie Leroy, in their home by the western end of the stockaded village site. A short distance west of the village, Jean Fournier was wounded but escaped, while his wife Marie Crépin was captured; in addition, two soldiers died and were buried there. Besides these victims, the dead buried within this area included about twenty native allies who had been felled there.

The other 21 victims (twenty French and one native) died in the western portion of the Lachine seigneury and in the adjacent La Présentation seigneury. It was in this area, extending along the shoreline for some four miles, that the raiders had directed their greatest fury. The deceased individuals here included seven men, three women, nine children, one soldier, and a fifteen-year-old native slave.

An estimated 79 settlers living in the attacked area were captured in the raid. However, an estimated 27 of these individual eventually made their way back to their homes, either by escaping or by being later exchanged or released. One of these fortunate returned souls was Catherine Renusson, the Brunets' neighbor who lived on the adjacent farm immediately to the west; she was cited in a document in April of 1691. (Much greater detail concerning the casualties, as well as full footnotes for this data, are included in the dual biography of François Brunet, Sr. and Barbe Beauvais.)

It is not known whether the Brunets' farm and livestock remained intact during the raid. Fortunately, all ten of their family members survived the onslaught (at least physically), including the eight children, who ranged in age from $15^2/3$ down to $2^2/12$ years. In any case, they decided to move to the security of Montreal for the present time. Since Senior had recently reaped substantial financial profits from his trading enterprise in the Illinois Country, he had considerable financial resources on hand. As a result, he could purchase a home outright, without needing to take out a loan. On September 13, 1689, five weeks after the August raid, the parents purchased a lot on Rue St. Paul in Montreal, on which stood both a house and a shop. Twelve days after purchasing this town property, on September 25, the couple also arranged to lease a piece of land which was located at a distance south-southwest of town, in the sub-fief of Pointe St. Charles. They intended to farm this parcel of leased land.

In the early spring of 1691, two months before Junior would turn nine, his maternal grandfather died. Jacques Beauvais dit Saint Gemme was laid to rest in the Montreal cemetery on March 20. That summer, two attacks on the outlying regions of Montreal clearly underscored that they were a people at war. First, on June 26, enemy forces raided the western area of the Lachine seigneury and the adjacent seigneury of La Présentation, killing six men. Six weeks later, on August 11, a combined force of about 400 English and Iroquois fighting men attacked Laprairie. This village and seigneury, located directly across the St. Lawrence from the Verdun fief, was about seven miles southeast of the Lachine village site, some six miles southeast of the Brunet farm, and about five miles south-southeast of Montreal.

Some $1^1/2$ years later, in April of 1693, François, Sr. was granted an additional parcel of land in the Lachine seigneury. This lot, measuring 768 feet in width by $7/10$ mile in length, angled northward from the inland end of their lot that fronted on the St. Lawrence. This acquisition clearly indicated that the family intended to permanently move back to this seigneury in the future, returning to their farm beside the Lachine Rapids, where they had lived for many years before the Iroquois raid of 1689. However, in spite of receiving this land concession, they would not return to their farm at Lachine for at least another year or more (probably not until the summer or autumn of 1694).

One week after registering their new rear lot behind their riverfront farm at Lachine, the parents leased a farm in the fief of Verdun. This area was located immediately south-southwest of the sub-fief of Pointe St. Charles, and occupied the riverside space between the Pointe St. Charles lands and the Sault St. Louis section of the Lachine seigneury. Some $3^1/2$ years earlier, the couple had leased a piece of land in the Pointe St. Charles area; they had eventually allowed this agreement to run out and had not renewed it. The new lease, commencing on April 12, 1693, would run for three harvest seasons, on property which was located just three miles or less away from their own Lachine farm. At this point, Junior was about to turn 11, while his older brother Jean was age 20; his sisters were 18, 16, 13, 13, 8, 6, and 2. After most of the family members would return to their own property at Lachine (in about the summer or autumn of 1694), certain of the children would probably remain on this Verdun property until the conclusion of the lease, after the harvests of the summer and autumn of 1695 would be completed.

During the entire five-year period while the Brunet family was absent from the Lachine seigneury, they continued to own their home on St. Paul Street in Montreal. They had purchased this town property in September of 1689, within five weeks of the Iroquois attack. However, they apparently wished to raise their own foods and other products, instead of living as traditional town-dwellers. Thus, during the planting, tending, and harvesting seasons, they probably divided their time between one or the other of the successive leased farm properties and their home in town. During the winters, they probably resided entirely on Rue St. Paul in Montreal, having made arrangements for the care of the farm animals in the countryside during their absence.

Near the end of the summer in this year of 1693, the family was plunged into deep grief. The newest baby of the family, little Joseph, arrived on April 30. However, he lived but four months, and was laid to rest in the Montreal cemetery on August 30. Until now, the

Brunets had been extremely fortunate concerning the survival rate of the offspring of the family. Previously, they had welcomed into the world nine children, and all nine of them were continuing to thrive. This survival rate, however, was an anomaly in the colony, where about a quarter of all children died before they had completed their first year, and almost 45 percent of them perished before they reached the age of ten.

During the first week of April in 1694, Jean Brunet, the eldest child of the family and Junior's only brother, celebrated his 21st birthday. Ten weeks later, on June 14, he signed a contract to serve as a voyageur-trader in the Ottawa Country. This engagement represented Jean's initial entry into the world of the fur trade. This first step would eventually lead him to spend his entire adult life in the Illinois Country, where their father had traded during 1688-1689. Over the course of his many years of working in the peltries commerce, François, Sr. had set a strong and positive example for his children, which would spread over time to all three of his eventual surviving sons as well as the spouses of his daughters. As a result, over the span of more than three decades, commencing in this year of 1694 and extending to at least 1725, all three of his sons and five or six of his seven sons-in-law would be employed at some point in the fur trade in the western interior.

By the time of the arrival of the next baby in the family, in late January of 1695, the Brunets had permanently moved back to their Lachine farm. Sadly, this second Joseph passed away on February 5, having survived for only seven days; he was buried amid many tears in the Lachine cemetery on the following day.

During the summer of 1696, when François, Jr. was $14^{1}/4$ years old, his parents purchased the entire lot which was located immediately west of their riverfront property. This new plot, also fronting on the St. Lawrence, measured 575 feet in width by $7/10$ mile in depth, exactly the same dimensions as their original riverfront property next door. Two months later, they sold their lot and buildings on Rue St. Paul in Montreal.

On November 26, 1696, Junior's eldest sister, Barbe (who was $21^{5}/12$ years old), married Georges Brault dit Pomainville. On this gladdening occasion, the official witnesses included the bride's sisters Marie Jeanne (age 19) and the twins Catherine and Anne ($16^{1}/2$), as well as her brother François, Jr. ($14^{1}/2$).

In the following spring, on May 29, 1697, Junior's last sibling joined the family. Little Louis, the tenth and final living Brunet offspring, arriving three days after François, Jr. had marked his 15th birthday. Five months later, on October 29, his second-oldest sister, Marie Jeanne, was married in the Lachine church.

On June 6, 1698, when he was 16 years old, Junior received the sacrament of Confirmation in the Lachine church. Among the twenty other persons who were also confirmed on this day were his sisters Élisabeth (age 13) and Marie (11). In the records of this occasion, the young man was listed as Jean François Brunet.[6]

Ten days later, he appeared as one of the official witnesses at a wedding in the same edifice. On this occasion, the groom was 25-year-old Louis Lory, who had grown up on the adjacent farm immediately to the east of the Brunet property. His bride was the widowed Marie Louise Beaune, whose husband Pierre Maupetit dit Poitevin had been killed nearly nine years earlier in the Lachine Massacre. (The biography of this latter couple's son Pierre Maupetit, Jr. and his wife Angélique Villeray is presented next in this work.) In the parish ledger, the priest recorded the name of this witness as Jean François Brunet.[7]

Later this summer, Junior's brother-in-law Georges Brault dit Pomainville and his sister Barbe purchased the double lot which lay immediately west of the Brunets' double lot. This newly-acquired land had a St. Lawrence frontage of 1,150 feet.

When the ships from the mother country arrived during this summer, they brought word that the war between France and a number of European nations had ended during the previous year. It was also in this same year of 1698 that the raids by Iroquois warriors against both the French colonists and their native allies finally ceased once and for all. However, treaty negotiations between the latter three groups would drag on for another three years, until the Great Treaty would ultimately be signed in Montreal during the summer of 1701. When a new war would break out between France and other European countries in 1702, the Iroquois would remain neutral, not siding with the English as they had previously done for decades.

In November of 1699, the children of the neighboring Boursier family who had survived the Iroquois attack of 1689 lost their family land, due to non-payment of seigeurial fees. This lack of payments went back twelve years, to when their parents had still been living. Shortly afterward, this property was divided into three parcels by the seigneurs (the Sulpician order) and it was acquired by three different individuals. The westernmost 384 feet of frontage went to Louis Mallet and his wife Marie Jeanne Brunet (Junior's sister); the middle 384 feet was acquired by Jean Baptiste Brault dit Pomainville (Georges Brault's brother, who would marry Junior's sister Élisabeth in 1703); and the easternmost 575 feet went to Louis Roy. Following these three transfers, the lots extending eastward from the Commons of the seigneury were owned by the following men, in sequence from west to east: Georges Brault dit Pomainville, 1,150 feet of St. Lawrence frontage; François Brunet dit Le Bourbonnais, Sr., 1,150 feet; François Lory, 575 feet; Louis Mallet, 384 feet; and Jean Baptiste Brault dit Pomainville, 384 feet. (After Jean Baptiste's marriage to Élisabeth in 1703, the eventual purchaser of Monsieur Lory's lot, Paul Lécuyer dit Lapierre, would be the only landowner within this stretch of 7/10 mile of frontage who would not be a member of the extended Brunet clan.)

In the middle of the summer of 1700, when he was 18 years old, Junior stood beside the baptismal font of the Lachine church, as the godfather of his two-day-old niece Marie Anne Couillard. She was the first child of his sister Anne and her husband Pierre Couillard, who had been married back in February of 1699. On this day of July 1, the officiating priest recorded that the sponsors were Jean François Brunet and Marie Buet (the future wife of Jean Baptiste Gros dit Laviolette). To the sadness of the entire family, the infant died and was laid to rest on the very next day.[8]

Five months later, on November 24, Junior appeared as one of the official witnesses at the wedding of long time family friends and neighbors Jean Baptiste Gros and Marie Buet (who were ages 26 and 22, respectively). Two of the other witnesses on this occasion were his sister Anne and her husband Pierre Couillard.[9]

By the following year of 1701, the Holy Angels church within the stockaded village at Lachine (nearly three miles west of the Brunet farm) had been in use for a quarter-century. Built of stout timbers, this first edifice measured about 36 by 20 feet. In the spring of 1701, plans were finalized for the construction of a much larger church here, which would be built of field stones; this new one would measure 60 by 30 feet. In pleasant anticipation of attending services in this grander edifice during the remainder of his life, François, Sr. arranged on April 11 to permanently lease a specific pew for himself and his family within it.

Three days before Christmas in this year of 1701, when Junior was 19 2/3 years old, he was chosen to stand as the godfather for an infant who had been born that same day. This baby was Marguerite Roy, the fourth offspring of the local residents François Roy and Marie Cécire. Junior's co-sponsor this time was the Lachine resident Marie Merlot, 17 years old and unmarried. Unfortunately, tiny Marguerite would perish just six weeks later, and her godmother would die at the Hôtel Dieu hospital in Montreal after four more years, without ever having married.[10]

By the spring of 1702, only two sons of the Brunet family were residing close by: François, Jr., who would turn 20 on May 26, and Louis (the baby of the family), who would turn 5 three days later. Jean, the eldest son, age 29, was away living and working in the Illinois Country. Junior's other seven siblings were all girls: Barbe, Marie Jeanne, and Anne who were married (ages 26, 24, and 22, respectively) and Catherine, Élisabeth, Marie, and Angélique who were still single (ages 22, 17, 15, and 11, respectively). Other than Jean and his family in distant Illinois, the entire clan all lived in the Lachine seigneury, including the parents, their nine children, their three sons-in-law, and their five grandchildren.

On the very day of his 20th birthday, François, Jr. traveled to Montreal to visit the office of the firm that held the beaver-exporting monopoly in the colony. There, he approved a contract to work as a voyageur hauling freight in both directions between Montreal and Ft. Frontenac, at the eastern end of Lake Ontario. This was the same labor that his father François, Sr. had carried out with his partner Jean Boursier dit Lavigne 26 and 27 years earlier, back in 1675 and 1676. At that time, the two men had been employed by La Salle, immediately after he had acquired the post and the surrounding area as a seigneury, and had commenced rebuilding and expanding the original facility.

In this instance, more than a quarter-century later, Junior would be working with two partners. One would be his brother-in-law Georges Brault dit Pomainville, age 34, who had been married to his sister Barbe for $5^1/2$ years. This couple owned the large double lot immediately west of the Brunet property; they had just commenced their fourth pregnancy. Junior's second paddling partner would be Pierre Tabault, age 26, who lived in the adjacent seigneury of La Présentation, some $3^1/2$ miles west of the Lachine village. He would become Junior's brother-in-law eleven months later, when he would marry his sister Catherine in April of 1703.
"Were present Georges Brault dit Pomainville, Pierre Tabault, and François

Brunet dit [Le] Bourbonnais, Junior, all habitants of this Island and voyageurs presently in this town, who have promised and promise by these presents, solidly one for the other and each of them for the whole, without division and renouncing [any such divisions], to Joseph Fleury, Esquire, Sieur de La Gorgendière, principal clerk of the Office of the Company of the Colony of Canada at Montreal and Sieur François Dumontier [dit Brillant], also a clerk of the said Office at Villemarie, who were present and assenting. The said named individuals have agreed to take, bring, conduct, and transport from this town to the Fort of Frontenac all of the merchandise, flour, and generally whatever other belongings that the said Sieurs de La Gorgendière and Dumontier will have for them to take or send to the said Fort of Frontenac, and to bring down all of the belongings and peltries which the said Sieur de La Gorgendière would like to ship from the said Fort Frontenac to the said Villemarie. Above all, particular care will be taken to be careful that nothing will become wet, either in going up or in coming down, so that the said belongings or merchandise will arrive without any loss or waste, under penalty of being accountable and held solidly responsible for the said waste of their said load if they allow it to become wet or wasted as a consequence of the above. A statement of each load will be delivered to them before their departure, to which they will give their acknowledgement before the notary. Under no pretext will they be allowed to open and unpack the bales of said peltries which will be consigned to them, under penalty of being accountable for everything which might be found to be missing or to have been altered according to the invoice which will be sent by the said Sieur de La Gorgendière. Neither a single one of the said entrepreneurs nor any part of them shall be permitted to do any trading with the natives, directly or indirectly, under any pretext, either at Fort Frontenac or on the route, whether in going out or in returning, under penalty of confiscation of the seized goods and the loss of the proceeds of one of their voyages. In case a violation might be discovered at any time, whether or not it be several years earlier that it would have been committed, and whether or not the violation was caught at the time, it will be able to be pursued during the following five years. Those present have consented to the said penalty, in case it be eventually discovered and proven that they have violated this article.

The said entrepreneurs will begin to do the said transporting from this day forward, and they will continue to do so without interruption as long as the said lessors will have cargo to transport. The said lessors promise to them first preference in doing the said transporting to the said Fort Frontenac, as much during the present summer and autumn as during the navigation seasons of the following years, as much as it will be in their power. To carry out these aforesaid transports and shipments, the said entrepreneurs will equip themselves at their own cost and expense with everything which they will need for the said shipments and for the protection of the said belongings. This agreement is made in consideration of and upon the following grounds. Ten francs [livres] will be paid for each hundredweight [100 pounds] which they will take up and ship to the said Fort Frontenac, and twenty francs [livres] in the currency of the country for each canoe load which they will bring down from the said Fort to the said Villemarie. The said Sieurs de La Gorgendière and Dumontier have promised and promise to the above-named individuals to pay or cause to be paid to the said entrepreneurs the said sums as they complete each of the said shipments, the last payment to be made immediately after all of the transporting [of this paddling season] has been accomplished. Against these fees the said entrepreneurs acknowledge that they have received before this time the sum of 145 livres in currency of the country for a canoe, which they agree will be deducted from that which will be owed to them for the first four voyages which they will make, under penalty, etc. Thus have they promised, obligated themselves, waived, etc.

[This agreement] made and drawn up at Villemarie in the office of the said Company of the Colony in the year 1702, on the 26th day of May in the forenoon, in the presence of Charles Alavoine and Dominique Bergeron, merchants at present in this town who have signed in the place of the said entrepreneurs, who have declared that they do not know how to write or sign, having been questioned after the reading was done, according to the ordinance. It has been agreed that the twenty words scratched out are null and void.

Signed,

La Gorgendiere, Dumontier, Alavoyne, Bergeron, and P. Raimbault, notary"[11]

It is extremely likely that, among the three paddling partners, at least Georges Brault and Pierre Tabault were highly experienced in dealing with the challenges of transporting freight by canoe, and that they had developed reputations as being very responsible in this business. Otherwise, the trio would not have been given the hauling contract, including the promise by the hirers of *"first preference in doing the said transporting to the said Fort Frontenac, as much during the present summer and autumn as during the navigation seasons of the following years, as much as it will be in their power."* However, all three of the men may have garnered their experience during earlier unlicensed, illegal ventures, since no documentation of their participation in the fur trade had been entered into public records before this particular day in 1702.

On the same day, another three-man crew was also hired by Monsieur Fleury to carry out cargo runs to and from Ft. Frontenac. One of these latter voyageurs was Louis Mallet, age 29, who had been married to Junior's sister Jeanne for nearly five years. They resided on the second farm east of the Brunet property. Their first child had died at the age of two weeks back in 1698, but their second one was now 25 months old and thriving. Louis' two partners during these multiple trips would be Louis Rose and Jean Baptiste Gros dit Laviolette. The latter man, 28 years old, was likewise a resident of Lachine. He and his wife Marie Buet, having been married for eighteen months (Junior had been one of the witnesses at their wedding), had one child who was eight months old.[12]

Two days later, Monsieur Fleury engaged an additional four voyageurs to paddle to and from Ft. Frontenac. These were Jean Gabriel Picard (from Lachine, age 33 and married), Toussaint Dardenne (from Montreal, 31 and single), Jean Baptiste Jarry (from Montreal, 36 and single), and Pierre Lat (from Lachine, 34 and married). It is highly likely that these four paddlers were hired to man two canoes, rather than a single craft. From the 1680s through the first decade of the following century, French cargo canoes were usually paddled by crews of three, and sometimes only two, voyageurs. It would only be during the 1710s and 1720s that crews of three, and more often four or five men, would become the norm. Over the course of these five decades, the canoes which were utilized would range up to a maximum of 32 feet in length; this latter size had been documented as early as 1670.[13]

In addition to these ten voyageurs who were engaged in May of 1702 to haul freight along the upper St. Lawrence River to and from Ft. Frontenac, another seventeen men were hired via Montreal notary contracts to paddle to other destinations in the west during this year. Hired between April 12 and May 13, these individuals included two men who were engaged by a single hirer to travel to Michilimackinac; another three men who were contracted by this same hirer to travel to the Illinois Country; and twelve men who were engaged by a single hirer to travel to the Mississippi River. Later in the summer, forty voyageurs were engaged by the Company of the Colony of Canada on July 16 to travel to Ft. Pontchartrain at Detroit, in order to retrieve the accumulated peltries there. (Robert Réaume, whose biography has already been presented in this work, was one of those paddlers.) On September 26, an additional five men were hired by the same Company to paddle to the same destination at Detroit.[14]

At this point, besides Ft. Pontchartrain (which had been established by Cadillac at Detroit in 1701), very few of the interior posts were being operated legally. Back in 1698, in response to the massive overstock of peltries (especially beavers) which were held in the storage facilities of the monopoly company in France, most of the posts in the west had been closed, and the French troops had been withdrawn to the St. Lawrence Valley. Trade was allowed to continue only at Ft. Frontenac, the post at Chicago and Ft. St. Louis in the Illinois Country, and Ft. Tourette/La Maune at the northern end of Lake Nipigon, north of Lake Superior. Late in 1701, shortly after the Detroit facility had been founded, the Company of the Colony of Canada had been formed by a number of wealthy investors and businessmen. This firm had then acquired the monopoly of the beaver exports of the entire colony, as well as the monopoly of the trade at Ft. Frontenac and Ft. Pontchartrain, along with the responsibility of covering the expenses of these latter two facilities.[15]

The paddling route on the upper St. Lawrence River between Lachine and Ft. Frontenac, consisting of about 210 miles of waterway, has already been described in considerable detail in the biography of François Brunet, Sr. Back in 1684, La Salle had thus described various aspects of the work of the voyageurs who had been handling the transportation for his Ft. Frontenac operations at that time:

"The [paired] canoe men now get [as a team] eight francs [livres] per hundredweight [of cargo hauled] in place of twelve [livres], the price which was paid before the barques were constructed. Two men carry, on each voyage, twelve to thirteen hundredweight, and ordinarily take twelve to fifteen days in going up [against the current] and four or five [days] in coming down [with both the current and the prevailing westerly winds]. Thus, they can make ten or twelve voyages [per paddling season], and consequently, transport from twelve to thirteen thousand weight from the opening of navigation in the month of April until the end of November, when it is closed by the ice at Montreal. When they are returning, they are obliged to bring back as much peltry as the canoes can hold without [additional] payment, so that the return does not increase the expense."[16]

Back in Senior's day on this route, during 1675 and 1676, he and his partner had together earned 110 livres for each round trip, hauling merchandise and supplies westward to this post and then peltries eastward to Montreal. However, the *barques* (relatively small ships propelled by sails) which had soon been constructed at Ft. Frontenac were sailed eastward from the fort for about eighty miles, on St.

Lawrence waters that lacked rapids, to a place where they met and took on the cargo of westbound voyageurs traveling in canoes from Lachine. These trips by the *barques* had shortened the distance that was covered by the paddlers, which in turn had enabled La Salle to negotiate a decrease in the canoe handlers' wages. As a result, the new pay scale had encouraged the two-man voyageur teams to transport more cargo on each journey, since they were then paid per hundred pounds of weight hauled. Compared to the 110 livres garnered by the Brunet-Boursier team for each journey, if a team of paddlers in the 1680s had hauled 1200 pounds of cargo to the fort, they would have together earned 96 livres. If they could manage 1300 pounds, their combined take would have increased to 104 livres.

By Junior's time in 1702, the pay scale had been averaged out at 10 livres per hundred pounds of cargo transported the full distance to the fort, compared to the former rates of 12 and 8 livres from the 1680s. Thus, if he, Brault, and Tabault would haul 1200 or 1300 pounds of freight west, they would garner 120 or 130 livres for that inbound leg of the voyage. Adding the 20 livres more for transporting a canoe load of peltries eastward on the outbound leg, they could earn a total of 140 or 150 livres per trip, to be split between the three paddlers. However, since this crew consisted of three men rather than two, they may have been able to haul more westbound merchandise and supplies, possibly utilizing a larger canoe, than the loads that the voyageurs had transported during the 1680s (thus generating more profit during their westbound leg of the journey). Their 1702 contract mentioned that they had paid 145 livres to purchase the canoe that they would use for carrying out this labor. However, this document did not indicate whether it was a new or used craft, nor did it provide any other descriptive information. As a result, it is not possible to determine the size of their canoe.

La Salle's assertion that a pair of voyageurs could carry out ten or twelve round-trip voyages to Ft. Frontenac during the seven-month paddling season was an exaggeration. According to his own information, an average round trip required three weeks to complete. Thus, it would have been technically possible to carry out about ten trips during the period between the spring thaw and the fall freeze, between April and November. However, such an intensely grueling schedule, with virtually no rest days during the entire period, would not have been sensible for any paddlers who intended to sustain long-term careers. Allowing for a few days of rest between voyages, during which the men would recuperate in the St. Lawrence settlements, would have created a time frame of nearly one month per trip. This would have allowed a maximum of about seven or eight journeys during the unfrozen months, at the most. Even the voyageurs who made round trips to the distant west during a single summer, laboring over the course of the span of six months, usually had a short period of lighter duty at their destination point in the interior, before they commenced their grueling return leg of the trip. However, more crucial in determining the number of journeys to and from Ft. Frontenac was the amount of cargo that was available to be hauled. Four different crews had been engaged to make these runs during this particular summer. Thus, their respective work loads would have been based upon the amounts of westbound merchandise and supplies and eastbound furs and hides which would be waiting at each end of the route. But it must be remembered that the Brunet-Brault-Tabault crew was promised "first preference" in this transport work, above the other three crews that had also been hired.

In examining the ten men who had been contracted for the Montreal-to-Ft. Frontenac route during this year of 1702, François, Jr. was by far the youngest, having been hired on his 20th birthday. The ages of the other *engagés*, which ranged from 36 down to 26, were 36, 34, 34, 33, 31, 29, 28, and 26. Not including the age of Louis Rose (which is not known) or the age of Junior, the average age of these other eight paddlers was 31.4 years. In addition, four of these men were married, and a fifth (Pierre Tabault) would soon marry Junior's sister Catherine. From these facts, it is clear that Monsieur Brunet dit Le Bourbonnais was by far the youngest, and probably also the least experienced, among this group of ten voyageurs. That dubious distinction may have earned for him a considerable amount of friendly ribbing from his colleagues.

Four weeks after signing on for this serial employment, Junior, his brother-in-law Georges Brault, and his soon-to-be brother-in-law Pierre Tabault all lost a major figure in their lives. For some time, François, Sr. had been afflicted with pleurisy, an inflammation of the pleura, the thin membrane that covers the lungs and also lines the chest cavity. Sufferers of this disease usually experienced difficult and painful breathing, which was often accompanied by the exuding of liquid into the chest cavity. Finally, on June 23, 1702, Senior passed away in his own bed at home. After his funeral at the Lachine church, the priest recorded in the parish ledger that "Burial was done in the presence of his wife, children, relatives, and friends." Since the names of the witnesses were not noted by the cleric, it is not possible to determine whether the three paddling partners were present on this sad occasion, or whether they were away on one of their journeys to Ft. Frontenac.[17]

Less than half a year later, additional deep grief gripped the clan, when a horrendous epidemic of smallpox swept through the St. Lawrence settlements during the latter part of 1702. This scourge continued at least through the following spring. At the Georges Brault household (immediately west of the Brunet farm), the disease caused François' sister Barbe to deliver her male baby two months early, on December 18, after just seven months of gestation (according to the priest's notations in the parish register). The tiny lad was either stillborn or he died after just a few hours; he was buried in the Lachine cemetery on the same day, a week before Christmas. Eighteen days later, on January 3, 1703, little Marie Josèphe, the youngest member of the same family, was felled by smallpox at the age of $18^1/2$ months; her funeral was held two days later. On April 22, the priest recorded in the parish ledger that he had just interred baby Louis Roy, age $4^1/2$ weeks, a victim of smallpox. His parents, François Roy and Marie Cécire, lived about $1^1/2$ miles northeast of the Brunet farm, near the border of the Verdun fief. (François, Jr. had stood as the godfather of their previous baby back in 1701.) Two days later, on the Louis Mallet farm (just east of the Brunet home), François' sister Jeanne delivered a baby girl, who was either stillborn or she died after a very short time; she was buried on the following day, April 25. The priest did not indicate whether the death of this infant had been caused by the raging smallpox epidemic. During the course of this vicious outbreak, some 250 residents of Montreal Island died of the disease, and about a quarter of the population of the town of Quebec.[18]

Eight days before the Mallet baby's death, on April 16, François' sister Catherine (two weeks short of her 23rd birthday) and his paddling partner Pierre Tabault were wed in the old wooden church at Lachine. Three months later, the brand new edifice built of field stones was dedicated, amid considerable festivities. Unfortunately, François, Sr. had not lived long enough to enjoy the prominently-located pew that he had leased in perpetuity for his family within this new building.[19]

For some unrecorded reason, when the contracts were drawn up on May 13, 1703 for the voyageurs who would carry out the trips to and from Ft. Frontenac this year, François Brunet, Jr. was not included. As before, one of the crews was headed by his brother-in-law Georges Brault dit Pomainville, who had lost the younger two of his four children in the previous autumn, during the fearsome epidemic. This year, his two paddling partners on these multiple runs would be his two Lachine-based brothers. The elder one, Jean Baptiste, age 29, owned the third farm east of the Brunet property; he would marry François' sister Élisabeth Brunet in six months. Younger brother Joseph, age 27, had been married to Marie Anne Marchand for five weeks. The other contract for Ft. Frontenac voyageurs which was approved by François Dumontier dit Brillant on this same day of May 13 engaged four men. These included three repeats from the previous year, namely Jean Baptiste Gros, Jean Baptiste Jarry, and Jean Gabriel Picard, plus the addition of the new man Louis Roy. Again, it is highly likely that these latter four paddlers would form the crews of two canoes.[20]

During the early summer of 1703, if François had been occupied hauling freight with his in-laws on the upper St. Lawrence River, he may not have had either the time or the energy to get into serious trouble. However, such was not the case, and he eventually did find himself in legal, social, ecclesiastical, and financial difficulties as a result of certain of his actions during this period. His offense: impregnating the young wife of an elderly trader who was off working in the distant interior.

The merchant-outfitter, investor, and trader Alexandre Turpin had been based for many years at Montreal, but he had been residing for the previous two years in the Bout de l'Île area, near the western end of Montreal Island. Earlier, he had been married to François Brunet's maternal aunt Marie Charlotte Beauvais for eighteen years, until her death on Christmas Day in 1700. (At the time of their marriage in October of 1684, François, Jr. had been $2^1/2$ years old.) Some fourteen months after her death, in February of 1702, Alex (about 61 or 62 years old) had married the Lachine resident Marie Gauthier, when she had been two months short of turning age 18. Through this marriage, this young woman had instantly become the stepmother of six children, who ranged in age from $16^1/4$ years down to 14 months. About seven months after the wedding, Monsieur Turpin had departed with the September brigade for the west, where he would work from his base of operations at St. Ignace during the following two years. It is extremely likely that he and his employees had left Montreal at this time without legal permission. Unfortunately, he owed to the prominent Montreal merchant Charles de Couagne several years worth of overdue annual payments on a long-term cash loan. At about the time of his departure, the Montreal Court had declared that he was obliged to pay the overdue amounts on this loan. As a result, the new bride Marie Gauthier had found herself having to handle not only her newly-acquired family of six children, but also this extra financial burden during her husband's extended absence.

In response, she had handed over the merchant creditor quantities of wheat and peas, a cow, and two mattresses as partial payment on the debt, after which she had leased out their land at Bout de l'Île. Then she had relocated with her children to the eastern section of the seigneury of Lachine, where her elderly father and most of her siblings lived, both those who were married and those who were still single.[21]

In about mid-to-latter June of 1703, some two months after she had celebrated her 19th birthday and about nine months after her husband Alexandre Turpin had departed for the interior, Marie became *enceinte*. On February 18, 1704, when she was about eight months pregnant, she traveled from Lachine to Montreal, in order to testify before the Montreal Court in a paternity case concerning her soon-to-be-born child. The records of the Court, written by the notary Antoine Adhémar, thus summarized her testimony and the resulting decisions of the judges:

"Marie Gauthier, wife of Alexandre Turpin, stated that her husband having deserted her to go to the Ottawa Country, she had the misfortune to become pregnant due to the unwelcome solicitation of François Brunet dit Le Bourbonnais [Jr.], son of the deceased other François Brunet dit Le Bourbonnais [Sr.], who seduced her while she was living at the home of her family at the Sault de St. Louis [section of the Lachine seigneury]."

After the judges had conferred, they sent a communication of their decisions to the King's Attorney at Quebec. These decisions demanded that Marie Gauthier care for the child, that François Brunet be summoned to respond to these charges, and that he pay for the expenses of the delivery and the feeding of the child. In addition, the Chief Judge, Jacques Alexis Fleury, Sieur de Deschambault, ordered Marie to care for the child, to have it baptized, and to report back to the Court concerning the delivery. (Between 1701 and 1760, the average rate of illegitimacy in the colony was $8/10$ of 1 percent, or 8 out of 1,000 births.)[22]

One month later, on March 20, Marie safely delivered the baby. After the tiny boy's baptism on the following day at the Lachine church, the priest recorded in the parish ledger various events that had taken place during March 20 and 21:

"Was baptized François, son of Marie Gauthier, wife of Alexandre Turpin, fencing master, by whom she was deserted for the past several [eighteen] months. The said child was born [yesterday]...at the cabin of Denise Marié, widow of Jean Quenneville, royal bailiff of Montreal, deceased...who with the said Gauthier took refuge at the fort of this church [Ft. Rémy, the stockaded Lachine village site]. The said Denise Marié, who had served as midwife and had assisted in the delivery, served as the godfather, and she also served as the godmother of the child. Following the request which she told me that the said Gauthier had made to her, she named this child François, the name of his father."[23]

In this entry, the cleric noted that the two women, carrying the baby, had left the midwife's home (on the third lot east of the palisade-enclosed village, which was called Ft. Rémy) and "took refuge at the fort of this church." However, he gave no explanation as to what concerns they may have felt which had induced them to seek this stockaded haven of safety. Attacks by marauding Iroquois war parties were not longer a concern, ever since the Great Treaty had been ratified nearly three years earlier. Might they have harbored concerns that either some members of Marie Gauthier's family, or certain members of the birth father François Brunet's family, might attempt to lay claim to the illegitimate baby for themselves? Both of these families resided at Sault St. Louis, which was the eastern section of the Lachine seigneury.

François Brunet, Jr., who was two months short of turning 22 at the time of the infant's arrival, must have paid the expenses as ordered by the Montreal Court. Support for this assertion is the fact that no further mentions of the case were entered into the official records of the Court.

Five months earlier, back in October of 1703, Junior's mother Barbe Beauvais had leased out the family farm to Joseph Brault dit Pomainville. He was one of the three Brault brothers who had undertaken the transport duties between Montreal and Ft. Frontenac during the shipping season of 1703. At the time of this lease, François' sister Élisabeth (age 18), was about six weeks away from her marriage to Jean Baptiste Brault, after which the couple would settle on his farm, which was the third lot east of the Brunet land. Thus, not counting

François, only his siblings Marie (age 16), Angélique (12), and Louis (6) were truly living at home by this point. So the addition of the second resident family there (Joseph Brault, his wife Marie Anne Marchand, and her four children from her first marriage) would not cause much crowding in a home that had once teemed with an entire array of active Brunet offspring. Since Barbe arranged this lease of the farm in the name of herself, her five underage children (including François), and her son Jean who lived permanently in the Illinois Country, all seven of them would divide the lease payments that would be made by Joseph Brault as the lease would proceed over time.[24]

On February 13, 1705, François purchased a piece of land that was located along the southern shore of Montreal Island. He acquired this property from the Lachine residents Jean Auger dit Lafleur et Liborne and his wife Élisabeth Dagenais, a young couple who had been married for seven years and had produced four children. However, it is unlikely that François ever applied much effort in developing this particular land, since he purchased a portion of the property that belonged to his brother-in-law Georges Brault and his sister Barbe Brunet three months later. In addition, seven years after buying the Auger-Dagenais lot, he would abandon it to the Sulpician seigneurs.

The property that François acquired from his relatives in 1705, purchased in partnership with his new brother-in-law Jean Baptiste Brault dit Pomainville (Georges' brother, and the third member of the Ft. Frontenac paddling crew of 1703) was located immediately west of the Brunet farm. This land, which was transferred to Junior and Jean Baptiste on May 21, consisted of a portion of the double lot containing 1,150 feet of St. Lawrence frontage that Georges and Barbe had bought seven years earlier, back in 1698.[25]

Nine days after arranging this land purchase, François signed on to make a round trip voyage to Ft. Pontchartrain, during which he would haul supplies and merchandise westward and then peltries back eastward.

"Were present...François Brunet dit Le Bourbonnais...Jean Tabault [who would marry François' sister Angélique five years later, in 1710]...[and 42 other men], for the one part, and Jacques Urbain Rocbert, Sieur de la Morandière, principal clerk for the Gentlemen of the Company of the Colony of Canada at Montreal, representing the Gentlemen of the Company, for the other part. These parties have voluntarily acknowledged and declared that they have made the contracts and agreements which follow. That is to say, the said...Brunet...Tabault [etc.]...have engaged themselves, promised,

and promise to go to Fort Pontchartrain on Lake Erie for the service of the Gentlemen of the Company, to depart from this town at the first request which will be made of them, to come back down in the present year, to obey and do everything for the service of the said Company during the said voyage which will be commanded of them by Monsieur De Jordy, who will command the said convoy, or those whom he may appoint for these ends, and to assist, in going up and returning, in taking the loaded canoes of the said Company, taking as much care as will be possible. If the said employees, or any of them, by their laziness, mischievousness, or ill will should not be obedient in doing what will be commanded of them in their service to the said Company, they shall be sent back, and according to the records of the clerk of the said Company, they shall have their wages reduced, after determining the portion of damage and detriment which has been done to the said Company. The said employees will not be permitted to leave or quit the said service nor be allowed to return to this said town without a written permit from the said Sieur De Jordy or someone who has been so instructed by him. Nor shall the said employees do any wrong in the gardening operations of the said Fort Le Pontchartrain, under the penalty that all expenses, damages, and interests shall be taken from the wages and salaries of those who caused the said damage. In addition, each of the said employees shall take one gun and one axe, which they shall purchase at their own cost and expense, and upon coming out, they will bring out their gun.

It is expressly agreed between the said Sieur de La Morandière and the said employees that the said employees will not carry out any trading for their own profit, either in going to the said Fort, while staying there, or during their return, in such a way that is either direct or indirect, under the penalty of the loss of their wages and salaries and the loss of the merchandise which might be found belonging to them and the peltries which they might have been able to trade, which will be for the profit of the said Company, to which the said employees have submitted and subjected themselves by these presents.

This bargain is made with the stipulation that the said employees shall be fed during their said voyage and their stay at the said Fort at the expense of the said Company, according to the customary manner of voyageurs, and in addition in consideration of the sum of 150 livres of the country for each of the said employees for their wages and salaries during the said voyage. The said Gentlemen of the Company will pay this sum to them upon their return, in letters of exchange on the Office of Beaver for France, with the retention of twelve percent for the support of their legal representatives, who work in particular for their benefit and by whom the said employees are represented to the said Sieur de La Morandière.

If the half-gallon of brandy which the Gentlemen of the Company give to each employee for his voyage to the said Fort is not sufficient for them to take, it will be requested of the said Sieur de La Morandière that each of them may be permitted to take at his own expense two [additional] half-gallons to drink during the said time. In addition, concerning the half-gallon which the said Company gives to them, to which the said Sieur de La Morandière has given permission, any of the said employees will be permitted to save the said brandy or part of it. But the said employees will not be permitted in any manner to either trade or sell it to the Frenchmen or the natives [in the interior], under the penalty of the loss of their wages and salaries and the loss of the peltries which might be found belonging to them, which will all be for the profit of the said Company. Thus, having reached agreement between the parties, they have promised, obligated themselves, waived, etc.

[This agreement] made and drawn up at the said Villemarie in the office of the said Gentlemen of the Company, in the year 1705 on the 30th day of May in the afternoon, in the presence of Sieurs Pierre Cabazier and Thomas Quenet, attorneys in civil cases as witnesses residing at the said Villemarie, who have signed below with the said Sieurs de La Morandière, [the voyageurs] De Couagne, Lacroix, Demers, Moreau, Rivard, Lécuyer, Frigon, Morisseau, Desbroyeux, [Jean Lemire dit] Marsolet, Filiatrault, Pierre Beauchamp, Roy dit Châtellerault, and the notary. The said others named above [including François Brunet and Jean Tabault] have declared that they do not know how to write or sign, having been questioned after the reading was done, according to the ordinance.

Signed,

François Desbroyeux, Lamorandiere, M. Demers, Robert Rivard, Edmond Roy, Pierre Lecuyer, Pierre Bauchans, J. B. Frigon, C. De Couagne, Jean Lemire, Joseph Moreau, Filiatro, Pierre Morissau, [Charles] Cabazie, and Adhemar, notary."[26]

According to the portion of this contract which was not quoted here (the list of names of all 44 of the men), these particular hirees hailed from Montreal, various other locales on Montreal Island, Laprairie, Contrecoeur, Champlain, Batiscan, and Ste. Anne. On this same day of May 30, an additional thirteen voyageurs were also hired to make the same run to and from Detroit. This second contract, which was drawn up by the same notary Adhémar, contained virtually the same terminology and stipulations.[27]

Several of the details of these two agreements are of particular interest. Probably the most important of these unusual stipulations was the one indicating that a full 12 percent of each man's earnings from this season of labor was to be relinquished "for the support of their legal representatives, who work in particular for their benefit and by whom the said employees are represented to the said Sieur de La Morandière." It was extremely rare for voyageurs or voyageur-traders to employ legal representatives when they officially drew up the details of their employment. However, in the case of Ft. Pontchartrain, large numbers of paddlers were engaged in massed groups for making summer round trips to this facility. In arranging this process, some devious and highly-placed individuals had decided that each of these *engagés* would be systematically bilked, by having a "legal representation fee" deducted from his wages.

The prohibition in the men's contract against causing damage to the *jardinages* (gardening operations) at Detroit was likewise very unusual in fur trade agreements. It must have been inserted as a standard phrase in the Detroit hiring documents after one or more paddlers had indeed caused such damage during their temporary stay at this interior settlement. The incident in question had most likely occurred when some voyageurs had been caught raiding the gardens or orchards for produce to consume or to sell.

Each of the hirees for the Ft. Pontchartrain convoy was obliged to carry a gun and an axe with him during the entire run. This stipulation transformed the party into a well-armed militia force. It was made abundantly clear in the contract that each man was to bring his gun out to the St. Lawrence settlements during the return leg of the voyage. No one would be permitted to trade or sell his weapon en route, in order to generate some additional profit. Oddly enough, the axe that each voyageur was required to take in was not specifically mentioned as something that he was obligated to bring out. However, each hiree was expressly prohibited from conducting any trading while in the interior. Thus, it is to be presumed that each man was barred from trading his axe during the journey.

Some 1 1/2 years earlier, back in latter 1703, the Company of the Colony of Canada had relinquished control of Ft. Frontenac and its fur trade. At that time, the firm had allowed this facility at the eastern end of Lake Ontario to return to the control of the Crown. This move had instigated a new mode of transportation between Lachine and this particular fort. Since all of the soldiers were employees of the King, certain selected men among them were thereafter drawn from this large pool of labor to undertake the duty of hauling cargo by watercraft. This transport, which had formerly been carried out by highly skilled voyageurs in birchbark canoes, was now conducted by semi-skilled troops in wooden *bateaux*, wooden boats which were propelled with oars. These craft were supplemented by somewhat larger *barques* (small sailing vessels) on the westernmost section of the route, the eighty-mile portion which contained no rapids. This loss of potential employment on the Lachine-to-Ft. Frontenac route had led numerous voyageurs (including François Brunet and various of his brothers-in-law) to switch their attentions to the Lachine-to-Ft. Pontchartrain route. This switch in focus was clearly illustrated by the hiring contracts of 1705, which engaged François and Jean Tabault to haul cargo on the latter route to and from Detroit.[28]

François returned home to the Lachine seigneury in about September or October of this year. At about this time, when he was $23^1/3$ years old, he must have decided that it was the appropriate time for him to take a bride and commence a family. At some point, either before or shortly after his labors with the Detroit convoy, he met and became infatuated with Marie Françoise David, a resident of the seigneury of Champlain, which was located to the east of Trois-Rivières, some 100 miles down the St. Lawrence from Lachine. This young woman, who would usually be called Françoise during her lifetime, had turned age 20 in November of 1704. She was the *petite-fille* (granddaughter) of Claude David, Sr., one of the pioneering traders of the western Great Lakes region, who had spent the period of 1660-1663 on Lake Superior (his biography has already been presented in this work). She was also the niece of her maternal uncle Pierre Couillard (likewise originally from Champlain), who had married François' sister Anne Brunet $6^1/2$ years earlier, back in February of 1699, and had settled with his bride in the Lachine seigneury. This particular uncle had also been Françoise's supplemental or deputy guardian all of her life. It was presumably this Brunet-Couillard family relationship that ultimately led to the mutual connection and commitment between François Brunet and Françoise David.[29]

Françoise had arrived in this world on about November 11, 1684, as the first child of Claude David, Jr. and Marie Jeanne Couillard, born some ten months after their wedding. However, within just a couple of weeks, Claude, Jr. had died suddenly, a few weeks before his 28th birthday. It is highly likely that his untimely demise had been caused by the virulent Spanish influenza which the men of the army had brought back with them from their Lake Ontario campaign against the Iroquois in August, which had then raged through the colony for months afterward. During this terrible time, it is entirely possible that the priests in the entire region had been so involved in innumerable ceremonies of Last Rites, funerals, and grave-site burials that they had postponed and eventually had overlooked entirely the baptism of the newborn lass. That is most likely why no record of her birth and christening may be found in any church documents in the colony. Likewise, no information concerning the death and burial of Claude, Jr. are to be found in the ecclesiastical records. Again, this may testify to the overextended condition of the priests during this months-long epidemic, when even the accurate recording of each burial in the church ledgers may have been occasionally overlooked. However, on December 20, 1684, probably within weeks of the demise of Claude, Jr., an inventory of the possessions of the young couple had been conducted at their farm at Bécancour, directly across the St. Lawrence from Trois-Rivières. In this document, the infant Marie Françoise had been described as "age one month and nine days or thereabouts." Two days before this inventory had been carried out, Claude David, Sr., the baby's grandfather, had been declared as her legal guardian by the Trois-Rivières Court, while her uncle Pierre Couillard had been declared as her supplemental or deputy guardian.[30]

Her widowed mother, Marie Jeanne Couillard, only about 15 years old at this time, had then apparently moved with her infant daughter back across the St. Lawrence to the Champlain seigneury, to reside with her parents and siblings. It was there that she had remarried in February of 1694, after more than nine years of widowhood, to the retired soldier Jacques Valois. Settling at Champlain, this couple had produced six younger half-siblings of Françoise between 1695 and 1704. At least four of these six latter children would survive and grow up to adulthood; however, the youngest had died at the age of just four weeks in May of 1704. Sadly, Françoise's mother Marie Jeanne herself had passed away two weeks earlier, from complications resulting from the birth of this lattermost baby. She had been laid to rest in the Champlain cemetery on April 20, at about 35 years of age. Two weeks before this mournful occasion, on the day of the infant's arrival on April 6, Françoise (then age 19 1/2) had stood as his godmother in the church at Champlain, along with Alexis Lepellé as the godfather. Seven weeks later, on May 27, these same two individuals had again appeared as godparents, that second time for the newborn daughter of Antoine Desrosiers and Marie Renée Lepellé.[31]

François and Françoise planned to exchange their nuptial vows in her home church, Notre Dame de la Visitation at Champlain, on January 25, 1706. In advance of this occasion, Fr. Rémy, the pastor of François' church at Lachine, published the first two banns of marriage at Lachine. The Bishop then dispensed with the third customary bann, which was usually obligatory. At the uplifting ceremony in her home parish in January, the official witnesses on the bride's side were her stepfather Jacques Valois and her grandfather Pierre Couillard from Champlain, and her cousins René David and Jean David from Bécancour. On the groom's side, the sole witness was his uncle the royal notary Jean Baptiste Pothiers, who was married to François' aunt Marie Étiennette Beauvais; this couple had relocated from Lachine to Trois-Rivières back in 1703.[32]

Shortly after the newly-married Brunet couple had returned to Montreal Island, twelve days after their wedding, they visited the Montreal notary Adhémar to make a land transfer. On February 6, they together sold a piece of property in the seigneury of Bécancour, which belonged to Françoise by inheritance from either her deceased father or her paternal grandfather, Claude David, Jr. or Claude David, Sr. The recipient of the land was her cousin Jean David dit Lacourse, a resident of this same seigneury, who had been one of the witnesses at their marriage. As a threesome, they had apparently agreed to conduct this transaction when they had all been assembled two weeks earlier, at the time of the wedding gathering at Champlain.[33]

In this document, the notary identified François and Françoise as residents of Sault St. Louis. This statement indicated that they had set up housekeeping on the piece of land immediately west of the Brunet family farm, which he had acquired from his sister Barbe and her husband Georges Brault nine months earlier, back in May of the previous year of 1705. François had made this purchase in partnership with his brother-in-law Jean Baptiste Brault, who was married to François' sister Élisabeth.

Five weeks before they would commemorate their first wedding anniversary, celebrations were in order for François and Françoise, as well as for the entire Brunet clan. On December 18, 1706, they were elated at the safe delivery of their first child, little Françoise. At her baptism in the Lachine church on the same day, the sponsors of the infant were her grandmother Barbe Beauvais and her great-uncle Pierre Couillard. This was the first Brunet-named grandchild whom Barbe had ever held. By this point, her eldest son Jean Brunet and his native wife Élisabeth Deshayes had produced one daughter in the

Illinois Country. However, it is very unlikely that Barbe and François, Sr. had ever had the opportunity to meet this distant daughter-in-law or this grandchild.[34]

Unfortunately, the newborn Françoise would not grow up to reach adulthood. The only documentation concerning her time on earth would be the record of her baptism, which was held on the day of her birth. Thus, it is not possible to determine just when this girl's parents were forced to endure the anguish of the death of their first child.

About six weeks after this baby had been born, on February 7, 1707, François' sister Marie, who was 19^2/$_3$ years old, was married in the Lachine church. Her husband was Pierre Caillé dit Biscornet, who had been born and raised at Laprairie, on the eastern shore of the St. Lawrence about seven miles east of the Brunet farm. Settling at Laprairie, these newlyweds would be the second couple within the extended Brunet clan to settle in some other seigneury than Lachine. (The other couple, Catherine Brunet and Pierre Tabault, resided about 3^1/$_2$ miles west of the Lachine village, in the seigneury of La Présentation.)[35]

Within weeks of this inspiring wedding, François and his brothers-in-law Georges Brault and Jean Baptiste Brault finalized their preparations for the coming trading season. These partners and their families all lived in very close proximity to each other beside the Lachine Rapids, within a span of ^{7}/$_{10}$ mile. Georges' property was located immediately east of the terminus of the Lachine-to-Montreal portage road and the Commons land. In adjacent succession to the east of his double lot lay the Brunet family land, followed by the plots belonging to Paul Lécuyer dit Lapierre, Louis Mallet (also a voyageur brother-in-law), and Jean Baptiste Brault. Further binding the three fur trade partners together, two years earlier, François and Jean Baptiste had jointly purchased a portion of Georges' land.

Until this point in the spring of 1707, when François was approaching his 25th birthday, the only legal fur trade employment that had been documented for him had been his labors as a salary-earning voyageur, hauling freight for his employers. According to his hiring contracts, he had actually been barred from carrying out any trading during his journeys to and from Ft. Frontenac in 1702, and to and from Ft. Pontchartrain in 1705. However, it is entirely possible that he and certain of his brothers-in-law had together conducted illegal, unlicensed peltries commerce in the interior during some of the years before, between, and after these publicly-recorded periods of employment. Now, he and two of his brothers by marriage determined that they would not only legally haul merchandise to the west but also publicly trade it with native customers there. In the process, they could generate considerably greater profits; but they would also bear the financial risks, which they had not done when they had worked as salaried employees.

Their plans for this year would involve hauling cargo westward to Ft. Pontchartrain for Captain Cadillac, trading their own merchandise during their stay at Detroit, and finally transporting out both the peltries belonging to the commandant as well as those which their own commerce had generated. If all went according to plan, these steps would all be completed during the coming five summer months, with a projected return to Montreal Island by August or September.

On April 5, the three partners acknowledged before the Montreal notary Le Pailleur their debt for the outfit that they had received from the merchant-outfitter Pierre Trottier, Sieur Desaulniers. This Montreal-based businessman, about 27 years old, had already been married for nearly eight years. He and his wife Catherine Charet were expecting their sixth child in about November.

"Before Michel Lepailleur, royal notary of the Island of Montreal, residing at Villemarie, undersigned with the witnesses named below, were present in person the Sieurs Georges Brault [dit] Pomainville, Jean [Baptiste] Brault [dit] Pomainville, and Sieur François Brunet, all three habitants of Lachine on this said Island. Being about to depart to go up to the Fort Pontchartrain at the Detroit [Strait] of Lake Erie, they have, in solidarity one for the other and each of them for the whole, without division or discussion, acknowledged and declared that they fairly and justly owe to the Sieur Pierre Trottier [Sieur] Desaulniers, merchant living in this town, present and assenting, the sum of five hundred livres for merchandise and good belongings which he has sold to them, as the goods which will serve as their outfit for their voyage, for which they are held accountable for its contents and with which they are satisfied. The said sum of five hundred livres the said debtors have promised and are obligated to render, give, and pay to the said Sieur Creditor or on his order upon their return from the said voyage, which will be at the latest during the entire month of August or the beginning of September next, in good peltries but without any beaver pelts, with the said peltries rated according to the current prices at the time of the said payment, or in currency, at the choice of the said creditor, all of this under the penalty of all

expenses, damages, and interests. This they have done in solidarity, as was mentioned, and they have obligated, given over, and mortgaged all of their belongings, both present and future...For the execution of these presents, the said debtors have selected as their [temporary] legal residence in this town [to which writs may be delivered] the home of Nicolas Pothier, baker, situated on St. Paul Street. Thus have they promised, obligated themselves, waived, etc.

[This agreement] made and drawn up at the said Villemarie at the home of the said Sieur Creditor, located on St. Paul Street, in the afternoon on the fifth day of April, 1707, in the presence of the Sieurs Jean Boudor, merchant bourgeois, and of Sieur Jean Baptiste Neveu, merchant, as witnesses living in the said Villemarie who have signed with the said Sieur Creditor and the notary. The said debtors have declared that they do not know how to write or sign, having been questioned according to the ordinance.
Signed,
Desoniers, Boudor, J.B. Neveu, and Lepailleur"[36]

During this same afternoon, the three partners also visited the office of the notary Adhémar, in order to draw up the record of their debt to the Montreal merchant bourgeois Antoine Pacaud. This outfitter, about 42 years of age, had been married to Marguerite Bouat for more than a decade; they were awaiting the arrival of their sixth baby in the coming December.

"Were present Sieurs Georges and Jean Brault [dit] Pomainville, brothers, and François Brunet dit Le Bourbonnais, habitants of the Sault St. Louis in the parish of Lachine on this Island, being at present in this town. They have acknowledged and declared that they owe, in solidarity one for the other and each of them for the whole, without division, discussion, or disloyalty, renouncing any such said divisions, to Antoine Pacaud, merchant bourgeois in this town, absent, the Sieur Pierre de Lestage [Sieur Despeiroux], his clerk, present and assenting for the said Sieur Pacaud, the sum of 256 livres 19 sols 4 deniers for the sale of merchandise which was sold and delivered to them by the said Sieur Pacaud on this day. This said sum...the said debtors have promised and obligated themselves to pay, in solidarity as mentioned above, to the said Sieur Pacaud or to the bearer during the course of the month of August next or at the latest when they will return from the voyage which they are going to make to the said Fort [Pontchartrain] of Lake Erie, in peltries or in currency but not in beaver pelts, at the choice of the said Sieur Pacaud, under the penalty of all expenses, damages, and interests, and under the mortgage of all of their belongings, both moveable and real estate and both present and future. For the execution of these presents, the said

debtors have selected as their [temporary] legal residence in this town [to which writs may be delivered] the home of the Sieur Nicolas Pothier, located on St. Paul Street. Thus have they promised....
Signed,
P. Delestage for Monsieur Pascaud, C. Villiers, A. Rivet, and Adhemar, notary"[37]

On the following day, the three partners apparently decided that they required certain additional articles from the store of Monsieur Pacaud. Thus, François, "both for himself and for Georges and Jean Brault dit Pomainville, brothers," returned to the same scribe's office, to acknowledge an additional debt of 115 livres 7 sols 6 deniers which they now owed to the merchant. This was the price "for the sale and delivery of merchandise to the said Brunet and to the said Brothers, which was done by the said Sieur Pacaud on this day." Virtually all of the other details of this document were identical to those within the agreement of the previous day. However, in this latter record, the notary identified the destination of the trio as "Fort Pontchartrain of Lake Erie." As on the day before, the two official witnesses were Charles Villiers and Alexandre Rivet. This second transaction increased the indebtedness of the three traders to Antoine Pacaud to a total of 372 livres 6 sols 10 deniers, which was due upon their return from Detroit.[38]

In total, they had acquired articles worth 500 livres from Monsieur Trottier and 372 livres plus change worth from Monsieur Pacaud. An outfit costing 872 livres was considered to be a rather modest one, by the usual standards, since a westbound crew would often spend up to 3,000 livres in assembling their entire outfit. However, the latter amount of expenses would typically include all of the equipment, supplies, and trade merchandise for a full venture of some 15 to 17 months in the west (including at least a year's worth of food supplies, before they would resupply at Michilimackinac for the outbound journey). It is entirely possible that the Brunet-Brault trio had already owned a considerable amount of the needed items before they had visited the two outfitters. In that case, they would have only required certain supplemental articles from the merchants, such as trade goods, to fill out their own possessions. In addition, the trio would have only a few weeks time to conduct all of their commerce at Detroit, before returning during the same paddling season with their garnered furs and hides as well as the commandant's peltries. Traders who spent up to 3,000 livres for their complete outfit typically had an entire year in the interior in which to trade all of their merchandise. Thus, without having the actual invoice listing the specific items that François and his partners had received from the two outfitters, it is not possible to determine just how extensive was the array of trade goods that they were to carry to the west.

During this same afternoon of April 6, all three of the partners again stood before Monsieur Adhémar, to ratify their employment contract with Captain Cadillac.

"Were present Sieur François Ardouin, merchant living in this town, conducting at present in this town the affairs of Monsieur Antoine de Lamothe Cadillac, Captain, Commandant for the King at the Fort Pontchartrain of Lake Erie, of the one part, and Georges and Jean Brault, brothers, and François Brunet dit Le Bourbonnais of the parish of Lachine on this Island, being at present in this town, of the other part. These parties have agreed to that which follows. That is to say, the said Brault brothers and the said Brunet have promised, in solidarity one for the other and each of them for the whole, without division, discussion, or disloyalty, renouncing any such said divisions, to depart from this town for the navigation which they will freely undertake in uprightness to the Fort Pontchartrain, and to take in the canoe in which they will go up for the said Sieur de Lamothe all of the weight of the merchandise that the said Sieur Ardouin will provide to them. When they will arrive at the said Fort Pontchartrain, they will place this into the hands and the possession of the said Sieur de Lamothe in good condition. In coming down, they will transport for the said Sieur de Lamothe to this town all of the weight of those peltries that the said Sieur de Lamothe will provide to them at the said Fort, returning it in this town to such person as will be ordered by the said Sieur de Lamothe, also all in good condition except for the rigors of the voyage. They shall not be permitted to request anything as their part from the transported [westbound] merchandise and [eastbound] peltries. [As remuneration] For going up, the said Sieur Ardouin has issued in their name a permit to trade the merchandise which they will transport for themselves, upon arriving at the said Fort Pontchartrain. Thus have they promised, obligated themselves, waived, etc.

[This agreement] made and drawn up at the said Villemarie in the office of the said notary in the year 1707, on the sixth day of April in the afternoon, in the presence of the Sieurs Charles Villiers, merchant, and Alexandre Rivet, witnesses living at the said Villemarie who have signed below with the said Sieur Ardouin and the notary. The said Brault brothers and the said Brunet have declared that they do not know how to write or sign, having been questioned after the reading was done, according to the ordinance.

Signed,
Ardouin, C. Villers, A. Rivet, and Adhemar, notary"[39]

It is particularly interesting to note the one sentence in this agreement which was originally written in by the notary but which was later lined out by him, when the contract was read aloud upon its completion so that all of the parties could hear the details and agree upon them. The sentence read: "The said Brault brothers and Brunet have promised to take as much care as is proper with the merchandise while going up and with the peltries while coming down." The elimination of this crucial sentence was a reflection of the lack of any salary being paid to the paddlers, and likewise the lack of any wages which could be reduced in case the cargo would be damaged en route.

It is of considerable interest that the three men agreed to receive no pay from Captain Cadillac, even though they would be hauling cargo in both directions for him. However, they did acquire a cost-free permit from his Montreal agent, which allowed them to trade at Ft. Pontchartrain. In addition, the commandant would not be charging them the fees which were customarily levied upon those traders who did not reside at Detroit but wished to conduct commerce there. (Those who did not own a lot within the community and have a house on it were usually required to pay a fee of 200 livres per round trip, or instead, to transport 300 pounds of merchandise in and 300 pounds of furs and hides out for the commandant.) Apparently, these two stipulations offered sufficient financial inducements for the trio to undertake this voyage, from which all of the proceeds from their trading activities would remain with themselves.

Starting with the previous year of 1706, the voyageurs and voyageur-traders who had been engaged to work at Detroit had been hired in individual crews of either two or three men, rather than by means of massed hiring sessions, as had previously been the custom. Thus, during this spring, summer, and autumn of 1707, the same new method of contracting individual teams of paddlers for each canoe was applied. From the Montreal notary documents, it is clear that the first brigade headed for Ft. Pontchartrain this year contained, besides the Brault-Brunet canoe, at least one other craft, which had three paddlers; these men were hired on April 13 to work at Detroit for the Sieur Bourgmont. However, based upon the dates of the later contracts, it is not possible to discern just how long these two craft waited before departing for the west. Nor is it possible to determine which of the later canoes were grouped together to form the later convoys.

Over the course of the summer, two three-man crews were hired on June 5 and 13 respectively, to work for Cadillac. These were followed by the contracting of other individuals for employment at Ft. Pontchartrain: one man on June 25, one man on July 15, a three-paddler crew on July 25, one man on July 31, and a two-man crew on August 2. Each of these contracts was drawn up by a different employer. For the final convoy of the season to Detroit, two crews were engaged to labor for Captain Cadillac: a two-man crew on September 22, and a three-man group on October 13. The date of this lattermost hiring underscores just how late into the autumn paddlers were sometimes able to set off on the more southerly St. Lawrence River route, headed for the interior by way of Lakes Ontario and Erie, compared to those voyageurs who traveled to the west along the more northerly Ottawa River route.[40]

As their three indebtedness contracts from 1707 indicated, the Brunet-Brault trio exited from the interior to the St. Lawrence settlements during the autumn of this same year. However, during the following summer, on June 20, 1708, the Detroit commandant granted to François a parcel of land within the stockade-enclosed community at Ft. Pontchartrain. This lot measured 20 feet along Rue Ste. Anne, which was the main north-south thoroughfare across the center of the settlement, and 22 feet in depth. According to Cadillac's records of his land grants between 1707 and 1710, this particular lot was flanked on both sides by properties that had not yet been granted to other individuals.[41]

Owning this lot would annually cost Monsieur Brunet 2 livres for the *rente* and 10 livres for other rights, particularly the right to carry out trade in the area. In a summary from September of 1708 of Cadillac's letters, the following paragraph presented the commandant's rationale for charging the residents of Detroit the lattermost fee, for the right to conduct commerce in furs and hides there:

"The King granted to him the trade of Detroit to the exclusion of all others. [Cadillac] believed that, for the advancement of this post, it would be expedient that he should give up his right [to this commerce] to everyone. And, as he was thus deprived of a certain revenue, he thought that he could impose a tax on all those whom he permitted to carry on this trade, to take the place of the favor which was granted to him by His Majesty."[42]

There is no documentary evidence which indicates that François Brunet was actually present in person at Detroit during this summer of 1708. None of the known hiring contracts drawn up by Montreal notaries indicate that he or his two Brault brothers-in-law were contracted to make a voyage there, nor did the trio make any arrangements with outfitters during this season.[43] In fact, François was definitely present at Lachine by November of this year, when he served as a wedding witness. Thus, it is highly likely that, during his former trading trip in 1707, he had expressed to Cadillac his wish to acquire a lot within the fort. He would have wanted to be considered a resident land holder, so that he would be permitted to conduct commerce at the facility during his future sojourns there, by simply paying the 12 livres in annual fees on his plot of land.

On November 6, 1708, François, his 17-year-old sister Angélique Brunet (who was still unmarried), and his brother-in-law Pierre Couillard (who had married François' sister Anne nearly a decade earlier, and was also the uncle of Françoise David) all stood as official witnesses at a wedding that was held in the Lachine church. On this occasion, the bride was the 27-year-old Lachine resident Geneviève Gignard, while the groom was René Couillard, Pierre's widowed older brother, age 41. In the seigneury of Champlain, he had been married for nine years and had produced three children, of whom two had survived and grown up. However, his wife had died back in 1699, after which he had lived as a widower for the next $8^1/2$ years, until this happy moment.[44]

Ten months later, François again stood as an official witness in this same edifice. However, this time it was not at the altar for a wedding, but instead at the baptismal font for a christening. On September 29, 1709, his sister Barbe and her husband Georges Brault had welcomed their seventh child into the world. On the same day, they traveled the $2^3/4$ miles westward from their farm to the Holy Angels church in the Lachine village. There, the baby's sponsors were his uncle François Brunet and the family friend Marie Perthuis, who was the wife of Vital Caron.[45]

Two months after this ceremony, Françoise took her turn as a baptismal sponsor, for yet another of the new babies who were being regularly born into the closely-spaced families of the Brunet clan living beside the Lachine Rapids. On *Ignolée* (New Year's Eve) of 1709, she stood in the Lachine church beside the two-day old daughter and second child of Élisabeth Brunet and her husband Jean

Baptiste Brault. The other sponsor on this uplifting day was Pierre Brault, the 27-year-old uncle of the baby, who had not yet married.[46]

During the winter of 1710, the severe weather was offset by a warmhearted celebration in the Brunet family: the wedding of François' youngest sister, who was also the last one to be married. On February 17, Angélique, who would turn 19 in April, was joined in matrimony to Jean Tabault, who was $27^1/2$ years old. They were already in-laws, since Jean's older brother Pierre had wed Angélique's older sister Catherine nearly seven years earlier, back in 1703. The newly wedded couple would soon relocate from Lachine to Montreal, where they would produce two children within the next seven years.[47]

It was not unusual in the smaller, closely-knit communities of New France for multiple siblings from one family to marry multiple siblings from another family. However, this phenomenon had occurred in double fashion in the Brunet dit Le Bourbonnais family. Not only had the Tabault brothers Pierre and Jean taken as brides the Brunet sisters Catherine and Angélique (in 1703 and 1710, respectively), the Brault brothers Georges and Jean Baptiste had married the Brunet sisters Barbe and Élisabeth (in 1696 and 1703, respectively). Besides these four men who were voyageurs or voyageur-traders, a fifth brother-in-law of François, Louis Mallet (who had married François' sister Marie Jeanne in 1697) was also employed in these same fur trade occupations. It was only his brothers-in-law Pierre Couillard and Pierre Caillé (who had married his sisters Anne and Marie in 1699 and 1707, respectively) for whom no clear peltries-related documentation has yet been found. However, the lack of public records concerning such activities certainly does not indicate that these individuals did not take part in the lucrative trade whenever it was possible for them to do so.

Throughout the colony, but especially in the regions of Montreal and Trois-Rivières, it was very common for a man to combine the labors of running his farm and working in the peltries commerce. These two occupations were often carried out in alternating seasons or years, based upon the opportunities for fur trade work that were either available or unavailable at various times. In a great many instances, men participated in illegal commerce in furs and hides whenever the opportunities presented themselves, as will be amply illustrated in future pages of this biography of François Brunet, Jr.

By this point, nine out of ten of the Brunet siblings had found soul mates and had married. The two older brothers and all seven of the sisters had spouses, and all but the newly-married Angélique had already produced offspring. Only Louis, the youngest sibling, who would turn 13 in May, was still living at home (he would remain single for another eleven years, until 1721).

Throughout nearly all of 1710, Françoise had been pregnant with their second child. However, the baby's arrival on October 17 did not bring great rejoicing to the little family or the clan. On the same day as her birth, the tiny lass died and was tearfully laid to rest without a name in the cemetery beside the Lachine church. (This lack of a name indicated that the child had not received an official baptism administered by a priest.) In the parish ledger, the cleric noted that the two official witnesses on this mournful occasion were François Quesnel and Monsieur Trudel.[48]

The grieving mother must have become pregnant again almost immediately, since she safely delivered their next baby just eight months and one week after the 1710 funeral. Little Marie Angélique was baptized on the day of her birth, June 23, 1711, with her uncle Louis Brunet as her godfather and her aunt Élisabeth Brunet as her godmother. (This girl, who would grow up to marry the voyageur Guillaume Lalonde Number 2, would provide the direct ancestral link between François and Françoise and the present author. The biography of this Lalonde-Brunet couple is offered later in this work.)[49]

In the Lachine parish register on this day, the officiating priest recorded that the newborn Marie Angélique was the daughter of "François Brunet, absent, and Françoise David." In this manner, the cleric was being both prudent and protective of his flock, not willing to publicly record the incriminating information that the father was away trading in the interior, quite possibly without official permission. No surviving documents reveal just where François traded for hides and pelts during this summer and autumn. As a result, it is not possible to determine whether he took advantage of his commercial rights at Detroit as a land owner there, or whether he instead headed for the Upper Country, traveling via the Ottawa River route to the regions that were far beyond the view and control of officials.

In the autumn, Françoise stood as the godmother for Pierre Couillard, the second child to be born to René Couillard and Geneviève Gignard. René was the brother of Françoise's uncle Pierre

Couillard, who was married to Anne Brunet. At the baby's christening ceremony on September 13, 1711, held in the Lachine church on the same day as his birth, the godfather was the Lachine resident Pierre Ozanne.[50]

François eventually returned to Lachine in time to spend the winter of 1712 with his little family on the farm. During the last week of February, he conducted two land transactions. First, on the 22nd, he purchased a portion of the Brunet family farm from his mother. Until this transfer, the double lot belonging to his parents, located immediately to the east of Georges Brault's property, had contained a total of 1,150 feet of frontage along the St. Lawrence River.[51] Three days later, on the 25th, François abandoned his rights to the property along the southern shoreline of Montreal Island, fronting on the shoreline of Lac St. Louis, which he had purchased nearly seven years earlier, back in May of 1705, from Jean Auger and Élisabeth Dagenais. On this date, since he had apparently done very little to improve this land during those seven years of ownership, he relinquished it to the seigneurs of Montreal Island, the Sulpicians.[52]

Both Françoise and François' younger brother Louis were ordered to testify before the Montreal Court in a case which ran from latter April until early August in this year of 1712. In this criminal case, four voyageur-traders were accused of having previously carried out illegal commerce at the Straits of Mackinac. According to the records of the proceedings, Jean Baptiste Réaume dit Le Borgne, Jacques Maret dit Lépine, Jean Magnan dit l'Espérance, and Jean Magdelaine dit Ladouceur were accused of having departed from the St. Lawrence without either a license or a permit, in order to "make a voyage to Michilimackinac" and "to the nations of the Upper Country, against the prohibitions of His Majesty." Their activities had allegedly also involved Pierre Juillet, who was accused of having assisted the four men by transporting from Montreal to Lachine a cart which was loaded with "considerable trade merchandise, in packing cases, bales, and boxes, plus black [imported] tobacco, three kegs of brandy, and one keg of wine."

Apparently, the Court officials strongly suspected that François Brunet was often involved in such activities at and around Lachine (*"Il n'y a pas de fumée sans feu,"* "There is no smoke without fire.") Yet they possessed no solid evidence which would link him to this particular case. The fact that François himself was not called to testify in this case clearly implies that he was off trading in the west at this time, either legally or illegally. However, on May 25, the officials did summon both his wife and his younger brother to appear on the following Monday at one o'clock in the chambers of Jacques Alexis Fleury, Sieur Deschambault, the *Lieutenant Général* (Chief Judge) of the Court. At that time, these two individuals would provide under oath whatever information they might be able to render concerning the activities of the five accused men during the period in question, which was probably back in 1711.

"Has appeared Marie Françoise David, wife of François Brunet, habitant of the Sault St. Louis, age twenty-six years [actually 27], who, after she had taken an oath to tell the truth, was asked and she declared that she is not related to nor allied as a servant or domestic with one or the other of the [accused] parties...She has said that, during the night before they [the accused four voyageurs] departed, she saw passing in front of her house a canoe conducted by one Réaume who lives near La Présentation [the respected trader Robert Réaume, older brother of the accused Jean Baptiste], which was going up the [Lachine] Rapids with another man whom she did not know. After two hours had passed, she also saw [walking] in front of her house [Jean Baptiste] Réaume [dit] Le Borgne, and after him a young blond man whom she did not know, who were going up to Lachine. This is everything that she has said. After her deposition was read to her, she has said that it is the truth, and she has declared that she does not know how to sign, having been questioned according to the ordinance. The pay to her [for her testimony] with tax is thirty sols [1.5 livres] of France."

Then it was Louis' turn to testify:

"Has appeared Louis Brunet, living at the home of François Brunet, his brother, at the Sault St. Louis, where he works as a farm laborer, age fifteen years or thereabouts. After he had taken an oath to tell the truth, he declared that he is not related to nor allied as a servant or domestic with one or the other of the [accused] parties...He has said that, on the evening that the above-named Réaume [dit] Le Borgne, Maret [dit] Lépine, Lespérance, and Ladouceur departed from this Island to go to the Ottawa Country, while he was coming from his work, he met Réaume [dit] Le Borgne, who was going toward Lachine. There was not anything which he could notice that was in his hands, nor was there any person with him. This is everything that he has said. After his deposition was read to him, he has said that it is the truth, and he has declared that he does not know how to sign, having been questioned according to the ordinance. The pay to him [for his testimony] with tax is twenty-two sols six deniers [1.15 livres] of France."

Ultimately, the verdict in this trial, which was announced on

August 8, decreed that each of the four voyageur-traders was to be employed on the King's galleys (laboring as rowers on his vessels in the Mediterranean Sea) for the rest of their lives. However, there is no evidence that this extreme sentence was ever carried out. Amnesty declarations for *coureurs de bois* had been quite common during the previous fourteen years, ever since the post closures of 1698, and they would continue to be equally common for the next several years. Thus, it is apparent that the sentences of these four traders were commuted at a later date. In fact, all four of them later participated in the trade legally, with their employment recorded publicly in notary contracts.[53]

François apparently did not return to the St. Lawrence settlements to spend the winter of 1713 with his family at Lachine. There are no church records which document his presence there during that particular period, and by the first week of May, when major legal difficulties arose with the authorities of the colony, he was nowhere to be found.

At this time, a number of his colleagues had been completing their final preparations in order to join him in the interior with an infusion of new merchandise. It is possible that their activities as *coureurs de bois* may have been a bit too overt. In any case, someone tipped off the officials about both their preparations and their apparent intentions. In response, certain administrators who were intent upon stopping unlicensed traders before they could depart for the interior set the forces of the legal system into motion.

François' confederates had assembled a large canoe, considerable amounts of traveling food supplies, and a significant amount of trade goods on the Brunet property at Lachine, in anticipation of their imminent departure. However, on May 6, all of these articles were seized by Lieutenant Bouat of the Provost Court in Montreal. On the same day, the officer submitted his detailed report to his superiors. Apparently, Françoise's cover story to him and his accompanying officials, offering a supposed explanation for the presence of these items on their land and in their buildings, was not entirely believed. Regardless of her story, however, the court officer had previously been issued his orders as to what activities he and his men were to carry out there.

"I, François Marie Bouat, Councilor of the King and his Lieutenant of the Provost Court of Montreal, by virtue of the ordinance of Monsieur the Intendant [Michel Bégon] dated the twelfth of April last, signed Bégon,

transported myself to the place of Lachine on this Island of Montreal, to the home of François Brunet dit [Le] Bourbonnais, assisted by Jean Petit [Sieur] de Boismorel, bailiff of the Provost Court, and two archers, and for me a sergeant and four soldiers. In talking with the one named Geneviève [actually Françoise] David, a young woman about twenty-eight years of age, I asked her if there were any birchbark canoes there. She declared that in the field was a six-place one which belonged to the Sieur Desroches. [She also stated that,] After expressing his goodbyes to Monsieur [Claude] de Ramezay, Governor of the said Montreal, the said Desroches planned to depart with two canoes to go to Detroit.

Since Monsieur de Ramezay had ordered me to draw up an inventory of the merchandise which had been brought in a cart conducted by the man Jean Cousineau [as the cargo of the said canoe], I had the merchandise for the canoe removed and transported to the home of the Sieur Vital Caron, Captain of the militia of the said Lachine, to whom it has been voluntarily entrusted, which contained the following. That is, four bales of fabric, two cases [of ironwares], seven rolls of tobacco, two sacks of lead, five kegs of gunpowder, six kegs of brandy, three bags of biscuit, one bag of side pork, one keg of salt, and one six-place birchbark canoe which is entirely new. I have placed the above articles into the charge and protection of the said Sieur Caron, with prohibitions against him doing anything with them that may be ordered by those to whom they belong. In witness thereof, we have signed in the presence of the Sieur [Pierre Dupuis dit] Saint Michel, Sergeant of the Troops, Sieur Jean Petit [Sieur] de Boismorel, royal bailiff of the aforementioned Provost Court, and the said Sieur Caron, who has declared that he does not know how to write or sign, having been asked after the reading was done, according to the ordinance.

[This statement] made at Lachine on May 6, 1713.

Signed,

Bouat, J. Petit, and Saint Michel Dupui"[54]

The initial list of the seized articles (upon which the above statement was based) had included certain pieces of additional information. It had also contained the specific marks which had been applied to most of the shipping containers:

"Statement of the merchandise which I have left in storage at the home of the Sieur Vital Caron, Captain of the Côte [of Lachine and Sault St. Louis]

2 bales of fabric marked .... FST
1 bale of fabric marked..FST x C
1 bale of fabric marked... marsac
1 case of ironwares marked .... FST

1 case of ironwares marked ....*FST x C*
6 rolls of tobacco in bales, weighing together around 150 pounds,
marked..*FST x C*
1 roll of tobacco weighing around 30 pounds, to be baled [thus without mark]
2 sacks of lead, weighing 50 pounds apiece, without mark
2 kegs of gunpowder marked.. *FST*
2 kegs of gunpowder marked..*FST x C*
1 keg of gunpowder marked .... *IM*
6 kegs of brandy containing 15 half-gallons apiece, marked.............*FST x C*
3 bags of biscuit weighing 50 pounds apiece [without mark]
1 bag of side pork [without mark]
1 keg of salt marked... *FST*
1 birchbark canoe with six large places, entirely new

*[This document] made at Lachine on May 6, 1713. Sieur Caron does not
know how to sign, having been asked according to the ordinance.
Signed,
Bouat and J. Petit"*[55]

These are very rare documents from the period of the French regime. Numerous lists of merchandise, equipment, supplies, and canoes that were supplied by specific outfitters to specific voyageur-traders have been preserved, particularly in the ledger books of certain merchants. However, a roster of materiel which was seized by the authorities from a group of *coureurs de bois* at a specific time and place is exceedingly unusual.

In spite of the presence of the large trading craft, along with the generous amounts of traveling food supplies and the extensive consignment of trade goods which were all seized at the Brunet property, this must have been considered to be only circumstantial evidence that François' colleagues were about to venture off to join him on an unlicensed commercial trip. In truth, it was not illegal for either Françoise or the unidentified men to possess these articles, and François did indeed own a lot within the stockaded settlement at Detroit. Thus, he would technically be permitted to conduct commerce there, if he were to receive permission in advance from the authorities in the St. Lawrence settlements to make the westward voyage. As a result, Françoise had utilized the cover story about "Sieur Desroches," who was supposedly poised to undertake such a venture, in an attempt to explain the presence of the assembled canoe, merchandise, and food supplies on her property. Since neither

François nor any of his unidentified confederates had been caught actually carrying out an unlicensed journey to the interior, they all apparently got off scott free in this instance, with possibly just the loss of the craft and the cargo. The lack of definitive evidence against Monsieur Brunet and his unnamed colleagues must have been the reason that no arrest warrants were issued, no arrests were carried out, and no subpoenas were issued to individuals which would have summoned them to appear before the Court for interrogation under oath. In fact, no further information concerning this case was filed amid the records of the Court.

It is not possible to discern for certain whether Monsieur Brunet's colleagues had been planning to travel to Ft. Pontchartrain to join him there for trading activities, or whether they were instead headed to meet him in the *Pays d'en Haut*, where they would have been based at St. Ignace. However, their amounts of assembled food supplies had included 150 pounds of biscuit and one bag of side pork, as well as certain amounts of salt and brandy that would have been drawn from what was nominally their stock of trade merchandise. These generous amounts of supplies strongly imply that François' accomplices had intended to travel to the much more distant Straits of Mackinac and the surrounding Upper Country. Such supplies would not have been readily available there, in sharp contrast to the settlement at Detroit, where large amounts of wheat and numerous pigs were raised and the place was often awash with brandy.

Five months after the canoe, food supplies, and merchandise of François' cohorts had been seized by government officials, he experienced a heart-wrenching loss: his sister Catherine, one of the twins, died at the untimely age of $33^1/3$ years. When she was buried in the Montreal cemetery on September 7, 1713, she left behind her husband Pierre Tabault and three children, who were 9, 7, and 5 years old.[56]

Before freezing weather set in solidly during the final months of 1713, François had returned to the Lachine seigneury, to winter with his family. On January 22, 1714, he was present in the Notre Dame church at Montreal, standing as an official witness at a wedding. On this day, the bride was his cousin Élisabeth Beauvais, age 21, the daughter of Raphaël Beauvais and Élisabeth Turpin, while the groom was Louis Hurtubise, Jr., son of Louis, Sr. and Jeanne Gateau. In addition to François, the other witness on the bride's side was her cousin Pierre Couillard; the two on the groom's side were his step father Louis Langevin and his brother Pierre Hurtubise.[57]

During the early months of this winter, Françoise and François settled certain details concerning her inheritance. A piece of land in the Champlain seigneury which had belonged to Marie Jeanne Couillard, her deceased mother, had been sold back in October by her stepfather Jacques Valois and his second wife Marie Marguerite Carpentier. This couple lived with Françoise's half-siblings, plus the Valois children whom they had themselves produced, on Île Dupas, offshore from Sorel in the St. Lawrence River. The proceeds from the sale of this property, which had been purchased by Marie Marguerite's unmarried brothers Étienne and Médard Carpentier, were to be divided between Françoise and the various underage descendants of the Valois-Carpentier couple.[58]

Some 4½ months later, Françoise and François reached a financial settlement with Monsieur and Madame Valois, when they all gathered on February 21, 1714 in the office of the Montreal notary Adhémar. First, all of the parties agreed that, at the time of the marriage contract of Françoise's parents Claude David, Jr. and Marie Jeanne Couillard on January 3, 1684, the prospective bride had been promised a prefixed dower of 300 livres. After the death of Claude, Jr., Marie Jeanne had received on March 31, 1685 the sum of 568 livres 16 sols, to cover this prefixed dower plus certain other advantages that had been expressed in the nuptial agreement. On October 14, 1706, after Marie Jeanne had died and five months after Jacques Valois had remarried, the Judge at Champlain had decreed that Monsieur Valois was to pay to Francoise David and her husband François Brunet the 300 livres that had belonged to Marie Jeanne via her prefixed dower. Valois had appealed this ruling to the Chief Judge of the Trois-Rivières Court. As a result, François had then sued him in the Montreal Court, to collect the prefixed dower plus certain of the proceeds from the properties which the deceased had owned. The latter suit was decided in favor of François, supporting the original decision of the Judge at Champlain. However, the Valois couple claimed that various expenses and debts of the estate justified them not paying, which meant that the situation still required a compromise in order to reach a final settlement. Thus, on this February day, Monsieur and Madame Valois finally promised to pay to Françoise and François the reduced sum of 150 livres. In return, Monsieur and Madame Brunet agreed to relinquish all claims to the various parcels of land which had once belonged to Françoise's mother and Jacques Valois. Although the Valois couple agreed to hand over this money by Christmas Day of 1714, Françoise would visit the notary by herself on August 13, to officially report that she had already received the full amount of the promised sum, more than four months ahead of the agreed-upon deadline date.[59]

In this year of 1714, the closure policy concerning most of the posts in the interior was still in effect. Thus, the hiring contracts for voyageurs which were drawn up by Montreal-area notaries were very limited in number. One man was engaged on April 6 to labor for the commandant of the Illinois Country, while another was hired May 25 by four individuals to travel to Michilimackinac. Those *engagés* who were bound for Detroit, hired between March 28 and April 13, included three men who would be working for one hirer plus three others who would each be laboring for three different hirers. (At the end of the summer, five more voyageurs would be engaged, between August 20 and September 9, to travel to Ft. Pontchartrain.)[60]

These various voyageurs and voyageur-traders were the ones who would be working above board this year, with official permission. However, there were numerous others who would head for the interior this season without either a permit or a license. François Brunet, four of his colleagues, and a number of their hired voyageurs would be among this latter group.

In preparation for his upcoming illegal trading trip, Francois received an outfit from the Montreal merchant Simon Réaume. He was the next-younger brother of the well-known voyageur-trader Robert Réaume (whose biography has already been offered in the present work), as well as being the older brother of Jean Baptiste Réaume, who had been convicted three years earlier of making an illicit commercial voyage to Michilimackinac. The merchant-outfitter Simon, 44 years old, had been married to Jeanne Thérèse Catin for four years; they already had two children (and two more would be in their future). He had been hiring voyageurs to work with and for him in the distant interior since at least 1693. According to their outfitting contract of 1714, which was passed before the Montreal notary Michel Lepailleur on April 20, the individual who received the consignment of merchandise on credit from the merchant Réaume was identified as "François Brunet, voyageur, from Lachine."[61]

Just eight days later, on April 28, the charge of "having stealthily departed from this town [Montreal] with several employees some days ago, without having taken with them a permit, to go up to the said place of Fort Pontchartrain," was officially registered against

Monsieur Brunet in the Montreal Court. This same charge was simultaneously leveled against his brother-in-law Jean Tabault (age 31, who had been married to his sister Angélique for more than four years; living in Montreal, this couple had one daughter who was about two years old); Joseph Cuillerier, Sieur de Ribercour; and the brothers Julien and Alexis Trottier, Sieurs Desruisseaux. The criminal allegations against these five men and their *engagés* had been lodged with the Court by Louis Lefebvre, Sieur Duchouquet. This merchant, age 42, married with nine children, served as the legal representative in Montreal of Captain François Dauphin, Sieur de La Forest. This officer had been the commandant at Ft. Pontchartrain since 1710, having replaced Cadillac upon the departure of the latter officer. (Captain La Forest, who had been married since 1702 and had produced only a single stillborn child, would retain his position of command until his death on October 15, 1714 at the Hôtel Dieu hospital in Quebec, at the age of 65.)

One of François' four trading partners, Joseph Cuillerier, 35 years old, had been born and raised in the Lachine seigneury about $1^1/2$ miles west of the Brunet farm. Having been married for six years, he and his wife Louise Guillory had already produced two children, who were ages 5 and 3 at this time. The unmarried Trottier brothers Julien and Alexis, born and raised at Batiscan and then at Champlain, northeast of Trois-Rivières, were 26 and 25 years old, respectively. No specific names of the partners' various hired voyageurs were recorded in the legal complaint. As a result, it is not possible to identify these latter men, or to even provide an accurate count of their number. Thus, the total number of canoes of the party and the number of paddlers in each one cannot be estimated.[62]

At this time, François was one month away from turning age 32. He and Françoise had been married for $8^1/4$ years, and during that period of time they had already produced three children. However, at least one of those offspring, the tiny girl born in 1710, had not survived. It is also possible that their first baby, born in 1706, had already perished by this point as well. Thus, among the five trading partners, Monsieur Brunet was the second-oldest; but he had been married the longest, and he and Françoise had produced the greatest number of children.

The legal charges that were leveled against these five voyageur-traders and their hired voyageurs decried not only their lack of acquiring official permission to travel to Ft. Pontchartrain, but also "their evasion of the agreed-upon payment for the said permit." These charges, plus the date of April 28, made it entirely clear that this illicit party had headed for Detroit, via the upper St. Lawrence River and Lakes Ontario and Erie. It was much too early in the season for the ice to have entirely cleared from the more northerly route of the Ottawa and Mattawa Rivers, Lake Nipissing, and the French River, and for the spring floodwaters on these liquid highways to have reduced to manageable levels. However, it is possible that, upon reaching Detroit in May or early June, the men may have encountered legal difficulties with Captain La Forest which could not be rectified by simply paying the obligatory fee for the trading permit plus the court costs. What is known for certain is that at least some of them, including Monsieur Brunet, subsequently traveled northward over the length of Lake Huron to reach Michilimackinac and the surrounding Upper Country. This fact is revealed by information that was included in the document presented below.

On March 18, 1715, Françoise visited the office of the Montreal notary Jean Baptiste Adhémar. (He was the son of Antoine Adhémar, who had been a prominent notary at various locales for 46 years, from 1668 until his death at Montreal on April 15, 1714. Jean Baptiste had officially become a notary one month later, on May 13; he would hold this position at Montreal for the next four decades, until his own demise in 1754.)[63] On this spring day in 1715, Madame Brunet officially registered the outfit of trade goods that she had received a short time earlier from a Montreal merchant, which she would soon send on to her husband in the interior.

"Was present Françoise David, wife of François Brunet, living at Lachine but being at present in this town, who has acknowledged and declared that she owes to Sieur Pierre You [Sieur] de La Découverte, merchant of this Island, accepted by Damoiselle Madeleine Just, his wife, the sum of 575 livres 5 sols for good trade merchandise which has been sold and delivered to her a short time before the passage of these presents by the said Sieur de La Découverte, to be sent to the said Brunet, her husband, at present in the Ottawa Country. This said sum of 575 livres 5 sols the said David, acting for her said husband, promises to pay and obligates herself to give and pay to the said Sieur Creditor or to the bearer during the entire course of the month of next June [1715], in beaver pelts at the price of the Office [of the export monopoly company] at Quebec and in [other] peltries at the prices which the merchants receive for outfitting, or earlier if the said Brunet or his belongings will come down from the said place of the Ottawa Country,

under the penalty of all expenses, damages, and interests, under the bond of all of their possessions, both moveable and real estate, at present and in the future...For the execution of these presents, the said David has selected as her [temporary] legal residence in this town [to which writs may be delivered] the home of Barbe Beauvais, her mother-in-law, located on St. Paul Street. Thus have they promised, obligated themselves, waived, etc.

[This document] made and drawn up at the said Villemarie in the office of the said notary on March 18, 1715 in the afternoon, in the presence of the Sieurs Louis Thomas Masson and Vincent Lenoir, witnesses living at the said Villemarie who have signed below with the said Demoiselle de La Découverte and the notary. The said David has declared that she does not know how to write or sign, having been questioned after the reading was done, according to the ordinance.

Signed,

M. Just, Masson, Lenoir, and Adhemar, royal notary"[64]

On June 15, 1715, the notary would insert an addendum to this document, on a supplemental page. This added statement would indicate that François himself had paid off the owed sum of 575 livres 5 sols to Demoiselle Just, some time on or before this date in the middle of June.

It is possible that, before his departure without permission in latter April of 1714, François and Françoise had agreed that she would dispatch additional merchandise to him in the west about one year later, during the following spring of 1715. However, it is much more likely that he had sent out a message to her with a party of voyageurs in the summer or autumn of 1714. In this latter scenario, he would have indicated that he had relocated northward from Detroit to Michilimackinac, and that he wished her to procure a new supply of trade goods for him. She was to ship these to him when the waterways would be clear of ice and floodwaters in the late spring of 1715. That is presumably why Françoise stated in the official acknowledgement of the debt on March 18 that she would be sending the merchandise to her husband in the Ottawa Country, rather than to him at Detroit.

From the above document, it is known that Françoise's acquisition of the merchandise was recorded on March 18, 1715, while François' payoff of those goods was recorded on June 15, just three months later. These two end dates are crucial in determining the likely series of events that took place during this spring and early summer.

In April of this year, only the southerly route to Detroit would have been available for shipping the goods to François. If they had been sent to him at Ft. Pontchartrain, he would have easily had time to receive them, to complete his business there, and to return to Montreal by June 15. In this first scenario, even though Françoise indicated that she intended to dispatch the merchandise to her husband in the Ottawa Country, she instead sent it to him via Detroit. This would have allowed him sufficient time to deal with the goods and then to travel out to Montreal by mid-June.

In the second scenario, Françoise waited until after the spring thaw had taken place and the dangerous floodwaters had receded before she dispatched the merchandise via the Ottawa River route to François at the Straits of Mackinac. However, in this second version of the story, there would definitely not have been enough time for him to receive the goods, to trade them, and finally to travel out from the interior via the northerly route, all by June 15. In fact, if the merchandise was sent by way of this route, it would not have reached Michilimackinac until probably about mid-to-latter June, at the earliest.

There is a third and much more likely scenario, which is both plausible and logical; it also matches Françoise's stated intentions in the notary document. In this version of events, she did indeed ship the goods westward to Michilimackinac (as the notary document indicated she would), sending them off in May via the Ottawa River route. However, in this instance, the merchandise was delivered to a pre-arranged associate of Monsieur Brunet's at Michilimackinac. This latter individual would then have traded the goods there, long after François had departed from the Straits, headed for Montreal with an eastbound brigade in May. In fact, the merchandise may have replaced that which had been loaned to François by this particular associate. In this third version of events, the westbound goods and the eastbound Monsieur Brunet would have crossed paths at some point, probably in about late May or early June, as they were each traveling in opposite directions along the northerly route.

Pierre You, the Montreal peltries merchant who had supplied this merchandise to Françoise, was a 57-year-old former military officer. While he had still been single, back in about 1694, he had fathered an out-of-wedlock child with a Miami native woman. By this year of 1715, Pierre and Madeleine Just had been married for eighteen years, since April of 1697. Their first child had arrived one day short of nine months after their nuptial celebration, to be followed by five more babies over the next eight years. The couple had not been fortunate in the survival rate of these offspring. Their fourth child had lived only for three days in April of 1702; a year later, their eldest had perished at the age of $5^1/3$ years in May of 1703, probably as a result of the virulent epidemic sweeping through the colony at that time; and their second baby would have no further documentation other than his baptismal record from November of 1699. Six weeks after their sixth and final child had arrived, in April of 1706, Monsieur You's second out-of-wedlock baby had been born, to 17-year-old Marie Madeleine Drousson at Laprairie. Some 28 months later, this same young woman had delivered another baby who had been fathered by Monsieur You, this time with the child arriving at Montreal. (Mademoiselle Drousson would finally marry in 1720, when she would be 31 years old.)[65]

By 1714, the wooden palisade walls which surrounded the town of Montreal had been standing for nearly three decades, and they were in need of a major upgrade. The initial stockade had been erected in 1685 or 1686, after which this first set of log walls had been reinforced in 1699. Over the course of the following nine years, the inhabitants had outgrown the area of this initial enclosure. This expansion of the population had required a commensurate expansion of the stockade perimeter, which had been carried out during the years from 1708 to 1710. Now, however, the King's Minister determined that all of the wooden walls of the palisade were to be replaced with much more durable ones, constructed of cut stone.

On November 6, 1714, Intendant Bégon decreed that these new and improved walls encircling the town would be built with contributions from all of the colonists who resided within the governmental district of Montreal (which extended to a point some thirty miles northeast of the town itself). This massive construction project would be carried out by means of the *corvée* system. This term referred to the amount of unpaid labor which each household was obliged to contribute every year to the seigneurs (in this instance, the Sulpicians), since the inhabitants were their *censitaires* or property-holders. In his pronouncement, the administrator declared that there would be drawn up "an allotment and tax of the number of days of labor which each of the said habitants will be obliged to furnish for the said *corvées*, in proportion to their possessions and abilities." The various tasks which they would carry out were planned to take place during those seasons in which most of the people were less busy, particularly after the autumn harvests had been completed. Thus, during the autumn seasons, they would be assigned to transport the rough-cut stones from the quarries to the assembly points, and during the winters they would haul these crude blocks to the workshops for further shaping. Other tasks of the habitants would entail hauling lime and sand to appropriate locales, for the fabrication of mortar.

However, instead of carrying out these assigned labors themselves, with their own teams of horses, each of the habitants had the option of paying for another individual to substitute for him. For each day of labor of a man, the levied tax was to be three livres, and for each day of labor of a pair of harnessed horses, the tax would be eight livres. These funds would be utilized to pay for replacement workers and teams of horses. For anyone who did not participate as ordered, with either direct labor or payments for substitutes, "the penalty for disobedience will be five hundred livres in fines for each of the contraventions, applicable to the King to be utilized for the expenses of the fortifications."

Between December 16, 1714 and March 25, 1715, the master roster of all of the colonists who were expected to contribute to this immense building project was drawn up. This document was entitled "List of the habitants of Montreal Island, Jesus Island, and the neighboring seigneuries who have been requisitioned to work on the fortifications of Montreal in 1715." After the 344 designated residents of the town and outlying areas of Montreal were listed, there followed the inhabitants (in this sequence) of Longue Pointe (37 listings), Côte de Vertus (27), Notre Dame de Liesse (42), Saint Michel (20), Saint Ours (50), Ménagerie des Pauvres (5), Boucherville (78), Côte de Verchères (25), Île Bouchard, Seigneury of Monsieur Dejordy (15), Côte de Varennes (21), Côte St. Michel (23), Côte Ste. Thérèse (15), Côte de Lachine (56), Côte St. Paul (14), Côte St. Pierre (5), Lachenaie (32), Rivière des Prairies (55), Île Jésus (46), Les Mille Îles (16), and Haut [Bout] de l'Île (74).

In the section of the roster pertaining to the Lachine seigneury, called "Côte de Lachine," a total of 56 land owners were recorded. They were headed by the Captain of the parish militia forces here, Claude Caron. Within the eastern or Sault St. Louis section of this seigneury, where the majority of the Brunet clan members resided cheek by jowl, four of the clan's families were listed. These included "The Widow Bourbonnais" (Barbe Beauvais, widow of François Brunet dit Le Bourbonnais, Sr.), "Brunet [dit] Bourbonnais" (Barbe's son, our François Brunet dit Le Bourbonnais, Jr.), "Jean [Baptiste] Pomainville" (husband of Barbe's daughter Élisabeth Brunet), and "The Widow Pomainville" (Barbe's daughter Barbe Brunet, the widow of Georges Brault dit Pomainville).

After a number of years of ongoing construction, the entire set of encircling walls would be completed. Rising more than twenty feet in height, they would feature a total of sixteen gates, most of which would be positioned in the south wall, which faced the St. Lawrence River. The western wall of the town enclosure was located at the present Rue McGill, while the eastern wall was positioned just to the east of the present Rue Berri; the north wall extended along the present Rue St. Jacques, and the south wall ran parallel to the St. Lawrence. These ponderous barriers of mortar-laid stone would protect the community for more than eight decades, until they would be razed in 1804.

At some point during or before 1714, François Brunet had received a loan of 500 livres from Captain La Forest, while both of them had been at the officer's post of Ft. Pontchartrain. However, the recipient had not yet repaid this debt, for which he had issued a promissory note to the commandant. In the autumn of 1714, the Captain's wife had died in the hospital at Quebec in September, and the officer himself had passed away in the same facility four weeks later; they had left no surviving children. Afterward, the individuals who were settling the officer's affairs sued certain of his debtors, in order to collect the monies which these people had owed to the Captain. Thus, on June 14, 1715, Pierre Derivon, Sieur de Budemont (whose wife was Marie Godé, the former widow of the prominent Montreal merchant Charles de Couagne, who was also involved in these financial affairs) brought suit against Monsieur Brunet. By this means, he intended to force François to pay off the 500 livres of his promissory note. According to the records of the Court, "François Brunet, habitant of Lachine, voyageur," did not appear before the Court on June 20, even though he had been ordered to do so on that date (and he had returned from the Ottawa Country by June 15). His failure to appear caused the case to be decided, by default, in favor of Monsieur Derivon. However, in spite of this legal decision, the defendant apparently still did not pay the owed money. As a result, seven weeks later, on August 5, 1715, he was again summoned to appear in the chambers of the Court. Since no further details were recorded in this case, the defendant must have soon paid off the debt of 500 livres, without having to receive any further legal prodding.[66]

At some point during 1715 or earlier, François lost his brother-in-law Georges Brault dit Pomainville, at the untimely age of about 47. This man had been for many years his adjacent neighbor to the west. In addition, François and Jean Baptiste Brault (Georges' brother, who was married to François' sister Élisabeth) had jointly purchased from Georges and his wife Barbe Brunet (François' oldest sister) a portion of their large double lot a decade earlier, back in 1705. These two Brault brothers and François had together formed a trio of voyageur-trader partners back in 1707, when they had made a trading trip to Detroit. Five years before that, back in 1702, François, Georges, and their future brother-in-law Pierre Tabault had together carried out numerous cargo runs to and from Ft. Frontenac, as a three-man voyageur crew. In other words, Georges and François had been very closely related and intertwined for a long time. Having been married for about nineteen years, Georges and Barbe had produced eight children, of whom at least three would grow up to adulthood. The grieving widow, 40 years old, eventually signed a marriage contract on January 16, 1716 with Martial Dumoulineuf; in their subsequent years together, the new couple would not produce any additional children.[67]

Ever since François' trading voyage to Ft. Pontchartrain with his Brault in-laws back in 1707, he had apparently conducted commercial ventures in the west whenever he wished to do so, whether he had received official permission or not. He seems to have taken to heart the old proverb *"Vouloir, c'est pouvoir"* ("To want, this is power," which is usually expressed in English as "Where's there's a will, there's a way.") This unfettered approach must have engendered in him a certain delight each time he did not bother to request clearance from the authorities. Another element for him was probably financial; he apparently relished not being obliged to pay for trading permits or licenses from government officials in the St. Lawrence settlements. In addition, Monsieur Brunet had managed to avoid paying the rather steep trading fees that had been imposed by Cadillac on non-resident traders at Ft. Pontchartrain. (These fees involved either paying 200 livres per sojourn there, or instead hauling 300 pounds of merchandise westward and 300 pounds of peltries eastward for the commandant.) He had accomplished this latter feat by acquiring a lot within the stockaded community at Detroit. In order to maintain this property, he was only obliged to pay an annual *rente* of 2 livres and an annual trading fee of 10 livres.

By weaving together the strands of scattered evidence that can be extracted from surviving documents, it is possible to discern the pattern of François Brunet dit Le Bourbonnais regularly working beyond the reach of governmental authority. In June of 1711, at the time of the baptism of his and Françoise's third child, he was recorded by the priest as being "absent." (This reflected the discrete manner in which the clerics avoided entering into the parish ledgers incriminating evidence concerning those parishioners who were away trading in the interior, often illegally.) In the following spring and summer of 1712, when four voyageur-traders were placed on trial in Montreal for making an illegal commercial trip to Michilimackinac, François was unavailable for interrogation under oath (his spouse and his younger brother were summoned to testify). In May of 1713, when officials from the Montreal Court raided his property and seized there a large canoe, along with plenty of traveling food supplies and trade merchandise, neither he nor his unidentified confederates were to be found in the St. Lawrence Valley. In April of 1714, he and four trading colleagues, along with a number of their hired voyageurs, were charged in the Montreal Court with having departed for the interior without receiving and paying for a permit.

At this point, the history of Frenchmen leaving the St. Lawrence communities to participate in the peltries commerce in the west and north without official permission was already some six decades long. It had commenced shortly after the departure for the upper Great Lakes region of numerous young colonists in 1653. In the *Jesuit Relations* of that year, the author had observed: *"All of our young Frenchmen intend to go trading, to find the nations scattered here and there, and they hope to come back laden with the beaver pelts of several years."*[68] The peltries that these men had sought were those which had been accumulated by the various native allies who, between 1649 and 1651, had fled far westward and northward from their home regions in an attempt to escape from the incessant depredations of the Iroquois. This was the very first instance in which Frenchmen had ventured into the distant interior specifically to trade. Before this, the native traders had paddled out to the St. Lawrence Valley, to conduct their commerce in furs and hides at certain locales there.

This radical departure from the time-honored method of waiting along the St. Lawrence for peltries to be delivered there by the native populations had prompted Jean de Lauzon, the Governor of New France, to issue a ruling during the following spring of 1654. He had declared that every individual was to obtain permission before departing for the interior, in order to determine the "number and character" of the traders; fines were to be imposed upon anyone who did not comply.[69] However, this regulation had done little to keep numerous colonists from slipping away to take part in this very lucrative business, in which much greater profits could be garnered by transporting merchandise directly to the native nations who resided in the distant interior. There, the prices which they charged were much higher. By 1672, Jean Baptiste Patoulet, a deputy to the Intendant Jean Talon, had noted that an estimated 300 to 400 men were trading in the interior without the approval of the authorities.[70]

In November of that same year of 1672, Governor Frontenac had complained to the Court about these illicit traders:

"[They] will finally become, if care not be taken, like the Banditti of Naples or the Buccaneers of Santo Domingo. Their insolence, as I am informed, extends even to the formation of leagues, and to the distribution of notices of rendezvous. [They are] threatening to build forts, and to go off to Orange [Albany] and Manatte [New York], boasting that they will be received and have protection there."[71]

The administrator's lattermost statement reflected the fact that the peltries of the *coureurs de bois* often made their way to the English and the Dutch of the New York colony. It was to Albany specifically, in the northern area of this colony, to which most of those furs and hides were usually transported. This community had been first established by the Dutch in 1614, with the name Ft. Nassau. A decade later, the facility of Ft. Orange had been constructed there, which soon came to be called Beverwyck, or Beavertown. After the English had seized the area in 1664, the name of the community had been changed to Albany.[72]

Furs and hides were carried there either by the illegal French traders themselves, or by native confederates. There were two primary routes over which these clandestine peltries were most often transported to Albany. One involved paddling eastward from the southeastern corner of Lake Ontario, via the Oswego and Mohawk Rivers. The other entailed traveling southward from the Montreal area, via the Richelieu River, Lake Champlain, Lake George, and the Hudson River. This latter route was regularly traveled by some of the Christianized Iroquois who lived in villages a short distance to the south, southwest, and west of Montreal. These allies had adopted the Roman Catholic religion of the French; they built considerable numbers of birchbark canoes for the French; they often supplied warriors to join with French forces in conducting military expeditions against the English; and they served as the southern and western guard posts for the entire Montreal region. However, some individuals among them had maintained relationships with their relatives and friends to the south, in the Iroquois homelands. It was often through these latter relationships with the original Iroquois nations, who were closely associated with the English and Dutch traders of Albany, that the peltries of illicit French traders were transferred to the south, out of the French sphere of commerce.

In fact, back in 1668, Fr. Dollier de Casson at Montreal had complained that a great many of the native allies of the French were transporting their peltries southward to Albany of their own initiative, in no way in association with illegal French traders. One of the main attractions of doing business in the south was the much better rate of exchange there:

"Our neighbors [in the English colonies to the south]...use so much skill both without and within their country that they secure the greater part of the peltries of Canada, and everyone there is comfortable at home, instead of being generally wretched as they are here. If the peltries [gathered by our native allies] were only worth a third less with us than they are among our foreign neighbors, all of the natives would come here and none would go to the foreigners. For not only do the natives like us better than they do them, but the hunting takes place in our country, and they have the task of transporting the peltries to foreign territory at great labor."[73]

In spite of the lengthy voyage to Albany, conducting business with the English and Dutch merchants there offered a number of distinct advantages, for both the illegal French traders and the native traders who were nominally allied with the French. First of all, these merchants to the south paid up to three times more for beaver pelts than did the French company that held the export monopoly on such furs. In addition, the Albany men paid in hard cash, rather than in post-dated bills of exchange. Thirdly, the monopoly company's office in Quebec refused to accept any beaver pelts after October 20 each year, so that the received peltries could be shipped across the Atlantic on the final vessels of the season, instead of having to be stored until the following summer. In contrast, the Albany merchants accepted beaver pelts in all seasons. Another major advantage of exchanging furs and hides at Albany was that the traders were not obliged to pay export taxes on them. In the St. Lawrence settlements, a tax of 25 percent on all beaver pelts and a tax of 10 percent on all moose hides was collected by the export monopoly company; these fees had been established back in 1664.[74]

In time, the authorities of New France had come to think of the facilities of Ft. Frontenac (at the eastern end of Lake Ontario) and Ft. Chambly (on the Richelieu River, southeast of Montreal) as simply bases for those individuals who conducted commerce illegally with Albany. One report from this period clearly laid out this belief:

"Fort Frontenac...was erected in the year 1673 by Count de Frontenac, apparently for the security of the country, but, in fact, for the purpose of trading with the Iroquois; to serve as a place of refuge and entrepôt for the coureurs de bois scattered among all of the Ottawa nations [throughout the upper Great Lakes region]; and to carry on from there a trade in beaver pelts with the Dutch and the English of Orange [Albany] and Manatte [New York]...

Fort Chambly is the second place by which quantities of beaver pelts are diverted to foreigners, that is to say, to Orange, Manatte, and even to Boston...There was formerly a pretty considerable number of settlers there, the greater portion of whom have removed, or are reduced to poverty because they have not been sustained, so that it has become the refuge of people who pay attention only to the Orange and Manatte trade."[75]

In their attempts to control the peltries commerce, the authorities of the colony had encountered two particularly vexing issues. One of these involved Frenchmen departing for the interior, with the intention of conducting trade there, without first receiving official permission. The other major issue involved Frenchmen taking their garnered furs and hides southward to Albany, rather than turning them in to the French export company in the St. Lawrence Valley.

As a result of these serious infractions, an edict had been issued in 1676 which had forbidden anyone from carrying on trade beyond the confines of the St. Lawrence settlements without permission from the authorities. One of the individuals who had received a legal permit in this same year of 1676 was Nicolas Perrot. He was one of the most prominent French traders in the region of Green Bay on Lake Michigan and the region which extended to the west and southwest from there. He had explained his permit, as well as the responses which had been engendered by the new edict against interior traders, in this manner:

"Monsieur [Governor Louis de Buade, Count] de Frontenac gave to various persons permits for the trading which was carried out in the Upper Country,

among the natives who are outside of the [St. Lawrence] colony. I also obtained one, through the favor and recommendation of Monsieur Bellinzany, secretary of Monsieur de Colbert [Minister of the Marine Department of the Court]. It was at about the same time that Monsieur [Jacques] Duchesneau, Intendant of the country, wrote letters against Monsieur de Frontenac, and sent word to the Court that he [Frontenac] was bestowing permits upon his own dependents only. His letters obtained credence, and it was forbidden to issue these permits to anyone thereafter.

The Canadians, seeing themselves deprived of these privileges, grew lax [in their obedience to the government], and believed that the privileges were rightfully theirs. And that is the reason why most of the young men in the country left it, and returned only by stealth to obtain trade goods, and to bring back peltries, which were secretly sold. This traffic opened the eyes of the merchants, who found it greatly to their own advantage. They advanced these young men the goods that were necessary for their voyage, some of them being opposed to the issuing of the orders mentioned above. As a result, these Canadians made themselves like unto the natives, whose dissolute conduct they copied so well."[76]

Since the edict of 1676 against unlicensed voyageur-traders had brought about few results, further ordinances to halt their activities had been issued on two occasions in 1678: in May by Governor Frontenac, and in September by Intendant Duchesneau. One of the provisions in both of these edicts had pertained to those merchants who were found to be dealing with illicit traders. In May, their fine had been established at 1,000 livres; in September, this amount had been increased to 2,000 livres.[77]

In the following year of 1679, Intendant Duchesneau had reported in considerable detail on the situation of unlicensed traders operating in the interior:

"I refer to what relates to the disobedience of the coureurs de bois...It has at last reached such a point that everyone boldly contravenes the King's interdictions. There is no longer any concealment; even parties are gathered with astonishing insolence to go and trade in the native country.

I have done all in my power to prevent this misfortune, which may lead to the ruin of the colony. I have enacted ordinances against the coureurs de bois; against the merchants who furnish them with goods; against the gentlemen and others who harbor them; and even against those who have any knowledge of them and will not inform the justices nearest to the spot. All of that has been in vain, inasmuch as several of the most substantial families in this country are interested therein, so that the Governor lets them go on, and even shares in their profits...

The coureurs de bois not only act openly, they carry their peltries to the English, and endeavor to drive the native trade there...The natives complained to the Governor, in the council which was held at Montreal, that the French were in too great numbers at the trading posts [in the interior]; he curtly rebuffed them...There is an almost general disobedience throughout this country. The number of those in the woods is estimated at nearly five or six hundred, exclusive of those who set out every day...

The great number of people who have gone to the native country to trade for peltries ruin the colony, because those who alone could improve it, being young and strong for work, abandon their wives and children, the cultivation of their lands, and the care of rearing their cattle; they become dissipated. Their absence gives rise to licentiousness among their wives, as has often been the case, and is still of daily occurrence. They accustom themselves to a loafing and vagabond life, which it is beyond their power to quit. They derive but little benefit from their labors, because they are induced to waste, in drunkenness and fine clothes, the little that they earn, which is very trifling, since those who give them licenses take the larger share, besides the prices of the goods, which they sell to them very expensively. The natives would no longer bring their peltries in such abundance to sell to the honest people [in the St. Lawrence settlements, at the trade fairs], if so great a number of young men went in search of them to those very barbarians...

In 1676, His Majesty forbade the Governor from giving licenses to trade in the interior and in the native country. The Sovereign Council...issued an edict by which...the ordinances would be made known to the French traders among the natives of the farther nations, enjoining them to return to their settlements by the month of August of the following year [1677], under the penalties contained in the said ordinance, which would be affixed in the villages of the Nipissings [north of Lake Superior], Sault Ste. Marie, St. Ignace on Lake Huron, and St. François Xavier on Green Bay. Meanwhile, the Governor, in order to elude the prohibitions which had been laid down in the King's ordinance, and yet not to appear in contravention of them, issued licenses to hunt, which served as a pretext to nullify those orders. His Majesty, as was just, again remedied this by his last ordinances [of 1678]."[78]

In the latter 1670s, René Robert Cavelier, Sieur de La Salle had held a monopoly on the commerce in the regions of the southern end of Lake Michigan, the Illinois Country, and the central and lower Mississippi Valley. As a result, the unlicensed traders had generally avoided those areas. Instead, they had continued to stream into the region of the upper Great Lakes, and to the north and west of the Lakes, with the Straits of Mackinac serving as their central base of operations.

In 1680, Intendant Duchesneau had again reported to the Court the activities of these illicit traders in the west. All of them had been illegal, except for those few individuals who were supposedly on official government business:

"There is not a family of any condition and quality whatsoever [in the St. Lawrence settlements] that has not children, brothers, uncles, and nephews among them...Governor Frontenac [at least publicly on the surface] and I have already commenced together the prosecution of the coureurs de bois and of those who outfit or protect them...Seven have been arrested, who are under interrogation, and will be judged at the earliest opportunity...[However,] the Governor...has again dispatched that famous coureur de bois La Toupine, whom I had arrested last year, and whose interrogation I sent to you. It is he whom [the Governor] employs to carry his orders and to trade among the Ottawa nations...There are eight hundred persons or more in the bush, whatever may be stated to the contrary. I have not been able to obtain the precise number, inasmuch as all those who are involved with them conceal it...

The country suffers so seriously from the scarcity of people that many farms lie uncultivated...On account of the absence of the coureurs de bois, it is not to be expected that the cultivation of the soil will be increased, nor that the cattle will multiply, owing to the unfavorableness of the seasons and the lack of people to take care of them. And, since it is to be presumed that each coureur carries a gun, there will be a decrease of at least eight hundred fusils [of the 1,840 fusils which had been enumerated in the census of 1679]...

The best means to oblige them to return...[would be] to notify them to return home, and that they make a sincere and frank declaration in court of the time that they have been absent, for which persons they have been trading in the native country, who has furnished them goods, how many peltries they have had, and how they disposed of them."[79]

Close examination of the facts reveals that a very considerable portion of the male work force of New France had been involved in the illicit fur trade during this period. In 1680, the total population of the St. Lawrence settlements had consisted of nearly 10,000 persons, counting all ages and both genders. Fully 10 percent of these, nearly 1,000 individuals, had been single or widowed men ranging in age from 20 to 54, the primary age span of the adult working population. There had also been a disproportionate number of children in the settlements at this time. In fact, slightly more than 50 percent of the children who would be born in the colony during the entire century between 1620 and 1720 would be born in the fifteen-year span between

1670 and 1684. Thus, in 1680, single and married men of working age had probably constituted, at most, some 20 to 25 percent of the total population, or a maximum of 2,000 to 2,500 individuals. It is highly likely that the Intendant's estimate of 800 *coureurs de bois* in that year had been somewhat inflated. However, even a conservative estimate of 500 illegal traders would have represented some 20 to 25 percent of the male work force of the colony. This figure did not include the many investors, outfitters, and other individuals who had assisted the men in carrying out their illegal commerce.[80]

In May of 1681, following the suggestions of the Intendant of New France, the King's Minister in Paris had issued a decree which had established a system of legal trade licenses or *congés*. In addition, an ordinance had granted an amnesty to all of the *coureurs de bois* who would come out from the interior regions. Thus, instead of the former ban on traders operating in the west, the Governor or the Intendant could now issue up to 25 official licenses each year. In addition to these licenses, the administrators could also grant an unspecified number of permits to worthy traders who had performed some special service for the government.[81]

In this same year, Intendant Duchesneau had described to the Court officials certain methods by which the illegal traders operated: *"There are two sorts of coureurs de bois. The first go to the original haunts of the beaver, among the native tribes of the Assiniboins, Dakotas, Miamis, Illinois, and others; these cannot make the trip in less than two or three years. The second, who are not so numerous, merely go as far as the Long Sault or the Petite Nation [both locales on the lower Ottawa River] and sometimes to Michilimackinac, to meet the natives and Frenchmen who come down, in order to obtain, exclusively, their peltries, for which they carry goods to them. These men sometimes bring nothing but brandy, contrary to the King's prohibitions, with which they intoxicate and ruin them. The latter coureurs de bois can make their trips in five or six months, and even in a much shorter period. It is not easy to catch either the one or the other, unless we are assisted by disinterested persons. And if they [the coureurs] are favored but ever so little, they easily receive intelligence, and the woods and the rivers afford them great facilities to escape justice."*[82]

On his own initiative, Governor Frontenac had decided to postpone the implementation of the new licensing policy until the following year of 1682. This happens to have been the very same year in which François Brunet dit Le Bourbonnais, Jr. had been born. Thus, his entire period of growing up had taken place while many people around him had been participating in the peltries business, either legally with a license or a permit or instead illegally, beyond the view of the officials. These participants, both in the Lachine area and beyond, had included not only his father François, Sr. but also many of his neighbors, friends, and acquaintances.

After the establishment of the program of legal licenses and permits, the term *voyageur* or traveler had come into common usage. It was applied to differentiate those individuals who had received official permission to trade in the interior from the *coureurs de bois* or illicit traders, who would continue to operate outside of the legal system during the entire French era. However, during the eighteenth century, the term *voyageur* would come to be applied to all canoemen who were hired by a licensed employer.

Even with the license system in place, considerable numbers of young men had continued to stream westward from the St. Lawrence communities, headed for the Straits of Mackinac and other locales in the interior, seeking to make their fortune. Although a certain percentage of them had been officially approved and licensed, many others had not. This had led the new Governor, Joseph Antoine Lefebvre de La Barre, and the new Intendant, Jacques De Meulles, to jointly make the following declaration on October 1, 1682:

"Due to the information which has been provided to us that various individuals, notwithstanding the express prohibitions of His Majesty, have continued to go into the woods to conduct trade with the natives without our permits...we have prohibited and we prohibit all persons of whatever quality and condition...to go to the woods and dwelling places of the said natives to carry out trade, under the penalty of the confiscation of the merchandise and canoes and under the penalty of being sent to the galleys, as decreed by the ordinance of His Majesty."[83]

Eighteen days later, on October 19, the two administrators had extended their prohibitions to also apply to the merchants who provided provisions, equipment, and merchandise to the illegal traders.[84]

By 1684, a number of *coureurs de bois* had altered their method of operations, with the overt encouragement of Colonel Thomas Dongan, the Governor of the New York colony. Instead of living in the St. Lawrence communities and hauling their clandestine furs and hides to Albany, these men had actually relocated, taking up residence in that English-Dutch community to the south. Before long, these renegade traders would lead brigades of Anglo traders to St. Ignace at the Straits of Mackinac, where they would provide the native customers with more merchandise per pelt than the St. Lawrence-based traders had ever given.[85]

In response to this new development, in April of 1684, the King had issued two edicts. The first one had "prohibited all French habitants of New France from withdrawing to Orange [Albany], Manatte [New York], or other places belonging to the English and Dutch without our permission." The leaders among such renegades would be condemned to death, while the others would be condemned to serve for the rest of their lives as oarsmen aboard the King's galleys in the Mediterranean. The second ordinance had "prohibited all merchants and habitants of Canada and New France from transporting any beaver pelts or moose hides to the English, Dutch, or other foreign nations under any pretext, under the penalty of a fine of 500 livres and the confiscation of the merchandise which might be found going to the places of the foreigners."[86]

Five months later, Governor La Barre had issued the following ordinance on October 5, 1684:

"Due to the widespread commotion in the country, and the reports that we have received from all parts that various individuals are intending to go to the Ottawa Country without either a permit or permission, and it being necessary to prevent very considerable disorder and actions which are very contrary to the intentions of His Majesty, we have made and are declaring it illegal for all people, of all qualities and conditions, to attempt to go up to the Ottawas or the Temiscamingues, or to equip any canoes to go to them, or to ascend the Grand [Ottawa] River, as they have done this winter, without a permit and permission of the proper form. This applies to all those who will go to trade, whether to the Ottawas [at the Straits], to Lake Superior, to Green Bay [and the adjacent Fox-Wisconsin Rivers region], or to the Sioux [in the upper Mississippi region], without a signed permit from us, sealed with our arms, and a passport from Monsieur the Intendant. It also applies to those who might go there to carry some important orders from us as well as munitions, without any merchandise, without our exact orders concerning what they are going to do in the said regions.

*In order to prevent them from committing any abuses in the execution of this order, we have ruled against all persons departing from the said town of Montreal or other places in this country, for the said voyages, without Monsieur [Louis Hector de] Callières, Governor of the said town, having seen their permit. **He will give them a pass, by virtue of which they will be able to pass by all of the guard posts that it will please him*** *to establish, whether it be at the [western] point of the island or at Lachine, whichever he will judge appropriate* (emphasis by the present author).

We make a parallel declaration against all merchants and others who involve themselves in commerce by delivering to certain people merchandise for the trade, without having seen beforehand our permits, under the penalty of having imposed upon them the penalty which was declared by His Majesty against coureurs de bois. We therefore grant [to the Governor of Montreal] the power to offer the necessary inducement, in order to prevent and reprimand these said undertakings, by declaring that half of the merchandise which will be seized and confiscated will belong to the denouncer and also to whomever will take the persons, canoes, and merchandise from the said coureurs de bois, and the other half will belong to those whomever it pleases Monsieur the Intendant and others to render judgement.

So that the present ordinance receives full and complete execution, we have committed and we commit Monsieur Callières, Governor of the said Montreal, to take, seize, and arrest the said coureurs de bois or those who will undertake the navigation of the Grand [Ottawa] River without permission, loaded with merchandise or brandy. We likewise commit him to seize, arrest, and make prisoners the merchants who will be found to have contributed to their outfitting, whether it be in merchandise or brandy, or in giving them information. This will be done by such judgement as seems to him to be suitable and appropriate, after which the said information will be sent to Monsieur the Intendant, for consideration by him and the Sovereign Council, to be followed by the judgement of the guilty parties according to the law that was decreed by His Majesty on May 24th, 1681. The said Governor will generally do all of the things provisionally that we would do if we were there in person.

To execute this order, we have given him all power and authority, and will have the present ordinance read, published, and posted at the said Montreal, as well as at Prairie de la Madeleine and other places. Done the 5th of October, 1684." [87]

In spite of this edict, however, numerous men had continued to head west, to carry out commerce without permission. This had spurred the Intendant to issue two additional rulings against illegal traders and their associates in 1685, one on February 26 and the second one on May 17. One of the provisions of the winter edict had forbidden parents from selling fur trade merchandise to their paddling-age children. A clause in the spring edict had declared it illegal to travel as far west in the settlements as Île Perrot without a permit, since such journeys might facilitate dealings with *coureurs de bois*.[88]

In May of 1685, the officer Lahontan had spent a number of weeks at Ft. Chambly, which was located southeast of Montreal beside the Richelieu River. While there, he had observed the clandestine trade links with Albany in action, and in his account he had explained one of the primary attractions of this commerce:

"While I was at Chambly, I saw two canows loaded with beaver skins pass privately by that way [headed southward up the Richelieu]; and 'twas thought they were sent thither by Mr. [Governor] de La Barre. This smuggling way of trade is expressly prohibited; for they are oblig'd to carry these skins before the Office of the [export monopoly] Company, where they are rated at an hundred and 60 per cent less than the English buy 'em at in their colonies."[89]

Later that year, in his report to Versailles, Governor Jacques René de Brisay, Marquis de Denonville, had complained about the continued activities of the *coureurs de bois*:

"I cannot emphasize enough the attraction that this native way of life, of doing nothing, of being constrained by nothing, of following every whim and being beyond correction, has for the young men...[Their departure from the St. Lawrence Valley is leading toward] the complete ruin of the colony. Those who have farms let them lie fallow...[and] married men desert their wives and children, who are [then] dependent upon the public for their living, or get into debt to the merchants."[90]

In January of 1686, Governor Denonville had issued a further set of regulations, which he had hoped would suppress the activities of unlicensed traders in the interior. The new rules had included the following four provisions, which had underscored the central role of the Straits of Mackinac in the trade:

A. Outfitters in the St. Lawrence Valley were to provide a statement of all of the merchandise and provisions which they supplied to each of the individuals who were involved in the trade.

B. During expeditions, traders were to have neither more nor less than three voyageurs per canoe.

C. At St. Ignace, these men were to be subject to the orders of the commandant, Olivier Morel, Sieur de La Durantaye.

D. When they returned to the St. Lawrence communities from the interior regions, the men were to bring a certificate of good behavior from Fr. Jean Enjalran at the Straits; this priest was the Superior of all of the interior missions.[91]

Four years later, in January of 1690, this same administrator had dispatched to the Court additional complaints about the behaviors of the illicit traders:

"It would have been much better...to have left all of the natives to come to the colony in quest of the merchandise which they require, rather than...carrying the goods to them in such large quantities as to have been frequently obliged to sell them at so low a rate as to discredit us among the natives and to ruin the commerce. For many of our coureurs de bois have often lost, instead of gained, by their speculations. Moreover, the great number of coureurs de bois has inflicted serious injury upon the colony, by physically and morally corrupting the settlers, who are prevented from marrying by the cultivation of a vagabond, independent, and idle spirit. For the aristocratic manners which they assume upon their return, both in their dress and in drunken revelries, wherein they exhaust all of their gains in a very short time, lead them to despise the peasantry, and to consider it beneath them to marry [the settlers'] daughters, though they are themselves peasants like them. In addition to this, they will condescend no more to cultivate the soil, nor listen any longer to anything except returning to the woods for the purpose of continuing the same avocations...

There is reason to believe that the wisest and oldest merchants [outfitters] of the country are tired of sending them into the bush. However, there will always be too many new and ambitious petty traders [merchant-outfitters], who will attempt to send ventures there, both with and without a license. It is very proper that an ordinance be enacted which will hold the merchants responsible for the faults of the unlicensed coureurs de bois, for if the merchants would not furnish them goods, there would not be any coureurs de bois...

Great precautions must be used against the restlessness of all of the coureurs de bois, whose spirit leads them always to a distance and to constant roaming...The missionaries whom we have among the Ottawas, who are very numerous, are greatly thwarted by the libertines and the debauched."[92]

In October of 1698, legal commerce had been closed in most areas of the west, and the military personnel had been recalled from nearly all of the interior forts. Thereafter, illegal trading had increased dramatically. For the next eighteen years, until the interdiction against open trade had been officially lifted in 1716, the lines between legal and illicit commerce in the Upper Country and along the St. Lawrence had remained considerably blurred. During this span of years, a number of amnesty proclamations had been issued by the government, urging the men in the interior to return to the eastern settlements, with no adverse consequences. Few had responded to these announcements.

In addition, little had been effectively done by the officials to stem the flow of illegal merchandise which had been transported westward and the resulting peltries which had been brought back eastward. Canoe crews that had been authorized to carry supplies in to the missionary stations had been particularly suspected of delivering illicit merchandise to the *coureurs de bois*, and also trading it themselves. Cadillac had noted that "many abuses went on among the people who brought them wine and wafers to say their masses, for their canoes were laden with very heavy loads of goods."[93] In defense of the priests, the Intendant Jacques Raudot had written in 1705:

"I have made inquiry as to what might have laid the Jesuit Fathers open to the suspicion of trading in beaver pelts, as they are accused of doing. What has given rise to this is that they are obliged to make use of servants or hired men to take up the canoes conveying to them their provisions and the other things which they have need of at their missions. Notwithstanding all of the precautions taken, these servants or hired men cannot be prevented from taking goods on their own account, which they trade for their own profit. And as they take them in the canoes belonging to these Fathers, people will believe that it is they [the priests] who carry on this trade."[94]

During the years of the closed posts, canoe loads of illegal trade merchandise had also been paddled into the interior by individuals who had been granted official permission to travel there under various pretexts. Some had been assigned to deliver the declarations of amnesty, while others had been sent to settle the disputes which occasionally arose between various of the allied nations.[95] In addition, the sanctioned trade of the Illinois Country, which was to have been carried out at Ft. St. Louis/Ft. Pimetoui and the post at Chicago, had had a tendency to spread out much farther afield. A number of canoe crews who had been authorized for Illinois had traded instead at the Straits of Mackinac, which lay along the primary route of travel to and from Montreal.[96]

Finally, some traders had simply departed from the St. Lawrence for the west with canoes loaded with trade goods, regardless of the possible penalties. The administrators of the colony had explained this constant exodus to the Minister at Versailles in 1697; they had also noted that much of the clandestine commerce flowed to and from Albany, rather than to and from Montreal:

"Will it be possible to prevent the departure [from the eastern settlements] of our coureurs de bois, who, being deprived of a trade to which they have been accustomed since their infancy, will most assuredly leave without permission, despite the orders of King and Governor? If any escape, notwithstanding all of the care which may be taken to prevent them, who will be able to arrest them in the woods, when they will be determined to defend themselves and to carry their peltries to the English?"[97]

Besides the economic attractions of this occupation, there were also other benefits which had led the men to leave their narrow strips of farmland bordering the St. Lawrence and depart for the west. An account which had been penned in about 1705 had referred to "settlers from the colony who get so accustomed to the business of voyageurs that they become incapable of devoting themselves to cultivating the land; and many of them do not return to their concessions [of land], and become coureurs de bois."[98]

In about the same year, another chronicler had been more specific in noting the attractions which were offered by this way of life:
"Since little time is required to carry out this trade, the life of a coureur de bois [in the interior] is spent in idleness and dissolute living. They sleep, smoke, drink brandy whatever it costs, gamble, and debauch the wives and daughters of the natives. They commit a thousand contemptible deeds. Gambling, drinking, and women often consume all of their capital and the profits of their voyages. They live in complete independence, and account to no one for their actions. They acknowledge no superior, no judge, no law, no police, no subordination."[99]

During the summer of 1699, the royal declarations concerning illegal commerce had been enforced more assiduously by the new Governor, Louis Hector Callières, who had replaced Frontenac after his death during the previous December. To show his firm stance, the new administrator had ordered the seizure of a number of canoes at Lachine, which had been loaded with merchandise bound for traders at the Straits of Mackinac. In the aftermath, the outfitters who had been carrying out this smuggling operation had received heavy fines for their aborted attempt. That same autumn, the administrator had also reported that numbers of *coureurs de bois* had been returning to Montreal in small groups, after their supplies of merchandise had become depleted, since they had made no arrangements for its replenishment.[100]

In the summer of 1700, the Governor had sent the first of many representatives into the interior to urge the exit of the *coureurs.*

However, for the most part, the renegade traders had been unresponsive to the offer:

"I dispatched Sieur [Alphonse] de Tonty, Captain of the troops, to Michilimackinac, in order to convey my orders, agreeable to those of the King, to persuade the Frenchmen who remained there to come down. He brought only 20 of them to me. The others, to the number of 84, adopted, for the most part, the resolution to proceed to the establishment on the Mississippi [the newly-founded Gulf Coast colony], to which 30 of them had already descended in ten canoes, loaded with beaver pelts which they owe to the merchants [outfitters and investors] of this country. [Pierre Lemoine,] Sieur d'Iberville [Governor and founder of the Louisiane colony] put this beaver on board his ship, and gave them 1,500 pounds of gunpowder, and some of his people also gave them other goods in trade. I have learned that, since he set sail [for France], ten other canoes loaded with beaver pelts have [also] gone there, and that other coureurs de bois are preparing to do likewise."[101]

During this particular period, it had been rather common for traders to be accused of having carried out illegal voyages to the interior. Accounts of the trials of three such cases have already been presented in this work, within the biography of Robert Réaume. Those court cases had been heard in 1701, 1702, and 1712.

During the summer of 1702, another governmental emissary had been sent to the Straits, to again offer amnesty to the renegade traders if they would return to the eastern settlements. In his subsequent report on the conditions which he had observed there, the Sieur de Boishébert had noted that the former faults of the inhabitants had become even worse. The entire western interior had become awash in brandy and other merchandise, which was being imported from both the St. Lawrence settlements and the Gulf Coast colony. The *coureurs de bois* had laughed at the officer delivering the amnesty declaration, and they had threatened his safety when he had attempted to enforce the Governor's orders. Boishébert had later reported to his superior:

"It is very fine and honorable for me, Monsieur, to be charged with your orders, but it is very vexatious to have only ink and paper as my sole force to carry them out."[102]

On August 30 of that same year, Fr. Étienne Carheil had written to the Governor from his mission at St. Ignace, where he had observed the native and French populations for some fifteen years:

"Since His Majesty has ordered that the voyageurs and the coureurs de bois be recalled, and has granted them an amnesty to facilitate their return, that recall has not pleased everyone. Several persons in authority [in the St.

Lawrence Valley] who [formerly] maintained various trading relationships here have not ceased to continue the same, by secretly sending every year to their fugitive agents supplies for carrying on a new trade...Those very persons who were sent here under the pretense of coming to bring the amnesty came, in reality, solely to trade during the entirety of that time...That is why, for so many years, new amnesties are continually being requested, because the previous ones were always rendered useless."[103]

In 1702, the year after Cadillac and his large party had established Ft. Pontchartrain at Detroit, the commandant had recorded his thoughts concerning the French traders who then inhabited the Straits (where he had formerly been in command). He had also voiced his sentiments on why and how they should be removed from there:

"Michilimackinac...is now the scene of all debauchery, serving as a retreat for all who are in rebellion against the orders of the King, and for the libertines who set out from Montreal every day, taking an enormous quantity of brandy there by way of the Grand [Ottawa] River, which they sell to the natives...
If [the St. Ignace and Gros Cap settlements at] Michilimackinac were not in existence, and there were no more provisions there, it would be impossible for deserters to take goods there, for there are 300 leagues [900 miles] of very difficult route between Montreal and Michilimackinac..."[104]

Two years later, during the summer of 1704, the newest amnesty announcement had been delivered to the French residents at the Straits, by Captain Nicolas d'Ailleboust, Sieur de Mantet. He had traveled west with two canoe loads of presents and trade goods for the native populations, while the missionary Fr. Pierre Gabriel Marest had brought in one loaded canoe in the same small brigade. At the end of the summer, the only men who had traveled out with the officer had been those few individuals who had gone up that season to collect peltries from the renegade traders who were indebted to them.[105]

By 1710, it had become clear that it would be necessary to reinstate the license system, and also to reactivate the post at the Straits of Mackinac, as both a military and a commercial facility. Clairambault d'Aigremont, who had conducted an extensive inspection tour of the interior posts two years earlier, supplemented his report with an additional letter to Versailles at this time:

"The man Petit Renaud dit Mitasses de Velours (Little Fox, nicknamed Velvet Leggings) came down from Michilimackinac last year [in 1709], with a great many furs, in which it appears that the secretary to the Governor General had a large share. He has gone up again this year, with the three

canoes which conveyed the property of the missionaries. The voyageurs were all men chosen by the Governor General. It is sufficiently well known that it is on the condition that they convey for [the Governor], or for his henchmen, a certain quantity of goods which are most suitable for trading.

It must not be expected that we can oblige all of the coureurs de bois to return to the colony, nor even retain in the settlements those who are obedient there, except by re-establishing the licenses. Those people, not being accustomed to tilling the soil, will never submit to doing so, however they may be punished. This country is composed of persons of various characters and of different inclinations. Each of them ought to be managed, and can contribute to making the country flourish. The coureurs de bois are useful in Canada for the fur trade, which is the only branch [of the economy] which can be relied upon."[106]

Although licenses authorizing traders to operate in the interior had still not been officially permitted in 1714, at least three parties had received permission that year to carry out commerce at the Straits of Mackinac. In addition, the Governor had sent a canoe there ordering Captain de Lignery to arrange for the participation of large numbers of allied warriors and *coureurs de bois* in the campaign against the Fox nation, which was scheduled to take place during the following summer of 1715. However, in that latter year, the proposed expedition would not come to fruition, as is discussed later. At any rate, the licensing system would be reinstated in 1716, the closure era of the interior posts would come to an end, and an entire series of posts would be established there. With these events, the numbers of illegal traders in the west would reduce drastically, as avenues for legal, licensed commerce would again be made available to large numbers of traders.

However, the restoration of the system of licenses and permits did not by any means totally eliminate the operations of numerous *coureurs de bois*. Such men would work beyond the scope of the authorities throughout the remainder of the French regime. Various of their activities would be described by Captain Louis de La Porte, Sieur de Louvigny, in a 1720 report to Versailles, based upon his experiences as the commandant of the *Pays d'en Haut*. In this missive, he would offer his insider's observations on the activities of illegal traders, who were still very much present at Michilimackinac and elsewhere in the interior. He would also describe the infractions that were being committed even by licensed traders:

"When the [new] posts were established in the Upper Country [after the *period of closures had ended]...it was with the intention that a certain number of licenses would be granted, under specified conditions, for trading with the natives of each place, which licenses would not be valid at other posts. In this manner, the Frenchmen who obtained these licenses would ensure the safety of the post to which each of them was assigned, without being allowed to roam with the natives in the woods and to infringe upon the limits of the other posts. These just regulations are transgressed by the greed of the coureurs de bois, a greed which is detrimental to the state, to good order, and to commerce. The impunity with which they have violated the law seems to constitute an authority for these voyageurs, against whom it will be necessary to fix a severe and exemplary penalty, to be visited upon all offenders based upon the valid accusation and report by the officers in command at the forts, and by the missionaries...*

The threats of the natives to go among the English [to trade] are often made to avoid paying their debts. The greed of the French traders leads them to lend [sell on credit] easily, and also in greater amounts than the natives can pay back. This gives rise to quarrels, and leads the French to run after their debts, and to pass the winter in the woods and to fix their abode in the Upper Country, which renders then undisciplined and like the natives. Therefore, in order to secure order, I think that it ought to be forbidden for the French to [sell on credit] clothing; they should be allowed to [sell on credit] only gunpowder and shot, to enable the natives to hunt and subsist. They should also be forbidden to pass the winter stealthily in the woods, roaming about with the natives. Instead, they should remain at the posts which are designated in their licenses. It is not for the natives to keep the French in order, but it is for us, who ought to be law-abiding, in order to bring the natives to be so by the persuasion of our example. Indeed, they would conform to these examples if they were not led astray by the coureurs de bois, who refuse to obey the orders which are given to them...

It would be necessary...to have a prohibition issued by the Council and published throughout the entire country, which would inflict material punishment -- either confiscation to the Royal domain of the property and estates of those violating the law, or some other severe penalty -- which will reduce to submission the coureurs de bois, who put their trust in the nearness of the English [to carry out their illicit commerce]"[107]

In 1724, as part of their ongoing efforts to control and restrict the activities of illegal traders, the colonial officials would announce a new regulation. As of December of that year, all of the habitants in the St. Lawrence communities who owned one or more birchbark canoes would be obliged to make a declaration of those craft to the secretary of the court jurisdiction which was closest to their domiciles.[108]

Three years later, in 1727, the Anglos would establish Ft. Oswego in the southeastern corner area of Lake Ontario, beside the mouth of the Oswego River. This facility, called Chouaguen by the French, would serve as a very convenient outlet for illegal peltries, delivered by both unlicensed French traders and their native counterparts. The location of this post would eliminate the need for them to paddle along the full lengths of the Oswego and Mohawk Rivers, thus shortening by about 170 miles the eastbound voyages that they had formerly made from the interior all the way to Albany.

A decade later, the presence of illicit French traders in the west would still be very much a part of the fur trade business. In an effort to convince the illegal men to return permanently to the St. Lawrence communities, another proclamation of amnesty would be declared by the King in 1737.[109]

Eleven years after that, in 1748, their presence in the west would still be a troublesome issue for the commanders at the interior posts and the colonial administrators in the St. Lawrence Valley. In that summer, the leader of the brigade that descended from the Straits of Mackinac would deliver to the Governor a roster from the commandant of Ft. Michilimackinac, Jacques Legardeur, Sieur de Saint Pierre. This list would include the names of the *coureurs de bois* who were still operating in the west. In response, the administrator would assure the officer that "we shall pay close attention" to the activities of those individuals and their associates.[110]

In May of 1750, Governor Jacques Pierre de Taffanel, Sieur de La Jonquière, would still be wrestling with abuses and misbehaviors by those who were working in the peltries commerce in the interior. As a result, he would issue an ordinance concerning various aspects of the trade, which he would summarize in this manner:

"To put an end to the infringements of the prohibitions which are inserted into the licenses; to prevent the lessees [of the posts] and the voyageurs from encroaching upon one another's rights; to stop the coureurs de bois; to forbid the trade which is carried out by certain voyageurs with the English; and finally to divert the native nations from the said trade [with the English]."[111]

Even as the French regime would be approaching its final years, there would still be numerous problems involving illegal activities in the west, which were being committed by both licensed and unlicensed traders. In an attempt to curb these illicit actions, in May of 1755, Governor Ange de Menneville, Sieur Duquesne, would issue a new series of ordinances concerning various aspects of this commerce. His document would be entitled "Regulations for Trade at the Upper Posts."

"It has come to our knowledge that many voyageurs who obtain licenses multiply the number of canoes as much as they please, without fear of inquiry regarding such abuse, or fear of inquiry regarding brandy, which they carry in excess of the quantity which is allowed. Therefore, we have deemed it indispensable to remedy all such abuses, which are based upon bad faith and independence, by means of the following rules:

Article 1.

When a canoe shall arrive at [a given post], the commandant at such post shall request that our permit be shown to him, and shall ascertain...whether the number of canoes is not in excess of that which is allowed by us. In the event of contravention, he shall seize and confiscate the entire cargo of the person who has committed the fraud, sell the same, and send the proceeds from it to us, to be distributed to the hospitals. He shall likewise send to us, under good and safe custody, the person who had charge of the said cargo.

Article 2.

We order the [commandant] to make an equally accurate inquiry regarding the quantity of brandy which is allowed, and we order him in the event of contravention, to inflict the same punishment under this article as under the one regarding the number of canoes in excess of a license.

Article 3.

We have been further informed that a number of the voyageurs who go to the Upper Country establish their residence there, without our permission, either to trade by stealth between one post and another, or to lead a dissolute life with the native women. Being desirous of remedying an abuse which is so prejudicial to the welfare of the colony in every respect, we order the [commandant] to send back to us all those who, within the extent of his post, are not acknowledged to be domiciled at [that post], and who are reputed to be coureurs de bois.

Article 4.

We further order the [commandant] not to send [any individuals] to trade at the posts which are outside of his jurisdiction, and to arrest all those who may come by stealth to trade within his jurisdiction. He is to send them to us under good and safe custody, confiscating the goods which are in their charge for the benefit of the hospitals...This regulation is a general one, which confines each commandant to the limits of his post with regard to ordinary and legitimate trade."[112]

Now we return to the activities of François Brunet dit Le Bourbonnais. In 1716, it would be very easy for him, along with large numbers of his fellow voyageur-traders, to travel legally to the Upper Country. In this instance, the men would paddle into the interior, equipped and fed at government expense, in order to first serve as militia fighters. After the military campaign had been completed, they would be permitted to remain in the west for a full year of commerce, at no cost to themselves except for their individual supplies of trade goods.

The military expedition against the native people of the Fox nation, who resided in the region of Green Bay on Lake Michigan, had actually commenced in the previous year, in 1715. (A detailed discussion of this entire martial campaign, including the multiple events which had led up to it, the aftermath, and detailed footnotes, has already been presented in the biography of Robert Réaume.) The combined forces who had paddled westward from the St. Lawrence communities that summer had included 24 regular soldiers, numerous militiamen-traders, and a party of native allied warriors from the St. Lawrence Valley. According to the plan, they were to travel via Detroit to the Straits of Mackinac, join the many *coureurs de bois* from the interior plus warriors from the northern regions who would have assembled there, and then travel southwestward as a massed army to reach the Green Bay region by the end of August. However, the forces from the St. Lawrence had apparently tarried for an extended period of time at Detroit, probably conducting the trading there that was supposed to have been postponed until after the campaign had been completed. Thus, they did not actually arrive at the Straits until September, too late in the season to carry out the campaign. As a result, the commandant had allowed about one hundred French traders who had previously gathered at the Straits to depart for Montreal, upon their request.

It was most certainly at this time that the new Ft. Michilimackinac had been constructed on the southern shore of the Straits, by the considerable force of men who had been assembled there. The numerous arriving traders had required extensive amounts of secured and sheltered storage space for their merchandise and supplies. In addition, the garrison of 24 soldiers who were now to be permanently stationed there had also required buildings in which to live, work, and store their supplies year round. Eventually, the commandant had allowed many of the traders to disperse, to carry out the commerce which had been promised to them, even though their services as militia fighters had not yet been called upon.

In the spring of 1716, preparations were made throughout the St. Lawrence settlements with the intention of successfully carrying out the Fox campaign which had not come to fruition during the previous year. It was at this time that the license system was officially reinstated (having been curtailed for eighteen years, ever since 1698). All of the voyageur-traders who agreed to travel to the interior to participate in the military expedition were granted free trading permits. This was done with the understanding that, after their martial service had been completed, they would be permitted to remain in the interior until the autumn of 1717. (Those men who had ascended to Mackinac during the previous year would be obliged to come down to the St. Lawrence settlements after the campaign, in the autumn of 1716.)

At this time, François Brunet heeded the adage *"Il faut battre le fer pendant qu'il est chaud,"* ("Strike the iron while it is hot," or paraphrased in English, "Make hay while the sun shines"). Preparing himself to join this expeditionary force and then take advantage of the associated commercial opportunities (which would be legal this time, for a change), he acquired a consignment of trade goods from the Montreal merchant Pierre You, Sieur de La Découverte. It was this individual who had provided the merchandise to Françoise, to be shipped westward to the Ottawa Country, back in March of 1715. (That year, François had exited from Michilimackinac to Montreal by June 15, in time to pay off this outfitter on or before that particular date. Thus, he could not have been one of the traders who had traveled northward from Detroit in August or early September of 1715, during the abortive campaign of that year.) On April 27, 1716, the outfitter and the trader together visited the office of the Montreal notary Michel Lepailleur, to officially register the debt which Monsieur Brunet owed to the businessman, for the merchandise that he had just supplied for the upcoming venture. In their contract, the recipient was identified as "François Brunet, voyageur, from Lachine."[113]

Four days later, on May 1, Captain Louis de Laporte, Sieur de Louvigny, and about 225 Frenchmen departed from Montreal, headed for Michilimackinac by way of the lower Great Lakes route and Detroit. Upon their arrival at the Straits, this eastern force, including the new additions from Detroit, was joined by the garrison soldiers at the fort and the legions of legal and illegal Frenchmen who were in the west. Ottawa warriors who resided at Michilimackinac and Ojibwa fighting men from Sault Ste. Marie also joined the army. These combined forces, containing some 800 men (including François

Brunet), then paddled westward to the southern end of Green Bay, where they soon located the primary settlement of the Fox nation, on the Fox River. The siege of their stout fort, which contained some 500 warriors and about 3,000 women, consisted of heavily bombarding its inhabitants with four cannons and a mortar day and night, and gradually advancing a trench toward the fortifications. All the while, the French and native attackers hoped that the neighbors of the Fox nation, the Kickapoos, Mascoutens, and Sauks, would not send warriors to assist their besieged friends. Finally, the Fox leaders sought a truce, and subsequently agreed to the presented conditions. These consisted of a general peace, restoration of all of the prisoners whom they held, replacement at a future date of all casualties with captured native slaves, and payment at a future date of reparations for all governmental expenses of the expedition. These amazingly easy terms have often been explained, both at the time and since, by noting that this campaign was primarily a profit-generating one, for both the military and civilian participants along with their backers in the St. Lawrence Valley. That is to say, the various participants were not as interested in subduing the Fox people as they were in benefitting from the commerce that took place in conjunction with the expedition.

It is very likely that François was able to complete his trading in the *Pays d'en Haut* before bitter cold and ice closed off the water navigation for the winter, and that he paddled out to rejoin his family on their farm at Lachine before the freeze. It is known that certain of the men who had carried out the Fox campaign did return to the St. Lawrence communities before winter. These individuals included Captain Louvigny, the overall commander of the entire operation. The evidence for the return of Monsieur Brunet to the east is simple: Françoise became pregnant at about the beginning of February in 1717. (However, an alternate explanation for the commencement of her pregnancy at this time would be that her husband remained in the Upper Country over the winter and spring of 1717, and that someone else fathered this baby.)

Wherever he did spend this particular winter and spring, François was present at Lachine in the third week of June in 1717. On the 22nd of this month, he stood beside the baptismal font in the church, as the godfather and name-giver of the baby who had been born on this day to the local residents Jean Bizet and Catherine Louise Gros. This was the seventh child of to be fathered by this craftsman, who was a master blacksmith and maker of edged tools. On this day, the godmother was 27-year-old Marie Angélique Girard, who had married Pierre Quesnel in this same edifice five months earlier.[114]

Three months before this christening ceremony, Françoise had also appeared in the Lachine church as a baptismal sponsor. On March 27, along with her co-sponsor Pierre Quesnel, she had stood beside her one-day-old nephew Pierre Couillard, who had been born as the seventh and final child of Anne Brunet and Pierre Couillard. The officiating priest had recorded in the ledger that the father, Pierre Couillard, Sr., was "absent." In this case, he was most likely away trading legally in the Upper Country, after having participated as a militia fighter in the Fox campaign. (No other documentation besides this one instance has yet been located for the likely participation of Pierre Couillard, Sr. in the fur trade.)[115]

Little Marie Louise Brunet entered the world at Lachine on November 4, 1717. The christening ceremony of this fourth child in the brood of François and Françoise was held at the church there seven days later, on the 11th. On this day, the baby's godfather was her unmarried uncle Nicolas Brault dit Pomainville, age 20, who had commenced his twelve-year career as a voyageur in April of this year; he was the eldest child of the deceased Georges Brault and François' sister Barbe Brunet. The infant's godmother was Marie Clémence Girard, age 23, the unmarried daughter of the Lachine residents Léon Girard and Marie Clémence Beaune, both of whom were deceased. (This young woman would not marry until she was 30 years old.) Interestingly, the priest recorded the male sponsor in the register as "Nicolas Pomainville," using only his *dit* name as his full family name.[116]

About five months later, François lost for the second time one of his adult siblings; this time, it was his youngest sister, Angélique. (His older sibling Catherine, the wife of Pierre Tabault, had died at Montreal five years earlier, at the age of 33.) On April 20, 1718, four days after having celebrated her 27th birthday, Angélique passed away and was interred in the Lachine cemetery. During their eight years of married life, she and Jean Tabault had produced two children; however, both of them had died at an early age, one at four years and the other at eleven months. The widowed Jean would remarry six years after Angélique's passing, but he and his second wife would not produce any offspring, and he would perish after just four years.[117]

During this summer of 1718, one of the most elderly of the residents of the Lachine seigneury was arrested and brought before the Montreal Court, accused of having sold brandy to native people without an official permit, which was strictly prohibited. Alexis Buet, a farm worker who was about 73 to 79 years old at this time (he stated to the Judge that his age was 75), had lived with his family in the easternmost section of the seigneury for more than forty years. His property commenced about $1^1/10$ mile northeast of the Brunet family land. The criminal charges had been leveled against him in Court by Fr. Jacques Tessier, the resident Sulpician priest of the Lachine parish. Having arrived in New France only thirteen months earlier, this cleric was apparently still possessed with a fiery zeal when it came to the obedience of the myriad rules and regulations. On June 18, one of the subpoenaed witnesses who testified in this case was Françoise David, who was identified as "wife of François Brunet, age 30". Interestingly, this was the age that she provided while under oath, yet she was truly five months short of age 34. Other local residents who were also summoned to give sworn testimony before the Court in this case included Françoise's sisters-in-law Élisabeth Brunet, "wife of [Jean Baptiste] Brault dit Pomainville, age 34," and Anne Brunet, "wife of Pierre Couillard, age 37." These two witnesses were actually 33 and 38 years old, respectively. The additional subpoenaed testifiers from Lachine were Marie Anne Marchand, age 47, the wife of Joseph Brault dit Pomainville, and Françoise Lecomte, age 35, the wife of François Gauthier. Apparently, these five local women were compelled under oath to provide damning evidence against the accused Monsieur Buet, since he was convicted of the criminal charge.[118]

In the year 1719, during which François would celebrate his 37th birthday, he served as an official witness in the Lachine church on three occasions within the span of $7^1/2$ months; two of these were for mournful interments, while one was for an optimistic baptism. First, on May 4, he attended the funeral of Jacques Paré, the 24-year-old husband of Anne Caron, age 20. After Monsieur Paré had completed the employment of his 1714 voyageur contract, the young couple had been married in the Lachine church in November of 1717. During their short eighteen months of married life, they had produced one baby; this son was now seven months old. The young widow would wait nine years before she would remarry. (The other funeral witness besides François who was recorded in the register was Jean Picard.)[119]

Three months later, on August 1, François stood as the godfather of Anne Marie, an Abenaki infant who had been born 55 days earlier, back on June 6. Her parents, who usually resided at the Abenaki mission of St. François du Lac (some sixty miles down the St. Lawrence), had been earlier given the baptismal names of Robert and Marie Louise. Standing beside François as the godmother and name-grantor was his unmarried niece Marie Anne Couillard, who was six weeks short of her 14th birthday; her parents were Pierre Couillard and Anne Brunet.[120]

Three days before the Feast of Noël, on December 22, it fell upon our François Brunet and Pierre Galien to witness the forlorn funeral of Catherine Louise Gros, age 36, the wife of the blacksmith and farrier Jean Bizet. François had stood as the godfather at the baptism of this couple's son Jean $2^1/2$ years earlier, back in June of 1717. Catherine's untimely death had resulted from complications following the birth of their next child, Guillaume, who had arrived at Lachine on November 25 in this year of 1719. The mother had lived for five weeks after the delivery; unfortunately, her tiny baby would follow her to the grave just nine days later. Jean and Catherine had been married and residing in the Lachine seigneury for sixteen years; during that time, they had produced a total of eight children.[121]

In the heart of the winter of 1720, François received a rather small piece of land from the seigneurs of Montreal Island, the Sulpicians. On February 26, he visited the office of the Montreal notary Pierre Raimbault to register this granted property, which was located near his other lands in the Lachine seigneury. In this document, the recipient was identified as "François Brunet, from the Côte de Lachine [Sault St. Louis] near the Commons land."[122]

During all of his years of working in the fur trade, Monsieur Brunet had always acquired his outfit of equipment, food supplies, and merchandise, or at least the supplemental items that he needed for that given venture, from a stay-at-home merchant-outfitter in advance of the journey. After completing his sojourn in the west, he had then paid for the supplied articles with some of the furs and hides that he had garnered in the interior. In the spring of 1720, he decided to switch to a slightly different approach, at least for the upcoming venture. On May 21, he formed a partnership with the 28-year-old Montreal voyageur-merchant Jacques François Poisset. In their business arrangement, which was recorded on this day by the Montreal notary Jacques David, Monsieur Poisset would provide the needed equipment, supplies, and trade goods. Both of the partners would conduct the commerce in the west, and afterward they would settle their finances accordingly.

Poisset represented the third generation of a family of businessmen in the colony. His grandfather, François Poisset, Sieur de La Conche, having emigrated from La Rochelle, had operated as a merchant in the Lower Town area of Quebec. Then his father, François Poisset, Sieur de La Conche et Dutreuil, had carried out his own business as a merchant bourgeois in the same section of the capital town. These two generations of businessmen had died in 1691 and 1697, respectively. Jacques François, the only surviving child of his parents, had relocated upriver from Quebec to the Montreal area in or before 1713, when he had been 21 years old. After marrying Élisabeth Quenet (the daughter of the businessman Jean Quenet and his wife Étiennette Hurtubise) at the Lachine church in July of 1713, the couple had then produced three children at Montreal by the summer of 1719. However, their first baby had died in August of 1716 at the age of ten months; the second one would only be documented by his baptismal record in 1717; and the third one, Jean François, Jr., would perish just three weeks after this business arrangement was ratified with Monsieur Brunet in 1720, which would be two weeks after the lad's first birthday. In their partnership agreement, Monsieur Poisset's associate was identified as "François Brunet, voyageur, from the parish of Lachine."[123]

After arranging this partnership, François may have postponed his departure for the interior for some seven or eight weeks, until after the fifth Brunet baby had arrived safely. Fr. Tessier, the resident priest of the Lachine parish, penned the following record into the church's ledger to mark that occasion:

"On the thirty-first day of July, 1720, has been baptized by us, the undersigned parish priest, François, born yesterday, son of François Brunet dit Bourbonnais, habitant of this parish, and of Françoise David, his wife. The godfather was Louis Brunet dit Bourbonnais, uncle of the child, and the mother was Marie Madeleine Girard, all of this parish, who have said that they do not know how to sign.
Signed,
J. Le Tessier, parish priest of Lachine"[124]

Since the cleric did not identify the father as "absent," it is highly likely that François, Sr. had not yet left for the west. The godfather on this day, his younger brother Louis, was 23 years old at this point; he would marry in this same church five months later, on January 4, 1721. The godmother of François, Jr., Marie Madeleine Girard, who was four months older than Louis, would be the woman whom Louis would join in matrimony on that January day. François would not be present for this jubilant celebration, since he would still be away on his trading trip at that time. In his stead, the official witnesses on the groom's side would be Louis' mother Barbe Beauvais, his uncle Raphaël Beauvais, and his brother-in-law Jean Baptiste Brault dit Pomainville.[125]

However, even though François was absent at the time of the young couple's wedding, he was back in time to stand as the godfather of their first baby, who arrived about eleven months after the couple had exchanged their vows. On December 12, 1721, one-day-old Marie Josèphe Brunet was christened in the Lachine church. On this happy day, her two sponsors were her paternal uncle François Brunet and her maternal aunt Marie Angélique Girard (who had married Pierre Quesnel nearly five years earlier).[126]

Two days later, on December 14, François was again in attendance at this same edifice, this time to officially witness the wedding of one of his nephews. Jean Baptist Brault dit Pomainville (age 22, who was apparently known only by his *dit* name of Pomainville), was the second child of the deceased Georges Brault and Barbe Brunet. He had grown up on the farm immediately west of the Brunet family property. His bride Marie Caron, age 19, had likewise been born and raised in the eastern section of the Lachine seigneury. At their wedding, besides François and Louis Brunet, uncles of the groom, and Nicolas Brault, brother of the groom, the other official witnesses were the bride's uncle Claude Caron and cousin Angélique Caron from Montreal as well as the couple's friends Jean Baptiste Paré and Marie Anne Paré from Lachine.[127]

In the following spring, Françoise and François' daughter Angélique, who was five weeks short of her eleventh birthday, appeared as the godmother at a christening ceremony at Lachine. On May 18, 1722, she stood beside the baptismal font with her co-sponsor and cousin Jean Baptiste Brault dit Pomainville, 17 years old, who was the son of Jean Baptiste Brault, Sr. and Élisabeth Brunet. The infant on this occasion was François, the one-day-old son and ninth child of Jean Leroux dit Rousson and Louise Chaussé.[128]

New Year's Day in 1723 marked the arrival of the next member of François and Francoise's family. On the same day on which the tiny lad arrived, his proud parents took him to the Lachine church so that Fr. Tessier could conduct his baptismal ceremony. Afterward, the cleric recorded in the parish register the christening of Claude Marie Brunet, son of François Brunet dit Bourbonnais and Françoise David. He also noted that the godmother was the baby's aunt Marie Caillé dite Biscornet (age 13), the unmarried daughter of Pierre Caillé and Marie Brunet of Laprairie. In addition, the cleric identified the godfather on this occasion as "Baptiste Brunet of Lachine, brother of the child," which was definitely an error. He most likely meant "Louis Brunet of Lachine, brother of the father."[129]

On the last day of this same month of January, a very large portion of the Brunet clan assembled in the Lachine church for the festive wedding of François' niece Françoise Angélique Brault; $17 2/3$ years old, she was the daughter of the deceased Georges Brault dit Pomainville and Barbe Brunet. Having grown up on the farm immediately west of the Brunet family property, the bride had known her uncle François all of her life. This day, she exchanged nuptial vows with the Lachine voyageur Pierre Noël Legault, Jr., who was age 23. The fourteen official witnesses who were registered by the priest included François, his mother, his brother Louis, his sister Marie, and his brothers-in-law Pierre Couillard, Jean Baptiste Brault, and Martial Moulineuf, along with the bride's brothers Nicolas and Jean Baptiste Brault and her cousin Baptiste Brault. On the groom's side, the witnesses were three of his brothers and a maternal uncle.[130]

Just sixteen months after having delivered their sixth child, Françoise brought their seventh offspring into the world, at the beginning of May in 1724. On the fourth day of this month, when little Marie Catherine was baptized in the Holy Angels church at Lachine, her sponsors were two residents of the parish, Pierre Valois and Marie Catherine Girard. This godfather was married to Marie Clémence Girard, the sister of Louis Brunet's wife (and thus the brother-in-law of François and Françoise), while this godmother was related to these two Girard sisters as well.[131]

Within the next few months, some time after celebrating his 42nd birthday on May 26, 1724, François decided to change occupations, at least temporarily. Probably during the summer or autumn, he accepted the position of agent/tax collector (*fermier*) at Senneville, which was located at the westernmost tip of Montreal Island. It was to this place, some 17 miles west of their farm in the Lachine seigneury, that he relocated with Françoise, who was $39 1/2$ years old at this time, and their five surviving offspring. (It is quite likely that their eldest child, Françoise, who had been born back in 1706, had died some time before this; no documentation for her other than her baptismal record has been preserved. In addition, their unnamed baby girl who had arrived back in October of 1710 had been buried on the same day as her birth.)

Senneville was the sub-fief which had been originally granted in 1672 to the officer Sidrac Michel Dugué, Sieur de Boisbriant, who had arrived in New France in 1665 as the Captain of his own company within the Carignan-Salières Regiment. He had established a trading post on this piece of land on the western point of Montreal Island, where the Ottawa River ended, flowing into the St. Lawrence River to form the broad Lac St. Louis. As the first place on the Island that would come into view for the convoys of native traders who paddled out from the Upper Country, it was an excellent spot to intercept them before they would reach the site of the trade fair at Montreal. In 1679, the wealthy and prominent Montreal merchants Jacques Le Ber and Charles Lemoine had purchased the land from Captain Dugué, and they had proceeded to conduct their own extensive trading there. Although their interception of customers had been decried as unfair by the other merchants and the residents of Montreal (and it would later be prohibited by the authorities for this reason), such commerce had often been carried out there, on the sly when necessary. Monsieur Le Ber had acquired full ownership of the property in 1685, following the death of his partner and brother-in-law Monsieur Lemoine. In the following year, he had hired craftsmen to construct a field stone windmill on this piece of land, which measured 1,920 feet in river frontage by $3/4$ mile in depth. This stone building had served as a handy defensive fort of refuge, during the many attacks that Iroquois war parties had launched against the local residents during the 1680s and 1690s. In response to these raids, the merchant had eventually had the site bolstered in 1703 by the construction of four stone walls with corner bastions; thus had been born Ft. Senneville. In time, as Jacques Le Ber had aged and retired, his son Jacques, Jr. had inherited the sub-fief from his father, and along with it the title of Sieur de Senneville. In addition to serving as a wealthy peltries merchant in Montreal, the son also had a military career, reaching the rank of Captain by 1716.

By latter 1724, when François Brunet dit Le Bourbonnais moved to the sub-fief to work as its agent/tax collector, Jacques, Jr. was 61 years old (he would die in 1735). Thus, many of the business affairs of Senneville were then being handled by his only surviving son, Joseph

Hippolyte Le Ber, Sieur de Senneville. This officer (about age 27, who would advance from the rank of Ensign to Major three years later), had been married to Anne Marguerite Soumande for nearly seven years. The couple was expecting their sixth child in late December of 1724. Unfortunately, three of their previous five offspring had already died; the two surviving children were ages 5 and 3 (and their sixth baby would only live for two weeks).[132]

It is not clear just what were the duties of Monsieur Brunet as the *fermier* (agent/tax collector) of Senneville. It is not known for certain with whom he dealt or from whom he may have collected fees, although it is quite likely that his contacts were with departing traders who were headed for the *Pays d'en Haut* via the Ottawa River route. The title of official agent/collector of taxes may have indicated that his primary role was to check the government-issued passes of all westbound traders. Four decades earlier, back in 1684 (as was quoted earlier), Governor La Barre had ordered the creation of such a pass-checking system:

"We have ruled against all persons departing from the said town of Montreal or other places in this country, for the said voyages, without Monsieur [Louis Hector de] Callières, Governor of the said town, having seen their permit. He will give them a pass, by virtue of which they will be able to pass by all of the guard posts that it will please him to establish, whether it be at the [western] point of the island or at Lachine, whichever he will judge appropriate."

In addition to checking passes, Monsieur Brunet was probably also assigned to watch for and intercept those individuals who did not follow the licensing policies. As a well-known and highly experienced *coureur de bois*, he may have been specifically chosen for this position because he knew intimately the many stratagems that were regularly used by voyageur-traders who did not hold trading permits. He was very familiar with avoiding the payment of fees for those permits, and with operating beyond the view of governmental officials. (However, choosing this man to play the role of enforcer of official policies might have eventually played out as a perfect example of "hiring the fox to guard the hen house.") Whatever his duties entailed, François would remain on this job for some six or seven years, until about the spring of 1731.

During the entire decade before his arrival here, there had occurred a tremendous surge in the amount of peltries commerce that was being carried out in the Upper Country. This process had started with the Treaty of Utrecht, back in April of 1713, which had ended the War of the Spanish Succession (also called Queen Anne's War), and had initiated a period of peace between France and England that would extend over the next three decades. Firstly, the treaty had declared that the French were obliged to relinquish their posts on Hudson's Bay; this had interrupted the commerce which they had been conducting with a wide array of native populations via that watercourse in the north. In addition, the treaty had stipulated that the Iroquois were British subjects; it had also permitted both the English and the French to trade with the native nations of the interior. Therefore, considering this newly altered situation, the Ministers at Versailles then felt the urgent need to reoccupy the former interior posts, and to construct additional ones as well. The personnel at these facilities would strive to block any invasion by Iroquois and British traders into those regions; they would also work to retain the native inhabitants as French allies.

Between 1715 and 1722, the establishment of forts and smaller posts throughout the Great Lakes region and beyond had generated a great deal of military, diplomatic, and commercial activity in those areas, which had continued thereafter. The creation of these new facilities had reflected the abandonment of the policy which had been attempted at Detroit, that of concentrating large numbers of native residents at selected major centers of commerce, where the inhabitants were induced to gradually adopt French ways. Instead, these new forts had reflected a return to the former policy of the previous century, in which a number of military/commercial facilities were scattered throughout the interior, in the home regions of various native groups.

The primary post and distribution center of Ft. Michilimackinac had been constructed at the Straits of Mackinac during 1715 and 1716, while a small post had also been established on the Maumee River south of Detroit in 1716. (The latter facility served the Maumee-Wabash-Ohio Rivers route, with its connecting Maumee Portage between the first two waterways.) The following year of 1717 had witnessed the founding of three major facilities, including Ft. St. Joseph on the St. Joseph River, Ft. La Baye near the southern end of Green Bay on Lake Michigan, and Ft. Kaministiquia on the northwestern shore of Lake Superior at the mouth of the Kaministiquia River. Ft. La Pointe, on Madeleine Island near the western end of Lake Superior, had been established in 1718, while the Nipigon post, north of Lake

Superior, had been reactivated by this time. In 1720, Ft. Ouiatenon had been constructed on the Wabash River, while Ft. De Chartres (sometimes called the Tamaroas Post) had also been built near the French and native communities on the Mississippi River in Illinois. In this same year, Joncaire's Post had been established on the Niagara River, at the southern end of the Niagara Portage. Ft. Miami, often called Ft. St. Philippe, had been constructed in the years 1721 and 1722, to guard the portage (varying from $4^{1}/2$ to 8 miles in length, depending on water levels) which connected the head of navigation of the Maumee River to the Wabash River. Thus, by the close of 1722, an entire series of posts had been added to Ft. Frontenac and Ft. Pontchartrain, whose operations had not been curtailed during the period of closures. Later in the 1720s, the Michipicoten Post on the eastern shore of Lake Superior as well as Ft. Temiscamingue on the upper Ottawa River had also been added, to intercept native traders who were bound for the Hudson's Bay Company posts on James Bay.

(The Sioux Post would be constructed in 1727-1728 on the upper Mississippi River, and between 1731 and 1741, Pierre Gaultier, Sieur de Laverendrye would establish various forts in the region stretching toward the northwest from Lake Superior. Other officers would establish posts on the lower Saskatchewan River between 1749 and 1753. Thus, the watershed of the Saskatchewan River would represent the maximum expansion point of the fur trade toward the northwest during the French regime. This entire expansion intercepted a great deal of the commerce which had formerly flowed to the Hudson's Bay Company facilities that were positioned along the shores of Hudson's Bay and its southern extension of James Bay.)[133]

As a result of all this activity, by the latter part of 1724, when François Brunet dit Le Bourbonnais was engaged as the agent/fees collector at the westernmost tip of Montreal Island, there was a huge amount of commercial traffic traveling from that place to the west, and later returning from there. His work for the authorities at this particular location most likely entailed keeping tabs on the myriad canoes and individuals who were involved in these moving business operations, which comprised the very core of the economy of New France.

On March 2, 1725, after François and his family had already relocated westward from their farm at Lachine to Senneville, he leased a plot of land in this sub-fief. The transaction, which was recorded by the Montreal notary Jean Baptiste Adhémar on this day, noted that the lessor was "Joseph Hippolyte Le Ber, Sieur de Senneville, Esquire, officer in the Troops of the detachment of the Marine Department and Aide-major at the Place d'Armes in the town of Montreal." In this same document, the lessee was identified as "François Brunet dit Bourbonnais, living at the top of Montreal Island."[134]

Three weeks later, on March 24, François stood as the godfather at a christening ceremony in the Ste. Anne church. Baby Jean, the first child of Jacques Renel dit Lebrun et Fleuridor and Marie Jeanne Lalande dite Langliche, had been born two days earlier in the nearby area which was called Côte St. Philippe. This couple had been married for fifteen months; however, she had been previously married for nearly seven years to Jean Brunet dit Létang, and had borne three children by him before his death in December of 1722. The priest recorded in the Ste. Anne register that the godfather on this occasion was "François Brunet dit Bourbonnais of this parish, agent/tax collector of Senneville," while the godmother was the St. Philippe resident Marie Thérèse Énaud dite Canada, the wife of Jean Martin dit Saint Jean.[135]

Back in 1685, when this parish had been originally founded (encompassing the entire western section of Montreal Island, which was called Le Bout de l'Île or Le Haut de l'Île), it had been dedicated to St. Louis. The original parish church had been erected on Pointe St. Louis, which formed the eastern end of Baie d'Urfé. Some 28 years later, in about 1713, the resident priest here had changed the dedication of the parish from St. Louis to Ste. Anne, who had been the mother of the Blessed Virgin Mary and was the patron saint of mariners, fishermen, and water travelers. At some later date, a new church was constructed about 1 1/2 miles west of the first one, which was also dedicated to Ste. Anne.[136]

After the Brunet family had been residing in the Bout de l'Île area for about a year, they suffered terrible grief upon the death of their youngest child. Little toddler Marie Catherine, who was 17 1/2 months old, was laid to rest in the Ste. Anne cemetery on October 15, 1725. At her funeral, the two official witnesses were Antoine Villeray and Pierre Maupetit, who lived with their families on the fourth and the seventeenth lots east of the church, respectively. Monsieur Maupetit had married Angélique Villeray, daughter of Antoine, seven years earlier. (The dual biography of the Maupetit-Villeray couple is presented next in this work.)[137]

One month later, on November 12, François was asked to sponsor and give his name to the brand-new baby and first child of Pierre Prieur dit Saint Léger and Marie Louise Saint Onge. This couple, who had been wed in the Lachine church 8^1/2 months earlier, lived in the area of Côte St. Philippe. The godfather was recorded by the cleric as "François Brunet, agent/tax collector of Senneville," while the godmother was Marguerite Jousset, the wife of Jacques Desgagnés.[138]

Nine days later, on November 21, François traveled about seven miles eastward to the church at Pointe Claire, to attend the wedding of his niece Marie Anne Tabault. The bride (the daughter of François' sister Catherine and her husband Pierre Tabault, who had been baptized with the given name Marie Marguerite) would turn age 20 in two months; the groom, Thomas Ranger, who was a Lachine voyageur, was 25 years old. In addition to the bride's uncle François Brunet, the other two official witnesses were Pierre Sabourin and Louis Sauvé.[139]

François was again asked to stand as the godfather at a ceremony that was held in the church at Bout de l'Île in March of 1726. Michel Marie Pagési was born on the 17th of the month to Jean Baptiste Pagési dit Saint Amand and Marie Anne Ondoyer, after which he was taken to the priest for baptism on the same day. Standing beside Monsieur Brunet as the godmother on this occasion was the local resident Marie Anne Girardin, the wife of Hubert Ranger dit Laviolette. François had witnessed the marriage of their son Thomas Ranger to Marie Anne Tabault at Pointe Claire, back in the previous November.[140]

On September 15, François traveled to Montreal, to officially record that he had made a partial payment to a young mason who was about to construct a new home for him and Françoise. *"Before [Jean Baptiste Adhémar,] the undersigned royal notary of the Island of Montreal in New France, living at Villemarie on the said Island, was present Paul Bizet, living in this town, who has acknowledged and declared that he has received before the passage of these presents from Sieur François Brunet [dit] Bourbonnais the sum of one hundred livres as an installment and a deduction from the sum of two hundred livres for a house which he is going to build for him of stone with lime and sand [mortar], eighteen feet long by forty feet wide, according to and in conformity with the agreement which they have said that they had [previously] made together. This sum of one hundred livres the said Sieur Bizet has registered as paid by the said Brunet and all others. The remaining one hundred livres the said Brunet promises to give and pay to the said Bizet when the work will be done and completed, which will be subject to his examination. Thus have they promised and obligated themselves.*

[This agreement] made and drawn up at the said Villemarie in the office of the said notary in the year 1726, on the fifteenth day of September in the afternoon, in the presence of the Sieurs François Harel [dit] Despointes and Étienne Trottier [Sieur] Desaulniers, witnesses who have signed with the said notary. The said parties [Bizet and Brunet] have declared that they do not know how to write or sign, having been asked after the reading was done, according to the ordinance.

Signed,

Desaunie, Despointes, and Adhemar, royal notary"[141]

For many years, François had known this young mason, Paul Daniel Bizet (age 28), as well as all three of his parents. Jean Bizet and his first wife Catherine Quenneville had relocated from Montreal to Lachine in about 1701 or 1702. Within one or two years of their arrival, Catherine and the two younger of their three children had died, during the vicious smallpox epidemic of 1702-1703. The mother and the 33-month old girl had both perished on January 27, 1703, one day after the birth of the next baby, a boy; unfortunately, this tiny infant had followed them to the grave ten days later. In November of that same year, Monsieur Bizet had taken a second wife, Catherine Louise Gros. Fourteen years later, François Brunet had stood as the godfather of their seventh child, in June of 1717. Then, some 2 1/2 years later, he had sadly witnessed her funeral, after her death due to complications following the delivery of their last baby.

Paul Daniel Bizet, the eldest child of Paul and his first wife Catherine, had learned the craft of masonry working, and had settled in Montreal to seek his fortune. At this point in 1726, he had been married for nearly eleven years. Paul Daniel and his wife Angélique Guérin (the illegitimate daughter of Marie Brazeau, who had also borne two sons out of wedlock) had already produced six children.[142]

The payment document quoted above mentioned that the two men, craftsman and customer, had previously drawn up a construction agreement. However, that earlier document has not yet been located in the archives of the colony. As a result, many of the details of their agreement, especially the specific community in which the house would be built, are not known. However, according to the surviving records, François had only been leasing property in the Senneville sub-fief at Bout de l'Île. Thus, he most likely had arranged to have their new stone home constructed by the mason on their own land in the eastern section of the Lachine seigneury, in the Sault St. Louis area beside the Lachine Rapids. It was there that François and Françoise had been living with their children before moving to Senneville. This was also the place where various of the other members of the extended Brunet clan had resided with their families for decades.

Three years after this field stone house had been constructed for François and Françoise, most likely on their property at Sault St. Louis, François received a grant of land in the brand-new seigneury of Soulanges. This seigneury, which was located southwest of Île Perrot on the north shore of the St. Lawrence River, had been originally granted to Pierre Jacques Joybert, Sieur de Soulanges, back in October of 1702. However, just three months after receiving this concession, Captain Joybert had died at Quebec. His funeral had been held ten weeks after he had married Marie Anne Bécard; exactly $8^1/2$ months later, their daughter Marie Geneviève had been born. A quarter-century later, when the young woman had wed Captain Paul Joseph Lemoine, Sieur de Longueuil in October of 1728, the seigneury had passed into her husband's possession. It was this officer who granted a lot along the Catarakoui River to François Brunet on April 5, 1729. When the transfer was recorded on this day by the Montreal notary Michel Lepailleur, the recipient was described as "living at the top of Montreal Island." In spite of receiving this property some miles to the southwest of Senneville, there is little evidence which would indicate that François and his family expended much time and energy developing it, during the two more years that they resided at the western end of Montreal Island.[143]

The final week of July in 1730 brought with it a momentous occasion for the Brunet family: the safe arrival of the last baby of the brood. On the same day that she arrived, the 26th, little Anne Renée was taken to the Ste. Anne church to be christened. Her godfather and godmother were Lieutenant René Godefroy, Sieur de Linctot, Esquire (age 55) and his second wife, Marie Catherine d'Ailleboust de Coulonges (age 38). Having been married for twenty months, this local Godefroy couple had welcomed their first child into the world just ten weeks earlier.[144]

Over the span of $22^1/2$ years, Monsieur and Madame Brunet had produced eight children, of whom five would survive to grow up and marry. (However, to these eight well-known offspring must be added another son and another daughter. The surviving documentation of son Antoine does not commence until his marriage at the Ste. Anne church in April of 1738. He was most likely born during the 76-month interval between the arrivals of their well-documented daughters Marie Angélique in June of 1711 and Marie Louise in November of 1717. Likewise, the records of daughter Marie Anne do not begin until her marriage at the Lachine church in November of 1749. At that time, her age was given as 24; thus, she was born in about 1725. This would place her birth during the 63-month interval between the arrivals of their well-recorded daughters Marie Catherine in May of 1724 and Anne Renée in July of 1729. For unknown reasons, the baptisms of these two Brunet offspring are not to be found in the church records.)

During their period of childbearing, François' age had increased from $24^1/2$ to 47, while the age of Françoise had gone from 22 up to $44^2/3$ years. The first one of their offspring had arrived five weeks before they had celebrated their first wedding anniversary. Thereafter, the intervals between the other seven clearly-documented babies had been 46, $8^1/4$, 76, 33, 29, 16, and 63 months, respectively. Within this series of births, there had been several lengthy intervals. These long spaces without pregnancies were in decided contrast to the typical birth patterns of those couples who resided together on a regular, long-term basis, year in and year out; they tended to produce offspring in a rather steady pattern, about every two years or so. In comparison, the wide intervals of time between a number of the Brunet babies may have reflected the many instances in which François had been away conducting trading ventures in the west. This assertion is probably applicable even after one factors into their sequence of births the two children for whom no records of birth and baptism have survived.

Just $5^1/2$ months after welcoming their final child into the family, the Brunet parents experienced a series of events which were unique for them, revolving around the marriage of their eldest surviving offspring. During the heart of the winter in 1730, daughter Marie Angélique was $18^7/12$ years of age. On January 15, she and her fiancé Guillaume Lalonde visited the Montreal notary Joseph Raimbault to draw up their marriage contract. The prospective groom, five weeks short of his 25th birthday, was the son of Jean Baptiste Lalonde, the Captain of the militia forces of the Côte Ste. Anne, and Jeanne Gervais (the dual biography of these parents has already been presented in this work). In the document, the scribe noted that the parents of the prospective bride were "François Brunet dit Bourbonnais, habitant, and Françoise David, of the parish of Ste. Anne at the top of Montreal Island."[145]

On the following day, the young couple, along with various of their friends and relatives, assembled in the Ste. Anne church for the wedding ceremony. Afterward, the officiating priest recorded the three official witnesses: Lieutenant René Godefroy, Sieur de Linctot, Esquire; Jacques Charbonnier, merchant bourgeois; and Raphaël Beauvais, Montreal innkeeper, who was 85 years old and a great-uncle of the groom. (The biography of the newly wedded Lalonde-Brunet couple is presented later in this work; in this study, the husband has been designated as Guillaume Lalonde Number 2.)[146]

This exciting occasion for the family was followed by an equally cheerful event sixteen months after the wedding: the safe arrival of Françoise and François' first grandchild, who was named François Amable Lalonde. On May 26, 1731, the day after his birth, the sponsors at the baby's baptism in the Ste. Anne church were his maternal grandfather François Brunet and his paternal grandmother Jeanne Gervais.[147]

Some time within the next three months, François relinquished his position of *fermier* (agent/tax collector) of Senneville, after which the Brunet family moved back to their home beside the Lachine Rapids, in the eastern section of the Lachine seigneury. It is not possible to determine whether Monsieur Brunet left his position so that he could return to active trading himself, or whether he returned to commercial peltries operations because he had been removed from his official role at the western tip of Montreal Island (a job which he had held for some six or seven years).

At any rate, at the age of 49, François again took up trading for furs and hides on a much more extensive scale than he had previously done (at least according to the surviving documents). During his preparations for his return to active commerce, he acquired nearly 5,000 livres worth of goods from a Montreal outfitter in August of 1731. In addition, he also took on a young partner, Jacques Boutin. This new associate, who was likewise a resident of the Lachine seigneury, was 25 years old and unmarried. The young man's first known hiring contract to work as a voyageur had been drawn up in June of the previous year. This time, however, he would be laboring as a full partner.

"Before [Joseph Raimbault] the royal notary, etc., were present in person the

Sieurs Jacques Boutin and François Brunet [dit] Bourbonnais of Lachine, at present in this town [Montreal], who have voluntarily acknowledged and declared that they well and duly owe to Sieur Jacques Quesnel [dit Fonblanche], merchant bourgeois of this town, present and assenting, the sum of 4,896 livres 13 sols 6 deniers, for good and saleable merchandise which was furnished to them by the said Sieur Creditor for the voyage which they are going to make from this town to Detroit. This said sum of 4,896 livres 13 sols 6 deniers, plus 40 sols [2 livres] as a fee for these presents, the said Sieurs Debtors have promised by these same presents, together and solidly, one for the other, to hand over and pay to the said Sieur Creditor at his home in this town, in good and saleable peltries [of other animals than beavers] at the prices of the merchant outfitters or in beaver pelts at the price of the Office [of the exporting monopoly company], or to the bearer, to be delivered during the course of the month of August of next year, 1732, all being done without division, discussion, or disloyalty, renouncing any such said divisions. They have placed under bond all of their possessions, both moveable and real estate, present and future, and especially the belongings which may be produced by the said voyage, as natural wages for the said Sieur Creditor, according to the nature of loans. For the execution of these presents, the said debtors have selected as their [temporary] legal residence in this town [to which writs may be delivered] the home of Gabriel Gibault, where Pierre Cardinal is presently living, located on St. Pierre Street. Thus have they promised, obligated themselves, waived, etc.

[This agreement] made and drawn up at the said Montreal in the office of the said notary in the year 1731, on the 16th of August in the afternoon, in the presence of Sieur Joseph Caron, attorney for civil cases, and Joseph Gouin, tailor of suits, living in this town, who have signed with the said Sieur Creditor, the said Jacques Boutin, and the said notary, but not François Brunet. He has declared that he does not know how to write or sign, having been questioned after the reading was done, according to the ordinance.
Signed,
Boutin, Fonblanche, J. Caron, Gouin, and Raimbault, Jr., notary"[148]

To form a general idea of the types of articles which were supplied by outfitters to Detroit-bound voyageur-traders at this particular time, it is informative to examine the ledgers of another merchant-outfitter of Montreal, Jean Alexis Lemoine, Sieur Monière. Some 22 months after François and his partner Boutin had received their outfit from Monsieur Quesnel, Monsieur Lemoine supplied the below-listed items to the trader Monsieur Cuillerier, for his journey to Detroit in June of 1732. The merchandise, supplies, and equipment are presented here in a simple summary fashion, without including any descriptive details, any specific amounts, or any prices for the respective listings. In total, the charges for this outfit came to 3,196 livres. Nearly half of this cost was represented by the fabrics, sewing articles, items of clothing, and blankets.

Woolen, linen, and cotton fabrics
Binding tape or gartering
Silk braid
False silver braid
Needles
Packing needles
Thread
Chemises for women
Shirts for young children
Hooded coats
Pump-style shoes
Blankets
Cradle blankets
Kettles
Axes
Tomahawks
Butcher knives
Crooked knives
Awls
Fire steels
Scrapers
Brass wire
Nails for flooring, roofing, and shingles or lath
Glass beads
Pearl necklaces
Dressing table mirrors
Vermilion paint pigment
Wooden combs
Soap
Calumet pipes
Playing cards
Paper
Guns
Gunpowder

Lead balls and shot
Gunflints
Gun worms
Tobacco
Pork
Biscuit
Flour
Salt
Pepper
Red wine
Brandy

Canoe
Sealant gum for canoe repairs
Cod line for towing lines
Birchbark strips to cover the pole frame of traveling shelter[149]

Certain portions of the supplies of pork, biscuit, flour, salt, pepper, wine, and brandy served as the provisions of the crew, both en route and during their sojourn at Ft. Pontchartrain. Likewise, the canoe, repair gum, towing lines, and bark strips for covering a traveling shelter were utilized by the trader and his employees during the journey to and from Detroit. It is to be assumed that the contents of the outfit that Messieurs Brunet and Boutin received from Monsieur Quesnel was very similar to the above listed materiel.

The voyageur-merchant who supplied these articles to the two partners, Jacques François Quesnel dit Fonblanche, was 47 years old. Having been born at Lachine to the master gunsmith Olivier Quesnel and Catherine Prudhomme, he had grown up there and at Montreal. After having married Marie Anne Truillier in 1715, the couple had produced eight children at Montreal in twelve years, before her death there in February of 1729. After spending twenty months as a widower with several young children, he had finally remarried in October of 1730, to Marie Anne Franquelin.[150]

After the Brunet-Boutin duo paddled along the upper St. Lawrence River and then over the lengths of Lakes Ontario and Erie, they reached Detroit in the autumn of 1731. It is highly likely that they then took up residence in the home that François had owned within Ft. Pontchartrain for some 23 years, ever since his lot on Rue Ste. Anne had been granted to him by Captain Cadillac back in 1708.

However, rather than remaining at Ft. Pontchartrain over the coming winter, François left his partner in charge of conducting their business operation there, while he returned to the St. Lawrence communities before the freeze set in. Two entries in church registers over the winter of 1731-1732 specifically document him on Montreal Island during the course of this frozen season. It is not known whether he later returned to Detroit, to assist Monsieur Boutin in carrying out their joint commerce and in transporting out to Lachine the resulting furs and hides. However, what is known for certain is that the two partners would not be able to pay off their outfitter in August of 1732, as they had agreed in the notary document. In fact, it would not be until September of 1734, a full 37 months after having received the outfit of equipment, supplies, and merchandise, that they would finally settle their debt with the merchant. This payoff would be recorded by the notary in an addendum that he would pen at that time at the bottom of the final page of their agreement:

"The present bond was cancelled by [Jacques Quesnel dit] Sieur Fonblanche when he acknowledged in person that he had been satisfied, and it was signed at Montreal on September 19, 1734.
Signed,
Fonblanche and Raimbault, Jr., notary"[151]

Both of the entries which definitely place François on Montreal Island during the winter of 1731-1732 were recorded in the register of the Ste. Anne parish. He, Françoise, and their six youngest children (ages 14 down to 2 years) had previously moved back to their farm in the Lachine seigneury. However, they still made periodic trips westward on the Island, to visit their relatives and friends in the Bout de l'Île area. December 21, 1731 was one of those occasions, when François stood beside the baptismal font in the Ste. Anne church along with his co-sponsor Marie Michaud. On this day, the infant receiving the sacrament of Baptism was Marie Josèphe Tabault, the one-day-old daughter of Joseph Tabault and Marie Josèphe Sauvé dite Laplante.[152]

Nine weeks later, on February 26, 1732, Monsieur Brunet again found himself standing in this same edifice near the western end of Montreal Island. However, this time the festive occasion was the wedding of the friends Jean Baptist Turpin, Jr. and Marie Louise Magdelaine dite Ladouceur. The groom, age 24, was the son of Jean Baptiste Turpin, Sr. and Marguerite Cousseau, while the 16-year-old bride was the daughter of Étienne Magdelaine dit Ladouceur and Jeanne Boursier. Besides François Brunet, the other four official witnesses were André Turpin, brother of the groom; Joseph Magdelaine dit Ladouceur, uncle of the bride; and Jean Baptiste and Jacques Neveu, first cousins of the bride.[153]

In the years that followed, it seemed that more and more of the ecclesiastical celebrations involving the Brunet family were taking place at the Ste. Anne church, which was located some 17 miles west of the Brunet farm at Lachine. One of these special ceremonies was held on November 21, 1736, when the newest grandchild of Françoise and François, little Guillaume Lalonde, was christened. Standing beside the godfather, who was the infant's 16-year-old maternal uncle François Brunet, was the godmother Marie Josèphe Hunault dite Deschamps. By this point, the young Lalonde-Brunet couple, who had been married for nearly seven years, had taken up residence on Île Perrot. (This baby, who was their fourth offspring, has been designated in this study as Guillaume Lalonde Number 4; he would grow up to marry Marie Charlotte Sauvé dite Laplante. The dual biography of this Lalonde-Sauvé couple is presented later in this work.)[154]

By the spring of 1737, it was time for the second-oldest of the offspring of Françoise and François to marry. At this point, when Marie Louise was $19^{1}/_{2}$ years old, she became engaged to the 39-year-old widower Joseph Émery dit Coderre, who resided in the Côte de Contrecoeur area of the Ste. Anne parish. Back in July of 1725, Joseph had married Marie Perrin, and they had produced two children before her untimely demise in January of 1729. When the Émery-Brunet couple exchanged their nuptial vows in the Ste. Anne church on April 30, the priest listed four official witnesses in the parish ledger: Jean Baptiste Dubreuil, Michel Brabant, Joseph Tabault, and Olivier Perrin.[155]

Nine months later, François and Françoise decided to sell their property which was located on the Catarakoui River in the seigneury of Soulanges, southwest of Île Perrot on the St. Lawrence River. He had been granted this lot by the seigneur there back in April of 1729, nearly nine years earlier. On February 7, 1738, the Brunet couple traveled to the office of the Montreal notary Lepailleur to officially register this land transfer. The buyer was Marie Madeleine Duboc, the widow of Joseph Chénier, as well as her underage children from this union. This family had been living in the Côte du Buisson section of the Soulanges seigneury for at least sixteen years. In the document of sale, the scribe identified the sellers as "François Brunet and Françoise David, his wife, of Lachine on the Island of Montreal."[156]

About nine weeks after they relinquished this land, the third offspring of the Brunets to be wed celebrated his marriage in the church of Bout de l'Île. Since Antoine had most likely been born during the 76-month interval between the arrivals of their daughters Marie Angélique in June of 1711 and Marie Louise in November of 1717, he was probably about 22 to 26 years of age at this time. On April 14, 1738, "Antoine Brunet of this parish, son of François Brunet dit Bourbonnais and Françoise David," took as his wife "Marie Angélique Boyer of this parish, daughter of Étienne Boyer and Barbe Lamoureux." This inspirational ceremony took place three days after the bride had celebrated her nineteenth birthday; she and her nine siblings (five older, four younger) had all been born and raised in the Ste. Anne parish. According to the priest's records, the four official witnesses on this day included Alexandre Boyer (the bride's 17-year-old brother), Jean Mallet, Jean Turpin, and Jean Dubreuil.[157]

Some 21 months later, the next-younger Brunet child was married, again in the Ste. Anne church near the western end of Montreal Island. This time, it was François, Jr., who would turn age 20 in July and was residing by this point in the Ste. Anne parish. It was a fellow parishioner, Marie Hunault dite Deschamps of Île Perrot, who had agreed to become his life partner. On January 25, 1740, when they exchanged their nuptial vows, François became the son-in-law of the voyageur Pierre Hunault dit Deschamps, a resident of Île Perrot and the Captain of the militia forces of the Ste. Anne parish, and Marguerite Suzanne Lefebvre. The official witnesses at this ceremony were Antoine and Pierre Hunault, Noël Lefebvre dit Lasisseraye, Pierre Miville, and Jean Dubreuil.[158]

Unfortunately, the patriarch François Brunet would not live long enough to either see or hear about any more of his children being married. On March 13 in this year of 1740, he was laid to rest in the cemetery at Ste. Anne, ten weeks before he would have celebrated his 58th birthday. The fact that he was buried at this locale rather than in the cemetery of the Lachine parish implies that he and Françoise were visiting one of their children who resided in the Bout de l'Île area at the time of his demise, or instead, that they were actually living at this time with one of those children. For some reason, the record of his interment was started in the parish register but was never completed. The priest indicated that the deceased was 56 years old (although his baptismal records from May 26, 1682 clearly indicated that his true age was just short of 58). In addition, the cleric also recorded that Monsieur Brunet was the son of François Brunet (his mother's name was not provided, but the venerable Barbe Beauvais was still living in the Lachine seigneury at age 83); and that his parents had been *"anciens habitants de la paroisse de Sts. Anges de Lachine"* (early settlers of the Holy Angels parish at Lachine). However, the priest did not finish the entry, but instead left a blank space in the ledger for its continuation, presumably with the intention of returning to it later. But no one ever did complete the entry; thus, neither the name of François' surviving spouse Françoise David, nor the names of the individuals who had served as the official witnesses at his funeral, were ever recorded. Nor was the entry in the register ever signed. Considering the incomplete condition of his funeral record, it is highly likely that François Brunet was felled by the epidemic of yellow fever that raged through the St. Lawrence settlements during this year of 1740. If the resident priest of Ste. Anne had been heavily taxed during this period with numerous cases of administering Last Rites and of conducting funerals, it would have been understandable if he had overlooked returning to and finishing this particular funerary record. The ravages of the epidemic might also explain why François had been buried in the Ste. Anne cemetery, rather than in the cemetery of his own home parish of Lachine.[159]

In this spring of 1740, at the age of $55^2/3$ and after 36 years and seven weeks of married life, Françoise found herself widowed with seven living children. In order from the oldest to the youngest, these were Marie Angélique ($28^3/4$ years old, married for ten years), Marie Louise ($22^1/3$, married for nearly three years), Antoine (married for nearly two years), François ($19^2/3$, married for two months), Claude Marie ($17^1/4$, single), Marie Anne (about 15, single), and Anne Renée ($10^2/3$, single).

During François' lifetime, the population living in New France had increased by about $4^1/2$ times, while the population of Montreal Island had increased even more, by a factor of about $5^1/2$ times. When the 1681 census had been enumerated, in the year before his birth, the total number of residents in the colony had been 9,742, while those living on Montreal Island had numbered 1,388. In 1739, the year before his death, the population of the colony had increased to 43,264, while the number of residents on the Island had grown to 7,736. It was no wonder, then, that the entire St. Lawrence Valley region seemed to be so much more crowded with settlers than it had been while François and Françoise had been growing up, in the Lachine seigneury and in the Champlain seigneury northeast of Trois-Rivières, respectively.[160]

Likewise, during François' extended career in the fur trade (which had spanned a full three decades of both legal and illicit commerce), he had seen a major increase in the amount of trade merchandise that was exchanged each year, and in the amounts of furs and hides that were garnered from native customers each year. Now, there was an entire series of posts scattered throughout the interior regions. The commerce that was conducted at these facilities was causing a huge drop in the numbers of native traders who paddled eastward each year, to participate in the trade fairs at Montreal and Trois-Rivières. However, certain native traders did continue to make this annual voyage out to the St. Lawrence settlements, in order to take advantage of the much lower prices there compared to the rates that were charged in the distant interior.

Seven months after her husband had passed away, Françoise was pleased to be asked to serve as the godmother of one of her new grandchildren, and to grant her name to that *petite-fille*. The christening ceremony was held in the Ste. Anne church on October 20, 1740, when little Françoise Gabrielle Émery was around one month of age. Her parents, Marie Louise Brunet and Joseph Émery dit Coderre, had been married for $3^1/2$ years. They had settled in the seigneury of Argenteuil, which was located northwest of Montreal Island, and fronted on the north shore of the Ottawa River immediately west of Lac des Deux Montagnes. According to the entry in the parish ledger, the parents were residing "in the area of Carillon Island." The priest also noted that the sponsors were Olivier Lemoine from Argenteuil and "Françoise David, widow of Brunet dit Bourbonnais."[161]

Although it is possible that Françoise may have been residing with one of their married children in the Ste. Anne parish at the time of François' death, and possibly for a period afterward, she had definitely returned to their farm beside the Lachine Rapids by the autumn of 1743. At some earlier point, the court had officially declared her to be the legal guardian of her underage children. These two facts were included in the document which was penned by the Montreal notary Jean Baptiste Adhémar on November 17, 1743. On this day, Madame Brunet sold a piece of property in the seigneury of Vaudreuil, which was located on the west side of the Ottawa River terminus, west of Île Perrot. In the transaction, she was identified as "Françoise David, widow of François Bourbonnais, of Lachine, acting both in her name and as the guardian of her minor children." (Interestingly, the scribe did not include the husband's family name

"Brunet," but only his *dit* name "Bourbonnais.") The purchasers were Joseph Bonaventure Legardeur, Sieur de Croizille (age 34) and his wife Marie Josèphe Maret de La Chauvignerie, who lived in the seigneury of d'Ailleboust.[162]

On January 25, 1746, Françoise's mother-in-law Barbe Beauvais passed away on the nearby family farm in the Lachine seigneury. Having lived to the very advanced age of $89^1/2$, she had outlasted her husband François, Sr. by more than 43 years.[163]

Within the span of the next 37 months, all three of Françoise's remaining children would be married. First came the wedding of Claude Marie, who exchanged nuptial vows with Marie Angélique Émery dite Coderre in the Ste. Anne church on February 14, 1746. At this time, he was 23 years old, while she was age $18^1/2$. This new bride was the daughter of Joseph Émery dit Coderre, who had taken as his second wife Claude Marie's sister Marie Louise Brunet nine years earlier, back in 1737.[164]

The next wedding in the family took place 33 months later, on November 24, 1749. According to the entry in the ledger of the Lachine church, "Marie Anne Brunet of this parish, age 24, daughter of François Brunet dit Bourbonnais, deceased, and of Françoise David" married on this day "Gabriel Mallet of this parish, age 26, son of Jean Baptiste Mallet and Barbe Milot." The sole official witness on the bride's side was her brother Antoine Brunet, while the three witnesses on the groom's side included Jean Baptiste Renaud, husband of Marie Lécuyer, the groom's grandmother; the groom's uncle Gabriel Mallet; and his uncle Jean Baptiste Legault dit Deslaurier. Also joining them as another witness was their friend Pierre Clocher dit Saint Pierre.[165]

This festive occasion was followed just nine weeks later by the nuptial celebration of the youngest offspring of Françoise and François. Anne Renée, who was 21 years old, was prepared to join in a lifetime partnership with Charles Daoust from Île Perrot, who was age 24; both of them were members of the Ste. Anne parish. On February 1, 1750, the engaged couple traveled to Montreal, to draw up their marriage contract with the notary François Simonnet. In this document, the scribe correctly recorded the prospective groom as Charles Daoust, son of Charles Daoust, Sr. and Marie Angélique Sauvé, of the Ste. Anne parish at the top of Montreal Island. However, he identified the bride-to-be as "Marie Renée Brunet, daughter of François Bourbonnais dit Brunet and of Françoise David, of the Ste. Anne parish at the top of Montreal Island." Interestingly, the family name and the *dit* name of her father were interchanged, and this parent was not designated as being deceased. It is also to be noted that the identification of being a resident of the Ste. Anne parish applied to the daughter Anne Renée, not to her mother Françoise David, who was a resident of the Lachine seigneury.[166]

On the following day, when the young couple was wed in their parish church, the resident priest identified the bride in the register as "Marie Renée Bourbonnais, daughter of François Bourbonnais and Françoise David." One of the official listed witnesses was "François Bourbonnais, brother of the bride," while the other witnesses included François Laplante, uncle of the groom; Pierre Pilon of Pointe Claire; Jean Baptiste and René Leduc of Ste. Anne; and Pierre Docile.[167]

Some $3^1/3$ years later, in June of 1753, Françoise was 68 years old. On the sixth day of the month, she and her son Antoine visited the Montreal notary Jean Baptiste Adhémar. By means of the document which the scribe drew up at this time, the mother transferred to her eldest son the ownership of the Brunet family property in the Sault St. Louis section of the Lachine seigneury. At this point, Antoine, who was probably about 35 to 41 years old, had been married to Angélique Boyer for more than fifteen years. In the document of transfer, the individual relinquishing ownership of the land was described as "Françoise David, widow of François Brunet dit Bourbonnais, of Lachine.[168]

When her daughter Anne Renée had married Charles Daoust in February of 1750, the bride could not have imagined that exactly one decade later, in February of 1760, she would find herself at the altar again, after having been widowed. This time, when Anne Renée was 31 years old, she married Guillaume Daoust, who was also a resident of the Ste. Anne parish. In the register under the date of February 4, the priest recorded that the groom was the son of Guillaume Daoust, Sr. and Catherine Énaud. The cleric described the bride as "Angélique Brunet of this parish, widow of Charles Daoust and daughter of François Brunet dit Bourbonnais, deceased, and of Françoise David." The three witnesses were the bride's brother François Brunet, the groom's grandfather Antoine Énaud, and Pierre Lafleur.[169]

A full decade after she had handed over the Brunet family farm to her eldest son Antoine, Françoise was still residing in the Lachine seigneury. Her long and eventful life finally drew to a close on September 25, 1763, after which she was laid to rest in the cemetery by the Lachine church two days later. In the parish register, Fr.

Delagarde recorded that he had interred on September 27 "Françoise David Bourbonnais, age 75;" however, in the margin was written "Françoise, widow Bourbonnais." The two official witnesses at her burial were Antoine Boyer and Pierre François Maccabee. A family member must have provided to the priest the information that the deceased was 75 years old. However, according to the inventory of her parents' estate, which had been drawn up back on December 20, 1684, Françoise had been described as "age one month and nine days or thereabouts." This statement clearly indicated that the date of her birth had been about November 11, 1684; this would have made her age at the time of her death six weeks short of 79. Having been married in January of 1706 at the age of 21, Françoise had been wed for more than 34 years; then she had lived as a widow for another 23 1/2 years.[170]

Jean François Brunet dit Le Bourbonnais, Jr.-Françoise David
Lineage of Timothy Kent

I. François Brunet, Sr.
(Antoine/
Philippe David)

11 July, 1672
Montreal, QC

Barbe Beauvais
(Jacques/
Jeanne Soldé)

II. **Jean François Brunet, Jr.**
(François, Sr./
Barbe Beauvais)

25 Jan, 1706
Champlain, QC

Françoise David
(Claude, Jr./
Marie Jeanne Couillard)

III. Angélique Brunet
(Jean François, Jr./
Françoise David)

16 Jan, 1730
Bout de l'Île (Mtl.), QC

Guillaume Lalonde #2
(Jean Baptiste/
Jeanne Gervais)

IV. Guillaume Lalonde #4
(Guillaume #2/
Angélique Brunet)

2 Feb, 1761
Bout-de-l'Île (Mtl.), QC

Marie Charlotte Sauvé
(François Marie/
Élisabeth Madeleine)

V. Angèle Lalonde
(Guillaume #4/
Marie Charlotte Sauvé)

27 Jan, 1812
 Vaudreuil, QC

Hyacinthe Achin
(Jacques/
Marie Amable Trottier)

VI. Élisabeth/Isabelle Achin
(Hyacinthe/
Angèle Lalonde)

17 Feb, 1835
St. Polycarpe, QC

Joseph Lalonde
(Joseph/
Geneviève Daoust)

VII. Joseph Lalonde
(Joseph/
Élisabeth/Achin)

ca. 1873
Curran, ON

Josephine Chatelain
(Étienne/
Marie Madeleine Taillon)

VIII. Élisabeth Lalonde
(Joseph/
Josephine Chatelain)

30 Jan, 1893
Carrollton, MI

Joseph Bouchard
(Philéas Joseph/
Adelaide Barbeau)

IX. Frances L. Bouchard
(Joseph/
Élisabeth Lalonde)

28 Apr, 1945
Detroit, MI

S. George Kent
(George Kapantais/
Eugenia Papadakis)

X. Timothy J. Kent
(S. George/
Frances L. Bouchard)

5 Sept, 1970
Ossineke, MI

Dorothy J. Minton
(Garnet J./
Elaine A. Reece)

Notes for Brunet dit Le Bourbonnais, Jr.

1. Detailed footnotes for all of this material are included in the Brunet-Beauvais biography.
2. H. Charbonneau and J. Légaré, 1978-1990, Vol, 5, Notre Dame de Montreal and Sts. Anges de Lachine recs; R. Jetté, 1983, p. 180.
3. H. Charbonneau and J. Légaré, 1978-1990, Vol, 5, Sts. Anges de Lachine recs; R. Jetté, 1983, pp. 197, 801, 974; F. Stanislas, 1950, p. 38.
4. Notary Michel Lepailleur, October 16, 1703, Archives Nationales du Québec à Montréal (ANQ-M).
5. All of this data is fully footnoted in the biographies of his parents, François Brunet, Sr. and Barbe Beauvais.
6. H. Charbonneau and J. Légaré, 1978-1990, Vol, 6, Sts. Anges de Lachine recs; R. Jetté, 1983, p. 180.
7. H. Charbonneau and J. Légaré, 1978-1990, Vol, 5, Sts. Anges de Lachine recs; R. Jetté, 1983, pp. 744, 792.
8. H. Charbonneau and J. Légaré, 1978-1990, Vol, 14, Sts. Anges de Lachine recs; R. Jetté, 1983, pp. 180, 280.
9. H. Charbonneau and J. Légaré, 1978-1990, Vol, 14, Sts. Anges de Lachine recs; R. Jetté, 1983, pp. 531, 183.
10. H. Charbonneau and J. Légaré, 1978-1990, Vol, 14, Sts. Anges de Lachine recs; R. Jetté, 1983, pp. 1020, 801.
11. Notary Pierre Raimbault, May 26, 1702, ANQ-M; R. Jetté, 1983, pp. 165-166, 1060, 423, 384, 6, 86.
12. E. Massicotte, 1929-1930, p. 207; R. Jetté, 1983, pp. 759, 531.
13. E. Massicotte, 1929-1930, p. 207; R. Jetté, 1983, pp. 911-912, 308, 594, 660; T. Kent, 2004, p. 94.
14. E. Massicotte, 1929-1930, pp. 206-207.
15. T. Kent, 2004, p. 148, 150, 155; A. Cadillac, 1719, p. 622.
16. R. La Salle, 1684, pp. 218-219.
17. N. Webster, "pleurisy;" H. Charbonneau and J. Légaré, 1978-1990, Vol, 14, Sts. Anges de Lachine recs.
18. R. Jetté, 1983, pp. 165, 1020, 759, 218; F. Stanislas, 1950, p. 27 and map inside back cover; L. Blair, 2000, p. 11; D. Hunter, 2002, p. 92.
19. H. Charbonneau and J. Légaré, 1978-1990, Vol, 14, Sts. Anges de Lachine recs; R. Jetté, 1983, pp. 181, 1060; F. Stanislas, 1950, p. 38.
20. E. Massicotte, 1929-1930, p. 208; R. Jetté, 1983, pp. 165-166.
21. R. Jetté, 1983, pp. 1101, 475; see the Turpin biography in this work for much greater detail, as well as numerous footnotes.
22. J. Holzi, 1995, Vol. 2, 1704-1713, Jud. Crim., February 18, 1704, Case No. 016-0747; R. Jetté, 1983, pp. 180, 182, 22-423; G. Stanley, 1968, pp. 209-210.
23. H. Charbonneau and J. Légaré, 1978-1990, Vol, 14, Sts. Anges de Lachine recs; R. Jetté, 1983, p. 954; F. Stanislas, 1950, p. 25 and map inside front cover.
24. Notary Michel Lepailleur, October 17, 1703, ANQ-M; R. Jetté, 1983, pp. 166, 435, 181.
25. Notary Pierre Raimbault, February 13, 1705, ANQ-M; R. Jetté, 1983, p. 33; Notary Michel Lepailleur, May 21, 1705, ANQ-M; Notary Antoine Adhémar, August 10, 1698a and August 10, 1698b, ANQ-M.
26. Notary Antoine Adhémar, May 30, 1705a, ANQ-M; E. Massicotte, 1929-1930, p. 210.
27. Notary Antoine Adhémar, May 1705b, ANQ-M; E. Massicotte, 1929-1930, p. 210.

28. A. Cadillac, 1706, p. 251; A. Cadillac, 1719, p. 622.

29. R. Jetté, 1983, pp. 312, 279.

30. Notary Antoine Adhémar, December 20 and 22, 1684, ANQ-M; Notary Antoine Adhémar, March 23, 1685, ANQ-M; R. Jetté, 1983, pp. 312, 279.

31. R. Jetté, 1983, pp. 312, 279, 1111, 717; H. Charbonneau and J. Légaré, 1978-1990, Vol, 12, Notre Dame de la Visitation de Champlain recs.

32. H. Charbonneau and J. Légaré, 1978-1990, Vol, 12, Notre Dame de la Visitation de Champlain recs.; R. Jetté, 1983, pp. 1111, 279, 312, 937.

33. Notary Antoine Adhémar, February 6, 1706, ANQ-M; R. Jetté, 1983, p. 313.

34. H. Charbonneau and J. Légaré, 1978-1990, Vol, 14, Sts. Anges de Lachine recs; R. Jetté, 1983, pp. 70, 280.

35. H. Charbonneau and J. Légaré, 1978-1990, Vol, 14, Sts. Anges de Lachine recs; R. Jetté, 1983, pp. 181, 191-192.

36. Notary Michel Lepailleur, April 5, 1707, ANQ-M; R. Jetté, 1983, pp. 1092, 142, 847.

37. Notary Antoine Adhémar, April 5, 1707, ANQ-M; R. Jetté, 1983, pp. 862, 725.

38. Notary Antoine Adhémary, April 6, 1707a, ANQ-M; R. Jetté, 1983, pp. 1129, 990-991.

39. Notary Antoine Adhémar, April 6, 1707b, ANQ-M.

40. E. Massicotte, 1929-1930, pp. 210-211.

41. A. Cadillac, 1707-1710, p. 378, Lot 57.

42. A. Cadillac, September 15, 1708, p. 393.

43. E. Massicotte, 1929-1930, pp. 211-212; E. Massicotte, 1921-1922, pp. 191-192.

44. H. Charbonneau and J. Légaré, 1978-1990, Vol, 14, Sts. Anges de Lachine recs; R. Jetté, 1983, pp. 279-280, 495.

45. H. Charbonneau and J. Légaré, 1978-1990, Vol, 14, Sts. Anges de Lachine recs; R. Jetté, 1983, pp. 165-166, 200.

46. H. Charbonneau and J. Légaré, 1978-1990, Vol, 14, Sts. Anges de Lachine recs; R. Jetté, 1983, pp. 165-166.

47. H. Charbonneau and J. Légaré, 1978-1990, Vol, 14, Sts. Anges de Lachine recs; R. Jetté, 1983, pp. 180, 1060.

48. H. Charbonneau and J. Légaré, 1978-1990, Vol, 14, Sts. Anges de Lachine recs; R. Jetté, 1983, p. 182.

49. H. Charbonneau and J. Légaré, 1978-1990, Vol, 14, Sts. Anges de Lachine recs; R. Jetté, 1983, pp. 180, 182.

50. H. Charbonneau and J. Légaré, 1978-1990, Vol, 14, Sts. Anges de Lachine recs; R. Jetté, 1983, pp. 280, 861.

51. Notary Michel Lepailleur, February 22, 1712, ANQ-M.

52. Notary Pierre Raimbault, February 25, 1712, ANQ-M.

53. J. Holzi, 1995, Vol. 2, 1704-1713, Jud. Crim., Case No. 025-1351, May 28, 1712; R. Jetté, 1983, pp. 970, 768, 751, 750, 614. 1702 land ownership map of Montreal Island by Vachon de Belmont: in Nos Racines, Vol. 22, 1979, pp. 430-431; M. Trudel, 1973a, pp. 172-173; recreation by G. Gallienne, 1977; and L. Dechêne, 1992, p. xxi.

54. Archives Judiciares de Montréal, May 6 and May 14, 1713, ANQ-M; R. Jetté, 1983, pp. 132, 74-75, 905, 963-964, 285-286, 200, 391-392.

55. ibid.

56. R. Jetté, 1983, p. 1060.

57. H. Charbonneau and J. Légaré, 1978-1990, Vol, 13, Notre Dame de Montreal recs; R. Jetté, 1983, pp. 70-71, 584.

58. Notary Daniel Normandin, October 3, 1713, ANQ-TR; R. Jetté, 1983, pp. 312, 1111, 202.

59. Notary Antoine Adhémar, February 21, 1714, ANQ-M.

60. E. Massicotte, 1929-1930, pp. 215-216.

61. Notary Michel Lepailleur, April 20, 1714, ANQ-M; R. Jetté, 1983, pp. 970-971.

62. J. Holzi, 1995, Vol. 3, 1714-1718, Jud. Crim., Case No. 029-1572, April 28, 1714; R. Jetté, 1983, pp. 1060, 295, 1092, 690, 310; F. Stanislas, 1950, pp. 17-19, 24, and map inside front cover.

63. R. Jetté, 1983, pp. xvi, 3.

64. Notary Jean Baptiste Adhémar, March 18, 1715, ANQ-M; R. Jetté, 1983, pp. 1136, 787, 714.

65. R. Jetté, 1983, pp. 1136, 364.

66. Montreal walls: Exhibits in Pointe à Callières Archaeological Museum, Montreal, 1994; ANQ, Ordonnances des Intendants, 1713-1720, Vol. 6, p. 54v., Archives des Colonies, C11A, Vol. 35, folios 330-352. La Forest loan: J. Holzi, 1995, Vol. 3, 1714-1718, Jud. Crim., Case No. 031-17, June 14, 1715; R. Jetté, 1983, pp. 310, 336.

67. R. Jetté, 1983, pp. 165-166, 384.

68. W. Fitzgerald, 1995, pp. 32-33; W. Fitzgerald et al, 1995, p. 121; J. Moreau and E. Langevin, 1992, pp. 37-47.

69. J. Lauson, 1654, pp. 383 ff.

70. W. Eccles, 1983, p. 110.

71. L. Frontenac, November 2, 1672, p. 90.

72. Funk and Wagnalls, 1990, Vol. 1, p. 336.

73. F. Dollier, 1928, p. 331.

74. W. Eccles, 1964, pp. 110, 148, 220.

75. P. Dubé, 1993, pp. 112-119.

76. L. Blair, 1911, pp. 227-231.

77. P. Roy, 1924, pp. 228-229, 237-238.

78. J. Duchesneau, 1679, pp. 131-135.

79. J. Duchesneau, 1680, pp. 140-145. Guns: J. Duchesneau, 1679, p. 136.

80. J. Hamelin, 1960, p. 55; H. Charbonneau et al, 1993, pp. 37, 81, 113.

81. W. Eccles, 1978, pp. 109-110; C. Skinner, 1996, pp. 49-50.

82. J. Duchesneau, 1681, No. 2, pp. 160-161.

83. L. Dubé, 1993, pp. 45-46.

84. ibid., p. 52.

85. W. Eccles, 1964, p. 148.

86. P. Dubé, 1993, pp. 134-136.

87. National Archives of Canada, Archives des Colonies, F3, Vol. 6, f. 143.

88. P. Roy, 1924, Vol. 2, pp. 86-88, 107-108.

89. L. Lahontan, 1905, Vol. 1, p. 91.

90. J. Denonville, 1685, pp. 45-47; A. Vachon, 1982, p. 148.

91. T. Pease and R. Werner, 1934, p. 93, n. 2.

92. J. Denonville, 1690, pp. 442-443.

93. A. Cadillac, 1702, p. 148.

94. J. Raudot, 1705, p. 249.

95. A. Cadillac, 1704, pp. 231-232; J. Marest, 1706, p. 267; D. Riverin, 1707, p. 317; A. Raudot and J. Raudot, 1709, p. 459.

96. J. Champigny, 1697, pp. 74-75; L. Callières and J. Champigny, 1701, p. 108.

97. M. Monseignat, 1696-1697, pp. 673-674.

98. Memorandum on the Posts, ca. 1705-1707, p. 243.

99. D. Riverin, 1705, p. 106.

100. W. Eccles, 1978, pp. 245, 267; C. Skinner, 1996, p. 68.

101. L. Callières, 1700, pp. 200-201.

102. W. Eccles, 1964, p. 245.

103. Jesuit Relations, 1896-1901, Vol. 65, pp. 190-253.

104. A. Cadillac, 1702, pp. 145-146.

105. L. Vaudreuil and F. Beauharnois, 1704, p. 761; A. Cadillac, 1704, pp. 231-232; R. Jetté, 1983, p. 5.

106. C. d'Aigrement, October 1710, p. 488, and November 1710, p. 266.

107. L. Louvigny, October 15, 1720, pp. 388-391; L. Louvigny, October 19, 1720, pp. 391-392.

108. Nos Racines, Vol. 22, 1980, p. 440.

109. Ft. Oswego: D. Miquelon, 1987, pp. 173-175. 1737 amnesty: F. Beauharnois, 1737a, p. 263.

110. J. Peyser, 1996, p. 109.

111. J. La Jonquière, September 29, 1750, p. 70.

112. A. Duquesne, May 29, 1755, pp. 154-155.

113. Notary Michel Lepailleur, April 27, 1716, ANQ-M.

114. H. Charbonneau and J. Légaré, 1978-1990, Vol, 14, Sts. Anges de Lachine recs; R. Jetté, 1983, pp. 111, 500, 956.

115. H. Charbonneau and J. Légaré, 1978-1990, Vol, 14, Sts. Anges de Lachine recs; R. Jetté, 1983, pp. 280, 956.

116. H. Charbonneau and J. Légaré, 1978-1990, Vol, 14, Sts. Anges de Lachine recs; R. Jetté, 1983, pp. 165, 500.

117. R. Jetté, 1983, pp. 180, 1060.

118. J. Holzi, 1995, Vol. 3, 1714-1718, Jud. Crim., Case No. 037-2246a, June 18, 1718; R. Jetté, 1983, pp. 183-184, 1066, 180, 165-166, 280, 479; F. Stanislas, 1950, p. 31 and map inside back cover.

119. H. Charbonneau and J. Légaré, 1978-1990, Vol, 14, Sts. Anges de Lachine recs; R. Jetté, 1983, pp. 873-874, 912.

120. H. Charbonneau and J. Légaré, 1978-1990, Vol, 14, Sts. Anges de Lachine recs; R. Jetté, 1983, p. 280.

121. H. Charbonneau and J. Légaré, 1978-1990, Vol, 14, Sts. Anges de Lachine recs; R. Jetté, 1983, pp. 459, 111, 531.

122. Notary Pierre Raimbault, February 26, 1720, ANQ-M.

123. Notary Jacques David, May 21, 1720, ANQ-M; Notary Antoine Adhémar, April 15, 1718, ANQ-M; R. Jetté, 1983, pp. 931-932.

124. Sts. Anges de Lachine recs, ANQ-M and H. Charbonneau and J. Légaré, 1978-1990, Vol, 14.

125. R. Jetté, 1983, p. 180, 183, 500; H. Charbonneau and J. Légaré, 1978-1990, Vol, 14, Sts. Anges de Lachine recs.

126. H. Charbonneau and J. Légaré, 1978-1990, Vol, 14, Sts. Anges de Lachine recs; R. Jetté, 1983, pp. 183, 500, 956.

127. H. Charbonneau and J. Légaré, 1978-1990, Vol, 14, Sts. Anges de Lachine recs; R. Jetté, 1983, pp. 165, 200.

128. H. Charbonneau and J. Légaré, 1978-1990, Vol, 14, Sts. Anges de Lachine recs; R. Jetté, 1983, pp. 182, 166, 720.

129. H. Charbonneau and J. Légaré, 1978-1990, Vol, 14, Sts. Anges de Lachine recs; R. Jetté, 1983, pp. 182, 192, 180, 183.

130. H. Charbonneau and J. Légaré, 1978-1990, Vol, 14, Sts. Anges de Lachine recs; R. Jetté, 1983, pp. 165-166, 698.

131. H. Charbonneau and J. Légaré, 1978-1990, Vol, 14, Sts. Anges de Lachine recs; R. Jetté, 1983, p. 500.

132. R. Jetté, 1983, pp. 379, 670-671, 710; Fort for Sale, p. 7; Y. Zoltvany, 1969c, pp. 374-376. 1702 land ownership map of Montreal Island by Vachon de Belmont: in

Nos Racines, Vol. 22, 1979, pp. 430-431; M. Trudel, 1973a, pp. 172-173; recreation by G. Gallienne, 1977; and L. Dechêne, 1992, p. xxi.

133. T. Kent, 2004, pp. 181, 220-221.

134. Notary Jean Baptiste Adhémar, March 2, 1725 ANQ-M.

135. H. Charbonneau and J. Légaré, 1978-1990, Vol, 14, Ste. Anne du Bout de l'Île recs; R. Jetté, 1983, pp. 979, 181-182, 782.

136. F. Dollier de Casson, 1928, p. 21; P. Dubé, 1993, p. 88; R. Harris, 1987, pl. 46; C. Hamp, 1988, p. 23; A. Yon, 1969, p. 350. 1702 land ownership map of Montreal Island by Vachon de Belmont: in Nos Racines, Vol. 22, 1979, pp. 430-431; M. Trudel, 1973a, pp. 172-173; recreation by G. Gallienne, 1977; and L. Dechêne, 1992, p. xxi.

137. H. Charbonneau and J. Légaré, 1978-1990, Vol, 14, Ste. Anne du Bout de l'Île recs; R. Jetté, 1983, pp. 182, 1129, 792.

138. H. Charbonneau and J. Légaré, 1978-1990, Vol, 14, Ste. Anne du Bout de l'Île recs; R. Jetté, 1983, pp. 947, 341.

139. H. Charbonneau and J. Légaré, 1978-1990, Vol, 14, St. Joachim de Pointe Claire recs; R. Jetté, 1983, pp. 1060, 965.

140. H. Charbonneau and J. Légaré, 1978-1990, Vol, 14, Ste. Anne du Bout de l'Île recs; R. Jetté, 1983, pp. 864, 965.

141. Notary Jean Baptiste Adhémar, September 15, 1726, ANQ-M; R. Jetté, 1983, pp. 111, 558, 1092.

142. R. Jetté, 1983, pp. 111, 537.

143. Notary Michel Lepailleur, April 5, 1729, ANQ-M; R. Jetté, 1983, pp. 611, 713.

144. H. Charbonneau and J. Légaré, 1978-1990, Vol, 14, Ste. Anne du Bout de l'Île recs; R. Jetté, 1983, pp. 510, 4.

145. Notary Joseph Raimbault, February 14, 1730 (the date of registration of the document, not the January 15 date on which it had been drawn up) ANQ-M; R. Jetté, 1983, pp. 182, 635.

146. H. Charbonneau and J. Légaré, 1978-1990, Vol. 25, Ste. Anne du Bout de l'Île recs; R. Jetté, 1983, pp. 510, 70.

147. H. Charbonneau and J. Légaré, 1978-1990, Vol. 25, Ste. Anne du Bout de l'Île recs; R. Jetté, 1983, pp. 183, 635.

148. Notary Joseph Raimbault, August 16, 1731, ANQ-M; R. Jetté, 1983, p. 956.

149. Montreal Merchants Records, Monière, Vol. 4, pp. 174-178; National Archives of Canada, MG 23/GIII 25: Microfilm M-848.

150. R. Jetté, 1983, pp. 955-956.

151. Notary Joseph Raimbault, August 16, 1731, ANQ-M.

152. H. Charbonneau and J. Légaré, 1978-1990, Vol. 25, Ste. Anne du Bout de l'Île recs.

153. H. Charbonneau and J. Légaré, 1978-1990, Vol. 25, Ste. Anne du Bout de l'Île recs.

154. H. Charbonneau and J. Légaré, 1978-1990, Vol. 25, Ste. Anne du Bout de l'Île recs; R. Jetté, 1983, pp. 635, 580.

155. H. Charbonneau and J. Légaré, 1978-1990, Vol. 25, Ste. Anne du Bout de l'Île recs; R. Jetté, 1983, pp. 182, 403-404.

156. Notary Michel Lepailleur, February 7, 1738, ANQ-M; R. Jetté, p. 244.

157. H. Charbonneau and J. Légaré, 1978-1990, Vol. 25, Ste. Anne du Bout de l'Île recs; R. Jetté, 1983, p. 162.

158. H. Charbonneau and J. Légaré, 1978-1990, Vol. 25, Ste. Anne du Bout de l'Île recs; R. Jetté, 1983, pp. 182, 580, 692.

159. H. Charbonneau and J. Légaré, 1978-1990, Vol. 25, Ste. Anne du Bout de l'Île recs; R. Jetté, 1983, pp. 180, 182; L. Blair, 2000, p. 11.

Jean François Brunet dit Le Bourbonnais, Jr. and his wife Françoise David

160. L. Dechêne, 1992, pp. 292-293.
161. H. Charbonneau and J. Légaré, 1978-1990, Vol. 25, Ste. Anne du Bout de l'Île recs; R. Harris, 1987, pl. 51.
162. Notary Jean Baptiste Adhémar, November 17, 1743, ANQ-M; R. Jetté, 1983, p. 697; R. Harris, 1987, pl. 51.
163. H. Charbonneau and J. Légaré, 1978-1990, Vol. 25, Ste. Anne du Bout de l'Île recs.
164. H. Charbonneau and J. Légaré, 1978-1990, Vol. 25, Ste. Anne du Bout de l'Île recs; R. Jetté, 1983, p. 404.
165. H. Charbonneau and J. Légaré, 1978-1990, Vol. 25, Sts. Anges de Lachine recs; R. Jetté, 1983, pp. 759, 978, 759, 698.
166. Notary François Simonnet, February 20, 1750 (the date of registration of the document, which had been drawn up on February 1), ANQ-M.
167. H. Charbonneau and J. Légaré, 1978-1990, Vol. 38, Ste. Anne du Bout de l'Île recs; R. Jetté, 1983, pp. 182, 307.
168. Notary Jean Baptiste Adhémar, June 6, 1753, ANQ-M.
169. H. Charbonneau and J. Légaré, 1978-1990, Vol. 38, Ste. Anne du Bout de l'Île recs.
170. H. Charbonneau and J. Légaré, 1978-1990, Vol. 25, Sts. Anges de Lachine recs; Notary Antoine Adhémar, December 20 and 22, 1684, ANQ-M.

XV

Pierre Maupetit dit Poitevin
and his wife Angélique Villeray

Voyageur-trader at Michilimackinac and in the Upper Country,
at the very end of the posts closure period and
the early rebuilding and expansion period

Pierre Maupetit was born to Pierre Maupetit dit Poitevin, Sr. and Marie Louise Beaune in the autumn of 1686. (The family name was also sometimes spelled in period documents Monpetit or Montpetit, since all three versions had very similar pronunciations.) The nickname of "Poitevin" or "Le Poitevin" ("One from Poitou") was derived from the fact that Pierre, Sr. had emigrated from Notre Dame parish in the town of Fontenay le Comte. This community, some thirty miles north-northeast of the port city of La Rochelle, was located in the province of Poitou. In his home town of Fontenay, Pierre Senior's parents had been the cloth seller François Maupetit and his wife Marie Pascalle. Before emigrating from the Old Country, Pierre, Sr. had himself worked in that town as a master handler of woolen fabrics.[1]

In 1683 or earlier, Pierre Maupetit, Sr. crossed the Atlantic to become a settler in New France. It is not known how long he had been in the colony before he settled in the Lachine seigneury, but it was definitely in the western portion of that locale in which he found his life partner. She was Marie Louise Beaune, who was about fifteen years old in the autumn of 1683. On October 24 of that year, the prospective bride and groom stood before the Montreal notary Bénigne Basset, in order to draw up their marriage contract. Three weeks after creating this nuptial agreement, on November 15, the Maupetit-Beaune couple exchanged their wedding vows in the church at Lachine, which was the home parish for both of them.[2]

Marie Louise, born in about 1668, was the eldest child of the farm worker Jean Beaune dit Lafranchise and Marie Madeleine Bourgery. Jean, from St. Cloud parish in Bellenaves (about 210 miles east of La Rochelle), had arrived in the colony during the summer of 1665, as a soldier in the La Varenne Company of the Carignan-Salières

Regiment. Shortly after retiring from military life, he had married 15-year-old Marie Madeleine Bourgery from Trois-Rivières, in August of 1667. After their wedding at Quebec, the couple had first settled in Montreal, where their first three children had been born. Then they had relocated southwestward to the Lachine seigneury, where an additional five offspring had arrived. In the census of 1681, this family had been enumerated on their farm, which was located about one mile west of the Lachine village site. This document had listed the parents (ages 48 and 30), along with Marie Louise (13) and the five younger siblings who had arrived by that time; these latter children ranged in age from 8 years down to 7 months.[3]

After their wedding in the autumn of 1683, Pierre Maupetit, Sr. and Marie Louise Beaune likewise found a place to settle down in the westernmost section of the Lachine seigneury, in the same general area in which she had grown up with her family. At some point, Pierre also acquired a piece of property that was located some nine miles toward the west, about two miles east of the westernmost end of Montreal Island. Fronting on the St. Lawrence, this lot measured 3 arpents (575 feet) along the river and 20 arpents ($3/4$ mile) in depth. This long, rectangular piece of land was the fourth lot east of the brand new church of St. Louis, which was built on Pointe St. Louis in 1685-1686. (Some 28 years later, in about 1713, the name of this parish would be changed to Ste. Anne, and a new church would eventually be constructed about $1^1/2$ miles further toward the west.) However, even if the Maupetit couple was able to clear a small portion of this distant property, they would never have an opportunity to build a home on it or move permanently onto it.[4]

Their first baby, little Jean, arrived on February 26, 1685, fifteen months after they had been married. When he was baptized on the following day in the Lachine church, his godfather and name-giver was the Lachine and Montreal businessman and hat maker Jean Quenet, whose distant lot was the fifteenth one east of the St. Louis church. The infant's godmother was Michelle Perrin, the wife of the Lachine tailor of suits Jean Gourdon dit La Chasse. This latter couple lived immediately east of the Beaune family farm. (The last record pertaining to Jean Maupetit would be his mention in a notary document from Pointe Claire dated August 24, 1718; at that time, he would be $33^1/2$ years old and still single.)[5]

Some 21 months after the arrival of baby Jean, Pierre Maupetit, Jr. (the male subject of this biography) was welcomed into the world.

At his heartening christening ceremony in the Lachine church on November 15, 1686, his godfather was identified by the priest as the farm worker Jean de Lalonde (or Lalande). This was most likely Jean de Lalonde dit L'Espérance; his farm was located a short distance west of the St. Louis church, thus making it the sixth lot west of Pierre's distant land. (However, there is a slight possibility that this individual was either Étienne Lalande dit Langliche, who resided with his family on the second lot east of the Beaune family, or Léonard Lalande dit Latreille, who would marry Louise's sister Gabrielle Beaune a decade later, after her husband Vincent Jean would perish). Standing beside the godfather at the baptismal font was Marie Madeleine Émond, the wife of the Lachine-based voyageur-trader Nicolas Dupuis dit Montauban. The distant lot belonging to Monsieur Dupuis was located immediately east of Pierre's distant property, thus making it the fifth lot east of the St. Louis church.[6]

Ten weeks after safely delivering this second child, Marie Louise lost her father, Jean Beaune dit Lafranchise, at the age of about 54. On January 25, 1687, he was laid to rest in the Lachine cemetery, on the day following his death. Marie Louise's mother, Marie Madeleine Bourgery, would remain a widow for the next 34 months.[7]

Baby Pierre's one other sibling joined the little Maupetit family 21 months after him, on October 12, 1688. On the following day, her parents took the tiny lass to the Lachine church to receive the sacrament of Baptism. During the ceremony, she received her double name Marie Clémence from Marie Clémence Beaune, who was her 17-year-old unmarried aunt. The infant's godfather was her uncle Vincent Jean, who had married her aunt Gabrielle Beaune during the previous year, when the bride had been $13^1/2$ years of age.[8]

Back in about 1686, warriors from several of the Iroquois nations had begun conducting sporadic raids against the residents of the St. Lawrence communities. Up until this time, peaceful relations had reigned between the French and the Iroquois during the previous two decades, ever since the peace treaties of 1666 and 1667. In 1687, in response to the resumption of their attacks, Governor Denonville had led a massive campaign against the Seneca homeland, which was located south of Lake Ontario. However, this expedition had involved only one battle with uncertain results, plus the destruction of huge amounts of both standing corn crops and stored parched corn at the Iroquois villages. In the aftermath of this campaign, raids by Iroquois war parties had actually increased, rather than decreased, both in number and intensity. Their raids fell not only upon the settlements of the St. Lawrence Valley, but also upon the Ottawa River route leading to and from the Upper Country.[9]

However, another threat, even more insidious than marauding Iroquois warriors, also endangered the lives of the people living along the St. Lawrence at this time. When the annual fleet of vessels from France had arrived during the summer of 1687, beginning on the first day of June, their cargoes had included not only people, merchandise, and supplies, but also fatal germs. Shortly after their arrival, a terrible epidemic of both measles and smallpox had begun to sweep through the French and native communities that lined the shores of the river, ranging from Tadoussac all the way upstream to the Montreal area. This scourge of sickness and death would continue unchecked for nearly a year, extending well into 1688. By the time it would finally abate, over a thousand residents, both French and native, would be dead.[10]

Two of its victims were the two children of Pierre, Jr.'s godmother, Marie Madeleine Émond, and her husband Nicholas Dupuis dit Montauban. Their eldest, Nicholas, was 37 months old at the time of his passing on October 31, 1687. Nine days later, on November 8, their toddler Louise died at the age of 17 months. These little ones were tearfully buried in the Lachine cemetery on the day of their death and on the following day, respectively. At the time that Marie Madeleine suffered these heart-rending losses, she was about six months pregnant. However, when Marie Catherine arrived three months later and was baptized in the Lachine church on February 16, 1688, the mother refused to declare to the officiating priest the name of the baby's father. The cleric recorded that the pregnancy had commenced "during the voyage of her husband to Michilimackinac." Sadly, the newborn infant only survived for eight weeks; she was laid to rest in the cemetery at Lachine on April 22, 1688. It is not known whether she perished as a result of the double-disease epidemic that was raging at the time, or from one of the many other causes that felled so many of the babies who were born in New France.[11]

As the depredations of the Iroquois escalated, stockades of refuge were constructed during 1688 at each of the exposed seigneuries. Along the southern shoreline of Montreal Island, from east to west, these included the fortifications at Verdun (about $3^1/2$ miles northeast of the Lachine village), Ft. Cuillerier on the property of René Cuillerier, Sr. ($^3/4$ mile east of the Lachine village site), Ft. Rémy (a palisade wall surrounding the village itself), and Ft. Rolland (1^3/4 miles further toward the west, at the western edge of the Lachine seigneury). The residents of the seigneury of La Présentation or Côte St. Gilles, extending for about 2^1/4 miles west of Ft. Rolland (to about the present community of Dorval), would use the latter stockade as needed. Thus, the settlers who were spread out along some nine miles of the shoreline in this southeastern section of the island, from the eastern end of Verdun to the western end of La Présentation, had four stockades to which they could flee for protection in case of attacks.

Across the Atlantic, in the spring of 1689, war broke out between France and the combined countries of England, Spain, the Dutch Netherlands, and the Hapsburg Empire. By late spring, ships had brought this news to the English colonies; unfortunately, word of it would not reach New France via French vessels until September. During the summer, the Iroquois nations were elated to receive this information, which meant that in their upcoming war with the French, they would have the military support of both England and her colonies. However, unaware of these perilous events, the colonists along the St. Lawrence had no idea of the fierce onslaught that was about to descend upon many of them.[12]

During the night of August 4-5, 1689, under the cover of darkness and a violent hailstorm, a massive force of about 1,500 Iroquois warriors crossed northward over the broad St. Lawrence. Silently spreading out along eight miles of shoreline, from the Côte St. Louis area beside the Lachine Rapids westward to La Présentation, the raiders remained undetected by the sentries in the various forts throughout the entire night. Waiting until dawn to launch their ferocious strike, the Iroquois, who numbered nearly 200 attackers per mile of shoreline, took the French completely by surprise. Soon, they had slain at least 24 French residents and had captured an estimated 79 others. They also destroyed by fire 56 of the 77 houses in the area, along with numerous stables, granaries, and other buildings, and killed a large portion of the livestock. In the immediate aftermath, most of the survivors of this first onslaught sought refuge within the four stockades. But some of them made their way to Montreal, where Governor Denonville was visiting at the time. Immediately, he sent Vaudreuil, the acting governor of Montreal, to the raided area with a force of about 300 soldiers. Their orders were to bolster the troops who had been manning the four forts, and to enforce the Governor's orders that all of the residents of the attacked area were to gather within these stockades of refuge and remain there.

After reaching Ft. Rolland, Vaudreuil sent word back to the Governor requesting additional reinforcements. In response, on August 6, the administrator dispatched about fifty solders and some thirty allied native warriors, under the command of Lieutenant Labeyre and Charles Lemoyne. This party covered the ten miles to Ft. Rémy without incident; however, after they departed from the fortified village and headed west toward Ft. Rolland (1 3/4 miles away, just beyond the western section of the Lachine seigneury), they were attacked by an Iroquois party. During the skirmish that followed, the enemy warriors killed and scalped about twenty of the native allies and captured about half of the soldiers, including Labeyre and four of his subaltern officers. In the fray, Lemoyne was wounded, but he and some of his companions managed to return to Ft. Rémy. During this debacle, which was taking place within sight of Ft. Rolland, the officers inside pleaded with Vaudreuil to be permitted to go to the aid of their comrades. But the commander refused, since his orders specifically stated that he and his forces were to remain within the forts! Previously, again taking his orders literally, Vaudreuil had denied permission to one of his officers to conduct a counter-attack upon a large party of Iroquois warriors. These enemies would have been easy prey, since they had become drunk on the liquor that they had seized in the homes. Thus, by remaining entirely in a defensive mode, the commander had lost at least two opportunities to fight back against the Iroquois raiders and inflict heavy casualties on them.

Numerous scholars have sought to identify the colonists who either died or were captured in this horrific raid, which was soon afterward dubbed the Lachine Massacre. The primary document for identifying those who perished on site in the attack was the official list that was drawn up by Fr. Rémy, who had been the resident priest of the Lachine parish since 1680. Not long after the raid, the deceased were hastily buried in the very places in which they had each been found. Five years later, Bishop Saint-Vallier declared that these bodies were to be exhumed and reburied in the consecrated ground of the Lachine cemetery. These mournful reburials were conducted during the last week of October in 1694. It was during this process that Fr. Rémy drew up a list of those 24 individuals who had perished in the raid of 1689. (This roster was signed by the priest; by Jean Paré and André Rapin, members of the church council; and by

Guillaume Daoust, the chanter of the parish and a direct ancestor of the present author.) Among the listed victims, nine of them had originally been buried in the area of the Lachine seigneury, while the other fifteen had been initially interred further to the west, in the adjacent seigneury of La Présentation, which was also called Côte St. Gilles. (A detailed discussion of many of the killed and captured individuals has already been presented in the biography of François Brunet dit Le Bourbonnais, Sr., accompanied by numerous footnotes.)

Although no members of the Maupetit family were recorded on Fr. Rémy's melancholy list, this household in the western section of the Lachine seigneury, containing two parents and three children, did not escape unscathed. Unfortunately, Pierre, Sr. was captured alive during the fierce raid. Since he was never heard from again, he apparently later perished while he was in Iroquois captivity, quite possibly by being tortured to death. There was a terrible irony in the fact that Pierre was seized in this raid by Iroquois warriors, since his father-in-law Jean Beaune had been a soldier in the Carignan-Salières Regiment. This body of troops had come to Canada back in 1665, and their campaign against the Mohawk nation during the following year had forced all five of the Iroquois nations to sign peace treaties, which had remained in effect for nearly two decades.[13]

During the 1689 attack, in the eastern two-thirds of the Lachine seigneury (the stretch of about $4^1/4$ miles that extended eastward from Ft. Rémy), one settler and two soldiers were killed, while ten other settlers were captured. According to the priest's list of reburials, the other 21 victims who had been killed (twenty French and one native) had been initially interred in the western portion of the Lachine seigneury and in the adjacent La Présentation/Côte St. Gilles seigneury. It was in this area, extending along the shoreline for some four miles, that the raiders had directed their greatest fury. The deceased individuals here included seven men, three women, nine children, one soldier, and a fifteen-year-old native slave who had belonged to René Chartier.

A span of $1^3/4$ miles of St. Lawrence frontage comprised the western section of the Lachine seigneury. This area extended from Ft. Rémy (the stockaded Lachine village) to Ft. Rolland, at the edge of the La Présentation seigneury. In this particular area, residents in at least nine of the households (including that of the Maupetit family) suffered either death or capture at the hands of the Iroquois raiders. The losses in three of these families included one or more direct ancestors of the present author, while the losses in a fourth family included a daughter and siblings of ancestors.

One of the hardest-hit households here, in terms of sheer numbers of dead or captured individuals, was that of Pierre Barbary dit Grandmaison and Marie Lebrun (both of whom are direct ancestors of the present author). Their home was located immediately west of the Beaune family farm (Marie Louise's place of growing up), which was about one mile west of Ft. Rémy and about $^3/_4$ mile east of Ft. Rolland. During the attack, both of the parents and all five of their living children were captured, while one of their two sons-in-law was slain. (Three months earlier, on April 28, the heavy-hearted Barbary couple had lost two of their other young children, in a tragic house fire; these little ones had been $4^2/_3$ and $2^1/_2$ years old, respectively.)[14]

Immediately west of the Barbary home, the household of Jean Michel (or Michau) and Marie Marchessault was the scene of bloody carnage on the morning of August 5. On that fateful day, Jean, as well as the couple's stepson and their eldest child were all killed on site. Marie was taken captive, as was possibly their second-oldest child as well.[15]

About a quarter-mile west of Ft. Rolland, in the La Présentation/ St. Gilles seigneury, lived Michel Prézeau dit Chambly, his wife Marie Chancy, and their four living children (this couple had earlier lost three other offspring at very young ages). During the course of the attack, both of the parents and their second-youngest child were taken captive.[16]

In summary, the majority of the known casualties of the raid took place along a stretch of at least $6^1/_2$ miles of St. Lawrence shoreline, extending westward from the Jean Roy household ($^1/_2$ mile west of Verdun) to at least the René Chartier home ($^3/_4$ mile west of Ft. Rolland). In addition to those 24 individuals who were killed on site, an estimated 79 settlers living in the attacked area (including Pierre Maupetit) were captured in the raid. However, an estimated 27 of these latter persons eventually made their way back to their homes, either by escaping or by being later exchanged or released over the years. Unfortunately, Pierre was not among those lucky souls who returned.[17]

In the aftermath of the brutal attacks, his shocked and grief-stricken widow Marie Louise Beaune surveyed the tattered remains of her life. She was about 21 years old, and she had three young children. These were Jean, age $4^1/_2$ years; Pierre, $2^3/_4$ years; and

Marie Clémence, 10 months old. Although they were badly shaken and scarred on the inside, these four family members had survived the ordeal unscathed, at least on the outside. It is not known whether the home in which the family had been living had remained intact. However, the western section of the Lachine seigneury, where they had been residing, had been one of the hardest-hit areas, sustaining especially heavy destruction of its people, livestock, and buildings.

The reburials of the 24 victims of the 1689 raid, ordered by Bishop Saint-Vallier, took place in the cemetery of the Lachine church in late October of 1694. This has misled many historians of the past into thinking that all of the surviving residents of this portion of Montreal Island abandoned their homes and farms for five years after the raid, before eventually returning in fear and uncertainty. It is undoubtedly true that the horrible events of death, capture, and destruction that occurred in August of 1689 must have scarred their psyches for the rest of their lives. However, a number of period documents clearly show that, soon after the horrific attacks, many of the residents of the area began courageously repairing and rebuilding both their farms and their lives.

As a testament to these activities, between August and the end of December in 1689, the priest performed five marriages, one baptism, and two burials in the parish church in Lachine. It was one of these marriages, the one celebrated on December 2, which joined Marie Louise's widowed mother, 38-year-old Marie Madeleine Bourgery, and Jacques Chasle dit Duhamel. The bride's first husband, Jean Beaune dit Lafranchise, had been gone for 34 months, since January of 1687. Before his demise, Marie Louise (their eldest child) had married Pierre Maupetit in 1683. Since Monsieur Beaune's departure, Gabrielle (their third offspring) had joined in matrimony with Vincent Jean in 1687, while Clémence (their second child) had married Léon Girard in 1688. In addition, Marie Madeleine (their sixth child) had perished on October 16, 1687, during the fierce double epidemic of that time, at the age of $6^{1}/2$ years. Thus, at the time of Madame Bourgery's remarriage to Monsieur Chasle in December of 1689, she had four children (Marie Louise's youngest siblings) who were still living at home. These were Jean (age 12), Marie Anne (11), Albert (6), and Antoine François (3). The groom at this wedding, Jacques Chasle, was a retired soldier; he had come to New France among the troops in the Du Cruzel Company.[18]

The Chasle-Bourgery couple was married in the Lachine church on December 2, 1689, just four months after the Iroquois raiders had struck so fiercely. This timing, as well as the location of their wedding at Lachine rather than at Montreal, implies that the Beaune-Bourgery home, along with its stable, granary, and other outbuildings, had survived the numerous fires that had accompanied the Iroquois onslaught. However, the family may have quickly reconstructed their buildings, if some or all of them had indeed been destroyed by the enemies' torches. At any rate, the blended family obviously had a place where they could live within the Lachine seigneury following the wedding, and this was likely the Beaune farm.

After the attack and the capture of Pierre Maupetit, it it highly likely that Marie Louise and her three young children moved in with her mother and her four younger siblings, or instead with one of her two married sisters. These latter two siblings, Gabrielle and Clémence, also lived in the Lachine seigneury with their respective husbands, Vincent Jean and Léon Girard. They may have extended their hospitality to their grieving sibling.[19]

During the months and years following the raid of 1689, the threat of lightning attacks by Iroquois war parties and their Anglo allies continued to hang over all of the residents of the St. Lawrence settlements. However, this threat was especially severe for those colonists who resided in the more thinly populated areas, such as the southern shore of Montreal Island and the adjacent areas on the mainland to the south. A hint of the dangers that they faced on a daily basis, as well as the precautions which the settlers in these areas were obliged to take in order to survive, was recorded by the officer Baron Lahontan in 1690. In late July, after native scouts had reported a large force of Anglo and Iroquois fighting men approaching the Montreal area from the south, this officer was among the contingent of French and their native allies who gathered at Laprairie to fend off the attackers. However, most of the enemy forces eventually abandoned the campaign and turned back without striking.

"The English being unable to encounter the fatigues of the march, and [being] unprovided with a sufficient stock of provisions, both they and the Iroquese were return'd to their own country. This account being confirm'd by other savages, our troops decamp'd, and march'd back to this place [Montreal], from which I was detach'd some days after to command a party that was to cover the reapers [harvesters] of Fort Rolland, which lies on this Island. When the harvest was over, I return'd to this place."[20]

However, having soldiers guard work parties of colonists when they left the confines of their homes to tend their crops still did not guarantee the safety of the people who lived in the Lachine area. On June 26, 1691, three settlers and four soldiers were slain here by an Iroquois war party.[21]

By 1698, the Iroquois nations had lost a considerable number of their fighting men from many years of campaigning. In addition, they had lost their offensive position in this protracted warfare, and had been forced into a defensive mode. To further their troubles, disease epidemics had weakened and decimated their populations from within. As a result, in 1698, the Iroquois ceased once and for all their attacks against the French and their native allies. However, treaty negotiations between the three groups would drag on for another three years, until the Great Treaty would ultimately be signed in Montreal during the summer of 1701. When a new war would break out between France and other European countries in 1702, the Iroquois would remain neutral, not siding with the English as they had previously done for decades.

With the constant threat of surprise attacks finally removed from their lives, the events of daily life of the French colonists returned to blessed normal. By the beginning of the summer in 1698, Marie Louise was about 30 years old, and her three children were continuing to grow. Jean was now $13^1/3$ years of age, Pierre was $11^7/12$, and Marie Clémence was $9^2/3$ years old. Marie Louise had lived as a widow for nearly nine years, ever since she had lost her beloved Pierre Maupetit, Sr. back in the raid of 1689. At some point during that period of time, she had met Louis Lory, who was about 25 years old in 1698. His father, François Lory, Sr., was the bailiff and royal sergeant of the Montreal Court. This official had recently purchased the farm in the Sault St. Louis section of the seigneury which was located immediately east of the lands of the Brunet dit Le Bourbonnais clan. Louis himself owned a long, slender piece of property which was situated some five miles west of Ft. Rolland, and about $3/4$ mile west of Pointe Claire.

On June 16 of this summer, the widow and Louis exchanged their nuptial vows in the Lachine church. According to the priest's records, the bride was "Marie Louise Beaune, widow of Pierre Maupetit dit Le Poitevin and daughter of Jean Beaune, deceased, and of Madeleine Bourgery." The witnesses included Gabrielle Beaune, sister of the bride, François Lory, Jr., brother of the groom, Jean Baptiste Gros, Nicholas Gros, Jean François Brunet (the Lachine voyageur-trader

François Brunet, Jr., whose biography has already been presented in this study), Jean Baptiste Pothier, notary of Montreal and Lachine, Catherine Aubry, and Nicole Filiatrault, who was married to Étienne Lalande dit Langliche and had lived immediately east of the Beaune family farm for decades.[22]

After the ceremony, the Lory-Beaune couple presumably settled with Marie Louise's three children on his property west of Pointe Claire. During their years of married life together, they would not produce any additional children. The third lot west of Louis' farm belonged to his older brother, François Lory, Jr. This proximity must have soon brought Marie Louise's younger sister Marie Anne, who was $19^1/2$ years old, into close contact with the elder Lory brother, who was about age 27. They were married in the Lachine church on November 4, less than five months after the bride's older sister had married the groom's younger brother.[23]

By the spring of 1700, it had been nearly two years since Marie Louise had remarried, and more than a decade since her mother had taken as her second husband Jacques Chasle dit Duhamel. On April 6, the Montreal Court called together various family members and friends of the Maupetit children, who were now 15, $13^1/2$, and $11^1/2$ years of age. On April 6, the participants in this hearing together determined that Monsieur Chasle, who through marriage had become the stepgrandfather of the three underage children and heirs of Marie Louise Beaune and Pierre Maupetit, would serve as their legal guardian. He would carry out this role until they would each reach the age of majority, which was 25 in New France. Jacques Chasle's property, located immediately east of Pointe Claire, was the eighth lot east of the land on which Louis Lory resided with Marie Louise and the three Maupetit children.[24]

After surviving the epidemic that raged through the St. Lawrence Valley late in 1700, the family again escaped death during the devastating smallpox scourge which ripped through the population in the latter part of 1701. During the course of the latter epidemic, over a thousand residents of the St. Lawrence Valley, both French and native, succumbed to the disease.[25]

By the summer of 1702, when Pierre was $15^7/12$ years old, he, his parents, and his legal guardian had decided that it was time for him to be engaged in an apprenticeship program. Thus, on June 24, his guardian traveled to the office of the Montreal notary Pierre Raimbault, to meet with the Montreal resident who would serve as

Pierre's master for the next three years. This was Claude Caron, Jr., who would turn age 30 in two months. He and Élisabeth Perthuis, age 25, had been married for seven years; during that time, they had produced four children. However, their second baby had died at the age of four days in May of 1698, and their third one had perished after six weeks of life in August of 1699. At this point, their two surviving offspring were 6 years and 18 months old, respectively. Claude's father-in-law was Pierre Pethuis dit La Lime, a prominent Montreal merchant bourgeois and hirer of voyageur-traders for the west. Claude himself had been employed as a legal voyageur-trader nine years earlier, back in 1693. Thus, it is possible that at least some of the labors that young Pierre Maupetit would be carrying out for Monsieur Caron during his three years of employment in Montreal would be related to the fur trade.[26]

"Before the undersigned royal notary was present Jacques Chasle dit Duhamel, guardian of the underage children of the deceased Pierre Maupetit dit Poitevin, who while living was an habitant of the Côte de Lachine, and of Marie Louise Beaune, at present the wife of Louis Lory. For the good and advantage of Pierre Maupetit, one of the said minors, about sixteen years of age and otherwise not being able to provide for his subsistence, the said Chasle has acknowledged and admitted that he has given and placed him into service for three years, which has commenced on the first day of this present month, to Sieur Claude Caron, Jr., present and accepting for himself and his own people during the said time. This has been done in consideration of one cow, which the said Caron promises to furnish to him and to deliver at the end of the first two years, which the said Maupetit will place wherever it will seem good to him. In addition, at the end of the said three years, the said Caron will furnish to the said Maupetit one hooded coat and breeches, stockings, French shoes, and tapabord cap, all new and made of Mazamet or rateen woolen fabric, at the discretion of the said Caron, and six new shirts made of hempen linen or Mélis linen [sailcloth], as well as his maintenance [room and board] during the said three years. In addition, the said Maupetit will also be permitted to take away with him the old used clothing [provided by the said Caron] which he will have at the end of the said three years. Thus have they promised, obligated themselves, waived, etc.

[This agreement] made and drawn up at Villemarie in the office of the notary in 1702, on the 24th of June in the afternoon, in the presence of Léonard Libersan [dit Laviolette] and Joseph Barbe, habitants who have declared with the said Caron that they do not know how to write or sign, having been questioned after the reading was done, according to the ordinance.

Signed,
Jacques Chale and P. Raimbault, notary."[27]

According to this contract, as remuneration for his three years of service, Pierre would receive room, board, clothing, one cow, and training in an unidentified occupation.

Within months of Pierre's commencing this employment, another horrendous epidemic of smallpox began to sweep through the communities along the St. Lawrence Valley. This wave of sickness and death broke out during the latter part of 1702, and it continued until at least the spring of 1703.[28]

It was during that death-laden spring that the wife of Pierre's employer died, after giving birth to their fifth child. On April 17, 1703, Élisabeth Perthuis delivered little Charles Caron; he was baptized in the Montreal church within hours of his arrival, but he perished and was buried on the same day. The mother, apparently having sustained physical damage during the delivery, survived for six more days; then she died and was laid to rest in the Montreal cemetery on the 23rd. Having two surviving children who were 7 and 2 1/2 years old, Claude Caron clearly needed a partner who would spend her life with him. Thus, six months and three weeks after he had buried his first wife, Claude remarried, on November 12, 1703. His new bride was the Montreal resident Marguerite Jeanne Boyer, who was 18 1/2 years old. This couple would produce twelve children in Montreal during the following 24 years. The first of these offspring would arrive during Pierre Maupetit's apprenticeship period with Claude, in September of 1704.[29]

By the time autumn arrived in 1706, eighteen months had passed since Pierre had completed his three-year term of service for Monsieur Caron. By this point, he was two months short of his 20th birthday, while his brother Jean was age 21 1/2. These two siblings were residing near the western end of Montreal Island, in the area that was called Le Bout de l'Île or Le Haut de l'Île. Their sister Marie Clémence, who would celebrate her 18th birthday in October, was engaged to the soldier Pierre Poirier dit Lafleur (however, the betrothed couple would not marry until the following June of 1707).[30]

In order to provide a dowry for their engaged sister, the two brothers visited a Montreal notary on September 18, 1706. On this day, they officially transferred to Marie Clémence ownership of the family property in the Bout de l'Île area, which was the fourth lot east of the St. Louis church. This land had belonged to their mother, and their deceased father during his lifetime, for more than twenty years, ever since the mid-1680s. However, even if the Maupetit-Beaune couple had been able to clear the forest cover from a small portion of this land, they had never built a home or any other structures on it. During their short 5³/4 years of married life together, they had never moved westward with their children from the Lachine seigneury to reside on this land. Ever since the death of Pierre, Sr., the property (as part of the family estate) had belonged to the three children and their mother.

"Before Michel Lepailleur, the undersigned royal notary of Montreal Island living at Villemarie, and the witnesses named below were present Jean Maupetit, age twenty-three [actually 21¹/2] and Pierre Maupetit, age twenty-one [actually 19¹⁰/12], brothers, children and heirs of the deceased Pierre Maupetit and of Marie Beaune, habitants of the Bout de l'Île on Montreal Island. According to their free will and good will, and for the good friendship and affection which they bear for Marie Clémence Maupetit, their sister, and in consideration of the marriage which she is ready to contract with Pierre Poirier dit Lafleur, soldier of the troops of the Marine Department in the Company of Monsieur de Lorimier, with Sieur Poirier present and accepting with the said notary for the said Marie Clémence Maupetit, they have made and they make by these presents a donation pure and simple to the said Marie Clémence Maupetit, their sister...of a piece of land contingent upon the said estate of the said deceased Maupetit, their father, located and situated on this said Island, containing three arpents [575 feet] of frontage [on the St. Lawrence] by twenty arpents [³/4 mile] of depth, without any buildings, along with its circumstances and dependencies...This land is adjoined on one side by [that of] the one named [Pierre Sauvé dit] Laplante and on the other side by [that of] the widow [Marie Madeleine Émond] and heirs of [Nicholas] Dupuis [dit Montauban], at the front by the St. Lawrence River and at the rear by the lands not granted. In addition, the said donators, in respect, give to the said recipient two cows which belong to them and which they have acquired by their labors and cares...The said donators promise to ratify these present as soon as they will attain the age of majority, each of them with their respect..."[31]

About ten weeks later, the guardian of the three heirs, Jacques Chasle dit Duhamel, entered a complaint with the Montreal Court against their stepfather, Louis Lory. He did this in order to force the latter man to cancel the sale of the above property, which Monsieur Lory had arranged with some other individual. On December 1, 1706, the Court decided in favor of the complainant, and declared that Monsieur Lory was to cancel the sale agreement, since the land belonged in part to the three underage children of Pierre Maupetit dit Poitevin and Marie Louise Beaune.[32]

Some 4^1/2 years after this court case had been settled, in the early summer of 1711, Pierre was 24^1/2 years old. On June 13, he was chosen to appear in the Lachine church as the godfather at the baptismal ceremony of his newborn cousin François Beaune. The parents of this two-day-old infant were Pierre's uncle and aunt Antoine François Beaune (age 25) and Marie Anne Lalande dite Langliche (age 24). This young couple, who would only produce this one child, had arranged their privately-signed marriage contract at Lachine on May 25, just three weeks before the arrival of the baby. No record of their marriage ceremony has survived in the church records of the colony. On this christening day, the baby's godmother was her aunt Marie Jeanne Lalande dite Langliche, the 21-year-old unmarried sister of Marie Anne.[33]

By the beginning of June in 1712, nearly seven months had passed since Pierre had celebrated his 25th birthday and had thus reached the age of legal majority. On June 5, he and his brother-in-law Pierre Poirier dit Lafleur visited the office of the Montreal notary Antoine Adhémar, to officially settle two legal issues. Monsieur Poirier and Pierre's sister Marie Clémence, now 23^2/3 years old, had been married for five years; during that interval, they had produced three children. In the first document which the two men drew up on this day, "Pierre Maupetit, Jr., one of the heirs of the deceased Pierre Maupetit, his father, habitant of the top of this [Montreal] Island, of majority age," acknowledged and ratified the donation which he and his brother Jean had made to their sister Marie Clémence nearly six years earlier, back on September 18, 1706. This earlier gift had entailed the piece of property fronting on the St. Lawrence River which contained 3 arpents of frontage and twenty arpents of depth. According to information which was included in this new document, during the intervening years since their gift, the lot had devolved into the possession of "Louis Lory and Marie Beaune, his wife, mother of the said Maupetit."[34]

The other piece of business that the two brothers-in-law conducted with the notary during this same afternoon entailed the cancellation of the guardianship of the three Maupetit children by Jacques Chasle dit Duhamel (who had earlier become their grandfather through the remarriage of their grandmother). This guardianship responsibility had been placed upon him by the Montreal Court back on April 6, 1700, when all three of the siblings had been of minority age. Although Marie Clémence was still sixteen months short of the full age of majority, she was now legally represented by her husband. According to the statements of Messieurs Maupetit and Poirier on this day, Monsieur Chasle had previously delivered to them an accounting of his administration of the Maupetit family estate during the period of the children's minority, and the two men now released him and all others from any further responsibilities in this matter. The document also noted an additional property transfer which had been involved in the settlement of the Maupetit estate, between the three children and their mother:

"...the release which was made by Marie Beaune, wife of Louis Lory and former widow of Pierre Maupetit, of one half of a land grant located at Grande Anse at the top of this Island in favor of the children of the said deceased Maupetit and her, which was passed in front of the undersigned notary [Antoine Adhémar] on June 27, 1706...and two discharge receipts for four years of seigneurial cens et rente *fees [on this property], signed by Monsieur Caillé and registered with Pierre Raimbault on February 28, 1710."*[35]

Grande Anse (Big Bay), on which this piece of land fronted, was a mile-wide bay that was located about one mile east of Pointe Claire.

As spring approached in 1715, Pierre Maupetit was $28^{1}/3$ years old. At this time, he decided that he would hire on as a legal voyageur-trader, to make a round trip journey to the Straits of Mackinac which would have a duration of six months or more. Since his contract of engagement from March 31 identified him as a "voyageur," it is highly likely that he had previously done this type of work. However, there is no earlier surviving documentation which portrays him in this business. Thus, either he had not participated in the fur trade before this time (which was not likely), or he had done so in illegal ventures, which did not have official permission and were thus not recorded publicly.

"Were present Louis Renaud dit Duval, living in this town [Montreal], both for himself and for Michel Hertel, Esquire, Sieur de la Fresnière, his partner, and Pierre Maupetit, voyageur, who have made the following agreements. That is to say, the said Maupetit has voluntarily engaged himself to the said Sieurs Duval and de la Fresnière to go to Michilimackinac and to come down to the said place next autumn [the word "this" was crossed out and replaced with the word "next"]. In case the said Sieurs Duval and de la Fresnière

will not be able to come down in this said autumn, the said Maupetit will be free at the said place of Michilimackinac [of all obligations to them until it is time to commence the return voyage in the following spring or summer]. He will assist in going up in taking a canoe loaded with merchandise, and in coming down in taking another canoe loaded with peltries, of which merchandise in going up and the peltries in coming down he will take as much care as will be possible. He will faithfully serve the said Sieurs de la Fresnière and Duval, obey them [the phrase "in everything that they will command of him" was crossed out], warn them of damages if it comes to his knowledge, and generally do everything which will be commanded of him by the said Sieurs de la Fresnière and Duval that is honest and legal. He will not be permitted to leave the said service during the said time without the consent of the said Sieurs de la Fresnière and Duval, under the penalties of the ordinance which were presented to his hearing by the said notary. This agreement is made with the stipulation that the said Maupetit will be fed at the expense of the said Sieurs de la Fresnière and Duval during the said time as it is customarily done among the voyageurs. In addition, it will be in consideration of the sum of four hundred livres of the country, of which sum the said Maupetit has received fifty livres and the remainder will be paid to him upon his return to this town. The said Maupetit will be permitted to carry in the canoe in which he will be going up one keg with sixteen pots [half-gallons] of brandy, and four pounds of vermilion [red paint pigment], all without having to pay anything [in freighting costs]. In coming down, he will be permitted to place in the canoe in which he will be two packs of peltries [derived from trading the said brandy and vermilion], also without having to pay anything. Thus have they promised, obligated themselves, waived, etc.

[This agreement] made and drawn up at the said Villemarie in the office of the said notary in the year 1715, on the 31st of March in the afternoon, in the presence of the Sieurs Louis Lefebvre [Sieur] Duchouquet and Charles Lepailleur, witnesses living at the said Villemarie who have signed below with the said notary. The said parties [hirer and hiree] have declared that they do not know how to write or sign, having been questioned after the reading was done, according to the ordinance.

Signed,

Charle Lepallieur, Duchouquet, and Adhemar, royal notary."[36]

Since each *pot* ("half-gallon") of brandy actually contained 1.64 English quarts or 41 percent of a gallon, Pierre's entire permitted stock of this beverage would total 6^1/2 gallons.[37] Legally, he would be allowed to consume this alcoholic drink himself during his round trip journey and his sojourn in the interior, or to trade it to other Frenchmen, but not to native people. However, it would probably not be very difficult for him to exchange his brandy with native customers surreptitiously, while he was trading his four pounds of vermilion with them publicly. During the course of this commerce, it is possible that Pierre might garner more than the two packs of furs and hides which were allowed to be transported out without paying any freighting fees. In that case, although it was not so stated in the contract, he would be able to have a colleague in another canoe who had been less fortunate in his own trading haul out Pierre's overage amount, in return for a portion of those extra *pelleteries*.

The first-mentioned one of Pierre's two employers was the Montreal resident Louis Renaud dit Duval, who was 31 years old and still unmarried. Back in 1703 and again in 1706, he had worked first as a voyageur-trader and then as a voyageur. The first of these legal trading ventures had taken him to the Illinois Country, while the second one had taken him to Ft. Pontchartrain at Detroit. Now, nine years later, he was making arrangements to again participate in the peltries commerce (although he may have done so during those intervening nine years in an unlicensed, illicit manner). This time, he would be working with a partner and two *engagés* who would be hired by the partners.[38]

Monsieur Renaud's business associate in this venture was Michel Hertel, who was usually known as Sieur de Cournoyer (the *dit* name of his father, Jacques Hertel), but in this contract he was called Sieur de la Fresnière (the *dit* name of his great-grandfather, Jacques Hertel). This young military officer was 22 years old and still single.[39]

As these two partners had carried out their preparations during the late winter of 1715, they had hired their first of two *engagés* on February 20. This was Louis François Brias dit Latreille et Lacombe, who was unmarried and about 26 years old; he had relocated from the Quebec area to the Montreal region so that he could take part in the fur trade.[40]

Six weeks after hiring Monsieur Brias, the two associates had engaged Pierre Maupetit. His contract specified that, if all went according to plan, he and his colleagues would exit from Michilimackinac with a load of furs and hides during the autumn of 1715. However, if the two partners would not be able to come down that season, they and Pierre would exit during the following spring or summer. In contrast, the contract of Louis François Brias indicated that he would serve "for one year, commencing on the day of his departure until the month of June in the year 1716." It is possible that, during the six weeks between his hiring and that of Monsieur Maupetit, the two partners had decided that the four of them might be able to complete their business and exit from the interior before the winter freeze, instead of definitely planning to spend the winter at the Straits of Mackinac. This would explain the difference in the length of the period of service that was expressed in the two contracts. However, there is also another possible explanation. Perhaps the two hirers intended that they and Pierre would travel out to Montreal before the winter freeze, as a three-man crew, while Monsieur Brias would remain behind at the Straits, to trade until the following spring. Then, he would paddle out with his gathered peltries in the canoe of some other traders.

As Messieurs Renaud, Hertel, Maupetit, and Brias completed their preparations for their upcoming voyage to the west, they were 31, 22, 28, and 26 years old, respectively. These four unmarried men would comprise the complete crew of their canoe. During this decade as well as the following one, crews of three, and more often four or five paddlers, were the typical sizes.[41]

According to the plans of these four men, before they would carry out their trading activities, they would participate in the upcoming military campaign against the people of the Fox nation, who resided southwest of Green Bay of Lake Michigan. The Governor had ordered that all of the voyageurs who were going up to the Ottawa Country this summer were to participate in this campaign. In order to recruit a large force of militia fighters for this martial expedition, the colonial administrators had unofficially reinstated the trade licenses during this spring of 1715. After participating in the campaign, all of the men would be permitted to trade in the interior for a year or more, based primarily at the Straits of Mackinac. After seventeen years of minimal legal commerce in the west, there was great eagerness on the part of the French citizenry to engage in this newly legitimized trading. Likewise, the native nations in the interior happily anticipated the return of sufficient supplies of merchandise, which would be delivered to their home regions by the French. Between February 20 (the contract of Louis François Brias) and May 22, at least 30 voyageur-traders were hired in the Montreal area, as recorded in notary documents there. Among these, the contracts of 17 men specified that they would be working at Michilimackinac, another 6 would be laboring in the Ottawa Country, and 7 would be conducting trade at Detroit. These 30 individuals were undoubtedly accompanied by many others who had not been registered with Montreal notaries, as well as those employers who were also traveling to the west with their hirees. All of these men received a trading permit, at no cost, in return for their participation in the campaign. (A detailed discussion of the events leading up to this military expedition, its unfolding during 1715 and 1716, and the events which followed has already been presented, along with numerous footnotes, in the biography of Robert Réaume.)[42]

In May of 1715, the large convoy of canoes, including that of Pierre Maupetit and his three colleagues, departed from Lachine, bound for the Straits of Mackinac by way of the southern Great Lakes route. Travel along Lakes Ontario and Erie was necessary in order to pick up a supply of corn from the Iroquois, which had been transported to the shore of Lake Ontario, and to take on at Detroit the shipment of corn which had been supplied by the Miami nation. The large brigade included the twenty rank-and-file soldiers who would be stationed at Ft. Michilimackinac after the campaign, who were led by four officers. These 24 regular soldiers were accompanied by a considerable number of militiamen-traders, as well as a party of native warriors from the St. Lawrence communities. The brigade was scheduled to reach Mackinac by mid-August, at the very latest. After being joined there by many *coureurs de bois* from the interior and warriors from the northern regions, the massed forces would then travel five or six days by canoe to reach the Fox River, just south of Green Bay, by the end of August. In order to save as many of the scarce provisions as possible, with the arrival in Fox territory not planned until the close of August, the St. Lawrence convoy was not dispatched from Lachine earlier than May. In addition, thinking that a shortage of time was not a crucial element, the party did not proceed hastily, by any means, toward Michilimackinac.

Conveying badly needed provisions, munitions, and presents for the native allies, the arrival of this convoy was eagerly awaited by Captain Constant Lemarchand, Sieur de Lignery, who was the commandant at Mackinac and the overall leader of this campaign. On August 30, he wrote from the Straits that these forces had not yet arrived there, although they had set out from Lachine during the month of May. Therefore, when this eastern army would eventually appear, it would be too late in the season to initiate the actual invasion.

As a result, the officer allowed about one hundred French traders who had previously gathered at the Straits to depart for Montreal, upon their request.

Ultimately, the St. Lawrence brigade did arrive at Mackinac in September. It was most certainly at this time that the new Ft. Michilimackinac was constructed on the southern shore of the Straits, by this considerable force of men. The numerous arriving traders (including Pierre Maupetit and his three colleagues) required extensive amounts of secured and sheltered storage space for their merchandise and supplies. In addition, the garrison of 24 soldiers who were now to be permanently stationed there also required buildings in which to live, work, and store their supplies year round. Eventually, Captain de Lignery permitted many of the traders to disperse, to carry out the commerce which had been promised to them, even though their service as militia fighters had not yet been called upon.

No explanation for the tardy arrival at Mackinac of the St. Lawrence convoy was ever conveyed to Versailles, according to the official correspondence which has been preserved. However, it is to be suspected that the majority of the men in this brigade tarried long in the region of Ft. Pontchartrain, in order to carry out the commerce which was to have been postponed until after the military campaign had been completed.[43]

Records of the Provost Court of Montreal clearly show that Pierre Maupetit did come down from Michilimackinac to the St. Lawrence Valley in late 1715, as did also one of his two employers, before ice closed the waterways for the winter. It is also clear from these records that, before departing from the Straits, these men and their colleagues had received permission to descend from Captain de Lignery. (A number of voyageur-traders who had paddled out to Montreal without the commandant's official attestation were jailed and tried for this infraction during the autumn and early winter of 1715-1716.) However, Pierre made the voyage down to the St. Lawrence ahead of his employer, rather than with him. This created a dispute between them, which apparently led the employer to refuse to pay Pierre the agreed-upon remainder of 350 livres of his salary.

In response, on November 29, 1715, "Pierre Maupetit, voyageur of Lachine," registered a complaint with the Court against "Michel Hertel, Sieur de la Fresnière, officer." On December 17 and 18, respectively, Jean Petit, the bailiff of the Court, personally delivered subpoenas to two Montreal residents, ordering them to appear on December 20 at nine o'clock in the morning, to testify before the Chief Judge. The first of these writs was given to the 38-year-old Montreal peltries merchant Jacques Campeau, while the second one was delivered to the 31-year-old Montreal-based *voyageur* Zacharie Boyer. Boyer had been a member of the convoy that had traveled to Michilimackinac by way of Detroit during the previous summer. He had been hired by Paul Guillet on May 5 to carry out a trading journey to the Straits.

On the appointed day of December 20, Monsieur Campeau did not appear before the Court, but Monsieur Boyer did. At issue in this hearing was the Sieur de La Fresnière's declaration that "he had never granted the liberty to Maupetit to leave [Michilimackinac] for [Lake] Nipissing without waiting for his [La Fresnière's] return to Michilimackinac." Pierre Raimbault, who served as the King's attorney and also as the clerk for the *Lieutenant Particulier* (Deputy Judge) of the Provost Court, conducted the hearing. The notary Jean Baptiste Adhémar recorded the proceedings, including a summary of Boyer's testimony, as well as the events which followed.

"Appeared the said Zacharie Boyer, thirty-three years of age or thereabouts, habitant living in this town, who, in order to represent to us his deeds, we took and received the oath of the said Boyer. After the oath was made in the customary manner to tell the truth, the facts mentioned at the said hearing on the said day of November 29 last were read to him. [Then followed his testimony:] Being at Michilimackinac, he heard it said that the said Sieur de La Fresnière, when he learned that the said Maupetit had left for [Lake] Nipissing without waiting for him [to return to Michilimackinac from a trading session at some distant place], he was very unhappy to have an employee who thus left. This obliged him [La Fresnière] to remain a longer time at the said Michilimackinac due to the fault of this man, who had made the great error of leaving, since he [Maupetit] had had sufficient provisions to wait for him, he [La Fresnière] having left for him three or four bags of wheat, he [Boyer] not remembering whether it was one or the other quantity. Effectively, the said Sieur de La Fresnière was obliged to take on a native in the canoe to help him come down [to Montreal], and he gave to him [the native paddler] at Lake Nipissing while going to Sable fifty beaver pelts as his payment for coming down to this town. The convoy of canoes which came down together with that of the said Sieur Hertel [de La Fresnière] numbered twenty-five or thirty canoes. Along the route, in talking with the said Sieur de La Fresnière, who was always complaining about the said employee, he

[Boyer] asked him one day if he had not the pleasure of having learned that the said employee had happily arrived safely in port with his peltries. The said Sieur de La Fresnière told him yes. This is all that he is said to know. The deposition was read to him, and he persisted [in the veracity of his statements]. After having received his salary [the fee for testifying], a tax of thirty sols [1.5 livres] of France was imposed upon him.

This being done, the said Maupetit stated to us that he had subpoenaed Jean Verger to appear on this day to be also heard, for verification of the facts which had been alleged by him [Maupetit]. However, he had not obeyed the summons, having given as the reason his indisposition. For this reason, we were required to grant to him a delay of fifteen days. The parties having been heard, we granted a default to the said Sieur de La Fresnière against the said Campeau for not appearing, whom we sentenced to a fine of three livres according to the ordinance and ordered that he be subpoenaed again. With the consent of the parties, we have granted to the said Maupetit a delay of fifteen days in order to bring the said Verger. With this delay, the parties will produce the witnesses whom they would like to serve, without any other delay or postponement."

In spite of the official postponement of fifteen days, progress in the case did not resume for more than three weeks. On January 13, the bailiff of the Court delivered subpoenas to both Michel Hertel, Sieur de La Fresnière and Jean Verger dit Desjardins. Both of these Montreal residents were to appear before the Chief Judge on the following Friday at nine o'clock in the morning. According to the Court records of these two subpoenas, they had been issued "at the request of Pierre Maufait (sic, for Maupetit), voyageur living at Lachine, who has chosen as his [temporary] legal residence at Villemarie [to which writs may be delivered] the home of the widow Bourbonnais [Barbe Beauvais, the widow of François Brunet dit Le Bourbonnais, Sr.], located on Rue Saint Paul." Jean Verger, who sometimes hired *engagés* to labor for and with him in the interior, had signed a contract on September 2, 1715 to labor in the Upper Country for the Montreal merchant Jacques François Poisset. (In fact, Verger was one of those men who had been imprisoned and tried for descending from the Straits without the Captain's permission.)

No later records concerning the case of Pierre Maupetit against Michel Hertel were entered into the Court papers. This implies that the issue was likely settled out of court, with no further involvement of the authorities being necessary to force Monsieur Hertel to remit to Pierre the full sum of his earned wages.[44]

After Ft. Michilimackinac was constructed and permanently staffed by troops in 1715 and 1716, the French labored assiduously to re-establish a series of posts throughout the interior regions. By 1718, these facilities included (besides Ft. Michilimackinac and Ft. Pontchartrain) a post among the Weas and Miamis on the Maumee River, south of Detroit (founded in 1716); Ft. Pimetoui, on the central Illinois River (in 1716 or 1717); Ft. St. Joseph, on the St. Joseph River (1717); Ft. La Baye, near the southern end of Green Bay, beside the mouth of the Fox River (1717); Ft. Kaministiquia, on the northwestern shore of Lake Superior at the mouth of the Kaministiquia River (1717); Ft. La Pointe, on Madeleine Island near the western end of Lake Superior (1718); and the Nipigon Post, north of Lake Superior (reinstated by 1718).[45]

The voyageur hiring contracts which were registered with Montreal notaries in the spring and summer of 1718 mentioned various of these posts as the destinations of the men. However, many of the contracts specified only a general locale in which they would be working. Thus, 12 men were hired to labor at Michilimackinac, 14 were engaged to work at Detroit, 2 were contracted to serve in the Illinois Country, and one was to be employed at La Baye. In addition, investors arranged expeditions to Kaministiquia and to Ouiatenon (the Wea post). Finally, 24 voyageurs were hired to work in the generalized Upper Country, while two more were engaged to labor in the similarly generalized Ottawa Country.[46]

When the census figures and the voyageur hiring contracts from this particular period are examined and compared, two important facts are revealed. First, some 12 percent of the men (ages 15 and over) in the entire population of New France worked at some point as voyageur-traders or *engagés*. In addition, a very high percentage of the individuals who were thus employed resided on Montreal Island. In 1716, the total population of the colony numbered 20,530; of these residents, 5,520 (26.8 percent) were adult males, ages 15 and higher. Within this group of males, 657 (11.9 percent of them) worked in these two occupations in the interior during the period from 1708 through 1717.

During this decade-long interval, among these 657 men who labored in the fur trade in the interior regions, the places of permanent residence of 622 of them are known. Within this latter group of 622 men, fully 337 (54 percent of them) lived on Montreal Island. Those other individuals who lived on the mainland surrounding Montreal

Island and off toward the northeast for some 30 miles may be separated into four geographical areas. The western section of the southern shore of the St. Lawrence River (Châteauguay, Laprairie, Chambly, St. Lambert, Tremblay, and Longueuil) provided 42 men (6.8 percent). The central section of the southern shore (Cap St. Michel, Boucherville, Varenne, and Trinité) supplied 66 men (10.6 percent). The eastern section of the southern shore (Verchères, Vitré, Contrecoeur, St. Ours, Sorel, Îles Bouchard, and Ste. Thérèse) provided 11 men (1.8 percent). The northern shore of the St. Lawrence (Île Jésus, Lachenaie, Repentigny, St. Sulpice, Lavaltrie, Lanoraie, D'Autré, Berthier, and Île du Pas) supplied 17 men (2.7 percent). Thus, those individuals who lived on Montreal Island plus those who resided in the rest of the Montreal governmental district totaled 473 men, or 76 percent of the voyageur-traders and voyageurs who were employed during this decade-long period. Of particular interest is the fact that these 473 individuals represented fully 22.7 percent of the 2,086 men ages 15 and over who lived in this district at this time. On Montreal Island itself, the percentage of westward-traveling men was even higher. The 337 voyageur-traders and *engagés* living there represented a full 27.4 percent of the 15-and-over males in the population of the Island.

In comparison, the entire Trois-Rivières governmental district supplied only 98 men, or 15.8 percent of the total number of voyageur-traders and *engagés* who were employed during these ten years. These individuals may be separated into three areas: 29 were from the town proper, 67 were from the seigneuries along the northern shore of the St. Lawrence, and 2 were from the seigneuries along the southern shore. Although the total numbers of these men were relatively small in the overall picture, they represented an amazingly large percentage of the males ages 15 and over who lived in this district. In the town of Trois-Rivières proper, the voyageur-traders and *engagés* represented a whopping 53.7 percent of the adult males; in the north shore seigneuries, fully 30.3 percent of the adult males worked in these two occupations.

The Quebec governmental district provided far fewer westward-paddling men during this decade, numbering 51, or 8.2 percent of the total. These individuals may be separated into four areas: 29 were from the town proper, 9 were from western section of the north shore, 9 were from the eastern section of the north shore (including Île d'Orléans), and 4 were from the western section of the south shore (from Lauson to the west). Apparently, none of the men working in these two occupations during this decade-long period lived in the region of the lower St. Lawrence.[47]

In 1718, a total of 55 voyageur-traders and *engagés* were hired via Montreal-area notary contracts to labor in the west. One of these individuals was Pierre Maupetit, who, at the age of 31 1/2, had been a resident of the southern shore of Montreal Island for nearly all of his life. On April 15, he visited the office of the Montreal notary Adhémar, to officially settle the details of his employment as a voyageur-trader during the coming year.

"Was present Pierre Maupetit, who has voluntarily engaged himself to Sieur [Jacques-] François Poisset, merchant of this town, to go up and to come down in one year, commencing on the day of his departure, to go to le Pays d'en Haut *(the Upper Country). He will assist in taking a canoe loaded with merchandise in going up and in coming down to take a canoe loaded with peltries, of which merchandise in going up and of the said peltries in coming down the said employee promises to take as much care as will be possible, to avoid damage for the said Sieur Poisset, to warn him if it comes to his knowledge, and generally to do everything which will be commanded of him by the said Sieur Poisset that is honest and legal. The said employee will not be permitted to absent himself from the service of the said Sieur Poisset without his command, under the penalties of the ordinances. This agreement is made with the stipulation that the said employee will be fed at the expense of the said Sieur Poisset as is customarily done among the voyageurs, and in addition in consideration of the sum of four hundred livres in the currency of the country. He will receive from the said sum of four hundred livres the sum of one hundred forty-six livres when he leaves the said Sieur Poisset and all the others [on this day]. In addition, the said Sieur Poisset promises him that he will pay to him the remainder of the said sum of four hundred livres, which amounts to the sum of two hundred fifty-four livres, in this town upon his return [text crossed out: "in beaver pelts at the price of the office [of the export monopoly company] or in [other] peltries at the prices of the merchant-outfitters"]. Thus have they promised, obligated themselves, waived, etc.*

[This agreement] made and drawn up at the said Villemarie in the office of the said notary in the year 1718, on the fifteenth of April in the afternoon, in the presence of the Sieurs François Moreau and Louis Lefebvre [Sieur] Duchouquet, witnesses living in the said Villemarie who have signed below with the said Sieur Poisset. The said employee has declared that he does not know how to write or sign, upon being questioned according to the ordinance. Signed,

Duchouquet, Moreau, and Adhemar [but not by Poisset]"[48]

Pierre's employer, the 26-year-old voyageur-merchant Jacques François Poisset, had been hiring employees to work for and with him in the west for at least two years, since at least 1715. He represented the third generation of a family of businessmen in the colony. His grandfather, François Poisset, Sieur de La Conche, having emigrated from La Rochelle, had operated as a merchant in the Lower Town area of Quebec. Then his father, François Poisset, Sieur de La Conche et Dutreuil, had carried out his own business as a merchant bourgeois in the same section of the capital town. These two generations of businessmen had died in 1691 and 1697, respectively. Jacques François, the only surviving child of his parents, had relocated upriver from Quebec to the Montreal area in or before 1713, when he had been 21 years old. After marrying Élisabeth Quenet (the daughter of the businessman and hat maker Jean Quenet and his wife Étienette Hurtubise) at the Lachine church in July of 1713, the couple had then produced two children by December of 1717. However, their first baby had died in August of 1716 at the age of ten months, and the second one would only be documented by his baptismal record from December 12, 1717. (This voyageur-merchant would also partner with François Brunet dit Le Bourbonnais, Jr. in 1720.)[49]

Pierre's contract with Monsieur Poisset did not indicate specifically where the unmarried voyageur-trader was residing at this time. He had spent his early years in the westernmost section of the Lachine seigneury, both before his father's death in 1689 and then during the ensuing years. When his mother had remarried in 1698 (when Pierre had been 11 1/2 years old), the three Maupetit children and their mother had moved west to the property of the new father of the family, Louis Lory. His long rectangular piece of land was located some five miles west of Ft. Rolland and about 3/4 mile west of Pointe Claire. It was here that Pierre and his two siblings had completed their years of growing up, until Pierre had commenced his three-year period of employment for Claude Caron in Montreal; this latter stint had begun when he had been 15 1/2 years old. When Pierre and Jean had gifted the family property near the St. Louis church in the Bout de l'Île area to their sister in 1706 (when Pierre had been nearly twenty years of age), the two brothers had been described as residents of "the [western] end of Montreal Island." Six years later, when Pierre had ratified this same land transfer in 1712, he had been likewise identified as an "habitant of the top [western end area] of this Island." Neither of Pierre's two voyageur hiring contracts, in 1715 and 1718, had indicated his specific place of residence. However, the official complaint and lawsuit which he had registered with the Montreal Court in December of 1715, against one of his two employers on that voyage, had noted that he had been a resident of the Lachine parish at that time.

The new parish of St. Joachim de Pointe Claire had been established in 1713, and its church had been constructed on or near to the prominent land feature on the St. Lawrence shoreline that was called Pointe Claire. (At about the same time, the St. Louis parish, which had been established in the Bout de l'Île area back in 1685, had been renamed in honor of Ste. Anne.)[50] Since Pierre's mother and her second husband Louis Lory resided about 3/4 mile west of the St. Joachim church, this was logically their home parish. And until such time as Pierre would marry, the parish of his parents would be considered to be his own parish as well.

On April 26, 1718, eleven days after he had drawn up his contract of employment for the next year, Pierre was selected to stand as the godfather at a christening ceremony in the Pointe Claire church. This event was held two days after the twins Louis and Léonard (Jr.) Lalande had arrived. These two boys, Pierre's cousins, were the eleventh, twelfth, and last children to be born to Léonard Lalande dit Latreille, Sr. and Gabrielle Beaune (who was Pierre's aunt, a younger sister of his mother Marie Louise). The farm of the Lalande family was located a short distance east of Pointe Claire, and about one mile east of the Lory-Beaune land.[51] On this celebratory day, the information that the officiating priest penned into the St. Joachim ledger included a number of particularly interesting details. First, the godfather was identified as "Pierre Maupetit dit Potevin of this parish, unmarried son of Jean Paul Maupetit and Marie [Louise] Beaune of this parish." Twelve years earlier, back in 1706, when Pierre and his brother had transferred the family land to their sister, the notary had clearly written that their deceased father was named Pierre Maupetit, not Jean Paul Maupetit. In November of 1718, this latter name, written simply as Jean, would appear again in another church record related to his son Pierre, Jr.

An even more fascinating piece of information was recorded at the conclusion of this baptismal ceremony in April of 1718. The godmother was identified as "Angélique Villeray of this parish, unmarried daughter of Antoine Villeray and Jeanne Quenneville, of this parish." Exactly five months later, Angélique and Pierre, the two christening sponsors on this joy-filled day, would become husband and wife.

Born and baptized on December 9, 1698, Angélique was 19¹/₃ years old on this April day. She was the third of ten children who had been produced by the Villeray-Quenneville couple, during the 22 years following their wedding at Montreal in February of 1694. (He had emigrated from either Chambon or Chambord, while she had been born and raised in Montreal and Lachine.) Among their ten offspring, at least two had died at very young ages. Their first child, Pierre I, had died on his second day of life in March of 1695, while their fifth baby, Pierre II, had died at the age of six months in January of 1704. Angélique's seven surviving siblings, in sequence, were Marie Louise (born on May 10, 1696, and baptized at the Lachine church on the same day), Michel (born on May 28, 1701, and baptized at the Lachine church on the same day), Jacques (born on January 3, 1705, baptized at the St. Louis/Ste. Anne church on January 18), Marie Madeleine (born in about 1710), Antoine (born on January 11, 1711, baptized at the St. Louis/Ste. Anne church on January 21), Marie Suzanne (born in about 1713), and Jean Baptiste (baptized at the Pointe Claire church on April 16, 1716; this lattermost christening took place some three years after this new parish had been founded).

The farm of the Villeray family was located about one mile west of Pointe Claire, and thus about ³/₈ mile west of the farm of Louis Lory and Marie Louise Beaune. Pierre Maupetit had lived on the latter piece of property from ages 11¹/₂ to 15¹/₂, and possibly again when he was older, after he had completed his three-year apprenticeship. The Lory plot was separated from the Villeray family land (where Angélique had apparently lived all of her life) by just three lots, which contained a total of 1,920 feet of St. Lawrence frontage. In June of 1702, when Pierre had been 15¹/₂ years old, he had departed from the family farm to begin his three-year apprenticeship program in Montreal; at that time, Angélique, living less than ⁴/₁₀ mile away toward the west, had been 3¹/₂ years old. Technically, these two young people had known each other for all of the girl's life; however, they were separated in age by twelve years and three weeks. In addition, while she had been growing up, he had been absent from the area of their two farms for a number of relatively long periods.[52]

On April 26, 1718, their serving as co-sponsors at the christening of the two-day-old Lalande infant must have kindled a serious mutual interest between them, now that she had grown to adulthood. It is to be remembered that, just eleven days before this ecclesiastical event, Pierre had signed a long-term contract to work as a voyageur-trader based at Ft. Michilimackinac. The date of his hiring implies that he and his voyageur-merchant colleague had intended to depart for the west with the May brigade, planning to be away for some twelve to fifteen months.

However, Pierre and Angélique would exchange their nuptial vows in the Ste. Anne church in the Bout de l'Île area on September 25, five months after these baptismal festivities. Thus, the groom would labor in the Upper Country for only five months, or depart almost immediately after their wedding, traveling via the Ottawa River route. However, for the sake of safety, this would have been a rather late date for heading off on the latter watercourse. It was closed by winter ice many weeks earlier than the more southerly route, which entailed the upper St. Lawrence River, Lake Ontario, and Lake Erie.

In anticipation of their September wedding, Fr. René Charles de Breslay published the first bann of marriage in the St. Joachim and Ste. Anne parishes. Afterward, Charles de Lagoudalie, the Grand Vicar, granted a dispensation of the other two banns, which were usually obligatory. (However, this dispensation apparently did not imply a premarital pregnancy. The couple would not welcome their first baby into the world until one year and three weeks after their marriage.)

At the conclusion of their nuptial ceremony on September 25, the priest recorded in the Ste. Anne parish register that the groom was "Pierre Maupetit of Île Perrot, age 30, son of Jean Maupetit and Marie Louise Beaune, wife of Louis Lory." Based upon his baptismal records in the Lachine church, Pierre was actually seven weeks short of turning age 32 at this time. As was mentioned earlier, the identification of his father as "Jean Maupetit" was parallel to the name "Jean Paul Maupetit" which had been applied to his father five months earlier, back in the spring when Pierre, Jr. had served as a baptismal sponsor. Of particular importance in this record is the information that the groom was already a resident of Île Perrot. This island, situated at the junction of the Ottawa and St. Lawrence Rivers, lay southwest of the Bout de l'Île area of Montreal Island; it measured about six miles in length by some $3^1/2$ miles in width. The Maupetit-Villeray couple would reside nearly all of their married life on this offshore landmass, only leaving it to live close to the Ste. Anne church for a period of about eight or nine years between 1722 and

1730. According to the cleric's records on this day, the bride was 19 years of age; this statement was correct, since she would celebrate her 20th birthday eleven weeks later, on December 9. The four official witnesses at the heartwarming ceremony were Pierre's sister Marie Clémence Maupetit and her husband Pierre Poirier; Pierre's cousin the voyageur Jean Baptiste Jean dit Vincent (age 27, who had grown up on the eleventh lot east of the Lory property; he would marry at Montreal in eight months); and the voyageur-farmer Pierre Sabourin, Jr. (age 24, who had grown up on the second lot west of the Lory farm; he had been married for nearly two years, and he lived with his wife and one child in the Pointe Claire parish).[53]

Three weeks after Pierre and Angélique's first wedding anniversary, baby Pierre joined the family. On October 12, 1719, he was baptized in the Pointe Claire church, to which both of his parents had belonged until their marriage. According to the priest's notations on this festive day, the parents were Pierre Maupetit dit Poitevin and Catherine (sic, actually Angélique) Villeray of Île Perrot. The godfather was the maternal grandfather Antoine Villeray, while the godmother was the paternal grandmother Marie Louise Beaune.[54]

As was mentioned earlier, Pierre did not paddle off to the Straits of Mackinac with his employer in the May convoy of 1718 and spend a year or more in the interior, as his April contract had specified. Instead, he had either labored for only five months or he had remained in the St. Lawrence settlements, after which he had married Angélique on September 25. However, it is possible that he might have set out for the west immediately after the wedding; but this would have been a risky proposition, departing for the interior via the more northerly route this late in the season. There is another piece of evidence which supports the supposition that he remained behind on Île Perrot, and spent the following winter with his new bride. Angélique became pregnant with their first child in about early-to-mid January of 1719. Thus, either Pierre had altered or cancelled his voyageur-trader contract with Jacques François Poisset, and had worked for only five months or not at all, or he had departed for the west very shortly after their wedding. If the latter scenario was the one that actually had occurred, someone else had fathered the first child to be borne by his wife. Oddly, the notary never penned an addendum onto the end of Pierre's April contract, which would have indicated that he had changed or cancelled his employment agreement and had returned to Monsieur Poisset the advance on his wages of 146 livres.

To the great sadness of all, little Pierre Maupetit lived for only one month. On November 13, he was tearfully laid to rest in the Pointe Claire cemetery. According to the record of his burial, the baby's parents resided on Île Perrot, and the two official witnesses were his paternal great-uncle Jean Beaune and his maternal grandfather Antoine Villeray. The latter individual had also been his godfather at the baby's optimistic baptism just four weeks earlier.[55]

About ten months after burying their first child, Angélique and Pierre welcomed their second baby into the world on September 27, 1720. As with their first offspring, although they resided on Île Perrot, they transported their brand-new baby some six or seven miles eastward to the Pointe Claire church for her baptism on the following day. At the christening ceremony for tiny Marie Thérèse on this optimistic and hopeful day, the godmother was Catherine Brunet. Standing beside her as the godfather was 27-year-old, unmarried Jacques Chasle dit Duhamel, Jr. (whose father, Jacques, Sr., was the second husband of Marie Madeleine Bourgery, Pierre's maternal grandmother). Since this baptismal record would be the only documentation for this child that would be preserved in the colony, it is highly likely that Marie Thérèse did not grow up to adulthood and marry. Due to this lack of records, it is not possible to determine just when Pierre and Angélique were obliged to endure the crushing sadness of her death and burial.[56]

During the following August of 1721, Angélique appeared in the Ste. Anne church as the godmother of two-day-old Marie Angélique Merlot. On the 19th, when she granted her name to the infant, her co-sponsor was Michel Brébant dit Lamothe. The proud parents of this baby were Joachim Merlot and Jeanne Martin, fellow residents of the parish, who had previously borne eight children. Sadly, this latest one would only survive for 4 1/2 weeks; she would be buried in the Ste. Anne cemetery on September 20.[57]

When the third Maupetit child arrived in May of 1722, Pierre and Angélique named him Pierre, Jr., as they had previously done with their very first baby 2 1/2 years earlier (the one who had only lived for one month). At his christening ceremony in the Ste. Anne church on May 25, the same day as his birth, the boy's godfather was Guillaume Lalonde (designated in this study as Guillaume Number 2, whose biography is presented later in this work), the unmarried 17-year-old son of Jean Baptiste Lalonde and Jeanne Gervais (the dual biography of these parents has already been presented). The child's godmother was Marie Josèphe Brébant, the unmarried 13-year-old daughter of Michel Brébant dit Lamothe and Marie Élisabeth Lafaye.[58]

By this time, Pierre and Angélique had already relocated a short distance toward the northeast, having moved across the water from Île Perrot to a location on the mainland that was immediately west of the cemetery of the Ste. Anne church. In the baptismal records of their first two children in 1719 and 1720, as well as in the burial record of their first baby in 1719, the priest had indicated that the parents resided on Île Perrot, which was included in the territory of the Ste. Anne parish. However, in the christening record of their third offspring in May of 1722, the cleric had simply noted that they were "of this parish," which signalled that they had left Île Perrot.

On August 7 in this year of 1722, Pierre traveled to Montreal, in order to receive a small supplemental piece of land from the Sulpicians (who were the seigneurs of Montreal Island) and to officially register his ownership of his main lot, which was located immediately west of the supplemental plot and the Ste. Anne cemetery. The primary lot had never been officially granted to him, although he and his little family had already been residing on it for some time.

"Before the royal notary [Pierre Raimbault]...were present Messieurs François Vachon de Belmont...Superior of the Gentlemen of the Ecclesiastics of the Seminary of Montreal [and two other Sulpician officials]...who have voluntarily acknowledged and admitted that they have transferred and ceded by title of seigneurial cens et rente, *now and for always, to Pierre Maupetit dit Poitevin, living at the top of this Island, present and accepting the said title for himself, his heirs, and assigns, of a supplemental piece of land which is located between the habitation [living site] which he possesses at the end of the top of this Island near the Ste. Anne chapel, and the cemetery of the said Ste. Anne chapel, along with the said living site for which the recipient has said that a contract of concession was never passed. This [primary lot] has three arpents [575 feet] of frontage and a depth which extends to the land of the Dame [Louise Charlotte Guillet, wife of Jean Baptiste] Cuillerier, having on one [west] side [the land of] Hubert Ranger [dit Laviolette], Jr. and on the other [east] side the said supplemental piece of land, joined to the said living site by these same presents. All of this property has the amount of sixty [square] arpents of surface area [51 acres], the entirety having at the front end the side of the St. Lawrence River and at the other end the lands granted to the Dame [Louise Charlotte] Guillet, wife of the Sieur [Jean Baptiste] Cuillerier, on one [west] side [the land of] the said Hubert Ranger [dit Laviolette, Jr.], and on the other [east] side the Ste. Anne cemetery, all*

comprising the amount of the said sixty [square] arpents of surface area...
[This agreement] made and drawn up at the said Villemarie in 1722, on the
seventh of August in the afternoon, in the presence of Messieurs Jacques
Pierre Paumereau, merchant, and Christophe [-Hilarion] Dulaurent,
attorney for civil cases. The said Maupetit has declared that he does not
know how to write or sign, having been questioned after the reading was
done.
Signed,
François Vachon de Belmont, priest, François Chèze, priest, Paumereau,
Dulaurent, and P. Raimbault."[59]

By accepting these two land grants, Pierre agreed to a number of
standard provisions, which were spelled out in the middle section of
this document. He would clear the two properties, occupy them, and
build structures on them within one year (he had already cleared a
portion, occupied, and built upon the primary lot), and permit the
construction of any and all roads that the seigneurs might deem
appropriate to build across them. In addition, he himself would
construct and maintain in a practical manner a road across the river
frontage of his property, at the location where it would be marked out.
He would have his grains ground at the seigneurial mill, and pay the
grinding fees to the miller there (under the penalty of the confiscation
of all grain that he might have ground elsewhere). He would also
relinquish to the seigneurs whatever stone and lumber found on his
land which they might require to construct their buildings, fences,
and public works. In addition, he would engage a licensed surveyor
to accurately measure his property, and he would register the
surveyor's report with the seigneurs. Each year, he would pay to the
Sulpicians at Montreal, either at their residence there or at the place
designated for making such payments, ten sols ($^1/_2$ livre) and a half-
bushel of good, dry, and saleable wheat for each twenty arpents (17
acres) of surface area of his land. These very modest fees of *cens* and
rentes, in his case totaling just $1^1/_2$ livres and $1^1/_2$ bushels of wheat,
would be paid annually on November 11, the Day and Feast of St.
Martin (who was the patron saint of France).

When the land grants in this region had been initially planned
out, a plot with 14 arpents or $^1/_2$ mile of St. Lawrence frontage had
been reserved for the St. Louis (later named Ste. Anne) church, the
presbytère (combination priest's residence and parish hall), and the
cemetery, when this parish had been established in 1685. Immediately
east of this ecclesiastical land was the lot, containing 768 feet of river

frontage, which had been granted in 1687 to Jean de Lalonde and his descendants, which was still owned by them (including Jean Baptiste Lalonde, whose biography has already been presented in this work). The property immediately west of the church land consisted of Pierre Maupetit's supplemental piece of land, and immediately west of that his large primary lot, with a total river frontage of 575 feet. These various details were portrayed on the land ownership map of Montreal Island which had been drawn up in 1702 by Fr. Vachon de Belmont, who would serve as the Superior of the Sulpician Seminary at Montreal from 1701 until 1732.[60]

The 1722 document which officially granted the two pieces of land beside the Ste. Anne cemetery to Pierre was the first known record penned by a notary in New France which identified him by both his family name "Maupetit" and his nickname "dit Poitevin." In the six earlier notarial documents that had involved Pierre (when his age had ranged from 16 to 31), he had been called only his given name and his family name. In the twelve other notary records which would come later, he would be identified by every one of his names in seven of them. In the numerous church documents mentioning him which were drawn up by priests, both during his lifetime and after his death, he was called his full name Pierre Maupetit dit Poitevin in only thirteen of them. Those thirteen records in which the priest used all of his names had commenced in 1719, at the baptism of his first child. In all of the other ecclesiastical records in which the man was mentioned over the span of many decades, he was identified as simply Pierre Maupetit.

It is interesting to note that Pierre, and his father Pierre, Sr. before him, utilized the *dit* name Poitevin (meaning "one from Poitou") even though these men represented the only known Maupetit family in all of New France. Thus, there was no need to use a nickname to separate the various lines within the family, or to clearly distinguish their Maupetit family from other Maupetit families who were not related. In fact, the nickname "dit Poitevin" was not very distinguished. It was rather common and widely employed in the colony, being used in association with at least 23 other family names before 1730.[61] One logical explanation for the use of this *dit* name by the Maupetit family is that it had earlier been applied to Pierre, Sr., or to one of his ancestors, when he or they had served as soldiers. Within military circles, the use of nicknames was extremely common and popular during this era.

In the spring of 1723, Pierre and his sister Marie Clémence (who resided with her husband Pierre Poirier and their children on Île Perrot) appeared in the Ste. Anne church as the christening sponsors for an out-of-wedlock infant. On April 16, Marie Suzanne Turpin (age 17²/₃, the youngest child of the deceased merchant-trader Alexandre Turpin, whose biography has already been presented in this work) brought her newborn baby to her own parish church. She had become pregnant by the Montreal butcher Antoine Poudret, who was 32 years old and still single. Six months later, on October 29, Marie Suzanne would marry the 24-year-old immigrant Jean Laroche in the Montreal church; the infant's birth father would be wed in December of 1724.[62]

Celebrations were in order for Angélique and Pierre upon the safe arrival of their fourth baby in the autumn of 1724. At his christening festivities in the Ste. Anne church on September 17, little Joseph's godfather was his uncle Michel Villeray (age 23 and single) of Pointe Claire. The infant's godmother was the 17-year-old local resident Marie Merlot, who was the daughter of Joachim Merlot and Jeanne Martin.[63]

Pierre took part in a much sadder occasion in the same church thirteen months later, when he served as one of the official witnesses at the interment of an 18-month-old toddler. Little Marie Brunet, the youngest child of François Brunet dit Le Bourbonnais, Jr. and Françoise David (whose dual biography has already been presented in this study) was laid to rest amid many tears on October 15, 1725. The other witness on this poignant day was Angélique's father, Antoine Villeray.[64]

The year 1727 brought a mixture of both gladness and grief to the Maupetit clan. First, Angélique was asked to appear in the Ste. Anne church as the sponsor of the fifth child of the local couple Pierre Lecomte and Marie Charlotte Fournier. On March 15, the same day as she had arrived, Marie Pélagie was held over the baptismal font, with Angélique and her co-sponsor and local resident Pierre Ranger standing close by. Unfortunately, the tiny lass died and was buried in the Ste. Anne cemetery on the very next day.[65]

Five weeks later, on May 20, Angélique safely delivered their fifth child, Marie Angélique. On the same day, her proud parents carried her to the nearby Ste. Anne church to be baptized, where her aunt Marie Madeleine Villeray served as her godmother and the family friend François Brazeau from Pointe Claire stood as the baby's godfather. (This infant would grow up to marry Albert Lalonde, and the two of them would provide the direct ancestral linkages between Angélique and Pierre and the present author.)[66]

However, it seemed that jubilant times in New France were almost always followed before long by mournful times. Just ten weeks after the heartwarming arrival of Maupetit baby number five, grief descended upon the clan when Pierre and Angélique's 16-year-old niece Marie Marthe Poirier passed away. After her death on Île Perrot, she was laid to rest in the Ste. Anne cemetery on August 7, 1727. At this time, the mother of the deceased, Marie Clémence Maupetit (age 38), was about three months pregnant with their tenth and final child. On February 7, 1728, the day following his birth on Île Perrot, tiny Louis Poirier was brought to the Ste. Anne church. There, his aunt Angélique Villeray and his maternal grandfather Louis Lory stood as his co-sponsors.[67]

Four months later, Pierre served as one of the official witnesses at the sad burial of a six-week old baby. On June 17, Marie Thérèse, the eighth child of Jacques Desgagnés and Marguerite Jousset, was interred in the Ste. Anne cemetery beside the Maupetit farm. The other witness on this day was 13-year-old Antoine Sauvé dit Laplante, who lived with his family on the third lot east of the church.[68]

As has already been shown on several occasions, since Pierre resided on the property immediately west of the Ste. Anne cemetery, he was regularly called upon to serve as an official witness at burials there. (Jean Baptiste Lalonde, living on the opposite side of the church, was often asked to serve in the same capacity.) However, during the winter of 1730, Pierre was obliged to shoulder this sorrowful role three times within the span of just two months, in each instance at the burial of a young child.

The first time took place on February 7, when Angélique Lalande, who was eleven months and two weeks old, was laid to rest. Her parents were Jacques Lalande dit Latreille and Judith Réaume. Judith was the daughter of the distinguished voyageur-trader Robert Réaume (whose biography has already been presented in this study). Thus, Pierre Maupetit served on this mournful occasion as the only official witness at the burial of Monsieur Réaume's granddaughter.[69]

Just eighteen days later, the funeral at which Pierre stood as the only official witness hit him and Angélique much closer to home. On February 25, their nephew Louis Poirier, who had celebrated his second birthday 2^1/2 weeks earlier, was laid to rest. Back in February of 1728, Angélique had stood as the godmother of this little lad in the same church.[70]

Their mourning was relieved slightly three weeks later, when Angélique safely delivered their sixth child and third daughter on March 18, 1730. On the same day, Marie Suzanne was christened and received her name from her aunt Marie Suzanne Villeray. The infant's godfather was the family friend Nicholas Robillard. Interestingly, when the priest recorded the details of this event in the parish register, he entered the name of the father correctly, but he identified the mother of the baby as Élisabeth Villeray, instead of Angélique Villeray.[71]

Three weeks later, Pierre was again reminded of just how tenuous life was for young children in the colony, when he was obliged to stand as the sole official witness at the burial of a ten-month-old girl. Born as the eleventh and twelfth children of the Île Perrot-based voyageur Pierre Hunault dit Deschamps and Marguerite Suzanne Lefebvre, Marie Madeleine and her twin sister Marie Thérèse had arrived on June 9, 1729. However, life had been too challenging for Madeleine, who was laid to rest on April 8, 1730.[72]

Before the end of this year, Pierre and Angélique decided that they would permanently return to Île Perrot, where they had resided for about the first four years of their marriage. Having lived immediately west of the Ste. Anne cemetery for some eight or nine years, Pierre now traded the land that he owned there for property on the island, which was separated from Montreal Island by a half-mile of water at the narrowest crossing. On December 29, 1730, he traveled to the office of the Montreal notary Guillet to officially register this land exchange. The trade was done with his stepfather Louis Lory, who, along with Pierre's mother, now resided in the seigneury of Soulanges. (This seigneury was located immediately southwest of Île Perrot, on the north shore of the St. Lawrence.) Monsieur Lory, who was about 56 years old at this time, had married Pierre's widowed mother Marie Louise Beaune 29 1/2 years earlier, back in June of 1698. During that span of nearly three decades, the couple had not produced any children together.[73]

Now, Pierre, Angélique, and their four or five living children moved back onto Île Perrot. (It is not possible to determine when daughter Marie Thérèse, who had been born a decade earlier, in the autumn of 1720, actually passed away.) The parents would spend the remainder of their lives on this island, and it would be here that their other five children would join the family and all nine of their surviving offspring would grow up.

Some eighteen months after they had permanently returned to the island, Pierre lost his only sister. (The last known documentation for his only brother, Jean, was a Pointe Claire notary record from August 24, 1718, when Jean had been 33 years old.) Marie Clémence, who had been a resident of Île Perrot for the previous several years and was identified in her burial record as still being from there, was for some reason laid to rest in the Montreal cemetery. Perhaps she had been on a trip to town at the time of her death, and her family decided to have her interred there rather than bringing her body back to her home parish of Ste. Anne for burial. This bleak event took place on July 18, 1732, when she was three months short of her 44th birthday. Having been married to Pierre Poirier for 25 years and five weeks, the couple had produced ten children. Their oldest child had already been married for eight years, while their youngest one had died at the age of two back in February of 1730.[74]

After enduring the painful loss of Marie Clémence, the Maupetit family was buoyed up considerably six months later, by the arrival of the next member of their family on January 2, 1733. At her christening ceremony in the Ste. Anne church two days later, the tiny lass was given the name Marie Thérèse Maupetit. This clearly indicated that the second child of the family, who had been granted this same name at the time of her arrival in September of 1720, had passed away some time before this date. The infant's baptismal sponsors were her 16-year-old uncle Jean Baptiste Villeray and her cousin Marie Angélique Poirier, who was age 23 and still single.[75]

This same year of 1733 also brought with it the marriage festivities of three of Angélique's siblings. Each of these celebrations was held at the Pointe Claire church, which was the home parish of the Villeray family. (It had been nearly twenty years since the first and only wedding of one of Angélique's siblings had taken place, back in December of 1713, when her sister Marie Louise had married François Quévillon. That had been $4^3/4$ years before Angélique and Pierre had themselves been wed, in September of 1718.)

The first of the three sibling weddings was held on January 10, when Marie Madeleine Villeray (about 23 years of age) married Jacques Beaune. The second one was celebrated three months later, on April 14, when Antoine Villeray (age 22) took as his wife Marie Madeleine Brunet. Four months after that, on August 11, Marie

Suzanne Villeray (age 20) exchanged nuptial vows with Jacques Prou.[76]

Fifteen months after the latter wedding, another of Angélique's siblings was married, this time at the Lachine church. On November 27, 1734, her brother Michel Villeray, who was 33 years of age, took as his bride Marie Charlotte Gros. At this point, among all of Angélique's brothers and sisters, only her siblings Jacques (age 29) and Jean Baptiste (age 18) were still single.[77]

The number of offspring in the brood of Pierre and Angélique increased by one in May of 1735, when their eighth child arrived safely. On the 21st, the same day as the baby had been born, the parents transported little Étienne across the water to the Ste. Anne church to be christened. At the ceremony, the sponsors were Joseph Leduc and Marie Françoise Trottier Desruisseaux. This godmother, 23 years old, was the youngest child of the deceased seigneur of Île Perrot, Joseph Trottier, Sieur Desruisseaux, who had purchased the island from the Lemoine brothers (sons of Charles) back in 1703.[78]

Nearly three years after the arrival of Étienne, Angélique and Pierre were pleased to welcome their next child into the family. However, this time, their bright and joyful mood did not last for long. On February 14, 1738, Marie Élisabeth was born on Île Perrot, and within hours she was taken across to the church for her baptism. Her godmother was Marie Angélique Lafleur, while her godfather was Pierre Énaud, Jr. However, just five days later, on the nineteenth, the tiny infant was interred in the Ste. Anne cemetery, within sight of the farm on which her parents and siblings had earlier lived for about eight or nine years. On this heart-wrenching day, the official witnesses were the baby's brother Pierre Maupetit, Jr. ($15^3/4$ years old) and the parish beadle or sexton Jacques Saint Julien.[79]

During the depths of winter in 1739, Angélique's youngest brother, Jean Baptiste Villeray (who was two months short of turning age 23), was married in the St. Joachim church at Pointe Claire. On February 3, he joined in matrimony with Marie Josèphe Séguin.[80] This would be the last of Angélique's siblings to be wed, since her one brother who was still single, Jacques (age 34 at this point), would not live long enough to take a bride.

In the autumn of this same year, one of the neighboring couples of the Maupetits on Île Perrot was René Leduc and Marie Élisabeth Fortier. Shortly after the arrival of the Leduc baby on October 5, 1739, the tiny lad's survival seemed to be in serious doubt. Thus, as an emergency measure, Pierre performed on him a provisional lay person's baptismal ceremony. Six days after his birth, on the eleventh, the infant was laid to rest in the Ste. Anne cemetery, with two official witnesses in attendance. These were the master blacksmith Jacques Diel and the parish beadle or verger Jacques Saint Julien. In the church ledger, Fr. Sartelon recorded the burial of "a son of René Leduc...born on the fifth of the present month and baptized provisionally at home by Pierre Maupetit dit Poitevin, due to the danger of death." (Since the child had never received the sacrament of Baptism officially from a priest, he was interred without a first name.)[81]

Six months later, the tenth child to be born to Angélique and Pierre joined the family. On April 3, 1740, his parents transported one-day-old Antoine Amable across the water from their island home to the Ste. Anne church. At his christening ceremony, the baby's godparents were Joseph Brébant and Marie Félicité Lafleur.[82]

As was typical in the lives of the colonists of New France, this encouraging and heartwarming event was followed soon thereafter by another event which produced deep melancholy. Just 25 days after the safe arrival of their new baby, Angélique lost her sister Marie Madeleine Villeray at the untimely age of thirty. Having been married to Jacques Beaune for seven years and three months, she was buried in the Pointe Claire cemetery on April 27. The official witnesses who were present were Antoine Villeray (the father of the deceased), Jacques Prou, Sr. (her brother-in-law), and Jacques Prou, Jr. Thirteen years earlier, back in May of 1727, Marie Madeleine had stood as the godmother of Pierre and Angélique's newborn daughter Marie Angélique. It is not known whether Marie Madeleine had been felled during this spring of 1740 by the massive epidemic of yellow fever that swept through the St. Lawrence communities during this year.[83]

Some time before March 2, 1741, Pierre crossed over to Montreal Island and traveled about six miles eastward to Pointe Claire, so that he could stand as the godfather of his brand new nephew Jean Baptiste Villeray, Jr. This baby, born on March 2 to Angélique's brother Jean Baptiste, Sr. and Marie Josèphe Séguin, was christened on the same day. His godmother on this festive occasion was Angélique Séguin.[84]

Instead of the happiness and optimism that had filled the church on this day in 1741, feelings of melancholy and sorrow pervaded the hearts of the Villeray-Maupetit clan in the same edifice one year later. On June 4, 1742, Angélique's brother Jacques, her only unmarried sibling, was buried at the untimely age of 37. On this mournful day, the official witnesses were Jean Beaune, Jacques Prou, Jr., and Joseph Charlebois.[85]

It was in this same year of 1742 that Angélique and Pierre welcomed their last child into the world. No entry indicating the dates of this lad's birth and baptism are to be found in the surviving church records of the colony. However, the age which was recorded for Michel in his marriage contract 23 years later, on October 26, 1765, implied that he had been born in 1742.[86]

Over the span of 23 years, Monsieur and Madame Maupetit had produced eleven offspring, including six boys and five girls. Their first baby had been born one year and three weeks after their wedding, after which the intervals between this child and the next ten had been about 11, 20, 28, 32, 34, 33, 29, 33, 26, and possibly about 24 months, respectively. During their child-bearing years, Angélique's age had advanced from six weeks short of 21 to almost 44, while Pierre's age had increased from one month short of 33 to almost 56. Of their eleven progeny, they had lost three at young ages. Their first baby, Pierre, Jr. I, had died after one month of life in 1719; their second child, Marie Thérèse I, had perished some time before her twelfth birthday; and their ninth baby, Marie Élisabeth, had survived for only five days in 1738.

In the early summer of 1743, Pierre was asked to serve as the godfather for the new baby of a couple who were fellow residents of Île Perrot. On May 31, Pierre Énaud dit Canada et Delorme and Marguerite Piet brought their son Pierre, Jr. to the Ste. Anne church on May 31 for his baptism, at which time Monsieur Maupetit granted the lad his own name; his co-sponsor on this day was Marie Josèphe Lalonde.[87]

Three weeks later came a significant day, particularly for the father of the Maupetit family. On June 22, Pierre Maupetit dit Poitevin, Jr., who had celebrated his 21st birthday a month earlier and was the eldest surviving child of the family, signed his very first voyageur contract. On this day, the young man stood in the office of the Montreal notary Louis Danré de Blanzy and officially agreed to labor in the peltries business. His employer was Marie Catherine Lériger dite Laplante, the widow of the Montreal peltries merchant René Bourassa dit Laronde. At the hiring session with the notary and the employee, she was represented by the Montreal merchant Louis Charly dit Saint Ange. Upon first glance, this contract might seem to imply that Pierre, Sr., at the ripe old age of 56¹/₂ years, was still working diligently in the west, as he had done as a young man. However, although the hiree was identified by the scribe as "Pierre Maupetit dit Poitevin of Île Perrot," with no "Jr." added to his name, it is very clear that this was Pierre, Jr. In fact, over the following decade, until at least April of 1753, Junior would continue to draw up similar hiring contracts for employment in the distant interior.[88]

During the five-month interval between late September of 1744 and mid February of 1745, Pierre Maupetit was recorded on four occasions as being the godfather at baptismal ceremonies which were held in the Ste. Anne church. However, in none of these cases did the officiating priest indicate whether the sponsor was Pierre, Sr. or Pierre, Jr. Further confounding the situation, these four events took place after Pierre, Jr.'s voyage of 1743 and before his journey of 1745. Thus, in each instance, it is not clear whether it was the father or the son who appeared as the godfather of these four babies.

The first of these occasions took place on September 26, 1744, when the baby was one-day-old Marie Élisabeth Lalonde, daughter of François Lalonde and Marie Josèphe Trottier (the father François was a son of Jean Baptiste Lalonde and Marguerite Masta). Standing beside Pierre Maupetit as the other sponsor was Élisabeth Réaume.[89] Three weeks later, the infant who was christened on October 15 was Marie Josèphe Lalonde, the daughter or Guillaume Lalonde (designated in this study as Guillaume Number 2, another son of the above-mentioned Jean Baptiste Lalonde) and Angélique Brunet, residents of Île Perrot. Along with Monsieur Maupetit, the godmother was Marie Josèphe Daoust. (Interestingly, Pierre Maupetit, Jr. and Marie Josèphe Daoust would be married in this same church in February of 1746. Thus, the two sponsors on this day would become husband and wife sixteen months later.)[90] After two more weeks had passed, on November 1, 1744, the next baptismal ceremony to be held in the Ste. Anne church was for Marie Clémence Raymond, the one-day-old daughter of Pierre Raymond and Isabelle Poirier. Standing beside Pierre Maupetit as the fellow sponsor was Marie Barbe Denis.[91] Finally, the fourth ceremony in the sequence took place on February 16, 1745. On this day, Pierre, the one-day-old son of Jean Legardeur, Sieur de Repentigny, and Marie Anne Lalande, residents of Île Perrot, received the sacrament of Baptism. Standing beside Pierre Maupetit as the godmother was Marie Josèphe Trottier, the wife of François Lalonde and the mother of the infant who had been christened in the previous September.[92]

On June 22, 1745, at the age of 23, Pierre, Jr. hired on for his second stint as a voyageur. On this day, he also arranged for the employment of his next-younger brother, Joseph, who would turn 21 in September. As before, Junior would be working for the Widow Laronde, and at the hiring session with the notary, she was represented by the merchant Louis Charly dit Saint Ange. According to the first contract of the day, Pierre was engaged to work for the widow; in the second contract, Joseph was hired to work for his brother Pierre and the widow.[93] As before, these events probably brought a considerable degree of satisfaction to Pierre, Sr., seeing his sons taking up the same employment that he himself had done in his younger days. This was a very typical scenario for families in the St. Lawrence Valley, having multiple generations of the men each working in their turn in the trade, in a sequence that often spanned well over a half-century.

In the heart of the winter of 1746, Angélique and Pierre, Sr. experienced the unique pleasure of witnessing the marriage of the eldest of their children. In fact, these pleasant feelings came in pairs, since both their oldest son and their oldest daughter each drew up their marriage contracts with their respective spouses on the same day, February 5; they were likewise each wed in the Ste. Anne church on the same day, February 7.

On the fifth day of the month, the two couples visited the office of the Montreal notary Louis Danré. First, Pierre Maupetit, age $23^{3}/4$, son of Pierre Maupetit dit Poitevin and Angélique Villeray, from Île Perrot, drew up his marriage agreement. His fiancée was Marie Josèphe Daoust, two months short of age 19, daughter of Charles Daoust and Marie Angélique Sauvé, who was likewise from Île Perrot.[94]

Then, Albert Lalonde, age $26^{3}/4$, son of Guillaume Lalonde (designated in this study as Guillaume Number 1) and Marie Madeleine Allyn, "of English nationality," from the seigneury of Soulanges at Les Cèdres, arranged the details of his marriage contract. His fiancée was Marie Angélique Maupetit, age $18^{3}/4$, daughter of Pierre Maupetit and Angélique Villeray.[95]

Two days later, on February 7, 1746, the two couples each exchanged their wedding vows in the Ste. Anne church. In his record of the Maupetit-Daoust marriage, Fr. Élie Déperet noted that the official witnesses on the groom's side were his maternal grandfather Antoine Villeray, his maternal uncle Jean Baptiste Villeray, and his maternal uncle Jacques Prou. On the bride's side, the sole official witness was her maternal uncle Jean Baptiste Lalonde, Captain of the militia forces of the Ste. Anne parish.[96]

Fr. Perthuis' record of the Lalonde-Maupetit marriage included the information that the official witnesses on the groom's side were his uncle Jean Baptiste Lalonde, Captain of the militia of Ste. Anne, and his brother André Lalonde. The witnesses on the bride's side were Antoine Lalande and Pierre Lafleur. (It was this couple, through their son Étienne, who would provide the direct genealogical linkages between Pierre and Angélique and the present author.)[97]

As was to be expected, it was not too long after these festivities that the first grandchild of Angélique and Pierre joined the clan. On January 10, 1747, eleven months after the wedding of Pierre Maupetit, Jr. and Marie Josèphe Daoust, the young couple safely delivered their first child on Île Perrot. At the christening ceremony in the Ste. Anne church two days later, *petit-fils* Pierre Maupetit IV received his distinguished name (the father of the living patriarch had also been called Pierre Maupetit, thus making this baby the fourth generation in New France to bear the name). The infant's godmother was his paternal grandmother Angélique Villeray, while his godfather was his maternal grandfather Charles Daoust.[98]

Unfortunately, these jubilant sensations turned to deep sadness nine weeks later, when Angélique's sister Marie Suzanne Villeray died at Pointe Claire, where she was interred on March 16. Only about 34 years old, she had been married to Jacques Prou for $13^{1}/2$ years, since August of 1733.[99]

Another significant loss to the clan followed just two months later, when Louis Lory passed away at Pointe Claire; he was laid to rest there on May 18. Louis had lived a particularly long life, surviving until about 74 years of age. He had married Pierre's widowed mother Marie Louise Beaune back in 1698, and then he had helped her to raise her three children to adulthood. At his burial, the official witnesses were Jacques Parent, Jr. and Jacques Beaune, both of them members of the St. Joachim parish.[100]

One week later, an event of some significance for the Maupetit family took place. On May 25, 1747, Pierre Maupetit dit Le Poitevin, Jr., Angélique and Pierre, Sr.'s eldest child, celebrated his 25th birthday. According to the Customary Laws of Paris, the legal code which was also utilized in New France, he had now reached the legal age of majority.

As time marched forward, the elderly members of the clan

continued to depart. On July 27, 1749, Antoine Villeray, Angélique's father and Pierre, Sr.'s father-in-law, was laid to rest in the cemetery at Pointe Claire. The official witnesses on this occasion were Michel Lasisseray, Noël Bonnet, and Joseph Charlebois. At the time of his funeral, one of his family members indicated to the priest that the deceased had been 90 years old. Although this figure may have been somewhat exaggerated, Antoine had indeed been a very old man: he and Jeanne Quenneville had been married more than 55 years earlier, back in February of 1694.[101]

Grand-père Villeray had lived a good long life, so it was understandable when it was time for him to depart. However, an event that was much more difficult for the clan members to bear was the death of the first Lalonde grandchild of Pierre and Angélique. Little Marie arrived on July 21, 1749, three years and three months after Albert Lalonde and Marie Angélique Maupetit had been married. However, the tiny lass survived but a few hours, after which she was buried amid many tears in the cemetery close by the Ste. Anne church.[102]

Fifty-one weeks later, after a considerable amount of trepidation, Marie Angélique and Albert were relieved and elated to safely deliver a healthy baby (who would live to adulthood and marry 21 years later). On July 13, 1750, Marie Françoise Lalonde was christened at the Ste. Anne church.[103]

Seven months later, Angélique conducted a provisional lay person's baptism on the newborn son of one of her neighbor couples on Île Perrot, Jean Baptiste Leduc and Marie Trottier Desruisseaux. Her feelings of imminent danger of death for the tiny boy were perceptive, since he was buried in the Ste. Anne cemetery soon afterward, on February 17, 1751. In the parish register, the officiating priest recorded the interment of "a male child who had been provisionally baptized by Madame Maupetit." He also indicated that the four official witnesses were Pierre Ranger, Joseph Tabault, René Larivière, and Joseph Brébant, all members of the parish. (More than eleven years earlier, back in October of 1739, Pierre had done a similar provisional christening of another ailing Leduc baby, who had been the child of René Leduc and Marie Élisabeth Fortier.)[104]

During the last week of April in 1751, Madame and Monsieur Maupetit saw clear indications that their eldest son, Pierre, Jr., having been married for more than five years, was advancing well in the world. On April 27, he was again engaged as a trusted voyageur, this time working for the Montreal resident Ignace d'Ailleboust, Sieur de Périgny.[105] On the following day, he purchased a piece of property on Île Perrot from Marguerite Legardeur de Repentigny, the widow of Captain Jean Baptiste de Saint Ours, Sieur Deschaillons. This couple had married at Montreal, and had produced their eight children there; however, now that Marguerite was 65 years old and widowed, she resided at Quebec.[106]

March of 1752 brought with it the safe arrival of another healthy Lalonde grandchild, bolstering everyone's happiness. On the fifth day of this wintery month, little Joseph Marie was taken to the brand new church at Soulanges for his christening festivities. This new parish, dedicated to St. Joseph, had been just established in the Soulanges seigneury during this same year.[107]

On October 14, 1753, Pierre Poirier III was born on Île Perrot to Pierre Poirier II and Marie Anne Daoust. At the boy's baptismal ceremony in the Ste. Anne church on the same day, Pierre Maupetit, Sr. served as his godfather, while Marie Angélique Sauvé, the wife of Charles Daoust and the baby's grandmother, appeared as his godmother. In the records of the event, Pierre (one month away from celebrating his 67th birthday) was identified as a great-uncle of the child. His brother-in-law Pierre Poirier I and his deceased sister Marie Clémence Maupetit had been the baby's grandparents, thus making Pierre, as the brother of Marie Clémence, the infant's great-uncle.[108]

Two weeks later, Angélique lost one of her siblings, Michel Villeray, who was 52 years of age. At the time of his interment at Pointe Claire, on the first day of November, he and Marie Charlotte Gros had been married for nearly nineteen years. At his funeral, the two official witnesses were Noël Brunet and Jacques Prou.[109]

As was so typical in daily life in the colony, this loss was offset seven months later by the safe arrival of another Lalonde grandchild. To the great gladness of everyone in the clan, little Étienne was christened at the baptismal font of the St. Joseph church at Soulanges on June 16, 1754. (No one who was present on that uplifting day could have known that this baby would grow up to marry Marie Charlotte Levac dite Leval. He and she would provide the direct ancestral linkage between his parents Marie Angélique Maupetit and Albert Lalonde, as well as his maternal grandparents Pierre Maupetit and Angélique Villeray, and the present author.)[110]

By the winter of 1755, it had been nine years since Angélique and Pierre had happily watched their eldest son and their eldest daughter each marry, on the same day, their respective spouses. Now, it was time for their third-oldest daughter, Marie Thérèse, who had just turned age 22, to take a husband. On January 19, 1755, she and her fiancé, Jean Baptiste Noël Lefebvre dit Lasisseray, visited the Montreal notary Louis Danré to draw up their marriage contract. The 25-year-old groom, likewise a resident of Île Perrot, was the son of Noël Lefebvre and Marianne Gervais. On the following day, the couple exchanged their nuptial vows in the Ste. Anne church, with six official witnesses observing. On the bride's side, these were her two older brothers Pierre, Jr. and Joseph Maupetit, while the witnesses on the groom's side were his brothers Michel and Joseph Lefebvre. In addition, Guillaume Daoust was present, as was also Jean Baptiste Leduc, the seigneur of Île Perrot. Oddly enough, in both the notarial marriage contract and the church marriage record, the mother of the bride was mistakenly identified as Marie Jeanne Villeray, rather than Angélique Villeray.[111]

The first three months of 1756 delivered a series of events that induced very mixed emotions in Angélique and Pierre. First came the inspiring marriage of their second-oldest son, Joseph, who was $31^1/_3$ years of age and still a resident of Île Perrot. On January 26 in the Ste. Anne church, he took as his bride Marie Anne Hunault, who was $26^1/_3$ years old. She was the sixth child of the voyageur Antoine Hunault dit Deschamps and his wife Marie Catherine Lefebvre. At their nuptial celebration, the four official witnesses were the groom's brothers Pierre and Étienne Maupetit and the bride's uncles Pierre Hunault dit Deschamps and Noël Lasisseray.[112]

Four weeks later, the fifth Lalonde grandchild of Madame and Monsieur Maupetit arrived; she was baptized in the Soulanges church on February 26. However, tiny Angélique survived for only two days, after which she was sadly laid to rest in the Soulanges cemetery on the 28th. This was the second baby whom Marie Angélique Maupetit and Albert Lalonde had lost during the span of $6^1/_2$ years. Their first child had perished in July of 1749, followed by their fifth baby during this winter of 1756.[113]

For Angélique and Pierre, this sad news was followed by equally tragic news just three weeks later. On March 20, Angélique's brother Antoine was buried in the cemetery at Batiscan, having been married to Marie Madeleine Brunet for 23 years; he was 45 years old.[114]

It was during this same year that Pierre Maupetit, Jr. purchased additional property on Île Perrot, further establishing himself. On

December 28, he bought land on the island from his 34-year-old first cousin Joseph Poirier dit Lafleur and his wife Marie Josèphe Lasisseray.[115]

During the winter of 1757, Angélique and Pierre had an entire series of reasons to celebrate, which involved the drawing up of marriage contracts and the wedding ceremonies of two of their children. The first of these brightening events took place on January 7, when son Étienne ($21^2/3$ years old) and his fiancée Amable Boyer (age 15) traveled to the Soulanges notary Vuatier to create their nuptial contract. Like the groom, the bride was also a resident of Île Perrot, being the daughter of the deceased Claude Boyer and of Marianne Riberville. On the following day, the engaged couple celebrated their wedding at the Ste. Anne church, with Pierre and Joseph Maupetit, the groom's two older brothers, along with Pierre Hunault and François Lalonde, serving as the four official witnesses.[116]

Four weeks later, on February 7, 1757, it was time for the second-oldest Maupetit daughter to be wed in the same church. On this day, Marie Suzanne Maupetit, six weeks short of her 27th birthday, took as her husband François Daoust, who was $31^1/4$ years old. Like the bride a fellow resident of Île Perrot, the groom was the son of Charles Daoust and Marie Angélique Sauvé dite Laplante. Appearing as their official witnesses at the ceremony were Pierre and Joseph Maupetit, the bride's two older brothers; Charles Daoust, the groom's brother; Augustin Lefebvre, brother-in-law of the groom; and Jean Baptiste Legardeur, Sieur de Repentigny, of Île Perrot. Taking things slightly out of order, five days after their wedding celebration, the newly wedded couple traveled to Montreal to belatedly draw up their marriage contract with the notary Danré.[117]

Now, only the two youngest Maupetit children were still single and residing at home. These were Antoine Amable, who would celebrate his 17th birthday in April, and Michel, who would turn 14 before long.

Shortly after the holidays that ushered in the year 1758, it was time for Angélique to say *adieu* forever to her mother. On January 10, Marie Jeanne Quenneville was laid to rest in the Pointe Claire cemetery, with three official witnesses in attendance. These were Mathieu Pilon, Joseph Denis, and Joseph Charlebois, who was the beadle or sexton of the parish. Based upon the records in the Lachine church, she had been christened 83 years and two days earlier, back on January 8, 1675. (However, her burial records stated incorrectly that she had been age 90 at time of her demise.) Marie Jeanne had been a widow for more than seven years, ever since her husband of 55 years, Antoine Villeray, had passed away back in July of 1749. She had outlived seven of the ten children whom she and Antoine had produced.[118]

Some 21 months later, Angélique was forced to endure an even more crushing loss, that of her husband of more than four decades. Pierre Maupetit had been baptized in the Lachine church 72 years and eleven months earlier, back on November 15, 1686. Thus, he had lived a very long and eventful life when, on October 5, 1759, it was time for him to finally depart from their home on Île Perrot. On the following day, he was transported for the final time across the half-mile expanse of water to Montreal Island, and he was gently laid to rest in the Ste. Anne cemetery. At his funeral, Pierre Ranger and René Rivière served as the official witnesses. This tearful day came ten days after Pierre and Angélique had celebrated their 41st wedding anniversary. (At the time of his burial, one of the family members had provided to the officiating priest the information that the patriarch of the clan had been 75 years old. This was an increase in his age of about two years).[119]

In Randle Cotgrave's 1611 *Dictionarie of the French and English Tongues*, the various definitions of the word *mau* were not very positive. The entry for this word as a noun read "an evil, mischiefe, dammage, annoyance, paine, griefe, sickness." Similarly, the entry for the term as an adjective was equally negative, reading "bad, ill, naughtie."[120] Our Pierre Maupetit bore the family name which meant the diminutive of each of these derogatory nouns and adjectives. However, even if one or more of his ancestors many centuries earlier had deserved this particular label, it appears that Pierre certainly did not. On the contrary, he seems to have lived a good life, in his various roles as a voyageur, voyageur-trader, farmer, son, husband, father, grandfather, colleague, neighbor, and friend.

At this point, Angélique was two months short of turning age 61. Six of her children, the oldest three boys and the oldest three girls, were married, and they were all living relatively close by with their spouses and children. In order to plan ahead for her future and that of her clan, five months after Pierre's demise, Angélique leased out for the rest of her life the Maupetit family lands on Île Perrot, to her two eldest sons. This act was officially registered with the Soulanges notary Vuatier on March 7, 1760. According to the document of *donation*, "Angélique Villeray, widow of Pierre Maupetit dit Poitevin, of Île Perrot," leased out the family properties on the island to "Pierre Maupetit [Jr.], habitant of Île Perrot, and Joseph Maupetit, habitant of Île Perrot." These two sons had already reached the age of legal majority; the younger three sons, in sequence, were ages $24^3/4$, $19^{11}/12$, and 18 years old. In return for her life-long lease of the lands, Angélique would receive a pension and lifetime annuity, which would entail care and support for the remainder of her days from the two oldest boys.[121]

In the Maupetit family, it had been a fun-filled custom for pairs of the children to celebrate their respective weddings in the Ste. Anne church on either the very same day or within a month of each other. First, Pierre, Jr. and Marie Angélique had each been wed on February 7, 1746. Eleven years later, Étienne had been married on January 8, 1757, followed four weeks later by the wedding of Marie Suzanne on February 7. Seven years after this, on January 23, 1764, a pair of Maupetit siblings would again celebrate their marriages on the same day and in the same church.

Son Antoine Amable Maupetit was ten weeks short of his 24th birthday. On January 12, 1764, he and his fiancée Marie Josèphe Lefebvre, a fellow resident of Île Perrot, made the trip to the Soulanges seigneury to have their marriage contract drawn up. Based upon information that was included in this document penned by the notary Vuatier, it is clear that the prospective groom's sister Marie Thérèse Maupetit had married the prospective bride's brother Jean Baptiste Noël Lefebvre nine years earlier, back in January of 1755. The parents of these two Lefebvre siblings were Noël Lefebvre dit Lasisseraye and Marie Anne Gervais. Eleven days after completing their nuptial agreement, the couple was married in the Ste. Anne church on January 23. At this festive occasion, the official witnesses were Pierre, Jr. and Joseph Maupetit, the groom's two oldest brothers, and Louis Amable Lefebvre from the bride's family.[122]

On the same day and at the same altar, Fr. Sartelon also performed the wedding ceremony at which Pierre Maupetit, Jr. remarried. He and his first wife, Marie Josèphe Daoust, had been married eighteen years earlier, back in February of 1746. However, after her death, it was time for the widower (who was now age $41^2/3$ years old) to move on with his life, with a new partner. His choice was the fellow Île Perrot resident Marie Charlotte Fortier, daughter of Joseph Fortier and Marie Josèphe Réaume. At the couple's nuptial ceremony, the official witnesses were the groom's brothers Joseph and Antoine Maupetit and the bride's brother-in-law René Leduc.[123]

Twenty-one months later, in the autumn of 1765, it was finally time for the youngest Maupetit offspring to be wed. Michel, now 23 years old, had chosen as his life partner Marie Josèphe Hunault dite Deschamps, a fellow resident of Île Perrot. Her father was Michel Hunault dit Deschamps, an officer in the militia forces of the Ste. Anne parish. On October 26, the affianced couple traveled to the Soulanges seigneury to have their marriage contract drawn up by the notary Vuatier. Interestingly, in this document, both the prospective bride and her father were identified only by the name "Deschamps," without any mention of the "Hunault dit" portion of the name. This was an example of certain branches of a family dropping the official family name and utilizing only the *dit* name. Oddly, the name of Marie Josèphe's mother, Charlotte Cuillerier, was not recorded by the notary in the contract. When the actual marriage ceremony was conducted in the Ste. Anne church nine days later, on November 4, the priest's records in the parish ledger were much more complete. First, he utilized the full "Hunault dit Deschamps" name for the father of the bride; in addition, he included the name of Charlotte Cuillerier as the mother of the bride. The official witnesses on this uplifting day were the groom's brothers Pierre, Jr. and Étienne Maupetit and the bride's cousin Pierre Hunault.[124]

Finally, all eight of Angélique and Pierre's children were married. Their respective weddings had taken place over a span of time that was just three months short of two decades. However, over the course of the following years, not all of the activities of the children and grandchildren brought contentment and happiness to the matriarch. The day of April 4, 1768 was an especially miserable one for her. On that day, she was obliged to endure the death and the burial in the Ste. Anne cemetery of her second-oldest son, Joseph. Passing away at the untimely age of $43^1/2$, he had been married to Marie Anne Hunault for twelve years.[125]

Some $5^1/2$ years later, Angélique was about to celebrate her 75th birthday. By this time, she had moved from Île Perrot, and she was residing with her daughter Marie Angélique, her husband Albert Lalonde, and their nine children. Their home was in the seigneury of Soulanges, which was located a short distance southwest of Île Perrot, on the north shore of the St. Lawrence. Back in 1760, she had granted to her two oldest sons a life-long lease of the Maupetit family properties on Île Perrot, which would extend until her death.

On November 23, 1773, the resident notary at Soulanges, Thomas Vuatier, traveled to the home of Albert and Marie Angélique, to draw up a legal document for the matriarch. On this occasion, they were joined by Pierre Maupetit, Jr., who traveled from Île Perrot, and Albert's older brother Édouard Lalonde, who lived in the Soulanges seigneury. By means of this document, Angélique intended to provide, in a rather modest way, some financial security for certain of her grandchildren, specifically the young children of her deceased son Joseph. (Christophe d'Arpentigny had been previously chosen by the Montreal Court to serve as the legal guardian of these minor-age children.) Madame Maupetit also wanted her heirs to be aware of her wishes concerning the eventual repose of her soul.

"Before the notary in the province of Quebec, residing at Soulanges in the [governmental] district of Montreal, and the undersigned witnesses named at the end was present Angélique Villeray, widow of the deceased Pierre Maupetit dit Poitevin. Of her own accord and her candid and free will, she has voluntarily made a donation pure, simple, and irrevocable between her and the children heirs of the deceased Joseph Maupetit dit Poitevin, these young children being represented by Pierre Maupetit dit Poitevin, their paternal uncle, habitant living on Île Perrot and being this day in this place of Soulanges, present and accepting for and in the names of the said children of the said deceased Joseph Maupetit. The said Villeray donates generally everything which will be found to belong to the said donator on the day of her death by Christophe d'Arpentigny [the guardian of the said children] as the balance of the pension et rente viagère *(pension and lifetime annuity) which is owed to her, which is to be used thriftily for the good and advantage of the said children. The sum of the aforementioned balance may be utilized and invested after the debts of the said donator have been paid, which will be accounted for by a receipt or a discharge receipt from the said d'Arpentigny, for the said recipients to enjoy in all propriety and to use and dispose of as it will seem best to them, by means of the present donation. The said donator has declared that, when it will please God to dispose of her, her linens and clothing from her own usage are to remain in the hands of Albert Lalonde, in whose home she is living, to be sold by him. The proceeds are to be utilized to have prayers said to God for the repose of her soul, with the children [who will have received the above donation] having no power to lay claim to them. Thus is the wish and intention of the said donator, without which these presents could not have been made or drawn up. Thus have they promised, obligated themselves, waived, etc.*

[This agreement] made and drawn up at Soulanges at the home of Albert

Lalonde [in the year 1773,] on the 23rd day of November in the afternoon, in the presence of Édouard Lalonde and of the said Albert Lalonde, witnesses expressly called, who have signed with us, the said notary. The above-named donator has declared that she does not know how to write or sign, having been asked after the reading was done, according to the ordinance. That is why she has made the ordinary mark which follows.
Signed,
+ mark of Angélique Villeray, + mark of Pierre Maupetit, Albert Lalonde, Edouard Lalonde, and Thomas Vuatier, royal notary"[126]

This represents the last known documentation concerning Angélique Villeray in the colony. No information concerning her death and burial has yet been located in any of the church records.

When she drew up this document of donation, she was just sixteen days away from turning age 75. Back in September of 1718, she had married Pierre Maupetit when she had been ten weeks short of her twentieth birthday. Then she had been married for two weeks more than 41 years, until Pierre's death in October of 1759. During that span of more than four decades together, she had borne eleven children, of whom eight had survived to adulthood and had taken spouses. After Pierre's departure, she had then lived for more than fourteen years as a widow, until some time after her donation agreement in the autumn of 1773.

Looking back over the span of their lives, Angélique Villeray and Pierre Maupetit had spent nearly all of their years residing on rather modest pioneer farms in the Montreal area. From this rural and small-scale perspective, they probably assessed their fortunes according to the old French proverb *Contentement passe richesse* (Contentment is better than riches). Indeed, there had been those various years of dire hunger, when nearly complete crop failures had occurred throughout the colony. And yes, there had been the seemingly endless series of epidemics that had raged along the length and breadth of the St. Lawrence Valley, wreaking sickness and death. And yes again, there had been those terrible years from 1755 through 1760 when the Seven Years' War had caused such food shortages and starvation, and a great number of settlers and their native allies had been either wounded or killed by Anglo forces. (Pierre had died on October 5, 1759, 23 days after the fall of Quebec to James Wolfe's army. Thus, he did not have to endure the loss of Montreal, and thus the capitulation of the entire colony, to the Anglos during the following year.) It was some consolation that the vast majority of the colonists had together endured these serious deprivations and these daunting challenges. In addition, the patriarch and matriarch of the clan had each lived to an unusually advanced age, and eight of their eleven children had lived to reach adulthood and had married. Perhaps these were Pierre and Angélique's accumulated riches, which had hopefully brought them much contentment.

marque ƚf dangelique Silvay

Mark of Angélique Vilray, November 23, 1773.

Pierre Maupetit dit Le Poitevin-Angélique Villeray
Lineage of Timothy Kent

I. Pierre Maupetit, Sr.
(François/
Marie Pascalle)

15 Nov, 1683
Lachine, QC

Marie Louise Beaune
(Jean/
Marie Madeleine Bourgery)

II. **Pierre Maupetit, Jr.**
(Pierre, Sr./
Marie Louise Beaune)

25 Sept, 1718
Bout de l'Île, QC

Angélique Villeray
(Antoine/
Jeanne Quenneville)

III. Marie Angélique Maupetit
(Pierre, Jr./
Angélique Villeray)

7 Feb, 1746
Bout de l'Île, QC

Albert Lalonde
(Guillaume #1/
Sarah Allyn)

IV. Étienne Lalonde
(Albert/
Marie Angélique Maupetit)

20 Jan, 1777
Les Cèdres, QC

Marie Charlotte Levac
dite Leval
(Martin/
Marie Josèphe Réaume)

V. Joseph Lalonde
(Étienne/
Marie Charlotte Levac)

30 Jan, 1809
Ste. Geneviève. QC

Geneviève Daoust
(Claude/
Ursule Jamme)

VI. Joseph Lalonde
(Joseph/
Geneviève Daoust)

17 Feb 1835
St. Polycarpe, QC

Élisabeth/Isabelle Achin
(Hyacinthe/
Angèle Lalonde)

VII. Joseph Lalonde
(Joseph/
Élisabeth Achin)

ca. 1873
Curran, ON

Josephine Chatelain
(Étienne/
Marie Madeleine Taillon)

VIII. Élisabeth Lalonde
(Joseph/
Josephine Chatelain)

30 Jan, 1893
Carrollton, MI

Joseph Bouchard
(Philéas Joseph/
Adelaide Barbeau)

IX. Frances L. Bouchard
(Joseph/
Élisabeth Lalonde)

28 Apr, 1945
Detroit, MI

S. George Kent
(George Kapantais/
Eugenia Papadakis)

X. Timothy J. Kent
(S. George/
Frances L. Bouchard)

5 Sept, 1970
Ossineke, MI

Dorothy J. Minton
(Garnet J./
Elaine A. Reece)

Notes for Maupetit

1. Notary Bénigne Basset, October 24, 1683, Archives Nationales du Québec at Montréal
(ANQ-M); H. Charbonneau and J. Légaré, 1978-1990, Vol. 5, Sts. Anges de Lachine recs; R. Jetté, 1983, p. 792.
2. Notary Bénigne Basset, October 24, 1683, ANQ-M; H. Charbonneau and J. Légaré, 1978-1990, Vol. 5, Sts. Anges de Lachine recs; R. Jetté, 1983, pp. 792, 70.
3. Notary Bénigne Basset, October 24, 1683, ANQ-M; H. Charbonneau and J. Légaré, 1978-1990, Vol. 5, Sts. Anges de Lachine recs; R. Jetté, 1983, pp. 70, 152; A. Lafontaine, 1986, p. 138. 1702 land ownership map of Montreal Island by Vachon de Belmont: in Nos Racines, Vol. 22, 1979, pp. 430-431; M. Trudel, 1973a, pp. 172-173; recreation by G. Gallienne, 1977; and L. Dechêne, 1992, p. xxi.
4. Notary Pierre Raimbault, June 24, 1702, ANQ-M; F. Stanislas, 1950, pp. 19-33 and maps inside front and back covers; Notary Michel Lepailleur, September 18, 1706, ANQ-M. 1702 land ownership map of Montreal Island by Vachon de Belmont: in Nos Racines, Vol. 22, 1979, pp. 430-431; M. Trudel, 1973a, pp. 172-173; recreation by G. Gallienne, 1977; and L. Dechêne, 1992, p. xxi.
5. H. Charbonneau and J. Légaré, 1978-1990, Vol. 5, Sts. Anges de Lachine recs; R. Jetté, 1983, pp. 792, 951, 521. 1702 land ownership map of Montreal Island by Vachon de Belmont: in Nos Racines, Vol. 22, 1979, pp. 430-431; M. Trudel, 1973a, pp. 172-173; recreation by G. Gallienne, 1977; and L. Dechêne, 1992, p. xxi.
6. H. Charbonneau and J. Légaré, 1978-1990, Vol. 5, Sts. Anges de Lachine recs; R. Jetté, 1983, pp. 792, 633-634, 595, 390. 1702 land ownership map of Montreal Island by Vachon de Belmont: in Nos Racines, Vol. 22, 1979, pp. 430-431; M. Trudel, 1973a, pp. 172-173; recreation by G. Gallienne, 1977; and L. Dechêne, 1992, p. xxi.
7. R. Jetté, 1983, pp. 70, 238.
8. H. Charbonneau and J. Légaré, 1978-1990, Vol. 5, Sts. Anges de Lachine recs; R. Jetté, 1983, pp. 792, 70, 595.
9. E. Blair, 1911, Vol. 1, pp. 249-252 and Vol. 2, pp. 20-23; L. Lahontan, 1703, Vol. 1, pp. 124-131, 144 and n. 1; W. Eccles, 1964, pp. 150-156; T. Pease and R. Werner, 1934, pp. 132-133; L. Kellogg, 1968, pp. 234-236; L. Kellogg, 1967, p. 311; P. Charlevoix, 1866, Vol. 3, pp. 280-287; W. Kane, 2002, p. 130.
10. W. Eccles, 1964, pp. 150, 155.
11. R. Jetté, 1983, pp. 390-391.
12. W. Eccles, 1964, pp. 155, 157-158, 163-165; F. Stanislas, 1950, pp. 44-50. 1702 land ownership map of Montreal Island by Vachon de Belmont: in Nos Racines, Vol. 22, 1979, pp. 430-431; M. Trudel, 1973a, pp. 172-173; recreation by G. Gallienne, 1977; and L. Dechêne, 1992, p. xxi.
13. W. Eccles, 1964, pp. 164-165; F. Stanislas, 1950, pp. 44-50; Y. Zoltvany, 1969b, p. 566; P. Moogk, 2000, p. 256; S. Colby, 2003, pp. 137-138; H. Lamarche, 1999, pp. 189-228; H. Lamarche, 2002-2003, pp. 1-4; A. Lafontaine, 1986, various Lachine households; R. Jetté, 1983, p. 70. 1702 land ownership map of Montreal Island by Vachon de Belmont: in Nos Racines, Vol. 22, 1979, pp. 430-431; M. Trudel, 1973a, pp. 172-173; recreation by G. Gallienne, 1977; and L. Dechêne, 1992, p. xxi.
14. R. Jetté, 1983, p. 44; H. Lamarche, 2002-2003, p. 2.
15. R. Jetté, 1983, p. 808; H. Lamarche, 2002-2003, p. 2.
16. R. Jetté, 1983, p. 946; H. Lamarche, 2002-2003, p. 3.
17. See the detailed discussion of the captives, and its associated footnotes, in the biography of François Brunet dit Le Bourbonnais, Sr.

18. R. Jetté, 1983, pp. 70, 238.
19. ibid., pp. 595, 500.
20. L. Lahontan, 1703, Vol. 1, pp. 239-241.
21. H. Lamarche, 2002-2003, p. 3.
22. H. Charbonneau and J. Légaré, 1978-1990, Vol. 5, Sts. Anges de Lachine recs; R. Jetté, 1983, pp. 70, 744, 633; F. Stanislas, 1950, p. 28 and map inside back cover. 1702 land ownership map of Montreal Island by Vachon de Belmont: in Nos Racines, Vol. 22, 1979, pp. 430-431; M. Trudel, 1973a, pp. 172-173; recreation by G. Gallienne, 1977; and L. Dechêne, 1992, p. xxi.
23. R. Jetté, 1983, pp. 70, 744. 1702 land ownership map of Montreal Island by Vachon de Belmont: in Nos Racines, Vol. 22, 1979, pp. 430-431; M. Trudel, 1973a, pp. 172-173; recreation by G. Gallienne, 1977; and L. Dechêne, 1992, p. xxi.
24. Notary Antoine Adhémar, June 5, 1712, ANQ-M. 1702 land ownership map of Montreal Island by Vachon de Belmont: in Nos Racines, Vol. 22, 1979, pp. 430-431; M. Trudel, 1973a, pp. 172-173; recreation by G. Gallienne, 1977; and L. Dechêne, 1992, p. xxi.
25. B. Weilbrenner, 1966b, p. 583; T. Kent, 2004, pp. 163-164.
26. R. Jetté, 1983, pp. 199-200, 902-903.
27. Notary Pierre Raimbault, June 24, 1702, ANQ-M; R. Jetté, 1983, p. 735.
28. L. Blair, 2000, p. 11; D. Hunter, 2002, p. 92.
29. R. Jetté, 1983, pp. 200, 161.
30. ibid., pp. 792, 931.
31. Notary Michel Lepailleur, September 18, 1706, ANQ-M; R. Jetté, 1983, pp. 1037, 390-391. 1702 land ownership map of Montreal Island by Vachon de Belmont: in Nos Racines, Vol. 22, 1979, pp. 430-431; M. Trudel, 1973a, pp. 172-173; recreation by G. Gallienne, 1977; and L. Dechêne, 1992, p. xxi.
32. J. Holzi, 1995, Vol. 2, 1704-1713, Jud. Civ., Case No. 016-0888, December 1, 1706.
33. H. Charbonneau and J. Légaré, 1978-1990, Vol. 14, Sts. Anges de Lachine recs; R. Jetté, 1983, pp. 70, 633.
34. Notary Antoine Adhémar, June 5, 1712a, ANQ-M; R. Jetté, 1983, pp. 792, 931.
35. Notary Antoine Adhémar, June 5, 1712b, ANQ-M.
36. Notary Antoine Adhémar, March 31, 1715, ANQ-M; R. Jetté, 1983, pp. 978, 566-567, 690, 716.
37. Michigan Pioneer and Historical Collections, Vol. 33, 1903, p. 791.
38. R. Jetté, 1983, p. 975; E. Massicotte, 1929-1930, pp. 208, 210.
39. R. Jetté, 1983, pp. 566-567; B. Pothier, 1969, p. 205.
40. E. Massicotte, 1929-1930, p. 216; R. Jetté, 1983, p. 169.
41. T. Kent, 2004, p. 94.
42. J. Peyser, 2008, p. 149; E. Massicotte, 1929-1930, pp. 216-217; T. Kent, 2004, p. 191.
43. T. Kent, 2004, pp. 191, 197-200.
44. J. Peyser, 2008, pp. 144-158; Bibliothèque et Archives Nationales du Québec, Pistard Archives (BANQ), Cote TL4, S1, D1835; J. Holzi, 1995, Vol. 3, 1714-1718, Jud. Civ., Case No. 032-1835, December 18, 1715; R. Jetté, 1983, pp. 161 163, 1118-1119, 932; E. Massicotte, 1929-1930, pp. 216-217.
45. T. Kent, 2004, pp. 220-221.
46. E. Massicotte, 1929-1930.
47. L. Dechêne, 1992, pp. 314-315, Graph 17.
48. Notary Antoine Adhémar, April 15, 1718, ANQ-M.
49. R. Jetté, 1983, pp. 931-932.
50. ibid., pp. xiv-xv.

51. H. Charbonneau and J. Légaré, 1978-1990, Vol. 14, St. Joachim de Pointe Claire recs; R. Jetté, 1983, pp. 634, 70.

52. H. Charbonneau and J. Légaré, 1978-1990, Vol. 5, Sts. Anges de Lachine recs; R. Jetté, 1983, pp. 1129, 954. 1702 land ownership map of Montreal Island by Vachon de Belmont: in Nos Racines, Vol. 22, 1979, pp. 430-431; M. Trudel, 1973a, pp. 172-173; recreation by G. Gallienne, 1977; and L. Dechêne, 1992, p. xxi.

53. H. Charbonneau and J. Légaré, 1978-1990, Vol. 14, Ste. Anne du Bout de l'Île recs; R. Jetté, 1983, pp. 168, 630, 931, 595-596, 1027. 1702 land ownership map of Montreal Island by Vachon de Belmont: in Nos Racines, Vol. 22, 1979, pp. 430-431; M. Trudel, 1973a, pp. 172-173; recreation by G. Gallienne, 1977; and L. Dechêne, 1992, p. xxi.

54. H. Charbonneau and J. Légaré, 1978-1990, Vol. 14, St. Joachim de Pointe Claire recs; R. Jetté, 1983, pp. 1129, 70.

55. ibid.

56. H. Charbonneau and J. Légaré, 1978-1990, Vol. 14, St. Joachim de Pointe Claire recs; R. Jetté, 1983, pp. 792, 238.

57. H. Charbonneau and J. Légaré, 1978-1990, Vol. 14, Ste. Anne du Bout de l'Île recs; R. Jetté, 1983, pp. 167, 801.

58. H. Charbonneau and J. Légaré, 1978-1990, Vol. 14, Ste. Anne du Bout de l'Île recs; R. Jetté, 1983, pp. 792, 635, 167.

59. Notary Pierre Raimbault, August 7, 1722, ANQ-M; R. Jetté, 1983, pp. 295, 965, 883, 379.

60. Notary Jean Baptiste Pothier, November 29, 1687 and January 19, 1688, ANQ-M; R. Jetté, 1983, pp. 1104-1105. 1702 land ownership map of Montreal Island by Vachon de Belmont: in Nos Racines, Vol. 22, 1979, pp. 430-431; M. Trudel, 1973a, pp. 172-173; recreation by G. Gallienne, 1977; and L. Dechêne, 1992, p. xxi.

61. R. Jetté, 1983, p. 1174.

62. H. Charbonneau and J. Légaré, 1978-1990, Vol. 14, Ste. Anne du Bout de l'Île recs; R. Jetté, 1983, pp. 931, 1101-1102, 937, 657.

63. H. Charbonneau and J. Légaré, 1978-1990, Vol. 14, St. Joachim de Pointe Claire recs; R. Jetté, 1983, pp. 1129, 801.

64. H. Charbonneau and J. Légaré, 1978-1990, Vol. 14, Ste. Anne du Bout de l'Île recs; R. Jetté, 1983, pp. 182, 1129.

65. H. Charbonneau and J. Légaré, 1978-1990, Vol. 14, Ste. Anne du Bout de l'Île recs; R. Jetté, 1983, pp. 679, 965.

66. H. Charbonneau and J. Légaré, 1978-1990, Vol. 14, Ste. Anne du Bout de l'Île recs; R. Jetté, 1983, pp. 792, 1129, 167.

67. H. Charbonneau and J. Légaré, 1978-1990, Vol. 14, Ste. Anne du Bout de l'Île recs; R. Jetté, 1983, pp. 931, 744.

68. H. Charbonneau and J. Légaré, 1978-1990, Vol. 14, Ste. Anne du Bout de l'Île recs; R. Jetté, 1983, pp. 341, 1037. 1702 land ownership map of Montreal Island by Vachon de Belmont: in Nos Racines, Vol. 22, 1979, pp. 430-431; M. Trudel, 1973a, pp. 172-173; recreation by G. Gallienne, 1977; and L. Dechêne, 1992, p. xxi.

69. H. Charbonneau and J. Légaré, 1978-1990, Vol. 25, Ste. Anne du Bout de l'Île recs; R. Jetté, 1983, pp. 634, 971.

70. H. Charbonneau and J. Légaré, 1978-1990, Vol. 25, Ste. Anne du Bout de l'Île recs; R. Jetté, 1983, p. 931.

71. H. Charbonneau and J. Légaré, 1978-1990, Vol. 25, Ste. Anne du Bout de l'Île recs; R. Jetté, 1983, pp. 792, 996.

72. H. Charbonneau and J. Légaré, 1978-1990, Vol. 25, Ste. Anne du Bout de l'Île recs; R. Jetté, 1983, p. 580.

73. Notary Nicholas Augustin Guillet de Chaumont, December 29, 1730, ANQ-M; R. Jetté, 1983, pp. 544, 744.
74. H. Charbonneau and J. Légaré, 1978-1990, Vol. 24, Notre Dame de Montreal recs; R. Jetté, 1983, pp. 792, 931.
75. H. Charbonneau and J. Légaré, 1978-1990, Vol. 25, Ste. Anne du Bout de l'Île recs; R. Jetté, 1983, pp. 1129, 931.
76. H. Charbonneau and J. Légaré, 1978-1990, Vol. 25, St. Joachim de Pointe Claire recs; R. Jetté, 1983, p. 1129.
77. H. Charbonneau and J. Légaré, 1978-1990, Vol. 25, Sts. Anges de Lachine recs; R. Jetté, 1983, p. 1129.
78. H. Charbonneau and J. Légaré, 1978-1990, Vol. 25, Ste. Anne du Bout de l'Île recs; R. Jetté, 1983, pp. 1092-1093, 710-712.
79. H. Charbonneau and J. Légaré, 1978-1990, Vol. 25, Ste. Anne du Bout de l'Île recs.
80. H. Charbonneau and J. Légaré, 1978-1990, Vol. 25, St. Joachim de Pointe Claire recs; R. Jetté, 1983, p. 1129.
81. H. Charbonneau and J. Légaré, 1978-1990, Vol. 25, Ste. Anne du Bout de l'Île recs; R. Jetté, 1983, p. 352.
82. H. Charbonneau and J. Légaré, 1978-1990, Vol. 25, Ste. Anne du Bout de l'Île recs.
83. H. Charbonneau and J. Légaré, 1978-1990, Vol. 25, St. Joachim de Pointe Claire recs; L. Blair, 2000, p. 11.
84. H. Charbonneau and J. Légaré, 1978-1990, Vol. 25, St. Joachim de Pointe Claire recs.
85. H. Charbonneau and J. Légaré, 1978-1990, Vol. 25, St. Joachim de Pointe Claire recs; R. Jetté, 1983, p. 1129.
86. Notary Thomas Vuatier, October 26, 1765, ANQ-M.
87. H. Charbonneau and J. Légaré, 1978-1990, Vol. 25, Ste. Anne du Bout de l'Île recs; R. Jetté, 1983, pp. 406, 915, 635.
88. Notary Louis Danré de Blanzy, June 22, 1743, ANQ-M; Notary François Simonnet, June 12, 1745a and June 12, 1745b, ANQ-M; Notary Jean Baptiste Adhémar, April 27, 1751, ANQ-M; Notary Louis Danré de Blanzy, April 13, 1753, ANQ-M; R. Jetté, 1983, pp. 147, 231.
89. H. Charbonneau and J. Légaré, 1978-1990, Vol. 25, Ste. Anne du Bout de l'Île recs; R. Jetté, 1983, p. 635.
90. ibid.
91. H. Charbonneau and J. Légaré, 1978-1990, Vol. 25, Ste. Anne du Bout de l'Île recs; R. Jetté, 1983, p. 969.
92. H. Charbonneau and J. Légaré, 1978-1990, Vol. 25, Ste. Anne du Bout de l'Île recs; R. Jetté, 1983, pp. 687-688.
93. Notary François Simonnet, June 12, 1745a and June 12, 1745b, ANQ-M.
94. Notary Louis Danré de Blanzy, February 28, 1746 (the day of registration, rather than the day of February 5 on which the contract had been drawn up), ANQ-M; R. Jetté, 1983, pp. 792, 307.
95. Notary Louis Danré de Blanzy, March 13, 1746 (the day of registration, rather than the day of February 5 on which the contract had been drawn up), ANQ-M; R. Jetté, 1983, pp. 635, 792.
96. H. Charbonneau and J. Légaré, 1978-1990, Vol. 25, Ste. Anne du Bout de l'Île recs; R. Jetté, 1983, pp. 336, 1129, 635, 949.
97. H. Charbonneau and J. Légaré, 1978-1990, Vol. 25, Ste. Anne du Bout de l'Île recs; R. Jetté, 1983, pp. 635, 634.

98. H. Charbonneau and J. Légaré, 1978-1990, Vol. 25, Ste. Anne du Bout de l'Île recs; R. Jetté, 1983, pp. 792, 1129.
99. H. Charbonneau and J. Légaré, 1978-1990, Vol. 25, St. Joachim de Pointe Claire recs.
100. H. Charbonneau and J. Légaré, 1978-1990, Vol. 25, St. Joachim de Pointe Claire recs; R. Jetté, 1983, p. 744.
101. H. Charbonneau and J. Légaré, 1978-1990, Vol. 25, St. Joachim de Pointe Claire recs; R. Jetté, 1983, p. 1129.
102. H. Charbonneau and J. Légaré, 1978-1990, Vol. 25, Ste. Anne du Bout de l'Île recs; R. Jetté, 1983, pp. 635, 792.
103. H. Charbonneau and J. Légaré, 1978-1990, Vol. 25, Ste. Anne du Bout de l'Île recs.
104. H. Charbonneau and J. Légaré, 1978-1990, Vol. 38, Ste. Anne du Bout de l'Île recs.
105. Notary Jean Baptiste Adhémar, April 27, 1751, ANQ-M; R. Jetté, 1983, p. 5.
106. Notary François Simonnet, April 28, 1751, ANQ-M; R. Jetté, pp. 1029, 697.
107. H. Charbonneau and J. Légaré, 1978-1990, Vol. 25, St. Joseph de Soulanges recs; R. Harris, 1987, pl. 46.
108. H. Charbonneau and J. Légaré, 1978-1990, Vol. 38, Ste. Anne du Bout de l'Île recs; R. Jetté, 1983, p. 307.
109. H. Charbonneau and J. Légaré, 1978-1990, Vol. 38, St. Joachim de Pointe Claire recs.
110. H. Charbonneau and J. Légaré, 1978-1990, Vol. 38, St. Joseph de Soulanges recs.
111. Notary Louis Danré de Blanzy, February 20, 1755 (the day of registration, rather than the day of January 19 on which the contract had been drawn up), ANQ-M; R. Jetté, 1983, p. 692.
112. H. Charbonneau and J. Légaré, 1978-1990, Vol. 38, Ste. Anne du Bout de l'Île recs; R. Jetté, 1983, p. 580.
113. H. Charbonneau and J. Légaré, 1978-1990, Vol. 38, St. Joseph de Soulanges recs.
114. H. Charbonneau and J. Légaré, 1978-1990, Vol. 38, Ste. Geneviève de Batiscan recs; R. Jetté, 1983, p. xv.
115. Notary Thomas Vuatier, December 28, 1756, ANQ-M; R. Jetté, 1983, p. 931.
116. H. Charbonneau and J. Légaré, 1978-1990, Vol. 38, Ste. Anne du Bout de l'Île recs; R. Jetté, 1983, p. 980.
117. H. Charbonneau and J. Légaré, 1978-1990, Vol. 38, Ste. Anne du Bout de l'Île recs; R. Jetté, 1983, p. 307; Notary Louis Danré de Blanzy, March 4, 1757 (the day of registration, rather than the day of February 12 on which the contract had been drawn up), ANQ-M.
118. H. Charbonneau and J. Légaré, 1978-1990, Vol. 38, St. Joachim de Pointe Claire recs; R. Jetté, 1983, pp. 954, 1129.
119. H. Charbonneau and J. Légaré, 1978-1990, Vol. 38, Ste. Anne du Bout de l'Île recs; R. Jetté, 1983, p. 792.
120. R. Cotgrave, 1611, "mau."
121. Notary Thomas Vuatier, March 7, 1760, ANQ-M.
122. Notary Thomas Vuatier, January 12, 1764, ANQ-M; H. Charbonneau and J. Légaré, 1978-1990, Vol. 38, Ste. Anne du Bout de l'Île recs; R. Jetté, 1983, p. 692.
123. H. Charbonneau and J. Légaré, 1978-1990, Vol. 38, Ste. Anne du Bout de l'Île recs; R. Jetté, 1983, p. 430.
124. Notary Thomas Vuatier, October 26, 1765, ANQ-M; H. Charbonneau and J. Légaré, 1978-1990, Vol. 38, Ste. Anne du Bout de l'Île recs; R. Jetté, 1983, p. 580.
125. H. Charbonneau and J. Légaré, 1978-1990, Vol. 38, Ste. Anne du Bout de l'Île recs; R. Jetté, 1983, p. 792.
126. Notary Thomas Vuatier, November 23, 1773, ANQ-M.

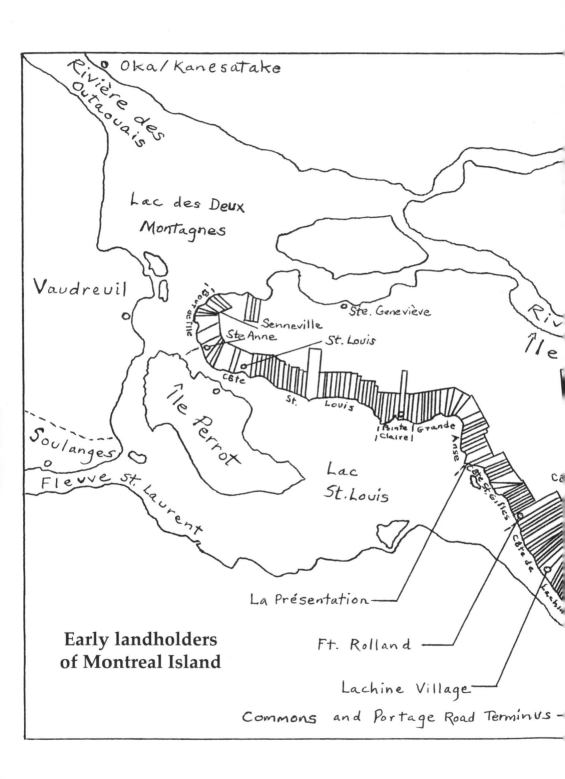

Oka/Kanesatake

Rivière des Outaouais

Lac des Deux Montagnes

Vaudreuil

Ste. Geneviève

Bout de l'Île

Senneville

Ste Anne

St. Louis

Côte

St. Louis

Île Perrot

Pointe Claire

Grande Anse

Côte Ste Anne

Côte de Lachine

Soulanges

Fleuve St. Laurent

Lac St. Louis

La Présentation

**Early landholders
of Montreal Island**

Ft. Rolland

Lachine Village

Commons and Portage Road Terminus